The United States
and World Sea Power

The United

and

AUTHORS . . .

Henry H. Adams   James A. Arnold   Ellery H. Clark, Jr.

R. W. Daly   W. M. Darden   J. R. Fredland

Edwin M. Hall   Neville T. Kirk   Winston B. Lewis

E. B. Potter   W. H. Russell   H. O. Werner

. . . UNITED STATES NAVAL ACADEMY

States

World Sea Power

E. B. Potter   *Editor*

J. R. Fredland   *Assistant Editor*

Englewood Cliffs   PRENTICE-HALL, INC.   1955

Preface

The United States and World Sea Power is not so much a history of the United States Navy as an analysis of the *emergence* of American naval power. The authors have endeavored to include within the scope of a single work a history of United States sea power and of international sea power, placing the former within the setting of the latter and both within the setting of world history. The rise of the American navy is preceded by the rise of the British navy, and this in turn is preceded by the rise of earlier navies. The evolution of sea power is presented as a continuing process with the various epochs linked together by developing concepts, traditions, and techniques, and above all by the relatively unchanging elements of naval strategy.

One effect of viewing the rise of United States sea power from the standpoint of world history is to reveal naval operations of the American Revolution, America's Quasi-War with the French, and the War of 1812 as facets of England's long struggle with France. Any other handling is bound to involve distortions of fact. Equally distorting would be any treatment that lessened the achievements of the United States Navy in World War II and later, when it clearly overshadowed the navies of the rest of the world. The authors are confident that American readers are prepared to view history thus in broad focus.

Because this is a history of sea power, with emphasis on the products of a long evolution, the distant past and periods of comparative peace have intentionally been neglected in order to emphasize the two great modern struggles for command of the sea. The naval aspects of the Wars of the French Revolution and Empire, and the Pacific theater of operations in World War II—the climactic conclusion of the Age of Sail and the greatest naval war of the Age of Steam—jointly occupy a third of the total space. But the authors have endeavored to achieve something more than a mere operational history. They have tried to make clear the interrelation between technological developments and naval strategy and tactics, between land warfare and naval operations, between national policy and naval doctrine.

The United States and World Sea Power develops six main themes: (1) the influence of sea power upon history, (2) the rationale of strategic decision, (3) the characteristics of successful leadership, (4) the development of naval weapons, (5) the evolution of naval tactics, and (6) the evolution of amphibious doctrine. Emphasis is placed on the problems posed in each period of history by new weapons and new conditions, and on the solutions worked out for each by the navies of the world. The reader will note that problems of a similar or parallel nature arise in each epoch and that these have to be solved in most instances by somewhat similar means. He will thus perceive the parallels of naval history and the value of studying the past as a guide to future action. At the same time he will note that the problems are never *precisely* the same and will perceive thereby the dangers inherent in trying to "fight the last war."

The occasion for writing *The United States and World Sea Power* was the need for such a single, unified treatment at the United States Naval Academy. The conception of a composite work written by the naval history faculty has been an organic process. The ideological framework, stemming basically from Clausewitz, Jomini, Mahan, and Corbett, has been refined by several years of discussion by the authors among themselves and with officers in the services, and by the wartime experiences of the individual authors, all of whom were on active duty, chiefly in the naval reserve, during World War II.

The participants thus have had the unusual advantage of treating the historical process from the same point of view. *The United States and World Sea Power* was fully organized in advance of composition, and the efforts of each author have been subjected to intensive analysis and criticism by his colleagues and to close supervision and control by the editors. It is believed that such means have produced in no sense a mere symposium. Though there are instances in which it would be difficult to specify where one writer's work leaves off and another's begins, the authors take primary responsibility for the various chapters as follows: Henry H. Adams, Chapters 34, 36, 48, and 50-52; James A. Arnold, 22 and 35; Ellery H. Clark, Jr., 23, 27, 30, and 31; R. W. Daly, 4-13; W. M. Darden, 3; J. R. Fredland, 16-18, 26, and 32; Edwin M. Hall, 14, 15, and 47; Neville T. Kirk, 24, 25, and 29; Winston B. Lewis, 37-39; W. H. Russell, 28 and 33; E. B. Potter, 1, 2, 41-46, and 49; and H. O. Werner, 19, 20, and 40. Chapter 21 is the work of Messrs. J. R. Fredland and H. O. Werner.

The maps and diagrams were drawn from the authors' sketches by William M. Shannon, assisted by James L. Phipps, Wilbur R. Phillips, and Albert R. Jones, all of the Naval Academy staff.

While taking full responsibility for errors of fact or interpretation, the authors wish to express their gratitude to all who have helped them complete this work. The unstinted assistance of Professor Louis H. Bolander, Head Librarian of the Naval Academy, and his staff have saved the authors many hours of bibliographical research. The United States Naval Institute has allowed the authors free access to materials written by themselves and published by the Institute for use at the Naval Academy. Dr. Henry H. Lumpkin, formerly of the Naval Academy faculty, generously provided access to his extensive research materials in ancient and medieval military history. The Civil War chapters owe much to the editorial advice of Professor Richard S. West, of the Naval Academy faculty, who improved their conception and corrected errors of detail. Much of the material for the chapters on the Dardanelles-Gallipoli campaign and on the evolution of American amphibious and aviation doctrine was made available through the assistance of the Historical Branch, G-3, HQ, USMC, which arranged for studies by Professor Russell at the Marine Corps Schools, Quantico, and at the Naval War College. Suggestions and information invaluable in developing the area of amphibious doctrine were also furnished by two Forrestal Fellows in residence at the Naval Academy, Dr. Philip A. Crowl, of the Office of Military History, Department of Defense, and Rear Admiral Walter C. Ansel USN (Ret.), who also gave helpful criticism of the World War II section. Captain Brooks J. Harral USN, Head of the Department of English, History, and Government at the Naval Academy, has helped the authors sharpen their ideas regarding campaigns of the Pacific theater in World War II and has been a mine of information on submarine operations.

So many persons have been of material assistance that a really comprehensive listing is impractical, but prominent among them are Fleet Admiral Chester W. Nimitz USN, General Thomas Holcomb USMC (Ret.), Admiral H. Kent Hewitt USN (Ret.), Vice Admiral Eliot H. Bryant USN (Ret.), Vice Admiral A. Stanton Merrill USN (Ret.), Major General R. W. Keyser USMC (Ret.), Rear Admiral Arleigh A. Burke USN, Commodore Howard H. J. Benson usn (Ret.), Mrs. Robert H. Dunlap of Washington, D. C., and Dr. Gerald E. Wheeler of the Naval Academy faculty. Thanks are also due Mr. David Vanderburgh of the Prentice-Hall staff for his careful scrutiny of the typescript which resulted in elimination of slips of fact and style that might otherwise have gone unnoticed. Mention should be made of the extensive use of Samuel Eliot Morison's multi-volume *History of United States Naval* *Operations in World War II,* which was the basic but by no means exclusive source for Chapters 34 and 36-45.

The authors wish to emphasize that *The United States and World Sea Power* is in no sense an official history. It was conceived and written as a private enterprise in the authors' own time and without official sanction, control, or guarantees of adoption. The opinions expressed are theirs alone.

E. B. Potter

ILLUSTRATION ACKNOWLEDGMENTS

The maps, charts, and diagrams used are necessarily the result of compiling information contained in many sources. In some cases however one source has furnished the primary basis for the illustration presented herein. The authors therefore wish to acknowledge these sources for the illustrations appearing on the following pages: Pages 48, 57, and 62, adapted from G. A. R. Callender, *Sea Kings of Britain* (London: Longmans, Green & Co., Ltd., 1911-1915); page 220, adapted from R. C. Anderson, *Naval Wars in the Levant* (Princeton: Princeton University Press, 1952); page 389, adapted from H. W. Wilson, *Ironclads in Action,* vol. II (Boston: Little, Brown & Company, 1896); page 448, adapted from Frank Theiss, *The Voyage of Forgotten Men* (Indianapolis: The Bobbs-Merrill Company, Inc., 1937); page 607, based on a chart in Anthony Martienssen, *Hitler and His Admirals* (New York: E. P. Dutton and Co., Inc., 1949); page 625, adapted from Rear Admiral Raymond De Belot, *The Struggle for the Mediterranean 1939-1945* (Princeton: Princeton University Press, 1951); page 657, adapted from Allen Westcott, ed., *American Sea Power Since 1775* (Philadelphia: J. B. Lippincott Company, 1952); pages 669, 736, 792, and 793, adapted with the permission of the author from Samuel Eliot Morison, *History of United States Naval Operations in World War II,* vols. 3, 4, 5, and 8 (Boston: Little, Brown & Company, 1948-1953); page 856, from Alfred Stanford, *Force Mulberry* (New York: William Morrow and Company, 1951); and page 860, from Dwight D. Eisenhower, *Crusade in Europe,* Copyright, 1948, by Doubleday and Company, Inc. The title page and cover decoration is adapted from a map by J. McA. Smiley in *The Geography of the Peace,* by Nicholas J. Spykman, Copyright, 1944, by Harcourt, Brace and Company, Inc.

Contents

Contents *continued*

1

The Origins

of Western Sea Power

THE VARIOUS ELEMENTS OF modern naval warfare have roots deep in history. The considerations which the modern commander takes into account as he plans a campaign, goes into battle at sea, or prepares to storm a beachhead are often the products of slow growth.

An inspired leader wins a victory by using his weapons to best advantage while his opponent fumbles. He thereby sets a precedent in *tactics* upon which other officers, preparing for later battles, can base their plans. Thus from generation to generation naval leaders, taking into account changing conditions imposed by changing weapons, have developed the tactical doctrines in use today.

The science of supply, transportation, and maintenance—known as *logistics*—has likewise been the product of gradual development based on precedent, and of intelligent disregard of precedent. As with tactics, the evolution of logistics has been conditioned by changes in weapons. The nearly self-contained sailing ship enjoyed a relative independence from bases that its oar-driven predecessor, the fragile galley, had never

known. The coming of steam propulsion, fueled first by coal and then by oil, tied ships again to their bases until developing techniques of servicing at sea restored to fighting fleets their old reach and endurance.

Understanding the principles of *strategy* has been less a matter of evolution than of gradual clarification. Strategy is, after all, only the application of informed common sense to the problem of where to place forces, and is therefore relatively stable. Yet the principles had to be thought out in scores of wars and in hundreds of theaters of action before Alfred Thayer Mahan could enunciate his simple yet profound axiom: "Communications dominate war." [1]

Lastly, the full meaning of *sea power* and its influence upon history has only by slow degrees come to be appreciated by historians and military leaders. When Captain Mahan in 1890 reinterpreted history so as to put the widespread effect of naval actions into proper perspective, he strongly impressed students of history with much that had been

------

[1] *Naval Strategy* (Boston, 1918), 166.

1

previously overlooked. Yet the facts had been there for all to see: how Greece and then Rome through naval actions won dominance in the ancient Mediterranean world; how England in the Oceanic Age that was inaugurated by the voyages of discovery in the 15th and 16th centuries achieved world empire and world-wide influence by first winning mastery of the seas. Similarly the United States in two world wars has been able to project power in wholesale quantities by controlling the oceans that washed her shores.

To understand modern sea warfare and the influence of sea power today the student must go very far back into history. He must take at least a brief look at the earliest recorded naval traditions of our western world as they originated in the ancient Mediterranean. Here early naval warfare differed from modern naval warfare chiefly because the weapons of antiquity were simpler, less powerful, and less varied than weapons of later periods.

The very simplicity of the ancient campaigns permits the reader to discern all the more clearly the basic principles of war at sea and to observe that, though specific practices have undergone striking transformations, these basic principles have not greatly altered through the ages. Themistocles and Sextus Pompey saw as clearly as Nelson and Halsey that a victory at sea could isolate and weaken an army by making its supply line untenable. Alexander the Great in the 4th century BC understood the techniques of amphibious assault no less clearly than Kelly Turner in World War II. By observing how the early Mediterranean commanders solved or failed to solve their problems, the reader prepares himself to see through the complications of technological warfare to the heart of today's naval problems.

EARLY NAVIES

The civilizations which developed around the Mediterranean basin found the inland seas less a barrier than an avenue of intercourse for the exchange of commodities and the spread of ideas. In the Middle East and in North Africa, deserts facilitated the establishment of caravan routes between populated areas, but in general water transportation was so much easier and cheaper than transport over land that major nations and city-states tended to rise in areas which had access to navigable rivers and seas.

The appearance on the seas of wealth in the form of trade goods inevitably produced piracy, and the increase of overseas commerce led to clashes between rival trade interests. The first battles afloat were therefore merely unorganized skirmishes between traders and predatory seafarers out to capture booty. Because merchant vessels loaded with goods and manned by their regular crews were ill prepared to defend themselves, organized communities early set aside certain vessels manned with warriors to patrol and guard the commercial sea lanes. Specialization of function soon led to specialization of type, as marine architects devised craft especially designed for fighting. So at the very dawn of history in the Mediterranean world we find two sorts of vessels: the broad, clumsy cargo carrier, driven primarily by sails; and the long, narrow man-of-war, or *galley,* propelled by oars in battle but provided with masts and sails for cruising or flight. Thus navies came into being to protect sea commerce, and the history of sea power is to a great extent the story of rivalries among nations resulting from their conflicting commercial interests.

Even when the causes of war were more complex and subtle, warships retained as their principal function the task of patrolling the sea lanes to protect their own shipping and to attack the enemy's. To put it a little differently, the primary mission of navies, especially during periods of armed conflict, has been to safeguard their own sea routes and to deny to the enemy the sea routes he requires. To the extent that a fleet has achieved this mission it is said to have command (or control) of the sea. The routes along which men and materials move on land or sea, and the routes for possible retreat which a fighting force must keep open between itself and its base, are called communication lines. The whole complex of routes and transport is called *communications*.[2]

The primary function of navies, then, has been to control sea communications, that is, to defend one's own and to disrupt the enemy's. Such control is generally attained by destruction of enemy sea forces; and often it has been achieved by a single decisive naval battle, in which one fleet by shattering the opposing fleet gained command of the sea in a stroke. Possessing command of the sea enormously facilitates the ability of a nation to project power, by transporting armies over water to distant shores and keeping them supplied there—and makes it difficult if not impossible for an enemy to send armies across the sea against one's own shores.

Organized naval battles were evidently slow in developing from the confused raids, with each individual ship fending for itself, which must have characterized the first fights at sea. By the 5th century BC however, when the naval history of the Mediterranean came to be recorded with some degree of accuracy, there had grown up a definite system of *tactics*—that is, organized handling of forces in battle. Whereas rowed galleys might cruise in column (line ahead) they almost invariably fought in line abreast. Though this formation was probably imitated from infantry tactics, it was certainly the most logical for galleys. In line abreast each galley protected its neighbor's vulnerable sides, where the banks of oars were exposed, and at the same time presented to the enemy its fighting part, the bow with its ram, its grappling irons, and its engines of war. Here is an early illustration of the axiom that the nature of one's weapons determines the tactics one should employ—from which it follows that changes in weapons generally require changes in tactics, and the nation which most quickly and realistically

adapts its tactics to its weapons gains thereby an immense advantage over its more conservative or less realistic opponents.

As two opposing lines of galleys approached each other, oars stroking in unison, archers stationed at the bow fired arrows, and sometimes catapults hurled stones or firepots. Then the lines collided, metal-shod underwater rams crunching into wooden hulls. Lastly, the galleys grappled one another, and warriors swarmed across decks, turning the sea fight into an infantry battle. Not all naval actions were such brute contests of strength. The Greeks, for example, employed the maneuvers of sideswiping, breaking the line, flanking, and slipping past an enemy vessel to ram her before she could complete her turn. For both shock and mobility the early navies continually sought means to combine speed, maneuverability, and striking power. To that end special galleys were developed: notably *biremes*, carrying double banks of oars; and *triremes*, typically 150 feet long, carrying 30 warriors, and propelled to maximum speeds above seven knots by 170 rowers, who manned oars in three banks. By the 5th century BC the trireme had become the capital ship in navies of the Mediterranean. Like all galleys, it was a fragile craft, unable to weather storms. By day the triremes hugged the coast, and by night or in foul weather they were usually hauled ashore.

The sea power of a nation is measurable not only by the number and quality of its fighting ships but also by the character and numbers of its population, the character of its government, its commercial shipping, the quality and numbers of its harbors, the extent of its coastline, its overseas bases and colonies, and its location with regard to major sea lanes. It is difficult to say what people first exercised extensive sea power in the Mediterranean basin, but clearly Crete was one of the earliest and most powerful. The reasons are obvious, for given a population of sufficient density, the Cretans must early have been forced by the mountainous, inhospitable geography of their island to seek their living on the sea. Here geography was more in their favor, for Crete sits squarely

---

[2] Not to be confused with another word of the same spelling which refers to the dissemination and exchange of information. In his axiom about communications dominating war, Mahan was referring of course to routes and transport; but communications in the other sense are also enormously important in warfare.

EASTERN MEDITERRANEAN SEA

athwart the major sea routes of the eastern Mediterranean, achieving thereby advantages which England was to enjoy centuries later by virtue of her position athwart the major sea routes of Western Europe.

The Phoenicians were the next wielders of pre-eminent sea power in the Mediterranean. Forced to take to the sea as they outgrew their narrow strip of seacoast between the mountains of Lebanon and the eastern Mediterranean, they established a flourishing trade which carried their ships into all the inland seas in their part of the world and even beyond the Pillars of Hercules (modern Straits of Gibraltar) to seek the tin of Britain, the amber of the Baltic, and the slaves and ivory of western Africa to exchange for the spices, gold, and precious stones of India. This East-West trade enabled them to establish the mighty ports of Sidon and Tyre at the termini of caravan routes from the Orient, and the search for new customers and new sources of raw materials impelled them to become the first great colonizers of ancient times. Their trading stations on the shores and islands of the Mediterranean became new centers of civilization, some of which outlasted the influence of the parent state—notably Carthage, which in course of

time developed a land empire embracing North Africa, Sardinia, Corsica, half of Sicily, and much of Spain.

It is of early Greek sea power that we are able to attain the clearest and most accurate picture, thanks to Herodotus and Thucydides, who wrote excellent contemporary histories of the Greco-Persian and Peloponnesian wars. By the time the Persians invaded Greece in the 5th century BC however Greek naval traditions were already old and their tactics had achieved a high degree of sophistication. Indeed, there is some reason to believe that Homer's *Iliad* is really a poetic description of prehistoric Greek sea power at work—that the siege of Troy was a commercial war, to secure control of the Hellespont (modern Dardanelles) and thus of the Black Sea trade.

THE GRECO-PERSIAN WARS

A landlocked nation, as it grows in power through exceptional leadership or other advantages, tends to push to the sea in order to obtain the benefits of sea commerce. Thus Persia, expanding from the Iranian highlands, reached the Mediterranean and the Aegean Seas in the 6th century BC. The Phoenicians, satisfied with the profits of trade and having no solidarity as a nation, submitted easily—as they had earlier submitted to the Assyrians and to the Egyptians— and readily provided fleets for the overseas conquests of their new masters. But the Greek cities of Asia Minor resisted, and even when conquered, rose against their conqueror with naval aid from Athens and Eretria across the Aegean. The Persians recaptured the recalcitrant cities, but suppressing the revolt cost them several years and gave the city-states of the Greek peninsula time to prepare for the inevitable attack. Herodotus explains the Persian assault on Greece as reprisal for the assistance that Athens gave the rebels in Asia Minor, but the fact is that Persia's absorption of populations with powerful maritime trade interests had long since brought her into direct competition with Greece. Hence a struggle for commercial domination of the eastern Mediterranean was sure to follow. Besides, the expanding Empire had already spread across the Hellespont and through Thrace and Macedonia as far as Thessaly. Conflict was inevitable.

The first Persian expedition against Greece in 492 BC succeeded in subduing revolt in Thrace and Macedonia, but the fleet, which accompanied and supplied the army as it marched around the northern shores of the Aegean, was heavily damaged in a storm off the promontory of Mt. Athos. With the fleet out of action, cargo vessels could not be protected while supplying the troops. Hence further advance was out of the question; loss of its communication line back to base stopped the first expedition in its tracks and might have served warning to the Persians of the special difficulties they were to encounter 12 years later.

In 490 however the Persians undertook a second and different sort of advance against Greece. This was to be an amphibious expedition, directly across the Aegean. Such an operation, especially when it involves landing a force on a hostile coast, can be one of the most complex and vulnerable in warfare. Certainly the Persians, for all their mastery of overland transportation and supply, were ill prepared for a large-scale advance by sea. For one thing, the small transport vessels of the period were inadequate to land and reinforce troops with enough speed to make a frontal assault against forces which the Athenians could assemble overland from their Greek allies. And even if they had had a navy and a naval transport force adequate to carry out the task, the Persians lacked bases in the theater to shelter, launch, and support the fleet needed for a major amphibious attack. Probably they intended merely to secure a base on the Attic peninsula where seaborne strength could slowly be built up to carry out their intended conquests.

Whatever the Persian plan, it did not work. From Cilicia on the southern coast of Asia Minor, the expeditionary force of 600 triremes set out, carrying probably 15,000 soldiers and 1,500 horses. When we consider that the Persians ten years later sent 12 times as many troops against Greece, we are forced to the conclusion that they did indeed regard the initial landing force of 490 BC as a mere first echelon, with more troops to be fed into the beachhead by successive naval expeditions. Be that as it may, the expeditionary force put in at Samos off the Aegean coast of Asia Minor, presumably for victuals and water, little of which could be carried aboard for lack of space, and then set out for the island of Naxos, there burning the chief town. From Naxos the expedition proceeded through the Aegean islands to Euboea, where they pillaged the city of Eretria, and then crossed the narrow strait to Marathon, 20 miles from Athens. Here as they landed they were met by 10–12,000 Athenians, who preferred to wait until their allies from Sparta arrived before giving battle. Nervously the Persian commander divided his forces, re-embarking part of the army for a direct attack on Athens, now emptied of garrison troops, before the Spartans should arrive.[3] This weakening of the force before

---

[3] The Persians, like the Japanese in World War II, were fond of divided force and envelopment tactics. When the divided forces failed to support each other through poor timing or otherwise they were sometimes defeated piecemeal.

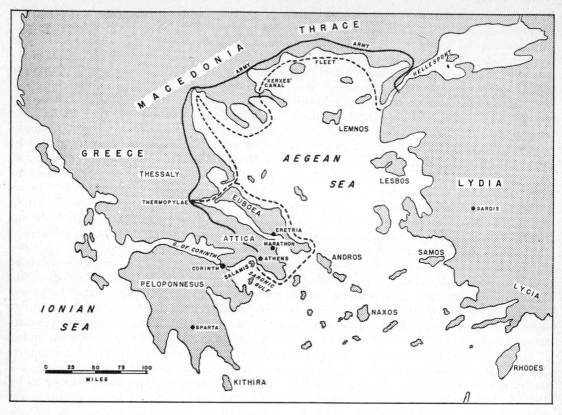

APPROXIMATE ROUTES OF XERXES' FLEET AND ARMY, 480 BC

them proved too great a temptation for the Athenians at Marathon to resist. Without waiting for the Spartans to arrive, they attacked at once and drove the invaders into the sea.

Not until 480 BC, ten years later, were the Persians prepared to renew their attack on Greece. Choosing the less vulnerable of the two difficult lines of approach, King Xerxes assembled 180,000 troops at Sardis in Asia Minor and marched them overland to the Hellespont, which they crossed by means of two pontoon bridges. Since the Persian army was far too large to live off the land, it followed the example of the first expedition by proceeding along the Aegean coast while hundreds of cargo vessels kept it supplied from Asiatic bases. Meanwhile, about 1,300 fighting ships, manned by some 175,000 soldiers, seamen, and rowers, protected the cargo vessels. To avoid the disaster which

had befallen the earlier expedition along this route, Xerxes had had a canal dug across the peninsula of Athos so that the fleet could avoid rounding it in stormy weather.

As the hordes of Persia advanced through Thrace and Macedonia and poured into Thessaly, the Athenians, together with the Spartans and their other allies, prepared to defend themselves. Luckily for Greece, Athens had produced an exceptional leader in Themistocles, who correctly saw that the Persian army, for all its size, was no stronger than the fleet which protected its communication line back to base. Themistocles persuaded his fellow citizens to invest increased capital from their silver mines in a fleet of their own, which with ships of their allies gave the Greeks a naval force of 380 triremes. In deference to Sparta, which had provided the major land forces, the Spartan

Eurybiades was given the top naval command; but Themistocles provided the vision, the intellectual acumen, and the driving force which held the shaky Greek coalition together and directed its energies toward the salvation of the Hellenic peninsula.

The Persians, advancing inexorably southward, were briefly halted at the narrow coastal pass of Thermopylae. Here a small advance force of Greeks under King Leonidas of Sparta had taken a stand—their left flank against a steep hill, their right covered by the Greek fleet so that they might not be outflanked by sea. But the Persians, sending a part of their force around Leonidas' left flank by way of a mountain pass, clamped the pincers on the Greek defenders and annihilated them. The Allied fleet, which had steadfastly covered Leonidas' right despite attacks from Persian triremes, now retired south to the narrow waters between the Island of Salamis and the mainland not far from Athens.

Meanwhile, a succession of storms had cost Xerxes some 400 of his galleys, ". . . the gods so contriving," wrote Herodotus, "that the Persian fleet might not greatly exceed the Greek, but be brought nearly to its level." Xerxes now took counsel whether he should detach 300 of his warships for an assault on Kithira, off the tip of the Peloponnesus. An attack here would doubtless draw the Spartans and their neighbors southward to protect their own lands and thus split up the unstable Greek alliance. But the Persian king rejected this alternative, for he now had scarcely enough naval force left to meet the combined Greek fleet and also to defend his seaborne communications. Instead he pressed with his army into Attica, laying waste everywhere, and at length plundered the city of Athens, while his fleet moved in a body to Phalerum Bay, the port of Athens, only a few miles from where the Greek fleet lay, under the lee of Salamis.

The Peloponnesians were for withdrawing with the fleet at once and taking a stand on the narrow Isthmus of Corinth. But Themistocles, exercising all his force of intellect and powers of persuasion, argued in favor of keeping the 300 ships still remaining to the Greeks in the narrow strait where they were. Here the Persians could not attack with their full force in line abreast and hence would lose much of the advantage of their superior numbers. The Persian fleet, he asserted, would not dare advance while a hostile fleet remained behind on its line of communications, but if the Greek fleet moved to the Corinthian isthmus, the Persians could outflank the Allied position by sending forces across the Saronic Gulf to attack the isthmian defenses from the rear. Eurybiades and his admirals were almost convinced when Xerxes played into Themistocles' hands by sending 200 ships of his diminished fleet south around Salamis to block the escape of the Greeks. Eurybiades now had no choice but to fight where he was, for the remaining 600 Persian ships were already advancing on the eastern entrance to the strait.

Under the eyes of Athenian evacuees watching from the heights of Salamis, and of Xerxes enthroned on the opposite shore, the Persian galleys moved north, presumably in several columns, to eastward of the island of Psyttalea. They then must have executed ships left and advanced in line abreast, ultimately six to eight ranks deep, against the Greeks, who we may suppose were in line abreast three or four ranks deep, with their flanks covered by the shorelines. The Persians thus could present no more bows to the enemy than the Greeks could, and though they possessed greater strength in depth, their rear ranks could do little more than feed fresh troops forward. The Persian advantage in number of soldiers afloat was probably offset however by the fact that the Greek oarsmen were all freemen who could when needed seize sword and shield and join the fight across decks. Among the Greek ranks there were no mercenaries or unwilling levies but men fighting for their lives and homes. Regarding the tactics at Salamis one can only speculate, though the poet-dramatist Aeschylus, who fought in the battle, has stated in a famous passage that the numerous Persian ships crowded inside the strait became jammed together in confu-

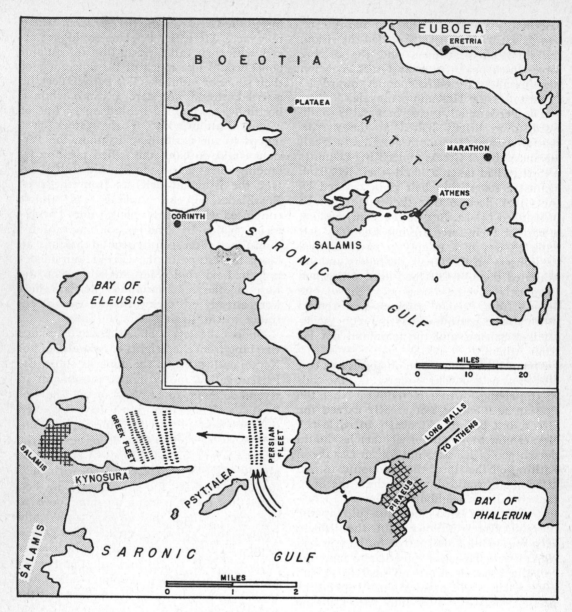

BATTLE OF SALAMIS, 480 BC

sion,[4] whereupon ". . . the ships of Hellas, with maneuvering not unskillful, charged circling round them."

At any rate the Greeks lost only 40 ships whereas the Persians lost 200 by sinking and an indeterminate number by capture. With his naval force thus cut down, Xerxes real-ized that his seaborne communication line was no longer tenable, and that his army was stranded with insufficient supplies for an extended campaign. So he dispatched what was left of his fleet across the Aegean to Asia Minor and returned the way he had come, leaving behind 50,000 troops to win-ter in Thessaly, where grain enough could be found to feed that many but no more.

[4] It would appear that the Persians were unaware that the strait narrowed west of Psyttalea.

The following summer, land forces of the Greek alliance—at last operating in unison, as the combined fleet had operated at Salamis—attacked and annihilated Xerxes' 50,-000 at Plataea, some 40 miles northwest of Athens. That same summer the Greek combined fleet demonstrated .the command of the sea it had won at Salamis by advancing across the Aegean to Asia Minor and there driving ashore and burning the remnants of Xerxes' armada.

The wars between Greece and Persia thus illustrate as clearly as any in history the truth of Mahan's axiom that "Communications dominate war." Themistocles saw well enough that an army which cannot live off the land is no stronger than its line of supply and that when supplies must come across water, a victory at sea can set the stage for a victory on land. In centuries to come, many another army commander— Montcalm at Quebec, Cornwallis at Yorktown, Napoleon in Egypt, Lee at Petersburg, Blanco at Havana, and Yamashita in the Philippines, to name a few—was to find himself isolated like Xerxes in Attica by naval operations which decisively cut his communications.

THE PELOPONNESIAN WAR

The Greek unity which had repelled Xerxes from Hellas did not long survive the Persian retreat. There was an interval of co-operation in which Athenians and Spartans jointly liberated Byzantium and Cyprus from Persian rule. But the institutions of Sparta and Athens contrasted too deeply to permit a permanent union. Sparta, a monarchy ruled by a military aristocracy, became increasingly suspicious of her democratic neighbor. While Athens, the sea power, looked more and more outward, extending her trade and influence over the eastern Mediterranean, Sparta turned ever more inward, fearful of her own slave population, distrustful of Athenian intentions, maintaining a highly-trained army, awaiting the war which appeared inevitable.

As tension grew between the two states, the smaller Greek communities grouped themselves through pressure or fear in one camp or the other. Sparta took under her leadership the Peloponnesian League of neighboring satellite states dependent upon the Spartan army; while Athens took full control of the Aegean, establishing an opposing maritime confederation known as the Delian League. Conflict finally broke out as the result of a clash between Athens and Corinth, a Spartan ally, over rival spheres of influence. Corinth appealed to Sparta, and in 431 BC the disastrous 30-year Peloponnesian War broke out.

As the two powerful Greek alliances bled each other white, Athens ceased to be a democracy, and the Delian League became not a union of allies but part of an Athenian empire. The Athens that succumbed at last to Sparta was no longer the great and free city of the days of Pericles.[5]

ALEXANDER OF MACEDON

A Greece already exhausted by three decades of war continued to be torn by more years of confused and fruitless conflict. This unhappy state of affairs was finally brought to an end by the emergence of a new power on the Hellenic political scene. At the Battle of Chaeronea, 338 BC, Philip II of Macedon, a semibarbaric kingdom in Macedonia, defeated the allied Greek armies. A Hellenic League, including all the important Greek states except Sparta, was set up under Macedonian leadership. Philip's son Alexander, who came to be known as Alexander the Great, in due course set out to invade and conquer the now-moribund Persian Empire.

Crossing the Hellespont in the spring of 334 BC with 35,000 disciplined troops, Alex-

[5] General of the Army George Marshall said shortly after World War II: "I doubt seriously whether a man can think with full wisdom and deep convictions regarding certain of the basic international issues today who has not at least reviewed in his mind the period of the Peloponnesian War and the fall of Athens." Quoted in Robert Campbell, "How a Democracy Died." *Life* (January 1, 1951), 96.

ander met and defeated a Persian army numbering 40,000. He then advanced into Asia Minor and captured Sardis. Behind him in the Aegean however a large Persian fleet denied him direct overseas communications with his Macedonian base, threatened to land an invasion force on the Greek peninsula, and interdicted the seaborne trade of any ports which submitted to him. To Alexander this was a nuisance which he could not hope to remove by seeking a decisive battle at sea, for he had no fleet to speak of.

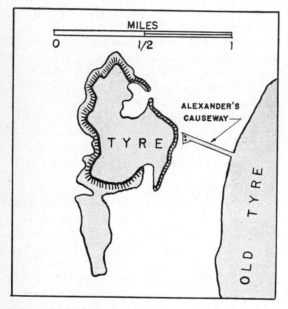

SIEGE OF TYRE, 332 BC

He therefore planned to conquer sea power by use of land power—through capturing all the ports rimming the eastern Mediterranean. The Greek cities of Asia Minor were, in general, glad to submit, for they were still restive under Persian tyranny, and Alexander promised them a democratic form of government. After another Macedonian victory over the Persian hosts, the cities of Phoenicia were ready to capitulate—all except Tyre, whose leaders preferred not to compromise themselves until it was clear who the final victor would be.

The main part of Tyre, on an island a third of a mile from shore, was surrounded by high walls of masonry and had two harbors and a squadron of 80 ships. The problem of capturing such a citadel strained the imagination and resources even of the ingenious Alexander, for he had no ships of his own to blockade the city or to bring siege machinery up against its walls. He first tried building a causeway out to the island from the shore, but the Tyrian squadron and archers on the city walls so harassed the workmen that he temporarily shelved the project and called on the "liberated" cities of Asia Minor and Phoenicia for ships, eventually assembling a fleet of 250. Though he was now able to complete his causeway, Alexander's siege of Tyre was in all essentials a true amphibious assault. Allowing for differences in weapons, the tactics he employed were strikingly similar to those used by United States naval forces nearly 23 centuries later in capturing fortified islands in the Pacific.

First, he had to send in sweeping vessels to sweep up boulders—forerunners of mines—which the Tyrians had strewed in the shallows about the city to pierce the bottoms of ships which ventured in close. Next, ships of the Tyrian squadron attacked, but the allied fleet under Alexander's personal command cut them off from their harbor and dispersed them. The Macedonians now set up huge catapults and other siege machinery on the causeway and on pairs of ships lashed together. Operating under cover of bowmen, who kept the Tyrian battlements cleared, the machines hurled stones against the walls of Tyre until they made a breach. While ships feinted at various points about the island city, the catapults enlarged the breach, whereupon special landing craft sped in and dropped gangways against the opening. With Macedonian archers firing arrows over his head to clear his path of Tyrian troops, Alexander himself led the assault forces as they rushed the breach and entered the city. At the same time, squadrons of Allied warships broke the chains guarding the city harbors and, after subduing what was left of the Tyrian fleet, the naval infantry advanced to meet Alexander's column. Thus after a seven-month siege the city fell in the summer of 332. Eight thousand citizens were killed in the battle through the streets and the rest were executed or sold into slavery.

Alexander now advanced south into Egypt, where he founded the port of Alexandria. By conquering or occupying naval bases from the rear, he had secured command of the sea. He thus, in the phrase of Sir Halford J. Mackinder, proponent of the land-power theory, made of the eastern Mediterranean a "closed sea," [6] that is, a sea over which commerce could move without strong naval protection because the shores were all held by one and the same power. The first cycle of sea power was ended. With the eastern Mediterranean secure behind him, Alexander turned east and advanced overland on Persia and India.

THE PUNIC WARS

Meanwhile, the supreme struggle for command of the *western* Mediterranean was about to begin. In these waters, ships of the Carthaginian Empire had lorded it for centuries, gradually taking over the trade and colonies of Phoenicia, the parent state, as the Phoenicians fell under Oriental domination. From the capital city of Carthage, located in North Africa at the narrows of the Mediterranean, warships set up a barrier, making all the seas to westward a Carthaginian lake. In Sicily, opposite the imperial city, the eastward-expanding Carthaginians had come into conflict with the westward-expanding Greeks. Here in 480 BC, instigated by Persia, the Carthaginians attacked the Greek cities in an attempt to divert Greek strength at the time of Xerxes' descent upon the Hellenic peninsula. But the Sicilian Greeks, for once uniting, signally defeated the Carthaginians at Himera—on the same day, it is said, that the Hellenic Greeks triumphed at Salamis. Thereafter the sea power of victorious Athens held Carthage in check for several generations.

By the time Athens went into decline as the result of the Peloponnesian War and the subsequent Macedonian conquest, Carthage had become weakened by internal cleavage. The large land-holding elements wanted a peaceful foreign policy emphasizing exploitation of North Africa in the area of the imperial city. The equally powerful commercial families favored a far-flung trade, development of colonies, and a foreign policy dominated by the protection of commerce—even at the price of war. In their ascendancy during the early years of the third century, the commercial elements strengthened the Carthaginian position in Spain and showed an increasing interest in the island of Sicily.

While Carthage was successfully limiting the Greeks' westward expansion, there was rising on the Italian peninsula another power which would not be stopped. After 500 years of conflict with neighbors and invaders, the Romans had expanded from the Tiber basin until they controlled all of peninsular Italy. This unique achievement, which gave Rome a numerous, sturdy, agricultural population, provided her with military power and started her on the road to world domination. The Carthaginians had early taken note of the rising Roman state by limiting Rome on the seas to direct trade with Carthage and specifically excluding her seafarers from other ports of North Africa and from the ports of Spain and Sardinia.

In 279 BC Carthage was willing to sign a treaty with Rome which stipulated that there should be no Carthaginian outposts on Roman soil. Within the next few years Rome established a series of coastguard colonies of her own citizens, guarded by a squadron of patrol cruisers responsible for protecting the Tyrrhenian coastline against foreign infiltration. As the expanding rivals crept toward each other, the situation grew tense. Since none of their treaties defined spheres of influence in Sicily, an outburst of disorder in Messana (modern Messina) brought in Carthaginian and Roman intervention on opposite sides and precipitated the First Punic War (264-241 BC).[7]

In Sicily, the Roman legionaries defeated

---

[6] *Democratic Ideals and Reality* (New York, 1942), 35.

[7] So-called from the Latin word for "Carthaginian."

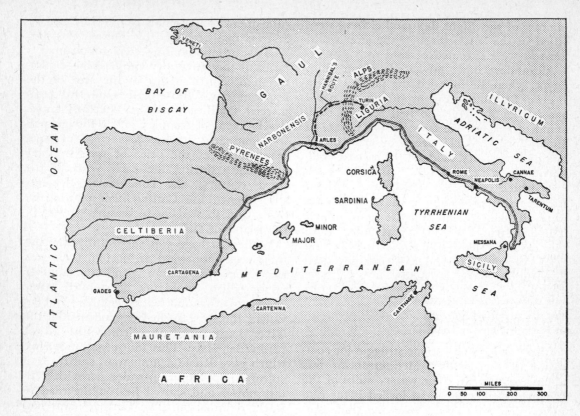

WESTERN MEDITERRANEAN SEA, 3RD CENTURY BC

the Punic forces and bottled them up in their fortified cities at the western end of the island. But the Carthaginians, exercising their command of the sea, virtually destroyed Roman commerce and pillaged the Italian coasts. Evidently Rome had to become a sea power quickly or else lose the war. Calling on her dependent Greek maritime cities of southern Italy and her allies in Sicily for ships and naval architects, she assembled and built a fleet of 160 galleys in record time. Rome thus by sheer industry soon equaled Carthage quantitatively on the sea, but dealing with Punic skill, based on centuries of seafaring experience, was another matter. The Roman galleys were heavy and sluggish, suitable for the "Syracusan" tactics of ramming, grappling, and boarding employed by the Italo-Greek subject states, while the ships of Carthage were light and nimble, best fitted for "Rhodian" tactics requiring seamanship and maneuver.

The Roman solution to the problem of dealing with the agile foe was the *corvus,* or "raven," a superior grappling device for seizing and holding enemy ships when they attempted to ram. Essentially a gangway 18 feet long, the corvus was pivoted to the deck near the bow at its inner end and bore a large iron spike or beak under its outer end. Normally held upright against a mast by a topping lift, it could be dropped forward or to either side to grapple any enemy vessel which approached too close. Over the gangway foot soldiers could then surge, converting the naval battle into an infantry battle across decks. In this manner the Romans planned to employ their specialty—the well-disciplined legionary—to offset the enemy's superior seamanship.

The corvus got its first test in action in 260 BC at the Battle of Mylae, off the north coast of Sicily, where some 125 Punic vessels engaged a slightly larger force of Romans.

Despising their lubberly foe, the Carthaginians bore down without much order, the first echelon of 30 ships far ahead of the rest. As these attempted to sideswipe or ram, the corvi came slamming down and grappled them firmly, whereupon the legionaries, bearing their shields before them, raced across and made short work of the Punic mercenaries. Seeing the fate of the first wave, now all captives, the Carthaginian rear adopted more wary tactics, attempting to sidestep the corvi and strike at the Roman sterns and broadsides. But increased disparity of numbers gave the ships of Rome such an advantage that they took 20 more vessels before the enemy, appalled by the success of their opponent's surprise weapon, fled with what remained of their fleet. From this time forward the Carthaginian naval forces felt constrained to employ cautious tactics which cost them more than one victory.

Their defeat at the hands of a neophyte naval power shocked the Carthaginians into building up their fleet; and their taste of victory at sea encouraged the Romans to do likewise. Rome believed however that the final decision would have to be reached on land and counted on her legions to put an end to the menace from overseas. By 256 she felt ready to invade North Africa in order to capture the city of Carthage, after which the Punic Empire, held for the most part against its will, must inevitably break up. The Roman plan to transport troops directly to Africa in the face of Carthaginian sea power was bold, not to say foolhardy; for a fleet burdened by a convoy puts to sea at its peril when an enemy fleet of approximately equal strength stands ready to dispute its passage.

Nevertheless the Roman fleet of 250 men-of-war plus numerous transports set out from Messana to pick up probably 20,000 legionaries from a base on the south coast of Sicily and convey them across the narrows of the Mediterranean. To intercept this expedition, Carthage dispatched Hamilcar with 250 ships to Heraclea, 35 miles west of the Roman army base. Hamilcar's task seemed easy. Since in those days ships invariably hugged the coast when they could, he had only to await the arrival of the Romans opposite his position. Then he could strike and smash their transports, without which the enemy would be powerless to invade.

After picking up the legionaries, the Romans put to sea again in four squadrons, the 1st, 2nd, and 4th forming the sides of a triangle, point forward, and enclosing the 3rd, which was towing the transports. At the apex of the triangle, leading the fleet, were the flagships of the consuls Regulus and Manlius. Critics have suggested that Hamilcar should have let the Romans pass him and continue along the Sicilian coast so that they would be off a hostile shore and he could place his fleet between the transports and their base. As it was, Hamilcar advanced to meet the enemy at a point near Mt. Ecnomus, where the coast was held by Roman forces. Thus, on contact, the transports departed hastily and headed back toward base along a friendly coast. Meanwhile, the warships fought the Battle of Ecnomus, which set a new high in tactical complexity. (See map on next page.)

While Hamilcar's two center squadrons engaged the Roman 1st and 2nd squadrons, his wings sped around the enemy flanks in an enveloping movement. But his left encountered the Roman 3rd with one flank against the shore, covering the fleeing transports; and his right found the 4th covering the Roman rear. Manlius and Regulus, by grappling and boarding tactics, soon defeated Hamilcar and put the remains of his center squadrons to flight. They then turned back to aid their lighter 3rd and 4th squadrons, which though hard pressed had saved themselves by the threat of their corvi. The Carthaginians lost 94 ships; the Romans lost only 24 and saved all their transports besides. Again the corvus had proved decisive, restricting the maneuvers of the Punic commanders by the constant threat of the descending iron beak and of the legionaries' implacable rush. That of course was not the whole story, for the Romans had shown what was for the time extraordinary teamwork and command control when the 1st and 2nd squadrons withdrew intact from their successful engagement with the Punic center and sped to aid the Roman rear.

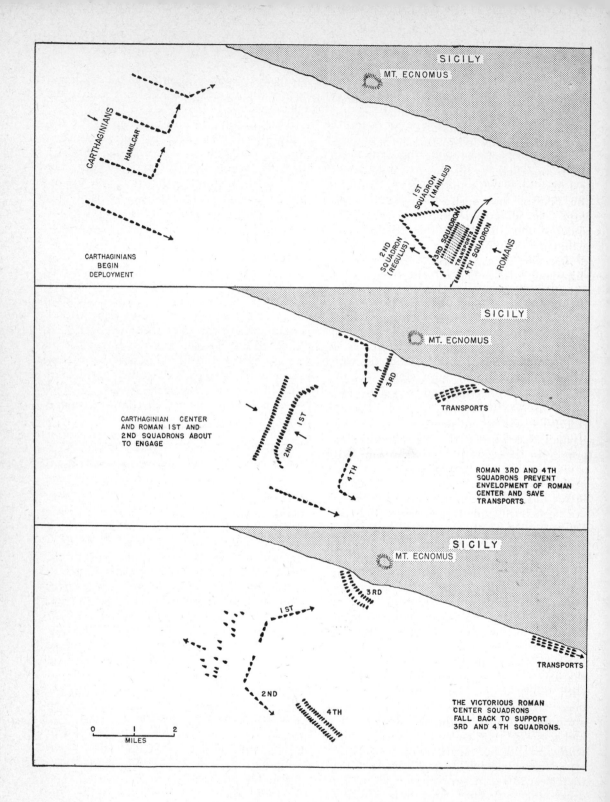

SICILY

MT. ECNOMUS

3RD

TRANSPORTS

2ND 1ST

4TH

CARTHAGINIAN CENTER
AND ROMAN 1ST AND
2ND SQUADRONS ABOUT
TO ENGAGE

ROMAN 3RD AND 4TH
SQUADRONS PREVENT
ENVELOPMENT OF ROMAN
CENTER AND SAVE
TRANSPORTS.

SICILY

MT. ECNOMUS

3RD

1ST

TRANSPORTS

2ND

4TH

THE VICTORIOUS ROMAN
CENTER SQUADRONS
FALL BACK TO SUPPORT
3RD AND 4TH SQUADRONS.

0   1   2
MILES

BATTLE OF ECNOMUS, 256 BC

With the Carthaginian fleet thus reduced in strength, the Romans invaded North Africa with impunity. In Africa however, mismanagement and premature withdrawal of part of their army led to Roman defeat and evacuation. The fleet which brought away the troops then ran into a gale off Sicily and lost most of its ships and men. This was only the first of four such disasters, in which large fleets with armies aboard were wrecked and lost. On top of this, the Carthaginians, achieving their only clear-cut naval victory of the war, in 249 BC captured 93 Roman ships and 20,000 men off Drepanum in Sicily. Rome was at long last paying the price of poor seamanship. Within five years a sixth of her citizens had perished, her treasury was exhausted, and her Senate had about decided to abandon the sea to the enemy.

At this point a new class of war-enriched citizens came forward and saved the day. These were associations of merchants and capitalists made wealthy by the overseas commerce which had developed as the first Roman fleets broke the Carthaginian monopoly in the western Mediterranean. With a vital interest in Roman sea control, they provided unsecured loans for building and fitting out a new fleet of 200 ships. This was the fleet, built and trained better than any before, which finally broke the Carthaginian hold on Sicily and brought the First Punic War to an end.

The new fleet, under the consul Catulus, proceeded in the summer of 242 to the western tip of Sicily, where Hamilcar was still holding several Punic strong points. Catulus did what he could to reinvigorate the long-drawn-out Roman siege, but he was careful to husband his forces because he knew that he would at length have to contend with hostile ships. The Carthaginians, for once taken completely by surprise, were astounded to learn of the new fleet, for they had felt sure that after her desperate losses Rome would not again appear upon the sea. Secure in their belief, they had kept their fleet idly at home, where it lapsed into decay and inefficiency. Something had to be done, so Hanno set out from Carthage, his ships manned by untrained oarsmen and military recruits, intending to run supplies in to his beleaguered fellow countrymen in Sicily and there pick up veteran troops before challenging the Romans at sea.

But Catulus, guessing the Punic strategy, placed his fleet in an intercepting position in the Aegatian Islands. Hanno, coming in from the west under sail with a stiff breeze at his back, tried to make a run for it, counting on the wind and the well-known Roman awkwardness at sea to get him through. But

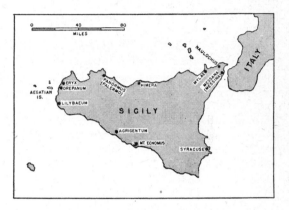

SICILY, 3RD CENTURY BC

Catulus was a new kind of Roman commander with a new kind of fleet. He neatly blocked Hanno, who was obliged to haul down his sails and take to oars. In the ensuing, one-sided Battle of the Aegatian Islands, the Carthaginians were quickly shattered, with a loss of 50 ships sunk and 70 captured.

For exposing his fleet to disaster and losing the battle, Hanno was crucified on his return to Carthage. With their Sicilian garrisons completely isolated, the Carthaginians at last sued for peace, agreeing to pay an indemnity and to evacuate Sicily forever.

Her victory over Carthage so nearly established Rome's dominance over the western Mediterranean that in 238 she cynically appropriated the Carthaginian base on Sardinia. The commercial-colonial faction still retaining control in Carthage refused to bow to Rome's Mediterranean domination. Led by Hamilcar, they set out to recapture the former prestige of their city by new trade and colonial developments in Spain. Roman efforts to limit Carthaginian Spain at length persuaded the Hamilcar faction that a second resort to arms was unavoidable. The First Punic War had made it abundantly clear that Carthage could not hope to conquer Rome by attacking on the sea, frontally or via Sicily. So Hannibal, most distinguished of Hamilcar's soldier sons, precipitated the Second Punic War (218-202 BC) by a flank attack on Rome over land.

With an army unequaled since the campaigns of Alexander the Great, he crossed the Ebro River, the Pyrenees, and the Alps and descended upon the Italian peninsula. His army, thus isolated in Italy, was at the beginning of his campaign in much the same situation as Xerxes' army *after* the Battle of Salamis. Nevertheless, the skillful Carthaginian won decisive victories at the River Trebia and at Lake Trasimenus. In 216 he won what has been called "the perfect battle" at Cannae [8] and from then until 204 maintained his army in southern Italy, its threat accentuated by an alliance between Hannibal and Philip V of Macedon.

By containing Hannibal after 216 and by defeating the relieving force his brother Hasdrubal brought over the Alps in 207, Rome's land forces maintained a stalemate until her superior navy assured final victory. A seaborne Roman invasion of North Africa obliged Hannibal to return home to defend Carthage. His defeat at Zama in 202 brought the war to a close.

Resurgence of Carthaginian commercial and agricultural prosperity in the course of the next century awoke old fears and envies among the Romans, who, on a trivial excuse, reopened the conflict. In the Third Punic

---

[8] Perfect, that is, from the Carthaginian point of view. The Roman consul Varro, with 75,000 legionaries against 25,000 Carthaginian foot soldiers, made the fatal mistake of letting himself be lured into a frontal assault on Hannibal's center, which was thrust out like an arch towards the Romans. The Carthaginian arch became more cohesive as it was forced inward by the legionaries, at length snapping back into a concave formation whose wings closed in on the Roman flanks. Hannibal's cavalry of 10,000 horses then fell upon the Roman rear and completed the encirclement, pressing the legionaries so tightly together that they could scarcely use their weapons. Roman losses were 60,000; Hannibal's, 6,000.

War (150-146 BC) they disarmed Carthage by treachery and then, after a four-year siege, razed the city to the ground. Except for troublesome pirates to be suppressed, Rome was now supreme in the central and western Mediterranean, which, like the eastern Mediterranean in the days of Alexander and his successors, had become a closed sea because all the shores were held by the same power.

THE ROMAN CIVIL WARS

Militarily strengthened rather than weakened by her long struggle with Carthage, Rome had already turned eastward where the Hellenistic monarchies, successor states to Alexander's empire, were becoming increasingly conscious of the Roman threat. In two major wars she defeated Hannibal's erstwhile ally, Macedon, and incorporated it as a province under a Roman governor the same year that saw the destruction of Carthage. She next defeated the Seleucid Empire, which controlled much of the Middle East, and thereby paved the way for bringing Syria into the expanding Roman hegemony. Meanwhile, quarrels among the Greek states were providing a continual invitation to foreign intervention from the East. This intermittent threat to her flank Rome at last found intolerable and so rather reluctantly brought Greece under her control. Rome thus emerged by the middle of the 2nd century BC as the dominant power in the Mediterranean world.

But the expanding Roman Republic had received a mortal blow. The devastation of Italy by Hannibal's army had broken up the small-farm economy upon which the republican power and the sturdy republican virtues had been based. The influx of slaves attendant upon the Roman conquests completed the process. The small farms were never re-established. In their place were founded huge cash-crop estates farmed by slave labor on the Carthaginian model. A pauperized peasantry, driven from their lands, remained in the city as a restless mob. Attempts to arrest these evils caused the breakup of the old republican system and led to political revolution and thence to civil war, until at length the Roman citizenry, exchanging their liberties for restoration of order, submitted to the imperial rule of the Caesars.

The Civil War began in 49 BC, when Julius Caesar, fresh from his conquests in Gaul, defied the consul Pompey and the Roman Senate by invading Italy with his victorious army. War was suspended during the period of Caesar's dictatorship but broke out again after his assassination in 44. Two years later the army of the assassins Brutus and Cassius was defeated at Philippi in Macedonia. The victors, Antony and Caesar's grandnephew Octavius, soon thereafter divided the Roman world between themselves, and Antony married Octavius' sister Octavia to seal the compact.

During the confusion following Caesar's death, Sextus Pompey, son of Caesar's enemy, made a bid for empire. With a great fleet he seized control of the western Mediterranean; captured Sicily, southern Spain, Corsica, and Sardinia; and cut off Rome's overseas food supply. Octavius in 36 BC set about removing this intolerable nuisance by leading an expedition against Pompey's headquarters in Sicily. Aware that he could not match Octavius' strength on land, Pompey planned to defeat the expedition at sea. He had more ships than Octavius, perhaps 155 to 120; his crews were more experienced and better trained; and his vessels were light and swift, built for the speed necessary to their semi-piratical operations.

The Roman ships as always were heavy and sluggish and now were built with high sides and with towers fore and aft to provide platforms for archers and javelin throwers. However Octavius had a priceless advantage in his naval commander, Agrippa. Off Mylae, site of Rome's first sea victory over Carthage, Agrippa's ships achieved success of sorts over their lighter opponents, but in a subsequent engagement they took losses. Though tactically worsted, Agrippa was the strategic victor, for he had carried out his primary mission of keeping Pompey's fleet occupied long enough for the Roman army to cross the straits to Sicily.

Pompey's only hope now was to isolate and starve Octavius' army by first destroying his fleet and then cutting his overseas communications back to Italy. He therefore challenged the Roman naval force off Naulochus on the north shore of Sicily. For this battle he had followed Agrippa's example by providing his ships with towers on the Roman model. But Agrippa had adopted a surprise weapon which was as much an advance over the corvus as the corvus had been an advance over the simple grappling iron. This was the *harpago,* a heavy timber with an iron claw at one end and a long rope attached to the other. Retaining one end of the rope on board, the Romans fired the harpago from a catapult, and when it hooked an enemy vessel they hauled her in by means of a winch and then dashed aboard. Finding their ships being thus reeled in like so many hooked fish, 17 of Pompey's captains threw their heavy towers overboard and escaped. The rest of his fleet was destroyed or captured, and Pompey fled to Asia.

Octavius was now ready to challenge Antony, who ruled in the East. Antony soon gave him the pretext he needed by canceling his political marriage to Octavia and taking to wife Cleopatra, Queen of Egypt, on whom he bestowed rich Roman provinces. Fearful that Antony was planning to subdue Rome and make Alexandria the capital of the Empire, the Senate deprived him of his command and his titles and declared war on Cleopatra. Instead of submitting to the senatorial decree, Antony accompanied by Cleopatra established his army and navy in Greece, taking up headquarters near Actium on the Gulf of Amvrakia.

Octavius, as champion of the West, thereupon set up an army base in the high, healthful ground north of Antony's position and clamped a tight naval blockade on the Eastern fleet and sea communications. He then encouraged the Greeks, disaffected by the high taxes Antony had imposed, to cut his communications over land via Thessaly. Then, having isolated his enemy, Octavius simply remained in his strong, defended position, declining Antony's offers of battle.

He could afford to wait, for time was on his side. Within Antony's camp food became scarce; then malaria struck; worse, his Roman followers fell to quarreling with Cleopatra's Egyptians, who favored a retreat to Egypt. Perceiving at last that they were serving an alien cause, the Romans began deserting to Octavius. So Antony was forced to

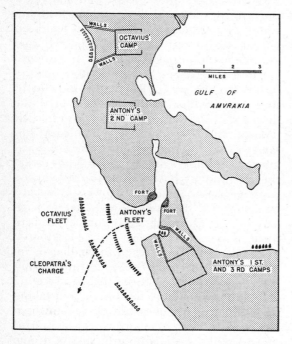

BATTLE OF ACTIUM, 1ST CENTURY BC

seek a battle at sea since he could not have one on land except under impossible disadvantages. If he were to win at sea, he might turn the tables and blockade Octavius. If he lost, he might at least escape to Egypt with the bulk of his fleet, leaving the army to follow as it could.

The fleet of 200 vessels which Antony took out of the Gulf to face Agrippa's 260 were burdened with troops, stores, and sails for flight in event of defeat. They were very large vessels, carrying four to ten banks of oars and towers several stories high for mechanical artillery and archers. Antony, attributing the Roman victory at Naulochus to Agrippa's bigger ships, had built still larger ships to meet Agrippa. Now the Ro-

man ships, which had overawed Pompey's by their size, were themselves dwarfed by the ships of Antony. So Agrippa, ever adaptable, decided to change his tactics. He discarded the harpago, which would now work to his disadvantage, for the enemy had legionaries aboard every bit as good as his. Instead, he would rely on his superior powers of maneuver and on new surprise weapons.

Through the morning the two fleets remained inactive facing each other, Agrippa's in three squadrons abreast, Antony's in a similar formation with Cleopatra's 60 vessels to the rear in reserve. At noon a breeze set Antony's left flank in motion and soon the fleets were engaged all along the line. Agrippa's ships now avoided compact formations of the enemy and sought to gang up on isolated units, darting in to sweep away oars or rudders and then, without pausing to permit boarding, backing off and striking swiftly again. At the crucial moment Agrippa made use of his new weapons, blazing arrows and pots of flaming charcoal and pitch hurled by mechanical engines.

Seeing the battle turning against Antony, Cleopatra, as capable a commander as any man, came charging through the center of both lines with the wind at her back and her reserve squadron under sail. The more agile Roman ships seem merely to have drawn aside and let her pass, leaving her separated from the main body of Antony's fleet. Since the wind did not permit her to repeat her maneuver on the opposite tack, she turned south and sailed away for Egypt. Antony boarded a light craft and managed to join her, but the rest of his fleet, under attack by Agrippa's fiery missiles, could not disengage and follow according to plan. Instead, they fought on until the flaming arrows and fire pots decided the issue in Agrippa's favor. At nightfall what was left of Antony's fleet withdrew within the Gulf, whereupon the Roman blockade again closed down. A week later fleet and army surrendered to Octavius.

His victories at Naulochus and Actium gave Octavius command of the whole Mediterranean, an indispensable preliminary to his subsequent conquest of Egypt and his assumption of imperial power as Caesar Augustus, first of the Roman emperors. For five centuries after Actium, commercial vessels moved freely throughout the Mediterranean basin, protected only by small fleets of police vessels to keep down piracy. The entire Mediterranean had become a closed sea with all coasts and naval bases controlled by Rome. Land power had again terminated a cycle of competition upon the sea.

THE DECLINE OF ROME

In 328 AD Emperor Constantine, impelled by new military requirements and imperial interests, shifted his capital from the city of Rome to Constantinople on the Bosporus. The unity of the Roman Empire did not long survive the shift. Sixty years later, the sons of Theodosius the Great divided the Empire between them; and the Western or Latin Roman Empire, with its capital at Rome, became independent of the Eastern or Byzantine Empire, with its capital at Constantinople. The subsequent decline of vitality in the Western Empire produced a power vacuum into which moved the barbaric and semibarbaric peoples of Europe—the Franks, the Vandals, the Goths, the Alans—themselves pushed by the Huns and other nomads who came pouring out of Central Asia.

Checked in Gaul, Attila the Hun in 452 invaded northern Italy, sacking its cities, from which fled fugitives to the islands and lagoons at the head of the Adriatic, where they laid the foundations of the future city-state of Venice. In 476 the German mercenary troops in Italy mutinied, deposed the last of the West Roman emperors, and choosing one of their number to be king of Rome, sent the imperial crown to Constantinople in notification that the Western Roman Empire was at an end.

THE EASTERN ROMAN EMPIRE

While invading hordes from the East were shattering the remains of Roman civilization in Western Europe, Constantinople and the Byzantine Empire stood firm against the onslaughts of Persians, Slavs, and Bulgars. The city of Constantinople, erected on a point of land where the Bosporus enters the Sea of Marmora, was guarded on its seaward face by its fleet and protected on its landward side by double walls and a moat. For almost a thousand years after the fall of Rome, Constantinople remained a bastion against invasion of Europe from the Middle East and a preserver of the cultural heritage of the ancient Mediterranean world.

The first serious threat to the Eastern Roman Empire came in the 7th century with the rise of Islam. Overpopulation and the drying up of oasis areas on the fringes of the Arabian desert sent the nomadic Arabs on land-seeking raids to the north and east. United and electrified by the eloquence of the religious leader Mohammed, the Arabs turned against the neighboring empires. The Persians and the Byzantines quickly gave way as the Moslem [9] forces advanced eastward to the Indus and thrust back the Romans to the Bosporus. Arab conquest of Egypt soon followed. Based securely upon the whole Middle East, the Moslems took to the sea, overrunning Cyprus and Rhodes and raiding southern Italy and Sicily. At the same time they pushed westward across North Africa, conquering by the sword and then winning adherents through their policy of low taxes and religious toleration. By 700 the movement had reached the Straits of Gibraltar, across which Berber converts to Islam under Arab leadership advanced to conquer Spain.

Early Moslem attempts to take Constantinople were frustrated by the city's maritime defenses, but in 717 the Arabs staged an attack of such proportions that it seemed almost certain the city could not survive. According to old records, possibly exaggerated, 80,000 Moslems crossed the Hellespont and invested Constantinople from the landward side, while a fleet of 1,800 galleys and sailing vessels entered the Sea of Marmora

[9] Moslem: believer in the faith taught by Mohammed. Islam: the whole body of Moslems, also the religion.

to supplement the blockade and to protect the seaborne supplies of the army. The Arab sea forces easily cut the city's communications with the Mediterranean. But when they attempted to complete the blockade by sending detachments up the Bosporus, the Byzantine fleet issued from harbor and attacked with a terrifying secret weapon, Greek fire, a forerunner of gunpowder and apparently of somewhat similar composition. Hurled in pots by mechanical artillery or mixed with pitch and sprayed from tubes by the force of its own explosion, it set fire to the Moslem vessels and burned the men, who found it almost impossible to extinguish.

After that, everything seemed to work against the besiegers. Unversed in the siege operations at which the Europeans later became so skillful, they could not breach or force the city walls. Wracked by cold and disease, deserted by the Christians whom they had pressed into service, living in dread of the terrible Greek fire, which the Byzantines were not slow to use, the Arab forces in 718 abandoned their campaign and withdrew. On retiring into the Aegean, the Moslem fleet ran into a storm which so reduced its numbers that the pursuing Byzantines made short work of what was left. Only five Arab ships, it is said, returned to home ports in Syria. With no fleet assistance and hence no overseas supply line, the huge Moslem army likewise melted away. Not more than 30,000 men survived the long retreat through Asia Minor. No doubt this great double disaster played an important part in the subsequent decline of Arab power.

The Byzantines, on the contrary, were so encouraged by their victory that within a few years they pushed their frontier once more to the Euphrates. Though they were never able to retake Egypt and Syria, and hence lost the southern routes to the Far East, the Eastern Romans for centuries remained wealthy and influential by virtue of their control of the northern route. Most Oriental goods shipped to Europe, even those arriving by way of the Red Sea, were normally directed through Constantinople for transshipment in mixed cargoes. The prosperity of Constantinople however was eventually to prove her undoing by arousing the envy of Venice, which aspired to be chief trader between East and West. Through Venetian incitement, the Fourth Crusade in 1204 diverted its efforts from freeing the Holy Land to sacking the ancient city which had stood against Oriental incursions for nearly a thousand years. Thus weakened, Constantinople gradually lost its outlying territories and in 1453 fell to the Ottoman Turks, imperial successors to the Arabs.

2

The Approach
to the Oceanic Age

WHAT THE MEDITERRANEAN was to the ancient Western World, the vast oceans of the earth are to the civilized world today. Across these waters have moved the goods, the people, and the ideas that have made dominant the civilization which arose in Western Europe after the collapse of the Latin Roman Empire. Yet for centuries following that collapse the Europeans, harassed by confusion at home and attacks from without, had few products or ideas to export and few ships to carry them in.

THE SIEGE OF EUROPE

Assaulted by invading hordes from the East, Western Europe clung precariously to the remains of Roman civilization. Semi-barbaric kingdoms and tribal principalities rose and fell. The civilized Ostrogoths and Visigoths in the South and the Franks at the mouth of the Rhine maintained a semblance of order, but even where the land was not devastated, the landscape began to take on an appearance which we think of as typically medieval, with walled cities and fortified strongholds. England's Roman civilization was overrun by Angles, Saxons, and Jutes from across the North Sea. Ireland, protected by geography, became for a while a haven for scholars and churchmen fleeing the ravaged Empire, but this center of culture was soon laid waste by inter-clan warfare and Viking invasion. Meanwhile, against divided West Europe, torn with conflict within, came three powerful antagonists.

Out of the East, Slavic and kindred peoples continued to make periodic forays. Most prominent among these, after the Huns, were the related Avars, Bulgars, and Magyars. The Magyars conquered and settled what is now Hungary, thence launching raids each summer into the more heavily settled areas to the west. Their great raid of 938 carried them burning and robbing through Germany and France, over the Alps into Italy, and back into Hungary.

Out of the North came the Northmen, or Vikings, in ships with rounded bottoms and sharp ends that were otherwise like the Phoenician, Greek, and Roman vessels that had long before traded with the Baltic. As Scandinavia became unified under kings, dissident and independent-minded bands, long used to piracy, descended upon Europe in search of spoils and new homes. They conquered half of England, obliging King Alfred to organize the first English navy to fend them off, and then invaded northern France. Pressing on southward, they entered the Mediterranean and established forward bases in Sicily and Southern Italy. Other Northmen worked their way up the rivers of eastern Europe and founded the Norse-Slavic kingdoms of Kiev and Novgorod, thereby establishing the basis for what is now Russia. Some of these adventurers pushed on down the southern rivers and emerged as pirates on the Black Sea and the Caspian Sea, and five times attacked the Eastern Christian stronghold of Constantinople.

Out of the South via Gibraltar came the Moslems, whose empire stretched like a great scimitar from Constantinople through North Africa and Spain to France, threatening to engulf the Christian world.

Europe's response to the threefold attack upon Christendom was unification against the dangers from without. The main unifying force was the Church, which had never ceased to carry on its monastic, teaching, and missionary activities. In a very real sense the Pope replaced the Roman Emperor as a focus for Western unification. The second unifying force was the feudal system whereby knights swore allegiance and owed military service to a superior lord or king. An expanding bond of loyalty, operating upward and downward, thus united areas of Europe as a means of maintaining order within and repulsing foes from without. Out of these two unifying forces emerged the third, the new Empire.

When the Moslems crossed the Pyrenees it appeared for a while that they must subjugate Gaul as readily as they had overcome Spain. But as they penetrated north they came at last against a barrier. This was the kingdom of the Franks, which had been consolidating for more than 200 years in northern France and along the Rhine. At Poitiers a Frankish army led by Charles Martel

hurled back the Moslem advance and brought it to a standstill. By 800 AD the grandson of Charles Martel, Charlemagne, had expanded the Frankish kingdom into an empire including most of civilized Western Europe, and on Christmas day of that year, he was crowned Emperor by Pope Leo III. Though the empire of Charlemagne was to disintegrate after his death, it was in part revived as the Holy Roman Empire, and even those areas of Europe which remained independent shared a unity in the general concept of Christendom that they had not known before the Frankish consolidation.

The menace of the Northmen ended as suddenly as it had begun. Having found homes in Western Europe and Russia, these invaders soon blended with the peoples whose land they had penetrated. At the same time the Slavs were settling down more or less peaceably in the Marches of the East. Here they were to serve as a barrier to the westward advance of the Mongols, who in the 13th century overran Russia and penetrated into Poland and Hungary. The Moslems continued to pick at the frontiers of Christendom, while their fleets turned the Mediterranean into a cockpit of raid and reprisal, piracy and counter-piracy.

By the 11th century, Europe was ready to strike back at its last besieger. It had now at least a tenuous unity, and its strong agricultural base and increasing manpower began to tell over the Moslems, who for the most part were meagerly based on desert, steppe, and oasis land. In 1035 Normans took southern Italy and Sicily from the Arabs and beat back their fleets in the central Mediterranean. At the same time Genoa and Pisa drove the Moslems from Sardinia, and in 1087 they sacked Tunis. With Italy, Sardinia, and Sicily under Christian control and with Christian navies dominating the central and western Mediterranean, Moslem sea power had passed its first peak.

The great Crusading movements which occupied Europe from the end of the 11th to the middle of the 13th century were a continuation of the western offensive against Islam. Taken as a whole, the Crusades may be considered a series of religio-commercial amphibious operations in which the resurgent West struggled to break Islamic control of the Christian Holy Places—as well as Moslem control of Mediterranean commerce. Led by northern warrior-aristocrats, carried in commercial shipping, and escorted by war fleets of the Italian cities, they fired Western imagination for 250 years. They were responsible for the prodigious growth of the Italian commercial cities, from which trade and industry had never quite disappeared. In the south, Amalfi, Bari, Naples, Salerno, and Taranto early re-established themselves as commercial centers. With the development of markets beyond the Alps, northern Pisa, Genoa, and Venice gradually overshadowed their southern rivals.

PERIOD OF INLAND SEAS, RIVERS, AND COASTS

In proportion as the threats from outside diminished, Western Europe broke from its confines and again appeared upon the seas. Centers of seaborne trade began to flourish on the coasts and navigable rivers.

As in ancient times, the area of greatest commercial activity was the Mediterranean; indeed, even in the darkest days of the siege of Europe, waterborne commerce in this area had not entirely died out. Stimulated by the Crusades, as we have seen, the Italian city-states gradually took over the bulk of the carrying trade between East and West, picking up spices and fine goods at the termini of the Oriental caravan routes in the Middle East and transporting them to the coastal cities of southern and western Europe.

Venice was especially fortunate in her central position, between north and south as well as between east and west. Situated at the head of the Adriatic, her merchants had ready access to the passes of the Alps as well as to the sea. During the Crusades the Venetians profited handsomely by keeping a foot in both the Christian and the Moslem camps—alternately hiring out their ships to the Crusaders and then coming to terms with the Arabs to obtain commercial advantages in the East-West trade. As a result of the sack of Con-

stantinople by the Fourth Crusade, Venice gained control of Crete, which sat athwart the principal arteries of Mediterranean commerce. Subsequently she increased her control over the sea routes by annexing Cyprus. The Great Arsenal of Venice, a sort of assembly-line shipbuilding yard, provided the fleets of galleys whereby she enforced her monopoly, particularly over Genoa, her principal rival for maritime supremacy. By the year 1400, when Venice was at the height of her power and grandeur, she had 3,000 ships and 38,000 seamen out of a population of 200,000.

From Venice and other Italian cities, goods of the Orient and the Mediterranean were transported over the passes of the Alps and down the rivers of Germany. Here commercial cities sprang up to distribute the merchandise to all the north country. The merchant guilds of these cities (Cologne, Hamburg, Bremen, Lübeck, Danzig, and some 70 others) pooled their resources to maintain their independence and to open the eastern Baltic. From this early association developed commercial combinations which by 1200 had merged into the Hanse, or Hanseatic League, of north German cities. The Hanse dominated north and west European economic development for more than two centuries, even joining in a successful naval war against Denmark to protect its commercial interests. Its chief aim was encouraging and protecting trade, to which end the Hanse adopted a code of maritime law, supplied capital and management for new enterprises, built lighthouses, set up systems of piloting and buoyage, and worked out improvements in ship construction. During the period of Hanseatic dominance, the Baltic and North Seas together became a sort of Mediterranean of the North, serving to link together the adjacent areas intellectually as well as commercially. By 1400 the Hanse, like Venice, was at the height of its power and prestige. Thereafter the cities both of Italy and of Germany went into a slow decline.

Venice, along with the other Italian cities, fell into economic distress with the rise of the Ottoman Empire. Political and religious feuds among the Arabs had opened the way for the Ottoman Turks, coming down out of the hills of central Asia, to take over the Arab world and its religion. Unlike their predecessors, the Turks were little interested in commerce, preferring the quick rewards of raid, piracy, and pillage. By the end of the 15th century they had conquered Constantinople, occupied the Balkans, and nearly dominated the Mediterranean from their bases in North Africa and the Middle East. No shore and no fleet was safe from their attacks.

The decline of the Mediterranean trade also cut sharply into the prosperity of the north German cities. On top of this, consolidation of an isolationist Russian state deprived the Hanse of its river routes to the East via the Black Sea. Then one by one the cities lost their freedom and commercial solidarity as they fell under the domination of German princes with little interest in trade.

The most damaging blow to the commerce and hence to the wealth and prestige of both the Italian and German cities came however from the great voyages of discovery which radically shifted the main trade routes of western Europe and turned the Mediterranean and Baltic seas into backwaters.

THE GREAT VOYAGES OF EXPLORATION AND DISCOVERY

The consolidating forces of European civilization had at length reached the ocean front. Rising commercial interests along the Atlantic seaboard not unnaturally looked with some envy upon the Italian and German monopoly of the rich trade from the Orient. The cottons, spices, dyes, perfumes, and jewels of the East found a ready market in Europe, although the cost of transport by caravan from the Persian Gulf or the Red Sea to the Mediterranean caused prices to quadruple in transit. When the rise of the Ottoman Empire threatened to cut off this trade, Europeans began to consider old legends and quasi-historical accounts of unbroken water routes to the East.

Herodotus had related, with some show of disbelief, how the Phoenicians of the 7th century BC circumnavigated Africa; and the ancient mathematicians had not only established that the world was spherical but had estimated its circumference with reasonable accuracy. With the Renaissance and its classical learning came a renewed interest in geography, replacing the imaginative and highly inaccurate theories held during medieval times by practically everyone except scholars. The invention of movable type in the 15th century made the writings of the ancients available to educated men everywhere, so that there developed a growing body of opinion that ships sailing from Europe could reach Asia either around Africa or across the unknown sea which washed the shores of Western Europe. No one of course guessed that yet undiscovered continents intervened to the westward between Europe and Asia.

The means were at hand, for though the sailing ships of the 15th century were slow and crank, they were reasonably seaworthy, and the art of navigation had so far progressed that mariners were no longer obliged to hug the coasts. For one thing, the compass had been brought to Europe by the Crusaders, who got it from the Arabs, who earlier had learned about it from the Chinese. This gave the seafarer his approximate direction in any sort of weather, and he had learned to measure his approximate speed by observing the time it took his ship to pass a bubble or a bit of flotsam—for the log-line had not yet been invented. Using these two factors he was able to find his way reasonably well by dead reckoning.

The ancients had known how to find latitude by measuring the altitude angle of the sun or the pole star above the horizon, but their methods were of little use at sea. The principal instruments for determining latitude in the 15th century were the astrolabe, a metal disk marked off in degrees with an arm pivoted at the center and containing peephole sights at each end; the quadrant, a quarter disk similarly marked and carrying fixed peepholes and a plumb line; and the cross-staff, with one or more crossbars, one end of which the observer lined up with the horizon and the other with a celestial body. But all such instruments required a steady platform and some slight knowledge of mathematics. Since the sea-tossed mariner rarely had either, the determining of latitude was usually performed on land by mathematicians, if at all. Even the learned Vasco da Gama went ashore and hung his astrolabe on a tree when he wanted to take the altitude of the sun. The 15th century sailor had of course no dependable means of reckoning longitude, for he had no sure way of measuring time. Indeed, the only possible method in those days was by timing an eclipse of the sun or the moon.[1] Later, a cumbrous method was devised for using the moon as a celestial clock by measuring its angular distance from certain fixed stars; but no really practical method for determining longitude was available until the late 1700's when John Harrison of England, Pierre Le Roy of France, and Ferdinand Berthoud of Switzerland at last developed accurate chronometers.

At the beginning of the 15th century, Portugal, isolated and out of the main stream of growing European prosperity, was only one of the several states occupying the Iberian Peninsula. It was this little out-of-the-way country however which took the lead in fostering voyages of exploration. She thereby established the first great colonial empire and a claim to half the world's seas. The impetus came from the third son of King John, Prince Henry the Navigator (1394-1460), whose imagination was fired when at the age of 21 he took part in the amphibious conquest of the Moorish trading center of Ceuta, in North Africa opposite Gibraltar. At Ceuta he saw richly laden caravans from distant parts of Africa and learned of realms wealthy beyond anything he had seen in Europe. Thenceforth he worked to establish an African empire for the extension of Christianity and the prosperity of Portugal.

Realizing that his only chance for achieving his aim was to outflank the Moors by way of the sea, Prince Henry established a naval

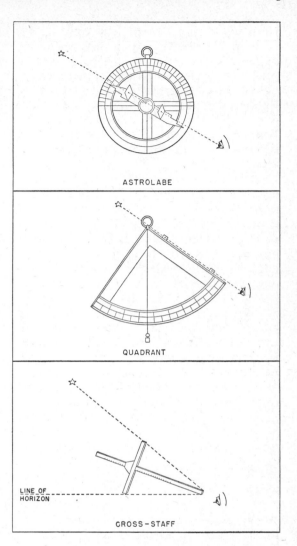

ASTROLABE

QUADRANT

LINE OF HORIZON

CROSS-STAFF

LATE MEDIEVAL INSTRUMENTS FOR FINDING LATITUDE AT SEA

college at Saigres near Cape St. Vincent and there gathered around him the leading cartographers, naval architects, and navigators of Europe. At the college, maps and travelers' records were studied and corrected, navigation instruments and tables were improved, and new types of sailing ships were developed, notably the light, broad-beamed caravel. From the nearby port of Lagos Prince Henry began sending out expeditions to explore the seas and to descend the coast of Africa. By 1450 Henry's explorers had dis-

---

[1] The mathematicians of Mexico City, working diligently and applying all their lore, made an all-out effort in 1541 to reckon their longitude by timing two lunar eclipses. They missed by 1,450 miles.

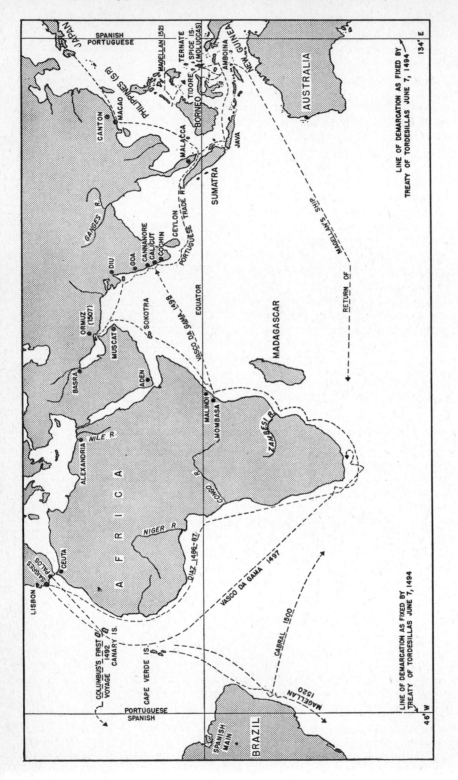

EARLY VOYAGES OF DISCOVERY and the PORTUGUESE TRADE EMPIRE

covered or rediscovered Madeira and the Azores and claimed them for Portugal, and at the time of his death they had rounded the westward bulge of Africa and captured black men, thereby re-establishing the old African slave trade.

For a generation after Prince Henry's death the Portuguese neglected exploration in favor of capitalizing on their discoveries by trading in the gold, ivory, and slaves of Africa. But King John II, who understood the importance of Henry's work, sent Pedro de Covilham via Cairo to the Indian Ocean to learn the source of the Venetian spice trade and Bartolomeo Diaz to seek a sea route around Africa. Although Diaz, beset by food shortage, mutiny, and foul weather, did not reach the Indian Ocean, he did round the Cape of Good Hope in 1487 and ascertained that he had reached the southernmost point of the continent. Pooling the findings of these two expeditions, the Portuguese were convinced that they could reach India around Africa.

There had been at Lisbon for several years a young Genoese mariner and chartmaker, Christopher Columbus, who had been pushing by every means at his command a project for reaching Japan and China by sailing to westward. King John had blown hot and cold on the matter until at length Columbus went in disgust to Spain, but here he had no better luck than in Portugal. He was back in Lisbon when Diaz returned from the Cape of Good Hope. Now that the way to India via South Africa had been discovered, the Portuguese king lost all interest in Columbus and his proposals. Back in Spain, Columbus cooled his heels at court three more years without getting a definite commitment from their sovereign majesties Ferdinand and Isabella. He was actually on his way to France to put his project before King Charles VIII, when Isabella called him back and granted him the three caravels and other equipment he needed for his westward voyage into the unknown.

Departing from Palos August 3, 1492, Columbus sailed down the African coast to the Canaries in order to reach, as he supposed, the latitude of Japan. He then sailed west-ward with the trade wind at his back and on October 12, seventy days and 2,600 miles later, touched at San Salvador in the Bahamas, far west of the longitude where he had expected to find the Asiatic coast. In this and three subsequent voyages Columbus discovered most of the West Indies and the coasts of Central and South America but died convinced that he had reached Asia.

By a papal bull of May 1493, reinforced and somewhat altered the following year by the Treaty of Tordesillas, Spain and Portugal fixed the line of demarcation between their areas of interest at 100 leagues west of the Cape Verde Islands. All discoveries made or to be made west of this line were to belong to Spain; all to the east were to belong to Portugal. On the basis of this agreement Portugal was to lay claim to the East Indies, India, and most of Africa; and Spain would claim the New World and the seas and lands beyond.

Columbus' discoveries spurred the Portuguese to continue searching the possibilities of circumnavigating Africa. In 1497 Vasco da Gama set out from Lisbon to complete the work of earlier Portuguese explorers. From the Cape Verdes he steered straight for the Cape of Good Hope, completing the 4,500-mile voyage in a hundred days. After hugging the east coast of Africa as far north as modern Kenya, da Gama engaged an Arab pilot who guided his little fleet across the Indian Ocean to Calicut, India. Here he received a poor welcome from Moslem traders, who recognized the imminent danger to their commercial monopoly. At Cannanore, farther to the north, however, he was permitted to engage in trade, and so returned home with a cargo valued at 50 times the expense of his voyage.

Both Portugal and Spain now set about turning their discoveries into profit.

In 1500 the Portuguese Pedro Alvares Cabral, following the route of da Gama, was blown westerly by the Atlantic trade winds and touched the eastern tip of Brazil, thereby establishing for the first time that a bit of America lay east of the Tordesillas line and hence belonged to Portugal. On reaching the Indian Ocean, Cabral like da Gama traded successfully, this time with Ceylon, and made fabulous profits for his king. In 1505 Francisco de Almeida went to the East with 16 ships and 16 caravels as "Viceroy of the Indies," with supreme authority from the Cape to the Malay Peninsula in the name of the King of Portugal. What he could not get by diplomacy he took with the sword, easily defeating the Arab traders in a series of naval engagements culminating in the decisive battle of Diu in 1509, which established Portuguese command of the Indian Ocean. Almeida's successor, Alfonso de Albuquerque (1509-1515), consolidated the Portuguese empire in the Indies by setting up headquarters at Goa in India and capturing Malacca on the Malay Peninsula and Ormuz at the mouth of the Persian Gulf. Operating from these points, he could control traffic all the way from the China Sea to the coast of Africa. The Viceroys, mere commercial agents for all their high-sounding title, made no attempt to take over the government of any entire country and planted no permanent colonies. There were, after all, fewer than two million Portuguese, and the Orient was already densely populated. What they did, rather, was to establish a commercial empire by setting up trading posts and bases all the way from Mombasa in East Africa to Yokohama in Japan. Europe had outflanked Islam. It had taken its foe in the rear, circumventing the land by way of the sea, as Xerxes, Alexander, and the early Crusaders had outflanked the sea by way of the land.

Spain was also pushing her explorations farther and at the same time exploiting her new possessions. She promptly colonized Haiti, Cuba, Puerto Rico, and Jamaica—all discovered by Columbus—establishing profitable plantations and setting up advanced bases for exploring North, Central, and South America. Advancing overland from a Spanish colony on the Isthmus of Darien (Panama), Balboa in 1513 discovered the Pacific Ocean. The conquest of Mexico (1519-1521) by Hernando Cortes and of Peru (1531-1532) by Francisco Pizarro opened up to Spain wealth accumulated over the centuries by the Indian civilizations; and the working of American gold and silver mines, which remained crown

property, assured such an influx of bullion that the far less productive silver mines of Europe were abandoned. In 1523 the first "plate fleet," bearing precious metal, set out from Mexico to Spain, and thereafter others of increasing value crossed the Atlantic year after year. Meanwhile, Ferdinand Magellan, a Portuguese mariner sailing for Spain, in 1520 entered the Pacific through the straits now bearing his name. Despite the ravages of disease and shortage of food and water he pushed on, claiming the Marianas and the Philippines for Spain. Though Magellan and most of his expedition lost their lives, one of his five ships with 18 survivors reached Spain late in 1522, having circumnavigated the globe. From bases in the West Indies the Spaniards surveyed the Atlantic coast from Labrador to the Gulf of Mexico, and Hernando de Soto explored Florida and the lower Mississippi Valley. From Mexico City expeditions surveyed the Pacific coast as far north as Oregon, and Francisco Coronado explored western North America. From Mexico sailed expeditions to survey and occupy the Philippines. Peru was the point of departure for explorations into Chile and Colombia and of Spanish ships which discovered the Solomon, the Marquesas, and the New Hebrides island groups.

In defiance of the papal bull and the Treaty of Tordesillas, English adventurers, following the lead of John Cabot in 1497, explored the Atlantic coast of North America; and Frenchmen under Jacques Cartier and others explored the St. Lawrence basin —thereby establishing claims upon which future empires were to be based. But all that came later, for England was still mainly an agricultural nation which had not yet conceived that its future lay upon the seas; and the French in the 16th century, along with the Dutch, were more interested in using the route around Africa to purloin a bit of the Portuguese spice trade with the Indies.

The hardy adventurers and explorers of the 15th and 16th centuries had at long last joined the East and the West by cheap, practical sea routes and had opened up a new world for European expansion. Prolific and industrious, operating from one of the world's most productive bases, the people of Western Europe after centuries of being hemmed in were on their way toward dominating almost the entire world by use of the world's seas. The Oceanic Age was launched; a new cycle of sea power was about to begin.

THE FIGHT FOR THE MEDITERRANEAN

The decline of the Mediterranean as a route for commerce did not lessen the alarm of the Christian princes at the growing control exercised by the Ottoman Turks. Spain was no less perturbed than Venice, for by the inheritance of King Ferdinand the Spanish dominions included southern Italy and Sicily (which together formed the Kingdom of Naples, or the Two Sicilies), and Sardinia. Her fleet and army captured points along the North African shore in an attempt to suppress Turkish piracy and to protect her extensive Mediterranean coasts.

For a while the disjointed efforts of Spain, Venice, and the other enemies of the Turk were given some degree of coordination by the Papacy, which had maintained a policy of opposition to the Moslems since the preaching of the First Crusade by Pope Urban in 1097. Further co-ordination was achieved when Charles of Hapsburg united a great part of Europe under a single crown. Born in Ghent in 1500, Charles inherited the throne of the Netherlands from his father in 1506, and ten years later he became also King Charles I of Spain on the death of his grandfather Ferdinand. In 1519 the death of his grandfather Maximilian gave him the Hapsburg territories, which comprised Austria and parts of Germany and Italy. The next year he out-bribed Henry VIII of England and Francis I of France to win the imperial election as Charles V, Emperor of the Holy Roman Empire, thereby bringing the rest of Germany into his domains. He thus commanded the wealth of America and controlled more of Western Europe than any man since the greatest days of Rome. As Emperor he was the traditional defender of Christendom, and as king of Spain and Na-

ples he was deeply concerned with regaining Christian ascendancy in the Mediterranean. In both capacities it was his duty to stop the Turk, a task made no easier by the fact that his reign coincided with that of Suleiman the Magnificent, ablest of the Turkish Sultans.

Pushing into central Europe, the Turks surged forward to the gates of Vienna, whence they were repulsed in 1529 by the mere threat of Charles's army. In the Mediterranean the Emperor was obliged to take active measures, for here the Sultan was ably represented by Barbarossa, who rose through piratical warfare to the throne of Algiers and supreme command of the Turkish fleet. It was Barbarossa who is reported to have said to Suleiman at their first meeting, "Sire, he who is master of the sea will very shortly become master on the land," a comment which might have won the assent of Mahan if not of Mackinder. The same year that the Sultan's European army faltered before Vienna, Barbarossa expelled the Spaniards from their last foothold in Algiers and then went on to capture Tunis. At this point Charles intervened. With a Genoese admiral, Andrea Doria, commanding his Spanish fleet, he recaptured Tunis by amphibious assault and placed a native ruler on the throne as a vassal to Spain.

Three years later Doria took the combined fleets of Spain and Venice—briefly and uneasily in alliance—to blockade Barbarossa's fleet, then lying at Prevesa on the west coast of Greece. Doria's fleet as it stood off Prevesa included 166 galleys and 64 sailing ships; largest of the latter was the *Galleon of Venice*, a high sided, deep-draft vessel armed with numerous guns. Barbarossa, though commanding a fleet of only 122 galleys, accepted the challenge and came out to give battle. The Turkish admiral had selected his time well, for the *Galleon of Venice* that day lay becalmed, 20 miles away from the rest of the Christian fleet. Seizing his opportunity Barbarossa closed in on the great galleon. At point blank range the Venetians opened fire with guns and small arms, causing heavy slaughter among the Turks. While Doria maneuvered uselessly ten miles to the south, the Turks attacked the *Galleon of Venice* all afternoon with increasing caution, and though they wrecked her deck structures and killed 13 and wounded 40 of her complement, they were obliged to withdraw at nightfall without a victory.

Here was clear evidence that in ordinary circumstances neither sailing ships nor galleys could win a decision when pitched against each other. The well-armed sailing ship was too strong defensively to be defeated by oar-driven craft, which had little space for guns; yet she lacked speed and maneuverability to operate offensively against galleys, for the galleys could always retire upwind out of her reach. When the sailing ship, with the modest spread of canvas then used, had wind enough to maneuver successfully, the water was generally too choppy for the fragile galleys to operate at all. Faced with a choice, the Mediterranean powers clung to the oar-driven warship long after it had disappeared from other waters.

Though the *Galleon of Venice* had magnificently survived attack by a whole Turkish fleet, the Venetians were bitter over Doria's conduct in not coming actively to her support. Distrustful of the Spaniards and distrusted in return, Venice broke the alliance and came to terms with the Turks, paying an annual tribute for meager trading privileges and freedom from piratical attack. For the next 30 years the Turks steadily tightened their control over the Mediterranean basin. Not until both Charles V and Suleiman the Magnificent were dead did the Christian powers again unite on the sea against the menace.

An attack on Cyprus in 1570 by Suleiman's son and successor, Selim "the Drunkard," led to the next combined naval action against the Turks. Though Selim's counselors advised him against such a move, pointing out that the mutual interests and common enemies of Venice and Turkey made them natural allies, the Sultan ordered his forces to invade the island and lay siege to its cities. Venice, lacking strength to fight the Turk alone, applied to her Christian neighbors for help, but her appeals fell on deaf ears. She found at last that her callous drive for wealth, in which she more than once served

the infidel cause for her own advantage, had left her friendless.

Help came for Venice from a quarter where she had least expected it. Though the Venetians had frequently defied papal authority, Pope Pius V called upon the Christian powers to forget their differences and take action against this new surge of Turkish aggression. Spain, more interested in protecting her interests in the western Mediterranean than in risking warships in distant operations, reluctantly joined forces with Venice and the Papal States. While the combined fleet was en route by easy stages toward Cyprus late in 1570, word came of the fall of Nicosia, the Cyprian capital. At this the Christian forces, already at odds among themselves for want of unified command, broke up for the winter. Sultan Selim offered peace terms to the dispirited Venetians, who might have accepted but for the crusading zeal of Pius V. The following spring the Pope succeeded in binding Spain and the Italian states together in a Holy League. Once more the Christian fleet began to assemble.

Meanwhile Famagusta, the main port of Cyprus, had surrendered to the Turks after a long siege. Assured of his conquest of Cyprus, Selim ordered his fleet, 250 galleys and galliots (smaller galleys) under Ali Pasha, to advance into Italian waters to lure out and destroy the Christian fleet. Ali thereupon rounded the Greek peninsula and entered the Adriatic, raiding the east coast and threatening Venice but avoiding the Spanish domains in Italy lest he thereby impel the Spaniards into firmer partnership with the Venetians. After harrying the Christian island base of Corfu, Ali fell back upon his own base within the Gulf of Lepanto (or Corinth) to revictual and replace casualties.

The Christian fleet, assembled at Messina, was weaker than the Turkish in numbers of ships and men but considerably stronger in firepower. Included were more than 200 galleys, mostly Venetian and Spanish, with a few from the Pope and from Genoa, Savoy, and Malta. They were long, slim, and flat-bottomed like the galleys of ancient Greece and Rome but carried an 18-foot spur above the water line in place of the classic underwater ram. While the Turks still clung to the bow and arrow, many of the Christian soldiers aboard were armed with the arquebus or hackbut, precursor of the musket. While the Turks carried only three guns at the bow, the Christians carried five—a heavy gun at the center line firing a 36-pound shot, flanked by two 9-pounders and a pair of 4½-pounders. The Holy League galleys for the most part also mounted smaller guns along the sides to repel boarders. In addition to the galleys, the Venetians also brought along six galleasses—heavy, sluggish vessels with a deck above the oarsmen and carrying up to 30 guns, mostly in broadside. Lastly there was a fleet train of 24 nefs, sailing vessels without oars, for carrying supplies. The total complement of the Christian fleet must have numbered at least 44,000 seamen, including rowers. In addition, there were about 28,000 soldiers aboard, some two-thirds of whom were supplied by Spain.[2]

The inevitable suspicion and cross-purposes of distrustful allies was somewhat mitigated by the choice of Don John of Austria as Commander in Chief. Don John, son of Charles V and half brother of Philip II of Spain, was at the age of 24 an experienced campaigner on land and sea. Fired with zeal for the Christian cause, he aroused general enthusiasm among most of his followers but caused his senior commanders some uneasiness lest he act rashly against the wily Turk.

In mid-September the ships of the Holy League set out from Messina, a special envoy from the Pope blessing each as it put out to sea. After crossing over to the coast of Greece, the armada worked its way south—with galleys towing the galleasses, which could make no respectable speed with oars, sails, or both. Early in the morning of October 17, 1571, the Christians rounded Point Scropha and entered the Gulf of Patras. Almost at once lookouts sighted Ali Pasha's fleet approaching from the east, for the Turks had decided to fight in open water. Even at this late hour

some of Don John's Spanish counselors advised him to retire. To this the young commander resolutely replied, "It is too late for counsel; it is now time for battle."[3]

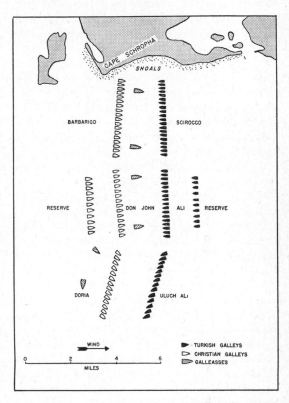

BATTLE OF LEPANTO, OCTOBER 7, 1571

The Battle of Lepanto is especially significant as the last of the great galley actions. As in the Battle of Actium, fought 16 centuries before only a few miles north of the scene of Lepanto, the ships of the opposing fleets were in three squadrons abreast. Both Turks and Christians held an additional squadron in reserve to the rear. Don John made an innovation in the ancient battle plan by placing the four galleasses which arrived on time ahead of his squadrons of galleys. When the Turks advanced to attack, they were obliged to sweep around these heavy fortress

---

[2] One of these Spanish soldiers was Miguel de Cervantes Saavedra, who commanded a squad of 12 men in one of the Genoese galleys. Cervantes lost his left hand in the Battle of Lepanto; with the right he later composed the immortal *Don Quixote*.

[3] Vice Admiral William L. Rodgers USN, *Naval Warfare under Oars, 4th to 16th Centuries* (Annapolis, 1939), 190.

ships, taking heavy losses from their broadside guns and falling into some confusion.

As the opposing lines came together each galley fired its bow guns two or three times. These guns were rarely used thereafter for they could be fired only dead ahead and hence had to be aimed with the helm. In this exchange of fire the Turks almost certainly had the worst of it, for the Christians were protected by an armor belt of thick planking about the bows and sides of their galleys and the Turks were not. After the opening shots the battle became, as always in galley warfare, a matter of grappling and boarding and fighting across decks.

In the center squadrons the hottest fighting was between the opposing flagships, or royals, and their supporters. Three times the Turks entered Don John's royal, and each time they were driven back as additional Christian soldiers came aboard the flagship from the reserve or from adjoining vessels. At length the Christians succeeded in severely crippling Ali Pasha's royal by ramming. Then Italians and Spaniards, including Don John himself, poured aboard the Turkish flagship and took possession, killing Ali and all his crew.

The Turks of the right squadron, under Scirocco, attempted to outflank the Christian left by putting in close to the shore, exploiting their superior knowledge of the shallows; but Barbarigo, the Christian squadron commander, concluding that where there was enough water for Turks there was enough for Christians, also closed the beach. At the same time Barbarigo's right wing, taking advantage of the Turkish shift to shoreward, enveloped Scirocco's left. The Turks, thus surrounded and forced against the coast, were defeated in an hour of fierce fighting, but many survivors escaped through the shallows to the shore.

A flanking attempt by Uluch Ali, commanding the Turkish left squadron, came nearer to success. To avoid being enveloped, Gian Andrea Doria, grandnephew of the Doria of Prevesa, swung south, thereby leaving a gap between his squadron and the Christian center squadron. Uluch Ali, seeing his opportunity, suddenly changed course and headed for the opening in order to out-

flank and roll up the Christian line. A little earlier the ruse might have succeeded, but by now Don John's center and reserve were so near to victory that they could release vessels to block the opening and force Uluch Ali into retreat.

When the battle ended late in the afternoon, the Gulf was red with blood and the Christians were unqualified victors. According to contemporary Christian accounts, possibly exaggerated, 30,000 Turks lost their lives and all but about 60 of their ships were captured or destroyed. The Christian losses were 12 ships and 7,700 men.

The Christians by their overwhelming victory had won a certain moral ascendancy in that their dread of the Turk was never again so great as it had been, and the Turks thereafter operated with greater prudence and discretion. But Lepanto by no means won control of the Mediterranean for the Christian states. By straining its resources the Ottoman Empire was able the next summer to put a fleet of 200 galleys to sea under Uluch Ali. In the ensuing campaign the Turks and Christians, though not lacking opportunity, never came to grips.[4] The following year Venice, disappointed at the static situation, distrustful of Spanish motives, and suffering from lack of trade, made a separate peace with Turkey in which she surrendered Cyprus and resumed payment of tribute for commercial privileges.

Though the Turks and their subsidiary states of North Africa never again threatened to dominate the Mediterranean, the "Barbary system" of piratical excursions and payment of tribute and ransom by Christian powers continued for centuries. Even when certain European states developed navies powerful enough to put an end to the nuisance, they willingly tolerated the corsairs for the damage they could do to their weaker commercial rivals. The United States was to pay tribute and become involved in two naval wars with the Barbary powers before Europe, at the

---

[4] In maneuvers that never quite produced a battle, the Christian fleet learned at last that sailing ships and galleys could no more operate successfully together than they could achieve a decision in combat against each other.

end of the Napoleonic wars, decided to crush the system forever.

SEA POWER IN THE ATLANTIC

Despite the early example of the oar-propelled Viking ships, galley warfare did not develop among the powers bordering the Atlantic coast of Europe. Probably the main reason was that the long swells of the Atlantic had a nasty way of capsizing the slim, shallow-draft galley. Another was the difficulty of finding oarsmen. Life in the rowing benches was about as near to hell on earth as anyone could devise. Certainly no man would choose such a profession of his own free will. Where we find freemen at the oars, as among the Greeks at the Battle of Salamis, it was for a brief period while the homeland was in imminent peril. A regular galley fleet had to rely upon slaves and convicts for motive power. In the Mediterranean, slaves were easily come by—captured Christians for the Moslem fleets; captured Moslems for the Christian fleets. But along the Atlantic seaboard one's captives in war were one's fellow Christians and not to be degraded by being chained to the rowing benches. Lastly, the king of England and his royal neighbors were necessarily frugal men who in the earlier days felt that they could not afford specially designed fighting ships. The cargo vessel—the crank, broad-beamed Round Ship—had to serve as warship when needed. The English king had a standing arrangement with his merchants to supply ships for fighting when called upon.

Tactics were of course out of the question with such unmaneuverable craft as Round Ships. When there was a fight at sea it was every ship for itself, and the usual method was grappling and boarding, with the defeated crew being tossed overboard to drown. Weapons, besides the usual grappling irons, pikes, swords, bows and arrows, and later, guns, included such materials as quicklime to throw in the adversary's eyes, soft soap to make the decks slippery, and pointed bits of metal scattered about for the enemy to fall

upon. The first real refinement consisted of the erection of temporary towers fore and aft, called forecastles and after- (or somer-) castles, to achieve the advantage of height. If the enemy succeeded in boarding and entering, the defenders simply withdrew from the waist of the ship into the towers. From these they rained down arrows, stones, or hot pitch, making things exceedingly unpleasant for the boarders. From the towers too, heavy stones could sometimes be dropped upon the enemy in ships alongside. The towers, or castles, proved so useful that in due course the merchant owners had them built permanently into new construction, for one never knew when he might have to deal with pirates or other raiders. By the middle of the 15th century raised structures at bow and stern had become a regular feature of ships in the north.

The introduction of the gun brought about considerable strengthening and enlargement of the castles. The guns were originally placed here because, like all the weapons that had gone before, they were aimed at men and not at ships—indeed, the early naval guns were much too small and feeble to do any important damage to ships even at close range. Guns were received with some trepidation by seamen, for their recoil was difficult to check and they had a bad habit of blowing up, especially during the period before breech loading was given up as hopeless. The only really safe method of attaching the breech to the barrel was by screwing the one onto the other, but then the heat of the explosion so expanded the threads that the breech could not be unscrewed until it had cooled off. Hence, at sea, where delay in firing could easily prove disastrous, the screwed-on breech was never even tried. Not for centuries would anyone hit upon the simple device of the screw with an interrupted thread, which permitted the breech to be engaged and disengaged by a quarter turn or less. Meanwhile the muzzle loader, with a touchhole in the breech to ignite the charge, became universal.

When peace was restored at last in England following the Hundred Years' War and the long-drawn-out civil Wars of the Roses, the nation began to prosper to the extent that King Henry VIII was able to build a few ships of his own, intended exclusively for fighting. His first battleships were huge, high-towered Great Ships such as the *Henry Grâce à Dieu* or, as she was generally called, the *Great Harry*. But the *Harry* was already obsolescent when she was built, for the big guns which became possible with the general acceptance of muzzle loading made ships top-heavy when they were mounted in the towers. Puzzling over the problem, Henry's carpenters cut gunports in the sides and mounted most of the guns in the waist. Thus the first broadsides came into being. When Lord Lyle after an action off Shoreham in 1545 reported to Henry that the broadsides had proved ship destroyers and not man killers only, he was announcing a new sort of warfare. The days of grappling and boarding were numbered. For centuries to come, the ship-destroying gun was to rule the seas.

With the introduction of guns in broadside and King Henry's decision that he would have a fighting fleet apart from the merchant marine, England forged ahead of all other nations in warship design. Down came the high fore- and aftercastles,[5] length increased relative to beam, and lighter ships were built specifically as gun platforms, with comparatively low freeboard. When Henry's daughter Elizabeth came to the throne in 1558, flush-decked, low-freeboard ships of three or more beams' length had become standard in the English navy, though a certain proportion of Great Ships continued to be built, partly because not everyone was convinced that the day of grappling and boarding was over and partly to overawe the enemy by sheer size. The Spanish, by way of contrast, adhered almost exclusively to the Great Ship for operations in the Atlantic. When they sought to improve maneuverability they went to the Long Ship or galley for their model instead of the Round Ship, and built galleasses. These however lacked strength to contend with the northern seas or with the strain of firing guns in broadside. Moreover, there always remained the problem of whether to place the guns above the rowing deck and accept a top-heavy vessel or to place them below and have their line of fire fouled by oars.

By the time of the Anglo-Spanish War, late in the reign of Queen Elizabeth I, English warships had adopted a rough line-ahead formation so as to avoid masking each other's fire, and they made a practice of seeking the windward position in order to have the initiative in attack. All fighting was to be done with the guns, and boarding and entering was forbidden except in unusual circumstances. By this time standard ordnance in the English navy was the culverin, a long gun of 28 to 34 calibers[6] firing a ball weighing 17 or 18 pounds, with ranges up to 1¼ miles, and even more by ricochet.

Thus by the latter part of the 16th century England had outdistanced all possible rivals in ship construction, naval ordnance, and tactical doctrine at sea. Though her navy still had much to learn, and would at times fall into serious neglect, it was basically the instrument by which England was to become Mistress of the Seas and ruler of the most far-flung empire in history.

THE SPANISH ARMADA AGAINST ENGLAND

When Charles V, Emperor of the Holy Roman Empire, laid down the heavy burden of his responsibilities in 1556, he divided his realms between his brother Ferdinand and his son Philip. The German and Austrian possessions of the Hapsburgs he gave to Ferdinand, who was chosen to succeed his brother as Emperor. To Philip went the Netherlands, Franche-Comté, Milan, the Kingdom of Naples, Spanish holdings in North Africa, America, the West Indies, and the Philippines, and above all Spain itself, where he was born and bred, and which he was to rule as Philip II. In 1580, by inheritance, bribery, and military pressure, he added Portugal to his domains, thereby unifying the Iberian Peninsula and acquiring a claim through the

---

[5] A vestige of the aftercastle was retained or restored as the raised quarter-deck, useful for observation and command.

[6] Caliber: ratio of the length of the bore to its diameter.

Treaty of Tordesillas to the entire heathen world.

Besides his national and imperial responsibilities, Philip II took very seriously his position as monarch of the most powerful Catholic nation, regarding himself as principal champion and defender of the Church of Rome. At the Pope's request, as we have seen, he sent the cream of his troops and his galley fleet along with the Italian and Maltese forces in the crusade against the Turks which culminated in the Battle of Lepanto in 1571. To Philip, the rising Protestantism of northern Europe was as detestable as anti-Christian Islam. When England more and more assumed leadership of the Protestant world, Philip began to consider the necessity of dispatching a fleet and army northward to dethrone the English monarch and return England to the Catholic Church.

The disaffection between Spain and England began in 1533 when Henry VIII divorced Catherine of Aragon, aunt of Charles V. Two years later Henry disavowed the Pope's authority and assumed the primacy of the church in his own country. At this, the Emperor and Francis I of France joined in protestations of horror and threatened an attack on England blessed by the Pope and backed by the sentiment of most of Europe. But mutual distrust between Charles and Francis and the readiness of the English to support their king brought the crusade to nought. After the death of Henry VIII and his Protestant son Edward VI, Catherine's daughter Mary Tudor reigned in England for five years, during which time the English Church was restored to papal control. Mary married her cousin Philip of Spain on the advice of his father the Emperor, who saw a chance thereby to bring England more firmly within the Catholic sphere and at the same time complete the encircling of his old enemy France with hostile powers. When Charles V abdicated, Philip left his wife and England in order to ascend the throne of Spain, but even after Mary's death he retained a shadowy claim to the English crown.

Under Elizabeth I, Mary's half-sister and successor, the English Church returned to Protestant practices and again denied the authority of Rome. For several years however neither the Pope nor Spain gave up hope of winning England back to Catholicism. Philip II even proposed marriage to the new English sovereign, and when his offer was refused, swallowed his pride and tried to interest Elizabeth in his younger brother. But Elizabeth, concluding that Philip's intentions boded England no good, allied herself instead with France in order to secure the balance of power which had been the policy of her father Henry. For 30 years she kept her hopeful suitors dangling in expectation and astutely played off Spain and France against each other without any intention of marrying or of returning to the Catholic fold. At length in 1570 Pope Pius V, despairing of converting England, excommunicated Elizabeth, branded her a heretic and usurper, and called upon the sovereigns of France and Spain to launch a crusade against her. This was the year, it will be recalled, in which Philip joined the Venetians at the Pope's behest in defense of Cyprus. However, neither he nor the King of France was ready at that time to attack England, for Elizabeth's bewildering yet ingenious diplomacy had succeeded in keeping them suspicious of each other and afraid of her. Moreover Philip had his hands full not only with the Turks but with the people of the Netherlands, who had rebelled against high taxes imposed by Spain and efforts of the Catholic Inquisition to suppress Dutch Protestantism.

Despite Elizabeth's pacifist inclinations and astute diplomacy, war was bound to come sooner or later between Spain and England. For one thing, Elizabeth enraged Philip by simply disregarding his claims to the New World and encouraging English seamen to engage in illicit trade with his overseas colonies. When Spain took countermeasures, such enterprising mariners as John Hawkins and Francis Drake sought reprisal by raiding Spanish bases and shipping. A dozen English sea raiders, considered mere pirates by the irate Spaniards, won fame and wealth through such attacks—and it was widely and correctly believed that Elizabeth shared in the booty. When Drake outperformed all the other raiders by returning from an expedition along the west coast of South America with 26 tons of silver, besides gold and precious stones, the English queen knighted him forthwith on his own quarter-deck. In 1585 Elizabeth openly authorized Drake to raid the Spanish Indies, and two years later she sent him with 23 ships to strike at the port of Cadiz, where he "singed the King of Spain's beard" by thrusting aside the galleys guarding the harbor and destroying some 18 cargo vessels. Besides at first covertly and then openly defying Philip on the seas, Elizabeth in her usual indirect manner actually went to war against him in 1585 by forming an alliance with his rebellious Dutch subjects and sending an army to Holland. If there was to be war, she considered, it was better to fight on foreign soil with the aid of an ally than alone in her own realm.

Philip, as indirect in his methods as the English sovereign, secretly conspired with the large Catholic faction in England to assassinate the heretic Elizabeth. Her death would vacate the throne in favor of her Catholic cousin Mary Stuart, Queen of Scots, whom Elizabeth had held captive since 1568, when Mary had been driven out of Scotland by the Calvinist faction. In 1584 English agents uncovered a plot against the life of Elizabeth involving the Spanish ambassador. The ambassador was promptly dismissed, and Philip disavowed the scheme by refusing to receive him on his return to Madrid. That same year however an assassin in Spanish pay struck down William the Silent, Stadtholder, or President, of the new Dutch Republic. Philip had thus issued his challenge, and Elizabeth responded early in 1587 by signing the death warrant of Mary Stuart. Philip thereupon openly claimed the crown of England and prepared for a campaign of conquest.

The Spanish king had already exchanged correspondence on the subject with the Duke of Parma, commanding the Spanish Army of Flanders against the rebellious Dutch, and with the Marquis of Santa Cruz, his Captain General of the Ocean Sea. Santa Cruz, who had adroitly led the reserve force of galleys at the Battle of Lepanto, suggested a descent upon England in overwhelming strength directly out of the ports of Spain. Philip shrank from the cost of such an enterprise however, for it would entail raising a new army, and the Dutch War had depleted his treasury. He directed instead that Parma strip his Flanders garrisons to provide most of the invasion troops. These were to invade England by crossing in flatboats from Dunkirk to Margate under cover of Spanish warships, which would fend off the English fleet. Spain's main naval force was the galley fleet that had made history at Lepanto, but Drake's 1587 raid on Cadiz made it abundantly clear that galleys were no match for the latest types of sailing ships. Even Philip had to concede that he would have to have a sailing fleet like England's if he intended to cope with England on the high seas.

So Philip piled even higher taxes on his Spaniards and other subject peoples and directed Santa Cruz to assemble an armada fit for the task at hand. From spies placed high in Elizabeth's government he obtained full data on England's ships and tactics. He adopted the broadside arrangement of guns but not the English plan of battle by long-range gunfire.[7] After all, the Spanish infantrymen were reputed to be the finest in the world. They had beaten the Turks at Lepanto by grappling and boarding; if only they could get aboard the English vessels they would certainly win another great victory for Spain. Accordingly Philip did what he could to make his fleet an efficient adjunct to the army. He fitted his ships with lofty fore- and aftercastles to give his soldiers the advantage of height, and he armed his fleet with heavy guns to cripple the English vessels so that they could not maneuver out of the Spanish reach. When Parma reported that he could raise only 17,000 amphibious troops instead of the 30,000 the King had asked for, Philip found 17,000 more soldiers to accompany the Armada and was even more determined to make any na-

---

[7] Philip's instructions to his admiral read in part: "The enemy will fight at long range to get the advantage of his artillery and artificial fires and you must close and grapple, taking them in your hand. This you must be sure to do."

val action against the English an infantry battle across decks in the Lepanto style.

In the midst of the vast preparations Santa Cruz, exhausted by overwork and mortified by the King's constant interference, took to his bed and died. To replace him, Philip chose the 38-year-old Duke of Medina-Sidonia, whose chief qualifications were that he was of the high nobility, that he had a vast fortune which he would be expected to risk in the King's enterprise, and that he had a reputation for piety and virtue. These were recommendation enough for the rank-conscious, poverty-haunted Philip, who conceived of the undertaking as first and foremost a crusade of the Church against the forces of heresy. "I kiss his Majesty's hands and feet for thinking of me for so great a task and wish I had the strength for it," replied Medina, "but I lack the necessary health and have been little at sea. I am seasick and rheumy. . . . I am sure I should do badly." On the King's insistence however he accepted the commission, saying gloomily, "May Our Lord be pleased to help the good intentions of your Majesty, and as it is His cause, I hope of His Mercy he will do so." [8]

The Armada put out of Lisbon on May 30, 1588 and worked its way up the coast of Portugal against head winds. By mid-June, when it stood off Corunna, Medina was complaining of spoiled provisions, leaking water casks, and general need of repairs. While the Captain General was debating whether to risk desertions by putting into port, a storm made his mind up for him and he entered the harbor. Because he had failed to signal his intention to the fleet, many of the ships became scattered. Most sought refuge from the heavy seas in the ports of northern Spain, but a dozen proceeded to the rendezvous near the Scilly Islands off the southwest coast of England. A month passed before the Armada was reassembled and reconditioned, and the soldiers and sailors had once more attended the wholesale masses and confessions which Philip required. At last on July 23 it was again under sail for

England. Included were 137 vessels carrying 2,400 guns and manned by 7,000 seamen. Besides the 17,000 soldiers aboard, there were 1,400 officers, servants, priests, and adventurers. About half the Armada was composed of warships; the rest were cargo vessels, dispatch boats, and other auxiliaries.

Philip had counted upon a rising of the Catholics in England to facilitate his plans, but when the English learned of his warlike preparations they composed their differences and rallied to their sovereign. Converted merchantmen and other craft from the seaport towns and artillerymen from all over England reinforced the Queen's navy of 34 warships to the respectable total of 197 vessels, carrying 16,000 men. Uncertain where the Spanish Armada intended to strike, the English divided their forces. A small squadron under Lord Henry Seymour watched Parma in Flanders while the bulk of the fleet operated out of Plymouth as a western squadron to cover Ireland and the south and west coasts of England. With the western squadron were the Lord High Admiral, Thomas Howard of Effingham, in the *Ark Royal,* with Francis Drake as Vice Admiral in the *Revenge* and John Hawkins as Rear Admiral in the *Victory.* Lord Howard, who held his position by virtue of his high nobility, was not without experience at sea but he recognized that in Drake and Hawkins he had the two foremost seamen of the age and generally followed their advice. In fact, Drake, with Howard's consent, virtually exercised command.

Because they were designed for different styles of combat, it is difficult to compare the strengths of the Spanish and English fleets. The English had more ships but they were in general smaller, carried less lofty deck structures, and were longer in proportion to the beams. In consequence they were swifter and more maneuverable and could carry more guns without overloading. The Spanish fleet carried more men and was in fact an army afloat; on reaching Flanders the soldiers aboard were to reinforce the Spanish invasion forces, and fleet and army would come under the direct command of the Duke of Parma. The table cited here, ad-

---

[8] Rodgers, *Naval Warfare Under Oars,* 262-3.

mittedly based on data of uncertain accuracy, illustrates the comparative advantages of the best 45 ships on each side, which bore the brunt of the fighting.[9]

	Tonnages:	Guns:	*Total Weight of Broadside:*	*Men Aboard:*
ENGLISH	17,000	1,600	7,000 lbs.	8,200
SPANISH	35,500	1,350	4,450 lbs.	15,200

The southwest wind which brought the Spanish Armada to the English Channel on July 30, 1588 caused Howard considerable embarrassment in beating out of Plymouth harbor. Some of Medina-Sidonia's admirals advised him to attack the English fleet at once, but orders from the King directed him to disregard the enemy and press on, fighting only if the English followed. So the Armada sailed on past Plymouth, and Howard fell in behind, thereby blocking the Spanish line of retreat back to Spain. Philip's directive displayed a curious lack of foresight, for obviously the English would not let themselves be invaded without forcing a battle. If Medina fought in Plymouth Roads, the Armada might indeed be heavily damaged or even defeated before reaching Flanders to support the assault on England, as Philip feared. But if the Spanish fleet did not defeat Howard in the Channel it would have to fight him in the Straits of Dover. Here the Armada would be encumbered by the task of protecting Parma's flatboats and barges, and Howard would be reinforced by Seymour's squadron and the Dutch fleet. Apparently the King did not fully appreciate the hazards of invading a hostile coast. Lacking surprise, an invasion fleet must either secure command of the sea in advance of landing operations by defeating or blockading the defending fleet—or it must be strong enough to support and cover the invasion simultaneously.[10]

Philip's Armada had been detected and it was not sufficiently superior to perform a defensive and an offensive function at the same time.

For a week the Armada moved slowly up the Channel while the English picked at its windward wing and forced three general engagements. At first the major Spanish combat vessels were in three squadrons abreast, each in line abreast, somewhat like the battle formation at Lepanto—an excellent disposition for galleys but very poor for ships with guns in broadside because thereby they masked their own artillery and at the same time exposed their bows and sterns to raking fire. After the second battle, Medina drew in his wings, which Howard had been attacking, and formed the Armada into a roughly circular mass, which the perplexed English called a "plump" or "roundel." For their part, the English attacked in crude line ahead, each ship firing a broadside as she passed the enemy. When the entire line had completed firing, it circled back in follow-the-leader style, fired the other broadside, and then hauled off.[11] After the second day, Howard's squadron began to operate in four divisions to achieve greater flexibility and better command control.

During the run up the Channel the Spanish fired more than 100,000 rounds and the English almost as many, yet neither fleet seriously hurt the other. A few Englishmen were killed, but none of their ships received any damage worth mentioning—and not a Spaniard boarded an English vessel. Three Spanish vessels were damaged and two of these the English captured, but loss of one was due to collision and loss of the other was due to an accidental explosion aboard. The third damaged ship, which was hit in the foremast, slipped into a French port. The English achieved little because their marks-

---

[9] *Ibid.*, 289-90.

[10] For example, in World War II, the Allies invaded Guadalcanal by surprise; Normandy and Iwo Jima, after securing command of the sea; Saipan, by simultaneous support and cover—while the combat vessels of the Fifth Amphibious Force supported the Saipan beachhead, the Fast Carrier Task Force fended off the Japanese fleet in the Battle of the Philippine Sea.

[11] The best explanation advanced for these curious tactics is that reloading was at that period time-consuming and hazardous. Because no method had then been devised for dealing with recoil, the guns during battle were lashed securely to the deck with the muzzles protruding through the ports. Ships entered an engagement with guns shotted. After firing, they withdrew out of range while the gunners leaned out of the ports to reload.

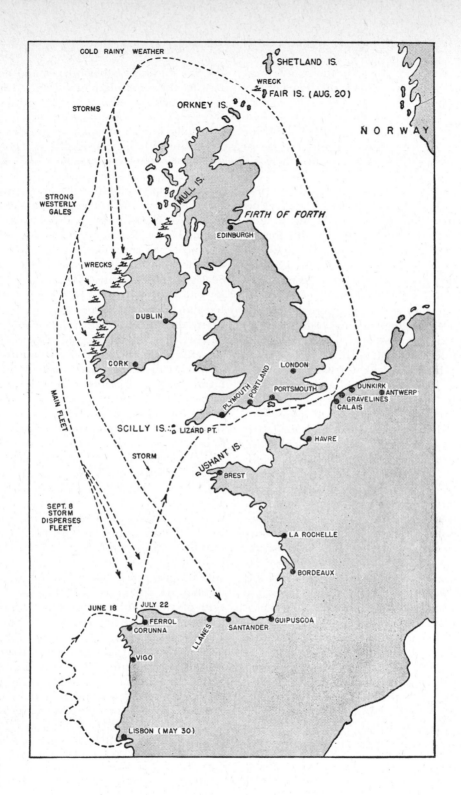

CRITICAL: *CRUISE OF THE SPANISH ARMADA, 1588*

manship was poor, because their guns were too lightly shotted, and because they held off at long range, both out of policy and to avoid the heavy but short-ranged Spanish shot.[12] The Spanish achieved almost nothing at all because they simply could not get at the English, who held off upwind and thereby determined the ranges.

For all his failure to hurt the English, Medina-Sidonia had achieved his tactical objective when he dropped anchor in the neutral port of Calais on August 7 with the Armada practically intact and his defensive formation unbroken. Strategically however he was in a poor situation, for he had fired off all his heavy shot and could get no more, whereas Howard could be supplied with ammunition from England and reinforced by the ships under Seymour. The Spanish admiral could think of nothing better to do than to call on the Duke of Parma for help. But Parma was tightly blockaded by the Dutch, and even if he could have got out, he had little besides flatboats to offer.

While Medina was still considering what to do next, Howard floated eight flaming hulks into Calais Roads on the tide, thereby forcing out the Spanish fleet in the middle of the night. Off Gravelines the next day the English attacked, with assistance from the Dutch fleet. Howard now closed the range with impunity because the Spanish, without ammunition for their big guns, could reply only with arquebus and musket. Had the Queen been less tight-fisted in providing Howard with powder and shot, he might have crushed the Armada then and there. As it was, the English fleet sank two Spanish ships and forced two more into the shallows, where they were captured by the Dutch. The rest of the Armada was badly battered however and had taken 1,400 casualties; besides,

the Spaniards were bewildered and demoralized by their complete inability to board the swift English vessels. With the wind against them and the English behind them, they had no choice but to retreat into the North Sea.

Medina-Sidonia considered the possibility of wintering in Norway or Germany but concluded at last that he must not keep the Armada so long away from home lest the English, flushed with their success at Gravelines, seize the opportunity to descend upon the Spanish coast. Because, as he supposed, there was no other route left open to him, he set out for Spain the long way around—north of Scotland and west of Ireland. Actually, had he but known it, the English fleet was now too short of ammunition and supplies to bar his retreat to the south—and it soon would be melting away as the plague struck. Though without means to fight another English-style battle, Howard pursued the Spaniards until August 12, when he stood off Newcastle, to encourage them to maintain their northerly course; but he kept his distance in order not to reveal his weakness. When at last he put into port to revictual, his men began to sicken. By September fully half his crews were dead or incapacitated. Luckily for England, the Dutch fleet was able to prevent Parma's crossing, for there were not 10,000 soldiers guarding the road to London.

When the Spanish Armada reached the latitude of the Orkneys on August 19, it was still in many respects the most formidable naval force in the world. But the humiliation of their failure and shortage of food and water had destroyed the men's spirits. After they entered the Atlantic, storms and poor navigation began to destroy their ships. Some 35 or 40 foundered at sea, and at least 20 were hurled upon the rocky shores, some on the coast of Scotland and more on the coast of Ireland, where such Spaniards as reached the beach alive were robbed by the Irish and massacred by English soldiers. In October Philip received back no more than half the naval and military power he had sent with such high expectations against England; some 70 vessels of all sorts, with 11,000 starving, feverish men staggered back

---

[12] The principal guns used by both fleets were the cannon, which could throw a 50-pound ball one mile; the mortar-like perier, which could throw a 24-pound ball three-quarters of a mile; and the culverin, which could throw a 17-pound ball 1¼ miles. According to a recent study, the English fleet was armed with 55 cannon, 43 periers and 1,874 culverins; the Spanish fleet, with 163 cannon, 326 periers, and 635 culverins. From Michael Lewis, "Armada Guns," *The Mariner's Mirror* (January 1943).

into the ports of Spain. *"Flavit Deus, et dissipati sunt"*—"The Lord sent his wind and scattered them"—thus went the inscription on the English victory medal. Yet it was the English fleet that wore down Spanish morale, battered the Spanish vessels into unseaworthiness, and forced the Spaniards in a defeatist frame of mind to undertake the long voyage home which proved their undoing.

Though the English had not achieved any great destruction of the enemy in combat, they had demonstrated superior adaptability of tactics to weapons. After the Armada campaign, grappling and boarding were practically abandoned in favor of long-range artillery battles. Sailing ships gradually replaced galleys even in the Mediterranean, arrangement of guns in broadside became the universal practice, and fleets thereafter tended to fight in column, or line ahead. Henceforth ships would fight ships in distinctively naval combat and not merely transport infantrymen over water to fight infantrymen in other ships.

Centuries later, historians could look back and see that the failure of the Armada marked the beginning of the decline of Spain. Philip at once lost some credit as defender of Catholicism, and England was stimulated into those ventures in commerce, exploration, and colonization which, together with the flourishing of the arts, mark the Elizabethan Age. Yet Europe did not immediately perceive that, without the wealth of Holland and the Holy Roman Empire to draw upon, Spain was no longer a first-class power. The bullion from the mines in America and the spice trade of the Indies were not enough to offset her lack of internal resources. Spain survived, and even retained her colonies for three more centuries, mainly because her enemies failed to recognize and take advantage of her inherent weakness.

So it was that the aftermath of the Armada campaign was as much an anticlimax as the situation following the Battle of Lepanto. Nothing was really changed. The English in 1589 and again in 1596 invaded Spain. Spanish troops landed in 1598 at Calais and in 1601 in Ireland. Yet the English were fearful of risking their forces to attain a final decision, and the Spanish lacked the forces to risk. The Anglo-Spanish War came to an end at last in 1603 with the death of Queen Elizabeth and the accession to the English throne of James Stuart of Scotland, son of Mary Stuart, whom Elizabeth had sent to the scaffold. James, more credulous than Elizabeth concerning Spanish power, promptly brought hostilities to an end and sought an alliance with Spain.

Because England was thus unrealistically allied with her erstwhile enemy, and France was divided by religious strife, the Dutch were the first to profit by Spain's decline. In the course of their struggle for independence, achieved in 1609, they had developed a formidable fleet, which they used to carve out a commercial empire. By the mid-1600's Dutch ships were handling more than two-thirds of Europe's carrying trade, and Holland had taken over Portugal's trade and empire in the Indian Ocean. Yet little Holland at the height of prosperity and influence was peculiarly vulnerable. It was inevitable that her powerful neighbors England and France, once they had suppressed their internal dissensions, would break the Dutch monopoly and employ their resources and geographical advantages to become the first nations of Europe and competitors for world trade and for empire beyond the seas.

3

Beginning

the Rivalry for Empire

AT THE COST OF SOME REPE-
tition, it is well at this point to survey certain aspects of European affairs at the dawn
of what we have called the Oceanic Age.

With the passing of the imminent danger
to Christendom posed by the Moslem World,
the fragile unity of medieval Europe had begun to disintegrate. The vague internation-
alism of the feudal system gave way to national feudalisms with a dominant monarch.
National monarchs were abetted in the extension of their power by the rising merchant
class, which wanted domestic peace, uniform
coinage, and a centralized government favorable to commerce and industry. Alliances
formed to offset the strong position of the
Holy Roman Emperor Charles V further defined the national state system and inaugurated the balance-of-power policy. Finally,
the only continuous and universal European
unity, that of the Church, broke asunder in
the Reformation. What had begun as a sort
of spiritual declaration of independence developed political aspects when national monarchs seized upon the Protestant movement

to defeat what they regarded as papal encroachment on their powers. In some nations, e.g., Spain and France, a workable
compromise was reached between papal
power and princely power. In others, e.g.,
England and the north German and Scandinavian states, national churches were established under the king.

But it was the opening of the new routes
to the East and the discovery of the New
World that did most to change the complexion of Europe and to usher in the modern period. The influx of precious metal
from Spanish America debased the value of
European currencies, while at the same time
raw materials from East and West came into
competition with European farm products.
Thus the costs of services and manufactured
articles rose out of proportion to income
from agriculture. This rise worked to the advantage of the city commercial classes but
tended to undermine the aristocracy, whose
wealth was drawn from the soil. The Age of
Discovery set in motion those economic
forces which were to transfer the wealth,

and therefore the power, from the nobility to the bourgeoisie and change Europe from a feudal to a capitalist society.

To account for the changes they saw but could not explain, Europeans developed the economic theory of mercantilism, which measures national wealth in terms of bullion. Since precious metal was limited in amount, it apparently followed that available wealth was limited and that a nation could grow richer only in proportion as it made some other nation poorer through capture by one means or another of part of its trade or possessions. This remorseless logic accounts as much as anything else for the post-medieval division of Europe into rival and competing states. It accounts for the trade wars which, along with other causes, kept the rivals in almost continuous conflict from the beginning of the modern age until after 1800. And the theory seemed proved by the fact that England, which devoted her wealth and energies single-mindedly to acquiring trade, colonies, and sea control, emerged supreme over all other competitors.

The breakup of Medieval Europe resulted in the establishment of five rival oceanic powers: Portugal, Spain, France, the Netherlands, and England. Of these, Spain was the first to emerge as a Great Power. But as we have seen, Spain in her Golden Age was already in decline. The causes were numerous: loss of North European resources with the division of Charles V's empire; expulsion of the Jews and Moslems, who were the backbone of Spain's commercial and industrial class; the cost in men and treasure of conquering Spanish America and maintaining Spanish dominance in Europe; and the influx of gold and silver from the New World, which debased Spanish money and set off uncontrollable inflation. Portugal, whose fortunes were tied to those of Spain at the time of the disastrous Spanish Armada against England, joined Spain in decline. Though it was not apparent at the time, early in the 17th century only England, Holland, and France remained as serious competitors for worldwide trade and empire. Of the three, Holland, because of her lead as

carrier for Spain in Spain's great days, because of her relatively stable government, and because of the strong position of her commercial class, quickly monopolized the carrying trade of Europe.

ENGLAND'S FITNESS TO RULE THE SEAS

An important thesis of Alfred Thayer Mahan's *The Influence of Sea Power upon History, 1660-1783* and subsequent works is that sea power is based upon sea commerce, that certain conditions or characteristics favor the development of sea power, and that England in the period of her great expansion on and beyond the seas possessed or acquired these characteristics to a greater degree than her rivals did. Briefly stated, the characteristics favoring the development of sea power are:

(1) *Geographic Position:*
   (a) central in relation to maritime neighbors
   (b) easily defensible from enemy land forces
   (c) not conducive to land expansion
   (d) giving easy access to the sea
   (e) controlling at least one major trade route
   (f) close to maritime rivals
   (g) providing good bases for naval operations
   (h) promoting concentration of naval forces

(2) *Physical Conformation*—providing:
   (a) *insufficient* agricultural and raw material resources
   (b) deep, defensible harbors with easy access to the interior
   (c) protected coastal waterways or easy internal transportation
   (d) undivided land area, or control of intervening water

(3) *Coastline*—relatively long and relatively populous

(4) *Population*—in excess of area and resources, and therefore available for:
   (a) manning seagoing vessels
   (b) industries that support sea power
   (c) colonization

(5) *National Character*—conducive to:
   (a) real aptitude for commerce

(b) aptitude for development of external areas

(c) investment of national resources in a navy

(6) *Government*—controlled by elements of the population dependent on external trade rather than by elements whose livelihood depends upon domestic consumption of agricultural or industrial products.[1]

England, driven to the sea by her sparse resources to seek a livelihood and to find homes for her burgeoning population, and sitting athwart the main sea routes of Western Europe, seemed destined by geography to command the seas. With no land frontiers to guard and little temptation to expand upon the European continent, she could spare herself the expense of massive land armies and devote her wealth to fleets for blockading her European rivals in their own ports and exerting her power in every quarter of the globe. In the process she acquired bases near terminal points (i.e., major ports) and focal areas (i.e., the waters near capes, straits, and canals), where sea routes tend to converge. Her eventual acquisition of such strategic positions as Gibraltar, Minorca, Cyprus, Suez, Aden, Cape Town, the Falklands, Jamaica, Ceylon, Singapore, and Hong Kong enabled her at length, as the old phrase has it, to "lock up the seven seas of the world."

The delay in England's rise to maritime dominance resulted mainly from her early lack of Mahan's sixth condition—a government favorable to maritime operations. As we have seen, James I, first of the Stuart kings, surrendered the strong lead England had won through the defeat of the Spanish Armada. By his treaty with Spain he put an end to English privateering and thereby obstructed the development of his navy. As a result the Dutch took what they liked of Europe's trade, French privateers flourished in English waters, and the corsairs of Algeria brazenly swept the Channel for booty and slaves. By 1616 "there were not ten ships of two hundred tons left belonging to the river of Thames fit for the defence of the kingdom." [2]

The second Stuart king, Charles I, recognized the need for a fleet but unfortunately got his navy embroiled with politics. His demand for "ship-money" was taken by the English people to mean that the King wanted money without grant from Parliament, and became an important cause for the Civil War, which broke out in 1642. It was not until the Commonwealth (1649-1660), when England was governed by commercial interests, that she could begin fulfilling her obvious destiny. Oliver Cromwell and his Puritan-business government restored the navy, which in a succession of three wars seized from the Dutch the greater part of that colonial and commercial empire which they had acquired largely from weakened Spain and Portugal. Once the Dutch collapse was complete, the English navy turned upon France and in another series of wars covering more than a century succeeded in overwhelming her sea power and seizing the best of her colonies. England's striking rise to mastery of the seas—and of many lands beyond the seas—was achieved through astute diplomacy, which generally allied Britain with the second strongest European power against the strongest and most aggressive power, and through emphasis upon her navy at a time when the great prizes of the world lay elsewhere than in Europe. The spirit of the contest was mercantilism, whose aim was crudely but aptly expressed by British General George Monk when he said, "What matters this or that reason for going to war? What we want is more of the trade which the Dutch have."

---

[1] Based on W. H. Russell, *The Fundamentals of Naval Strategy* (Annapolis, 1950), 8, which in turn is based on Alfred Thayer Mahan, *The Influence of Sea Power upon History, 1660-1783* (Boston, 1898), 28-89. It may be argued with some assurance that Mahan's six conditions, though unquestionably valid in the 17th and 18th centuries, are no longer prerequisites of dominant sea power, particularly since naval personnel are not today drawn to an important degree from the merchant marine.

[2] M. Oppenheim, editor, *The Naval Tracts of Sir William Monson,* 5 vols. (London, 1902-1914), III, 431.

EARLY COLONIAL RIVALRY

Despite the confusion of religious war in France and a sometimes hostile royal attitude in England, French and English private interests in the early 17th century set out to compete with the Dutch for the empires which Spain and Portugal claimed but could not hold. The fact that the competitors were mainly private companies, however heavily taxed for the benefit of the national treasuries, resulted in a curious attitude carried over into the 18th century: violence in the colonies was rarely regarded as an act of war—a whole colony might be massacred by a foreign rival and the matter would be written off as a bad business venture.

The bitterest of the early contests was in the East Indies, where the British and Dutch East India companies became sharp rivals for the Portuguese colonies and trade. The British company, lacking the active support of its government, failed to establish bases in the area, whereas the Dutch garrisoned the former Portuguese strongpoints and developed new fortified positions besides. The massacre of the British merchants at Amboina in 1623 marked the culmination of the conflict. England undertook no official reprisal for this outrage but the bloody affair was not forgotten and served to heighten the growing hostility between English and Dutch that had begun over their dispute concerning the part played by each in their joint war against Spain during the reign of Elizabeth I.

As a result of Holland's unshakable grip on the East Indies the English East India Company and a similar French concern shifted their activities to the mainland of Asia, whence they helped expel the Portuguese from all but a few small enclaves such as Goa in India and Macao in China. In India in particular the English and French gradually built up interests that were to come into conflict in the 18th century.

Holland's capture of the eastern spice trade impelled the English and the French to look to the West. In 1607 adventurers of the London Company established the colony of Jamestown on the American river which they named the James after their king and set out to exploit the resources—notably tobacco—of Virginia. Thirteen years later Puritans hounded from England by King James's persecution founded Plymouth colony in Massachusetts in order to provide themselves with homes where they could worship as they pleased. Meanwhile in 1608 the great French explorer Champlain had founded Quebec and thereby staked off the valley of the St. Lawrence for development by France. In 1626 the Dutch West India Company founded the colony of New Amsterdam on Manhattan Island and claimed the Hudson River Valley. In North America, and in the lush sugar islands of the West Indies, where all the rivals were out for what they could seize and hold, conflicts were bound to arise among the colonial interests of England, France, Holland, and Spain.

CROMWELL'S "NEW MODEL NAVY"

The small fleet that Charles I built with the ship-money wrung unwillingly from his subjects was in a sense the nucleus of the national navy of England, for it was the first fleet paid for by *all* England—not merely by the king's treasury and by the coastal shires. When the Civil War broke out, the Ship-Money Fleet promptly deserted the royal cause and sided with Parliament. Had it not, Charles might have obtained help from his fellow monarchs overseas. Certainly the court of the child-king Louis XIV of France was in complete accord with the English king's pretensions. France had the most powerful army in Europe, but despite a patently unneutral attitude which amounted to undeclared war she lacked the sea power actively to intervene. Ironically, the fleet Charles had built guarded the Channel, insulating him from outside aid while he was defeated, tried, and beheaded by his own subjects.

When Charles had lost his fight the winning side split asunder, thereby dividing the English navy into two opposing forces.

Charles's nephew, Prince Rupert, took a part of the fleet to sea in order to disrupt the anti-royalist merchant marine and to organize resistance. He did not lack bases for his operations, for still adhering to the royalist cause were Ireland, the Isle of Man, the Scilly and the Channel Islands, Virginia, and Barbados, England's only possession in the West Indies. To add to the touchy situation the Lord High Admiral of the parliamentary fleet had become suspect. So Oliver Cromwell, acting on behalf of Parliament, made a clean sweep of the naval high command and selected as admirals three trusted colonels from his New Model Army. These "Generals-at-Sea," as they were officially called, were to guarantee the loyalty of the fleet, defeat Rupert, and assure the safe crossing of Commonwealth troops to put down the rebellion in Ireland. Of the three, Robert Blake (1599-1657) soon displayed qualities of leadership which gave him a position of dominance at sea not inferior to that of Cromwell ashore.

Blake, whom many Englishmen consider their greatest admiral, was 50 years old when he first hoisted his flag in 1649. After ten years at Oxford, where he had sought a teaching fellowship, he took over his father's merchant shipping business and probably crossed the seas many times in his own vessels. Elected to Parliament in 1639, he sided against the king and served in the army of the Commonwealth, where he greatly distinguished himself. While defending Taunton he withstood siege by royalist forces for nearly a year; to demands for surrender he spiritedly replied that he had four pairs of boots left and would eat three pairs before the besiegers should enter the town. At length Taunton was saved, Blake ate no boots, and a grateful Parliament voted him a gift of £500. Short, plump, modest, and grave, Robert Blake possessed the rare combination of intuition, assurance, and vigor that in the last few years of his life brought him fame among English sea fighters unsurpassed even by that of the great Lord Nelson.

Blake's first task as general-at-sea was to assist in chasing Rupert's marauding force out of the Channel and into the Irish port of Kinsale. Here despite bad weather he kept the royalist fleet tightly blockaded while Cromwell's army crossed to Dublin Bay. The Commonwealth's campaign against the recalcitrant Irish was almost complete when a tempest blew Blake off station, allowing Rupert to escape to Lisbon, where Blake soon bottled him up in port. When King John of Portugal, disdaining to recognize the Commonwealth, refused to order Rupert out of the Tagus, Blake captured seven vessels of an approaching Portuguese convoy and so brought the king around to his point of view.

Rupert, ejected from Lisbon, slipped into the Mediterranean with Blake not far behind.[3] Harassed by their pursuer and tossed by storms, a part of the royalist fleet foundered upon the rocky coast of Spain. The fragment which managed to regain the Atlantic ran into more storms off the Azores, where Rupert lost his flagship. Reaching the West Indies, the Prince met further misfortunes and returned to Europe a beaten man.

Impressed by this clear evidence of the resurgence of English sea power, Portugal and Spain hastened to send ambassadors to London. To induce France to break off her undeclared war and follow suit, Blake captured one French man-of-war, sank another, and later scattered a French convoy off Dunkirk. With Rupert disposed of, he captured the Scillies and headed the naval forces in the invasion of the Channel Islands. Thus he crowned his efforts at unifying the British people and winning recognition for the Commonwealth. For reward he was elected to the Council of State and appointed commander in chief of the fleet.

Cromwell and the Commonwealth government, their eyes opened to the possibilities of sea power, early set about creating a "New Model Navy" as formidable in its way as the New Model Army which had unseated the king. Altogether they added 207 new ships, improved the pay and victuals of the sailors, and instituted an honest and efficient administration. Customs had so changed since

---

[3] Blake's advance through the Straits of Gibraltar was instrumental in establishing the English policy of maintaining a permanent naval station in the Mediterranean.

the roaring days of Elizabeth I however that they did not see fit to revive privateering in the semi-piratical style of Hawkins and Drake; instead they substituted a system of prize money whereby the ship's company received half the value of each enemy vessel captured, or 20 pounds sterling for each gun of all enemy vessels sunk. Cromwell thus acquired a loyal, well-organized fleet more formidable even than that of Holland. His warships were not so powerful as the great three-deckers [4] of Nelson's day, but they were bigger and stronger than contemporary Dutch men-of-war, which had to be kept relatively small to enter Holland's shallow harbors. In Blake moreover he had an admiral to compare with the renowned Martin Tromp, commander in chief of the Dutch fleet and accounted the best sea fighter in Europe.

Having brought England into tenuous unity by force, Cromwell, like other dictators before and since, found it expedient to pursue a strong foreign policy in order to distract his countrymen from their domestic differences. His instrument was the fleet, which enabled him to operate from strength. His obvious target was Holland, hated by England's merchant class because of her arrogant monopoly of the European carrying trade. By three acts he alienated Dutch attempts at rapprochement and brought on hostilities: he continued the Stuart custom of demanding a tribute of all herring caught within 30 miles of England, he insisted that all ships plying the Channel salute English warships by dipping their ensigns, and he put through a Navigation Act whereby goods could be brought into England only by English ships or by ships of the country where the goods originated.

The Navigation Act, a direct blow at Holland's cherished monopoly, caused the Dutch to mobilize their sea forces, and the demand for a salute brought on war. In May 1652 Tromp with 40 warships and instructions not to dip his flag to the English encountered Blake with 23 men-of-war off Dover. When Tromp refused to salute, Blake opened fire

[4] Meaning that they carried three covered gun decks.

and in a battle which lasted from early afternoon till nightfall succeeded in sinking one Dutch ship and capturing another.

THE FIRST ANGLO-DUTCH WAR, 1652-1654

Holland was absolutely dependent upon the sea for a livelihood. Yet because of threats from her continental neighbors she was obliged to divert much of her substance to the upkeep of a standing army. In consequence the fleet she was able to maintain was inadequate to support her far-flung commitments, particularly since her oceanic lifelines were dominated by England. Recognizing the enemy's weakness, the English navy correctly devoted its main effort to commerce raiding. Holland's desperate efforts to protect her merchant and fishing fleets precipitated a series of naval battles as fierce as any in history.

In July 1652 Blake broke up the Dutch herring fleet and seized the catch. Tromp, hastening in great strength to intervene, had his force scattered in a storm and so achieved nothing at all. Though it was none of Tromp's fault, an angry Dutch public demanded his removal. He was succeeded by Admiral de Witt, a courageous, hot-tempered man but no match for Blake, who so severely defeated him off the Thames estuary the following September that Tromp was promptly restored to command. Two months later, when over Blake's protest the British Council of State had shortsightedly diverted English ships to the Mediterranean and the West Indies, Tromp with 101 ships met Blake with 42 off the Thames and won a victory, capturing two English men-of-war. Thus through 1652 fortunes at sea fluctuated between the English and the Dutch, favoring first one, then the other.

In 1653 fortune almost wholly favored the English. The Dutch States-General had decided that Tromp's fleet should simultaneously carry out a defensive and an offensive strategy—escort convoys of merchantmen through the Channel or around Scotland and also seek out and destroy British warships. Only an overwhelmingly powerful fleet could successfully have performed such a double mission. Yet Holland had no choice, for she was not self-sufficient enough to keep her merchant ships in port while Tromp, unencumbered, won command of the sea by decisively defeating the English fleet.

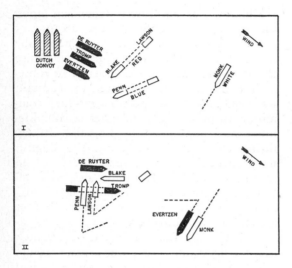

BATTLE OF PORTLAND, FEBRUARY 1665
(symbols stand for groups of vessels)

The magnitude of Tromp's problem came to the test in mid-February. With some 75 warships he was escorting nearly 200 merchantmen up the Channel when the English fleet darted out to intercept him, thus bringing about the Three Days' Battle, or Battle of Portland. Though the English squadrons were rather badly scattered, Blake attacked at once, disregarding his leeward advantage which permitted him first to fall off downwind and mass his forces, had he chosen to do so. Tromp's squadrons had nearly boxed Blake in when the other English commanders tacked to his support and with sturdier ships and greater weight of broadside broke through the Dutch line and put Tromp between two fires. Thus threatened, and handicapped by his convoy, Tromp was obliged to tack his fleet together and beat upwind to save his warships and merchant-

men. During the next two days Tromp, sailing generally in a defensive crescent formation, concerned himself solely with escape into the shallow waters off France, where the deeper-draft English vessels could not follow. Employing all his guile and agility, he managed to escape with the bulk of his fleet and convoy, but he left some 50 merchantmen and a dozen warships in English hands.

Though Blake was wounded and many of his ships had been badly battered, there was no doubt that he had won a victory. Yet he had little reason to be satisfied, for against an enemy encumbered with a convoy his victory should have been greater. The scattered condition of the English squadrons at the opening of the engagement had put him at a severe disadvantage. Moreover, the Battle of Portland, like the preceding battles, had been a bludgeoning affair, disintegrating into a melee of ship-to-ship duels. Evidently some more orderly system of naval tactics was needed. The English fleet, to be sure, was organized in squadrons—the Red, the White, and the Blue, commanded respectively by an admiral, a vice admiral, and a rear admiral. And continuous fire had become possible through a system of handling recoil which permitted guns to be reloaded inboard. What was required was a means of giving coherence to the fleet so that it would fight as a unit.

Perhaps some such considerations passed through Blake's mind as he lay recuperating from his wound, for in March 1653 along with his fellow generals-at-sea he issued a new set of *Fighting Instructions* which were to prove a milestone in the evolution of naval tactics. Article 3 specified: "All ships of every squadron shall endeavour to keep in line with the Chief. . . ." This directive established the *fleet line ahead* that was to be maintained with certain significant variations until World War II, when antisubmarine and antiaircraft defense required entirely new formations.

Obviously line ahead, or column, had at least been tried earlier with some success or it would never have found its way into the *Instructions,* for Cromwell's naval commanders were practical men, not visionaries.

Once ship guns had been arranged in broadside and naval battles had become mainly gunnery engagements, development of the column had become inevitable. Any other formation caused ships to mask each other's fire and exposed bows and sterns to raking fire from the enemy.[5] More important, line ahead enabled the fleet to achieve unity of action and massing of fire which line abreast or mere bunching of ships could never have attained.

When the fleets clashed again in the Battle of the Gabbard (June, 1653), Blake, still suffering from his wound, was in the Thames with a small squadron. The main English fleet was under the command of Generals-at-Sea George Monk and Richard Deane. Deane was killed at the first exchange of broadsides, whereupon Monk took the command wholly into his own hands. In conformity with the *Fighting Instructions* the English were in line ahead, while the Dutch, under Tromp, were still using their three-squadron, line abreast formation for mutual support against boarding. For better control and to avoid collisions, Monk had his ships spaced at regular intervals of about 100 yards, or half a cable's length, between vessels. Though there were about a hundred ships on each side, the English had more guns, and their column formation unmasked them all simultaneously. Moreover on hearing the guns Blake brought his squadron out of the Thames to join Monk.

Tromp in desperation attempted to offset the English advantages by forcing a melee at close quarters and reverting to boarding tactics. He actually entered the flagship of Vice Admiral William Penn,[6] but the Britons repulsed the Dutch and entered Tromp's flagship. Believing that all was lost and preferring death to surrender, Tromp retreated below decks and set off an explosion, determined to die in the holocaust. However only the upper deck of his ship was destroyed and

with it most of the Englishmen aboard. Tromp miraculously escaped death, but he was obliged to retreat to the shallows of the Flemish coast leaving behind 25 warships and 1,500 Dutch captives.

The Dutch, recognizing a good thing when they saw it, temporarily abandoned their line abreast squadron formation and adopted the fleet line ahead. But the English were already tactically several steps ahead. Their line had shattered a little too easily at the Gabbard when a shift in the wind had given the Dutch the windward position. So they adopted the close-hauled line. That is to say, they would set their sails so as to sail as nearly against the wind as possible. In those days that meant a little better than at right angles, for even the best of the old square-riggers could sail not much closer than six points into the wind. Sailing close-hauled made the individual ships more responsive to the helm and gave better control all down the line. Moreover, the English fleet would seek to gain and maintain the windward position.

From the earliest days of broadside gunfire all navies had recognized certain advantages in having the weather gage, i.e., the position to windward of the enemy. The wind would drift gunsmoke into the enemy's eyes and float fireships into his battle formation. With the ships heeled over by the wind, the windward fleet could fire faster because its guns would recoil uphill and roll quickly back into battery without much manhandling. Enemy shots penetrating at the waterline would be less likely to sink ships to windward, for when they came about on the opposite tack the shot holes would be raised above the surface, whereas shots between wind and water in the leeward fleet would be plunged under water as the ships came about. On the other hand, in a strong wind the leeward fleet enjoyed a gunnery advantage over the windward for then the ships would be so far heeled over that the windward fleet could not risk opening the lowest row of gunports on the engaged side and so would be deprived of the use of its heaviest guns.

To the English however all these consid-

[5] Raking fire was of course to be avoided insofar as possible, for an enemy vessel across one's bow or stern could not be reached by one's broadsides, and shot from a vessel so placed would range the *length* of the ship, killing more men and doing far more damage to spars and rigging than fire across the beam.
[6] Father of the founder of Pennsylvania.

erations were secondary to the fact that the weather gage was the *offensive* gage. The windward fleet held the initiative. It could decide when and where to attack, for it could move downwind on the enemy when and as it chose, whereas the leeward fleet could not beat upwind to give battle except under greatly disadvantageous conditions. The windward fleet could attack but it could not very well retreat. It could not take only so much of the battle as it liked; it was in for a decision. Because the British navy almost invariably followed an offensive strategy, it generally strove for the wind in any engagement.

The leeward position favored the *defensive*, for the fleet in the downwind position could keep open its line of retreat, and disabled ships could retire without drifting into the enemy. Moreover while the enemy to windward was bearing down for an attack, the leeward fleet could use its broadsides while the attacking fleet could not. In consequence the windward fleet usually arrived in line of battle with its rigging rather shot up and its mobility impaired. This last advantage was to prove particularly attractive to England's enemies on the Continent, who with armies to support could never expend ships as recklessly as England could.

Because Blake's wounds, aggravated by his efforts in the Battle of the Gabbard, kept him at home through the summer, Monk retained command of the English fleet. At the end of July Tromp, in a last great effort, eluded the English blockade, assembled 125 men-of-war, and attacked Monk's 130 ships, bringing about the Battle of Scheveningen. The Dutch as well as the English were now in column, but Monk's close-hauled line under superior control was able to break through the Dutch formation. Overwhelmed by English firepower and outclassed by English tactics, many of the Dutch captains flinched and ran for the shallows of their own coast. The gallant Tromp did not live to witness the final Dutch humiliation and defeat, for he had been struck by a musket ball early in the battle. His fleet lost from 30 to 40 ships; Monk's, only two. Dutch losses in men were five times those of the English.

The fleet line ahead was now so thoroughly established in the English navy, at least for the approach to the enemy, that its use was not questioned for more than a century. Henceforth English capital ships, i.e., warships which by virtue of their size and gunpower were fit to lie in the line of battle, were distinguished from smaller types by being designated *ships of the line*.[7]

Holland held out until April 1654 but her situation had long since become hopeless. The English had captured more than a thousand of her merchant ships, and the rest rode idly at their moorings in the Zuider Zee and the Rhine mouth. Business in Dutch ports was at a standstill and the Seven Provinces were feeling the pinch of direst want. At length the Dutch agreed to Cromwell's terms, which were not so harsh as they sounded, for they in no way interfered with Dutch independence and left her all her territories. Cromwell could afford to be generous, for the war had won him acclaim at home, it had broken the Dutch monopoly and launched English merchants upon the profitable carrying trade, and it had provided him with an incomparable fleet to further his ambitions for England.

THE SECOND ANGLO-SPANISH WAR, 1656-1659

Not since the defeat of the Spanish Armada had England been so stirred by national pride. The stubborn Dutchmen had been taught their lesson, and Britons were at long last able to share in Holland's source of wealth. In the courts of Europe English representatives were treated with renewed respect. While most of his countrymen were exulting in the inviting present, Cromwell was thinking in terms of England's place as future world leader. He saw clearly that commerce and colonies were the key to world eminence and that sea power was the means

---

[7] Or *line of battle ships* or *battleships* or more simply *ships*. Smaller types were frigates, sloops, and brigs. In naval parlance not even the ship-rigged frigate was referred to as a ship.

of acquiring more of both. Even before the defeat of Holland he had been considering how next to use the weapon that Blake had forged. It was mainly a question of whether to wage naval war on France or on Spain, for England had grievances against each.

In the end, Spain was elected to be the next adversary. Her strict monopoly of the Caribbean trade was almost as much an affront to commerce-hungry England as Holland's carrying-trade monopoly had been. Cromwell demanded a share of Spain's American commerce and received the brusque refusal he must have expected, for he was prepared to seize what Spain would not give. "Providence," said he, "seems to lead us to an attack on the West Indies," and promptly sent thither a fleet of 38 ships under Admiral Penn, with 6,000 troops under General Robert Venables, to pilfer what they could of Caribbean trade and territory.

Venables' troops were raw recruits, and he and Penn began badly by quarreling over command relationships. Operating out of the English base at Barbados they had a try at capturing Santo Domingo. It was a fiasco. Penn put Venables' motley force ashore and then did not bother to use his fleet guns against the Spanish fortifications. In short order, Venables and his men were put to flight by a small but well-trained body of Spanish cavalry and barely made it back to the ships. To salvage some fragment of honor out of the generally disgraceful proceedings, Penn and Venables took possession of lightly-defended Jamaica and then sailed back to England to face the wrath of Cromwell. Cromwell clapped them both into the Tower for achieving less than he expected, but he knew a good strategic position when he saw it and quickly set about fortifying Jamaica and developing its excellent harbor.

Meanwhile Blake had proceeded with 24 ships through the Straits of Gibraltar to "show the flag" and assure the safety of British commerce in the Mediterranean. For a demonstration of Britain's new sea power he elected to overawe the piratical states of North Africa, which hitherto had not hesitated to capture English merchant ships and enslave Englishmen. Selecting Tunis, largest and most formidable of the Barbary states,[8] Blake demanded of the Dey guarantees of immunity from capture for English ships and citizens. The Dey's reply was to draw his fleet of nine vessels inside his fortified base of Porto Farina and bid the English admiral defiance. To the Tunisian ruler's amazement and consternation, the English fleet sailed into the supposedly impregnable harbor and engaged the Tunisian ships and forts. As Blake had calculated, the wind which blew him in also rolled gunsmoke upon the enemy forces and left them blinded while English ships pounded down their fortifications and English boarding parties set fire to the Dey's cruisers. When he had destroyed the Tunisian navy and silenced all the forts of Porto Farina, Blake sailed with great equanimity out of the harbor, his ships virtually unscathed.

Following this extraordinary exploit, the North African states of Algiers and Tripoli hastened to offer Blake the assurance he demanded. Thereafter at every Mediterranean port where he was pleased to touch, Blake and his squadron were received with uncommon demonstrations of civility not unmixed with fear. The long eclipse of English sea power was ended, for English fleet guns had again spoken with authority on distant seas. "Blake's cruise did so much for English prestige in the Mediterranean," wrote Sir Geoffrey Callender, "that he deserves to be regarded as the creator of British influence within the Straits." [9]

Outraged by the attack on Santo Domingo and the capture of Jamaica, the King of Spain in 1656 declared war on England. It now became Blake's task to blockade Cadiz. This in itself was no great problem against decadent Spain, but Blake again created history by maintaining his blockade for six months at a stretch. The feat was later repeated by British admirals in the war against Napoleon but that was after the English had learned to copper the bottoms of their ships and had acquired a base at nearby Gibraltar.

---

[8] So called from the Berbers, principal tribe of North Africa.

[9] *Sea Kings of Britain: Hawkins to Blake* (London, 1912), 187.

In the spring of 1657 Blake learned that a treasure fleet was en route to Spain from Mexico and set out to intercept it in the Canary Islands. When he arrived in the Canaries the six treasure galleons and their ten escorting warships had already anchored in the narrow-mouthed harbor of Santa Cruz, the port of Teneriffe Island. The probability of Santa Cruz being entered by ships with hostile intent seemed almost negligible, for the entrance was difficult even for friendly craft and the harbor was guarded by no fewer than seven forts. Nevertheless, after carefully studying the situation, Blake went in on a rising tide, hugging the shore so closely that the forts at the entrance could not sufficiently depress their guns to hit his ships. Once inside he so positioned his force that gunsmoke blinded the enemy, as at Porto Farina, and the galleons and their escorts masked the fire of the shore batteries. With the loss of only 50 men he destroyed the Spanish fleet, battered the fortifications, and then under the smoke of the conflagration slipped out of the harbor on the ebb tide. With this attack, one of the most skillfully executed in history, Blake crowned his fabulous career. Lord Nelson, endeavoring 140 years later to duplicate the feat, not only failed but lost his right arm in the attempt.

Having demonstrated Spain's weakness to the world and left the Spaniards impoverished through blockade and loss of treasure, Blake sailed home on his last voyage. The poet Edmund Waller expressed the sentiment of all England:

The sea's our own; and now all nations greet
With bending sails, each vessel of our fleet.

Tired to the point of utter exhaustion and never really recovered from his old wound, Robert Blake died as his flagship, the *George,* entered Plymouth Sound. Cromwell, who better than most men knew Blake's worth, gave him a funeral befitting his greatness and buried him in Westminster Abbey. The Lord Protector did not long survive his great and loyal admiral.

With the death of Blake and Cromwell Englishmen began to lose the vision of British sea power as a means for winning command of the sea and of the lands beyond. A hundred years later William Pitt was to revive the vision and use the fleet realistically as the key to world power. In the meantime the English navy would have its ups and downs and more than once be reduced to impotence.

In the chaos following Cromwell's death it fell to honest George Monk to restore order with his troops. Instead of grasping the reigns of government himself, he reconvened Parliament and in 1660 brought over from Holland the exiled son of Charles I to be King Charles II. Far from blind to the importance of sea power, if a little uncertain how to maintain it, Charles restored his royalist followers to the naval service but also retained the veteran Commonwealth officers. He loaded Monk with honors and titles, the most exalted of which was Duke of Albemarle. The fleet now became the Royal Navy, the title it has borne ever since.

The new government dropped the rank of General-at-Sea in favor of Admiral and set out to develop a corps of officers especially trained for service afloat. To that end young gentlemen [10] were sent to sea to grow up with the fleet in preparation for command. The effect, while excellent in many respects, tended to make the Royal Navy the property of the nobility and to bar gifted commoners from naval command. No system moreover could offset the weakening effect of introducing Charles II's self-serving adherents to high naval position or insulate the fleet from the influence of his majesty's incurable dishonesty.

THE SECOND ANGLO-DUTCH WAR, 1665-1667

Holland's seafarers and traders were far too industrious and enterprising to abandon

---

[10] Called King's Letter Boys because they were issued a royal letter in lieu of a commission. Assigned the duty of leading parties up the ratlines to reef sail, these agile young fellows also became known as Reefers. But their most lasting title was Midshipman—from their station amidships, whence they relayed the captain's orders forward.

any part of their commercial empire merely because they had been beaten once by the English. A stepped-up shipbuilding program soon replaced all the merchantmen that England had captured and destroyed, and under Admiral de Ruyter, worthy successor to Martin Tromp, a powerful Dutch fleet once more plied the seas. The Dutch, still resentful of the Navigation Act, became increasingly annoyed at the incursions of England's revitalized trade. Englishmen were wrathful at being undersold by the Dutch in the West Indies slave trade. The simmering hostility came to a boil when an English squadron in the fall of 1663 captured two Dutch trading posts on the West African coast and the following summer crossed the Atlantic and seized New Amsterdam, renaming it New York. De Ruyter soon reconquered the African posts and then crossed over and attacked Barbados in the West Indies. In March 1665 Charles II declared war on Holland.

For naval historians the chief interest of the Second Anglo-Dutch War is the part it played in solidifying the tactical ideas tried out in the First War. In 1665 a new set of *Fighting Instructions* was issued in the name of the Lord High Admiral, James, Duke of York, brother to the king. The new instructions were mainly a warmed-over version of those laid down by Blake and his colleagues in 1653, but there were significant additions based on experiments tried in the battles of the Gabbard and of Scheveningen. Now the close-hauled line ahead was definitely prescribed, at least for the leeward position, and the hundred-yard interval between ships in column was laid down as an order.

As old soldiers and sailors will, the veterans of the First Anglo-Dutch War had engaged in much discussion about the tactics employed. Nobody seems to have disputed the value of the fleet line ahead, but by 1665 there had arisen in the Royal Navy two rival schools of thought concerning *how far* the line should be maintained. These groups have been called the *Formal* school and the *Melee* school, and the names aptly suggest the point of view held by each. Both believed in a formal line ahead *approach;* where they

disagreed was in what should happen after *contact* with the enemy. The Formalists insisted that the line ahead should be maintained throughout the battle in order to achieve full impact, develop maximum use of gunfire, and maintain command control. From such a battle, should matters turn adversely, the commander with full control might extricate his fleet with minimum risk. The Melee school believed that optimum results could be achieved by departing from the line at a favorable opportunity and forcing a melee in which the commander would inevitably lose control, and the conclusion would depend upon the initiative of the individual captains or subordinate commanders. It was mainly a question of the relative emphasis to be put upon the defensive and the offensive. The great debate over these divergent tactical views raged for 40 years, and the matter was not actually settled until the period of the Napoleonic wars and the last days of sailing-ship warfare.[11]

The Formal school, headed by the Duke of York and Sir William Penn, advocated the "Conterminous Line of Battle." Their ideal engagement would begin with the British fleet seizing the windward position and then maneuvering until it was in close-hauled line ahead with its leading ship exactly opposite the leading ship of the enemy, who would be in close-hauled line ahead under easy sail to leeward. The British, holding off out of gun range, would adjust intervals until the parallel fleets were conterminous, i.e., van to van, center to center, and rear to rear. Now if the leeward fleet were wise it would back sails and come as nearly as possible to a halt, for then the windward fleet, in order to come down into gun range,

---

[11] As we shall see, the debate was revived with the introduction of steam propulsion, reaching a climax in discussions following the Battle of Jutland in 1916. It was revived once more in 1942 over how best to use cruiser-destroyer forces in night actions in the Solomons campaign. The best brief narrative of the original debate appears in Michael Lewis, *The Navy of Britain* (London, 1948), which this book follows. A more detailed and technical discussion is to be found in Sir Julian Corbett, *Fighting Instructions* (London, 1905), published by the Navy Records Society.

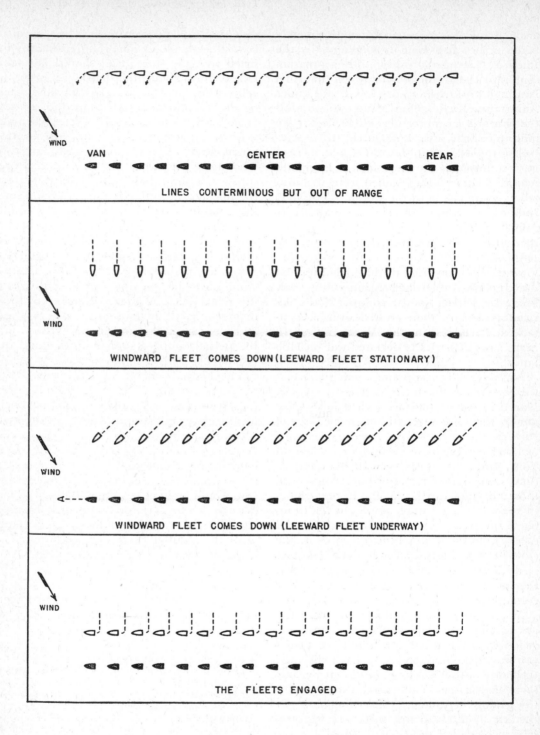

WIND

VAN   CENTER   REAR

LINES CONTERMINOUS BUT OUT OF RANGE

WIND

WINDWARD FLEET COMES DOWN (LEEWARD FLEET STATIONARY)

WIND

WINDWARD FLEET COMES DOWN (LEEWARD FLEET UNDERWAY)

WIND

THE FLEETS ENGAGED

FORMAL TACTICS

would have to turn together eight points of the compass and advance in line abreast (see diagram, opposite). During this advance the leeward fleet could of course rake the windward ships as they came within range bows-on, thereby weakening the windwards and cutting down their mobility by shots through the sails and rigging. This was a serious disadvantage for the British but had to be accepted as the price for taking the weather gage. If the leewards were less wise, they would continue in motion; this would permit the windwards to come down more obliquely in line of bearing, perhaps using their broadsides against the leewards on the approach.

Once the windward fleet, whatever the approach, had come within gun range (for the British this was almost invariably close), they would turn together once more into close-hauled line ahead, paralleling the enemy ship for ship. Only under exceptional circumstances was the windward line to be broken, even if one or more of the enemy ships should drop away and fall off to leeward. Later versions of the *Fighting Instructions* were precise on this point: "None of his majesty's fleet shall pursue any small number of the enemy's ships before the main body of their fleet shall be disabled or run." Such was the formal battle advocated by the Duke of York and by Penn. It was a battle which was never fought however, for invariably the enemy had some ideas of his own; these and difficulties of ship handling tended to throw the formalist plans into confusion.

It is noteworthy that the Duke of Albemarle (i.e., Monk) and Prince Rupert, chief protagonists of the Melee school, had done most of their fighting ashore. It is not surprising that they should desire to apply to sea battles the age-old techniques of concentration that had proved effective in land engagements.[12] The principal military objective in warfare is to mass superior force against some *part* of the enemy, and to defeat him in detail by bringing one's whole force, or most of it, against successive enemy fractions. The Meleeists objected to the formalist battle plan precisely because it sacrificed concentration by spreading its gunpower thin along the whole of the enemy line instead of massing more guns against fewer guns at some selected point. The formalist battle thus tended to become a mere contest of endurance, with the victory going to the side that could longest take punishment without flinching. Surely, said the Meleeists, brute staying power should not alone determine the outcome; cleverness should count for something. So they advocated adoption of the army tactics of massing, flanking, and breaking through the enemy line. Applied to sea battles, such tactical results were to be attained by the following maneuvers (see diagrams, page 56):

(1) *Massing*—decreasing the interval between one's ships so as to bring a preponderance of ships and gunfire against some part of the enemy line.

(2) *Doubling*—shifting part of one's fleet to the far side of the enemy line by first overlapping the enemy ahead or astern and then crossing his track so as to put his van or rear between two fires.

(3) *Breaking*—passing one's fleet *through* the enemy line instead of doubling around the end. This maneuver had the added advantage of permitting the attacking ships to fire double broadsides while breaking through.

---

[12] The terminology here used is derived from the writings of Alfred Thayer Mahan and hence belongs to a later period. Much of Mahan's work is devoted to applying to sea warfare the military practices of Napoleon as analyzed in Antoine Henri Jomini's *Summary of the Art of War*. According to Mahan, *concentration* is a complex concept applicable to strategy as well as to tactics. It has three aspects. To achieve full concentration a fleet or other force must: (1) Be coordinated by (a) unified command, (b) pursuit of a single objective, and (c) mutual support among participating elements; (2) Be disposed with regard to the strategic center, that point where a blow can most seriously affect the outcome of a battle, campaign, or war; and (3) Bring its main attack against *part* of the enemy force while the enemy is held at *all other points*. Means of holding the enemy outside the area of the main attack include: use of secondary forces, surprise, feints, distance, wind, geographic features, use of interior and exterior position, and so on. Mahan made a clear distinction between *concentration* and mere *massing*. A force can be divided without loss of concentration, provided the foregoing requirements are adhered to.

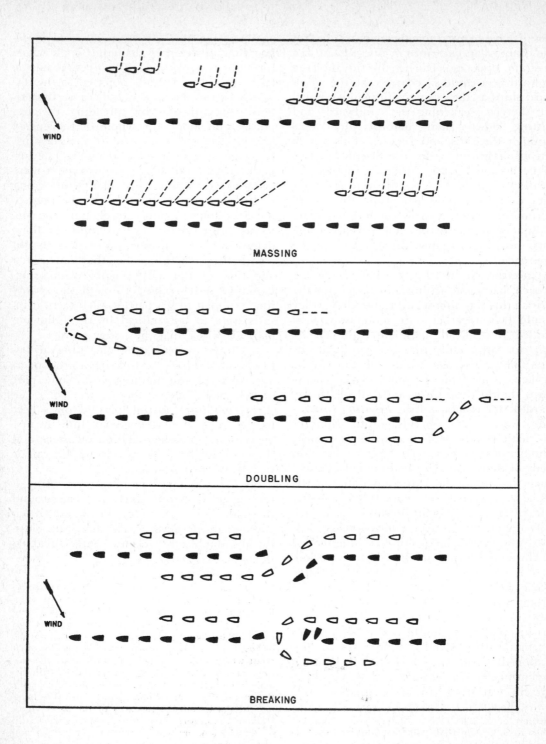

MELEE TACTICS

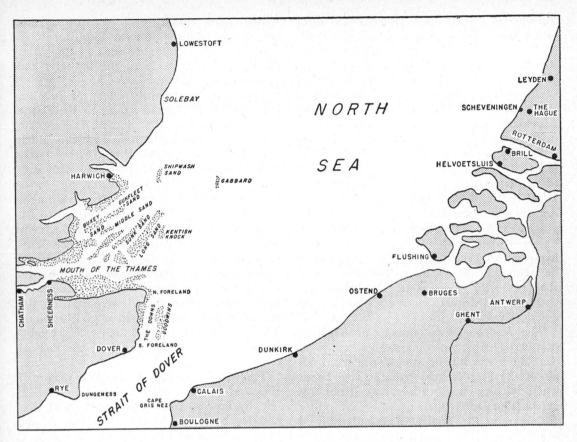

LOWER LATITUDES OF THE NORTH SEA

Presumably any of these maneuvers, if successful, would cost the enemy so heavily at the point of attack that the rest of his force could readily be overcome or put to flight. At best, such tactics produced a melee of ship-to-ship duels. At worst, they might give the enemy an excellent opportunity to spring a few tricks of his own.

The first engagement of the Second Anglo-Dutch War, the Battle of Lowestoft of June 3, 1665, gave the Formalists a chance to test their theories, for the Duke of York was in command and Penn was Captain of the Fleet (i.e., chief of staff). The British fleet numbering some 80 ships in a preliminary skirmish took position to windward of the Dutch fleet of about equal strength under Admiral Obdam (de Ruyter was still on his cruise against West Africa and Barbados). Precisely in conformity with formalist notions, the British then bore down line abreast and engaged. What happened next is not altogether clear from the rather confusing contemporary narratives, but it is apparent that the Dutch refused to fall in with the formalist plans. They reversed course, a procedure which cut down the effective firepower of both fleets by increasing relative speeds. Three times the Duke of York tried to attain his cherished conterminous line, but each time the non-cooperative Dutch came about so that the two long lines passed each other on opposite tacks, firing steadily at close range. At the third passing Obdam's flagship blew up, and some of his captains in panic fell off to leeward, leaving a wide gap in the Dutch line. Seeing his opportunity the Duke of York at once dispensed with his formalist theories and broke through. By this maneuver he not only forced the enemy to retreat but cut off a great many Dutch ships, 18 of which he took captive. For all that, the Duke had clearly not taken full advantage of the situation, and the Meleeists could with some justification accuse him of too much maneuvering and not enough fighting. At any rate, the king brought his brother ashore and put Albemarle and Prince Rupert in command of the fleet.

Exactly a year later these two leading Meleeists, in joint command, had an opportunity to try out their contentions in the Four Days' Battle, beginning June 1, 1666. It was not a really fair test, for Albemarle made the grave mistake of dividing the fleet, detaching Prince Rupert with 20 ships to look for a hypothetical French naval force reputed to be advancing to join forces with the Dutch. Rupert's wild goose chase left Albemarle with only 59 ships to engage a hundred under de Ruyter.

The first day, even though greatly outnumbered, Albemarle massed his forces on the Dutch van but because of the shoal water of the French coast had to come about when victory was apparently within his grasp. The Dutch then massed their center and rear on the English rear and inflicted heavy losses. The second day of the battle Albemarle again attacked the enemy but the odds were so much against him that he shifted to the defensive. The third day he retreated back toward England using the Dutch line abreast formation. Rupert and his fresh ships, returning from their bootless cruise, combined forces with Albemarle on the fourth day and once again the English attacked. Albemarle performed the extremely difficult maneuver of breaking the Dutch line from to leeward, but de Ruyter had his fleet in two parallel lines and eventually caught many of the British ships between the fires of both his lines. Because not all of the British ships had been able to break the enemy's lee line however, some Dutch ships found themselves between the fires of two British lines. De Ruyter retired first, but the English losses were much the greater: 5,000 casualties against half as many Dutch, 20 English ships captured against only seven Dutch vessels destroyed. The For-

malists made much anti-Melee propaganda out of the result, but most Englishmen allowed for the formidable odds against Albemarle and took pride in the fight he had put up.

Less than two months later, on July 22, the rival fleets clashed again, in the Battle of the Gunfleet, or of St. James's Day. Again, apparently, Albemarle massed on the Dutch van. This time, because the opposing forces were more nearly equal and the English were not embarrassed by shoal water, he won a victory. But it was not so decisive as it might have been because the Dutch replied to Albemarle's maneuver by breaking through the English line and cutting off the rear. This gave the Formalists additional ammunition; they pointed out that massing ships opposite one sector of the enemy line left the rest of one's line weakened and so permitted the enemy to mass or break through elsewhere. Thus the Meleeists for all their spirited fighting had lost the first round of the tactical contest.

The war, in addition to the great plague of 1665 and the destructive London fire of 1666, had by now so impoverished England that Charles began to look with a bilious eye upon the cost of maintaining a large fleet. He had long since disbanded the army with no adverse effect; why not whittle down the Navy? Convincing himself that the Dutch had been so chastised by the Battle of the Gunfleet that they would give no more trouble, he proceeded over the strong protests of Albemarle and Rupert to lay up much of the fleet in ordinary.

By the king's direction the Royal Navy now limited its operations to *guerre de course,* i.e., commerce raiding, sending out small squadrons of frigates to harry the Dutch trade routes. Charles was well aware of the building and refitting going on in the ports of Holland, but he was in such dire financial straits that he refused to see any danger in these activities. The following year he paid the price of his shortsightedness. On June 7, 1667, de Ruyter suddenly appeared off the mouth of the Thames with a hundred ships and proceeded to inflict upon England the deepest humiliation of her history. Entering the river unopposed he captured a large supply of naval stores at Sheerness, bombarded Chatham, burned seven large men-of-war and captured the *Royal Charles,* flagship of Albemarle and before him of the Duke of York and of Blake and the ship which had brought Charles II in triumph back to England in 1660. Only the intricacy of the channel and unfavorable wind and tide prevented de Ruyter from attacking London, whence the court fled like so many frightened chickens. The Dutch departed as suddenly as they had arrived but they clapped so tight a blockade upon English shipping that in a few weeks the London government asked for terms. The result was the Peace of Breda, whereby England relinquished all claims to the East Indies and agreed to modify the Navigation Act in favor of Holland. In return, the Dutch recognized the West Indies as a British sphere of influence and confirmed the British occupation of New York.

The Dutch had demanded no more because they were as anxious for peace as the English were. The armies of France had invaded the Spanish Netherlands (Belgium) and were pushing on toward Holland, evidently determined to advance to the Rhine.

LOUIS XIV'S ADVENTURE IN IMPERIALISM

In 1661, the year after the restoration of the House of Stuart in England, Louis XIV, then 22 years old, took into his own hands the reins of the French government. France had by then arrived at the peak of power and influence on the Continent. Her internal religious wars were long concluded, the last attempt of the nobility to share the kingly power had been suppressed, and she had recently signed victorious treaties of peace with the German states and with Spain. Though Louis acted as his own prime minister, he was at first much influenced by his minister of finance, Jean Colbert, who organized French finances and rid the country of debt.

An economic thinker as well as a financier, Colbert was very much a mercantilist, and within the limitations of mercantilist theory he set out to increase France's wealth and prestige. He fostered agriculture, manufacture, and commerce, improved roads and canals, and stimulated colonial progress in Canada, India, and the West Indies. To develop and protect France's growing commerce and colonial empire, he enlarged both the merchant marine and the navy. He made Toulon a naval base, established shipyards in the major ports, set up naval officer training schools, and by means of a national conscription made sure that there would be enough sailors for the fleet. Under Colbert's patronage, French ship construction became a fine art, far superior to the rather casual shipbuilding practices of the English. By the time of Colbert's death the *Marine Française* was the equal of any navy on the high seas.

It is perhaps idle to speculate upon the probable course of French history had Colbert's system been adhered to. As it was, King Louis, inordinately vain, insatiable for glory, and somewhat lacking in imagination, transferred his affections from the navy, whose silent influence upon France's neighbors won him no encomiums, and prepared to use his army to expand the boundaries of his kingdom. Thereafter he passed the rest of his life in almost continual warfare, turned all Europe against him, plunged France again into debt, and prepared the way for the French Revolution.

Louis's first military adventure was against the Spanish Netherlands. This as much as anything else brought the Second Anglo-Dutch War to a sudden close. Holland, fearful of an expanding France, now exercised artful diplomacy to form an alliance with Sweden and her erstwhile enemy England. Confronted by this combination of powers, Louis backed down, contenting himself with a strip of frontier territory.

The French king now embarked upon a diplomatic campaign of his own. First he lulled the Swedes into complacency with meaningless guarantees. Next he purchased the cooperation of the profligate Charles II of England by means of an immense bribe (Secret Treaty of Dover, 1670). When all was ready he combined his fleet with that of the English for a sea campaign against the Dutch and sent his army via the Rhine valley to invade Holland.

THE THIRD ANGLO-DUTCH WAR, 1672-1674

England's alliance with an expanding France was as contrary to her time-tested balance-of-power policy as her sudden attack on Dutch sea commerce was unjustified. Holland responded to the peril of the double attack, on land and on the sea, by opening her dikes to check Louis's army of invasion and by straining every resource to equip a fleet able to meet the combined naval forces of France and England. The British, for their part, sorely felt the absence of such leaders as Blake and Albemarle and found the French squadrons more of a hindrance than a help, for they tended to abandon their British allies whenever the fighting became hot.

The third naval war between Holland and England found the Duke of York in command of the British fleet and a new set of instructions in force. The *Fighting Instructions* of 1672 added nothing to the old ones except to make official certain maneuvers which Albemarle had put into practice in the Second War: fighting van to rear, center to center, and rear to van, instead of in the usual order, when the fleets approached from opposite directions, and the tricky maneuver of breaking through the enemy's fleet from to leeward. This last looks like a meleeist regulation, but it was nothing of the sort, for the British line was to be kept intact at all times; the purpose was merely to permit part of the fleet to seize the weather gage and employ the windward advantage.

In the first of four engagements with the Dutch, the Battle of Solebay in late May 1672, the Duke of York tried a formal line ahead against de Ruyter and failed. He then tried doubling on the head of the Dutch column and failed again. The second and third so-called battles were mere indecisive skirmishes, but the fourth, the Battle of the Texel of mid-August 1673, was a full-dress engagement involving 130 ships. The British forces in this battle, under the command of Prince Rupert, tried frankly meleeist tactics and had somewhat the worst of it. In all four engagements de Ruyter had proved himself the master of the situation and the first tactician in Europe. Moreover he had saved his country from seaborne invasion and broken up every attempt at blockade.

The failures of Britain's vaunted fleet and the reticence of the French squadron to fight increased the dissatisfaction of the English people, with whom the war had never been popular. At last, bowing gracefully before the rising storm, Charles II gave in and early in 1674 made peace with Holland. Already fear of imperialist France had drawn Spain and several German states to the Dutch cause. Finding himself isolated against a growing coalition, Louis XIV in 1678 acknowledged his failure and made peace with the Dutch, from whom he had not extracted a foot of territory. England for all her poor showing turned out to be the principal beneficiary of the war, for more and more of the lucrative carrying trade had passed from exhausted Holland to British merchants.

So ended England's wars with Holland. With them ended a kind of naval warfare. Not again would England wage war on the sea for so limited an objective as control of the Channel and the narrow waters of the North Sea. Not again would she deal with an opponent so determined to fight for a decision. Gradually too, as ships of the line became bigger and heavier and more sharply differentiated from merchantmen, battles would be fought with fewer ships on each side, and tactics would become more precise and orderly. Nevertheless out of the conflicts with Holland the Royal Navy was born, developing tactical doctrines that were to influence all sea warfare for a century and more.

THE WAR OF THE LEAGUE OF AUGSBURG, 1688-1697

The continued aggressions of Louis XIV and his hounding of the Protestant Huguenots in France caused such alarm among his neighbors that Holland, Spain, Austria, and several German states banded together against him in a defensive alliance called the League of Augsburg. In 1688 the English people, disgusted with the House of Stuart, deposed and sent into exile King James II, the former Duke of York and brother and successor of Charles II. They then invited Holland's stadtholder, William of Orange, and his English wife to become joint sovereigns of England as William and Mary. With the pro-French Stuarts out of the way, William had little difficulty persuading England to join the anti-French League. This inaugurated the first of a series of Anglo-French wars covering more than 125 years, beginning with the threat of Louis XIV to dominate Europe and ending with the downfall of Napoleon. As a result of this long-continued conflict France, lavishing her treasure on huge continental armies, lost an overseas empire and gained nothing, while England, devoting her military resources mainly to her navy, established an empire of worldwide proportions. Britain's single important loss, the American colonies, resulted in part from temporary neglect of her fleet.

The chief naval interest in the first Anglo-French war centers about Louis's attempt to seize command of the Channel preliminary to landing troops in England, Ireland, Holland, or wherever he chose. For that purpose the Comte de Tourville, commanding the French fleet, appeared off the Isle of Wight towards the end of June 1690 with 70 ships of the line. To oppose him the English admiral, the Earl of Torrington, had only 55 ships, because a good part of his fleet was off Ireland supporting King William, then engaged in suppressing adherents of ex-King James, who had landed there to stir up trouble.

Torrington was in a dilemma. The boldest course, and the one which he would evidently have preferred to follow, would be to go out in the spirit of Blake and Albemarle and engage the superior French fleet, whatever the odds. But there was an excellent chance that Torrington would himself be beaten and his fleet destroyed. In that event there would be nothing to prevent a French invasion of England. On the other hand if he did nothing at all, merely keeping his force intact as a fleet-in-being, the French would hesitate to engage in so vulnerable an operation as an amphibious assault. If they did the English might sortie and wreak havoc on their forces while they were half afloat and half ashore. Weighing the alternatives, Torrington concluded that the wisest course was one of defense—at least until reinforcements could arrive from Ireland. So he avoided an engagement, kept Tourville guessing, and incidentally added the term "fleet-in-being" to the lexicon of naval terminology.

The British public however became aroused at the presence of a hostile force in the Channel. Recalling with an apprehensive chill de Ruyter's invasion of the Thames 23 years before and having little understanding of passive defense, they loudly demanded action. Queen Mary, left at the head of the government in William's absence, called a council and asked advice. Whether the advice she received emanated from jealousy of Torrington or from genuine patriotic concern for England's welfare is still a matter of question. At any rate the Queen in great agitation wrote the Admiral a letter peremptorily ordering him to go out and fight. The result was the Battle of Beachy Head of June 30, 1690.

The engagement is of special significance because it pitted together the two best tacticians of the day. Torrington had inherited the fleet line ahead from the Anglo-Dutch Wars but he gave it added flexibility by dividing his Red, White, and Blue squadrons each into a van, a center, and a rear division which could be detached and rejoined as the occasion required. Faced with a superior enemy fleet, he sought and obtained the windward position and prepared to carry out the least risky attack open to him in the

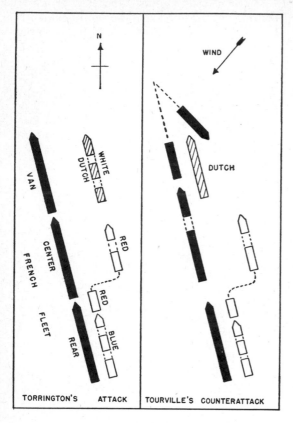

BATTLE OF BEACHY HEAD, JUNE 30, 1690

circumstances—massing on the enemy's rear. To that end he strengthened his rear squadron at the expense of his center and then sent his strengthened rear with reduced intervals between ships against the French rear. He thus attained a preponderance of force in that quarter. At the same time he "refused" his van and the rest of his center, i.e., he held them off out of gun range of the enemy.[13] Now if Tourville's van and center were to come about in an attempt to succor his embattled rear, Torrington's van and center could attack while the French ships were in some confusion and perhaps masking each other's fire. Or if Tourville's van and center were to shorten sail and deliberately lose speed for the same purpose, Torrington's van could double on the French van. Thus by the English admiral's refusal of his van and center, the French were practically obliged to leave their rear to its fate.

In view of Torrington's inferiority no serious flaw can be found in his plan. However, an unforeseen development spoiled everything. Torrington's van squadron was composed of Dutch ships that had only recently joined and were perhaps unfamiliar with the English signal system. At any rate instead of refusing they came down on the enemy almost as soon as the rear squadron did. This gave Tourville his opportunity. He pounded the sails and rigging of the Dutch ships to impair their mobility and then, deliberately extending his van, doubled back and put the Dutch between two fires, mangling them fearfully.

Torrington saved his fleet from destruction by ordering his ships suddenly to drop anchor with sails set. The French, taken by surprise, were quickly carried out of range by wind and tide. The English admiral then set fire to a dozen of his most disabled vessels and with the rest fled eastward. Tourville never caught up, for instead of signaling General Chase he kept his line intact, thereby reducing his speed to that of his slowest and most damaged ship. Arriving at the Thames, Torrington pulled up the buoys and took shelter inside the river. By what his enemies called ignominious flight he had tarnished his reputation but preserved his fleet-in-being and saved England. He was cast into the Tower for his failure and subsequent retreat, but a court-martial absolved him of all blame. King William however could never quite convince himself that Torrington had not deliberately sacrificed the Dutch. At any rate he never again gave him a command.

Luckily for England, James and his Irish supporters were defeated by William in the Battle of the Boyne the day following Torrington's defeat, and an unfavorable turn of events on the Continent dissuaded Louis XIV from exercising his control of the Chan-

---

[13] Here is a clear demonstration of concentration as defined by Mahan, for Torrington was bringing his main attack against *part* of the enemy force while the enemy was held at *all other points*. In Chapter 11 we shall see that Nelson successfully achieved much the same sort of concentration in the first phase of the Battle of Trafalgar in 1805.

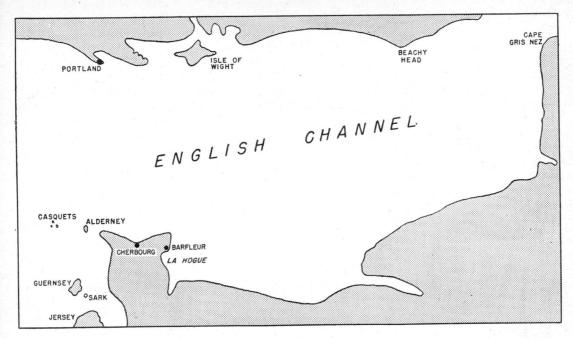

THE ENGLISH CHANNEL

nel before the English fleet could be reassembled.

The most important long-range result of the Battle of Beachy Head was that it shifted naval opinion definitely in favor of formalism. The *Fighting Instructions* of 1691 reflect the new attitude. Out went the old instruction about "dividing the enemy from to leeward"; in went two new articles (numbers 17 and 18) requiring a line conterminous with the enemy in all situations and a third (number 19) forbidding doubling on the van: "If the admiral and his fleet have the wind of the enemy, and they have stretched themselves in line of battle, the van of the admiral's fleet is to steer with the van of the enemy's and there to engage them."

English tacticians had come to the conclusion that when the enemy's strength was equal, or nearly equal, to your own it was inadvisable to concentrate against any part of his line, for that might give him an opportunity to concentrate against part of yours.[14] In their view the primary aim was

no longer to break the enemy's line but to keep him from breaking one's own line. The purpose of the increasingly stringent instructions however was to maintain control of the line in the hands of the commander rather than to shackle the commander with a set of written regulations. The commander could signal his divisions or individual ships to make independent maneuvers, but the only sets of signal flags in the fleet were in the flagship and in the signal relay vessels.[15]

The soundness of the new instructions seemed confirmed by the Battle of Barfleur in mid-May 1692 when Tourville broke his line in the presence of a superior English fleet and was soundly beaten. The victorious British chased the defeated French into the port of Cherbourg, and La Hogue Bay, and

[14] The English had solved only half the technique of concentration. They had learned how to bring their main attack against part of the enemy force, but they had not learned in all circumstances how to hold the rest of his force. Until they had solved the *holding* part of their problem, they were dubious about attempting the *hitting* part.

[15] Usually frigates which operated alongside the line of battle to repeat the admiral's signals for the benefit of ships out of visual range.

there captured or destroyed 12 ships. After that England had undisputed command of the Channel, and the French were compelled to limit their activities on the seas to commerce raiding.

By 1697 all participants in the war were exhausted and ready for terms. By the Peace of Ryswick Louis lost everything he had gained in nine years of conflict, but England confirmed her cherished project of closing the port of Antwerp. The use of Antwerp as a natural port for the Rhineland would have minimized the importance of London as the entrepôt of German trade carried to Hamburg. Quite apart from treaty commitments, England had by 1697 taken a strong lead over all possible rivals in the carrying trade and in seaborne commerce in general. Her erstwhile rival, Holland, through the drain on her resources and energies had declined to the rank of secondary power.

THE WAR OF THE SPANISH SUCCESSION, 1702-1713

An attempt by Louis XIV to put a Bourbon on the throne of Spain caused warfare to break out again. In the War of the Spanish Succession, Louis, commanding the resources of France and Spain, faced most of the rest of Western Europe. England entered the conflict not only to curb the power of France but to preserve her trading privileges and to wrest from Spain some of her American colonies. As it turned out she gained a great deal more.

Britain's naval activities consisted mainly of convoy and diversionary maneuvers; France's, of desultory commerce raiding. While the Duke of Marlborough campaigned on the Continent, the Royal Navy operated in the Mediterranean in order to draw French and Spanish forces away from northern Europe. Louis XIV, advised by his economists that he could not afford both a formidable army and a formidable fleet, had permitted the French *Marine* to fall into serious neglect. Partly for this reason British

sailors and marines,[16] with fleet support, were able to capture Gibraltar in July 1704 by amphibious assault.

The Toulon fleet, coming out to contest the capture, met a combined British-Dutch fleet under Admirals Sir George Rooke and Sir Cloudesley Shovel and brought on the Battle of Malaga. This time the allies adhered as closely as possible to the *Fighting Instructions* and kept at it until the French sailed away with neither side quite sure who, if anybody, was the tactical victor.

Malaga was the first battle in which the British made strenuous efforts to maintain a conterminous line throughout. It proved two things: that an engagement fought in accord with formalist doctrine between opponents of similar strength was not likely to be decisive for either side, and that the shock or impact on the enemy which the windward fleet was supposed to achieve was almost impossible of attainment because the attacking ships could not manage to come down together. In the turn from line ahead to line abreast the second ship would put its helm over only as it saw the first coming around. The third would follow the second, and so on down the line. As a result the van came into gun range of the enemy ahead of the rest of the line and took heavy punishment from his concentrated fire (see diagram).

The *Fighting Instructions* which Rooke fought under in the Battle of Malaga were his own, issued in 1703. They were simply Torrington's instructions slanted a little more in the direction of formalism, but they are of special importance because in the relatively long period of peace following the War of the Spanish Succession they became the *Permanent Fighting Instructions*. As such they stultified British tactical progress for 80 years. One reason was that these instructions emanated not from the fleet commanders but from the Admiralty and hence had the force of Standing Orders. Moreover, virtually the only flag signals in use during that period were numbers referring to articles in the *Permanent Instructions*; the admiral

---

[16] The first marines, i.e., true naval infantry as distinguished from soldiers serving temporarily afloat, were organized in the Royal Navy in 1702.

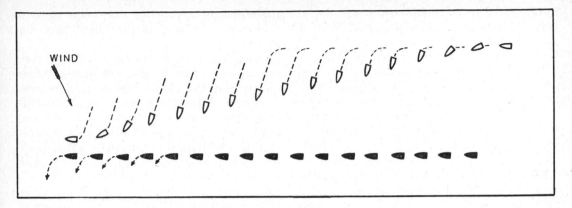

TENDENCY OF WINDWARD SHIPS TO STRAGGLE INTO ACTION

thus had no voice of his own but could speak to his fleet only in the words of dead Torrington and Rooke. Lastly, in the peacetime years the instructions acquired a sacrosanctity never intended by their authors; what had begun as doctrine, subject to experiment and change, ended as inviolate dogma. As a result, between the Battle of Barfleur (1692) and the Battle of the Saints (1782) the English fleet did not win a single clear-cut decision in any sea engagement in which the enemy was prepared and willing to fight a regular battle.

By the terms of the Treaty of Utrecht, concluding the War of the Spanish Succession, England acquired from France the Hudson Bay Territory, Nova Scotia, and Newfoundland. Spain, allied to France, lost Gibraltar and Minorca to England and had to grant an *"Asiento,"* a concession legalizing a small amount of English trade at the focal point of Puerto Bello in Panama. Britain's possession of Gibraltar and Minorca not only made her for the first time an important Mediterranean power, it also rendered it difficult for the French Brest and Toulon fleets ever to join forces during wartime to threaten the Channel. Immediately following the war however England ceased being able to hold aloof from Continental disputes, picking her time and allies, for in 1714 King George of Hanover became George I of England, and his German state became a millstone hung on British foreign policy.

THE WAR OF THE AUSTRIAN SUCCESSION, 1740-1748

British merchants grossly abused the limits placed upon their legal trade with Spanish America. Spain permitted one ship of 500 tons annually to trade at Puerto Bello, but the goods presumably landed from that ship would have sunk the *Normandie*. Such irregularities inevitably led to a rupture. The pretext occurred in 1739 as attested by the appearance in Parliament of one Captain Jenkins carrying an ear he claimed had been sliced off him by an irate Spanish customs officer. The War of Jenkins' Ear soon merged into the War of the Austrian Succession when France moved to capture Antwerp. The long war was terminated by exhaustion rather than victories, and the settlement of Aix-la-Chapelle left things approximately as they had been before hostilities began. England succeeded in keeping Antwerp closed but had to accept a cash settlement in lieu of the *Asiento*. Spain's monopoly had been irretrievably injured however, for Spanish Americans had become habituated to English manufactures, and the subsequent smuggling continued to enrich England at Spain's expense.

Naval interest in the War of the Austrian Succession centers chiefly about the Battle of Toulon, fought in February 1744, because it illustrates to what extent the dead hand of formalism had been laid upon the Royal Navy. A combined French-Spanish fleet of 28 ships broke out of Toulon and headed for Gibraltar in an attempt to join forces with the French Brest fleet. Admiral Thomas Mathews, commanding the British blockading fleet, also of 28 ships, instantly gave chase. He secured the windward position but, because he had been long out of port and his vessels were foul and slow, he could not overtake the enemy van with his own van division. Determined at all costs to prevent the juncture of enemy forces, Mathews decided to disregard Article 19 of the *Permanent Fighting Instructions:* "The van of the admiral's fleet is to steer with the van of the enemy's and there to engage them." Still flying the signal for line, he went down on the enemy just as he was. Thus he brought his van division against the enemy's center and his center against the enemy's rear and left his own rear division with no enemy at all.

The commander of the British rear division was Vice Admiral Richard Lestock, an experienced officer of courage and skill but a surly, jealous man whom Mathews had superseded in command of the Mediterranean. For this and other reasons Lestock bore his commander in chief no love. Mathews had expected the rear division to do the obvious thing: press on all sail and advance into the battle, supporting the British fleet wherever support was needed. Lestock did nothing of the sort. He chose instead to obey Mathews' signal for line quite literally; in very dilatory fashion (because of light airs and adverse currents, he claimed) he came down just where he was—against an empty sea. As a result the overmatched British van and center were badly battered and

succeeded in capturing only one ship, a Spaniard. The rest of the allied fleet got away.

After the battle Mathews put Lestock under arrest, but in the subsequent court-martial the tables were turned—Mathews was cashiered and Lestock was acquitted. This extraordinary decision had a profound and pernicious effect upon subsequent British tactics. The impression, not altogether justified, got abroad that Mathews was broken for failing to follow the *Fighting Instructions.* Thereafter it was a courageous officer indeed who would break his line or fail to fight van to van, center to center, and rear to rear, whatever opportunities for concentration presented themselves. The conterminous fleet line of battle had become inviolate.

The French meanwhile were developing a tactical reply to growing British formalism. Because the army was absorbing so much of France's resources the *Marine* was directed to conserve its ships. So French naval officers, if they could not avoid battle altogether, deliberately sought the lee, or defensive, position. Then as the British came down in line abreast, or line of bearing, the French would begin firing at sails and rigging, concentrating on the enemy van since that ordinarily came first into range. Because the British normally fired at hulls, the French tended to suffer more casualties, but they could hope to end the action by falling off to leeward after rendering the British powerless to chase. These French tactics did not sink enemy ships or make captives but they often as not obliged the British to return to base for repairs. Meanwhile the French possessed local command of the sea and were thus able for a time to carry out operations unmolested.

4

The Seven Years' War

No FACTION WAS SATISFIED with the settlement of Aix-la-Chapelle, least of all the British colonists in America, who had captured Louisburg, the key to the St. Lawrence River, and had seen it returned to France in exchange for far-off Madras in India. Only a few years were needed to lick wounds and prepare for another conflict. This was the Seven Years' War (1756-1763).

The Seven Years' War is a classic example of a world war that was won by expert command of the sea. It is particularly interesting today because the British exploited their superior naval strength by initiating numerous "conjunct expeditions," which were tactical ancestors of modern amphibious operations.

In the struggle for colonial supremacy that was largely decided by the Seven Years' War, France had the serious disadvantage of being compelled to expend most of her military effort fighting on the Continent, while England's effort was concentrated upon the sea. French armies could defeat England's armies, but the Royal Navy usually captured enough French commerce to finance Britain's friends and enough French colonies to more than redress British colonial defeats. France was gradually being leeched white. Her economy was deteriorating into the chaos that would ultimately produce her Revolution.

BACKGROUND OF THE WAR

The French had gone into the New World for gold and had stayed to develop the fur trade, while the British had sought homes. Thus by 1750 there were only 65,000 Canadians to oppose the expansionist drive of 2,000,000 British subjects penned by the mountains in a narrow strip of coast from New England to the Carolinas. Rivers were highways in America, and of these, the Ohio gave access to the wild, rich land of the Middle West, which was an essential part of France's fur empire. In 1753 the French began to guard their heartland of America by building a chain of fortifications from the Great Lakes to the Ohio and thence down the Mississippi to New Orleans. The salient of this chain was to be placed at the site of present-day Pittsburgh, well within land claimed by both Virginia and Pennsylvania.

The Virginians sent George Washington, then a young militia colonel, with a detachment of 400 men to eject the trespassers. His defeat in May 1754, after a sharp battle against heavy odds, led eventually to the Seven Years' War. All of the colonists were alarmed by the construction of Fort Duquesne at Pittsburgh, for they regarded the French fort as a haven and supply base for the Indians, whose tomahawks and arrows were the deadliest barrier to westward movement. Various disagreements prevented the British colonies from uniting their abundant resources for defense, but all united in appeals to the Crown.

However England's Prime Minister, the Duke of Newcastle, was reluctant to take any steps that the economy-withered Royal Navy could not support. The safety of the German state of Hanover, the home of England's king, had to be a prime consideration in British policy. Hostile moves could not be initiated until some Continental ally could be induced to protect Hanover by checkmating France. While Newcastle negotiated with Prussia and Russia to fight France in Europe, Parliament goaded him into sending General Edward Braddock and 1,000 men to capture Fort Duquesne. France promptly sent a small reinforcement of 3,000 men to Canada but, desiring to avoid full-scale war, refrained from any hostile move on the Continent.

As soon as Newcastle had successfully negotiated for a Russian army, he was free to aid the colonies and satisfy the demands of the war party in Parliament. His first move was to release the Royal Navy for raids on French communications at sea. Vice Admiral Edward Boscawen with 24 ships of the line [1] attempted to prevent the French reinforcement from entering the St. Lawrence. He succeeded in overtaking only two ships, but Admiral Sir Edward Hawke, cruising off Cape Finisterre to intercept the annual convoy returning from the French colonies, captured some 300 vessels.

Disturbed by the belligerence of his British subjects, King George went to Hanover to expedite the treaty, which provided for the hiring of 55,000 Russian troops to defend his natal kingdom. The treaty with Russia was overshadowed however when Frederick the Great in January 1756 allied Prussia with England to finance his impending war with Austria.

France was slow to declare the war into which she had been provoked; she was debating an invasion of the British Isles planned by Louis, Duc de Belleisle. Belleisle's plan was to strike a hard blow which would produce a swift and acceptable peace. He argued that conquest in America was difficult because of British naval superiority and to seize Hanover would mean a fight with Frederick of Prussia. But England was close at hand, and with luck could be breached while her naval superiority was dissipated by diversions. He believed that the capture of Minorca would make England scatter her navy in order to protect her far-flung possessions. When England had only the Home Fleet to protect the British Isles, Belleisle, with the combined Brest and Rochefort squadrons and 100,000 troops, hoped to attack England at three different places simultaneously and immediately reinforce whichever expedition gained a foothold. He realized he was violating security by committing his land force to the uncertainties of a disputed sea but he felt that the deplorable condition of the British Army compensated somewhat for his rashness. France had to postpone her invasion plans however until her land frontiers were secured against possible hostilities with Prussia, so Belleisle's dream was shattered. Thus the pattern of the war was foreshadowed: France was to be preoccupied on the Continent while England roamed the seas, carrying the war as far as the Philippines.

---

[1] In 1755 the largest ship of the line carried 100 guns and 841 men. The two-decked 74 with 644 men was most popular. The class extended down to the 50-gun ship, which by the end of the war was used in frigate squadrons as a flagship, while the two-decked 64 was the smallest ship. Frigates ranged from 20 to 44 guns. Square-rigged sloops-of-war had 12 to 18 light guns. Prior to the American Revolution, as ships with 120 guns and nearly 1,000 men were constructed, the division between sloop and frigate was set at 28 guns. The large crews for vessels which rarely exceeded 2,500 tons were required to manhandle the cumbersome cannon. Seven men were needed for a 12-pounder, and 15 for the 42-pounder occasionally found on the largest ships.

Only a vestige of the plan remained: France decided to capture Minorca.

THE BATTLE
FOR MINORCA

By seizing Minorca, which was England's only Mediterranean base, the French not only expected to throw the Royal Navy back upon the resources of Gibraltar but also to gain something which might lure Spain into an alliance.

Despite a year's warning, England was not ready for initiating actual, full-scale hostilities. Mindful of the heavy cost of the recent War of the Austrian Succession, Newcastle was reluctant to press for war, contenting himself with readying England's mothballed fleet to stop Belleisle's rumored invasion. Even though Port Mahon was known to be threatened, a year had actually lapsed since Boscawen's breach of the peace, and France had not retaliated. Consequently Newcastle was very slow in correcting the virtually helpless condition of the British garrison on Minorca.

The 2,800 effective men at Port Mahon were commanded by 84-year-old Lieutenant General William Blakeney because the Governor was on leave, as were many officers whose absence was to be desperately felt. In April 1756 Newcastle scraped together a squadron of ten ships under Admiral Sir John Byng to send belatedly to the Mediterranean. Byng's orders were vague, making him responsible for not only Minorca, but also, as he explained at his later court-martial, for Gibraltar as well. Unhappy about the paucity of his undermanned, meager force, Byng requested more of the ships being commissioned at Spithead and was assured that the French could have no more than six or seven ships to match him at Toulon.

The British Admiralty was overly optimistic. The day after Byng weighed anchor, a strong French armament left Toulon. Twelve well-found ships commanded by the Marquis de la Galissonière escorted 150 transports bearing 16,000 troops under the

Duc de Richelieu. Ten days later, Richelieu landed without opposition on Minorca as Blakeney concentrated his small garrison in Fort St. Philip dominating Port Mahon.

On May 2, Byng reached Gibraltar and learned of the attack from the commander of the Mediterranean detachment, whose handful of ships had been unable to cope with the French fleet. Everyone at Gibraltar assumed that Blakeney could not resist very long. There were few troops to be spared from the Rock to take to Minorca, even had transport been available. Pausing only to replenish and to embark a token relief force of one battalion, after five days Byng pushed on with 13 ships into what is possibly the most tragic controversy in British naval history.

On the morning of May 19, almost within the three-mile extreme range of his cannon, Byng was becalmed in a slight easterly wind by the land mass of Minorca, close enough to see Blakeney's flag valiantly flying over the beleaguered fort. No French ships were in sight. At his trial, Byng was censured for not seizing the opportunity to land his handful of troops and the missing officers of the Minorca garrison. However, because of his short-handed condition, he had upon entering the Mediterranean been obliged to strip seamen from his frigates and to draft soldiers to fill the guncrews of his battle line. Rather than expose his men in boats, Byng wanted to sail into Port Mahon. Unfortunately for him, square rigged men-of-war could sail no closer than six points into the wind, and before the wind veered from the east to favor him, Galissonière appeared on the windward side of the island.

With the aggressive spirit that has characterized British admirals, Byng thought only of coming to grips with the French. Turning away to the south to fill his sails, he began maneuvering to get the windward position. Byng won the weather gage about noon of the 20th, some ten miles southeast of Minorca. The wind being southerly, Galissonière moved between Byng and Minorca. Thus, each admiral had the position he desired. Easily able to replace ships, British leaders fought whenever possible, knowing

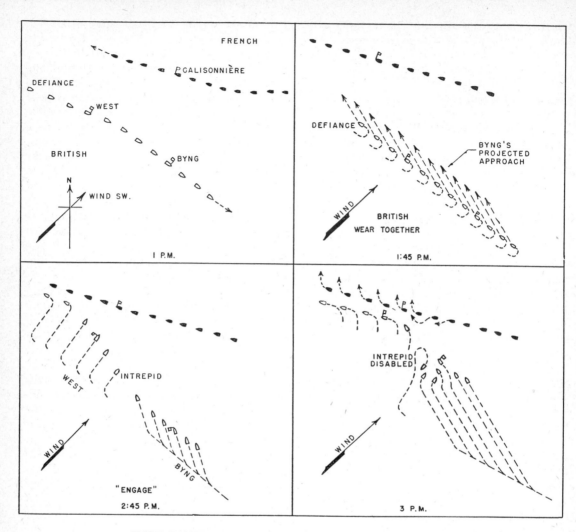

THE BATTLE FOR MINORCA, MAY 18, 1756

by increasing proof of experience that the destruction of enemy organized forces ultimately meant the attainment of whatever objectives were dependent upon command of the sea. On the other hand, French admirals as poor relations of the army did not enjoy the privilege of fighting at will. Battle was usually thrust upon them. When French ships were lost, the French Treasury demanded a good explanation. Since a bit of land like Minorca constituted a valid physical objective, something tangible to offer in exchange for shattered ships, Galissonière was willing to fight to preserve his prize.

Having one more ship in his line than Galissonière's 12, Byng detached a 50-gun ship to a signaling station with his frigates to windward. This curious action was to prevent any of the confusion that had occasionally risen because of disparate numbers and the better to conform to the conterminous line required by the *Fighting Instructions.*

Byng's fleet was in two divisions, himself with the van and Rear Admiral Temple West with the rear. The French came slowly on a westerly course, sailing easily under topsails. Going southeasterly to meet and parallel the French, Byng closehauled to reach south and open a wide angle between himself and Galissonière. He deliberately stood on past the French rear so that when he shifted to the port tack he could come down on the French in line of bearing, which would permit his broadsides to bear during his approach. Byng desired his captains to meet their customary foes but did not want them to go down helplessly into raking fire, unable to reply until the time to swing parallel ship to ship at musket range. Unhappily for him, such a maneuver was not prescribed in the *Fighting Instructions* and was not understood by his officers.

When Byng finally turned together, Galissonière had thrown his sails aback, killing way, so that relative movement would spoil the effect of Byng's stratagem. The English captains were completely confused by their admiral's unorthodox evolution. The captain of the *Defiance,* leading West's division, cracked on sail to pull abreast of his proper adversary instead of steering the reciprocal of Byng's opening course. Other captains likewise sought to retrieve what they considered their admiral's blunder, and Byng's tight line began to open. Without an adequate signal in the *Fighting Instructions* to clarify his intentions, Byng had to accept the bungling of his tactical innovation, and made the signal to engage. This slowed West and turned his ships into courses perpendicular to the French van. By this time, West's division had lost the position that Byng had obtained, and were raked three times in their head-on attack. The Admiral continued his slanting advance as the quickest means of getting within support distance before resuming line ahead parallel to Galissonière.

As West came under fire, the Admiral attempted to support him at long range. In the dense black smoke of his first broadside, Byng's ships lost their battle order and the Admiral killed way rather than let his division go slovenly into action. In the midst of this re-forming, West's rearmost ship, the *Intrepid,* completed the day's mishaps by losing her foremast and going out of control right across Byng's line of advance. This brought the leading vessels of Byng's division almost to a halt to avoid collision and threw the following ships into further disorder. Byng's flag captain (chief of staff), seeing West's division undergoing heavy punishment, now urged the Admiral to run down in all haste to his support without regard to the condition of his line.

The Admiral was shocked at the suggestion, for as Captain Byng he had sat on the fateful court-martial that broke Mathews after the Battle of Toulon—in part for taking his line down in imperfect order. "You would not have me, as admiral of the fleet, run down as if I were going to engage a single ship," he replied. "It was Mr. Mathews's misfortune to be prejudiced by not carrying down his force together, which I shall endeavor to avoid." [2]

So West fought Galissonière alone and suffered from French gunnery practice while Byng struggled to re-form his line. West's guns forced five of the ships he was fighting to give way, but by then Galissonière was satisfied he could safely withdraw to the haven of Port Mahon and easily broke off action. Heavily damaged aloft, West was in no condition to hinder the escape, and Byng was still out of effective range. All of the French ships had suffered casualties, but only one of Byng's division was harmed. West's division, which had borne the brunt of the fighting, was heavily damaged.

Byng jury-rigged repairs and waited fruitlessly two days for another chance at Galissonière, who was content merely to cover the siege. The British ships needed yard facilities, available in Port Mahon, but Byng and his council of war decided the siege could not be raised and so returned to Gibraltar. When Byng reached the Rock he found a reinforcement of four ships, but repairs and casualties occupied him for almost a month until Admiral Hawke arrived to supersede and send him home for trial. By then it was too late to aid Blakeney, who had surrendered on June 28, 1756.

[2] Quoted in Alfred Thayer Mahan, *The Influence of Sea Power upon History, 1660-1783* (Boston, 1898), 287.

It was his retirement from the Mediterranean which brought Byng to his death at the hands of a firing squad. His contemporaries thought, and posterity has agreed, that Byng had been in the rare situation for a British admiral where it was better not to have fought. So long as his fleet was loose, threatening communications with Toulon, the siege was a gamble. Byng's hovering had nearly panicked the French troops worn down in the face of Blakeney's magnificent resistance. When Byng disappeared, Richelieu steeled himself to accept the losses of a grand assault before he was rendered powerless to make any assault at all. In his trial, Byng accused the Newcastle government of using him as a scapegoat to conceal England's unpreparedness. He cleared himself of the charge of cowardice but his peers judged that he had not done his utmost. Under the current Articles of War, that was a capital crime, and so on March 14, 1757 Byng knelt before a marine firing squad. Following his death, English admirals looked more critically at the *Fighting Instructions* and ventured to make corrections and additions. Formalism began to wane.

PITT'S PLAN

The loss of Minorca was a terrific jolt to the Newcastle ministry, for it followed news of the infamous Black Hole of Calcutta and Braddock's defeat; on the Continent, Frederick had taken full advantage of his English treaty to begin the European phase of the War by invading Saxony. To save himself, Newcastle had to combine with his opponent, William Pitt. Newcastle believed that Hanover had to be preserved and that France had to be met and defeated on the battlefields of Europe. To the Royal Navy he assigned the role of a mobile defense force, to thwart all attempted invasions of England. Such a policy was incredible to William Pitt. He denounced the folly of putting England's feeble army within reach of the superb French Continental armies while chaining Britain's powerful fleet. His opin-

ion that Hanover was not a fundamental concern for shaping English policy did not endear him to George II, and prevented his being Prime Minister. Instead, Pitt became the Newcastle ministry's Principal Secretary of State with authority to conduct the war.

Pitt possessed a rare understanding of strategy, with which he integrated diplomacy and the armed services into an invincible team. His overall plan was simple. Except for British troops serving in Hanover, the Continental war would be left to subsidized allies, with an occasional amphibious expedition to provide a diversion. England's real effort would be in the colonies, aiming principally at conquering French America. In broadest terms, Pitt proposed to keep England on the strategic defensive in Europe and on the strategic offensive in the colonies. The French, also choosing to use their finer service, unwittingly cooperated with Pitt by concentrating their military effort against Frederick.

Seeing the war as a whole, Pitt was sanguine about the loss of Minorca, for the Royal Navy was thereby relieved of the defense of anything in the Mediterranean, and could apply maximum effort to the aggressive blockade of Toulon. This supplemented the blockade of Brest maintained by the Home Fleet based on Portsmouth and made it obvious to the French that, if they wished to use the sea, they must first fight. To soothe the anxieties of those who feared invasion, Pitt established frigate squadrons of observation to stand inshore from time to time to discourage the accumulation of boats and personnel at the French Channel ports.

The war on the Continent found Frederick of Prussia fighting alone, except for the aid of a small British force in Hanover, against most of the European nations, principally Austria and France. France was allied to Austria with the hope that as a reward she would receive the port of Antwerp from the Hapsburgs. Russia, Poland, Sweden, and Saxony were fighting with the aim of acquiring Prussian territory. In the last stages of the conflict, Spain entered for an opportunity to injure England. It was Pitt's

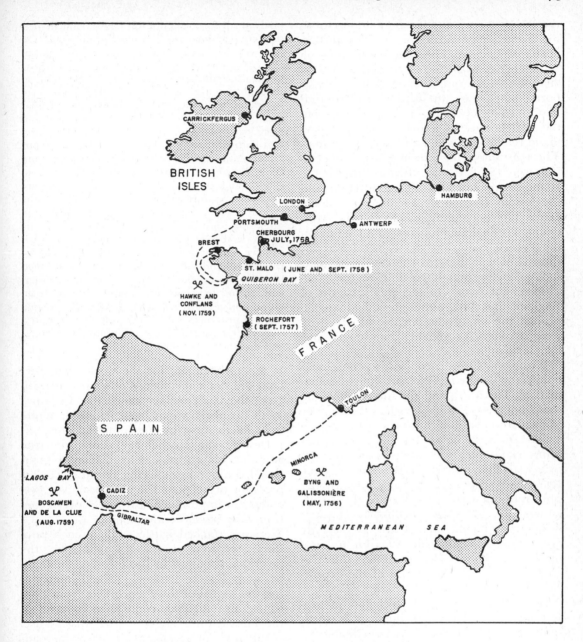

THE SEVEN YEARS' WAR IN EUROPEAN WATERS

plan to engage the British navy and army in amphibious, or conjunct, expeditions against the coast of France so that French military forces would be diverted from Germany, thus relieving the pressure on Frederick.

"CONJUNCT EXPEDITIONS"

The first such diversion was against Rochefort in September 1757. Rochefort was a major shipbuilding city and naval arsenal in the Bay of Biscay, and far more important to the French navy than the stations at Bordeaux or Lorient. The expedition sailed on September 8, with 9,000 men under General Sir John Mordaunt, embarked in 49 transports escorted by 19 ships under Admiral Hawke. The operation was a failure from the start because of a lack of clear-cut command relationships and a plan of operations. The two redeeming features of this expedition were the battering, then capture, of the Island of Aix by Captain Richard Howe and the lessons learned by Lieutenant Colonel James Wolfe, chief of staff to General Mordaunt. Wolfe drew up plans for a landing on the French coast but the General and his council of war came to the conclusion that such a landing was impossible. So the expedition went home, to the great chagrin of England and Pitt, although it had accomplished the important purpose of diverting some ten French regiments from starting out for Germany.

Wolfe was humiliated in his professional opinion of himself at the subsequent court-martial. He was asked questions which he could not answer exactly, such as the number of men who could have been simultaneously embarked in the boats. The drawn-out, rambling trial, which ultimately exonerated the principals in contrast to the fate of poor Byng, was an education for Wolfe. In the process of questioning, he learned the lessons he was later to apply so brilliantly. Hawke's hearty recommendation of him as the only army officer worth his salt secured him a promotion to colonel. Though he was thus singled out from all the officers of the expedition, Wolfe did not gloat.

Instead, he thought of Rochefort in professional terms. His sober judgment is worth quoting as evidence of his perceptiveness:

I have found out that an Admiral should endeavour to run into an enemy's port immediately after he appears before it; that he should anchor the transport ships and frigates as close as he can to the land; that he should reconnoitre and observe it as quick as possible, and lose no time in getting the troops on shore; that previous directions should be given in respect to landing the troops, and a proper disposition made for the boats of all sorts, appointing leaders and fit persons for conducting the different divisions. On the other hand, experience shows me that, in an affair depending upon vigour and dispatch, the Generals should settle their plan of operations so that no time may be lost in idle debate and consultations when the sword should be drawn; that pushing on smartly is the road to success, and more particularly so in an affair of this nature; that nothing is to be reckoned an obstacle to your undertaking which is not found really so upon trial; that in war something must be allowed to chance and fortune, seeing it is in its nature hazardous, and an option of difficulties; that the greatness of an object should come under consideration, opposed to the impediments that lie in the way; that the honour of one's country is to have some weight; and that, in particular circumstances and times, the loss of a thousand men is rather an advantage to a nation than otherwise, seeing that gallant attempts raise its reputation and make it respectable; whereas the contrary appearances sink the credit of a country, ruin the troops, and create infinite uneasiness and discontent at home.[3]

It was unfortunate for the world that England did not remember Wolfe when it initiated the Dardanelles campaign in 1915. With his observations fixed in mind, Wolfe went off to America and immortal glory.

Despite the Rochefort failure and the gibes of his enemies, Pitt displayed great moral courage in adhering resolutely to his program of keeping the European war secondary in importance. His first concern continued to be the enticement of the French fleet into pitched battle while French reinforcements were prevented from altering the favorable situation in the colonies. In October 1757 Hawke narrowly missed intercepting the return of the French fleet from Louisburg, but Pitt was content to have all of the French units at last under surveillance.

When warm weather again made the roads passable, the campaign in Germany was renewed; Pitt also renewed his diversionary attacks on the French coast. Since Rochefort, the Admiralty had made progress in planning. The escort fleet had only five small two-deckers, with the main strength

---

[3] Robert Wright, *The Life of Major-General James Wolfe* (London, 1864), 396-397.

in ten frigates and 37 smaller bombardment vessels whose shallow draft would permit a close approach to the shore. The escort was commanded by Captain Richard Howe; the objectives were the privateer nests on the Normandy-Brittany coast.

In June 1758 the first target was St. Malo, attacked by 13,000 regulars under the Duke of Marlborough. Howe's guns silenced token resistance by weak coastal batteries and drove away a small body of French troops posted near the shores of Cancale Bay, eight miles east of St. Malo. Disembarkation was swift. In perfect line, the boats pulled inshore, touching together, so that troops formed regimental front and dug in to secure their beachhead within an hour. The steep coast, soaring to a plateau above, impeded movement and allowed the governor of St. Malo to lock up his fortress town. St. Malo was built upon a granite promontory nearly a mile offshore, connected to the mainland village of St. Servan by a causeway, which the French blew up. Marlborough had to be content with burning more than a hundred raiders nestled in the port of St. Servan. Retiring in good order after eight days ashore, Marlborough remained a week at anchor in Cancale Bay, shattering French complacency. With the French countryside trembling in anticipation, the expedition demonstrated against ports in Brittany and then returned to England.

In August, Lieutenant General Thomas Bligh, replacing Marlborough, and Captain Howe sailed to attack strongly defended Cherbourg. Keels touching, Howe's armada of shallow draft bombardment vessels thundered at the town and works, while the transports assembled at a beach a few miles away and loaded their boats. These boats were new special landing craft similar to World War II LCVP's, with forward ramps for easy transference of horses and vehicles to the shore. A determined force of 3,000 French who had assembled to contest the landing were pinned down by Howe's furious volume of shot, grape, and howitzer shells. The famous British Guards hit the beach, formed line as the bombardment lifted, charged, and in a display of perfect

coordination took the beachhead at bayonet point. Cherbourg, whose fortifications like Singapore's in 1941 covered only the sea approaches, surrendered meekly when taken from the landward side. For a week, the British destroyed fortifications and shipping. But Bligh's troops got out of hand; looting and drunkenness destroyed the efficiency of

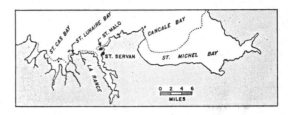

ST. MALO AND ENVIRONS, 1758

his once magnificent force. Howe had to assume responsibility for planning the re-embarkation of the demoralized troops, after they had virtually put Cherbourg out of the war.

Leaving Cherbourg, Howe transported the expedition to St. Malo to complete the job begun by Marlborough. Landing six miles east of the port at St. Lunaire to dislocate coastal pursuit, Bligh dawdled for three days, thereby providing the Duc d'Aiguillon, military governor of Brittany, ample time to prepare his defenses. When a rising westerly wind suddenly forced Howe to shift his anchorage eight miles west to the friendly lee of St. Cas Bay, Bligh gave up his plans for St. Malo. Refusing to be deprived of naval gunfire support, he marched along the coast after the fleet, and began to re-embark. Bad discipline straggled his troops. The consequent delay allowed d'Aiguillon to catch Bligh at St. Cas with one foot on the beach and the other in the water, and without a good re-embarkation plan. Two-thirds of the British were afloat when the French appeared on the heights covering the beach and deployed out of reach of Howe's guns. The rear guard of 1,400 men of the Guards lived up to their great tradition. Fighting off envelopment and frontal assault until their ammunition failed, the Guards extricated the last of Bligh's stragglers. Then, alone on the beach, they ran for the boats, where Howe by personal example was fishing soldiers out of the churning water, but it was too late. D'Aiguillon cut down or captured the Guards almost to a man. From her proudest regiment, England lost nearly a thousand killed or wounded, and another six hundred were prisoners.

Thus, Pitt's conjunct expeditions fell into disrepute. Development of a system of amphibious warfare so promisingly begun by actual trial and error had to await another time, for Wolfe was the only ardent army advocate of combined operations, and he was soon to fall on the Plains of Abraham.

Ironically, despite St. Cas, Pitt's diversion scheme helped enormously to produce the naval crisis he and his admirals desired.

THE FRENCH
COUNTERATTACK

The epochal year 1759 justified Pitt's war plan. France, unable to defeat Frederick, losing ground in the colonies, hurt and harassed by the raids on her ports, revived Belleisle's project of hitting the heart of her principal foe. The year was ideal for invasion. The British Army was away either on colonial conquest or supporting Ferdinand and the Hanoverians, then in the field with Frederick. Nothing stood in the way of humbling England except the Channel and the Royal Navy. These proved more than adequate.

As detailed by the Duc de Choiseul, 50,000 veterans would storm ashore at Suffolk in England, while 10,000 landed in Scotland to confuse the defense and perhaps form a second thrust at London. Taking a lesson from Pitt, they would stage diversions before and during the actual invasion. Choiseul recognized that success hinged upon temporary naval superiority in the Channel, which he hoped to achieve by bringing the Toulon fleet to Brest. Choiseul's plan was a model for Napoleon 50 years later, but not even the great Emperor solved the key problem of getting the Toulon fleet safely to Brest in the face of British watchdogs. Neither Choi-

seul nor Napoleon saw in peacetime the folly of violating strategic concentration by splitting the French fleet between the Mediterranean and the Atlantic.

Since a major part of their purpose was to frighten the English into recalling troops from distant enterprises, the French made small efforts at secrecy. Flatboats of the new English type were openly built at the Channel ports. At Le Havre and Dunkirk, invasion troops ostentatiously practiced getting in and out of boats under the scrutiny of the frigates patiently cruising offshore and reporting every new development to Pitt. These activities had the reverse of the effect desired. All hands in the Royal Navy were delighted rather than alarmed. With frigates warily checking the invasion ports, the British Admiralty put well-founded reliance upon the ability of Hawke to deal with the Brest squadrons, while Boscawen coped with Toulon.

Boscawen's turn came first at the Battle of Lagos (see map, page 73).

Contrary to French hopes, the capture of Minorca had not made the Mediterranean their lake. Losing Port Mahon severely strained British logistics in supporting the blockade off Toulon, but Gibraltar proved adequate. However, in those bygone days of the graceful ships of the line, wooden construction entailed maintenance problems for hulls that got wormy as well as foul. Therefore in August 1759, after an eventful summer of frigate actions, Boscawen had to take his fleet to the Rock for careening and repair before the winter gales. A leader of more than ordinary excellence, he prudently left behind him a chain of small, fast vessels to warn him if the enemy sortied in his absence.

Impatiently waiting at Toulon to execute orders to run for Brest, Admiral de la Clue regarded Boscawen's disappearance as his own opportunity. Leaving hurriedly with 12 ships and three frigates, de la Clue approached the Straits of Gibraltar in the night of August 17-18. Fortune seemed to favor him. Haze, darkness, and a strong east wind astern were as perfect a combination as he could have prescribed. Then he discovered the professional competence of his adversary. Off in the gloom, an orange flash lighted up an English frigate firing signals to warn Boscawen.

Fortune had only flirted with de la Clue. Putting out his lights, he pressed on toward Portugal. In thickening haze he gradually lost sight of his three frigates and five ships of the line, which dared not display lanterns. The number was unlucky. At sunrise, sighting eight sail to windward, de la Clue naturally assumed they were his missing captains, who had actually made for Cadiz. He shortened sail and waited. The ships were Boscawen's.

As Boscawen stood down toward a puzzling enemy who had obligingly killed way, he was unable to answer a recognition signal. De la Clue was thereby disabused of his error and immediately filled away to struggle for the weather gage. Unhappily for him, seven of his ships were hamstrung by one slow sailer which held them back from the speed necessary to outreach Boscawen. The best that de la Clue could do was to dress his line and try to protract the westward chase throughout the day.

Had Boscawen sacrificed individual speed to keep a rigid column, de la Clue might have escaped, but he did not hamper himself with the niceties of the *Fighting Instructions*. Luckily, a loophole had long since been found by way of one of the oldest and apparently most restrictive of the formalist provisions, which had reappeared as Article 21 in the *Permanent Instructions:* "None of the ships in the fleet shall pursue any small number of the enemy's ships till the main body be disabled or run." Article 25 made the loophole even more apparent: "If the enemy be put to the run, and the Admiral thinks it convenient the whole fleet shall follow them, he will make all the sail he can himself after the enemy, and . . . every ship in the fleet is to use his best endeavour to come up with the enemy and lay them on board." In other words, if the enemy fleet is disabled or on the run and "the Admiral thinks it convenient," he might signal General Chase and dispense with the line. The onus of course was put on the admiral himself, for it was up to him to decide if the enemy was disabled or running. If he so decided and won a victory nobody was going to inquire too closely about the state of the enemy when the signal for Chase was given. On the contrary, if he signaled Chase and lost, then he would almost certainly have to prove to a skeptical court-martial that the enemy was indeed disabled or on the run. Thus the decision for a chase was the touchstone distinguishing those British admirals possessing merely physical courage, which seems to have been the common possession of the breed, from those possessing the rarer quality of moral courage. Yet during the long stagnation of British line tactics, between 1692 and 1782, every clear-cut English naval victory was attained by use of General Chase.

As officers experimented with Chase, there gradually grew up a body of *Additional Instructions* which tended to convert pursuit from a mere free-for-all into something more scientific. One maneuver, based on an experiment by Admiral Hawke, provided for a sort of leap-frog attack. In this attack the pursuing fleet endeavored to maintain at least a semblance of a column until its van had overtaken the enemy rear. Then the leading ship of the attacking fleet engaged the rear ship of the enemy. The following attacking ships passed on the disengaged side and took under fire the enemy ships one after the other as they came into range. Ideally this maneuver would result in a battle line-to-line, with the attackers in reverse order from their original line. Complications of seamanship and enemy reaction prevented the perfect achievement of such an order of battle,[4] but such plans helped bring order into pursuits that might otherwise have degenerated into mere scrambles. Unhappily for Boscawen, Hawke's concept had not yet been incorporated into the *Additional Instructions* when de la Clue slipped past Gibraltar.

In the morning of August 18 Boscawen, perceiving that de la Clue meant not to stand his ground, signaled General Chase.

[4] Unless we except Nelson's attack on the anchored Danish fleet in 1801.

At 2:30 PM the somewhat scattered British van caught up with the French rear. Boscawen evidently wished at this point to execute Hawke's leap-frog attack, but he lacked a signal to make his intention clear to his captains. To his consternation, his leading ships all concentrated fire on the *Centaur,* 74 guns, commanded by de Sabran, at the end of de la Clue's line. Heroically accepting the function of rear guard, de Sabran tried to give his admiral a chance to escape by hotly challenging the British as they came up one by one. The *Centaur's* well-served guns fired high and slashed the rigging of five adversaries, rendering them incapable of effectively supporting the determined attack which Boscawen's flagship led on the rest of the French fleet. Although de la Clue could not save the *Centaur* from capture or de Sabran from a gallant death, the botching of Boscawen's tactics allowed the French to survive into the night. Firing ceased at eight o'clock.

De la Clue no longer had an organized force. Two severely damaged 74's disappeared into the darkness, leaving him in the 80-gun *Ocean* with only four of the 12 ships he had so confidently taken from Toulon. Through the night, Boscawen grimly jury-rigged his battered masts and spars and kept under easy sail to windward, tracking his quarry. At dawn, suffering from a badly wounded leg, aware of the consequences of his defeat, de la Clue studied Boscawen's fleet of 14 ships and bitterly concluded that further fighting was useless. Rather than give up his ships, he decided to burn them on the nearby coast of neutral Portugal. Heading for Lagos Bay, de la Clue made his intentions clear to his remaining subordinates by ramming the *Ocean* aground so hard her masts all went by the board. His subordinates were not made of the same tough fiber, timidly anchoring and providing an irresistible lure for Boscawen. In the spirit of British admirals when an enemy is in sight, Boscawen ignored the warning shots from a nearby Portuguese fort. Relentlessly entering the bay, he fired until the three French ships surrendered in full sight of their miserable admiral.

With the dispersal or capture of the Toulon fleet, France lost her chance to fight for superiority in the Channel, but her miseries were not at an end. Giving up the full scale project against England, Choiseul recklessly persisted in carrying through the Scottish phase. The Brest fleet was given the option of starting the operation whenever weather forced the British away from their blockade. In November, weather did drive Hawke back to England. Shortly after he left, the French West Indian convoy he had been hopeful of seizing slipped into Brest. Hawke's loss of prize money was more than offset by the assurance given to Admiral Conflans that the coast was clear, because Conflans put to sea, thereby offering Hawke a greater prize. Conflans headed southeast to drive off the heavy frigate squadron watching the transports for d'Aiguillon's troops assembled at Quiberon Bay. The day that Conflans sailed, Hawke was flying back with all of his expert seamanship, and was soon swiftly plowing the French wake.

On the morning of November 29, Conflans was a little to the southwest of Belle Île, watching a fresh, rising westerly wind driving on an array of sails he mistook for a fleet train sent down to revictual the British frigates at Quiberon. Enjoying the luxury of having a van detachment off scattering the British frigates, Conflans prudently formed his 21 ships in line of battle. Notwithstanding this automatic reaction to strange sails, Conflans was astonished when the approaching vessels proved to be black ships of the line flying the white ensign. Not having dreamed that Hawke could be so near, Conflans was surprised in the true military sense. Too rattled to improvise a battle plan, he thought only of escape.

Conflans did not believe that Hawke would dare to follow him into Quiberon Bay, for the wind was beginning to lash the sea into moving mountains; he misjudged the man who had been patiently waiting two years for a fight. As the British frigates off Belle Île scattered like rabbits on the approach of the magnificent French ships, Conflans regarded the rising gale as a tremendous ally, which would compel Hawke to sheer away from the sunken reefs choking the entrance. It is possible however that Hawke had charts of the entrance as good as those of the French, for his frigates had often boldly stood into the bay. To him, a great storm meant as little as sacrosanct neutrality had meant to Boscawen when the enemy was at sea. On seeing the French take to their heels, he had immediately signaled General Chase but had also flown signal for line ahead. He had seen to it in advance that his captains understood his intention. In the course of pursuit the British ships would gradually form column in order of speed with the fastest sailer at the head of the new line. This ship should at least be able to stick closely behind the enemy, following him through the intricacies of the reefs and serving as guide for the succeeding British ships.

Hotly pursued by the British, Conflans cherished the notion of getting into the bay, hugging the western shoals, and thence by some legerdemain slipping back across the entrance to bottle up Hawke tightly within the terrible reefs. But Hawke's close pursuit prevented Conflans from organizing even the semblance of a military defense. Pursuer and pursued pounded pell-mell through the crashing waves towards the black foaming bay of Quiberon. There was neither room nor time for an orderly battle.

Hawke's van caught the French rear as Conflans, himself in the lead ship, was rounding into the bay. When an outnumbered French 74 valiantly opened her lower deck gunports to use her main battery, the rushing sea filled and sank her with 800 men. Another challenged Hawke's 100-gun flagship *Royal George,* and was blown to pieces by one broadside from the mighty three-decker. Hawke's terrified pilot warned him about the certain death waiting among the great rocks in the spuming valleys of the charging sea. "You have now done your duty in apprising me of the danger," Hawke replied. "Lay me alongside the French admiral!"

The pilot was unable to obey, because Conflans did not tarry in his panic and there was too little light on a short winter's afternoon for Hawke to halt his prey. In the gloom, Conflans scudded off for the river Vilaine. Darkness and gale at last imposed caution on Hawke, who put down his anchors

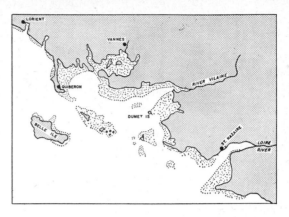

QUIBERON BAY

near the isle of Dumet and grimly waited out the night for a chance to complete the destruction of a fleet that dared to use the oceans he thought belonged to England. He had two fine prizes to replace the two ships he lost upon passing the reefs. These were all he was to have.

In the morning, there was no French fleet. In the confusion and darkness, seven vessels had slipped away to Rochefort, where they remained for the rest of the war. Seven more jettisoned their guns and used the storm's crest of water to ride up into the shallow Vilaine, where they were stranded for more than a year until dredging and ditches could free them. Finding himself alone, Conflans deliberately crushed his 80-gun flagship *Soleil Royal* upon the rocks.

France's navy was broken. England had won command of the sea. Occasionally the French sent out detachments of frigates or ships on some desperate, foredoomed enterprise. They continued their privateer war —indeed, a dashing privateersman named Thurot in 1760 actually held for a brief time the town of Carrickfergus in northern Ireland. The Royal Navy could not stop every French raider that left port, but they had achieved complete security for all of England's military movements afloat and denied the same security to their foes.

It was a display of uncontestable power when Pitt in the triumphs of his war plan was permitted to have another conjunct expedition to relieve hard-pressed Frederick and chose to capture and hold Belle Île. The British flag was thus arrogantly planted on soil that overlooked the very waters where France had lost her colonial empire. For with command of the sea, England took her pick of the French domain overseas.

THE ASSAULT ON LOUISBURG

For two years after Braddock's massacre, the French and their Indian allies enjoyed success in America. In 1756, the year of Minorca, French official indifference to the colonial aspect of the war seemed to be justified when the able General Montcalm set the British back on their heels by the capture of Oswego. This wilderness town on the shore of Lake Ontario had been the British salient on the flank of the French communications with the Lakes country, and was to have been the British base of operations. In 1757 Montcalm improved his position by moving down Lake Champlain from Montreal to capture Fort William Henry at the foot of Lake George near the head of the Hudson. On the New England coast, a British conjunct expedition sailed from Halifax to capture Louisburg in order to unlock the St. Lawrence and thus open the way to an attack by water on Montcalm's base at Quebec. The venture was a more miserable failure than Rochefort.

In 1758, when Pitt's plan went into full operation, a first class team of young colonels was placed in the critical American theater, nominally commanded for the sake of military form by an over-age incompetent named Abercromby. Commissions of rank valid only in the colonies made the outstanding, 40-year-old Lord Jeffrey Amherst a temporary major general, with vigorous and experienced brigadiers in Lawrence, Whitmore, and Wolfe. Another young brigadier named Forbes jarred Montcalm by storming Fort Duquesne and renaming the place Pittsburgh, but it was at Louisburg that the British Army won the respect of their proud foes.

Situated on the east coast of Cape Breton Island, which together with Newfoundland closes the Gulf of St. Lawrence, Louisburg was a town on a rugged promontory enclosing an excellent harbor which served a fleet of 3,000 boats fishing the Grand Banks. The post commanded by Chevalier de Drucour consisted of 3,800 men and more than 200 cannon. To these during the siege were added 3,000 seamen from 12 naval vessels caught in the harbor. Amherst had 14,000 men and 150 field and siege guns. The transport fleet was covered by Boscawen with 23 ships and 18 frigates. This was the most powerful and best planned conjunct expedition of the entire war, and reflected Pitt's passionate desire to have America.

Arriving early in June off Gabarus Bay, some two miles down the coast from Louisburg, the British were confronted by 20- to 60-foot perpendicular cliffs, a rocky, irregular coastline, and deadly shoals. Within easy march of their fortified base, the French could readily man the entrenchments and 40 guns at Gabarus, which afforded the only possible way ashore next to a *coup de main* against the town itself. The continental shelf of the Grand Banks formed a prodigious swell which made landing one boat risky, and landing hundreds for an assault costly enough to discourage a stout-hearted commander. Anxious to vindicate Pitt's confidence in them, Amherst, Boscawen, and Wolfe resigned themselves to considerable losses, reconnoitered and adopted as the only feasible plan of operations a direct frontal attack on the shore of the bay. With these officers there was no council of war. Wolfe's post-Rochefort opinion that it was better to lose a thousand men than to sail ignominiously away was the spirit of the assault.

On the night of June 7, 1758 the troops entered longboats from the transports manned by Boscawen's seamen. Aligning throughout the night, the British extended in three brigades on a two-mile front at dawn, Wolfe to the left leading the main attack into Fresh Water Cove, Lawrence in the center to create a diversion against the strong battery at Flat Point before supporting Wolfe, and Whitmore on the right to demonstrate against White Point. Boscawen's frigates went in as close as they dared, to lay down a covering fire, while at first light of dawn the ships of the line in deep water hurled a brief, massed barrage.

When the fire lifted the boats headed for the beach. Nearly the entire garrison of Louisburg waited to receive them, confident of the protection afforded by the hidden dangers of the coast. Drucour wished to withhold his fire for a tremendous volley when the boats were well entrapped by the surf, but the implacable, steady progress of an orderly line bearing four times his number unnerved him into shooting too soon for full impact. The French volley proved less murderous than the breakers. Tossing about, the boats spilled their occupants into the sea, which drowned many more than the French killed.

Dismayed, Wolfe signaled his brigade to sheer off, but some agile light infantrymen weathered the surf and found a cranny on the rocks which was safe from the plunging French shot. Wolfe promptly capitalized on the toe-hold and directed his brigade to follow him. Unarmed, cane in hand, he splashed ashore through knee-deep foam, imperturbably rewarded each of the first men to land with a guinea, and set about to form his arriving troops. Heedless of splashing projectiles and the fierce firefight raging on the cliff above between the detachment of sharpshooting skirmishers and the defenders hurrying to the threatened area, the British regulars dressed into regimental front. A flanking battery on a 20-foot-high slope pounded in a devastating fire. The regulars calmly closed ranks, fixed bayonets, and charged in an irresistible surge, taking the battery and all before them and reaching the plateau.

The French who did not die, fled. Wolfe wheeled into column as Lawrence made a beachhead to support him, then stabbed east in a hard effort to cut off Drucour's retreat to nearby Louisburg. Stunned by a lodgement they had considered impossible, the French became fugitives, proving faster as individuals than Wolfe's disciplined regiments double-timing in order. Wolfe pursued to the massive fortifications, halting only when a furious cannonade warned him of the limits of the French arcs of fire. The British lost 111 men and 100 boats in making the landing. The French lost 121 men.

Positive that Hawke and Anson would never permit reinforcements to relieve Louisburg, Amherst prudently substituted entrenchment for bayonet charges. He took his time in order to save the lives of his well trained men, and his reliance upon the

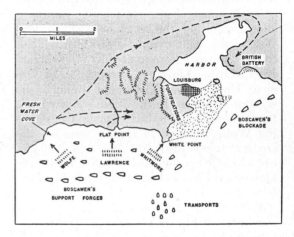

ASSAULT ON LOUISBURG, 1758

Royal Navy proved sound as Hawke drove ashore in Aix Roads the ships that were to have strengthened Drucour. For the latter, isolated from France, there could be no other choice but surrender. Amherst's patient siege came to its inevitable conclusion on July 27, 1758. Drucour's able if doomed defense did delay Amherst from attempting a campaign against Quebec, but the fall of Louisburg signified the beginning of the end of French rule in Canada. England was enabled to lock up the gate to the St. Lawrence.

THE CAMPAIGN AGAINST QUEBEC

Wolfe showed himself at Louisburg to be the commander that Pitt needed to guarantee attainment of his principal objective. Amherst generously accepted a subordinate role in the campaign of 1759 to capture Quebec. The plan envisaged a threefold movement to a concentration about Quebec by using the available water routes. First and most important, Wolfe and 8,500 men were to ascend the river with a naval covering force sufficiently strong to deal with either the Brest or Toulon fleet should either one evade blockade. Second, Amherst and 12,000 men were to seize Ticonderoga and Crown Point on Lake Champlain and descend the Richelieu River to await juncture with Brigadier Prideaux before by-passing Montreal and descending the St. Lawrence to join Wolfe and assume command. Third, Prideaux's 5,000 men were to capture Niagara and enter the St. Lawrence through Lake Ontario. Unavoidable delays kept Amherst, the greatest organizer in the British Army since the famous Duke of Marlborough, from joining Wolfe in time to receive some of the credit that was justly his. As it was, Amherst isolated Quebec by land for Wolfe as truly as Admiral Charles Saunders isolated Quebec by sea.

With his 23 ships and 13 frigates, Saunders was instructed to get Wolfe's transports safely into the St. Lawrence and to guard his communications, lending such cooperation as the Army might require. The duty laid out for Saunders was minor, but Saunders was not a minor man; he exercised his discretionary orders to take the Army to the very beaches of Quebec. During the confused days of the ensuing siege, it was the fleet that gave Wolfe the additional firepower and mobility that attained victory. In the absence of unequivocal orders defining their command relationship, the union between Wolfe and Saunders was to be as effective as that between powder and shot.

Such cooperation was missing among the responsible officials in French Canada, whose military commander despised the civil Governor. Montcalm's apparently strong force of 14,000 men and 300 emplaced guns had been weakened by corruption tolerated by Governor de Vaudreuil. Military supplies had been pilfered or wasted or spoiled by neglect. An ambitious man, Vaudreuil conspired against Montcalm, writing secret letters to Versailles urging his recall. In the administrative structure of New France, the Governor was invariably an army or navy officer who was able to assume military command if all the militia were called out. A naval captain of considerable merit, Vaudreuil was positive he could defend Quebec better than Montcalm could, and wished to have command.

Montcalm, an excellent soldier with his hands full training the raw militia already under him, resisted Vaudreuil's schemes to invoke the calamity clause that would raise every man capable of bearing arms. Appreciating the need for more troops, Montcalm sent his friend Bougainville to Versailles to appeal for a modest leaven of regulars in addition to his 2,000. Bougainville was refused on the grounds that building up the Canadian establishment would only result in Pitt's sending greater reinforcements to maintain British superiority. Versailles did take cognizance of Montcalm's unquestioned ability and quashed Vaudreuil's machinations. Bougainville returned with fewer than 500 men, the majority of them recruits, and a sparse amount of supplies gleaned from the German campaign. On his voyage, he barely missed capture by Admiral Durell, who was blocked by ice in the Gulf of St. Lawrence.

Many of the ministers at Versailles justified their preoccupation with the war against Frederick on the assumption that Wolfe's expedition would duplicate the Rochefort fiasco. The strange shoals and 20-foot tides of the broad St. Lawrence were expected to dampen the spirits of British officers, who were all under 30 except for Wolfe and a general in his early 40's. These optimistic French ministers did not realize that with such superb navigators as Master James Cook in Saunders' fleet, the St. Lawrence was an open highway. Besides, Admiral Durell pursued Bougainville as far as the Basin of Quebec and partly amended his failure to overtake the French by surveying a considerable part of the river.

Durell's failure however gave Montcalm a tremendous advantage. A French frigate on the high seas had stumbled upon a British dispatch sloop carrying a copy of Amherst's campaign plan. Montcalm thus knew exactly what Amherst had in mind. Not only did this give the French general time to devise countermeasures, but the knowledge that Quebec was the real point of attack allowed him to concentrate all of his regulars for its defense. Since the columns of Amherst and Prideaux had to traverse country where their camps would be exposed to Indians, he could rely upon the deadly integration of warriors with small French units to harry or stop them.

Montcalm entrenched on the high banks of the St. Lawrence immediately below Quebec. Thinly stretching 10,000 militia and 1,000 Indians to the Montmorency on his left and to the St. Charles on his right, he based himself and his regulars at Beauport in a central position. Converting merchantmen into floating batteries or fire ships to send blazing into the British armada, Montcalm blocked Quebec by a boom of chained logs. The few small naval vessels present were moved well up-river and their 1,000 seamen put into the batteries.

Wolfe seized the undefended Isle of Orleans on June 27, 1759; from here he had an excellent view of his objective, six miles away. The Upper Town was a hundred yards above the Lower Town, which was crowded into a depression of the St. Lawrence valley at a point where the river was constricted to less than a mile. To Wolfe's left as he studied the rugged terrain, the heights of Levis rimmed the diminishing valley of the river. To his right, the smoke from ready matches curled above the long French entrenchments stretching along the bluff northern shore to the high, crashing falls of the Montmorency.

Wolfe was depressed by Montcalm's apparently perfect dispositions. By taking the field instead of crowding into the fortifications of the city, Montcalm looked down upon the very beaches where Wolfe had planned to land. Paradoxically, and indicating the extent that tradition had stultified military initiative, Wolfe, who was pre-eminent among his contemporaries for employing the mobility of sea power, accepted Montcalm's dispositions. Instead of forcing the passage of Quebec and landing above the city, more quickly than Montcalm could follow, Wolfe was hypnotized by Montcalm's deliberately over-extended line, and elected

to attempt rolling up Montcalm's left flank.

First, to give Quebec itself some attention, Wolfe seized the heights of Levis and moved down the point of land to a place where his heavy guns could shoot across the river into the city and harbor. With the view from Levis, Wolfe changed his mind, and chose to storm ashore at the Anse du Foulon, after

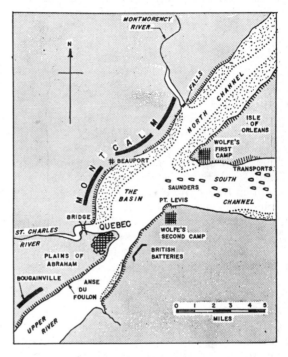

SIEGE OF QUEBEC, 1759

Saunders in a conspicuous display of naval capabilities pushed a detachment of ships up-river. To deceive Montcalm, Wolfe reverted to his original project against the left of the French line. After Cook made a precise survey of the tidal flats, Wolfe, on July 9, landed a brigade on the east bank of the Montmorency. Then, once actually within sight of his foe, Wolfe was hypnotized again by Montcalm's apparently weak left, and planned his major attack at the Montmorency anyway!

For nearly a month, Wolfe ran through a bag of tricks to persuade Montcalm to stand up out of his entrenchments and fight without exposing the British to the losses of a direct assault against concealed marksmen. Montcalm husbanded his strength and refused to move, his wary eyes on the transports that contained the bulk of Wolfe's force. Finally, on July 31, Wolfe in exasperation sent his boats in to attack in conjunction with an effort to cross the Montmorency with the brigade already ashore. The attack was badly managed, missing the high tide, so that the perfect order of the Louisburg approach disintegrated on mudflats. The attack force lost unity. Companies straggled ashore. The grenadiers, landing first, refused to wait and impetuously charged at the trenches above them. They took part of the first line, but the French on higher ground held steadily and broke the grenadiers by volleys of withering musketry. Sloshing about, futilely trying to organize coherent support for the rash grenadiers, Wolfe was suddenly showered by a heavy summer storm that ruined his gunpowder. Suffering a loss of 500 men, he limped back to the stranded flatboats and got off with the help of naval gunfire, having gained nothing except respect for the steadiness that Montcalm had instilled into the polyglot French militia.

At last giving up the blindness of allowing a static enemy to dominate his movements, Wolfe looked again at the Anse du Foulon as his best means of landing. Raiding above Quebec where Bougainville and 900 men kept watch, Wolfe tested the flexibility of Montcalm's defense. It soon became obvious that the Anse du Foulon afforded a difficult but practical access to the plains outside Quebec. And then, his plans matured, Wolfe fell seriously ill for several weeks. His subordinates carried on, passing a flotilla of flatboats by Quebec and loading them with troops marched down from Point Levis. Montcalm immediately raised Bougainville to military respectability by a detachment of 3,000 men with which to keep off the boats moving about in obvious search of a landing site. The British simply wore out Bougainville by floating some dozen miles up- and down-river with the tide, until Wolfe was on his feet.

All was ready on September 12. Off Beauport, Saunders cooperated by moving in at sunset with empty transports as though ready to attack. The fire from 30 great ships and frigates abruptly shattered the peaceful twilight. Seamen and marines pretending to be soldiers conspicuously manned the flatboats and completely deceived Montcalm, who alerted his force at Beauport to repel a landing that was actually taking place elsewhere.

Wolfe slipped ashore at Foulon, where he knew the sentries were expecting somewhat optimistically the arrival of a provision convoy from Montreal. Silencing the sentries, the British filed up a steep path to the plateau and routed the detachment encamped to cover the Anse du Foulon. Montcalm did not know until after dawn that the British general had boldly placed himself and 4,500 men within reach of Quebec. Wolfe had thrust himself into a position to be assailed front and rear but trusted to the fatigue of Bougainville's countermarching troops to allow him to beat the French in detail. Selecting the grassy ground of the Plains of Abraham, a mile outside the walls of Quebec, Wolfe formed a long line three deep, ready to fight in front or rear.

Rattled by the mocking collapse of the Beauport diversion and Wolfe's magical appearance, Montcalm made no attempt to concert operations with Bougainville. Hastening by a forced march to the Plains of Abraham, Montcalm rushed into battle before all of his units were on the field. The battle lasted less than an hour. Unruffled by the whoops of skirmishing Indians, the steady British regulars lay prone until Montcalm's true attack developed in the classic regimental front. At 200 yards, the British rose and waited for the line of gaily-faced white coats to advance behind fixed bayonets to a hundred feet. Then in a single great volley, Quebec was conquered. Dense powder smoke covered the plains, and when it cleared the French were in full flight. Firing a second volley, the British charged with bare steel to complete the rout. Within an hour of that fateful shock of arms, Montcalm's brocaded white coat spurted a brighter red than the uniforms of his foes, and Wolfe stumbled in death onto the ground he had bought for Pitt.

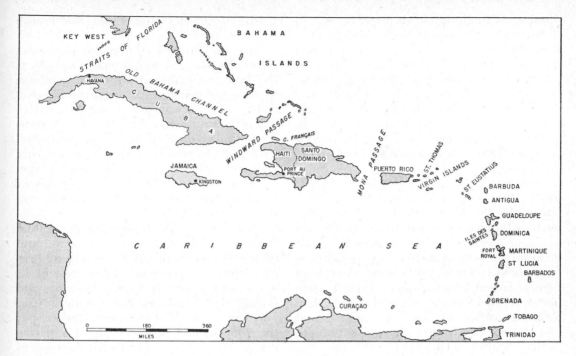

THE WEST INDIES

Vaudreuil was not the man to rally the French; he fled with other survivors circuitously to Montreal, his flight angrily covered by Bougainville. Quebec taken, Amherst assumed command and with quiet efficiency completed the conquest of Canada, doomed by the victories of Boscawen and Hawke. A long, hard year was needed to pry Montreal loose from Vaudreuil, yet thanks to the Royal Navy no one could have held the city. Of her vast American empire, France was to retain only the tiny islands of St. Pierre and Miquelon as havens for her fishing fleet. With all the rest of French America his, Pitt reached out for the West Indies and India.

THE WEST INDIES

During the 18th century, sugar, cotton, coffee and cocoa gave the lush Caribbean islands an economic importance out of all proportion to their small area. The trade was twice as valuable as that of India and constituted fully a quarter of all British and a third of all French seaborne commerce. Each country here employed at least 600 vessels, which were vulnerable to privateers. England's principal possession was Jamaica, guarded by naval stations or bases at Antigua, St. Christopher, and Barbados. For the French, Guadeloupe was slightly more important than Martinique, Santo Domingo, or the Grenadines, which together formed the most valuable colonial possessions in the world. As illustrative of this value, Santo Domingo alone produced more sugar than all of the British West Indies.

The Antilles were called the Windward and Leeward Islands because of the prevailing easterlies. Antigua was the pivot of the islands, those south of Antigua to Trinidad comprising the Windward chain, and those westward to Cuba, the Leeward chain. In sailing ship days, the wind was the dominating factor in West Indian strategy. The easterlies that blew a ship from Antigua to Jamaica in a week, on a return trip necessitated long tacks that lengthened the voyage to more than three weeks (see map). Because of geographic location, Barbados should have been the key to the area, but, lacking a good harbor, it was used primarily as a first port of call and a staging ground for expeditions. Except for the perfect harbor of Castries in St. Lucia, the West Indies provided little shelter against the seasonal hurricanes of summer and autumn, so that merchantmen and men-of-war alike cleared for home in the late spring.

The piracy that had begun in the earliest days of the Spanish Main had by 1756 flowered into the licensed system of irregular warfare known as privateering. In the absence of naval equality, the French nation embraced private warfare at sea, investing in swift, heavily-manned vessels to prey on England's 20,000 merchantmen. French commerce raiding was concentrated in the Channel approaches, in the West Indies, and along the East African coast on the route to India. Against such raiders the ships and frigates of the Royal Navy proved too cumbersome; only in convoy could the navy protect much of the trade. In the West Indies French privateers were largely manned by Negro slaves, whose viciousness in battle was stimulated by promises of freedom. The 50 per cent of French slaves supplied by British traders in peacetime ended during hostilities, and Pitt effectively hit at France's own supply in 1758 by having small squadrons capture the island of Goree as well as Senegal on the West African coast. The privateers originally operating in the French West Indies however remained a serious menace, those of Martinique alone taking a thousand merchantmen in only two years.

Thus after the fall of Louisburg assured the success of the subsequent campaign against Quebec, Pitt decided to extend operations to the West Indies, where he had three big objectives. First, he wished to legitimatize the actual trade defiantly carried on with the enemy by the North American colonies, whose economy was a natural complement to that of the West Indies. Second, he wished to crush the privateers, which were dangerously undermining the British financing of the war. Third, he wanted to establish British supremacy throughout the French holdings in the New World.

Since the outbreak of war, the commanders of the Antigua and Jamaica squadrons had been unequally pitting small squadrons of ships and frigates against swarming privateers. In January 1759 the arrival at Barbados of a strong conjunct expedition enormously raised British prestige in the Indies. The French planters were depressed, not knowing that Commodore Bompart and a squadron of nine ships had slipped out of Brest with troop transports in a winter storm that blinded Hawke.

Commodore John Moore and Colonel John Barrington, who commanded the naval and military elements of the newly-arrived British conjunct expedition during most of its operations, made a team as harmonious and skillful as that of Wolfe and Saunders. After practicing landing procedures, Moore put the troops ashore on a wing tip of butterfly-shaped Guadeloupe, and then proceeded to cut the French defenses in two by sending his marines and a handful of Highlanders to capture Fort Louis at the narrows. Then learning that Bompart had arrived at Martinique, he took his 11 ships to Dominica to intercept any sortie by the French fleet. In Moore's absence Barrington improved his reputation by nimbly using his armed transports and a few frigates as an amphibious force to nullify the great numbers of the French militia. Raiding in force along the coast, always striking at the rear of a defensive unit, he worried the French into exhaustion. Despairing of relief from the dilatory Bompart, they surrendered to Barrington's inferior numbers on May 1, 1759. The next day Bompart, having eluded Moore, arrived with a reinforcing army stronger than that of the haggard British. Luckily for Barrington, Bompart did not feel capable of reversing the surrender. Contenting himself with a demonstration, he sailed away to Santo Domingo.

Bompart's happy facility in evading British ships recurred in November 1759 when he successfully brought the 300 vessels of the Santo Domingo convoy to the French coast. His arrival, it will be remembered, heartened

Conflans into dashing out of Brest to initiate the planned attack on Scotland, and this sortie culminated in Hawke's pursuit and the decisive battle of Quiberon Bay. After Quiberon Bay, there were no more Bomparts to shake British control of the Caribbean. In succeeding years the British leisurely reduced all the French islands except Santo Domingo, where privateering gradually became a suicidal gamble.

The contemporary importance of the West Indies was reflected in the Peace of Paris, 1763. French successes in Germany entitled France to the recession of some British conquests. In the Western Hemisphere the French government without a qualm ignored the vastness of North America, and chose to have the little islands of Guadeloupe, Martinique, and St. Lucia! The British established title to Grenada, the Grenadines, St. Vincent, Dominica, and Tobago. Their factious colonists in New England immediately resumed the smuggling trade with the restored French islands.

INDIA

In India a decade of fighting for supremacy between the British East India Company and the more powerful French East India Company had so worn down the resources of both that their governments were constrained to assist such significant taxpayers by loans of naval squadrons and small bodies of troops. Rear Admiral Charles Watson's arrival at Madras in late autumn 1754 with four ships and a regular infantry regiment was soon counterbalanced by a reinforcement of 3,000 French regulars sent to nearby Pondicherry. Shortly afterwards, during a lull in Anglo-French hostilities, an Anglophobic prince inherited Bengal and committed the atrocity known as the Black Hole of Calcutta, in which only 33 Europeans survived out of 146 packed for a night into a tiny, unventilated room. Disregarding orders to return to England, Watson supported Robert Clive, commanding general of the East India Company's private army, in a retaliatory campaign against Bengal.

Using the broad waters of the Ganges delta for swift amphibious movements, Watson and Clive harried the natives until they concentrated for a decisive battle at Plassey. There in June 1757 Clive's scarlet-clad men stood to arms against tremendous odds and won, saved by a sudden rainstorm that drenched the combatants. Clive's foresight in providing tarpaulins for his powder, and his craft in seducing some of his adversary's subordinates, combined to give the British their most resounding victory in a galaxy of victories in India. From it resulted British dominion over the teeming provinces of Bengal, Orissa, and Behar, whose revenues put the British East India Company at last on financial parity with the French.

Rewarded with the Presidency of Bengal, Clive displayed his understanding of the need to control the sea by helping Watson to eliminate the French naval supply base at Chandernagor. As a result, a squadron of nine French ships under command of the Comte d'Aché had to be based upon the island of Mauritius, 2,100 miles away. While Clive was slowing the aggressive march on Madras of a French army under General Lally, Admiral George Pocock, Watson's successor, was making sure that Lally should not be supplied by sea. In two battles against d'Aché's superior force, he so battered the French ships that d'Aché was obliged to retire to Mauritius to repair damages and hasten the recovery of his irreplaceable wounded.

Deprived of naval support, Lally could not open the siege of Madras by land communications until the December monsoon sent Pocock to the haven of Bombay. Knowing they would be easily re-equipped by Pocock, the defenders of Madras lavishly used their ammunition to beat off all of Lally's attempts, until Lally, low in munitions and cursing his naval partner, lifted his two-month siege as Pocock reappeared with reinforcements and threatened to level Pondicherry to the water.

Lally's withdrawal from Madras ended the last French offensive in India. Too late, d'Aché returned in April to be tracked by Pocock from the Ceylon Straits towards Pondicherry. The chase became a running battle that inflicted 1,500 casualties upon the French, finishing d'Aché's capacity for further operations. As soon as he could refit for the long voyage, d'Aché departed for home, deserting India to the British, contributing further to the epochal year of 1759, which was witnessing the triumphs of Quebec, Lagos Bay, Quiberon, and Guadeloupe.

With undisputed command of the sea, Clive and his colleagues began an offensive that crushed the French Company's troops in the Battle of Wandiwash and did not end until the last French stronghold had hauled down its colors. The Treaty of Paris restored nominal trading privileges to the French, but this was in an India that had become British.

SPAIN PAYS FOR THE WAR

In 1761 Choiseul thought he had found the naval force he needed in the untouched squadrons of Spain. Madrid, alarmed by the successes of the British so close to her monopoly in South America and infuriated by arrogant British violations of Spanish neutrality and laws, readily listened to Choiseul's proffer of an offensive-defensive alliance. Pitt welcomed Spain's entry into the war; now he could plan the conquest of Cuba and Louisiana to bring all of North America under the British flag. He was ready to act long before the Spaniards mobilized their 56 ships.

In addition to the strong conjunct expedition being outfitted for the reduction of Martinique and another en route to take Belle Île, Pitt's superb management had established a reserve which could furnish a third conjunct expedition for simultaneous service.

The ambitious project of pouncing upon Havana and New Orleans required a mighty armament. The Earl of Albemarle was given 12,000 soldiers and marines. Pocock, who had made it possible for the British East India Company to win, was placed in command of 19 ships and 18 smaller men-of-war whose crews totaled 14,000 seamen.

In the spring of 1762 this armada, by approaching Havana from the east through the dangerous reefs of the Old Bahama Passage, succeeded in surprising the Spanish garrison. Early in June Albemarle put his troops ashore near the city with a sureness and power that showed the high degree of efficiency attained by British amphibious practice. For two months the invaders laid formal siege to the Morro, Havana's main fortification. At the end of July they succeeded in demolishing a wall of the fort by mining. Through the breach the British charged at the concussion-shocked, haggard defenders and cut them down before they could form in fighting units. Unable to expect succor from Spain because of Britain's command of the sea, Havana surrendered ten days later. Malaria and yellow fever so decimated Albemarle's force that the survivors had to be sent home before completing their Caribbean conquests.[5] The goods and gold of Havana however exceeded a whole year's profits from normal trade in the British West Indies, and more than defrayed the entire expenses of the British Army for 1762.

The war stretched all the way to the Philippines. Pitt chartered troops of the British East India Company under Brigadier William Draper to accompany eight ships under Vice Admiral Samuel Cornish on an expedition to capture the fountainhead of Spanish silver at Manila. As at Havana, the appearance of the British was the first notice the Spanish had of a state of war. On September 24, 1762 the Manila garrison valiantly tried to contest Draper's landing. By this time British amphibious practice had the precision and power of habit. The Spanish shrank away from the bombardment laid down by Cornish's ships and inshore frigates. Draper's force outnumbered by three to one the Spanish regulars, but the Spaniards were assisted by 10,000 loyal Filipinos, who proved to be respectable foes. British skill and superior arms however conquered Manila in only 12 days, and more treasure went to Pitt—enough

---

[5] In colonial times before the advent of vaccines, West Indian tropical diseases, principally yellow fever and malaria, invariably killed about half of a force fresh from Europe in their first year, and an annual five per cent in succeeding years.

to pay half of England's foreign subsidies for the year.

Everywhere triumphant, the English sense of invincibility and private initiative reached absurdity in September 1762 when a group of English merchants in Lisbon outfitted a small expedition of 1,350 men to capture Buenos Aires. Lacking the professional knowledge of conjunct expeditions, the adventure came to a sorry end. The Spanish authorities, more amused than alarmed, treated the survivors kindly and helped them to return home.

SUMMARY

In Europe the military genius of Frederick the Great dominated the Seven Years' War, but in its broader character as a world conflict the war was dominated by William Pitt. Formulating the strategy of keeping England as free as possible of the European theater so that the bulk of her strength could be devoted to colonial conquest, Pitt masterfully used Frederick and German allies to entangle France's warmaking capacity in a wasteful series of campaigns across the Rhine. For him the European war was a titanic diversion. He weathered all criticism and disaster until he had set England straight on the course of establishing colonial supremacy. Because his opponents drove him from power before hostilities ended, he did not become the architect of the Treaty of Paris of 1763, in which England ransomed Hanover and Frederick by renouncing much more than France and Spain expected.

At Paris England exchanged Belle Île for Minorca; Havana and Manila, for Florida and a bit of Honduras; and Goree, off Dakar, for Hanover. France got back Guadeloupe and Martinique but was obliged to demolish the fortifications at Dunkirk. From Pitt's plan England gained Canada, Florida, all the area east of the Mississippi except New Orleans, several islands of the West Indies, a grip on Senegal, and an acknowledgment of the British East India Company's primary possessions as won up to 1763. These huge gains fostered jealousy, and the English by their lack of moderation did not make themselves beloved.

In the realm of naval tactics the Seven Years' War initiated a trend, at first imperceptible, away from the rigid formalism that had long barred the Royal Navy from decisive victories. With his blood the unhappy Byng purchased for his colleagues a measure of freedom from the *Fighting Instructions* and opened the way to the full initiative that finally produced Nelson. Unfortunately, the discrediting of the *Fighting Instructions* also discredited the idea of establishing other doctrines. The long list of amphibious victories at Louisburg, Quebec, Guadeloupe, Martinique, Belle Île, Havana, and Manila had produced a practice well understood by the participants, but these generals and admirals died without consolidating their experience into precepts to guide their successors. British officers inherited the tradition of confidence from the Seven Years' War without learning any of the amphibious lessons which had made such confidence a measure of true ability rather than mere pride. These lessons had to be relearned again and again, always at tragic cost.

Thanks to Pitt, England had a tremendous empire, but France did not passively accept humiliation. The spirit of the French people responded to the exhortations of Choiseul, and before diplomats had picked up their copies of the Treaty of Paris, shipwrights were hammering away in Brest, Rochefort, and Toulon. Planning for revenge, French strategists put aside the tempting chimera of invading England and realistically planned for the next heaviest blow of seizing Jamaica. Their opportunity came too soon, for the necessary fleet was not complete when the American Revolution exploded amidst England's sprawling empire.

There had been a flaw in Pitt's perfect plan after all. He had removed the threat of the French in America. Fear of the French had made the 13 cantankerous colonies dependent upon British arms. Now, with the French gone, and only the Indians and a few Spaniards to face, the colonies were angered by their share of the cost of empire and marched to fulfill their destiny.

5

The American Revolution, Part I

FOLLOWING THE BRILLIANT success of British arms in the Seven Years' War, British forces during the American Revolution proved so inept that British historians have tended to gloss over the events of 1775-1783 in favor of more glorious eras. As a result, according to the foremost naval historian of the period, "the story of the Armada of the sixteenth century is familiar, but the story of the insolent threat to the British flag when the French and Spanish fleet sailed unchallenged up channel in 1779 fills a comparatively obscure page in English history. Never were these shores in greater peril from an invader." [1]

From the broad view of the history of sea power, the war should be considered a resumption of the struggle between France and England for colonial domination. The efforts of American Continental and State navies, together with privateers, had little effect on the outcome of the Revolution. For richness of tradition, the names of Barry, Jones, and Wickes may be cherished by the United States Navy, but it was the French navy that broke the hold of King George upon the rebellious colonies.

In studying the war, one should keep uppermost in mind the paramount importance of water communications—not merely across the open Atlantic, but on the rivers and bays of the American coast. Another generation would witness the introduction by Macadam of a road surfacing which by 1800 would give England, and eventually the world, reliable land communications, but in 1775 water transport predominated. A glance at a map of the colonies will show how closely the population clung to the shorelines of the ocean or of rivers. To illustrate the conditions then prevalent, it will suffice to point out that travelers between New York and Philadelphia preferred a long voyage to a short ride in coaches which jostled along rutted or muddy dirt roads. Communications were confined to water routes. Whoever could control the coast would have a stranglehold upon the colonies. This does not mean that individual vessels could not elude the British sloops and frigates. It does mean that the Royal Navy was able to shatter the regular commerce and way of life in the colonies, if the Crown so chose to do.

The Crown however was not in the best of hands for British interests. In English history, the war proved to be a constitutional struggle testing the fitness of George

---

[1] Captain (later Admiral) W. M. James RN, *The British Navy In Adversity: A Study Of The War Of American Independence* (London, 1926), vi.
N.B. Chaps. 5-13 herein Copyright 1954 by Robert W. Daly.

III to be more of an actual king than Parliament had permitted since the days of Elizabeth I. Thanks to Tory support and judicious bribes, George III was given great latitude in managing colonial affairs but as a consequence succeeded merely in crystallizing the supremacy of Parliament. He was a Briton born and bred, but he did not understand the sea. With his German background, he preferred an army to a navy. To get funds for troops, he economized on the naval establishment, endorsing cheap ships such as the 64-gun ship of the line. This unfortunate type of battleship epitomized the King's naval mentality; small in size, four 64's could be built from the material required for three 74's and could be manned by fewer men. In firepower however a 64 could pit only 600 pounds of broadside metal against the 900 pounds from the standard 74. The 64 represented a step backward at a time when the foes of England were increasing the size and strength of their 74's.

The ambition of George to be King was not the only factor which caused the British war effort to be comparatively feeble. Three other factors were involved. First, Pitt was not in power and no minister equal to him rose to unify the strategy and conduct of the war. Second, corruption in the Admiralty under the Earl of Sandwich resulted in rotten ships and empty storerooms. Lastly, the combined French and Spanish navies for a long time outnumbered the naval force that England could muster from her nominal 150 ships. Thus, England could not resume the system of blockading enemy ports that had been initiated in the previous war; the French and Spanish moved at will.

Politically, the quarrel with the 13 colonies developed slowly. Among other vexatious clauses, the Treaty of Paris in 1763 obliged England to suppress smuggling into the Spanish colonies. Having engaged in such activity since England won the *Asiento* in 1714, Americans felt that two generations had legitimized the trade. They resented being stopped by patrols of the Royal Navy at a time when the Crown also attempted to assert the right to tax colonists. The Stamp Act of 1764, the Revenue Act of 1767, the Boston Massacre of 1770, the tea riots of 1773—these marked a steady increase in provocations which ultimately in 1775 demanded redress by arms. Too late did King George moderate his demands and attempt conciliation.

War was not unanimously desired by either side. Perhaps a third of the American population wished independence, another third did not, and the remainder prudently awaited the outcome. In England, Tories supported the war and Whigs opposed it. Such division of purpose on both sides restrained either from mobilizing full weight to force an early decision. Indeed, a substantial part of the English people so opposed what they deemed to be civil war, that troops mutinied when ordered to America, and George was compelled to turn to his German cousins for help.

Clearly, the British government was in a poor situation to conduct full scale land operations in distant colonies that could contribute little to logistic needs even had the colonists been friendly. In view of the lack of roads in America, naval blockade should have sufficed. The Crown became involved in land operations through the honorable folly of announcing that persons loyal to the King would be protected by His Majesty's troops. This policy could not be repudiated and so the British perforce called upon their weak army to do a job it could not do and relegated their powerful navy to minor support missions when it could have coerced the colonies with ease. Economic starvation would have been an unspectacular though positive means of reviving the King's authority, and much of the bitterness resulting from bloody conflict would have been avoided had troops been used only to hold bases for mounting a naval blockade. As British soldiers went ashore to meet the rebels on rebel terms, Pitt bluntly said in Parliament, "You may ravage, you cannot conquer. It is impossible. You cannot conquer the Americans." But Pitt, who had placed the most brilliant gems in England's scepter, was out of favor—as were long range, unified plans. Patchwork strategy, misguided opportunism, and simple obstinacy characterized the British conduct of the war, while sporadic zeal, selfish profiteering, and armed opposition vitiated the colonial effort. Soon mired in military stalemate, the conflict was drifting towards political compromise rather than armed decision when France entered the war and tipped the balance in favor of the colonists. At that point, the war became European. As we shall see, the French navy really established American independence.

THE COLONISTS FIGHT ALONE

The military resources of the colonies were meager, thanks to the mercantilist theories of the British government which had forbidden any colonial manufacturing which competed with British industries. Firearms were made primarily on the frontier, where the Allegheny watershed fed the Mississippi tributaries. Only Connecticut had an iron foundry. War had flamed too spontaneously for any stockpiling of finished goods and such war material as existed in the colonies was largely inherited from the militia organizations that had fought the French and Indians. The naval resources of the colonies were much more important. The extensive American merchant marine had provided a valuable auxiliary body of privateers in England's wars of empire. Guns had changed little in a hundred years, so that families which had in the past taken to privateering when England quarreled with France, were now armed for the struggle with the Mother Country. Gunpowder and shot were the chief munitions necessary, and these were easily procured in the West Indies, at times from English merchants, for the British West Indies were heavily dependent upon the continental colonies for subsistence. If coordinated, the hundreds of privateers were capable of commerce destruction that might have injured London merchants to the extent of inducing a favorable peace.

Coordination however implied a strong government, and this the rebels did not have. Each of the colonies operated as a sovereign state. A framework of mutual interest produced the Continental Congress, to which none of the member states surrendered much if any power. The Congress was more than a forensic society, in that it spoke for the American cause and issued commissions recognized from Massachusetts to Georgia. Congress could order—but Congress could not compel. States obeyed only if they saw fit. With such a loose organization, the colonies could not exert maximum strength. In order to have a dependable minimum force, Congress established a regular army, navy, and marine corps, to which states rarely contributed their full quotas, so that the Continental Army could rarely muster 20,000 men. Nearly every state had its own military and naval structure, which cut deeply into the forces available to Congress. In effect, each state participated in two wars: one in conjunction with Congress and the other on its own behalf. State militia readily cooperated with the Continentals when the British invaded their territory, but disbanded when the enemy moved on to another state. In consequence, American planning was cautious, fortunately paralleled by the hesitation of British Whig generals, who tended to view the conflict as a constitutional test of King George's right to be the executive head of the British government instead of being just a figurehead.

The land phase of the war opened with colonial victory at Boston, which General George Washington compelled General William Howe to evacuate in March 1776, after Howe had been jolted into respect for American fighting qualities at Bunker Hill. Concurrently, Generals Richard Montgomery and Benedict Arnold failed with 1,200 men to conquer Canada, which was defended by General Sir Guy Carleton with a slightly inferior force. On New Year's Eve, 1775, Montgomery was killed in a desperate assault on Quebec. Arnold, badly wounded, assumed command and continued the siege of the key to Canada until early May 1776, when a British ship forced her keel through thick ice floes to bring relief to Quebec. Arnold then raised the siege and retreated.

The British, having absorbed the first offensive blows of the rebels, now took the initiative. Having all the advantages of preponderant sea power, the British began three campaigns: the first, based on Quebec, was designed to drive Arnold out of Canada and invade New England; the second was a diversion in the Carolinas in support of the main effort, which, based on Halifax, was directed against New York.

On July 4, 1776, Congress issued the Declaration of Independence. Prior to the Declaration, France had covertly assisted the American cause; after the Declaration, French aid became open. It was made clear that France would become an actual ally as soon as the colonies could indisputably prove they could maintain the character of an independent nation. The summer and autumn of 1776 did not seem likely to produce such evidence, as Arnold rashly attacked the forces collecting under Carleton and was beaten to the extent of being obliged to quit Canada.

Retiring along the Richelieu River into Lake Champlain, Arnold paused at Crown Point to carve a tiny fleet of 15 small vessels from the virgin timber. A soldier, he became a sailor and awaited the enemy advance on the natural invasion route from Montreal. The British patiently built a superior force of 28 small vessels and a full-rigged sloop-of-war mounting eighteen 12-pounder guns. On October 11, 1776, the pigmy fleets began a three day battle near Valcour Island. When firing ceased, Arnold had been crushed, lucky to be among the survivors escaping to the wooded shore. It was a tactical defeat but a strategic victory that proved to be the essential foundation for ultimate victory: his men left the British too battered to continue their advance. Carleton retired to winter quarters where he was superseded by General John Burgoyne. Arnold's sacrifice had won the Americans a breathing space of a year in which to collect forces to stop the next British thrust.

The second part of the British 1776 plan, the diversionary movement to the Carolinas, was hurled back by the colonists. On June 4 a light-draft squadron appeared off Charleston. Some 2,000 troops under General Sir John Clinton were landed on a spit of land beyond the town while Rear Admiral Sir Peter Parker undertook to demolish a log and sand fort hastily constructed on the tip of Sullivan's Island, commanding the main entrance into the fine harbor. Parker expected to have little difficulty with Fort Moultrie as he placed four heavy frigates into bombardment positions. The South Carolina troops silently endured naval gunfire until the British had anchored. When the thundering British frigates were immobile, Colonel William Moultrie opened fire. The fort had absorbed British shot with little damage. American shot was deadlier. For nearly ten hours, Parker futilely endeavored to silence the fort, while Clinton found himself unable to cross to Sullivan's Island to storm the place from the rear. After losing some two hundred killed and wounded to the rebels' less than two score casualties, Parker retired. Clinton agreed the attempt should be abandoned and so the shot-torn British ships vanished.

The third and important part of the 1776 British plan was much more successful. General Howe left Halifax in mid-June and landed his army on Staten Island early in July. Washington, having correctly foreseen this move, was entrenched on the western heights of Long Island. Howe marked time for a month until a heavy reinforcement of Hessians reached him and Clinton had returned from the rebuff at Charleston. Howe thus had some 25,000 men; Washington had 18,000 distributed about the vulnerable parts of New York harbor, the major portion being 9,000 men in fieldworks on Brooklyn Heights. On August 22, Howe landed at Gravesend Bay against minor opposition. After a week of skirmishing, Washington used a fog to slip across the East River to Manhattan. His militia had not stood up well to British bayonets, so Washington preferred maneuver to fortification. Unable to preserve New York City, he retired north and then southwest across New Jersey, not too vigorously pursued by Howe. His force dwindled before Howe's plodding pressure and by early December, when he crossed the Delaware into Pennsylvania, he had only 3,000 men. Howe went into winter quarters while Clinton and Parker went off to seize Rhode Island to serve as an anvil for the following spring

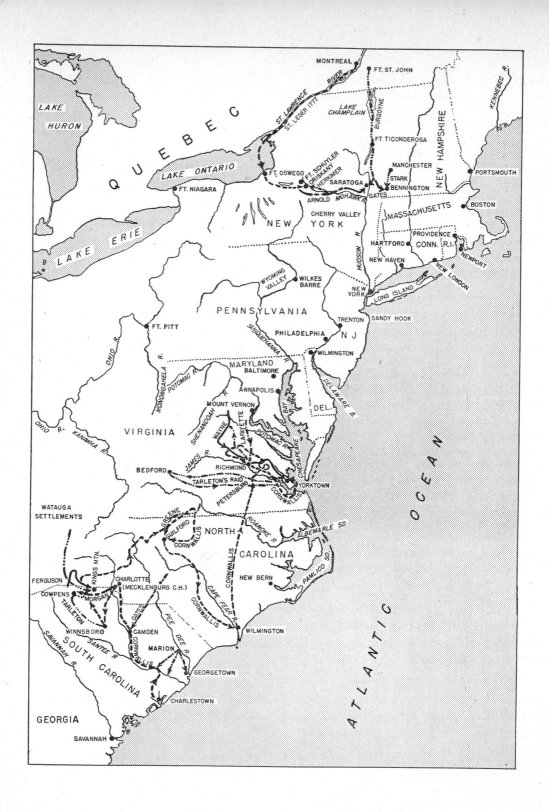

AMERICAN REVOLUTION: BRITISH INVASIONS FROM NORTH AND SOUTH

campaign that would drive through Connecticut and shatter New England.

All seemed to be going well for the Crown. The colonists had apparently expended their strength. Parliament voted funds for 89,000 troops and the commissioning of 16 more ships, which on paper was supposedly more than enough to quash the revolt. Congress retorted with a vote for 81,000 troops, who were to exist only in the minds of debaters. Washington disturbed British complacency by his Christmas capture of 1,300 Hessians at Trenton, and went on in a daring winter campaign to revive the depressed spirits of his countrymen. It was in these hours that Washington became the Father of his Country, for it was then that he saved the cause of independence.

For 1777, the British planned decisive campaigns. New England was to be stabbed after a three-pronged attack through its hinterland. From Montreal, Burgoyne was to follow the Lake Champlain route to Albany, where he would join a diversionary column of 700 men under Colonel St. Leger. St. Leger was to start from Oswego with Indians and terrorize the frontier so that buckskinned riflemen would be confined to their forests. Leaving New York in time to receive Burgoyne and St. Leger at Albany, Howe was to have over-all command and prepare the operational plans for driving east towards Rhode Island. Unfortunately for the British, orders for the elaborate combination never reached Howe, who left New York to capture Philadelphia as Burgoyne was moving through Canada. St. Leger crashed into obdurate rebels at Fort Stanwix and had to retire, and so Burgoyne plodded alone into a fateful debacle that proved to be the turning point of the war.

The time that Arnold had won the previous year by the defeat at Valcour Island had more than sufficed for the Americans to gather regulars and militia to stop Burgoyne. Much skirmishing that began in early July 1777 carried Burgoyne wearily by late September to the vicinity of Saratoga. The American General Horatio Gates, seconded by Arnold, was beaten by Burgoyne in a costly victory that left the British too en-feebled to go on. American columns raided British transport on Lake Champlain and marooned Burgoyne in an extremely hostile countryside. On October 7, Burgoyne gambled his remaining strength in a violent attack that Arnold blunted and stopped. Surrounded, with no news at all from New York, Burgoyne stubbornly hung on for another ten days before surrendering at Saratoga.

This was the most important victory of American arms. It provided the proof of American toughness for which France had been waiting. In early February 1778, France signed a treaty of amity and commerce with the Continental Congress, thus bringing a true navy into the lists against King George's fleet.

REVIVAL OF
THE FRENCH NAVY

If the people of Great Britain were stunned by the capture of a complete British field army for the first time in their history, the people of France rejoiced. Rankled by the loss of Canada and India in the Seven Years' War, the French thirsted for revenge. Even more important, the French recognized that their indifference to sea power had cost them the bulk of their empire and, after 1763, a great spontaneous enthusiasm swept city and farm to rebuild a fine, new navy upon the ruins of the old one. Gabriel de Sartines became Minister of Marine in 1774 and harnessed the naval energy of his country. The splendid new ships slipping down the ways were formed into training squadrons that revolutionized French thought by actually going to sea to practice the business of developing naval proficiency. Noble officers applied themselves diligently to the writings of Père Hoste and Bigot de Morogues, who taught the need for a tight, line-ahead formation but misemphasized absolute obedience to orders. French captains strove for technical perfection while scrupulously eschewing initiative in action upon the belief that flawless, cohesive tactical formations made decisive actions impossible.

In effect, the French were unconcerned

with building sea power sufficient to execute broad offensive plans but sought a naval organization which could survive another war with the redoubtable British. There was to be no repetition of the loss of 37 ships and 56 frigates to enemy action. The French were unable to build towards decisive superiority anyway because of their relatively small maritime population. Prudently therefore they planned a fleet which would gain or lose little for France. Their admirals were brought to realize that their beautiful ships were too precious to be expended in actions that had no other object than the elimination of enemy forces. Age was esteemed in a French admiral, because age presumably brought caution in judgment. Thus, the 50 ships available to French policy in 1778 were not going to be lightly gambled in penny-packet combat.

The French treaty of February 1778 with the Americans was accepted by the British as a glove thrown in the face. France, dreaming beyond her own naval resources, began successfully to involve Spain in the war. This was not too difficult; Spain wished to recover Minorca and Gibraltar. Thus, by June 1779 a naval superiority was produced that ranged some 90 Allied ships against 72 Britons. Nor did the French intend to abuse their good fortune. Only a dozen ships were to be diverted to the American theater; the bulk would be used to launch an invasion of England.

The British had ample warning of French disposition to enter the war but did little to reduce the actual shock. If parsimony had whittled at the impressive number of ships on the Navy List so that barely half could be commissioned, the situation was made worse by previous victories which had enormously expanded the empire. For each ship, there were a dozen squadrons in which it could be employed. Faced with the prospect of enemy blows in every quarter, Lord Sandwich kept ships at home, assuming the strategic defensive until the enemy declared his intentions. Sandwich did not follow his predecessors' policy of sending squadrons of observation to watch enemy ports; thus throughout the war enemy movements were almost entirely un-opposed. For a consistent, offensive strategy, Sandwich substituted a game of trying to guess what the enemy had in mind. Initiative was handed to the French and Spanish, who proved unable to use it. Committed to a supine policy of warding off enemy thrusts, the British evolved nothing that approached the aggressive lucidity of Pitt's War Plan in the Seven Years' War.

The Brest fleet was the first concern of the British Admiralty. Augustus Keppel was in command of England's Channel Fleet. An admiral of the old school, Keppel longed to have at the enemy, and was finally turned loose after four months of fuming. In mid-June 1778, he left Portsmouth with his 20 ships to carry out the two-fold duty of preventing a juncture of the Brest and Toulon fleets while escorting past the latitude of Ushant a troop convoy en route to relieve Gibraltar. War had not been formally declared but Keppel's orders gave him full authority to shoot if the French came under his guns. Thus, Keppel's fleet fired the first shots of the Anglo-French war in capturing a pair of French frigates that had shadowed his movements. From his prizes, Keppel learned that Admiral d'Orvilliers had 33 ships ready in Brest. Formal tactics automatically made it mandatory for Keppel to retire until he had approximately an equal number. In early July, Keppel was again at sea, this time with 30 ships, ready to fight.

THE BATTLE OF USHANT, JULY 27, 1778

D'Orvilliers sortied with 32 ships under peculiar orders to cruise for a month while avoiding action with superior forces. The purpose was ostensibly one of training, although protection was also afforded to trade homeward bound from the shrunken French empire. On the foggy afternoon of July 23, some 60 miles west of Ushant, Keppel and d'Orvilliers found each other. The discovery pleased Keppel more than his French rival, for the British fleet by good fortune happened to stand between d'Orvilliers and Brest. D'Orvilliers had the wind, so he did

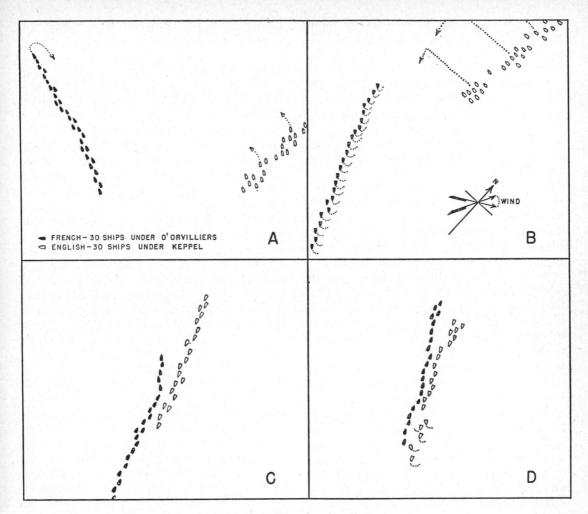

FRENCH — 30 SHIPS UNDER D'ORVILLIERS
ENGLISH — 30 SHIPS UNDER KEPPEL

A

WIND

B

C

D

BATTLE OF USHANT, JULY 27, 1778

not have to fight, even if he had not considered himself bound by his orders to slip away. He was short two ships that had parted company at night, three other ships had proved too weak to take position in a line of battle, and the captains of the remaining 27 had not impressed their admiral by their efficiency. Keppel frustrated all efforts to get past him and by the morning of July 27 made collision unavoidable. By then the wind was showing signs of shifting from the west. D'Orvilliers viewed an eager enemy to leeward, struggling into the wind to pounce upon some French stragglers. Both fleets steered a northerly course, separated by some

six miles, until d'Orvilliers felt impelled to do something about the ships obviously reaching for his stragglers. Wearing in succession onto a southerly course, d'Orvilliers was tightening his formation when the wind backed to the north. Keppel deftly steered into the wakes of the French, who still were to windward but had become exposed to a stern chase in which the fastest ships of the British van could hope to double upon the slowest ships of the French rear. To escape the hazards of being the prey in a stern chase, d'Orvilliers wore his fleet together onto a close-hauled northerly course. The British and French then drove at each other at the maximum range rate, the French only slightly to windward. Wishing to avoid short-range action, d'Orvilliers ordered his van to close-haul as tightly as possible, thereby opening the distance at which the fleets would pass. The first three French ships thus got well clear of the British preferred battle range of 300 yards, and the fourth Frenchman received the first fire. The French aimed high, as usual, to dismast, and in the passing exchange of broadsides, disabled five Britons. Before perceiving this in the haze of gunsmoke, Keppel ordered a turn to follow the French and carry the attack to their rear. The wind shifted to the southwest and gave him the windward position. The game was in his hands, had his ships been intact.

As it was, d'Orvilliers thought that the odds had been broken in his favor, 27 effective French vessels against 25 British, so he discarded the role of rabbit to turn upon the hounds. He signaled for a turn in succession to the south. The maneuver however was one to be executed swiftly. By the time the signal was repeated in the French van, Keppel had been given time to see his disabled ships. So he gave up the chase to turn south to guard his unfortunate captains and the maneuver broke his line. One of the frequent freak accidents that occur in battle found the flagship of the van admiral, Sir Hugh Palliser, unable to answer her helm properly. The ship worked up into the wind, and the ships of Palliser's division, which kept station according to his movements, faithfully followed him. The British became dangerously split as the two fleets converged again on a southerly heading. The French were tantalizingly to leeward but Keppel was helpless to force action. Part of his force under Palliser steadily moved away to windward and another part of his force, ahead of him, could not move at all. Frantically sending private signals to each captain in Palliser's division, Keppel at last corrected their dangerous divergence. D'Orvilliers, seeing the British slowly re-form their line, decided not to force the issue. The way to Brest was now open and the British were in poor condition to give chase. Shortening sail, d'Orvilliers perfected his line, waited for night, and then steered for his base.

The cannonade off Ushant had killed or wounded 1,200 men without contributing anything significant to a campaign. It was celebrated as a victory at Versailles and a victory it was, of sorts. A French fleet had been in sight of a British fleet for four days and had come home with its ships intact. That was unusual. It proved to have far greater significance in England. The British nation was disgusted. A parallel was popularly made with Byng's action off Minorca, which had opened the Seven Years' War. The press and Parliament at length demanded a court-martial, which began in early January 1779. Four counts were laid against Keppel, each charge carrying the death penalty if proved. The shade of Byng haunted the proceedings, which continued with great circumspection through six weeks. In the end, Keppel was honorably acquitted on all counts. In itself, the Battle of Ushant was trivial but the resultant court-martial was of enormous consequences in developing the free exercise of initiative by British admirals. Thenceforward, the fate of Byng was no longer an albatross hung upon the neck of a British commander. An admiral's professional judgment was acknowledged to be sufficient to overweigh absolute conformity to petrified tactical concepts. The verdict of Keppel's court tacitly proclaimed that there could be more than one given means to a given end.

The Age of Nelson had become possible.

FIRST CLASHES IN AMERICA, 1778

In mid-April 1778, a fleet of 12 ships under Admiral Charles le Comte d'Estaing sailed from Toulon, bound for New York and cooperation with the Continental Army. The news of d'Estaing's departure disturbed the British on both sides of the Atlantic. In London, the Admiralty realized there was nothing to stop his combination with the Brest fleet because the French hostilities had been a surprise and at least four months was necessary to take a ship out of "ordinary"—the contemporary equivalent of "mothballing" —and commission her for service. A squadron of 13 ships independent of the Channel Fleet was scraped together under Vice Admiral John Byron and held in sailing readiness at Plymouth. Anxious weeks finally produced a frigate in early June which had tracked d'Estaing past Gibraltar on a westerly course until her enterprising captain was positive the French were steering for America. Byron immediately shook out sail.

In the colonies, news of the French alliance demonstrated at once the impact of sea power. Shortly after General Howe seized Philadelphia and then sailed for England, General Clinton had succeeded to command. In view of French interference, Clinton was ordered to evacuate Philadelphia in favor of New York as an operational base. In addition, to tempt the French into fractionalizing their forces, Clinton was directed to send a third of his troops to operate in Florida and the West Indies. If Clinton was worried about the safety of his army, Admiral Lord Howe, General Howe's elder brother, had more reason to fear for his fleet. Lord Howe's command consisted of minor men-of-war, admirably suited to dealing with American raiders but worse than useless in opposition to a genuine naval force. Scattered along the coast, he had six of the economy 64's, seven 50-gun ships,[2] 43 frigates, and 17 sloops.

Clinton was respected in his profession as a stolid, methodical soldier; Lord Howe was idolized throughout the Navy as a daring, energetic seaman. It was fortunate for their King that they were in command at the critical time of preparing to receive the shock of French entry into the war. Clinton decided not to transfer the army to New York by sea, since they would be exposed to enemy interception. Instead Lord Howe undertook to carry the army's heavy material while Clinton made a quick march from Philadelphia. Washington was alert to the chances offered by improvised movements

and soon began to harry Clinton, who doubtless would have been trapped into another Saratoga had he been encumbered by supplies. As it was, Clinton had to shift his line of march towards New York in order to seek refuge with the fleet at Sandy Hook. Lord Howe, on the other hand, relieved of the need to collect troop transports, sailed much sooner than would otherwise have been possible. He beat d'Estaing to Sandy Hook by a mere four days.

It had been a close business but simply reaching the sea buoys of New York did not provide security. Howe anchored across the channel off Sandy Hook, on which Clinton had thrown up batteries. D'Estaing arrived on July 11, dropped anchor within easy sight of the British line shielded by the hump of Sandy Hook, and exchanged letters with Washington. American pilots boarded the great ships. All waited tensely for a fair wind. American hopes were high. The war seemed practically won. Excepting the small garrison of Rhode Island, British power in the colonies was within easy reach of stout-sided French ships whose weight of metal tripled that of Lord Howe. On the morning of July 22 a combination of wind and tide proved perfect for d'Estaing to attack. Instead, he spent the golden moments ostentatiously sounding the approaches to the bar. Then, in the afternoon, he sailed away, to the joy of the British and the fury of the Americans. The reasons put forward to explain d'Estaing's desertion of the field usually revolve around the fact that he was not a true admiral but a general appointed to command a fleet. It is much more probable that the French did not seek to end the war at a blow before seizing some land from their ancient rival. France had not underwritten an unlimited American victory. The treaty with Congress precluded assistance in conquering Canada, for it was not France's desire to create a monstrous state in the New World. Whether he had secret instructions or not—whatever his motive—d'Estaing shaped course for Rhode Island.

There, French performance proved equally disappointing. Arrangements with the Americans besieging the 5,000 British troops at

---

[2] The 50-gun ship was an intermediate type that served as flagship for a frigate squadron. It was usually a "razee"—an old 74-gun two-decker with the upper deck cut down.

Newport had scarcely begun when Lord Howe appeared to offer battle. Howe was living up to his reputation for daring, since he had been reinforced by only one of Byron's ships: the rest of the reinforcement had been scattered by storm. Although six of his seven ships were insignificant, and his enemy had 12, Lord Howe was ready to dispute command of the sea. But the sea interfered. It was August 12 and a harbinger of the Caribbean hurricane season suddenly swept over the intended battlefield. The two fleets were scattered. The British made for Sandy Hook and the French for Boston.

So ended the first efforts of the French navy to aid the colonists. Action for the year was over. The scene, as customary in sailing ship days, shifted to the West Indies for the good weather of winter months.

THE WEST INDIES, 1778-1779

It will be recalled that the West Indies in colonial times had an importance that seems inordinate in our times. None of the islands was self-sufficient, for they specialized in sugar crops which represented a substantial third of the imports into the European countries which owned them. The islands were divided into the Windward and Leeward groups by the phenomenon of the prevailing easterly winds. Since one week was needed to make the passage from Antigua to Jamaica and three weeks to return, the strategic importance of the most windwardly position is obvious. England possessed such an island in Barbados, but it did not have a harbor, so that the island of St. Lucia, some hundred miles north and west, was the preferred base. St. Lucia offered a chance to control access to the next island north of it, Martinique, and even Dominica and Guadeloupe still further north. The war for the islands, then, was economic to the extent of removing a third of a nation's trade, and strategic to the extent of attempting to occupy an island to windward of an enemy possession. The British had relatively poor harbors; the French had many good ones.

In days when marine growth was an extremely serious problem, the French facilities for cleaning the bottoms of ships gave a tremendous advantage. The desire to obtain a safe careenage probably motivated more British admirals than anything else.

Sailing from Boston in November 1778, d'Estaing reached Martinique early in December. He had 9,000 troops and a plan for capturing Barbados, Grenada, and St. Vincent. He had originally intended to take Dominica, between Martinique and Guadeloupe, but found that the governor of Martinique had already succeeded in this project. Before d'Estaing could initiate his own campaign, he had to prevent the capture of St. Lucia by Rear Admiral Samuel Barrington and General James Grant. Barrington had five ships, three of them 64's, and five smaller vessels. Grant had 5,800 men, detached from Clinton's army at Philadelphia.

British regulars made quick work of defeating the French on St. Lucia, but Grant had barely raised his colors when a British frigate was seen running down from the north with the signal for "enemy in sight." Barrington had a seaman's eye and in a little bay took a position that would make the wind work for him. Stretching his small squadron across the mouth of a basin which kept the transports safe from enemy hands, Barrington had much less than half the firepower available to d'Estaing. The situation resembled the one which d'Estaing had met at New York and he experienced the same lack of success. On December 15, d'Estaing did all in his power to deploy his heavy line against Barrington and failed twice. Lacking the seamanship to get at his foe, d'Estaing reverted to the profession he knew. Going north of the principal town of Castries to a broad anchorage, d'Estaing landed his troops and went at the British sword in hand. The terrain was difficult, Grant was able, and the fighting was bloody. At the end of a week which cost him 400 killed and 1,100 wounded, d'Estaing fell back in acceptance of defeat. Re-embarking his troops, he returned to Martinique, leaving the British an anchorage at Castries that Rodney considered the finest in the West Indies to

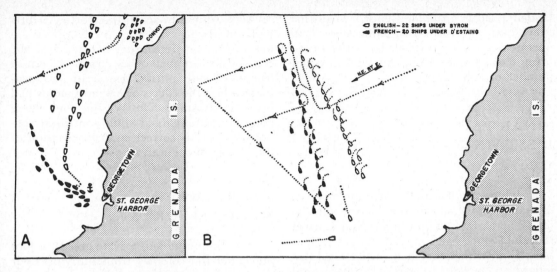

BATTLE OF GRENADA, JULY 6, 1779

stand as a sentry only 30 miles from Fort Royal.

Licking his wounds, d'Estaing now set his original plans in motion. He captured Grenada after a reinforcement raised his fleet to 20 ships. In the meantime, Byron had arrived in the West Indies to give the British a slight superiority with 22 ships. Byron was looking for the French and found them on July 6, 1779, as they left Grenada in a light wind. Since the French were in confusion, Byron signaled General Chase and drove down from the north upon d'Estaing. The Battle of Grenada opened with long-range gunfire. Three British ships in the van fell to leeward and were virtually deserted by Byron, who, upon seeing the French flag firmly planted on Grenada, turned to parallel d'Estaing's course in the manner prescribed by the *Fighting Instructions*. As Byron reached along the French line, d'Estaing's high-aimed shot disabled four British ships. D'Estaing tacked to bear down upon the cripples and Byron, who had the weather gage, cautiously conformed to the enemy movement but did not close. On a southerly course, d'Estaing cannonaded the cripples in passing and withdrew from the battlefield without any capture other than the island itself. To him, the retention of Grenada was more important than the de-

struction or capture of enemy ships. Since Byron did not force an issue, d'Estaing was content. Both nations claimed victory. The French however held Grenada and it was for Grenada that d'Estaing had fought. Byron was too shattered to be a further threat to French plans and retired to St. Kitts for repairs. D'Estaing consolidated the hold on Grenada before following his recent adversary. Therein, of course, was the fundamental difference between a French and a British commander. In the same situation at the same period of history, a British commander would not have slept until a wounded foe had been brought to decisive action.

At St. Kitts, d'Estaing found Byron lined up at anchor, awaiting attack, too crippled aloft to sally out. D'Estaing had had more than enough of anchored Englishmen, so, after sailing insultingly to and fro off the roadstead, he bethought himself of the approaching hurricane season and sailed for Haiti, the last French port of call in the Indies.

Letters awaited d'Estaing at Cap Français that enabled him to plan his summer movements in the North American theater. He learned from Washington that the British had exploited the absence of the French fleet to invade the southern colonies. After failing again to take Charleston, the British had landed 4,000 men under General Augustine Prevost at Savannah. D'Estaing agreed to operate against Prevost, pledging himself to bring 6,000 French troops to join an equal number of Americans.

FINAL FAILURE: D'ESTAING AT SAVANNAH, 1779

Arriving off Savannah on September 1, d'Estaing conferred with the Continental Major General Benjamin Lincoln and learned that the French had indirectly liberated Newport, from which they had earlier been dislodged. The British, sure that he would renew his attack there with the advent of summer, had prudently evacuated Rhode Island before d'Estaing could return. Joining Lincoln, d'Estaing now subjected Savannah to formal siege. Prevost resisted stoutly through two steaming months, inflicting losses favorable to him in the ratio of six to one. As winter approached and brought another good sailing season to the Caribbean, d'Estaing at length felt duty bound to withdraw from Georgia. Splitting his ships so that half could begin a campaign in the West Indies, he returned to France. Dispirited, General Lincoln marched to Charleston, where he was in turn besieged and compelled to surrender.

It is easy to understand how d'Estaing's reputation suffered because of his American performance. Colonists felt that the French had betrayed them, exploiting the American cause for their own purposes. For them, d'Estaing had done nothing except raise false hopes. But it was clear that France had made three distinct gains through the work of d'Estaing's fleet: (1) Dominica had been captured, (2) Grenada had been captured, and (3) France had successfully tested her new navy in overseas operations and found it a dependable instrument. The American gains should have been equally apparent. D'Estaing's cruise had contributed four advantages to the rebel cause: (1) his sailing from France had forced the evacuation of Philadelphia;

(2) his readiness to act in the North Atlantic had forced the evacuation of Newport; (3) his presence in the theater had lessened the grip of British men-of-war upon American commerce and spurred American privateering; and (4) the effects of his movements had been keenly studied by Washington, whose knowledge thus gained would contribute substantially to his correct strategic decision at the climax of the war.

AMERICAN NAVAL EFFORTS

As previously noted, private greed for loot prevented the colonies from unifying their considerable commerce raiding potential. At the siege of Boston in 1775, Washington had led the way in demonstrating the need for a regular service. On his own responsibility, he raised a light squadron of armed schooners that captured some 35 British supply vessels whose military cargoes were of inestimable value to the rebels. In November 1775, Congress established a Naval Committee with responsibility for founding Continental naval and marine forces. Administration of the Continental Navy began with a cumbersome 13-man committee whose responsibilities by 1781 devolved upon one man, Robert Morris. The first vessels of the navy were two sloops converted from merchantmen: the 24-gun *Alfred* and the 20-gun *Columbus*. The first squadron commander was Esek Hopkins, who, in February 1776 with five vessels raided Nassau and captured from the somnolent garrison extensive quantities of military goods. This constituted the only significant employment of a squadron by the Continental Navy; thereafter, its vessels operated on independent missions or as mere commerce raiders, distinguishable from privateers only by Congressional commission and prize law.[3]

State navies were akin to militia and per-

---

[3] American combat vessels, public and private, captured more than 200 British merchantmen or privateers a year from the outset of the war. The figure more than doubled when the French and Spanish entered the war in support of the colonies. By the

formed duties more or less in direct support of their respective governments. That of Connecticut, for example, regularly attempted to bring sulfur from the West Indies which ultimately made it possible for Connecticut to fill General Washington's gunpowder needs.[4] That of Virginia perished in futile efforts to keep small enemy men-of-war from infesting Virginian waters. The Navy of Massachusetts became involved in the most ambitious colonial amphibious operation, the disastrous Penobscot expedition of 1779.

As an illustration of the waste of colonial power for state rather than Continental Congress objectives, the Penobscot expedition is classic. Loyalists driven from Boston in the first months of the war had settled at the site of Castine, on Maine's Penobscot Bay some 200 sea-miles north of Boston, where they commenced privateer operations under British commissions. A strong element of civil war colored the decision of Massachusetts to attack its former citizens. Personal hatreds evoked a response among the citizens of Boston that the distant Continental Congress had reason to envy, for no less than 3,000 men came forward to man 20 vessels and supply a landing force. A member of the Congressional Marine Committee endorsed the project and authorized Captain Dudley Saltonstall of the Continental Navy to accept command of the little fleet. Saltonstall's frigate, the 32-gun *Warren,* was joined by two minor vessels to make a substantial contribution by the Continental Navy. New Hampshire contributed a brig and the rest came from Massachusetts, three from the state navy and 13 from privateers temporarily inducted into the state navy. Reaching the Penobscot River late in July 1779, State Gen-

eral Solomon Lovell courageously assailed the British garrison but was beaten off through Saltonstall's failure to support him. The British Navy, tensed for the arrival of d'Estaing from the West Indies, spared a detachment of a 64, two frigates, and six sloops, to relieve the besieged troops and loyalists. Commodore Sir George Collier terrified the little American fleet with this small force on August 13. Firing scarcely a shot in defense, Saltonstall's command disintegrated in panicked flight upriver. Running aground, the Americans burned their vessels and disappeared into the forests. Some 500 Americans died in this debacle; Collier lost only 13 men. The expedition all but ruined the financial stability of Massachusetts and in this respect alone tremendously injured the cause of freedom. Saltonstall was court-martialed at Boston. Blame for the failure was laid upon his lack of energy and skill, and he was dismissed from the Continental Navy; but that verdict could not undo the damage. The colony that had produced the *casus belli* now wearied of the war.

The willingness of men to gamble for personal profit however made privateering an unremitting war. Prospects of a rich prize were more attractive to the bulk of American seamen than the privilege of wearing uniforms. The lords of the British Admiralty were not greatly concerned about the little state and Continental navies, but they displayed their respect for the 2,000 or so American privateers by convoying essential troop movements. Operating in American coastal waters, in the West Indies, on the Atlantic sea routes, and even in British and European waters, the privateers in the course of the Revolution are estimated to have captured prizes valued at $18,000,000. The privateer *Rattlesnake* in one Baltic cruise made captures worth more than a million dollars. If all the cargoes taken by the privateersmen had been made available to the Continental Army, Washington's supply problem would have been appreciably lightened; but the sorry fact is that the cargoes as readily ended up in British hands when Congressional agents were unable to pay in hard cash. If this smacks of treason, as in a sense it was,

time of peace negotiations, the British had lost 3,176 vessels in all; the Americans, French, and Spanish, only 1,351. Of these, the British recaptured 893 vessels, and the allies, only 28, leaving a rough balance of about a thousand vessels in favor of the allies. This triumph over British commerce was not duplicated in naval actions: the Continental Navy was practically destroyed.

[4] For the most complete account of a state navy, see Louis F. Middlebrook, *History of Maritime Connecticut During The American Revolution,* 2 vols. (Salem, Massachusetts, 1925).

one must remember that the American Revolution was a civil war, with more colonists serving in regular regiments for the King than for Congress. Even if all privateersmen had been dedicated patriots, their work would not have amounted to a regular system of supply. What the Continental Army desperately needed was usually to be found in vessels escorted by frigates; and few privateers were disposed to attack protected enemy vessels.

This was the most striking difference between American privateer captains and officers of the regular Navy. While privateers usually steered clear of any well-armed vessel, naval captains, given chances at anything approaching a fair fight, sought to reach close quarters. To be sure in the course of the entire war only 53 vessels, none larger than a frigate, flew the colors of the Continental Navy. It is improbable that this tiny force appreciably shortened the Revolution, yet it took enough prizes to alarm British shippers. If only because they established the earliest traditions of the United States Navy, the achievements of the Continental skippers deserve mention.

Captain Nicholas Biddle in the 32-gun frigate *Randolph,* for example, while cruising east of Barbados in March 1777, allowed the 64-gun British ship of the line *Yarmouth* to approach within hailing distance. Then, hoisting his colors, Biddle fired a broadside. There followed a 30-minute running battle in which the *Yarmouth* was roughly handled, but the *Randolph,* taking a freak hit in her magazine, suddenly blew up with the loss of all but four of her crew of 315. Of this battle, the British naval historian Joseph Allen wrote: "The temerity of Captain Biddle in thus engaging a ship so much superior to his own, deserved a better fate." [5]

Captain Lambert Wickes of the brig *Reprisal,* while transporting Benjamin Franklin to Paris in the fall of 1776, captured two prizes which he sold privately at Nantes. Early the next year he was at sea again and in a few days made five more captures of merchantmen, which he took into Lorient.

When Lord Stormont, the British ambassador, protested at this unneutral use of French ports, Paris ordered Wickes to get out within 24-hours—and then looked the other way while he stayed where he was and endeared himself to French merchants by selling his prizes to them at a seventh of their value. As soon as British protests had died down, the *Reprisal* was out again, accompanied by two more American vessels. In a month's cruise off the British Isles, this little squadron took 18 prizes. That same spring Captain Gustavus Conyngham in the lugger *Surprise,* purchased at Dunkirk by American agents in Paris, captured two British prizes, including a mail packet out of Harwich. By this time Lord Stormont was so incensed at France's unneutral conduct in harboring American raiders that he took his protests directly to the French premier. Unable any longer to gloss over the matter, the government at Paris at last obliged Wickes to leave the country and even temporarily jailed Conyngham, whom the British called "the Dunkirk pirate." In July however Conyngham was at sea again, this time in the cutter *Revenge.* Eluding chase by frigates, sloops-of-war, and cutters, he took more prizes in British waters, disposing of them in Spanish ports.

John Paul Jones, in some respects the most successful and certainly the most daring of American raiders, arrived in Quiberon Bay in February 1778, after the French had allied themselves with the rebellious colonies. Here in the new 18-gun *Ranger* he flew the flag of 13 stars and stripes and heard the first authorized salute to the American colors by a foreign vessel. In April he was out on the first of the two cruises that are his greatest claim to fame.

Heading into enemy waters, Jones captured a merchantman off the Scilly Islands and then proceeded into the Irish Sea, where in three days he produced something like a panic along the British coasts by nearly succeeding in setting fire to the port of Whitehaven, raiding the castle of the Earl of Selkirk, and capturing the sloop-of-war *Drake,* the first vessel of the Royal Navy to be taken as an American prize.

The next year Jones was out again with a

---

[5] *Battles of the British Navy* (London, 1900), 259.

squadron of five vessels: his flagship *Bonhomme Richard,* a converted East Indiaman mounting 32 guns which he had rechristened in gratitude to his patron Franklin; the new frigate *Alliance,* 32 guns; the *Pallas,* 32; the *Cerf,* 18; and the *Vengeance,* 12. After circumnavigating the British Isles and taking prizes as he went, Jones's squadron, reduced to four by separation of the *Cerf,* sighted off Flamborough Head the main object of his cruise, the rich Baltic convoy of 41 sail bound for England. While the British merchantmen scattered in the gathering twilight, Jones went after the escorts, the new 50-gun frigate *Serapis* and the *Countess of Scarborough,* mounting 20 guns.

So different are British and American accounts of the ensuing battle, fought under bright moonlight before throngs of Englishmen gathered on the nearby shore, that it is probably impossible ever to reconstruct the exact tactics employed. It is clear however that the *Bonhomme Richard* attacked before the rest of Jones's force could beat up wind to join, that somehow Jones succeeded in lashing his flagship to the *Serapis* in order to offset the new frigate's superior sailing qualities, and that Jones continued to fight long after his subordinates regarded his situation as hopeless. When one of them begged him, "For God's sake, Captain, strike," he replied, "No, I will sink; I will never strike." A little later the *Richard*'s master gunner, believing reports that both the captain and his first lieutenant, Richard Dale, had been killed, loudly cried for quarter. To the query of Captain Pearson, commanding the *Serapis,* whether the *Richard* had indeed struck, Jones shouted back, "I have not yet begun to fight," [6] a cry which has remained the watchword of the United States Navy.

In spite of several initial advantages and the sinking condition of the *Richard,* the British gradually found the battle turning against them. The *Pallas* captured the little *Countess of Scarborough,* and the *Alliance* worked up to within range of the main antagonists. The ill-aimed volleys of the *Alliance* seem to have done at least as much damage

---

[6] So reported by Dale and certainly Jones's meaning if not his precise words.

to the *Richard* as to the *Serapis,* but the mere presence of a fresh frigate was enough to shake Pearson's resolution. The decisive blow however came from the 40 marines and sailors whom Jones had early sent aloft. Fighting their way through the tangled rigging of both ships, they won the tops and very nearly cleared the main deck of the *Serapis* with grenades and musket fire. One grenade, dropped through an open hatchway, set fire to a cartridge. The flames then flashed from cartridge to cartridge, causing an explosion which put several British guns and gun crews out of action. Shortly afterwards the *Alliance* took a raking position off the stern of the *Serapis.* At this, Pearson, having carried out his major duty of saving the convoy, surrendered in order to put an end to the carnage. On the way to port in Holland, Jones finally gave up his attempt to save the battered *Richard* from sinking and shifted his command to the *Serapis.*

The ultimate tribute to the courage of Jones, who would not acknowledge that he was beaten, was given by Pearson himself, who said at his court-martial: "Long before the close of the action it became apparent that the American ship was dominated by a commanding will of a most unalterable resolution, and there can be no doubt that the intention of her commander was, if he could not conquer, to sink alongside."

Humiliating as such exploits might be to English pride, the Admiralty was far more concerned about the movements of the grand fleets of France and Spain. As Jones fought his gallant battle, 68 ships of Spain and France sailed home from the English Channel after weeks of being at large in English waters.

FRENCH INVASION PLANS, 1779

While the officers of the Royal Navy frantically worked in dockyards and harbors to undo the harm of a decade of decline, the need to commission more ships was suddenly doubled. Spain declared war on June 16, 1779. The people of England were not at first disturbed. Hostilities with Spain had been synonymous with rich booty since the days of Elizabeth I. However, the British government was properly alarmed. Excellent intelligence had disclosed that the French had long been concerting an invasion plan with Spain. General le Comte de Vaux, commanding two divisions of 20,000 men each at Havre and St. Malo, was ready to land them at Portsmouth for a thrust at London as soon as the Brest and Cadiz fleets together had defeated the British Home Fleet and secured command of the Channel. To mystify the British, supporting diversions were to be launched against Scotland and Ireland, while expeditions captured Minorca, Gibraltar, and Jamaica. Keppel, following his court-martial, had voluntarily withdrawn from service, and so the defense of England's moat was put into the trembling hands of Admiral Sir Charles Hardy. Old for his years, uncertain of his ability to wield a fleet of 37 ships, Hardy took refuge in austere silence, spurning the excellent counsel tactfully offered by his juniors. Fortunately for England, Hardy's incapacity was matched by discord between the French and Spanish. Spanish pride recoiled from serving under French orders and demanded that the Brest fleet come south for a rendezvous off Corunna.

Accordingly, d'Orvilliers left Brest early in June, two weeks before Hardy was ready for sea. Arriving at the appointed rendezvous with 32 ships and nine frigates, d'Orvilliers waited some 50 days before being joined by 36 ships under Don Luis de Córdoba. D'Orvilliers had dashed out of Brest with undermanned ships poorly supplied, because the Spanish had insisted upon haste. His enforced idleness at the rendezvous had cut heavily into his provisions besides inducing sicknesses of almost epidemic proportions. Attempting to use the time in training, d'Orvilliers learned that he could employ only the simplest of tactical maneuvers because too many of his ships were incapable. The Spanish ships did not raise his spirits. Sluggish, ill found, and wretchedly short of good seamen, the combination of 68 ships was impressive principally in number. Maneuvers other than small changes of course were too

risky for d'Orvilliers to contemplate. His grand fleet was the heir of the ill-fated Armada of 1588, which had sailed on a similar mission to carry invasion to England.

Delayed by translation of signal systems and integration of tactical concepts, the cumbersome force finally reached the latitude of Ushant on August 7. D'Orvilliers had no knowledge of Hardy's location, which was at a convoy receiving point some 30 to 60 miles west of the Scilly Islands. The door was open to the Channel but d'Orvilliers had come to fight. Reaching the Lizard in mid-August, d'Orvilliers was baffled by the absence of British resistance. His was the first French fleet to sail unopposed into the Channel during wartime, and he was uneasy. Fortunately for England, the wind died and left the Franco-Spanish fleet drifting aimlessly off Plymouth, long enough for d'Orvilliers to receive new orders from Paris. Once again, as so often happened in French planning, ministers in Paris changed their minds when a project was well underway. The descent on the Isle of Wight and the capture of Portsmouth was now to be abandoned in favor of a landing on the Cornwall coast at Falmouth Bay. Horrified, d'Orvilliers consulted his charts and pilots, confirming the fact that the beachhead desired by the Ministry of Marine did not afford adequate holding ground for the fleet to anchor.

D'Orvilliers began a long correspondence with his superiors explaining difficulties which would have been obvious at a glance to a seaman. From their mastery of land warfare, the French had derived concepts of sea warfare which ignored the realities of natural conditions. After a few days off Plymouth, an easterly gale sprang up and d'Orvilliers had to look to the safety of his command. The same wind held Hardy well away to the west. Blown out of the Channel, d'Orvilliers finally learned where Hardy was, and toward the end of August arrived at the Scillies in search of a decisive action that would enable the government at Paris to take its time about settling upon a sound invasion plan.

On the last day of August, Hardy sighted the great fleet to westward of him, and gave the allies the unusual view of a British admiral in full retreat. Hardy struggled to race the foe to the Channel and his ships had faster bottoms than the fouled hulls of the enemy. D'Orvilliers gave chase but could not catch the agile British. Dangerously reduced by sickness, low on water and stores, d'Orvilliers disgustedly decided to return to Brest. He had done his best. Resigning from the navy, he retired to seclusion.

As in the days of the Spanish Armada, weather had again blocked enemy plans. In 1588 however Howard had been aggressive in the defense of the English Channel, and the guns of his ships had injured the Spanish fleet before a rising wind delivered the *coup de grâce*. England had resounded with praise for a job well done. In 1779, there were few cheers. The professional men of the Royal Navy felt shame. Among the ministers, there was great worry. Previously, the enemy had based his plans upon hopes of avoiding the British fleet, and those plans were therefore fundamentally unsound. This time, the enemy plans were based upon the condition that the British fleet would first be met and destroyed. If this cruise of 1779 represented a basic change in French strategic thought, England was entering the most dangerous years of her existence.

Elsewhere in the world, Britons received the Spanish declaration of war as an invitation to attack the sprawling empire of Spain. Expeditions were prepared hastily, among them one directed against Nicaragua, to sever land communications between Mexico and South America. The commander of the naval escort for the Nicaraguan venture was a young, ardent, newly-made captain named Horatio Nelson.

6

The American Revolution, Part II

Sir Charles Hardy died in the spring of 1780. His successor in the command of the British Home Fleet was Admiral Francis Geary. Another man too old for his years, Geary endured the weight of responsibility for scarcely three months before reporting himself too sick for duty. Then at last a leader in full intellectual and mental vigor stepped aboard the 100-gun *Victory* to hoist the flag of Commander in Chief; this was Vice Admiral George Darby. From August through October, Darby with 30 ships stood sentry duty at the entrance to the Channel awaiting assault from the combination of 67 Franco-Spanish ships commanded by Don Luis de Córdoba. But Córdoba was content to loiter in the latitudes of Spain and gobble up a fat British convoy bound for East Indian campaigns. British outcry against their navy for permitting this heavy financial disaster to occur was quieted by ominous diplomatic developments. England foolishly provoked Holland into declaring war in December 1780, at a time when Catherine of Russia was forming an "Armed Neutrality" with Denmark and Sweden to assist the American cause. The Dutch came to war with 30 ships, manned by seamen as good as the British. The Armed Neutrality had 84 ships in commission. England stood alone against an alignment of all the important navies of Europe. The time was overdue for her to send fighting admirals to sea.

Sir George Brydges Rodney was the type of admiral able to redeem England's tarnished primacy. Not too admirable in his personal life, Rodney proved to be one of the finest leaders in British history. Late in 1779, he was appointed to the West Indies and given a fleet of 22 ships. He did not proceed directly to his new post. The Spanish had been blockading Gibraltar since the middle of 1779. Rodney carried a convoy to relieve the hard-pressed garrison of General Eliott.

RODNEY'S MOONLIGHT BATTLE, JANUARY 16, 1780

Capturing a convoy of some 16 Spanish merchantmen in the Bay of Biscay bearing naval stores to Cadiz under the escort of six frigates, Rodney learned that the Spanish fleet was active. A few days later, he learned definitely that a Spanish division was at sea somewhere in the vicinity of Lisbon. Rodney thoroughly prepared for battle. His ships were copper-bottomed, a recent innovation intended to frustrate marine worms as well as to retard fouling. As a consequence, old ships were rejuvenated. The entire British navy acquired a significant speed advantage that more than matched the advantages the French had enjoyed from their superior design and construction.

Anxious for a test of his ships and captains, Rodney rounded Cape St. Vincent in line of battle on January 16. Some four leagues south of the Cape about noon, he sighted a fleet to the southeast and swiftly maneuvered into line abreast. Admiral Don Juan de Langara was astonished by the appearance of ships of the line. The Spanish had retired to winter quarters and posted de Langara with eleven ships to intercept the supplies that had to be sent to Gibraltar. Ambush at sea, always difficult, is embarrassing when the enemy unexpectedly employs an escort double in strength to the ambuscade, as the British did in this instance. On a strong westerly wind, de Langara prudently ran for Cadiz and its 24 ships.

Rodney had only four hours of daylight and little time to waste. It was a situation for a general chase and melee. Releasing his swiftest ships to overtake the enemy, Rodney restrained them only by the order to drive to leeward, so as to stand between the Spanish and the shore. De Langara might have escaped through outright flight but he chose to escape in a military formation, thereby chaining himself to the speed of his slowest ship. The wind was rising to gale strength toward sunset when the leading British ships came within range.

Guns thudded into the night, illuminated by the explosion of a Spanish 70-gun ship, from which the British picked up a single survivor. With the old deftness and daring of Hawkins and Hawke, Rodney's men fastened upon Spanish opponents, hurling deadly broadsides. Clouds of gunsmoke and churning seas permitted four Spaniards to get away. The remaining six were in British hands at dawn and de Langara dined with Rodney aboard the 90-gun *Sandwich*.

Without further incident, Rodney supplied Gibraltar and sent relief to Minorca.

News of his victory was ecstatically received in an England that had begun to suspect that French and Spanish ships could sail the seas with impunity. Morale and tone in the Royal Navy, depressed by months of fumbling ineptitude, now revived. It was true that de Langara had been hopelessly outnumbered, but the professional ease with which the Spanish had been cut down made the average Briton certain that the victory would only have been greater had de Langara been in company with half or all of the 24 ships in Cadiz.

The British nation made Rodney a hero and placed their glory in his hands. He vindicated their trust in a climactic battle against the French in the West Indies.

FLEET CLASHES IN THE WEST INDIES, 1780-1781

The French ships based on Martinique had a fine new commander, the Comte de Guichen. A practical seaman as well as a thorough master of his nation's naval concepts, de Guichen had the skill to preserve his fleet against an opponent of Rodney's high caliber. Rodney arrived at St. Lucia in March 1780 and assumed command of 20 ships that had been overlong in the Indies. By early April Rodney was at sea, in position to intercept de Guichen's attempt to take 3,000 troops south to capture Barbados.

Since de Guichen's 22 ships were attempting to beat into the trade wind through the passage between Martinique and Dominica, they did not progress far before Rodney's frigates brought news of the French sortie. Rodney had given much thought to the French gunnery tactics of firing high and proposed to circumvent dismasting by reducing the interval between ships in his line of battle so as to have two of his own firing upon one of the enemy. As a departure from the *Fighting Instructions,* this massing of fire was in direct contradiction to the concepts which had established ship-to-ship matching in lines of equal strength. It was the first gi-

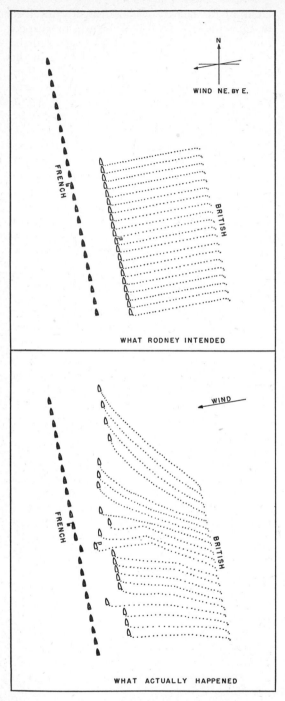

RODNEY AND DE GUICHEN, *APRIL 17, 1780*

but in 1780 the inertia of tradition benumbed Rodney's captains and admirals from fully supporting his views.

By dawn, April 17, 1780, Rodney had de Guichen in battle view and was dressing his line by signals that did not clearly convey his intentions. Rodney had the wind, so that de Guichen was helpless to decline action. Nearly 70, de Guichen did not believe in battle for the sake of battle. Narrowly watching Rodney's maneuvers, de Guichen countered skillfully but fell into the trap of Rodney's plans. By 11 AM the fleets were headed north and Rodney had succeeded in bringing his whole line opposite the center and rear of the French fleet, which was arrayed at normal interval. The wind became too gentle for de Guichen to have time to shorten sail and close up, so he took the risk of slight disarray by signaling his force to wear, intending to receive the British blow on his new van and center, enabling his new rear to press up into action. At this moment however Rodney turned to attack and de Guichen canceled his order. If some French captains were confused and turned away from the wind, some British captains served their admiral worse. The captain of Rodney's leading ship led Rodney's van in a long slant toward their opposite enemy numbers.

In a few moments, Rodney's carefully devised plan of battle began to disintegrate as his admiral in the van division carried his ships away, and his line stretched out to match the French one for one. The signals of the *Fighting Instructions* had proved completely inadequate to impart Rodney's initial intentions and now proved equally inadequate to correct the situation. Committed to his attack, Rodney went down with a heavy heart on the enemy, knowing he could not force a decision.

The end of the battle was predictable. Individual actions were close and heavy. The French shot high and the British shot to kill. After some three hours, de Guichen sailed away and Rodney could not follow. As usual, the French lost half again as many men. They had demonstrated anew that they had learned a method to save their ships,

ant step toward the tactical concentrations which were ultimately to defeat the French, and although England claimed victory on the grounds that the descent upon Barbados had been averted, the French were proving themselves disconcertingly adept at eluding the catastrophes of the past.

A month later, off St. Lucia, Rodney had another chance at his agile foe. On May 15, de Guichen partially capped Rodney's "T" and delivered the fire of 15 ships into three. The fleets sparred at jabbing distance for three days, de Guichen keeping out of range until May 19, when a shifting wind offered Rodney an opening to attack. De Guichen was on a southerly course and to windward of Rodney, who was on a northerly course within close-hauled reach of the French. The leading British ship struck at the middle ship in the tight French line, and the fleets filed past each other in swift cannonading. By this time, the three ships posted in the British van had received considerable structural damage and were leaking badly. Rodney did not dare risk them in another action and, perforce, abandoned further efforts to make de Guichen stand for a decisive engagement.

Venting his spleen on his subordinates, Rodney, in his own words, "taught them to be what they had never been before—Officers." His van admiral, Sir Hyde Parker, went home in anger and vindicated his reputation for bravery in a bloody fight with the Dutch. Rodney's troubles with the enemy increased in June. Intelligence arrived that twelve Spanish ships covering a troop convoy of 11,000 men were en route to join de Guichen. Determined to crush this force, Rodney posted himself to the east of Martinique, but the Spanish eluded him. Already afflicted with gout, Rodney raged about seeking battle which the Allies declined to offer him. The Spanish were interested in strengthening their colonial posts, such as New Orleans, whose commander had daringly led an expedition against the British in the region of northern Lake Michigan, and Nicaragua, which had flung back in broken health the men that Horatio Nelson had brought into its jungle. The French, ever conscious of their fine, new ships, wanted the fleet to leave the Indies before the hurricane season. De Guichen had such positive instructions on this point that he did not feel free to comply with the requests of Washington and Lafayette to operate in North Atlantic waters for the summer. In addition, the French and Spanish fleets were struck by epidemics that rendered them incapable of strong offensive action. Two minor brushes by detachments occurred, the British being led by Commodore William Cornwallis, but the great enemy fleets simply disappeared from the British range of action. Rodney at last took ten ships to New York in September. He left the Caribbean none too soon. A great hurricane smashed at the fleet he had left in the Indies, inflicting more damage than all of the engagements with de Guichen. Nine ships were dismasted and two sunk, and ten frigates and sloops were lost. It was a miserable end to an inglorious campaign.

Rodney returned to Barbados in early December. The hurricane had ruined a critical amount of naval stores at British bases. Anxious to accomplish something before being forced home, Rodney was circumvented by French forehandedness in his effort to recapture St. Vincent. The bootless expedition reduced to nine the ships he could carry to sea on other ventures, and so he rejoiced at a timely reinforcement of eight ships under a new and able second-in-command sent to replace Sir Hyde Parker. This was Rear Admiral Sir Samuel Hood, a conceited officer whose conceit was founded upon very real ability. Cannibalizing some of Hood's stores, Rodney was readying a force of 21 ships when in late January 1781 there arrived a welcome dispatch which solved his logistics problem. Informed that a state of war existed with Holland, he was directed to attack Dutch possessions in the Caribbean. Of these, St. Eustatius was the most alluring.

A small island north of St. Kitts, St. Eustatius had been waxing rich as the seat of neutral trade during the war. There, Americans had been procuring vital naval munitions and stores. There, the French sent their islands' produce to be shipped under a neutral flag. There, too, some Britons found a means to do business with the enemy. All things considered, including the custom of prize money and the great quantities of naval stores to be had, Rodney was pleased to pounce early in February upon the unsuspecting island. The booty was valued at the tremendous sum of £3,000,000, which unfortunately diverted Rodney from his offensive and defensive duties. Notoriously impecunious, Rodney sought to refound his fortune at St. Eustatius, which King George graciously made over to its captors. Three months were consumed in reckoning the accounts of booty. Rodney postponed the attacks upon Dutch Curaçao and Surinam until his opportunity passed with the return of a French fleet to the theater.

Doing his admiral's work, Hood was posted in the eastern approaches to Martinique on the morning of April 28, 1781, when 20 ships and a large convoy appeared to windward of him in the east. This was the fleet of the Comte de Grasse, who had learned seamanship under the tutelage of the Knights of Malta. Joined by four ships from Martinique, de Grasse accepted the invitation to battle implied by Hood's shortened sails. However, mindful of orders to conserve ships, de Grasse was not needlessly reckless. He kept at long range. All ships engaged for two hours in a futile, formal battle which verified French beliefs that no one could win when both adversaries had skill. The vans were close for a brief time during which heavy damage was received by three British hulls. As these vessels signaled they were leaking badly, Hood's zest for a standup fight evaporated. Having a faster fleet, Hood was able to stand away from de Grasse. For his part, de Grasse was amiably disposed to continue peacefully to his destination.

Rodney was shocked by the news. Befuddled by greed, he had overlong neglected his duty. Offensive opportunities were gone and he had a broad area to defend. Hastening away from St. Eustatius, Rodney found that his negligence had been exploited by the French to mount expeditions against St. Lucia and Tobago. St. Lucia was preserved by the crews of three frigates who manned shore batteries at a crucial time, but Tobago

fell. Shaken by the energy of the French, Rodney in early June caught up with de Grasse in the vicinity of Grenada. Although de Grasse was caught to leeward near shore, Rodney refrained from testing his tactical theories. Professing to be restrained by navigational hazards, Rodney showed de Grasse the unusual spectacle of a British admiral hanging back from an attack until too late. Needlessly worried about the safety of Barbados, Rodney let de Grasse go unmolested to Martinique.

This proved to be one of the most costly moments of vacillation in British naval annals: a few months later, de Grasse and his ships guaranteed victory in the Yorktown campaign which won independence for the United States. Rodney's subsequent annihilation of de Grasse could not restore the thirteen colonies to the crown.

THE YORKTOWN CAMPAIGN, 1781

In the thirteen colonies, British military effort had from the first been weakened by the insistence of the British government upon directing operations from London. Clinton, in command of 30,000 troops at most, watched one opportunity after another fade away when he might have concentrated against the waning strength of Washington and ended the rebellion. Instead, the scatter-gun strategy of the British War Office allowed Washington to survive. Clinton was not permitted to resign, since he was known to be a loyal and dependable soldier, and his protests against dribbling diversions were quietly filed and ignored. A more or less realistic strategy became mandatory. With the French as an American ally, the British considered withdrawing from the continent to Halifax. Such a move however would give American offensive power full scope, and Canada had once been threatened. Therefore Clinton was ordered to remain at New York as the main entrepôt of British supplies, principally as a threat to American aspirations against Canada. In itself, Clinton's occupation of New York would be static, doing little to affect the outcome of the war. Obliged to consider genuine military efforts, the British selected the theater of the southern colonies, whose cotton and tobacco, rice and indigo were the only American exports desired by European markets. These crops could provide the financial sinews for American life and constituted an attraction to French businessmen.

Consequently, Clinton sailed south in the spring of 1780 and in May captured Charleston. Having a base for southern operations, he returned to New York, leaving General Charles Cornwallis with 8,000 men to initiate campaigns against the arteries of American economic life. Supported by such dashing cavalry commanders as Tarleton and Hanger, Cornwallis marched through the Carolinas, meeting indifferent success in demolishing Major General Nathaniel Greene. Battles were won by each side as Cornwallis gradually worked north toward Chesapeake Bay.

In the spring of 1781, the war against the colonies seemed no closer to successful conclusion than it had in any previous year. British strategists concluded that the communications between Washington in the north and Greene in the south had to be cut. Light-draft vessels operating on the Chesapeake and its tributaries could drive American communications north and south up into the high ground beyond the tidewater region and perhaps prevent the Continental Army from further timely shifts of strength. Campaigning along the James River in pursuit of elusive American forces, Cornwallis was recalled from the vicinity of Richmond to find a suitable base for naval operations. Retiring along the southern bank of the James, he inspected Norfolk, which had been ravaged the year before by the traitor Benedict Arnold, and took ship across Hampton Roads to the peninsula between the James and York rivers. Here, at Yorktown, he found a harbor that seemed ideal for the purposes of the navy and stacked arms to wait for the tall ships of England. Facing the water, Cornwallis felt at ease for the first time in many months of tramping

through the hostile, tangled counties of Carolina and southern Virginia.

In the summer of 1781, then, as de Grasse entered the powerful base of Cap Français on the northern coast of Haiti, British forces in North America were split into two segments, the bulk at New York and a force of campaigning strength at Yorktown. Letters to de Grasse from Washington and from Rochambeau, who had landed at Newport with 5,000 French troops to cooperate with the Continentals, explained the situation. Washington wished to attack Clinton, but yielded to Rochambeau's preference to attack Cornwallis. The help of the French fleet was absolutely necessary to isolate Cornwallis. Inasmuch as de Grasse planned at the advent of the next sailing season in the Indies to combine with a Spanish fleet to capture Jamaica, operations in the sheltered Chesapeake appealed to him more strongly than the comparatively exposed New York theater. He agreed to come to the Chesapeake by the end of August.

Leaving light forces to screen their withdrawal and deceive Clinton, Washington and Rochambeau began the long march from the north. In the meantime, to deceive Rodney, de Grasse steered through the treacherous channel along the northern coast of Cuba to the Straits of Florida instead of following the customary direct route north. It was not Rodney however with whom de Grasse had to contend. Sick in a sickly climate, Rodney had learned that the British merchants he had injured in their illicit trade at St. Eustatius were villifying him at home, and he deemed his health and honor sufficient reasons to shift command to Hood. Because Rodney took to England the ships that needed repair and refitting, Hood had only 14, which would however be appreciably strengthened by the squadron of six stationed at New York. Hood pursued de Grasse, but, going by the customary course north made better time than his quarry. Hood believed, on the basis of British experience, that de Grasse would have with him only half of his force, at most 14 ships. Hood pinned his hopes for glory in a running fight at sea before he had to submit to

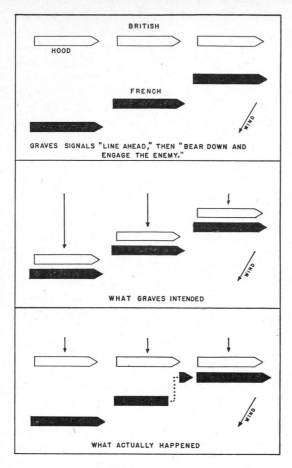

BRITISH

HOOD

FRENCH

WIND

GRAVES SIGNALS "LINE AHEAD," THEN "BEAR DOWN AND ENGAGE THE ENEMY."

WIND

WHAT GRAVES INTENDED

WIND

WHAT ACTUALLY HAPPENED

DIAGRAM:
BATTLE OF THE VIRGINIA CAPES

Symbols represent divisions

the seniority of Admiral Thomas Graves at New York. The sea proved empty, as did Chesapeake Bay, whose entrance Hood inspected on August 25. Grimly, Hood pushed on to Sandy Hook, dropping anchor on August 28, satisfied that he had won the race from the Indies and placed the Royal Navy in an extremely favorable interior position. The French had a division of eight ships at Newport under the Comte de Barras. These would have to move to unite with de Grasse, but Hood fondly believed that Graves and he could smash de Barras and then deal with de Grasse at leisure.

Having news that de Barras had sailed

and anticipating that de Grasse was coming toward New York, Graves put to sea to defeat first one portion of his enemies and then the other. Hood had assured Graves that de Grasse probably had only twelve ships, so that their combination of 19 ships was more than enough for victory. In the meantime, de Grasse reached the entrance to the Chesapeake five days after Hood had called there. Completely unsuspected by the British naval commanders, de Grasse rounded Cape Henry, anchored at Lynnhaven Bay in some disarray, landed 3,000 French regulars from the Indies, sent boats up the Chesapeake to assist Washington and Rochambeau, and detached two pairs of ships to block the James and York Rivers and cooperate directly with the Allied forces present under Lafayette. If Cornwallis was startled to find himself under siege, cut off from the sea, Graves was overwhelmed on a September morning to stumble upon de Grasse's whole fleet rather than a part.

During the morning of September 5, 1781, in fair weather with a NNE wind, Graves in rough line abreast confidently approached the entrance to the Chesapeake. Seeing a swath of sails on the horizon, Graves expected to pounce upon a small squadron fluttering closehauled into the wind and pin them onto the lee shore of Cape Henry. His own force was deployed for maximum shock attack, awaiting the signal of General Chase. Such attack however was not a safe tactic to employ against a superior enemy since control would soon disappear in general melee. Consequently, Graves was sorely tried when his lookouts reported a total of 24 French ships. Frantically thumbing through the *Fighting Instructions*, Graves did his best to devise a series of signals which would dress his line and allow a well-directed attack. The *Fighting Instructions* failed him.

De Grasse was caught in a weak position. A large number of his seamen were ashore assisting Lafayette or had gone up the Chesapeake with boats to transport Washington and Rochambeau. Details of taking on wood and water had disarranged the original anchorage dispositions of the ships. Unable to present a solid line of broadsides to repel as-

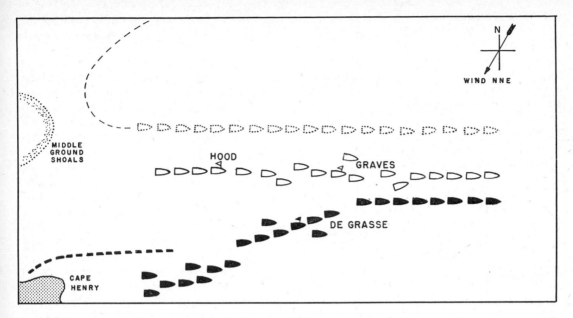

BATTLE OF THE VIRGINIA CAPES, SEPTEMBER 5, 1781

sault and short-handed for working ships and fighting underway, de Grasse chose to weigh anchor. This was done hastily, out of order, and presented Graves a situation "almost beyond the wildest dreams of a sea-commander."[1] Had Graves possessed the revolutionary signal system then being carefully perfected by Admiral Richard Kempenfelt for use in the Home Fleet, it would have been possible for him to drive de Grasse ashore. Instead, Graves had to turn to port into the conventional line ahead, shorten sail, and permit de Grasse to get to sea.

Saved from immediate disaster through no effort of his own, de Grasse blundered into a situation that offered Graves a second chance for decisive action. De Grasse permitted his captains to sail in order of speed rather than form line in assigned stations. The result was three separated clusters of French ships, each group struggling into line. The van close-hauled to the wind and formed an advance guard to cover the center and rear, but being composed of the swiftest sailers the van opened a great gap with the center, which, in turn, stood considerably away from the

rear. The three groups were stepped toward the north, the van being within easy reach of Graves. The two divisions astern and in the lee valiantly closehauled to come into line with the van, which fell off the wind to assist the juncture. However, the French fleet could not attain tactical integrity before Graves could interfere.

Unfortunately for England, the *Fighting Instructions* once again failed to give signals that Graves needed to clarify his intentions. He wished each of his divisions to attack its opposite, thus breaking the action into three separate battles. As the fleets lazed along on slightly converging easterly courses, Graves had to waste precious minutes correcting his line and extending it to equal that of the French. At 3:45 PM, he concluded that his signals were understood by his subordinates and ordered the attack. To his infinite disgust, he discovered that his signals had not been understood at all. His van went down on the French van and his fleet followed in the traditional manner. The efforts of Graves to halt the erroneous movement merely confirmed the opinion of his subordinates that they had correctly unraveled his confusing signals. Hood interpreted the sig-

[1] James, *British Navy in Adversity*, 290.

nals to suit himself and remained out of action entirely. Firing went on until sunset, when de Grasse fell away to perfect his line. As usual, the British were too damaged aloft to prevent the withdrawal. Casualties were relatively light, but two to one against the British.

For five days the fleets moved to the east within sight of each other until the wind shifted and favored de Grasse. Graves in mortification had by this time lost sight of his original purpose of protecting the beleagured Cornwallis at Yorktown, but de Grasse had his primary mission fixed in mind. At his first chance, de Grasse sped back to the Chesapeake and found that Barras had arrived. This raised his strength to 36 ships, far too many for Graves to contend with, and so Graves abandoned Cornwallis.

The doughty British general hung on for a month with his 7,000 men against 9,000 Americans and 8,000 French. Shortages and sickness and casualties gradually brought him low. On October 19, 1781, Cornwallis surrendered with the honors of war. For the second time in the war, a British field army had been captured intact. The British people recoiled against their King's ambition, and the supremacy of Parliament was reaffirmed in the resignation of Lord North and the appointment of Lord Rockingham to be Prime Minister in March 1782. Rockingham had opposed the war from the first and among the conditions of his acceptance of office was the king's promise to recognize the independence of the American colonies. Thus, the war in North America virtually ended at Yorktown, although the terms of alliance with France precluded Congress from signing a separate peace.

With its sterile Battle of the Virginia Capes and its tedious weeks of siege warfare, the Yorktown campaign did not produce events of great military glory. It merely affirmed anew the silent, tremendous power exerted by controlling sea communications. It did have the possibility of a great battle, as General Clinton scraped up ships and troops for a desperate amphibious assault in relief of Cornwallis, but Clinton arrived at the Chesapeake five days after Cornwallis surrendered, so he dejectedly returned to New York.

To Graves and his fellows, the Battle of the Virginia Capes was only another futile brush which proved the inadequacy of the *Fighting Instructions* and the urgent need for a clear, simple system of tactical communications. For Graves, there was hope for another year and another battle, which he would win. To Washington and his fellows, the Battle of the Virginia Capes was a further example of French reluctance to lose ships in action. To de Grasse, the Battle of the Virginia Capes was something he had to accept. Few of the participants considered the battle to be of any greater significance than a score of similar clashes. But trivial though the battle appeared at the time, it helped lay the foundations of what was to become the most powerful nation in the world.

The decision of de Grasse to bring his entire fleet into the Yorktown campaign was the critical decision of the war. The immense strength thus unexpectedly thrown against the British in America covered the concentration about Cornwallis, raising a shield for the American-French army which British sea power proved unable to brush aside.

CLIMAX IN THE WEST INDIES, 1782

Hood had no sooner left the Indies in pursuit of de Grasse than the energetic governor of Martinique captured St. Eustatius. This portent of French offensive capabilities alarmed Hood when he returned to Barbados after Yorktown to guard British islands until Rodney brought a fresh fleet into the theater. De Grasse had followed Hood back to the Indies, determined to capture every bit of land that flew the British flag. On January 9, 1782, de Grasse with 31 ships landed 8,000 troops on St. Kitts, whose garrison promptly withdrew to the defenses of

Brimstone Hill and defied demands to surrender.

On January 23, Hood quietly approached the besieged frigate base. He had 22 ships, most of them worn and foul from long months at sea, but commanded by officers who supported Hood because he habitually took them into his confidence. By such familiarity, Hood effectively freed himself of the hampering *Fighting Instructions,* because his subordinates came to know him well enough to anticipate his commands. With knowledge of his own ability, he had the advantage of being able to make a shrewd guess about the reaction of de Grasse to the appearance of a threatening, inferior fleet. Hood wished to dislodge de Grasse from the anchorage in Frigate Bay so that he might occupy it himself.

On the morning of January 25, de Grasse saw a weather-beaten fleet timidly approach St. Kitts and suddenly ripple with signal flags before putting about in hurried confusion. Hood's *ruse de guerre* was successful. De Grasse hastily weighed anchor and pursued, for with this fleet destroyed, he could break his own into detachments to cover a half-dozen simultaneous descents on other islands, bagging the lot before Rodney came from England. Driving south into the night, de Grasse was unable to preserve order, for his captains thrilled to the prospect of a general chase. Magically, during darkness, Hood's ragged line tightened, beat to windward, and headed north, back towards St. Kitts. In the morning, de Grasse bitterly watched Hood's fleet crack on full sail and with superior seamanship speed away. De Grasse gave free rein to his fastest ships, which, in mid-afternoon came within gunshot of Hood's rear, where Hood had foresightedly stationed three of his best captains. These held back the French van as Hood steered NNW into the anchorage, brilliantly tacked in column, and came back on the reciprocal course so that his van and then his center could fire in support of his heavily engaged rear. The maneuver was so swiftly and ably executed that de Grasse in effect merely exchanged a passing cannonade at an anchoring fleet. De Grasse had been boldly evicted. More than this, he had been pinned down where Hood could watch him until Rodney arrived, because honor would not allow de Grasse to abandon the troops who were attempting to reduce Brimstone Hill.

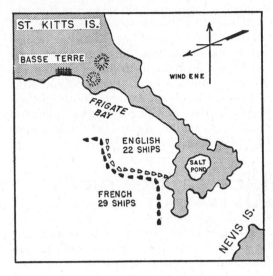

HOOD AND DE GRASSE, JANUARY 26, 1782

Anchored with an angle presented to the enemy, with sides approximately six points into the wind, Hood secured his van against doubling by placing his lead ship as close as possible to land. His rear was defended by the three captains led by Commodore Cornwallis, brother of the General, who had personal reasons for being exceptionally valiant. The next day, de Grasse attacked and was compelled by Hood's use of the constant trade wind to drift along the face of the British line. De Grasse led the attack in the magnificent 110-gun *Ville de Paris,* receiving the fire of each British ship in succession without shaking Hood's hold upon Frigate Bay. In the afternoon, after plugging shot-holes, de Grasse tried and failed again.

In cold anger, convinced that further attacks would uselessly shed blood, de Grasse pulled away from Hood's position and set up a vigil, waiting for the French army to win. The outnumbered British garrison on Brimstone Hill succumbed on February 12 and the island fell into French hands. For

Hood, the picture abruptly changed. There was no news of Rodney, and French soldiers ostentatiously began construction of a mortar battery close to the head of his line. On the night of the 13th, Hood's ships deftly cut cables in succession, left lights burning on anchor buoys, and slipped away from the anchorage, eluding de Grasse's lookouts.

Hood had not saved St. Kitts but he had paralyzed de Grasse through three long weeks which sufficed to bring Rodney to Barbados. In late February, Hood and Rodney joined forces off Antigua. With 36 ships together, the British were now powerful enough to hunt down the troublesome Comte de Grasse.

THE BATTLE OF THE SAINTS, APRIL 12, 1782

The French capture of St. Kitts and similar projects had been planned only to pass time until the Spanish could assemble forces in the Indies to cooperate in the major allied project of 1782, the attack on Jamaica. The Spanish sent 15 ships under Admiral Solano to Cap Français, while de Grasse was reinforced to a strength of 36 ships, thus making possible a joint fleet of 51 to cover the landing of 14,000 troops on England's richest island.

As he refreshed his fleet at Martinique in preparation for rendezvous with Solano at Cap Français, de Grasse determined to avoid battle with Rodney. Two years of campaigning had worn out his ships and men. His experienced admirals had returned home to be replaced by de Vaudreuil, who was new to fleet tactics, and Bougainville, who was an excellent explorer but not a divisional commander. Twenty miles away at St. Lucia, Rodney counted among his 36 ships a dozen straight from English dockyards. The balance of his force was being completely refurbished in the careenage, so that all coppered bottoms were clean and ready for utmost speed. Furthermore, Rodney's flag captain, Sir Charles Douglas, had made major gunnery reforms which gave

Rodney a vast superiority in firepower.[2] In addition, the weatherdecks of Rodney's ships were studded with carronades, invented in 1779, which were a species of lightweight artillery that at ranges up to 300 yards added a fourth to a ship's broadside weight of metal. De Grasse had more than sufficient reason to desire a peaceful voyage to his rendezvous.

Rodney willed otherwise. By 3 AM on April 8, de Grasse sent a convoy of 150 merchantmen out of Fort Royal and got his fleet underway at 10 AM. On the heights of St. Lucia, sharp-eyed lookouts signaled news of the French sortie to Rodney, whose 36 ships were under sail before the last French ship cleared port and set course to the northwest. Unencumbered by convoy protection, British frigates were in touch with the French by mid-afternoon, and by sunset Rodney could see enemy mastheads.

De Grasse ordered his convoy to seek sanctuary in Guadeloupe as he worked clear of the blanketing effects of Dominica and started to beat to windward through the Saints' Passage. He wished to draw Rodney

---

[2] The reforms of Douglas were the first noteworthy improvements in naval ordnance since the Dutch wars. Each was simple in itself, but the combination placed Rodney's broadsides in the category of surprise from secret weapons. Douglas introduced (1) wetted wads between shot and cartridge to minimize the dangerous sparks frequent in the use of dry wads; (2) use of flannel instead of silk in making powder cartridges, thus eliminating an operation known as "worming" which had been necessary to remove smoldering fragments of cloth; (3) use of priming tubes made of quills filled with molded gunpowder, which obviated both the gun-captain's use of a powder horn to fill the priming vent to the gun chamber and the opening of the cartridge by a long needle; (4) reduction of recoil violence by expending force through friction in mounting a corrugated, inclined plane built on the deck beneath the gun carriage; (5) an improved rigging of gun tackle by which guns could be trained four points fore and aft of the beam, for a field of 90 degrees instead of the usual 60-degree limit of gunports; (6) steel springs in gun-tackle to take up some of the initial force of recoil instead of all being absorbed by manpower; and (7) substitution of a pistol flintlock mechanism to fire vents by a shower of sparks instead of touching with a burning slowmatch. These seven developments were to enable Rodney's ships to fire two to four times faster than the French.

east away from the convoy, outsail him, and double back to pick up the convoy and continue his journey. Hood's division however, leading Rodney's fleet, had also worked clear of Dominica, and so on the morning of April 9 de Grasse attacked the British van with his own, hoping to inflict sufficient damage aloft to discourage Rodney from continuing the chase. De Grasse made the error of committing only a portion of his force instead of the full weight that might have smashed Hood. Hood prudently backed sail to kill way as Rodney struggled to his support and de Vaudreuil kept at long range during two passages along Hood's line. It was respect for the small but mighty carronades that prevented de Vaudreuil from justifying de Grasse's hopes. A light wind enabled Rodney to move and de Vaudreuil withdrew.

In the meantime the French convoy made Guadeloupe and de Grasse was free to beat eastward into the wind. By daylight on April 10, de Grasse was a dozen miles east of Rodney, who ordered a general chase to free his fastest ships. Two years at sea had made seamen of the French, who succeeded in opening their distance advantage by nightfall. Good fortune deserted de Grasse on the 11th. A pair of de Vaudreuil's ships, damaged in the skirmish with Hood, slowly fell behind. This reduced de Grasse to 30 ships, counting those with the convoy and one that had crawled to Guadeloupe after meeting Hood. As Rodney's foremost ships leaped towards the cripples, de Grasse honorably abandoned his eastward movement, put about and formed line of battle, sending frigates to assist his unhappy subordinates.

As April 12 dawned, de Grasse without fear awaited Rodney. De Grasse had the wind and confidence in the maneuvering skill of his captains. De Grasse believed that he had acquired moral ascendancy in his clashes with the British and expected another inconclusive brush. The day opened with de Grasse bearing N by E of Rodney, some ten miles away. In that position, if chased, de Grasse could hold the windward advantage. However, one of his cripples under tow still labored in the area between the

fleets and de Grasse turned on a southerly course, closehauled to the wind. This maneuver discarded the security of his northward position and gave Rodney a chance to race for the weather gage at the estimated point of collision of the converging fleets. In his three-decked *Ville de Paris,* de Grasse masterfully conducted his force to windward of the oncoming British. Rodney gave way, accepting the leeward position, and action commenced at 8 AM, the fleets slowly filing past on opposite courses, pounding at short range.

Such an action was traditionally inconclusive and at best gave Rodney only two hours to work his will upon the elusive de Grasse. Adopting French tactics, British captains did not disdain to fire high, hoping to stop enough enemies to immobilize the fleet for a stationary fight to the finish. Slowly the fleets moved along, until Rodney's leading ship came up with de Grasse's last ship. At this moment—9 AM—nature intervened. Suddenly the wind veered four points to the south, driving the French bows on a slant into Rodney's ships. As each French captain, panic-stricken, wrestled to keep his heavy hull in its assigned station, the French line disintegrated. Close to Rodney, a British ship unexpectedly found itself to windward of the French.

This was the turning point of the battle. Rodney's next decision produced a flood of ink sufficient to float Rodney's 98-gun flagship *Formidable;* he had long sought a way to pin down the French and it had come to hand.[3] He swung his flagship through the French line and others, seeing his example, followed. The result demonstrated the folly

---

[3] Sir Charles Douglas, for example, was credited with respectfully insisting upon cutting through the French line at the moment the heaven-sent opportunity offered. Another gentleman, not even on the scene, laid claim to credit; this was a retired Scottish businessman, John Clerk, who in 1782 had privately printed his *Essay on Naval Tactics,* which proposed to attain victories by breaking an enemy's line and crushing a section of it. Rodney did not have an opportunity to read Clerk's work before the Saints battle, but it was an important work, carefully studied by Nelson, who derived from it several fruitful concepts. Rodney's decision was unpremeditated, a sailorman's impulse correctly seized.

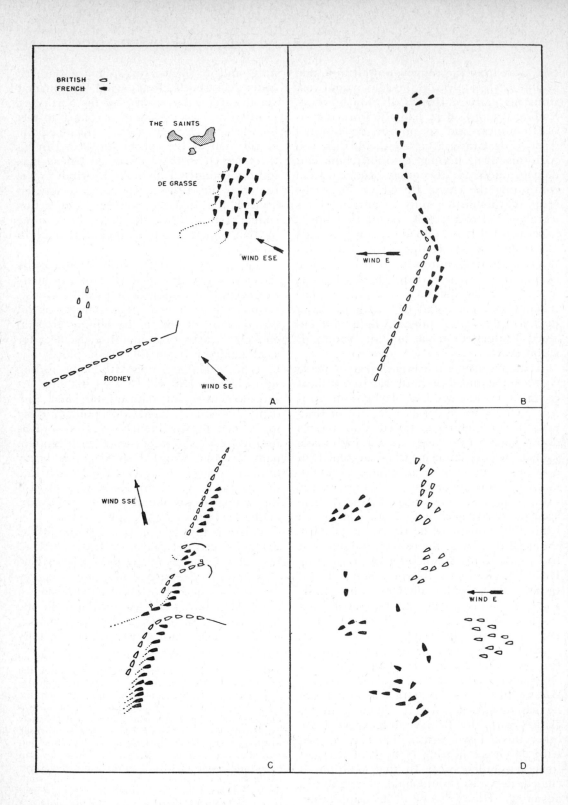

BRITISH
FRENCH

THE SAINTS

DE GRASSE

WIND ESE

RODNEY

WIND SE

A

WIND E

B

WIND SSE

C

WIND E

D

BATTLE OF THE SAINTS, APRIL 12, 1782

of prescribing rigid axioms of war. French theorists had again and again emphasized the paramount importance of maintaining an unbroken line. Mutual support and tactical integrity were, in their teachings, essential to proper conduct of fleet actions. The line had to be preserved. These views however were predicated upon the conviction that naval actions could not be decisive so long as fleets were large and in line, as well as upon the mandate that ships had to be preserved. There was thus no mental preparation for adapting to the unexpected, such as the critical shift of wind right into the teeth of de Grasse's line. There was no willingness to accept the melee, because the melee was not supposed to occur. When the conditions for a melee were forced upon de Grasse's fleet, none of the French leaders was ready to heave to and fight.

The force that de Grasse had so skillfully carried through two long years of campaigning, now dissolved into scattered fugitives. Abandoning three dismasted comrades, the French captains fell off the wind and cracked on sail in full flight to the west. The British aggressively pursued, here and there overtaking individuals, and finding a pitched battle in the vicinity of the *Ville de Paris*. The carronades and Douglas's reformed gunnery gear had their way. By nightfall, Rodney had five prizes in hand, among them the proud, three-decked flagship of de Grasse, who was spiritually and physically crushed. Part of the French under de Vaudreuil made Cap Français; part under Bougainville made Curaçao; two ships fell prey to the relentless Hood a week later in the Mona Passage.

England went mad with the news, which came at a welcome time to offset discouragement in the European theater. Rodney was hailed as another Drake, who had reasserted British primacy at sea. In the Indies however the French licked their wounds, quietly gathered with the Spanish, and vengefully continued at Cap Français to lay plans for seizing Jamaica. Sickness among the Spanish rather than want of spirit in the French postponed the use of 43 ships and 20,000 troops until the advent of the hurricane season obliged the French to sail for Boston. By this time, Rodney had been recalled by the new Rockingham government for political reasons, only to meet with a hero's welcome. The extent of Rodney's victory was as grossly magnified by the British people as it was in France. D'Estaing was ordered to prepare a joint force of French and Spanish ships and troops to join those already in the Indies to create a tremendous concentration of 75 ships and 30,000 troops for a great thrust at Jamaica in the spring of 1783. But this venture was canceled by the Peace of Paris.

Rodney's victory was the last fleet action in the Caribbean theater but he had not thereby won indisputable command of the sea.

WAR IN EUROPEAN AND ASIATIC WATERS, 1781-1782

Gibraltar and Minorca were the focal points of Spanish interest in the war. From the outset of Spain's declaration of war in 1779, Gibraltar was invested by land and sea, being occasionally supplied by efforts of the British Home Fleet. In June 1781, de Guichen was sent from Brest with 24 ships to cooperate with 25 Spanish ships against Minorca. By mid-August, a force was landed on Minorca consisting of 8,000 men led by a famous French expert of siege warfare, the Duc de Crillon. The British, commanded by Sir James Murray, swiftly withdrew to Fort St. Philip. Murray was a good soldier and with his 2,600 men held de Crillon at bay for four months, even though the besiegers were doubled in number by the landing of 8,000 French troops. As long as Gibraltar was invested by the Spanish however England could not maintain a fleet in the Mediterranean, so no friendly squadrons appeared to succor Murray. Quietly, the Spanish-French blockade sapped the vigor of the British defense, denying the harried garrison fresh vegetables and healthy meat that abounded in the countryside. An exclusive diet of salt provisions eventually resulted in an onslaught of scurvy which swept in epidemic proportions through the dank galleries of Fort St. Philip. At last Murray could not maintain sentry posts, much less withstand assault. De Crillon did not force action, preferring to let scurvy fight for him. On February 4, 1782, scarcely a fifth of the original garrison was able to stumble out to surrender. The victors were compassionate in triumph, according full honors of war, hospitalization, and passage to England. The British trident was blunted; the Mediterranean was closed; Spain had finally regained her precious island of Minorca.

British thoughts of relieving Minorca while under siege were discouraged in late August 1781 by the sudden appearance at the Channel approaches of the combined Spanish-French fleet. Admiral Don Luis de Córdoba was in command but incapable of offensive decision when the British fleet was discovered at Torbay under the command of Admiral George Darby. Córdoba vetoed de Guichen's urgent wish to attack, preferring instead to snap up British trade. With 25 ships, Darby followed the 50 ships of Córdoba but was misled by reports that Córdoba was standing off the southwest coast of Ireland. In September, the Combined Fleet broke up, stimulating the British Admiralty into dispatching ships and orders in anticipation of blows that never fell. Córdoba returned to Cadiz; de Guichen, to Brest.

The only fighting that season occurred on the Dogger Bank, when Vice Admiral Sir Hyde Parker on August 3, 1781 with five ships attacked a Dutch force of six ships protecting a convoy akin to that Parker was escorting from the Baltic. In line abreast, Parker ran down bows-on to Admiral Zoutman, formed column close to the Dutch and fought for four hours. At the end, killed and wounded were nearly equal on each side, neither admiral had made a prize, and both convoys had disappeared. All that was proved was something that needed no proof: Dutch seamen were as tough as Englishmen. The principal significance of the battle is that it constituted the sole naval action of any size in which the Dutch participated during the war.

A greater battle might have occurred in December. Rear Admiral Richard Kempenfelt was at sea with twelve ships hunting the French East and West Indian convoys, and found one some 150 miles southwest of Ushant. De Guichen's fleet of 25 ships was in escort and attempted to close with Kempenfelt. For his part, Kempenfelt was content to cut out a handful of prizes and slip away, his force adroitly handled by means of his revolutionary signal system. His agility was not appreciated by the English nation, who hungered for a smashing victory like those of Hawke and Boscawen. It was deeply disturbing to have British fleets in all quarters of the globe show reluctance to fight the French.

At the advent of 1782, Lord Howe was obliged to seek a decision with the combined fleets of France and Spain. The war, never popular, was worse than wearisome to the British people after the news of Yorktown. Feeling against the government began to turn against the Navy, which seemed powerless to avert disaster after disaster. With Jamaica threatened, Gibraltar and Minorca under siege, and the enemy fleets roaming at will upon the oceans, the British now learned that the Dutch intended to contribute ten ships to the next concentration of the Allied fleets.

Howe kept his head as he had during the dark days of New York. Intimidating the Dutch with a show of force, he sailed in late June with 25 ships and Kempenfelt's signals to bring in the precious annual convoy from Jamaica for which the enemy was searching with 40 ships. Near the Scilly Islands, Howe sighted the enemy and daringly sought to get to windward of them by carrying his fleet between the Scillies and Land's End at night. Córdoba and de Guichen, in line of battle, assumed that Howe was running away and continued towards the Channel. Fortunately for England, a gale blew the combined fleet from the Channel entrance before the Jamaica convoy arrived. Unfortunately for England, the same gale displaced Howe as he beat towards England in search of an action, with himself standing between the enemy and their bases.

Patiently accepting this setback of nature and thankful that the enemy had obviously given up intentions of invading the British Isles, Howe was rewarded in late August with orders to take relief to Gibraltar. Freed thus from the defense of England and sent at last into enemy territory, Howe hoped for the great victory which his country needed. The hysterical outburst following news of the Saints battle had faded as the Rockingham ministry opened peace negotiations and found the enemy too confident of further success to agree to ending hostilities. Howe prepared carefully, leaving as little as possible to chance, particularly in view of the tragic loss of Kempenfelt's 100-gun *Royal George,* which in late August broke and sank with all hands while being slightly careened. With the legacy of Kempenfelt's signals to give him a range of flexibility never before possessed by a British commander, Howe on September 11 left Spithead with 34 ships and a great convoy.

By then Gibraltar was in serious case. Following his success at Minorca, the victorious Crillon was given the task of reducing the Rock, which had stubbornly withstood continuous bombardment for 13 months. Crillon was given the biggest force massed by the Allies during the war. In early September 1782, he began operations with 47 ships, ten floating batteries certified to be unsinkable,[4] and hundreds of supporting vessels, cooperating with 40,000 troops serving 200 heavy guns. By this time, General Eliott could muster only 7,000 men in his defenses.

---

[4] These batteries were a milestone in the spasmodic inventions of naval architects to stop the penetration of shot. Full-rigged, they sailed almost as handily as they had before being converted from 600 to 1,200 ton merchantmen. They had one or two decks mounting 7 to 21 bronze 24-pounders and carried a total of 5,300 men. The exact nature of the conversion features is unknown. An extant plan shows one that had a sloping casemate some five feet thick presented to the enemy. This was built over the ship's regular structure. A roof four feet thick, hinged to facilitate rolling off enemy hot shot, covered the weatherdeck, whose disengaged side was sandbagged against shot and sparks. The roof was covered with wet hides and held water tanks that fed piping through the exposed side to stifle any fires which might develop. Colonel d'Arçon of the French Engineers, who devised these batteries, considered them indestructible. See C. F. Duro, *Armada Española,* 9 vols. (Madrid, 1895-1903), VII, 323-328.

At dawn September 13, 1782 the novel batteries sailed into position to the west of Gibraltar, a thousand yards from the British. Assigned the mission of making a breach in the fortifications on the isthmus, the batteries were supported by Allied siege artillery. The fleet cruised in the distance, all hands eager to watch the invincible batteries do their work. Ignoring the enemy fire from the isthmus, the British concentrated upon the floating batteries, meanwhile heating shot in furnaces that Eliott had foresightedly procured. Through some six hours of shooting, small damage was done by either side. Then the British started to hurl red-hot shot at the ungainly vessels hovering off the Rock. At first, there were no visible effects. Suddenly, about 2 PM, smoke wisped up from the flagship battery. Then another showed evidence of distress. By 8 PM, the fire from the batteries was slackened considerably, as the British battered away, succeeding in smashing by impact the intricate water system designed to fireproof the batteries. Shortly after midnight, the flagship battery burst into flame. By 4 AM of September 14, half a dozen crackled in blazes that brilliantly illuminated the roadstead and gave the British ample light for aiming more accurately. By noon, three batteries had burnt to the water's edge, five had blown up, and two still burned. The invincible flotilla had failed completely.

Furious, Crillon redoubled his efforts on the isthmus, steadily creeping toward the Rock. A daring dispatch boat cheered Eliott with news of Howe's coming, but Howe's arrival on October 11 was bedeviled by a westerly gale that drove him through the Straits into the Mediterranean. Admiral Córdoba took his 44 ships in pursuit. Grimly, Howe declined action until he could see his convoy safely delivered to Eliott's hands. Adroitly outmaneuvering Córdoba's clumsy efforts, Howe landed his troops and supplies. This was accomplished by October 19, and Howe was free to seek his great battle.

On October 20, Howe formed in line of battle to the west of the Straits, Córdoba to windward a dozen miles further west. Howe's fleet bristled with excitement, certain that the enemy with a superiority of ten ships would accept a challenge truculently offered. An ardent French admiral, La Motte-Picquet, attempted to persuade his Spanish senior to grasp the laurels of immortality. Timidly, Córdoba consented. Towards sunset, La Motte-Picquet bore down on Howe's van and opened fire at long range, waiting for Córdoba to support him. Howe's rear came under fire but his center was untouched. La Motte-Picquet lacked the assurance to carry the brunt of action alone, and so the engagement was merely a cannonade which Howe was helpless to shape into a battle. Scattered firing went on into the night, then died as the Allied fleet worked clear. Dawn disclosed the Allies leaving the scene. Disappointed, Howe had to let the enemy retire to Cadiz while he set sail for Spithead. He returned to England empty-handed except for the satisfaction of delivering the means to Eliott of preserving Gibraltar against all further assaults by de Crillon.

This was the last series of movements by great fleets. In late January 1783, England, France and Spain signed provisional articles of peace.

Halfway around the world in Indian waters, the war continued between a handful of ships commanded by the Bailli de Suffren and a squadron under Sir Edward Hughes. News of the work of Suffren came too late to Europe to affect the terms of peace or the decisions made concerning India. However, Suffren's campaigns merit mention because they became the chief pride of French historians. For dauntless aggressiveness and indefatigable resourcefulness, Pierre André Suffren is a model for all naval officers. Without a base, without a source of supplies, Suffren fought five battles off the Indian coast and recuperated his strength through captured enemy stores. His captains were such inferior seamen and indifferent officers as to prevent him from annihilating his adversaries. Despite the feeble comprehension and cooperation of his subordinates, who had been more or less rejected from participating in the main operations of the war, Suffren was on the verge of reversing the humiliations of the Seven Years' War when hostilities ceased. Returning home to tumultuous ovations, he

received his finest tributes at Cape Town, when he was waited upon by the British admiral and captains he had fought so well. It was unfortunate for France that he was too junior to command one of her great fleets.

SUMMARY

Aside from the American colonists, who obtained the independence for which they had rebelled, only Spain gained much from the war. While Gibraltar and Jamaica remained in British hands, Spain had recaptured Minorca and was given back the whole of Florida. Spain lost claim only to the Bahama Islands and conceded to England the privilege of cutting mahogany in Honduras. Numerous islands and trading posts were exchanged between England and France, generally reflecting a return of all conquests made during the war. Holland lost the most, receiving nothing to compensate for the losses at St. Eustatius and the captures of her merchantmen at sea.

Except in the American theater and at Minorca and Gibraltar, European armies contributed little to the war, which was naval in character. Beyond renting to England 30 of the 87 regiments sent to fight General Washington, the German states held aloof from the struggle, so there was literally no war in Europe. In naval history, then, there are few wars more productive when studied. As the British historian, David Hannay, wrote:

The American War is perhaps mainly fertile in that kind of instruction which Sir William Napier said was to be derived from a study of the operations of the Spanish generals in the Peninsula— examples of what *not* to do. The French never understood that the best way of defeating us abroad was to crush us at home. We again never seem to have had a glimpse of the truth that the best of all ways of preventing the French fleet from appearing in the West Indies was to keep it shut up in Brest. We did the second best thing —we scattered our forces, we attempted to protect everything, and came dangerously near protecting nothing.[5]

[5] David Hannay, ed., *Letters Written by Sir Samuel Hood in 1781-2-3* (London, 1895), xlvi.

Apart from the repudiation of basic strategy, the Royal Navy proved comparatively ineffectual because it had been victimized by politics. Notwithstanding the paper list of 150 ships of the line, the Navy's potential had been so reduced by economy, graft, corruption, and indifference that after the outbreak of war it was never able to commission enough ships to meet the multiplying demands made upon it. British strategy perforce was one of expediency rather than long range planning.

In the conduct of the war, mistakes were carelessly frequent. No clear-cut chain of command was established for the American area, thus leading to Hood's resentment of Graves and the consequences of that in the climactic Battle of the Virginia Capes. Ministers in London attempted to keep control of operations in their hands, thereby destroying initiative in the field, as well as reacting far too slowly to the shifting conditions of a campaign. On the positive side, the Royal Navy made three great advances, which, in view of the following war to begin in 1793, possibly offset the frequent mistakes. First, thanks to Sir Charles Douglas, British gunnery started to become a science rather than a haphazard trade for petty officers. Second, Richard Kempenfelt's signal system at last gave a commander a swift, efficient means to make his wishes known in an unusual situation. Lastly, the ghost of Byng was laid to rest by the exoneration of Keppel and the countenance of departures from the *Fighting Instructions* by Rodney. With these three advances and the advantage of being one nation against a coalition of conflicting objectives, England muddled through the war without extensive harm.

On the side of France, the amazing rejuvenation of her navy was negated by departure from the original, sound plan to employ the navy as a massed whole. France had the greatest opportunity in her history to invade the land of her foe. Never again would the Royal Navy be so weak and the Admiralty so confused. The battle effectiveness of French fleets was tremendously reduced by the enforced reluctance of French admirals to hazard their ships for a decision. More than any-

thing else lack of tactical aggressiveness made the maneuvers of French fleets little more significant than parades, although at the time they proved most alarming to the British. Always excepting Suffren, too much trust in the complete validity of axioms of war cost the French many opportunities and led to one shameful defeat. The French admirals however should not be judged too severely. They were fighting the only naval war in their history. For more than a century, their navy had been subordinated to military operations. Traditions are hard to shake and French admirals had learned in infancy that their king could spare only a few francs for his ships, and so those ships should not be idly cast away. The defensive concepts that handcuffed French admirals had a long and valid history. Under the circumstances their achievements in the American Revolution were enormous.

Spain perhaps harmed France more than she helped, because the only common denominator between the two Allies was their opposition to England. The fundamental weakness of the Allies was the impossibility of agreeing upon objectives. The French plan to invade England at the outset of the war was supported only through one timid effort by the Spaniards. Thenceforward, Spanish interests predominated in dictating the deployment of Allied forces. Spain shifted the emphasis of the European war from the sound objective of invasion to the eccentric objective of recovering Minorca and Gibraltar. Even the descent upon Jamaica was inspired by Spanish interests. Thus, although Spain extended the scope of British countermeasures, her entry into the war would have best served France had the Allies each planned and executed their own operations. Mutual cover instead of combination, had France adhered to her original strategy, might well have broken England's power.

Desiring to be strategically offensive and, in fact, tactically defensive, the French were fatally inconsistent. They emptied their treasury, weakened their government, and set a precedent attesting the right of a people to discard the rule of their king. This last soon had grave effects.

7

Wars of the

French Revolution and Empire:

Opening Events

THE AMERICAN REVOLUTION had revealed that in several vital respects Britain's Royal Navy still outclassed *La Marine Française*—the navy of France. The battles with Graves and Rodney had shown that French ships required copper-bottomed hulls to restore the original speed advantage conferred by their superb design and construction. Carronades, more heavily shotted yet lighter than long guns, were needed to equalize the weight of broadside metal in ships of nominally identical rates. Such shortcomings Marshal de Castries, the French Minister of Marine, was attempting to overcome while the discontent of the people of France was gathering force for revolt against their Bourbon monarchy. From tight-fisted Ministers of Finance, de Castries could pry money to repair material deficiencies of the fleet, but battles had also demonstrated that French naval officers had to be brought up to the British level of professional attitude and skill.

Judicious and patient, de Castries studied France's naval requirements and in 1786 issued an ordinance that thoroughly reorganized the *Marine* in almost every field except the concept of remaining on the tactical defensive. The fleets of Louis XVI were to consist of 81 ships, an equal number of frigates, and 121 minor vessels, based upon greatly improved facilities at Brest, Rochefort, and Toulon. Obligatory service for seamen was more equitably applied to the maritime population. While the ships, bases, and men of the *Marine* were being systematically renovated, de Castries tactfully went to work on the real problem, that of competent leadership at sea. Rewarding officers who sought to perfect their professional knowledge rather than their swordsmanship or dancing, he attempted to weed out all those to whom the service was merely an avocation. Spurred by his spirit and enthusiasm, the *esprit de corps* that had vitalized the *Marine* in the days of Colbert slowly returned.

Across the Channel, the British Admiralty did not fail to take note, especially when fortifications began to rise at Cherbourg, a strategically central position opposite Portsmouth. To the average Briton however war seemed remote in 1786. Louis XVI amicably signed a treaty of commerce with England that applied the radical concepts of Adam Smith to foreign trade by reciprocally reducing tariffs. The treaty favored England greatly, providing one of the springboards that vaulted British traders into economic domination of the Continent. As France also withdrew from the colonial race, another area of friction was removed. No Bougainville was encouraged to compete with the score of new Cooks who were busy rounding out England's empire.

French diffidence was a humiliating consequence of the ferment bubbling in France. Facing rebellion, Louis could not risk provoking a foreign war. His grandfather, Louis XIV, had undermined France's financial stability by his thwarted attempts to expand the realm to its "natural" boundaries. His father, Louis XV, had fallen into fruitless colonial conflicts that in the Seven Years' War completed the ruination of Colbert's dreams. Louis XVI had himself gambled: his support of the 13 colonies during the American Revolution had completed the destruction of his fiscal resources. By 1789 the government of France tottered into economic chaos. Only new taxes could preserve the monarchial system, but new taxes required the consent of the Estates-General, which had not met for 175 years. When the representatives of the nobility, the clergy, and the middle class were summoned, they were more in a mood to dictate fiscal and political reform than to submit meekly to the impost of a new tax structure.

Desperate for funds, the King and his ministers yielded some of the kingly powers. A transition from absolute to constitutional monarchy began peacefully and ended in anarchy as the people slowly realized their power. As control slipped from the King to the middle class, the momentum of revolution, now well started, gradually swung tax-conscious moderates out of control and elevated radicals into that Reign of Terror popularly associated with the French Revolution. By the summer of 1793, full civil war had broken out and no one in France was safe, for even a king could be tried and executed.

REVOLUTION AND THE FRENCH NAVY

Absorbed in salvaging a remnant of feudal prerogatives, Louis XVI and his court wasted little effort to preserve the navy. The force that de Castries had lovingly constructed was allowed to disintegrate. No one tended material, seamen deserted, saws and adzes and hammers fell silent in the great arsenals, rats multiplied in the holds of abandoned ships and frigates. Few voices of authority were raised to halt the ruin. The officer corps came almost entirely from the nobility and most chose voluntary retirement or exile when Paris took cognizance of the situation and began to republicanize the *Marine*. Some officers could abide the first stages of bourgeois transformation; very few remained when the influence of the Paris mob briefly assumed executive functions in the collapsing government. These few who compromised their class for patriotism were later extravagantly rewarded. Eighteen of France's 20 principal admirals in the period 1790-1815 came from this cadre, which unfortunately for France was too small to maintain the officer standards of the navy.

At first, professional eagerness to pit their refurbished ships against Britain made French naval officers loath to leave their country's service, even though they were openly encouraged to quit. Remote from the capital, the seaports were for a time unaffected. The tricolor of rebellion was inconspicuously tucked into a corner of the *Marine*'s white battle flag. But as notions of equality gradually intoxicated the seamen, the illusion of normality disappeared. The wildest aspirations of the lower deck were realized in the decree of April 1791, which obliterated the entire monarchial system of administration and command. A new order was created wherein political purity was more important than skill. For the next two years the Jacobins, most radical of the revolutionists, would be supreme.

The traditions of discipline and professional competence were submerged to depths that contemporary observers were positive would drown those traditions forever. Bravery would never be lacking in the French fleet, but bravery alone was insufficient to produce victory. Centuries had gone into the building of discipline, and it could not be brought back by mere decrees when its lack was grievously felt. In the ensuing years of external war, captains could not always rely on their crews, nor admirals on their captains. Nor was the command relationship the sole casualty of anarchy. Under the Bourbon monarchs, special regiments of artillery and infantry had furnished gunners and marines to the fleet. Under the Republican theorists, service in the ships of France was deemed a privilege that should be open to all soldiers. The special regiments were sent off into the regular army and their duties were assumed by veterans from the army's volunteers. Not only was French naval gunnery thus brought down to the effectiveness of saluting batteries but seasickness among the landlubberly gun crews threatened to deprive French commanders of the ability even to fire a gun or two in hopeless situations *pour l'honneur du pavillon*—for the honor of the flag. The introduction of large numbers of landsmen in ships also too often made French officers temporize with duty rather than risk antagonizing crews among whom they had little reliable support and even less sympathetic understanding. It is perfectly clear why the redoubtable Bougainville declined the rank of vice admiral in 1792 on the grounds that it "would be a title without function."

The Republic endeavored to make officers from worthy enlisted men or merchant marine veterans, provided they were politically pure. Even if such a man had native ability however, the nebulous principles of liberty, fraternity, and equality prevented him from becoming a true officer. His former messmates would not let him develop into an au-

tocrat akin to those of the *ancien régime*. Soon disillusioned, the more ambitious of the expert noncommissioned officers and men disgustedly transferred into the army. There, essential discipline was being instilled by the brilliant, tireless Lazare Carnot, who was virtually a Minister of War. The navy sadly needed a Lazare Carnot, but none was forthcoming until insubordination had been regularized as a matter of pride instead of shame. The seasoned men whose patriotism had kept them in the navy despite all affronts were foolishly subjected to a decree of "purification" which directed all loyal citizens to report officers suspected of disloyalty to the Revolution. Those who survived malice and revenge through charges of *incivisme* were insulted by a policy of recruiting officers from the merchant marine in preference to naval seamen. The argument was advanced by self-styled civilian experts that the details of tactical evolutions were trifles that an experienced seaman could be taught in a week or so. One such expert, André Jean Bon Saint-André, who was destined to talk himself into an important if damaging prominence in naval matters, persuaded his colleagues in the National Convention that "learned evolutions" should be despised. True Frenchmen, in Saint-André's opinion, would eschew geometrically perfect maneuvers and close the enemy to win by boarding. Such amateur pronouncements ignored, of course, the skill required to carry a fleet into close action, and no naval officer dared risk the charge of cowardice entailed in ridiculing such brave glibness.

Within three years from the summoning of the Estates-General, the *Marine* was left with the remnants of splendid material but had few captains fit to operate in divisions and fewer flag officers willing to undertake the training of a rabble commanded by inexperienced juniors and intransigent merchant marine sailors. In time, experience did produce capable ship commanders. Even these usually lacked the spirit of the old navy. Worse than that, they were scorned by their own people as inferior to the officers of the army. When the army produced the dominant personality of Napoleon, who seized control of the nation, the navy was still further deprived of opportunity to serve the common cause. Throughout the entire period to 1815, men of ambition preferred the army as the path to glory.

FRANCE GOES TO WAR

As the French middle class in 1789 took advantage of their king's financial embarrassment to assert their rights to a share in government, the crowned heads of Europe were not immediately alarmed. For more than a century, a strong France had been a troublemaker. Presumably a weak France might be a blessing. Furthermore, monarchs were dubious about establishing a precedent of international interference in the internal affairs of a sovereign state. However, the steady encroachment upon royal power and the rising murmurs of the mob which had tasted blood at the Bastille, finally persuaded the rulers of Austria and Prussia that the Revolution had to be arrested. At Pillnitz in 1791, the rulers of the two Germanic countries joined in a bellicose warning to the French to honor the person and authority of their monarch. The threat was ill advised. Added to natural resentment of German presumption, the contending factions in France were thereby presented with an opportunity to submerge differences in the unifying pressures of a foreign war. Louis was persuaded in April 1792 to declare war on the meddlesome German powers and the bold little kingdom of Savoy which supported them. By summer the Royalist cause in France was lost. The Paris mob rose and butchered the King's Swiss Guard. By September civil war, epitomized by the guillotine, had burst out in full fury. Aristocrats and friends of the *ancien régime* were massacred. Accused of "traitorously" trafficking with the German princes, Louis himself was no longer safe.

Since Austria, Prussia, and Savoy did not have fleets, the French enjoyed command of the sea by default during their first Italian campaign. The extent of naval disintegra-

tion was attested by the fact that the Toulon arsenal was hard pressed to commission a small squadron of five ships while Brest put out four—a total of nine ships of the 80 inherited from de Castries. Six others were made ready by Christmas 1792, so that Captain Latouche-Tréville could have ten ships to give his country a furtive taste of the fruits of sea power by intimidating the would-be hostile King of Naples. All 15 ships were combined under Rear Admiral Truguet for a proposed amphibious conquest of Sardinia in January 1793, but winter storms proved superior to French seamanship. After a promising start, Truguet and his 15 ships crept ignominiously back to Toulon. The affair would be worth scant notice except for the presence of a seasick young Corsican, an artillery officer whose father had hoped to place him in the French navy. As the British failure at Rochefort during the Seven Years' War had an effect upon history because Colonel Wolfe reached maturity in analyzing the mistakes made there, the French failure at Sardinia was perhaps more significant. Captain Napoleon Bonaparte had little but scorn for the naval incompetence which had prevented him from employing his beloved guns, and the scorn endured into his days as Emperor.

Had the French Republicans remained unchallenged at sea, a tolerable degree of efficiency might have been restored to their squadrons. Unfortunately, the French army enjoyed unexpected success. Emigration and civil strife had dispersed the magnificent troops of the monarchy. Only a comparative handful of regulars remained to build forces that would hold back the German professionals. In desperation, the Republic introduced the *levée en masse,* drafting Frenchmen indiscriminately from every class of society because it was a privilege to serve the nation. The problem of converting heterogeneous recruits into genuine military strength was solved by substituting mass for drill. Ironically, the Austrians and Prussians marched to suppress revolution with armies finely trained in the elaborate close order drill instituted by the French General Martinet in the days of Louis XIV. Lacking time to give their levies of men military precision, the Republicans fought compact German formations with bewildering hordes of fleet-footed skirmishers who fired and ran, always giving way before bayonet charges and reforming when pursuit slackened. When a German soldier fell, ten years of training were necessary to replace him; for every French patriot who fell, there were ten to pick up his musket. Soon the Germans were checked and then harried into retreat beyond the frontiers of France, where their tacticians hoped for leisure to devise methods of combating French unorthodoxy. Sparked by Lazare Carnot, the French won a victory of sorts at Valmy. Triumphant, the Republican leaders opportunistically decided to carry their ideals into neighboring lands and defiantly killed their royal family for treason to the new regime. A horrified world watched the regicide French sweep into helpless Belgium.

Here the Republicans overreached themselves: regicide and the prospect of having the French in Antwerp prodded England into war.

Since 1789, a few Englishmen like Edmund Burke had been warning their complacent countrymen about the menace of Jacobinism. So little impression did Burke make however that in February 1792 the Prime Minister, William Pitt the Younger, actually reduced appropriations for the British armed services, optimistically predicting that England would have a decade and a half of peace. The French push into Belgium, then called the Austrian Netherlands, mocked Pitt's optimism. England was concerned at the economic threat of having a free port at Antwerp, an easy entry to the Rhine and Germany. Several times, England had gone to war to keep Antwerp closed to trade. The additional shock of Louis' execution induced the British government to break off diplomatic relations. France replied with a declaration of war in February 1793 and abolished the Ministry of Marine, creating a special committee to carry on a naval war in imitation of the British Admiralty.

The Royal Navy was not as ready as Brit-

ain's leaders for hostilities. Only 26 of her 113 ships of the line and barely half of her cruisers were in commission. Four months minimum would be needed to fit the others for sea. The British army, traditionally the Navy's poor cousin, was even less prepared. But the least prepared of all was the British government. No minister was strong enough to integrate the complex of operations into a strategic entity. There was indeed a Pitt at the helm, but this Pitt was the second son of the great statesman who had so masterfully directed the Seven Years' War. Outstanding in public finance, Pitt the Younger had absorbed little of his father's martial genius. Any suggestion that seemed reasonable was adopted by him with no attempt to create a consistent pattern that would lead to victory. Operations derived from previous wars were launched without the same strategic objectives, and failed for want of a clear understanding as to where the operations would fit into the grand strategy presumably guiding Pitt's orders. There was no grand strategy, principally because no responsible minister believed that the war would last long.

Nor was there any way of knowing that this war with the French would be the longest and bitterest of all those that stemmed from the ambition of Louis XIV. No one would have dared to predict that more than 20 years would be required to demolish the edifice of Jacobinism. The conflict was unlike any that had gone before, for France had introduced the concept of a whole nation at arms. Small armies of professionals were replaced by great armies of recruits. The limited objectives of the colonial wars of moderation disappeared in the belief that the struggle was for survival. The gentlemanly retirement of naval vessels to winter quarters went by the board as blockades were maintained month after month, year after year, close to French ports.

The French did not foresee the 20 years ahead any more clearly than the British did. Zealots welcomed the war with the confident conviction that they had devised the best of all political systems and would brush all anachronistic systems away. Within weeks of declaring war, numerous Republicans came forward with proposals like Tom Paine's to load hordes of patriots aboard fishing smacks to carry liberty, fraternity, and equality across the Channel to the benighted English. An ambitious ship-building program was voted amidst oratory predicting that French audacity and impetuosity would drive the Royal Navy from the seas.

The Royal Navy was soon busy. By trial and error, three traditional missions had evolved as minimum strategy. First, the tight little kingdom had to be insulated against invasion. Second, British seaborne trade had to be protected against privateers. Third, French trade had to be cut off. To these, during the Revolutionary period, was added a fourth: the Revolution had to be stifled and a decent government restored to France. Such objectives were instinctive rather than reasoned, summarizing the experience of more than a century. During Pitt's ministry, although the traditional objectives were hampered by opportunism, England was fortunate to find that the disordered French did not have any consistent naval objectives. As the Republic stabilized and passed into Napoleon's hands, a strategic program developed, but by then it was too late. The French did not recognize their opportunities while the British steadied into the war and easily reasserted their physical and moral ascendancy at sea.

In 1793, England's initial deployment of major naval forces put a Channel fleet to sea under Lord Howe to challenge the Brest fleet. Another force of 21 ships was collected piecemeal under Lord Hood to close with the French at Toulon. Willing to accept a decisive action with the Republicans, the Royal Navy did not neglect collateral duties. To protect trade, frigate squadrons were established off minor stations and privateer ports in the Channel and the Bay of Biscay. These frigates also reduced France's naval potential by cutting heavily into the import of Baltic wood and naval stores necessary to supplement the modest domestic resources supplying French shipyards. Ultimately in 1798, a convoy system was to be adopted by the British Admiralty; prior to that frigates and sloops cruised at large upon the shipping routes. The Admiralty had need of every vessel that could be sent to sea, but Pitt found further duties. Covering squadrons were needed to escort the bulk of the British army under the Duke of York to campaign against Antwerp. The remainder of the army was hastily readied for expeditions against Corsica and French colonial possessions. Such missions threatened to dissipate the numerical superiority that the Royal Navy enjoyed, but Pitt went still further. Although unwilling to employ French naval officers in his ships, Pitt was willing to listen to the suggestions of *émigrés* who urged expeditions to the French coast to support bands of Royalists fighting hopelessly against the Republic. As a result, Pitt undertook too much with too little, and within a year brought England closer to disaster than France realized. Had the resources scattered about the world been brought to bear upon the campaign of the Duke of York, the extra weight might have brought an early end to Jacobinism.

As it was, an early end seemed likely for the French navy. Two months before Lord Howe was ready to cruise, the Brest fleet under Morard de Galles truculently moved to an anchorage off Belle Île, which the Republic thought was about to be attacked to provide a base for British coastal operations and supply in favor of Royalist partisans in the Vendée. On August 1, 1793, Howe was finally at sea and sighted de Galles cruising clumsily near Île de Groix. Although nearly identical in nominal force—17 British to 19 French—neither commander lusted for battle. De Galles was experienced and able, the sole flag officer seduced from the monarchy by the Republic. Having put to sea at this time primarily to train fanatics whose principal virtue was overconfidence, de Galles did not intend to be aggressive. He would accept battle if forced upon him but he did not seek a decisive action. Howe, for his part, was nearly 70, and the haste and bustle of preparing his fleet had drained his energy. He refused to accept the initiative pointedly extended to him and made only minor efforts to halt the French retirement towards Belle Île.

By tacit consent, the summer drifted away without a clash in the Atlantic. Howe got his force shaken down and the old ardor returned to him. De Galles did not oblige his adversary with an opportunity to fight, for he had his own problems. His men soon lost interest in learning their duties and grew increasingly disgruntled about the preventive blockade of the Vendée while fortunate comrades in cruisers grew rich from the prize money looted from British merchantmen. Poorly fed and worse supplied, the men finally defied all authority, threatening to kill their officers unless they were returned to the comforts of Brest roads. From the day of his appointment, de Galles had deprecated his ability to be a *"bon général"* at the head of such crews. He yielded wearily at last to the men's insolent deputations and returned to base, in the hope that he could call on the army for assistance in restoring order. The army had been happy to take French marines but wanted no real share of marine duties. De Galles and most of his officers were curtly dismissed from command, because the government found it more convenient to ignore flagrant mutiny and to pretend that loyal seamen had actually uncovered as they claimed a plot by their Admiral and his subordinates to deliver the fleet to the British.

This was not too preposterous a charge—it had occurred at Toulon.

DESTRUCTION AT TOULON

When Lord Hood reached the Mediterranean in August 1793, his ships were unchallenged. Toulon had been seized by the Royalist element of its population, who had been inflamed into participating in the general civil war that broke out in June when the radicals of the Convention brutally purged their conservative colleagues. The Revolutionists who had swaggered with cockades through the town scurried into hiding. The years of their dominance however had made of the Toulon fleet nothing more than a collection of decaying ships and despondent men, split in sentiment between the old and new orders. The fleet was like the wounded lion in the statue dedicated to the valiant Swiss guard of Louis XVI—dying but still dangerous. With precarious control of the Toulon arsenal, the Royalists anxiously invited Hood to take protective custody in the name of Louis XVIII, who was imprisoned in Paris.[1] By this singular proffer, 32 of France's fourscore ships were put into British hands without firing more than a few pounds of gunpowder to salute a king without a throne. The gift was an illusion. Half of the ships were nearly ready to take to sea; the rest were refitting or in ordinary. Hood's ships were extremely short-handed, having been sent off in haste, so that he was unable to furnish prize crews which were necessary because the great majority of the Toulon seamen were Republicans. Even those few who were Royalists doubted the wisdom of letting the English take the ships. Led by the rear admiral who was second-in-command, the seamen belligerently defied attempts to transfer the ships peacefully. Sending home for reinforcements, Hood determined to seize the ships, hold the town, and hope for time to rig the fleet for sea.

While landing his two regiments of troops to capture the forts commanding the harbor, Hood's situation was intolerably complicated by the sudden appearance of 17 Spanish ships under Rear Admiral Juan de Gravina. The Spanish government did not intend to sit passively while the Toulon fleet went to augment Britain's navy. Complimenting Hood upon his successful intimidation of the surly French, de Gravina politely suggested that Spain had a substantial interest in the proceedings. To Hood, Gravina's troops were as welcome as those opportunistically sent by Naples and Savoy. An extensive defense perimeter thrown up in the hills circling the harbor was thinly manned by the allies. Unfortunately Hood was not a diplomat, and allies irritated him.

He was soon more worried than irritated. "The Marseillaise" was the marching song of

---

[1] Louis XVII, the young son of Louis XVI, presumably died in captivity. Louis XVIII was the younger brother of Louis XVI.

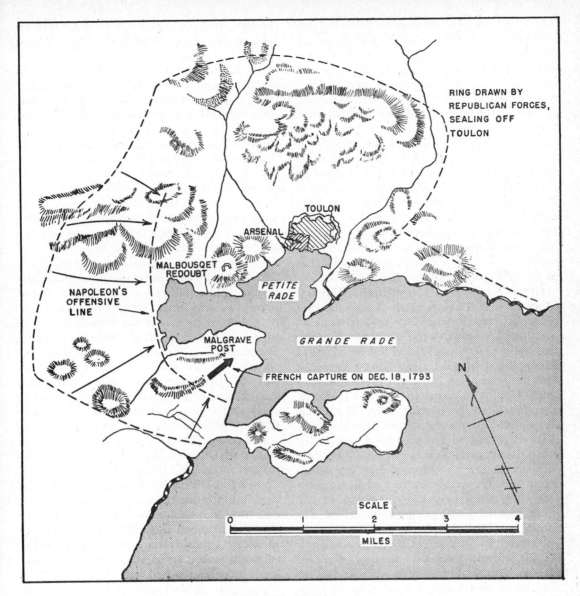

TOULON AREA, 1793

the Revolution, and from Marseilles came a powerful army of 45,000 determined to recapture the ships. They had the strength of unity and purpose in contrast to the language and policy barriers dividing Hood's polyglot command of 2,000 English, 7,000 Spanish, 6,500 Italians, and 1,500 Royalists. His forces too weak to erect and defend necessary fortifications adequately, Hood was also hampered by the need to control the 5,000 French seamen he had dispossessed. They had become a fifth column. Fighting out of his element, Hood nevertheless managed to hold Toulon for three months until the Republicans won heights that compelled him to abandon the Harbor or lose his fleet.

This campaign, which forced the illustrious Hood into retirement, started the most illustrious of French soldiers upon his path to fame. Striking a pose on the parapet of a battery, Napoleon Bonaparte looked down contemptuously at the awkward ships scrambling away from his plunging red-hot shot. The opinion he had formed about naval officers during the abortive Sardinian venture now included the vaunted British. Bonaparte's skill in placing the guns that expelled the invaders brought him to the notice of the Convention. At the age of 23 he was exalted to the rank of brigadier general; within three years he had his own army to campaign in Italy. While Toulon thus made it possible for an unknown officer to start towards the crown of "Emperor of the French," Toulon perhaps also confirmed in Napoleon Bonaparte those strategic and tactical misconceptions about naval matters that in the end eroded all he was to win.

Hood's evacuation of the harbor did not conclude the Toulon affair. Safely beyond range of French batteries, he anchored in position to command the channels. Prouder than most proud men, Hood was mortified at having been hurried away before he could raze the arsenal and tow out more than five ships. Unable to succor the piteous Royalists abandoned to revengeful fury, Hood felt duty-bound to do something about the 27 ships that had so recently been within his grasp. Bombardment was impossible because of extreme ranges enforced by Napoleon's guns; fireships could be shunted off long before they could penetrate the vitals of the inner harbor; and finally, there was no amphibious assault force that could return to the arsenal in the teeth of French opposition. At this point in Hood's meditations, Captain Sir William Sydney Smith volunteered to lead a few boatloads of seamen in to burn the ships, and took the luster from Napoleon's triumph by coolly destroying a third and damaging another third of the French Mediterranean fleet.[2] Hood accepted this as

the best that could possibly be done and reluctantly sailed off to make Corsica a fit base for watching Toulon.

Thus, for the French, the first year of hostilities ended with military triumph and naval ruin. Without a decisive battle at sea, the French *Marine* had been staggered by the loss of 15 ships, including two wrecked through incompetence. Anarchy lasted in Toulon into 1795 and few repairs were made because materials had to cross an ocean subject to search by British cruisers. The morale of the *Marine* reached its nadir.

Finally jarred out of idealism, the Convention took a fresh look at the sea service. To restore discipline, special deputies like Saint-André were given the fearful power of death. The violence of the Revolution was suddenly turned against the very seamen devoted to its precepts. Saint-André supported the authority of officers by means of the guillotine. Nor were officers exempt. It was decreed a capital offense for a captain to surrender to the enemy, no matter what the odds against him. But the guillotine could not create in naval leaders the aggressiveness France needed to carry ships to victory in battle. For a century, French commanders had fought only when compelled to do so and then their tactics were designed to preserve their own ships rather than inflict crushing damage upon a foe. Rarely had they been encouraged to seek battle for the sake of such an ephemeral trophy as command of the sea. The new decree reinforced the old conservatism. Republican captains naturally tended to be even less ardent in seeking close action than their predecessors had been.

The first naval battle of the war offered the French their best chance for success, for it took place before leaders like Nelson were emancipated from the dead tactics of the past. Yet the French were bested even in this action because an aging British admiral, veteran of the American Revolution, was not too old to be inspired by the tempo of the times, and essayed a bold change in ponder-

---

[2] Smith had been at Constantinople visiting his brother, who was the British minister to the Sultan. While en route to England after the outbreak of war, Smith had come to the sound of the guns booming at Toulon. Being on half-pay, the inactive duty status of that period, Smith did not have legal authority until reappointed to duty by the Admiralty. This was later made the pretext for treating him as a political rather than a military prisoner when he was captured

in a reckless exploit at Le Havre. The distinction infuriated him into a personal vendetta with Napoleon, with unhappy consequences for the latter, as we shall see.

ous line-ahead, ship-to-ship tactics. Thereafter, as Nelson's generation rose to supremacy in the black-hulled fleets, change was dynamic and the French were hopelessly outstripped.

THE BATTLE OF THE GLORIOUS FIRST OF JUNE, 1794

In the spring of 1794, the men of Lazare Carnot rested on their arms at the Rhine, all of their enemies in flight. England worried about the Duke of York, who was dragging along sullenly to evacuation at Bremen, while Austria and Prussia, whose rulers had precipitated the war, turned their backs on the Revolution and sought to restore the delicate balance of power in eastern Europe. Catherine of Russia had quietly annexed a part of Poland while Europe's attention was focused elsewhere. The rulers of Austria and Prussia then found compensation for their humiliation in the west by appropriating the rest of Poland.

Left alone in the war with the regicides, England had through greed rendered herself almost defenseless against military reprisal. Almost automatically a substantial part of the British effort had been devoted to the old game of seizing French sugar islands in the West Indies. The game had seemed simplified by an urgent plea from the Royalist planters of Santo Domingo to protect them before their Negro slaves took up the Revolution. A stern but just old veteran named Sir John Jervis was given four ships of the line and a light force to operate with 6,000 regulars under Lieutenant General Sir Charles Grey. An exceptional officer, Jervis was destined to make a benchmark in the Royal Navy for the measurement of disciplinarians. The West Indian campaign of 1794 brought him inescapably to the attention of his superiors, who were discomfited by his stern concept of duty. Jervis worked well in harness with Grey, training seamen to act as infantry companies with marines to supplement the military effort of Grey's command,

whose small numbers indicated the indifference of the British War Office toward amphibious warfare.

Grey's troops were too few for the dual mission of capturing and holding all of the French islands. In the miasmic climate, men expended their vigor in assault. Martinique, St. Lucia, and even Guadeloupe fell, and Santo Domingo was garrisoned, but the ravages of tropical diseases swiftly wore down and decimated the soldiery. By summer, when a small enemy force arrived from France to dispute the conquests, Grey could not prevent the recapture of Guadeloupe. His efforts to retake the island forts merely wasted lives because the French reinforced their troops in time and the British did not. At last, Grey and Jervis abandoned Guadeloupe to the Republicans, who brought to the New World a taste of the Terror already going out of fashion at home.

Islands had been cheaply won by the British with 35 killed and 102 wounded. Three months of vain efforts to retake Guadeloupe, however, cost 155 killed and 493 wounded, and bitterly underscored the tactical folly of undertaking conquest without providing the means of consolidation. Then Pitt compounded his strategic folly of divided effort. Though the Duke of York desperately needed every man in Holland for Britain's only chance to suppress the Revolution in its infancy, Pitt scraped together a mighty force of 12,000 troops under Sir Ralph Abercromby to restore British prestige in the West Indies. The major benefit of this 1795 campaign was the amphibious training of Sir Ralph and his gallant subordinate, Sir John Moore. But the cost was too high, for by early 1794 England had been very nearly stripped of military defense.

May of that year found England defended only by her ships. Scarcely a corporal's guard of the regular army could be mustered to repel invasion. Across the Channel, the ground was drying out from winter storms and the Jacobins, after a peaceful winter, stirred restlessly.

There was one ray of hope for the English. The French had won respect for their new order at a heavy toll. The masses of troops who wore the gay cockade had swarmed by draft from all classes of people. War had bitten deeply into French families. The most costly casualties for France were those in the ranks of her farmers. War and internal strife and unusually bad weather reduced the harvests of 1793, while the losses among farmer-soldiers critically deprived the nation in arms of those experts who might have managed to avoid famine in such regions as the Vendée. The countries that France in time of disaster could normally ask for help had become implacable foes. Only the United States, despite an insolent French decree of contraband which would in a few years produce an unofficial war, was willing to sell food to carry western France through the lean months until the harvests of 1794.

But American food had to go by sea and the sea was England's natural arena. Here her sailors could deal those heavy concentrated blows which her soldiers could not. The French, for their part, had to ensure the safe arrival of American grain, and so the stage was set for the first great collision of fleets.

Louis Thomas Villaret-Joyeuse had succeeded de Galles as commander of the Brest fleet. Despised by Old Navy officers for his expedient friendship with the Terrorist Saint-André, to whom he owed his promotion to rear admiral, Villaret had been a blue water lieutenant under the redoubtable Suffren. In his forties, he had seen close relatives guillotined, and his brother was with the Duke of York's army, but Villaret had cast his lot with the Revolution. For fullest cooperation from his subordinates, he was too close to Saint-André, who established himself aboard the 120-gun flagship *Montagne* and behaved like the model for 20th century political commissars. However, not even Saint-André with his tiny guillotines aboard each ship to remind everyone of his cruel penal code, had been able to give Villaret squadrons comparable to those which had sailed with de Grasse. The ships had been neglected during the intoxication of revolt; improperly maintained rigging gave way too easily in battle and weakened, dry-rotted masts went swiftly by the board. Gunfire recoil started

leaks in the slimy bilges and cannon broke loose from their rotten breechings. Half of Villaret's captains came from merchantmen and did not appreciate the niceties of station-keeping. The other captains had been junior officers—some proved to be rash from overconfidence, others timorous in responsibility. The crews were scarcely leavened by veterans. Most were seasick underway; those who were not were unskilled in seamanship and gunnery.

In April 1794 Villaret was alerted to receive a grain convoy of about 150 French and American merchantmen assembling at Norfolk under the dubious protection of Rear Admiral van Stabel, who had two ships and four frigates to ward off prowling cruisers. It was impossible to keep the existence of the convoy from the British.

Well aware of conditions in the Vendée and the change that could be wrought by the arrival of some 40,000 tons of grain, the British Admiralty ordered Lord Howe to intercept the convoy. Although lacking the boldness to send Howe to Cape Charles, where the convoy could be shattered before clearing into the Atlantic, the Admiralty was prepared for war with the United States as a result of seizing American merchantmen in European waters.

The ensuing campaign illustrates anew the fallacy of assuming that superior numbers ensure automatic command of the sea. A respectable if inferior foe can dispute nominal command of the sea at will. By spring 1794, the British had commissioned 75 ships for the European theater, distributed in their customary deployment of a third in reserve based upon Spithead to ward off invasion, another third for cruising against Brest out of Portsmouth, and the remainder in the Mediterranean. Superior in aggregate, the Royal Navy was diminished in total effectiveness by this fragmentation. England periodically and, for the most part, needlessly feared invasion and insisted upon maintaining the Spithead force as basic insurance against sudden attack. The cruising Portsmouth command was continually plagued and fractionalized by pressure from merchants to escort trade within the approaches to the British Isles. The Mediterranean fleet was similarly required to keep Gibraltar as secure as the Thames. It has been suggested that British business elements too often interfered with the ideal strategic objectives of the Royal Navy by insisting that trade protection was its paramount mission.

With the riches of the world's greatest empire funneling towards London, the home squadrons were not allowed to stray far from home waters. Freedom of action was indeed thereby curtailed, yet this policy progressively strengthened the financial sinews with which England subsidized Continental allies through two decades, and, after eight years, the Royal Navy's constancy was rewarded by expansion to numbers that permitted the aggressive close blockade that eventually foiled even Napoleon's efforts to mass a naval force for invasion.

In 1794 however the Royal Navy had yet to be even partially freed of its albatross. Lord Howe had first to escort some 150 merchantmen safely away from the Channel approaches when he sailed on May 2 in response to reports that the Brest fleet was bending on sail. Tied to the slowest merchantman as he went past French privateer nests, Howe was weakened by having to detach eight of his 34 ships to carry the trade safely past the latitude of southern Spain. Those eight ships could have given Howe the strength to annihilate Villaret; but at the time of action the detachment was still cruising in the Bay of Biscay.

Lord Howe was one of Britain's finest admirals. Distinguished for courage in a navy of brave officers, he was thoroughly experienced. Unfortunately for England, Howe's ardor and vigor had been spent in previous wars. This had appeared in 1793 when he failed to force de Galles into action. Nearly 70, haggard from responsibility instead of comfortable retirement, uncertain about the quality of the Republican navy, Howe manifested his age in uncharacteristic timidity. He would have preferred to remain in port for training, and weighed anchor reluctantly when ordered to find and destroy the American convoy.

Howe's orders were directly opposed to those given to Villaret, whose instructions could have been written during the *ancien régime*. Villaret was to rendezvous with van Stabel 100 leagues west of Belle Île and escort the convoy to ports in the Bay of Biscay: he was to avoid action with the British, fighting only if he could not avoid it. Villaret himself had little enough enterprise, and Saint-André sailed with him in the flagship *Montagne* to guarantee there would be no idle quest for *la gloire*. The Brest fleet was forbidden to dispute command of the sea except for a narrow avenue of retreat. Thus, if Howe wanted a battle to win, he had to force action upon an adversary disposed and ordered to be reluctant.

Howe was bedeviled by two objectives—the convoy he was ordered to intercept and the fleet that someday had to be brought to action. Ideally he could combine the two, but that presented a dilemma. He could sweep within easy reach of Brest, allowing Villaret ample sea-room to sortie, before pouncing. However, should Howe thus lock himself in position, Villaret could execute his instructions satisfactorily without leaving port. Fast frigates from Lorient or Bordeaux could redirect the convoy well south of Brest while Villaret showed tempting signs of coming out to fight. Howe manfully avoided temptation and cruised well out to sea in a position across the probable trackline of the approaching convoy. After two weeks however he began to doubt the wisdom of his decision. Peeking at Brest on May 19, he was horrified to discover that Villaret had slipped out during foggy weather past Howe's sentry frigates. Neutral merchantmen however soon put Howe in Villaret's wake.

Thus, at dawn on May 28th, some 400 miles west of Ushant, Villaret was happy to see a sweep of sail on the squally horizon to his lee in the northeast. He had long been cruising through his rendezvous area and the convoy was overdue. He could be excused for mistaking the identity of a fleet coming from the right direction. By 9 AM, Villaret had recognized Howe and began to recover from the shock.

Numbers were equal, 26 to a side, but this

was Villaret's only equality. During the cruise from Brest, he had indefatigably drilled his raw captains, but a few weeks of tactical training could not compare with the years of preparation that stood between a British officer and captain's rank. Even so, Villaret had succeeded in infusing a degree of understanding and confidence in his subordinates that enabled them during the following days to maintain the posture of a fleet.

Confronted by the enemy, Villaret kept his head, though Robespierre had threatened that he would forfeit it if anything went amiss with the convoy. Raggedly forming into the classic line ahead, Villaret fixed his strategic objective uppermost in his mind. Using his windward advantage, he fled the rendezvous area to decoy Howe, shifting as the wind permitted him to a westerly course. Subscribing to the axiom about a bird in the hand, Howe filed the convoy for future reference and went after Villaret.

As the French shuffled into line, Howe sloughed off the fatigues of the chase. Detaching a flying squadron of six 74's to catch the enemy rear, Howe and the rest of his fleet reached into the wind to shorten distance. His flying squadron of trim, clean-bottomed two deckers had well-indoctrinated captains who justified his expectations, expertly closehauling into the wind to reach extreme gunshot of the French rear. The ship at the end of the French line however acquitted itself far beyond Villaret's wildest optimism.

Captain Van Dongan of the powerful 110-gun *Révolutionnaire* was Horatius at the bridge, savagely fending off uncoordinated thrusts by the flying squadron throughout the day of flight. Howe's most determined efforts to come to grips were frustrated. Villaret escaped virtually unharmed into the night. By then the gallant *Révolutionnaire* was a shambles commanded by her third lieutenant, who was the senior survivor. Howe disgustedly broke off action to form a night cruising disposition. The last of Van Dongan's adversaries, the 74-gun *Audacious,* was so badly mauled that like the *Révolutionnaire* she was left on the battlefield to

shift for herself. The fleets were still nominally equal, 25 to 25, but Villaret had gained confidence.

Contrary winds and heavier seas deranged Howe's force during the night. The British had to spend the morning of the 29th re-forming their line. Howe stubbornly repeated his attack upon the French rear shortly after noon and succeeded in passing his flagship, the 100-gun *Queen Charlotte,* ahead of the sixth from the rear of Villaret's line. Other close-hauled Britons followed their doughty admiral and surrounded three of the French rear.

Villaret was confronted with a decision to be made. With his disengaged line still in good order, he could retain the wind by pulling away from Howe before the British could re-form in that tight line deemed absolutely essential by the tactical conceptions of that period. Or he could relinquish the wind, falling off to leeward to present a friendly haven for his battered subordinates. Choosing to rescue his cripples, Villaret came about so briskly and well that Howe was momentarily intimidated and congratulated himself with having won the weather gage. Jean Bon Saint-André watched these evolutions with uncomprehending eyes and later declared to the Convention: "The slowness in the maneuvers, the continual mistakes, the tiny efforts when it was necessary to plan with boldness and execute with audacity, that is what robbed us of the success which we had a right to expect." Howe's opinion was different. He was finding the French tolerably well handled.

There was no further fighting on the 29th; the time was spent by the slow-sailing ships in disengaging and reforming lines close ahead. Villaret's hapless cripples, unfit for further service and a hindrance to the other ships, were left safely behind as he calmly resumed at sunset his game of drawing Howe to the west. On May 30, merciful fog gave the French a peaceful day of repair and Villaret was unexpectedly rewarded for fidelity to his command by stumbling upon a fresh detachment of four French ships which restored him to his full strength and puzzled Howe when the fog lifted and he counted 26

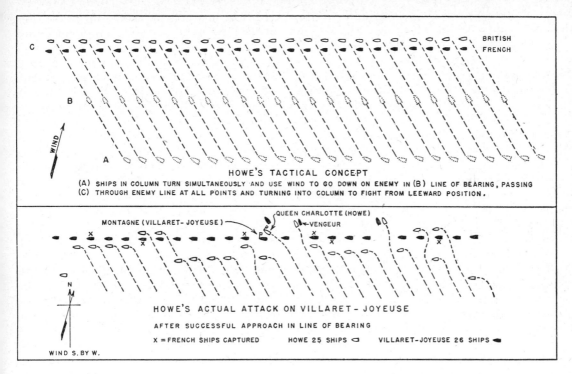

HOWE'S TACTICAL CONCEPT
(A) SHIPS IN COLUMN TURN SIMULTANEOUSLY AND USE WIND TO GO DOWN ON ENEMY IN (B) LINE OF BEARING, PASSING
(C) THROUGH ENEMY LINE AT ALL POINTS AND TURNING INTO COLUMN TO FIGHT FROM LEEWARD POSITION.

HOWE'S ACTUAL ATTACK ON VILLARET - JOYEUSE
AFTER SUCCESSFUL APPROACH IN LINE OF BEARING
X = FRENCH SHIPS CAPTURED   HOWE 25 SHIPS ◁   VILLARET-JOYEUSE 26 SHIPS ◀

BATTLE OF THE FIRST OF JUNE, 1794

foes. Howe still had the wind but the day cleared too late for him to want to use it. He wanted a full day to take care of the will-o'-the-wisp French.

The climactic First of June broke upon a swelling sea, whitecapped by a stiff wind ideal for combat under sail. The sun was brilliant. Howe fussily rearranged his 25 ships to match them with their firepower equals in the French line. With the game in his hands, he became the aggressive, brilliant Howe of old. He had given much thought to the traditional French preference for being to leeward in action. It will be remembered that in this position, the French could edge away to protract the time of contact, firing high at long range to cripple attackers coming from windward. If extended over a sufficient period of time, high firing often enabled the French to fall away from a headlong attacker too damaged aloft to prevent escape. Howe could not stop the French from shooting to dismast, but he was determined to pin Villaret to the battlefield.

Howe's solution to the tactical problem that had vexed his predecessors was brilliantly simple if extremely risky. Still subservient to the doctrine of ship-to-ship combat of opposite numbers, Howe moved down slowly in perfect line of bearing akin to Byng's slanting approach. His ships could return enemy fire at long range.

Howe's maneuver was meant to do more than just minimize the effects of raking. *He ordered his captains to pass astern of their respective foes and to fight from the leeward position.* He was willing to gamble on the superior mobility of his force by passing right through the enemy. He proposed to have his cake and eat it too. He used the windward position to force Villaret to fight and then discarded the windward for the leeward so that Villaret, to get through him, had to cut through his re-formed line. Howe's tactical innovation was so simple and obvious that the question naturally arises: why was it not done long before? The answer lies partially in the dead weight of the *Fighting Instructions,* partially in the loss of command control in those days when black powdersmoke blotted out signals, and partially in the individual competence of captains in the old *Marine.* It was far too risky against a well indoctrinated foe. Howe had been studying his opponent for several days however and had concluded that these French were just as brave as their predecessors but not as finely trained. England was desperate for a victory, for reassurance that invasion was impossible, and would forgive Howe any departure from prescribed practice that was even partially successful. Howe felt compelled to gamble his reputation and everything else for a crushing success. And so he went down on the French with plans that in his youth might have brought him to dishonor and execution.

Ideally all the British ships should have penetrated Villaret's thundering line. Instead, by 10 AM only five had followed the *Queen Charlotte* to the leeward position. Adhering to the courtesy of the period, Howe personally engaged Villaret, whose friend Saint-André abruptly found excuses to take himself belowdecks. The engagement became a melee in which ship-to-ship action destroyed the tight integrity upon which French tactics depended. At close range, French valor and the gunnery doctrine of shooting at rigging was unequal to British valor and the doctrine of shooting at hulls. Ton after ton of exploding gunpowder blackened the air above flame-stabbed heavy hulls, so that neither admiral had a clear view of the four-mile-long battle nor the means of directing ships. The outcome had been placed in the hands of subordinates. Here, the inroads of the Revolution became evident. The French had the spirit, but not the skill, to conquer. Villaret was plagued like all French commanders before him by "prudence to conserve material."

The battle was heavy in the center and rear. The French van was largely untouched. Amidst the confusion, the members of the French van instinctively reverted to French practice. Falling off the wind, they formed a reserve to leeward, unable or unwilling to see Villaret's signals demanding their instant

return to duty. The defection of this division enabled the British to attain unplanned and therefore uncoordinated doubling upon Frenchmen held against the wind by the six Britons that had pierced the line.

Shortly before noon, Villaret slipped clear of the *Queen Charlotte* and gave way towards his self-appointed reserve with those ships able to follow his example. He left behind a dozen Frenchmen, nine of whom were completely dismasted. Stonily holding in check his fury at his faithless subordinates, Villaret formed a line afresh with his blooded veterans and timorous van. When ready, he grimly put about as he had on the 29th to recover his wounded, who valiantly strove to hold off the Britons exultantly surrounding them. At this juncture, Saint-André returned to the weatherdeck of the silent *Montagne* and reminded Villaret—who needed little reminding—of the prohibition against needless fighting.

Villaret therefore had to be content with truculently heaving to for several hours on the lee of the battlefield, sending frigates and corvettes to tow down the five cripples who were within easy reach. The other seven, all dismasted, had been put to windward by a British line hastily formed by Howe to forestall rescue and to counter the unusual obstinacy shown by the French. Having the weather, Howe had also the initiative. Further combat was his option and he decided to be content with seven battered prizes. The battle was over.

Both nations claimed victory and both had cause to do so. Howe had tangible evidence in the form of six lolling hulks, but 11 of his ships were in nearly as bad condition, although French gunnery had inflicted only a quarter of Villaret's losses of 5,000 killed and wounded. The French casualties best remembered by history were aboard the captured 74-gun *Vengeur,* which suddenly sank before the eyes of British boarding parties. As the men of the *Vengeur* were swept down to their doom, they spontaneously cried, *"Vive la République!"* That defiant shout somewhat lessened the moral triumph of Howe's tactical victory.

And despite Howe, Villaret had accomplished his mission. The grain convoy passed safely some 70 miles south of the battle scene. England, heartened by the six prizes towed triumphantly to Portsmouth, showered extravagant honors upon Howe and his men for their tactical success. To the average Englishman, alarmed by the seemingly invincible sweep of Jacobinism across the Continent, the matter of a grain convoy was secondary. Britons scoffed at the French for celebrating a strategic victory. But there was little mockery in the Royal Navy, for the new French *Marine* had proved worthy of respect.

THE
BRITISH EXPEDITION
TO QUIBERON BAY, 1795

General Lazare Hoche was one of the most implacable enemies of England. A man of extraordinary military ability, rivaled before his death in 1797 only by the repute of Napoleon, he cherished from the first the dream of carrying the war across the Channel. To that end he assembled 20,000 men at St. Malo, but the outcome of the Battle of the Glorious First of June deprived him of the naval support necessary to carry out his project of capturing the Isle of Wight. Refusing to relinquish his plans entirely, Hoche shifted to an interim program of training a small corps of *Chouans,* desperate men recruited from prison and criminal haunts, eager to earn gold and full pardon by landing in small guerilla bands on the British coast to kill and burn.

The British learned of Hoche's plans and sought to divert him by a counter-landing. In earlier wars England had had few friends in France; now the Royalists were natural allies and were constantly asking for help. In 1795, the *émigré* Comte de Puisaye easily persuaded the British government that the predominantly Royalist French of the Vendée needed only the appearance of a friendly naval force and a few reinforcements to rise in revolt. This accorded well with British plans, which had already named Quiberon

Bay in the Vendée country for the landing. Trouble here would draw Hoche's troops southward from St. Malo and throw his invasion scheme into confusion. So in the summer Sir John Warren sailed from England with three ships and six frigates carrying de Puisaye's mixed force of 4,500 *émigrés* and disillusioned Republican captives. The expedition nearly came to disaster because Villaret had broken out of Brest.

Villaret, instead of cowering in port after the previous summer's experience, had surged out at Cornwallis' blockading squadron of frigates, which was attacking a French coastal convoy. Thanks to superior seamanship Cornwallis escaped in a rising gale that compelled Villaret to anchor. Not having been notified about Warren's expedition, or that Lord Bridport was at sea with the Channel fleet, Cornwallis did not warn anyone that Villaret was out of port and lying athwart Warren's path.

Thick weather blinded Warren during his approach. When the sun broke through, he was astounded to discover Villaret and at first thought that his expedition had been betrayed. Coolly he formed his insignificant force in line of battle and sent his fastest frigate in search of Bridport. Standing between the French and his transports, Warren prepared to sacrifice his little squadron for the glory of England, and his bold attitude saved him. Villaret, recalling the flying squadron of 74's in the First of June Battle, assumed that Warren was fulfilling the same function ahead of the transports which were hulldown and could be easily mistaken for a battle force by an admiral who was not overanxious for an engagement.

Villaret hauled away to the northern shoals, opening Warren's way undisputed into Quiberon Bay. The comedy of mistaken identity ended for Villaret when he encountered Bridport running to Warren's aid near the Île de Groix the following day. With no tangible strategic objective to attain, Villaret was content to escape in a running fight. Before winning an entry into Lorient, Villaret paid three ships for his temerity, but this was a much cheaper price than he might have paid in the full dress fleet action that could have taken place had the Admiralty troubled to keep Cornwallis informed of movements in his area. Such administrative failure was not repeated in the following years and marks the real contribution of the Quiberon Bay expedition to the climactic campaign of Trafalgar.

The amphibious operation itself was a failure. Stiffened by British marines, the *émigrés* got ashore at Fort Penthièvre ideally placed at the tip of a long, narrow sandspit curving into the bay. De Puisaye confidently waited for the countryside to rally to his white standard, for the expedition was too weak to venture beyond the range of shipborne gunfire. In England, news of the foothold produced rash plans of sending 17,000 British regulars there, but Hoche arrived first. With one hand, he crushed the Royalists incited by de Puisaye; with the other, he struck Fort Penthièvre so swiftly that Warren had time only to embark his marines and less than a thousand *émigrés*. The grandiose plan of exploiting Quiberon Bay as a base of strong operations against the Republic was another victim of too little and too late.

TRUGUET
AND THE *MARINE*

Following the Quiberon Bay affair, a new Minister of Marine sought to stamp out the lack of discipline which Villaret loudly blamed for the failure of the Brest fleet to smash Howe and Bridport. Admiral Truguet, an ambitious, strong-minded blue water veteran, had a firm hand and a rare opportunity. British cannon and French lack of seamanship had almost cut the *Marine* in half in three years. Billets for officers were correspondingly reduced. Truguet set up a program designed to weed out the unfit while attracting *émigrés* to return to duty. With a dozen new laws that were based upon his experience, Truguet returned to the old system that had been discarded in the madness of revolution.

Materially, Truguet's reforms were excellent. The ships came back to standard. Unfortunately, the old strategic and tactical concepts were also reasserted. Truguet was not Lazare Carnot. He deified the past of de Grasse and Suffren and aimed at their system as the greatest perfection. Instead of channeling the vigor of the Revolution into tactics suited to the enthusiasm of men who asked only for opportunity to excel upon the sea as their comrades did on the land, Truguet bridled impetuosity. In contrast to the galaxy of brilliant young generals rising in the French army to rival the fame of young British admirals, French naval officers were reminded to have "prudence to conserve material." The *Marine* took refuge in the traditionalism that had proved inadequate in the clashes of the American Revolution and was to prove hopeless in combat with a Royal Navy finally liberated from the *Fighting Instructions*. As the French army repudiated the conservative tactics born in the wars of moderation and made their foes conform to their system, so the British navy leaped a war ahead of the *Marine*. Aggressiveness in the French army was not matched in the *Marine,* because not even Napoleon possessed a system for finding and training leaders who were willing to lose ships just to win a battle. In effect, there had simply been an interruption in the program of de Castries.

When, in 1796, Lazare Hoche was given full support for a large scale invasion of England, the Army was ready.

The *Marine* was not and never would be.

8

England at Bay, 1797

IN THE WARS WITH THE BOUR-
bon monarchs, the British had usually been
able to follow a simple strategic program,
but anything like Pitt's Plan was impossible
in the wars with the French Revolution and
Empire. During this period, two new conditions were imposed upon British planning.
First, Great Britain no longer had a choice
about maintaining a major battle fleet in the
Mediterranean. It was necessary to protect a
swelling number of important possessions as
well as to afford direct support to allies.
Largely because of constantly changing Mediterranean demands, the Admiralty was often
unable to provide in home waters that comfortable margin of superiority which the
average Briton had come to consider a birth-
right. The second condition altering traditional strategy unexpectedly resulted from
the successful annihilation of French and
Dutch trade. French and Dutch seamen
gladly swarmed into privateers in preference
to vulnerable merchantmen, leaving their
trade problems to neutral ships from the
Scandinavian countries or the United States,
whose shipping quickly tripled in tonnage.
For the undermanned Royal Navy, the requirement of a Mediterranean fleet and the
predilection of the Allies for privateering
continually demanded a judicious juggling

of men between cruisers and battleships. Had
the French been habitually aggressive, England would several times have invited disaster
by being too weak in some critical area.

THE MEDITERRANEAN
THEATER, 1794-1795

In the Mediterranean, the progress of the
Revolution seemed to justify the uneasy
warning of Admiral Sir Hugh Palliser that
"there is no knowing what such an enthusiastic, mad, ferocious nation as the French
now are may attempt." The Admiralty was
upset by the rapidity with which Toulon
was restored to consequence as a naval base.
Indeed, while Hood was engaged in pacifying Corsica in the summer of 1794, six ships
untouched by the holocaust of Sir William
Sydney Smith boldly sortied from Toulon.
The detachment was led by Rear Admiral
Pierre Martin, who had been born 40 years
before in Canada. In the old navy Martin
had been a "blue water" lieutenant with little hope of advancement. The Revolution
however had brought him the promotion
that his humble birth and crude manners
had earlier denied him. Although untrained
for flag rank, he had some skill and was re-

solved to acquire more. Cheerfully accepting responsibility, he proclaimed the heretical doctrine that French fleets must fight the British for command of the sea before seeking territorial conquest beyond French shores.

More a man of action than of words, Pierre Martin set out to train himself and his ships in the hard school taught by British cannon. Astounded by such impudence, Hood was quick to send a tutor. Vice Admiral Lord William Hotham was soon on Martin's track with 28 British and Spanish ships. Well east of Toulon, Martin anchored in a small bay, set up shore batteries at either end of his line, and for five months resisted all of Hotham's efforts to annihilate him. Then, having imparted some knowledge of discipline and gunnery to his men, Martin returned to his base in an October storm that blew Hotham out of his way. At Toulon, Martin found eight ships readied for him by the zealous Saint-André, who had been sent from the triumph of the Glorious First of June to work a similar miracle in the Mediterranean.

Encouraged by his own modest success and the French reports of Villaret's battle with Howe, Martin persuaded his superiors to let him fight the British before launching a combined attack upon Corsica. He expected to offset British technical superiority by valor and a secret weapon, red-hot shot heated in special furnaces. After the Spanish had returned to their home ports, Martin went out in March 1795 to contend for command of the sea.

Steering for Corsica with 15 ships and seven frigates, Martin stumbled upon a storm-crippled British 74, the *Berwick,* off Cape Corso. From the *Berwick* he learned that Hotham had succeeded to Hood's command and was operating in the Gulf of Genoa with 14 ships, including a Neapolitan two-decker. Martin turned north and on March 12, 1795, a few leagues south of Genoa, found Hotham to leeward in a light wind. The British were in disorder—a group of four ships was close to Martin's van. The light southerly wind and general ineptitude of his captains kept Martin from maneuvering his clumsy force to cut off the four ships. Thereby he lost an opportunity to sink

or capture the little 64-gun *Agamemnon* and her captain, Horatio Nelson, famous at the time only for his gallantry during the sieges of Bastia and Calvi on Corsica, which had cost him his right eye.

The day drifted away with Martin powerless to prevent Hotham from forming line. The wind freshened too late and too much, during the night carrying away a mast of a French ship, thereby reducing the fleets to equality. With daylight on March 13, 1795, Martin was preoccupied with righting the ravages of the increasing wind and was in no wise able to exploit his windward advantage. Hotham impatiently signaled for a general chase and the skillful British belligerently closehauled into squally weather to close the gap between the forces. Trying to form and hold line, the French could not manage their ships as well in the rising seas. About 8 AM, the 80-gun *Ça Ira* crashed into the 80-gun *Victoire* in a tangle of masts and rigging. Seeing the accident, British frigates supported by the alert Nelson cut into the wind to attack the *Ça Ira* as she was towed by a frigate. For more than three hours, Nelson hung off the quarter of the plodding *Ça Ira,* in the midst of a partial, long-range engagement involving five ships, until Martin managed to wear and cover his cripple. Nelson discreetly withdrew. Action ended for the day.

As much disgusted with himself as disappointed in his subordinates and chances for victory, Martin put the now-dismasted *Ça Ira* in tow of the 74-gun *Censeur,* and headed for home. Hotham adeptly seized the weather gage. During the night, the windward advantage returned to Martin as the wind veered to the north, but to offset this, his only three-decker left him after sunset and the *Ça Ira* and her consort dropped far astern. By dawn, the wind was dying out. Martin had a difficult time getting about to head for his stragglers, who were stubbornly battering into helplessness a pair of British two-deckers that had ranged ahead of their fellows. Clumsiness and the feeble breeze kept Martin from arriving before Hotham's superior seamanship effectually interposed the British van to windward of the embattled *Ça Ira* and *Censeur.* At last becalmed within medium range, the French and British vans drifted for some six hours of cannonading. Shortly after 2 PM, the breeze freshened. Martin promptly signaled his leading ship to bear down towards the *Ça Ira*. Either unable to read the admiral's signal or to understand the orders verbally delivered, the leading French captain held the wind and the rest of the line followed him. Despite Martin's chagrin at abandoning two subordinates whose valor was extravagantly complimented by their captors, the battle was over.

Having two prizes in hand and with four of his own ships nearly dismasted during the formless fight about the *Ça Ira* and *Censeur,* Hotham was willing to call an end to the Battle of Noli. Young Horatio Nelson however was not content. Boarding the flagship to urge his admiral to pursue Martin, he was coolly told to be content, that the British fleet had done well enough. The spirit that would produce the Nile and Trafalgar flamed in Nelson's account of the interview: "Had we taken ten sail, and had allowed the eleventh to escape, when it had been possible to have got at her, I could never have called it well done."

As Hotham doubtless perceived, he had not seen the last of the unusual Pierre Martin. During their meeting off Genoa, a detachment of six ships loaded with naval stores slipped into Toulon from Brest. The little squadron was commanded by Renaudin, the captain of the famous *Vengeur,* who had been promoted to rear admiral upon his triumphant return to France from British captivity. Renaudin buttressed the spirit of Martin, who went to sea again on June 7, 1795 with the combined force of 19 ships and seven frigates. Martin wished to drill his officers and crews so that they would prove more worthy of their foes. After a month's aimless cruising that was equivalent to shakedown, he turned towards the Gulf of Genoa under orders to support the French army there. A long southerly tack brought him within view of the British anchorage at San Fiorenzo Bay in northern Corsica. Martin knew he was not ready for the battle that Hotham and 23 ships obviously sought in the speed with which they came in pursuit.

The ensuing action on July 13, 1795 was even less distinguished than that of March 13-14. The French had improved and Hotham was cautious, missing opportunities to do more than capture a ship that had been set afire by her own red-hot shot. For his part, Martin was chagrined at still being unable to wield a fleet. He had to be satisfied with extricating his force, and returned to Toulon determined upon more training and another chance.

Pierre Martin had run through his chances. The Revolution came back to the control of the middle class, who established a supreme committee known as the Directory to rule France. The Directory appointed Truguet as Minister of Marine. Under Truguet, as we have seen, orthodoxy reigned supreme, and Martin was unorthodox. For having lost three ships in ventures justified merely by a desire to fight for command of the sea, Martin was relieved by Rear Admiral Brueys. With Martin went the will to undertake offensive fleet operations, even had Truguet's ministry tolerated departures from traditional French strategic concepts.

The Toulon fleet was forbidden to embark upon cruises that merely invited useless destruction. Small squadrons were permitted to make commerce-raiding sweeps but there were no repetitions of Martin's audacity. Admittedly, the Toulon fleet had been carried beyond its true capacity by Martin. Years of hard work lay ahead to rebuild the arsenal to the extent required to sustain great operations. The supplies brought from Brest by Renaudin had not been enough even for Martin's use. However, the important factors at Toulon were less material than moral. Under Martin's adventuresome leadership, the French Navy had promised to duplicate the ability acquired by the French Army. When he was publicly disavowed, his spirit of the naval offensive, never truly French, vanished in a welter of busywork that aimed at the soundness of ships rather than the soundness of the officers who would sail them.

Martin received his true appreciation in the councils of the British Admiralty, where he had a profound effect that lasted many years. British hope that the Revolution would completely ruin the French navy had been shaken by Villaret's performance during the action with Howe and his subsequent cruise into the Bay of Biscay. Villaret had proved capable of maneuvering a fleet but he had subscribed to the defensive tradition; Martin had not manifested ability commensurate with that of his colleague. The British could understand the good reasons which had sent Villaret to sea; they chose to misunderstand the motives of Martin. Could the skill of a Villaret be joined to the aggressiveness of a Martin, the Royal Navy would face a foe worthy of more than mere respect. Complete uncertainty about the quality of French squadrons influenced British strategy until Trafalgar revealed that the French navy had become even more subordinated to the army of Napoleon than it had been in the days of the Bourbons. Until Trafalgar, many Englishmen thought the frequent changes among French admirals was a search for a Villaret-Martin. British strategy therefore aimed at furnishing at least equal numbers of ships against any possible French naval force, not altogether in the confidence of producing victory but also to prevent decisive defeat. Only experience taught the British how thoroughly Martin had been repudiated within the French navy. In the meantime, England did not gamble: her steadiest admiral was ordered to relieve Hotham. In the autumn of 1795, back from the West Indies, Admiral Sir John Jervis took his flag to the Mediterranean.

THE SPANISH MONARCHY JOINS THE JACOBINS

Jervis assumed unenviable responsibilities. Spain and Prussia had made peace with France, and Austria was wavering. Jervis had to prop up the Austrians, who were facing the Republicans along a front in northern Italy. He had to reassure the small Italian states. He had to defend his Corsican base, while watching a detachment of six French ships at Cadiz and the fleet in Toulon. Lastly, he had to be on guard against surprise hostilities by Spain. To execute these scattered missions, Jervis had 18 ships in poor condition. Hotham had dangerously depleted naval stores without creating a regular system of supply nor had he seen to adequate provisioning. Jervis was obliged to scour the markets of the Mediterranean in a political climate rapidly cooling towards the British; despite his fleet, Tunis afforded harbor to two French corvettes with a British frigate in tow. Under such circumstances, Jervis found morale more of a problem than supplies. Others besides Nelson had been dejected by Hotham's failure to press combat upon his willing but awkward foe.

Eradication of prevalent laxity and carelessness was the primary task Jervis set for himself. His high standards of discipline and seamanship slowly built that team of young officers who would become the boast of England. Jervis gave outlet to ambition in active missions, such as recapturing the British frigate at Tunis. Detaching Rear Admiral Mann with seven ships to watch Cadiz, Jervis posted himself with ten to watch Toulon, thereby providing cover for small operations along the Riviera in direct support of the Italians and Austrians. These light squadrons were directed by Nelson, who had begged Hotham to undertake the measure, since the French had access to Italy only by roads exposed to gunfire from the sea. Nelson's outspoken enthusiasm had earned him recognition and a commodore's pennant. Cutting up coastal traffic here and silencing French batteries there, Nelson had much to do, for the French army in Italy had been given a man of destiny. Napoleon Bonaparte was exercising his first command, opposing an overwhelming force of Sardinians and Austrians carelessly deployed along the Riviera.

Allied numbers were only figures to juggle in the brain of the brilliant Corsican as he cleverly feinted and drove in mass against portions of his foes. His campaign became a rout that ended with a peace signed in proud Vienna. As the campaign developed, the Allied forces went limp with astonishment. Jervis did his best to aid them but ships could not wheel against Napoleon into the Lombardy plain. Within a year, Jervis had to think of himself.

Spain had made peace with France in July 1795, seeing no reason to continue a war that roused little enthusiasm in the Spanish people, and had brought French troops into the Pyrenees. For peace, Spain received half of turbulent Santo Domingo and considered the bargain good. French diplomats adroitly suggested that war with England might prove even better, if only to recover Gibraltar and to avenge the arrogance of Lord Hood during the siege of Toulon. Little persuasion produced the spectacle of the Spanish Bourbon king allying his state with the people who had executed his cousin. News of the Spanish alliance chilled Jervis, for he could only hope to gain the active support of some 12 dubious Portuguese ships, which would be more of a handicap than a help. While Jervis dreaded the juncture against him of the 25 Spanish and French ships in Cadiz, the seven in Cartagena, and the 12 at Toulon in a grand force of 44, the British government looked in alarm to the West Indies where 13 Spanish ships were presumably ravening to fall upon English colonies.

The aspirations of Lazare Hoche to invade Britain were well known in England, but the official attitude in London is well summarized in a letter from Henry Dundas of the War Office to his colleague in the Admiralty, Lord Spencer. The occasion was the departure from Cadiz by Richery and his six French ships. His destination was Newfoundland and the fisheries. Dundas feared otherwise: "The loss of Jamaica in the present moment and state of the country would be complete ruin to our credit and put you at once at the feet of the enemy. I have no hesitation in saying that I would much rather hear that 15,000 men were landed in Ireland or even in Great Britain, than hear that the same number were landed in Jamaica with a fleet there superior to ours." Dundas smarted from criticism for his preoccupation with the West Indies, but the reason for his concern lay in his loyal adherence to Pitt's policy of putting the war on a "pay-as-you-go" basis. Jamaica and India were the treasuries of England, providing the wealth both to finance hostilities and to buy allied armies. Jervis realized that most available aid would speed to the In-

dies, where enterprising Britons used Spain's declaration of war in October 1796 as an invitation to acquire Trinidad and its four ships. Plans were then put afoot to take Puerto Rico. Such conquests were doubly beneficial in British strategy: wealth was not only cut off from England's enemies but was put to use against them. With emphasis upon the colonial war, Jervis had to shift for himself.

The quality of the Spanish navy was a mystery. It had been reorganized recently by José de Mazarredo, the admiral most respected by the British. Mazarredo was a superb seaman and fleet commander, proved during the American Revolution. He was also an eminent astronomer and writer on naval matters. Professionally, he was the equal of Howe, and Jervis could only guess how well he had succeeded in making the Spanish fleet effective. The time was not too distant when a British squadron would imperturbably keep the Mediterranean when simultaneously opposed by ships of France, Spain, Turkey, and Russia. In 1796 however Sir John Jervis was alarmed and called in his detached elements.

Rear Admiral Mann was quietly summoned from the blockade of Richery in Cadiz before Spain went to war. Worn by the tensions of a year blockading a port containing quadruple his numbers, and which might sortie any day, Mann neglected to provision at Gibraltar and came empty to Corsica. Jervis ordered him to return to Gibraltar for stores. In the interim, Spain decided to send her fleet to Toulon before declaring war. Thus, as Mann came within sight of Gibraltar, he encountered what he had dreaded for a year: Admiral Juan de Langara with 19 ships. Mann considered himself lucky to escape into Gibraltar with the loss of a few small vessels. Shaken by the experience, he summoned his captains to a council of war which supported his decision to take his seven ships home to England. As de Langara picked up his Cartagena detachment to make a combined Allied potential of 38 ships, Mann's defection deprived Jervis of a third of his force.

When confirmation of the Spanish-French

alliance reached London, the British government made a bitter decision. Such overwhelming numbers made adequate supply of Jervis impossible when available extra strength had to be sent to the Indies. Consequently, Jervis was ordered to evacuate the Mediterranean. Had Jervis been reluctant, Napoleon left him no option, sending troops from Italy to seize the Corsican bases from the rear. Blockading Toulon to provide cover for withdrawal from Corsica and Elba, Jervis entrusted Nelson with the duty of extricating their troops and military supplies. The swiftly advancing French prevented Nelson from finishing the job before he rendezvoused with Jervis in a protected anchorage in northern Corsica. Jervis expected Mann. Late in October, de Langara arrived instead.

High in morale, the British cleared for action, but de Langara had only come to locate and count the British before proceeding to Toulon. Although the French and Spanish outnumbered him 38 to 14, Jervis remained for two weeks until convinced that something had happened to his errant subordinate, Mann. Early in December, Jervis arrived at Gibraltar. Here, chained by adverse winds, he was galled to see five ships of the Brest fleet under Rear Admiral Villeneuve sail past. As soon as possible, Jervis established a base at Lisbon and took up a blockade of Cadiz to await de Langara's return. The Cadiz blockade was intermittent because the Directory was applying pressure to Portugal, and Jervis occasionally had to bring his full force to the Tagus to preserve Portugal's loyalty.

The British evacuation of the Mediterranean gave Italy and the Adriatic to France, while furnishing Austria an excuse for seeking peace. England entered upon a dark year. Except for a Russian squadron of 12 ships cooperating with Admiral Adam Duncan in the North Sea, England had no friends.

HOCHE REVIVES
HIS INVASION PLAN

Prior to peace with Austria in the summer of 1797, the French Directory could not seriously countenance proposals for full-scale invasion of England. Even though the help of the Dutch and Spanish fleets might suffice to control the Channel, the French army could not spare the number of troops that would be needed. However, small scale operations were feasible, such as that against the Isle of Wight for which Lazare Hoche had been patiently training and building. Irish patriots persuaded the Directory that Ireland needed only a token force of French troops bearing an arsenal of small arms to rouse the country and expel the British. Hoche was therefore ordered in the autumn of 1796 to shift his preparations against the Isle of Wight to attack northern Ireland. Averse to the idea, Hoche exacted as a price the replacement at Brest of Villaret by his own friend Morard de Galles.

In mid-December, Hoche was at last ready when heavy weather drove off the blockading squadron of Vice Admiral Colpoys. The success of French expeditions was predicated upon opportunity for evasion rather than combat. This little choice of time to sortie required a caliber of seamanship that the French could rarely display. Thus, weather and incompetence broke up Hoche's force of 17 ships and 46 minor vessels carrying 17,000 troops before it gained the open sea. The force never got together, despite Hoche's detailed instructions for rendezvous points. The startled British hunted everywhere but in the right area so that the French had only storms to obstruct their juncture, but storms made a sufficient obstacle. Elements of Hoche's command straggled into Bantry Bay, did nothing, and individually sailed home. By mid-January 1797, all were back in Brest minus two ships and four vessels lost to the sea.

Hoche had to postpone his eagerness to apply the lessons he had learned. Striking north from Italy, Napoleon was near victory if the Austrians on the Rhine could be distracted. Within a week of returning to Brest, Hoche was en route to the Army of the Sambre et Meuse. Within three months, his troops had driven deep into the Hapsburg domain and joined the left flank of Napoleon's exultant Army of Italy. Austria had no choice but surrender. Hoche was happy during this period because the Directory hinted that he could soon take charge of a tremendous project dear to his heart: the invasion of England. With the Dutch and Spanish fleets added to the 30 ships at Brest, he was assured of a safe passage for his flotillas. Unfortunately for him, something happened to the Spanish before he had time to draw up plans. The Spanish were not too enthusiastic, anyway, as a naval minister, Urquiza, pointed out; the Cadiz fleet, he said, "might be employed upon some useful expedition which will promise some good results, striking wherever it may be judged suitable, and avoiding naval battles which result only in shedding blood and destroying ships uselessly, obliging them to return to harbor for repairs and to remain there in inactivity, sometimes blockaded; while we have to fight a nation whose strength lies wholly in a formidable fleet, whose measures must be countered by wisdom and appreciation of how to strike in the vulnerable parts." With such an attitude, the Spanish fleet sailed from Toulon in obedience to the Directory's orders. José de Córdoba had replaced de Langara, who had been promoted to duty in Madrid. Córdoba was loath to leave the Mediterranean to the mercy of Admiral Brueys, who too cheerfully undertook to extend French power undisputed into Italy and the Adriatic. In the huge, 4-decked, 130-gun flagship *Santísima Trinidad*, Córdoba set sail with 27 ships for Gibraltar. Like Medina-Sidonia of the Armada, Córdoba was recommended by little except bravery. He scorned Mazarredo's warning that his fleet was only "a shadow" of a naval force, but battle found him irresolute and without capacity for the great responsibility entrusted to him.

THE BATTLE OF
CAPE ST. VINCENT,
FEBRUARY 14, 1797

In early February 1797, nearing Gibraltar with a strong, following wind, Córdoba detached three ships to escort a convoy into Al-

geciras. Another of his ships was loaded with Sardinian quicksilver and unable to use her main batteries. Thus, as the wind blew him far out into the Atlantic, Córdoba had 23 effective ships for a line of battle. Learning that he had been blown to the westward of Jervis, Córdoba lacked the imagination to see that the fates had bestowed upon him an advantage that he would have had to fight Jervis to obtain otherwise. Already beyond Cape St. Vincent, Córdoba had only to make for Brest, well ahead of Jervis, to carry out the basic part of his orders. However, he had been ordered by his superiors to put into Cadiz and he dared not risk their displeasure by pushing on to France. When the wind moderated and shifted to the west, he headed for Cadiz on February 13, expecting little trouble from Jervis, whom he believed to have no more than ten ships. The British Admiralty was known to be hard-pressed and Córdoba believed the scout who reported having seen Jervis with only nine ships.

Unfortunately for Córdoba, this report was no reason for complacency, since it was based upon a temporary division of Jervis's force. For the battle, Jervis had all of the 15 ships allowed him by the West Indian policy. Of the 15, Captain Troubridge's 74-gun *Culloden* was in serious condition from a recent night collision with a mate. Although outnumbered, Jervis was more than ready for action which would at once assuage the humiliation of being forced from the Mediterranean and reassure England. "Notwithstanding the disparity of force," he calmly told a cruiser captain who had correctly reported Córdoba's strength, "with such stuff as I have about me, I shall attack them, and England shall hear of them." Jervis had faith in ship commanders like Nelson and Collingwood, trained in his exacting school, and took them supremely confident through hazy weather towards an interception calculated from the reported position of the scattered, seasick Spanish. "A victory," he is reported to have said, "is very essential to England at this hour."

Shortly after first light on February 14, the thud of gunfire through the luminous fog broadcast the news that British scouts had

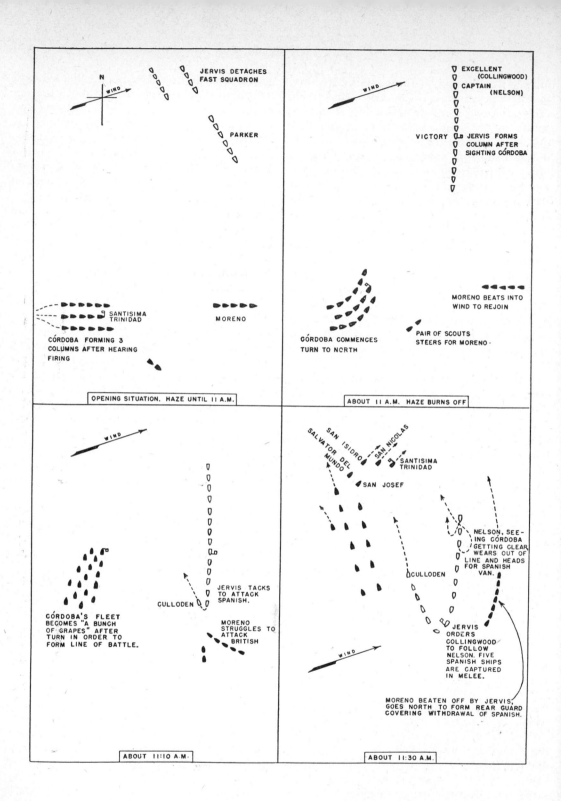

BATTLE OF CAPE ST. VINCENT, FEBRUARY 14, 1797

located the Spanish to the southward of Jervis. The wind was still in the west. In an open cruising formation of two columns, Jervis swung south into the mist. For his part Córdoba saw the gunflashes. Still deluded about the number of ships seeking him somewhere on the gray, clouded sea and unable to see all of his own ships, Córdoba signaled his fleet to form three columns abreast. This unusual formation provided awesome defense in depth should Jervis be tempted to attack and it also nullified Howe's tactical penetration of a single line. Córdoba prudently intended to avoid useless fighting and also to have better control over stragglers. Before the formation was attained by captains busy with their quadrants, sails were detected in the haze to the south, and at 8 AM Córdoba detached two 74's to investigate.

Córdoba's complacency vanished with the clearing fog: only 17 ships were about him. The other five were in column more than a mile ahead. At 10 AM, before Córdoba could signal this group, the British appeared, not in the south but in the north, big black hulls steering for the gap between Córdoba and his van. As the horizon cleared and numbers could be counted, Córdoba lost his composure: the situation was not the one for which he was mentally prepared. Jervis was thus given the advantages of tactical surprise.

By 11 AM Jervis had handily shifted into line, the Culloden in the lead, relentlessly driving perpendicularly south towards the split in the east-bound Spanish. Córdoba frantically called his force about him. His superiority meant little when scattered into elements of 17, 2 and 5 ships. Relative motion favored Jervis. The Spaniards could not combine before the Culloden could reach gunshot. Dreading the consequences of being raked in a crossing situation and intent upon at least recovering his van, Córdoba ordered a turn to the north to create a passing situation. A minute before Troubridge opened fire at 11:30 AM, Córdoba lost his head, giving an order that might have meant salvation an hour earlier but now resulted in fatal confusion. Under fire, Córdoba's fleet read a signal to form a single line of battle without regard for assigned stations. The result was best described by the Spanish historian Duro: Córdoba's 17 ships became "a bunch of grapes." The tight British column was presented with an almost helpless mass to shoot into, although the Spanish van under Juan Joaquín Moreno promised to be troublesome by loyally beating back towards the cannonading fleets. The pair of Spanish 74's to the south headed for Moreno to give him a respectable force of 7 ships.

Jervis had three options: he could be content with engulfing Moreno, he could turn north together and form to leeward to engage Córdoba, or he could tack in column towards Córdoba and endeavor to keep the Spanish separated long enough to break the main body into pieces to be chewed at leisure. This last course of action could be dangerous if the Spanish had a good commander, but Jervis had taken his foe's measure in the slovenly handling of the approach phase. This was not Mazarredo and Jervis was willing to risk battle with both broadsides.

Upon reaching the rear of Córdoba's group shortly after noon, Jervis signaled his fleet to tack in succession. It was too late for proper effect and Troubridge had been impatiently waiting for something like it. Before the flags were fairly shaken out on the Victory's halyards, the Culloden's helm was over and her bow swinging toward the enemy. Jervis was proud of Troubridge's promptness, although soon distracted from full attention for Córdoba by the intrepidity of Moreno. With the British line turning into the shape of a fishhook, Moreno's force was spared from annihilation. Instead of being grateful, Moreno flung his 7 ships at the Victory as she rounded into the knuckle of the British turn.

Had Córdoba had the perception and ability to use the opportunity presented by Moreno's gallantry, he would merely have fallen off the wind, destroying the tactical integrity of the British in a general melee and smothering 15 ships with 23. Instead, Córdoba continued north. The Victory and her consorts threw back Moreno, who did not press the attack that was disregarded by his chief. Moreno gave way to continue north towards the juncture astern of the British so obviously considered paramount by Córdoba.

By contrast, the manner in which the British navy came to enjoy naval supremacy in the period may be descried in the ensuing action. As the British marched through the *Culloden's* wake, Córdoba's van gradually drew north of the British rear and began to turn east. It was apparent to the captains in the British rear that the evolution then underway would bring them about far too late to throw their weight into the action finally begun by Troubridge against Córdoba's rear. Their venerated Jervis had turned too late; the Spanish were getting clear. At 12:51 Jervis signaled his force to take suitable stations and to engage "as arriving in succession." The meaning was clear, but flying his commodore's pennant in the *Captain,* third ship from the last, Nelson interpreted the order to suit the requirements of the situation. With enormous moral courage, he flouted the *Fighting Instructions* by wearing out of line and crossing ahead of his friend Collingwood in the *Excellent,* the last of the British ships. Like a true Horatio, Nelson went to block the bridge of Córdoba's escape, striking into the Spanish center. Córdoba abandoned the effort to meet Moreno and hauled tightly to the wind.

In the Royal Navy only flagships at the time carried complete signal bags, so there was no way for Nelson to explain his reasons for forging directly across to aid Troubridge, who had been fighting alone for ten minutes. As Jervis saw his young commodore stand into the mass of Spaniards, he needed no explanation. Instead, he directed Collingwood to join Nelson. Collingwood was reputed to be "the hardest hitter of the fleet" and his fast, well-served broadsides were tremendously effective against the last half of Córdoba's force. Crossing the stern of one Spaniard, Collingwood's *Excellent* fired a broadside that killed or disabled a third of her crew.

With British ships moving up to help Troubridge, Nelson, and Collingwood, the tail of the Spanish fleet was overwhelmed. Sword in hand, Nelson boarded the 80-gun *San Nicolas,* which had been shattered by Collingwood, and used her as "Nelson's Patent Bridge" to enter the 112-gun *San Josef,* entangled alongside in an effort to dodge the *Excellent's* murderous guns. These were two of the five Spaniards which surrendered, including Córdoba's flagship. The great *Santísima Trinidad,* afire below, and with a side masked by fallen sails, was obliged to haul down her colors to prevent further punishment from a swarm of British ships. Her assailants, including Collingwood, thought that the flag had perhaps been carried away and did not cease firing. Córdoba then hoisted British colors, which were unseen in the battle smoke. However, Jervis was cheated of this triumph as the indefatigable Moreno smashed a way to his commander and coolly held out a shield of eight ships behind which Córdoba was able to limp away with the other fugitives. Moreno followed in good order when Jervis broke off the action after more than three hours of heavy combat.

Thanks to Moreno's persistence, the Spanish had come together, 20 ships to windward of Jervis. The issue could be debated on the morrow. Moreno urged his admiral to redeem the honor of Spain. Instead, Córdoba listened to the majority of his officers who wished only to reach Cadiz. The Spanish had 404 killed and 1,089 wounded, including the casualties aboard the four prizes that compensated Jervis for his 73 killed and 227 badly wounded. Moreno was vindicated by the court-martial that harshly punished Córdoba and his adherents. When night came Jervis was not at all certain that he had won. With four of his ships seriously damaged, he ordered his prizes to be burned should the Spanish attack the following day.

Not until early afternoon on February 15 did Córdoba manage to form line. The British were disarranged. Córdoba eased off the wind as though to attack. The British snapped into a column in a display of alert seamanship that dispelled any notion about combat that Córdoba might have entertained. Ignoring a Spanish flag mockingly hoisted by Troubridge over the battered *Culloden,* Córdoba closehauled to the wind on a southerly course and left the field. Jervis pointedly unblocked the way to Cadiz by heading north to Lagos Bay.

The Battle of Cape St. Vincent was not a great victory compared to those that Nelson and his fellows would soon win. However, the Spanish tacitly withdrew from the half-formed plan to invade England. The Spanish fleet was far from destroyed. Mazarredo's frankness had been vindicated and he was placed in command to prevent recurrence of the disaster he had foreseen. Thus, Jervis was not at liberty to reenter the Mediterranean even in response to Austria's desperate appeals. The watch on Cadiz was resumed.

Honors were showered upon Jervis and his captains, for their news arrived when Pitt's "pay as you go" policy and fear of invasion had caused the closing of the Bank of England and a general suspension of cash redemption of government securities. Pitt's party gratefully made Sir John Jervis the Earl of St. Vincent with an annual income of £3,000. His two admirals were made baronets. Nelson became a Knight of the Bath and a rear admiral.

The defeat of Córdoba had importance far beyond the views officially expressed in exaggeration intended to bolster public confidence. It was the *Fighting Instructions* that had really been defeated. Shortly after the battle, Jervis's Flag Captain, Sir Robert Calder, commented that Nelson's maneuver had been unauthorized. Jervis cheerfully replied, "It certainly was and if ever you commit such a breach of your orders, I will forgive you." This attitude expressed by an admiral of Jervis's professional stature virtually gave full initiative to Nelson's generation. The way was opened for what was hailed as tactical daring but which was actually a sound reversion to emphasis upon the principles of war, especially that of concentration.

In April, the glory of the victory at Cape St. Vincent was blighted. Total disaster threatened England from a most unexpected quarter: the Home Fleet mutinied.

THE MUTINIES OF SPITHEAD AND THE NORE, 1797

The naval mutinies of 1797 resulted primarily from inadequate pay, insufficient leave, poor food, and general living conditions. Harsh discipline and officer abuses and officer privileges were secondary. The primitive armament then in use was indirectly the chief cause of the complaints. Each cannon on a ship of the line needed a dozen or so men to act as human recoil mechanism, so that a two-decked 74 with a tonnage slightly greater than that of a modern destroyer escort, had a crew of 713 for her broadsides. A tenth of this number actually sailed the ship; the rest were kept occupied by traditionalized busywork until rare moments of battle. A warship was almost as cramped as the infamous Hole of Calcutta. The wonder is not that mutinies exploded in 1797, but rather that mutinies were the exception rather than the rule in the Royal Navy.

In 1797, the British had in commission 131 ships, 159 frigates, and 108 sloops besides a multitude of smaller craft. This gigantic navy was supplied with men and materials through haphazard methods unworthy of being called a system. Corruption and graft of every conceivable type had been legalized by long toleration which even Jervis proved incapable of scuttling. Except for the seamen, almost everyone connected with the Royal Navy made money and much of this money was taken from the pockets of helpless sailors. The crew's pay, for example, was kept on the books throughout the entire period of a ship's commission—which might be as long as 14 years—until the ship was no longer needed and she was "paid off." Paying off was done by "tickets" which had to be presented at a special office in London. In theory, married seamen could allot half of their pay to their wives. In practice, payment was blocked by indifferent officials, so that the families of seamen usually had to seek the meager relief of the Poor Laws. Even full payment of a seaman's wages to his dependents however would still have thrown them upon public relief, because pay was less than a shilling a day, unchanged since the Duke of York had been Lord High Admiral of England in the Dutch Wars. The public had turned a deaf ear to all petitions for pay increases because the public believed mistakenly that seamen got rich on prize money for wartime captures. The amount of such money was insignificant after coming through the filter of officer shares. The richest distribution of all, it will be remembered, was made after the capture of Havana in 1762: Admiral Pocock received £122,700 in serious contrast to the common sailor who received less than £4. Nor was England generous if a sailor died on active service; his widow received a settlement of her husband's wages and an extra year of his pay. If he was merely wounded, he had a payless period of six weeks in which to recover or be discharged. A substantial pay increase and a pension system were long overdue in 1797, and this issue triggered the mutiny at Spithead. The other four mutinies of April and May were complex in origin, founded upon all that needed correction in the ships that kept the French from English soil.

Had the crew jammed into a warship been composed of volunteers, the disciplinary system of flogging might have been as mild as that prescribed for the navy established by the United States in the year of the British mutinies. However, only a small fraction entered the Royal Navy by choice; the bulk of the crews came involuntarily from many sources and these were of mixed virtue. Many were impressed; many were sentenced by magistrates to expiate crimes by serving at sea; many more were sentenced merely to fill quotas imposed upon the inland counties by law in 1795; and many came from the orphaned poor. Fear was considered to be the only means of controlling such disparate elements, and fear there was, even in ships commanded by the humanitarian Nelson and Collingwood. Had there been liberty and leave to afford some slight escape, the cat-of-nine-tails might have been endured, but with a quarter of the navy managing to desert annually even without leave, few captains looked with favor upon permitting men to go ashore except on duty.

Food could offer a palliative. The finest admirals, notably those trained by Jervis, forever strove to procure the best provisions available. The staples of diet however were salt beef and pork often kept pickled too long in brine casks to be recognizable. Dried peas and beans, oatmeal, and hard biscuits rounded out a day's menu. The value of fresh vegetables in preventing and curing scurvy was known; the means of bringing an adequate supply of them to a cruising fleet was not. On a foreign station, ships might secure freshly killed meat and sufficient vegetables—indeed some of Nelson's force missed the Battle of Trafalgar for this very reason—but then, water might prove unsafe. Bad food, contaminated water—these took their toll. As one seaman said, "Where we had one man died by shot in the Navy we had ten died by means of bad provisions." For those who had money, there was an alternative; they could buy relatively good food from the purser's private store. Since the purser also purchased ship's supplies, no more need be said.

One commodity did afford temporary relief: grog was issued daily. Not even alcohol however could make a man totally unconcerned with the conditions of shipboard life. Congestion and dampness were spurs to the spread of any contagious disease. The personnel figures for the Seven Years' War tell the story: out of 183,900 men enlisted, fewer than 50,000 were paid off. The battles of the war killed only 1,512. Deserters and those who died of sickness numbered 133,700.

This, then, is a brief suggestion of what it was like within the wooden walls of England's fleet.

Lord Howe, revered as the sailor's friend, was acquainted with the impending trouble when in early March he received several anonymous petitions from Lord Bridport's Channel Fleet. The petitions were identical, asking Howe's influence in securing an increase in pay, a leave system, and decent food. Despite Howe's conscientious efforts, the government did not act, other than to order Bridport to return to Spithead, where, early in April, the seamen after two expectant weeks openly refused a signal to return to sea. Within a week, the government yielded, granting much that was asked, and pardoning all mutineers. Public sentiment was with the seamen and redress of grievances was popularly supported. With cheers, Bridport's squadrons dropped down to St. Helens to await a favorable wind. Unfortunately, governments move slower sometimes than circumstances warrant. Bridport's men saw only promises and no deeds at the end of a week. The fleet mutinied again. Blood was spilled and officers sent ashore. On May 15, Lord Howe had the satisfaction of justifying the sailors' confidence in him. He arrived in Portsmouth with a convincing Act of Parliament and the King's Pardon. The mutiny vanished and the fleet returned to duty. The whole matter, lasting six weeks, was characterized by respectful disobedience. This was not true of the revolt which broke out in Duncan's North Sea Fleet.

Since the privileges won at Portsmouth extended to the whole Navy, Pitt and his confreres believed that disaffection had been eliminated. When a few ships at the Nore raised the red flag of rebellion on May 12, just as Howe was composing the disturbance at Portsmouth, the government was as exasperated as it was alarmed. By May 27 the plague infected the entire North Sea Fleet. This fleet was desperately needed because the enemy was known to be extemporizing an invasion plan to capitalize upon England's distress, and only the 33 ships of the Dutch were in condition to cooperate with the French fleet at Brest.

For the past two years, Admiral Adam Duncan, a tough Scotch veteran of 66, had been watching the Dutch. Described as the biggest and strongest officer in the navy, he suppressed mutiny aboard a 50-gun razee by picking up the crew's spokesman with one hand and holding him over the side while urging the fascinated seamen to remember their duty. Unfortunately, he could not board his rebellious ships without risking open conflict. Duncan preferred to sail to his post with only his 74-gun flagship *Ven-*

erable and his loyal razee,[1] leaving his fleet to be dealt with by his superiors. Lest it be thought that Duncan was a coward who shirked his duty, on June 1 he entered the narrow Texel and anchored athwart the channel within easy view of an expeditionary force of 50 transports, 20 frigates, and 16 ships commanded by Vice Admiral de Winter. "I have taken the depth of the water," he said to the captain of the *Adamant,* "and when the *Venerable* goes down, my flag will be flying still." His only frigate was kept busy on the horizon relaying signals to divisions that were not there. Baffled by this version of the boy holding his finger in the dike, the Dutch did not budge. For more than two weeks, Duncan remained in the throat of the Texel channel until the mutiny at the Nore had been crushed by force and his ships rejoined him. By the end of June, the crisis passed in the execution of a score of mutineers. Disaffection still flared in the cruiser squadrons at Plymouth and Falmouth, and cropped out in single ships for the remainder of the war. Seriously shaken, the British government sought peace. Lord Malmesbury went to Paris on a secret mission which foundered upon the French demand for recognition of their annexation of Belgium. The English merchants could not abide the French in Antwerp, so Malmesbury came empty-handed home.

Mutiny stirred in the fleet of Jervis (who will hereafter be called St. Vincent), but was firmly and promptly obliterated with such efficiency that the Admiralty when doubtful of ships' loyalty "sent 'em to Jervis." The new Lord St. Vincent's only compromise with sheer imposition of discipline was to seek more active employment for idle hands. In early July, Nelson and an inshore squadron twice bombarded the approaches to Ca-

---

[1] The *Venerable* and *Adamant* were not all that would have obeyed Duncan's orders. Three ships and five frigates remained from the original Russian squadron of 12 ships and six frigates, but two years of commanding Russian subordinates inclined Duncan to dispense with their services at this time. The Russians had been ordered home in May but loyally remained at Duncan's disposal until the mutinies ended. They sailed for the Baltic in July and thereby missed being present at the Battle of Camperdown.

diz until Mazarredo erected defenses which precluded anything short of full-scale assault. St. Vincent then turned to a project which under more settled circumstances he might have ignored. Principally to put some extra money in the purses of his favorites, Nelson and Troubridge, rather than to strike a useful blow, St. Vincent sent a small force under Rear Admiral Sir Horatio Nelson to capture Santa Cruz in the island of Teneriffe, Canary Islands. The silver galleon from Manila was reported to have arrived there and to be awaiting orders from blockaded Cadiz. On July 24, 1797, Nelson with 1,100 seamen and marines in boats attacked Santa Cruz. The venture failed and Nelson was seriously wounded. Troubridge averted the disgrace of complete surrender only by threatening to burn the town. Contemptuously, the Spanish governor permitted the beaten British to leave. The ignoble affair, a close cousin to piracy, cost Nelson his right arm and England 221 dead and 123 wounded.

But England's interest was focused on Holland rather than Spain. The implacable Hoche had been freed from the Army of the Sambre and Meuse to talk the Dutch into a sensible invasion plan to exploit the opportunity afforded by the mutinies. Irritated by French control, the proud Dutch declined to do more than send out an all-Dutch expedition, preferably to Scotland. They also stubbornly clung to the concept that troops should not be landed anywhere in the British Isles until adequate command of the sea had been obtained. Dutch obstinacy killed Hoche's recurrent ambition to invade England itself and he reverted perforce to the Irish campaign plan. The Dutch at last agreed to send out an army of 16,000 men escorted by 16 ships. By then, the opportunity had passed.

Undaunted, still eager for action against the enemy he hated, Hoche returned to France. His driving hate had consumed him. For years he had literally worked feverishly; tuberculosis claimed him on September 19. At the age of 29, nearing the pinnacle of his glory, Hoche was forever cut off from ambi-

tion. The one French general inexorably dedicated to the invasion of England was dead.

Perhaps as a tribute to his memory, the Directory exerted pressure upon the Dutch to honor their compact. There was neither plan nor purpose when de Winter left the Texel on October 8. Making the best of a foolish situation, de Winter sought to clarify the issue of command of the North Sea. Duncan desired the same objective.

THE BATTLE
OF CAMPERDOWN,
OCTOBER 11, 1797

Close to the coast of Holland, de Winter on the night of October 10 sighted a few ships of Duncan's fleet and unsuccessfully gave chase. Nature imposed limitations upon Dutch ships which handicapped them against the British. Shallow coastal waters put a premium upon shallow draft design, which, in turn, put emphasis upon small ships. None of the Dutch battleships carried more than 74 guns, while Dutch admirals put in line of battle vessels that in other navies were considered extra-heavy frigates. De Winter had four 74's, seven 64's, and four 50's for his line, and four frigates to scout. Instead of a total of 15 ships, the British would have said he had only 11, the four 50's being disregarded. In contrast, Duncan had seven 74's, seven 64's, and two 50's, all with thicker sides than Dutch vessels of the same rates. All other factors being equal, superior firepower and shot resistance were bound to bring victory to Duncan.

Duncan and de Winter found each other nine leagues off the town of Scheveningen, as de Winter was hove to seeking information from a group of friendly merchantmen. The wind was from the northwest and Duncan had it. De Winter lost valuable searoom by forming line upon his ships farthest to leeward, and was dangerously close to shoal water when he presented his force on a northeast heading. Seizing any means of minimizing enemy superiority, de Winter did not race closehauled to the southwest in an effort to win the weather gage, but hoped to enlist shoal water as an ally against the heavier British ships. Suspecting de Winter's intentions, Duncan prudently went on soundings, which fell below nine fathoms before the battle ended.

When Duncan sighted de Winter at 8 AM, the weather was misty and squally, the northwest wind driving him at four knots as he closed the Dutch on a rough reciprocal of their course. The British were in two columns, somewhat off station, but Duncan did not waste time forming line, because de Winter might then change his mind about struggling for the windward position if tempted by British delay. The fleets were about ten miles apart, with Duncan bearing about N by E from the Dutch, who, by holding their NE course, steadily moved themselves to the eastward. About 9:15 AM, aided by the Dutch, Duncan reached a position to the west where he stood between de Winter and the wind.

Firmly grasping the weather gage, Duncan rounded onto a southeast heading and bethought himself of tactics. He led the northern column in the *Venerable,* and Vice Admiral Richard Onslow led the southern column in the 74-gun *Monarch.* Duncan began a series of signals to bring his ships into line abreast on a NE-SW axis. This would make his ships approach parallel to the Dutch course, each ship steering straight into Dutch guns. Duncan thereby accepted the dangers of being raked when helpless—which Byng had tried to avoid at Minorca —but in compensation, if his line was perfect, all his ships would simultaneously strike into the enemy column.

Sailing large at three knots, the approach phase lasted two hours, during which Duncan made more than 20 signals to attain his tactical formation. The ships' logbooks give few clues as to why his captains failed to understand him. The signals seem clear enough, yet the British fleet went down more or less in their original two columns, thereby inadvertently anticipating Nelson's

deliberate attack in the climactic Battle of Trafalgar. Perhaps the story told of Captain John Inglis of the 64-gun *Belliqueux* tells all: "He had neglected to make himself master of the signal code and could not quite follow all that was in Duncan's mind. At

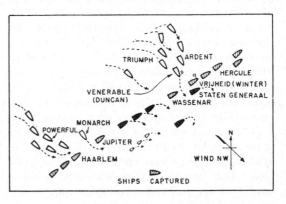

BATTLE OF CAMPERDOWN,
OCTOBER 11, 1797

last he closed the book and hurled it on the deck. Then shutting his telescope with a vicious snap he sang out to the master, 'Dang it, Jock! Up with the hel-em and gang recht into the middle o't!' " [2] Whatever the reason—British eagerness, the squally sea, the mist, the number of signals—Duncan had the courage of mind to abandon the role of drillmaster about 15 minutes before the action began.

His next order was an inspired improvement upon Howe's maneuver. He would throw his division upon the Dutch center, while Onslow attacked the rear: all British ships would break through and fight from the leeward position. Duncan got the necessary signals into the air but not into his subordinates' heads. His purpose was not understood. The British captains chafed under raking fire and thought only of using their own broadsides.

At 12:30, Onslow led his force into the Dutch rear. His *Monarch* passed under the stern of the 74-gun *Jupiter,* fourth from

[2] Geoffrey Callender, *Sea Kings of Britain,* 3 vols. (London, 1911-15), III, 194.

the Dutch rear. Only Onslow's *Monarch* obeyed the order to fight from leeward in support of Duncan's *Venerable,* which cut through the Dutch behind de Winter's flagship *Vrijheid.* The battle itself need not be lengthily described. The British were alongside their toughest enemies and fortune was on the side of the biggest battalions. The thinner bulwarks of the Dutch ships yielded to point-blank shot. Unlike the French and Spanish, the Dutch aimed at hulls, so that this was the bloodiest engagement of 1793-1815, as the British lost 228 killed and 812 wounded out of a total complement of 8,200 men. The Dutch loss was even heavier.

The action ended in general wreckage at 3 PM. Duncan had captured de Winter, who had wounds that were to prove fatal in London. The British ensign flew over 9 ships and two frigates, all so riddled that none could be added to the Royal Navy. If any proof be needed of stronger British construction, all of Duncan's fleet continued in commission, after damage such as 98 shot in one ship had been repaired. In contrast to the results of fighting the French or Spanish, no British ship had lost a mast, although all of the prizes had been virtually dismasted in a successful use of French gunnery to fix the foe to the field.

England rejoiced. The French were now thrown upon their own resources; both of their naval allies had been injured without gain for their common cause. Duncan became Baron of Lundie and Viscount of Camperdown, and Onslow a baronet, with corresponding rewards for the rest who had done their duty. Quietly, amidst the jubilation, the Admiralty court-martialed a captain who had not done his best. Duncan had to abide public acclaim until his fleet was repaired, when he gladly put to sea to resume his guard upon the Texel. Strategically and tactically, Duncan had control of the North Sea.

After nightmarish months, Englishmen breathed more easily and counted their blessings. First, to their satisfaction, the enemy had been rendered incapable of invasion.

Second, enemy colonies, including the Dutch settlements at Cape Town and in the East Indies, were steadily coming into British hands. Third, the Royal Navy had presumably become thoroughly trustworthy. Fourth, the fanatic Lazare Hoche was dead. And lastly, public confidence supported Pitt.

On the adverse side, the Spanish fleet had come into the hands of a capable admiral, enemy privateers were increasing their tax upon British shipping,[3] the West Indian campaign had killed 100,000 troops and had to be canceled, and the French were obstinately persisting in preparing an invasion flotilla. British strategy underwent a major change. If only because the sacrifice of troops in the West Indies had become intolerable, Dundas yielded. Henceforth, the colonial war would be subordinated to the European theater. The disposition of the Navy would continue as before; instead of having the objective of covering distant operations and protecting trade, it would now have the mission of covering continental expeditions and protecting trade. A limited naval offensive was to be mounted with support from the few troops available in England. Trade governed the choice of enemy privateer ports as the first targets for joint operations. Four light squadrons were formed to operate from Holland to the Spanish border in hit-and-run raids that in practice and purpose resembled the commando raids of

---

[3] Captures of English and French merchantmen were:

Year	English losses	French losses
1793	261	63
1794	527	88
1795	502	47
1796	414	63
1797	562	114

The disparity was due to the greater number of British ships at sea. In subsequent years, the disproportion was greater as fewer French merchantmen went out and the number of French privateers increased. The figures given serve to point up the strategic meaning of command of the sea: British squadrons could safely sail all waters save the Mediterranean, while British merchantmen were subject to capture.

World War II. The British army could not participate in significant operations until recuperation and recruitment restored it to respectability.

Until troops could be readied, Pitt's cabinet was confident after Cape St. Vincent and Camperdown that the strategic situation was stabilized. Little perturbation resulted from the news that the French a few weeks after Duncan's victory had formed an "Army of England" on the Boulogne coast. The British had come to live with the threat of invasion, but their calm did not last long.

The strategic situation was not at all stable: the new Army of England was placed in the hands of General Napoleon Bonaparte.

9

England Re-enters

the Mediterranean

DURING 1789, THE YEAR OF
the Bastille and the commencement of those
political adventures in France that produced
the phenomenon of Napoleon Bonaparte,
the erstwhile British colonies in America
consolidated their future with a republican
constitution. A modest infant in a world of
bickering adults, the United States wanted
only to be left alone to pursue the destiny
implicit in the vast virgin land stretching
toward the Pacific. With the attainment of
independence, Americans ceased to be preoccupied with European affairs and looked
west to the domestic barrier athwart the
routes to the Mississippi. Confronted by Indian warriors, fewer and fewer Americans
gave thought to the sea and the protection
of their swiftly expanding trade, which was
beginning to range as far as China. The
last vessel of the Revolutionary Navy, the
Alliance, was sold in 1785 just as Barbary
pirates in the Mediterranean noticed that
American merchantmen were no longer protected by British passports.[1]

---

[1] As late as 1798, the year of Nelson's great victory

BIRTH OF THE
UNITED STATES NAVY

Before the Treaty of Paris, 1783, Americans had enjoyed the immunity conferred by
British passports in the Mediterranean. Independence removed the protection of the
Royal Navy. Two American merchantmen
were soon captured by Algiers and the prisoners held for ransom as an invitation from
the Dey for the quondam British colonies to
join the Barbary System. While thrifty Americans in 1786 favored tribute as the cheapest
solution to the difficulty, red-headed Thomas
Jefferson insisted upon building a cruiser
navy. His colleague John Adams disagreed,
principally because of expense: a 32-gun frigate would cost $300,000 to build and $100,-
000 annually to maintain. So 21 countrymen
languished in slavery while Americans fruitlessly debated means of saving them. Formu-

---

at the Nile, Tunisian pirates completely depopulated
an island near Sardinia, carrying off a thousand captives.

160

lation of the Constitution was of greater moment.

When Jefferson became the first Secretary of State in the new government of the United States, he resumed his efforts for a navy. In 1790, he submitted to Congress an incisive indictment of the Barbary pirates and demanded a means of protecting the American flag at sea. The Senate was induced to concur, especially when George Washington remarked, "Would to heaven we had a navy able to reform these enemies to mankind or crush them into nonexistence!" In the House of Representatives however economy prevailed, if only because the urgent Indian problem demanded as much money as possible. Proponents of a navy steadily lost support and Congress in 1792 voted to pay ransom and tribute.[2] Before treaties could be satisfactorily negotiated, the French Revolution exploded. England, turning to her oldest ally, persuaded Portugal to abandon intermittent patrol action that had kept Barbary pirates bottled up in the Mediterranean. Corsairs ranged again into the open Atlantic, and Algerians in the autumn of 1793 captured 11 American ships.

News of this reached Congress on the heels of a French decree that authorized French warships and privateers to capture neutral vessels carrying food or goods to enemies of the Republic. Congress finally felt impelled to heed Washington's recommendations. The United States Navy was founded by a two-vote margin in an act of March 27, 1794, which provided for the construction of six frigates. Opposition of frontier and agricultural representation however had been so strong that the Naval Act carried a proviso that building would cease should diplomacy produce a satisfactory treaty with Algiers.

Naval affairs were placed under the jurisdiction of the Secretary of War, Henry Knox, who shrewdly distributed orders for construction materials throughout the different states. Knox thus succeeded in establishing some self-interest in support of a naval force, yet

even so a strict party vote was all that saved the embryo navy in April 1796, when a humiliating treaty with Algiers was successfully negotiated. Although the United States agreed to pay ransom and tribute to the Dey, three frigates were nearly complete and the administration successfully prevented them from being broken up for sale. The 44-gun frigates *Constitution* and *United States* and the 36-gun *Constellation* were authorized. A definite future was finally held out to veterans of the Continental Navy.

As Americans had thought for themselves in designing their government, so, too, their new frigates were not mere imitations of European models. Joshua Humphreys, William Doughty, and Josiah Fox pooled their considerable talents to produce 44-gun frigates with batteries of 24-pounders and the sides of conventional 74-gun ships of the line. In heavy weather, the *Constitution* was capable of engaging a two-decker in fair fight; in weather that permitted a two-decker to employ her main battery, the *Constitution* could speed away. Clean in design, exceptionally strong throughout, the big American frigates outclassed all rivals. Ironically, they were destined to hurl their first shot at ships manned by seamen from the country whose navy under de Grasse had been the essential factor in winning the crucial Yorktown campaign.

When Revolutionary France declared war on England, the United States proved loath to honor the terms of the 1778 alliance. With President Washington acting as the spokesman for neutrality, missions such as that of Citizen Genet foundered upon the rocks of early American isolationism. In the eyes of French government officials, American neutrality favored England. French privateersmen were encouraged to consider as British the 500,000 tons of American shipping carrying on a $60,000,000 foreign trade. The United States sought to define its peaceful position by diplomatic missions to Paris and London. When the "XYZ Affair" showed French intransigence, John Jay was able to write a tolerable treaty in London. The American ratification of Jay's Treaty led by the summer of 1796 to a formal rupture with France. By the summer of 1797, more than

---

[2] John Paul Jones, then in Paris, was appointed to ransom the 13 Americans who remained in Algiers, but Jones died on July 18, 1792, before receiving his first commission in the service of the United States.

300 American ships had fallen under French prize law. Then, in January 1798, the French Directory authorized the seizure of neutral vessels carrying anything of English origin. Such a position was tantamount to war, which the United States acknowledged on April 30, 1798 by the creation of a Navy Department. Amidst the paradoxes of politics, Thomas Jefferson had now become the leader of the party opposed to a navy, while his erstwhile colleague, John Adams, had become President through the support of the party pledged to a navy.

The first Secretary of the Navy, Benjamin Stoddert of Maryland, carried sound business acumen into his duties. When French privateers during the summer of 1798 boldly captured American merchantmen within the territorial waters of the United States, Stoddert received almost a blank check from an aroused Congress. Rushing to completion the six frigates of the 1794 Act, strengthening the crews of eight revenue cutters,[3] converting suitable merchantmen, Stoddert within a year had 49 miscellaneous vessels under his orders.

From July 1798 to September 1800, these vessels were gradually formed into four squadrons that protected American trade in the West Indies. The theater of operations was deliberately chosen to exploit geographical advantage. Furthermore, since Great Britain was equally concerned with trade protection in that productive area, United States squadrons were soon treated as British allies. Not only were United States squadrons made welcome to the facilities of the frigate bases at St. Christopher and Antigua, they were also welcomed as working partners. Thus, in its important formative months, the United States Navy had the tremendous benefits of working in conjunction with the finest navy in the world. Observing and adapting British practice, American commanders exchanged signal systems with the Royal Navy and alternated escort of mixed convoys north to the latitude of Bermuda.

Captain Thomas Truxtun, commanding the force based on St. Christopher, was the outstanding American officer in the "Quasi-War With France." [4] In the 36-gun *Constellation,* Truxtun on February 9, 1799 proved the superiority of American frigate design. Meeting the French *Insurgente,* whose 36 guns were nominally equal to his own, Truxtun had an actual broadside advantage of 432 pounds against 282. This disparity of fire power and Truxtun's superb seamanship compelled the *Insurgente* to haul down her colors after a half hour of fighting. The *Constellation* had only four casualties to the 70 of the French. The action was applauded even in London, whose merchants gave Truxtun a piece of silver plate.

Almost a year later, on February 1, 1800, Truxtun's *Constellation* encountered the slightly smaller 40-gun frigate *Vengeance* off Guadaloupe. A five-hour midnight engagement was inconclusive. The French gunnery practice of aiming for rigging crippled the *Constellation,* so that Truxtun was unable to close and board. Truxtun suffered 40 casualties; the French had half again as many.[5]

Truxtun's engagements were the most noteworthy among those by which the United States Navy divested the French of 98 minor vessels. Far more important than Truxtun's cool example of skill however was his founding of a realistic disciplinary structure. Truxtun critically abstracted the best from the British system, added his own thoughtful improvements, and gave his subordinates regulations, standing orders, and a sense of dis-

---

[3] These were the ancestors of the present United States Coast Guard. Originally formed in 1790 as a maritime police force for the Treasury Department, the service was at first loosely referred to as "Mr. Hamilton's system of cutters." The first formal name was the Revenue Marine, which evolved into the Revenue Cutter Service. The name Coast Guard resulted from the amalgamation in 1915 with the Lighthouse Service. In peacetime, the Coast Guard operates under the Treasury Department in a wide range of duties. In wartime, the service comes under the Navy.

[4] So called because no war was declared, Congress merely authorizing the capture of armed French vessels, but not merchantmen.

[5] Heavily damaged, the *Vengeance* made the Dutch island of Curaçao. Repaired, she was captured in August by the British 38-gun frigate *Seine* in the Mona Passage, after a running fight of some 18 hours. Towed to Jamaica, the battered *Vengeance* was surveyed and broken up.

cipline which were destined to endure. Truxtun was largely responsible for the professional training and pride of early American naval officers. His high standards enabled his colleagues in the West Indies to earn the approbation of their British contemporaries. In seamanship, Truxtun was the Lord Exmouth of the American navy; in leadership, he was the St. Vincent. Through Truxtun, the United States acquired an officer corps capable of more than independent, ship-to-ship engagements.

This did not escape Secretary Stoddert, who was a fervent advocate of the fleet battle instead of the *guerre de course* so popular in those days as the principal recourse of weak maritime nations. While Jefferson's partisans insisted that privateering was both the cheapest and most efficient means of coercing a maritime enemy, Stoddert foresightedly attempted to build a modest naval force which could provide respectable support for American policy. Arguing that logistics would make it awkward for a European nation to maintain a powerful fleet off the American coast, could such a fleet be spared by a potential enemy from the strategic requirements of the European and colonial theaters, Stoddert asked Congress in December 1798 for twelve 74-gun ships, twelve more frigates, and a commensurate cruiser force and shore establishment. After much heated debate, Congress compromised and authorized the construction of six ships.

Accepting the measure as a tacit endorsement, Stoddert boldly let contracts for eight ships of the line, hoping to find the funds in his budget for extra construction. With Stoddert's perceptive enthusiasm to supply capital ships and with Truxtun's demonstrated ability to organize squadrons, the United States Navy seemed ready to attain serious consideration in Europe. Stoddert's program was proved in value when Napoleon Bonaparte seized control of the French government in November 1799 and promptly put an end to the undeclared war with the United States.

A year later however Jefferson was elected President and his anti-navy party was swept into control of Congress.

THE BATTLE OF
THE NILE, AUGUST 1, 1798

The trifling hostilities between the United States and France were of small consequence in the over-all course of the war conducted by monarchs against France.

We left Napoleon Bonaparte, fresh from his triumph over Austria, assuming command of the French Army of England, which had been erected upon the hopes of the late Lazare Hoche. In December 1797, Napoleon approved plans for building gunboats sufficient to bear 30,000 troops. With great fanfare, in February 1798, he inspected the progress made in the Channel ports and boasted that the invasion would be launched in the spring. His intentional indiscretion perturbed the British far less than the news that the arsenal of Toulon had begun to bustle with the first real vigor since the days of Admiral Martin. The British Admiralty tended to ignore the ostentatious activity in the Channel ports because French capital ships had to win command of the narrow seas before invasion gunboats could sail. The Brest fleet was insufficient to defeat the British home fleet and the Spanish and Dutch navies had been prevented from coming to France by the battles of St. Vincent and Camperdown. Thanks to Napoleon's careful carelessness, it was reported that ten ships were to transfer from Toulon to Brest and, if possible, to bring the Spanish from Cadiz. Faced with such a potential concentration, the British were expected by Napoleon to mass their ships with fear and trembling in the Channel, while he quietly set off undisturbed to capture Egypt for a bridge to British wealth in India. Undeceived, the British Admiralty in May 1798 ordered Jervis at Cadiz to choose between sending a squadron to Toulon and going there himself with his fleet.

Preoccupied with watching the quiescent Mazarredo in Cadiz, the new Earl of St. Vincent had to weigh the possible objectives of the Toulon armament. The most damaging to the English sea war would be the loss of Portugal, where St. Vincent based his fleet. Closure of the Tagus River facilities would

THE MEDITERRANEAN

render the British unable to sustain major operations south of the Bay of Biscay. At all costs, St. Vincent had to avert such disaster. Like the Admiralty, he never suspected Egypt as a French objective. Ireland or Jamaica perhaps, but not the land of the pyramids. St. Vincent had already sent Nelson with a few ships to reconnoiter Toulon. With the moral courage which distinguished him in a navy of courageous men, St. Vincent accepted the consequences of dividing his force. Choosing to continue watching Mazarredo, he sent ten of his best ships, fully provisioned, to join Nelson in a virtually independent command.

Thus, after a costly absence of two years, the British flag was seen again in the Mediterranean. Of the Italian states, only Naples remained free of the French. Proud, ancient Venice had been coerced into giving France nine ships and five frigates, while Genoa had become little more than an appendage of Toulon. Naples was important to England principally because Naples was important enough to Austria for that country to consider renewing the war against France, if properly encouraged by British sea supremacy. Naples soon held more than military interest for Nelson, for it was there that he met Lady Hamilton.

A gale that dismasted Nelson's 74-gun flagship *Vanguard* drove his three ships to the lee of Sardinia. Profiting by the enforced absence, Napoleon's force sailed on May 19, 1798 in the wake of the gale. Napoleon's 38,000 troops were principally veterans of the Army of Italy, with which he had won his initial fame. The members of the middle-class Directory were more than happy to see the glorious general and his cohorts depart on an overseas conquest that was strategically unsound. Once again, success of a major French venture depended upon evading the British navy rather than upon winning command of the sea, but many Frenchmen who loved France were resigned to the probable loss of a potential dictator. The Directory thriftily did not risk too much. The naval escort consisted of 13 ships and nine frigates, plus 26 supporting vessels. Some of the ships had been condemned; all had material deficiencies. Crews were a quarter below proper complements. Supplies were barely sufficient to reach Egypt. The quixotic organization was headed by Vice Admiral François Paul Brueys, who was destined soon to give his life in his devotion to the magnetic Bonaparte. Subordinate admirals who survived the expedition were to find precedence in the new France of the Little Corporal's forging. The stars of Honoré Ganteaume and Pierre Villeneuve were to rise with Napoleon's, but the star of Captain Denis Decrès was to shine brightest of all, even though Decrès proved more deadly than Nelson in the role of Napoleon's naval nemesis.

Nelson proved to be deadly enough, although his start was unpromising. By May 28, Nelson and his three ships had returned to Toulon and discovered that the French had vanished. So, too, had the pair of frigates Nelson had left to continue the watch. Compelled to wait for reinforcement momentarily expected from St. Vincent, Nelson was in a state of frenzied uncertainty. Troubridge brought him ten more 74's on June 7 and news that the French had not passed Gibraltar. Indeed, on that day, Brueys was steering for Malta, his convoy swollen by additional transports from Genoa and Corsica. On June 19, after Napoleon had taken Malta, the French started for Egypt. Brueys imposed a blackout of news for Nelson by seizing all vessels that he encountered on his way.

The delay at Malta actually prevented a battle at sea. On June 14, Nelson was off Civita Vecchia, learning that the French had gone to Malta. On June 22, Nelson was off Cape Passaro learning that the French had left Malta and were steering to the east. Bold and direct, Nelson sailed straight for Alexandria, so positive about the correctness of his estimate that he did not bother to deploy his ships in a screening line. Unencumbered by transports, the 13 British ships of the line and single 50-gun ship made a swift passage. Presumably in hot pursuit, Nelson was actually ahead of the French, who were headed for Crete. During the night of June 25, Nelson crossed the French line of advance some 60 miles ahead. Consequently, he arrived at

Alexandria on June 29 to find that port still serene.

A better tactician than a strategist, Nelson instantly decided he had been too impulsive in weighing the evidence that had led him to Egypt. Fearing that he had left Naples to the mercy of the French, he hastily reversed course and made full sail. As he had been positive about Egypt, he was now certain about Naples, again to the costly extent of neglecting to deploy his ships in line abreast. While he sped towards Naples, the cumbersome French expedition was sprawled two days due west of Alexandria, creeping along the coast and quite safe from Nelson's flying column.

On July 1, 1798, Napoleon reached Alexandria, depriving history of a conclusive answer to what might have happened had Nelson and Napoleon collided at sea. English historians confidently hold that Napoleon was lucky; French historians as confidently hint that there would never have been a Trafalgar. In any event, Napoleon and his veterans reached the land of the Pharaohs, quickly shook off their seasickness, and swept down the Nile towards Cairo, their heavy equipment transported by a naval flotilla.

Unable to carry all his heavy ships into the shallow, cramped channels of Alexandria, Brueys went a dozen miles east to Aboukir Bay. Here he could still support the army during the critical days of establishing a firm foothold. Expecting momentary attack, Brueys preferred to fight at anchor, so that his unskilled crews could devote themselves to gunnery. Freed of transports, the fleet on July 7 anchored in column on a northerly heading less than two miles from the sandy, palm-studded hillocks of the Bay. The van ship, the *Guerrier,* was a mile and a half south of Bequières islet, on which Brueys mounted a puny battery of two mortars and four six-pounders which were optimistically intended to dissuade the British from attempting to double upon the anchored column. Clearing seaward broadsides for action, Brueys was at his height of battle readiness in the first few days of taking his position. Fresh from the spell of Napoleon, the fleet had high morale. However, Nelson did not

return to Alexandria from his foolish dash to Syracuse until August 1. By then the French fleet, in the words of a French historian, "had lost its soul."

Time, privations, sickness, heat, and lassitude steadily ate into the French ships. Harassed by a multitude of cares in the service of the army, Brueys came to neglect elementary precautions. Men were allowed to forage ashore, so that any ship could scarcely man a full broadside. Many other men were absent on duty with the army. Those who were left aboard felt that the English had forgotten them. Frigates on picket duty abandoned their stations at will and were not reprimanded for failure to chase strange sails. Gun drill was forgotten. Brueys became not so much complacent as convinced he could do no better than stay where he was.

When Nelson's arrival was reported to Brueys at 2 PM on August 1, 1798, he convened a council of war aboard his 120-gun flagship *Orient.* The council almost unanimously agreed that it would be foolhardy to risk combat under sail. Ganteaume, Villeneuve, and Decrès endorsed their commander's judgment that the stationary French fleet was well placed according to the experience of the American Revolution. "The reasoning of Brueys," wryly comments a modern French historian, "would perhaps have been good if the English squadron had for its leader one of those admirals who handled their ships as a *corps de ballet,* more preoccupied with maneuvering elegantly than destroying the enemy. Nelson had changed all that." [6]

Nelson had indeed changed all that—and more. In the two months of hunting Brueys, Nelson had also demolished the traditional barrier that set an admiral apart as a god from his subordinates. Loquacious, persuasive, and inspiring, Nelson descended from the isolation of Olympus. Captains dined at his table whenever possible. Endlessly discussing tactics, Nelson planted his views deeply into the minds of his officers. Something beyond duty to an admiral began to motivate the group of leaders who would be known to British hagiolatry as "Nelson's

[6] A. Thomazi, *Napoléon et ses Marins* (Paris, 1950), 51-52.

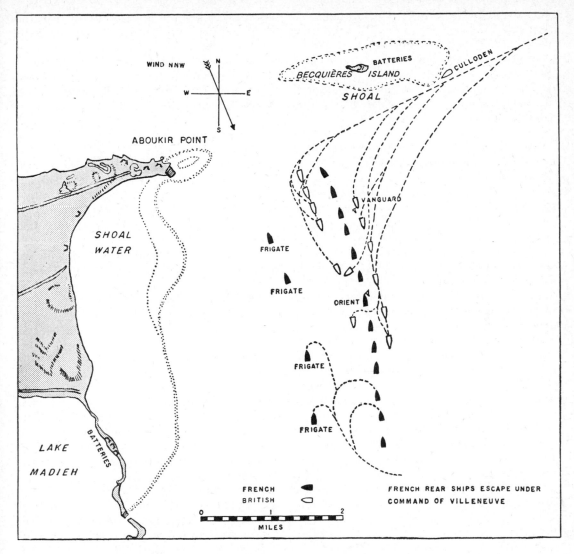

BATTLE OF THE NILE, AUGUST 1, 1798

Band of Brothers." Nelson's captains soon needed few signals to understand and execute his orders. Mahan defined doctrine as "the formation of a similar habit of thought." By the time of the Battle of the Nile, Nelson's captains could confidently exercise initiative and know they would be correct if they thereby damaged the enemy. With the insight that distinguishes great commanders, Nelson demolished one of the principal reasons for chaining ships into rigid column for battle. Previous admirals had perforce adhered to the limitations of the close line ahead because their command control vanished in clouds of powder smoke. Night or day, fog or sun, Nelson was spiritually on the quarter-deck of each ship under his flag. This was brilliantly demonstrated in the Battle of the Nile, which was fought under the usually blind conditions of night.

Nelson with his thirteen 74's sighted the French of equal number at 4 PM on August 1, 1798 and without hesitation pressed sail to enter battle. "By this time tomorrow," he said to his officers after a hasty dinner, "I shall have gained a peerage or Westminster Abbey." The wind was from the north-north-west, right into the teeth of the French had they desired to get underway. It was perfect for the tactics that the British now almost instinctively employed. Shortly after 6 PM, Captain Thomas Foley in the *Goliath* led the British column around Becquières. Nelson, having emancipated himself from usual tactics, had planned to concentrate two of his ships against each Frenchman. If shoal water permitted, this was to be done by forming a line on either side of the enemy; if that maneuver was impossible, then the doubling of firepower would be attained by tightening column to half the intervals of the French. Ships were to pay out on stern anchors in order to preserve some degree of mobility. Because all the British captains knew what to do, the battle, despite nightfall and shoals, developed as smoothly as though it had been rehearsed for months.

Ignoring the battery on Becquières, Foley majestically sailed across the bow of the *Guerrier,* eased to port, and commenced an engagement for which Brueys was wholly unprepared. Four ships followed Foley. The others, less Troubridge's *Culloden,* which went aground on Becquières shoal, crept into position on the seaward side. As the expert British settled into their work, darkness fell. The French fought blindly. Abruptly, about 10 PM, amidst the roar and flash of cannon, the *Orient* was set afire and exploded, carrying to eternity the bulk of her crew and the gallant person of Brueys, who had just died from his fourth wound. The shock of the great explosion was the climax of the battle. French resistance ebbed and in the confusion, Villeneuve at the rear of the line slipped away with two ships. He ultimately reached Malta, where he surrendered when the island fell to Nelson's blockade.

At dawn on August 2, Nelson, suffering from a severe scalp wound, was consoled by the sight of nine captured ships. Two more had been destroyed. The British had lost 218 killed and 677 wounded. French casualties could only be estimated at 1,700 killed or drowned, 1,500 wounded, and 2,000 captured.

The victory was the greatest attained in the long war. It proved to be even greater in its ultimate effects. Denis Decrès was going to be Minister of the Imperial Navy, in which Ganteaume and Villeneuve would command fleets. None of them forgot the horror of the Nile: "They preserved indelibly the memory of that fatal night, illuminated by the explosion of the flagship. All their acts henceforth would bear its seal." [7]

The victory indirectly gave the Royal Navy an indisputable moral ascendance when Napoleon, after rising to control of France, naturally but shortsightedly put his navy into the hands of the sailors he had known in the Mediterranean. The Battle of the Nile, then, was the turning point in the naval war that had yet another 17 years to run.

The political effects of Nelson's victory were enormous. The enemies of French Republicanism were heartened. Russia, whose navy had cooperated with the British since 1795, now sent an army to Italy and prepared another for an invasion of Holland. Austria joined Russia in the reconquest of Italy. To these formidable allies, Pitt was able to add Turkey, Portugal, and Naples to form the Second Coalition against France and Spain. Temporarily, before the weight of the new combination could be felt, the French held the upper hand in Italy, forcing King Ferdinand of Naples to flee to Sicily. Thanks to Nelson's personal concern for the welfare of the Neapolitan court, British sea power soon came to bear on the western side of Italy. The Adriatic fell to the interest of Russia, whose Admiral Ushakov with nine ships and seven frigates began operations against the Ionian Islands in November 1798. Ushakov was joined by four Turkish ships. Thus, in addition to cooperating with the Russian army that had marched to Italy via the Germanies, Ushakov was able to detach ships to assist the British, notably in the siege of Malta.

In Egypt, Napoleon watched developments in Europe and consolidated his own conquest. Stubbornly refusing to acknowl-

[7] René Jouan, *Histoire de la Marine Française* (Paris, 1950), 217.

edge the subtle, silent pressures of naval blockade, Napoleon made light of his increasingly impossible logistic situation. He was content that India was within his reach by land should he, at 29, choose to follow his star as a latter-day Alexander. However, Turkey compelled him to postpone the prospect of wresting India from the British. Egypt was tributary to Turkey, whose government declared war on the French Republic and began to collect armies in Syria and on the island of Rhodes. An exponent of the maxim that a good offense is the best defense, Napoleon decided to dictate a peace in Constantinople as he had in Vienna. Selecting 13,000 picked troops, Napoleon set out along the shore of the Near East to meet the Turkish army in Syria. At El Arish in February 1799, he defeated the Turkish vanguard and paroled prisoners only to find them again among the 4,000 Turks he captured at Jaffa in March. Having few supplies, he thereafter massacred his prisoners on a plea of military necessity and succeeding in creating a war unto death. After Jaffa, the Turks did not expect either to ask or to give quarter, and their ferocity was fully exploited by Napoleon's old enemy from Toulon, Sir William Sydney Smith.

Shortly before the Battle of the Nile, Smith escaped from his prison in Paris. During the years of his captivity, he had succeeded in convincing himself that Napoleon was responsible for his treatment as a political prisoner rather than one subject to military exchange. Arriving in London, Smith asked only to be sent to fight Napoleon. The British government gave him two ships and an extraordinary commission as joint Minister Plenipotentiary to Turkey with his brother. With the burning haste of a fanatic, Smith found his way to Napoleon's operations in Syria. Fate brought them together in March 1799 at the Crusaders' city of St. Jean d'Acre, where 3,000 Turks grimly awaited the French.

The old walled city was a box sitting on a corner of land, its south and west battlements washed by the sea. Ships could not be placed in a much better position to fight

an army which lacked artillery to drive them off. Nor did Napoleon, the professional artillerist, have enough of his favorite tools at hand. Sand and fatigue had induced him on his coastal march to entrust his heavy equipment to a naval flotilla of the kind that

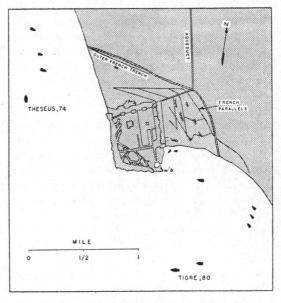

SIEGE OF ST. JEAN D'ACRE,
MARCH–MAY, 1799

had been so helpful on the Nile. Smith captured the little convoy and incorporated Napoleon's guns into the fortifications of Acre. The 80-gun *Tigre* was posted to fire along the eastern wall of the town and the 74-gun *Theseus* covered the northern approaches. Not content to remain at a distance from his foe, Smith took 500 marines and seamen into the town, and assumed command of the defense.

The siege began on March 18 and ended on May 20, 1799, after two score assaults had been personally directed by Napoleon and repelled by Smith's ubiquitous energy and courage. The deadliness of broadsides from the ships of the line was ultimately minimized by the parallels [8] of formal siege

---

[8] Parallels: trenches dug to shield siege engineers from artillery as they approached and undermined the walls of a fort or fortified position.

operations, but nothing could minimize Smith's ingenuity and determination. After 63 days, Napoleon accepted a loss of 5,000 men and set the battered remainder of his army into retreat. In putting this indelible stain upon Napoleon's military reputation, Smith sacrificed 66 killed and 113 wounded from his crews. The Sultan awarded him the same honors as those given to Nelson for the Nile, while Parliament voted him an annual pension of £1,000. Smith continued on active duty for the remainder of the war but he had reached the zenith of his glory.

"The fate of the Orient is in that paltry little town," Napoleon said to his devoted subordinate, Murat. Perhaps it had more correctly been the fate of Great Britain that rested in Acre. Ambition had led Napoleon to spurn the chance to lead Hoche's Army of England in favor of the Egyptian adventure. He had been able to explain, to his own and France's satisfaction, the loss of Brueys' fleet. Brueys had simply disobeyed Napoleon's orders. The humiliation of Acre, Napoleon explained away as only a reconnaissance in force. Despite his casuistic pen, Napoleon in a few short months had been sharply instructed in the capabilities of British sea power. After the Nile and Acre, it is dubious if he ever again seriously planned to expose his destiny to the full weight of the mighty ships that had withered the flower of his army before his eyes.

At the very least, Napoleon realized that there was no longer a future for him in Egypt. For a brief time, he was given cause to hope when, in response to his appeals after Nelson's victory, the Directory in January 1799 ordered the Brest fleet to the Mediterranean. The resulting performance merely amplified Napoleon's reasons for restraining his ambition to the shores of Europe.

THE CRUISE
OF ADMIRAL BRUIX, 1799

In response to urgent orders from the Directory, Vice Admiral Eustache Bruix stepped down from the office of Minister of Marine and personally assumed charge of preparations in Brest. On April 26, Bruix got to sea undetected when a heavy wind blew away the sentry frigates posted by Lord Bridport, who was then in command of England's Home Fleet. Bruix had 24 ships and ten frigates, hastily manned and more hastily equipped. His orders were ambiguous except in the strict injunction to enter the Mediterranean *sans combat*. The orders to Bridport, on the other hand, were too explicit. Upon learning that the Brest fleet had escaped, Bridport promptly sailed to the entrance to the Irish Sea, for the British government feared an invasion of Ireland. Thus, Bruix was allowed to get away safely.

On May 4, Bruix appeared to windward of Lord Keith, who maintained the Cadiz blockade with 15 ships while St. Vincent was ill at Gibraltar. As Keith formed a close-hauled line and hoped that the wind would continue to hold Mazarredo's 18 ships in port until the Brest fleet could be crippled, Bruix had a golden opportunity to test his strength against inferior numbers caught to leeward. Handcuffed by his orders however, Bruix held tantalizingly aloof until a sudden gale enabled him to pass the Straits peacefully. St. Vincent had assumed that England had absolute command of the Mediterranean. He had scattered his force into detachments to take Minorca, attack Malta, guard Sicily, and blockade Alexandria, while others cooperated with Ushakov. The British and Russians were thus exposed to defeat in detail by a swift, aggressive foe.

Fortunately for Allied interests, Bruix was not aggressive. Storm and collisions during the entry into the Mediterranean induced him to throw away the precious boon of strategic surprise, although he thereby anticipated a change in his basic orders. On May 13, he limped into Toulon, far from Egypt, allowing ample time for British cruisers to spread the alarm. He found new instructions from the Directory. Affairs were so deteriorating in northern Italy that while Napoleon was making his last assault upon Acre, Bruix was sent on a trifling logistic mission to Genoa. This delay obviously made it prohibitively dangerous for Bruix to revert to his original mission of succoring Napoleon's expedition, although St. Vincent did little to merit the French compliment to his efficiency. Of all Britons who should have appreciated the need to mass in the face of a potential French-Spanish force of 40 ships, St. Vincent split his 33 ships with Nelson at Naples. Of all Britons who should have envisaged the enormous consequences of successfully tracking down the Brest fleet, St. Vincent paradoxically behaved like a French traditionalist, clinging to his newly-won foothold upon Minorca as the point most likely to be threatened by the combined enemy. When illness obliged him to go ashore at Minorca, he did not entirely relinquish command to Lord Keith, who hunted Bruix into the Gulf of Genoa. Sighting was only a matter of a few hours more when Keith received unequivocal orders from St. Vincent to put about. Mazarredo had shifted from Cadiz to Cartagena to facilitate juncture with Bruix, and St. Vincent chose to leave his favorite, Nelson, with 18 ships at Sicily in favor of recalling Keith to stand between Bruix and Mazarredo. Keith was almost certain that Bruix was just beyond the horizon, but a lifetime of subordination bade him return to Minorca. On June 15, shortly after dropping anchor at the new British base, Keith had to summon all of his sense of loyalty, for St. Vincent finally admitted physical collapse and formally relinquished command. St. Vincent returned in his flagship to England and adulation, having given his country two victories by allowing Nelson to exercise initiative. By denying Keith a measure of the same tolerance, St. Vincent possibly missed an opportunity to rid England of the Brest fleet as further luster to his well-earned glory. At last unfettered, Keith retraced his steps, but only succeeded in capturing a squadron of three frigates and two brigs, which were remnants of Brueys' shattered force.

Every hour that Keith scoured the Riviera and the Italian coast, he went further from Bruix, who made rendezvous on June 22 with Mazarredo at Cartagena. The calamity that St. Vincent had feared had taken place: the French and Spanish had joined 40 ships against Keith's 19 and Nelson's 18 (which in-cluded three Portuguese). If the French and Spanish proved to be indifferent allies, Keith proved to be unable to make the hero of the Nile forsake dalliance in Sicily. Although Russian-Austrian armies brilliantly led by Suvorov were herding the French into the Alps, Nelson disobeyed Keith's orders to join, obstinately persisting in devoting his strength to the minor matter of assisting the King of Naples in a civil war that ensued upon the French evacuation of southern Italy. Only a reinforcement of twelve ships from England enabled Keith to proceed with assurance.

Happily for the reputations of St. Vincent and Nelson, Bruix and Mazarredo could not agree on a course of action in the Mediterranean, and so did nothing. Since the British were thoroughly aroused, Bruix and Mazarredo elected to retire to Cadiz, which they reached on July 10. Then, in an aberration of Spanish policy, Mazarredo was ordered to go with Bruix to Brest. Thus, unmarred by British shot, 40 ships and 15 minor warships on August 5, 1799 accomplished what St. Vincent had prevented two years before in the battle which earned him his title. The French and Spanish fleets were snug in Brest, with the indefatigable Keith one unlucky day behind. What the British Admiralty had two years before expected to be catastrophic was now thankfully accepted as a stabilization of the naval situation. Enemy fleets, although combined, were at least pinned down under close observation.[9] Nelson's insubordination was mildly rebuked by the Admiralty and Keith consented to assume the duties of Commander in Chief of the Mediterranean.

The episode represented a tremendous waste of naval effort, from which only Keith derived any stature. Although uneventful, Bruix's cruise did have important consequences. Napoleon was a keen observer. If he noted the lack of enterprise in French admirals, he saw no less the effect upon the British of a French fleet at sea. In view of Nelson's two-month chase of Brueys and Keith's equally long, futile pursuit of Bruix,

---

[9] For an interesting account of the stay of the Spanish fleet in Brest, see J. M. Carlan, *Navios En Secuestro: La Escuadra Española del Oceano en Brest (1799-1802)*; Madrid, 1951.

Napoleon could not be too severely condemned for forming a contemptuous opinion of the strategic abilities of British admirals. It was upon his opinion of Britsh reactions to French movements that he based the plans that culminated in the Trafalgar campaign of 1805.

In the meantime, disgusted by Bruix's failure to send even a frigate to Alexandria, Napoleon conceded that all was lost in Egypt. On August 23, 1799, he abandoned his faithful army. With 400 carefully chosen subordinates aboard a handful of small vessels, he slipped away from Egypt. Eluding enemy cruisers, Ganteaume cautiously groped towards France, finally landing Napoleon at Fréjus on October 9. By the 16th, Napoleon was in Paris, where he learned of France's defeats on all fronts, except in his own theater. Having exercised strict censorship over communications from Egypt, Napoleon was saluted as the only victorious general serving the Republic. Popular acclaim also hinted that the oligarchic Directory had outlived its usefulness. The people of France hungered for unified leadership. Members of the bourgeoisie plotted to give France peace and stability, and a man of military glory was needed to cloak their plans. Courted, Napoleon quickly consented, and on November 10, 1799 a *coup d'état* made him the First Consul of three men who constituted themselves the executive power of France. The other two individuals proved to be insignificant: Napoleon had come to the height of power.

England was now confronted with war to the death—when Napoleon was ready.

PERFECT
AMPHIBIOUS ASSAULT
AT ABOUKIR, 1801

The French Army marooned in Egypt had a brief history after Napoleon deserted it. Command devolved upon Jean Baptiste Kléber, who, able and brave, made the best of an impossible situation. Cut off from military supplies, decimated by pestilence, the

Army of Egypt rapidly lost ability to fight. Kléber sensibly opened negotiations with Turkey, offering to evacuate Egypt if repatriated by Turkish ships. Sir William Sydney Smith, overstepping his authority, opposed acceptance of the offer because it slighted England's alliance of January 1799 with Turkey and Russia. As a nondescript Turkish army gathered in Syria, Smith impetuously landed 3,000 Turks at Damietta. These were easily crushed by 1,000 French regulars, who displayed ominous superiority by capturing twice their own number and driving the rest into the sea. His confidence somewhat shaken, Smith completely reversed himself and sponsored the Treaty of El Arish, which accepted Kléber's terms. The treaty was signed late in January 1800.

Lord Keith, worried about the stubborn resistance of blockaded Malta and personally cooperating with Austrian operations reducing Genoa, was aghast at the news of Smith's activities. Keith promptly repudiated the treaty when it came into his hands, because the British government was determined that no Frenchman would return to France from Egypt except as a prisoner. Furious, Kléber routed the Turks arrayed against him, and then was assassinated by Egyptian insurrectionists. General Menou succeeded Kléber and undertook to punish perfidious enemies who signed treaties only to disavow them. Keith was willing to take up the challenge by landing a British army in Egypt but was held in check until Genoa capitulated in June 1800.

The British government eagerly accepted Keith's suggestion for offensive action, if only because the British army needed a victory after being driven out of Holland for a second time in 1799. If anyone could carry the army to victory, Keith was the man. Almost as though he had been born for amphibious operations, Keith had acquired experience that enabled him to grasp military problems. As a captain during the American Revolution, he had led a marine battalion in the capture of Charleston. Still a captain, he had brilliantly served ashore during the siege of Toulon in 1793. Responsible for embarking the Allied troops and Royalists when Lord Hood evacuated the town, Keith won a reputation in England as the hero of the defense equivalent to the reputation won by Napoleon in France as the hero of the assault. Well rewarded, and promoted to rear admiral, Keith had been a natural choice in 1795 for commander in chief of the expedition that descended upon Cape Town. The British army knew and trusted Keith. It was not an accident that the defeat of Menou in Egypt began with his flawlessly executed amphibious assault upon the very shores of the Bay that had witnessed Nelson's annihilation of Brueys.

However, the Egyptian expedition was slow getting underway. Napoleon's dazzling victory at Marengo on June 14, 1800 broke the fighting spirit of the Austrians, and Italy was again overrun by the French. Keith was obliged to duplicate his feat at Toulon by evacuating Genoa. Then the jackals of North Africa, sensing a decline in England's fortunes, began to nibble at British commerce. Keith was preparing to demonstrate against Algiers when orders reached him in August 1800 to attack Cadiz with the troops that had been collecting at Minorca and Gibraltar for the Egyptian venture.

Somewhat dubious about the practicality of attacking Cadiz at the advent of the bad weather season, Keith on October 4, 1800 brought 21,000 troops before the ancient seaport. General Sir Ralph Abercromby, a veteran of the colonial wars and Holland, was in command. An epidemic of yellow fever was rampant in the town and the Governor asked the British in the name of humanity to leave the suffering populace in peace. However, the Governor refused to surrender the remnants of Mazarredo's fleet as the price of British compliance. Abercromby and Keith were unable to enforce their demand when the weather turned against them. With an onshore wind blowing, Keith hesitated to risk the unpracticed troops in a landing from ships that had to lie out several leagues from the shore. Inasmuch as the army had become hypersensitive about prestige, relations between the British commanders were strained until the steadily increasing surf justified Keith's reluctance. The frustrated expedition

returned to Gibraltar and learned that the decision to break off operations at Cadiz happily anticipated orders to do so. The original destination was to be reached as soon as possible. Napoleon had consolidated his position on the Continent and was showing a strong intent to extricate Menou. London wished the French army in Egypt to be destroyed.

As in the instance of the Rochefort expedition in 1757, participants in the Cadiz fiasco turned the experience to good account. Keith and Abercromby studied their failure with a view to eliminating any repetition and at length relearned the old lesson that success in amphibious assault requires the utmost thoroughness in preparation and training. The expedition was delayed briefly as a result of Malta's surrender in September 1800, but the British hold on the rocky island was soon secure. Malta was used as a staging area, although unsuited to the training exercises that Keith and Abercromby had in mind. Finally 17,000 troops in 100 transports escorted by 19 men-of-war set out for a rendezvous with the Turks. On January 1, 1801 the expedition skillfully slipped through the narrow channel into Marmorice Bay, which was situated in Turkish territory some 30 miles north of Rhodes. The great land-locked bay, ringed with wild, forested shores, was ideal for secret landing. The British made the most of their privacy.

The descent upon Egyptian soil was not to be haphazard. The blunders of previous amphibious operations became the foundation of a sound operations plan. Seven weeks of continual debarkation and landing practice evolved a three-wave attack system. The first wave consisted of 58 flatboats that were deployed on a 3,000 yard front and carried 3,000 infantry. The second wave carried 2,700 infantrymen in 90 cutters. The third wave had seamen in 37 launches towing 14 launches loaded with field artillery units. Signals, control ships, guides, and gunboat fire support were all carefully developed. All that could be foreseen was tested in drill and crystallized into an elaborate series of instructions. The troops and seamen drilled until everyone clearly understood what

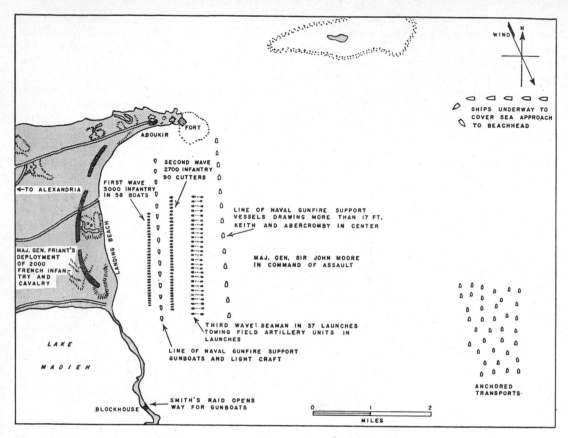

WIND N

SHIPS UNDERWAY TO COVER SEA APPROACH TO BEACHHEAD

FORT

ABOUKIR

SECOND WAVE 2700 INFANTRY 90 CUTTERS

FIRST WAVE 3000 INFANTRY IN 58 BOATS

←TO ALEXANDRIA

LINE OF NAVAL GUNFIRE SUPPORT VESSELS DRAWING MORE THAN 17 FT. KEITH AND ABERCROMBY IN CENTER

MAJ. GEN. FRIANT'S DEPLOYMENT OF 2000 FRENCH INFANTRY AND CAVALRY

MAJ. GEN. SIR JOHN MOORE IN COMMAND OF ASSAULT

THIRD WAVE: SEAMAN IN 37 LAUNCHES TOWING FIELD ARTILLERY UNITS IN LAUNCHES

LAKE MADIEH

LINE OF NAVAL GUNFIRE SUPPORT GUNBOATS AND LIGHT CRAFT

ANCHORED TRANSPORTS

BLOCKHOUSE

SMITH'S RAID OPENS WAY FOR GUNBOATS

0   1   2
MILES

AMPHIBIOUS ASSAULT AT ABOUKIR, MARCH 8, 1801

would happen about him. The force had the further blessing of homogeneity because the Turks had neither the patience nor the desire to go to war in such a manner.

Keith had only seven ships to cover the expedition because Napoleon had sent the Brest fleet to sea again under the command of Ganteaume, and Keith had prudently left the bulk of his fleet under the command of Rear Admiral Sir Richard Bickerton at Minorca. Ganteaume had the seven fastest ships of the Brest fleet and 5,000 troops to land in Egypt, but Keith was correct in assuming that nothing would come of the attempt to reinforce Menou.[10] Russian am-

bition in the Adriatic worried him far more.

On March 2, 1801, Keith brought Abercromby into Aboukir Bay. A strong, northerly wind built up a sea-swell and made landing impossible until the early morning of March 8. The week's delay provided ample time for the French to mount a strong defense and deprived the British of a *coup de main*. There was no question of a surprise landing; there had to be an assault. Sir Wil-

[10] Ganteaume's cruise was a repetition of the indecision that had marred the chances of Bruix. Sailing from Brest on January 23, 1801, Ganteaume captured a British packet after entering the Mediterranean in early February. Learning of Keith's

presence off Egypt, Ganteaume irresolutely made for Toulon. Three times Ganteaume was sent by Napoleon to execute his orders and finally, in early June, came within view of Alexandria, which by then had fallen to the British. Attempting to land his troops well to the west of Alexandria, Ganteaume was frightened by British cruisers and made for Toulon. His chief success consisted in skillful evasion of the detachments hunting him, while he captured a handful of small warships and a lone 74-gun ship of the line.

liam Sydney Smith led a daring raid which opened a way for gunboat entry into Lake Madieh. Menou having lost his head upon receiving news of the British arrival, left the defense in the hands of Major General Louis Friant, who did his best with the garrison of Alexandria. Leaving the city to be guarded by seamen and invalid soldiers, Friant placed 2,000 troops on the hills overlooking the beach. The heights concealed the defense positions from gunboats and the situation was one in which a respectable force might have thrown back an attack.

Aboukir beach was at the end of a leg of land running west to Alexandria. The beach was scarcely 4,000 yards long, curving in the north into a slender hook of land some thousand yards out in the bay. This was Aboukir Point, which mounted a castle whose guns obliged Abercromby to plan to land on the southern 3,000 yards of the beach. A lofty sandhill in the middle of the hilly, wooded shore was the natural objective for the attack, which started to assemble at 2 AM on March 8.

At dawn, the three waves halted some two miles from the beach to rest and to perfect their alignment. Each man carried 60 rounds of ammunition, an entrenching tool, and a full canteen. Major General Sir John Moore commanded the force and at 8 AM gave the order to advance. Not since Louisburg and Quebec had British troops undertaken such a frontal assault, but Moore had been cast in the mold of the dedicated James Wolfe.

Keith's ships were restrained by shoal water to a distance too great to assist the assault without endangering Moore's troops.[11] Taking a position to guard against the unlikely possibility of being interrupted by Ganteaume's rumored squadron, Keith entrusted close gunfire support to gunboats, which began to bombard the unseen enemy.

The advancing waves encountered bounding shot and soaring shells from Aboukir

Castle and five batteries emplaced in the sandhills. As the range closed to that of grape and canister, splattering the gently swelling sea and close-packed boats, Friant left cover and formed his infantry on the beach to greet the attackers with dragoons. In fine fashion applauded by the British, Friant's troops delivered their volleys and withdrew steadily to their prepared positions, the maneuver screened by the dragoons, who here and there galloped into the surf to cut and thrust at the red-coated soldiery cramped in battered boats.

Despite Friant, Moore's first wave grounded almost simultaneously. Stubborn French were driven off and units formed as smoothly as they had in the peaceful seclusion of Marmorice Bay. Closing ranks about fallen comrades, the British stolidly studied the broken ground before them, searched out the spitting flashes of enemy muskets, and waited to be turned loose. When the first wave was ready, Moore personally led a charge up the central sandhill. The French fought well but British bayonets sufficed. Moore attained the height from which he could view the central plain and found Friant organizing a retreat to Alexandria. With the British ashore, Friant did not propose to continue a hopeless fight against superior numbers. Some of his subordinates however hotheadedly clung to their positions, and desperate fighting continued in the hills, gradually dying into the flickers of sniping and then into silence. For their beachhead, so smoothly won by sunset of March 8, the British paid 124 dead and 587 wounded. Friant's casualties were less than a hundred.[12]

Too late, Menou sent reinforcements to the invasion area. Two battles lay before the British and Alexandria, and the second cost the life of Sir Ralph Abercromby, but the end was inevitable. The British had strong communications across the Mediterranean; the French had only an occasional small craft

[11] Heavy guns of the period might attain a range of three miles, but did so in a series of bounces known as "grazes." The first graze for a 32-pounder would be something like 1,500 yards. Shoal water kept Keith from coming closer than 3,000 yards at best; hence his shot would have bounced through Moore's assault waves.

[12] Eyewitness accounts of the assault on Aboukir are generally excellent. For a British version, see Sir John Fortescue's edition of Sir Henry Bunbury's *Narrative of Some Passages in the Great War With France* (London, 1927). For a French version, see *Histoire de l'Expédition Française en Égypte,* 10 vols. (Paris, 1830-1836), VIII.

that slipped through enemy cruisers. Menou was shut up in besieged Alexandria, while the British went up the Nile to Cairo. By early June 1801, Cairo capitulated; by early September, even French fanatics agreed to surrender.

The entire campaign had been a magnificent success, coming as a climax to eight long years of wearying defeats, reverses, and failures of the British Army. The results were tremendous. As a participant, Sir Henry Bunbury said, "It revived confidence and an honourable pride in our military service. The British nation, exulting in the proved valour and the triumphs of their army, felt once more that they might rely upon their officers and soldiers as securely as they had long relied upon their seamen." Thus, the British war machine had found itself in battle on sea and land, and was ready for the challenge of the Corsican.

For his part, Napoleon had the marooned army in Egypt on his conscience. Ganteaume's failure on the heels of Bruix's bootless effort did not end Napoleon's plans to rescue his faithful friends. As the British troops hunted down random units of enemy garrisons and tightened the noose about Menou in Alexandria, Napoleon in August 1801 collected 20,000 troops at Otranto to be carried to Egypt, where their fresh strength would overwhelm the audacious redcoats. Bruix was given a second chance at command. With five ships from Rochefort, combined with six purchased from the Cadiz fleet and manned by Frenchmen, Bruix was to call three ships from Toulon to Cadiz. The 14 French ships were to be joined by six Spaniards. Bruix was to have a respectable fleet of 20 ships to execute his mission. However, the preliminary moves toward the naval concentration in Cadiz early in July at last came within range of British guns, whereupon the project was abandoned. Because the French fleet had twice sent elements harmlessly about the Mediterranean, Napoleon may have been justified in assuming that the game might continue forever, but a junior British flag officer, Sir James Saumarez, proved more fortunate than his seniors.

Rear Admiral Durand Linois, an officer of the Old Navy who had lost an eye proving his courage in battle, left Toulon in mid-June 1801 with three ships and a frigate. On July 4, having learned from a captured sloop that a British squadron was loose in the Straits, Linois anchored in line in the roadstead of Algeciras, some six miles west of Gibraltar. Throwing up batteries on the nearby shore and enlisting the help of Spanish gunboats, Linois awaited the onslaught of British pursuers. Saumarez, cruising before Cadiz, where a division of six ships under Moreno (the Spanish hero of the Battle of Cape St. Vincent) was bending on sail, hastened to attack Linois while there was a chance to crush him with so small a force.

Shortly after 8 AM on July 6, Saumarez anchored in line off the French position and opened fire. Craftily, Linois had given himself some sea room. When the action was well-joined and British shot had hit home, Linois warped his ships about closer to the shore and presented undamaged broadsides. The wind was feeble and afforded little control, so that when Saumarez attempted to duplicate the maneuver and keep the range closed, he had the mortification of seeing one of his ships go helplessly aground beyond the range of assistance. This was the 74-gun *Hannibal*, commanded by a captain who had been at the Nile, and who attempted to duplicate Foley's doubling of the line. With the *Hannibal* hard aground beyond the head of the French line, Saumarez broke off action at 1:35 PM and grimly made for Gibraltar, where the action had been watched with astonishment by the officers and men of the garrison.

It was a shock to learn that the despised French could bite and Saumarez coldly pressed repairs so that he could wipe the shame from his reputation. On July 9, Moreno's squadron sailed into Algeciras. The enemy now had nine ships plus the captured *Hannibal*, and Moreno was well respected by the British as an excellent commander under sail. Two of the Spaniards carried 112 guns each and were considered by the reckoning of the period to be equal to four 74's.

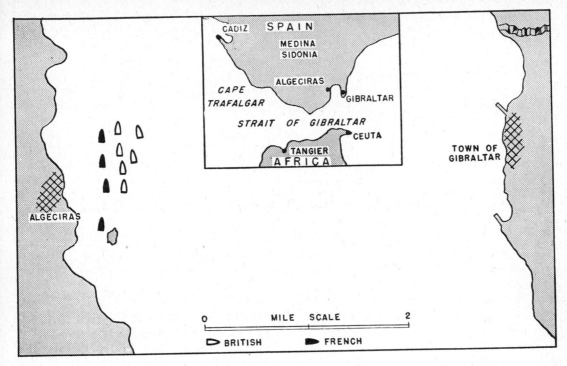

BATTLE OF ALGECIRAS, JULY 6, 1801

Saumarez's largest ship was the 80-gun *Caesar,* but he willingly faced odds of two to one.

Waiting for the French-Spanish force to make for Cadiz, Saumarez was ready in the evening of July 12 when Moreno sortied. About midnight in a running chase, Saumarez came within gunshot. The action was confused. The Spanish 112's mistakenly began firing into each other, causing fires in both. Moreno proved unequal to controlling his force in a night battle and when morning came, Saumarez was triumphant. The *Hannibal* remained in French hands, but the British had captured a 74 to replace her.

Seven ships straggled into Cadiz, their officers doubtful about making another trial with British arms. Saumarez returned to a jubilant Gibraltar.

This pair of engagements concluded, for a time, naval activities in the Mediterranean. Napoleon turned his back on his beleaguered troops in Egypt and reluctantly endorsed the opinion of the late Lazare Hoche that France's difficulties with the British could best be resolved by invading England. Hoche's Army of England was reconstituted. An invasion force known as the Boulogne Flotilla was begun on the foundations of Hoche's well-laid plans.

10

The Atlantic Front, 1798-1802

NELSON'S VICTORY OF THE Nile had enabled Pitt in the autumn of 1798 to form the Second Coalition consisting of England, Russia, Austria, Portugal, Turkey and the Kingdom of the Two Sicilies. The new allies concerted three major blows at France. The first was a drive through Switzerland by the Austrian army under Archduke Charles. The second was an invasion of the northern Italian states by a Russo-Austrian army under the Russian Marshal Suvorov. The third was an Anglo-Russian amphibious invasion of Holland.

This last operation grew out of British fear of the Dutch fleet's potential in invasion attempts against the British Isles. There was legitimate cause for concern. In the summer and autumn of 1798, the French Directory prepared no less than seven expeditions to execute such missions as stimulating and supporting rebellion in Ireland. Only one of these expeditions reached its destination. In late August 1798, General Humbert landed at Killala with 1,000 men and a corps of officers to provide leadership for Irish volunteers. On this occasion, the Irish displayed amazing docility, shunning Humbert, who skirmished with redcoats for a month before disgustedly surrendering to the 30,000 men of General Cornwallis, the loser at York-

town. The size of the force given to Cornwallis exemplified British anxiety.

In the face of such minor threats, the British had been active. A young naval captain, Home Riggs Popham, glowed with ideas, one of which was to enlist fishermen and smugglers into a loose militia organization known as "Sea Fencibles." Rugged individualism made a mockery of the Fencible project, but Popham was a man of action. Bonaparte was pressing the exhausted Dutch to supply hundreds of gunboats for various raids. Completion of a 14-mile, broad canal from Bruges to Ostend made it possible to assemble gunboats without British interference. Popham had resided in Flanders for many years, and on the basis of his knowledge of the coast proposed to destroy the locks and sluices at Ostend. The British army, being shaken down by reforms, sought offensive activities and supported Popham's proposal despite Admiralty indifference. Accordingly, Major General Eyre Coote was supplied 1,400 men, including a heavy backbone of Guards companies, and sent with a small, light squadron under Popham to execute a commando raid.

In the small hours of May 19, 1798, Popham hove to off Ostend and landed Coote. The movement was discovered towards dawn and Popham commenced shelling the small town with bomb-vessels, enabling Coote to make his way against minor interference to the vital locks. Planting 150 barrels of gunpowder, the raiding party blew up the locks and withdrew towards the beach with only one casualty. Unfortunately for Coote, wind had lashed the surf too high for re-embarkation. The British entrenched in the sandhills on the beach and steeled themselves for counterattack. The following dawn, columns of French troops assailed Coote's position. For more than two hours, the steady British regulars held their own, unaided by the helpless Popham, until Coote was wounded. Colonel Burrard, the second-in-command, was unwilling to sacrifice life uselessly. When two hundred casualties sprawled in the British trenches and hope for victory had passed, Burrard surrendered. The project was tantamount to a failure, costing far more than it permanently achieved. The canal soon functioned and enabled enemy preparations to continue. Popham attempted to shrug off the failure by proposing raids to burn masses of gunboats at Flushing and Calais.

Popham's voluminous letters were shelved, and the British government shortly after the Ostend raid made a momentous decision. Prior to the summer of 1798, British strategy had been deeply rooted in the commercial dictates of the Seven Years' War and the American Revolution. The British Army had been employed in the colonies instead of in Europe. With the evacuation of Santo Domingo in 1798 Dundas in the War Office returned the major effort of the army to continental affairs. Henceforward, the British army was to be used in direct support of the British navy. Dundas wished to capture and demolish naval facilities in Europe, and drew up a sample plan for sending 12,000 men on such a mission to Ferrol. The Admiralty, delighted by the change from the man-killing emphasis upon the West Indies, requested leave to exploit the command of the sea in the Mediterranean following the Nile Victory. In November 1798, Dundas proposed an operation easier to support than one in Spain: since the Dutch, as well as the Spanish, could lend naval power to the French, Dundas urged his colleagues in the cabinet to invade Holland. The Admiralty reluctantly assented. Holland was the only real competitor to Great Britain in wealth and industry, and so an invasion would be popular with British businessmen. Mercantile interests however insisted that neither Ceylon nor Cape Town be offered to the Dutch as an inducement to submit peacefully to the seizure of their ships. Upon such a basis, the project was doomed from its conception. Where the French had been pinning hopes for invasion success upon side-stepping the British naval forces which French ships could not match, the British had come to compensate for their lack of an adequate army by cherishing the illusion that the people of an invaded country would immediately flock to their standard. Certainly, the alliance with revolutionary France was repugnant to most Dutchmen, but the British who had captured and wanted to keep Ceylon and Cape Town did not appear as noble liberators to the sorely taxed Dutch. Since the Helder Expedition of 1799 depended for success upon Dutch cooperation, it could not succeed.

BRITISH REBUFF IN HOLLAND, 1799

Even though Britons began to come forward voluntarily for service in their army when emphasis upon campaigning in the deadly West Indies was shifted to more healthy climes, the British army had too many garrison commitments to furnish a field force of 30,000 men upon short notice. An ally was needed. Accordingly, a treaty was negotiated with Paul of Russia late in 1798 to furnish 45,000 men under subsidy. In addition, Paul was to attempt to revive the Armed Neutrality of 1780 with Prussia, Denmark, and Sweden aligned against France. Captain Popham arranged the transport details for the Russian troops, whose number was finally reduced to 18,000 in recognition of heavy Russian commitments to the Italian campaign. The British were obliged to furnish the major portion of manpower, which

Dundas accomplished by enlisting militia, ultimately sending 38,000 men into Holland. Had the militia response been foreseen as well as the ensuing difficulties with the Russian contingent, the expedition could easily have been exclusively a British venture, and the whole might have had happier results.

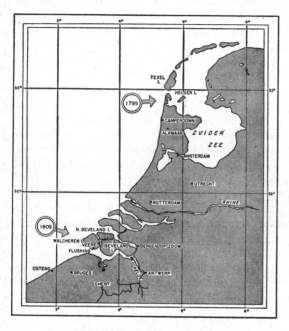

THE DUTCH COAST

Dundas laid down three objectives. First, a diversion was to be created in favor of the Austrians and Russians fighting in Switzerland and Germany; two, the Prince of Orange was to be restored and the French expelled; and lastly, the Dutch navy was to be impounded. Despite the grave forebodings of seasoned generals who forecast an inglorious, bogged-down operation and the outright opposition of Admiral Duncan, the expedition was organized. Lieutenant General Sir Ralph Abercromby was appointed to command during the initial phase of establishing the troops ashore until the Duke of York should arrive to supersede him. A small naval force, including two Russian ships, was placed under Vice Admiral Sir Andrew Mitchell with authority to draw upon Duncan for support during the landing. Aber-

cromby was considered the best professional soldier of his rank; Mitchell was not his equal. In Lord St. Vincent's trenchant opinion, Mitchell was "a bullet-headed centurion, and never would have been higher in the best times of the Roman Republic."

Anxious for a swift, powerful campaign, Abercromby wanted to wait for the Russians to arrive. Delays seemed endless to Pitt, who had a political view of the matter, and as the summer melted away, he finally insisted on action. Pitt was positive that Abercromby would have little fighting to do, because the arrival of British troops would presumably explode a revolt in favor of the Prince of Orange. Consequently, in mid-August 1799, two hundred ships set sail for a covering rendezvous with Duncan off the Helder.

Unseasonably bad weather descended upon the amphibious force, which was held for six days unable to land. More than enough time was presented to the Franco-Dutch defenders to assemble opposite the threatening fleet. General Daendels collected 10,000 men to meet Abercromby, but not in pitched battle on the beaches. Since Mitchell's broadsides could sweep the landing area, Daendels dug his force into the ridges of sandhills overlooking the beaches. The wily Dutch general preferred to conserve his force for a fight on his own terms in the sand dunes.

Early in the morning of August 27 the weather proved suitable for disembarking, whereupon Mitchell's force commenced firing blindly at the shore. Abercromby could not complain about the enthusiasm of his gunfire support. He could complain, and did, about the abruptly revealed inadequacies in Mitchell's preparations for landing the troops. There were not enough flatboats nor was there a well-defined organization. England's first major amphibious assault in the war bumbled ashore in cheerful confusion. Troops were thrown on the beach without any regard for company or regimental structure. A Russian ship of the line went aground. Heavy surf tumbled flatboats and drowned heavily-laden troops. British officers set a high standard of resourcefulness in snapping their bedraggled redcoats into improvised units before attacking the ridge above them.

The Dutch had a chance to smash the British where they stood but in accordance with plans, their center was withdrawing to leave an invitingly soft spot to lure the British beyond reach of naval gunfire support. Strong Dutch forces waited on either flank to participate in a later-day Cannae. Abercromby's men scrambled up the sand slopes out of sight of Mitchell's guncrews. Musketry rattled throughout the day in the rolling, scrub-patched hills. Daendels did his best; Abercromby did better. At sunset, Daendels disengaged his center and left, withdrawing four miles to the south. Some 2,000 men were left in the batteries commanding the Helder until their commander decided to escape while he could. The patrols of Major General John Moore reported the evacuation of the key batteries and Moore energetically marched through the night to occupy the position.

At dawn, the way to the Zuider Zee was open. Mitchell cautiously sounded his way through the shallow sea in chase of the small Dutch fleet. On August 30, he demanded that the Dutch fleet be surrendered in the name of the Prince of Orange. The Dutch Admiral capitulated instantly, treating as an ally instead of as an enemy. Mitchell's acceptance of the Dutch attitude embarrassed Pitt and Dundas, who wanted the Dutch fleet without any hampering restrictions. In any case, ten ships and 14 frigates and 6,000 prime seamen passed from French control into British custody, and Dutch sea power was temporarily obliterated. Duncan's ships could be distributed among the other British fleets, for there was no longer need for vigil in the North Sea.

The naval objective of his expedition completely fulfilled, Abercromby might have evacuated the Helder peninsula and claimed a modest success. The political and strategic objectives remained however, and so he patiently stood to arms waiting for the Dutch to rally to him in the name of their Stadtholder. The Dutch belied Pitt and Dundas, refusing to follow the example set by their seamen. Indeed, Dutch troops remained loyal to the French, and by early September began a campaign to drive the British out of Holland. In mid-September, Abercromby was relieved in command by the Duke of York, who was superb in an office and irresolute in the field. The Russians arrived to complicate British maneuvers and battle plans. By October 18, 1799, the weary British were compelled to quit campaigning and ingloriously left Holland, having turned the Dutch against them and driven a wedge into relations with Russia.[1] As the last Briton sailed home, Napoleon seized France.

The chief value of the entire operation was the training received by Sir Ralph Abercromby on the very first day. We have seen how his training flowered in the flawless landing at Aboukir in 1801.

For Napoleon, who wished to consolidate his power as First Consul, British humiliation in Holland seemed to offer an opening for peace overtures. Besides, with Bruix and the Spanish fleet in Brest, he had steel to suggest an unmentioned alternative in the letter he penned to George III on Christmas Day 1799. However, Pitt and his cabinet did not appreciate the gesture. Pitt had found a new instrument to implement his pay-as-you-go doctrine of waging war and had inaugurated an income tax graduated to ten per cent. Armed with this new fiscal strength, Pitt was emboldened to insist that any peace would have to be on British terms, which meant retention of all British conquests in the war. To this, Napoleon could not agree and he went ahead with his plans to crush Austria.

The busy brain of Henry Dundas, Secretary of State for War, was also alive with plans. Far from being alarmed by the presence of Bruix and Mazarredo in Brest, Dundas saw only a joyous opportunity to clarify the entire naval situation by a single blow—an attack on Brest itself.

---

[1] Through the incompetence of their commander, 3,000 Russians were captured by the French. Napoleon, when he became First Consul, treated these prisoners magnanimously, refurbishing their uniforms and gear and sending them home to their Czar as a gesture of friendship. The other Russian troops of the expedition were foolishly quartered by the British for the winter in the Channel Islands.

BRITISH INDECISION OFF FRANCE AND SPAIN

The course of the Helder expedition made it impossible for the British to take advantage of the rumor that the *Chouans* were again on the rampage in the Vendée, other than to send a furtive frigate or two with arms and gold. The Brest project would have been made easier by large bands of rebels operating in the hinterland of the great Atlantic arsenal. When the Duke of York finally left Holland, a respectable field force was released, but General Sir Charles Grey resolutely vetoed the plans of his superior, because Grey refused to countenance any more projects whose success depended upon the chimera of revolt. Dundas reluctantly accepted the professional criticism of his Brest project but stubbornly persisted in exploiting the *Chouan* situation.

The Second Coalition was in the process of dissolution, principally because of friction in Italy between the Austrians and Russians. Dundas cherished the illusion that a strong diversion on the west coast of France might relieve the dangerous tension developing in Italy. He disregarded the fact that the unfortunate Helder expedition had been expelled by local forces and pointed to the favorably altered naval situation resulting from the elimination of the Dutch fleet. At length, civilians and officers in the British government yielded to Dundas, who now saw in the island of Belle Île a powerful base for inciting a flaming civil war in western France.

Unknown to British planners, Napoleon took as one of his first tasks after becoming First Consul that of eliminating disunity in France. Consequently, early in January 1800, Napoleon made peace with the *Chouans,* whose recent sporadic demonstrations had been set off by a hostage policy desperately initiated by the Directory. As the British fondly studied their maps and charts, France was internally at peace for the first time since the outbreak of the Revolution. Having achieved this harmony, Napoleon then mustered strength for a dazzling attack on Austria which soon culminated in the shattering victory of Marengo in June.

Against this background, Dundas refreshed 13,000 troops under Lieutenant General Sir James Pulteney and attempted to persuade Czar Paul to release the troops in the Channel Islands for cooperation in a common cause. Since one of Paul's conditions was the flat insistence that the Duke of York be denied any role in the operations, Dundas made final plans without the Russians, who shortly afterward were recalled to St. Petersburg. The naval officers assigned to Pulteney's project tacitly disapproved the whole concept of the Belle Île attack by making a general rule that British forces would not march inland further than three miles nor be gone more than two hours into France.

Operations began on June 2, 1800, when Captain Sir Edward Pellew with seven 74's appeared in Quiberon Bay with transports bearing 5,000 troops. Briskly silencing the forts on the southwest of the Quiberon peninsula, Pellew landed troops who razed the fortifications. A few days later, emboldened by success, the British sent troops into the Morbihan basin and seized a handful of small vessels, took 100 prisoners, and blew up the fortifications and magazines. The immediate resources on the coast being ruined, the British contemplated attacking Belle Île. Learning that the island was garrisoned by 7,000 troops, the advance party of Pulteney's expedition decided to wait for the balance of their force, in the meantime taking two little islands some ten miles east of Belle Île, which was thereby effectually cut off from relief. Lord St. Vincent with the Channel Fleet covered the operation by cruising off Brest, openly challenging Bruix to interfere.

Bruix did not have to stir. News of Marengo reached Brest and London almost simultaneously and against the elimination of Austria as a fighting enemy, the presence of Britons on two small islands in a bay of France was only a trifling irritation. Dundas, deprived of his motivation for assisting nonexistent *Chouans,* now flexibly reverted to attempts upon enemy naval bases. Thanks to the lingering visit in Quiberon Bay, France was too thoroughly alerted for any chance of surprise. On the other hand, Spain, Dundas was informed, chafed under the yoke of France and longed for freedom. In Spain, the British army would be hailed as liberators. Accordingly, the troops gathering in the Mediterranean under Abercromby for the assault upon the French in Egypt were diverted to a descent on Cadiz, timed to strike in conjunction with Pulteney's thrusts at Ferrol and Vigo in northwest Spain.

Thus, on August 25, 1800, an English squadron under Rear Admiral Sir John Warren brought Pulteney to the seacoast approaches to Ferrol. A broad stretch of water reaches into the rugged Spanish coast and flicks a tongue to the north, whereon sits the fine town of Ferrol. The harbor was perfect in sailing ship days, with a channel broad enough for beating into an adverse wind upon entering or leaving port. Both sides of the channel were protected by batteries. The British avoided a direct approach, preferring to land west of the city to take the northern batteries in the rear, before bringing full force to bear upon the Spanish.

Ferrol harbored six ships under the redoubtable Admiral Moreno, and quartered some 6,000 astonished troops. Warren demolished a battery defending a landing beach on the seacoast near Doninos and lent seamen to Pulteney to assist in manhandling 16 field-guns. The Spanish met the British in the rough country, skirmished, and withdrew to the fixed defenses of Ferrol. Pulteney, who had been wounded in each of his four limbs during his service, was a brave but not a foolish man. After careful study of the enemy works and a council of war, Pulteney decided to abandon his foothold and hope for better luck at Vigo.

Having lost a hundred men and gained nothing more than exercise, Pulteney's troops re-embarked. They fared no better at Vigo, where an offshore inspection of the defenses persuaded Pulteney it was foolish even to land. Consequently, the force sailed on to join Abercromby, ultimately finding successful action in the assault at Aboukir. Pulteney's failure was not a total waste. Historians have speculated on the course of European history had the Austrians welcomed British troops in the encounters that terminated at Marengo, but the shifting, driblet program of Dundas produced humiliations that taught Abercromby and the British army the mistakes to avoid in amphibious operations. Without the Helder and Cadiz and Ferrol and Vigo, Aboukir in 1801 could well have been a massacre. From these operations Abercromby learned to base success upon his own resources, to amass correct and complete intelligence, to practice ship-to-shore movements, and to move swiftly and with assurance.

Notwithstanding public taunts and insults, the British army had become ready for full partnership with the senior service. Maturity came none too soon. After Marengo, Napoleon contrived to sentence the British navy to slow death at the hands of Czar Paul. To screen this metamorphosis of an ally into an enemy, Napoleon endeavored to fix British attention upon the Channel.

NAPOLEON TAKES OVER THE FRENCH NAVY

In consolidating his power after November 1799, Napoleon did not forget to turn his talents for organization towards the French navy. With the eternal hope of the vanquished in seeking to find the key to the success of a victor, he established a commission to study the British Admiralty system with a view to replacing the French ministerial system. Bruix, heading the commission, had been Minister of Marine, but nonetheless urged the adoption of the British system. A clue to Napoleon's later troubles in sea warfare may be found in his instant rejection of his commission's recommendation. Napoleon intended to control the navy and did not want to depart from a rigid chain of command. Subordinates were expected to guess his desires and applaud his decisions, rather than advise him competently and honestly. With his genius to guide him, he preferred sycophants over men who spoke their minds. Unfortunately for France, Napoleon's genius could not make ships march like soldiers.

Pierre Forfait became Napoleon's first Minister of Marine. An old Mediterranean acquaintance, Forfait was an excellent naval engineer, who grasped at once what had to be done to restore the physical strength of the navy. Plagued by his master to send relief to the troops marooned in Egypt, Forfait uneasily dispatched Bruix and Ganteaume, feeling much happier when grappling with the problems of rebuilding the fleet. Incisive in manner, he had many enemies and made more when he attempted to triple the size of the navy. He was a good minister, although denied a share in formulating his country's naval strategy. In that area, Napoleon alone made the decisions.

Early in July 1800, the British altered one of the classic foundations of French strategy by incorporating Ireland in an Act of Union with England and Scotland. The Irish thereby shifted from the status of an offshore colony to the importance of a junior partner. The Act proved to be one of bloodless pacification that made unreliable a once fertile ground for disrupting British offensives or misleading them in defense. Often the threat of inciting civil war in Ireland had enfeebled British campaigns or diverted blockading squadrons from proper reaction to French sorties from port. Whenever the French had the means for a limited thrust at the British Isles, Ireland was the first objective to be mentioned in their councils. The Act of Union removed Ireland from the board as a potential ally of France. Napoleon had to find a substitute for shackling or weakening the British fighting capacity.

The area that could be considered a new Ireland was disclosed by British diplomatic blunders, while Napoleon perceived from the efficiency of Lord St. Vincent what the consequences of success would be should France succeed. St. Vincent had brought the Cadiz system of close blockade to Brest and so effectually stopped coastal convoys to the fleet of Bruix that all supplies for the upkeep of that French force had to be carted overland.[2] Bruix was being slowly crushed.

Few shots were exchanged except between shore batteries and small British men-of-war, yet the Brest fleet suffered progressive deterioration worse than the effects of battle. Studying the reports of Forfait, Napoleon saw that logistics was a two-sided problem involving critical shortages in wood and naval stores. If Bruix could not hold together without a constant supply, the tall, great ships of England cruising off Brest would wither from a similar blight. Therefore, Napoleon amid his many activities adroitly maneuvered to deprive the British of their access to naval replenishment.

Insofar as the ships of George III were concerned, the worst effect of the American Revolution was the loss of Maine and the Carolinas. The virgin forests of Maine grew tall, straight, stout pines fit for masting the greatest men-of-war, whose hulls were sealed and preserved with the turpentine and pitch of the Carolinas. The Americans after the war had raised prohibitively the price of these essential articles, so the British had turned to the Baltic forests to fill their needs. A tremendous trade had been established with Sweden and Russia, of mutual interest and advantage, with money flowing into the Baltic and naval stores into England.

The members of the Second Coalition however did not submerge their individual ambitions in a common interest. Each pursued his own aims, and very little was needed to drive wedges into these natural lines of cleavage. When Napoleon came to power,

---

[2] St. Vincent also brought his strict concepts of discipline to the Brest blockade, thoroughly expunging from the officers and men any trace of the mutinies of 1797. Punishing incompetence and careless performance of duty, he could not do enough for the men who met his standards. His methods may be judged from his treatment of a subordinate admiral who protested that his divisional flagship was stationed too close to a shoal for safety. St. Vincent quietly sailed the entire fleet around the flagship of his discomfited junior and shortly afterwards replaced him with an admiral of more steadfast courage. The blockade conducted by St. Vincent was one that required alert young men, and he constantly pressed the Admiralty to promote into retirement the cautious old men who obstructed the rise of officers with the fire of Nelson and the iron of Collingwood. The blockade of Brest was actually a training school which brought the British navy back to high proficiency. The fleet that Nelson took to Copenhagen in 1801 was drawn from ships trained in St. Vincent's regimen.

Austrian avarice in Italy had already estranged Russia. The army under Suvorov awaited orders to march home. Shrewdly, Napoleon professed to be friendly to Czar Paul and seized upon British errors to prove his good intent. Paul was irritated by the mishandling of the Helder expedition, which left thousands of prisoners in French hands. He was impressed when Napoleon graciously gave these troops back without exacting any ransom or favor. Napoleon went further. He had taken Malta while en route to Egypt. He could not hold the island; yet he made excellent use of it before it passed into Nelson's hands. In 1798, the Knights of Malta had placed themselves under Paul's protection and elected him Grand Master. The ancient order of knighthood became fashionable in St. Petersburg, for Paul took the honor seriously. Napoleon ostentatiously offered the island to Paul, who viewed it with the romantic fancies of a disordered mind. Nelson, whose ships were reducing the French garrison, viewed Malta with the professional clarity of a sailor interested in bases. At Nelson's insistence, the British government refused to deliver the keys of Malta to the Russian admiral present in the Mediterranean, and Paul was embittered.

Paul was not the only Baltic ruler who was losing a friendly attitude towards Great Britain. Sweden and Denmark wished to use the high seas as neutrals, selling their products to anyone who would pay. In the face of high-handed British interference at sea, the Swedes and Danes began to escort convoys of their merchantmen, resulting in incidents that shed blood in July 1800, when a Danish frigate gallantly tried to prevent the search of its convoy in the English Channel. Belatedly, Pitt took cognizance of the deteriorating relations with the Baltic states and sent Lord Whitworth in August to affirm friendship with Denmark, while asserting England's right to stop neutral ships dealing with France. In this impossible diplomatic mission, Whitworth's velvet glove encased a glass hand, consisting of ten ships, which were outnumbered two to one by the truculent Danes, who defied the British squadron

to make an untoward movement. Whitworth returned in failure.

In December 1800, Paul followed an embargo on British ships by reviving the Armed Neutrality that had been so injurious to England in the American Revolution. Russia, Denmark, Sweden, and Prussia leagued in common interest to keep England out of the Baltic. Not content with halfway displays of hostility, Paul proposed a joint offensive to Napoleon. British India, which Napoleon had hoped to reach through Egypt, was vulnerable to a Russian drive through the Himalayas. Paul invited Napoleon to send an army down the Danube to rendezvous in the Caucasus. Napoleon went through the motions of cooperating but did not take extraordinary precautions to keep the project secret from ubiquitous British intelligence agents.

Indeed, to screen his true interest in Baltic developments, Napoleon reverted to the threat of invasion as a further element of confusion. From the Directory, Napoleon had inherited the Army of England under General Kilmaine. During his attempt to make peace with Pitt, Napoleon redesignated this force the "Army of the West" and used it to intimidate the short-lived *Chouan* uprising. When Pitt's adherence to the war aims of the Second Coalition made continuance of hostilities necessary, Napoleon noted that England had boldly stripped the British Isles of regulars for Pulteney and Abercromby. Since there were only volunteers and militia to oppose his landing, Napoleon professed to listen to Forfait's insistent suggestion that England was ripe for assault.[3]

---

[3] Napoleon was not quite as receptive to a revolutionary invention that might have destroyed the Royal Navy. For three years, an American, Robert Fulton, had been attempting to interest the French in his submarine. Bruix, when Minister of Marine, approved Fulton's plans after a strong recommendation from d'Arçon, the designer of the ill-fated "unsinkable" batteries used at Gibraltar in 1782. The *Nautilus* was finally completed for tests in July 1800, at Brest. Fulton's submarine was successful in tests but encountered traditionalistic disapproval. Fulton received no answer from a direct appeal to Napoleon. Discouraged, he then attempted to interest the British in his invention. Naturally, the British displayed little desire to sponsor a type of vessel which

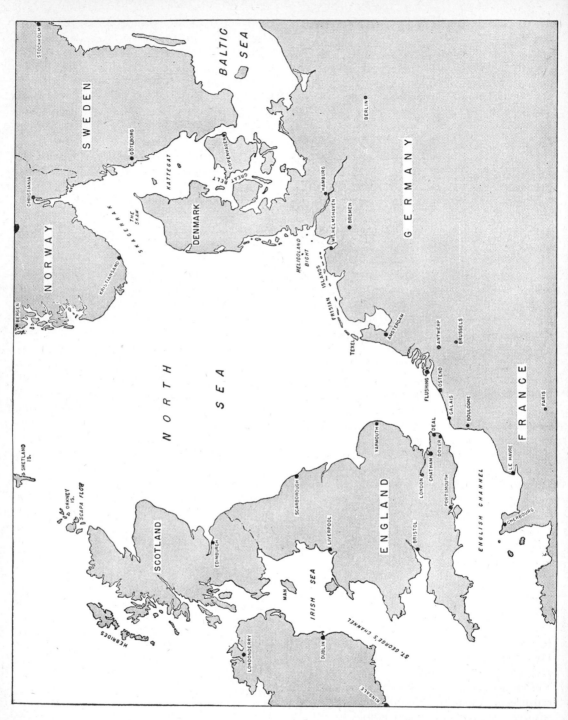

THE NORTH SEA

By March, 1801, Kilmaine's army had been redeployed in a dozen seaports from Quiberon to Flushing and the old vessels of the abandoned Boulogne Flotilla were being repaired. Command of the naval flotillas was put in the hands of Latouche-Tréville, described by a countryman as a *"véritable homme de guerre."* Altogether, the preparations for invasion were pointedly ominous.

In the face of Napoleon's devious plotting, Pitt clearly grasped the greatest threat to England and warned the Baltic states that ratification of the Armed Neutrality treaties would be accepted by Great Britain as a declaration of war. With Napoleon's recognition of the Armed Neutrality and the claim to freedom of the seas, the Baltic states stood firm and commenced mobilization of their navies. Pitt promptly ordered a strong fleet sent to the Baltic before the allied powers could combine. Before Pitt's decision could be executed, he was turned out of office by a trivial domestic quarrel arising from the matter of Irish Catholics and their status under the Act of Union. The Speaker of the House of Commons, Henry Addington, was called to form a cabinet which proved to be an enormous blessing for England. Addington made Lord St. Vincent the First Lord of the Admiralty in February 1801, and British strategic planning at last came into steady, able hands. The fleet that St. Vincent sent to the Baltic in March knew exactly what had to be done.

NELSON'S BATTLE OF COPENHAGEN, APRIL 2, 1801

Lord Spencer had selected and his successor St. Vincent had confirmed Admiral Sir Hyde Parker as commander of the Baltic expedition with Rear Admiral Lord Horatio Nelson as his second. Should diplomacy be required, the Admiralty hoped that Parker would show the wisdom of his years; should

battle develop, the Admiralty trusted to the proved skill of Nelson for a favorable outcome. Parker had been a dashing young frigate captain in the American Revolution and had a fair share of his father's bulldog courage, but age had made him cautious. To St. Vincent's disgust, Parker worried about dark nights and fields of ice instead of shaping his course of action. To St. Vincent's delight, Nelson was full of fire, panting to reach Copenhagen before a dozen Swedish ships and 33 Russians joined the 20 ships the Danes could send to sea. Only 40 of the enemy ships were ready to set sail. Ten of these were Danes. Nelson proposed to smash the Danes and then attack the Swedes and Russians. The British force consisted of 21 ships and 32 smaller men-of-war, strong enough to engage the allies in detail and homogeneous in face of an enemy combination. From his Mediterranean experience, Nelson had formed a poor opinion of Russian officers, and his views were shared by those who had seen the Russian ships cooperating with Duncan in the North Sea. For the Danes, the British had considerable respect based upon the 20,000 Danes then serving aboard British warships and the other Danes who carried British commerce to India. Regret rather than hatred animated the men of Parker's fleet, but this in no way diminished their resolution to do their duty. Parker carried with him a 48-hour ultimatum to the Danes to disavow their unnatural hostility, and few in Parker's fleet wanted the Danes to refuse.

On March 19, 1801, Parker anchored in the Kattegat and sent Nicholas Vansittart to Copenhagen with the demand for Denmark to withdraw from the Armed Neutrality within two days. Vansittart returned on March 23, informing Parker that the Danes had not only rejected the ultimatum but were working around the clock to create defenses far stronger than previously reported. In Vansittart's opinion, successful attack had become impossible. Copenhagen, on the eastern side of the large island of Zealand, had a harbor instead of a roadstead because of the small island of Amag which nestled close to the city. Shoals reached out

---

could best be employed against them. The submarine as conceived by Fulton had to await the Crimean and Civil Wars for use in navies.

from the two islands to deep water which was split into two north-south channels by a Middle Ground that compelled sailing ships to form line ahead in approaching the city. There was little room for maneuver or carelessness in making the channel into the harbor between Amag and Zealand. A powerful battery of 68 guns named the Trekroner Fort, squatted on pilings near the northwest tip of Amag shoal. From the Trekroner, a line of 18 dismasted hulls stretched nearly two miles southeast along the edge of Amag shoal. Another two miles of land batteries covered the rear of the line. Just north of the Trekroner, five vessels were stationed in the throat of Copenhagen channel, backed by the powerful citadel of Copenhagen.

When Vansittart finished describing these works in which apparently all the men of the city stood to arms, Parker called a council of war. In British annals, councils of war almost invariably preceded ignominious withdrawal. If Parker had had full rein, Copenhagen might well have been another Rochefort. However, Nelson was the embodiment of English resolution and he did not betray those who had suggested him as a counterweight to Parker. With spirited logic, Nelson transformed the gloomy defeatism of his colleagues into an ardent debate over the relative merits of going directly down the Sound to attack Copenhagen from the north or of using the Great Belt passage to round Zealand and come at the city's defenses from the south.

Perhaps these were Nelson's finest hours as a leader. On the one hand, he had to avoid offending a senior who might resent an unguarded slur upon his ability or bravery. On the other hand, he had to inspire juniors among whom many were jealous of his renown or scornful of his youth or critical of his infidelity to his wife. He was not addressing the Band of Brothers he had formed in the Mediterranean; here were a score who viewed him as St. Vincent's pet. Nelson's self-confident zeal blazed in the cabin of the 98-gun *London,* melting the shells of doubt and malice and envy. He did not that day entirely win the fleet but he set in train a positive attitude that within a week firmly imprinted his personality upon the captains of the ships he would use.

On March 30, with a fair, following wind, the British finally got underway in the Sound. Kronborg Castle on Zealand guarded the channel in conjunction with batteries on the Swedish coast. The Danes in Kronborg opened fire. The British looked at the Swedish batteries, which were silent. Nelson, commanding the van, edged to the Swedish side of the channel and shot from Kronborg splashed harmlessly short. The Swedes had the fleet within range but did not fire and so the British proceeded without incident to an anchorage a few miles north of the Middle Ground.

Nelson personally supervised the charting of the channel east of the Middle Ground, working under cover of darkness to blind the Danes to his intentions. Parker gave Nelson a force of ten ships, two 50's, and 18 small craft to engage the hulks in the Danish defense line. During the day of April 1, Nelson moved his force down the eastern side of the Middle Ground, while Parker with the balance of the fleet covered the north. Anchoring at the southern tip of the Middle Ground, Nelson invited his juniors to a jubilant dinner-party and impatiently awaited a favorable wind. During the night, the northerly wind which had helped him take his position shifted to the south, so that as April 2 dawned, he could move into action. Parker was to have cooperated in the attack but the wind was in his teeth.

Nelson was too impatient to await a wind favorable to both Parker and himself. He could move and that sufficed. He called his captains to breakfast and explained his plan of attack. The *Edgar,* his leading ship, was to pass five Danes and then anchor, thus leaving open targets for the rest of his column to engage as they crept to their reverse-order anchorages. The plan had the merit of crushing the Danish rear with successive broadsides from Nelson's whole column as they came to positions one by one ahead of the *Edgar.* By the time Nelson's last ships had passed along the disengaged side of the anchoring British line, he expected the Danish rear to be silenced. Thus his last

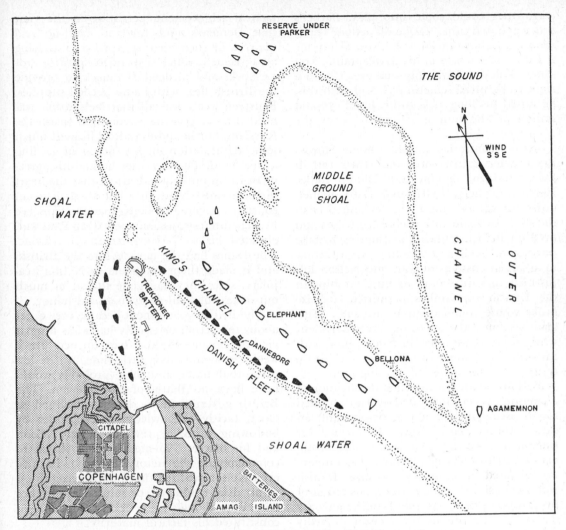

BATTLE OF COPENHAGEN, APRIL 2, 1801

ships would come unharmed and ready for action in range of the Trekroner. Nelson in the 74-gun *Elephant* placed himself seventh in line so that he could exchange iron with the 62-gun *Danneborg*, which flew the pennant of Commodore Olfert Fischer.

The *Edgar* smartly went into action about 10:30 AM but three of the ships which followed her struck on the Middle Ground, thereby considerably reducing Nelson's strength and throwing a disproportionately heavy load upon his small craft. As the British ships singly glided to a halt and anchored, springs on cables, the battle became a mere contest to reveal which side had more fortitude. Science and seamanship went by the board; rate and weight of fire was everything. For some three hours the Danes and British pounded at each other, seemingly to no conclusion.

Lying helpless to the north, trying to warp down within long range of the Trekroner, Parker peered with mounting anxiety into the flashing, thundering cloudbanks of gunsmoke. Finally, Parker's nerve broke. At 1:30 PM, he signaled Nelson to discontinue the engagement. At the time, Nelson was flying a signal for closer action, so that British carronades could come into play. Parker's order agitated him. "Leave off action?" he is reported to have exclaimed. "Now, damn me if I do!" He turned to his flag captain. "You know, Foley, I have only one eye. I have a right to be blind sometimes." And with this, he raised his long glass to his blind eye and smiled at the bunting fluttering over the *London.*

Action continued another hour. Slowly, the heavier British guns took their toll in the thin-sided, shallow-draft Danish hulks. Here and there, a battered Dane hauled down his colors, only to be remanned from the shore by zealots who rehoisted colors and fired on British launches attempting to take possession. Such a proceeding was contrary to accepted customs of war, and Nelson felt justified in threatening to hurl fireships in the Danish line unless permitted to seize hulks whose commanders capitulated. With grim vigilance the opposing forces fell silent when Nelson sent a flag of truce ashore with his threat and was answered by a Danish inquiry about his motive in ceasing fire.

Nelson confidently assumed the attitude of a conqueror, certain he had at least attained moral ascendancy if not a victory, and assumed that a parley had been opened for surrender. Asserting that Danes were brothers of Englishmen, he declared that humanity dictated a cease-fire to take Danish wounded ashore, while he took possession of his proper prizes. As the Danish emissary desired further discussion, Nelson shrewdly referred him to Parker, distant some four miles, and used the time so gained in freeing his grounded ships and carrying his column safely past the unharmed, powerful Trekroner. Nelson had had quite enough battle to satisfy him for a day; another bout could finish his shot-riddled squadron. The Danes had lost some 2,000 men; the British, about 1,200. Numbed and uncertain, as negotiations commenced in the *London,* the Danes suffered ten hulks to be towed off as trophies.

A week went by in discussion of armistice terms, the Danes belligerently shaking off the shock of battle to mend their defenses. During that time, Nelson disclosed unsuspected ability as a diplomat. Minimizing his tactical achievement, persisting in the view that Denmark and England had no real quarrel, he succeeded on April 9 in drafting an agreement which suspended hostilities for 14 weeks and pledged Denmark to provide the British fleet with badly needed supplies. Fourteen weeks was all that Nelson felt was needed to subdue the Swedes and smash the Russians, but he did not allow himself much self-congratulation for his success in gaining a free hand. The day after he had his agreement in his pocket, he learned that the heart of the Armed Neutrality had died. Russian courtiers, angered by being made to subserve French interests, assassinated Czar Paul and elevated his son Alexander to the throne. The Danes had the news before the British, and it made them amenable to Nelson's cajolery, since they had gone to war as much out of fear of Paul as for national honor.

The British government became very quiet about the action originally hailed as a great victory, because Nelson had opened fire a week too soon. Only a little time, a little less precipitate haste, and there probably would have been no Battle of Copenhagen. The British government in decency declined to gloat, tacitly acknowledging a blunder by bestowing minimal rewards upon Nelson and his officers. No medals were struck to commemorate the victory. Proud as he was, even Nelson realized that public recognition of his deed could not be saluted as another Nile, even though his action at Copenhagen constituted his tactical maturity.

Aside from demonstrating the paramount importance of possessing a superior will to win, Copenhagen had the beneficial effect of silencing those who claimed that Nelson had been merely lucky in the Mediterranean. The favoritism manifested by St. Vincent was now accepted as premature recognition of Nelson's qualities as a great leader. His primacy in the Royal Navy was firmly established. Henceforward, Nelson would command in the area of greatest danger. Few grumbled when Parker was peremptorily recalled and Nelson was given the Baltic fleet.

There was no further fighting that year in the Baltic. Much of the 14-week armistice passed in repairing battle damage and by then there were no enemies. From the first, the Swedes had displayed reluctance to be agents of their ancient Russian foe, and the Battle of Copenhagen confirmed their wisdom. As for the Russians, Czar Alexander did not share his late father's madness. The Armed Neutrality collapsed. So, too, did the threat to British India.

Napoleon had been checked.

AGAIN THE BOULOGNE FLOTILLA

Europe was weary of war but could not find a formula for peace. Moreau at Hohenlinden and Napoleon at Marengo had broken Austria and made the French army predominant in Europe. British admirals had made their Royal Navy predominant at sea. The land power of France was diplomatically balanced by the sea power of England. It seemed clear to Napoleon that the only way to cut the Gordian knot of British stubbornness in peace negotiations, was to range his magnificent army against the splendid ships of England. As British negotiators stiffened their demands after Copenhagen, Napoleon resorted to a public display of all-out effort with the Boulogne Flotilla. Encamping on the coast, he established rigorous, realistic training for the troops and seamen who would man the hundreds of small craft building in the yards of Holland, Flanders, and France. He harangued his troops as was his wont and promised them action when the summer brought favorable weather.[4] His gasconading fed fat to a fiery war of nerves and slowly wore away his enemy's resolution.

From every quarter, details of the French preparations reached London. Suspecting a gigantic hoax, Addington's cabinet was compelled by public fear alone to raise the alarm along the coasts of Britain. With the army gone on colonial expeditions or serving with Abercromby's venture in Egypt, Addington had few regulars to deploy against invasion.

Should the French bulldoze a path through the Royal Navy and land their thousands of veterans, the British could not stand up to them in the field, but would have to turn to hopeless guerilla war. Even though Napoleon flourished the Boulogne Flotilla to intimidate and shrank from gambling all that he had gained, Addington's cabinet shrank even more. If Napoleon had no stomach for a tangled melee on the tossing waters of the Channel, his reputation for daring and swiftness would still induce him to launch his assault if disaster elsewhere weighted the odds heavily in his favor. Egypt was in doubt but Napoleon could have positive control elsewhere, and threatened the British not only with invasion but with capture of Britain's traditional ally, Portugal, unless his terms of peace were accepted.

Addington breathed an atmosphere of uncertainty. It was impossible to save Portugal from a Spanish invasion, and, in the summer of 1801, he knew only that Abercromby had landed and died in Egypt. As French squadrons sporadically broke loose with reinforcements for the French in Egypt, one might succeed at a critical juncture. Sailing ships carried news slowly, too slowly for Addington's equanimity. His serious view of the invasion possibility was revealed when he called Nelson from the Baltic to take command in July 1801 of the light squadrons hovering watchfully off the Boulogne coastline. Magic accompanied Nelson. All eyes turned to see what he would do.

Ever direct, Nelson turned to the offensive. "It is necessary to attack the invaders on their own soil," he wrote to St. Vincent and got underway with 37 mixed vessels. On August 3, he bombarded at long range a line of 30 gunboats anchored in shallow water directly across the entrance to Boulogne. Nelson's bomb vessels arched 900 shells at the little French warships but damaged only two. Mortified, Nelson hauled away, finding in his pen the victory denied his guns. Having reassured the British public that after his raid the Boulogne division was incapable of participating in an invasion, Nelson privately informed St. Vincent that shelling was ineffectual. The only way to break up the

---

[4] This was counter to his professional belief that shock assault could only succeed in the turbulent winter months, which deranged the cruising arrangements of the Royal Navy.

enemy flotillas was to sail in and seize them. Fully aware of the inaccuracy of crudely-fused, high trajectory shells, St. Vincent gave his favorite everything he desired.

In the meantime, Latouche-Tréville had also learned lessons from the first clash of arms. Securing either end of the line with bomb-vessels and strongly reinforcing his land-batteries, he presented a far more formidable front when Nelson reappeared on the night of August 15. Nelson planned a large-scale cutting-out attack, organizing 53 boats into four divisions. Impetuously and without regard for mutual support, the British dashed off into the darkness at the waiting enemy. At midnight, the darkness was dazzled with flashes and roared with the shocks of hand-to-hand combat. At dawn, the French line was intact. Nelson's force was in full retreat minus a dozen boats and eight-score men, creating a legend that the French had chained their boats together.

The jittery people of England heard only of another heavy blow against the French flotillas and hoisted their glasses to Lord Nelson's health. Rocking on the decks of the 32-gun *Medusa*, Nelson's health was undermined by his chronic enemy, seasickness. Nonetheless, grimly aware of the need to carry the war to the French, Nelson busied himself with plans against the flotillas of Calais and Flushing. His enthusiasm had been considerably dimmed by Latouche-Tréville however, and he kept finding difficulties in the way of again closing with the enemy. By the end of September, he had reverted to the fireship tactics of Drake, and was preparing to burn the bristling flotilla at Brest when his hand was stayed by the welcome news that the war was over.

TEMPORARY PEACE, AMIENS, 1802

On October 1, 1801, as Latouche-Tréville urged Napoleon to take heart from the repulse of the British and mass the flotillas for a descent on England, preliminaries of peace were signed in London. Addington's cabinet had been unable to hold out for definite news from Egypt. Nelson's failures at Boulogne and subsequent inactivity had burst the bubble of Addington's confidence. In the formal peace drawn up at Amiens in May 1802, the British virtually repudiated their victories, pledging the restoration of colonial conquests except Spanish Trinidad and Dutch Ceylon.[5] Worse than this in the minds of Addington's opposition was the agreement to evacuate Malta and Egypt. In exchange, France did little more than revert to the status quo of Turkey and Portugal, pledging only to quit Italy and the Dalmatian Coast. However bad the Peace of Amiens appeared to the British public, one tremendous gain overshadowed the concessions.

Eight years of war had not been wasted. England had stayed in the ring with Jacobin France, sometimes aided by many allies, more often fighting alone, until fanaticism was replaced in France by respectable nationalism. Largely because of the bulldog English, the Revolution withered. Napoleon remained, but he was one man, not a nation. Both sides viewed the peace as a breathing space vital to regroup forces for a decisive war. Napoleon needed tranquility to lay an iron hand on the French people. England needed time to reflect upon past errors and to devolop a sound strategy under the guidance of St. Vincent. Napoleon needed the respite far more than his foes.

In bumbling along to a belated realization that this war was not an echo of the colonial struggles of the century, England had done fairly well from the standpoint of holding her trident. Commissioned in her blue water navy as of 1802 were 126 ships and 505 minor men-of-war. Fifteen ships had been lost through causes other than enemy action,

---

[5] The extent of British success in eight years of colonial war is measured in the territories returned. France received her fishing islands of St. Pierre and Miquelon, the West Indian islands of Martinique, St. Lucia, and Tobago, and her Indian and African trading posts at Goree, Madagascar, Pondichérry and Chandernagore. To the Dutch were returned in the West Indies, her islands and posts of Surinam, Berbice, Curaçao, Essequibo, and Demerara; in Africa, the Cape of Good Hope; and in the East Indies, Malacca and its dependencies. In the colonial war England had lost nothing.

which accounted for a paltry five. Losses were more than replaced by captures from France and her allies. Indeed, as of 1802, France scarcely had a navy, certainly in no way a rival of England's. The Jacobins had begun with 83 ships and 74 frigates; ten years later, Napoleon could muster only 46 ships and 37 frigates. France and her allies—Holland, Spain, and Denmark—had 61 ships captured by the British, who sank an additional 24 in battle. Poor seamanship cost the French nine. After provoking British naval action, the Russians alone escaped unscathed and then simply because Nelson had been unable to get at them in time.

Nor had the French been more successful in their favorite *guerre de course*. Their privateers had captured less than three per cent of British shipping, which expanded in war a full quarter to reach the unprecedented total of 20,000 vessels in British registry. Conversely, the French merchant marine was practically annihilated. Some 5,600 French trading vessels fell prey with 600 privateers to British cruisers, delivering 42,000 seamen to British prisons. War was a financial boon only to the British and the Americans, who at one period linked together in the West Indies in common cause against the French. Thanks to Pitt's fiscal policies and his insistence upon paying for the war out of current income, England was enormously ahead of the other hostile nations. Subsidies could be paid with a lavish generosity when the war was renewed. The way was open for a sound, well-considered strategy instead of the potpourri of belligerency, fear, reaction, and opportunism that had marked the previous years.

To this, Addington's cabinet gave full thought. Both armed services had grown in stature, although St. Vincent held the opinion that his country would do well to disband the army and leave such soldiering as was needed to the Royal Marines, who had won that name just prior to Amiens. After Egypt, the British army was no longer negligible, and General Sir John Moore was working on a new drill to defeat Napoleon's columns. England harked back to the days of Marlborough, when British troops were respected on the Continent.

The Royal Navy however remained England's primary weapon, and naval developments were therefore more significant. In the struggle with the Revolution, the Royal Navy had finally broken its chains: the *Fighting Instructions* had now become a mere point of departure for commanders with initiative. Ships and equipment had improved in such matters as substitution of metal water tanks for wooden casks, giving fleets more endurance as St. Vincent taught admirals and captains to keep the sea throughout the year. The ability to maintain close blockades offered a solution to the dilemma of Spencer and Dundas, who had to mount offensives while protecting colonies and commerce from furtive privateers and minor operations. Constant cruising had perfected the performance of officers and men unattainably beyond any of their potential adversaries. The Royal Navy was as fine and deadly as a Damascus blade. It had found great young leaders and one genius, Nelson. Best of all, it had attained a professional attitude. No longer would there be naive trust that all was well when a superman took the helm. Not after Nelson's failures off Boulogne. In the war to come, Nelson would have full freedom, but the Admiralty would not let him bear alone the weight of England's life or death. Strategic safeguards would envelop Nelson's movements. St. Vincent saw to that.

Merry in their strength, officers of the Royal Navy watched the French take to sea when the Peace of Amiens allowed them to chastise Toussaint L'Ouverture, who had snatched Santo Domingo from the Revolution. The independent Negro government was beset by 30,000 troops grandly escorted by 41 ships under Villaret-Joyeuse, who carried Ganteaume and Latouche-Tréville with him to enjoy the open Atlantic. Not all the ships reached home. The Peace of Amiens died in infancy.

11

Climax at Sea:
the Trafalgar Campaign, 1805

WHILE FRANCE AND ENGLAND moved toward a truce, the United States drifted into its first overseas war. The treaties with the Barbary coast had not ended the demands of Barbary rulers. The Bashaw of Tripoli was soon discontented, for his terms of tribute were much less rewarding than those of Algiers. The American consul at Tripoli, James Cathcart, had been one of the prisoners ransomed by treaty from Algiers, and knew the ways of corsair despots. When the Bashaw suggested that a sloop-of-war and a few score guns should be presented to him, Cathcart transmitted the demands to Congress. At the same time, Cathcart warned the American consul at Gibraltar that hostilities could begin at any moment, so that by the winter of 1801 no American ships entered the Mediterranean.

AMERICAN INTERLUDE: WAR WITH TRIPOLI

Unable to understand the function of Congress in the American system of govern-ment, the Bashaw steadily pressed Cathcart to yield more tribute. Eloquently describing this pressure Cathcart begged Congress to send a squadron of frigates to help him. His appeals could not have been more opportune for the destiny of the United States Navy. As the Quasi-War with France reached an amicable settlement, the anti-Navy Jeffersonian party swept the elections of 1800. The Navy that had fought so well in the West Indies was threatened with extinction as a costly luxury, but in view of the Tripolitan situation, Secretary Stoddert was able to persuade the "lame duck" Congress to pass on March 3, 1801 a Peace Establishment Act providing for the retention of 13 frigates. Six of these, with two-thirds wartime complements, were to be kept on active duty, officered by a corps of nine captains, 36 lieutenants, and 150 midshipmen. The other seven frigates were laid up in ordinary and the balance of the navy was sold for some $300,000.

With Cathcart's correspondence supplemented by similar forebodings from the consuls at Tunis and Algiers, even Jefferson upon assuming the Presidency did not feel justified in meddling with the Navy Department. An expedition to the Mediterranean was clearly necessary. Waiting two months for Albert Gallatin to take up the duties of Secretary of the Treasury, Jefferson and his cabinet in late May 1801 decided to send "a squadron of observation" to Cathcart's assistance. Commanded by Richard Dale, the onetime lieutenant of John Paul Jones, the little force of four vessels left Hampton Roads about June 1, escorting two vessels carrying tribute payments for Tunis and Algiers. The Bashaw declared war on the United States by the formal procedure of chopping down the flagstaff of the consulate on May 10. Thanks to Cathcart's foresight, the Bashaw's corsairs could only hope to find American warships. The first clash of the war occurred near Malta on August 1, when Lieutenant Andrew Sterrett's 12-gun schooner *Enterprise* captured a 14-gun Tripolitan corsair after three hours of fighting. Since Congress had not yet declared war, the corsair was disarmed and allowed to return to the Bashaw with the news that the United States really had a navy.

Dale did little else to impress the Bashaw, who was contemptuous of blockades. The Bashaw knew, as Dale soon learned, that squadrons without storeships could not long remain off the unhospitable Barbary coast. There was no need for the Bashaw's corsairs to fight Dale's warships, even had good business practice permitted such a foolish waste of manpower. Generations of Christian slaves had built high, thick fortifications to protect Tripoli. With the harbor channel blocked by a chain of moored corsairs, the Bashaw's seamen relaxed in an enforced holiday, waiting for the Americans to exhaust their supplies. Baffled by a quiescent enemy, Dale frittered away the one-year enlistment time of his crews and accomplished nothing.

A new squadron was being readied in the United States and Jefferson turned to the hero of the Quasi-War to settle the Tripolitan question. Thomas Truxtun accepted the commission as a chance to further the interests of a blue water fleet, which was then under attack in Congress in connection with Stoddert's old program for building 74-gun ships of the line. Consistent with his aim of creating a true navy, Truxtun requested and then demanded a captain to command the 44-gun frigate in which he was to hoist the pennant of a Commodore. Truxtun insisted that a squadron commander had to be freed from shipboard routine. The precedent had been set by Dale's squadron, but unfortunately for Truxtun's position, Dale had sailed in peacetime when the navy had a few surplus captains. Now, with war, the parsimonious Republican government lacked sufficient captains to command 13 frigates, much less furnish Truxtun with the pretensions of a British or French flag officer. As a matter of principle, Truxtun resigned from command of the second Mediterranean squadron and it was accepted as a resignation from the Navy. Thus, not yet 50 and with 20 years of life ahead of him, Thomas Truxtun was lost to the service he had done so much to mold.

The officer who replaced Truxtun did little with the second squadron to further the American cause, but the Commodore of the third squadron sent out in 1803 had been trained in Truxtun's West Indian school. This was Edward Preble, who sensibly compromised the flag-captain issue by appointing his First Lieutenant as acting Captain of his flagship, the 44-gun *Constitution*. In everything else, Preble merely reasserted and embellished Truxtun's teachings.

Scarcely 40, Preble was a veteran seaman, with experience in privateers, the Massachusetts Navy, merchantmen, and revenue cutters. Incompetence infuriated him. In the collection of vessels that came under his command, there was much to trigger his hot temper, and at first few men with experience to understand the errors that produced his tirades. Preble always strove to show that a regulation was founded upon wisdom. The young gentlemen who served him were swiftly disillusioned if they believed that handsome uniforms endowed them with the knowledge of a seasoned lieutenant or captain. Preble sought to break the lone-wolf, privateering instincts that had served Americans at sea as they had the lawless, undisciplined frontiersmen. Like Truxtun before him, Preble aimed at a regular service. His problem was to bend his subordinates to a system of instant obedience while simultaneously cherishing their innate aggressiveness. To do this, he set an example of uncompromising devotion to duty, and, passing the Straits of Gibraltar at night, showed a disposition to fight an insolent British vessel under circumstances that displayed the highest moral and physical courage. This incident broke the resentment displayed against him by his young gentlemen. Thenceforward, knowing that Preble practiced what he preached, his officers obeyed him wholeheartedly, proud to be known to history as "Preble's Boys."

Entering the Mediterranean, Preble found bad news. The 36-gun *Philadelphia* under William Bainbridge had preceded him. An energetic commander, Bainbridge had forestalled a disposition of Morocco to prey on American commerce by seizing a Moroccan corsair committing piracy. Preble had to follow up Bainbridge's action and was thus diverted to Tangier for successful negotiations, while Bainbridge went on to Tripoli with the *Philadelphia* and the 14-gun *Vixen*. While Preble was pacifying Morocco, Bainbridge lost his ship. In hot pursuit of a corsair slightly east of Tripoli, Bainbridge struck an uncharted shoal. The Tripolitans swarmed about him, compelling him to surrender before flood tide. Bainbridge had done his best before hauling down his colors to protect his crew from useless bloodshed and he had the bitterness of seeing the Tripolitans free his ship and carry it into harbor long before Preble's arrival.

This calamity reduced Preble's strength to one frigate supported by five small brigs and schooners. His force had been pitifully inadequate to begin with, when compared to the detachments of ships of the line employed by the European nations on similar missions. Even worse than the loss in strength however was the power placed in the hands of the Bashaw by the possession of more than 300 captives from the *Philadelphia*. Preble was restrained from full measures by fear of violent retaliation against helpless men, which is ever the handicap of a civilized state

in conflict with barbarians. The *Philadelphia* herself he could reach, and reach her he did.

Tripoli was a walled city, built on a slight hill, facing the sea to the north and the east. A roadstead rather than a landlocked harbor, it had the security of extensive shoals as natural breakwaters. The northern face of the city, impressive with massive walls, descended gradually to the east into a thin finger of land slightly above sea level. Small islets stretched along the line of this finger to enclose the roadstead from the north. Vessels entering Tripoli did not dare approach from the east, where lay the reefs on which Bainbridge had met disaster, but entered from the north close to the finger of land, thereby coming under the guns of powerful Fort Mandrach.

The *Philadelphia*, which had been dismasted in Bainbridge's efforts to free her, floated mockingly well within the harbor behind a swarm of corsairs. Her presence was a stain upon the American flag which Preble's Boys wished to eradicate. Lieutenant Stephen Decatur won the privilege. On the night of February 16, 1804, Decatur entered the harbor with some fourscore men aboard a small, captured ketch renamed the *Intrepid*. Posing as a Maltese vessel, Decatur's ketch succeeded in getting alongside the *Philadelphia* unsuspected. Within a few moments, the American boarding party was slashing through the startled sentries. Fire trains were laid and ignited and Decatur's party was back in the *Intrepid* before the alarm was given and understood ashore. Dried by the Mediterranean sun, the *Philadelphia* readily took fire, lighting Decatur's safe return—to a spot promotion to captain.

This was the outstanding episode of the war; the rest was futility. Assisted by gunboats hired from Sicily, Preble initiated a series of bombardments in which his men clashed many times in hand-to-hand combat with corsair crews. Shot and shell rained on the defenses and shipping of Tripoli. Victory was always in sight and always proved elusive. Tripoli was simply too strong to be intimidated or defeated by a light squadron. Against his will, Preble had to begin haggling terms of ransom for Bainbridge, and

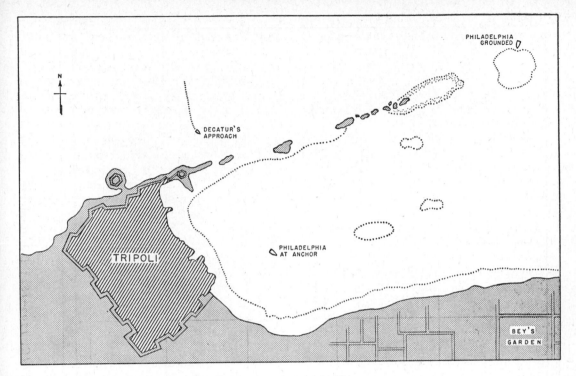

HARBOR OF TRIPOLI, 1804

his operations began to be little more than an instrument for moderating the Bashaw's demands. Informed that Captain Samuel Barron was en route with four frigates to assume command of the united force, Preble made every effort to attain a decision, including the desperate expedient of employing a tiny fireship. This was made by stuffing the little *Intrepid* with eight tons of gunpowder. On the night of September 4, 1804, Lieutenant Richard Somers with a crew of 12 volunteers, including Lieutenants Israel and Wadsworth set out in it, but the *Intrepid* exploded prematurely without damaging the defenses of Tripoli. Gloom dampened the spirits of Preble's Boys, for the *Intrepid* had no survivors. A week later, Commodore Barron arrived and Preble went home, having failed in his primary task. To his credit however was the now solid foundation of the United States naval officer corps.

Neither Barron nor his successor, John Rodgers, improved upon Preble's efforts, other than to countenance a political venture to unseat the Bashaw, who had usurped the throne from his elder brother Hamet. The American Consul at Tunis, a firebrand named William Eaton, located Hamet hiding in Egypt. Persuading Hamet that the Americans longed to assist him in regaining his rights, Eaton scraped together a legion of a thousand mercenaries spearheaded by a few United States Marines under Lieutenant Presley O'Bannon. Marching through the desert to a rendezvous near Derne, Eaton captured this Tripolitan town in late April 1805 with the assistance of the 12-gun *Nautilus* and 10-gun *Hornet*. The importance of this puny expedition was reflected in the successful peace negotiations in June, when the Bashaw insisted that his brother and Eaton be compelled to leave the borders of Tripoli. By this time, the Bashaw agreed to abandon his pretensions to tribute, settling peace for a mere $60,000 ransom to be paid for Bainbridge and his crew.

Within the limitations of conducting war on a hostile coast several thousand miles re-

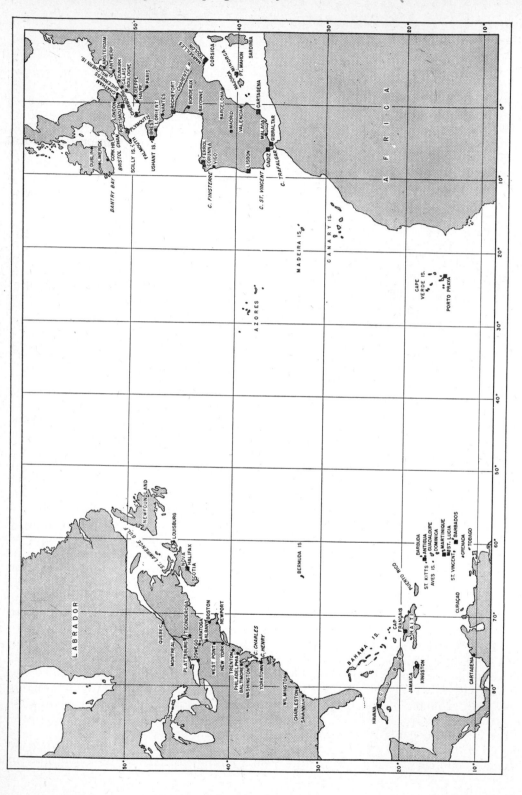

NAVAL BASES ON THE NORTH ATLANTIC, 1700–1815 (squares indicate bases)

moved from home bases, the United States Navy had performed well. Unfortunately, success was pregnant with disaster. Jefferson and his party wished to remain aloof from European quarrels, and a navy that displayed offensive potentialities made the Republicans uneasy. A navy capable only of defending the American coastline could offend no one, and so Jefferson turned his back on the blue water concept. In early 1803, fifteen small gunboats were authorized, each to carry one or two guns, which had to be stowed on the keel for stability if the vessels ventured into deep water. Another 25 were authorized in 1805. Since this was the only American naval construction in the war period, Jefferson's pacific intentions were advertised to the world. If anyone doubted his sincerity, the final disposition of the authorized 74's was conclusive proof. In 1804, a Mediterranean Fund had been raised from a 2½ per cent tax on imports. In December 1805, Secretary of the Navy Robert Smith called the attention of Congress to the materials collected for 74's by the previous administration. The wood was now seasoned. Suggesting that the surplus from the Mediterranean Fund could be used to start building the big ships, Smith also pointed out that one ship cost $329,000 to complete and an annual $192,000 to maintain.

The Senate tabled the bill for the 74's and so the great, tough timbers were sawed into planking to make more gunboats. Preble's Boys had to wait until 1813 and another war before Congress again approved ships of the line. The first of these to carry the flag was the 74-gun *Independence* of Captain William Crane, flying the pennant of Commodore William Bainbridge, who commanded a squadron in conjunction with another under Captain Stephen Decatur. With real might in 1815, Bainbridge and Decatur made a swift peace with troublesome Algiers.[1]

---

[1] To understand the navy of the Tripolitan period, see Captain (later Commodore, Ret.) Dudley W. Knox USN, editor, *Naval Documents Related to the United States Wars with the Barbary Powers*, 7 vols. (Washington, D. C., 1939-1945).

RUPTURE OF THE PEACE OF AMIENS

The relief felt by Britain's Addington ministry was short-lived. It soon became obvious that the terms of the Treaty of Amiens had settled none of the sources of conflict between Great Britain and Napoleon, for Napoleon apparently acted on the premise that he had split the world with the British, who were to have the sea while he became master of the land. Pitt and his followers raged at Addington's pledge to restore Malta, Minorca, Egypt, and the Cape of Good Hope, especially since Napoleon ruthlessly extended his sway into Switzerland and northern Italy. The charges of bad faith passing between London and Paris intensified when Napoleon not only refused to loose his hold upon Holland but showed a disposition to annex that rich territory. Addington obstinately retained Malta to compel Napoleon to honor his end of their bargain. The possible incorporation of Dutch naval potential into the French naval structure was intolerable to the British. When British intelligence verified that Napoleon intended to convert Antwerp into Europe's greatest naval base, peace became impossible. Antwerp commercially had been threat sufficient to drive England into bloody wars with Louis XIV just to seal the port from trade. Antwerp strategically made invasion feasible. Reluctant to precipitate hostilities, Addington saw no alternative when Napoleon not only refused to leave Holland but brazenly upbraided the British ambassador for England's delay in evacuating Malta. On March 13, 1803, Napoleon said flatly, "Malta or war!" On May 18, 1803, England stunned Napoleon with a formal declaration of war.

Having publicly stated that ten years of peace were necessary for France to build a navy able to challenge England at sea, Napoleon had entrusted Denis Decrès with the long range task of developing such power. Decrès had scarcely begun and would never finish. Personally brave, a slavish imitator of Napoleon, Decrès was detested throughout the French navy. He ceaselessly and slyly undercut the admirals of outstanding ability, lest he be replaced by one of them as Minister of Marine and Colonies. He pushed forward mediocre officers for great responsibilities, knowing they would fail but being indifferent to their failures because he cynically doubted that French fleets could ever accomplish anything in the face of English rivals. To his inferiors, he was a mocking skeptic who blunted enthusiasm and initiative. To Napoleon, he was a fawning courtier who instantly comprehended what was desired and deftly explained why little could be done at the moment. Decrès was ever ready to endorse his master's projects—if planned for next year. It is a mystery that Napoleon, with all his knowledge of men, was unable to understand Decrès, whom he retained in power even for the Hundred Days that ended at Waterloo. Perhaps in their attitude toward the capabilities of the French navy, they were in fundamental harmony. It is conceivable that Napoleon maintained a navy only to have squadrons-in-being that would oblige England to divert funds to the Royal Navy which could have been better used to raise Continental armies against the French. In any case, Denis Decrès was not the man for the task of fitting the French navy for victory at sea. After the first year, Napoleon expressed displeasure with the performance of his naval minister, and yet retained him for a dozen more.

During the brief peace, Decrès displayed great energy. Shipyards worked night and day to send 45 new ships down the ways. Aside from the Santo Domingo expedition, a small force was sent out to Mauritius to make ready for war in the Indian Ocean. Then in March 1803 Napoleon gave orders to revive the Boulogne Flotilla—this would revive the fear of invasion in the British, who were proving stubborn about Malta. Decrès set up a program for building landing craft and gunboats in every small yard from the Seine to the Elbe. Merchantmen shuttled to and from the Baltic to replenish the exhausted warehouses of Brest and Toulon. Seamen were cajoled to enlist in a navy that Napoleon needed to chastise the meddlesome English. The navy began to be something of

a fad—triumphant invasion seemed possible. The magnificent army was being brought to face England on a front whose right flank could be covered by the Dutch fleet and ships building at Antwerp, and whose left flank was anchored on Brest. The marvels of the semaphore telegraph enabled orders to sweep between Brest and Antwerp in five hours, so that the slightest flaw in British dispositions could be utilized to launch an assault. All looked well in the plans and papers carefully drafted for Napoleon's approval.

The British declaration of war in May 1803 punctured the gaudy balloon. As usual the *Marine* was scattered. One ship was at St. Malo, 21 at Brest, five at Lorient, six at Rochefort, one at Bordeaux, and 12 at Toulon. One was en route to Mauritius and nine were returning from the West Indies. The British Admiralty, with St. Vincent's hand at the helm, moved into war with confident speed. Before sunset on the day the French ambassador received his credentials, 60 British ships weighed anchor to establish a close blockade of the enemy ports, hunt down the French West Indian detachment, and commence campaigns in the West and East Indies. So swiftly did the British move that Admiral William Cornwallis and his ten blockaders appeared off Brest before the port commander knew that war had been declared. A detachment of five ships watched Lorient and Rochefort, and Lord Nelson went to stand guard over Toulon with ten. It was in the Narrow Sea however that the British held the bulk of their resources. Here Lord Keith watched the Dutch while efficiently organizing squadrons of minor men-of-war to interrupt the coastal traffic essential in mustering enemy flotillas. Although professionals like St. Vincent discounted the invasion menace, the British nation did not. The fright of 1801 was too recent, and Nelson's inability to destroy the enemy small craft had been too alarming to permit complacency. Britons rose to arms. Parliament voted a huge expansion of the army, while volunteers flocked into the militia and fencibles. Sturdy Martello towers were raised at all commanding positions on the exposed coast. St. Vincent could tell his peers in

Parliament, "I do not say they cannot come, milords; I only say they cannot come by sea," but the average Briton made ready even should the French fly over in their newfangled balloons. Addington assiduously strove to create a Third Coalition, whereby Russia finally promised to field 500,000 men with the help of Prussia and Austria. Sweden was induced to grant England the use of naval bases in the vital Baltic.

Thus in 1803 England went to war with resolute vigor totally different from the fumbling awkwardness of the previous decade.

THE BOULOGNE FLOTILLA

His bluff called long before he was ready, Napoleon was in the serious straits of a challenged bully. The French looked to him to make good his boast of crushing the people who had "oppressed France for 40 generations." He was expected to win quickly. There was neither spirit nor wealth for a long conflict. The French wanted triumph in one campaign and peace in which to recuperate from the ravages of revolution and enjoy the sweets of liberty. For a swift peace, they gave freely to voluntary funds for building gunboats as passionately as they had contributed to the renaissance of the navy after the Seven Years' War. A consummate politician, already maneuvering to exchange his republican toga for an imperial crown, Napoleon used the Boulogne Flotilla as an outlet for the fervor of his people. A master of logistics, already singed by venturing upon a sea his country could not command, Napoleon had confessed to the British ambassador that an invasion attempt had only a chance in a thousand of succeeding. Given time, he meant to improve his chances, to outbuild the Royal Navy. His threats had applied to a vague future. In the fashion of dictators, he had naively assumed that his victims would be paralyzed with fright until he deigned to devour them, that with his one-man control he automatically had the initiative. The British in 1803 not only disillusioned him,

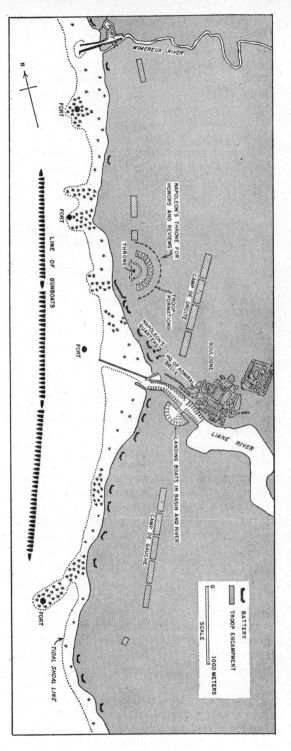

THE CAMP AT BOULOGNE, 1803–1805

they balanced him on the horns of a dilemma: his people were entirely with him for a short war but he could only hope to win in a long war. In this situation, deliberately or otherwise, Napoleon sought a scapegoat. Above all else, he had to preserve the myth of his infallibility. Someone, something had to bear the onus should the grand assault be canceled.

Ever an opportunist, Napoleon threw himself headlong into the invasion project. Establishing headquarters at Boulogne, he ostentatiously rushed preparations. It was just possible that something could be done, even under hawkeyed British surveillance. The number of craft along the flotilla coast doubled and tripled in short weeks to nearly a thousand units by July 1803 and two thousand in August. With typical French thrift, the vessels were designed by Forfait for easy conversion to merchantmen when the invasion was over. Bruix, commanding the flotilla, had the courage to object to some of his master's endlessly contradictory and confusing orders and was finally permitted to organize the force on a sound basis. Ironically, Napoleon's assembly and training of amphibious troops never quite attained the readiness of the naval commanders he despised; by the summer of 1805, he had only 90,000 trained men to put in boats that could have carried twice as many. Long before then, British light squadrons deployed by Keith had proved the folly of launching the invasion without providing the protection of great ships. Though British frigates and sloops and bombs failed to destroy detachments of French boats that were covered by land batteries, they did attain sufficient success to worry even the most violent French patriots who burned to cross the Channel.

For the French, hammering away at their great project, the year 1803 had a bright spot: all save one of the Santo Domingo squadron slipped through the fingers of the British to fetch up in Spanish ports. Elsewhere, the news was discouraging. In other theaters, the British acted with sureness to protect the founts of gold they needed. In the West Indies, privateer nests were cleared out of St. Lucia, Tobago, Demerara, Esse-

quibo and Berbice. Independent Santo Domingo was virtually a British ally. In the East, the French expedition sent to take Pondicherry arrived too late for a surprise descent and continued on to Java, where its leaders later deflected Napoleon's thoughts briefly to a fantastic scheme of colonial conquest. Pursuing the war against French and Dutch privateer strongholds, the British Captain Bligh of *Bounty* fame captured Curaçao and Surinam in early 1804.

St. Vincent's efficient officers settled patiently into a flexible blockade system that baffled Napoleon by early 1804. Keith held the Channel and faced the invasion flotillas. Fulfilling the primary mission of controlling the western approaches to the Channel, Cornwallis commanded the Western Squadron off Brest. Subordinate to him, detachments watched Rochefort and the Santo Domingo ships in Ferrol. Sir John Orde with five ships cruised in the vicinity of Cadiz waiting for Spain to be dragged into the war. In the Mediterranean, Nelson rested at Magdalena north of Sardinia and invited the Toulon fleet to sortie.

Keith was the real key to England's defense. Clinging to the flotilla coast through fair weather and foul, he prevented any coasting vessels from entering Boulogne until May 1804. With his 11 ships and seven-score smaller craft, Keith's vigilance became an absolute guarantee against surprise, whether Napoleon sought to use winter fog or summer calm. Napoleon learned from experience that the Boulogne Flotilla needed five days to file out of harbor, assemble, and dress line. Experience also taught him that within three days Keith could mass sufficiently to drive the flotilla back into port. Napoleon sought to circumvent Keith by establishing a permanent line of gunboats outside the harbor but weather and sea made this too dangerous, even if the British eschewed attack. If an invasion force was to have a fair start, Keith had to be either neutralized or destroyed. Gunboats alone were unable to brush him aside; ships were needed.

Power to defeat Keith could come from three bases: Antwerp, Brest, or Toulon. Antwerp could not guarantee sufficient strength for certainty until 1808. Brest was too closely watched by Cornwallis. The most favorable prospect was to bring the Toulon fleet into the Channel behind Cornwallis' back. With only 11 ships, Latouche-Tréville at Toulon could barely match Keith, should he evade Nelson. Latouche had to be made decisively stronger. To Napoleon, this suggested combination by Latouche with the scattered elements in the minor ports of France and Spain. Once the idea of combination occurred to Napoleon, it expanded into mania.

Unfortunately for France, his other manias precluded wholehearted cooperation from his naval subordinates. In May 1804, precisely twelve months after the British declaration of war, Napoleon made himself Emperor of the French, founding a dynasty of his blood and an aristocracy of his choice. Publicly exalting his army, he made a poor relation of the navy. Creating the Legion of Honor to reward brave men, he conferred the highest degree of the order upon 14 generals but only upon two admirals, the obsequious Decrès and the outspoken Bruix.

If French naval officers took heart from the recognition of the latter, Napoleon disillusioned them in July. Sending word from Paris for the Boulogne Flotilla to be readied for a review underway, Napoleon arrived at the port to find the flotilla still moored. Bruix had countermanded the orders from Paris, explaining that a heavy storm was brewing. In a violent scene during which Bruix put hand to sword, Napoleon insisted that the review take place. Upon Bruix's refusal, another admiral eagerly did the Emperor's bidding. Bruix was vindicated by a flash storm which sank 50 vessels and drowned hundreds of men. Napoleon's apology was one of silence—he suffered Bruix to remain in command at Boulogne. This was not for long; Bruix died the next March. Napoleon had lost a man of great administrative skill, fleet command experience, and high moral courage, who could have given him a fine navy if made Minister of Marine. The episode goes far to explain the relative ineffectiveness of Napoleon's navy: he arbitrarily refused to accept professional wisdom.

In seeking to outwit the Royal Navy,

Napoleon trusted only himself to formulate plans. As his mind switched opportunistically from one scheme to another, Napoleon had to contend with the formidable figure of William Cornwallis, whom he considered to be the chief obstacle to his success.

CORNWALLIS AND THE BLOCKADE OF BREST

Sixty, portly, and beloved by officers and men, Cornwallis personified the aggressiveness of the Royal Navy. He had a well-earned reputation for courage and daring. Perhaps the best all-around British admiral of the period, he was destined to retire without fighting a fleet action under his own flag. This was not for want of trying. His system of close blockade at Brest was to push an inshore squadron of observation tantalizingly close to the shore batteries, while his fleet cruised offshore. The inshore commander had orders to permit the French full freedom to come out at any time to fight, offering only enough action to keep them in check until Cornwallis appeared. Such an arrangement was necessitated by the collateral duty of watching the enemy in the Bay of Biscay ports, as well as keeping in readiness to move into the Channel approaches should the Toulon fleet evade Nelson. With an able, diplomatic subordinate like Sir Edward Pellew to ensnare the French detachment in the nominally neutral Spanish harbor of Ferrol, Cornwallis preoccupied himself with Brest.

By midsummer 1803, naval commando-type raids had destroyed the semaphore communications from Ushant to Brest, depriving Admiral Truguet of easy information about the movements of Cornwallis. In turn, Cornwallis had established an excellent intelligence system that soon discovered Truguet's orders to ready 20 ships and 32,000 men at Brest for a November expedition. Cornwallis forwarded the news to London. Addington's cabinet decided that Ireland was Truguet's probable destination, as a diversion in support of the Boulogne Flotilla. Unfortunately, the King's continued refusal to sign the Irish Catholic Emancipation Bill had revived the

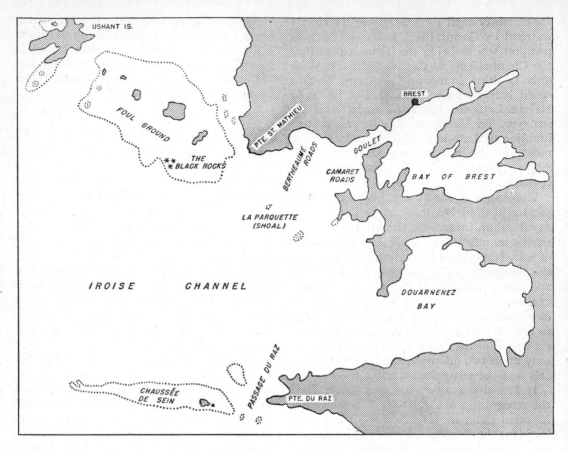

BREST AND APPROACHES

old antagonisms and Ireland was ripe for a French landing. Within a few months, thanks to an encampment near Toulon that Napoleon had established to bemuse the victor of the Nile, Addington's cabinet thought Truguet might be destined for Egypt. Such strategic concerns did not overly disturb Cornwallis. His eyes were on Truguet, who was not going to sail anywhere until he broke through the fleet of Cornwallis.

Unusually bad weather for the first two months of 1804 forced Cornwallis to raise his blockade, but he was correctly certain that weather which drove him into port would not let Truguet out. Besides, his intelligence agents reported that the enemy ships were far from ready, despite gigantic exertions, because all supplies had to be carted into Brest. At this time, also, sporadic sabo-

tage was initiated by *Chouan* extremists who had formed an underground and started fires on a ship or two. Lastly, Cornwallis correctly assumed that Truguet's fleet would not be wasted in an Irish or Egyptian venture when common sense required maximum naval cover for the Boulogne Flotilla. Heavy seas that were dangerous for big ships were death for gunboats, so there was no sound reason for Truguet to stir. Under these conditions, Cornwallis might have made a holiday in England. Instead, he and his men remained aboard ship, setting sail the instant he judged the stormy season to be moderating.[2] His

[2] At this time, Pellew's tactful regard for Spanish neutrality found him a safe anchorage. Proceeding on the assumption that the Spanish were irritated by the presence of a French group from Santo Domingo, Pellew was firm in keeping watch on the French but

weatherworn force was back on station while great breakers were still shifting the channels of Brest.

The early months of 1804 were stormy not only at sea. In England, Pitt suddenly began attacking the Admiralty for mismanagement. St. Vincent was personally exempted from culpability but his colleagues were maligned for failure to destroy the French invasion threat. The dispositions made by St. Vincent were mocked by Pitt because Napoleon was daily waxing stronger. The movement was political. Pitt's own record was less than noteworthy. However, he voiced the anxieties of the nation who could not be with Keith near Boulogne or Cornwallis at Brest or Nelson off Toulon. Addington was colorless; Pitt had a magic name. In May, Addington was obliged to turn the reins of government back to Pitt. St. Vincent was replaced as First Lord of the Admiralty by Henry Dundas, who only a few years before had managed as head of the War Office to run England to the brink of disaster.

Cornwallis soon felt the effects of the change in administration. With everything under control at Brest, his fleet gradually grew restive. In June, Captain Peter Puget [3] came to Cornwallis with a proposal to attack the Brest fleet with fireships. The plan was carefully detailed and Cornwallis thought it had more than a fair chance of success. Imposing secrecy in the fleet, Cornwallis sent the plan to the Admiralty with a requisition for ten fireships. The Admiralty approved in accordance with the practice of supporting a field commander's judgment. Privately however Dundas threw cold water on the project, delaying preparation of the fireships until he could truthfully write to Cornwallis that

the secret was known to the French. Inasmuch as the plan hinged upon surpise, Cornwallis was deftly presented with the onus of canceling an operation whose success would have precluded the Trafalgar Campaign.

Dundas had more arrows in his quiver. Having for reasons or weaknesses of his own recoiled from diminishing enemy naval power, he gave an order certain to add to the ships at Napoleon's bidding. In September 1804, Dundas ordered Cornwallis to have the Ferrol squadron intercept the annual Spanish treasure fleet from the West Indies. Pellew had been relieved by Rear Admiral Cochrane, who undid Pellew's work in a brisk act of piracy which netted a million pounds for England's war chest and obliged her to spend many more in fighting a new enemy. Spanish pride could not abide the insult of having four ships stolen in peacetime. On December 13, 1804 a Spanish declaration of war answered Dundas and his antiquated colonial ideas.

With 32 more ships to move on his chessboard, Napoleon was enabled to plan great combinations. Dundas, seeing intensified activity on the French coast, warned Cornwallis that Ireland was doubtless the enemy objective. Dundas further thought that the time had come to relax the close blockade of Brest, expressing worry over the use of ships for an inshore squadron. Cornwallis politely ignored the letters from the Admiralty. Conducting his blockade as he saw fit, Cornwallis deprived himself of a great battle, but by his stubborn hold on Brest he set in train the Trafalgar Campaign.

NAPOLEON'S PLANS FOR COMBINING A FLEET

Amidst a welter of contradictory ideas and orders, Napoleon had one central purpose: to control the Straits of Dover long enough to pass the Boulogne Flotilla to English soil. His estimate of the time he needed varied from hours to days. Prohibiting his admirals to fight except in the Channel, he expected his ships to march with something like the regularity of disciplined troops. His secret

---

consistently courteous in all his dealings with the port authorities. In short time, the Spanish displayed greater preference for him than for their unwelcome guests. Pellew had no trouble in victualing and drawing essential supplies from the naval arsenal. When the storms began, his occupation of an anchorage near the throat of the Ferrol channel was gracefully accepted by the Spanish, although his flagship was thereby placed only three miles from his enemy.

[3] As a subordinate of Captain Vancouver, Puget explored the sound in Washington state that bears his name.

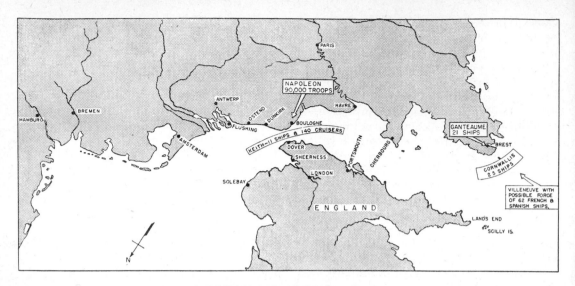

INVASION FRONT, 1805

service was excellent. He had almost precise information about the Royal Navy's strength and counted only fourscore effective ships instead of the ships listed on paper. Printing false reports in European papers, he hoped to confuse the British about his own strength and ship movements. However, the British Admiralty was fully aware that nine ports from Holland to Toulon contained a greater line-of-battle potential than England's. One order to British blockaders consequently overrode all other instructions: should an enemy detachment escape and be lost to pursuit, the blockading detachment was to hurry to the Channel. Had this order been obeyed and had all of Napoleon's squadrons slipped away to a successful rendezvous, blockaders and blockaded would have met again in the Channel. Thus, from the first, a sensible British policy inaugurated by St. Vincent would have frustrated Napoleon. Therefore, it is pointless to review Napoleon's plans in detail.

The first noteworthy project evolved in the summer of 1804. Latouche-Tréville was directed to take the 11 Toulon ships past Nelson's loose blockade, free the 5 ships at Rochefort under Villeneuve, and, swinging wide to the west to get clear of Cornwallis, report to Cherbourg for duty. At this time,

Napoleon declared he needed to control the Straits of Dover for only six hours. In August however, resurgent illness contracted in the West Indies killed Latouche-Tréville.

The selection of an admiral to replace Latouche at Toulon brought to an end the employment in top commands of officers who had established their reputations without Napoleon. Bruix had died a few months before and Truguet had committed career suicide by opposing Napoleon's self-elevation to emperor. Villaret-Joyeuse was forgotten as Governor of Martinique. There were admirals young and old who had a touch of Latouche's fire, but their destinies were in the hands of Denis Decrès. There was vigorous Pierre Martin, who had tried to train a fleet in combat with Hotham; Decrès considered him to be an uncouth Republican, and Martin was lucky to be employed as the yard admiral of Rochefort. There was Edmond Missiessy, whose aristocratic origins had debarred him from taking a Republican fleet to sea; Decrès feared his rumored skill and relegated him to insignificance with the tiny squadron at Rochefort. Unknowns had no chance, unless they had served in the Mediterranean with Decrès, and even then they had no chance if they had displayed promise of eclipsing him. Mediocrity alone had a claim to favor in the eyes of Decrès, who had no fear in putting Ganteaume in Truguet's place at Brest and Villeneuve in the cabin of Latouche-Tréville's flagship.

Villeneuve exemplified the difference between physical and moral courage. Fearing no man, he dreaded decisions. He lacked confidence in himself and any plan to foil the ubiquitous British, and his attitude soon filtered down to the crews whose morale had been militant under Latouche. In September 1804, Villeneuve quailed at orders that directed him to raid St. Helena and British Guiana, unite with Missiessy at Martinique, break the blockade at Ferrol, and sweep up the Channel with 23 French ships, while Ganteaume led the British home forces on a chase about Ireland. The orders were changed before Villeneuve could study his charts but the essential feature of combination in the West Indies remained in the numerous modifications of Napoleon's plans. The entry of Spain into the war only complicated the orders flowing from the Emperor's busy pen as he tried to produce the greatest possible mass off Calais.

The plan under which Villeneuve sailed, after a false start in January 1805 sent Nelson scuttling uselessly off to Egypt, was a plan easily prepared in an office. Napoleon designated Martinique as a rendezvous for some 70 French and Spanish ships to unite under the command of Ganteaume for a grand return to the Channel. Villeneuve was to evade Nelson, pick up the ships at Cartagena and Cadiz and bear away for the West Indies. Ganteaume was to evade Cornwallis, break the blockade of Ferrol, and proceed to the rendezvous which Missiessy had already reached with the Rochefort squadron. There was to be no waste of ships and men in useless fighting. The British were expected to puzzle over the mysterious disappearance of their foes and be astonished by the sudden appearance of a mighty force in the Channel.

Very doubtful that the British would be deceived, unaware that the plan had been changed in several important particulars, Villeneuve took advantage of Nelson's loose blockade to sail unopposed on March 30, 1805. On learning this, Nelson took station south of Sardinia to block the way to Naples and Egypt, thereby giving Villeneuve full freedom to go the opposite direction to Spain. Villeneuve, after waiting two uneasy days off Cartagena for the six Spanish ships therein to join him, had his first concrete evidence that Napoleon's staffwork was not foolproof: the commander of the Cartagena detachment refused to move because he had no orders to do so. Pausing for a few hours off Cadiz, he had more success: a lone Frenchman and six Spaniards under Rear Admiral Gravina came under his flag. The British blockading detachment of five ships under Sir John Orde was unmolested and, consistent with orders, Orde retired to the Channel, causing considerable consternation among those who had pinned their hopes upon Nelson. The hero of the Nile did not emerge from the empty Mediterranean until May 7; by then, Villeneuve was only a week away from Martinique. Nelson pursued on May 12, after ascertaining that Villeneuve had not been seen to the north.

On May 16, Villeneuve brought his seasick, weary crews to anchor at Fort de France, Martinique and found further evidence that something was awry with Napoleon's planning. Missiessy had left for Rochefort three weeks before Villeneuve left Toulon. After a brief, brilliant campaign that wrested Dominica and three small islands from amazed British garrisons, Missiessy had received orders to return home because Villeneuve had been unable to sail. In the comedy of errors besetting the French, Missiessy reached France only a few days after Villeneuve reached Martinique. Missiessy was stunned by official displeasure and asked to be relieved, which Decrès readily granted, because Missiessy had magnificently trained his little five-ship squadron and was obviously the great admiral that Napoleon lacked. Years later, Napoleon turned to him; then it was too late.

Villeneuve was not too long in an agony of doubt. On May 20, the last two ships of the Rochefort arsenal arrived with a new plan. The Boulogne Flotilla was to make an August crossing. Villeneuve was to wait until June 20 for Ganteaume, whom he now superseded in command of the joint force. If Ganteaume did not appear on schedule, it was to be assumed that the stubborn Cornwallis would not let him depart without a disastrous fight. In this case, Villeneuve was to proceed to Ferrol, thus raising his force to

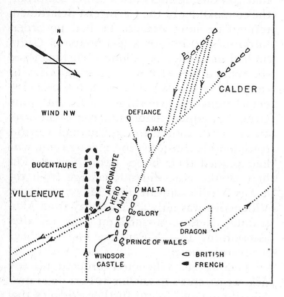

ACTION OFF FERROL, JULY 22, 1805

Calder vs. Villeneuve

35 ships, and then attack Cornwallis to allow Ganteaume's 26 ships to get clear. The joint force of 61 ships, after dealing with Cornwallis—although fighting was to be eschewed if possible—was to arrive at Cherbourg for the triumphal passage of the flotillas. Napoleon did not inform Villeneuve that England and Russia had signed an agreement which founded the Third Coalition, or that Austria was stirring.

Villeneuve had his own worries. In early June, he learned that the indefatigable Nelson had been sighted near Barbados. Villeneuve considered himself acting within the spirit of his orders by sailing 11 days early, since he would most certainly be forced into battle by Nelson if he delayed departure until June 20. Reaching high above the latitude of Bermuda before steering for Ferrol, Villeneuve's movements again deceived Nelson. Although the two forces were actually on

parallel tracks a few degrees apart on July 2, Nelson steered for Gibraltar. Thus, Nelson was far away when Villeneuve's broadsides fired their first shots in action.

Fortunately for England in these unsettling weeks, an experienced, decisive, energetic old admiral, Lord Barham, had replaced Dundas[4] as First Lord of the Admiralty. The hour that a brig captain reported sighting Villeneuve in mid-Atlantic steering a course for the Bay of Biscay, Barham ordered Cornwallis to send the Rochefort blockaders to Ferrol and himself cruise to the southwest on an interception sweep. It was Sir Robert Calder with the Ferrol force who made contact with Villeneuve on a reach to westward of Cape Finisterre, some 300 miles from the Spanish coast.

Cruising in double columns, worried that the unblocked 15 ships in Ferrol followed him, Calder with his 15 ships sighted Villeneuve to windward southwest of him about noon of July 22. The wind was NNW and Calder had the disadvantages of the leeward position. Flowing into line ahead, he stood south to stand in the way of passage to Ferrol. Villeneuve brought to and formed his 20 ships in line. Haze in the afternoon thickened into heavy fog as the opposing fleets slowly got under way to pass each other on opposite tacks along a north-south axis. Visibility closed amidst cannonading until ships could not see the next ahead or astern. Calder lost all control. Blind battle ruined his brilliant attempt to mass on Villeneuve's center and rear by reducing his interval to half those of the enemy. Night imposed caution. The action ended.

Two Spanish ships from Villeneuve's rear were in Calder's hands. He longed for more, but morning and a clearing sky disclosed his fleet scattered and Villeneuve still to windward. There was no sign of the Ferrol squadron, which Calder began to fear had dashed

---

[4] A Commission of Enquiry into Abuses in the Navy reported to Parliament that Dundas had misappropriated funds while earlier holding the office of Treasurer of the Navy. Dundas was impeached on ten counts in April 1805 and compelled to resign. Although he ultimately cleared his name, Dundas never again held office, despite Pitt's great friendship for him.

to Brest, where Cornwallis held the fort with 20 ships. Slowly reforming, Calder waited for Villeneuve to drive towards Ferrol. Villeneuve however was morally defeated and almost physically broken. What will he had to execute his orders had withered in the deadly twilight of ghostly broadsides. When the Franco-Spanish force got under way, it was on a southerly course for Cadiz. Shadowing for a day or so to make certain there was no trickery, Calder cracked on sail to hurry to Cornwallis. As Calder left, Villeneuve was heartened into shaping course for Vigo and, finally, for Ferrol, once he learned that Calder had vanished. On August 2, exhausted from long months of being harried, Villeneuve's men dropped anchor in a friendly haven.

Calder's skirmish was not a great British victory from the standpoint of destruction. He was satisfied he had done well under impossible weather conditions when threatened by another force equal to his own in his rear. An anxious nation harshly criticized him and Nelson was one of the harshest. Calder's maneuvers were smothered in opprobrium thicker than the fog that had blinded him, but they actually represented the last tactical advance prior to Nelson's masterpiece of Trafalgar. Indeed, Nelson made silent apology to Calder by incorporating Calder's massing concept in his own battle plan. Calder demanded a court-martial. This, sitting after Nelson had crushed Villeneuve at Trafalgar, severely judged Calder and reprimanded him while exonerating him from any guilt other than failure to do his utmost to renew action. Actually, by attaining moral ascendancy over Villeneuve, Calder deserved thanks from his country for ruining Napoleon's opportunistic plans. It was Cornwallis however who was recognized as the man who squelched Napoleon's hopes for 1805.

As Cornwallis cruised off Ushant, he was joined on August 14 by Calder's 15 ships and on the next day by Nelson with his Homeric squadron of 14. Cornwallis suddenly had a total of 50 ships, the defensive concentration at the entrance to the Channel that St. Vincent had envisioned at the outset of the war as the correct answer to French schemes. England was safe. A powerful force, crushingly superior to either element of the enemy, held a central position between Ganteaume and Villeneuve. With magnificent courage and even greater insight, Cornwallis broke up the defensive concentration after a day, reasoning that the French had been darting about precisely to focus British attention on the Channel while the true French objective was in the Mediterranean. Cornwallis could not believe that Napoleon would cross the Channel while Austria was rising to arms in his rear. In this he was correct, although he erred about Napoleon's naval aims. Correct for the wrong reason in deciding that the Boulogne Flotilla would never sail, Cornwallis chose to check Ganteaume and to blockade Villeneuve. Eleven ships from the different fleets needed refitting, and these Cornwallis sent with Nelson to England. Twenty ships he gave to Calder to carry down to Spain. Eighteen he kept to watch Brest.

The decision of Cornwallis to divide his force was ridiculed by military savants, including, in later years, Napoleon himself. In theory, perhaps, Cornwallis violated the principles of concentration; in practice he sent a fleet after Villeneuve which terrified that gentleman into giving up all pretense about an offensive. On August 10, Villeneuve was goaded into leaving Ferrol with the 29 ships that could sail. Many of his ships limped from Calder's mauling and none were well-handled. Steering due west to reach far out for a broad sweep north towards Brest and vague cooperation with Ganteaume, Villeneuve sighted strange sails to the north of him. It was the Rochefort squadron trying to locate him, but on the night of August 15 Villeneuve turned and fled for Cadiz. Not until the following day did Calder reach south from Ushant for him. Villeneuve in flight passed a French ship being brought in triumph from the West Indies by British captors and did not pause to rescue an old comrade. On August 19, he scurried into Cadiz past the four ships of Vice Admiral Cuthbert Collingwood, who imperturbably set up a blockade over 35 enemy ships until strengthened by Calder at the end of the month.

Napoleon attempted to shift the blame onto Villeneuve for the failure to make good the rash boast of conquering England in a few hours. The admirals instead of the Emperor of the French had to accept the blame for the tremendous waste of money and energy on the Boulogne Flotilla. In reality, Villeneuve had little to do with Napoleon's scuttling of a project already rendered hopeless by the emergence of the Third Coalition subsidized by Pitt's gold. Napoleon could master enemy armies, and he gladly assumed the offensive in a medium he understood. His arrogation of the title of King of Italy in May had infuriated Austria, whose ministers lent ever more attentive ears to Pitt. As Villeneuve scurried for Cadiz, Napoleon renamed the soldiers of the Boulogne Flotilla the *"Grande Armée"* and on August 26 broke camp to march swiftly to the Danube. The Flotilla was officially disbanded on August 30, after giving Napoleon his best-trained army, fully mobilized and ready for the lightning war which dazzled the Austrians and Russians on the field of Austerlitz.

There was still something that the ships of Villeneuve could do under a new commander whom Napoleon was quick to name. Part of Pitt's compact with Russia pledged England to cooperate militarily in the vicinity of Italy, where Czar Alexander had designs upon the Dalmatian coast. In mid-April 1805, a force of 8,000 men under Lieutenant General Sir James Craig left England prior to knowledge of Villeneuve's escape. The Admiralty feared for Craig's safety but the expedition was warned about its danger near Ferrol and proceeded cautiously along the Iberian coast to Lisbon, where Villeneuve's course to the West Indies heartened Craig to proceed to Malta. In November, an Anglo-Russian force of 22,000 captured Naples, but evacuated upon hearing news of the Battle of Austerlitz.[5] Napoleon, foresee-

ing these amphibious operations, ordered Vice Admiral François de Rosily-Mesros to relieve Villeneuve, proceed to Naples, disembark all troops serving aboard the fleet, and retire to Toulon. Once safely home, Rosily was to form raiding squadrons, each composed of five ships, two frigates, and a brig.

With six of these, Decrès assured the Emperor, France could provide opportunities to develop admirals.

THE BATTLE OF TRAFALGAR, OCTOBER 21, 1805

On September 28, Nelson arrived at the Cadiz blockade to take command from Collingwood, his old shipmate and best friend. At once he began to form another "Band of Brothers." Endlessly discussing tactics until his subordinates were thoroughly imbued with his views, on October 9 he drew up the famous Memorandum embodying his ideas. The essence of his philosophy was contained in the statement, "in case Signals can neither be seen or perfectly understood, no Captain can do very wrong if he places his Ship alongside that of an Enemy." With this aggressiveness underscored, Nelson's system of tactics was little more than a reversion to Elizabethan simplicity. He reintroduced (1) the organization of the line of battle into integral divisions, which were (2) commanded by divisional admirals entrusted with initiative in carrying out (3) a massing on the enemy rear before (4) forcing a melee. He stressed firing at targets of opportunity rather than reserving fire for assigned opponents in formal battle. He discarded entirely that concept of concentration which rested upon mutual support in rigid line ahead. In his system, the will to win was everything. He fought to the death, all or nothing. Confident that each captain would beat down a foe, he cheerfully abandoned punctilious control. It was a system for tre-

---

[5] Nelson met Craig's expedition in early May at Gibraltar and courageously ordered his only three-decker to escort the force through the Straits to Malta. Operations in the Italian area were covered by the Russian Admiral Dmitri Seniavin with 12 ships of the line.

mendous victory or cataclysmic defeat. It was really a serene expression of faith that British captains had no peers.

In Cadiz, Villeneuve held a council of war on October 8 aboard his 80-gun flagship *Bucentaure*. Having carefully studied Nelson's battles, he anticipated a massed attack on his rear and expounded the view that the formal line ahead afforded the best defense. French and Spanish harmony was ephemeral, if only because the Spanish felt that the French invariably placed them in position to bear the brunt of British gunfire. Villeneuve ultimately eased this tension by proposing alternate stations for French and Spanish ships, so that both nations would equally share the weight of battle. The council had a depressing effect, inasmuch as all present accepted the attitude of defense. There was little else to do. Worn by voyage and action, the French ships were in poor condition. The Spanish were worse; many had not been to sea and most were feebly manned, principally by riff-raff.

By October 18, Villeneuve had imperative orders to carry his troops to Naples. He also learned through newspapers the humiliating news that Rosily had reached Madrid en route to replace him. Goaded into action, he consulted with Admiral Federico de Gravina aboard the latter's magnificent 118-gun flagship *Principe de Asturias* to make final plans for a sortie. Nelson's fleet was stationed nearly 50 miles southwest of Cadiz, kept informed by a frigate squadron of observation posted close to the Spanish harbor. Having learned that the British had been reduced to 27 ships when six went for supplies to Gibraltar, Villeneuve and Gravina agreed that there was a good chance to carry their 33 ships into the Mediterranean. Napoleon's ban against fighting had been lifted, but there was nothing to be gained but honor if battle was deliberately invited. Gravina saw no merit in allowing Nelson to close; Villeneuve was indifferent, determined if need be to die bravely. Giving Gravina six French and six Spanish ships to form a van squadron of observation in two columns, Villeneuve proposed to form the remaining 21 ships into three columns. These dispositions,

intended to provide flexibility in forming line equal to the British while leaving a mobile column in reserve for defense at the point of attack, resulted in fatal confusion.

Light wind enabled only part of the fleet to leave Cadiz on October 19, so a free voyage to the Straits became impossible. British frigates warned Nelson, who attempted to recall his Gibraltar detachment while getting under way. On the 20th, Villeneuve brought out the rest of his force and attempted on a SSW course during the day to form the prearranged cruising formation. French and Spanish captains found the sea too much for them after long idleness and by nightfall, the allies were hopelessly confused, as Villeneuve in sudden concern belatedly ordered a single column. All the while, Nelson and Collingwood brought their ships closer in deceptive disarray: the experienced British captains were primarily concerned with blocking the Allied move toward the Straits, not with elegant maneuvers.

On the morning of October 21, the wind was light and from the WNW, giving the British the weather gage as the straggling Allied mass ranged along the eastern horizon on a southerly course. The day was clear but a westward swell warned of an impending gale. Shortly after 6 AM, Nelson hoisted the signal to form two columns in order of sailing and set a northeasterly course to cut off the Allies from retreat to Cadiz. Before 7 AM, Nelson altered course to the east, steering directly for the enemy some eight miles away. In the interim, Villeneuve signaled his force to form line ahead in normal sequence. Dangerous shoals were close to leeward and Cape Trafalgar only 12 miles distant. The light wind astern of the British gave them two to three knots speed. The same wind, being abeam of the Allies, gave them little more than steerageway.

By 8 AM, Villeneuve perceived that his force could not possibly form line in time to round Trafalgar and fill away for the Straits. Unwilling to submit in disarray to the perils of a stern chase, especially when a strong detachment of enemy ships was ahead of his line of march, Villeneuve decided to return to Cadiz and try again another day. Signaling his fleet to wear together onto a reciprocal course, he disintegrated his force into fatal chaos. Had he maintained his original course, he would have attained a semblance of a line. In the gentle wind, a well trained group of captains would have required upwards of two hours to complete the turn. Villeneuve's captains were not well trained. The allied fleet became a long bow, van and rear closest to the enemy, here and there two and three ships deep, in a semblance of defense which Collingwood, for one, considered to be premeditated and skillful answer to Howe's tactic of penetrating from windward to form line-of-battle to leeward.

As Nelson approached, Villeneuve ironically permitted a zealous subordinate to parade the crew's imperial eagle through the *Bucentaure.* Aboard the 74-gun *San Juan Nepomuceno,* Don Cosme de Churruca was possibly more realistic in calling his men to prayers, for they were the last ship of the Allied line. Aboard the 100-gun *Victory,* Nelson stood resplendent in his best uniform bedecked with his medals and orders, his famous Memorandum discarded in a Duncan-like exploitation of an unexpected opportunity. Collingwood, in the newly refitted 100-gun *Royal Sovereign,* set studding-sails to keep ahead of his eager captains, and remarked, "I wish Nelson would stop signaling. We all know what to do." He regretted his impatience when the signal was read to him: "England expects that every man will do his duty."

Nelson's 12 ships approached in a rough column to penetrate the allied line. Collingwood's 15 ships struggled to form a line of bearing parallel to the last 12 ships of the enemy. In creeping, ponderous approach, neither British division attained parade-ground alignment. There was none of the precise station-keeping decreed by the *Fighting Instructions,* for precision tied a formation to the speed of its slowest member. Having a clumsy foe to leeward, Nelson made for him as fast as he could, certain his captains would press forward with the same eagerness. Intending to engage the flagship of the enemy commander, whom he incorrectly thought might be Decrès himself, in

the gigantic four-decked 136-gun *Santisima Trinidad,* which was directly ahead of Villeneuve's *Bucentaure,* Nelson did not at once steer for the center of the Allied line. With inspired guile, Nelson headed for the flagship of Rear Admiral Pierre Dumanoir Le Pelley, commander of the Allied van. Villeneuve too vividly recalled the manner in which Nelson had doubled on the van at the Nile. He hesitated overlong to call Dumanoir's division back to assist the center and rear. When it became impossible for Dumanoir to turn about in time to help his chief, Nelson gave up his feint and altered course for the *Santisima Trinidad* in the center of the enemy line. Even when Villeneuve perceived the true direction of Nelson's attack, he declined to order Dumanoir to him. Instead, he hoisted a general signal for all unengaged ships to maneuver to meet the enemy. Given this latitude, Dumanoir chose to remain aloof beyond the time of honor.

Although the British approach produced a "pi" situation or a double capping of the "T," the risk was not excessive. The French and Spanish were indifferent gunners at best. Rocking in a heavy sea-swell did not improve their accuracy. Nelson had correctly evaluated the ability of his foe. Few shots raked British hulls. Collingwood's *Royal Sovereign* was the first under fire as he reached a thousand yard range at noon. Replying only to let smoke from his broadsides blow downwind to cover his ship, Collingwood had his men lie flat on the decks, while he brilliantly maneuvered to pierce the enemy rear. Nelson's *Victory* received shot 15 minutes after Collingwood, whose ship was embedded in the enemy rear for five minutes before receiving immediate support from his next astern.

Nelson's last signal was an order to prepare to anchor after action, for a haze at noon and the rising strength of the sea-swell betokened a heavy onshore wind by nightfall. Briton after Briton drove into close range. Action became general. The British will to win was again pitted against the enemy's desire to avoid defeat. Courage

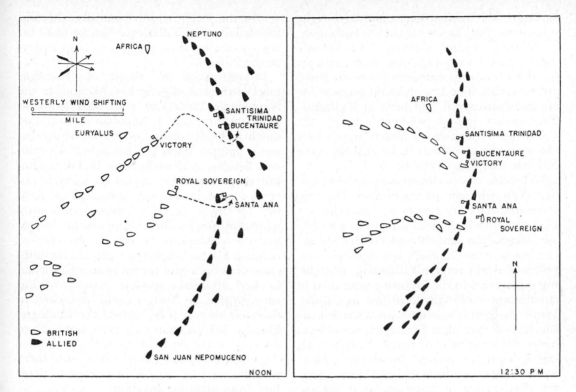

BATTLE OF TRAFALGAR, OCTOBER 21, 1805

abounded on both sides, but the British had more than courage. While being raked, the *Royal Sovereign* sustained some 60 casualties; Collingwood's first broadside into the stern of the 120-gun *Santa Ana* delivered at pistol shot range struck down 250 men. The *Victory* in similar case had only 50 killed or wounded, while Nelson's first broadside laid 200 men low in the *Bucentaure*. With superior gunnery, sublime confidence, and moral ascendance, the British had their way.

About 1 PM, after an hour's fighting, the Spanish 74-gun *Monarca* had half her crew cut down and she fell away from Collingwood's division. Fighting was then getting heavy in the center. At 1:15, a Frenchman in the mizzen top of the 74-gun *Redoubtable* fired a fatal bullet into the chest of England's greatest admiral. Carried below to die with a background chorus of hammering guns, Nelson's finest tribute was paid by his admirals and captains who without him fought through to tremendous victory. Bat-

tle in the center sputtered out an hour after Nelson was wounded, although Dumanoir had at last put about and was in a threatening position with eight fresh ships, his other four having gallantly gone to the sound of the guns. Villeneuve surrendered at 4:30. Dumanoir contented himself with acting as a receiving force for such friends as could escape from the debacle, but British truculence frightened him away with only four ships to the SSW. Gravina, mortally wounded, proved to be the rock of salvage, rallying 11 vessels to him for successful retirement to Cadiz as the unlucky 74-gun French *Achille* exploded.

Eighteen shattered prizes rested in Collingwood's hands. Rather than anchor so close to shoals, Collingwood tried to claw the prizes clear of shallow water. A gale in the succeeding days compelled Collingwood to think first of his own battered ships and in the end only four prizes reached Gibraltar, and but one of these proved serviceable.

In Cadiz, as Gravina died, there were eight ships, two alone fit for repair. On November 4, limping toward Corunna, Dumanoir's four fugitives were captured in a smart action by a four-ship squadron under Sir Richard Strachan. The British could account for all the ships which had been at Trafalgar. The victory was stupendous, capping the golden age of British sea power. Stupendous too were the casualties: 1,700 British, 2,400 Spanish, and 3,500 French.

Napoleon was in Moravia in late November when informed of the disaster. His rage was buried in his victory at Austerlitz on December 2, which checkmated any immediate benefits the British could derive on the Continent from Nelson's last triumph. Napoleon did not forgive Villeneuve, who, being repatriated in the following year, died in circumstances officially classified as suicide. While the Spanish government rewarded the survivors of Trafalgar for having upheld the honor of Spain in hard battle, Napoleon all but ignored his heroes. Dumanoir insisted upon being court-martialed and cleared himself on the basis of being unable to maneuver in the feeble wind. Ironically, this was the defense that Villeneuve had invoked for not coming up from the rear to help Brueys at the Nile.

In retrospect the Battle of Trafalgar marked the end of great naval actions in the Napoleonic War. Ten more years were to pass however before Napoleon was pulled down from the throne of France. Austerlitz was a damper upon jubilance in Pitt's cabinet. Besides, as the echoes of Trafalgar gunfire died, the Brest fleet had survived 11 years almost intact and Antwerp as a partner for Brest began to loom significantly with nine great ships nearing completion on her ways. Napoleon made no pretense of turning his back upon sea power. He indicated that he would try invasion again when he had attained complete mastery in Europe, so that no Austria could be incited to threaten his rear if he revived the Boulogne Flotilla. British strategy became a matter of denying Napoleon the ships to essay another Trafalgar campaign while making sure there would always be trouble in Europe to deter him from planning invasion.

12

Post-Trafalgar: the British
Come to Grips with Napoleon

During the Seven Years' War, the strategy of the elder Pitt had been welded to George's small kingdom of Hanover. Early in the War of the French Revolution, Pitt the Younger was freed from his father's albatross. Thanks to the solid support of Lord Cornwallis, the unfortunate but highly esteemed general of Yorktown, Pitt was enabled in 1795 to override George's desire to maintain British troops in Hanover. The King petulantly and with well-founded suspicion refused to place his German patrimony in the custody of Prussia, preferring to cut the little kingdom adrift until the smoke of battle lifted and it could be recovered. Pitt the Younger proceeded to imitate the form of his father's strategy without completely comprehending its purpose. The British army was pennypacketed into greedy grabs at colonies or impulsive parries of French minor offensives. His mania for fragmenting the effort of the British army engrossed England but wasted troops and prolonged hostilities in Europe which might have terminated much earlier had the Army been landed *en masse*.

A great opportunity arose in 1805 with the advent of the Trafalgar campaign and the formation of the Third Coalition. Austria was the keystone of the Third Coalition, to which Russia, Sweden, and Prussia gravitated, while Sicily offered a staging area for Mediterranean operations. Fearful of the well-trained troops in the encampments of Boulogne, who waited fruitlessly for Villeneuve and Ganteaume to storm England, the Austrians demanded military support. England could operate on either the northern or southern flank. On the map, Napoleon could be confronted with a solid line from the Baltic south to the tip of Italy, if the members of the Coalition had time to agree and to mobilize. England, exercising sea power, could cooperate with Russian troops to duplicate the feats of Suvorov in Italy, while Prussia took the field in the north, aided by Sweden. Napoleon could not be everywhere at once. If he fought in the center against Austria, either or both of the Allied flank attacks might well penetrate France. If he fought against either flank, Austria in the center could stand across his rear to cover the advance of the unengaged flank forces.

Such is the seductive lure of winning wars on maps. In practice, Napoleon moved far too swiftly for the Third Coalition to unite as he had feared. Nor was Napoleon in great danger. Prussia bickered overlong for maximum terms for her allies, while Pitt and the Russians committed only token forces to the southern flank. It was Hanover, innocently lethal to the best interests of England, that diverted Pitt's eyes from the vulnerable Mediterranean. By September, when Calder had shunted Villeneuve into Ferrol and Pitt's cabinet could scoff at the Boulogne Flotilla, Pitt confirmed an agreement to send 70,000 British troops to the Elbe River to cooperate with 50,000 Russians and 10,000 Swedes in direct support and supply of the Prussian army. Pitt did not have 70,000 troops or even half that number, but he hoped to eke out what he had with Hanoverians and mercenaries. Then by controlling the Elbe, Weser, and Ems, the British army would be in admirable position to assert British primacy in Hanover and, if opportunity offered, to invade the Netherlands. Late in October 1805, as an earnest of British faith, 11,000 troops under Major General George Don left Yarmouth.

BRITISH EXPLOITATION OF TRAFALGAR

Don's force landed unopposed at Cuxhaven in mid-November, because Napoleon had recalled his troops from northern Europe to mass against Austria. As news of the disbanding of the Boulogne Flotilla was confirmed in London, Pitt hastily threw together a second force to go to Cuxhaven under the British Commander in Chief, Lord Cathcart. The passage of these detachments was covered by attacks on the vessels of the French flotillas in which the new rockets of Colonel William Congreve performed indifferently. By December, Cathcart had 27,000 troops and was cautiously reaching towards the Ems. On December 2, however, long before the Prussian army mobilized, Napoleon at Austerlitz shattered an Austro-Russian

force. The Third Coalition was staggered. Austria promptly asked for an armistice. Cathcart had little desire to duplicate the Duke of York's misfortunes in the early stages of the war. Demanding either to be reinforced in strength or to be withdrawn, Cathcart prudently concentrated on Bremen, from which he was soon withdrawn, for he had with him the bulk of available British troops.

Austerlitz killed Pitt before he had a chance to savor Trafalgar. Seriously ill, uneasy about the progress of his great continental combination, he withered beneath the rumors about Austerlitz. Locating the little Czech town on a map, Pitt was sustained by hope that Napoleon was up to his old tricks of planting lies in newspapers. When the fact was at last confirmed beyond hope, legend would have it that Pitt told his secretary to roll up the map of Europe because it would not be needed for another ten bitter years. Whatever Pitt may have said about Austerlitz, he soon died, shrouded in gloom. To his successors he bequeathed a feeling that England had been lucky to escape unscathed from the Continent. While Napoleon went on to smash Prussia and compromise with Russia, Pitt's successors reverted to colonial expeditions and minor eccentric operations in Europe.

English operations in Europe were launched in anticipation of French threats to the strength of the Royal Navy. On the heels of Austerlitz, the court of Naples evacuated to Sicily. Collingwood, commanding the Mediterranean theater, was vitally concerned about Sicily because that island victualled his fleet. As Napoleon's brother Joseph marched down the peninsula to assume the title of King of Naples, Collingwood reinforced the squadron commanded by Sir William Sydney Smith on the Italian coast. Joseph had 50,000 troops and met little opposition from the Neapolitans except at the seaport fortress of Gaeta, which held out under Prince Hesse-Philistadt against the best siegecraft of Marshal Massena. Smith had energy, if not the finest strategic sense, and when Joseph scattered troops in detachments, Smith persuaded his superficial colleague, General Sir John Stuart, that something should be undertaken with the small force of British troops on Sicily. After Smith replenished Gaeta and captured the tiny island of Capri, Stuart on July 1, 1806 landed with 5,400 men a mile from the village of St. Euphemia at the ankle of the Italian boot. The landing was undisputed. A small enemy force offered slight resistance in the woods before St. Euphemia but quickly gave way. British experience in minor expeditions had not always been felicitous and as heavy surf delayed the landing of supplies, the troops grimly threw up sandbagged fortifications on the beach to form a safe embarkation point should disaster strike them. Their purpose was to encourage Neapolitan guerillas by striking a heavy blow at a French detachment. Swiftness was essential. Surf however delayed Stuart's train for two days, providing time for General Reynier to march up from Reggio, gathering a force of 6,500 French veterans on the way.

Stuart was able to move on the morning of July 4. Marching south along the coast, his right flank covered by frigates, he reached a river in a few hours and with some misgivings swung left to penetrate the gentle hills rising to the plain of Maida where Reynier was hastening to meet him. The day was intensely hot as the rival forces debouched upon the plain. Stuart's force was organized into three brigades under competent commanders. Reynier was considered a good general, whose principal failing was an unwarranted contempt for British troops. The battle reflected Reynier's attitude, for he confidently essayed nothing more elaborate than a frontal assault. The British, formed in two ranks, offered a line that brought every musket into action. Maida was a test of the British army's tactical system, which emerged stunningly triumphant. Stuart was little more than a spectator as his brigadiers each won an individual battle by superior musketry. Had British cavalry been present, Maida might well have been a French Cannae. Instead it was a rout, one third of Reynier's force being killed, wounded, or captured, and the terrified remainder scat-

tered to the four winds. The British had suffered scarcely 300 casualties.

Stuart was too sluggish to pursue his advantage, and Smith was too short-sighted to formulate an aggressive strategy. Indeed, Smith preoccupied himself with foolish efforts against isolated French garrisons in Calabria while Gaeta in the north was needlessly starved into submission. Strategically, the Battle of Maida altered nothing in Italy, for by November Napoleon had crushed Prussia and was about to humble Russia. Tactically however Maida gave the British professional soldier renewed faith in his superiority. Maida, where a thin red line first stood firm and hurled back the "invincible" French, was the harbinger of Waterloo. Maida, when it was at last believed in London, fostered a strategic boldness that made the British army count heavily in the ultimate defeat of Napoleon.

Unfortunately, the reputation of the British army was tarnished in 1806 by a defeat in the colonial war. This had begun auspiciously when 6,400 men under General Sir David Baird were conveyed to South Africa by a small squadron under Commodore Sir Home Riggs Popham. Reaching Table Bay on January 4, 1806, Popham energetically put Baird ashore in a heavy surf ingeniously minimized by running a transport aground to form a breakwater. Naval gunfire expeditiously silenced Dutch resistance, so that only two soldiers were wounded during the landing. As Baird marched along the coast to Cape Town, Popham landed marines on the flank and rear of the 2,000 Dutch defenders. Broken in the field, the Dutch shortly thereafter surrendered. Thus the British ensured control of the sea route to India, whose native rulers incited by the French had just been pacified by generals of the stamp of Sir Arthur Wellesley.

Inspired by the almost bloodless capture of Cape Colony, Popham persuaded Baird to countenance a freebooting expedition against Buenos Aires. Presumably the Spanish colonists would be easily and quickly overwhelmed. Baird loaned Popham a regiment for the enterprise. When a heavy storm blew a transport with 200 troops away from

Popham's convoy, he altered course for St. Helena, whose Governor donated 400 men to the expedition. Popham was reputed to be mercenary, but he took excellent care of his men and was popular in the army for his resourcefulness in amphibious operations. The legality of Popham's adventure was somewhat dubious. In his defense it may be stated that he was aware that his government had been toying with the idea of attacking Spain in South America and that he had presented Pitt and Dundas with a memorandum outlining his views. His estimate that South America meant an annual twenty million pounds in the Spanish treasury had possibly inhibited Dundas from categorically disapproving of the memorandum, and for Popham silence was assent.

On June 25, 1806 Popham landed Colonel William Beresford and 1,600 troops eight miles below Buenos Aires. Shoals kept Popham's squadron from providing close gunfire support but the landing was unopposed. The following day, Beresford drove off 20,000 attackers by well served artillery. The day after, Buenos Aires, a city of 55,000 inhabitants surrendered to the puny British force. However, on both sides of the River Plate, some 6,000 colonial volunteers flocked to join 2,000 regulars who were not included in the terms. Under the aggressive leadership of Juan Pueyrredon and Santiago Liniers, a naval captain, creoles and Spaniards responded to the indignant shame of the city. Beresford, whose force had been raised to 2,200 men by Baird, was unable to catch Pueyrredon in the open field and finally withdrew to the cramped citadel of Buenos Aires to await attack. Popham failed to prevent the massing of enemy forces when Liniers crossed the river in early August. On the 11th of that month, Beresford was brought to bay in the market square behind the fort. The populace joined their troops in the sport of firing from rooftops at the exposed redcoats, whose only shelter was the open market building. Covering the evacuation of his sick and dependents, Beresford at noon of the 12th called a halt to the slaughter of his men by hoisting a white flag. Popham, still kept by shoals from bombarding the town, lay helplessly offshore and wrote letters home.

News of the original capture of Buenos Aires had been well received by the commercially-minded British. A reinforcement of 3,000 men was sent out to Beresford, who was absolved by his government from any complicity in the affair even if he should be overwhelmed before the reinforcement arrived. Great vistas unrolled before the Cabinet, which was then disquieted by rumors about Napoleon's Austrian campaign. Gold was the sinew of war to the British who, if they captured South America, could expand new markets to offset the imminent loss of old markets in Europe. A project was set in train to exploit Popham's initiative by descending upon Chile with 4,000 men. Another project envisaged a combination of 14,000 men on the heights of Mexico. Wellesley, fresh from Indian triumphs, was set to work planning an attack on Venezuela. In January 1807 these bubbles were burst by news of Beresford's humiliation.

British reaction bitterly magnified the disaster into another Saratoga or Yorktown. Virulence was in direct ratio to disappointment. Popham was peremptorily replaced and compelled to pay his own passage home in a merchantman. Almost exactly a year after Popham carried Beresford to Buenos Aires, Rear Admiral Charles Stirling, adequately supplied with light craft, landed a retaliatory expedition of 10,000 troops under Lieutenant General John Whitelocke a few miles below the city. Whitelocke had troops blooded in the successful storm of Montevideo and confidently advanced into winter morasses to penetrate Buenos Aires from the rear while Stirling's gunboats bombarded the river front. Laid out in precise rectangles from the river's edge, Buenos Aires suggested a simple plan of operations to Whitelocke. To attain maximum deployment, Whitelocke split an attack force of 6,000 men into 15 parallel columns, each assigned a specific objective within the city. A reserve of 4,000 seemed adequate to deal with any emergency inasmuch as Liniers was reported to have scarcely 9,000 troops. The city was still, even dogs silenced, as the British began marching into the city. Unfamiliar shoals prevented Stirling from carrying out his share of the attack and Whitelocke had practically no naval gunfire support ahead of him. July 5, 1807 proved to be a nightmare for the British. Suddenly the flat roofs of the city were alive with the troops of Liniers. By dawn the following day, Whitelocke had lost nearly 3,000 men with no prospects of victory. Short of senseless annihilation, he had no choice but to show a white flag. The Spanish generously agreed to a truce, releasing Beresford and his men in exchange for British abandonment of Buenos Aires and Montevideo. Whitelocke left with his arms and the honors of war.

Thus ended British dreams of conquest in South America, which Englishmen since the days of Drake had advocated. The stubborn toughness of Spanish colonials shocked British patriots who had forgotten the similar result of an earlier piratical expedition against the same city in the Seven Years' War. The prestige of the army suffered tremendously, the two defeats in Argentina seeming to give the lie to Maida. Few Britons considered the different conditions of fighting against an ambushing enemy and against an enemy in the open. Few weighed the extreme difficulty of the orders that Whitelocke sought to execute. Fewer still wondered why it had not been known before Whitelocke sailed that effective naval gunfire support was impossible. National honor was deemed indelibly stained. Whitelocke was pilloried, for his disaster came at a time when the British yearned for reassurance. Not only was Napoleon preparing to attack Russia, after subduing Austria and Prussia, but off in the Mediterranean the vaunted Royal Navy had been chastised.

This was not the fault of Collingwood, who commanded the Mediterranean fleet. Collingwood was fixed close to Cadiz by the surprising energy of the Spaniards in readying a dozen ships after Trafalgar. Off in the Adriatic, Russian troops supported by Admiral Seniavin were steadily inching up the Dalmatian coast against bitter French resistance. Napoleon's diplomats abruptly swerved Turkey away from the tottering Coalition, gradually promising the cooperation in the Black Sea of a squadron of six French ships. The British, loyal to the interests of their last major ally, in February 1807 sent a squadron of eight ships to the Dardanelles. Vice Admiral Sir John Duckworth was instructed to demand the surrender of the Turkish navy, as well as the expulsion of French agents and the reversion to friendship with Russia. Hastily initiated and clumsily executed, the project was a resounding humiliation.

Seniavin's eight ships were hastening from the Adriatic at the request of Collingwood, but Duckworth disdained to wait for them. Impetuously entering the Dardanelles on February 19, Duckworth's column was challenged at Point Nagara by a motley group of Turkish vessels. Sir William Sydney Smith with three ships made short work of the would-be enemy. Within an hour, most of the Turkish vessels, including a ship, four frigates, and six small craft, were aground and ablaze. The survivors, a sloop and a gunboat, Smith took as prizes. This brisk beginning did not intimidate the Turks because light wind in the Sea of Marmora induced Duckworth to anchor some eight miles from Constantinople. His threat to bombard the city if his demands were not agreed to within a half hour was rendered patently ridiculous by his physical inability to come within range promptly upon the expiration of his time limit. As the wind died, leaving him becalmed, Duckworth could see feverish work make Constantinople far too strong for him to attack. Hundreds of guns were thrown into battery and a hundred thousand men manned the defenses of the Dardanelles in his rear. By March 1, when a wind sprang up, Duckworth hoped only to escape from the trap, and thought no more of the 19 ships and 19 frigates he had demanded a week before.

Pushing through the narrowing channel of the Dardanelles under almost constant fire, including stone projectiles weighing 800 pounds, Duckworth on March 3 at length reached the Aegean Sea, having suffered almost 300 casualties in his flight. Near Tenedos, Duckworth met Seniavin, who suggested that their combined force of 16 ships make another try at coercing Turkey. Having imminent business in Egypt, Duckworth refused and sailed on. Seniavin promptly seized Tenedos as a base for blockading the Straits and hopefully waited for a fleet battle.

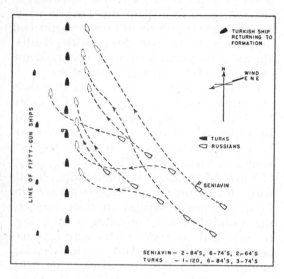

BATTLE OF LEMNOS, JUNE 30, 1807

Russian patience was rewarded in June 1807, when Seniavin lured the Turks from the Dardanelles by deliberately splitting his force in the presence of the enemy, and then cleverly reuniting his ten ships in time for battle. Seniavin had been trained as a lieutenant in the Royal Navy and British influence is clear in the following excerpt from his battle orders: "Open fire at musket range. If the enemy is under sail, shoot to dismast; if he is at anchor, fire into his vitals. Engage combat by pairs upon the same ship. If one vessel is forced to cede its place to another, it will only be under the excuse of moving further down the line. On the manner in which combat is closed depends the outcome. Continue action with the same foe until he is sunk or taken. In the impossibility of foreseeing all particular eventualities, I confine myself to the preceding instructions, and expect that each son of our country will do his duty with honor." [1] From Seniavin's pro-

[1] N. Monasterev and Serge Trestchenko, *Histoire de la Marine Russe* (Paris, 1932), 128.

posed concentration of two ships upon one, it will be noticed that he was a thoughtful student rather than a mere imitator of British tactics. Unfortunately, he did not have captains of British caliber. His subordinates were brave but clumsy, justifying Nelson's maxim, "Close with a Frenchman, but outmaneuver a Russian."

Seniavin's first brush in May with an equal Turkish force had occurred within sight of the Dardanelles forts, ending with three enemy ships broken on shoals. Anxious to be unhampered by forts, Seniavin exposed his Tenedos base to capture. The Turks took the bait, coming out with ten ships, nine frigates, and 70 galleys to attack the island. On the evening of June 29, with an easterly wind favoring him, Seniavin had his foe fleeing before him. At daybreak of June 30, the Turks were caught to leeward some six miles north of Lemnos. Forming two columns of five ships, Seniavin bore down almost perpendicular upon the Turks, who, steering due north with ships in line and five frigates to leeward, duplicated the conditions of Trafalgar. Seniavin chose to preserve his command control by stationing his ship next to last in his starboard column. Perhaps to avoid the charge of copying Trafalgar, Seniavin elected to attack the Turkish van and center. The battle was brief. The Turks quickly fell off to leeward and the Russians chased in rough line abreast, striving to herd the Turks onto the shore of Mount Athos. Unfortunately, the wind died and then with the fortunes of war sprang up in the northwest, favoring the Turks. Seniavin grimly pursued for three days, as the Turks gave up an 84-gun flagship and burned on various shoals two more ships, four frigates, and a sloop.

The Battle of Lemnos was not a great victory by Russian standards, which had as an ideal the total annihilation at Tchesme in 1770 of 21 Turkish ships and frigates by fireships sent in from Count Orlov's inferior fleet. However, the limited Russian victory was galling to British pride after Duckworth's failure. Nor was that all that affected British prestige. Further humiliation came at Alexandria.

Obsessed with the belief that Napoleon still had designs upon Egypt, the British mistook activity in the minor Atlantic French ports as preparation for a Mediterranean venture. To forestall capture of the land bridge to India, a force of 6,000 men under Major General Alexander Mackenzie Fraser was sent from Sicily in early March 1807. By March 20, Fraser had possession of Alexandria. Two days later his position was secured by the arrival of Duckworth from the Dardanelles fiasco. Fraser was a popular general, mediocre in ability, but seemingly able to carry out the simple order of holding Alexandria as an encouragement to the British faction in Egyptian politics and as a deterrent to French invasion. Fraser however was incapable of remaining idle. Considering it wise to live upon the resources of the country, Fraser felt constrained to control Rosetta, 40 miles distant, because Rosetta controlled the flow of cereals to Alexandria.

An expedition of 1,600 men sent to Rosetta was ambushed by the Turks. The British got clear with a loss of 460 men. Fraser promptly took the field and in skirmishes was making good progress until Turkish irregular cavalry in late April cut up and captured a detachment of 800 men. A month later, reinforcements began to replace Fraser's wastage of men. Chastened, he confined himself to Alexandria. The Turks thereupon ignored him and in September 1807 Fraser evacuated the entry port of Egypt, having brought British prestige in the East to its lowest point in a century.

St. Vincent had fought against the complacency engendered in the Royal Navy by Trafalgar, and the sorry results of England's offensive efforts—excepting Cape Town—justified the old disciplinarian's concern. England's exploitation had been badly bungled, discrediting the British army and embarrassing the Royal Navy. The defensive operations of the same two years however somewhat encouraged the British public. If decisive victory seemed impossible, a compromise peace was at least in sight—until Napoleon reached his apogee of European hegemony at Tilsit in 1807.

NAPOLEON'S NAVAL PROGRAM UNTIL TILSIT, 1807

After Trafalgar, Napoleon melted down the invasion medals prematurely struck for distribution to the troops of the Boulogne Flotilla at a grand review in London. The French army set about the task of supplying their Emperor with an invincible navy composed of all the fleets in Europe. Napoleon proposed to control every shipyard from St. Petersburg to Trieste and to make a puppet of every ruler on the Continent. In his own navy, Napoleon stressed reforms while officers and men gained necessary sea experience in squadrons preying upon British commerce.

Headed by Decrès, Napoleon's old Mediterranean seamen were in the top commands of the shaken navy. For an officer corps, naval schools were established aboard old ships. Napoleon insisted upon practical training rather than repetition of Bourbon tradition, and in time these schools began to produce good junior officers, although too few and too young to be important before his empire crashed. Striving to popularize the navy, Napoleon discarded the traditionally lax organization, creating 50 battalions of 800 men, who lived as units in barracks or served as units aboard a ship or were broken into detachments under their own officers to man frigates or corvettes. The rigid discipline of the army was instituted as a means of instilling self-respect. Lavish honors were heaped upon the seamen battalions of the Imperial Guard, who served him well as amphibious engineers on his campaigns. To raise morale, he placed an imperial prince or high personage aboard each ship authorized to carry his eagle in her bows.

Not even Napoleon however could solve France's perennial problem of raising enough seamen for her fleets. The navy battalions were raised to strength by drafts of soldiers, whose proportion increased as the war continued. Despite Napoleon, volunteers were rare, privateers claiming the loyalty of real seamen. Press gangs were necessary to provide minimum numbers of experienced men, and Napoleon resorted to press gangs even in Holland, where sailors were numerous.

Antwerp was to be the great naval base in Napoleon's revised program, but he tirelessly strove to improve all of France's minor ports. Money and labor poured into building dikes and locks, deepening channels, and throwing up fortifications. Shipyards were created wherever pontoons could be used to carry ships to deep water. In ship design, Napoleon favored reduced dimensions both to conserve material and to utilize more inland facilities. For tactical superiority he suggested building ships to carry batteries mounting guns of one caliber. As an artillerist, he further suggested using shells in horizontal gunfire, but at this his subordinates passively rebelled because shells in long guns had caused too many fatal accidents.

The foregoing reforms occupied only a tiny fraction of Napoleon's time. He was much more interested in the progress of his squadrons of raiders. His spies informed him that no less a person than St. Vincent was alarmed by the slackness in the blockading squadrons, as the British nobility made a fashion of assuming command of the great, weatherbeaten ships in which first lieutenants became virtual captains. At the height of the Trafalgar Campaign, Allemand had succeeded in leading a squadron to the West Indies and back. Napoleon thought that Allemand's feat could be duplicated, with ships returning to Toulon to reconstitute the Mediterranean fleet that Villeneuve had lost.

Accordingly, in mid-December 1805, 11 ships and four frigates slipped out of Brest and split into two squadrons. The first, composed of six ships and two frigates under Jean Baptiste Willaumez, had the ambitious objectives of (1) relieving Cape Town, (2) capturing British Indian convoys off St. Helena, (3) relieving French garrisons in the West Indies, (4) destroying British fisheries in Newfoundland, (5) destroying British whalers off Iceland and Spitzbergen, and (6) returning when empty to Toulon. One of Willaumez' ships was commanded by Napoleon's brother Jerome, who did not bring the family's magic to sea. Willaumez had toler-

able success until he reached the West Indies in June 1806, for he remained clear of pursuit until he had captured a score of enemy merchantmen. In August however Willaumez was deserted both by fortune and by Jerome Bonaparte, who tired of the cruise and quietly sailed home without permission. Shortly thereafter, Sir Richard Strachan, who had mopped up Dumanoir's rabble after Trafalgar, came into the Indies with seven ships. Willaumez and his squadron started for Newfoundland, one ship limping for repairs into Havana, and Strachan hove into view near the Virginia Capes. Fleeing, two Frenchmen found safety in the Chesapeake and a third entered the Delaware, but the fourth was chased aground at Cape Henry and burned by British boatcrews in violation of American territorial waters. Only two of the Willaumez squadron eventually reached France.

This raiding squadron thus had more success than the sister force of five ships, two frigates, and a corvette commanded by Vice Admiral Corentin Leissègues, who was directed to relieve Santo Domingo. Leissègues was found off Santo Domingo in early February by Sir John Duckworth, whose six ships in a sharp, smart action destroyed two Frenchmen and captured three. Only one of the prizes was salvable and was commissioned in the Royal Navy as the *Maida,* 74. The French frigates escaped, but the corvette was captured shortly afterwards.

Except for an episode in 1809, these disasters ended the French use of ships of the line as raiders.[2] Napoleon's military juggernaut however attained his goal of stripping major allies from England. In 1805, the victories of Ulm and Austerlitz eliminated Austria: in

---

[2] Two frigate squadrons had mixed success in 1806. In March, Captain le Duc left Lorient with three frigates and a brig, which was promptly captured. Le Duc proceeded to Spitzbergen and captured 39 prizes, losing the 40-gun *Guerrière* to the British before getting safely home in September. That month a squadron of five frigates and two brigs left Aix Roads to take reinforcements to Martinique. The alert blockaders off Aix snapped up four frigates and chased the survivors back into port. This ended for several years attempted forays even by light squadrons.

1806, Jena and Auerstadt ruined Prussia; and by July 1807, Eylau and Friedland had brought Czar Alexander to an armistice conference with Napoleon on a raft in the Niemen River near Tilsit. Napoleon did not have to campaign into Russia. Alexander yielded, consenting to become a partner of France. In exchange for trifling help in Turkey, the Czar joined Napoleon in inviting Denmark, Sweden, and Portugal to make common cause against England's maritime arrogance. In November 1806 at Berlin, Napoleon had amused the British by declaring the British Isles to be in a state of blockade, and the British Order in Council of January 1807 had been a flat warning to neutrals that Europe was blockaded by ships instead of paper. Within two weeks of the meeting at Tilsit, the excellent British intelligence system had detailed knowledge of the agreements between Napoleon and Alexander. Cabinet members no longer smiled. The Embargo Act that President Jefferson slapped upon American shipping until the combatants abroad could make sense with their Decrees and Orders, faded into insignificance when the possibilities of Tilsit were considered. If Napoleon succeeded, every port from Constantinople to Lisbon to St. Petersburg would be closed to British ships and cargoes. Deprived of trade, England would wither on the vine.

Confronted with a definite threat, the British acted swiftly and strongly.

BRITISH COUNTER TO TILSIT: COPENHAGEN, 1807

Concerned by the threat to naval supply inherent in Napoleon's successes in northern Germany, England since March 1807 had been negotiating with her feeble friend Sweden for some sensible plan of operations in Swedish Pomerania, which the invincible Corsican threatened with 30,000 Dutch and Spanish allies. In mid-July, Lord Cathcart arrived at Stralsund with 8,000 men, a quarter of the force to be put at his disposal for cooperation with the Swedes. News of Tilsit had just staggered Sweden. Bitterly recalling his inglorious withdrawal from Bremen two years previously, Cathcart prudently kept the transports for his troops while requesting instructions.

From the British point of view the agreement of Tilsit was a more serious blow than Napoleon's victory at Austerlitz, for Tilsit gave Napoleon potential control of Denmark's navy. Cathcart therefore was ordered to seize the Danish fleet in conjunction with Admiral James Gambier, who secretly sped to the Baltic with 22 ships, 60 light vessels, and a reinforcement of 20,000 troops. Thus, before French clerks had fairly copied the momentous papers of Tilsit, a powerful British amphibious force entered the straits guarded by Elsinore. The Danes had proudly refused to hire out their navy to the British, and so Cathcart and Gambier demanded "temporary deposit of the Danish ships of the line in one of His Majesty's ports." When the Danes refused, the British began landing troops a dozen miles north of Copenhagen.

There could be no repetition of Nelson's speedy victory. In 1801, defenses had been extemporized with little belief that the British would really dare to attack a peaceful nation. In 1807, there were no doubts. Danish defenses were formidable and neither an army nor a navy operating alone could capture the city. Cathcart and Gambier worked smoothly together. Although ships could not come close enough to offer effectual fire support, Gambier's light flotillas ably supported Cathcart's slow encirclement. Cathcart moved carefully, conserving his men, preferring to dislodge opposition by skillful flanking movements rather than frontal attacks. Day after day, the flotillas battered away at the outlying fortifications of Copenhagen, beating off gallant gunboat attacks, and gradually wearing down the Danish powers of resistance.

By August 28, after 12 days of incessant fighting, Cathcart's troops had encircled the city and pushed within a few hundred yards of the last defenses. Gambier remained steady despite a disturbing rumor that the Russian fleet was en route to attack him, and let

Cathcart take until September 2 to complete bombardment preparations and summon the Danes to surrender within 24 hours or suffer the destruction of the city. The Danes spurned the demand. Cutting off Copenhagen's water supply, the British at 7:30 PM mercilessly began to rain shot, shells, and rockets on the unhappy city, ceasing at dawn to give the Danes an opportunity to save lives. Fires of the first day were scarcely brought under control when nightfall brought a resumption of the bombardment. The Danes stubbornly endured the terror into a fourth night, when a great fire threatened to level the city unless men could be spared from the defenses.

On the night of September 5, the Danes gave up conditionally. The entire navy was surrendered as prizes of war, if the British could carry them to sea within six weeks. No Englishmen were allowed ashore to gloat over the effects of the bombardment. Under the eyes of a bitter population, British seamen labored night and day to fit out 19 ships, 14 frigates, and a few small craft. During this time, Cathcart belatedly received orders to occupy the island of Zealand, on which Copenhagen was situated, but he wisely adhered to the terms of the capitulation and withdrew. (See map, page 251.)

With 250 casualties afloat and ashore, Cathcart and Gambier had bought the Danish navy. While only four of the ships were sufficiently sound to be commissioned by the Admiralty, the Royal Navy was greatly assisted by the naval stores that filled a hundred transports. Tactically, the operation was a smooth, almost bloodless success. Strategically, it had been hastily conceived. Too narrow an objective had been assigned to Cathcart. Long after he demanded delivery of the Danish fleet, the ministers in London realized that Copenhagen could serve as a base for the Russian fleet, so that Zealand itself was at least as important as the Danish fleet. The second Battle of Copenhagen converted the Danes into zealous friends of Napoleon, seamen volunteering *en masse* for service in the French navy, so that many ships were three-quarters manned by Danes. The heavy-handed aggressiveness against Denmark jeopardized the security of England, insofar as naval stores from the Baltic area had to be convoyed through Danish waters. To insure themselves against deprivation, the British swallowed their pride and turned to their former colonists in America to establish a dependable—although high-priced—supply that could be expanded in an emergency to meet all the Royal Navy's needs.

Accepting the challenge to maintain financial strength by selling to old markets, the British in early September 1807 took the tiny Danish island of Heligoland, which soon became a great warehouse for smuggling into northern Germany as well as a base for cruisers watching the entrance to the Baltic. The prompt capture of the Danish fleet and island of Heligoland both dazed and angered Napoleon. He retorted by reaffirming the essential features of his "Continental System" of blockade-in-reverse and pointedly ordered the Boulogne Flotilla revived with transportation for 100,000 troops. Putting pressure upon Czar Alexander to declare war against England in November 1807, Napoleon signed an alliance with Denmark that was immediately directed against Sweden.

The British felt honor-bound to send an expedition to the Baltic in 1808 to assist Sweden. As in 1801, no medals had been struck commemorating the bombardment of Copenhagen, but the Danes were implacable and the British were anxious to have at least one friendly power in the Baltic. Left alone, Sweden would have made peace with Napoleon; as it was, she displayed little desire to join the war against him when Sir James Saumarez with 11 ships convoyed Major General Sir John Moore and 12,000 troops to Göteborg in May. Losing ground to the Czar's troops in Finland, the Swedes refused to let the British land at Göteborg, insisting instead upon immediate operations against the advancing Russians. Moore, the prime practitioner of amphibious operations in the British army, was unable to agree upon a sound plan. Fortunately, affairs in Spain caused his recall in early July and British commitment to the Baltic became purely naval, placed in the steady hands of Saumarez.

Flying his flag in the famous *Victory*, Saumarez was completely confident that his 11 ships could deal with the 20 Russians based on Kronstadt. Eleven Swedish ships were nominally cooperating with Saumarez to give him a slight edge of superiority on paper, but he could have managed without them. Off and on for a decade, the Russian Baltic fleet had cooperated with the British in the North Sea, and Saumarez fully shared his countrymen's low opinion of Russian seamanship. The Russians however seemed indisposed to sacrifice themselves for Napoleon. Only one opportunity for a fleet action was created by Admiral Hanichof, who in August 1808 came out with nine ships to reconnoiter the Anglo-Swedish fleet. Upon being sighted, Hanichof immediately made for Ragerswik (now Baltiski), closely pursued by two British ships under Rear Admiral Sir Samuel Hood. Saumarez had the balance of the British force in the southern Baltic at the time. Hood was in company with the Swedish fleet, whose uncoppered ships were too slow to support him. Hanichof chose to continue flight instead of turning on the isolated pair of British ships.

The 74-gun *Vsevolod*, rearmost of Hanichof's disordered column, was crippled by the British, who had to give way when Hanichof put about to send a frigate to tow the disabled two-decker. As the Swedes came up, Hood resumed the chase but the delay enabled Hanichof to reach the protection of the Ragerswik batteries. The *Vsevolod* unfortunately grounded on an outlying shoal and cast off her frigate. Boats sent by Hanichof from Ragerswik managed to work the *Vsevolod* free just as Hood ran alongside her and grappled. The Russian Captain Rudno dropped anchor so that the battling ships hovered at the edge of the shoal. Small arms fire broke up attempts to board. Neither Hood nor Rudno gained significant advantage until the second British ship came into action. Rudno fought until half his crew had fallen and then hauled down his colors. The *Vsevolod* was so broken that the British had to burn her on the spot.

This proved to be the only big-ship action with the Russians. When Saumarez arrived to bring the strength of the fleet off Ragerswik to 16 ships, Hanichof defied him with a compact formation thrown athwart channel behind well moored booms. Saumarez attacked with fireships, which failed. Further

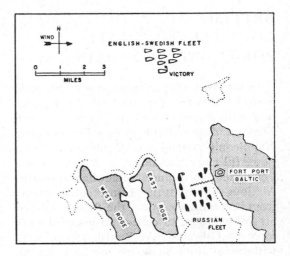

RAGERSWIK, SEPTEMBER, 1808

study convinced Saumarez it was futile to try to dislodge Hanichof and he raised the blockade after a month. Hanichof then hurried to Kronstadt, which Saumarez blockaded without incident until the Russian army forced a decision with Sweden in September 1809, whereby the Swedes gave up Finland.

England's war with Russia thereafter continued on a formal basis, disturbed only by frigate and gunboat actions about convoys. Saumarez proved an able diplomat and contributed much to the eventual rupture between Alexander and Napoleon. He had shown much skill in supplying news of the Spanish rebellion of May 1808 to the Marquis de Romana, commanding the Spanish troops in the Baltic, and successfully extricated the bulk of Romana's troops for service against Napoleon in Spain. His conduct of relations with Russia was the right mixture of firmness and understanding, placing Saumarez in the forefront of the diplomatic admirals England would require during the century-long *Pax Britannica*.

Trusting Saumarez, the British government, just to be on the safe side, sent an expedition in May 1809 to capture the island of Anholt. Situated in the heart of the Kattegat, Anholt was strategically located for control of all traffic in and out of the Baltic.

BRITISH COUNTER TO TILSIT: PORTUGAL AND SPAIN

In late July 1807, Napoleon gave Portugal a choice between rupture with England or war with France. Ancient friendship with England disposed the Portuguese to reject Napoleon's demand to close their ports, but a powerful army assembling at Bayonne made Portuguese resistance somewhat quixotic. Anxious to prevent the "Continental System" from becoming complete, the British ordered Sir John Moore to collect an expeditionary force at Gibraltar. As British troops were withdrawn from Sicily for use in Portugal, Napoleon opportunistically ordered a corps of 15,000 men to get ready at Toulon for an invasion of Sicily under cover of a naval concentration that would include the Rochefort detachment. Collingwood however was fully alert and Sicily was safe.

As an offshoot of the Tilsit agreements, Russian Admiral Seniavin suddenly found himself in a quasi-belligerent status with his good friend Collingwood. However, Collingwood satisfied himself that Seniavin was not disposed to support Napoleonic operations in the Mediterranean and, pending a declaration of war, let Seniavin leave the Mediterranean with nine ships, three unseaworthy Russians finding haven at Trieste, where their commander passively resisted Napoleon's subsequent orders. Seniavin reached Lisbon in early November 1807 and could go no further when a British squadron blockaded him at the formal outbreak of war.

The squadron of Sir William Sydney Smith did not go to Lisbon simply to watch Seniavin but in conformity with an earlier agreement to cover the King of Portugal in carrying out the unprecedented decision to transfer his family and court to the colony of Brazil.

Should the king refuse to abide by the arrangement, Smith was prepared to demand custody of the Portuguese navy. When the French invaded Portugal in mid-November 1807 however, the king promptly embarked.

Napoleon's army had moved too fast for the British, who had to be content with taking Madeira into protective custody until a respectable army corps could be fielded. In late January 1808, King George III publicly challenged Napoleon to a fight to the finish. Fortunately for England, a strategist had finally succeeded to the post of Dundas. This was Robert Castlereagh, who worked tirelessly to raise the British army to its greatest strength. The lesson of Maida was reasserted against the humiliations of Buenos Aires and Alexandria. Castlereagh proposed to put a mass of British troops directly in the field against the French, but this strategy had to wait until England parried the blows designed by Napoleon after Tilsit.

For the spring of 1808, Napoleon calculated on having a naval force of 110 ships, counting those of his satellites, and busied himself with planning expeditions for Ireland, the West Indies, India, Brazil, Tunis, Algiers, Egypt, and Sicily. As before, Antwerp, Brest, Cadiz, and Toulon were cornerstones of his operations, which got off to a good start when Atlantic detachments succeeded in entering the Mediterranean and reconstituting the Toulon fleet at a strength of 15 ships. In January 1808, Ganteaume sailed from Toulon with the two-fold mission of revictualing Corfu and covering the invasion of Sicily by Joseph Bonaparte, King of Naples. Collingwood, refitting 12 ships at Syracuse, failed through two months to overtake Ganteaume, who succeeded in relieving Corfu but failed to convince Joseph it was safe to invade Sicily while Collingwood was undefeated. In strategy, Collingwood resembled his friend Nelson. Tarrying overlong at Sicily while Ganteaume was in the Adriatic, he left for Corfu as Ganteaume steered for Naples. Their tracks crossed within a few hours. Tactically, Collingwood rejected Nelson. His Battle Plan reverted to Howe's concept of attacking from windward, breaking the line at all

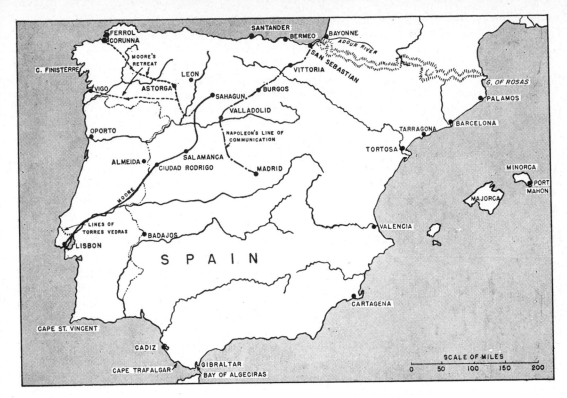

PENINSULAR WAR, 1808–1814

points, and reforming to fight from leeward. Ganteaume did not afford Collingwood another full dress opportunity, although more than a year later Collingwood had the satisfaction of destroying a detachment of three ships and two frigates bound for Barcelona.

In the spring of 1808, Napoleon postponed his ambitious program, partially because of Ganteaume's unproductive cruise, principally because the Spanish people rebelled against his arrogant confiscation of their throne. In an excess of triumphant exuberation, Napoleon had used a secret agreement with King Carlos IV, permitting the passage of French troops to attack Portugal, to fill Spain with French divisions that suddenly deposed the king. Since Spain had been France's most faithful ally for a decade, it was madness for Napoleon to promote his brother Joseph to the Spanish crown. Napoleon's reckless opportunism brought him into conflict at last with a nation instead of mercenary armies. In May, the citizens of Madrid rebelled against

French rule and rebellion burned through the countryside. In July, raw Spanish soldiery compelled 18,000 French troops at Baylen to lay down their arms. For a year, the Spanish did well against the scattered French endeavoring to hold Spain until Napoleon succeeded in uniting his detachments. Then the Spanish lost the taste of victory.

Castlereagh, who had been anxious to reenter the Iberian peninsula, needed little urging from generals like Sir Arthur Wellesley to send all available troops to Spain and to Portugal, whose people had also risen in revolt. British professional eagerness had been well displayed by General Brent Spencer, who in June 1808 began to employ 5,000 troops from Gibraltar in amphibious operations along the southern coast of Spain. Landing arms and ammunitions for eager patriots, Spencer correctly anticipated the wishes of his government, which, ironically, had a few months before been revengeful about Whitelocke and Buenos Aires. Whitelocke's defeat became a testimonial to the valor of the Spanish as the British scuttled their plans against South America and held out a friendly hand to revolutionary juntas in Spain. Spencer's troops made rendezvous with 10,000 under a general with whom Wellesley as second-in-command had a relationship akin to that of Nelson and Parker at Copenhagen. The mobility of sea power permitted the British to choose their own base of operations against the 26,000 troops of Marshal Junot in Lisbon, and Oporto was selected. Landing in July, the British kept close touch with the fleet of Sir Charles Cotton and moved south. On August 21, 1808 Wellesley at Vimeiro justified Castlereagh's faith in the British army by smashing a piecemeal attack contemptuously delivered by Junot. The victory liberated Portugal. Junot managed to escape with his broken regiments because the British were awaiting the troops of Sir John Moore's Swedish expedition. When Lisbon fell, Admiral Seniavin surrendered his nine ships to England for the duration of the war. A considerable squadron of the Royal Navy was thereby freed for further offensive operations.

There was delay as service politics muddied the process of selecting a commander for the 25,000 troops at last assembled in Lisbon. In late September, the choice fell on the strong shoulders of Sir John Moore. Not merely another Wolfe in his ability to inspire men, Moore was a teacher who perfected British linear tactics and introduced rifle regiments to augment the deadliness of the soon famous "thin red line." England's finest amphibious general, a sound disciplinarian, Moore had rare physical and moral courage. Obliged to predicate operations upon the assumption that Spaniards who could once win at Baylen could repeat their victories, Moore envisaged a thrust at Napoleon's communications with France as his soundest strategy. Moore realized that the Spanish army was nearly expended, ready to fragment into nuclei for partisan warfare. He faced 100,000 trained Frenchmen under the personal leadership of Napoleon and he could not hope to do more than win a winter's respite for the harried Spaniards. In October 1808, Moore intrepidly turned his back upon the sea and began his march to Salamanca, hoping to unite there with 18,000 Britons marching from Corunna.[3]

The subsequent campaign became one of the classics of British military history. The Spanish proved as unreliable as Moore had suspected and he was entirely alone against a Napoleon angered by the impudent stab at his communications. On November 13, Moore reached Salamanca and endeavored for three futile weeks to find a Spanish force worthy of being considered an army with which to cooperate. His cavalry meanwhile established touch with Napoleon's 100,000 troops. Full well realizing the danger of exposing England's only expeditionary force to annihilation, Moore outwaited hope and then ordered the Corunna column, which had been delayed by lack of wagons, to retire to the safety of the sea, leaving supplies along the way for his use. In mid-December, Moore shifted his headquarters northward to Alaejos, where captured enemy dispatches informed him of Napoleon's moves and of the complete submission of Madrid to French arms. Calling in his reconnaissance force, Moore ran for the hospitable sea. Napoleon's advance guard was ever in touch with Moore's rear guard, as the Emperor sought to take Moore in flank.

Moore's skill and speed frustrated Napoleon's combinations until Napoleon lost patience and gave up, turning command of the pursuit over to Marshal Soult. Moore's troops spoiled for a fight as the mountains afforded ideal defensive positions, but Moore was too conscious of his great obligations to allow himself to be pinned down. Brilliantly holding off the French, Moore safely brought his force into Corunna on January 11, 1809. At last the ragged, disgruntled British had a chance to fight. Contrary winds had delayed the arrival of their transports.

---

[3] At the same time, the French conquered the island of Capri in a smoothly executed amphibious operation, which light winds prevented British frigates from disrupting. The loss of Capri finished among the Neapolitans any respect for the British that lingered after the inertia following Maida.

Carefully tracing a defense line in the hills leading into Corunna, Moore on the 14th began to embark his sick, crippled, and wounded in the tardy transports. Soult made it plain that the main body of the British could not evacuate without a fight. The wastage of pursuit had whittled Soult down to 16,000 tough troops who exulted in the sight of their elusive quarry brought to bay. Moore had 15,000 troops in line when Soult attacked on the 16th. The battle was short and vicious until British marksmanship blunted French élan, but no profit could be made of Soult's shock, for Moore was shot from his horse by a cannonball. Moore's left arm was almost ripped from his shoulder and he died in the night. The numbed French had no more stomach for assault and the British boarded their ships. Soult paid generous tribute to a great soldier by raising a monument over Moore's grave.

This was more than Moore's countrymen were disposed to do when his ragged, filthy troops proudly marched down gangplanks into Portsmouth. In the public mind, a great British army had marched into Spain only to be ignominiously driven out. Castlereagh, who was to blame for the vagueness of Moore's orders, fervently defended the reputation of the fallen general. Hue and cry villified Moore, but history has accorded him credit for two solid achievements. First, his daring drive prevented Napoleon from reconquering Portugal, which later became the base for Wellesley's triumphs. Second, Moore proved to British and French professionals alike that Maida had not been a freakish accident; thereafter the redcoats moved confidently and the French respected them.

Napoleon's inability to crush Moore was the turning point in his successful career. Henceforth, his Continental System was permanently breached and his strength steadily drained by what has been called "the Spanish ulcer"—the deadly guerilla war of the Spanish people. Sporadic revolts erupted throughout his loose empire, notably in Prussia, and Austria was heartened into another brief, disastrous war in which Archduke Charles won a few victories.

FIRESHIP ATTACK IN AIX ROADS, APRIL 11, 1809

Shortly after Corunna, the British nation was diverted by scandalous charges against the Duke of York, who was compelled to resign as Commander in Chief of the army. An indifferent campaigner, the Duke was a superb administrator. His loss to the government necessarily delayed the employment of massed troops advocated by Castlereagh. The Admiralty, primarily charged with the defense of British shores, was not at all pleased by an opening to plead for use of troops closer to England. Following Copenhagen, Napoleon's rearming of the Boulogne Flotilla had been a petulant gesture, but the Admiralty was seriously concerned. Antwerp, Napoleon said in 1808, was "a pistol aimed at the heart of England." In 1809, the boast became reality. At the mouth of the Scheldt, Rear Admiral Missiessy had ten fine, new ships ready for sea, while ten more were building on the ways of Flushing and Antwerp.

The Admiralty viewed with grave concern the sea front presented by Antwerp, the Boulogne Flotilla, and Brest, linked together by the efficient mechanical semaphore system. Against this threat, the British commissioned the greatest establishment of the period 1793-1815, sending to sea 127 ships supported by 718 minor warships. Although Napoleon was suspected of bluffing, he was at last acquiring the capacity to launch a successful invasion whose covering squadrons would not have to rendezvous in some distant area. Napoleon was unpredictable and before he suddenly shifted weight into an invasion, the Admiralty wished to deprive him of naval support. Urging a strong combined operation against either flank of the Brest-Antwerp line, the Admiralty found that the recommendation fitted in with the government's desire to create a diversion in favor of Austria's imminent declaration of war. Naturally Pitt's heir, George Canning, preferred to act against Antwerp, which was a commercial as well as a strategic objective.

Castlereagh's views were represented in the decision only to the extent of making the Antwerp expedition the greatest combined force in the history of the war.

While troops collected and Moore's veterans were being patched up, the Admiralty was startled in late February 1809 by the abrupt sortie from Brest of eight ships and two frigates under Rear Admiral Willaumez. Unknown to the Admiralty, the mission of Willaumez was defensive rather than offensive and in no way threatened the English Channel. Minor operations in the West Indies in 1808 had given the British possession of St. Lucia, Marie-Galante, and Désirade. French Guiana fell early in January 1809, Martinique fell as Willaumez sortied, and Santo Domingo and Guadeloupe were under investment. Willaumez had instructions to pick up three ships and three frigates under Captain Troude off Lorient, rendezvous with three ships and two frigates from Rochefort, and carry relief to the Indies, afterwards bringing his fleet of 14 ships and seven frigates to Toulon for participation in Napoleon's grandiose schemes against Sicily and North Africa.

Willaumez did none of these things. A light, contrary wind prevented the Lorient detachment from coming out to him when he passed on February 22, and the Rochefort division was not at the rendezvous. Puzzled, Willaumez retired on February 24 to Aix Roads, where he found the Rochefort division still at anchor. His anger was surpassed by that of Napoleon, who replaced him with Allemand. However, Allemand could do no better, because the first stirring of the Brest fleet had produced instant response from the British. Lord Gambier clamped a stranglehold upon the entrances to Rochefort.[4]

Under the circumstances, Allemand deemed it prudent to take the best possible posture for defense and hope that Gambier would leave him undisturbed. Correctly guessing that Gambier would have to use fireships in any kind of attack in the constricted waters of the roadstead, Allemand anchored within pointblank range of the southern tip of Aix, on which he mounted 30 heavy guns. His ships were formed in two checkerboarded lines about a half mile long on a north-south axis. Striking topmasts and unbending sail to diminish fire hazard, Allemand made a mile-long floating boom of chain-linked spars. Firmly anchoring the boom about a half-mile to the west of his ships, Allemand laid it in a blunt wedge pointed towards the British. Frigates and brigs were stationed close to the boom to destroy approaching fireships. Those fireships which eluded the frigates were to be dealt with by five divisions of grappling parties aboard 70 launches.

Allemand had done the utmost within his means to be ready when Gambier used a strong northwest wind and a running sea on the dark night of April 11 to attack. Captain Thomas Dundonald, Lord Cochrane, was in command of eight frigates and 30 fireships that rode in on the gale. The boom was a complete surprise to the British, whose powder trains on the fireships had been finely calculated to explode them in the French lines. Hung up on the obstruction, exploding fireships cleared the way. The heavy seas prevented the French launches from being effective and the frigates gave way in a general *sauve qui peut* that panicked Allemand's command. In fearful disorder, all save two of Allemand's ships captains cut their cables in the wild night.

At dawn on April 12, Cochrane mustered his frigates. Seven of the enemy ships were aground while two had succeeded in reaching toward the Charente River. Signaling Gambier that half the fleet could destroy the stranded enemy, Cochrane gallantly attacked. Gambier moved towards Allemand's recent

---

[4] Troude sailed February 26. His squadron was the last of the raiding detachments created after Trafalgar. By the time he arrived in the Indies, Martinique had fallen and Guadaloupe was under attack. Troude took shelter in the harbor of the Saints Islands, whose heights were occupied by a landing force of 2,500 British on the night of April 14, forcing Troude out to sea. In a running fight, Rear Admiral Sir Alexander Cochrane's four ships captured Troude and his 74-gun flagship *Hautpoul*. The other two

---

French ships reached Cherbourg. The frigates were ultimately captured.

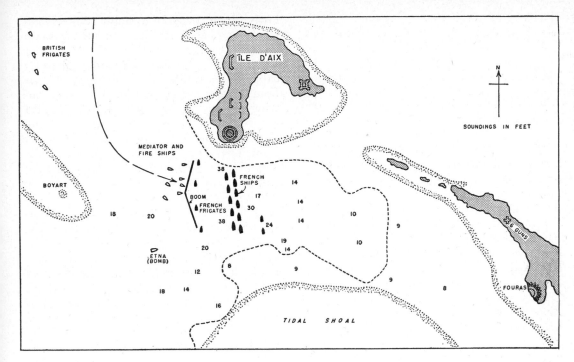

ATTACK ON FRENCH FLEET AT AIX ROADS, APRIL 11–12, 1809

anchorage, whereupon the two remaining French ships gave way, but as Cochrane blew up three helpless French ships and two frigates, Gambier refused to risk his heavy units negotiating a narrow channel which had a tide ebbing 20 feet. Aside from navigational hazards, the citadel and batteries of Aix had red-hot shot. Gambier contented himself with anchoring beyond range of Aix and providing cover for Cochrane, who retired in hot-tempered disgust when the undamaged French began to work clear and headed for the Charente. Gambier's subsequent efforts to stop the French near the entrance to the Charente were frustrated by shoals that grounded his ships. However, only two of the harried French ships were serviceable.

Allemand's command had been virtually wiped from the board but Gambier had behaved like a French admiral. There was in the eyes of the British people an unwelcome substitution of a limited objective in battle for the annihilation that Nelson personified. Cochrane, who was a member of Parliament,

angrily precipitated a demand for court-martial by Gambier, stating that he would oppose any motion to thank the quondam victor of Copenhagen. The Admiralty felt impelled to grant Gambier his trial. Heard on the charge that he had failed to do his utmost to demolish a helpless enemy, Gambier offered sound professional reasons for his decision. In the days of Byng, Gambier's reasons would have been brushed aside, but his peers now felt free to acquit him most honorably. The public did not share the professional view. Thanks were unanimously passed for Gambier's men. For him, there were dissenting votes. He was maintained on duty for a discreet period to display government confidence in him and then retired.[5] On the other side of the Channel, Allemand was not only vindicated but promoted to command the Toulon fleet.

---

[5] Lord Gambier's last public service was as head of the British Commission that at Ghent, August 1814, began negotiating with American representatives to end the War of 1812.

THE GREATEST
AMPHIBIOUS OPERATION
OF THE WAR:
WALCHEREN, 1809

Instead of viewing the Battle of Aix Roads as an oblique yet effectual blunting of the Brest fleet for use in any invasion plan, the British government inflexibly persisted in forwarding the operation against Antwerp. As Wellesley stoutly did his best with 26,000 men to clear the French out of Portugal, no less than 39,000 men, including Moore's veterans, left England for a blow at the Franco-Dutch fleet. The Earl of Chatham was convoyed in perfect safety by Rear Admiral Sir Richard Strachan with an armada of 37 ships, 28 frigates, and 180 minor warships. The expedition was not a surprise. Operations in the Germanies prevented Napoleon from reinforcing the threatened area, whose defense rested entirely in the hands of local garrisons. (See map, page 180.)

In the absence of the Emperor, Decrès attempted to direct the defense of Antwerp from Paris. He had been thoroughly shaken by the Battle of Aix Roads. Timid, if not worse, Decrès issued a stream of contradictory orders, which Rear Admiral Missiessy intelligently ignored. As Chatham and Strachan came to anchor on July 28, 1809 a few miles from Walcheren Island, Missiessy worked his ten ships up to Antwerp and energetically landed cannon and men for defense of the city. Most of his crews had large proportions of former soldiers, who eagerly returned to their old trade and soon made Antwerp formidable.

The details of the campaign need little discussion. Against light resistance, the British on July 30 landed a wave of troops in the north of Walcheren Island. Since amphibious assault had not been anticipated, the landing was conducted in a slovenly fashion, observing the form of Abercromby's Aboukir orders but devoid of practice. Chatham was now in position to begin carrying out his orders: first, to destroy the naval force and facilities of Antwerp, Flushing, and Terneuse; second, to reduce Walcheren; and

lastly, to make the Scheldt unnavigable. Cautiously moving south, plagued by inundations of water as the retreating French cut the cobweb of dikes, Chatham on August 16 captured Flushing in combination with bombardment from seven ships. The left wing of his army, operating on the island of South Beveland, was less fortunate, falling victim to the onset of swamp fevers. Although Sir Home Popham ably buoyed the channel of the West Scheldt leading to Antwerp, the army was soon paralyzed by epidemic disease. With some 14,000 troops sick or dying, Chatham at last decided to evacuate his lodgment without even coming close to his primary objective of Antwerp. By the end of December, the British had sailed home, having done little more than destroy a few small vessels, capture a 38-gun frigate, and enough timbers to build a 74 back in England.

Napoleon, studying reports of the British misadventure, personally designed more formidable fortifications for Antwerp and perfected a system of flooding the various islands in the Scheldt. In Portugal, licking his wounds after a Pyrrhic victory at the Spanish town of Talavera in July 1809, Wellesley read the reports with even greater interest. Certain that the British army's war against Napoleon had to be fought in the Iberian Peninsula, Wellesley was embittered by the Walcheren fiasco. Moreover even with the friendly help of Collingwood, Wellesley was unable to enlist the help of the 15,000 troops in Sicily, which Stuart used to reduce the Ionian Islands instead of contributing to the campaign in Spain.

British power was wasted by dispersion. Even the navy's efforts were too sporadic for Wellesley's approval. The initiative of Captain Robert Mends in harassing French coastal defenses on the Biscay coast of Spain was duplicated by the work of Rear Admiral Sir Charles Cotton in defending Cadiz. Spain had a long coastline however which Wellesley thought could be exploited by British mobility. The Sicilian establishment could render great assistance to the common cause by descending on the coast near Barcelona, as Collingwood futilely suggested to

Stuart. Instead, Stuart, like almost all his contemporaries in positions of responsibility, saw only what was before him.

England's fumbling could not continue. The four years subsequent to Trafalgar merely made victory more remote and a compromise inevitable. No less a personage than St. Vincent felt constrained to leave retirement for a withering speech in the House of Lords. Excoriating the Walcheren expedition, St. Vincent said, "The conduct of His Majesty's Government has led to most frightful disasters, which are nowhere exceeded in the annals of our history. The country is in a state which makes peace inevitable; and it will be compelled to make peace, however disadvantageous, because it will be unable to maintain a war so shamefully misconducted, and so disastrous in consequences." [6] But St. Vincent underestimated the power of his voice raised in support of the opposition to the government. The ministry fell, including Castlereagh, who was made to bear the brunt of criticism for an expedition he had only grudgingly approved. To take the place of Castlereagh in forwarding the mass employment of the army in British strategy, Wellesley's elder brother took over the management of foreign affairs and naturally stressed the importance of the Iberian Peninsula. An even more important change occurred, quietly and without public notice. The new ministry decreed a reduction in naval power from the peak of 1809. Henceforward, the army was given an increasing emphasis in the enlistment of men from the British population of ten million. Slowly, as ships sailed with ever lighter complements, soldiery increased in the Peninsular War. The usual peripheral operations in other theaters continued but the Peninsular War came to dominate all.

The Mistress of the Seas thus finally accepted land war with the Master of Europe

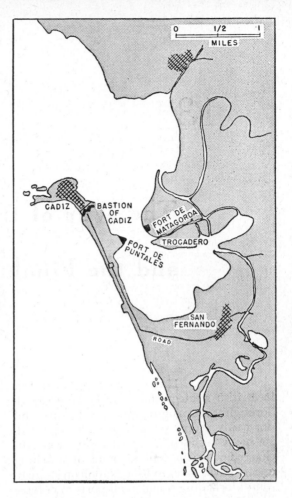

CADIZ, 1810

in an area logistically difficult for Napoleon and logistically simple for Wellesley. Napoleon gladly accepted the challenge, for the English were finally fixed in position and he had come to fear above all the mobility conferred by sea power. His adversaries never seemed able to comprehend the strategy implied by his comment about the Walcheren expedition: "With 30,000 troops in transports at the Downs the English can paralyze 300,000 of my army."

---

[6] Admiral Sir William James RN, *Old Oak, The Life of John Jervis* (London, 1950), 217.

13

The War of 1812
and the Final Defeat of Napoleon

HAVING BEEN PREDOMINANT in British strategy since the Duke of Marlborough's campaigns, the Royal Navy did not easily accept subordination to the British army in 1809. The Admiralty was still charged with the four missions of watching enemy naval bases to stifle Napoleon's squadrons, blockading commercial ports to enforce the Orders-in-Council, protecting merchantmen to ensure a steady stream of wealth into the British Isles, and conducting colonial war to deprive Napoleon of overseas revenue. None of these responsibilities was altered, and to them was added the duty of providing logistic and naval support to army operations in Europe. This increase in operations was accompanied by a reduction in the Navy list because emphasis upon building up military strength reached deeply into the manpower that had sustained the Navy. Ships and frigates had to be decommissioned so that what was left could put to sea with minimum complements. The efficiency of the Navy suffered to an extent that became humiliating when United States cruisers in the War of 1812 easily won nearly a score of ship-to-ship actions. Confronted with increasing requests from the War Office, the Admiralty did not dare to reduce the detachments watching enemy bases, for Napoleon persisted in building ships wherever he could. British admirals at sea were hopeful that next year would bring another Trafalgar.

Preoccupied with the objective of the decisive fleet battle, sea commanders operating under multiple directives tended in doubtful situations to do whatever favored naval interests. Any army complaints that resulted were dismissed as being founded upon ignorance of naval capabilities. By and large, the Royal Navy considered its subordination to the army as an unfortunate although temporary diversion of true strategy. Content with attempting to do what was asked by the War Office, the great majority of sea officers conservatively believed it was the business of ships to sweep the enemy's ships from the ocean. This limited view of sea power wasted tremendous resources when an enemy either could not or would not send ships to sea. A handful of naval officers

234

groped towards an amphibious concept of sea power, but they did not permanently influence the Royal Navy. Their efforts were too impulsive and dispersed to congeal as policy, or too inconspicuous and monotonous to merit much notice from their contemporaries. However, they did bring ships directly against Napoleon's land power and thereby materially accelerated his fall.

NAVAL OPERATIONS IN PORTUGAL AND SPAIN, 1809-1812

In the Peninsular War, naval and military history become entangled. Some discussion of military developments is necessary. When the British finally decided to strive for military significance at the expense of the Royal Navy, the French conscription system had been producing an army far beyond the potential of the British people. Napoleon's 1809 organization called for 800,000 men. Such quantity was needed to hold his empire but quantity had diluted the quality of his regiments. He had built his reputation in Italy leading a compact force whose mobility, maneuver, and coordination had made him decisively superior at the point of his choosing. The great army of Boulogne had been trained in the same system, only to be decimated on many battlefields. Expansion of power had taken Napoleon beyond the limits of training and flexibility. Conscription gave him the recruits he needed. England however was successful in rousing Continental trouble that kept Napoleon from peaceful interludes needed to convert recruits into good soldiers. Conscription, especially when imposed upon subject peoples, compelled Napoleon to abandon maneuver and resort to the simplest tactics. He revived the phalanx of ancient times, marching recruits in dense columns at an enemy line, preparing the way by bombardment from massed artillery. Columns won for him at Wagram in July 1809 against the Austrian Archduke Charles, but Charles was driven from the battleground by bloodshed rather

than skill. Napoleon's enemies took heart. The enormous losses inherent in his new system promised quick exhaustion.

Napoleon's columnar system was designed to punch through the conventional linear system. British generals were confident that the double rank formation that had triumphed at Maida over the French triple rank formation, would be even more successful against French columns. The British line employed every available musket at Maida. Since that time, rifle regiments had been introduced in Wellesley's army, so that the veteran officers and men leading enemy columns could be shot down before disciplined volleys tumbled French recruits. In addition to musketry, the British artillerists began to use an exploding canister projectile invented by Lieutenant Henry Shrapnel, which could be fused to detonate above advancing columns. By keeping a strong grip upon British missile tactics, General Sir Arthur Wellesley won the victories that made him the Duke of Wellington and destroyed Napoleon's power forever on the gentle slopes near Waterloo.

The beginning was in Spain. The British government had wanted Cadiz to be Wellesley's base of operations. Fortunately for him, the junta of Cadiz was uncooperative and Wellesley had to look elsewhere.[1] He was only too happy to select Lisbon, whose topography was ideal for defense during the period of his growth to an offensive strength of 60,000 men. Having naval supremacy,

---

[1] Cadiz sits on the tip of a long sliver of the island of Leon running north along the coast to enclose a harbor area. The Royal Navy maintained a force of light craft and gunboats to prevent the French from crossing the Bay to the strand below the city. In March 1810, when French besiegers on the mainland became too troublesome, the Royal Navy exploited sea mobility to land a combined force at Algeciras. Commanded by the Spanish General La Pena, the Allies marched north, defeated the French General Victor at Barrosa, and took the French batteries in the rear. Destroying the enemy works facing the island of Leon, La Pena's little army crossed to Leon and triumphantly re-entered Cadiz. The city was effectually liberated by the distant Battle of Salamanca in July 1812, which resulted in the French evacuation of southern Spain. Throughout the siege, the British gunboat flotilla was constantly engaged.

Wellesley viewed Lisbon as protected by a peninsula formed on the west by the Atlantic and on the east and south by the broad Tagus River. This peninsula was studded with mountains which Wellesley converted into a vast fortress that filled 500 square miles between the Tagus and the ocean. These defenses became famous as "The Lines of Torres Vedras," which was the name of a village in the first line some five miles in from the coast on the swiftly flowing Zizandre River. (See map, page 227.)

Skillfully employing natural obstacles, the defenses were in three successive lines. The first was secured at Alhandra on the Tagus by a powerful gunboat flotilla and ran in a series of connected strong points through Torres Vedras to the sea. The Alhandra Flotilla ranged upriver to break up enemy attempts to pass the river, engaging in frequent brushes with batteries and cavalry patrols. In the Atlantic, the squadron of Rear Admiral Sir Charles Cotton guarded the left flank against surprise descents by troops that might be escorted by ships from one of the French Atlantic ports. The second line backed up the few weak points of the first. The third, drawn about Lisbon itself, was held by British marines deployed to cover any enforced embarkation aboard 25,000 tons of transports held in constant readiness. The posts in the first and second lines were lightly manned as sentinel stations. Wellesley kept the bulk of the army massed in the center of the first line.

When tentative operations in the field against Marshal André Masséna proved too risky, Wellesley withdrew to the lines of Torres Vedras and defied Masséna to dig him out. Throughout the winter of 1810-1811, Wellesley anticipated and stopped every offensive movement of his excellent adversary. Masséna's supplies came overland from France through mountains beset by fanatic patriots. Wellesley was supplied from the sea. Slowly, Masséna's offensive capacity was arrested. Simultaneously, Wellesley's resources increased. The besieger grew gaunt while the besieged waxed fat. It was the Royal Navy which really arrested the French offensive, as naval defense made flanking attacks impossible in a situation where penetration was suicide. It was the inglorious tedium of convoys however that steadily brought Wellesley to superiority.

In the spring of 1811, Masséna was obliged to take his ragged, starving army back upon his communications line. Thereby his strength should have proportionately increased as Wellesley in pursuit grew weak. Instead, Wellesley remained strong. The sea bounding the arena offered innumerable new communication lines for supplying the advancing British. Wellesley cautiously followed Masséna into Spain, turning towards the lines of Torres Vedras whenever the balance of power was temporarily against him. Masséna was replaced by Marmont but no general could contend against the odds in Wellesley's favor. While Spanish guerillas mercilessly attacked French wagon trains, Spanish patriots eagerly helped forward British supplies from new magazines such as Corunna. In anticipation of denying the free use of the coast to the British quartermasters, the French had batteries and garrisons in every little harbor. That cumulative strength would have been better employed directly against Wellesley, because the Royal Navy took by storm whatever facilities were needed on the shores of Spain. Conversely, the Royal Navy interdicted the French attempts to use coastal waters.[2]

Although Napoleon was principally concerned at the time with enforcing his economic war against England, he did not passively accept the new role of the Royal Navy. Napoleon much preferred to have British power invested in ships rather than troops and took pains to maintain squadrons

---

[2] Coastal shallows and shoals favored French convoys but Britain's seamen attacked whenever possible. The raid on Palamos in 1810 by Captain Francis Fane was typical of hundreds of minor operations. A convoy bound for the French troops at Barcelona took daytime refuge at the mole of Palamos, some 60 miles short of its destination. Fane, commanding a light squadron, landed 600 seamen and marines with two field guns and sank the convoy at the mole. In the action, the French garrison inflicted 120 casualties and took 90 prisoners, including Fane himself, but the desperately-needed supplies did not reach Barcelona.

as potential naval support for stabs against the British empire. The success of British overseas expeditions had clarified French naval responsibilities by 1810, because at the end of that year France did not have a single colony left to serve as a base for cruiser warfare. The British blockade of Napoleon's empire had obliged him to resort to price-fixing of essential commodities and made it politic for him to pay public attention to his navy. Establishing a Council of the Navy headed by Ganteaume to expedite naval progress, Napoleon methodically surveyed the forests under his control and estimated that France could construct 4,800 ships. He wished to have only a fraction of these ready for 1812, when with 150 ships he planned to "conquer a maritime peace" with England. In the interim, he resorted for the last time to the device of reviving the Boulogne Flotilla to divert British strength from the Iberian Peninsula. In September 1811 enough craft had been readied to transport 70,000 troops. Napoleon ostentatiously staged an imperial review which a British frigate watched curiously until driven off by a sortie of the Flotilla. Within 48 hours, the frigate returned with sufficient reinforcement to force the Flotilla back into the defenses of Boulogne. Observing the poor performance of his sailors, Napoleon turned his back forever on Boulogne, whose vessels rotted into firewood to warm the hearths of the Bourbon restoration.

None of Napoleon's naval energy altered the inexorable progress of Wellesley, who by the summer of 1812 won the Battle of Salamanca and liberated southern Spain. Concurrently, British squadrons in the Mediterranean dared to capture prizes in the harbor entrance of Marseilles and landed marines to destroy batteries emplaced on the soil of France itself. By this time, Napoleon could do nothing to prevent petty insults, for he was too busy invading Russia, whose Czar Alexander had renounced the agreement of Tilsit and the Continental System. To his surprise, Napoleon found himself somewhat relieved of his naval problems by an unexpected adversary for the Royal Navy.

In June 1812 the United States declared war on England.

THE WAR
OF 1812 AT SEA

Trapped as a neutral between England and France, the United States had fished in troubled waters with some success. Between 1790 and 1812, American population doubled to a figure of 7,200,000 people, while trade and shipping tripled to $61,000,000 and 1,400,000 tons. Such growth however had not been unpenalized. Clashes with the economic policies of the French Republic had produced the Quasi-War that proved to have settled nothing when Napoleon inaugurated his Continental System. Napoleon's decrees roused some resentment in the United States but Americans by and large felt that those of their countrymen who cared to risk trading with Europe had only themselves to blame if caught within the vagaries of French law. It was England that had the sea power to hurt Americans, who were increasingly irritated by two issues: first, the matter of impressment of American seamen by British warships and, second, the legality of a blockade that ostensibly encircled Europe. The blockaders prior to the issuance of the Orders-in-Council seized 528 American ships on one pretext or another; after 1807 and until 1812, 389 American merchantmen fell prey. The United States contended that the blockade, especially from Brest to the Elbe, existed principally on paper, and tried to establish the position that a blockade to be binding had to be effective. The British continued to do as they pleased. American retaliation by the Embargo Act of 1807 and the Non-Intercourse Act of 1809 proved far more effective than diplomatic notes, inasmuch as deputations of British businessmen whose products were principally consumed in the American market persuaded their government to renounce the Orders-in-Council. The United States however had declared war before the decision reached Washington. Had the news come in time, it is doubtful if it could have stifled the bellicosity of the expansionist "War Hawks" in the American Congress, who thought Canada would prove an easy conquest. In any event, the issue of impressment remained.

Plagued by a manning problem in the Royal Navy, the British refused to acknowledge American citizenship conferred upon British-born subjects, particularly seamen. Man-hungry British captains took some 6,000 seamen from American ships. Adding insult to injury, British captains impressed men from American warships. In November 1798, during the height of the Quasi-War, five men were impressed from the U.S.S. *Baltimore* off Cuba. Just before the Battle of Trafalgar, one of Collingwood's captains took three men from an American gunboat steering for the Tripolitan War. The most notorious episode, and one that temporarily united the factions in the United States, occurred in June 1807, when the 50-gun *Leopard* attacked James Barron's 36-gun *Chesapeake* near Cape Henry, inflicting 21 casualties to carry off four men. In 1810, Lieutenant John Trippe in the 12-gun *Vixen* exchanged shots with a British frigate, and in a night action in May 1811, John Rodgers in the 44-gun *President* killed or wounded 31 men aboard the 24-gun British sloop *Little Belt*.[3] American officers had orders to resist to the utmost any repetition of the *Leopard-Chesapeake* affair and American opinion supported them.

The United States Navy had little more than spirit to carry into a war with the Royal Navy. Of the 19 vessels nominally in the American service, only 14 were fit for sea duty. Of these, six were frigates and eight had fewer than 20 guns. There was no fleet organization and virtually no shore establishment. Commerce-raiding was the gospel, each captain more or less as he saw fit operating to inflict as much destruction as possible upon British lifelines. Against the puny American navy, the Admiralty had on routine stations at Halifax and in the West Indies 11 ships, 34 frigates, and 38 sloops-of-war. These were promptly placed under the

command of Admiral Sir John Borlase Warren, who did not even count Jefferson's 164 gunboats when assigning squadrons their cruising stations.

British officers and men welcomed the war as a break in the monotony of blockading Napoleon and supplying Wellington. American commerce offered rich prize money and the handful of American naval vessels provided a chance to teach outspokenly confident Yankee officers a sharp lesson in respect. Actually, the Royal Navy had become dangerously slack since St. Vincent's time. More attention was paid to polishing guns than shooting them. Complacency became a substitute for experience and drill. The Admiralty was less optimistic, knowing from the friendly cooperation of the Quasi-War that American frigates were extraordinarily strong. To meet the well-designed *Constitutions,* the Admiralty laid down a special class of 50-gun ships and in the interval cut down the weatherdecks of some 74-gun ships to improvise a group of thick-sided 50-gun ships capable of meeting the *Constitution* on even terms. Minor classes of sloops were hurried to completion to contend with the powerful little *Hornets*. Simultaneously, the big navy group in the American Congress successfully passed a bill authorizing four 74's and six 44's, none of which were finished in time to fight in the war.[4]

Faced with the problems eternally confronting an inferior naval power in conflict with a vastly superior naval power, the American Secretary of the Navy, Paul Hamilton, asked his captains for their opinions on the best mode of annoying the trade of England. There were two schools of thought in

---

[3] The *Little Belt* was one of the prizes taken by Gambier at Copenhagen in 1807.

[4] The Secretary of the Navy, Paul Hamilton, originally recommended 76-gun ships "in honor of the year of our Independence." The class was designed to carry a main battery of twenty-eight 42-pounders, a secondary battery of thirty 24-pounders, and weatherdeck carronades numbering four 68-pounders, twenty-four 42-pounders and two 24-pounders. Broadside weight of metal would be 1,612 pounds of metal against the conventional 1,012 of a British 74. The Seventy-Sixers were to have hulls equivalent to British three-deckers, thus carrying to logical conclusion the American habit of surpassing foreign rates. Unfortunately for tradition, American conservatives modified the 76 plan into strong 74's.

American naval circles. One, founded upon the experience of the American Revolution and reading lessons from the French navy's war with England, believed in single-ship commerce-raiding. Captain Stephen Decatur was the leading exponent of this view. Replying to Hamilton, he wrote: "The plan which appears to me to be the best calculated for our little navy to annoy the trade of Great Britain in the greatest extent, & at the same time expose it least to the immense naval force of that Government, would be to send them out with as large a supply of provisions as they can carry, distant from our coast, & singly, or not more than two Frigates in company, without giving them any specific instructions as to place of cruising, but to rely on the enterprise of the officers." [5]

What might be termed the Truxtun-Preble view, founded upon squadron operations in the Quasi-War and the War with Tripoli, was vigorously advanced by Captain John Rodgers. Replying to Hamilton, he said, after counting the British force stationed regularly at Halifax and Bermuda, "Should war be declared and our vessels get to sea, in squadrons, before the British are apprised of it, I think it not impossible that we may be able to cripple & reduce their force *in detail* to such an extent as to place our own upon a footing until their loss could be supplied by a reinforcement from England." [6] To Rodgers, fighting enemy men-of-war was the soundest means of injuring England and protecting American trade.

Rodgers had an early opportunity to demonstrate the validity of his professional opinion. In sailing ship days, the outbreak of hostilities exposed merchantmen at sea to capture by cruisers they did not know were hostile. The readiness of the American navy in 1812 considerably minimized the impact of war upon American shipping. Three days after Congress declared war, Rodgers in the 44-gun *President* left New York in company with two frigates and two smaller vessels.

The moment was ideal for a diversionary cruise because the British convoy from Jamaica was just leaving the West Indies. When Rodgers disclosed the presence of his squadron on the high seas by chasing a British frigate into Halifax, the powerful British naval forces in the western Atlantic automatically assumed a temporary defensive. The central Atlantic was relatively stripped of British cruisers, allowing homeward bound American merchantmen peaceful passage. In southern latitudes, the British deployed to protect the Jamaica convoy; in the north, cruisers chased Rodgers, who steered a bold course to the east and the British Isles. Coming within a day's sail of the Channel, Rodgers ranged south to the Madeira Islands and swung westward home to Boston. His cruise lasted three months and produced few prizes, considerably vexing his subordinates and men, who learned that Isaac Hull in the 44-gun *Constitution* had handily captured the 38-gun *Guerrière* in an action so deadly that the riddled *Guerrière* sank the day after the engagement.

While Rodgers did not meet with popular appreciation, his work was the basis for Hamilton's planning of subsequent operations. In early September 1812, Hamilton created a paper organization of three squadrons, never completed, to consist each of two frigates and a brig. The first, under Rodgers in the *President,* was to hunt British commerce in the central Atlantic, steering toward the Canaries, dropping south to the latitude of Antigua, turning due west to longitude 50° and then homeward to Boston. The outward leg of the second squadron under Decatur in the 44-gun *United States* was to be on a course a little to the southward of Rodgers' but the homeward legs were to be identical. Bainbridge in the 44-gun *Constitution* had the third and only complete squadron, which was to steer directly for the Cape Verde Islands, swing towards Brazil, and then head NNW towards the last leg of the other squadrons.

This plan was the only concerted series of cruises which Hamilton was able to project with any hope of success before the Royal Navy blockaded American harbors. The

---

[5] MS *Captains' Letters* (1812), United States Naval Academy Library microfilm naval documents.

[6] *Ibid.*

squadron concept was not popular and Hamilton wisely included discretionary clauses in his orders which Decatur and Bainbridge invoked to detach their consorts on independent cruises. Rodgers kept his companion frigate with him. In view of the force

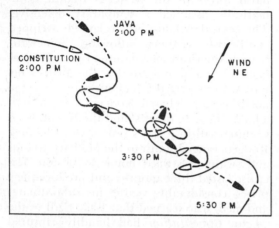

THE CONSTITUTION *AND THE* JAVA, *DECEMBER 29, 1812*

arrayed against the seven Americans who set out, Decatur and Bainbridge should have been humbled in defeat while Rodgers sailed on to victory after victory. Instead, sharply pointing up the dangers of being dogmatic in war, Rodgers cruised 11,000 miles and did not meet an enemy warship, while Decatur snapped up the outgunned *Macedonian,* 38, James Lawrence in the 18-gun *Hornet* took the 18-gun *Peacock,* and Bainbridge subdued the 38-gun *Java* in a display of seamanship and gunnery unsurpassed by any of his colleagues in the War of 1812.

Blighted by misfortunes during his career, Bainbridge had persevered against bad luck and discouragement to final triumph. To some degree, Captain Henry Lambert of the *Java* was a victim to superior American construction and armament. To a greater degree, Lambert was simply unable to outmaneuver Bainbridge. In more than two hours of intricate parry and thrust for weather gage and raking position, Bainbridge stripped the *Java* of fighting power, until she wallowed helplessly, her commander mortally wounded, paying a heavy price for smug neglect of gunnery training. The *Java* was sunk at sea. Bainbridge returned home to a well-earned ovation.

The stunning, easy captures of the *Guerrière, Macedonian,* and *Java* raised the American navy high in popular esteem, especially in view of army reverses in the poorly conducted campaigns on the Canadian frontier. A legend was founded that claimed the American navy had won the War of 1812, until Mahan's careful study a century later destroyed the illusion. The loss of the three frigates stung the British people, who had grown accustomed to endless victories. The Royal Navy was mortified and sloughed off its carelessness. The fine professional attitude and skill of the pre-Trafalgar years was restored and a deadly blockade was clamped upon the American coast. No longer could Hamilton send out coordinated squadrons. Single vessels occasionally broke the blockade to find prizes at sea, but one by one the vessels of the American navy were either taken at sea or locked up ingloriously in port.

British pride returned in June 1813, when Captain P. B. V. Broke in the 38-gun *Shannon* captured the slightly superior 38-gun *Chesapeake* of Captain James Lawrence. An officer in the Collingwood tradition, Broke was dedicated to his profession and alert to improvements. Having commanded the *Shannon* for some seven years, he had a flawless crew. At the time, few captains paid much attention to gunnery, much less fire control. Broke was a gunnery genius. Having perfected a primitive but practical method of fire control, he could direct the elevation and train of every gun under his command. To make such control useful, he held almost daily drills. The *Shannon* was in every respect a crack ship, possibly the finest frigate in the world in her day. By contrast, the *Chesapeake* had a new crew and captain, whose ardor exceeded his judgment. Given time, Lawrence could have shaken the *Chesapeake* down into an efficient man-of-war. Instead, when he saw the *Shannon* cruising alone outside the port of Boston, Lawrence rashly sallied forth to attack. Broke accepted the challenge to a broadside-on, close-range

action. Only 15 minutes were needed to reduce the *Chesapeake* to shambles. The action ended with Broke standing sword in
hand on the American's littered forecastle.
Lawrence was below, mortally wounded,
feverishly repeating "Don't give up the
ship!" He died before reaching Halifax.
Broke won a smart ship-to-ship duel; the
American navy won the second of its inspira-
tions, a motto fit to carry into the ages with
the "I have not yet begun to fight!" of John
Paul Jones.

The fate of the 32-gun *Essex,* Captain
David Porter, graphically illustrates the relentless superiority which smothered the
American navy. Originally assigned to Bainbridge's squadron, Porter sailed alone in the
fall of 1812 to the Cape Verde Islands, and
then went on around Cape Horn to attack
the British whalers in the Pacific. Unopposed, Porter virtually destroyed the British
Pacific whaling industry, doing damage he
estimated at $2,500,000 and living on sup-
plies from his captures. In time, British
cruisers were certain to come after him, and
Porter was as ready as he could be when
found in the Chilean harbor of Valparaiso
by Captain James Hillyar in the 36-gun
Phoebe and his consort, the 18-gun *Cherub.*
Hillyar was on his way to destroy the American fur trade depot at Astoria, on the Columbia River, but proved more than willing
to do his duty in the presence of the ravaging
Essex. The *Phoebe* and *Cherub* had conventional main batteries of long guns, supplemented by carronades. The *Essex* was an
unfortunate experiment in main battery
armament of 32-pounder carronades, supplemented by six long 12-pounders. Hillyar only
temporarily observed the neutrality of Valparaiso. When Porter unluckily lost his
main topmast trying to slip out of port, Hillyar attacked him. Unable to move effectively, Porter fought gallantly with three
long guns when the two Britons took position off his stern just beyond the effective
range of his carronades. The end was mathematically inevitable; when Porter's losses exceeded 60 per cent, he reluctantly surrendered.

So it went. The American navy could only
win glory, not the war. The Royal Navy's
blockade gradually stifled the waterborne
life of the United States and the American
navy was powerless even to protect American coasting trade. Before peace, idle ships
rotted in every cove and creek, among them
the remnants of the navy. The table of major naval captures at sea (pages 242-3) shows
that in general (1) superior force won, (2)
losers had heavy casualties, and (3) the margin of victory in seven instances was affected
by the death or mortal wounding of a captain. Contemporary British writers were
heated in explaining away the handful of
British defeats, compiling statistics to prove
that the Americans were almost invariably
grotesquely powerful in the battles they won.
These writers implied that it was unsporting
to have 44-gun frigates able to fire broadsides of 846 pounds. Their American breth-
ren however realistically applauded the tactical soundness of outclassing British types.
In its modest success, the American navy
could claim something that none could
claim before: the power of American men-
of-war had forced a radical rearming of
British vessels from 74-gun ships down to
cutters.

British cutters and sloops had a war of
their own, as they sought to deal with some
250 strong, swift American privateers.[7] No
less a person than Sir Arthur Wellesley paid
tribute to the effectiveness of American privateers, as a few months after the war began
he started an outraged correspondence with
the Admiralty demanding that something be
done to stop that swarm of Yankee leeches
that fastened onto his troop and supply transports. The Peninsular War was placed in
jeopardy until the Royal Navy managed to
assign sufficient escorts to ensure safe passage
of essential convoys. Bold American privateers were not always discouraged by convoy
escorts, some captains making a game of luring frigates or sloops into chases, then losing
pursuit by superior speed and doubling back

---

[7] These sailed from almost every American port.
Baltimore led with 58. New York had 55; Salem, 40;
Boston, 31; Philadelphia, 14; Portsmouth (New
Hampshire), 11; and Charleston, 10. More than 500
were registered but only half ranged out to sea.

MAJOR NAVAL CAPTURES AT SEA DURING THE WAR OF 1812

In each pair of ships listed, the first (name capitalized) is the captor,
the second (name italicized) is the prize

DATE:	SHIPS:	METAL:*	MEN:	LOSS:
1812				
Jul 16	H.M.S. SHANNON, 38**	538	330	0
	U.S.S. Nautilus, 14	*84*	*106*	*0*
Aug 13	U.S.S. ESSEX, 32	676	328	0
	H.M.S. Alert, 16	*132*	*86*	*3*
Aug 19	U.S.S. CONSTITUTION, 44	768	468	14
	H.M.S. Guerrière, 38	*517*	*272*	*78*
Aug 22	H.M.S. BARBADOS, 28	264	197	0
	U.S.S. James Madison, 14	*30*	*65*	*0*
Oct 18	U.S.S. WASP, 18	268	138	10
	H.M.S. Frolic, 18	*292*	*110*	*70*
Oct 18	H.M.S. POICTIERS, 74	1012	590	0
	U.S.S. Wasp, 18	*268*	*128*	*3*
Oct 25	U.S.S. UNITED STATES, 44	846	478	13
	H.M.S. Macedonian, 38	*561*	*301*	*104*
Nov 22	H.M.S. SOUTHAMPTON, 32	270	221	0
	U.S.S. Vixen, 14	*84*	*130*	*0*
Dec 29	U.S.S. CONSTITUTION, 44	846	475	55
	H.M.S. Java, 38	*529*	*377*	*81†*
1813				
Jan 17	H.M.S. NARCISSUS, 32	300	220	0
	U.S.S. Viper, 12	*117*	*93*	*0*
Jan 24	U.S.S. HORNET, 18	300	135	5
	H.M.S. Peacock, 18	*219*	*122*	*38†*
Jun 1	H.M.S. SHANNON, 38	538	330	83
	U.S.S. Chesapeake, 38	*590*	*391*	*176†*
Aug 14	H.M.S. PELICAN, 18	274	116	7
	U.S.S. Argus, 16	*228*	*125*	*24†*
Sep 5	U.S.S. ENTERPRISE, 14	135	102	14†
	H.M.S. Boxer, 14	*126*	*72*	*21†*
1814				
Feb 14	U.S.S. CONSTITUTION, 44	704	460	0
	H.M.S. Pictou, 14	*132*	*72*	*0*
Mar 28	H.M.S. PHOEBE, 36**	862**	421**	15
	U.S.S. Essex, 32	*676*	*255*	*155*
Apr 20	H.M.S. ORPHEUS, 36**	506	310	0
	U.S.S. Frolic, 18	*332*	*171*	*0*

NAVAL CAPTURES AT SEA *(continued)*

Date:	Ships:	Metal:*	Men:	Loss:
Apr 29	U.S.S. PEACOCK, 18	332	160	2
	H.M.S. Epervier, 18	*274*	*117*	*23*
Jun 22	H.M.S. LEANDER, 50	954	480	0
	U.S.S. Rattlesnake, 16	*204*	*131*	*0*
Jun 28	U.S.S. WASP II, 18	332	173	26
	H.M.S. Reindeer, 18	*198*	*118*	*67†*
Jul 12	H.M.S. MEDWAY, 74	1012	590	0
	U.S.S. Siren, 16	*300*	*137*	*0*
Sep 1	U.S.S. WASP II, 18	344	160	3
	H.M.S. Avon, 18	*262*	*117*	*42*
1815				
Jan 15	H.M.S. ENDYMION, 40**	3094**	1550**	25
	U.S.S. President, 44	*916*	*477*	*79*
Mar 20	U.S.S. CONSTITUTION, 44	728	470	15
	H.M.S. Cyane, 20	*469*	*180*	*38*
	H.M.S. Levant, 22	*309*	*156*	*39*
Mar 23	U.S.S. HORNET, 18	332	131	12
	H.M.S. Penguin, 18	*274*	*132*	*38†*

* Represents broadside weight of metal. The widespread use of carronades in this war accounts for the apparent inconsistencies between rated gun force and broadside weight of metal. For example, under Decatur the *United States*, 44, carried 30 long 24's on her main deck and 22 42-pounder carronades and two long 24's on her weather decks for a total of 54 cannon instead of her rated 44. It should be noted that a new commander often as not changed armament; this is the case with the *Constitution* in her first three engagements listed.

** Received surrender in the presence of consorts who contributed to the capture. Total broadside weight of metal and total on board are shown when consorts either fired or were within effective range.

† Includes captain killed in action.

N.B. Statistics for these actions are greatly disputed. Those given reconcile the best evidence.

to snap up prizes in the undefended convoy. Some privateers actually fought escorts, taking the 14-gun *Dominica,* the 4-gun *Ballahou,* the 4-gun *Landrail,* and the 12-gun *St. Lawrence* and blowing up the 10-gun *Alphea.* The most notable episode of privateer versus men-of-war occurred in September 1814, when Captain Samuel Reid in the privateer *General Armstrong* was attacked at Fayal in the Azores by boatloads of seamen from a small British squadron. Unprotected by Portuguese neutrality, Reid beat off boat attacks until the British commodore had to resort to bombardment, whereupon Reid sank his ship and escaped into the hills of the island, having inflicted eight-score casualties on the British, who were bound for Barbados and the mounting of an expedition to attack New Orleans. Altogether, the privateers captured 991 vessels.[8] This uncoordinated yet serious effort worked great hardship upon the British people, who were soon anxious for a decent peace with the United States.

[8] The American navy took 165 merchantmen. In the three-year period before the War of 1812, French privateers had captured 1,660 prizes. Thus, the combined loss for 1812-1815 of 2,500 merchantmen succeeded a period of heavy loss which made the War of 1812 lie very heavily upon the British economy.

Before peace could come however the American War Hawks had to have a try at conquering Canada.

THE WAR OF 1812 ON THE CANADIAN BORDER

In discussing the war on the Great Lakes, Mahan spoke of the St. Lawrence as the trunk of a tree, with the Lakes as its branches. True strategy, then, would consist of striking as close to the roots of the Canadian tree as possible. British power was based on Quebec and diffused through Montreal. Stoddert's program of building 74's, had it not been canceled by Jefferson, would have provided the United States with a fleet of a dozen ships for starving Quebec and thus all Canada. In the absence of a fleet, American power had to reach overland. Even this strategy however was vitiated by sectional interests. Where western border states feared Indian uprisings if troops should be concentrated in the east, people in the eastern border states feared a revival of the British 1777 invasion plan and wanted their militia kept for home defense. The end result was virtual paralysis of a great number of Americans under arms. At the outbreak of hostilities, General Isaac Brock in Canada had scarcely 7,000 troops, yet such was the division of purpose among American military leaders that Brock's tiny force was able to hurl back every attempt to cross into Canada, notably at Detroit, where General William Hull was induced to surrender in July 1812. By the time reinforcements from England reached Quebec, Brock had the situation well in hand.

It soon became clear that naval control of the Lakes was important, and control of Lake Ontario most important. Captain Isaac Chauncey became over-all American naval commander on the Lakes and naturally chose Lake Ontario for his own theater of operations, delegating Lake Erie to Lieutenant Jesse D. Elliott and then to Master Commandant Oliver Hazard Perry. Chauncey was an able officer and strategist. Indeed it was his tree analogy about the Canadian war which Mahan later elaborated. However, Chauncey was never seriously supported by his army colleagues and the war on Lake Ontario proved insignificant. Chauncey was opposed by Captain Sir James Lucas Yeo, who was an exceptionally able officer. Aside from a few indecisive brushes, the interest on Lake Ontario centered upon a naval building race. Yeo laid down and launched the 112-gun ship *St. Lawrence,* which Chauncey countered by commencing a pair of 74's. These, in turn, induced Yeo to start a 74 of his own and a frigate. The flotillas of light craft threatened to give way to full scale ships of the line but the war proved to be too brief for the *St. Lawrence* and her rivals to meet in battle.[9]

In view of mutual unreadiness, it was upon Lake Erie, the next branch of the Canadian tree, that the naval war was fought in deadly earnest. Niagara Falls prohibited the passage of bulky cargoes, so that British and Americans alike had to hew their ship timbers from the virgin forests. Water transport, interrupted by portage past Niagara, enabled the British to arm their vessels with as many long guns as they chose. Lack of good roads forced the Americans to haul in the lighter-weight carronades for principal armament. Thus, Perry's two big vessels, the 500-ton brigs *Lawrence* and *Niagara* each carried eighteen 32-pounder carronades and two regular 12-pounders. The preponderance of British armament was in long guns. The accompanying table shows the disparity.

The lack of uniformity in British batteries was a combination of misused opportunity to bring in overwhelming armament from Lake Ontario and haphazard planning of construction. Even so, the British enjoyed superiority in long guns which should have brought victory against the lightly built American squadron. Victory and defeat in the Battle of Lake Erie was a matter of commanders.

[9] The Lakes were disarmed until World War II, when the Rush-Bagot Agreement of 1817 was relaxed to permit naval training on the Great Lakes.

FORCES AT THE BATTLE OF LAKE ERIE

AMERICAN

VESSEL	RIG	LONG GUNS:								CARRONADES:			
		32:	24:	18:	12:	9:	6:	4:	2:	32:	24:	18:	12:
Lawrence	Brig				2					18			
Niagara	"				2					18			
Caledonia	"		2							1			
Ariel	Schooner				4								
Scorpion	"	1	1										
Porcupine	"	1											
Tigress	"	1											
Somers	"		1							1			
Trippe	"		1										
	Totals	3	5		8					38			

BRITISH

VESSEL	RIG	32:	24:	18:	12:	9:	6:	4:	2:	32:	24:	18:	12:
Detroit	Ship		2	1	6	8					1	1	
Queen Charlotte	"				3						14		
Hunter	Brig						2	4	2				2
Lady Prevost	Schooner					3							10
Little Belt	Sloop					1	2						
Chippeway	Schooner					1							
	Totals		2	1	9	13	4	4	2		15	1	12

Oliver Hazard Perry was 27 when he arrived at Presque Isle in the winter of 1812 to build his fleet. He had good seamen brought from the ships blockaded on the coast. Across Lake Erie at Malden, Robert Heriot Barclay arrived in May 1813 to assume command of the British force. Barclay was 26, had fought at Trafalgar, had lost his left arm, and scorned the skill of Americans. Wiser and better officers had declined command of Lake Erie, which was supplied with the leftovers from Yeo's buildup on Lake Ontario. Barclay's little fleet was manned by 250 soldiers and 140 French-Canadian militia, who received a leaven of 50 mediocre seamen in June 1813. Barclay commenced an increasingly desperate correspondence with Yeo, pleading for better guns and seamen in the face of Perry's well-trained and outfitted squadron. Yeo did not consider it safe to gamble on the tenuous security of Lake Ontario and so Barclay's requisitions went unanswered.

The inevitable collision between Barclay and Perry occurred on September 10, 1813. Perry sailed from Put-In Bay and Barclay from Malden, where he had just finished outfitting the *Detroit* by taking the guns from Fort Amherstburg. The little fleets were in column on a SW heading, Perry favored with the wind. Trafalgar permeated Perry's battle plan but dominated Barclay's intelligence. As the Americans drifted in on a light wind, Barclay's obvious tactics were to keep the range open by falling off the wind so that he could nullify Perry's carronade superiority and shoot the Americans to pieces with long guns. With such a reversal of British tradition, Hillyar had mastered Porter's *Essex,* but if pride could have allowed Barclay to use such tactics, his polyglot guncrews would not. Long range gunnery was an art little cherished in the Royal Navy even in ships properly manned. The general inaccuracy of smooth-bore cannon made British preference for short ranges realistic. Had

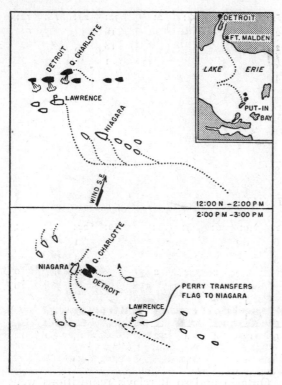

BATTLE OF LAKE ERIE,
SEPTEMBER 10, 1813

Barclay trained his people instead of writing complaints to Yeo, he might have been able to handle Perry's approach, for Perry was very poorly supported by Elliott in the *Niagara.*

Opening fire against the leading Americans at 11:45 AM, Barclay did his best. Fate seemed to favor the British as Elliott failed to obey Perry's signal to close with the enemy. For nearly two hours, Perry's *Lawrence* fought alone at short range with the *Detroit* and *Queen Charlotte,* until all the guns of the *Lawrence* were silenced and 60 per cent of her 142 men killed or wounded. Perry calmly took his commodore's pennant and battleflag emblazoned with James Lawrence's words "Don't give up the

ship!" and went in an open boat to take command of the almost undamaged *Niagara,* whose fresh broadsides of 32-pounder carronades proved too much for the gallant British, for they had lost 135 men in the shapeless melee. Every British captain and his second in command were either killed or seriously wounded. Barclay, struck in a leg and his remaining arm, broke before the hurricane of shot, giving Perry occasion to inform his colleague, General William H. Harrison, "We have met the enemy and they are ours; two ships, two brigs, one schooner, and one sloop."

Barclay's court-martial exonerated him because (1) he had defective means to equip his vessels, (2) Yeo had not honored the repeated requests for seamen, (3) the Americans had a broadside weight of metal advantage of 928 pounds to 478 pounds, and (4) leadership failed when the officers fell. On the heels of Perry's victory, General Harrison crossed into Canada and won the decisive Battle of the Thames on October 5, ending through the death of Chief Tecumseh the pretensions of the British plan for creating an Indian buffer state between the United States and Canada.

Perry's victory was the result of intrepidity and the will to win that had hitherto been the hallmark of British naval leaders, well underscoring the judgment of an eminent historian that in the War of 1812 "Great Britain had to meet the most capable naval foe she had ever encountered."[10]

The Battle of Lake Erie did not end hostilities on the Canadian border. Wellington had reached Bordeaux in 1813 and could detach some of his best troops for use against the United States. For the spring of 1814 therefore, Major General Sir George Prevost found himself with 18,000 seasoned soldiers to employ in a manner best suited to improve England's position in the peace negotiations that had begun at Ghent. In the summer of 1814, two thousand British troops seized eastern Maine. Prevost proposed to capture Lake Champlain as the western limit of territory to be ceded to England at the

---

[10] William Laird Clowes, ed., *The Royal Navy,* 6 vols. (London, 1900), V, 18.

FORCES AT THE BATTLE OF LAKE CHAMPLAIN

AMERICAN

Vessel:	Rig:	Long guns:					Carronades:			
		24:	18:	12:	9:	6:	42:	32:	24:	18:
Saratoga	Ship	8					6	12		
Eagle	Brig		8					12		
Ticonderoga	Schooner		4	10				3		
Preble	Sloop				7					
6 gunboats, each	Cutter	1								1
4 " "	"			1						
	Totals	14	12	14	7		6	27		6

BRITISH

Vessel:	Rig:	Long guns:					Carronades:			
		24:	18:	12:	9:	6:	42:	32:	24:	18:
Confiance	Ship	27						4	6	
Linnet	Brig			16						
Chubb	Sloop					1				10
Finch	"					4				6
2 gunboats, each	Cutter	1						1		
1 " "	"		1					1		
4 " "	"			1						
3 " "	"							1		
	Totals	29	5	16		5		10	6	16

peace. The usual line of advance along the Richelieu River was followed from Montreal, but the objective was more modest than Burgoyne's in 1777. Unlike Burgoyne, Prevost did not encounter a Saratoga. Instead, his naval support was annihilated and he meekly withdrew to Montreal.

There was little to stop the advance of Prevost's 11,000 regulars, for mistaken American strategists had ordered a concentration on the shores of Lake Ontario, leaving only 3,300 militia stiffened by four companies of regulars at Plattsburg, the key to Lake Champlain. The real defense of northwestern New England rested in the capable hands of 30-year-old Master Commandant Thomas Macdonough. As on the Great Lakes, the contending fleets on Lake Champlain had to be hewn from the timbers lining the shores. On the day of the Battle of Lake Champlain on September 11, 1814, the opposed vessels had the armament shown in the table.

The British squadron was commanded by Captain George Downie, who, it will be noted in the table shown, had the bulk of his strength in the 830-ton Confiance.[11] Unfortunately, Downie did not have the strength of character to resist the uninformed, impatient insistence of General Prevost that the American squadron be driven from Plattsburg. The Confiance was launched, rigged, equipped, fought, and captured within 17 days, providing a parallel to the unreadiness of Lawrence's Chesapeake. As in Barclay's squadron, Downie had only a handful of seamen among his crews of soldiers and French-Canadian militia, and they could not produce a miracle—if time did not allow miracles, neither did Macdonough.

Conscious of his superior men, Macdonough deliberately chose to discard the

---

[11] Although the Confiance was later rated as a frigate in the American navy, she was merely a sloop-of-war compared with the 36-gun Constellation of 1,250 tons (British measurement).

advantages of an engagement underway, preferring to select a powerful position at anchor under the cover of Cumberland Head, close to the shore where his broadsides helped the handful of troops under Brigadier General Alexander Macomb in defying Prevost to cross the Saranac River. Loath to encounter ship-fired grape and canister, Prevost arranged a combined attack with Downie, whereby Macdonough would be rendered too

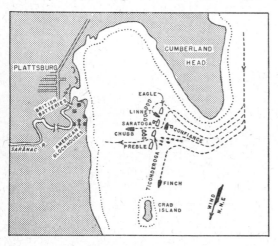

BATTLE OF LAKE CHAMPLAIN,
SEPTEMBER 11, 1814

busy to support Macomb. Prevost was supremely confident of his ability to crush Macomb, but saw little sense in unnecessary loss of life. Unknown to Downie, Prevost changed the time of the land assault, and the British troops actually sat down to breakfast garnished by the spectacle of a naval battle. Prevost did not dream of the possibility that Downie could be defeated; such things did not happen to squadrons of the Royal Navy —except in unusual circumstances as at Lake Erie. Unfortunately, Downie headed the equivalent of a naval militia force and engaged a regular force under a commander who had left nothing to chance.

A hundred times Macdonough had fought the Battle of Lake Champlain in his mind and he made thorough preparations, the most important proving to be the routine measure of anchoring with spring lines on his bow and stern anchors. On the morning of September 11 when Downie rounded

Cumberland Head on a NNE wind, the situation had a paper resemblance to the Battle of the Nile. Signaling to Prevost to commence the land assault, Downie proposed to duplicate Nelson's Nile maneuver by doubling on the American van. However, Cumberland Head choked the wind and the short British column lost way, only succeeding in coming within carronade range where the impact of heavy American shot blunted the resolution of British captains to push across the American van. The little bay rolled with banks of gunsmoke and echoed thudding broadsides. Downie was abruptly killed in the first 15 minutes of the action by a dismounted 24-pounder which smashed his groin. His little fleet stoutly worked in close to the Americans, the *Confiance* engaging the *Saratoga* at pistol shot range. The *Chubb* was disabled and drifted to leeward of Macdonough, where she hauled down her colors. The *Finch* was driven onto Crab Island, while the *Preble* was compelled to seek haven under Macomb's batteries. The gunboats proved negligible, the issue resting with the comparatively giant *Saratoga* and *Confiance*. When the last gun in the *Saratoga's* starboard broadside was disabled, Macdonough adroitly wound ship to present his undamaged port battery of heavy carronades to the enemy. In effect, it was a duplication of Perry's shift to the fresh *Niagara*. Commanding the *Confiance,* Lieutenant John Robertson attempted to duplicate Macdonough's maneuver and unhappily worked the British flagship into a position to be raked, giving him no alternative to surrender. The *Finch* and *Linnet* also surrendered; the gunboats escaped.

The British lost 129 of their 714 men; Macdonough lost 110 of his 882. Prevost stopped his attack and withdrew. In the name of the Royal Navy, Sir James Lucas Yeo was infuriated and precipitated the unusual situation of a naval commander demanding a court-martial of his army colleague. Prevost died before he could appear before the court convened to allow him to answer charges of having induced Downie to attack in cooperation with a land assault that proved too late and too irresolute. The court that tried Downie's officers most honorably acquitted those who had done their duty because they had been incontinently hastened into battle by Prevost before the major strength of the flotilla had been trained. Regardless of the acrimony arising in the British service, the Battle of Lake Champlain accelerated a favorable peace treaty for the United States.

The war took a serious turn when Napoleon was brought to his knees in mid-1814. At Bordeaux, Wellington was able to detach Major General Robert Ross with 5,000 veterans under escort of Vice Admiral Sir Alexander Cochrane to operate in Chesapeake Bay and retaliate for an injudicious American raid on the Canadian town of York (now Toronto) on Lake Ontario. In August 1814, Ross landed at the mouth of the Patuxent River to begin his famous raid on Washington. His naval colleague, Rear Admiral Sir George Cockburn, expressed amused relief when Captain Joshua Barney USN withdrew his squadron of gunboats blockaded in the river.

Washington was unfortified, defended by 7,000 bayonets in the hands of militia and regulars commanded by Major General William H. Winder, a political appointee of dubious talents. Barney proved to be the stoutest defender of the American capital. Destroying his useless cockleshells, Barney landed five 18-pounders and 400 seamen to hurry to join Winder's nervous troops at Bladensburg. Before Barney arrived, Ross coolly shattered Winder's army. With demoralized soldiers streaming past him, Barney halted on a height dominating the Bladensburg road into Washington and threw up a battery, which was incomplete when the British came in view. For a bloody half hour, Barney checked the British pursuit, giving precious minutes to the American government for evacuation of Washington. Then redcoats inundated the gallant battery of seamen. The wounded Barney was shown marked kindness by his captors, who hurried on to burn the Capitol, White House, and Department buildings, while President Madison, his young son, and his cabinet fled ingloriously into the environs.

Barney had roughly found a use for Jefferson's toys, but the country had very little to show for the $4,500,000 that Jefferson had obstinately lavished on his concept of naval defense.

The citizens of Baltimore took a lesson from the disgrace at Washington and threw up strong entrenchments about that major port of American shipping and privateers. When Cochrane and Ross approached the city in mid-September 1814, Baltimore was ready, well protected by fortifications and 13,000 men under Brigadier General Samuel Smith. The British probed for weakness and found none. The rebuff of the British at Fort McHenry inspired the writing of the American national anthem, and that was all that had been accomplished when the British wisely sailed away from Baltimore.

Peace was signed at Ghent on Christmas Eve 1814, but another battle was fought in America before the news was known. At New Orleans, on January 8, 1815, General Andrew Jackson with 4,500 regulars and frontiersmen repulsed a frontal attack by 6,000 British veterans, whose general, Sir Edward Pakenham, died among the third of his force mowed down by American riflemen. The United States Navy played an important role in the campaign. The 14-gun *Carolina* was destroyed in the skirmishes prior to the decisive clash, during which the 16-gun *Louisiana* under Master Commandant Daniel T. Patterson firmly anchored the right flank of Jackson's line on the Mississippi.

So ended the War of 1812, which American tradition converted into triumph, although the issue of impressment was discreetly ignored at Ghent. That issue died at Waterloo, after which England no longer had to kidnap men for her fleet. Economic wounds were healed by mutual need. The Canadian border was stabilized and the way was open for the peaceful march of the American people to their "Manifest Destiny." The United States Navy made enormous strides, thanks to the war. First and foremost, the virtues of having a professional officer corps was significantly set off by the conspicuous failures of politically appointed militia generals. Secondly, the folly of Jefferson's

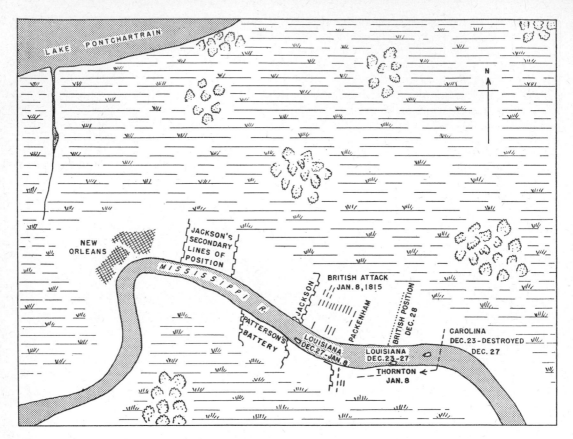

NEW ORLEANS CAMPAIGN, 1814 - 1815

politically inspired naval concepts were proved, and 74-gun ships of the line at last carried the American flag to sea on a mission against the Barbary States. The nation had not yet wholly subscribed to the big-ship concept of offshore defense, but the four 74's on the 1815 Navy List were the ancestors of the great capital ship navy that emerged from World War II.

Thirdly, the quality of American naval officers was now a matter of well-founded public pride. Ironically enough, the senior naval officers were all assigned to blue water commands, with the exception of Chauncey, but it was master commandants assigned inferior stations on inland waters who proved what American squadrons could accomplish in battle. Fourthly, the soundness of the American principle of building tactically superior classes of warships was amply dem-

onstrated, while, lastly, American commanders displayed startling aggressiveness in seeking and exploiting any tactical advantage. The deadly swiftness of many American victories, both at sea and on the lakes, led British apologists to stress the manner in which their countrymen were overmatched, thereby paying tribute to American foresight. All in all, the little American navy had done very well against the Mistress of the Seas, and was securely established as a significant instrument of American policy.

EPILOGUE: DOWNFALL OF NAPOLEON, 1812-1815

For the summer of 1812, Napoleon had dreamed of having naval forces ready to cooperate with amphibious troops numbering

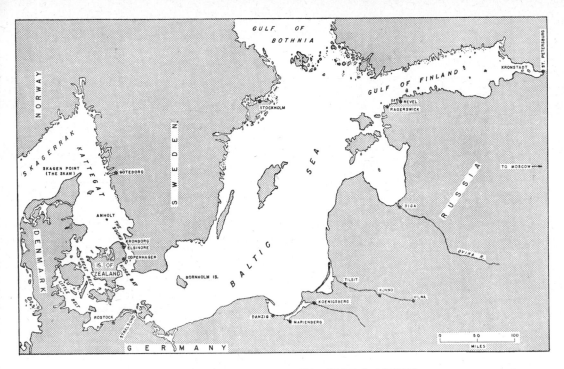

THE BALTIC AND ITS APPROACHES

180,000, to strike at England, Egypt, and Sicily. Unfortunately for him, his Continental System hurt Russia more than England. Russia had enjoyed a 10-to-1 trade advantage in selling England corn, hemp, flax, iron, and masts; and Russian merchants were not sufficiently Gallicized to endure endless years of financial sacrifice for Napoleon. When the British, who preserved entry into the Baltic by the careful skill of Sir James Saumarez, smuggled goods into Russian Baltic ports and offered to buy all that Russian merchants would sell, the Continental System was seriously breached. Alexander at first attempted to keep faith with his promises to Napoleon; then, as Napoleon left his own promises unfulfilled, Alexander winked at the illicit traffic. This led in turn to an ultimatum, the most significant in Napoleon's career, as he mobilized 680,000 men in the Germanies and Poland. A portent could be read into the unexpected alliance formed between Alexander and Napoleon's quondam Marshal Bernadotte, now King of Sweden:

this was the first open defection of a Napoleonic favorite.

Since Alexander was embroiled in war with Turkey, Napoleon knew the Russian army could not muster enough strength for an offensive, and possibly not enough manpower for more than token defense against the mighty horde raised up by the Emperor of the French. Distance would be the greatest military strength of Russia, imposing a very long line of communications upon Napoleon. Well aware of his logistics problem, Napoleon amassed great stores at Danzig and Koenigsberg and turned to his navy for a corps of seamen to establish a river supply line into Russia, ultimately to use the Neva at St. Petersburg. Napoleon bristled with ideas for canals, portages, and dredging, and in the end settled for what nature provided. The Niemen became the principal eastward route, converting Vilna into a tremendous magazine of supplies about 400 miles from Moscow. In February 1812 Napoleon issued orders for the seaman division to be formed from the cadre of the Boulogne Flotilla. Ganteaume declined the command, which was given to Rear Admiral Pierre Baste, an old merchant sailor who had not been to sea since 1803 but had served with increasing distinction in the logistic missions assigned the seamen of the Imperial Guard. Baste took four battalions into Poland in March 1812, and his 4,000 men had a firmly established supply line to the Niemen when Napoleon crossed the Russian frontier in June. Baste promptly pressed forward with his light craft to Kovno and Vilna.

The seaman battalion with the van of the army was busy building bridges beyond Vilna, while the greater part of Baste's corps toiled to bring supplies forward to the wagons of the regular transport system. As is well known, Napoleon defeated an inferior, stubborn Russian army at Borodino in September and entered Moscow, which the Russian government evacuated and set afire. After futilely waiting in the capital for an emissary from Alexander acknowledging defeat, Napoleon in October was obliged to retreat. Cold, snow, mud, and harassing Russians whittled the French expedition into staggering stragglers, devoid of discipline except in a few regiments whose commanders surmounted everything to preserve military order. Baste's work saved the remnants of the tattered, emaciated army, when the magazine of Kovno proved capable of supporting all who managed to reach it.

Napoleon's contemplated use of the Baltic coast as part of his supply system was denied him, as well as a chance to confiscate the Russian fleet, whose 18 ships sailed for refuge in England when that country renewed the alliance with Alexander. Saumarez, commanding ten ships in the *Victory,* was able to deal easily with the gunboats of Napoleon's naval ally, Denmark, and promptly saved Riga from French troops, while slowly interdicting the Baltic coast all the way to Danzig. Napoleon was unable to rest upon the sea for the 400-mile advance from Vilna, and army wagons were far less efficient than Baste's boats. Sea power enabled Saumarez to make Napoleon's operations even more tenuous as Rear Admiral Byam Martin with

26 vessels commenced bombarding the principal depot of Danzig in September 1812, effectually neutralizing shipments from that port to Baste's entries farther up the Baltic coast.[12]

While Napoleon overextended himself in the northeast, the new Marquess of Wellington rashly advanced beyond his land transport in Spain. He was almost trapped by the alert Marshal Soult, and had to return to the Lines of Torres Vedras as Napoleon dejectedly reached Paris after his Russian winter. While Napoleon scraped together a last army of old men and boys to astound his myriad enemies in the Germanies, Wellington reverted to the virtues of Sir Arthur Wellesley. If he was merciless in evaluating himself, he was insultingly blunt in criticizing the Royal Navy, which he accused of knowing nothing beyond fighting sea battles. In effect, the Royal Navy acted as though it had finished the job at Trafalgar and now only waited for Napoleon to topple. Nettled by American privateers that snapped up 50 of his precious supply ships in a few months, Wellington demanded a battleship force, frigates that would maintain patrol stations instead of cruising about after prize money, and lighter craft that would interdict the extremely important supplies that crept by sea from France to Soult's forces. Enemy intermediate bases on the coast could be captured by full and intelligent cooperation.[13]

---

[12] The following summer, the Royal Navy experimented with bombardment by improved Congreve rockets. The attack in August 1813 failed; the attack in September was partially successful; and the bombardment of October succeeded. Danzig surrendered on November 27, virtually ending French power in northern Europe.

[13] Sir Home Riggs Popham was instrumental in devising an answer to the problem of small enemy bases. Partly through his influence, two battalions of marines were formed in 1812 as a crude ancestor of the United States Fleet Marine Force established in 1933. The battalions numbered 672 men each, were commanded by majors, and were intended to be amphibious assault forces. They began operations on the Biscay coast with Popham in May 1812. The sudden declaration of war by the United States diverted them to the American theater, where they were brigaded into the army as regular infantry. Wellington despised marines and did not help Popham in

Rear Admiral Byam Martin, fresh from his knowledge of the shallow Baltic, was sent to explain the naval difficulties in trying to use heavy ships on the treacherous Biscay coast, as well as to enumerate the hazards of employing square-rigged vessels near the bight of Spain and France. Wellington reiterated his demands and the Admiralty at last sent him Lord Keith with 14 ships and 20 minor men-of-war.

With naval assistance that never measured up to his expectations, Wellington again moved from the Lines and irresistibly advanced. By May, he had Santander as a base of supplies. The coast from there to Bayonne was almost impossible to blockade, although in truth the nettled captains did not overexert themselves in Wellington's behalf, despite Keith's assistance. All hands itched for a shot at American frigates or merchantmen, and the dull business of supporting the army seemed endless. Nonetheless, Wellington doggedly went forward and by November stood in the Pyrenees watching Soult drag out of Spain to muster a last stand at Bayonne. Standing in winter snows, Wellington was more disgusted than ever with the navy, for the greatcoats of his shivering troops were stored in transports that waited four months at Oporto for naval escorts to protect them from American raiders.

Napoleon was retiring to the Rhine after the ruinous Battle of Leipzig, sometimes styled the Battle of the Nations because of the number of countries whose soldiers gathered to defeat him there. His hold on France was shaken. His troops had died in all the reaches of Europe, and their countrymen were weary of the slaughter. The countryside of France was ominously restrained as he headed for Paris. Thus, at the southern border, Wellington had a chance to shake Napoleon from his throne by invading France. Skirmishing down the foothills of the Pyrenees, Wellington in February 1814 was stopped from encircling Soult at Bayonne by the Adour River. Rapid, turbulent currents precluded the use of pontoons. Wel-

lington had to call on the navy or strike off into the east away from Soult.

In this juncture, Rear Admiral Charles Penrose vindicated the Navy. The mouth of the Adour was choked by sand that shifted continually under the onslaughts of 20-foot breakers crashing into the eddies of a 12-foot tide. On the morning of February 23, 1814, Penrose sent a flotilla of 70 boats at full sail through the foaming entry of the river. Thanks to incomparable seamanship, only a few boats were lost. The rest made a bridge for Wellington. Four days later, Soult was routed and the way opened to Bordeaux. Exactly a month later Penrose took his flagship up the Gironde River to Bordeaux as the Allied armies entered Paris.

Napoleon abdicated in April and was exiled to Elba, while the victors gathered at Vienna to divide the spoils. Veterans of Wellington's army were hurried off to chastise the Americans. Thus, in March 1815, when Napoleon cast off the yoke of Elba captivity and returned for the Hundred Days of desperate rule in a country already sick of Bourbon arrogance and hungry for Napoleonic glory, England was caught unprepared. With her army dispersed in America or off on leave visiting the peaceful Continent and her navy being laid up in ordinary, she could find comfort only in the destruction of the tremendous facilities at Antwerp by Admiral Martin. Wellington, scratching together an army, paid tardy tribute to the virtues of marines by demanding that 10,000 be landed immediately at the mouth of the Seine to divert Napoleon's preparations for renewal of hostilities. This was precisely the type of emergency that St. Vincent had foreseen and Popham had anticipated, but the marine battalions were in America and the police guards of the ships in home waters could not provide sufficient numbers to commit to such an operation.

Wellington in April 1815 had only 10,000 British troops with him in Belgium. In mid-June, he still had but 30,000 veterans, while Napoleon had massed 125,000 enthusiastic followers. The Allies joined 180,000 men under Wellington's proved leadership, but with such a small sprinkling of British under his

---

his efforts to retain them, else he might have had less cause for complaint about naval cooperation.

command, Wellington was less optimistic than his talents entitled him to be. Near an obscure Belgian village called Waterloo, on Sunday, June 18, 1815, maneuvers brought Napoleon with 74,000 troops into battle against 67,000 under Wellington. Each had reinforcements within a few hours' march. The battle was one of column and line in which the line triumphed. Wellington stood firm against all Napoleon's thrusts until late afternoon brought Wellington's subordinate General Blücher towards Napoleon's right flank. The battle was over and won. The ubiquitous Sir William Sydney Smith, who was present as a curious onlooker, was the first to shake Wellington's hand.

On July 15, Napoleon surrendered to the captain of one of the great black ships that had thwarted him, H.M.S. *Bellerophon*, which was anchored at Rochefort. He then passed into the hands of Lord Keith, who held him until the British Government decided to send him to St. Helena while his fate was being determined by the interrupted Congress of Vienna. The Allies were content to leave the Emperor of the French on his bleak rock in the South Atlantic where he died in May 1821.

SUMMARY, 1793-1815

The lesson of the wars of the French Revolution and Napoleon is the need for a properly calculated balance of force. A predominant sea power was brought into conflict with a predominant land power. After a dozen years of war, the sea power at Trafalgar emerged incontestably triumphant in its own element but another ten years of warfare were needed for the sea power to link efforts ashore with sufficient allied army strength to defeat the land power in its own element. The traditional disinclination of the British to develop and sustain an instrument for shifting national strength from sea to land produced a vacuum of four years after Trafalgar. Wellington's operations in the Iberian Peninsula developed more by accident than design into an effective amphibious effort; his campaign owed most of its

opportunity for success to powerful allied operations elsewhere in Europe that allowed Napoleon to use only a fraction of his strength in Spain. The Royal Navy lived for the fleet battle; when this was won British naval leaders were left somewhat puzzled about further operations.

Viewed strictly from the success or failure of naval effort, the Royal Navy performed magnificently. In the period, the British captured or destroyed 156 ships, 382 frigates, 662 sloops, and 2,506 armed vessels, public and private. Under the mantle of sea power, England's exports quadrupled and her shipping more than doubled to a registry of 24,000 ships. Cruisers brought insurance rates down to negligible figures as exemplified by the decrease for East Indian cargo insurance from 25 per cent in 1793 to 6 per cent in 1810. Captures of French vessels cut deeply into French maritime manpower, no less than 120,000 seamen being in British prisons by 1815, only slightly less than the number of seamen manning the Royal Navy in 1809, its year of greatest expansion. Because of these captures, Napoleon could not effectively man the fleets he kept planning to build.

From the naval viewpoint, Napoleon's errors were legion. First and most important, he did not seriously strive to build morale. No matter what he might profess when speaking at naval reviews, he made a thousand generals but only three vice admirals and 14 rear admirals. Promotions in lesser grades were proportionate. He said he wanted men of ability and daring for his navy; such men noted his actions rather than his words. Vain and easily flattered, he elevated favorites whose mediocrity he clearly recognized. Secondly, because he was a master of military strategy, he was dogmatic about naval strategy. He did not understand the capabilities of ships or of the British Admiralty, forever basing his judgment upon deductions from limited experience. He had a closed mind and could not be instructed by naval inferiors. To the end, he fondly believed that by maintaining an average establishment of 60 ships he compelled the British to commission double the number, which constantly wore out cruising before his harbors. Lastly, although he lived by the offensive in tactics, he did not seek to alter the defensive traditions of the French *Marine*. Like Louis XIV, he had a costly army and did not seriously encourage commanders to lose ships in combat for the sake of combat. These three defects overshadow the rest in Napoleon's management of his navy. Unless these were changed, he could not win at sea.

The aftermath of the Napoleonic Wars in Europe found Exmouth bombarding the Barbary System into extinction. In the Americas, the former Spanish colonies were so heartened by the repulse of the British at Buenos Aires that in the furor of the Peninsular War they struck for independence from Spain. International Congresses subsequent to that of Vienna toyed with the idea of uniting to restore Spain's colonies. The British, who had profited by the lapse in Spanish control to establish a strong trade, did not relish a return of Spanish monopoly and the conditions of the *Asiento*. When President Monroe in 1823 issued the Doctrine that bears his name, England supported the inviolability of the Western Hemisphere by ostentatiously strengthening her Jamaica naval force to numbers greater than the ships available to France and Spain. Thereupon the proposals died aborning.

Thus began the *Pax Britannica*.

14

The New Technology to 1861

LIKE ALMOST ALL OTHER ASpects of human activity, the navies of the world were profoundly affected by the Industrial Revolution, whose most characteristic aspect was the widespread adoption of relatively complex machinery. During the 200 years preceding the Napoleonic wars, ships and guns had not changed radically; the armament and construction of Hawkins' *Victory* in the Spanish Armada campaign were not unlike those of Nelson's *Victory* in the Battle of Trafalgar. After 1815 however changes came so swiftly that a new warship could become obsolete before she was launched. The extent of the changes that took place in fighting ships and in naval warfare is immediately apparent in the contrast between Nelson's *Victory* and the *Monitor* of the American Civil War period. The *Victory* and the *Monitor* were altogether unlike in motive power, in armor, in armament, and in construction materials; and fighting the "cheesebox on a raft" required techniques undreamed of by captains of lordly ships of the line. Even before the traditional warship began its startling transformation however, a new dimension was being added to naval warfare with the development of the mine, the torpedo, and the

submarine. To the age-old hazards of the naval service—wind, weather, fire, and projectiles—was added the underwater explosion.[1]

TECHNOLOGICAL DEVELOPMENTS BEFORE 1815

The inventive genius of Americans has furnished their defense establishment with good claims to having made the first practical use of the marine mine, the submarine, the screw propeller, and steam propulsion in warships. The first three were employed by David Bushnell during the

[1] Because this chapter emphasizes naval applications and the contributions of naval men, two extremely important developments receive scant attention: watertight integrity and slower burning gunpowder. Extensive compartmentation of the hull, the basis of watertight integrity, was at first chiefly a concern of the merchant service. The British passenger liner *Great Eastern*, designed by Isambard Kingdom Brunel, was in this feature far ahead of any naval vessel of her day. The chief contributor to the development of slow-burning powder was Captain Thomas Rodman USA, with the assistance of Lammot du Pont of the firm of E. I. du Pont de Nemours.

Revolutionary War; the fourth, by Robert Fulton in 1814-15.

Bushnell, an officer in the Continental Army, designed and built a one-man submarine that made history in that it and its operator survived a war patrol. Called the *American Turtle,* it contained in rudimentary form the essentials of the modern submarine: ballast tanks, a depth gage, a self-contained means of propulsion, and a detachable torpedo or mine. One "oar formed on the principle of a screw" could be rotated by the operator to move the boat horizontally; another assisted its vertical motion. There was also a device for attaching the mine to the hull of an enemy ship. In 1776 the *Turtle,* manned by sergeant Ezra Lee, attempted a night attack on H.M.S. *Eagle,* 64 guns, in New York harbor. The attempt was a failure only because the British were coppering their underwater hulls. The auger device for attaching the mine to the wooden bottom could not penetrate the copper.

The next year Bushnell made two moderately successful experiments in mine warfare. With a towed "machine" loaded with powder and set to explode on contact by means of a gun-lock, he attempted to sink H. M. frigate *Cerberus,* at anchor near New London, Connecticut. He missed the frigate but blew up a prize schooner at her stern, killing several men. The following December, in an attempt to destroy British shipping in the Delaware River, he set adrift several powder-filled kegs set with crude contact fuses. The kegs were held tightly by ice through the night, but the morning thaw set them floating once again in full view of the enemy. "One of them blew up a boat with several persons in it, who imprudently handled it too freely," wrote Bushnell afterwards, "and thus gave the British that alarm which brought on the 'Battle of the Kegs.' "

The next inventor to experiment extensively with undersea warfare was another American, Robert Fulton. Having gone to England originally to study art, he became interested in engineering. Resentful of what he considered British arrogance, he crossed to France and offered his ideas to Napoleon, then First Consul. In 1801, Fulton's submarine *Nautilus* (equipped with a sail for surface cruising) carried a four-man crew on several successful submerged trips in the harbor of Brest. Mines devised by Fulton also blew up several old hulks in French waters.

When the French government remained unimpressed, Fulton swallowed his pride and returned to England, where he proposed a form of mine warfare not unlike the modern use of the midget submarine. One man on a small raft would tow a mine into an enemy harbor, lash the mine to the anchor cable of a ship, pull a pin that started a clockwork mechanism and get away as fast as possible. Five such craft entered the harbor of Boulogne one night in October 1805 and made attacks which the British regarded as total failures, unaware that one had destroyed a pinnace with a crew of 21 men. A few days later Fulton favorably impressed observers by blowing up an old Danish brig by means of an underwater explosion. But British victory in the Battle of Trafalgar, which occurred that same month, caused the Admiralty to abandon further interest in undersea warfare.

Returning to America in 1806, Fulton gained wide fame by developing the *Clermont,* his successful commercial steamboat. In 1810 he persuaded Congress to appropriate $5,000 for experiments in undersea warfare. He was allowed to attack the brig *Argus* with his "harpoon torpedo," but Commodore John Rodgers USN, who had been assigned to defend the ship, arranged so many booms, nets, and spars overside that the *Argus* proved invulnerable; she was also, incidentally, immobilized. At about the same time Fulton developed the first moored contact mine. When a firing lever was struck, a musket charge was fired into a hundred pounds of gunpowder. The mine could be set to stay under water for a specified time, after which it would rise harmlessly to the surface with the firing lever locked.

Next Fulton produced what the British called a turtle boat, designed, like the later Confederate "Davids" and the Union monitors, to operate virtually awash. Drawing six feet of water while rising only a foot above the surface, its purpose was to tow mines into action. It was in fact the first American iron-clad, as the following contemporary British description makes clear.

She is intended to carry twelve men inside; the bottom of it is similar to that of a boat, and its top arched like a turtle shell. She is built nearly [to] the scantling of a 100-ton ship, and plank[ed] outside with 8-inch stuff, cased over with plate iron of half an inch thickness, and is, on the whole, considered so strongly and well constructed that a shot cannot penetrate it, nor can anything grapple with it.[2]

One such boat, having been driven ashore on Long Island by a gale, was destroyed by the British in June 1814.

Fulton's last contribution to the United States Navy was designing and building the world's first steam warship, the *Demologos*, later renamed the *Fulton*. By the time she was ready for her trial run the War of 1812 was over and she was no longer needed; she was so far in advance of her time that she was never imitated. Because her single paddle wheel ran in a sluiceway between twin hulls, her motive power was less vulnerable to shot than that of any other paddle-wheel man-of-war.[3] Unlike most of her successors, she carried her machinery low in the hulls. In a sense she was the first steam armor-clad, for her scantlings, almost five feet thick, made her impervious to contemporary ordnance.

During the War of 1812 Yankee ingenuity applied itself without much success to blowing up enemy ships, mainly by attaching mines to their hulls. All such methods of warfare were regarded as underhanded and uncivilized by the British commander on the North Atlantic station, Commodore Sir Thomas Masterman Hardy, who had been Nelson's flag captain at Trafalgar. When H.M.S. *Ramillies* had a narrow escape while blockading off New London, he sent proclamations ashore threatening reprisals. He also

introduced a primitive form of minesweeping into the Royal Navy by ordering that the hull of the *Ramillies* was to be swept with a cable every two hours while she lay off New London.

UNDERSEA WARFARE TO 1861

Despite the promising beginning made before 1815 in the development of submarines and mines, there was little further progress in this field until the period of the American Civil War. In 1853, after some years of experimenting, Colonel Samuel Colt (inventor of the famous revolver) fired a mine electrically from the shore and destroyed a moving ship five miles at sea. When the German states went to war with Denmark over the Schleswig-Holstein question in 1848, a Professor Himmly of Kiel University, with no knowledge of American developments, devised a system of defensive mining in Kiel harbor. Since the Danes did not attempt to force a passage, the effectiveness of Himmly's mines was not tested. Kiel harbor was also the scene in 1851 of the unsuccessful trial of a submarine constructed by Wilhelm Bauer. The submarine sank, drowning its crew.

During the Crimean War (1854-6) the Russians used a great many mines to defend their Baltic harbors. Those controlled from shore, like Colt's, were uniformly ineffective. The contact mines did little better, for their main charge was only 25 pounds of gunpowder, but their ingenious trigger mechanism deserves mention. A lead tube protruding from the mine proper was filled with a mixture of potassium chlorate and sugar, in which was embedded a glass tube containing sulfuric acid. When the hull of a ship bent the lead tube, the glass tube broke, and the mixture of chemicals generated enough heat and flame to detonate the main charge.

For the Russians Bauer built a second submarine, which was launched too late to take part in hostilities. A special feature of this boat was a pair of gutta-percha gloves built into the sides to permit the operator to attach his mine to an enemy hull. Compared

---

[2] Quoted by W. R. Rowbotham, Commander RN, Ret., "Robert Fulton's Turtle-Boat," *United States Naval Institute Proceedings* (December 1936), LXII, 1746-7.

[3] Except possibly the U.S.S. *Sea Gull*, mentioned below. Originally a New York ferry boat, she may also have been built to Fulton's plans.

to his 1851 project, Bauer's new submarine was a tremendous success, for it made several underwater trips without drowning anyone.

PADDLE-WHEELED NAVAL VESSELS

U.S.S. *Sea Gull*, which operated with the West Indies Squadron in its efforts to suppress piracy in the early 1820's, has been called the first naval steamer to engage in warlike operations. She was a tiny converted ferryboat, and her "warlike operations" were largely police duties. The first steamer to engage in actual warfare was the *Karteria*, which served against the Turks in the Greek War of Independence in the 1820's. Frank Abney Hastings, a young English officer in the Greek service, designed her, supervised her building in Britain, and commanded her in action. She destroyed at least one enemy brig-of-war and one transport and did some damage to shore installations. She was also one of the first ships to employ shell-guns effectively.

Steam power entered the Royal Navy in 1821, when the Admiralty purchased one small steamer, the *Monkey*, and ordered the building of another, the *Comet*. From that time forth, both British and French navies made some use of steamers, but these early wooden-hulled paddle-packets were small and lightly armed. They were auxiliaries, dispatch vessels, and tugs, rather than fighting ships. When France invaded Algeria in 1830, seven small steamers operated in these capacities with the fleet and apparently did excellent work. Small naval steamers were valuable at the bombardment of St. Jean d'Acre in 1840, and the East India Company's iron-hulled *Nemesis* impressed the naval officers who saw her performance in China in 1841.

The second steamer built for the United States Navy was the *Fulton II*, launched in 1837, twenty-three years after its namesake. She was a smaller and more conventional paddle-wheeler than the first *Fulton*, but she was speedy for her time; until 1850 she remained one of the fastest ships of the American navy. Her most important service, as it turned out, was in interesting her first captain, Matthew Calbraith Perry, in the possibilities of the steam warship.

Partly because of Perry's enthusiasm, the navy built and launched in 1841 two big side-wheelers of 1,700 tons, the *Mississippi* and the *Missouri*. The *Missouri* burned at Gibraltar in 1843, but her sister ship was Perry's flagship in the Mexican War, went with him to Japan in 1853, and remained a valuable fighting ship until the Civil War.

Simultaneously with the adoption of the screw propeller came a curious interlude in the history of the naval steamer. Lieutenant W. W. Hunter USN managed to convince somebody that the ideal steamer would be one with submerged *horizontal* paddle wheels rotating in slots in its wooden hull. The result was the U.S.S. *Union*, launched in 1842, a costly failure whose maximum speed was four or five knots. Two smaller ships later built to Hunter's specifications failed as dismally as the *Union*. Apparently nobody clearly grasped the obvious and fundamental error in such construction: that the wheels could hardly be efficient as long as the inner and forward thrust was displacing water at the same rate as the outer and backward one.

THE PROBLEMS OF CONVERSION

On learning that almost 40 years elapsed between the first successful commercial steamboat and the widespread adoption of steam as a means of propulsion for naval vessels, the modern reader is likely to decide impatiently that the naval officers of that time were stupidly unprogressive. The truth was less simple. There were many valid arguments against extensive reliance on steam.

The first and foremost was the diminution of a ship's cruising radius. Once laden with the necessary stores, a sailing warship could go around the world, but an early steamer could cruise less than a hundred miles under steam alone. The cruising radius was somewhat increased by the fuel changeover from wood to coal,[4] but this was not enough to offset the inefficiency of early low-pressure engines. From the time of James Watt to the present, there have been only three major types of steam engines: the low-pressure reciprocating,[5] the high-pressure reciprocating, and the steam turbine. Both the modern steam turbine and the high-pressure reciprocating engine use the expansive power of steam under high pressure to move a turbine wheel or piston. In the low-pressure reciprocating engine, which was standard in the early paddle steamers, the pressure of the steam was barely more than that of the atmosphere—one can think of the piston as being pulled or sucked rather than pushed. The pulling or sucking of the piston was produced by creating a vacuum at one end of the cylinder by first introducing steam and then condensing it by rapidly lowering its temperature. In retrospect, it is obvious that this was not the most efficient way to use steam power.

For naval vessels there were other drawbacks that prevented the early adoption of steam. Before Sir John Seppings made his famous report to the British Admiralty in 1814, no one knew how to build an efficient ship much more than 200 feet long. Virtually every timber in the frames of the traditional warship ran either vertically or horizontally. Until Seppings pointed out the additional rigidity that could be gained by the use of diagonal members and his views were applied to frame design, a ship more than 200 feet long tended to "hog" or to "sag"—that is, the keel was likely to arch either concavely or convexly. Either way, its sailing qualities were impaired. The ship of the line and the frigate were highly developed craft. With a 200-foot maximum length, the installation of engines and bunkers meant

the loss of necessary working spaces; and a 200-foot steamer could mount fewer guns than a 200-foot sailing ship, for the paddle wheels masked as much as a third of the broadside. Moreover, while in a battle between a sailing ship and a steamer of equal length the superior maneuverability of the steamer might count for something, one lucky shot could disable her paddle wheel or engines and leave her outsailed and outgunned.

So the widespread use of steam in navies was considered impractical until technology solved certain problems. A more efficient mechanism than the low-pressure engine had to be found. To make that possible, boilers capable of containing steam at relatively high pressures had to be developed. To build such boilers required major improvements in metallurgy and machine tools. The vulnerable paddle wheel had to give way to the more efficient screw propeller. If the guns were to be fewer they had to be larger and their ammunition more deadly. Such a development in armament would in turn require the adoption of defensive armor. And if wooden hulls could not be used in efficient modern warships, the iron hull must be adopted. By 1861, partial solutions had been found for every one of these problems.

THE HIGH-PRESSURE ENGINE

Engineers gradually overcame the obstacles to the use of steam at high pressure. As they did the low-pressure engine was virtually abandoned. As early as 1837 the United States Navy installed a high-pressure engine (30 pounds per square inch) in the *Fulton II*. The principal hurdle had been overcome, but the adoption of high pressure left numerous problems to be solved and raised some more of its own.

Of the three major parts of the steam engine (the condenser, the piston and cylinder, and the boiler), the condenser presented the fewest problems and underwent the least change. The steam was recondensed by cool-

---

[4] Fulton's *Clermont* and probably the *Demologos* used wood to fire the boilers. Because wood was readily available along the inland rivers, so did many of the American river steamers until the Civil War. Readers of *Huckleberry Finn* will recall the frequent references to the woodyards at which the boats stopped.

[5] A reciprocating engine is one in which the initial motion is imparted to the machinery by means of a piston which moves back and forth in a cylinder.

ing through surface condensation (chilling the outside of the apparatus) or by jet condensation (squirting a jet of cold water into the interior). What had worked well enough for low-pressure engines was apparently satis-factory for the new high-pressure engines.

The early boilers however were far from satisfactory. Many used sea water, but this practice led to constant incrustation and fouling. Ships using salt water had to "blow out" their boilers, i.e., empty the entire contents, about once a day. The solution of this difficulty came with the development of evaporators for distilling sea water. Another knotty matter to be solved was how to transfer heat from the fuel to the water with minimum loss. Early box boilers consisted merely of a water compartment set directly over a fire compartment. Later improvements were the "return flue" boiler, in which the heat flue passed twice along the water container; the water tubular boiler, in which much greater heating surface was provided by passing the water through the flame in numerous tubes or pipes; and what may be called a fire tubular boiler, in which tubes carrying heat were run through the water compartment.

The earlier steamers had vertical cylinders, with the piston rod connected to the paddle-wheel crank by means of a pivoted overhead "walking" (i.e., working) beam, to which it imparted a seesaw motion. This apparatus continued to be used in many river steamers and ferry boats well into the 20th century. A modification was the side-lever engine, with a modified walking beam pivoted on the side of the engine itself. Later variations were horizontal or inclined cylinders, with the cylinder axis parallel to that of the ship and the piston-rod applying power to the paddle-wheel crank through a connecting rod; and the oscillating engine, in which the cylinder itself was set on trunnions so that the piston-rod could be fastened directly to the crank.

The introduction of the screw propeller confronted engineers with new problems, for with the crankshaft running lengthwise there was no room to accommodate a horizontal piston and cylinder athwartships. The ultimate solution was the readoption of the vertical cylinder, but many compromise solutions were tried first. One was the back-acting engine, in which cylinder and piston rod were set athwartships above the crankshaft, with the connecting rod extending back and down from the end of the piston rod to the crankshaft. U.S.S. *San Jacinto* had its cylinders inclined on the principle of the modern V-8 automobile engine. U.S.S. *Monitor* had what were called trunk engines; these employed cylindrical pistons to which the connecting rods were directly connected by a pivot, somewhat as in modern gasoline engines.

THE IRON HULL

Because both the iron hull and protective armor developed during the period 1815-1861, people are apt to regard the two changes as synonymous. But in fact the first French ironclads had wooden hulls, as did C.S.S. *Virginia* of the American Civil War. The adoption of the iron hull had an importance of its own for without it the length of a ship could never have greatly exceeded 200 feet. Moreover, the traditionally great naval nations, Britain and France, were running out of suitable timber.[6]

The first iron vessel in history apparently was John Wilkinson's canal boat the *Trial,* which began operations at Birmingham, England in 1787. The first iron-hulled steamer may have been the paddle-wheeler *Aaron Manby,* assembled in Staffordshire. In June 1822 she sailed directly from London to Paris, the first ship to do so, and the only one for 30 years. The first iron-hulled ship to cross the Atlantic was the British merchantman *Ironsides,* which crossed in 1838.

---

[6] The United States, still possessing what seemed like limitless forests, was slower than her foreign rivals to change to iron construction. For several years American merchants had an advantage over their European competitors, who were obliged to build costly iron steamers. The swift clipper ships designed by Donald Mackay of Boston could outspeed many steam-driven vessels.

In 1836 John Laird, of the celebrated firm of William Laird and Sons, submitted to the British Admiralty a design for an iron-hulled steam frigate. The Admiralty rejected the Laird plan, but the East India Company seized on the idea and ordered from the Lairds the two iron-hulled steamers *Phlegethon* and *Nemesis,* which operated with great success in the First Opium War of 1840-42. The *Nemesis* in particular, by performing some of her feats under the eyes of naval officers, aroused new interest in iron construction and steam propulsion for warships.

In the early 1840's strained relations between the United States and Mexico quickened the interest of both countries in iron-hulled warships. Apparently the first nation to possess iron-hulled frigates was Mexico, for whom the Lairds in 1842 built the paddle-frigates *Guadelupe* and *Montezuma.* At about the same time the United States Navy contracted with the Stevens Brothers of Hoboken to construct a fast, ironclad, iron-hulled steamship, but as we shall see, this "Stevens Battery" was never completed.

Meanwhile two small iron-hulled naval vessels, one British and one American, appeared on the Great Lakes. The British *Mohawk* had been built and delivered to the Admiralty in sections, which were then shipped to Canada, assembled there, and launched early in 1843. U.S.S. *Michigan* was the American navy's first iron-hulled warship. Her builders made her more powerful than the *Mohawk* by simply ignoring the Rush-Bagot Agreement limiting tonnage and armament on the Lakes. The *Michigan,* later rechristened the *Wolverine,* served on the Great Lakes from 1844 until 1923, when she was converted into a historical memorial at Erie, Pennsylvania.

Beginning in 1839 with the paddle steamer *Dover* the British navy had purchased or built several small iron-hulled steamers like the *Mohawk,* and the French navy had followed suit. Britain's first iron-hulled ships large enough to be designated as steam frigates were ordered by the Admiralty in or about the year 1844.

Just as it began to seem that iron might be universally adopted for naval hulls, British Admiralty tests, conducted in 1840 and 1846, demonstrated that iron, in its current state of metallurgical development, was even more vulnerable to shot than oak. Consequently iron hull construction was virtually abandoned by all countries for several years. By the time of the Crimean War (1854-56) however, tougher iron had been developed. Defensive armor was now being employed, and the improved iron hull was better able to carry it than a wooden hull. The French "floating batteries" that fought at Kinburn had wooden hulls, it is true, as did the first ones built by Britain, but Britain switched from wood to iron for the hulls of its next ironclads. After that, the iron hull quickly became standard.

THE SCREW PROPELLER TO 1853

The reluctance of naval officers to adopt steam propulsion was lessened by the advent of the screw propeller in the early 1840's. Even then it was many years before steam became more than an auxiliary of sail in the seagoing ship (as opposed to the coast-defense vessel and the floating battery, which were not expected to make long cruises). For several years after the Crimean War the British flagship on the North American Station was a sailing ship of the line, which was accompanied by a steamer. In blowing weather the ship towed the steamer; in calms the steamer towed the ship.

In principle the screw propeller was very old; it will be remembered that Bushnell's *American Turtle* possessed two of them, both hand-operated. About a year before the success of Fulton's *Clermont,* Colonel John Stevens of Hoboken (whose sons undertook to build the Stevens Battery) had operated a small twin-screw steamer in American waters. Many other inventors from various nations had proposed screw steamers of one kind or another, but the first practical ones were developed in England during the 1830's, almost simultaneously by Francis

Pettit Smith, a farmer with no training in engineering, and by Captain John Ericsson, the Swedish engineer and inventor. Smith's first propeller, which he considered an adaptation of the screw of Archimedes, had a double full turn and looked somewhat like the drive in a worm-gear.

The Admiralty was suspicious of such new-fangled devices. Ericsson built a 45-foot boat whose screw propeller towed the Lords of the Admiralty in their barge at a speed of ten knots. But Sir William Symonds, a gifted designer of sailing ships, apparently refused to believe the evidence of his own senses, for he assured his colleagues, and apparently convinced them, that a ship whose motive-power was applied at her stern could not be steered. It was not until the *Archimedes,* fitted with Smith's screw, circumnavigated Great Britain and Ireland that the Admiralty began to change its mind.

Meanwhile the services of Ericsson had been secured for the United States. Francis B. Ogden, the American consul at Liverpool, had become interested in his work, and had in turn interested Captain Robert F. Stockton USN. History has been less than fair to Stockton. He seems to have been an excitable and quarrelsome man with a streak of flamboyance in him that sometimes made him look ridiculous. Nevertheless, there are two positive achievements on his record, and many men have become national heroes for less: during the Mexican War he commanded the forces that consolidated the conquest of California by the United States, and he persuaded the United States Navy to build the first screw warship ever launched.

Independently wealthy, Stockton ordered from Ericsson a small iron-hulled screw steamer which so pleased him that he persuaded the Swedish inventor to sell out his business and come to the United States. Here Stockton, by his insistence and political influence, got the Navy to authorize the building of a screw steamer to Ericsson's specifications. This was the U.S. sloop-of-war *Princeton,* a remarkable ship, ahead of her time in many ways. In addition to being the first screw-propelled naval steamer, she

was the first warship to have all her machinery below the water-line and thus out of reach of shot. She burned anthracite (hence smokeless) coal, and her funnel was telescopic, so that an enemy might be fooled into thinking her a sailing ship without auxiliary power.

The first screw steamer in the Royal Navy was H.M.S. *Rattler.* She was begun before the *Princeton,* but while she was on the stocks it was decided to convert her from paddle to screw propulsion, and for that reason the hull was cut in two and lengthened. As a result of the consequent delay, the *Princeton* was launched first (1843).

In 1839, Smith's *Archimedes* had lost a tug-of-war to the paddle-tug *William Gunston.* When the *Rattler* was launched, the Admiralty arranged a similar test for her against H.M.S. *Alecto,* a slightly smaller paddle-wheeler with the same horsepower. The results of these 1845 tests were convincing. Not only did the *Rattler* tow the *Alecto* backwards at $2\frac{1}{2}$ miles per hour, but she also beat her rival in three races, one in a calm, one in a moderate breeze, and one in a headwind. After that the future of screw propulsion was assured.

France's most successful unarmored screw-steamer was the *Napoléon,* designed by Dupuy de Lôme and launched in 1850. Even though she mounted 92 guns, she was capable of 14 knots. In 1853, when the Anglo-French fleet was unable to pass the Dardanelles because of headwinds and adverse currents, the *Napoléon* not only steamed triumphantly up the straits but towed behind her the French flagship *Ville de Paris,* 112. The *Napoléon* and the other unarmored screw steamers that took part in the Crimean War looked like traditional ships of the line, with their several tiers of guns and their full suits of canvas. A reincarnated Nelson, seeing one of them, might have been struck by their greater size and the funnel amidships; otherwise he would have noticed little difference unless he had gone below.

About 1856 the United States Navy began launching the *Merrimack* class of fast steam frigates equipped with exceptionally powerful ordnance capable of firing both shell and solid shot.

ORDNANCE: THE PROJECTILES

During the period 1815-1861 shells came into widespread and deadly use, and guns became bigger and more efficient. Use of shells in naval warfare was not new; for many years fleets that intended to operate against shore installations employed small craft called mortar-boats or bomb-ketches, whose function was to lob bombs (i.e., shells) into the enemy fortifications. The important change was the development of guns that could fire shells with the same trajectory as solid shot.

Lieutenant Colonel Robert Melville had developed in 1759 a new type of naval ordnance shorter than a long gun of equal caliber and only about a third as heavy. Because Melville's gun used a light charge of powder and hence had very little recoil, it could be mounted on a slide rather than on a fixed carriage. This was the famous *carronade,* so-called because it was first manufactured by the Carron Company of Carron, Scotland—though Melville had suggested "smasher" as an appropriate name for his invention. He had expected his gun to fire shell with the same ease as shot, but naval officers found the carronade's large solid shot so useful for splintering wooden hulls at close range that they neglected its possibilities as a shellgun—except during the siege of Acre in 1799, when two 68-pounders from H.M.S. *Tigre,* 74, threw shells into the storming French columns with destructive effect.[7]

Next to turn his attention to the problem of horizontal shellfire was Major George Bomford USA, who during the War of 1812 developed the "columbiad," named for the quasi-epic poem written by his friend Joel Barlow. This gun was a compromise in length, weight, and diameter-of-bore between the standard long gun and the carronade. In planning the *Demologos,* Fulton seems to have meant to mount two columbiads with their muzzles underwater in order to hull the enemy. Experiments carried out in the North River convinced him that such underwater fire could be effective. The columbiad, as modified and improved by Captain Thomas Rodman USA, later became a standard gun of the United States Navy (c. 1845).

The man whose name is most often associated with horizontal shellfiring however was a French army officer, Major (later General) Henri-Joseph Paixhans. A veteran of the Moscow campaign of 1812, Paixhans resented the secondary role in European politics for which France seemed destined after Waterloo. The biggest obstacle to the resurgence of France's glory, he believed, was the British fleet; he therefore set himself to finding ways and means to destroy it. Horizontal shellfire seemed to be the answer. General use of shells, he reasoned, would make the battle fleet obsolete. The navies of the future would be made up of small gunboats, each mounting one Paixhans gun, and France could produce as formidable a fleet of such gunboats as England could. In 1821 Paixhans published his conclusions in an epochal paper, *Nouvelle Force Maritime,* and in 1824 he gave a convincing demonstration of the value of shellfire by virtually blowing out of the water an old ship of the line, *Pacificateur,* 80. The gun which Paixhans invented had much in common with the carronade and the columbiad. Like them, it was shorter and lighter and used smaller propelling charges than guns of the same caliber designed for solid shot. Paixhans' ordnance began to appear on men-of-war about 1827. In 1837 the French navy officially adopted the gun; two years later Britain followed suit.

At this time the shell, as well as the solid shot, was spherical in shape. The standard fuse for these round shells was a hollow wooden cylinder filled with a hardened combustible mixture of gunpowder or some other combination of niter with sulphur and

[7] J. A. Dahlgren, Commander USN, *Shells and Shell Guns* (Philadelphia, 1856), 11.

charcoal. This cylinder, having been cut to burn for a length of time roughly consistent with the range of the target, was pounded into a hole in the shell until the after end of the fuse was flush with the outer surface. Steadied in the bore by a leather or wooden collar called a sabot, the shell was inserted in the gun so that the fuse pointed outward toward the muzzle. When the gun was fired, the flame of the explosion passed over the top of the shell and ignited the fuse as the projectile began its journey. Paixhans improved on this standard fuse by inventing a metal one which could be screwed rather than driven into the shell, but the old wooden fuse continued in use for many more years.

Meanwhile interest in elongated projectiles began to develop. Shortly after the War of 1812 Colonel John Stevens and his sons carried out experiments by which they found that such projectiles, when thrown by a smooth-bore gun, tended to tumble end-over-end in flight. Although Paixhans and other experts scoffed at the idea of elongated shot as impractical, the project had considerable appeal to some artillerists, for an elongated shot with the tumbling eliminated would have greater range and accuracy than a round one. With the widespread acceptance of shells, interest in elongated projectiles increased, for with them a percussion fuse could be employed. Round shells with the standard fuse tended to explode too long before or after they hit the target; some concussion fuses were invented, but they suffered from the obvious defect that any fuse which would detonate a charge on contact with a target was very likely to detonate the charge in the barrel of the gun at the moment of firing.

The problem of eliminating tumbling was reduced to the problem of imparting rotation around the long axis of the projectile. Even an arrow with no feathers at the end will tumble in the air; the feathers, which are not quite in line with the shaft, impart a spin that makes the arrow fly true. The answer to the problem of the elongated projectile was rifled ordnance, and rifling was ultimately introduced.

THE BUILT-UP GUN AND THE LARGER SMOOTH-BORES

Before rifling could be developed, stronger guns had to be made. Many of the major ordnance developments of the first half of the 19th century involved simply the improvement and enlarging of smooth-bored ordnance.

Until Paixhans' shell-guns were accepted, the standard ship gun was the 32-pounder, usually made of cast iron in a single homogeneous casting. In 1834 however Captain A. de Thiery of the French army published a book in which he described his recent experiments in the improvement of artillery and recommended a gun produced by shrinking a wrought iron envelope, while it cooled, onto a cast iron barrel. This shrinking of an outer band or tube onto an inner one (without regard to whether cast or wrought iron is used) is the principle of the built-up gun, which was one of the revolutionary ordnance developments of the 19th century.[8]

An explosion aboard U.S.S. *Princeton* on her trial trip in 1844 alarmed ordnance men about the future of homogeneous wrought-iron guns. Among Ericsson's inventions installed on the little ship was an enormous wrought iron 12-inch gun, the "Oregon." Not to be outdone, Captain Stockton designed a somewhat similar one, the "Peacemaker." During demonstration firing on the trial trip, the "Peacemaker" blew up, killing several dignitaries including the Secretary of State and the Secretary of the Navy.

The first built-up guns purchased for any military establishment were those of Professor Daniel Treadwell of Harvard University, who in 1843 built a small number for the United States government. Later he built some larger ones for the American navy, but by that time the *Princeton* explosion had occurred and the government was unwilling to

---

[8] In the sense that they had been cast or shaped in two separate sleeves, there had been earlier built-up guns, but the shrinking-on process was new in the 19th century.

accept guns made of wrought iron, no matter how well constructed.

In the early 1850's Commander John A. Dahlgren USN became interested in the development of naval ordnance. His first smooth-bores were cast solid and were cooled slowly from the exterior. The distinguishing feature of the Dahlgren gun however was its shape, which Dahlgren had worked out carefully after thorough study of the pressures generated in the barrel of a gun as it was fired. As a result of Dahlgren's derived "curve of pressures," his guns were very thick at the breech with considerable taper toward the muzzle, so that they looked like stubby black bottles. Meanwhile Captain Thomas Rodman USA was developing a casting method which was similar in principle to that of the built-up gun: the Rodman gun was cast hollow, around a sand core, and the interior was cooled first, so that the outer metal cooled gradually onto a shrunken and hardened inner core. By combining his own design and Rodman's method of casting, Dahlgren was able to produce some fine smooth-bore ordnance. Since the Dahlgrens fired shell and solid shot with equal efficiency, they quickly replaced the Paixhans guns, which were useful for shell alone. Frigates of the *Merrimack* class were unique among warships in that every gun they carried, all Dahlgrens or Rodman-cast columbiads, could fire shell.

The first navy to order built-up guns in any quantity was the British when toward the end of the 1850's it was alarmed by the threat of the nearly-completed French ironclad *Gloire*. The Royal Navy therefore placed with William Armstrong (later Sir William) a large order for his built-up rifled guns, which at the time threw 40-pound and 70-pound projectiles. This Armstrong gun had one unique and valuable feature: the tubes were essentially long coiled bars, and thus the metal received the strains and stresses of firing along its length rather than across its width.

By 1861 steel guns were in existence, but only the French navy had ordered any of them. The Krupp works in Prussia had produced a gun with a steel tube as early as 1847, and in 1851 such a Krupp gun had attracted much attention when it was on display at Britain's Great Exposition.

The Parrott rifle, the principal military rifled gun used by both sides afloat and ashore during the American Civil War, was something of an anachronism in that, unlike the British Armstrongs, it had only a partial outer reinforcement in the form of a heavy wrought-iron band shrunk around the breech. The notorious tendency of the Parrott to blow away its own muzzle was caused in part by this failure to reinforce the inner gun-tube along its whole length.

RIFLING

Just before the Crimean War (1854-56) an Englishman, Charles William Lancaster, invented a gun with a twisted elliptical bore. In cross-section the outer surface of the barrel was circular, and this outer circle and the inner ellipse were always concentric; but in successive cross-sections the long axis of the inner ellipse was inclined to the horizontal at progressively greater angles. (The bore was so nearly circular that its elliptical shape was hardly apparent to the eye.) When an elongated projectile, also somewhat elliptical in cross-section, was fired from this gun, the twist of the bore rotated it around its own axis. Thus, to the modern gunner the Lancaster would be a paradox, for it was a smooth-bore rifle, having no lands or grooves.

These Lancasters were the first naval rifles to be used in actual warfare. They played a part in the siege of Sevastopol during the Crimean War. Ships fired them at land fortifications, the naval battery ashore employed several of them, and apparently the army used others. Opinions as to the efficiency of these guns varied, but it is clear that out of the eight used in the siege three burst. Commander (later Admiral Sir) Leopold George Heath RN wrote home:

They say that the Lancaster gun which was to have done such wonders is all humbug. You may perhaps be aware that it was always known that it shot like an Irish gun, round a corner, and that in the range table supplied with it you are told that at one thousand yards distance you must point so many yards to the left; at two thousand yards so many more, etc., etc. But it turns out that you can never be sure which corner it is going to turn, and if you point carefully fifty yards to the left it is an even bet that it will strike fifty yards to the right of the object aimed at, and that in fact it is most uncertain.[9]

Rifled small-arms had developed earlier than rifled ordnance, but the performance of the British Enfield of 1853 was so disappointing that the British army turned for help to England's most celebrated "mechanician," Joseph Whitworth, who succeeded in improving the small arms and in the process developed an interest in larger weapons. After exhaustive experiments and tests, Whitworth reached the conclusion that the ideal shape for the bore of any rifle, large or small, was hexagonal. In the same sense in which it may be said that the Lancaster had a twisted elliptical bore, the Whitworth gun had a twisted hexagonal one. The sides of a Whitworth projectile were six long flat planes, all of them somewhat skew to the axis of the bullet.

This hexagonal system of rifling (still without lands and grooves) did produce considerable accuracy. Opening an exposition in 1860, Queen Victoria, who could hardly be called a sportswoman, steadied a Whitworth hand-rifle against a mechanical rest and, to the amazement of everybody who watched, made one of the most nearly perfect shots recorded up till then in the history of small arms.

Other Englishmen, working independently at about this time, adopted systems of rifling with lands and grooves. Sir William Armstrong, the most influential gun designer during this period, developed a service gun using grooves alone, forming what was called a "fluted bore." Because Armstrong was an official of the War Department, his enemies insisted that he used his position to prevent the guns of his rivals from obtaining serious consideration by either the army or the navy. Whether the charge is justified or not,

[9] Sir Leopold George Heath, Admiral RN, *Letters from the Black Sea During the Crimean War, 1854-1855* (London, 1897), 87.

the Armstrong gun had one decided advantage over its rivals: it was a breech-loader. There was a removable vent-piece which could be lifted up along vertical grooves. A huge non-interrupted screw closed the breech, but there was a hole in it as large as, and in line with, the bore of the gun. Shot and powder were pushed into the bore through this hole; the vent-piece was dropped back into place; and the screw, on being turned, acted as a vise to hold the vent-piece steady. One trouble with all previous ordnance had been a tendency to wear out and crack near the touch-hole. The Armstrong solved that difficulty by putting the touch-hole in the removable vent-piece; when one touch-hole showed signs of wearing out, it was simply thrown away and replaced by another. These Armstrong guns were becoming fairly standard equipment in the Royal Navy in the early 1860's.

In 1861 however the French tested two guns which were far more advanced in their engineering than anything Britain had invented. These two guns, called the "Nivernaise" and the "Marie-Jeanne," were breech-loading rifled guns of 16 centimeters. Like the earlier Krupp guns, they were made of steel and reinforced by steel hoops. Probably the greatest innovation was the fact that the breech of each gun was closed by an interrupted screw of six sectors. When guns similar to these were later adopted by the French army and navy, the rest of Europe regarded the interrupted screw as a French invention. Actually it appears to have been an American one. The system had been patented in the United States as early as 1853 by two otherwise obscure Americans, John P. Schenkl and Adolph S. Saroni.

EARLY IRONCLAD PROJECTS

The idea of so strengthening the decks or sides of a ship as to make her invulnerable to enemy shot was an ancient one. The "tortoise ship" with which the Korean admiral Yi Sun defeated the Japanese in 1592 had an ironplated turtleback deck. At the siege of

Gibraltar in 1780-82 the French and their Spanish allies used protected gunboats and floating batteries; the gunboats clearly used iron plates as a part of their defensive armor, and the batteries may have done so. Whether they did or not, the sloping side that was to face the enemy was composed of heavy timbers about five feet thick. It is a commentary on the slow development of ordnance that Fulton's *Demologos,* built more than 30 years later, had wooden sides of approximately the same thickness.

An interesting ironclad project that never got past the blueprint stage in the War of 1812 was that of the energetic Colonel John Stevens of Hoboken, who proposed a circular, saucer-shaped floating battery plated with iron, which was to be anchored in a river or harbor and then rotated like a merry-go-round by means of a screw propeller, in order that each gun in turn might be brought to bear on the enemy. This proposed firing of guns from a rotating platform is a curious anticipation of the way in which the turret-enclosed guns of U.S.S. *Monitor* were to be handled almost 50 years later.

In 1843, when there was tension between the United States and both Mexico and Britain, the three sons of Colonel Stevens were given a contract to construct an ironclad screw steamer according to their plans and specifications. The armor, four to six inches thick and inclined at an angle of 45 degrees, had been shown by actual tests to resist the fire of the largest naval ordnance then in use. The ship was to have such unusual features as an iron hull, a complete absence of rigging (since she was intended primarily for coast defense), and large-caliber, breech-loading, rifled ordnance throwing elongated shells which would explode upon penetration. Like the *Princeton,* launched in the same year, she was to burn anthracite coal, and her engines and boilers were to be beneath the water line, out of reach of shot.

This Stevens Battery was never completed, for it lost the race with ordnance. Ericsson's "Oregon" gun began its downfall, for the "Oregon" could pierce the armor of the battery. Plans were made to install heavier ar-

mor, but by that time still better ordnance was available. As late as the Civil War, Edwin A. Stevens was still trying unsuccessfully to get Congress to vote funds to complete the ship.

THE FLOATING BATTERIES OF THE CRIMEAN WAR

In 1850 there were no naval ironclads. By the outbreak of the American Civil War, France and Britain were beginning to build up ironclad fleets.

A major cause of this vastly-increased interest in armor was the Battle of Sinope (1853), in which a Russian fleet destroyed a Turkish squadron. The tactical lesson that contemporary military men drew from the battle was the devastating effect of shellfire against wooden ships. Old General Paixhans, probably gloating a little because his guns had done the work, wrote an article for the *Moniteur* (February 21, 1854) in which he commented on the effectiveness of shell guns and the obvious vulnerability of wooden ships. Having studied the situation, Napoleon III asked for plans of floating batteries.

When it became apparent that French ironworks could produce only enough armor for five ironclads in time for the 1855 campaign, the government suggested that Britain cooperate by producing five more, and this, after extensive tests, Britain agreed to do. In spite of the considerable head start of the French, their five ironclads and the four British (one having burned on the stocks) were launched within three months of each other, beginning in March 1855. These ships were similar in most respects. The armor was about four inches thick, the hulls were of wood, the displacement was about 1,500 tons, the length about 170 feet, and the mean draft under nine. The French ships carried sixteen 50-pounder guns, the British fourteen 68-pounders. The complement of each ship was about 280 men.

Three of these French ironclads (*Dévastation, Tonnante,* and *Lave*) were towed out to the Black Sea in time to win acclaim for their part in the bombardment of Kinburn. Britain was so impressed that she ordered the building of four more batteries, three of which were to have iron hulls; France built no more wooden line of battle ships after 1855.

SEAGOING IRONCLAD STEAMERS

France was lucky, once the race for ironclad navies began, in having as its *Directeur du Matériel* (what today's American navy would call Chief of the Bureau of Ships) Dupuy de Lôme. Although he wished to try several designs, he set his standards so high that only his own design and that submitted by Camille Audenet satisfied his requirements, among which were that the ships must displace over 5,500 tons, that the gunports must be at least two meters above the water line in order that the guns might be fought in heavy weather, that the armor must be sufficient to repel shot from existing ordnance at probable ranges. Yet the ships had to have speed and maneuverability equal to those of Dupuy de Lôme's famous unarmored *Napoléon*. In 1858 three ships on the design of Dupuy de Lôme (*Gloire, Invincible,* and *Normandie*) and one on that of Audenet (*Couronne*) were laid down. The first three were to have wooden hulls sheathed with copper; the *Couronne* was to have an iron hull.

The *Gloire,* launched late in 1859, was the first seagoing ironclad. Her sides, of 4½-inch iron plates backed with 17 inches of wood, were invulnerable to the best ordnance of the day and remained so for about two years—a signal achievement for her designer, since the American Stevens Battery had been vulnerable from the blueprint stage and the later British *Warrior* was vulnerable the day she was launched. The *Gloire* displaced over 5,600 tons and mounted 36 guns. Her maximum speed was 13.1 knots; she once averaged over 12 knots for ten hours. She was one of the first warsteamers to regard sail as an auxiliary motive-power rather than as the primary one; her sail area was relatively small, and it was estimated that she could carry enough coal to let her cruise for a month at slow speeds.

Since many Americans still accept the mistaken legend that the *Monitor* and the *Virginia* were the world's first ironclads, it may be well to state that, late in 1860, France approved a building program that gave her 16 seagoing and 20 coast-defense ironclads either built, building, or authorized.

The British, who were becoming increasingly distrustful of Napoleon III during the late 1850's, let the contract for their first seagoing ironclad in 1859; the ship was launched and commissioned as H.M.S. *Warrior* in 1861. A sister ship and two smaller ironclads soon followed. These ships had iron hulls, but their armor, unlike that of the French ships, did not run completely from bow to stern; instead, it formed a sort of rectangular box around the vital midships section. As a result of this vulnerability forward and aft, the designers of the *Warrior* had given great attention to matters of compartmentation and watertight integrity. The ship displaced 9,000 tons. Her armor was 4½ inches of iron backed with 18 of teak. She mounted 26 68-pounder smoothbores, as well as four 70-pounder and ten 110-pounder Armstrongs, presumably all rifled and breechloading.

Ever since steam had been introduced, naval officers, observing the destructive force of steamers in collisions, had given thought to the reintroduction of the old galley-warfare tactic of ramming, but the adoption of this method of fighting had to be postponed until the development of strong enough defensive armor to permit the ramming ship to approach bows-on. The *Gloire* and *Warrior* classes were thus the first to be designed with emphasis on the possibility of their being used as rams; one of Audenet's arguments for the use of an iron hull in the *Couronne* was that it would facilitate ramming.

As matters turned out, steamers soon became so fast that ramming was as dangerous to the attacker as to the attacked, but ramming was still regarded as a major offensive tactic all during the American Civil War and for some years afterwards.

SUMMARY

The United States Navy at the outbreak of the American Civil War was still relatively unprogressive, but Britain and France had already solved the major problems of conversion. There were now ships afloat in which sail was a secondary source of power. Some of them were big ships, displacing thousands of tons. The essential elements of steam power were below the water line, safe from shot. A few ships mounted rifled breech-loading ordnance; shell was replacing solid shot. Armor was being adopted; Britain and France had adopted extensive ironclad building programs.

The war-steamer had come a long way in 40 years—and yet in a sense it had come no distance at all. The stout oaken sides of the frigate *Constitution* had been invulnerable to the fire of her contemporaries at ranges of a thousand yards. As a result of all the technological developments of half a century, the ship of the 1860's had become vulnerable at the same range.

15

Naval Operations, 1815-1861

WITH THE FINAL DEFEAT OF Napoleon and the restoration of a state of peace among the major powers, the United States, Britain, and France turned their attention again to those perennial nuisances the Barbary corsairs. Algeria, strongest and most troublesome of the Barbary states, received the closest scrutiny.

DECATUR'S TREATY
WITH ALGERIA

The United States, it will be recalled, had once before been on the verge of war with Algeria. It was for the purpose of chastising the Algerian corsairs that the U. S. Navy had begun the frigates which fought in the Quasi-War with France. Although the Dey signed a treaty to avoid hostilities, the corsairs had never completely halted their depredations. Between the period of the war with Tripoli and the War of 1812, Algerian ships had interfered increasingly with American commerce in the Mediterranean. From 1812 to 1815, although there was of course little American merchant shipping at sea, a few minor indignities occurred, and with the return of peace Congress declared war on Algeria as a means of getting a more favorable

and more explicit treaty. In May 1815 Commodore Stephen Decatur sailed for the Mediterranean with his flag in the new 44-gun *Guerrière,* accompanied by the frigates *Constellation* and *Macedonian* and several sloops-of-war and gun-brigs.

Learning as he entered the Mediterranean that the Algerian squadron was at sea, Decatur made a careful search. At length the American squadron located and captured the Algerian flagship *Meshouda,* 46, after a spirited engagement in which the *Guerrière* did most of the fighting. Two days later the lighter American ships took the brig *Estedio,* 22. Proceeding to Algiers with his squadron, Decatur opened negotiations which led to the signing of a very satisfactory treaty, putting the United States on a "most favored nation" footing in many respects and giving her special privileges in others. Next Decatur visited Tunis and Tripoli, where he demanded and got indemnity for unfriendly acts committed during the War of 1812.

Shortly after Decatur's visits to the three principal corsair cities, Commodore William Bainbridge underscored the warning by appearing with another squadron, his flag in the *Independence,* 74, the first ship of the line to fly the American flag at sea. Twice in the year following Decatur's cruise, American squadrons appeared off the Barbary Coasts. On the second occasion Commodore Isaac Chauncey's flag was in another new ship of the line, the *Washington,* 74. The United States Navy now decided to maintain a permanent Mediterranean squadron and leased facilities in Port Mahon, Minorca for a base.

EXMOUTH'S BOMBARDMENT

By this time the major powers of Europe had come to the belated decision that it ill became civilized nations to tolerate piracy and slavery merely for commercial advantage. An international commission of the Congress of Vienna concluded that the time had come to put an end forever to the lawless practices of the Barbary corsairs. Britain,

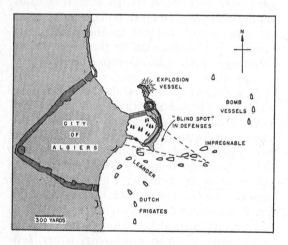

EXMOUTH'S ATTACK ON ALGIERS, 1816
(as actually carried out)

which had profited most from Algerian raids against her commercial rivals, undertook to execute the decision and in 1816 demanded that Algeria abolish slavery of Christians forthwith. The Dey replied by mockingly enslaving some Neapolitan fishermen who were under British protection. At that, the Admiralty dispatched Admiral Viscount Exmouth with a punitive force to end the nuisance once and for all. Offered an over-

whelmingly powerful fleet by Parliament, Exmouth contented himself with five ships of the line, a 50-gun "fourth rate," and a few frigates, considering that these were more than enough for the business at hand. He did however accept the assistance of a squadron of frigates from the Dutch, who had suffered for centuries from the corsairs and were anxious to be in on the final dissolution of the hated "Barbary system."

The port of Algiers was protected by a strongly fortified mole, behind which lay the Algerian fleet in a highly unseaworthy condition. Exmouth knew that there was a spot of minimum firepower near the southern end of the mole, and here he concentrated his ships of the line. He planned that four of them would engage the defenses while his flagship, the *Queen Charlotte,* 100, took position off the end of the mole and enfiladed it. The *Leander,* 50, would engage the shipping in the harbor, while the frigates kept the mainland forts occupied.

The plan worked almost according to schedule, except that one ship, the *Impregnable,* 98, anchored much too soon, well within range of a triple-banked battery on the mole. The 210 casualties she suffered brought the average for the ships of the line to 106, a far higher figure than the Royal Navy had sustained in any of Nelson's battles. The operation nevertheless was a success in that the Algerians, after seeing their city bombarded, their fleet burned, and a part of their fortifications silenced, accepted the British terms.

Though the formal system of regular protection money was ended by Exmouth's attack, the heavy price in British lives did not purchase final immunity from piratical raids in the Mediterranean. In the long run Exmouth accomplished little more with his five ships than Decatur had with his three frigates. Decatur had reduced the Dey to abject submission, and the Dey had crawled again for Exmouth; but the profits of piracy were too rich for the Barbary monarchs to restrain themselves for long. European and American squadrons had to pay several more calls along the Barbary Coast. In 1830, the Bourbon government of France set out to conquer Algeria, giving as one of its principal justifications the necessity of abolishing piracy. Actually the nuisance was not entirely wiped out until the 20th century, when the almost universal use of steam propulsion permitted merchantmen to outrun any raiding vessels the backward Barbary powers could send to sea.

THE UNITED STATES NAVY AFTER THE WAR OF 1812

Before the War of 1812 the Secretary of the Navy and four civilian clerks had handled the entire administration of the naval forces of the United States. After the war President Madison created a Board of Navy Commissioners, composed of three naval officers who had direct authority over material and advised the Secretary on all other naval matters. For the next 20 years Commodore John Rodgers, generally senior member and chairman of the Board,[1] was the dominant figure in the Navy. A few years after his retirement the Board was abolished, and the Navy in 1842 adopted something like the present bureau system—originally with five bureaus. A bureau system of some sort had become a necessity to handle the complexities of a fleet revolutionized by technological advances, but did not provide any means of coordinating the operations of the bureau chiefs, except through the usually inexperienced civilian Secretary of the Navy.

Before the Navy became seriously interested in steamers, it built a number of sailing ships of the line. The first three were the 74's *Independence, Washington,* and *Franklin,* a class that sacrificed comfort and seaworthiness for speed and firepower. None of the three saw much service in the line, but the *Independence,* as a 54-gun razee, was the flagship of the Pacific Squadron in 1847. More satisfactory were the 74's *Ohio* and *North Carolina,* launched in 1820. The *Pennsylvania,* 120, was the largest warship in the world at the time of her launching in 1837.

---

[1] Except for a short period of sea duty.

Meanwhile the protection of American commerce demanded the presence of the Navy in various parts of the world. Semipermanent squadrons were established—the West Indies Squadron, the African Squadron, the Mediterranean Squadron, the Brazil Squadron, the Pacific Squadron, and the East India Squadron. A Home Squadron later absorbed the West Indies Squadron.

In the 1820's the African and West Indies Squadrons were the busiest, the former being concerned with controlling the slave trade; the latter, with combating piracy. The African Squadron also had the duty of maintaining the immunity of American ships to search by British naval vessels. The anti-slave-trade patrol was chiefly British; its usual procedure was to order a suspected ship to lie to while an officer boarded her and examined her papers and possibly her cargo. With such incidents as the *Chesapeake-Leopard* affair in mind, the United States denied the right of the patrol to search ships flying the American flag. Most slavers therefore took to flying the Stars and Stripes except when they were in the presence of an American warship.

In the early 1820's the African Squadron rendered assistance in establishing the country of Liberia. The Navy furnished the sloop-of-war *Cyane* to escort the first Negro colonists on their voyage from the United States. A year later Lieutenant Robert F. Stockton visited the colony and secured for it a much healthier site, on which the capital city of Monrovia now stands.

The West Indies Squadron was at its greatest strength in the early 1820's, successively under Commodores James Biddle, David Porter, and Lewis Warrington. Small-scale piracy had become a serious nuisance in the West Indies and the Gulf of Mexico; the work of the Squadron under these leaders ended this menace to American commerce. During Porter's incumbency there occurred the unfortunate Foxardo affair in which Porter avenged what he considered an insult to the American flag by Spanish officials. When a court-martial found that he had exceeded his authority, Porter resigned from the United States Navy and accepted a commission as commander in chief of the navy of Mexico. As a result, his son, the future Admiral David Dixon Porter, began his naval career in the Mexican service.

THE BATTLE
OF NAVARINO

During the 1820's Greece was fighting for and achieving her independence from Turkey. The struggle had many interesting naval aspects, such as the revived use of fire ships and the first appearance of a steam warship armed with shell-guns, but in both the naval and the diplomatic sense, the most important incident was the Battle of Navarino in 1827.

The diplomatic situation was a curious one. Since 1815 the reactionary counsels of Prince Metternich had controlled European policy, and displays of armed force had crushed incipient revolts directed against "legitimate" rulers. Consistency therefore demanded general European support of the Turks against the Greeks, but popular feeling demanded the opposite course. Russia, even then adept at complicating international situations, was loudly proclaiming her sympathy with the Greeks in their struggle with the possessors of the Dardanelles and the Bosporus. The diplomats, unwilling to offend Metternich on the one hand or the Czar and public opinion on the other, tried to straddle the issue. At first, while it looked as if the Greeks might win by their own unaided efforts, Britain and France assumed an official attitude of strict neutrality. When Mehemet Ali, the viceroy of Egypt, made his efficient little army and fleet available to his overlord the Sultan of Turkey, the likelihood of single-handed Greek victory disappeared. Britain, France, and Russia thereupon formed an international fleet under British Vice Admiral Sir Edward Codrington, veteran of the Glorious First of June and of the campaign against New Orleans, and sent it to the Mediterranean with the ambiguous task of preventing the spread of hostilities. Among the ships under Codrington's command there were ten of the line—three British, three French, and four Russian.

The combined Turkish and Egyptian fleet, outnumbering Codrington's by three or four to one but including only three ships of the line, was lying in the Bay of Navarino on the southwest coast of Greece. Codrington went there, conferred with Ibrahim Pasha, the Turco-Egyptian military commander in chief, and obtained a sworn promise from Ibrahim and several of his principal subordinates that they would abstain from all aggressive military activities for a specified period. Relying on this oath, Codrington scattered his forces in order to attend to a secondary objective of his expedition, the suppression of Greek piracy.

The obvious weakness of the arrangement with Ibrahim lay in Codrington's inability to extract a similar promise from the Greeks. When a Greek force under Lord Cochrane showed an intention to extend the war south of the Gulf of Corinth, the Turks requested permission to counter the move. Codrington refused permission, whereupon the Turkish fleet defiantly put to sea. The only ships then available to Codrington were his flagship *Asia*, 84, a frigate, a corvette, and a brig. Nevertheless he unhesitatingly threw this little force, mounting 172 guns as against 1,270 for the Turks, across their course and ordered them to turn back. To his considerable relief, the Turks obeyed him and returned to Navarino.

Believing on the basis of this incident that the Turks would not fight, however great the provocation might be, Codrington now made a decision that does more credit to his courage and his sense of duty than to his diplomatic foresight. He decided that he could best immobilize the Turks by re-assembling his forces, sailing right into Navarino harbor, and anchoring alongside the Turkish fleet.

To prevent such a move, the Turks had drawn up their fleet in a horseshoe formation around the mouth of the harbor. The line was several ships deep, with the more powerful vessels forming the inner arc (i.e., nearest open water). To deal with these ships if hostilities broke out, Codrington assigned his British vessels to anchor near two Turkish

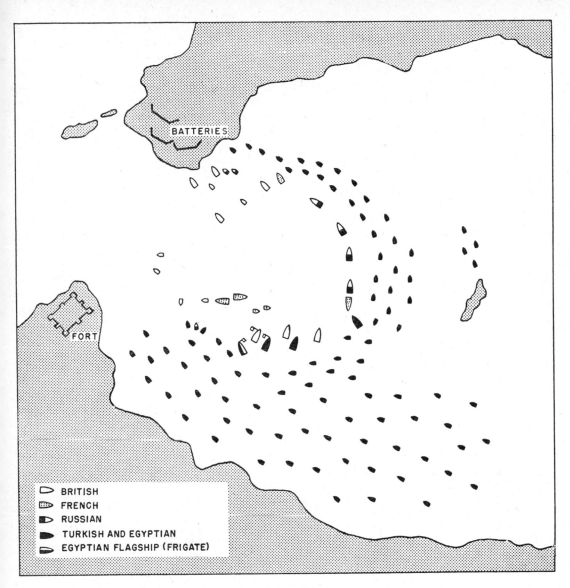

BATTERIES

FORT

▭ BRITISH
▱ FRENCH
◗ RUSSIAN
◆ TURKISH AND EGYPTIAN
▱ EGYPTIAN FLAGSHIP (FRIGATE)

BATTLE OF NAVARINO, OCTOBER 20, 1827

ships of the line and some of the more powerful frigates, the Russians to oppose one Turkish ship of the line and the remaining Turkish frigates, and the French to handle the small but efficient Egyptian squadron.

Codrington's fleet entered the bay without opposition, and, though the wind was light, many of his ships reached their assigned stations and anchored before any shots were fired. When the frigate *Dartmouth* sent a boat to request a fire ship on the Turkish left to shift its position, the boat received some small-arms fire, to which the *Dartmouth* replied in kind. An Egyptian ship then fired a cannon, and the engagement became general.

The result of the battle was the virtual annihilation of the Turkish fleet. The only unusual tactical feature was the effective use which Codrington's forces made of spring-lines on their anchor cables, a use which was almost as effective with the huge ships of the line as it had been with Macdonough's tiny vessels on Lake Champlain 13 years earlier. Codrington's flagship *Asia,* for example, having silenced the Turkish flagship, then swung through 90 degrees and brought the devastating force of its fresh port broadside to bear on the large frigate serving as flagship to the Egyptian squadron.

The British government, at least, had not wanted war and would have been glad to disavow Codrington's actions, even though he had been acting under unrealistic orders. In 1828 they relieved him of command and recalled him to England to answer certain charges, none of which related specifically to his battle. The charges did not stand up, and Codrington later commanded the Channel Fleet.

Greece gained her independence, partly because of Navarino, for the crushing of the Turkish fleet led to the withdrawal of a strong Egyptian army. Once more, landpower unsupported by adequate sea power had proved inadequate to sustain a campaign in hostile country.

THE NAVIES IN THE DOLDRUMS: FROM NAVARINO TO THE MEXICAN WAR

During the 1830's and early 1840's the major navies fought no important battles. They operated on decreased budgets, uncertain whether the future of naval warfare lay with sail or steam propulsion, with solid shot or shell ammunition. Nevertheless, the sea services were extremely busy. They protected commerce, conducted voyages of exploration and scientific research, and, in the language of the day, "showed the flag" and "chastised native insolence."

A typical incident was that of the American navy at Quallah Battoo in Sumatra. In 1831 the inhabitants plundered an American merchantman and killed a number of her crew. A year later Captain John Downes USN

brought to anchor off Quallah Battoo the frigate *Potomac,* 44, disguised as a Danish merchantman. Under cover of night Downes put ashore a landing party of seamen and marines. With the support of the frigate's guns this party assaulted the native fortifications and killed the principal chief.

In addition to punitive expeditions, the navies assisted with diplomatic negotiations. In 1833, for example, the U.S. sloop-of-war *Peacock* took a diplomatic agent to Siam and Arabia, where the agent obtained valuable treaties.

The scientific expedition of most importance to the world as far as its ultimate results went was that of H.M.S. *Beagle* in the early 1830's. While the 235-ton ship was surveying the coast of Patagonia, the Falkland Islands, and the west coast of South America, a civilian naturalist attached to the expedition, Charles Darwin, was collecting many of the geological and zoological specimens and data on which he later based his theory of biological evolution. Another expedition of considerable importance was that of Lieutenant Charles Wilkes USN, the officer who, 20 years later, was to precipitate the *Trent* affair. The Wilkes expedition cruised for four years (1838-1842), during which time it explored part of the Antarctic and surveyed what is now the western coast of the United States. Wilkes' book about the expedition became a best seller and gained the Navy much favorable publicity.

From 1836 to 1842, the United States Navy cooperated with the Army in its war against the Seminole Indians of Florida. Some naval personnel and most of the Marine Corps took part in land operations. The Navy also provided a "mosquito fleet" of canoes and larger boats to operate against the Indians in the shallow waters of the Everglades.

During the "Pastry War" between France and Mexico in 1838,[2] the French used their shell-guns effectively against land fortifications, bombarding and capturing the fortress of San Juan de Ulloa in Vera Cruz harbor. The destructive effect of shell tremendously

[2] So called because a major cause was the reparations demanded by France for the destruction of a Frenchman's bakery by riotous Mexican soldiers.

impressed an American observer, the future admiral David Glasgow Farragut, whose subsequent report stressed that point above all others. If the United States Navy had paid more heed to Farragut or if the Royal Navy had realized the significance of the fall of the fortress, Vera Cruz might have marked the beginning of the age of the ironclad, as the Battle of Sinope ultimately did, 15 years later. But perhaps because the shell guns had destroyed a fortress rather than a ship, the navies failed to realize the vulnerability of unarmored wooden hulls.

This French triumph at Vera Cruz in 1838 caused some embarrassment to the United States Navy during the Mexican War of 1846-1847, since many people felt that if the French navy alone had been able to take the fortress the United States Navy could do the same thing. Commodore David Conner decided against an all-naval attack on the fortress, apparently on the basis of reports, which may have been authentic, that the Mexicans had greatly strengthened the walls of the fortress since 1838, adding much granite to the original coral.

In 1840 the Royal Navy, together with an Austrian fleet, bombarded St. Jean d'Acre. Mehemet Ali, the viceroy of Egypt, was fighting his overlord, the Sultan of Turkey, with the support of France and the opposition of Britain. Small steamers that accompanied the British fleet convincingly demonstrated their usefulness in warfare, serving effectively as both dispatch boats and tugs. During this bombardment, which climaxed the campaign, Sir Charles Napier, second in command of the expedition, put his flagship *Powerful*, 84, in a position of great jeopardy, whereupon one of the steamers towed him to safety.

In the following year, during the course of the Opium War with China, the East India Company's iron-hulled steamer *Nemesis* participated in naval operations and greatly impressed the British navy. Her shallow draft and her maneuverability in light airs made her able to perform operations that were impossible for the other ships.

During 1842 there occurred three incidents involving the American navy, each of which had some historical importance. They were Commodore Jones' seizure of Monterey, Commodore Kearny's negotiations with China, and the mutiny of the brig *Somers*.

Commodore Thomas ap Catesby Jones USN, commanding the Pacific Squadron based on Callao, Peru, knew that American relations with Mexico were strained and also that his government was concerned about possible British designs on California. When the American consul at Mazatlan, Mexico wrote warning him that hostilities might have already begun and at the same time the flagship of Britain's Pacific Squadron left Callao with every appearance of haste, Jones decided that the time to act had come. Hastening northwards, he entered the harbor of Monterey, Mexican provincial capital of California, and took possession in the name of the United States. Two days later, on the basis of more accurate information, Jones hauled the American flag down; no war had begun after all. Although he apologized to the Mexican authorities, the United States government had to show outward disapproval of his actions, so the Secretary of the Navy relieved Jones from command of the Pacific Squadron and ordered him home.

The Opium War having interfered with American commerce, Commodore Lawrence Kearny went to the Far East in 1842 with the *Constellation,* 36, and the *Boston,* 18. When he arrived in China, the war was virtually over. Because Britain had acquired substantial commercial privileges thereby, Kearny set out to obtain equal privileges for Americans. By alternating tact and courtesy with a show of force, much as Perry was to do in Japan a decade later, Kearny obtained the unprecedented right of opening direct negotiations with Viceroy Ke. Kearny not only obtained the assurances he wanted, but the Viceroy offered to make a treaty with him. Kearny lacked authority however and could only lay a foundation for the subsequent negotiations of Caleb Cushing. On his way back to the United States, finding that the Hawaiian Islands had ceded themselves to Britain, Kearny added his power and his government's prestige to the forces that eventually revoked the cession and restored sovereignty to King Kamehameha III.

The mutiny of the brig *Somers* in 1842 brought to a head the general dissatisfaction with the training of young American naval officers. For years they had simply gone to sea and learned by experience, augmented in the larger ships by the teaching of an underpaid civilian schoolmaster or chaplain. Dissatisfied with the results of this method, Congress established schools for midshipmen at Philadelphia and Norfolk. Since midshipmen attended these schools only between voyages however, this new method proved unsatisfactory. Commodore Matthew C. Perry, who was becoming prominent as one of the most influential young flag-officers, urged the manning of small ships by naval apprentices, who would thus learn together at sea. As an experiment along this line, Commander Alexander Slidell MacKenzie, Perry's brother-in-law, took the brig *Somers,* 10, to sea with a crew consisting largely, but not exclusively, of naval apprentices. One of these apprentices, Philip Spencer, was the son of the Secretary of War.

On the voyage home from Africa, a sailor informed MacKenzie that Spencer was inciting his shipmates to mutiny, with the purpose of seizing the ship and setting up business as a West Indies pirate. The evidence suggests to a thoughtful reader that Spencer was mentally unbalanced and that MacKenzie was not much more stable himself. Even after clapping Spencer and two other supposed mutineers into irons—which, since the *Somers* lacked a brig, meant handcuffing them to the taffrail—MacKenzie managed to convince himself, on the basis of some curious evidence, that it was necessary for the safety of the ship to hang Spencer and the two enlisted men at the yardarm. This he presently did. When the *Somers* made port, the hullaballoo over MacKenzie's action was tremendous, but a court-martial ultimately absolved him of blame.

The *Somers* tragedy had one good result. By discrediting the best of the alternative solutions to the problem of training officers, it demonstrated the need for a naval academy comparable to the Army's academy at West Point. The historian George Bancroft, who became Polk's Secretary of the Navy in 1845, obtained a report from the Naval Board of Examiners in which they recommended the establishment of such an academy at Annapolis, Maryland. In his capacity as Acting Secretary of War during the temporary absence from Washington of Secretary Marcy, Bancroft signed over to the Navy Fort Severn, an old army post at Annapolis. By the time Congress returned from recess in the fall of 1845, the United States Naval Academy was in smooth and efficient operation. Since war with either Mexico or Britain seemed imminent, Congress had no wish to haggle over military expenditures. It accepted Bancroft's actions and appropriated funds for the Academy.

THE MEXICAN WAR: BACKGROUND

Historians have regarded the war between the United States and Mexico (1846-1848) as both a crusade on behalf of misruled people and an unprincipled land-grab. This is not the place to try to decide between these two interpretations. However, on two facts there is no room for dispute: the Mexican government was not effectively governing in Texas and California, and there was strong expansionist sentiment in the United States.

The weakness of the central Mexican government had been apparent for years. Texas and California were not the only areas that had at least temporarily achieved real or virtual independence. The provinces of Zapetecas and Yucatan had done the same, and the subjugation of Yucatan in particular had proved a long and difficult process. In 1836 Texas had achieved *de facto* independence by defeating the Mexican Army at San Jacinto and capturing the President-General, that extraordinary political phenomenon Antonio Lopez de Santa Anna. Although Mexico had repudiated Santa Anna's treaty and had never officially recognized Texan independence, the Mexican Army had not managed to make any serious attempt at reconquest. Even the tiny Texas navy under

Commodore Edwin Ward Moore had held its own against the forces of Mexico. When Mexico City had announced a blockade of the Texas coast Moore blockaded Mexico instead. His little fleet, operating in virtual alliance with Yucatan, closed the port of Vera Cruz, captured the town of Tabasco—levying a $25,000 ransom—and even attacked and defeated Mexican naval squadrons in surface combat.

California was almost as free from the control of Mexico City as Texas; she had driven out the last official representative of the central government by armed revolt. In 1845 the two chief officials were Californians, virtually self-appointed to office. The military commandant, General José Castro, maintained his capital at Monterey; the civil governor, Pio Pico, ruled southern California from Los Angeles, then a town of about 1,500 people. Antagonism between Pico and Castro, plus factional strife between the natives and the American settlers, so complicated the governmental situation that intervention by the United States probably prevented a small-scale civil war.

The desire of the American Southerners to extend slave territory was probably a less important reason for the expansionism of 1845 than a subconscious belief in the minds of many Americans that expansion was inevitable. It was "manifest destiny"; if ultimately, why not at once? The Democratic party in particular held this view, and the Democratic party was in power in 1845. Three leading expansionists were key figures in the government: James K. Polk, the President; Thomas Hart Benton of Missouri, a leader in the Senate; and George Bancroft, the Secretary of the Navy.

Many favored expansion for its own sake. Others, more moderate, believed it the lesser of two evils. This was the time of the Oregon dispute, and feeling against Britain was high. If the United States did not fill up the power vacuums of Texas and California, the moderates reasoned, Britain—or even France— might do so. Commodore Jones' dash to Monterey in 1842 had been chiefly for the purpose of forestalling the British. Modern historians deny that there was a serious British threat, but many Americans then sincerely believed that there was. In the closing days of Tyler's administration (March 1845) Congress had voted the annexation of Texas. The first task of Polk's administration was therefore to deploy the armed forces of the United States for maximum effectiveness in the event of war.

Bancroft issued most of the key orders. As Acting Secretary of War, he ordered General Zachary Taylor to advance into Texas and to take position "on or near the Rio Grande." When, in obedience to this order, Taylor crossed the Nueces River, which Mexico claimed as its northern boundary, hostilities soon began. Meanwhile, as Secretary of the Navy, Bancroft saw to it that Commodore David Conner's Home Squadron gave active support to Taylor by convoying supply ships, protecting Taylor's bases, and transporting troops. When war broke out Bancroft ordered Conner to clamp a tight blockade on the Mexican coast. In June 1845 Bancroft sent secret and confidential orders to the Pacific Squadron under Commodore John D. Sloat that, in event of war, Sloat must occupy San Francisco (then called Yerba Buena) at once, and such other ports as he could. In consequence of these orders, Sloat moved his base northward from Callao, Peru to Mazatlan, Mexico.

The only obvious step that Bancroft did not take was to send troops to support the Navy in California, and that was because Taylor needed every soldier that was available in 1845. Even so, Bancroft may have tried to remedy the deficiency. These facts are clear: Senator Benton had a son-in-law, John C. Frémont, a brevet captain of army engineers, who had gained some reputation as an explorer. During the summer of 1845, Bancroft and Benton had a number of talks with Frémont. The Senate Military Affairs Committee, of which Benton was chairman, arranged that Frémont should lead another exploring expedition across the Rockies into the California-Oregon area. Within a month Frémont was in Arkansas, in command of an expedition of 60 men. They were civilians, it is true, but their number included Kit Carson and other notable scouts and "mountain men." In speaking of Bancroft's part in the expedition, Frémont later said, "His mind was alive to the bearing of actual conditions, and he knew how sometimes skill and bold action determine the advantages of a political situation." There is no direct evidence that Bancroft arranged the expedition in order that there might be a quasi-military force to cooperate with Sloat in 1846, but the implications seem obvious.

Thus Bancroft arranged for every major military move of 1846 except Brevet Brigadier General Stephen W. Kearny's expedition into New Mexico.

MEXICAN WAR: THE NAVY TAKES CALIFORNIA

The conquest of California was a small-scale affair so far as military operations were concerned. Only a few hundred combatants were involved, and though the war was at times grim enough to the participants and ultimately added to the United States some of its richest territory, the history of the campaign has for today's reader a faintly comic-opera flavor. Much of the confusion and uncertainty that marked the conquest, and much of the tarnishing of reputations that followed, resulted from absence of clear channels of command and from doubts regarding relative rank. The absence of clear channels may be attributed in some degree to the informality of the command structure. Doubts regarding rank arose out of a complicated situation affecting rank and seniority which prevailed in the American armed forces at the time.

Although the Army had generals, the Navy had no officer higher in rank than a captain. Commodore was a courtesy title given to a captain who had commanded a squadron. Thus the veteran naval commanders of the War of 1812 who were still on active duty held only seniority but no actual rank over naval officers whose commissions dated from 25 years later. To deal with the complex situation that resulted, the Army adopted a clumsy system of assimilated rank: a naval officer who had held the rank of captain less

than five years ranked with a lieutenant colonel; during his next five years he ranked with a colonel; the next five, with a brigadier general; from then on, with a major general. The existence of brevet rank however introduced a problem which this rule of thumb could not clarify. There had recently been a protracted controversy between a brevet brigadier general and a colonel in Taylor's army, the colonel claiming that since his commission as a colonel antedated the general's commission as colonel he outranked the general. The Secretary of War decided the question one way and General Taylor the other.

Since one of the leaders of the American conquest of California was a brevet brigadier general, another was a commodore, and a third was son-in-law of the chairman of the Senate Military Affairs committee with the eventual rank of lieutenant colonel and aspirations to be governor, there were possibilities aplenty for cross purposes and confusion.

Captain Frémont's expedition reached California in the winter of 1845-46. The following spring, when it was about to withdraw at the request of General Castro, the expedition was overtaken by a courier from Washington, Lieutenant Archibald Gillespie USMC. Possibly in addition to his official dispatches Gillespie brought secret orders for Frémont. At any rate, the explorer turned back into California and began to agitate for revolt among the American settlers north of San Francisco. In June 1846 these settlers took military possession of the town of Sonoma and held a convention, as a result of which, on the 4th of July, they proclaimed California an independent republic, elected Frémont governor, and hoisted a flag carrying the picture of a bear. Learning soon afterward that Commodore Sloat had taken possession of Monterey, Frémont marched the Bear Flag army, 160 strong, to join him.

General Taylor's forces had begun fighting Mexicans in late April and early May. On hearing of these engagements, Commodore Sloat sent the *Portsmouth*, 20, to observe conditions at San Francisco and the *Cyane* and *Levant*, 18 guns each, to do the same at

Monterey; he himself tarried so long at Mazatlan that Bancroft sent him a sharp reprimand. Before the reprimand arrived however
Sloat had gone north with his flagship, the
Savannah, 44. Entering the harbor of Monterey on July 2, he paid the customary call
on the California authorities. On the 6th he
sent orders to the *Portsmouth* to seize San
Francisco, and on the following day he sent
a landing party ashore to hoist the American
flag over Monterey and to post a proclamation of annexation. Neither at Monterey nor
at San Francisco was there any military opposition. On July 15 Sloat's forces were augmented by the arrival of the *Congress,* 44,
aboard which was a commodore junior to
Sloat, Robert Field Stockton.

When the Bear Flag army reached Monterey, Frémont and Gillespie had a fruitless
interview with Sloat. The Commodore was a
sick man, and he had no idea of undertaking
any further warlike operations. "He told
them," Stockton testified at Frémont's court-
martial, "that he did not intend to move
from Monterey; that he had no use for their
services, and would have nothing to do with
them." Discouraged, the young men went
aboard the *Congress* to talk to Stockton, who
gave them an enthusiastic reception.

Sloat had told Stockton that he intended
to turn over command of the squadron and
return to the United States for medical attention. After the talk with Frémont and
Gillespie, Stockton went to Sloat and urged
that the transfer of command should take
place at once. Sloat characteristically hesitated to take so drastic a step, but agreed to
transfer immediate command of the forces
ashore and of U.S.S. *Cyane* to Stockton.
Thereupon, as Stockton later testified at the
court-martial:

I immediately sent to Captain Fremont to inform him of what had occurred, and to let him
know that, if he and Lieutenant Gillespie, with
the men who were with them, would volunteer
to serve under my command, as long as I was in
possession of the territory and desired their services, that [sic] I would form a battalion, and
would appoint Captain Fremont the major and
Lieutenant Gillespie a captain, and all the other
necessary officers. This was all done in the course

of the day and the next morning; and they were
ordered to embark on board the United States
ship Cyane, to be landed at San Diego. In this
way was the naval battalion of California mounted riflemen formed, and brought into the service
of the United States. I call it navy battalion, because it was not brought into service under the
laws of the army. . . . The law authorizing the
formation of this battalion was the law of necessity.

The *Cyane,* with this newly formed "navy
battalion" aboard, sailed for San Diego July
26, 1846 and arrived there without incident.
On the 29th Commodore Sloat turned over
full command to Stockton and sailed for
home in the *Levant.* Soon afterward Stockton took the *Congress* south to San Pedro,
drilled her crew in a few elementary military
maneuvers, and marched them inland to a
juncture with Frémont. The combined force
then marched without opposition into Los
Angeles.

THE NAVY
HOLDS CALIFORNIA

Meanwhile the Army was also getting
ready to conquer California. Brevet Brigadier General Stephen W. Kearny USA had
left Fort Leavenworth in June 1846 with the
primary purpose of capturing Santa Fe and
annexing the province of New Mexico. Having taken Santa Fe by a brilliant and rapid
march, he proceeded, in accordance with his
orders, to cross the mountains into southern
California. He took with him only 300 men,
ordering Colonel Doniphan with a much
larger force southward on a spectacular but
militarily worthless expedition to El Paso del
Norte and Chihuahua. While crossing the
mountains, Kearny met Kit Carson, who was
taking Frémont's and Stockton's dispatches
to Washington. Reading the dispatches and
understanding from them that California
was completely subdued, Kearny sent back
200 of his troops.

But California, far from being subdued,
was by this time in the throes of revolt.
Armed forces headed by José Maria Flores
and other Mexican-Californian officers who

had broken their parole to Stockton had defeated Gillespie, then commanding at Los Angeles, and forced him to withdraw. Captain William Mervine USN, leading a small relief column, also suffered defeat and withdrew to the squadron. Stockton held San Diego, but the Californians besieged him there; Frémont was absent somewhere in the north. The siege of San Diego must have been a nominal one however for when Stockton received word of General Kearny's coming he promptly sent Gillespie with 35 men to escort him to San Diego.

On December 6, 1846 Kearny and Gillespie attacked an enemy detachment at San Pasqual. If the Americans won a victory, as Kearny later insisted, it was a Pyrrhic one: 18 Americans died, a number (including Kearny and Gillespie) were wounded, and Kearny's second in command wrote to Stockton suggesting "the propriety of dispatching, without delay, a considerable force to meet us." Three days later three separate messengers arrived at San Diego in a state of exhaustion to report that the Californians were besieging General Kearny on San Bernardo Hill. As soon as he could spare them Commodore Stockton sent 215 more men, and this second detachment brought Kearny safely into San Diego.

No dispute as to the relative rank of the commodore and the general arose at that time, though it is probable that neither Kearny nor Stockton was quite sure which was senior.[3] In fact, while they were planning the expedition to retake Los Angeles, each of them offered before witnesses to serve as the other's aide-de-camp. According to Stockton, Kearny "said no, that the force was mine, and that he would go as my aide-de-camp, or accompany me." When the expedition was getting ready to march late in December 1846, Kearny came up as Stockton was about to mount his horse and asked who was to command the troops. On learning that it was a navy lieutenant, Kearny asked for the command. Stockton gave it to him, saying to several of his officers, as Kearny himself testified, "Gentlemen, General

Kearny has kindly consented to take command of the troops on this expedition. You will, therefore, consider him as your commander. I will go along as governor and commander-in-chief in California." Although Kearny seems to have regarded this statement as a formal abdication, Stockton continued to give orders and Kearny to obey them.

Early in January 1847 the little force met and defeated the enemy, crossing the San Gabriel River under fire and then withstanding an attack in the open. After that, enemy opposition ceased, and the Americans triumphantly re-entered Los Angeles. Some of the retreating enemy however encountered another advancing American column, that of Frémont, who by now held the rank of lieutenant colonel. Apparently hoodwinking Frémont as to the extent of their defeat, these men arranged a treaty with him, the Treaty of Cahuenga. Its terms were extremely liberal, far more liberal than Stockton wanted to grant, but he accepted them grudgingly to save American face. With the Treaty of Cahuenga, organized resistance ended in California.

Because the subsequent events, over which there has been much controversy, belong more closely to Frémont's biography than to naval history, the summary here will be brief. Swallowing his anger over the treaty, Stockton appointed Frémont governor of California in his place. On the same day Kearny gave Frémont an order which the latter refused to obey, answering that his authority emanated from Stockton. At about this time, Commodore W. Branford Shubrick USN arrived on the coast to supersede Stockton, bringing with him a set of orders for Stockton which cut the ground from under Frémont. George Bancroft had resigned as Secretary of the Navy; his less bellicose successor commanded Stockton to surrender all civil authority to the Army and to regard himself as ranking only with an army colonel. Since the orders gave Stockton an option between serving under Shubrick and returning home, he went home overland. Kearny managed to remove Frémont as governor and bring him to Washington under virtual arrest. A subse-

---

[3] Kearny definitely was not, according to W. H. Russell's testimony at Frémont's court-martial.

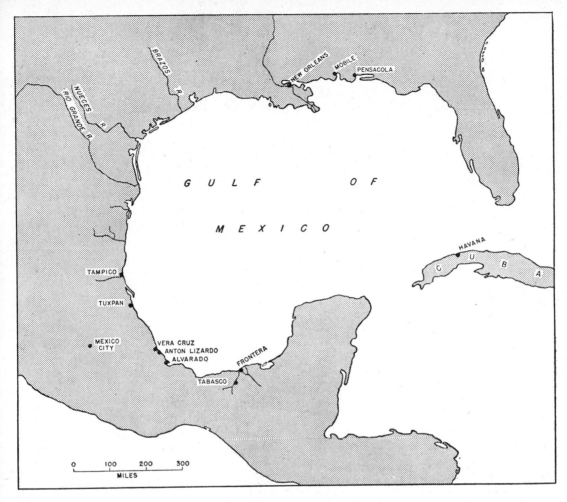

THE GULF OF MEXICO

quent court-martial found Frémont guilty on charges of disobedience and conduct prejudicial to good order and military discipline; it cleared him of a charge of mutiny. President Polk remitted the sentence of dismissal from the army, but Frémont resigned his commission.

Though some historians have pictured Commodore Stockton as merely insubordinate and impetuous, it is clear that he had some real achievements to his credit. He had acted aggressively rather than passively; he had been decisive and prompt; he had perceived the necessity of integrating the tiny armed forces that were available to the

United States in California; he had trained sailors to do efficient infantry service ashore. More than any other person, he has a right to the title of conqueror of California.

MEXICAN WAR: BLOCKADE ON THE EAST COAST

During all of 1846 and much of 1847, the chief job of the United States naval forces in the Gulf of Mexico was maintenance of a close blockade. The commander of these forces was Commodore David Conner until March 1847, when his former second in command, Commodore Matthew C. Perry, relieved him.

The Pacific Squadron of Sloat and Stockton necessarily included only sailing vessels because no coaling bases existed on the Pacific Coast. Conner had the steamers as well as a number of sailing ships, but even so close to home ports the steamers of that day were a logistic problem. The base of Conner's Home Squadron was Pensacola. If a steamer refueled there and returned to the squadron under steam, its coal supply was low as soon as it began blockading operations —and, since the Mexican coast is an area of light airs and calms, the steamers usually did return under steam. Conner solved this problem by establishing a secondary base of operations at Anton Lizardo, on the Mexican coast south of Vera Cruz.

Except for Vera Cruz itself, which was far too strong for the navy to take single-handed, Mexico had no good ports. Those that she did have were, from north to south, Tampico, Tuxpan, Alvarado, and Tabasco, two of which are north of Vera Cruz and two south of it. Obviously the blockade would be much more effective if the Navy closed these four ports; before the war ended it succeeded in doing so. But the work could not begin until a few small steamers joined the squadron; the draft of the bigger ships was too great, and the light sailing craft could not maneuver well enough, especially if the port lay on a river with a strong current, as Tabasco did. It was therefore August 1846 before Conner made his first attempt at one of the ports.

His first two efforts were against Alvarado, and both were failures. Late in October Perry led an expedition against Tabasco which was more successful. He took the port of Frontera with its shipping, including one small American-built steamer that was later to prove valuable to the Navy. Proceeding 75 miles upriver, Perry bombarded the town of Tabasco, but, having no troops to garrison it, he then withdrew. Next came a bloodless capture of Tampico by the whole squadron. Again there were no occupation forces available, but Conner held on until troops arrived. In December Perry occupied the town of Laguna on an island off the coast of Yucatan. In March 1847 Vera Cruz fell to General Winfield Scott's army, at which time Perry relieved Conner as commander of the Home Squadron. Shortly afterwards Alvarado fell to the steam gunboat *Scourge,* Lieutenant C. G. Hunter commanding. Ordered to Alvarado to blockade while strong land and sea forces closed in, Hunter discovered that the town garrison was very weak. He steamed in and received the town's surrender. He then proceeded up-river and took another town, with the result that when Perry and General Quitman arrived at Alvarado they found it governed by an American midshipman and five sailors. The chief purpose of the expedition had been to capture some horses and mules, the Army being low on mounts and draft animals. Furious at Hunter's success, the humorless Perry insisted on the lieutenant's court-martial and dismissal from the service, the principal charge being that Hunter through his excessive zeal had frightened the horses and mules away.

Before attacking Tuxpan and Tabasco, which the Mexicans had re-occupied as soon as Perry left, the commodore, like Stockton in California earlier, proceeded to organize and drill a naval brigade for landing operations. Throwing this brigade ashore and attacking with his gunboats, he took Tuxpan in April 1847. In June the second Tabasco operation occurred. Finding the river obstructed at one point, Perry went ashore with his naval brigade and cleared the banks between that point and Tabasco. With the danger of snipers removed, the gunboats, now under the command of Lieutenant David Dixon Porter USN, were able to clear the obstacle and proceed upstream, covering Perry's flank. With the second capture of Tabasco, maintenance of the blockade became a matter of routine.

Two lessons are implicit in all these operations of Conner and Perry. One was the need of naval small craft as well as capital ships, since a navy has other functions than fleet actions at sea. The second was the necessity of a landing and occupation force to cooperate with the navy in warfare against shore establishments. These truths seem obvious enough, yet the British and French navies were to ignore them in planning their Baltic campaigns during the Crimean War a few years later.

THE LANDING AT VERA CRUZ, MARCH 1847

The strategic center of land warfare against a geographically small country is usually the capital city. Even though General Taylor had penetrated deeply into northern Mexico during 1846, it became increasingly obvious that, since he was too far away from Mexico City, additional victories in that theater could contribute hardly anything to ending the war. President Polk and his advisers therefore decided to send another expedition to land at Vera Cruz and march inland to Mexico City. The commander of this new force was Lieutenant General Winfield Scott, senior officer of the United States Army.

To take an army of 10-12,000 men, with all its equipment, so far by sea and to land it in the face of probable opposition was an enormous undertaking for those days. It obviously would have been impossible if the United States Navy had not held undisputed command of the sea, just as Wellington's Peninsular Campaign was impossible until after Trafalgar.

At first the Army thought of the landing as primarily an army job. The quartermaster's department arranged for the construction of special landing boats. A fleet of transports, most of them belonging to the Army, would carry the troops to the landing place, whereupon the troops would enter the special landing boats and row ashore. The navy, if it did anything at all, would presumably watch, and perhaps fire at any shore opposition that might develop.

Somebody, probably Commodore Conner,

convinced General Scott that such a haphazard landing was inadvisable and that the planning should be extensive and careful. As a necessary preliminary, Conner, Scott, and their staffs embarked on the little prize steamer *Petrita,* which Perry had just brought back from his first Tabasco raid, and reconnoitered the coastline. They decided to land on a strip of mainland beach near an island called Sacrificios, three miles south of Vera Cruz and about ten north of the naval base at Anton Lizardo.

Conner's meticulous planning set a high standard for future American amphibious operations. At Anton Lizardo most of the troops left their transports and boarded the ships of the Navy, which then proceeded to Sacrificios. The captain of the frigate *Raritan* was in tactical command of the whole operation. The larger navy ships furnished crews for the surfboats, seven seamen and one junior or petty officer per boat. A Navy lieutenant commanded each division of ten boats. Each soldier knew in which boat to embark and with which of the "lines" (i.e., waves) his boat would go ashore. Each military company embarked in two boats. Since the boats were of three different sizes for stowage in nests on the voyage to Mexico, the companies that were not at full strength got the smaller boats.

The steamer *Princeton* anchored as close to the beach as she could, and the surfboats were stationed on her quarters in double lines parallel to the beach, each company and therefore each pair of surfboats being in its prescribed order of battle. Between these lines and the beach there were seven light-draft gunboats armed principally with 32-pounder shell guns. Like the LCI gunboats of World War II in the Pacific campaigns, these vessels shielded the lines of surfboats and stood ready to provide gunfire support to the landings if necessary.

As it happened, the landings were unopposed, partly because of a rising against the government in Mexico City at that time. They went off like clockwork; by leaving nothing to chance, Conner had provided an excellent model for future American am-

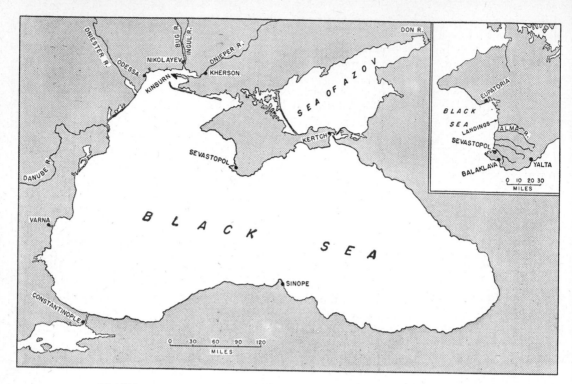

MAIN THEATER OF THE CRIMEAN WAR, 1854-1855

phibious operations. It was not his fault that the Navy overlooked or forgot that model for many years.

The Navy had some share in the subsequent taking of Vera Cruz. Perry, who had relieved Conner in command of the squadron, furnished Scott with some heavy naval guns for service ashore when Scott's own siege artillery failed to arrive in time. At Perry's insistence, naval gun crews went ashore and worked these guns under the general supervision of Captain Robert E. Lee USA.

When Vera Cruz fell, Scott marched inland on Mexico City, and the navy's direct participation in his campaign ended. But 300 United States marines went with Scott and at Chapultepec fought their first inland battle. When Mexico City fell to Scott, he chose the marines to mount guard in the halls of Montezuma, aware that of all his forces they were best fitted to impress the populace.

THE CRIMEAN WAR: BACKGROUND

Of all naval activities in the mid-19th century none were on a larger scale than the operations in connection with the Crimean War of 1854-55. The causes of the war are complex, not to say obscure. A dispute over who should administer the Christian shrines in the Holy Land strained relations between Roman Catholic France and Eastern Orthodox Russia. Napoleon III probably believed that he needed military glory to consolidate his dynasty. Czar Nicholas I was casting covetous glances at the Dardanelles and the Bosporus, and Britain was casting anxious looks at the Czar. At any rate, a Russian army violated Turkish territory by marching into what is now Romania, and hostilities between Russia and Turkey began in 1853. For a time the Turkish armies, under a brilliant general, Omar Pasha, held their own.

In accordance with the excellent 19th cen-

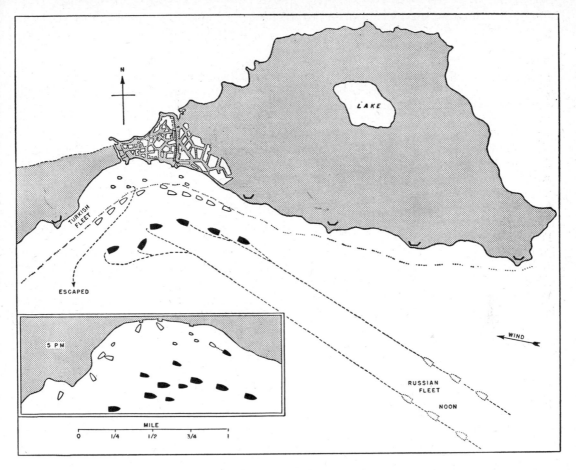

BATTLE OF SINOPE, NOVEMBER 30, 1853

tury custom, a congress of the major European nations met at Vienna to discuss the Russo-Turkish situation, but, largely because the government of Austria was grateful to Russia for her intervention in the Austrian revolution of 1848-1849, the powers reached no mutually acceptable solution. To prevent any sudden Russian descent on Constantinople, strong British and French naval squadrons proceeded thither and, on the invitation of Turkey, entered the Sea of Marmora. Believing that their presence would be sufficient to discourage any Russian naval operations in the Black Sea, they spent their time looking as menacing as possible. They soon learned that their mere presence was not enough.

SINOPE

The Battle of Sinope (November 1853), in which six Russian ships of the line annihilated a Turkish squadron of seven frigates and some smaller craft, shocked western Europe out of all complacency. Part of the shock came from the Russian failure to feel awe at the proximity of the powerful western fleets. Part came from the overwhelming demonstration of the destructive power of shell-guns in naval warfare. Part came from the ruthlessness of the Russian attack, for it had hitherto been naval tradition that ships of the line did not attack frigates [4] and that

---

[4] It must be admitted that this tradition had not been observed at Navarino.

no one ever fired on survivors in open boats or in the water.

When war broke out, Turkey began sending supplies to a Circassian guerilla named Tschamyl, who had for years been fighting the Russians in the Caucasus. About the time that four Turkish steamers began unloading supplies for Tschamyl at the eastern end of the Black Sea, the winter squadron of the Turkish navy began to beat up from Constantinople in a gale. As high winds began to scatter the squadron, the Turkish commander, Osman Pasha, ordered his captains to rendezvous at Sinope, the most northerly outcropping of the southern or Turkish shore of the Black Sea. This port, into which the battered squadron finally straggled, was an open roadstead with some obsolete shore fortifications. Russian Vice Admiral Pavel Stepanovich Nakhimov, cruising with three ships of the line, discovered the Turkish squadron there. Unwilling to risk an encounter under the circumstances, Nakhimov sent a small steamer to obtain reinforcements. Prince Menchikov, commanding at the naval base of Sevastopol, sent him three 120-gun three-deckers. The main batteries of these Russian ships comprised 68-pounder shell-guns. By this time shell-guns were standard equipment in the major navies, but no other nation put as much confidence in them as the Russians did.

Before he was willing to attack, Nakhimov stationed a line of dispatch vessels and other auxiliaries most of the way from Sinope to Constantinople, so that he could have immediate word if the British and French fleets came through the Bosporus. Thus secured against a surprise attack by the western navies, he took his six ships of the line into Sinope under cover of fog and rain that let him get to within half a mile of the Turks before they saw him.

It was between nine and ten in the morning when Nakhimov got under way; at 4 PM he broke off action, after having sunk all the Turkish frigates, silenced the shore batteries, and set fire to the town. Within 20 minutes after coming to anchor, the Russian *Grand Duke Constantine,* 120, silenced a shore battery and destroyed a frigate. At first the light breeze helped the Turks by blowing the smoke from the Russian guns over them. As soon as the breeze freshened, the slaughter of Turks progressed more rapidly. Nakhimov killed as many as he could, whether they were in ships, in boats, in the water, or ashore.

The Turks, who had fired the first shot, fought valiantly in a hopeless situation. They poured a tremendous amount of shot into Nakhimov's flagship, the *Empress Maria,* 84, but this was solid shot, not shell, and it did relatively little damage. While the Turks killed 37 Russians and wounded 229, the Russians killed 2,960 Turks and captured 150.

Since Britain and France had informally undertaken to protect Turkey, Sinope made their declaration of war inevitable. Thus, in the same sense that Pearl Harbor was a Japanese tactical triumph but strategic blunder, Sinope won Russia a brief advantage but brought against her forces which made a Russian defeat inevitable. Nevertheless, one fact became clear to all the navies of the world: somehow the hulls of warships must keep out shells. The age of the ironclad had to begin.

CRIMEAN WAR: BALTIC CAMPAIGN OF 1854

After the British and French declaration of war, a small British steamer that had arrived off Odessa to take away the British consul was fired upon by some shore batteries. Late in April 1854, the Allied fleets retaliated by bombarding Odessa. Because there was a "blind spot" in the city's seaward defenses at a point to which heavy ships could not go, the admirals entrusted the task to their smaller steamers. The bombardment was only moderately successful as a punitive measure; the principal significance of the whole expedition was the adoption of a new tactical method. The first division of four small steamers attacked while they sailed a circular course, each ship firing as it came nearest to the fortifications and then withdrawing so that the next in line astern could fire. Such tactics had been impossible under sail. They were not enormously successful under steam, for when the second division of small steamers came in, the squadron abandoned these tactics and anchored, to insure more accuracy of aim. Nevertheless, it is possible that the circular course of the steamers at Odessa suggested the oval or elliptical course steered later by American ships at Port Royal and Manila Bay.

Meanwhile the British Admiralty was confronted with the problem of who should command the Baltic fleet. The term "Crimean War" obscures the fact that nobody thought at the beginning of hostilities that the chief theater of conflict would be in the Black Sea. Britain had sublime confidence in her navy, which she expected to win laurels in the Baltic. Hence she planned to send many of her largest and most formidable steamers there.

What complicated the selection of commanders for the Crimean War was the advanced age of the ranking officers, a situation brought about by the tremendous expansion of the services during the Napoleonic wars. Vice Admiral Sir James Whitley Deans Dundas, commanding in the Mediterranean and Black Seas, was in his sixties. General Fitzroy Somerset, Baron Raglan, commanding the troops in the Black Sea theater, had served on Wellington's staff in the Peninsular Campaign; he sometimes embarrassed inter-allied relations in the Crimea by forgetting that "the French" and "the enemy" were no longer synonymous. Rear Admiral Henry Ducie Chads, who had so little relative seniority that he finally accompanied the Baltic expedition as fourth in command, had 40 years earlier struck the flag of H.M.S. *Java* to U.S.S. *Constitution.*

The final choice to command the British part of the expedition was Vice Admiral Sir Charles Napier, another veteran of the Napoleonic wars, and the man whose insubordination at Acre in 1840 had placed the *Powerful* in a position of jeopardy. Everything in Napier's record suggested that he was a dashing, aggressive officer, perhaps not the ideal subordinate (any more than Nelson had been) but an ideal commander in chief. Un-fortunately some of the dash and aggressiveness had seeped out of the old gentleman by 1854. Furthermore the Admiralty handicapped him by issuing a set of orders that were vague, ambiguous, and overcautious.

When Napier and a powerful French fleet under Vice Admiral Alexandre-Ferdinand Parseval-Deschênes joined forces in the Baltic, the admirals faced the problem of what to do next. In the face of such overwhelming force, the Russian fleet prudently remained in harbor. Lacking ships to fight against, Napier considered the destruction of shore installations. The obvious ones were Kronstadt, the big naval base off St. Petersburg (now Leningrad) and Sveaborg, a fortress protecting the city of Helsingfors (now Helsinki), but reconnaissance reports convinced Napier that they were impregnable. The Russians had built strong fortifications in the Åland Islands, which control the entrances to the northern end of the Baltic; the admirals finally decided to capture the islands. To do so they had to have a landing force, so they requested and got 10,000 French troops. In August 1854 the army and the fleets attacked and took Bomarsund, the principal fort, whereupon the Russians blew up the other fortifications on the islands. A month or so later, fearing that, with the coming of winter, the Russians could march over the ice and retake the islands, the Allies withdrew from the Baltic, having accomplished nothing except the destruction of some forts and the temporary maintenance of a blockade. Both in Britain and in France there was a public outcry against Napier's failure. It is probable however that his expedition, operating so near the strategic center of Russia, prevented many troops from going to the Crimea.

Three tactical lessons emerged from these operations: if a navy was to operate against shore installations, a landing or occupational force must accompany it; a navy engaged in such operations needed small, light-draft vessels as well as capital ships; and the sailing ship of the line no longer had military value, for time and again during the campaign the larger steamers (chiefly British) had undergone exasperating delays while they awaited the sailing ships (chiefly French).

In the following year another fleet went to the Baltic and won at least a propaganda victory by a successful bombardment of Sveaborg. This fleet encountered the little Russian mines and swept about 30 of them. The planners of the expedition, ignoring the first tactical lesson, sent no troops, but they did furnish the commanders (Rear Admirals Richard Saunders Dundas and Charles Penaud) with some small ships for inshore work, and the fleet consisted entirely of steamers.

FROM VARNA
TO THE CRIMEA

Meanwhile fighting was continuing in the Balkans. A Russian army had crossed the Danube and besieged the town of Silistria. To relieve pressure on the Turkish armies of Omar Pasha, the British and French sent an expeditionary force of about 60,000 men to Varna, near the mouth of the Danube, whereupon the Russians raised the siege and retreated to the Russian frontier.

While cholera was decimating the Allied troops at Varna, the generals and admirals pondered their future strategy. Although there were still some Russian forces in Asiatic Turkey, the two western allies had already achieved their major strategic purposes of securing naval control of the Black Sea and driving Russian troops out of the Balkans. The trouble was that Russia remained unwilling to sign a peace treaty. The failure of the Baltic expedition showed clearly that if peace was to come in 1854 the Black Sea forces would have to strike some telling blow. The only obvious place where the blow would hurt Russia at all was the big naval base of Sevastopol in the Crimean Peninsula. The destruction of Sevastopol would humiliate Russia and would partially avenge Sinope. Therefore, after many conversations not only at Varna but at London and Paris as well, the Allies made the decision to land in the Crimea early in September and try to take Sevastopol before

winter set in. The navies therefore assumed the task of transporting 60,000 men from Varna to the vicinity of Sevastopol and putting them ashore in the face of probable opposition.[5] Rear Admiral Sir Edmund Lyons RN, second in command of the British naval forces, assumed general direction of the big operation.[6]

"The work of transportation, though it was accomplished with success," says Sir William Laird Clowes, the British naval historian, "was done in a bungling and foolhardy manner." The French ships were loaded and ready to sail four days before the British. After two days of swinging at anchor, 14 French sailing ships put to sea unconvoyed, with their decks so crowded with soldiers that they could hardly have fired a shot in self-defense. These 14 ships were separated from the rest of the fleet for three days, easy prey for any Russian sortie from Sevastopol. The French steamers also took aboard so many troops that they could not fight a naval action, leaving all responsibility for the safety of the fleet with the British warships, only two of which were steam ships of the line.[7] Admiral Dundas, who had steadily opposed the whole operation, commented glumly, "If the Russians have the spirit of mosquitoes, they will now leave their harbor and try the issue."

Throughout the Crimean War, British military intelligence appears to have been almost nonexistent. Nobody among the Allied forces knew anything of consequence about Sevastopol or about the Crimea generally. Indeed, one reason for the appointment of Admiral Lyons was that he had once commanded a frigate in the Black Sea and had touched at Sevastopol. Preceding the expedition he and other officers had scouted the

---

[5] The strength of the Russian garrison was estimated at 45,000.

[6] He left the working out of specific details to his flag captain, W. R. Mends, who apparently did a brilliant job.

[7] It may seem inconsistent to praise the American Commodore Conner for having done the same thing and then condemn the French for it, but Conner knew that there could be no naval opposition to his move, and Admiral Hamelin knew that there very well could be to his.

Crimean coast in a little paddle steamer and returned with the recommendation that the landings be made at the mouth of the River Katcha, almost in the northern outskirts of the city.

During the voyage across the Black Sea the French began to worry about the wisdom of landing so near the guns of Sevastopol. Consequently the Allied leaders took the whole matter under consideration again. Arriving off the Crimean coast, the Allied fleets anchored in 20 fathoms of water, out of sight of land. Here the crowded sailors, soldiers, and horses waited for their leaders to reach a decision. After cruising up and down the coast and examining maps of uncertain accuracy, the commanders at last selected for their landing a point marked Old Fort, some 15 miles north of Sevastopol on the west coast of the Crimea.

Old Fort as a landing point presented advantages and disadvantages. The terrain was flat, and the beach where the British went ashore was backed by a salt water lake with an outlet to the sea. On such a beach the first forces landed would be able to hold back an enemy attack long enough for other troops to come ashore, but an enemy sufficiently numerous and determined could easily bottle up the invaders. The chief disadvantage of Old Fort however was the obvious fact that, in those days before the development of artificial harbors, it could not possibly serve as a satisfactory base of operations. This later became painfully apparent to the Allied generals and had much to do with making them change their basic plan of campaign. The American landings at Vera Cruz had also been on a strip of beach with shoal water in front of it, but Conner and Scott chose a beach within three miles of Vera Cruz, their first strategic objective. The Crimean Allies landed more than 15 miles away from Sevastopol, which they meant to besiege, thereby complicating their transport problems.

Once the actual landings began, when high decisions of ranking commanders no longer tied the hands of Admiral Lyons and Captain Mends, things went much more smoothly. There are some interesting and instructive features of the landings. The French had obtained special landing craft for getting their artillery ashore; the British did almost as well by decking-over the space between two large boats [8] and by employing "paddle-box boats," small steam paddle-launches. The French furnished inshore support for their troops by drawing up a line of rocket-firing boats.

But there were also mistakes. There is the story that the French forced the British to land on a sandspit by misplacing a buoy which would have allowed the British more room for their landings. General Sir George Brown got ashore too soon, rode inland too far, and almost got himself captured by Cossacks. Commander Leopold George Heath RN, who was (in modern terminology) beachmaster for half the British beach, wrote home in one of his journal-letters:

By noon of the 18th everything was landed, and then began what must happen more or less in such extensive undertakings, viz., undoing what had been done. The army found that they had not pack horses enough, and we had to re-embark the tents: then, after long discussion, they had fully decided to leave the packs and their contents on board and to carry a blanket, a great coat, a shirt, pair of shoes, towel, and the traditional bit of soap, and no more, and all the troops had been landed with this allowance on their backs, but further experience proved that these things would be more easily carried in their knapsacks, which were therefore sent for, but there was some confusion about them owing to this change of view, and many knapsacks were not recovered until the transports had reached Balaklava.[9]

That was about September 26, twelve days after the landings began.

[8] Conner had used a similar device but had abandoned it because the boat-rafts proved unmanageable.

[9] Admiral Sir Leopold George Heath, *Letters from the Black Sea during the Crimean War, 1854-1855* (London, 1897), 55. Note the date Heath gives, implying that landing operations were in progress from September 14 to 18 inclusive. Note also the remark about re-embarking the tents; the other witnesses tend to deny that tents were ever landed.

THE NAVIES
AND THE SIEGE
OF SEVASTOPOL

Soon after the completion of the landings, the Allies started to march south toward Sevastopol. At the River Alma the Russians waited for them and gave battle. The Allied armies stormed the heights which the Russians had thought impregnable and routed the defending army.

After the Battle of the Alma, the Allies were slow to move. While they hesitated, Prince Alexander Sergeievich Menchikov, commander of both military and naval forces at Sevastopol, made two unusual but effective decisions. He sank five ships of the line and two frigates across the entrance to Sevastopol roadstead, and leaving Sevastopol in the hands of a small garrison, including principally the 15,000 sailors thus made available for shore duty, he withdrew his army in a northeasterly direction.

If General Lord Raglan and Marshal Leroy St. Arnaud had any clear plan, it must have been to occupy the north side of Sevastopol, to employ a combined attack by their siege ordnance and the navies' guns to drive all effective Russian fighting ships out of the long, narrow roadstead; then either to withdraw, claiming a decisive victory, or to cross the roadstead with naval aid and occupy the southern side. The sinking of the ships spoiled this convenient solution by denying the Allied navies access to the roadstead.

Perhaps because of a lack of aggressiveness on the part of the Allied commanders, therefore, the Russians accomplished something virtually unprecedented in naval history. A passive fleet achieved more than an active one; a partially sunken fleet achieved more than a fleet-in-being. The sinking of ships in channels is a notoriously undependable way of preventing ingress or egress, for the ships may roll over or move with the tide; it is quite possible that Menchikov sank the ships primarily to free their crews to serve on shore during the defense of the city. But he accomplished much more; the Allies abandoned any idea of attacking the north side of the city. They marched around the eastern end of the roadstead to the south side of the city, cutting through the rear guard of Menchikov's withdrawing army as they did so; and they failed to assault the city until Colonel Franz Eduard Ivanovich Todleben, an engineering genius in the Russian army, had built adequate fortifications. The British now began to use the narrow, landlocked harbor of Balaklava as their base; the French found a much better base somewhat uncomfortably near Sevastopol in Kamiesch Bay. If the decision to establish these bases was strategically sound, it is hard to understand why the Allies did not land south of the city in the first place.

During October 1854 the Allies tried one combined army and naval assault, which failed. From the naval point of view, its only significance was another demonstration of the value of steam in naval warfare. The small steamers lashed themselves alongside the sailing ships of the line and towed them into position.

The failure of the assault doomed the Allies to spend the winter in the Crimea. Before the cold weather came, the Russians, now about as strong as their enemies, attacked first Balaklava, eliciting the magnificent but futile charge of the Light Cavalry Brigade, and then the Allied right flank, where the Allies won the Battle of Inkerman. Then winter came. During the whole grim siege, both the British and French navies had contingents ashore fighting as artillerymen, and of course the Russian navy ashore contributed vastly to the defense of Sevastopol. As a floating gun platform, the Russian steamer *Vladimir,* moving around the blockaded roadstead, proved an effective annoyance.

CRIMEAN WAR:
CONCLUSION

A tremendous storm in November 1854 destroyed many transports, including one laden with winter clothing, and enormously complicated Allied logistics. As a result of this gale plus abominable logistic planning, the winter of 1854-1855 was a winter of agony for the Allies. From this time on, the part played by the navies was essentially a logistic one. An Allied expedition to the Sea of Azov in the spring of 1855 hindered the flow of supplies to the besiegers at Sevastopol.

When at last Sevastopol fell to an army which reinforcements had made overwhelmingly French in its composition, the navies had one final job to do. An estuary called the Liman of the Dnieper River received the waters, not only of the Dnieper but of the Bug and Ingul Rivers as well. The important naval base of Nikolayev lay at the juncture of the Bug and Ingul; Kherson, on the Dnieper, was a rich commercial center. The entrance from the Black Sea proper into the Liman was a channel which ran northeast; it passed close to its south bank, a long sand-spit extending southwest from the Russian mainland, and at the southwest end of this spit there was a fortress called Kinburn. The Allies decided to take Kinburn and close the Liman.

The only thing remarkable about the taking of Kinburn is the emergence of the iron-clad steamer. Three "floating batteries"—ironclad ships with sufficient steam power to propel themselves short distances to the scene of action—the French *Tonnante, Lave,* and *Dévastation,* demonstrated their worth by lying within a thousand yards of the fort and pounding it while they themselves were proving invulnerable. With this action, much more truly than with the action between the *Monitor* and the *Virginia,* the age of the ironclad began. As for Kinburn, it fell to the combined naval and land forces, but the Allies achieved little by occupying it.

The whole story of the Crimean War is one of tragic frustration. Men on both sides lived and died with incredible bravery and accomplished very little by their deaths. The Russians lost the naval installations of Sevastopol and gained much credit for an effective defense; the Allies won the war and lost their military reputations. The curse of the Crimea was incomplete planning and inadequate Allied cooperation. It is to the credit of the British and French navies that they suffered somewhat less from these faults than the armies did. As for the Russian navy, its sailors fought magnificently ashore,[10] but that is not where navies gain reputations. When a navy is better off without its ships than with them, it is hardly an element of sea power.

And yet sea power played its part in the Crimean War. Without naval command of the Black Sea, the armies could not have gone to Varna and thus have raised the siege of Silistria, and it is probable that the Russians would have remained in the Balkans; the Allies could never have gone to the Crimea; they could never have stayed there during the winter; they could never have withdrawn. Without Allied sea power Turkey might have become a Russian satellite, and soon there might have been a Russian Mediterranean fleet.

---

[10] Among many others, Admiral Nakhimov, the victor of Sinope, died at Sevastopol.

16

The American Civil War:

Opening Events

THE REPUBLICAN VICTORY IN the American Presidential election of 1860 brought to a head the growing hostility between the northern states and the slaveholding South. In December South Carolina seceded from the United States, and six other neighboring states promptly followed her example. A month before Abraham Lincoln took office as President, delegates of the seceding states met in Montgomery, Alabama and formed the Confederate States of America. The stage was set for armed conflict.

The root causes of the American Civil War include cultural antipathy, economic hostility, the slavery issue, the struggle for political dominance, and the right of secession, but guns began firing over the immediate and practical question: Who has a right to the federal property in the territory of states which elect to secede from the Federal Union? By firing on the *Star of the West* and bombarding Fort Sumter, the impatient Secessionists began the war they were fated to lose, closed the door to peaceful conciliation, and sacrificed something at the bar of world public opinion. In the seven states that had first seceded there were the Pensacola Navy Yard, 15 forts guarding harbors, six federal arsenals, three mints, four custom houses, and three revenue cutters on duty. In addition, there were in Texas 18 military posts, with substantial quantities of weapons. Though hoping to avoid war, the Southerners were by no means oblivious to its possibility, and to secure these positions and their considerable armament became for them an immediate and pressing objective.

The position of the advocates of secession was that the new sovereign states were thereby merely exercising the well-established prerogative of eminent domain. Recompense in money would be granted to the United States government after suitable negotiation. For the most part, the custodians of this Federal property surrendered it peaceably—partly because those in charge were in many instances sympathetic with the Secession movement; partly because for the most part they possessed inadequate strength for a fight; partly because President James Buchanan gave no clear, unequivocal orders demanding resistance. Fort Pickens at Pensacola, Fort Taylor at Key West, and Fort Jefferson on the Tortugas, because of their remoteness and strength, remained in Federal hands. Also the forts in Charleston Harbor, under the command of Major Robert Anderson USA, were not immediately surrendered.

Because of the early importance of Charleston as a center of the Secessionist movement, the forts in the harbor—Castle Pinckney, Fort Moultrie, and Fort Sumter—assumed a symbolic significance to both the North and the South as soon as it became clear that they would not be peaceably surrendered by their tiny garrisons. Through the latter weeks of 1860, Buchanan let it be known that he would not order reinforcements unless Fort Moultrie were attacked,[1] but on December 26, 1860 Anderson on his own initiative moved his detachment to the much more defensible Fort Sumter. The South Carolina government forthwith seized and occupied Castle Pinckney, Fort Moultrie, the arsenal, the post office, and the customs house, and raised the Palmetto Flag in place of the Stars and Stripes.[2] Anderson's company found itself a beleaguered garrison in a hostile harbor. Governor Francis W. Pickens ordered the erection of supplementary batteries in order to command more thoroughly the water approaches to the city.

Secretary of War John B. Floyd, a Secessionist himself, had helped to hamstring all military preparations. After his resignation on December 31, 1860, Joseph Holt, his successor, did much to stiffen the spine of the President. Reinforcements and supplies were promptly dispatched to Anderson: the merchantman *Star of the West* with 250 men left New York for Charleston on January 5, 1861. As was almost invariably the case with secret missions in the early part of the war, intelligence of this effort reached the South long before the ship did.[3]

When the *Star of the West* entered Charleston Harbor on the morning of January 9, the new "sand batteries" on Morris Island opened fire on her. The ship received one or two hits, but quickly moved out of effective range. However, the course of the channel would have required her to pass under the ready guns of Fort Moultrie. The captain, having lost the advantage of surprise, thought better of making the attempt. He turned and steamed out through the fire of the Morris Island batteries, and Major Anderson got no reinforcements. Thus the first shots of the Civil War were fired in a bloodless naval encounter.

The policy of conciliation and compromise was to have one final trial. During a drawn-out tacit "truce" in Charleston Harbor, a committee composed of Senators Benjamin Fitzpatrick, Stephen R. Mallory, and John Slidell carried on a dilatory correspondence with President Buchanan, who welcomed any opportunity to postpone unpalatable decisions, but who was by now indisposed to retreat any farther.

Meanwhile General Pierre G. T. Beauregard, wearing the brand-new stars of a general officer in the Confederate States Army, arrived in Charleston to prepare for the capture of Sumter if it could not be won by negotiation.

THE SURRENDER OF FORT SUMTER

Fort Sumter was, considering the ordnance of the day, a very strong position, the capture of which by assault would be feasible only if the fort were very lightly garrisoned. It is situated on a man-made island in the middle of the channel about half a mile from the narrows between Cummings Point and Fort Moultrie. Its hewn stone walls, eight feet thick and 40 feet high, formed a pentagon enclosing a space about 300 by 350 feet. Its two tiers of casemates and barbette gun positions were designed for 140 guns.[4] A full garrison would have been 650 men, nearly ten

---

[1] At the time of South Carolina's secession, Fort Moultrie alone was garrisoned—by Major Anderson's little command of nine officers and 69 men.

[2] See map, page 367.

[3] Contemporary sources ascribe the leak to Jacob Thompson, the conspiratorial Secretary of Interior. It is probable however that a leak also occurred in New York, which was filled with Confederate sympathizers.

[4] At the time of the bombardment, only 48 guns were emplaced.

times the number of Anderson's slender force.

Beauregard, a skilled military engineer, designed and constructed defenses against expected reinforcements and mounted batteries to breach the fort. On April 1 he was able to telegraph President Jefferson Davis in Montgomery that he was ready. On April 2 supplies from the mainland were cut off, and all traffic to and from the fort was prohibited. A relief expedition organized by Gustavus V. Fox, consisting of the transport *Baltic* (with reinforcements), the *Pawnee,* the *Pocahontas,* the *Harriet Lane,* and three tugs, left New York on April 9, with orders to rendezvous ten miles east of Charleston two days later. On the 11th Beauregard demanded the surrender of Sumter and Anderson refused. Other proposals and counterproposals delayed the conflict until early morning of April 12.

At dawn on the 12th, the assembled Charlestonians, who were out in force to witness the spectacle, saw the first mortar shell curve through the air and fall into the parade of Fort Sumter. One after another the various Confederate cannon responded to this signal and in a matter of minutes Sumter was under general bombardment. Anderson chose to wait until daylight made his more difficult targets on shore visible. At about seven o'clock Captain Abner Doubleday [5] fired the first gun in Sumter at the Cummings Point batteries. Soon Sumter was spiritedly returning the Confederate bombardment. The cannonade continued for two days and a part of a third, during which Anderson, by keeping his men from the exposed barbette positions and the parade, prevented any casualties in his force.

A combination of unlucky circumstances prevented the relief expedition, part of which actually witnessed the bombardment, from fulfilling its mission. Through a high-level confusion of orders, the prospective flagship of the squadron had been detached from this duty and sent to the Gulf of Mexico. A severe storm delayed some of the vessels and prevented the tugs from reaching

[5] Better known as the half-legendary "father of modern baseball."

Charleston before the surrender. The success of Fox's plan, which was simply to engage the forts in Confederate hands while a supply vessel ran in to Sumter, depended on having heavy gunnery units available. Unknown to the Navy Department, a secret expedition for the relief of Fort Pickens, organized by Secretary of State William H. Seward and Lieutenant David Dixon Porter USN, had received from Lincoln permission to use U.S.S. *Powhatan* at this time. Fox had counted heavily on the big guns of the *Powhatan* in the Sumter expedition. This classic example of interdepartmental meddling, though salutary in that it enabled Secretary of the Navy Gideon Welles to demand a clearer definition of cabinet areas of authority, rendered the success of the Sumter relief expedition doubtful from the beginning.

On April 13 the administration buildings in the fort were fired by hot shot. The magazines thereby threatened, it became necessary to jettison most of the powder through embrasures into the sea. Without prospect of relief, with limited supplies, and no longer with any effective power to fight back, Major Anderson—who had been authorized by Lincoln to surrender when in his judgment no useful purpose would be served by prolonged resistance—bowed to the inevitable and capitulated. The flag of the United States was hauled down on April 14, and Sumter was evacuated.

Up to this time public opinion in both the North and the South was not consciously prepared for the dreadful contingency of civil war—nor were the leaders of either side. In purely military terms it is difficult to imagine more inadequate preparations for a death struggle than those of either the Federal government or the newly-formed Confederacy. But the events in Charleston harbor made war inevitable. What had, often as not, seemed to the man in the street a dry, metaphysical dispute over constitutional law now became a matter of life and death, for Lincoln's response was prompt and firm. In a proclamation on April 15, he called for 75,000 state militia and convened Congress.

The promise of coercive action by the

Federal government led the other four Southern states to join the Confederacy. Seeing the middle position between Secession and Federalism melt away, Virginia, Arkansas, North Carolina, and Tennessee passed ordinances of secession. There was strong Secessionist sentiment in the slave-holding border states, Missouri, Kentucky, and Maryland, but a combination of geography and loyalist majorities kept them in the Union.

LOSS OF THE NORFOLK NAVY YARD

The surrender of Fort Sumter, except as a blow to Northern pride, was a much less serious loss than the nearly contemporaneous abandonment of the Norfolk Navy Yard. The Norfolk Yard, biggest in the country, had one of the two large naval drydocks and was a storage arsenal for the Navy's reserve ordnance. Here were stored 300-odd modern Dahlgren guns, 50 or more of which were 9-inch weapons of the latest design. Here too were a number of vessels under repair, including the 50-gun screw frigate *Merrimack*.

While matters were coming to a head in Charleston harbor, the city of Norfolk seethed with Secessionist sentiment. Though Virginia had not yet joined the Confederacy, recruitment for the Virginia militia was being actively pressed, many of the officers stationed at the Yard were resigning, and desertion and petty acts of mutiny were becoming common. On April 10, Secretary Welles warned the aging Commandant, Commodore C. S. McCauley, to exercise "great vigilance." On the 12th, Engineer in Chief Benjamin F. Isherwood was ordered to Norfolk to supervise the reassembling of the *Merrimack's* machinery so that she could be shifted to Philadelphia. Isherwood quickly complied, but McCauley, reduced to a panicky irresoluteness by the distressing march of events and fearing to provoke an armed clash by any purposeful activity, finally ordered Isherwood to draw the boiler fires. By this time Virginia had just passed her secession ordinance. Secretary Welles lost no time

in dispatching Commodore Hiram Paulding to relieve McCauley and to evacuate or destroy all naval material and shipping at Norfolk.

Equipped with combustibles, Paulding took U.S.S. *Pawnee* to Norfolk, arriving the evening of April 20. Here he discovered the *Merrimack* and three other ships, scuttled by McCauley's order, gradually sinking in the anchorage. Paulding would have to hurry to complete his mission of destruction. Though reinforced by a troop contingent from Fortress Monroe, across the James River, he lacked an adequate force to defend the sprawling Navy Yard if the Virginia militia assembled outside were to storm the gates.

The marines and bluejackets from the *Pawnee,* dividing into small work parties, mined the drydock, spread turpentine-soaked cotton waste and gunpower around the wooden buildings and the tophamper of the sinking ships, and made unsuccessful efforts to sledge off the trunnions of the big guns in storage. In a matter of hours preparations were as complete as they could make them, and a little before dawn the powder trains were lighted off. As the firing parties rowed from the shore, the whole yard turned into a solid sheet of flame.

The work of destruction proved far from complete, for when the fires burned themselves out, the Confederates found undamaged among the ruins the largest cache of modern ordnance in the Western Hemisphere. Since at this time the entire South had no facilities for producing such weapons, this was good fortune beyond price. These were the guns that would arm the new forts defending Southern harbors. Moreover, a reckless band of Virginia militia had rushed into the yard in the nick of time to save the drydock by flooding.

MILITARY RESOURCES OF THE ADVERSARIES

The Union and the Confederacy were not, except in area, at all well matched. The population of the Union exceeded that of the seceded region by a five-to-two ratio.[6] The disparity in material resources and particularly in developed industry was much more marked. Even in textile manufacture, the South was far from self-sufficient.[7] In heavy industry, the basic component of economic war potential, the superiority of the North was overwhelming. The South lacked not only foundries and metal works to make guns and supply her railroads but also the skilled workmen and experienced engineers to run such plants. Her transportation system was hardly adequate to handle her peacetime needs; in relationship to her area, her railroads were relatively few, and these were not planned as a system. In the North, on the other hand, the 1850's had seen a boom in rail construction, and the great trunk line systems were already in operation.

In 1860 the exports of the South were valued at $31,000,000; [8] those of the North, at $331,000,000. Furthermore northern shipowners monopolized the carrying trade; there was not in the entire Confederacy an adequate number of experienced merchant seamen to man a navy—even if there had been the industrial wherewithal to build one. The United States Navy began the Civil War woefully unprepared, but the Confederacy had no navy at all.

Drugs and surgical instruments, and even such commonplace materials as harness leather, were to become unprocurable in the South as the Northern blockade became effective. Though it was an agricultural region, the South was not well supplied even in basic foodstuffs because of the large areas devoted exclusively to raising cotton. The South's peacetime economy was grounded on cotton export. When the war cut off this source of foreign exchange, the foreign credit of the Confederacy was gradually destroyed. The incursions of Northern armies, especially the splitting of Texas and Arkansas from the rest of the Confederate states, combined with the breakdown of transportation and inflation of the currency to produce near-starvation. In the last months before Appomatox, the value of the Confederate dollar shrank almost to the vanishing point, and flour and shoes were scarcely procurable in Richmond at any price. Even if Lee had saved the Army of Virginia, the South would have been starved into submission within a year. In summary, the North had the economic wherewithal to fight a war, and the South did not.

In the face of these facts, how did the Southern leadership dare to provoke a war? There is no single answer to this question. In the first place, nobody planned the Civil War: secession was planned, but for a combination of reasons, plausible at the time, very few even of the leaders of the Southern population believed that force would be necessary to accomplish its purpose. Secondly, the educational level of the South was low: a great many ignorant and unreflecting people gave serious credence to the demagogic assurance that the "Yankees are cowards." There was no general understanding of the economic demands of modern war, and there is considerable evidence that even Jefferson Davis and his cabinet did not at first realize the problem they faced. Third, there was some reliance on the hope that Northern "politics" would make the successful prosecution of the war by the North impossible. The Democratic party in the North still had many adherents, and, as the Vallandingham Conspiracy was to show, Southern sympathizers were in fact active (though ineffectual) in some Northern states.

Fourth, it was widely believed that to cut off "King Cotton" from British and French mills would ruin their industry and compel Britain and France to intervene in the war, or at least to breach the blockade. Fifth, the South counted on simple war weariness and the mounting cost of the war in casualties and treasure to prompt the people of the North to demand a peace. Sixth, in spite of all her handicaps, the South enjoyed certain real advantages: she had a proud and virile

---

[6] The North had a population of 22,000,000 (1860 census); the South, 9,000,000, of whom approximately 3,500,000 were slaves.

[7] The South had 150 textile plants, mostly small, with an annual output valued at $8,000,000. The North had 900 textile factories, including some huge industrial complexes, with an annual product valued at $115,000,000.

[8] Mostly cotton and tobacco.

rural population, accustomed to the use of firearms and possessed of a tradition of violence;[9] she had a ready-made officer corps in the large number of officers of the United States Army who resigned their commissions to take new ones in the Confederacy; furthermore in Lee, Jackson, Joseph Johnston, Beauregard, and others, she had some of the ablest military men of the day. The territory of the Confederacy was extensive and could be successfully invaded and held only by vast armies campaigning through years of fighting. Also, the bulk of the Southern population was passionately loyal to the cause. By concentrating on the few Southern strengths, and minimizing the many Southern weaknesses, it was possible for even shrewd men in the South to believe in the prospect of ultimate victory.

WAR PREPARATIONS

Both the North and the South anticipated a short war, and when the issue was joined after months of vacillation and negotiation, there was an almost pathological eagerness for battle. From the middle of April, war preparations went on rapidly on both sides.

The Confederate government, which already had 10,000 to 12,000 men in arms at Charleston and at Pensacola, had on April 8 called for a contingent of 20,000 from the seceded states; on April 16 there was a further call for 34,000 volunteers. In the seized arsenals the South found much military equipment, including over 100,000 stands of arms. Other weapons were secured by purchase from abroad. The forts, especially those of Charleston, furnished heavy guns, and the occupation of the Norfolk Navy Yard made available heavy artillery that the South could not herself have produced. Southern-born army and navy officers in the Union service resigned their commissions and offered their services.[10] Agents were

dispatched to Europe, both to work for diplomatic recognition and a line of credit, and to procure military stores and naval shipping. Further fortification of the Southern coast was undertaken; plans were made to blockade the Mississippi River as far north as Columbus, Kentucky (see map, page 334). At the special session of the Confederate Congress, President Davis announced that he "had in the field, at Charleston, Pensacola, Forts Morgan, Jackson, St. Philip, and Pulaski, 10,000 men, and 16,000 are now en route for Virginia." He also promised the immediate organization of an army of 100,-000 men.

Corresponding preparations were made by the North. Lincoln's call for volunteers on April 15 brought an enthusiastic response from all the free states, and from nearly every prominent citizen in the North. The governors without exception immediately set about recruiting and exceeding their quotas. Nearly double the 75,000 volunteers sought presented themselves for induction.

It takes some time to enlist, assemble, equip, and transport recruits, but in three months both sides had taken these first steps in the creation of citizen armies. Such was popular demand, and such was the inexperience of the general officers (commanding comparatively large forces for the first time in American history) that these untrained innocents were thrown at each other at the first opportunity, a discreditable performance known as the first Battle of Bull Run (July 12, 1861). Since the Union disorganization was the greater, and many of the blue-clad troops panicked in retreat, the South hailed it as a great victory. The North was correspondingly cast down. Southern officers also lost control of their troops in the field however, and the professionals on both sides were content to withdraw to train their forces into armies of soldiers. There were no further land engagements of consequence in 1861.

For the Union capital, the Battle of Bull Run was simply the culmination of a series of alarms and frustrations in the panicky

---

[9] The duel, for example, which had disappeared in the North, was still an integral part of a Southern gentleman's "code of honor."

[10] In order to avoid asking too much financial sacrifice on the one hand and the imputation of "buying

loyalties" on the other, the Confederate government wisely offered identical rank and pay to "transfers" from the United States regular forces.

spring and summer of 1861—the loss of Fort Sumter, the disgraceful abandonment of Norfolk, the quite reasonable fear that Maryland would secede and leave Washington a beleaguered city in a hostile land. Yet, though there were to be four long years of bloodshed and heartache before the Army of the Potomac could march in the victory parade down Pennsylvania Avenue, the foundations of a victorious grand strategy were already being laid.

NAVAL SECRETARY GIDEON WELLES

In a cabinet that included William H. Seward, Edwin M. Stanton, and Salmon P. Chase, Gideon Welles, the new Secretary of Navy, a Connecticut politician and newspaper editor, was far from being the most prominent member. Yet in many ways he was Lincoln's aptest choice. For one thing, he had had experience as a naval bureau chief. For another, he was passionately loyal to Lincoln, whom he recognized from the first to be a great leader. Finally, he possessed most of the qualities of a great administrator, possibly all except the capacity to delegate responsibility. This failing he compensated by an enormous capacity for hard work. His extensive diaries reveal a man of first rate intelligence and great firmness of purpose—with an uncanny eye for character weakness in his peers.

Welles was ably assisted by Gustavus V. Fox, a former naval officer who had resigned from the service in 1856 in order to become a cotton mill executive. After the unhappy Sumter Relief Expedition, Fox had been appeased by his appointment as Chief Clerk in the Navy Department; shortly afterwards he became the first Assistant Secretary of the Navy.

Welles and Fox through the summer of 1861 were endeavoring to implement the policy of blockade that was early recognized to be the proper function of the Navy in war. They set up the squadron organizations, procured and trained recruits, bought all vessels available that could be converted to the purpose of the blockade, placed on order many more to be built, planned in conjunction with professional advisers the preliminary operations that were necessary to make the blockade effective. From the slender resources initially available to them, these two men created the formidable naval organization that was at last to seal off the Confederacy from contact with the outside world. Crank and makeshift though most of its vessels were, the wartime Navy was well adapted to its tactical purposes. In a period of profound change in the basic nature of naval material, they succeeded in harnessing the superior industrial might of the North to the purposes of war.

17

The Blockade and the Cruisers

THE HISTORY OF THE FEDERAL Navy in the American Civil War is an account not of winning sea supremacy but of exercising it, of making potential control actual control. Except locally and under atypical conditions, the South made no effective challenge to the superior Northern sea power. Nevertheless, it required arduous service by hundreds of ships and thousands of men to make this superiority a heavy weight in the balance of victory and defeat. Offensive operations of great diversity were undertaken by the Union Navy. Coastal forts were bombarded, joint amphibious assaults were effected, Confederate commerce raiders were hunted down. Above all, the ceaseless patrol off the Southern ports was maintained. It may be said that every Confederate naval effort was an attempt to breach the blockade, while nearly every operation undertaken by the Union Navy was related to the constant effort to strengthen the blockade. The blockade of the South was first aptly characterized by General Winfield Scott as the "Anaconda Policy." Just as a python's coils grasp its prey loosely at first, then grip tighter and tighter until the victim is squeezed to death, so the improvised navy of Gideon Welles gradually extinguished the commercial life of the Confederacy.

The South was peculiarly vulnerable to blockade because of the specialization of her prewar economy, as we have noted. Having relied for nearly all of her manufactures on imports from the North and from Europe, she lacked industrial economic strength in every major category—capital goods, financial institutions, technicians and engineers, and above all, manpower, in view of the demand for men in the armies. Cotton bales accumulated on docks and in warehouses. The blood stream of foreign exchange dried up. The credit of the Confederacy in Europe, never good, became progressively worse as the war wore on.

The demands of war and the effect of the blockade created a critical shortage of consumer goods and a concomitant rise in prices in the Confederacy where the misguided government answered the popular outcry against high prices by simply issuing more currency. As prices spiraled steeply, "printing press" inflation caused the Confederate dollar to decline to $1/225$ of its worth in one year and by September 1864, one gold dollar exchanged for $2000 in Confederate currency.

An inflation of this kind demoralizes an economy and destroys all incentive for orderly production. All purchases automatically become a speculation. Farmers cease bringing food to market. Frantic government regulations and harsh penalties necessarily fail in their purpose, since even if ruthlessly enforced they can be effective only as prohibitions and cannot engender the motivation to production necessary to a cure of this disastrous economic malady.

PROCLAMATION OF THE BLOCKADE

Paradoxically enough, it was the South that started economic warfare. On April 17, 1861, Jefferson Davis issued a proclamation offering letters of marque and reprisal to armed privateers of any nation. Two days later Lincoln replied with a counter-proclamation, instituting a blockade of Southern ports from South Carolina to Texas and threatening privateers with execution as pirates.[1] Secretary Welles in a heated Cabinet quarrel argued that it had been a mistake to proclaim a blockade as such, since this had the effect of conferring belligerent rights on the South and was in fact a kind of tacit recognition of the Confederacy's claim to being a separate nation with all rights of sovereignty. Welles, with Congressional support, argued that the proper procedure would have been to "close" the ports of the South —a legalistic difference aimed at identifying the struggle as a domestic matter in which the rest of the world could have no proper interest. A law was finally passed requiring the President to proclaim a closure of the ports. He did so proclaim, remarking wryly that it would be "like the Pope's bull to the comet." Since the previously proclaimed blockade was not explicitly canceled, no real purpose was served by the second proclamation.

The immediate task facing the United States Navy was a formidable one. Under international law, neutrals are not bound by a "paper blockade." To secure foreign recognition of the blockade, it had to be made effective. And following the high water mark along shore from Alexandria, Virginia to Brownsville, Texas, the Confederacy had 3,550 miles of coast, much of the Atlantic portion of it a "double coastline." There were 189 harbors and navigable river mouths to watch. For this task, the Navy in early 1861 had 7,600 men and 90 warships,[2] of which 42 were actually in commission; 21 of the remainder were reckoned as "unserviceable." Many of those in commission were sailing vessels of a type that proved to be of little actual value. To cap this poor preparation, three of the vessels were in the East Indies, and 22 ships (236 guns total) were in the Pacific. On the other hand, eight of the ten navy yards were in the Union,[3] and Norfolk was regained in 1862. Extensive shipyards and machinery-fabricating facilities existed in the North. Besides, the golden age of the American merchant marine was just drawing to a close, and numerous merchant vessels and trained seamen were available.

Welles immediately ordered home all ships but the Anti-Slaver Patrol in the Guinea Gulf. All seaworthy craft were put in commission. Presently there were 76 vessels rated at 1,783 guns available for naval orders. In the same initial burst of activity the Navy purchased and adapted over a hundred vessels, including grain barges and ferry boats— anything stable enough to be a satisfactory gun platform. Construction was pushed in private yards and navy yards. By December 1861, 264 vessels—in aggregate 218,000 tons— were in commission. This figure was added to at a somewhat less frantic pace as the war progressed. The North was also to build 74 ironclads during the War.

Recruiting for the wartime service was initiated promptly, and by December 1861 the Union Navy had a strength of over 20,000. There was no "boot camp" in 1861, and the new "naval volunteers" were often standing

---

[1] This threat was never actually carried out. The limits of the blockade were extended to include Virginia and North Carolina as soon as they seceded.

[2] *United States Navy Register*, 1861.

[3] Kittery, Portsmouth, Charlestown, Sackett's Harbor, Brooklyn, Philadelphia, Washington, Norfolk, Pensacola, Mare Island.

watches at sea within a few days of taking their oath. Though the veterans of the "spit-and-polish" traditions of Matthew Perry's navy shuddered at their lack of smartness and their occasional ignorance of ceremonial observances, the new men were nearly all trained seamen from the merchant marine, soon indistinguishable from the men of the "Old Navy."

Once the blockade was initiated, it became obvious that its full implementation would require logistic support of a scale and variety not previously contemplated. The inshore patrol would be steam-propelled, and colliers and coaling stations, preferably near the blockading stations, would be required. As more ships joined the squadrons, more and larger base facilities would be necessary. Though there were adequate bases in the North, there was an evident need for others close to the Southern ports the Navy was attempting to seal. Possession of a base near Charleston and Savannah, for example, would greatly increase the number of Federal ships on station by eliminating the need for individual blockade vessels to return periodically to Washington or Philadelphia. Furthermore, ships taking on coal or undergoing repairs at such an advanced base would always remain available as a ready reserve for speedy reinforcement of the ships on patrol.

So the Navy planned to capture strategic sites for advance bases as soon as adequate amphibious forces could be assembled. With the ships and troops available in 1861, any attempt to seize fortified ports such as Charleston, Savannah, or Wilmington, N.C. was out of the question. Yet the sites to be occupied would have to provide good, deep anchorages and the possibility of developing docking facilities. Furthermore, they had to be near the Confederacy's major ports and at the same time be easily defensible from the landward side. Luckily, the length and convoluted nature of the Southern coastline, which made blockade so difficult, facilitated capture of the sort of bases the Navy required. With thousands of miles of coast and almost 200 harbors, the Confederacy could hardly manage to fortify in advance every place the Navy might strike.

HATTERAS INLET

The Strategy Board,[4] headed by Captain Samuel F. Du Pont, selected as the first coastal "key position" to be seized, Hatteras Inlet, a break in the offshore sand barrier between the Atlantic and Pamlico Sound, off the North Carolina coast. This inlet, and the low-lying sand dunes on both sides, was believed suited to the special needs of the blockade, for it was easily defended and yet reasonably close to Beaufort and Wilmington, which were good ports and railroad terminals.

On August 26, 1861 Flag Officer S. H. Stringham with seven ships, and Major General Benjamin F. Butler with 860 soldiers sailed from Fortress Monroe against Forts Clark and Hatteras, guarding Hatteras Inlet. These log and sandbank forts, armed largely with antique 32-pounders, were lightly manned and inadequately supplied. After a gunnery duel on August 28 between the ships and the outranged shore batteries, 300 of Butler's men landed behind Fort Clark, which was abandoned by her defenders. The next day the unequal contest concluded with the capitulation of Fort Hatteras. Its commander, Samuel Barron, had till a few weeks earlier been senior officer on the United States Navy List. As a base for the blockaders, Hatteras Inlet proved a disappointment. The shoal waters and shifting channels made it unsatisfactory even as an anchorage, and subsequent operations in this general section had to be undertaken later. The action is mainly notable as being the first amphibious assault of the war.

PORT ROYAL

Of much greater strategic and tactical significance was the Port Royal operation, which was undertaken less than a month later. Besides Norfolk, Beaufort, and Wilmington, the only Atlantic ports in the South with rail

[4] This was one of three officer boards appointed by Welles that helped the Secretary in his most important decisions. The others were the Retirement Board and the Ironclad Board.

connections to the rest of the Confederacy were Charleston and Savannah, both of which were stoutly defended by stone and masonry forts with numerous heavy guns. But Port Royal Sound, which lay between them on the South Carolina coast, though far more

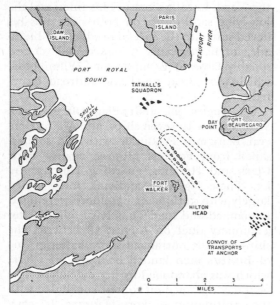

PORT ROYAL ATTACK,
NOVEMBER 7, 1861

formidably fortified than Hatteras Inlet, offered a suitable objective. In virtually all respects it would make an ideal blockade base, for there was ample deep water, it was close to major Southern ports, and counterattack from the interior would be difficult because the country back of Port Royal was so swampy as to be almost impassable. On the other hand, Forts Walker and Beauregard, at the entrance to the Sound, were strong enough to make the issue by no means the foregone conclusion the Hatteras Inlet action had been. In 1861 the Union Navy could not afford to lose many ships, and there had been till this time too little experience involving wooden steamers against forts for any one to be able to say what the gun power afloat had to be to insure the overpowering of a given number of guns ashore.[5]

[5] Traditionally, one gun in a fort was reckoned

Under these circumstances, Captain Du Pont, designated "commodore" to lead this expedition, delayed sailing until he was joined by the first of the "Ninety-Day Gunboats" [6] Welles had ordered built, and until he had collected a truly formidable flotilla of warships, transports, and supply vessels. Not counting a collier and supply convoy of 25 ships that sailed separately under naval escort, Du Pont's force, when it weighed anchor in Hampton Roads, comprised 11 large warships, 36 transports carrying 13,000 men under Brigadier T. W. Sherman, and a number of smaller gunboats.[7]

Heavy weather off the Carolina coast scattered this armada badly. Two supply vessels were driven ashore, and a transport was broken up at sea, though the 300 marines embarked were providentially saved. The expedition had been planned as a joint operation, but the loss of many of the landing boats in the storm compelled Du Pont to change the plan to a purely naval offensive. On November 4, 1861 the flagship with about half of the force crossed the bar that lies about ten miles off Hilton Head and anchored out of range of the forts to wait for the stragglers. Meanwhile boat parties took local soundings and reset channel markers, which the Confederates had everywhere moved or altered as a defense measure.

The entrance to Port Royal Sound lies between Hilton Head and Bay Point, which are 2.2 miles apart. Because Fort Walker, on Hilton Head, was the stronger fort, Du Pont determined to concentrate his attack on it first. Reconnaisance indicated that Fort Walker was strong on its seaward (eastern) front. On its northern face, fronting the Sound, it was armed with but two obsolescent guns. The

"equal" to four or five guns of similar caliber afloat in a sailing vessel. The problem in its new form was essentially a question of the degree to which the greater vulnerability of steam vessels, which could be disabled by a single shot, was compensated by their superior maneuverability.

[6] Vessels of 507 tons, 4 to 7 guns.

[7] The warships included several screw sloops of the "tribal" class (*Pawnee, Iroquois,* and so forth) carrying 11-inch Dahlgren smooth-bores. The transports were mostly chartered vessels, including big packets from the transatlantic run.

Commodore therefore elected to run up into the Sound and bombard the flank of the defenses.

On November 7, 1861 Du Pont led 14 of his strongest vessels up the center of the channel in two columns. The stronger column of nine ships steamed to port of a flanking division made up of five of the gunboats. These last would initially conduct diversionary fire on Fort Beauregard on Bay Point, while the 11-inch guns of the heavier sloops-of-war dueled with Fort Walker.

Some small improvised Confederate warcraft made a gesture of resistance until chased back up the Sound by the flanking division. The main Union force steamed two miles past Fort Walker; then the battle squadron turned to port and approached its target at close range, while the gunboat division remained inside the Sound and delivered a galling, deliberate fire on the weak northern face of the fort. The battle squadron, slowed by the flood tide, steamed slowly past the fort and poured in a devastating fire at point blank range. Fort Walker and Fort Beauregard replied as best they could, causing casualties to both personnel and material in the fleet; but the five-to-one superiority in volume of fire which the ships enjoyed over both forts together was very nearly overwhelming. About a mile beyond Fort Walker, Du Pont turned to port, and steamed up the channel again on a northwesterly course. While the gunboats continued to enfilade the fort on its flank, Du Pont's column repeated its elliptical run and started a third. By this time the defenders of Fort Walker had had enough and abandoned the works. Fort Beauregard surrendered by nightfall.

In terms of casualties suffered the Port Royal action was only a minor action comparable to a skirmish of patrols in the land war. The fleet had 8 killed, 28 wounded; the forts, 11 and 48. Ten of the 13 guns on the channel face of Fort Walker were dismounted, but the fort was abandoned only when powder was running out. In terms of strategic importance however it was a notable victory, enormously raising Northern morale. Port Royal promptly became a major base and supply depot for the blockaders, and was so used throughout the war.

Du Pont's careful planning and judicious exploitation of the enemy's weakness, coupled with his overpowering superiority in guns, make the victory appear deceptively easy. But by demonstrating that wooden ships could stand up to forts on land Du Pont became the pioneer who showed the way to his more celebrated colleague David Glasgow Farragut.

The Port Royal expedition has been described in some detail because of its place in the history of naval tactics and also because it is the archetype of numerous other expeditions undertaken later in the war. Similar in purpose, these differ only in detail from Du Pont's operations. Some were uncontested; others were resisted with much spirit by the local defenders. Operations against Roanoke Island and Elizabeth City, and the capture of New Bern in early 1862 by amphibious forces under Flag Officer L. M. Goldsborough and General S. E. Burnside gave the Union control of Albemarle Sound. As a result North Carolina's military strength was largely diverted to local defense, and the transport of the abundant provisions of the Carolina country to the Army of Virginia was thrown upon the completely inadequate railroad system. Du Pont's concurrent occupation of Amelia Island and Jacksonville, Florida, and the Union recovery of St. Augustine and Norfolk, reduced Confederate control of the Atlantic seaboard to the port of Savannah and the stretch of blockaded coastline between Wilmington and Charleston. The recapture of Pensacola (where Fort Pickens had never been surrendered) was an important preliminary to the seizure of New Orleans and Mobile and the closing of the Gulf coast to blockade runners.

CONFEDERATE NAVAL STRATEGY

So evident to the Southern leadership was the danger to their cause offered by the Union blockade that their major naval strategy was directed at breaching it. Because the Confederate Secretary of Navy, Stephen Mallory, was all too aware of the South's hopeless inferiority in ships and industrial facilities, he pinned his hopes on the success of one or more of three policies: (1) the solicitation of diplomatic and possibly naval intervention by England or England and France; (2) the use of commerce raiders to compel the Union to use its vessels in convoy and search away from the coasts of the Confederacy; (3) the building and purchase of ironclads abroad. In addition, the Confederacy experimented with mines, spar-torpedoes, and primitive submarines.

It will be observed that each of the principal hopes of the Confederacy depended wholly or in part on the attitudes and actions of foreign nations, notably England and France. Both nations in 1861 had much larger navies than did the Union. Furthermore, their navies were technologically advanced: they already had fleets of ironclads building. There can be little question that Britain and France acting conjointly, or even Britain acting alone, could early in the war have easily prevented an effective blockade. It is probable that at any time in the war up to 1864, British intervention would have rendered Union victory impossible.

From the first, informed public opinion in the South confidently looked forward to European intervention—possibly initially in a proffer of mediation, but then, if the United States rejected such offers, with naval assistance. A number of reasons were plausibly adduced why the British would intervene, the most frequently cited and most generally accepted being that the cutting off of the Southern cotton by the blockade would depress British industry to the point of bankruptcy.[8] This would presumably compel British intervention at least to the extent of raising the blockade. Furthermore, any major blockade might impinge on neutral rights and create an incident leading to war. Though Confederate agents worked early and late in the European capitals to promote intervention, Southerners believed that the inherent logic of the developing situation would

produce it anyway. The sympathies of the English aristocracy, from which the British government was largely recruited, were powerfully with the South, whose upper classes had copied as closely as possible their fox-hunting, country-house manner of life. Influential segments of the British press (e.g., the *London Times* and *Punch*) were articulately pro-Confederate.

"King Cotton" however was to prove a grievous disappointment to those who enthroned him. In the early stages of the war, when naval intervention was more likely and could undoubtedly have been decisive, the very inefficiency of the blockade would alone have prevented any painful shortage at the European mills. But, as a matter of fact, the record cotton crop of 1860, coupled with the threat of trouble, had resulted in inflated inventories in England and France.[9] It took substantially two years of mill operation to work off this raw material backlog; the reduced volume of production was compensated to the manufacturers by the high unit profits they received. The textile workers, who before the end of the war were hard hit by the cotton shortage, were not enfranchised as yet. Furthermore, actively and effectively propagandized by Northern abolitionists, they remained sympathetic to the people of the North, to whom they were bound by blood and culture.[10] Throughout the war some cotton reached Europe from the South, both through blockade-running and through licensed shipments from ports in Union hands. However, as a rough indication of the efficiency of the blockade, port records of Liverpool and Le Havre show that in 1862, 1863, and 1864, the American cot-

---

[8] Britain's export trade at this time was heavily dependent on American raw cotton.

[9] More than three million bales were shipped in the period September 1, 1860 to August 31, 1861. This was about three times the average annual export in the preceding decade. For a full discussion of "cotton diplomacy," see F. L. Owsley, *King Cotton Diplomacy* (Chicago, 1931).

[10] The native British Nonconformist clergy were strongly pro-Union because of the slavery issue—especially after the Emancipation Proclamation, January 1, 1863. The influence of Methodist preachers in the industrial Midlands of England was great. The Northern abolitionists did not depend wholly on the power of the spoken word; they also sent money and food to the mill workers.

ton received annually was only about one tenth that for the pre-war years.

It may be wondered why Great Britain, the world's strongest sea power, did not at once enforce a very strict interpretation of neutral rights. For, as always in economic warfare, there was a clear dichotomy of interest between the belligerent naval power and all neutral carriers whatsoever. Practically speaking, Great Britain was adamant only in cases involving "the honor of the flag." She acquiesced in some strained interpretations of international law, and allowed the United States Navy to set new precedents therein. The answer to this apparently paradoxical surrender of selfish interest was partly her tradition of defining belligerent rights broadly, and partly a far-sighted realization that these precedents might some day be of value to her in future wars.

In spite of the efforts of the Declaration of Paris (1856) to spell out belligerent rights, authorities in 1861 still did not agree as to what constituted a legal blockade, which neutrals were bound to respect. Some insisted that it had to prevent utterly all ingress and egress from the blockaded ports. Others maintained that to "offer a clear and present danger" to attempted blockade-running was enough. All however agreed that a "paper blockade"—a blockade that could not be reasonably enforced—was not legal. Yet in her Proclamation of Neutrality that so inflamed the North, Britain did recognize the blockade and set the pattern that the other European states followed. Even more to the point, the Admiralty promptly issued instructions to British units on American stations that they were to act with a scrupulous neutrality, permit search and seizure, and so on. By the Proclamation, the British also denied to the belligerents the right of setting up prize courts in British ports, home or colonial—a fatal blow to Davis' hope of a swarm of privateers flying the Stars and Bars.

The Union Navy and United States prize courts developed at this time the doctrine of "continuous voyage." [11] Advocates of "neutral rights" had generally insisted that an in-

tention to break the blockade was provable only if the ship's documents showed clearance for a blockaded port, or if such intention could be established constructively by the nature of her cargo coupled with close proximity to a blockaded port. A vessel under neutral flag on the high seas, cleared for a neutral port, whether carrying contraband or not, was regarded as untouchable.[12] During the Civil War however the islands of New Providence, Bermuda, and Cuba became great entrepôts for the contraband trade with Southern ports. Cotton was run out of Savannah and Charleston to Nassau, Hamilton, or Havana, and there transshipped to Le Havre or Liverpool. The blockade-runners would take on cargoes of war materials and luxury goods for the Confederacy.

After a time the Union Navy Department ordered search on the high seas, and indignant captains of contraband-carrying craft cleared for Nassau found Navy prize crews taking their ships in to Key West, New York, or Philadelphia for adjudication. In the *Bermuda, Springbok,* and *Peterhof* cases, United States courts held such seizures legal and the ships good prize. The refusal of the British Foreign Office to protest this doctrine of "continuous voyage," which was an extension of accepted belligerent rights, facilitated the work of the blockaders. As the war went on Nassau and Bermuda themselves came to be virtually blockaded by the Union Navy. It may be noted that such seizures on the high seas were judged to be legal only if the vessel were carrying contraband—then rather narrowly defined as "materials of war."

THE *TRENT* AFFAIR

The Confederacy, disappointed at not receiving full-fledged recognition in Europe—the right to maintain a ministry, to negotiate a state loan, and so forth—designated two of her most prominent statesmen, former

---

[11] A U. S. District Court may be constituted a prize court.

[12] This is the "broken voyage" doctrine. The United States insisted on this "right" during the Wars of the French Revolution and Empire.

United States Senators James M. Mason and John Slidell, as plenipotentiaries to advance her cause in Europe. No secret was made of this intention; it was widely advertised in the press, and, characteristically, the plan was as widely known in the North as in the South. The emissaries, with families and secretaries, successfully ran the blockade to Havana, where they embarked on the British mail-packet *Trent,* bound for England. Without orders, the redoubtable Charles Wilkes, then captain of the screw sloop *San Jacinto,* took pains to intercept the *Trent.* On November 8, 1861, he compelled the packet to heave to by firing twice across her bow, and sent a boarding party over. After a *pro forma* show of force, Mason and Slidell were taken off to the *San Jacinto.*

This simple and apparently effective thwarting of the will of the Confederacy made Wilkes a national hero all over again to a public surfeited with the frustrations and disappointments of that black year. There is irony in the fact that the United States had fought Britain in 1812 for the principle that the flag conveys its nationality to the ship that flies it, that the ship's deck is a floating piece of the country where it is registered. Now the shoes had changed feet! But the British public, who knew perfectly well who actually owned the high seas, failed to see any glory in Wilkes' challenge to their flag. Quite simply, the British viewed it as a rude and deliberate affront. They expected and desired war. The fondest hope of the Confederate leadership seemed about to be realized.

A variety of circumstances conspired to thwart this stroke of fortune—the common sense of Lincoln (who pointed out that the act had not been sanctioned by the government), the timely intervention of the British Prince Consort, and the slowness of trans-atlantic communications, which permitted a lapse of time to cool the hotheads on both sides of the Atlantic. After acrimonious debate in the United States Cabinet, Seward penned a conciliatory note to Lord Lyons, the British Minister, and Mason and Slidell were released from their clammy dungeon in Boston Harbor.

Early in the war, Lord Russell, British Foreign Secretary, William Gladstone, Chancellor of the Exchequer, and Lord Palmerston, Prime Minister—the three leading members of the British Cabinet—all favored mediation. But the time never seemed ripe for it. Napoleon III of France favored mediation also, and finally tired of waiting for the British to lead the way. In January 1863, after the tragic defeat of the Army of the Potomac at Fredericksburg, he actually offered himself as a peacemaker. The Union firmly declined, and that was as far as European intervention ever got.

SOUTHERN PRIVATEERS

It was Davis' idea originally, as is evidenced by his Proclamation of April 15, 1861, cited above, to broadcast letters of marque and reprisal. Recognizing that the South lacked the ingredients of a navy, Davis and Mallory hoped that foreign adventurers would be attracted by the profits of privateering. Merely by establishing legal sanction to freebooting, merely by extending the protection of the flag, the South hoped to strike at the sources of Northern economic strength, and, equally important, to destroy the blockade by compelling the Union Navy to scatter its ships in high-seas search for the privateers. Once Confederate sovereignty was fully recognized, consular prize courts could be established in foreign ports and prizes disposed of far from the home ports of the Confederacy.

In the light of the naval tradition of the United States, it was natural for the Southern leaders to think first of the *guerre de course*—commerce warfare—as basic naval policy. In both the American Revolution and the War of 1812, privateering had been the principal American offensive strategy on the high seas. However, the drift of the times was against this practice as a medieval survival. It had in fact been outlawed by the Declaration of Paris of 1856, to which the United States was not a signatory. The Confederacy itself, and also certain of its member states as individual sovereignties, actually commissioned a number of privateers, mostly small, ill-armed vessels. But very few ships were available and there was no sea-faring population to man ships. Furthermore, after the first few weeks of the war, it proved extremely difficult to get prizes in through the blockade. England refused to allow prize courts anywhere in her far-flung territories, and France felt constrained to follow the lead of her recent ally. Foreign capital and foreign adventurers hence found the slender prospects of reward incommensurate with the risks, and were not attracted.

All told, there were only about 30 privateers sent out by the Confederacy and the several states combined. In the first year of the war these were not wholly unsuccessful. For example, the brig *Jefferson Davis,* five guns, 74 men, 230 tons, in a seven-week cruise ranging from Cape Cod to Trinidad captured ten merchantmen. The Union Navy at one time had eight vessels assigned to running her down—suggesting that enough like her would have materially reduced the effectiveness of the blockade and other naval operations. Few as the privateers were, in the first five months of the war they captured between 50 and 60 merchantmen, with a loss of two of their own number. Marine insurance rates went up; transfers to foreign registry by United States vessels became common. On August 10, 1861, the *New York Herald* editorialized, ". . . twenty million dollars worth of property [has] been lost in various ways through the operations of these highwaymen of the seas . . . our shipping interest is literally ruined."

Yet as one by one the privateers were captured, no others came forward to take their places. Anyone with the necessary capital and a taste for this kind of speculation was drawn into the somewhat less hazardous and distinctly more profitable business of blockade-running. By mid-1862, privateering had virtually disappeared.

BLOCKADE-RUNNING

Up to the time of the fall of New Orleans, blockade-running was not unduly hazardous.

Vessels of all types were loaded with cotton bales to make the run to Havana, Nassau, Bermuda, or St. Thomas. As the blockaders became more efficient and more numerous, it became no longer feasible to run through in small sailing vessels. Only fast steamers were left in the trade. Even so, the risks of capture became progressively greater as the war went on. By the summer of 1863, the Union Navy had captured 850-odd blockade-runners, and already specially-built craft were being employed.

The laws of scarcity and demand being what they are, the more efficient the blockade became, the greater were the rewards to those who could run goods through. Joint-stock companies were formed in Britain; Clyde-built ships especially adapted to blockade-running and commanded by British officers were sent out to Nassau and Bermuda.

These blockade-runners were fast, wooden-hulled, shoal-draft vessels of about 450 tons. For the most part they were paddle-wheelers, burning anthracite to avoid smoking. They had fine lines, a length-beam ratio of eight or nine to one being common. They were, above everything, fast. Some could make 17 knots or better. Many of them had telescopic stacks; there was little tophamper; the masts were mere sticks. Painted gray, possessed of low freeboard, proceeding "blacked out" at night, they were nearly invisible.

In a typical run, the blockade-runner would load at St. George's (Bermuda), be piloted out the intricate channel at nightfall, and dodge the Union vessels lying in wait outside the reefs. Through the night she would steam at something less than her best speed, maintaining a sharp lookout for Union cruisers. Navigating carefully, she would try to make a precise landfall two days later in the early evening at, for example, Savannah. She would make her approach after dark, hugging the shore, and exchanging light recognition signals with the coast stations and the forts. Then came the final dash at top speed, past the "inshore blockade." At the pier the crated munitions and such luxuries as liquors, Paris gowns, linens, laces, corsetry, tea, and coffee were quickly unloaded and the company's agent took charge of speedily moving them to a ware-house. Without delay, bales of cotton were stacked in the hold and tiered on deck, with a few extra bales on top on the captain's personal account. The ship would then be fumigated with sulfur to smoke out any stowaways. At nightfall, the ship's officers got a fix on any blockaders visible and plotted them on their chart. Since the blockaders usually anchored at night, it was sometimes not too difficult to steam silently between them in the dark. Strict silence on board the blockade-runner was of course the rule, and sometimes the outward dash was altogether undetected. If discovered, the blockade-runner could still rely on her superior speed.

Even after escaping the inshore blockade, there was still the chance of being sighted by one of the faster Union ships at sea. But on any one given voyage, the odds favored the blockade-runner as long as there was a port in Confederate hands to run to. Up to January 1865, 84 specially-built steamers were regularly employed in blockade-running. Of this number, 37 were captured, 25 were lost by grounding, collision, and accident, and 22 survived the war.

In the period 1863-1864, the profits of the trade were so large that two or three successful round trips, which might be accomplished in as many weeks, would more than pay off the cost of the ship. Coffee, for example, worth 12¢ a pound in Nassau, brought $2.75 (in gold) in Richmond. As early as December 1862, the accepted freight rate from Nassau to Savannah was $500 per ton. Owners of a single lucky ship could easily clear over a million dollars a year. As the risks multiplied, even the officers and crews came to enjoy what were then deemed fabulous returns. A merchant skipper who in 1860 earned perhaps $140 to $160 a month received $5,000 a month for commanding a blockade-runner—and this was supplemented by opportunity for private speculation. Ordinary seamen received base pay of $100 a month, a bonus of $50 for each successful round trip.

It must not be supposed that the blockade-runners in any significant sense defeated the strategy of blockade. Indeed by draining off the South's slender supply of trained sea-men, by attracting capital that might otherwise have gone into further development of the South's war industries, by stimulating the gold flow out of the country and hence further demoralizing the currency, the blockade-runners weakened the South.[13] Their total carrying capacity was inadequate to move any but a small fraction of the cotton grown, and the higher profits in carrying expensive luxuries made a disproportionate share of the incoming cargoes frivolous items of no possible benefit to the war effort. The "blockade auctions" featured bolts of silk, jewelry, and French brandy while industry was in desperate need of chemicals and boiler iron and while the hospitals utterly lacked opiates and other drugs. The resentment stirred by the speculative few who amassed fortunes while the Army of Northern Virginia fought in rags compelled the Confederate Congress to pass an act (March 1, 1864) which forbade the importation of luxuries. This law was apparently not generally enforced however since editorial denouncings of the "speculators" were as frequent in the Southern press afterwards as before.

CONFEDERATE CRUISERS

The most effective naval effort by the South remained commerce-raiding after all; but instead of privateers, national cruisers became the instrument. These Confederate Navy vessels—most often foreign-built and foreign-manned, though officered by Southerners—inflicted enormous injury on the Northern merchant marine. Some notion of the "direct damage" done is furnished by the fact that the Geneva Tribunal adjudicating the "*Alabama* Claims" later awarded the United States $15,500,000 for merchantmen destroyed by cruisers built in British yards.[14]

---

[13] It is of interest that the Confederate government itself entered this field of unrestricted "private enterprise," being the secret owner of four blockade-runners, and having a part interest in a number of others through the agency of Fraser, Trenholm, and Company, Liverpool subsidiary of a Charleston firm.

[14] A modern reader has difficulty in appreciating the magnitude of this figure in terms of the 1865 mone-

Moreover, the indirect costs occasioned by the raiders were vastly greater. Marine insurance costs were of course much raised. American shipping firms sold many of their vessels, some even abandoning the business altogether. One hundred twenty-six United States ships were transferred to foreign registry in 1861, 135 in 1862, and 348 in 1863, when the *Alabama* was at the height of her depredations.

Of greater importance to the Southern cause was the large number of Union naval vessels diverted from the blockade and scattered over the oceans in "needle in a haystack" searches for the elusive commerce-destroyers. The *Alabama,* for example, had a squadron of seven vessels looking for her in the Caribbean alone. Inasmuch as some ocean-going cruising by the United States Navy would have been necessary in any event, it is impossible to cite a precise figure for the number of ships pulled off the Southern coasts and away from inshore operations by the necessity of tracking down Confederate raiders. But it can be no exaggeration to say that the Confederate cruisers, few in number as they were, so diverted at least ten times their own tonnage. This rather than mere aimless destruction was the principal objective of the Confederate government. Recent histories have generally dismissed the commerce-destroyers as "having no significant effect on the outcome of the war," and hence playing an unimportant role. Only in the sense that nothing that the South did had any significant effect on the outcome of the war is this a fair judgment.

Considering the poverty of naval resources in the South, the strategic decision to send forth commerce-raiders was perfectly sound. They accomplished more than their most sanguine proponents could reasonably have anticipated. They certainly rendered the task of the Union Navy in strengthening the blockade tremendously more difficult. It is

quite possible that if the blockading squadrons had had available the sloops and other units that were pursuing the raiders, the Union timetable of amphibious operations might have been advanced and the war concluded sooner.

The first of the regularly commissioned naval vessels to undertake commerce-raiding was the *Sumter,* a screw steamer of 500 tons converted from a peacetime packet. Bought by the Confederate government from a New Orleans shipping firm, she was refitted for war and armed with an 8-inch pivot and four short 24-pounders in broadside.

Captain Raphael Semmes took her down the lower Mississippi in June 1861 and played hide-and-seek with the blockading *Brooklyn,* which was too deep-drafted to get over the bar. The favorable moment for escape finally came when the *Brooklyn* went off on a local chase. The *Sumter* made a dash for it and outdistanced the *Brooklyn* when the latter attempted to retrieve her lapse. Cruising in the Caribbean and off the coasts of Spain and Portugal, the *Sumter* took 17 prizes, of which six were burned, two recaptured, and two ransomed. Seven that had been sent to Cuban ports for disposition were seized by the Spanish authorities and later released to their Northern owners.

After the *Sumter*'s escape from the *Brooklyn,* the *Niagara* and the *Powhatan* were detached from the Gulf Squadron, and joined the *San Jacinto,* the *Iroquois,* the *Richmond,* and the *Keystone State* to scour the Caribbean in what proved an aimless search. In January 1862 the *Sumter* was finally run to earth at Gibraltar by U.S.S. *Tuscarora,* which was presently joined by the *Kearsarge* and the *Ino.* Apart from the obvious danger of being blown out of the water if he ventured forth from his neutral sanctuary, Captain Semmes was bedeviled by a number of other problems. He could get no coal at Gibraltar, his boilers were rusted through, and his engines needed repairs, so Semmes had the *Sumter* surveyed and sold. But she continued to work for the Confederacy, for her British owners converted her into a blockade-runner.

The brief career of the *Sumter* as a raider

---

tary situation. To put these damages in historical perspective, consider that the average annual *total receipts* of the United States government for the period 1861-1865 was $161,000,000. For a comparable economic effect today, these claims would have to run to hundreds of millions.

is fairly typical of other cruisers. Its principal significance is that it was the apprenticeship of the master-raider of them all, the redoubtable Raphael Semmes. From the cruise of the *Sumter,* Semmes learned to avoid such frequented roadsteads as Gibraltar, to destroy his prizes rather than risk losing by diplomacy in neutral ports what his guns had captured. And he so perfected the timing of his cruises that he was apparently able to anticipate every move of his pursuers.

The *Sumter* was unusual in being a Southern-owned steamer converted to a war-vessel. Lacking facilities for building ships, the South was obliged to rely largely on the efforts of her agents abroad in purchasing vessels and in having them built. Shortly after the firing on Fort Sumter the Confederate Congress authorized the purchase of, and made appropriations for, six sail-steam cruisers to cost $165,000 each, and two million-dollar ironclad rams. James D. Bulloch and James H. North, both former officers in the United States Navy, were sent to England to try to procure these vessels. This assignment was to involve a great deal of intrigue and peculiarly British red tape, problems with which the able and persistent Bulloch proved quite capable of coping. The American Minister to Britain, Charles Francis Adams, and the American consuls in the British shipbuilding ports attempted by every possible expedient of diplomacy and British law to circumvent the Confederate agents' efforts.

The British neutrality laws, like those of all civilized nations in 1861, specifically forbade the "equipping, furnishing, fitting out, or arming" of a ship intended for making war on a friendly state. The manufacture and sale of arms or other contraband to either belligerent was permitted, though this could be done only at the subject's own risk. So far as the courts of England were concerned, proof of the vesssel's warlike character had to be established to warrant seizure of the vessel. This provision opened the possibility that commerce-raiders could be constructed in British yards, then as unarmored vessels be cleared to a dummy foreign purchaser. The Confederacy had agents in many European and Caribbean ports. Some of

these were foreign nationals. Meanwhile ordnance could be manufactured in England and transported to a previously agreed-on rendezvous. There the raider would be armed and commissioned. She need never have seen a Confederate port from first to last. Guided at every step by British legal counsel, Bulloch successfully followed this procedure to the end of the war, sending forth the *Florida,* the *Alabama,* and the *Shenandoah,* among others.

The purchase of British-built ironclads was another matter, since the warlike purpose of such vessels would be established by the details of their construction. Even the ingenuity of Bulloch proved unavailing. The firm of Lairds of Birkenhead contracted to build two "rams" carrying a battery of 9-inch rifles, ostensibly for the French government, later for the Pasha of Egypt, then for a French private firm. Lord Russell, Foreign Secretary, ordered them seized in 1863 shortly before their completion. Had they actually been delivered to the Confederacy, they would have posed a terrifying problem for the Union Navy.

The *Florida* was completed in March 1862. She sailed to Nassau, where through the connivance of the colonial authorities she was armed with two 7-inch rifles and six 6-inch smooth-bores, and commissioned under the command of Commander John N. Maffitt csn. She had an eventful and successful career, being finally captured in October 1863 by U.S.S. *Wachusett* in the harbor of Bahia, Brazil. This barefaced violation of Brazilian neutrality was later apologized for very handsomely by the United States. But the *Florida* herself was unfortunately sunk in an "unforeseen accident" at Hampton Roads, before she could be delivered back to Brazil.

THE CRUISE OF THE *ALABAMA*

The *Alabama* was justly the most famous of the raiders. Barkentine rigged, she was 230 feet by 32 feet; loaded she drew 15 feet. Her 300 horsepower engine gave her a trial speed of 13.5 knots. Cruising, she normally depended on her sails to conserve coal. Because of the danger of seizure by the British authorities, the *Alabama,* once she was launched, simply never returned from her trial trip, proceeding rather to a rendezvous in the Azores where arms, coal, and her prospective officers were sent by Bulloch to fit her out. While the Portuguese port officials in Porto Praya were encouraged to believe that the *"Enrica"* was merely coaling from the chartered *Agrippina,* a battery consisting of six long 32-pounders in broadside, a rifled 100-pounder and an 8-inch shell gun were winched into place on the cruiser. Eighty-three of the sailors who had brought the ship from England, mostly British and Irish adventurers from the Liverpool waterfront, volunteered as a skeleton crew to be filled out with volunteer recruits from prizes. Raphael Semmes took his ship outside territorial waters to perform the commissioning ceremony: mustering the crew, reading his orders, and raising the Confederate ensign. The *Alabama* was past her period of masquerade. She was a ship-of-war, ready to fulfill her mission.

The *Alabama* spent the first two months in the North Atlantic, making 20 captures in this time. Profiting from his experience in the *Sumter,* Semmes took what he wanted from the prizes, then put them to the torch. When the accumulation of prisoners aboard the *Alabama* became too much of a problem, Semmes stripped a captured vessel and made a cartel ship of her, on which the superfluous passengers could make their way to land. Semmes was a stern and able disciplinarian; no lesser man could have handled his crew of Liverpool toughs.

After cruising as far as the Grand Banks, the *Alabama,* her coal nearly exhausted, made for Fort de France, Martinique, which was a previously arranged fueling rendezvous. The *Agrippina* awaited her, but before refueling could be accomplished the U.S.S. *San Jacinto,* a more heavily armed vessel, appeared off the harbor and began patrolling just outside the marine league limit. Unhappily for the Union, Semmes succeeded in taking his ship out at night without being ob-

served, though with her considerable speed advantage it is likely that the *Alabama* would have escaped anyway.

The Confederate cruiser next headed for the obscure little port of Blanquilla in Venezuela, where she completed coaling from her tender. Hoping to intercept one of the California "treasure steamers" with gold in her cargo on the run from Colon to New York, Semmes now cruised south of the Mona Passage between Haiti and Puerto Rico.[15] Out of a number of captures in this area, the most valuable was the large passenger steamer *Ariel,* outward bound from New York.

Semmes next moved through the Yucatan Channel into the Gulf of Mexico, with the object of interfering with an expected Union amphibious operation against the Texas coast. Off Galveston, which a Northern squadron was bombarding, the *Alabama* steamed slowly, inviting the attention of a Union cruiser. Presently the gunboat conversion U.S.S. *Hatteras* came out to investigate the suspicious-looking stranger. At a point about 20 miles away from the support of the rest of the squadron, the *Hatteras* hailed the *Alabama,* which first identified herself as the British ship *Petrel.* When the Union vessel sent off a boarding party to inspect the *Petrel's* papers, the *Alabama* broke out the Confederate colors. Semmes bellowed through his megaphone, "This is the Confederate States steamer *Alabama!*" and immediately ordered a broadside. The action was fought in growing darkness at point-blank range. The superior armament of the *Alabama,* which had riddled the little gunboat at the first unexpected broadside, made short work of the Union steamer. In a sinking condition, the *Hatteras* struck her colors and fired a gun to leeward to signify surrender only 13 minutes after the first gun was fired. Semmes quickly transferred the surviving members of the crew of the *Hatteras* to the *Alabama.* In a matter of minutes the flaming hulk of the defeated

---

[15] The crew of the *Alabama,* which had unsuccessfully mutinied at Fort de France, had gone a long time without pay. Semmes hoped to meet his payroll with captured California gold.

vessel sank hissing in a cloud of steam. The *Alabama* then made a quick run to Kingston, Jamaica to put its prisoners ashore on parole before the alarm was spread.

For another 18 months Semmes played cat-and-mouse with the Union cruisers scouring the sea lanes of the world in fruitless pursuit. Operating successively in the Caribbean, the South Atlantic, the Indian Ocean, Sunda Strait, the South China Sea, and the Bay of Bengal, the *Alabama* gradually became the victim of her own successes. As Semmes worked farther and farther afield, he found progressively fewer Northern merchantmen. Doubling back to the South Atlantic again, the *Alabama* made two final captures as she cruised north to Europe to refit. On June 11, 1864 Semmes took his ship in to the port of Cherbourg and requested docking facilities from the French government.

THE *ALABAMA—KEARSARGE* ACTION

Operating earlier in the broad oceans, Semmes had been able to forestall pursuit by timing his moves to anticipate Union vessels sent out to intercept him. Because there were no transoceanic cables, he normally had several days or even weeks of leeway. But when the *Alabama* anchored in Cherbourg, the United States consul was able to telegraph Captain John A. Winslow of the U.S.S. *Kearsarge,* anchored off Flushing on the Dutch coast. So it was that three days later the Union cruiser appeared off Cherbourg. Without anchoring, the *Kearsarge* took up a patrol station just outside the port.

It had been Semmes' plan to dock his vessel and send his crew off on a well-deserved leave. However, it soon became apparent that he was unlikely to be granted the dock facilities he had requested, and the practical alternatives open to him were to accept internment in Cherbourg or to go out and fight. Because the *Alabama* and the *Kearsarge* appeared to be evenly matched,

Semmes allowed his temperamental bias in favor of the bold course to have its way. Through the United States consul he challenged Winslow to a single ship duel as soon as the *Alabama* had refueled.

Filling the *Alabama*'s bunkers not only provided the wherewithal to escape if fortune favored her, it also provided protection to the vital machinery of the ship. In accordance with a common practice of the day, Winslow had gone one step farther in protecting his engine and boiler spaces by faking chain up and down the sides of the *Kearsarge,* and sheathing it over with boards to hold it secure. This practice caused Semmes later to claim that the combat was "unfair" because the *Kearsarge* was "practically an ironclad." Otherwise the vessels were of nearly identical length and tonnage. The *Kearsarge* carried seven heavy guns with a total broadside of 432 pounds; the *Alabama,* eight guns with a 360-pound broadside. The *Kearsarge* had a 163-man crew; the *Alabama,* 149. The *Kearsarge* had a slight speed advantage.

On the slightly hazy morning of June 19 the *Alabama* headed out the West Pass. The *Kearsarge* steamed ahead to clear French territorial waters. The new French ironclad *Couronne* followed, and anchored at the three-mile limit. The private yacht *Deerhound,* of British registry, hovered about to witness the impending action. Thousands of spectators lined the coast.

When about seven miles from the shore, the *Kearsarge* reversed direction and bore directly down on the *Alabama,* which sheered off to port to present her starboard battery. The *Alabama* fired the first broadside at about 2,000 yards. Most of the shot fell short, but one or two cut into the *Kearsarge*'s top-hamper. Winslow held his fire as his ship bore down on his opponent. Reloading with great rapidity, the Confederate got off another broadside at about 1,000 yards. Only then did the *Kearsarge* in turn sheer off to port, present her starboard battery, and begin firing.

The ensuing action took place with both ships turning in a clockwise direction about a circle with a diameter of perhaps a half mile, while each vessel worked its starboard battery. The object of this maneuver was to endeavor to achieve a raking position on the adversary. Since there was a three-knot tidal current toward the WSW, the vessels were gradually set down toward the French coast west of Cherbourg.

The firing of the *Alabama,* though rapid and well-sustained, was wild, especially in the early stages of the battle. The more deliberate fire of the *Kearsarge* was a great deal more accurate and damaging. Moreover the powder, and particularly the fuses in the Confederate shells, appear in some instances to have been defective. A 100-pound shell which lodged in the sternpost of the *Kearsarge* failed to explode. However, of 370 shot and shell fired by the *Alabama* in the action, only 14 hulled the *Kearsarge;* perhaps twice as many went through her rigging. Considering the point-blank range, the results achieved indicate poor shooting. As the comparative damage to the ships showed, the 173 projectiles fired by the *Kearsarge* were obviously much better directed, though the actual number of hits can only be surmised. The guns of the *Kearsarge* blew gaping holes in the hull of the Southern raider, shot off whole sections of her bulwarks, dismounted guns, and splintered her decks. On the seventh rotation on the circular track, a shell from one of the *Kearsarge*'s 11-inch Dahlgren pivot guns crashed into the engine room of the *Alabama,* causing her to lose all power. Semmes ordered headsails set and attempted to beach his ship on the coast. But with all maneuverability lost, the *Alabama* was a beaten ship. The *Kearsarge* cut across her bow and hulled her time after time until Semmes struck his colors and streamed a white flag.

A boat from the *Alabama* brought over some of the wounded to the *Kearsarge.* When the stricken ship was seen to be sinking, both victor and vanquished launched boats quickly, and the *Deerhound* came up to help in the work of rescue. Semmes flung his sword into the sea from his quarterdeck and then plunged overboard. At 12:24 the bow of the *Alabama* rose perpendicular in the air as she sank stern first. The fight had lasted a little over an hour, and the raider had sunk about 20 minutes later. The *Kearsarge,* which suffered only trifling damage, had lost but one man and had two wounded. The *Alabama* lost 19 by gunfire and drowning and had 21 wounded. Semmes, together with 13 of his officers and 26 of his men, was picked up by the *Deerhound* and taken to Southampton. In Union eyes his avoidance of capture was the only flaw in the news of the victory. Winslow received the thanks of Congress and was promoted to commodore.

Between September 5, 1862 and April 27, 1864, the *Alabama* had captured 71 Union vessels, destroying most of them at sea. Semmes' epic cruise is by all odds the most successful in the history of commerce-raiding. Besides the direct damage inflicted, the *Alabama* caused enormous indirect losses to Union shipowners—higher marine insurance premiums, delays and cancelations of sailings, and spoilage of cargoes. The necessity of keeping a fleet of cruisers at sea searching for the raider was a serious drain on the resources of the Union Navy.

THE *SHENANDOAH*

Including captured vessels armed at sea as raiders the Confederate government sent out 19 commerce-destroyers in all; this figure however includes several vessels that had neither the speed nor the armament for the task. The *Shenandoah,* purchased by Bulloch to take the place of the *Alabama,* was armed in the Madeira Islands by a tender in October 1864. She sailed at once for the Pacific and began her depredations in November 1864. Operating chiefly in the North Pacific around the Aleutian Islands, the *Shenandoah* captured a total of 36 vessels, most of them whalers, and gave the American whaling industry a blow from which it never recovered. Because news of the Confederate surrender did not reach Captain James I. Waddell until August 2, 1865, two thirds of the *Shenandoah*'s captures came after the end of the war. The destructiveness of the *Shenandoah*'s cruise was second only to that of the *Alabama.*

As suggested earlier, there is some question as to the importance of the commerce-raiders in the total war picture. Certainly they were too few to constitute a counter-blockade such as the German submarine campaigns were almost to achieve in the world wars of the 20th century. Nevertheless their effect was not negligible. For their numbers, the commerce-raiders were very effective. It appears possible that a dozen *Alabamas* operating simultaneously could have destroyed Union sea commerce completely and thereby have disrupted the Northern war effort.

18

The Battle of the Ironclads

THE YEAR 1861 HAD BEEN one of surprise and bitter disappointment for the Union. The war had come to climax a disastrous policy of drift. The ignominy of Bull Run, and later of Ball's Bluff, had made the faint-hearted wonder if perhaps the reconquest of the South might not be beyond the capacity of the Lincoln government. The Confederate States of America was seen to emerge with an apparently stable and efficient government, evidently well able to maintain armies and wage war.

UNION STRATEGY

Yet the Union had made real progress. First and most important, Lincoln had demonstrated a determination to wage the war to a finish, and in spite of spotty political opposition from the "Copperheads," the people of the North rallied to his support with real patriotic intensity. Second, a workable grand strategy had been hammered out: (1) The Army of the Potomac would simultaneously cover Washington and threaten Richmond; (2) in the West, an effort would be made to secure the line of the Mississippi, thereby splitting off the Southwest from the

rest of the Confederacy; (3) the border areas —Missouri, Kentucky, West Virginia, and Maryland—would, if necessary, be occupied and held in the Union; (4) the Navy, which had already occupied Port Royal, would continue amphibious operations along the coast in support of its major mission of blockade, and the strength of the blockade would in all ways be improved; (5) foreign intervention would be obviated by a judicious combination of show of force, diplomatic ingenuity, and willingness to compromise.

The economic preponderance of the North was gradually mobilized in support of the Union as it became increasingly plain to all that a sustained war was going to be necessary. The Civil War was the first in history in which the steam engine, the railroad, and the industrial process generally were to have a decisive role. It was the good fortune of the North that in this vital area she was overwhelmingly superior.

In November 1861 the talented but unstable George B. McClellan succeeded elderly, ailing Winfield Scott in command of the Army of the Potomac. Supremely competent as a drillmaster, "Little Mac" trained his soldiers to a new excellence in the encampments around Washington. Urged by Lincoln to press directly south against the outnumbered Southern force around Manassas, McClellan favored a grand flanking operation against Richmond via the peninsula between the York and the James Rivers.

This plan had the advantage of providing secure lines of water-borne communication defended by superior Union sea power. Since the Union already held the extreme lower peninsula—Newport News and the area around Fortress Monroe—the troop movement could be accomplished without enemy harassment. The success of the earliest stages of the operation would incidentally insure the evacuation of Confederate forces from Norfolk. McClellan of course hoped that the tempo of the advance would produce major results before General Joseph E. Johnston could realign his forces to meet this unanticipated threat.

A principal disadvantage of the plan was that it involved uncovering Washington. This danger required splitting off a considerable force (McDowell's corps), to be held in northern Virginia. Secondly, McClellan was soon to reveal that he lacked the sturdy and decisive personality to command an "all or nothing" campaign. Thirdly, the element of secrecy, which was highly desirable if not absolutely essential to the success of the operation, was apparently unobtainable in those days. Richmond knew of his plans about as quickly as McClellan's own division commanders. Finally, the absolute control of the Potomac, York, and lower James Rivers, and of Chesapeake Bay—on which McClellan's lines of supply and reinforcement depended—was seriously threatened at the very time the first great adventure of the Army of the Potomac was to begin.

THE IRONCLAD *VIRGINIA*

At Norfolk the scuttled *Merrimack* had been raised by the Confederates and crudely converted into an ironclad. Should she prove impervious to the fire of the wooden Union blockaders, the essential precondition of Northern naval supremacy in the lower Chesapeake and on the Virginia rivers

would be destroyed. Even more disastrous, the blockade would be ruptured.

Stephen R. Mallory, Confederate Secretary of the Navy, had been chairman of the Naval Affairs Committee in the United States Senate. He brought to his job an intelligent awareness of the impending technological revolution in naval material. Two months before Secretary Welles had diffidently recommended an "Ironclad Board" to the U. S. Congress, Mallory had addressed the Chairman of the Confederate Naval Affairs Committee thus:

I regard the possession of an ironclad ship as a matter of the first necessity. Such a vessel at this time could traverse the entire coast of the United States, prevent all blockade, and encounter, with a fair prospect of success, their entire navy. If, to cope with them upon the sea, we follow their example, and build wooden ships, we shall have to construct several at one time, for one or two ships would fall an easy prey to their comparatively numerous steam frigates. But inequality of numbers may be compensated by invulnerability, and thus not only does economy, but naval success, dictate the wisdom and expediency of fighting iron against wood without regard to first cost.

Naval engagements between wooden frigates, as they are now built and armed, will prove to be the forlorn hopes of the seas, simply contests in which the question, not of victory, but of who shall go to the bottom first, is to be solved. Should the committee deem it expedient to begin at once the construction of such a ship, not a moment should be lost.[1]

Plans were speedily drafted on the general style of the new British ironclads. In early July 1861, Mallory formally approved the project of raising the frigate *Merrimack*,[2] repairing the hull and engines, clearing away

[1] Dated May 8, 1861. Cited by William C. Church, *The Life of John Ericsson* (New York, 1891), I, 245.
[2] U.S.S. *Merrimack* had been commissioned in 1856 —the first of a class of six steam frigates, then generally regarded as the finest of their type in the world. She was 300 feet over-all, 250 feet on the keel, and had a beam of 51 feet, 4 inches. She drew 28 feet. She displaced 4500 tons. She had two 600-horse-power engines of new design, four tubular boilers, a variable pitch screw. Like all such vessels in her day, she was ship-rigged. She carried a battery of 40 Dahlgren guns, including two ten-inch pivots, 14 eight-inch, and 24 nine-inch in broadsides.

the burnt-out superstructure, and replacing it with an armored casemate.

Work was started at once. Only the appalling shortage of metalworking industries in the South prevented it from securing a prompt and possibly decisive advantage in the technological race. There was at that time only one rolling mill in the South capable of turning out the two-inch iron slabs for side armor. The only source of iron was used rails from the railroads, which the constructors were obliged to scour the countryside to procure.

In spite of the best efforts of the engineers in charge, the work progressed slowly. And through the summer, fall, and winter of 1861, Northern spies brought through the lines detailed accounts of its progress. These reports speeded the tardy countermeasures of the Union Navy.

In conversion, the *Merrimack* was cut down to the waterline, and provided with an armored superstructure with sides sloping from the vertical about 35 degrees. The deck length of this casemate was 170 feet. The hull had only about two feet of freeboard forward, and rather less astern—under way at her plodding four knots, she carried her after deck virtually awash.

The casemate was framed with 20-inch pine beams overset with four-inch oak planks. The armor was two layers of iron plates, the first bolted on horizontally, the second vertically. The sloping sides of the casemate were to be smeared with tallow before the ship went into action, so that solid shot would tend to ricochet off harmlessly. The top of the casemate was protected by a heavy iron grating, 120 feet by 20 feet, which would permit ventilation of the gun deck beneath.

For a battery, the Confederates were entirely dependent on the heavy ordnance captured from the United States naval stores at the Norfolk Navy Yard; these however included about 50 large new Dahlgrens, as well as numerous older pieces. Four of the Dahlgrens were rebored as rifles. The *Merrimack,* recommissioned as C.S.S. *Virginia,* mounted three 9-inch Dahlgrens and two 6-inch rifles in broadside, and had in addition two 7-inch rifled pivots. A heavy iron wedge was affixed to her bow as a ram. A crank, unseaworthy craft, of awkwardly deep draft for the shoal inland waters in which she was to operate, the *Virginia* was nevertheless an ingenious adaptation of the materials at hand and a tribute to her builders' skill at improvisation.

When the vessel was nearly completed, Commander Franklin Buchanan, an able former United States naval officer,[3] was designated to command her. Since the agrarian South had no merchant marine, finding a crew of trained seamen was more difficult. Eighty sailors were discovered in a New Orleans regiment at Yorktown; seamen from the city of Norfolk and inexperienced army volunteers made up the rest of the crew of about 350 men.

The Confederate authorities were actuated by a terrible sense of urgency, for espionage and ill-advised revelations in the Northern press kept them informed not only of McClellan's invasion plan but also of the construction of U.S.S. *Monitor,* a mysterious countermeasure to the *Virginia.* If the *Virginia* could be gotten underway in time, the five wooden ships of the Union Navy blockading Norfolk and the lower Chesapeake could be smashed like matchwood for all their 222 guns. Interrupted transatlantic traffic would once more flow to Norfolk. The position of the Union troops in Newport News and Fortress Monroe would become untenable. The threat of the flanking operation against Richmond would of course evaporate. Well might the patriotically inspired workmen, laboring nightly to rush the *Virginia* to completion, feel that on them might depend the success of the Confederacy.

The temperate Mallory in his orders to Buchanan revealed the magnitude of his hopes from the *Virginia:*

The *Virginia* is a novelty in naval construction; and hence the department will not give specific orders as to her attack on the enemy. Her powers

---

[3] Buchanan, the first superintendent of the United States Naval Academy (1845-1847), was one of a handful of outstanding naval leaders who resigned from the Union service in order to serve the Confederacy.

as a ram are regarded as very formidable, and it is hoped that you will be able to test them. Like the bayonet charge of the infantry, this mode of attack, while most destructive, will commend itself to you in the present scarcity of ammunition. . . .

Could you pass Old Point Comfort, and make a dashing cruise in the Potomac as far as Washington, its effect upon the public mind would be important to our cause.

The condition of our country, and the painful reverses we have just suffered, demand our utmost exertions; and convinced as I am that the opportunity and the means for striking a decisive blow for our navy are now, for the first time, presented, I congratulate you upon it, and know that your judgment and gallantry will meet all just expectations . . .[4]

Buchanan and his hastily assembled, untried crew were eager to fulfill the expectations of the Secretary.

THE IRONCLAD BOARD

The United States Navy was not quick to realize the danger created by the early Confederate decision to build an ironclad or attempt to purchase one or more abroad. The subject of ironclad construction, discussed in the Navy Department in May 1861, was tabled in the face of the more pressing problem of finding more wooden vessels to implement the blockade. In early July the Secretary in a message to the extra session of Congress requested authority to constitute an Ironclad Board and asked an appropriation. On August 3, Congress authorized the board and appropriated $1,500,000 for the "construction or completing"[5] of iron- or steelclad steamships or steam batteries.

The ironclad board selected by Welles and Fox did not seem especially qualified by background or experience. In Commodore Joseph Smith, Commodore Hiram Paulding, and Commander Charles H. Davis, the Department had apparently selected officers of "the old school," hardly adapted to judg-

ments in the new warfare of scientific innovation. The board itself was mindful of its technical limitations, and in its report officially deplored the fact that, though they had requested a qualified naval constructor as a consultant, "they [were] all so employed on important service that none could be assigned to this duty."

Nevertheless the board reviewed more than a hundred ironclad proposals submitted to the department and prepared a detailed and precise report, which was submitted in September 1861. In summary, this important document, which established ironclad policy in the United States Navy for the Civil War period and for some time thereafter, stated: (1) Armored ocean-going cruisers are, for the time being, impractical. (2) For coast defense and operation in sheltered water—harbors, bays, and rivers—armored gunboats of relatively shallow draft are feasible; such vessels should be constructed at once. (3) Armored vessels of this type cannot successfully cope with masonry forts. (4) Wooden vessels will always be faster than ironclads, of whatever description. (5) At the current stage of technological development, smooth-bore cannon firing spherical shot are superior to rifled ordnance and shell. (6) Though the United States could doubtless get armored vessels cheaper and more expeditiously by purchase in England, it would be better policy to build them at home. (7) Three contracts for armored vessels are recommended—with the firms of Merrick and Sons and C. S. Bushnell and Co., and with John Ericsson.

These contracts were undertaken with comparatively little delay, and three vessels were duly produced. The *New Ironsides* (Merrick and Sons), a broadside type of ironclad, was to do good service at Charleston. The *Galena* (Bushnell) was a rather lightly armored gunboat that was mercilessly pounded at Drewry's Bluff and was regarded as a failure. By far the greatest historical interest centers in the *Monitor* (Ericsson): she was the Union ironclad first in naval action, by her arrival in Hampton Roads she frustrated the Confederate counterstrategy, she was the first of a succession of "Mon-

[4] Cited in John T. Scharf, *History of the Confederate States Navy* (New York, 1887), 155.
[5] An obvious reference to the unfinished Stevens battery.

itors" in the U.S. Navy, and she was probably the most influential American innovation in naval design in the 19th century.

THE *MONITOR*—A STUDY IN INNOVATION

John Ericsson, Swedish-born builder of the *Monitor,* was by 1861 already an internationally famous inventor and engineer. He had pioneered in locomotive design, had invented a screw propeller, and had made significant innovations in heavy ordnance. Justly chagrined at the parsimony of the United States Congress after the building of the *Princeton,* Ericsson had left Washington with an eloquent declaration that he never meant to return.

But the Civil War touched both his patriotic enthusiasm and his professional instincts; it was easy for his friend Bushnell to persuade him to present his original designs for an armored battery, and to explain to the less agile minds in the Navy Department just why it would work.

In mid-September 1861 Welles promised him a contract, and Ericsson began work at once. In 101 working days the *Monitor* was afloat—perhaps the most original design in the entire history of naval architecture. The design and supervision of the entire project were Ericsson's contribution. The hull, the turret, and the engines and other machinery were contracted to various firms in the New York area.

The building of the *Monitor* was a remarkable *tour de force*. There was never any comprehensive complete design or detailed model. Yet Ericsson prepared well over a hundred detailed drawings to guide the workmen. Nearly everything about the ship was radically new and untried. The first engineer of the *Monitor* estimated that the ship contained at least 40 patentable innovations.

The major distinctive features of this new instrument of warfare were: she was designed to have very little reserve buoyancy, so that she offered only a foot or so of freeboard— and consequently a very small target area;

her battery was concentrated in two guns of largest size, mounted side-by-side in a heavily armored turret; all exposed vertical surfaces were heavily armored; the deck was plated also, and an overhang protected the screw and rudder; all nonessential tophamper was dispensed with. Such a vessel, Ericsson reasoned, would offer a minimum and

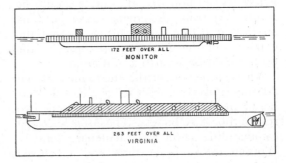

U.S.S. MONITOR *AND* C.S.S. VIRGINIA

impregnable target to the enemy, while packing tremendous offensive strength on a moderate draft and displacement.

The *Monitor* idea, which Ericsson always insisted constituted a new method of naval warfare, was by no means an improvisation of the moment. It had been maturing in the inventor's mind for almost a lifetime. Indeed in 1854 his typical Swedish hostility to all things Russian prompted him to submit a somewhat less elaborate design of a monitor to Napoleon III, who returned it with a courteous note, but who may well have been thereby stimulated to his early experiments with ironclads of French design.

The finished *Monitor* was a hull 124 feet long, on which was riveted a raft-like deck 172 feet by 41½ feet, the vertical sides of which carried 4½-inch iron armor. This deck was protected from plunging fire by one-inch armor on its horizontal surface. The 9-foot-high turret, 20 feet in diameter, was set on a brass ring laid into the deck. Eight layers of one-inch rolled iron plates made up the laminated sidewalls of the cylindrical turret. The turret cover was a grating of iron road rails. The 140-ton turret rested on a spindle which extended down to the keel.

This spindle was cogged to a steam auxiliary engine that could turn the turret through a complete 360-degree revolution.

The battery consisted of two 11-inch Dahlgren smooth-bores. When their muzzles were inboard of the ports (as for cleaning and loading), the ports were automatically shielded by heavy iron "port stoppers" which swung over like pendulums. It was Ericsson's opinion that the turret should be revolved to bring the enemy under fire only an instant before actual firing, so that the exposure of the gun crews in opening the ports would be kept to a minimum.

The engine was of the then conventional double-trunk type, with its 36-inch cylinders bored in a single casting. There were two return-tube box boilers. The *Monitor's* first commanding officer was Lieutenant John L. Worden USN—a brave man and a beloved leader, though rather lacking in the technical background this novel type of ship was to demand. The *Monitor* was commissioned on February 25, 1862 and after brief testing was ordered to Hampton Roads.

THE BATTLE OF HAMPTON ROADS

In early March the fortunes of the North and the South appeared to be hanging in unstable balance. McClellan believed that in the Army of the Potomac he had at last the well-oiled fighting machine needed to win the war in a single crushing campaign. His carefully worked out plan for advance up the peninsula appeared almost foolproof. The inferior Confederate armies would be pinned to their positions by the necessity of defending Richmond to the last. Only the latent threat offered by the presence of the *Virginia* in the Elizabeth River clouded the rosy expectations of the Union commander. If in fact the Confederate ram could impair the absolute sea control of the Union Navy, the transports could not venture into Hampton Roads, and McClellan's whole strategy would have to be modified or abandoned.

The events of March 8 and 9 in Hampton

Roads constitute one of those rare "set pieces" of history—not only in the dramatic reversal occasioned by the *Monitor,* but in that they occurred in a kind of natural naval amphitheater. The anchorage is essentially the lower James River, here broadened to six miles in width before its confluence with Chesapeake Bay. The north shore was held by Union forces: Fortress Monroe on Old Point Comfort, and Newport News Point to the west, where newly emplaced batteries covered the approach to the James River proper. The Confederates held the entire south bank: they had heavily fortified Sewell's Point, six miles almost due south of Fortress Monroe, and they had less formidable works at Pig Point to the west. So restricted were the dimensions of the battleground that thousands on both sides—Union troops, and a good part of the population of Norfolk—were able to witness the events related below.

Flag Officer Louis M. Goldsborough, commanding the North Atlantic Blockading Squadron, had concentrated in Hampton Roads what by earlier standards was a formidable blockading force—the 50-gun screw frigates *Minnesota, Roanoke,* and *Congress* (sister ships of the original *Merrimack*), the sailing frigate *St. Lawrence,* 52, and the sloop *Cumberland,* 24. Goldsborough correctly assumed that when the *Virginia* was first brought into action she would head for the *Congress* and the *Cumberland,* which were anchored farthest to the west, blockading the James. Goldsborough's plan was to run down the Confederate ram with the *Minnesota* (flagship) and any other vessels that might happen to be in the anchorage. His aim was, above all, to prevent the *Virginia's* retreat back up the Elizabeth River. The plan involved an underestimation of the defensive strength of the *Virginia;* it also took too little account of the shoalness of the water, which seriously restricted rapid maneuver by any of his deep-draft vessels.

On March 8, 1862 Flag Officer Buchanan took his new command out from the Navy Yard into Hampton Roads. Her officers and crew were still strangers to each other. Workmen were still putting on the finishing

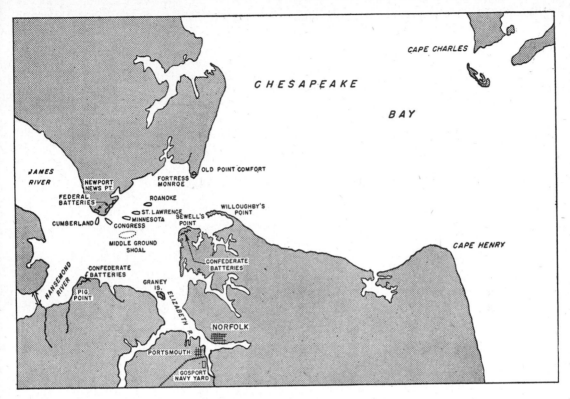

THE NORFOLK AREA, MARCH 8, 1862

touches as the *Virginia* was warped by armed tugs down the Elizabeth River. There were no engine run-ups and no gunnery drills. This, her trial voyage, was to be directly into action. Cheers went up from the crowds on the wharves and rooftops of Norfolk.

The deficiencies of the hybrid vessel became apparent as she steamed into deeper water by Sewell's Point. In calm water, her engines could manage at best a sluggish five knots. She answered her helm so reluctantly that it took over a half hour to turn her completely around.

Some small converted gunboats constituting the Confederate "James River Squadron" were blockaded up the river at Newport News by the *Congress* and the *Cumberland,* which lay at anchor at the northwestern extremity of Hampton Roads. Buchanan therefore turned first on these latter ships, intending by his attack on them to enable the Confederate gunboats to enter the anchorage.

The *Virginia* chugged ponderously northwest toward her adversaries. The Union vessels had hardly expected action that day. The commanding officer of the *Cumberland* was absent at a board of inquiry in the *Roanoke,* and on both *Congress* and *Cumberland* boats were at the booms, and laundry was drying in the lower rigging. Hastily the ships were cleared for action, and when the *Virginia* passed at about 1,500 yards range, she and the *Congress* exchanged a broadside. The heavy shells from the *Virginia*'s guns crashed through the oak planking of the *Congress,* whereas the hail of solid shot from the 25-gun port battery of the Union vessel bounced and ricocheted harmlessly from the greasy, sloping sides of the *Virginia.* The ram continued on toward the *Cumberland,* anchored farther to the west, ignoring the rapid and well-directed fire from that vessel.

With maximum way on, the *Virginia* crashed her ram into the *Cumberland's* starboard bow, crushing the wooden hull like an eggshell. At the moment of impact she fired her bow pivot into the stricken vessel, killing ten men at the number one gun. The *Cumberland* settled so rapidly that the *Virginia* barely escaped being dragged down with her victim, but the ram structure broke off as the vessel backed clear. The *Virginia*, still under heavy fire from the guns of the sinking vessel, slowly circled under her stern ports and raked her at 200 yards with a broadside which harvested a long windrow of dead and mangled on the decks of the wooden ship. The devotion and courage of the officers and crew of the *Cumberland* in continuing the hopeless fight is a splendid example of what the Old Navy meant by "iron men in wooden ships." With a third of her crew dead or wounded, with water surging into a hole in her side big enough to drive a horse and cart through, the *Cumberland* kept firing with every gun that would bear. As she sank, deck by deck, the gun crews simply joined the depleted crews on the deck above, until at length the magazines were flooded out and the vessel careened crazily to port. The last remaining gun crew fired its final shot and leaped into the water. Coming to rest on the shallow bottom, the *Cumberland* still had her mastheads above the water, and the flag of the sunken vessel still fluttered at her peak.

Meanwhile the *Virginia*, which had suffered only superficial topside damage and two casualties, turned her attention to the *Congress*. That ship, her officers realizing the invulnerability of the *Virginia* to their guns, had gotten under way with jib and topsails, and with the aid of a tug was run in near Signal Point to get the support of the land batteries. The *Congress* grounded in the shallows, but at least the *Virginia* with her great draft could not follow to ram. During this movement the *Congress* was attacked by the *Virginia's* tiny consorts, the armed tugs *Beaufort* and *Raleigh*, each of which carried one heavy rifled gun. These unarmored vessels were careful however to keep out of the way of the *Congress's* broadsides.

The *Virginia* was with some difficulty turned around in the shallows off the Union batteries on the lower James, which dueled the ship without much effect. But finally the ironclad lumbered down to a raking position off the stern of the *Congress* and at 150 yards threw shell after shell into the doomed vessel. These were devastating in their explosive effect; they also set her on fire. The acting commanding officer was killed. His successor saw his ship a flaming slaughterhouse, with not a single gun which could be brought to bear. He ordered the colors struck.

The Confederates attempted to accept the surrender and take off prisoners. But a regiment of troops ashore who had waded out in the shallow water kept up a galling musketry barrage, supported by artillery, which killed and wounded several of the Confederate boat party. Buchanan in a rage recalled the boarders, and ordered the *Congress* bombarded with red hot shot. Climbing topside to observe this operation, Buchanan was drilled in the leg by a Minie ball from an infantryman's rifle. Lieutenant Thomas ap Catesby Jones succeeded to the command of the *Virginia*.

During the two hours while the *Virginia* was destroying the *Cumberland* and the *Congress,* the James River squadron joined the *Virginia* and her diminutive escorts. The *Minnesota,* the *Roanoke,* and the *St. Lawrence* all had attempted to come to the aid of the stricken Union vessels. All had grounded before coming into effective range —the *Minnesota* so firmly that she was not successfully floated for four tides.

The *Virginia*, accompanied by the *Patrick Henry* and the *Jamestown,* now turned her attention to the helpless *Minnesota.* Fortunately the shoalness of the water prevented a near approach by the *Virginia,* and her marksmanship at 2,000 yards was such that only one shell struck its target at this time. The rifled guns of the smaller Southern gunboats did much more damage, but the single gun that the *Minnesota* was able to bring to bear finally drove them off. After about three hours of trying to approach nearer the *Minnesota,* the *Virginia* and her consorts steamed triumphantly back in the gathering dusk to an anchorage under Sewell's Point. In a single afternoon the Confederate ram had sunk a heavy frigate and a large sloop of war and had damaged another Northern vessel. Two hundred and fifty Union sailors had been killed or drowned. Including injuries to the boarding party, the *Virginia* had 21 killed and wounded. The *Patrick Henry* had four men scalded to death when her boiler was struck by a ball from the Newport News batteries.

Except for the loss of her ram, which occasioned a bad leak forward, the *Virginia* had suffered only superficial damage. The muzzles of two of her guns were smashed, and the tophamper was riddled and partly shot away. But her armor was not penetrated at any point, and she was ready for action on the following day.

Yet it was not so much in her accomplishments that the Confederates exulted. It was rather in the illimitable opportunities that seemed to be opening up. There appeared to be no reason why the *Minnesota,* the *Roanoke,* the *St. Lawrence,* and the host of little Union gunboats which remained in Hampton Roads could not be readily destroyed or driven away. The blockade would be broken. Foreign intervention was now, so it seemed, infinitely more likely. All the fondest hopes of Secretary Mallory seemed fully justified by the invulnerable *Virginia.* Bonfires of celebration were lighted off all over the South as the telegraph spread word of the victory.

ARRIVAL OF THE *MONITOR*

Yet even while the *Virginia* was wreaking havoc in the Union squadron off Norfolk, Ericsson's strange-looking little *Monitor* was laboring down the coast to get to the scene of the battle. Towed by a tug, and convoyed by the wooden steamers *Currituck* and *Sachem,* she had left New York after perfunctory trials on March 6. About noon on the 7th she ran into rough weather off the Delaware capes. Waves surging over the vessel flooded through the badly stoppered

hawse-pipes into the hull and down the stack and blower pipe. With the blowers disabled, the furnaces had insufficient draft, and the engine spaces filled with gases. The engineering force narrowly escaped asphyxiation: they were dragged topside unconscious to revive on the turret top. With all machinery inoperative, the water in the bilges was a serious worry to Lieutenant Worden; an awkwardly long bucket brigade attempted to maintain the vessel's small positive buoyancy. Toward evening the weather and sea improved, and it was possible to start the engines again. However, in the early morning of the 8th, the blowers were again flooded out. To render the volunteer crew even more miserable, the wheel-ropes jammed, so that the safety of the ship depended entirely on the manila hawser connecting her to the tug. This nightmarish voyage concluded about 4 PM on March 8, when the *Monitor* rounded Cape Charles and started up the bay toward Hampton Roads, from whence could be heard the sound of cannonading.

To a large extent the seagoing deficiencies of the *Monitor* stemmed from small, easily corrected defects of workmanship, and from the inexperience of her personnel. (The Executive Officer in particular was negligent in failing to provide adequate stoppering for her hawse-pipes.) The voyage is an eloquent reminder of the need for careful and detailed trials, for which there was no time with the *Monitor.*

Worden cleared his ship for action as he conned it up to Old Point Comfort. About nine in the evening he reported to Captain John Marston, Senior Officer Present, on the *Roanoke.* Marston ordered the *Monitor* to protect the grounded *Minnesota.*[6]

Her way was lighted by the flaming *Congress,* whose magazines finally exploded a little after midnight. The *Monitor* anchored just west of the *Minnesota,* and her exhausted crew attempted to get some sleep. Efforts continued all night to get the *Minnesota* afloat, but in vain.

About 6:30 AM on March 9 the morning

---

[6] Marston had received Navy Department orders to have the *Monitor* proceed to Washington. These he wisely disregarded.

fog had thinned just enough for the seamen in the Union vessels to see the exhaust steam of the *Virginia* as she came out of her anchorage under Sewell's Point. An hour or so later the sun appeared. By now the huge black ram had come south of the Middle Ground, and fired a shell into the rigging of the *Minnesota*. It was evident that she intended to turn into the channel north of the Middle Ground shoal. The *Minnesota* fired ineffectually with her stern guns.

Worden upped anchor and steamed around the *Minnesota* to approach the ram directly and engage her as far as possible from the nearly helpless frigate. Although the Confederates at first took it to be a mere floating buoy, or a "cheese box on a raft," the *Monitor* was nevertheless soon recognized by Jones and his officers as the radically designed Union ironclad of which they had read in the Norfolk papers. The *Virginia* opened fire with a rifled gun, and missed. Conserving her fire to point blank range, the *Monitor* swung her turret to bear at the moment she came alongside and rattled the frames of her adversary with two 11-inch shot, which struck the sloping casemate without penetrating. The *Virginia* turned to starboard sufficiently to bring her three-gun broadside to bear, and fired again, this time striking the *Monitor's* turret. The Confederate gunners were chagrined to see their heavy shell break up like ripe melons against the *Monitor's* plates, without discernibly denting them. There ensued a two-hour gunnery duel at very close range. Like a terrier baiting a bull, the *Monitor* kept close to her larger adversary, so that the *Virginia* could sometimes hardly bring a gun to bear. The *Virginia* was working badly, and in any event her 23-foot draft made her awkward to maneuver in the shallow waters of the Roads. The *Monitor* was operating as Ericsson had dreamed, and her mere 12-foot draft gave her much more working room. It was Worden's hope by repeated hits at pistol shot range to batter the *Virginia's* plates loose if he could not penetrate her hull through the armor. Blinding clouds of steam and black powder smoke enveloped the vessels most of the time during this duel at 40 yards or less.

Realizing the futility of trying to penetrate the armor of the *Monitor,* Jones determined to ram his opponent or to board her. After an hour of discouraging maneuvering with this end in view, Jones thought he saw his opportunity and ordered, "Full speed ahead!" But as the *Virginia* lumbered down upon her, the *Monitor* turned nimbly so that the blow was a glancing one, damaging the *Monitor* not at all, and springing another leak in the *Virginia's* own bow. The far greater maneuverability of the *Monitor* made boarding similarly infeasible. The Union vessel was virtually able to pick and hold any position relative to the *Virginia* that her commanding officer wished.

Resolved at any rate to destroy the *Minnesota,* Jones turned suddenly away from the *Monitor* and attacked the wooden frigate with the rifled bow gun of the *Virginia*. The *Minnesota* sought to defend herself with her broadside and her 10-inch pivot. This exchange had the expected result. The *Virginia* was apparently undamaged, and the battered *Minnesota* was set on fire. The tug *Dragon,* which had been futilely trying to pull the *Minnesota* off the bar, was destroyed by a shell through her boiler.

As quickly as possible, Worden brought the *Monitor* between the *Minnesota* and the enemy. In maneuvering for position, the *Virginia* now grounded. Both the *Minnesota* and the *Monitor* pounded their immobile adversary, and at this moment it seemed safe to predict the ram's destruction. But now occurred one of those chance events which so often upset the odds in battle. While the *Monitor* was standing in at 10 or 15 yards to try to deliver a *coup de grâce,* the *Virginia's* officers shifted their point of aim from the invulnerable turret of the *Monitor* to the tiny pilot house on the foredeck.

The pilot house, projecting only four feet above the deck, was made of 9-by-12-inch cast iron bars with a narrow eyeslit under the topmost bar. Inside were the stations of the conning officer, the pilot, and the helmsman. About 11:30 a lucky shell from the *Virginia* struck the front of the pilot house, and in its explosion drove powder fragments through the eyeslit into Lieutenant Worden's eyes—blinding him temporarily and otherwise wounding him seriously about the face. Worden sent for Lieutenant Samuel D. Greene, the Executive Officer, who was in the turret, but Greene did not assume the con of the ship for about 20 minutes. During this time the helmsman, lacking immediate direction, followed Worden's last order, which was to "sheer off." The effect was that the *Monitor* withdrew to the east toward Fortress Monroe.

The *Virginia* profited from this withdrawal to put out boats with kedges, by means of which she was successfully warped off the bottom. Seeing his iron protector apparently in retreat, the commanding officer of the *Minnesota* grimly made preparations to blow up his vessel rather than to allow her capture by the *Virginia*.

But the position of the ram herself was far from comfortable. Her leak forward had been made worse by her grounding. Furthermore her bow was so lightened by the loss of her prow and anchors that the water in her greatly increased her draft at the stern, whereas her bow tended to ride up so that her shield was almost out of water. When her pilots reminded Lieutenant Jones that the tide was falling, he decided that the risk of remaining on the scene was not justified by the slight advantage to be gained by destroying the battered *Minnesota*. The *Virginia*, leaking badly, her tophamper utterly shot away, chugged slowly back to her Sewell's Point anchorage. The fight had lasted more than four hours.

Meanwhile Lieutenant Greene, having at last taken the con, wheeled the *Monitor* about and came back to the *Minnesota*. He threw two or three long-range shots at the departing *Virginia* but made no further attempt to pursue. Thus indecisively ended the most celebrated single-ship duel ever engaged in by American vessels.

Damage to the *Monitor* was slight, and that entirely confined to the pilot house. The *Virginia,* though no shot penetrated her casemate, was struck by nearly all of the 41 solid shot that the *Monitor* fired at her; these cracked her plates, and in some instances fractured the wooden backing. Damage to her superstructure and hull required extensive repairs in drydock.

AFTERMATH OF THE BATTLE

The usual conclusion of historians is that the battle was a tactical draw but a strategic victory for the *Monitor*. Yet the thoughtful student is left with certain tantalizing questions that can be answered only with careful reservations: Why was the engagement so indecisive? Why did the *Monitor* fail to pursue her adversary toward Norfolk? Why was the duel never renewed? How could the evident structural superiority of the *Monitor* have been made the basis of the complete victory which Ericsson had a right to expect from his invention?

A partial answer to several of these questions can be summarized as inadequate testing of material, and inadequate training of personnel. This in turn stemmed not so much from oversight or carelessness as from the precipitate need of the *Monitor* in Hampton Roads as the single adequate weapon to cope with the *Virginia*.

The new 11-inch battery of the *Monitor* was restricted by Bureau of Ordnance order to 15-pound charges. Yet later experience was to make 25- and even 30-pound charges common. On seeing their shot fail to penetrate the *Virginia's* casemate, Worden and Greene must have been sorely tempted to increase their charges. Yet with the two guns mounted side by side, to burst a barrel would have been to destroy completely the offensive power of the ship. To disobey a categorical order and thereby to risk the destruction of an unfamiliar engine of war entrusted to them is surely too much to expect of junior officers.[7] There can however be no question that the *Monitor* would have

---

[7] The celebrated explosion of the "Peacemaker" aboard the *Princeton* was a fresh enough memory in the minds of naval officers to insure double respect for bureau restrictions against overcharging.

destroyed her antagonist if she had used sufficient powder charges.

The officers and crew of the *Monitor,* as the above account indicates, began the fight nearly exhausted from the harrowing voyage down the coast. This helps to explain why Greene did not see fit to pursue the *Virginia.* He doubtless felt he would be better advised to take a rested crew in under the guns of the Confederate shore batteries. Gustavus Fox, Assistant Secretary of Navy, who was at the scene of the engagement in a tug, apparently was not altogether satisfied with Greene's performance: he immediately relieved him of his temporary command of the *Monitor.*

Washington was still jittery over the threat of the *Virginia,* and on March 10 Gideon Welles, either on his own initiative or on the advice of the President, issued peremptory orders that the *Monitor* was not to be taken under the fire of the shore batteries. Too much depended on her continuing to exercise control of the Roads to risk her injury or destruction. The grand strategic offensive of McClellan's army could best be served by a tactically defensive object on the part of the Navy.

The *Virginia* was badly enough damaged to require much repair work. In addition, her officers realized she was no real match for the *Monitor.* Nevertheless, Josiah Tatnall, her new commanding officer, took her out into the Roads on April 11, May 8, and May 9. The Confederate command had worked out a scheme by which the *Monitor* would be boarded by crews of the wooden gunboats while the *Virginia* kept her closely engaged. This desperate plan was frustrated by the arrival of substantial reinforcements to the Union blockading force, including the ironclads *Galena* and *Naugatuck.* Goldsborough had moreover acquired a large fast vessel, the *Vanderbilt,* which was to be used as a ram against the *Virginia,* if that vessel could be enticed out into deep water. Both sides exercised caution in their use of their strongest naval weapons, since the risk of loss of either the *Virginia* or the *Monitor* seemed to outweigh the advantage of destroy-ing the adversary. The loss of the *Monitor* would seriously impair McClellan's land campaign now developing on the peninsula. On the other hand, the Confederate Government deemed Norfolk safe from assault as long as the *Virginia* stood at its water gates. The ram was a one-ship fleet-in-being.

By April 5 some 121,500 blue-coated soldiers of the Army of the Potomac, with all their equipment, had been landed on the peninsula. In spite of overwhelming numerical superiority, McClellan dallied before the thinly held Confederate line anchored on Yorktown until Johnston quietly abandoned it on the night of May 3. Pursuit brought on a partial and indecisive engagement near Williamsburg on May 5, after which the Confederates continued their withdrawal unmolested. The effect however was to leave the whole lower peninsula from the York to the James River, up to the line of the Chickahominy, in Union hands, and to open the James River to Union gunboats. Thus Norfolk and Portsmouth were between two Union forces—the Army of the Potomac and Burnsides' command, which was advancing north from North Carolina. Finding their position no longer tenable, the Confederate forces on May 10 rather precipitately abandoned the Norfolk area with its invaluable Navy Yard. Almost at once Union troops from Fortress Monroe moved in.

An effort was made to lighten the *Virginia* enough to take her up the James River to Drewry's Bluff, but the scheme had to be given up as impracticable. On the other hand her general lack of seaworthiness and her undependable engines made it impossible for her to try to fight her way out into the bay and to the open ocean. Regretfully, Commander Tatnall ordered her blown up.

The crew of the *Virginia,* together with those of the *Patrick Henry* and the smaller gunboats, manned the Confederate batteries at Drewry's Bluff, where they were to stop the Union gunboats in their efforts to fight their way up the James to Richmond. After a number of severe battles (Seven Pines, Fair Oaks, Seven Days', and so on), McClellan's force—though its farthest advance reached almost to the suburbs of Richmond—was withdrawn. McClellan, the magnificent drillmaster, had created an unconquerable army. But he had demonstrated all too clearly that he lacked the perseverance and moral courage that his army deserved in its commander. The Federal occupation of Norfolk was the only permanent harvest of the campaign.

Later in the year the *Monitor* foundered in a gale off the Carolina capes, taking with her a part of her crew. In her brief life she had by stopping the *Virginia* not only averted a serious threat to the blockade; she had also by her presence in Hampton Roads made possible the carrying out of the Army's offensive in the Peninsula. And her design fathered a numerous class of improved models, which were to perform notable service in the war. She was an important influence in ship design for more than 40 years—both in the United States and abroad.

OTHER IRONCLADS

The Confederates built a number of other ironclads, none of which enjoyed the early success of the *Virginia*. This partly stemmed from the fact that the South was never in a position to profit from the technological lessons of the *Virginia-Monitor* engagement, and partly from the fact that it never again had the initial advantage of surprise and novelty.

Early in 1863 two small ironclads (roughly of the *Virginia* model) sortied against the wooden blockaders off Charleston and inflicted some injury. But these were contained by superior Union ironclads which were sent down for the purpose. Later the same year Savannah sent out the *Atlanta,* an ironclad in most respects more formidable than the *Virginia.* She was immediately engaged by the monitor *Weehawken,* which with just five shots compelled the Southern vessel to surrender. Two solid shot from the monitor's new 15-inch Dahlgren gun smashed through the four-inch armor belt of the *Atlanta* and devastated the interior of the ship. Another Confederate ironclad, the *Albe-*marle, was the occasion of a dashing exploit by a junior officer. This vessel was built in 1864 for service on the North Carolina sounds, with the object of interfering with the blockade and Union amphibious activity in the area of Plymouth. Since no Union ironclads could be spared immediately to cope with her, Lieutenant William B. Cushing USN volunteered to destroy her at anchor with a spar torpedo rigged to the bow of a launch. One night in late October 1864 he went in with a picked crew and succeeded in getting his boat under the counter of the ram just as he was discovered and fired upon. Cushing exploded his "torpedo" successfully, blowing the bottom out of the *Albemarle,* which immediately sank. The launch was also sunk by the explosion, but Cushing and one of his men, who plunged into the chilly water, swam downstream to safety.[8]

"SUBMARINES"

Not only in armored vessels was the Civil War the incubator of modern naval material. Efforts were made by the Confederacy to produce successful submarines. A compromise model, known as a *David,* was a steam-driven vessel, wholly submerged except for her funnel and hatches. For offense she carried a spar torpedo. The first of these vessels was built at New Orleans, but never got an opportunity for a combat trial. Another, built in Charleston, attacked the *New Ironsides* in October 1863. The attack was unsuccessful. Another attack, on the *Wabash,* failed also, apparently by reason of an insufficient explosive charge in the torpedo.

An effort at a true submarine was also made: a tiny cylinder of boiler plate propelled by hand-cranks geared to its screw. This vessel drowned no fewer than five separate volunteer crews before General Beauregard, in command at Charleston, forbade her being operated submerged again. In February 1864 she made a surface attack on U.S.S. *Housatonic,* which she succeeded in tor-

---

[8] Two of Cushing's men were killed; 19 were captured.

pedoing. The unlucky craft sank with her victim.

Most of the technological innovations attempted by the South were well conceived, but the lack of enough trained engineers and above all the lack of an adequate industrial base prevented much success. It was the misfortune of the South that it was compelled to fight in the first modern war—a war in which economic war potential was quite as important as personal bravery and skill in command.

19

The Mississippi Valley Campaign,

Part I: the Road to Vicksburg

"THE MISSISSIPPI IS THE BACK-bone of the Rebellion," said Abraham Lincoln in 1861; "it is the key to the whole situation." Subsequent events proved Lincoln right, for the Federal victories that won control of the river and split the Confederacy made possible the ultimate preservation of the Union.

The significant details of the first year of the war in the Mississippi Valley fall chronologically into four major divisions: (1) political and military preparations for open warfare; (2) the series of engagements by means of which Union forces broke through the Confederacy's first line of defense—the "Northwest Barrier," as it is sometimes called —and withstood the Confederacy's desperate counterattack; (3) the Union navy's capture of New Orleans, made relatively easy because Confederate strength was concentrated on the up-river defenses; and (4) the collapse of the Confederacy's second line of defense on the Memphis and Charleston Railroad. At the end of this first year of fighting Union forces briefly controlled all of the Mississippi.

THE MISSISSIPPI VALLEY PREPARES FOR WAR

In the spring of 1861 the Mississippi River and its tributaries drained a confused, disjointed land. The up-river states were as firmly loyal to the Union as the down-river states were to the Confederacy, and each area provided the greatest reservoir of manpower and foodstuffs available to its side. Between them lay the four border states—Missouri and Arkansas, Kentucky and Tennessee— and those counties of Virginia tied to the economy of the Ohio Valley. Divided loyalties, divisive interests, and all the political pressure the North and South dared to bring finally split this border country asunder. Arkansas and Tennessee seceded to join the Confederacy; Missouri fell into civil strife which continued for over a year before the state was brought entirely under Union control; Kentucky's legislators declared their state "neutral"; and Virginia's 50 western counties formed the new state of West Virginia as part of the Union. These fateful acts marked the breakdown of strenuous efforts to prevent war.

From the beginning the down-river Confederate states had assured the Northwest that the Mississippi would be kept open to free navigation. Common sense dictated however that Confederate artillery should control the heights at Vicksburg as a precaution against invasion. Such seemingly warlike acts led to rumors that river boats were being stopped for customs payment at each of the seceded states. These rumors, in turn, contributed to prophecies of economic disaster for the up-river farmers, much of whose produce had usually been shipped through New Orleans. Events and rumors alike stemmed from the fact that control of the Mississippi was a vital necessity to each of the adversaries.

The natural strongpoint which the Confederacy desired as the northern anchor of its river defense positions was the shipping center of Columbus, Kentucky's main Mississippi River port and terminus of railroads extending south all the way to the Gulf. But Columbus was in Kentucky and Kentucky was at that time neutral. Confederate leaders recognized that if only Kentucky would join with them their entire river position would be immeasurably strengthened, giving them the broad Ohio as a natural northern boundary. Both sides had been accepting volunteers from Kentucky; each was hopeful that it could be won over. Finally, in September 1861, the Confederacy risked sending General Leonidas Polk north with forces to occupy Columbus as a countermove to Federal activity on the Missouri shore across the river. "The necessity," said President Jefferson Davis, "justifies the action." As a consequence of this Southern invasion the Kentuckians officially declared for the Union and excused the Federal occupancy of Paducah that shortly followed. At last the struggle for the Mississippi Valley was to be resolved by force of arms.

In the west as in the eastern theater of operation, neither the North nor the South was prepared for war. Each government had to improvise, placate, postpone, and yet somehow get a properly trained, led, and supported force into the field. Each government suffered from a plague of military amateurs and the popular belief, particularly prevalent in the North, that victory would be quick and cheap. Further, the Mississippi Valley campaign was without precedent. Transportation, communications, and logistics of this first "modern" war presented entirely new problems, magnified by the complications of joint and amphibious operations.

The river system itself held a unique position of importance, for steamboats still provided the primary means of transportation in this region.[1] Besides "Ole Man River," flowing 1,000 miles to cover the 500 between Cairo, Illinois and New Orleans, there were its navigable tributaries, the Ohio, the Tennessee, the Cumberland, the Arkansas, and the Red. Each river was an avenue for commerce, but it was also a barrier to overland transportation. Whoever controlled these rivers enjoyed four major advantages: (1) the best available line of logistic support, (2) control of the economy of the area drained by the river, (3) denial of those two advantages to the enemy, and (4) a barrier obstructing normal use of the railroads and highways which crossed the river. Though such control could be exercised and exploited only with the aid of naval forces, there was not a single warship on the Mississippi when hostilities began.

---

[1] The railroad, available for the first time in a major war, provided the second most efficient means of transportation. A single line might easily replace the 2,000 wagons and 10,000 horses required to supply a Civil War army of 50,000 men at a distance of three day's march from their nearest base. There were disadvantages as well: rolling stock was in short supply; trackage became an obvious target for guerillas and cavalry raids; in unfriendly territory, large numbers of troops had to be withdrawn from the combat forces for guard duty. The movement of men and materials on the inadequately developed Southern railroads proved more expensive and less reliable than transportation by means of the rivers. A third means of communication, the telegraph, likewise profoundly influenced the war. The mischief of interference with the commander in the field by telegrams from the higher level commander in the rear—all the way up to the President, whether Lincoln or Davis—has been better publicized than the greater efficiency and the possibility of centralized direction that it fostered.

The Confederacy had neither the facilities, the skilled labor, nor the material to build an adequate naval force for the inland waters. No Southern mill west of Richmond, Virginia could roll iron plates thick enough to stop anything heavier than a rifle bullet. Through heroic efforts and great ingenuity the Confederacy eventually produced three ironclads—the *Manassas,* the *Louisiana,* and the *Arkansas*—which saw action on the Mississippi, and a small fleet of wooden gunboats converted from river steamers. By contrast, the industrial North was able to build a formidable flotilla of ironclad gunboats, the nucleus of a steadily augmented fleet of river warships which were supplemented at times by the ships of the seagoing navy.

The first Union gunboats on the Mississippi were the *Tyler,* the *Lexington,* and the *Conestoga,* converted from wooden side-wheeled steamers. They were about 180 by 42 by 6 feet. Each was protected against musket fire by a five-inch oak bulwark and was armed with a mixture of 32-pounders and eight-inch guns. These were soon followed by the seven Eads ironclads, four of which were built at Carondelet, near St. Louis, where 4,000 men worked day and night, seven days a week, under the contract awarded in August 1861 to the river industrialist, James B. Eads. The *De Kalb, Carondelet, Cincinnati, Louisville, Mound City, Cairo,* and *Pittsburg,* as they were named, had casemates at a 35-degree angle, plated with 2½-inch iron sheet and pierced for three bow guns, four guns to a broadside, and two stern guns—a total of 13 heavy guns. Two single cylinder engines turned a 22-foot sternwheel protected by the after casemate, and drove these ponderous craft (175 by 51½ by 6 feet) at about seven knots. Most powerful of all the river warships was the *Benton,* Eads' conversion of a twin-hulled snagboat, which was to become flagship of the fleet. She measured about 200 by 75 feet, carried 16 guns, and was somewhat more heavily armored than the other ironclads. Ninth and last of the original ironclads was the *Essex,* a conversion of approximately the same dimensions as the *Benton.*

The Western Flotilla, as these ships were officially called, was actually the Union Army's navy and was under army control. The ships were commanded by regular naval officers however and the very existence of the flotilla as a fighting force must be credited to its flag officer, Captain Andrew Hull Foote USN. Secretary Welles had ordered Foote in September 1861 to report to the army and to direct the preparation of an inland fleet. In the midst of the war-born chaos of Union mobilization, Foote had a task to accomplish that demanded the utmost of his experience, perseverance, and courage. Overcoming every obstacle created by an ambiguous command relationship and by shortages of money, material, trained personnel, and supply, he scored the greatest if least heralded victory of his career by bringing into being the naval force with which he later spearheaded the first major Union offensive in the Mississippi Valley.

THE FIRST LINE OF CONFEDERATE DEFENSE

In all the Confederacy there was no natural line of defense connecting the Mississippi and the Alleghenies. Without the Ohio River as a barrier, the best the South could do in preparation for the inevitable Union attack was to substitute a makeshift line of strong points anchored on the Mississippi at Columbus, Kentucky, and on the Alleghenies at Cumberland Gap. Between the Confederate left flank, where General Polk's artillery denied the use of the river to the Northerners, and the right flank, where a Confederate army at Mill Springs guarded the approaches to the pass through the mountains, there were two possible invasion routes. One was via the Tennessee and Cumberland Rivers, each of which was navigable into the very heartland of the South. To plug this route the Confederates erected forts on the rivers where they flowed only 12 miles apart just south of the Kentucky border. The other invasion route was via the Louisville railroad, which branched at Bowling Green to provide connections with all the main rail lines in

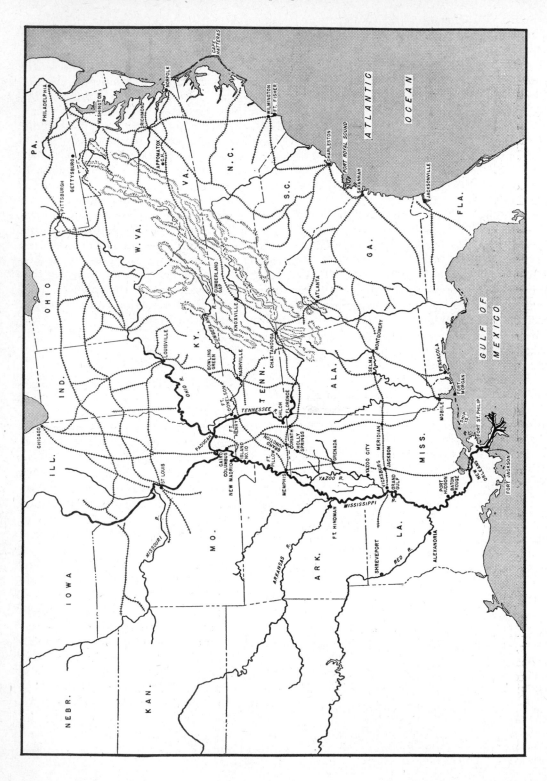

INLAND TRANSPORTATION IN THE CONFEDERACY

the South. To safeguard that route, a Confederate army occupied Bowling Green and proceeded to fortify its position.

A glance at the map opposite will show the critical weakness of the Confederate line of defense. Taken together, the western extremes of Kentucky and Tennessee form a peninsula, bounded on the west, north, and east respectively by the Mississippi, Ohio, and Tennessee Rivers. If the Tennessee were in Northern hands, the Confederate first line of defense on the Mississippi could be outflanked by water and made untenable. It should also be noted that the Tennessee River is paralleled in part by the Cumberland and that via the Cumberland Northern gunboats could sever both of the rail lines supplying the Confederates at Bowling Green. In short, against properly coordinated Union naval and military power, the so-called "Northwest Barrier" would be most difficult to defend.

Flag Officer Foote and the Union army commander in that area, Brigadier General Ulysses S. Grant, fully appreciated this situation. They believed that a rapid thrust, with water-borne logistic and gun-fire support, could drive a salient through the Confederate line while the South was just beginning to prepare its defenses. Grant had already demonstrated initiative and a rare understanding of what was the proper Union objective. He had established a base at Cairo, Illinois when General Polk occupied Columbus. And it was he who had occupied Paducah—which commands the lower Ohio, Tennessee, and Cumberland Rivers—before the Confederate forces could carry out their plan to occupy it themselves. Furthermore, Grant and Foote knew how to work together, or apart, as necessary. They had gained experience in a skirmish with the Confederates on the Missouri shore opposite Columbus, in the so-called Battle of Belmont. No other action of consequence ensued until a Union army defeated the Confederates at Mill Springs in January 1862. Then, with great difficulty, Grant and Foote gained permission to launch their joint operation with seven gunboats and 17,000 troops against the forts on the Tennessee and Cumberland.

THE GUNBOATS CAPTURE FORT HENRY

Fort Henry, hastily constructed by the Confederates on low, partially flooded ground on the east bank of the Tennessee river about 60 miles upstream from the Federal base at Paducah, was the initial Union objective of this campaign. Its few guns and small garrison could offer only token resistance against Flag Officer Foote when he arrived with the seven gunboats on February 6, 1862, four days after his departure from the main Union river base at Cairo, Illinois. The action that followed was short and decisive. Foote did not wait for the Federal army, delayed by muddy roads and high water, to make the simultaneous attack from the rear that the official plan had called for. As soon as the gunboats were within range, he opened fire, closed to 600 yards, and within two hours pounded Fort Henry into surrender. Most of the 3,000-man Confederate garrison had withdrawn to Fort Donelson, 12 miles away on the west bank of the Cumberland River, leaving General Tilghman and fewer than 100 men to delay the Union offensive. Of the 11 Confederate guns, seven had been rendered useless. Casualties were light on both sides, the greatest damage being suffered by the ironclad *Essex,* which lost 32 men, most of whom were scalded to death when a shot pierced her middle boiler. The brief action illustrated clearly the advantages that accrued to the Union from its gunboat flotilla.

Naval power permitted the joint operation against Fort Henry to achieve surprise and gain tactical success. It demonstrated that in the Mississippi Valley heavy artillery—the gunboats' batteries—might be moved more rapidly by water than even infantry could move by land. It opened and controlled an avenue for adequate logistic support. Further, it allowed for a speedy exploitation of the victory, keeping the enemy off balance. Union gunboats immediately proceeded up-river and penetrated into the Confederacy's heartland as far as Muscle Shoals at the head of navigation near Florence, Alabama. They compelled the Confederates to blow up several shiploads of military stores and captured the large steamer *Eastport,* which was being converted into a gunboat. Their landing parties ripped up the rails and destroyed the bridge of the only railroad connecting Columbus and Bowling Green. By disrupting enemy communications and by making an advance base at Fort Henry immediately available to Grant, they enabled the Union forces to turn promptly to their next major objective. The Union army's appreciation of its navy's activities is reflected in the renaming of Fort Henry as Fort Foote.

UNCONDITIONAL SURRENDER AT FORT DONELSON

Fort Donelson had been constructed to guard the river route to Nashville. It stood above a great bend in the Cumberland on the high ground of the west bank. There Brigadier General Gideon J. Pillow CSA with about 15,000 men elected to resist the Union attack. The Confederate army had its back to the river, its right flank made unassailable by flooded Hickman Creek, and its front established on a series of well fortified ridges paralleling the river. On its left flank, a road leading south through Charlotte to Nashville was its only line of retreat.

While Foote's gunboats made the long passage down the Tennessee and then up the Cumberland, the Union troops marched across the barren winter countryside without interference. By February 13, 1862 Grant's lines formed an arc running south from Hickman Creek and then east toward the Cumberland. When the first of the gunboats, the ironclad *Carondelet,* arrived, Grant ordered her to provide diversion by firing on the fort so that the Union troops could advance to cut the Charlotte road. The other Union gunboats, convoying 5,000 fresh troops and all necessary supplies, arrived next morning to strengthen the army, some of whose members had frozen to death that night in a snow and sleet storm and 12-degree

temperature. The ironclad gunboats then led the way upstream against Fort Donelson's water batteries. A heavy artillery duel followed. Only two of the fort's guns had a range equal to that of the gunboats' heavy armament, but instead of bombarding from an advantageous distance, Foote advanced to within 400 yards. He concentrated on the water battery, hoping to pass by it and then destroy the fort on the bluff by enfilade fire, but plunging shot from the fort soon disabled his two best ironclads and a bursting gun forced the *Carondelet* out of the action. Wounded himself, Foote reluctantly ordered his ships to withdraw. The flotilla had suffered more than 50 casualties as well as serious material damage.

In spite of this Union reverse, the Confederate forces were trapped by Grant's army, and the mere presence of the Union gunboats helped to make a mass escape across the Cumberland inconceivable. At a staff meeting that night the Confederate leaders decided to open the next day's battle with a desperate attack in an effort to recapture the Charlotte road as a line of retreat. Early the next morning, while Grant conferred with Foote aboard the *St. Louis,* 8,000 Confederate soldiers broke the Union hold on the Charlotte road so easily that General Pillow forgot about withdrawal and attempted to roll up the Union line. Grant rallied his numerically superior forces. With some aid from the *Carondelet,* he inflicted 2,000 casualties and forced Pillow's army back into its original position. The Confederate general with a small force escaped up river during the night in the two steamers available, while Colonel Nathan B. Forrest's cavalry stole away through the frozen marshes. The next day Fort Donelson's 10,000 surviving defenders accepted Grant's demand for "unconditional surrender."

The North was jubilant. Grant became the popular hero, "Unconditional Surrender" Grant. Union gunboats controlled the Cumberland and the lines of communication crossing it. The Confederate forces that had already withdrawn from Bowling Green to Nashville now withdrew from the Tennessee capital before Foote's gunboats could destroy the great railroad bridge there. The state government officials dashed away from the undefended city, which was soon occupied by Union troops.

Repercussions of the victory immediately made themselves felt on the Mississippi. At Columbus, Confederate General Polk had to move fast to prevent being trapped himself. He sent much of his artillery to Island No. 10, the nearest Confederate strong point downstream, and retreated with most of his army all the way to Corinth, Mississippi, a junction where major east-west and north-south railroads crossed and which was to become the key position in the second line of Confederate defense.

With control of the Tennessee, and the Nashville flank secured, Grant and Foote with available reinforcements could have overwhelmed all Confederate defenses on the Mississippi above and including Memphis. By maintaining the initiative they might have prevented the regrouping of Confederate forces for a counterattack. Instead, Grant's victorious army was kept inactive for almost two months while Major General Henry W. Halleck, commander of the Department of Missouri and Grant's immediate superior in the chain of command, pursued various secondary objectives and indulged in personal accusations against his successful subordinate. During the opening year of the war neither the North nor the South could be made to realize that a military victory had to be fully exploited if a final decision was ever to be reached.

ACTION ON THE MISSISSIPPI—ISLAND NO. 10

Union victories in Missouri as well as at Fort Donelson necessitated a general Confederate withdrawal on both sides of the Mississippi to a strong defensive position 60 miles below evacuated Columbus. Here the river made two 180-degree turns and carved two thumb-shaped peninsulas out of the river-bottom country. The more easterly of these peninsulas extended south from the Missouri shore. It was heavily wooded and almost entirely flooded by the high water of early spring. Off its tip lay Island No. 10, the tenth island down river from Cairo. On that

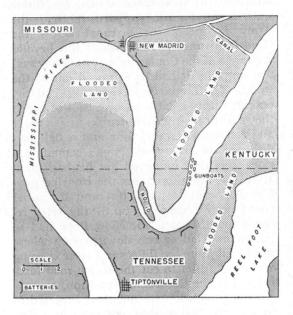

ISLAND NO. 10

island and on the high ground of the westerly thumb, which extended north from the Tennessee shore, 7,000 Confederate soldiers and 130 guns withdrawn from Columbus were reinforced by a garrison that, after spiking its guns, had abandoned New Madrid on the Missouri shore. Six gunboats and several support ships augmented these forces. These wooden gunboats the Confederates considered practically irreplaceable; they were not to be used against Federal artillery, or ironclad gunboats, except in the gravest emergency.

Opposed to them was Union Brigadier General John Pope in Missouri with a Federal army of 20,000 men and the support of part of the gunboat flotilla. Pope's problem was to get at the enemy. Reelfoot Lake, marshes, and spring floods made it impossible for the Federals to march along the east bank of the Mississippi in an encircling movement, and it was just as much out of the question to cross the river below Island

No. 10, where the Confederate warships could make short work of destroying the rafts and small boats to which the Union army would be limited.

Pope first occupied New Madrid and established his base there. Then, for direct water-borne logistic support, he had the Army Engineers cut a canal across the flooded Missouri peninsula on a line beyond the range of the Confederate guns. The canal was not dug; it had to be sawed out of the woods. The Engineers devised a special rig, operated from a flat boat, by means of which they cut through the tree trunks under water and cleared a channel four and a half feet deep for the transports. Pope's communications were thus improved but his basic situation was not altered, for the ironclad gunboats drew at least six feet and the canal could not be deepened until the river receded months later. Somehow Pope had to get an ironclad or two down stream where their heavy guns could cover a river crossing and enable him to cut the single road leading out of the Confederate position.

Even ironclads were not then expected to survive the hail of shot and shell in a daylight run past the Confederate defenses; nor was it thought that a cumbersome ironclad could possibly be navigated at night through the wayward currents of that torturous gantlet without grounding—and grounding while trying to stay in the deep water on the Conferedate side of the bend would mean capture. But among Foote's gunboat commanders Captain Henry Walke of the *Carondelet* was of a different opinion. He believed that his ship could make it under cover of darkness, with heavy chain faked down on deck for protection against plunging shot and a coal barge lashed alongside to protect the unarmored midships section. Since no one had a better alternative suggestion, he was given permission to try.

Walke made his departure on the night of April 5, 1862 while a furious thunderstorm was roaring down the river. Lightning flashes, he hoped, would aid his pilot and might blind the Confederate gunners. The *Carondelet's* crew, armed with cutlasses to repel boarders and reinforced by a contin-

gent of volunteer army sharpshooters, was ready. The shielded ironclad steamed slowly out into the wild night. Running so close that the Confederate guns fired too high, she swept around Island No. 10 without a single casualty. Proof that it could be done encouraged the ironclad *Pittsburg* to navigate the gantlet two nights later, also in a timely thunderstorm. Together the two gunboats gave Pope all the fire support he needed.

The complete Union victory that followed was an anticlimax. The Confederate ships scurried out of harm's way down river, so that there was no serious opposition to Pope's crossing below the Confederate defenses or to his seizure of the single line of retreat. Once more a Southern force was hopelessly trapped. The Confederate troops surrendered the next day with their heavy guns and a great quantity of supplies and ammunition. Thanks to the *Carondelet,* the victory had not cost the life of a single Union soldier.

This victory had little influence on the course of the war beyond effecting an immediate reduction in Confederate strength. Within a few days a great battle was to be fought on the banks of the Tennessee and the ironclad gunboats would be left with the task of clearing the Mississippi all the way south to Vicksburg.

THE CONFEDERATE COUNTERATTACK: THE BATTLE OF SHILOH

Although most of the details of the bloody Battle of Shiloh belong in the realm of military rather than naval history, an understanding of the Union conquest of the Mississippi demands some appreciation of what happened at Shiloh and of the part played there by naval power. The surrender of Fort Donelson had deluded the North into the expectation of a quick, final victory in the west. Presumably the Union forces would continue on the offensive with their immediate objective the defeat of the Confederate army covering the railroad junction of Corinth, Mississippi. Halleck planned to lead the attack in person. He could supplement Grant's army with Buell's, brought from Nashville, and reinforce them both with newly recruited troops from the North. Supplies could be shipped up the Tennessee River to Pittsburg Landing, on the west bank, only 20 miles northeast of Corinth. But administrative work in St. Louis caused Halleck to delay leaving his headquarters.

Meanwhile divisions of the Union army gradually assembled. Grant established his headquarters nine miles downstream from Pittsburg Landing at Savannah, the point on the east bank of the river where Buell's forces were expected to arrive on their way from Nashville. The bulk of Grant's army advanced to Pittsburg Landing and deployed almost exactly as General Pillow's Confederate forces had at Fort Donelson. The Union force was backed against the Tennessee. However, the river was a source of Union strength—a broad highway for supplies, reinforcements, and, if necessary, withdrawal, not a barrier as the Cumberland had been for the Confederates at Fort Donelson. The Union army's flanks were covered by two creeks large enough to be of natural defensive value. Its front extended a short distance along both sides of the road leading to Corinth. There, just beyond the rough, wooded terrain near the river, stood the Shiloh meeting house, a simple log structure from which the battle takes its name.

The Confederate leaders, perfectly aware of what Halleck intended to do, had begun an energetic concentration of their own forces under the skilled leadership of General Albert Sydney Johnston, who held a command position in the South analogous to Halleck's in the North. In a little over a month's time he assembled 50,000 men at Corinth. By moving fast, he planned to strike the Federals at Pittsburg Landing before Buell's army had time to join Grant's. He would strike as soon as possible, break the Union left flank in a surprise attack, capture Pittsburg Landing to prevent escape via the river, and pin the disorganized defenders in a bend of the creek that covered their original right flank. As events proved, Johnston was gambling his life and almost won.

Grant's division commanders, anticipating their own offensive, had taken only routine precautions against an attack on their troops. There was no plan for fire support from the gunboats. The troops were merely camped, not properly deployed. When the Confederate attack came on the morning of April 13, 1862 Grant was down-river at Savannah. There, just the previous evening, he had informed the commanding general of the first of Buell's divisions to arrive that his troops would be taken to Pittsburg Landing by boat some time the following week. Although Grant later denied that he was tactically surprised, certainly he thought that Johnston was patiently waiting for him at Corinth.

During the first day's battle the Confederates crushed the Union left flank and almost reached Pittsburg Landing, as planned. That night the river boats brought up Buell's 20,000 troops and artillery from Savannah. During the second day Union counterattacks regained all lost ground. Early the third day the Confederate forces withdrew. Casualties exceeded 20,000 out of a total of approximately 90,000 combatants on both sides. Strategically Shiloh was a Union victory, for the South had failed in its effort to repulse the invaders. In other respects it was a draw which left the Union army in possession of the field, too stunned by slaughter and too battle-weary to pursue the retreating Confederate forces to their fortified positions at Corinth.

The turning point in the battle had occurred toward the end of the first day's fighting. After the Union left flank collapsed, victory was just beyond the Confederates' grasp. One immediate objective remained. Johnston's troops had to break through the Union rear, seize Pittsburg Landing, and thus sever Grant's river-borne line of communications. It was just at that point that two of the original wooden gunboats, the *Tyler* and the *Lexington,* made a crucial contribution to the battle. There is no evidence that they scored many hits, but their booming guns discouraged the weary Confederates and put heart into the retreating Union troops. The Union naval commanders concentrated on Confederate artillery batteries and sent shells screaming up the ravines that the attackers would have to cross. After the assault was repulsed, the gunboats fired fused shells at intervals all night long and caused the Southern troopers to withdraw as far as the abandoned Federal camps where the action had been begun. "In this repulse," reads Grant's official report, "much is due to the presence of the gunboats."

The entire campaign and in particular the outcome of the battle of Shiloh hinged upon control of the rivers by naval power. Had the *Tyler* and *Lexington* been in Confederate hands or had there been even a single Confederate ironclad—a ship like the *Carondelet,* for instance—Shiloh might well have been a Confederate victory. As it was, only the rapid reinforcing of the Union army by Buell's river-borne divisions and artillery determined that it was the Confederate, and not the Union, forces that broke off the encounter.

After Shiloh most of western Tennessee was secure in Union hands. The Confederacy's northwest barrier was lost, the strongest counterattack that the South could launch was repulsed, and Halleck would himself assemble an overwhelming army with intent to crush the second line of Confederate defense. Shiloh was a defeat for which the Confederacy would continue to pay. Defenses elsewhere had been dangerously reduced in complying with Johnston's urgent request for forces to turn back Grant before it was too late. As an immediate result, Shiloh contributed to the outcome of the major campaign, essentially naval, that was about to wrest New Orleans, the "Queen City of the South," from the Confederacy.

NEW ORLEANS AND ITS DEFENSES

Commercial enterprise and 170,000 inhabitants made New Orleans the Confederacy's richest and largest city. Trade was her life, guaranteed to her in abundance because of her unique geographical position. Lying in a bend of the Mississippi about 100 miles above the Head of the Passes, where the river divided to enter the Gulf of Mexico through three major channels, New Orleans controlled all the lower Mississippi Valley. From the decks of river steamers and ocean packets, passengers could look down into her bustling streets and prosperous business houses, secure behind the levee. It is true that railroads were changing transportation patterns and that the farmers of the Northwest were diverting more and more of their grain to New York for transshipment abroad, but New Orleans had fattened on almost 50 years of steamboat trade and still prospered.

The outbreak of actual hostilities and the appearance of the *Powhatan* and *Brooklyn* on blockade duty in the Gulf ended abruptly the hopes for a free Mississippi and a free port that New Orleans' citizens had held when Louisiana seceded. For a short time war seemed a glorious thing to them. The more optimistic assumed that the fate of the Northwest lay in their hands; the young men eagerly enlisted, delighting in exotic uniforms and marching to military bands. They viewed the Union blockade with contempt. The many-mouthed Mississippi and adjacent waters gave blockade runners an advantage over any blockading squadron the Union had ships to maintain. Their commerce-raiders would make the Yankee merchantmen pay dearly for the war. They hardly noticed the city's businesses closing one by one for the duration, as though for a holiday.

In September 1861 the Union Navy seized Ship Island. This island, about midway on the coastal route between New Orleans and Mobile, had been partially fortified by the Confederates and then abandoned. In Union hands it increased the efficacy of the blockade by supplying a sorely needed advance base. In October a Union squadron of four ships—*Richmond, Vincennes, Preble,* and *Water Witch*—occupied the Head of the Passes. They were intended to exert a strangle-hold on all ocean shipping to and from New Orleans; instead, the Confederates made a laughing stock of them. Shortly before dawn on October 12 the Confederate ram *Manassas,* a football-shaped ironclad armed with one gun, led the attack, supported by some fire rafts and, at a safe dis-

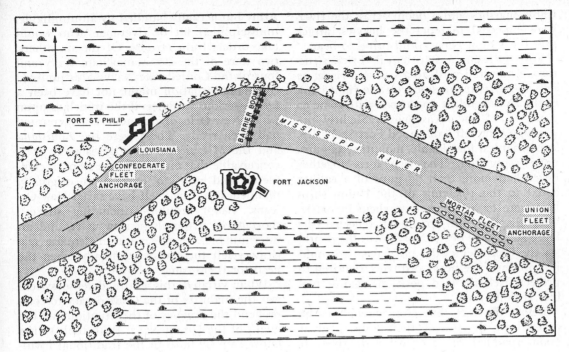

UNION AND CONFEDERATE FORCES BELOW NEW ORLEANS, 1862

tance, a little flotilla of wooden boats. Approaching unobserved, the *Manassas* rammed the *Richmond* and stove in three planks of the Union warship but lost her own smokestacks and the use of one engine. While she retreated up-stream, the panic-stricken Union fleet made a frantic effort to get out of the river. The *Richmond* grounded, and the *Vincennes* not only went aground but was abandoned with a slow fuse lighted to explode her magazines. Later, when it was apparent that the fuse must have spluttered out, the large ships were refloated; the Union squadron thereupon deserted the river for the more navigable waters of the Gulf. Reporting on these events, the British and French consuls in New Orleans questioned the ability of the Federal government to maintain the blockade.

Nevertheless by the beginning of 1862 the Confederate leaders felt serious concern for the safety and welfare of New Orleans. Cotton was piled high awaiting shipment. The rotting wharfs were falling into the river. Hard money had gone into hiding. Worst of all, the Confederate government's policy of giving priority to the defense of the Tennessee Valley kept drawing men, equipment, and supplies away from New Orleans. As a result, work progressed haphazardly on the city's defenses.

In theory, those defenses were excellent, comprising as they did an interior and an exterior line. The interior line consisted of fortifications thrown up around the city, extending from Lake Ponchartrain to the Chalmette Battery on the river, where Jackson had defeated the British in 1815. Such defenses would be unnecessary if the exterior line held. It was thought, and correctly, that the swamps around the city would discourage an overland approach. The weakest point was the river itself, and so the exterior defenses were concentrated on blocking the Mississippi about 90 miles below New Orleans at the Plaquemine Bend, where the river made one final turn before flowing into the Gulf. On that narrow front two forts, supported by the Confederate naval forces and with their flanks protected by impenetrable marshes and a boom across the river, were expected to repel the heaviest attack that the Union Navy could bring to bear.

Fort Jackson, a star-shaped, brick structure, a hundred yards to a side and rising 22 feet above its moat, stood on the right bank of the river bend. It was armed with some 90 guns, 16 of them casemated. Slightly upstream on the left bank stood Fort St. Philip, somewhat less formidable, mounting 52 guns, none casemated. The two forts together never had more than 39 guns of a caliber equal to the 165 guns of the Union ships that were to be opposed to them in battle. This disparity in armament reflected the basic advantage of the North over the South, for the Confederacy did not have, and could not produce, the heavy ordnance required to protect itself in fixed positions against mobile Union attack.

Below the forts but close enough to be covered by the fire of their guns, a great boom spanned the 700-yard wide river. It was constructed of the trunks of cypress trees, 40 feet long and five feet thick, held a few feet apart and parallel to the stream by large crosswise beams and by heavy chains, the bitter ends of which were secured on the banks of the river. A score and more of 3,000-pound anchors were attached at intervals along the boom to hold it against the current. Only some cataclysmic force, it was supposed, could penetrate such a barrier. No enemy ships could ram their way through it against the 4-knot current, and all efforts to sever the boom would be subjected to the fire of the forts and of the Confederate naval patrols. But winter storms, floating down thousands of tons of debris in spite of all Confederate efforts to tow the drift ashore, finally accomplished what was thought to be impossible. The boom broke, leaving a gap that was plugged as well as possible with dismasted schooners chained together, bows upstream.

In addition to these fixed defenses there were a dozen unarmored gunboats and the ironclad *Manassas* with her single 32-pounder carronade. Six of the gunboats belonged to the River Defense Fleet, nominally under the command of the Confederate

Army but actually handled by an unreliable, undisciplined lot of river-men who would take orders from no one. Of the six others, two were of the Louisiana State Navy and four of the Confederate Navy. This jumbled command situation might not have been a fatally serious weakness if the ironclads upon which New Orleans' defenders really counted had been ready. These were the *Louisiana* and the *Mississippi,* of 16 guns each. It is conceivable that either of these ships, if completed and able to operate as originally planned, could by itself have saved New Orleans. Labor troubles (including strikes), shortage of materials, a slow start, and an interminable struggle with inadequate machinery left these vessels unready when the need for them came.

What vitiated this entire defense system was the inability of the Confederacy to comprehend the urgency of the situation and the might of the Union Navy. With their spirits buoyed up by faith in the traditional invulnerability of New Orleans, Southerners generally believed that any real danger to the city was bound to come, if at all, from the north. Chains that might have repaired the shattered boom were being strung across the river north of the city as a protection against Foote's ironclad gunboats based at Cairo. The popular confidence has been well summed up in two sentences: "Nothing afloat could pass the forts. Nothing that walked could get through our swamps." [2] But Major General Mansfield Lovell, Commander of Confederate Department Number 1, with his headquarters in New Orleans, had very little with which to back this feeling of confidence. When Pensacola was abandoned, its guns went to Mobile, not to New Orleans as Lovell requested. Even when a major Union naval expedition appeared in March 1862 and began working large warships over the bars and into the Mississippi, Confederate troops and guns were being ordered out of New Orleans to the Tennessee Valley. By early April, with attack imminent, all regular troops had departed for the fighting north of Corinth. Lovell's entire

[2] *Battles and Leaders of the Civil War,* 4 vols. (New York, 1887), II, 19.

force consisted of the garrisons for the forts —less than 1,500 men—and in the city, 3,000 ninety-day militiamen, 1,800 of them armed only with shotguns, and a couple of companies of sharpshooters.

UNION PREPARATIONS FOR THE NEW ORLEANS CAMPAIGN

The Federal War Department originally estimated that the capture of New Orleans would require an army of at least 50,000 men with full naval support in a major campaign. Union army commanders assumed as a basic military truth that wooden ships, confined to a narrow channel and reduced by the current to a maximum speed of about four knots, could not survive an attempt to pass a heavy, casemated fortification such as Fort Jackson. That is why they turned a deaf ear to Assistant Secretary of the Navy Gustavus Fox when he insisted that a fleet alone could destroy Forts Jackson and St. Philip and compel the city to surrender. But Fox's opinions found ardent support from a naval officer who had become thoroughly familiar with the New Orleans area as a steamship captain in peacetime and who in November 1861 had just returned to Washington from duty with the Gulf Blockading Squadron. This officer was Fox's good friend Commander David Dixon Porter, the second son of Commodore David Porter of *Essex* fame in the War of 1812. He espoused Fox's plan for a naval attack on New Orleans with enthusiasm, ingenuity, and a wealth of descriptive detail, as shown in conferences with Secretary of the Navy Welles, President Lincoln, and George B. McClellan, then General in Chief of the Union Armies. The Army's objections were overcome by providing for a special mortar flotilla (Porter's idea) with which to silence the forts and by the Navy's willingness to undertake the expedition with only 13,000 troops, about to become available under Major General Benjamin Franklin Butler, as occupation forces.

Appropriately, the proposed mortar flotilla was commanded by Porter himself. Now 48 years old, he had the vigor and enterprise of a much younger man. He probably considered himself the Union Navy's most capable officer—an opinion shared by many of his juniors. Ambitious and self-confident, he frequently irritated his seniors, especially by habitually short-circuiting them in his voluminous personal correspondence with Gustavus Fox. For over-all command of the expedition however, Secretary of the Navy Welles had to find a senior officer, a man of action and of character, one who had the sound judgment of maturity, unflagging energy, and the respect of his officers and men. The success or failure of the expedition might well be determined by this choice.

In Welles' view, not one of the first 36 officers on the list of captains was both available and qualified. Number 37 was David Glasgow Farragut, a native of Tennessee and Porter's foster brother, 60 years old at this time. In Norfolk at the outbreak of the war, like Robert E. Lee at Arlington, Farragut had had to choose between his state and the Union. He and his wife considered themselves Virginians, but on the day that Virginia seceded, he embarked with his family for New York. Like Lincoln, he placed the Union first. Many in the South considered him a traitor; some in the North distrusted him, fearing that an underlying sympathy for the South might interfere with the rigorous execution of his duty in the war. But Farragut was Gideon Welles' choice for the command. The Secretary of the Navy recognized Farragut's loyalty, professional competence, and character; moreover, he sensed the rightness of having the expedition led by a man who had already felt the heartache of the struggle. As events proved, Welles could not have made a better choice. Later he was to refer to "the innate fearless moral courage of Farragut."

During the winter of 1861-62 the expedition was outfitted with unusual dispatch. In January Farragut received his orders naming him commander of the Western Gulf Blockading Squadron and designating the *Hartford* as his flagship. By the end of the month he sailed from the Chesapeake for the Gulf.

He was to await the arrival of the "formidable mortars," collect all ships that could be spared from the blockade, "reduce the defenses which guard the approaches to New Orleans," take possession of the city, and "hoist the American flag thereon." His orders, dated January 20, 1862 and written before any of the successes in the Tennessee Valley, also ingenuously stated: "If the Mississippi expedition from Cairo shall not have descended the river, you will take advantage of the panic to push a strong force up the river to take all their defenses in the rear." For good measure, Secretary Welles added: "You will also reduce the fortifications which defend Mobile Bay and turn them over to the army to hold." [3]

The mortar flotilla departed right on Farragut's heels. Porter had employed his "restless energy" to good cause. He supervised the purchase of 21 schooners in the New York-Philadelphia area, had them reinforced with heavy timbers amidships for service as mortar boats, and managed to get the 13-inch mortars, one for each boat, manufactured in Pittsburgh along with 30,000 rounds of ammunition. By the end of February the entire flotilla was holding target practice at Key West under Porter's direction, and Farragut was establishing his operational base at Ship Island.

The Union assault fleet consisted of four first-class steam sloops, *Hartford, Richmond, Pensacola,* and *Brooklyn;* the veteran sidewheeler *Mississippi;* and 12 smaller steam sloops, usually referred to as gunboats. The flagship *Hartford* was almost new, 225 feet long, of 2,900 tons, and capable of a maximum speed of 13 knots under sail and power but only eight knots when driven by her propeller alone. Under Farragut she usually carried 22 nine-inch Dahlgren shell guns and two rifled 30-pounders fore and aft. The other first-class sloops were similar in general dimensions and armament. Three of the smaller ships (*Oneida, Varuna,* and *Iroquois*) were 1,000-tonners with an average armament of nine guns and classified as screw corvettes; the nine others (*Cayuga, Itasca, Katahdin, Kennebec, Kineo, Pinola, Sciota, Winona,* and *Wissahickon*) were 500-tonners armed with two guns and classified as screw gunboats. Though built of wood and not armored, all 17 vessels were stanch, seagoing ships.

In early March 1862 Farragut had written Fox from Ship Island: "The moment Captain Porter arrives with his Mortar Fleet, I will collect my vessels, which are pretty close around me, and dash up the river, but I do not wish to make a display before I am ready, as I wish to keep up the delusion that Mobile is the first object of attack." [4] The Mississippi mud canceled this plan. Between the Confederate positions and the large ships of the assault fleet with their 16-foot draft the sand bars which had built up during the past year lay across the mouths of the river, so that the unused channels had in places only about 15 feet of water even during the early spring flood stage. Those obstructions held up the fleet for a full month. After repeated tries the *Brooklyn* plowed through mud into the deeper water at the Head of the Passes on March 12. The *Hartford* passed over the next day, but the *Richmond* took another ten days of trying. After two weeks of pulling and hauling, interrupted by a return to Ship Island for the removal of all possible weight, the *Pensacola* and the *Mississippi* finally worked their way through the mud on April 8. The *Colorado,* the largest of Farragut's ships, with a draft of 23 feet, never did get into the river and so cannot be numbered in the assault fleet. The smaller sloops and mortar boats were of sufficiently light draft to come and go as they pleased.

Farragut made good use of this month to collect intelligence and prepare his plans for the attack. He had been supplied with detailed descriptions of Forts Jackson and St. Philip. These were brought up to date by deserters who divulged the strength of the garrisons and reported that the Confederates were "sending every man they can to the northern army." [5] A Union raid on Biloxi brought him captured newspapers deplor-

---

[3] *Official Records of the Union and Confederate Navies in the War of the Rebellion,* Series I (Washington, 1904), XVIII, 8.

[4] *Ibid.,* 47.
[5] *Loc. cit.*

ing the fall of Nashville. Secretary Welles warned him of the ironclads under construction in New Orleans, for C.S.S. *Virginia* had just demonstrated at Hampton Roads what an ironclad could do against wooden ships. The added burden of administrative details in connection with maintaining the blockade from Mobile to the Mexican border and problems of supply forced Farragut to spend long hours at his desk. He had to borrow coal from the Army, only one of his ships had solid shot for use against an ironclad, and his requests for extraordinary supplies brought loud protests from the bureaus in Washington, where estimates were still based on a half century of peacetime frugality.

THE BATTLE OF NEW ORLEANS

In 1862 the Confederacy's confidence in the defense below New Orleans received the full support of orthodox military opinion, but the events of the week of April 18-24 were without modern precedent—Farragut's fleet accomplished the "impossible." Taken together, the actions of that week have long been referred to as "The Battle of New Orleans," although they occurred far from sight or sound of the city; severally, they include (1) the bombardment of the forts by the mortar flotilla, (2) the opening of the boom, (3) the fleet's run past the forts on the night of April 24, and (4) the near annihilation of New Orleans' naval defense forces.

Most of Farragut's captains were so impressed by the vulnerability of wooden ships against forts that they too believed the success of the attack depended upon the mortar flotilla. And many were firmly convinced that to run by the forts, leaving them in Confederate hands, was to place the fleet in a trap. Flag Officer Farragut did not concur. He had always been mildly skeptical of the mortars, but was willing to see what they could do and to let them distract the enemy while he prepared for the main assault. He expected that the forts, if by-passed, would soon surrender.

Porter's mortar boats moved into position on the night of April 17. Fourteen of them, their masts camouflaged with bushes, moored around the bend below Fort Jackson where they were screened from the fort by woods. The six others anchored out in the stream where they could fire on Fort St. Philip. Members of the Coast Survey, who had determined the exact position of the forts, gave the mortar boat captains their proper range and bearing. When the bombardment opened on the 18th, fused shells were accurately lobbed into the forts at an easy two-mile range. That day the citadel and quarters in Fort Jackson were burned out and the magazines temporarily endangered, but the Confederates put up a well-aimed counterfire, scored hits on the mortar boats out in the stream, and forced that group to retire around the bend. On the second day, while the mortar flotilla threw a shell a minute into Fort Jackson, Farragut ordered his gunboats to take turns offering themselves as moving targets out in the stream in order to distribute the Confederate fire. One mortar boat was sunk by a direct hit; otherwise the bombardment was maintained day and night without the loss of a ship.

Thousands of mortar shells buried themselves deep in the mud before exploding. Physical impairment to the military value of the forts was slight, but that proved less important than the effect of the bombardment on the morale of the defenders. High water and breaks in the levee turned Fort Jackson into a swamp, and the day and night shelling forced the disheartened garrison to live in the casemates, more like muskrats than men, whereas Farragut's sailors, over-estimating the effectiveness of the mortar fire, were confident of victory.

The night of April 20 marked important developments on both sides. While the mortars fired away, two of the gunboats, the *Itasca* and *Pinola,* attempted to open a breach in the Confederate barrier across the river. With masts removed, the ships made very difficult targets as they steamed up on the schooner hulks in the boom. After plans to blow up one schooner miscarried, it was found possible to cast off the chains holding another. In maneuvering, the *Itasca* went hard aground. Eventually pulled off by the *Pinola,* she found herself in a position to surge upstream through the gap, spin around, and steam down on the boom at full speed. She drove down between two of the hulks, rode high out of the water before her weight snapped the chains holding them, and left behind her a hole amply wide for the large ships of the fleet. During the hours that the *Itasca* and *Pinola* worked against the boom, the Confederate ironclad *Louisiana* was being towed into place under the guns of Fort St. Philip. She had left New Orleans loaded with workmen, her machinery practically inoperable, an inefficient floating battery (for her gunports were too small) rather than a fighting ship. The Confederate Army commander wanted her moved down nearer the boom where she would attract some of the mortar fire away from the forts, but her captain insisted she should be protected by the forts until her guns and machinery were ready.

By this time Commander Porter hoped that 48 hours of additional bombardment would take care of Fort Jackson, leaving only Fort St. Philip, which was virtually undamaged, for the ships to contend with. These last hours were spent in perfecting preparations. Masts were removed from five gunboats. Most ships daubed mud for camouflage on topsides, faked anchor chains over the midships section, piled sand bags around machinery spaces, readied howitzers in guntubs in the fore and main tops, strung splinter nets, and in some instances painted decks white to assist in handling the guns in darkness. All ships were trimmed by the bow so that, if run aground, they could back off with the help of the four-knot current. The 48-hour bombardment had so little effect that Porter himself became somewhat discouraged. Farragut, unperturbed, made his last tour of the fleet "to know positively," as he said, "that each commander understood my orders for the attack and to see that all was in readiness." [6] At two in the morning of April 24, two red lanterns, the signal to get

underway, were hoisted in the mizzen rigging of the *Hartford.*

Farragut had divided the assault fleet into three divisions, originally planning to have two heavy divisions of ships advance together on parallel courses, each concentrating its gunfire on the fort on its side of the river, and a third division of gunboats bring up the rear, presumably in a safe position because of the damage the lead divisions would inflict on the forts. The entire movement was to be supported by the mortar boats and Porter's auxiliary craft, which were to close up within range of the forts. This plan was followed except that the narrowness of the opening in the boom required the fleet to proceed in one long column.

The Confederate defenders had noted the placing of certain markers and were expecting the attack. Piles of brush were ready for lighting on the banks of the river to silhouette the Union ships, and fire rafts were prepared to throw them into confusion when under the guns of the forts. That some of the defenders recognized the urgency of the situation is shown by the prophetic answer to the Confederate captain who said that he could not move the *Louisiana* to a position near the boom for another 24 hours, "Tell Captain Mitchell that there will be no tomorrow for New Orleans, unless he immediately takes up the position assigned to him with the *Louisiana.*" [7]

The little gunboat *Cayuga* led the way, followed closely by the *Pensacola,* the *Mississippi,* and five more gunboats of the first division. The general battle began as soon as the *Pensacola* passed through the barrier. Porter's mortar shells arched like skyrockets against the dark sky. Both forts opened fire, and the ships replied with broadsides of grape and canister as soon as their guns bore on a target. Moving very deliberately, the *Pensacola* almost stopped opposite Fort St. Philip to deliver two broadsides at close range, close enough so that Union sailors and Confederate soldiers could swear back and forth at each other. The *Mississippi,* paddling leisurely through the smoke of

---

[6] *Official Records,* Series I, XVIII, 156.

[7] Alfred T. Mahan, *The Gulf and Inland Waters* (New York, 1883), 70.

battle so as to maintain her station astern of the *Pensacola,* was dealt a glancing blow by the ram *Manassas* while engaged with Fort St. Philip and was then swept across the river where she threw a broadside at Fort Jackson before drawing out of range upstream.

By this time the second division, *Hartford, Brooklyn,* and *Richmond,* was crowding through the boom. The *Hartford* had an exciting encounter with a fire raft off Fort St. Philip. "In trying to avoid it," Farragut wrote, "I ran the ship on shore," and then the Confederate tug *Mosher* "pushed the fire raft on to me and got the ship on fire all along one side. I thought it was all up with us, but we put it out and got off again and proceeded up the river fighting our way." [8] Shells rolled from the deck of the flagship had destroyed the raft and a single broadside sank the unarmed tug. According to her log, the *Hartford* spent less than half an hour under fire.

Of the large ships, the *Brooklyn* received the greatest damage. She collided with the gunboat *Kineo* of the first division while trying to pass through the boom, but after a struggle both vessels got clear and back on course. Off Fort St. Philip she was rammed by the *Manassas,* which had waited concealed against the shore after the attack on the *Mississippi.* Several of the *Brooklyn's* planks were stove in. A survey after the battle revealed that the ramming came much closer to having fatal results than the ship's crew had realized in the heat of the encounter.

Most of the other ships passed through the gantlet without heavy damage. Most severely shot up was the gunboat *Iroquois,* which blundered into collision with the stationary ironclad *Louisiana* and lost eight killed and 24 wounded before she got on course again. She was the last of the Union ships to pass the forts. Three gunboats had to turn back —the *Itasca,* with a shot through a boiler, and the *Winona* and *Kennebec,* which were fouled in the obstruction at the boom. The entire action between fleet and forts lasted a little over an hour. All of Farragut's ships took hits, but none was sunk.

In the early dawn several sharp ship-to-ship encounters took place above the forts. The *Manassas,* like a submarine stalking a convoy, tried to get in a final blow. But she was discovered by the *Mississippi* and ran herself ashore in trying to avoid the charging old paddlewheeler. The leading Union gunboats, sprinting ahead, made short work of their Confederate opponents. Only the *Governor Moore* put up a real fight. Bearing down on the *Varuna,* she fired through her own bow to rake the Union ship, which was forced ashore and destroyed. Other Union gunboats soon accounted for the *Governor Moore.* All Confederate warships except two which found temporary refuge under the guns of the forts were captured or destroyed, as eventually were the Confederate auxiliary ships that fled to New Orleans.

By afternoon the Union fleet was anchored off Quarantine, preparing to continue up the river to New Orleans the next day. Farragut did not worry about the forts behind him. "I think if you send a flag of truce and demand their surrender, they will do it," he wrote Porter, "for their intercourse with the city is cut off." [9]

Total casualties had been light on both sides: Union, 39 killed and 179 wounded; Confederate, 84 killed and 110 wounded. The Confederacy could find little consolation in those figures; the defense had failed. Only the *Manassas* had made repeated efforts to stop the Union ships. The *Louisiana* could have been of more use anchored in midstream as a navigational hazard. Someone failed to light important beacon fires. The scurrying Confederate gunboats had allowed themselves to be picked off in detail upstream, whereas their only conceivably profitable employment would have been down at the boom as the Union ships were trying to find their way through. The gunners in the forts had generally fired high, for they were not experienced artillerists and no match for the naval gunners of the Union fleet.

---

[8] *Official Records,* Series I, XVIII, 142.

[9] *Loc. cit.*

THE CAPTURE OF
NEW ORLEANS

Only token resistance and the formalities of negotiating surrender intervened between the battle and the occupation of New Orleans by General Butler's troops on May 1, 1862. The Union fleet anchored off the city on the afternoon of April 25, having smothered the Chalmette Battery with a few broadsides from the large ships. Farragut was appalled by the sight before him. Fires raged through all property that might be of value to the Union, including 13,000 bales of cotton. The river was ablaze with the debris of burning ships and stores, and in the midst of it all floated the smoldering hulk of the unfinished ironclad *Mississippi*. Farragut's representatives went ashore through the hysterical mobs with a demand that the city surrender. As soon as General Lovell withdrew his handful of troops to save the city from bombardment by the guns of the fleet, negotiations were opened with the civilian government. These parleys were somewhat protracted by the mayor's insistence that as a civilian official he did not have the authority to make a military surrender. Consequently, Farragut had some difficulty showing the American flag on the city hall, as Gideon Welles had ordered. But with the help of 250 marines and a howitzer, even that was accomplished. Actual Union seizure of the city had to be postponed until the arrival of General Butler's occupation troops.

Down river, Commander Porter worried about the forts and the *Louisiana*. "You will find the forts harder to take now than before, unless their ammunition runs out," he wrote Farragut; adding, "I hope you will open your way down, no matter what it costs." [10] But rumors of the surrender of New Orleans and the fact that General Butler's troops were now entrenched across the levee roads leading from the forts to the city caused the demoralized troops in Fort Jackson to mutiny, leaving the Confederate army commander no choice in the matter. He surrendered on the 28th. When the Confederate naval commander learned of the army's capitulation, he set fire to the *Louisiana*, which drifted out into the stream and exploded, killing a man in Fort St. Philip and almost taking down Porter's ship with it.

Victory in the New Orleans campaign was the greatest triumph, both in its military and in its political consequences, that the Union had won in more than a year of war. Farragut had demonstrated, as so many commanders on both sides had not, what could be accomplished by prompt, vigorous action based on sound judgment. It was he who took advantage of the South's incapacity to meet the threats poised simultaneously, like a classical pincers movement, from north and south. If he had delayed as much as a month, low water and Confederate ironclads could probably have frustrated the best Union effort. Instead, the entire lower Mississippi River was open to Federal warships.

Perhaps the true significance of the fall of New Orleans can be most readily appreciated by its effect on the international situation. Under Napoleon III France had thinly veiled ambitions in the Caribbean area. The Emperor's schemes might prosper if there were a Confederate States of America, friendly and indebted to him. England sat on the fence, but France would recognize the Confederacy as soon as the South gave clear indication that it could maintain its independence from the North. If the Union attack on New Orleans failed, that might be the time for France to act, but when New Orleans fell, French recognition of the Confederacy was indefinitely postponed.

The early Federal conquest of the entire Mississippi Valley and of Mobile, the one major Confederate port of the eastern Gulf Coast open to blockade runners, might well have followed on the heels of the New Orleans campaign. Instead, May and June 1862 saw numerically superior Union forces fritter away almost every opportunity for decisive action. From the point of view of the Blockading Squadron, Mobile was a plum ripe for plucking, its defenses ill-prepared and undermanned. The *Hartford* class sloops, supported by a division of mortar boats and a small force from Butler's army,

---

[10] *Official Records*, Series I, XVIII, 143.

would have had little difficulty at that time in capturing the forts guarding the entrance to Mobile Bay and sealing off the blockade runners from the city of Mobile. From the point of view of Lincoln and his cabinet however, clearing the Mississippi had to come first. In truth, both objectives were then attainable. Everything that Farragut's large ships could accomplish on the river in the spring of 1862 could be achieved equally well by his gunboats, leaving the large vessels to operate against Mobile. Once again Union naval power was to be operationally limited to blockade and to those functions which it could perform in support of land power.

THE COLLAPSE OF THE SECOND LINE OF CONFEDERATE DEFENSE

The Confederate plan to hold a second line of defense between Memphis and Chattanooga along the Memphis and Charleston Railroad—the only direct rail connection in the Confederacy between the Mississippi River and the Atlantic coast—was born of necessity out of the Fort Donelson disaster. Neither the Battle of Shiloh nor the Union occupation of New Orleans had altered the basic strategic pattern. The Federal campaign against the rail junction of Corinth was renewed under the direct command of General Halleck who, dismayed by the fearful bloodletting at Shiloh, felt bound to use his armies with caution. Only after assembling 100,000 men did he undertake his irresistible, grinding advance. Confederate General Beauregard had no more than 50,-000 troops with which to delay the Union forces. He had to save his army while the Confederacy rallied its full strength, even at the cost of abandoning Corinth. Brilliantly impeding Halleck by every means short of a major battle, Beauregard capitalized on Halleck's caution to prolong the 20-mile advance for a whole month. When Federal soldiers finally entered Corinth on May 29, 1862, they found the fortifications empty. Beaure-

gard's entire army had slipped south to Tupelo, 60 miles away. In the meantime, Union naval activity on the Mississippi largely depended upon the progress of Halleck's campaign.

After the capture of Island No. 10 in early April 1862, the Union gunboats steamed down-river to lead the Federal attack against the next Confederate strong point. That was Fort Pillow, on the east-bank bluffs of the Mississippi, the sole river fortification between the Union forces and Memphis. General Pope's 20,000 men landed above the fort but had made little progress before they were ordered to join Halleck in the Corinth campaign. In the absence of strong army support, the Union ironclads took turns guarding mortar boats which were brought down to bombard the Confederate position, for only the high arching trajectory of mortar fire could reach the fort from the river. Such activity had become routine by May 9 when Flag Officer Foote, incapacitated by the wound he had received at Fort Donelson, turned over his command to Captain Charles H. Davis. The very next morning a surprise attack by the rams of the Confederate River Defense Fleet produced a spirited engagement at Plum Point Bend above Fort Pillow. After the Union ironclads *Cincinnati* and *Mound City* were sunk, the attackers withdrew with several of their ships damaged but able to drift downstream to the protection of the fort.

The action was humiliating to the North, even though both sunken gunboats were soon raised and repaired. The enemy had dashed in for a telling blow, taking advantage of Northern laxity, and had escaped from superior forces on which they had inflicted greater damage than they themselves had received. However this Confederate success did not save Fort Pillow. The Federal bombardment was resumed and continued for another three weeks until the Union victory at Corinth gave the Confederates in their outflanked position a dubious choice: either abandon the fort or remain to be captured in it. Explosions heard on the night of June 4 notified the gunboats that the fort was being evacuated. Burning their stores and destroying their precious artillery, the Confederate defenders withdrew.

Captain Davis, his force augmented by four maneuverable rams commanded by Colonel Charles Ellet of the Union Army Engineers, now had an opportunity to avenge the humiliation of Plum Point Bend. His fleet steamed down to Memphis. The townspeople lined the heights along the river to see the show, confident in the eight rams of the Confederate River Defense Fleet, which were formed in a double line before the city. As Davis' five ironclads approached within range, two of Ellet's rams, *Queen of the West* and *Monarch,* darted ahead of the attackers to deliver the first blows. The surprised Confederate vessels, expecting to fight only sluggish gunboats, were thrown into disorder. The *Queen of the West* rammed and sank her first opponent, while the *Monarch,* slipping between two others, saw the Confederate rams crash into each other. Then the big Union gunboats closed in. In an hour's melee four of the River Defense Fleet were sunk and three captured. Only one escaped downstream. None of the Union ships was lost. Flag Officer Davis accepted the surrender of Memphis, reported four large river steamers seized as prizes, and, by 11 o'clock that morning, turned the city over to Colonel Fitch for occupation by a detachment of the Indiana brigade. The Mississippi was now open to Federal gunboats as far south as Vicksburg.

FROM NEW ORLEANS TO VICKSBURG

Neither Farragut nor the captains of his fleet were at all happy in their irregular advance up the Mississippi during the month following the occupation of New Orleans. If the *Hartford* had been a great sperm whale from the Pacific, she could not have been more out of her element—fighting the mud, snags, driftwood, current, and unending corkscrew bends of the river. "The elements of destruction to the Navy in this river are beyond anything I ever encoun-

tered, and if the same destruction continues the whole Navy will be destroyed in twelve months," Farragut lamented. "More anchors have been lost and vessels ruined than I have seen in a lifetime, and those vessels which do not run into others are themselves run into and crushed in such a manner as to render them unseaworthy . . . their sides are smashed in, their cutwaters entirely broomed up and removed. . . . They all require more or less repairs to their machinery, but the hulls all require docking—ribs broken, plank sheer gone, stems torn off to the wood ends, etc." [11]

Baton Rouge, then a town of 7,000 people, was occupied, and the ships pressed on. Even with the large Federal sloops in danger of being trapped hundreds of miles above New Orleans when the spring flood waters subsided, Farragut had no choice but to carry out his original orders. He sent the gunboats ahead and followed after them. On May 12 the *Iroquois* accepted the nominal surrender of Natchez, and by May 18 the *Oneida* was off Vicksburg demanding its surrender. The Military Governor there boasted, "Mississippians don't know, and refuse to learn, how to surrender to an enemy." [12] Farragut transferred his flag to the *Kennebec* and was himself off Vicksburg four days later to determine the best course of action. "There is very little use in attacking Vicksburg," he wrote General Butler, "as the guns on the height are so elevated that our fire will not be felt by them." He decided to leave the gunboats to blockade Vicksburg "until the battle of Corinth shall decide its fate," [13] and returned to New Orleans with the heavy ships.

Instead of waiting for Halleck's army to move, Farragut would willingly have taken prompt action against Mobile. Porter was all for it, but a message from his friend Fox showed how the wind blew in Washington. The Assistant Secretary wrote in a dispatch to Porter on May 17, while Farragut was in fact at Natchez, "Someone has made a most serious blunder in persuading the Flag Offi-

[11] *Official Records*, Series I, XVIII, 521.
[12] *Ibid.*, 492.
[13] *Ibid.*, 507.

cer to go at Mobile instead of obeying his instructions to go up the Mississippi River." He added rather hysterically and on the strength of nothing more than the Plum Point Bend fracas, "Davis has repulsed the iron rams of the enemy, but they are going at him and if they should be successful, Halleck would have to fall back and we should lose St. Louis, Cairo and everything." [14] The Confederate rams were of wood, not iron, and they made no second try, but Fox's message serves to underscore the official recognition of control of the waterways as *sine qua non* for successful Federal military operations in the Mississippi Valley.

From New Orleans Farragut sent in a full-length report to Secretary Welles, beginning almost wistfully: "I have just arrived here from up the river as high as Vicksburg, at least 300 miles farther than I was ever from sea water before since the days of my childhood." [15] Clearly he considered it quixotic to ascend the river again. Nevertheless, after suggesting to Welles that a monitor would be a more appropriate ship, he obediently set the *Hartford* to shepherding a flock of Porter's mortar boats and a segment of Butler's army north toward Vicksburg.

Midway between Memphis and New Orleans, Vicksburg occupied the naturally strongest point on the river and the only one that was then fortified by the Confederacy. Halleck's 100,000 men were now idle victors at Corinth, 300 miles away, but only

80 miles by rail from Memphis whence steamers could easily transport a large army, its artillery and supplies, to Vicksburg. If 20,000 troops under Grant had been sent down at this time, they would certainly have captured the city. But Halleck was taking no chances—and winning no further victories.

When Farragut arrived for the second time off Vicksburg, the cooperating land forces were still far too weak to attempt a frontal assault. On June 28 he ran past the Vicksburg batteries with eight of his ships, three turning back in the confusion of battle. Davis had come down the river from Memphis without hindrance and at last the inland and the sea-going navies were joined. In vain Farragut wrote Halleck for army reinforcements. The Federal offensive had stalled in its tracks. A year and a week would pass after Farragut's rendezvous with Davis before the Stars and Stripes flew over Vicksburg.

As President Lincoln with prophetic foresight had told Commander Porter in November, 1861, when they were discussing plans for the capture of New Orleans: ". . . we must have troops enough not only to hold New Orleans, but to proceed at once toward Vicksburg, which is the key to all that country watered by the Mississippi and its tributaries. If the Confederates once fortify the neighboring hills, they will be able to hold that point for an indefinite time, and it will require a large force to dislodge them."

[14] Richard S. West, Jr., *The Second Admiral,* (New York, 1937) 149.

[15] *Official Records,* Series I, XVIII, 519.

20

The Mississippi Valley Campaign,

Part II: Vicksburg and After

WHEN THREE OF FARRAGUT'S ships failed to follow the *Hartford* around the horseshoe bend of the Mississippi past the guns of Vicksburg, the Admiral's troubles had just begun. Ostensibly of course July 1, 1862 was a day of Union triumph. That was the day when the fresh water and salt water navies joined forces and anchored together above the city. Only a narrow neck of land separated them from the warships and troop transports that remained below. Casualties inflicted during the run past had been very light. General Halleck now informed Farragut that he would be able to send down troops in a few weeks, even though none were available at the moment. The three Union commanders at Vicksburg—Farragut, Davis, and Brigadier General Thomas Williams, whose 3,000 soldiers from Butler's army had been escorted up the river by the navy—agreed that no assault should be attempted until reinforcements arrived from Corinth. In the meantime, to harass Major General Earl Van Dorn and his 15,000 men working on the city's fortifications, four of

Davis's mortar boats above Vicksburg supplemented 16 of Porter's below in lobbing their shells into the Confederate positions. Lookouts in the rigging of the *Hartford* reported occasional hits. At the same time the Union Army turned to digging a canal across the narrow neck of land between the two segments of the fleet. A new channel which would by-pass Vicksburg beyond range of the city's guns might even make a direct assault on the Confederate position unnecessary. Neither undertaking progressed very far. The mortar bombardment was no more than started when orders arrived from Secretary Welles transferring Porter and 12 of the mortar boats 2,000 miles to the aid of McClellan in Virginia. The canal diggers, stricken by steaming heat and malaria, soon had over a third of their number on the sick list. The navy's binnacle lists were almost as long. By mid-July the Union position off Vicksburg was clearly becoming untenable. At last Halleck admitted that he could not send an army. Farragut was worried, for his large ships, needed on blockade duty in the Gulf, might be trapped in the river by low water. Action, when it came, was a result of the audacity of a single Confederate iron-clad gunboat, the *Arkansas.*

During those critical weeks of June and early July, one of the many Confederate defense projects was completion of the ram *Arkansas,* which to escape capture at Memphis had been towed to an improvised navy yard at Yazoo City on the Yazoo River north of Vicksburg. The ship was much like the Union ironclads in size, appearance, and armament. In lieu of armor plate, railroad rails covered her casemate. Her engine drove two propellers, but her machinery was entirely inadequate and never dependable. When she was completed in mid-July, the Confederates set in motion a grandiose plan for her to run down the Yazoo and through the Union fleet to Vicksburg, help liberate New Orleans, and eventually join the Confederate defense of Mobile.

On July 15, the very day that the *Arkansas* steamed down the Yazoo, the ironclad *Carondelet,* the wooden gunboat *Tyler,* and the ram *Queen of the West* set out on a reconnaissance up the Yazoo. When the Union ships encountered the Confederate, they turned and ran. What followed, Secretary Welles described as "the most disreputable naval affair of the war." [1] After forcing the *Carondelet* aground and pursuing the others right into the midst of the Union fleet where she received numerous hits, the *Arkansas* steamed at a majestic two knots—her crippled engines could drive her no faster—through the completely surprised Union ships and to temporary safety under the guns of Vicksburg. With "deep mortification," Farragut officially reported, "none of us had steam or could get it up in time to pursue her, but she took the broadside of the whole fleet." [2] Battered though she was, the *Arkansas* now threatened the mortar boats and transports below the city. That night Farragut took his fleet and the ram *Sumter* past Vicksburg in

an unsuccessful attempt to sink her. A few days later the ironclad *Essex* and the ram *Queen of the West* participated in an equally unsuccessful daylight attempt. Just at that juncture Farragut received orders giving him permission to withdraw downstream. The ships of the salt water fleet, with the *Essex* and *Sumter* and General William's army (by this time 75 per cent incapacitated by illness), departed with alacrity. Shortly afterwards, Davis took the fresh water navy 300 miles upstream to base at Helena, Arkansas. Thus, by default, 500 miles of the Mississippi were reopened to the Confederacy.

Delighted by this turn of events, General Van Dorn immediately dispatched part of the Vicksburg garrison to join other Confederate troops under Major General John C. Breckenridge in an effort to recapture Baton Rouge. To make a simultaneous attack, as planned, the *Arkansas* cast off her lines at Vicksburg and had steamed within sight of Baton Rouge when her engines broke down. The Confederate army's assault was repulsed, thanks in good part to the *Essex* and two Union gunboats, which fired over the town and into the Confederate ranks as directed by a naval officer who had a clear view of the action from the top of the Louisiana State House. The *Arkansas'* crew worked all that day and night to get their ship back into operation. When the *Essex* led a rein-forced Union fleet upstream against her the next day, the *Arkansas* steamed out, but her engines immediately broke down again and she drifted helplessly ashore. Her crew, at last forced to abandon ship, set her afire to prevent capture by the Union flotilla. The *Essex* threw in shells from a safe distance until the *Arkansas* was destroyed by the explosion of her own magazines.

General Williams had been killed in the battle and the outnumbered Union troops were soon afterwards withdrawn from Baton Rouge. In the meantime the defeated Confederate forces began to fortify Port Hudson, on the east bank of the Mississippi a few miles upstream from Baton Rouge. Port Hudson's fortifications were intended to stop Union offensives from the south, as Vicks-

[1] Charles Lee Lewis, *David Glasgow Farragut: Our First Admiral* (Annapolis, 1943), 123.
[2] *Official Records of the Union and Confederate Navies in the War of the Rebellion* (Washington, 1904), XIX, 4.

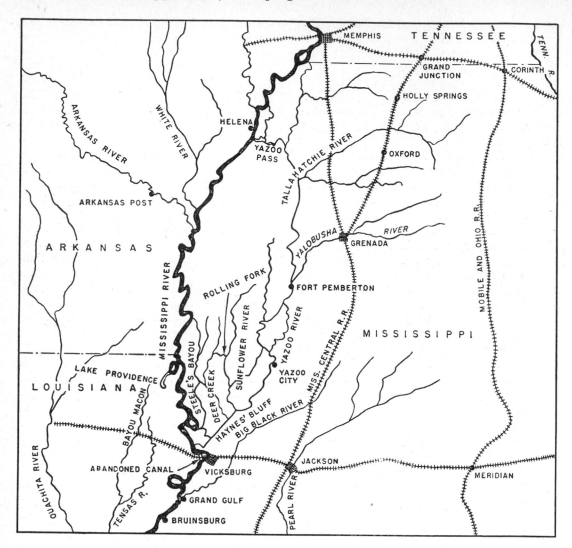

SCENE OF UNION OFFENSIVES AGAINST VICKSBURG

burg had so successfully stopped those from the north.

THE VICKSBURG-
PORT HUDSON BASTION

As the geographical advantage had favored the North in breaking the first and second lines of Confederate defense, now the advantage shifted to the South. At one time in the geological history of the Mississippi Valley, a long arm of the sea had extended up from the Gulf of Mexico even beyond present-day Cairo, Illinois. The bay thus formed, filled with sediment from many rivers, finally became an alluvial plain, so flat that the Mississippi meandered along in numerous, shifting coils. Wherever the river ricocheted against the foot of the bluffs—the shoreline of the ancient sea—that bounded the plain to east and west, it created what became in the Civil War a natural strongpoint for the Confederate defenders. Columbus, Fort Pillow, Memphis, Vicksburg, Grand Gulf, and Port Hudson were all such natural strongpoints on the east bank. Of these Vicksburg was paramount. (See map, page 334.)

Geography left Vicksburg vulnerable to attack only from the firm ground east of, or behind, the city. On the north the Yazoo basin, an elliptically shaped flood plain bounded on the east by the bluffs and on the west by the Mississippi, extended for 200 miles to Memphis. On the south another basin extended from Vicksburg west of the Mississippi all the way to the Gulf, and on the east bank the town of Grand Gulf and the Big Black River covered the city's southern flank. Where the Mississippi made almost a 180-degree turn in front of Vicksburg, the sloping east bank reached its greatest height of 264 feet, the high point of a 30-mile ridge extending north to Haynes' Bluff on the Yazoo and south to Grand Gulf on the Mississippi. During the second half of 1862 the Confederates made this entire ridge part of an integrated system of fortifications and the northern anchor of their defense bastion.

Port Hudson, 150 miles south of Vicksburg, commanded a similar bend of the river from similar heights. Because it was never threatened by forces as powerful as those the Union brought against Vicksburg, its defenses were less fully developed. Port Hudson's importance as a southern anchor for the Confederate defense was not so much in denying the Mississippi to the Federal government as in preserving for the Confederacy its last line of east-west communications via the Red River. The Red River flowed into the Mississippi just above Port Hudson from deep in the Confederacy's southwest. Down it came Confederate meat and grain in vast quantities and European products shipped via Mexico. So long as the Confederacy held this line of communications with the outside world, there persisted the hope that the war could be pursued until foreign intervention or Northern war-weariness brought hostilities to an end. But if either Vicksburg or Port Hudson fell, the Red River would be blocked, and the fall of the remaining strong points must shortly follow. With the Missis-

sippi firmly in Union hands, the "backbone of the rebellion" would be broken.

FAILURE OF THE FIRST ATTACK ON VICKSBURG

The successful Confederate counterattack under General Braxton Bragg which had penetrated almost as far as Louisville, Kentucky during the summer of 1862 had thoroughly alarmed the Federal government. There was a consequent reshuffling of armies and commanders. Grant's forces holding the Memphis-Corinth line were so reduced in numbers that they had all they could do to maintain their position while awaiting reinforcements through the summer and early fall of 1862. A clash at Iuka, southeast of Corinth, resulted in a concentrating of Confederate forces and gave General Van Dorn hope that he might be able to defeat Grant's divided army in detail and force the Union troops all the way back to Fort Donelson. Van Dorn's attack in October accomplished just the opposite result. The Confederates lost 5,000 men—casualties and prisoners—and Van Dorn was replaced by the more cautious John C. Pemberton. Grant was at last free to resume the offensive.

Since retiring to Helena after the *Arkansas* fiasco, Flag Officer Davis' gunboats, on the defensive, trying to hold what had previously been gained, had been fighting guerillas and convoying supplies on the Ohio, Cumberland, Tennessee, and Mississippi rivers. In October the 15 river gunboats were transferred from the Army to the Navy and, as the "Mississippi Squadron," were placed under the command of David Dixon Porter, now back from Virginia. Porter immediately reorganized his force along navy lines, had the older ships repaired and more heavily armed, and began adding new ironclads and "tinclad" patrol craft to the fleet until eventually he had more than 60 vessels of various sorts. Meanwhile he established himself on his flagship, the large river steamer *Black*

Hawk, with adequate facilities for administering his command.

In November 1862 Grant at last received permission from Washington to launch an offensive. His main base of supply at this time was at Columbus; his operational base, at Grand Junction; and his advance supply base, at Holly Springs. His army depended for communications on a single rail line joining those points (see map, page 334). His objective was the major Confederate base at Jackson, the capital of Mississippi, which flanked Vicksburg just as Corinth flanked Memphis. He knew that the Confederate Army, after withdrawing as far as Grenada, was preparing to contest his advance. Grant's plan was to trap the Confederate forces by making a double attack: a combined operation of some 32,000 men under Sherman, supported by Porter, would depart from Memphis by ship for a direct attack on Vicksburg; in the meantime Grant himself would attack Grenada, expecting to fight a holding action which would keep so many Confederate soldiers occupied that Sherman would have no trouble. If the Confederate forces at Grenada retreated to Vicksburg, Grant would pursue and trap them there. If they retreated only to Jackson, he would pursue and be joined by Sherman's troops from Vicksburg. Grant's plan, for all its ostensible logic, was wrecked by its dependence on an inadequate line of communications.

The Confederate defense plan was perforce flexible and opportunistic. Likelihood of a Federal offensive had caused President Davis to visit both Jackson and Vicksburg in early December. He recognized their weakness and, in attempting to find a remedy, may have committed one of the great blunders of the war. Instead of ordering reinforcements from the secondary Arkansas theater of operations, as advised by General Joseph Johnston, who was now in command of all Confederate forces between the Mississippi and Alleghenies, the Confederate President had 10,000 men transferred to Pemberton from eastern Tennessee. This was just 11 days before the great battle of Stone River that ended the East Tennessee campaign in Confederate defeat. Even with these reinforcements, Pemberton had strength only for a delaying action. But the winter rains favored the defense as roads turned to mud, and the railroad down which the Confederates retreated, tearing up rails and ties as they went, would require time-consuming repairs before it would be of much use to the Union invaders.

Making excellent use of their interior position and knowledge of the terrain, the Southern generals proceeded to teach Grant some lessons. First, a raid by Forrest's cavalry cut the telegraph and wrecked the rail line between Grant's advancing army and his main base at Columbus. For exactly those 12 days (December 19-30) during which Sherman took his army down-river and attacked Vicksburg, Grant had no communication with the outside world. The fatal blow was struck by Van Dorn with 2,500 men on a cavalry raid around Grant's flank. Catching the 1,500-man guard at Holly Springs completely by surprise, Van Dorn's men destroyed the entire $1,500,000 supply dump. With no logistic support, Grant's army ignominiously retreated 80 miles to Grand Junction, living off the land. Not only did Grant's holding action collapse, but the Confederate regiments that faced him at Grenada were shifted by rail to Vicksburg in time to parry the second Union blow.

Sherman and Porter meanwhile had reached the Vicksburg area via the Mississippi. Porter's task now was to convoy the transports into the Yazoo and protect them during the debarkation. First however the gunboats had to clear the lower Yazoo of mines, one of which sank the ironclad *Cairo.* The river fleet continued minesweeping until the Yazoo was cleared from its mouth, eight miles above Vicksburg, to Haynes' Bluff, where Confederate batteries controlled the river. The day after Christmas Sherman's troops, virtually unopposed under cover of the gunboats, landed on the flats between the Mississippi and the high ground to the east. By this time Sherman had good reason to suspect that Grant was meeting resistance, but he had no way of learning what actually had happened. He could only proceed on the assumption that the "holding action" was not so unsuccessful as to expose his own Vicksburg attack to certain defeat.

In drenching December rain, the Union forces deployed for assault along the five paths that led through swamplands to the Confederate fortifications on the bluffs. Though Sherman's troops outnumbered the Confederates three to one, the defenders' strongly entrenched position on the heights gave them an immense advantage, for the Union columns, confined to narrow approaches, could not bring their numbers to bear on a broad front. In the Battle of Chickasaw Bluffs on the 29th, every Union attempt to storm the well-placed Confederate fortifications crumpled under massed artillery and rifle fire. At the end of the day Sherman had lost 2,000 men; the Confederates, only 187.

Sherman nevertheless planned a second attack for the new year. This time it was to be a night assault by 10,000 troops farther up the Yazoo, where the Confederate batteries were within range of the heavy guns of Porter's fleet. Dense fog delayed the troop-laden gunboats so long that only a suicidal daylight attack would have been possible. By this time it was clearly evident to both Sherman and Porter that Grant's plans had gone awry and that in view of the rising river waters and the continuous rain, the only sensible choice was to withdraw.

In their first attempt to capture Vicksburg, Grant, Sherman, and Porter thus tasted the humiliation of defeat by numerically inferior forces.

THE WINTER CAMPAIGN AGAINST VICKSBURG

Mud, politics, and common sense finally compelled Grant to transfer his base of operations to the Mississippi in the winter of 1862-63. The heavy rains of an unusually wet season turned all roads into quagmires. If the Union Army was to advance in strength with artillery support, it must be by ship. After the failure of the Chickasaw Bluffs attack, Admiral Porter and General Sherman had cooperated in a secondary, face-saving operation against Arkansas Post, where taking 5,000 Confederate prisoners had cost a thousand Federal casualties. This undertaking was commanded by General John A. McClernand, an Illinois politician who had talked President Lincoln into allowing him to raise troops in Illinois for an independent expedition against Vicksburg. To his everlasting credit, Halleck thwarted this threat to a unified command; the upshot was that McClernand took a position over Sherman but subordinate to Grant. The Arkansas Post victory removed a nuisance from the Union flank but did not justify a general diversion of about 30,000 men to a trans-Mississippi campaign. Grant ordered an end to that "wild goose chase," as he correctly called it, and by the end of January took command on the Mississippi himself as the only way of controlling both McClernand and the Vicksburg campaign. He established his combined army on the west bank at Milliken's Bend just above Vicksburg with his rear base at Memphis 400 miles upstream.

Too strong to be stormed, the Vicksburg defenses had to be flanked. The problem was: how? High water made it impossible to march an army past Vicksburg through the cypress swamps and flooded underbrush of the west shore, and even supposing the troops could get past, no line of communications could be maintained on the river under Vicksburg's guns. Grant seems to have believed that nothing decisive could be accomplished until the land again became dry enough for marching, but he was willing to try any likely alternatives that would keep his forces occupied and satisfy the impatience of his superiors. Actually, four ingenious schemes were undertaken during the winter of 1862-63, and these together constitute the second campaign against Vicksburg.

(1) *Grant's "Big Ditch."* While Admirals Farragut and Foote dallied above Vicksburg in July 1862, General Williams' troops had actually made a good beginning on their canal across the finger of land pointing towards the Confederate stronghold. The falling level of the Mississippi and the Federal government's opinion that the fate of Vicksburg was going to be settled by a great

Union victory under Halleck in the vicinity of Corinth made completion of the canal less important than saving the lives of the malaria-infected soldiers. Now, in the winter of 1863, this project was revived, for it was remembered that a canal had succeeded at Island No. 10. The new ditch was to be a little over a mile long, 60 feet wide, and nine feet deep. The Northern press played up the progress the Army Engineers were making, trumpeting great expectations. By March 8 the goal was almost reached and flood waters were sweeping down the Mississippi to break through the last barrier. But instead of gouging out the last of the canal, the tumultuous waters flooded the peninsula, drowned horses and mules, swept away tents, destroyed machinery, made men flee for their lives to high ground, and plugged with silt and debris what canal there had been. The opponents of the canal who from the first had considered it an unholy interference with nature felt that their opinion had been vindicated. The project was abandoned.

(2) *Lake Providence and the Tensas Basin.* There was another possible way around Vicksburg. By cutting through miles of cypress swamp a route 400 miles long could be constructed from Lake Providence, on the west bank of the Mississippi about 75 miles north of Vicksburg, via the Bayou Baxter cypress swamp to Bayou Macon, then down the Macon, Tensas, and Ouachita rivers to the Red, and finally down the Red River to the Mississippi. Presumably the route could be used for Grant's troops to coordinate with Banks' in the capture of Port Hudson, which would in turn become the base for an attack from the south against Vicksburg. Union troops hacked away for two months at this nightmarish project before Grant withdrew them to take part in his spring offensive.

(3) *The Yazoo Pass Expedition.* A more promising possibility for a joint expedition consisted of opening a route that would outflank Haynes' Bluff, the northern point of the Vicksburg outer defense line. Just south of Helena, Arkansas and convenient to the Memphis base lay Yazoo Pass running from the Mississippi to the tributaries of the Yazoo

River. Some steamboats had regularly taken the route until it was plugged by a flood-control levee in 1853. Shortly after Grant established his headquarters at Milliken's Bend, Porter broached the subject of this 700-mile outflanking expedition and received the General's approval. The levee was blasted open and the waters of the Mississippi poured through. Two ironclads, six "tin-clads," and two rams led the way. They were supported by 4,500 Union troops embarked in 13 transports. The alert Confederates had felled huge trees across the channel, some as much as four feet in diameter and reaching from bank to bank. In the two weeks it took the expedition to hack its way through the Pass, a combination of narrow channels, overhanging trees, cypress stumps, and debris, abetted by Confederate sharpshooters, was unable to stop the slow progress of the Union fleet. At the end of a month's struggle the ships were approaching the final bend of the Tallahatchie where it joins the Yalobusha to form the Yazoo. There the desperate Confederate defenders were in the process of throwing up an earthwork and cotton-bale fortification, Fort Pemberton, armed with two heavy guns and supported by infantry. Occupying a flooded peninsula, the fort could not be attacked by anything short of amphibious infantry or ships painfully restricted by the narrow, tortuous channel. This was the "roadblock" that stopped the Union advance. During repeated attacks made over a period of several weeks, each ironclad gunboat was severely damaged. Since the Navy's gunboats failed to silence the fort and the Army was unable to stage an attack over the flooded countryside, each service found fault with the other. Reinforcements were brought up, but by then the Union leaders had become more interested in another alternative. On April 10 the entire expedition was back in the Mississippi with nothing to show for the two months' effort.

(4) *The Steele's Bayou Fiasco.* At the very time that the Union forces were attempting to batter down Fort Pemberton, Admiral Porter himself had launched a final expedition aimed at opening a route from the Mis-

sissippi to a point on the Yazoo between Yazoo City and Haynes' Bluff. If successful, this attack would place the navigable, upper stretches of the Yazoo in Federal hands, bring about the abandonment of Yazoo City (and, of course, of Fort Pemberton, which was in essence a northern outpost of the Yazoo City defenses), and secure a good advanced base in Yazoo City for outflanking Vicksburg from the north. The route was even narrower and more tortuous than that of the Yazoo Pass. Porter was able to push five of the old Eads ironclads through the forest of cypress and willows, but the lighter warships and transports did not have power and weight enough to fight their way through the willow-choked channel. Overhanging branches knocked off smoke stacks, cypress trees had to be pulled up by their roots, and the willows had to be chopped down one by one. Finally the flotilla ground to a halt within sight of clear water but in a tangle of felled trees. Confederate sharpshooters kept the Union crews behind the protection of the casemates, and the ironclads, walled in by the levee on either side, found their big guns useless. When Southern slaves were forced to fell trees behind the gunboats, the expedition stood on the brink of disaster. Only the prompt arrival of the Army saved the ships. General Sherman himself accompanied the major relieving force, its way lighted in a fantastic night march by candles. Porter's feelings of relief found expression in his official report: "I do not know when I felt more pleased to see that gallant officer. . . ."[3] As it was, it took 11 days for the ironclads to extricate themselves. The channel was so narrow that the ships could not be turned around. Rudders were unshipped and, "rebounding from tree to tree,"[4] the ironclads reached the Mississippi again on March 27.

Porter was thoroughly discouraged. "With the end of this expedition ends all my hopes of getting into Vicksburg in this direction. . . . There is but one thing now to be done, and that is to start an army of 150,000 men from Memphis, via Grenada, and let them

go supplied with everything required to take Vicksburg."[5]

Grant, influenced by recent developments on the Mississippi and the political temperature in Washington, had other and more daring ideas. Advance through the Yazoo basin was hopeless, as Porter said, but returning to Memphis would look like defeat, and an attack via Grenada to be successful would require protecting a long line of communications and rebuilding a railroad line as the army advanced. Grant knew what that meant only too well from his bitter experience of the past December. He had to get behind Vicksburg; if he could not do it from the north, he would have to do it from the south.

THE WINTER'S NAVAL ACTIVITY ON THE MISSISSIPPI

General Banks had replaced General Butler in New Orleans at the end of 1862. More troops had arrived. The grand strategy now called for a joint expedition under Banks and Farragut to reduce Port Hudson, but neither the Army nor the Navy was ready. Banks' position was very complex and entirely thankless. He had earned the nickname of "Dancing Master" through his efforts to win over the influential citizens of the occupied city. He was plagued by speculators with political backing who demanded that the Army make it possible for them to get out the upland cotton. He was gravely concerned for the safety of New Orleans, threatened more than once by Confederate armies in the general vicinity. His strength was thus largely absorbed by a multitude of tasks that had little to do with getting on with the war.

For Farragut too the year began badly. On New Year's Day two Confederate cotton-armored steamers with a single gun apiece captured the gunboat *Harriet Lane* and either seized or drove away the other Union ships blockading Galveston, Texas. In reporting to Welles, the Admiral admitted that it would

[3] *Official Records*, XXIV, 477.
[4] Alfred Thayer Mahan, *The Gulf and Inland Waters* (New York, 1883), 150.

[5] *Official Records*, XXIV, 479.

be difficult "to conceive a more pusillanimous surrender of a vessel to an enemy already in our power. . . ." [6] Three weeks later the Confederates also opened the blockade off Sabine Pass, when two of their cotton-clad gunboats took advantage of a calm day to capture the two Union sailing ships stationed there. All efforts to re-establish the blockade at those points failed.

On the Mississippi, the most important enterprise either Porter or Farragut could undertake was to dispute control of the river between Vicksburg and Port Hudson and raid the South's Red River source of supply. Porter tried it first.

On February 1 Colonel Charles Ellet received orders to run the ram *Queen of the West* past the Vicksburg batteries, sink the steamer *Vicksburg* moored there, and then raid the Red River commerce. The Union ram was hit repeatedly by solid shot and shell but got by the city in broad daylight on the morning of the 2nd without a single casualty. En route she damaged but did not sink the *Vicksburg.* Within the next few days the *Queen of the West* captured several valuable prizes, including a steamer with 110,000 pounds of pork and 500 hogs and another with 20 barrels of molasses, 10 hogsheads of sugar, and 30,000 pounds of flour. Both vessels had been bound with their provisions for the Confederate army at Port Hudson.

Porter sent the new ironclad *Indianola* past Vicksburg on the night of February 13-14 to join Ellet. That impetuous 19-year-old colonel had been raising havoc up the Red River, but the *Queen of the West* grounded and was captured on the very day that the *Indianola* steamed down to join her. Then the Confederates completely turned the tables. Using the *Queen of the West* to head a flotilla, they pursued the *Indianola* and caught up with her just below Vicksburg, where she was defeated, run aground, and captured. The last, if wry, laugh was Porter's. Because his other ironclads were bulldozing the willows and cypress of the Yazoo Basin or patrolling up river, the *Indianola* and *Queen of the West* in Confederate hands

posed a real danger. So the Admiral had a coal barge equipped with barrel-pile smokestacks and log guns to look like a monitor and floated her past Vicksburg at night. She grounded below the city on the west bank but was pushed back into the stream by the Union troops stationed there. News of her coming caused the apprehensive captors of the *Indianola* to blow up their stranded prize, and the *Queen of the West* retreated to the Louisiana waterways where she was eventually sunk by Farragut's gunboats.

The goings-on around Vicksburg struck Farragut as so much tomfoolery. If Porter intended to hold his ironclads for such time-wasting operations as the abortive Steele's Bayou expedition, Farragut considered it was up to him to regain control of the Mississippi. When he learned of the capture of the *Queen of the West* and the *Indianola,* he lost all patience. "I am all ready to make an attack on or run the batteries at Port Hudson," he wrote Secretary Welles, "so as to form a junction with the army and navy above Vicksburg." [7] The fact that Banks was ready to stage no more than a diversionary attack did not stop him. "The time has come," said Farragut, "there can be no more delay. I must go—army or no army." [8]

Once again Farragut directed the detailed preparations for taking a fleet past fortifications. This time he had the *Hartford, Richmond, Monongahela,* and *Mississippi,* with the gunboats *Albatross, Genesee,* and *Kineo.* The large ships were to proceed in that order past Port Hudson, each of the screw-sloops with a gunboat lashed to her port quarter and the side-wheeler *Mississippi* bringing up the rear. A flotilla of mortar boats and the ironclad *Essex* were assigned to shell the fortifications while the fleet steamed by. "I expect all to go by who are able," Farragut wrote in his general order to his fleet, "and I think the best protection against the enemy's fire is a well-directed fire from our own guns—shell and shrapnel at a distance and grape when within 400 or 500 yards." [9]

Leading the way in the *Hartford* on the

---

[6] *Ibid.,* XIX, 440.

[7] *Ibid.,* 644.
[8] Lewis, *Farragut: Our First Admiral,* 168.
[9] *Official Records,* XIX, 669.

dark, quiet night of March 14, Farragut was probably in the best command position to accomplish his difficult undertaking. Besides a score of heavy Confederate guns and half again as many field pieces, he had to contend with the five-knot current, a 150-degree bend in the river, and the ingenuity of the defenders, who spotted the ships with locomotive headlights from the east bank and silhouetted them against huge bonfires on the west bank.

While making the sharp turn under Port Hudson's batteries, the *Hartford* was thrown against the shore, but with the aid of the *Albatross* alongside, she returned to the channel and proceeded upstream. Not another ship got past. The *Richmond* lost power when her steam safety valves were opened by a freak hit, and the *Monongahela* went off course in the smoke and spent 25 minutes aground under fire. Both screw-sloops managed to escape downstream with the help of their escorts. The *Mississippi* however went aground on the west bank directly opposite the Confederate batteries. Here as she caught fire from enemy shells her crew abandoned ship. The next morning she floated free, blew up, and sank.

Although only two of his vessels had succeeded in running the gantlet, Farragut set about determinedly patrolling the river between Vicksburg and Port Hudson so as to deny Red River supplies to both Confederate strong points. Meanwhile Grant was completing preparations for his spring offensive.

THE CAPTURE OF VICKSBURG AND PORT HUDSON

In early April the falling level of the Mississippi finally made an overland route down the west bank available to the Union forces, and Grant began marching his army south. His plan was to cross the river, capture Grand Gulf, the southern outpost of the Vicksburg defenses, send 20,000 troops down-stream to assist Banks in capturing Port Hudson, and then use the combined armies in the even-

tual overwhelming of Vicksburg. He expected Porter to run the ironclads past Vicksburg to support his crossing with their heavy guns.

On the night of April 16 the Union fleet got under way. Flares and roaring bonfires lighted up the Federal ships for the Confederate gunners, and the vagaries of the current threw each of the larger ships into at least one 360-degree turn while passing the city. Remarkably enough, not a single Union sailor was killed and not one ironclad was critically damaged. Of the three supply-laden transports, one was sunk. A few nights later additional supply ships ran past Vicksburg to join the Union forces.

When prolonged bombardment from the ironclads failed to knock out the batteries at Grand Gulf, Grant and Porter shifted army and ships south and staged a practically unopposed crossing at Bruinsberg, six miles farther downstream. At the same time, to divert Confederate attention, Sherman staged a mock landing near Haynes' Bluff at the opposite end of the Confederate defenses just above Vicksburg. Sherman put on such a realistic show that the Confederates thought that his was the main thrust and Grant's the diversionary move.

Thus were initiated the most brilliant operations of Grant's career. By his success in moving his army to the east bank of the Mississippi he acquired the initiative, and did not relinquish it until he had captured Vicksburg. Moving first on Port Gibson, where the Bruinsberg-Vicksburg and Grand Gulf-Jackson roads converged, the Union van on May 1 defeated a small Confederate force and thereby made Grand Gulf untenable. When the Union ships returned to Grand Gulf, they found it already evacuated, and Grant's army marched in from the east on May 3.

Grant had originally planned to move a part of his force south at this time, cooperating with Banks against Port Hudson. But Banks was not ready. Although Grant's army of 45,000 (including Sherman's men) was confronted with Confederate forces in Mississippi numbering more than 65,000, Grant elected to keep the offensive. The essence of his strategy was to concentrate all his force against segments of the enemy one at a time.

Pemberton with 45,000 men was in the Vicksburg perimeter. Johnston was assembling a force of 20,000 at Jackson. If Grant moved east against Johnston, Pemberton would sever his line of communications from Grand Gulf. On the other hand, if Grant moved north against Pemberton, Johnston could come in behind him. But the Union cavalry commander, Colonel Benjamin H. Grierson, had already been dispatched with a thousand men on a 600-mile raid through Mississippi: between April 17 and May 2 he had destroyed 60 miles of telegraph lines, cut three railroads, and disrupted Johnston's communications from the north, east, and south. Disregarding the cautious advice of his principal subordinates, Grant cut loose from his base on the river and marched on Jackson.

Grant brushed aside a small Confederate force at Raymond, and struck directly at Johnston's little army in the state capital, driving the Confederates out. In the meantime Pemberton was expending the energy of his troops in grim determination to cut the nonexistent line of communications between Grant and the Mississippi River. Johnston, vainly attempting to unite the divided Confederate forces, ordered Pemberton to join him at Clinton, northwest of Jackson. He was too late. Grant had already turned west toward Vicksburg, and on May 16 intercepted and routed 18,000 of Pemberton's troops at Champion's Hill. Continuing in hot pursuit, Grant on the following day brought to bay a 5,000-man Confederate force, smashing it and capturing a third of the men. Johnston was by now frantically ordering Pemberton to abandon Vicksburg. But Sherman's corps surged northwest to engulf Haynes' Bluff from the rear, and to compel the evacuation of all defenses along the Yazoo north of Vicksburg. Firing from the gunboats on the river, the Union sailors watched Sherman's cavalry chasing the enemy from Chickasaw Bluffs, where his men had suffered defeat five months earlier. Pemberton and his decimated army were surrounded in Vicksburg. Grant's hungry men could once more be supplied from the fleet.

With supporting fire from the gunboats, Grant tried to storm Vicksburg but was repulsed. The Union force entrenched for a protracted siege. Time was on Grant's side: a steady stream of reinforcements poured into his camp; the steady bombardment from land artillery and the gunboats in the river was reducing Vicksburg to rubble. Cut off from supplies, the garrison was ultimately bound to be starved out.

After six weeks of siege, the end came. On July 4, 1863 Pemberton surrendered; his 37,000 men marched out, stacked their arms, and departed on parole. Falling on the day following the defeat of Lee's army at Gettysburg, the capture of Vicksburg shares with it a climactic position in the history of the Civil War.

Grant gave generous credit to the Navy for its vital role in the campaign. For not only did the Union ships maintain the army's single line of communications—the Mississippi River between Cairo and Vicksburg—at the end of which the army was suspended like a Federal bucket in a Confederate well, but the Navy by its control of the river cut Pemberton off from reinforcement from, or escape to, the west. Operating at once as mobile heavy artillery and troop ferries, the gunboats ranged over the whole navigable waterway system in the theater of operations, destroying Confederate supplies, supporting Union garrisons under attack, and cutting off all enemy water-borne traffic.

Meanwhile Farragut's squadron had been performing similar services downstream. Urged on and closely supported by the Admiral, General Banks began the long-postponed offensive against Port Hudson in mid-May of 1863. An assault on May 27 failed, and the pattern of bombardment and siege began. The Confederate garrison was still holding out when news of the fall of Vicksburg reached them, convincing them that protracting the struggle no longer conferred a military advantage. On July 8 they surrendered.

The river was clear at last to merchant shipping from the Northwest and Ohio Valley. The Confederacy was split, in effect extending the "Anaconda" from the Gulf to Cairo. The Union's right flank was secured from any major enfilading threat from the west. The sweeping right wing offensive that was to carry Sherman's troops through Atlanta to the sea to cut off the retreat of Lee's army in 1865 was now a strategic possibility.

THE RED RIVER CAMPAIGN

After the fall of Vicksburg and Port Hudson, the next logical objective for joint army-navy operations was certainly Mobile. Both Grant and Farragut favored an expedition whereby the armies of Banks and Grant, with the support of Farragut's squadron, would invest the last remaining Confederate port on the Gulf. The Gulf blockade would thus be completed, and the Union forces could then advance north to trap the Confederate army being driven down from central Tennessee.

But instead Grant was obliged to give his personal direction to the fighting at Chattanooga, and Banks became involved in eccentric operations in Texas. Although from a purely military point of view campaigning west of the Mississippi was a needless dissipation of Union forces, there were reasons for it. The war was being fought to restore the authority of the Federal government, and it was going to be necessary ultimately to occupy all Confederate territory. Furthermore, military successes in Texas would cut down the trickle of traffic in foreign goods that reached the western part of the Confederacy from Mexico. But most important, Napoleon III of France had been using his armies to intervene in Mexican affairs. French policy favored an independent buffer state between Mexico and the United States: if the Confederacy could not maintain its independence, then perhaps Texas could be reconstituted an independent republic. Successful Union occupation of positions in Texas might forestall serious postwar difficulties. Halleck accordingly ordered Banks to try.

Banks' first effort was a badly executed amphibious attempt against Sabine on the Louisiana-Texas boundary. This was an ignominious failure. Next Banks with naval support occupied Brazos Island at the mouth of the Rio Grande and moved inland to capture Brownsville. The expedition then leapfrogged up the coast with various minor triumphs until it reached Galveston. When Banks requested additional forces to reduce the Confederate defenses there, Halleck continued to favor the Red River route. If Banks cared to enter Texas via Shreveport, he could have the support of Major General Frederick Steele's Arkansas army and the loan of a detachment from Sherman's force to assist him. So the New Year found Banks back in New Orleans, where he was as much occupied by making arrangements for the inauguration of civil government in Louisiana in March as by planning the Red River campaign.

Banks' army was to march overland to rendezvous at Alexandria on March 17, 1864 with Sherman's 10,000 men under Brigadier General A. J. Smith, who would come up the Red River with Porter and the gunboats. The combined force would then advance 350 miles on Shreveport from the south via the river while Steele's army would leave Little Rock to descend on Shreveport from the north. Since Smith's corps was on loan for only the 30-day period when the water in the river would be high enough for the gunboats, the expedition had to be executed swiftly.

The campaign got off to an uneven start. Only Admiral Porter and General Smith carried out their assignments on schedule. With 18 gunboats, including the *Essex, Benton,* and the four remaining Eads ironclads, Porter had waited off the mouth of the Red River until Smith's transports arrived on March 11; then the joint expedition ascended the river to Alexandria, Louisiana in five days. The Union Army quickly captured Fort de Russy, the only prepared Confederate position between the mouth of the river and Alexandria; the Union Navy swept aside obstructions in the river and made raids up the navigable tributaries. By contrast, Banks' army started late, marched slowly, and did not reach Alexandria until the end of the month.

The progress of the combined force was greatly retarded by unseasonably low water in the river, which necessitated dragging the larger ships over the rapids at Alexandria, transshipping supplies from heavier transports below the "falls" to lighter transports above, and leaving behind a sizable garrison to safeguard the supply line. Marching overland, Banks' army had covered half the distance to Shreveport before running into heavy Confederate resistance in the vicinity of Pleasant Hill on April 8. At that time Porter was working up the river with some of the lighter gunboats and part of Smith's corps. By April 10 he had reached Springfield Landing, two-thirds of the way to Shreveport, where the river was so narrow that the Confederates had succeeded in blocking it by sinking a ship athwart the channel from one shore to the other. News then reached Porter that Banks' army was in retreat. The troops with him were ordered to return down river at once.

Blame for the Union rout that ensued rests unequivocably on Banks. Although the Confederate attack at Pleasant Hill had thrown the poorly organized Union column into confusion, a second Confederate attack the next day failed completely. For reasons best known to himself, Banks decided to retreat. This decision caused General Smith and Major General William B. Franklin (the latter a corps commander under Banks) to consider removing Banks and continuing the expedition on their own responsibility, but the situation deteriorated too rapidly for them to do more than make as orderly a withdrawal as possible. Porter was in a particularly precarious position. The water was falling, transports and gunboats were repeatedly grounding, and Confederate troops were severely harassing the ships. The *Eastport* and several smaller vessels were lost with heavy casualties.

By the end of April the entire expedition was back in Alexandria, where the Union Navy was faced with disaster. Instead of the normal 12 feet of water over the rapids at that time of year, there was little more than three feet. Ten gunboats (including the Eads ironclads drawing seven feet of water) and two tugs were trapped. Porter wrote despondently to Secretary Welles, urging a major relief expedition and recommending that command of the army be turned over to General Smith. He had neither hope nor expectation of getting his vessels out and no prospect except the destruction of the best part of the Mississippi Squadron. But later he was able to write: "There seems to have been an especial Providence looking out for us, in providing a man equal to the emergency. Lieutenant Colonel Joseph Bailey, acting engineer of the Nineteenth Army Corps, proposed a plan of building a series of dams across the rocks at the falls and raising the water high enough to let the vessels pass over. This proposition looked like madness, and the best engineers ridiculed it, but Colonel Bailey was so sanguine of success that I requested General Banks to have it done, and he entered heartily in the work." [10]

Bailey, who had had experience with log dams in his native Wisconsin, knew what he was doing. Valiantly assisted by a regiment of "down Maine" lumbermen who happened to be among the troops, he constructed his dam of trees, their trunks parallel to the current, and large log cribs. He weighted and filled in this skeletal structure with any material available, even the machinery of a nearby sugar mill. Under his direction 3,000 men in eight days built a structure that raised the water level high enough for ships to get through. Then the dam gave way in one section. Several of the lighter craft managed to run down in the rush of water. Next, Bailey constructed wing dams at the upper falls within three days, thus creating a total rise in the river level of over six feet and finally making it possible for the entire lightened fleet to pass through the gap. Backwater from the Mississippi had filled the lower Red River sufficiently to enable the ironclads to make good their escape.

That dramatic episode marked both the end of the Red River expedition and the

---

[10] *Official Records*, XXVI, 130.

last major campaign of the Mississippi River Squadron. By midsummer Porter was transferred to more important duty on the East Coast. The Mississippi Squadron went on patrolling the rivers and keeping them open for the support of the armies. The many spirited minor engagements fought between gunboats and Confederate troops or guerillas have little historic significance. The war was obviously entering its final stages, and any threat from the outside, French or otherwise, could be best answered after termination of the war between the North and the South.

21

Closing the Confederate Ports

FROM THE VERY BEGINNING OF the war, the North looked forward to the time when Fort Sumter would be recaptured and Charleston, hotbed of secession, occupied by Union troops. After the capture of Port Royal (November 1861) blockaders based on Hilton Head had made blockade-running from Charleston hazardous, but a trickle of traffic from Nassau and Havana continued to leak through. It was part of the Anaconda strategy to set about the capture of the important port cities of the South as soon as an adequate force could be mustered. Though possessing far less strategic value than New Orleans or Wilmington, Charleston had such symbolic value to both sides that it was inevitable that the North should attempt to occupy it at the first opportunity.

THE DEFENSES OF CHARLESTON HARBOR

The Navy believed this opportunity had arrived when it could send the first considerable number of improved monitors to Rear Admiral Samuel F. Du Pont, commanding the South Atlantic Blockading Squadron. Analogizing the problem of passing the Charleston harbor forts to the hazards of-

fered earlier at Port Royal and in the lower Mississippi below New Orleans, Secretary Welles encouraged Du Pont to try a purely naval bombardment. The powers of the Navy Department were well aware that the obstacles were far more formidable than in the earlier campaigns, but reasoned that the advantage of heavy armor should largely compensate for the greater exposure to enemy fire. Thus, as at Port Royal, it fell to the lot of Admiral Du Pont to be an innovator. At Port Royal he had successfully made the experiment of pitting wooden steamships against land fortifications. At Charleston he commanded the first considerable force of ironclads to duel heavy masonry forts.

As the chart indicates, the sea approaches to Charleston gave little room for an attacking force to maneuver. Distances between the various Confederate forts and batteries were measured in hundreds of yards rather than in miles. A column of naval vessels could approach only via the main ship channel, which would bring them successively under the fire of Fort Wagner (on Morris Island) and Battery Gregg; then between the formidable fire of Fort Sumter to port, and the various defenses on Sullivan's Island to starboard —Fort Beauregard, Battery Rudledge, Fort Moultrie, Battery Marion, and Battery Bee.

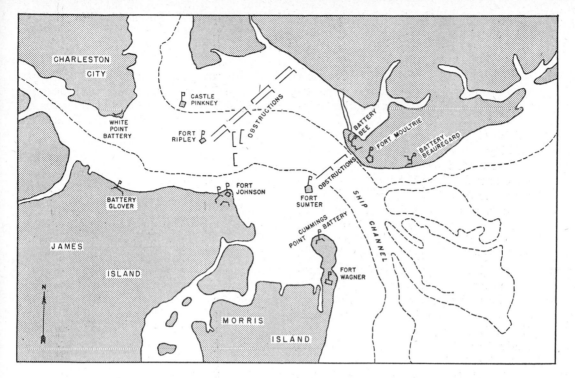

CHARLESTON HARBOR FORTIFICATIONS, 1863

If an attacking fleet succeeded in passing the barrier booms between Fort Sumter and Battery Bee, it still would face Fort Johnson, Fort Ripley, and Castle Pinckney, as well as numerous improvised batteries all along shore around the harbor. Furthermore, the harbor was so small that after passing into the anchorage area, attacking ships would still remain in effective range of the outer forts. Charleston Harbor was, in effect, a cul-de-sac. Merely passing the outer forts would not be enough. These forts had to be substantially silenced.

In addition to the masonry forts (Sumter, Moultrie, and Castle Pinckney), the wartime extensions of the defensive system (such as Fort Wagner) were triumphs of military engineering. Indeed the demonstrated value of the sandbag- and earthwork-protected battery in the Civil War spelled an end to the much more expensive and less efficient masonry fort. General Pierre G. T. Beauregard, who had designed the system and who was in command of the military district, and Briga-

dier General Roswell S. Ripley, who in 1863 was in tactical command of the defenses, were both military engineers of great skill. Assuming from the beginning that ultimately they would be attacked, they followed a policy of constantly strengthening their works. The forts mounted a total of 149 heavy guns (9-inch minimum), besides a much larger number of smaller weapons. Most of the ordnance was of latest design; much of it was rifled—firing cored conical shot of great penetrating power.

Underwater and surface obstacles in the channel were of several varieties: heavy piles driven into the bottom, a log and chain boom, rope barriers designed to foul propellers, and frame, cask, and electrically-fired torpedoes.[1] Considering the strong currents

[1] Frame torpedoes were explosives attached to heavy frames which lay on the bottom. Cask torpedoes were mines made by filling pitch-lined beer kegs with gunpowder and adding weights, flotation chambers, and contact detonators. Electric torpedoes were mines fired from shore positions by galvanic current. The extent and success of Confederate

and narrow channels of the harbor approaches, and the poor maneuvering qualities of ironclads generally, it is not surprising to learn that these obstacles were entirely successful against the Union vessels. Ceaseless Confederate vigilance guarded against reconnaissance by Union boat parties. The principal line of obstructions, between Fort Sumter and Battery Bee, was designed to arrest an attacking formation at the point at which the defense batteries had maximum fire potential. General Ripley had planned interlocking zones or cycles of fire: range stakes were set out, range and deflection errors were predetermined by test-firing each piece of ordnance. All things considered, the path of an attacking column of ships would lead directly through the most devastating heavy artillery fire that could then be directed at any spot on the globe. Every defensive arrangement available to an intelligent and well supplied adversary was developed, tested, and ready. In addition to the shore batteries and forts, the Confederates also had two formidable ironclads inside the harbor, the *Palmetto State* and the *Chicora,* which had—in January prior to the arrival of the United States monitors—sallied out and damaged the gunboat *Mercidita* and the steamer *Keystone State.*

Apart from the maintenance of an effective blockade, Northern efforts against Charleston for the first two years of the war were neither concerted nor particularly effective. At first an attempt was made to close the port by a "stone blockade," i.e., by sinking schooners laden with granite across the ship channels outside the harbor. This precipitated a flurry of diplomatic exchanges, the South indignantly protesting to England the illegality of "permanently" destroying a port, under international law. Presently however the tides swept open new channels, and the scheme was abandoned as impractical. Only in early 1863, as the *New Ironsides,* the monitors *Passaic* and *Nahant,* and later other ironclads were added to Du Pont's fleet, did

it become possible to consider direct attack on the shore fortifications.

Du Pont first tried out his new ships against Fort McAllister, a Confederate earthwork guarding the upper reaches of the Ogeechee River, digested the technical lessons of this test attack,[2] and readied his flotilla for a grand attack on the Charleston forts on April 7, 1863.

THE FIRST
MAJOR ATTACK ON
CHARLESTON HARBOR

Admiral Du Pont's plan of attack was a simple one. His nine ironclads, with the monitor *Weehawken* (Captain John Rodgers) in the van, would proceed in column a cable's length apart up the main ship channel, holding fire until at a point 600 to 800 yards north and east of Fort Sumter, which was to be the primary gunnery objective, to be reduced by deliberate, aimed fire. Once Sumter was silenced, the next objective would be the Morris Island batteries. The flag was to be in *New Ironsides,* fifth ship in line, the only casemated ironclad; the eight others were monitors. Five wooden ships were to constitute a support squadron outside the bar.

The problem offered by the mines and underwater obstructions was to be met by a specially designed raft, fitted with explosive "submarine shells" to blow out piles and log booms and with trailing grapnels to foul the anchor lines of the torpedoes. This device was to be pushed into the barrier by the *Weehawken*. It is evident from the official reports that the seagoing Navy viewed it with lack of confidence, if not with suspicion, and Du Pont's battle plan apparently did not contemplate going beyond the barrier in the first day's fighting.

The planned approach was delayed for about two hours by the *Weehawken's* get-

---

mine warfare in the Civil War is generally little known today—upwards of 20 United States Navy vessels were sunk.

[2] Among other conclusions it was determined that the fuse-settings provided by the Bureau of Ordnance were operationally unsatisfactory, the shells exploding at irregular and unpredictable intervals.

ting one of the grapnels from the "submarine shell raft" fouled in her anchor chain. The cumbersome *New Ironsides* proved so awkward to handle in these narrow waters that she twice had to anchor to avoid running aground. The head of the Union column reached the barrier boom about mid-afternoon, at which time the pre-aimed Confederate guns opened up with all their fury. For about 50 minutes the entire Union force was subjected to a blanket of fire till then unparalleled in weight of metal and accuracy. After the battle Captain Rodgers counted 53 shot marks on the *Weehawken* alone, 47 projectiles struck the *Patapsco,* and the other vessels reported numerous damaging hits. Hundreds of rounds of heavy and well-directed shot were fired at the Union ironclads, while the fleet, firing slowly, got off a total of only 139 shots, nearly all of which were directed against Fort Sumter, the principal Union target. According to the Confederate reports, 55 of these struck the walls and parapet, others falling inside the works. Considerable damage was done to the masonry and the officers' quarters in the parade were demolished, but Sumter's fighting efficiency was not materially impaired.

In order to get back over the bar before dark, Du Pont at 4:30 signaled recall and shepherded his battered line out into deep water. He planned to renew the engagement the next day, until the damage reports from his captains caused him to change his mind.

The ironclad *Keokuk* was injured worst, having been struck more than 90 times. Nineteen shot pierced through her at and just below the waterline. She successfully withdrew from action, but sank the following morning. The damage done to the monitors and to the *New Ironsides* was not severe. Armor plates had been jarred loose, turrets had jammed, and bolt heads, sheared off by concussion, had hurtled lethally about inside the turrets. Yet, despite the fury of the battle, only one man had been killed and few were wounded in the nine vessels. Clearly, the new ship armor was more than adequate defense against the artillery of the times. Among the monitors, only the *Passaic* required immediate yard overhaul.

On the other hand it was evident that the forts could not be silenced in a duel of this sort: the captains in their reports unanimously recommended against a renewal of an attack fraught with risks and without prospect of commensurate gain. The Navy Department and the President reluctantly concurred with the judgment of the Admiral and his subordinates. The capture of Charleston was acknowledged to be beyond the means of a fleet unsupported by amphibious troops.

Admiral Du Pont was presently relieved of command of the South Atlantic Blockading Squadron after nearly two years of arduous duty skillfully performed. Though he failed, it was in attempting the impossible. He deserves to rank with the best of his contemporaries—both for his services to the Navy and for his contributions to naval science.

THE SIEGE OF CHARLESTON

With the arrival of Rear Admiral John A. Dahlgren as Du Pont's relief came a change in plans. Charleston would be invested by a regular siege. Brigadier General Q. A. Gillmore of the Army Engineers would conduct the land phase, and the function of the fleet would be to support the operation.

Troops were moved to Folly Island in July 1863. Here Gillmore constructed batteries to command the Confederate works on the south end of nearby Morris Island. On July 10 he attacked across Lighthouse Inlet, strongly supported by the fire of four ironclads. These vessels paralleled the advance of the troops on the beach, laying down a barrage immediately ahead of them as they progressed to the outer defenses of Fort Wagner, which they reached after 14 hours. The *Catskill* (flag), coming under severe fire during this support operation, was struck some 60 times by fire from Fort Wagner and considerably damaged. The other vessels were less severely treated.

The next day Gillmore's division tried to storm Fort Wagner, but was repulsed with considerable losses. Again on July 18 a more deliberate and carefully planned infantry assault was repulsed. The Navy served as mobile heavy artillery; joined by guns ashore it took Wagner under a ferocious crossfire which drove the Confederate gunners to their underground bombproofs. But as the attacking columns moved up, the Southerners rushed to the parapets once more and poured grapeshot and canister into the assault parties. This murderous action cost 1,530 Union soldiers, killed, wounded, and missing. The 600 yards of sandy beach between the Union rifle pits and the walls of Wagner were so carpeted with blue-clad bodies that the fleet withheld fire on the fort until the wounded were removed.

After this, General Gillmore contented himself with establishing siege parallels and erecting heavy batteries on the south of Morris Island, both to take Fort Wagner under fire and also to deliver fire on Fort Sumter and on the city of Charleston itself, about 10,000 yards away. By mid-August the Army had 60 heavy guns mounted, and periodically thereafter the fleet joined in the incessant barrage kept up on Forts Wagner and Sumter and Battery Gregg. Fort Sumter was reduced virtually to rubble, with most of its guns dismounted. Fort Wagner and Battery Gregg were evacuated before an anticipated assault on September 7. Gillmore had the satisfaction of being able to turn some 19 of the Confederates' own guns on Charleston's remaining harbor defenses.

Hoping at this time to exploit the enemy's disposition to retreat, Dahlgren improvised a plan of night assault by boats upon Fort Sumter. The pounding from the guns of the fleet and from Gillmore's batteries had destroyed or dismounted all of its guns, and the Admiral evidently thought it nearly defenseless. Besides the symbolic value of its capture, Union possession of Sumter would facilitate the lifting of the underwater barriers that blocked the channel to the harbor.

Unfortunately Dahlgren showed bad judgment both in his estimate of the situation, and in failing to consult in advance with the troop commander. Late in the evening of September 8, the night planned for the Navy's assault, the Admiral learned for the first time that Gillmore was also planning a night attack. Allegedly because of a lack of inter-service signals, even then no effort was made to coordinate the separately planned assaults.

About 10 PM, a tug steamed off toward Sumter, with a long tandem tow of ships' boats loaded with volunteer "boarders." The monitors *Passaic* and *Montauk* moved up behind in close support. The hastily evolved plan was to send in a small diversionary force which would attack first near the northwest angle of the fort. Commander T. H. Stevens, in over-all command, intended to withhold the bulk of his force until the defenders' attention had been distracted from his chosen attack point, the southeastern corner. So imperfectly was this plan understood by the boat officers and coxswains that as the diversionary party swept forward, many of the main attack force did likewise. Since surprise was essential, Stevens refrained from shouting orders over the water in easy earshot of the fort. Instead, he quietly passed the word to the remaining boats to advance at best speed.

The Confederates lacked heavy guns in the fort, but there was no lack of garrison and no lack of small arms. Nor were they unprepared. Withholding fire until they could see the dark shape of the boats on the water beneath them, the defenders finally let loose a fusillade of rifle fire, grenades, grape, and canister. A signal rocket arched up from the parade. On the instant Fort Moultrie and the Confederate rams inside the harbor opened up with heavy guns zeroed in on the base of Sumter. Instead of the easy victory Dahlgren had hoped for, the attacking force had run into an ambush.

The attack was nevertheless relentlessly pressed home. Many boats were sunk, but several gained a landing—only to find in most instances a smooth vertical stone wall with no visible means for making fast or scaling. It is a tribute to the courage of the rank and file in that fleet that 133 men succeeded in getting into the fort. These of course were speedily killed or captured. Most survivors of the holocaust at the base of the fort succeeded in escaping in the darkness.

The lessons of this small-scale defeat are

too obvious to require much elaboration: the possible strategic advantages to be gained were not worth the risks; there was a needless lack of coordinated action between Army and Navy; there was inadequate advance briefing of the assault parties; there is good evidence that the Confederate garrison had advance word of the attempt. Dahlgren was a generally capable, even brilliant, officer, whose work both as Chief of the Bureau of Ordnance and as commander of a combat fleet are a source of pride to the Navy. However, the episode of the night of September 8, 1863 adds nothing to his reputation.

After this fiasco, there were not for some time any substantial offensive operations in the vicinity of Charleston. Gillmore banged away with his heavy batteries ashore, and the ironclads occasionally cooperated. Over Fort Sumter the Confederate flag continued to flutter on the stump of the flagstaff.

A joint effort in October 1863 to force evacuation of Sumter through sheer weight of bombardment also failed. Through the next 12 months there were a variety of minor episodes: bombardments, Confederate attacks with their "Davids," landing party reconnaissances up and down the coasts, and "cutting out" expeditions in the rivers, but no major efforts were made to breach the harbor defenses. "Brave Charleston" came to be a Southern watchword: news of the unyielding garrison was telegraphed daily all over the Confederacy.

ATLANTA IS THREATENED

After the simultaneous Union victories of Gettysburg and Vicksburg in July 1863, military activities came virtually to a standstill in the Virginia area and along the Mississippi; central Tennessee became for a time the principal theater of the Civil War. When General William S. Rosecrans USA forced General Braxton Bragg CSA below Chattanooga on the Georgia border, Longstreet detached his corps from Lee's army and rushed by railroad to reinforce Bragg. At the same time Hooker entrained two Federal corps to reinforce Rosecrans. Longstreet arrived first, and at the Battle of Chickamauga (September 1863) the Confederates won a partial victory, forcing the northern army back into Chattanooga. Grant, now given supreme command in the West, relieved Rosecrans and came in person to take charge. He succeeded in restoring the Federal line of communications, and in the Battle of Chattanooga (November 1863) chased Bragg from his entrenchments and into Georgia. Grant now left Sherman in command of the western army and proceeded to Washington to assume supreme command of the Union forces and to exercise direction in the field of the Army of the Potomac.

Now at last a unified land strategy was to be carried out. Grant would strike hard at Lee in Virginia, destroying or at least containing the Army of Northern Virginia, while Sherman headed into Georgia in a great flanking movement, the first major stage of which would be the investing and capture of Atlanta.

The advance on Atlanta gave a new sense of urgency to Farragut's long-cherished scheme to close the port of Mobile. For Sherman reasoned that if a demonstration were made against the Confederacy's only remaining Gulf port, the garrison of Mobile might be reinforced by detachments from the army of General Joseph E. Johnston (who had now replaced Bragg). In any event no assistance from Mobile would be available to the defenders of Atlanta. So in July 1864, the monitors Farragut had previously requested in vain were made available, and a troop contingent was provided to besiege and capture the forts.

CONFEDERATE DEFENSES AT MOBILE—1864

Mobile, Alabama, which had been the leading cotton-shipping port of the United States before the war, lies at the head of a shallow bay in delta country some 25 miles from the open waters of the Gulf of Mexico. To reach the city, large ships were forced to use the single deep-water channel that entered the southwest corner of the bay between Mobile Point and Dauphin Island, while vessels of six-foot draft or less might also employ a secondary channel, north of Dauphin Island, which connected the bay with Mississippi Sound. Thus geography determined that the Confederate defense of Mobile, as of New Orleans, was to consist of forts distant from the city guarding the water approaches and supported insofar as possible by naval vessels.

The fixed defenses at the time of the Union attack consisted of Fort Powell controlling the lesser entrance and Forts Gaines and Morgan flanking the main channel on either side. Extending from Fort Gaines on Dauphin Island were submerged pilings to form an obstruction almost two miles long between the island and the edge of the ship channel. A triple line of moored "torpedoes" (i.e., mines) extended the barrier to within a quarter of a mile of Fort Morgan on Mobile Point. About a fifth of the total were powerful and durable cask torpedoes; the rest were powder-filled metal cones, easily corroded by salt water. The eastern end of the minefield was marked by a buoy, between which and Fort Morgan the Confederates had left open a 150-yard wide channel for blockade runners. As a consequence Fort Morgan—a casemated, pentagonal structure with a water battery and a total of 45 heavy guns—was the key defense work for Mobile Bay.

Again, as at New Orleans, the hope of the defense rested to a great extent on completing an ironclad powerful enough to sink any Union ships able to fight their way past Fort Morgan. This ship, the *Tennessee,* had been building for more than a year at Selma, 150 miles up the Alabama River from Mobile, under the supervision of Admiral Franklin Buchanan, first commander of the *Virginia.* Not so long as the *Virginia,* which she closely resembled, the *Tennessee* was a new ship from the keel up. Her slanting casemate extended below the waterline and then back to the hull to form a "knuckle," making her impervious to the ramming of any likely opponent. Around the bows the knuckle be-

came a ram of unusual strength, a marked improvement over the beak carried by the *Virginia.* Her armament was six 8½-inch Brooke rifles fore and aft, firing 110-pound solid shot, and two 6-inch rifles firing 90-pound solid shot on each broadside.

Events were to demonstrate that the *Tennesee's* strength in armor and armament was offset by defects of construction. Equipped with engines that had previously driven a river steamboat, she could make no better than six knots when loaded for battle. As the result of an oversight her steering chains, instead of being concealed beneath, led over her stern deck where they might be severed by gunfire. Finally, her gunport shutters easily jammed closed when hit. Thus she could use her powerful ram only by lucky chance and readily lost steering and gunpower in battle.

To her builders such matters seemed less important than getting her completed and into the deep waters of Mobile Bay. The wooden hull was towed down to Mobile in March 1864 for the installation of machinery, armament, and armor. This completed, she had to be raised by means of caissons to be shifted over the bar which separated the city from the bay. At last in mid-May the *Tennessee* reached deep water and began holding gunnery practice off Fort Morgan. There she was joined by three light gunboats, the *Selma, Gaines,* and *Morgan.* These four ships with a total of 16 guns were all the Confederacy could muster to contest Farragut's assault fleet of 18 ships and 159 guns.

FARRAGUT PLANS THE MOBILE CAMPAIGN

As soon as Admiral Farragut returned from leave to the West Gulf Squadron in January 1864, he made a reconnaissance at the entrance to Mobile Bay and found that the Confederates had made little progress with their defenses in the 20 months since the fall of New Orleans. "I am satisfied that if I had one ironclad at this time," he reported to Secretary Welles, "I could destroy their whole force in the bay and reduce the forts at my leisure by cooperation of our land forces, say, 5,000 men." [3] His estimate of the situation was accurate enough, but so many Union ships were assigned to the expedition against Charleston or earmarked for the spring campaign in the Red River that he was obliged to wait until the defenses of Mobile Bay had achieved their greatest strength before he could lead an assault against them.

All during the seven months' wait Farragut kept himself informed of every Confederate move through captured Southern newspapers or the reports of deserters. Meanwhile his blockading squadron had its hands full, for the entire Gulf coast from Brownsville to Pensacola still abounded with blockade runners, many of them old foxes who had shifted their operations from the Atlantic coast. To one of Farragut's nature, routine success in blockading could not relieve his chagrin at his inability to get troops or monitors before the *Tennessee* reached Mobile Bay.

On July 8 the first of the Federal monitors, the *Manhattan,* was reported at Pensacola; three more were to follow: the *Tecumseh* from the Atlantic, and the *Winnebago* and *Chickasaw* from the Mississippi. Then the Admiral also learned that he could count on obtaining the required number of troops under Major General Gordon Granger by the end of the month. Within a few days he developed his basic plan for the attack. He decided on an early morning assault when he could count on a flood tide to help carry the ships past Fort Morgan into Mobile Bay and on a southwest wind to carry the smoke of battle away from the ships and into the fort. The wooden ships would be lashed together in pairs as at Port Hudson. The flagship *Hartford,* with the *Metacomet* on her port side, would lead the way through the open channel between the mine field and Fort Morgan. The *Brooklyn* and the *Octorara,* the *Richmond* and the *Port Royal,* the *Lack-*

awanna and the *Seminole,* the *Monongahela* and the *Kennebec,* the *Ossipee* and the *Itasca,* and the *Oneida* and the *Galena* would pair up and follow in that order.

The battle plan was later modified to include the four monitors, which were to pro-

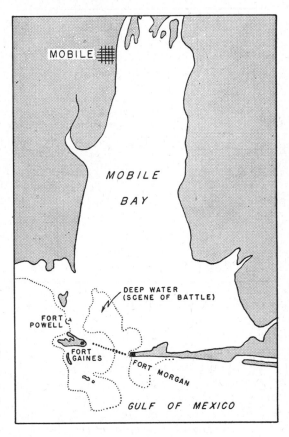

MOBILE BAY, 1864

ceed in a parallel column between the wooden ships and the fort. "The service that I look for from the ironclads," said Farragut, "is, first, to neutralize as much as possible the fire of the guns which rake our approach; next to look out for the [Confederate] ironclads when we are abreast of the forts; and, lastly, to occupy the attention of those batteries which would rake us while running up the bay." [4] A second modification, which Farragut made with great reluc-

---

[3] *Official Records of the Union and Confederate Navies in the War of the Rebellion* (Washington, 1888), XXI, 52.

[4] *Ibid.,* 404.

tance, placed the *Brooklyn* and her consort in the lead, the *Hartford* in second place. This change, urged upon him because of the *Brooklyn's* greater forward firepower and a torpedo-cowcatcher arrangement on her bows, he was to regret. The late arrival of

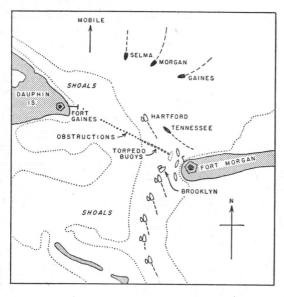

BATTLE OF MOBILE BAY, AUGUST 5, 1864

the monitor *Tecumseh* caused a 24-hour postponement which prevented the fleet from making its attack simultaneously with the army's landing on Dauphin Island to lay siege to Fort Gaines; otherwise the Union attack was launched according to plan.

The four monitors were well equipped for the role assigned them. The single-turreted *Tecumseh* and *Manhattan* were 1,000-ton craft armed with two 15-inch guns which could throw a 440-pound steel-headed bolt as an armor-piercing projectile. The rotating turret was protected by 10-inch armor; superimposed on it was the pilot house, which could be entered only through the turret. The *Winnebago* and *Chickasaw* were shallow-draft, double-turreted river craft protected by 8½-inch armor and armed with four 11-inch guns apiece. No faster than the *Tennessee*, they had heavier armor and larger guns.

PASSING FORT MORGAN

At 5:30 on the morning of August 5, 1864 the Federal fleet got underway for the entrance to the channel. Every protective device that had proved valuable at New Orleans or Port Hudson was employed and, if possible, improved upon. The *Tecumseh* steamed slowly along the Fort Morgan side of the channel, somewhat in advance of the *Brooklyn* pair on a parallel course. The first shots were exchanged just after seven o'clock, the *Tecumseh* firing twice at the Fort; she then reserved her fire for the *Tennessee,* which was discovered moving slowly into the bend in the channel beyond the Confederate mine field. While a general cannonading was joined behind him, Captain Craven of the *Tecumseh* devoted his attention exclusively to the Confederate ram. Her position and the narrowness of the channel between the mine field buoy and Fort Morgan made him doubt his orders from Farragut: "The vessels will take care to pass to the eastward of the eastern-most buoy, which is clear of all obstruction." [5] Craven turned his monitor to head for the *Tennessee* on a collision course, and passed about 300 yards ahead of the *Brooklyn*. His 15-inch guns loaded with 60-pound charges and steel bolts, he bore down on his opponent. On the Confederate ship the officers and crew braced themselves for the shock, for Admiral Buchanan ordered them to hold fire until the two ships actually came together. At this tense moment when they were little more than 100 yards apart, the *Tecumseh* ran upon a mine which exploded and ripped out her bottom. The monitor sank bow first almost instantly, her stern rising out of the water so that her propeller was seen turning in the air as she plunged to the bottom. Of her complement of over 100, only 21 survived.

Fortunately for the Union attack this catastrophe did not prevent the other monitors from maintaining their proper stations and carrying out their assigned duties, but a disastrous situation was rapidly developing

_____

[5] *Ibid.,* 398.

among the wooden ships. The *Brooklyn*'s captain, hearing a confused report of objects in the water ahead, stopped his ship and then backed her down against the current. Within a matter of minutes the *Brooklyn* and her consort lay across the channel, bows on and abreast the fort, while the other wooden ships bore down on them.

Farragut had sent his pilot into the maintop for a clear view above the smoke of the guns; he himself had taken a station in the port main rigging, climbing higher as the smoke rose and maintaining a position of easy communication with the pilot, with the captain of the *Metacomet* on the paddlebox of his ship alongside, and with the captain of the *Hartford*. When the *Tecumseh* sank, the Admiral had ordered a boat from the *Metacomet* to rescue survivors in the water. Now, with the *Brooklyn* barring his way and threatening to congest his entire fleet where the channel passed close to Fort Morgan's guns, Farragut ordered the *Hartford* to pass to port around the stern of the *Brooklyn*, through the mine field, and into the channel again. It was on this occasion according to certain postwar accounts that Farragut shouted "Damn the torpedoes! Full steam ahead!" [6] Although her crew reported hearing the primers of the torpedoes snapping, the flagship passed through. As the Admiral had suspected all along, most of the torpedoes were harmless through long immersion.

The *Hartford* proved too nimble for the clumsy *Tennessee*, which finally turned back to attack the other Union ships. The flagship meanwhile suffered heavy casualties from the enfilading fire of the Confederate gunboats until she had room to maneuver and bring her guns to bear on them. Her broadsides then quickly repulsed the gunboats, and the *Metacomet* cut loose and went after them. The fastest ship in the Union fleet, she succeeded in overtaking the *Selma* and forcing

her to surrender. She had also damaged the *Gaines* so badly that her crew beached and destroyed her. Only the *Morgan* made good her escape to the fort and eventually to Mobile.

After blocking the rest of the Federal ships under the guns of Fort Morgan, the *Brooklyn* at length got back on course and led the column through the mine field a mile behind the *Hartford*. Several vessels were hit but only the *Oneida*, at the end of the line, was disabled. Even she got past the fort with the help of her escort and the flood tide. As these ships trailed into the bay they were met by the *Tennessee*, which ran through the fleet, exchanging broadsides with ship after ship but seriously damaging none and in return receiving no injury worse than a perforated smokestack. After passing the last ship, the *Tennessee* made a long, slow turn within range of Fort Morgan's guns before returning for a second attack on the Union fleet.

It was now 8:30 AM. Four miles up the bay the *Hartford* anchored and Farragut sent his crew to breakfast. The other Union ships soon anchored nearby. The captain of the flagship summed up the battle at that point by remarking to the Admiral: "What we have done has been well done, sir; but it all counts for nothing so long as the *Tennessee* is there under the guns of Morgan." [7]

THE END OF THE *TENNESSEE*

The Confederate admiral had decided to use the six hours' fuel remaining to him in an unexpected attack on Farragut's ships. After doing all the damage she could, the *Tennessee* might in his opinion serve as a floating battery in the defense of Fort Morgan. Characteristically Buchanan wanted above all else to have another chance at the *Hartford*.

When Farragut was told that the *Tennessee* was returning, he could not believe it. "I did not think old Buck was such a fool," [8]

[6] Farragut himself records that he sought Divine guidance through prayer and heard an inner voice tell him to go forward. Eye-witnesses agree that the Admiral did signal for full speed ahead. For a discussion of this point, see Charles Lee Lewis, *David Glasgow Farragut: Our First Admiral* (Annapolis, 1943), 469.

[7] *Ibid.*, 274.

[8] *Battles and Leaders of the Civil War*, 4 vols. (New York, 1884-88), IV, 407.

he exclaimed, for he had feared the *Tennessee* might attack the light ships he had left outside the bay or wait to make a night attack on the fleet. Instead, Buchanan was playing directly into his hands.

What followed was a wild melee. First the *Monongahela* and then the *Lackawanna* rammed the Confederate, each attacker taking far greater damage than she inflicted. At last the two flagships came together obliquely, collided at the bow, and ground past each other port side to port side. The *Hartford*'s shot, fired at a ten-foot range, bounded off the *Tennessee*'s casemate, while the Confederate, plagued throughout the battle by bad primers, was able to fire only one shot, her last, into her opponent. Then the *Lackawanna* steaming at full speed for the *Tennessee* crashed instead into the circling *Hartford* near where Farragut was standing.

The monitors now moved in on the *Tennessee*. The *Chickasaw* followed behind the ram as though being towed, her shot jamming port shutters, cutting the steering chains, and wounding Admiral Buchanan. The only shot that penetrated the ram's armor however was a steel bolt from a 15-inch gun of the *Manhattan*. One of the Confederate officers reported that it "admitted daylight through our side, where, before it struck us, there had been two feet of solid wood, covered with five inches of solid iron." [9]

Almost dead in the water, three port shutters jammed, her steering gone, stacks shot away so that her gun-deck was filled with suffocating heat and fumes, the *Tennessee* was in a hopeless position. As the entire Union fleet was moving in for the kill and the Confederates could bring no guns to bear, Captain Johnston, with Admiral Buchanan's consent, climbed out onto the casemate top to show the white flag. It was then 10 AM.

The Confederate naval forces had lost a total of 12 killed and 20 wounded in the entire battle, and only two were killed and nine wounded in the *Tennessee*. Union casualties for the battle were 52 killed and 170

wounded, not counting those lost when the *Tecumseh* sank. The *Hartford* alone had 25 killed and 28 wounded.

FINAL STAGES OF THE MOBILE CAMPAIGN

Fort Powell was evacuated and destroyed by its garrison on the night of the naval battle. The next day Fort Gaines surrendered. General Granger's troops were then transferred to Mobile Point, and Fort Morgan capitulated before the end of the month.

These victories brought to an end Mobile's traffic with the outside world. The city's military importance to the Union had already passed, for Mobile was no longer needed as a Union base for a land campaign. No serious attempt was directed against the city itself until the spring of 1865, when six Union ships and a launch were sunk by mines while the Navy was cooperating in siege operations undertaken by the Army. With the fall of outlying fortifications, Mobile was finally occupied by Union troops on April 12, three days after the surrender of Lee at Appomatox.

SHERMAN'S MARCH

In the meantime, Sherman had forced Johnston back on Atlanta. Using Fabian tactics, the weaker army of Johnston obliged Sherman to take 74 days to achieve a 100-mile advance. But President Davis, demanding action, replaced Johnston with Hood, who went on the offensive and was beaten three times in succession. Sherman now broke loose from his line of communications and circled Atlanta, cutting rail lines and obliging Hood to evacuate the city to avoid being bottled up and captured. The near coincidence of the Battle of Mobile Bay and the fall of Atlanta (September 2, 1864) marked the beginning of the end for the Confederacy.

Leaving General George H. Thomas in command of a force adequate to defeat Hood, Sherman himself set out with 60,000

[9] *Official Records*, XXI, 582.

men on his celebrated march to the sea. Living off the country, his army laid waste to a strip 60 miles wide through the one remaining major granary of the South. He emerged at Savannah in late December, 1864, captured the city, and headed north into the Carolinas, where a small Confederate army under Johnston was unable to make effective resistance.

As word of Sherman's advance reached Dahlgren off Charleston harbor, the admiral formed a naval brigade equipped with two field howitzers, which was to do good service in General John G. Foster's command, campaigning between Savannah and Charleston. In addition, the navy's shallow-draft gunboats were employed to good advantage in providing logistic and gunfire support to Sherman's army as it marched north from Savannah. The doom of Charleston was sealed as Sherman's victorious Westerners closed in behind the city, which the Confederate garrison had to evacuate on February 18, 1865 in order to avoid capture.

And so at long last the officers of the fleet walked the nearly deserted streets of the city which had so long defied their guns.

The last act in the tragic drama of the Civil War was about to begin. Discounting Johnston's small force operating independently, Grant envisioned the final strategy as a pincers movement on Lee's army, tied to Richmond by the determination of the Confederate government to hold the capital at all costs. As Sherman's legions pushed inexorably north, Grant suddenly shifted the bulk of his forces to reinforce the Army of the James operating to the south and east of Richmond. Petersburg came under siege; the Petersburg-Richmond area became a gigantic fortress, covered by over 40 miles of entrenchments and dependent on rail connections to the south and west for supplies and reinforcements. The Weldon railroad line, connecting Richmond with Wilmington, North Carolina, 225 miles to the south, was of special importance to the Confederacy, for Wilmington was by now the principal port of entry for foreign supplies brought through the blockade. Through the summer and fall of 1864, various Federal operations against the Weldon line and the other railroads leading into Richmond and Petersburg achieved partial success. But by breaking bulk below Petersburg and transhipping by wagon, the defenders of the last Confederate bastion continued to bring in a trickle of war supplies from overseas.

THE FORT FISHER CAMPAIGN

As early as the winter of 1862, Secretary Welles had unsuccessfully petitioned the War Department to provide troops for a joint Army-Navy attack on the Confederate defenses at the mouth of the Cape Fear River in North Carolina. Wilmington, at the fall line of the river, was already a principal port for the blockade runners. The dual approaches to the river mouth, the notoriously dangerous Frying Pan Shoals off Smith's Island, and the comparative remoteness from Union bases made the maintenance of a close blockade here especially difficult. The excellent rail connections between Wilmington and Richmond and other points in the interior of the Confederacy gave Wilmington a vital strategic importance—far greater than that of Mobile, second only to that of New Orleans. But with the multitude of demands for troops Secretary of War Stanton for nearly three years could never seem to spare even the modest contingent required. Meanwhile the principal fortification at the mouth of the river, Fort Fisher, was gradually developed by the Southern command from a scantily manned "sand battery" to a very formidable complex of well protected ordnance.

In September 1864 Secretary Welles renewed his proposal for an amphibious operation. Grant was interested in the operation as a step in isolating Lee from all outside supplies, and promised an adequate force by the first of October. Because of failing health and near exhaustion, Farragut declined the proferred naval command. Admiral Porter, eager to regild his somewhat tarnished laurels after the fiasco of the Red

River, embraced this new opportunity with his characteristic enthusiasm.

THE FIRST FORT FISHER EXPEDITION

The plan of campaign as originally conceived was simple. A fleet mounting 150 guns would bombard Fort Fisher, which was known to be defended by about 75 pieces of ordnance. An army force to consist of not less than 8,000 troops would be landed under covering fire on the open beach north of New Inlet. This force would throw a trench line across to the Cape Fear River, thereby cutting off the fort from reinforcement and supply from the city. Capture of the fort by assault or siege could then be hazarded.

By mid-October a heterogeneous fleet of over a hundred vessels was mustered at Hampton Roads; it included everything from the latest screw frigates and ironclads down to makeshift gunboats converted from harbor ferries. It was the largest fleet to be assembled under the United States flag in the 19th century. Drilling of this awkwardly large and varied force in simple maneuver and gunnery presented an unusual command problem, which Porter cheerfully faced. The naval commander adopted an improved and more precise set of blockade instructions to govern interim operations off the mouths of the Cape Fear River, [10] set about getting to know his captains better, and had lithographed for general distribution a chart of the projected bombardment showing the position of each of the 55 gunnery vessels.

There ensued a period of tiresome waiting: the bombardment force had been concentrated by dangerously stripping the blockading force all up and down the coast. Both Porter and Welles feared that any protracted delay might jeopardize the operation.

Yet with Army and Navy serving only as cooperating entities without an over-all commander, a coordinated plan required a high measure of compatibility between Army and Navy seniors. This was notoriously lacking between Porter and General Benjamin Butler, who was to furnish the troops from his force at Bermuda Hundred. Moreover Butler was disposed to be dilatory.

After what appeared to Porter to be maddening procrastination, General Butler appeared on board his flagship, the *Malvern,* at Hampton Roads in late November. Instead of simply sending the agreed-on assault force, Butler further exasperated the impatient Porter by propounding a pet project he had conceived to make the job easy. This was to mine Fort Fisher by exploding a powder-laden ship near its walls immediately prior to the landing. Though dubious of the probable effects of this giant "torpedo," Porter, a born innovator, listened to the tepidly favorable opinion of certain civilian scientists and decided it was worth a try. In any event it would get the expedition under way, and that was the big thing.

Into the steamer *Louisiana,* weakened by dry rot and eligible for survey, was stuffed 150 tons of black powder. Fuse trains were laid about, and a clockwork device was improvised to set off the explosion after the volunteer crew had placed their strange weapon in position. Gathering the powder from various army and navy magazines, embarking the troops, and a spell of severe gales caused further delay so that it was mid-December before the Union armada left Hampton Roads. By this time of course the South knew almost as much of the Union plan, including the powder-ship, as did the Union commanders. Any possible advantage of surprise had long since been frittered away.

As the transports were making rendezvous with the fleet, another gale blew up, causing the attempt to be postponed again. The Navy vessels simply cast anchor and rode it out, but the transports scurried back to Beaufort. The bold venture was finally arranged for the night of December 22.

The *Wilderness* towed in the doomed

---

[10] These involved three concentric semicircles of patrol—one close inshore, one 12 miles out beyond Frying Pan Shoals, one 130 miles offshore. No blockade runner could hope to pass all three patrols at night.

Louisiana, which was finally anchored with some difficulty close to the beach. The crew of the powder-ship then started a pine-knot fire on the deck in the cabin, lit candles set in trains of loose powder, and rigged the clock that was the primary exploder. During the approach and afterwards—though the night was dark—there was a constant danger of a premature explosion from accident or from a ranging shot from the Confederate stronghold. At length the volunteers began to appear at the rail of the *Louisiana,* to be checked off by the boatswain as they slipped into the waiting boats. Presently Commander A. C. Rhind, in charge of the operations, gave the order to pull away to the *Wilderness,* waiting at a discreet distance.

There was an unexplained delay in the explosion. The clocks were set for 1½ hours, but apparently it was the fire that finally set off the powder, 20 minutes past the scheduled time. After the painful suspense of the risky preparations, the explosion proved to be a disappointing failure. The ship disintegrated with a flash and a roar like a thunderclap. The sea was illuminated for miles around. But the shock was scarcely felt in the fleet, and bothered the well-protected Confederates not at all.[11]

At daylight, the fleet stood in to their scheduled bombardment positions and opened a terrific cannonade. About 115 shots a minute registered on or within the walls of the fort. Two Confederate magazines were blown up by the Union shells, and wooden structures were set on fire. So quickly were the defenders harried to the shelter of bombproofs that they inflicted no casualties whatever in the fleet. In a little over an hour the fort was completely silenced. Though the bombardment was continued throughout the day, no transports appeared. At sundown the bombardment ships withdrew from range, having at least established that they could at will overpower the guns ashore.

The next morning, Christmas Day, the transports finally arrived. Porter dispatched 17 gunboats to cover the landing and provided 100 ship's boats for putting troops ashore. At long last the assault was to be made.

Once more the fleet stood in and took the fort under slow, deliberate fire, while the soldiers were landed five miles to the north. Porter was delighted to see the blue-clad skirmish line reconnoitering and sharpshooting near the outer works of the fort. One bold infantry officer coolly clambered up the parapet and seized a Confederate flag that had been shot away by naval gunfire.

Then came the incredible news that the 3,000 troops put ashore were being re-embarked. Not knowing the circumstances of this decision, Porter assumed the attack would be made the next day, and detailed the ironclads to keep the fort under fire through the night. But he presently received word from Butler that the assault was impracticable—"as it [Fort Fisher] was left substantially uninjured as a defensive work by the navy fire."[12] Contented with 300 prisoners captured in some outposts, Butler firmly announced his decision to return to Hampton Roads at once.

Porter's exasperation at this turn of events was matched only by Grant's. Butler was put on waiting orders at home, and Brigadier General Godfrey Weitzel succeeded him in command of the Army of the James. Porter pressed for a renewal of the attack under a bolder army command. Meanwhile, he returned the fleet to Beaufort to replenish ammunition.

THE SECOND FORT FISHER EXPEDITION

If the North had learned a lesson in the first expedition, so had the South. Fort Fisher had been entirely repaired and considerably strengthened. Heavy reinforcements enlarged the garrison. General Braxton Bragg was placed in command.

---

[11] It is probable that most of the powder simply burned, rather than exploded. In view of the Halifax (N.S.) disaster during World War I and other unscheduled explosions of munitions ships, it is possible that Butler's plan—in theory—was better than generally credited.

[12] *Official Records,* II, 251.

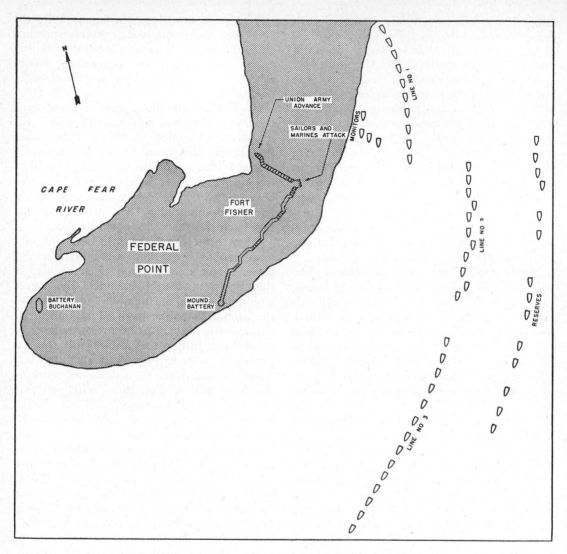

THE SECOND ATTACK ON FORT FISHER, JANUARY 13-15, 1865

Meanwhile Brigadier General A. H. Terry USA had arrived to take command of the troops, and on January 13, 1865, the Second Fort Fisher Expedition got under way. Terry well knew Grant's determination that there should be no delay. As soon as the transports anchored, he prepared to land the troops.

With close inshore support from the shoal draft gunboats, Terry's men poured ashore as fast as a shuttle service of 120 boats could transport them. Within an hour after they had landed, they had "dug in" all the way across the peninsula, cutting the fort off from support from the mainland. The fleet meanwhile kept up an avalanche of fire on the fort.

General Terry kept his men busy entrenching through most of the night, and on the morning of January 14 his position was reckoned by General Bragg as too strong for attack. Rapidly extending their positions, the Union infantry pushed their outposts to within 500 yards of the fort. The 2,500 defenders were cut off completely, closely be-leaguered, and hammered mercilessly by the massed floating artillery of Porter's ships. Porter had his divisions carefully organized and positioned for maximum bombardment effectiveness. A firm believer in the efficacy of mass and volume of fire, he never neg-lected precise planning and accuracy. The monitors and the *New Ironsides* kept up a night bombardment as well.

The entire fleet renewed its barrage at day-break, and maintained it up to the scheduled time of assault, which was 3 PM. The Navy was to be represented in the storming of the fort by a force of 1,600 bluejackets and 400 marines, who would attempt to "board" the naked sea face of the works. Simultaneously, the Army infantry would attack from their trench line, and take the enemy in the flank and rear.

The initial phase of the operation went as scheduled. The "Mound Battery" returned the ships' fire with some effect at first, but the defenders were soon driven from their guns to the bombproofs, and the ships' boats with their landing parties were scarcely fired on. The sailors and marines "dug in" just above the beach, and ditched their way for-ward to within 200 yards of the sea face of Fort Fisher.

The signal for the final rush was given at 3 o'clock. The ships raised the curtain of fire to the upper batteries. Every steam whistle in the fleet was blown. The race for the para-pets began. Led by division officers, the sailors, armed with revolvers and cutlasses, dashed gallantly forward. The plan had been for the marines, lying in the advanced rifle pits, to deliver covering small arms fire, and keep the enemy from the parapet. In the inevitable confusion of this unrehearsed operation, the marine party was not prop-erly stationed, and enemy troops stood up on the parapets and poured a withering musketry fire into the advancing blue line. Three times the surviving officers rallied their men to try the assault again. A very few of the sailors reached the parapet, only to be clubbed and bayoneted by the de-fenders. In a matter of minutes the brave effort was over, an evident failure. Leaving

nearly 300 of their number on the bloody sand, the survivors streamed back to their rifle pits.

Meanwhile the Army was having better luck. Profiting from the distraction offered by the sailors' assault, Terry's men stormed and captured two traverses. As the Confed-erate defenders on the parapets saw the sailors' attack break off, they paused to give three cheers—only to receive a volley of rifle fire in their backs as the Union infantry wave swept in behind them. Each of the traverses was a separate little fort in itself. The infantry methodically set about storm-ing them one by one, while the fleet kept its support fire just ahead of their advance. Finally the Mound Battery was reached and successfully assaulted. The surviving Con-federates fled down the beach toward the end of Federal Point. Realizing the hope-lessness of their position, they finally threw down their arms and surrendered—1,800 men. More than 700 Confederates had been killed or wounded.

Union Army losses were 691. The Navy lost 309. In terms of the numbers involved, this was one of the bloodiest battles of the war.

Tactically, the Second Fort Fisher Expedi-tion has a special interest as being the only successful large-scale amphibious attack against a strongly fortified position made by the Army and the Navy in the whole course of the war. It demonstrated the value of heavy, aimed support fire by ships. It showed the feasibility of bold, well coordinated as-saults on even the strongest and best engi-neered defenses.

Strategically, the capture of Fort Fisher and the consequent sealing of the port of Wilmington completed the "Anaconda," and may be said to have finished the Navy's primary role in the war.

THE FINALE

With his seemingly inexhaustible rein-forcements and supplies, Grant was in a posi-tion ultimately to outflank the defenses of the Richmond-Petersburg bastion to the north and to the south. Striking in first one sector, then in the other, he went on applying pressure to the depleted Confederate forces. Lee was finally forced to evacuate Richmond (April 2, 1865) to avoid encirclement. As the Army of Northern Virginia headed west with the object of joining forces with Johnston in the mountains, Grant made his final, checkmating move. Shifting his main force parallel and to the south of Lee, Grant placed himself in an intercepting position. With Sheridan's cavalry directly athwart his line of retreat, Lee surrendered at Appomatox (April 9). A week later Johnston surrendered to Sherman. The war was over. At the cost of nearly a million casualties, the Union was preserved and the institution of slavery destroyed.

The significance of the Civil War in the development of military strategy and tactics has been enormous. Coming as it did in a comparatively peaceful period of the world's history and in a time of rapid industrialization and technological development, the war immediately became a principal study of war colleges and general staffs all over the world. In many respects it was a "modern war": railroads were first utilized to move large bodies of troops; armored vessels were first employed on a substantial scale; the telegraph, submarine mines, rifled ordnance, and breech-loading small arms were first used extensively. Above all, it was the first war in which industrial capacity itself became a major (if not in fact the decisive) weapon.

In the Union grand strategy the navy performed a subordinate but essential role. Lacking substantial naval opposition, the Federal Navy did not need to *achieve* sea supremacy. It could at once begin to *exercise* it. By blockade it cut the South off from imported supplies and foreign assistance. By shore bombardment and support to amphibious operations it enormously aided the Union armies. To Gideon Welles' ferryboat navy goes a good share of the credit for the ultimate victory.

22

Naval Developments
in the Late 19th Century

THE SUCCESS OF U.S.S. *Monitor* in the Battle of Hampton Roads led the United States Navy to construct many small single-turreted monitors and some big, seagoing monitors for coastal service in the Civil War. Immediately after the war two of the large monitors made what were considered remarkable ocean voyages for ships of their type. The *Monadnock* steamed from Hampton Roads to San Francisco, and the *Miantonomah* from New York to England and Russia. As early as 1860 an English naval designer, Captain Cowper P. Coles RN, had invented a better turret than Ericsson's, and three years later he built for Denmark a double-turreted monitor, the *Rolf Krake*, which withstood 150 hits from Prussian batteries of Krupp rifles. But until 1866 ironclads, seagoing or otherwise, had seen action only in coastal and inland waters. In that year an English shipyard completed the 4,000-ton turret ship *Affondatore* for the Italian navy just in time for the first high sea battle of ironclads off the Austrian island of Lissa in the Adriatic.

LISSA: THE FIRST SEA BATTLE BETWEEN IRONCLADS

If the ships of the Italian navy in 1866 had been soundly built, properly equipped, and effectively manned and commanded, Italy would have had the most powerful navy in the world. Her fleet included 12 seagoing armored ships, of which seven were steam-and-sail frigates. The newest of these, the *Re d'Italia* and the *Re di Portogallo,* were protected by 7-inch armor and mounted 36 and 28 guns respectively, most of them large Armstrong rifles up to ten inches in caliber. The turret-ram *Affondatore,* expected momentarily from England, mounted two 10-inch Armstrong rifles in two turrets and carried a 26-foot iron ram. The principal wooden ships of the Italian navy were seven frigates of from 32 to 54 guns and four corvettes of from six to 20 guns ranging in caliber up to seven inches. All the Italian ships were steam-propelled; most were screw-driven; and none of the ironclads was more than five years old.

Nevertheless this navy had serious weaknesses. The new ironclads were hastily built and inadequately fitted out. The Italian sailors who manned them were enthusiastic but untrained. And the flag officers who commanded the fleet and its subdivisions lacked aggressive spirit. In particular the commander in chief, Admiral Count Carlo di Persano, seemed to have little enthusiasm for the war or the naval campaign in which he was about to engage.

The war had begun on June 14, 1866, when Prussia attacked Austria as a part of Bismarck's plans for winning control over the rising nation of Germany. Bound by an agreement with Prussia, Italy had declared war on June 20 with hopes of recovering Venice from Austria. The Prussian army was quickly successful on land and by July 3 had won a decisive victory at Sadowa. Meantime the Austrians had badly beaten an Italian army at Custozza on June 24. To counterbalance their defeat on land and increase their bargaining power at the peace conference, the Italian government desired some success at sea.

All that stood in the way of a victory for the Italian navy was a much inferior Austrian fleet under the command of Rear Admiral Wilhelm von Tegetthoff. The Austrian commander had only seven ironclad ships to oppose the 12 of Admiral Persano. All of them were frigates, and none had armor exceeding five inches in thickness. Although they mounted from 18 to 30 guns, most of these were of smaller caliber than the Italian guns; about half were muzzle-loading smooth-bores. Tegetthoff's principal wooden ships were the *Kaiser*, a line of battle ship of 92 guns, five frigates of 31 to 51 guns, and one corvette of 22 guns. Only two or three guns on each of the wooden ships were rifles.

On the day Italy declared war, the Ministry of Marine ordered Admiral Persano to move his fleet from Taranto at the heel of the Italian boot to Ancona about halfway up the Italian Adriatic coast, where it would occupy a more central position for offensive

operations against the Austrian fleet at Pola, some 90 miles across the Adriatic to the north. Twelve days before, Persano had been ordered "to sweep the enemy from the Adriatic and to attack and blockade them wherever he should find them." Since the Austrians were gaining on land and with their inferior fleet stood to lose at sea, Tegetthoff's orders quite properly were less aggressive. When he requested permission of the Archduke to take the offensive, he was directed not to extend his operations beyond Lissa to the south and to keep the mouth of the River Po and the coast of Venice covered.

During the first few weeks of the war Persano carried out his aggressive orders by avoiding action off his own fleet base with an inferior squadron under Tegetthoff and engaging in useless maneuvers in the central Adriatic, during which he did not even exercise his untrained gun crews. Finally came orders from the king himself "to attempt against the hostile fortresses or fleet what operations may be thought convenient to obtain a success." In consultation with the Minister of Marine, Persano decided to attack and seize the small Austrian island of Lissa, 130 miles from Ancona across the Adriatic to the southwest. On July 16 his fleet sortied, and the next afternoon it was off the island.

During two days of bombardment operations, directed principally against the defenses around the town of Lissa, the 600 guns of Persano's ships were unable to silence all of the 88 smaller caliber guns of the Austrian forts. Meantime Persano's vice admiral made only a half-hearted attempt at a landing north of the town, the failure of which he blamed on adverse sea conditions. The fire of the shore batteries killed 16 men and wounded 114 aboard the ships and put one ironclad frigate out of action. The fleet had fruitlessly shot away a large part of its ammunition, and none of the ships had much more than a two-day supply of coal left aboard. Nevertheless, on the morning of July 20 Persano resumed his amphibious assault. His wooden ships were about to land troops north of Lissa and his ironclads to resume

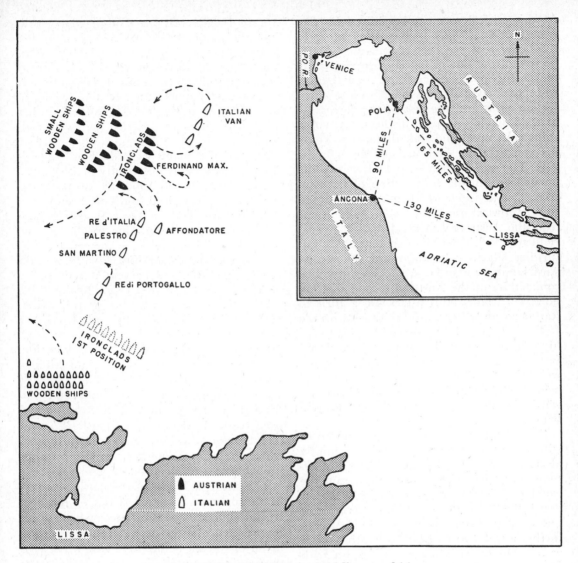

BATTLE OF LISSA, JULY 20, 1866

the bombardment of the forts around the town when the Austrian fleet was sighted steaming down from the northwest at its full speed of eight to ten knots.

Tegetthoff's ships were in three wedge-shaped divisions with the divisions in column. In the first wedge were his seven ironclads led by his flagship the *Ferdinand Maximilian* at the point. The second wedge contained his wooden frigates and one corvette, led by the wooden line of battle ship *Kaiser*. His remaining smaller vessels formed the third

wedge, which brought up the rear. These modified line-abreast formations were intended principally to facilitate ramming.

Caught in the midst of an amphibious operation with his force divided, Persano first ordered his ships to form line abreast, evidently also planning to make use of his ships' rams. As the Austrian fleet approached however, he formed his immediately available ironclads in column and steered across the head of the enemy formation, probably with the intention of attacking its left flank.

At this critical moment he shifted his flag from the *Re d'Italia* to the *Affondatore* in the belief that the fleet commander should be free of the line of battle to supervise the movements of his other ships. As a result a wide gap opened between the first three Italian ships and the rest of the force. Tegetthoff, having signaled his fleet, "Armored ships rush upon and sink the enemy," took his van division, of ironclads, through the gap. The van Italian ship had meanwhile opened fire on the port section of the Austrian first division, which in answer turned to port toward the Italian van. At the same time the Austrian starboard section turned right to attack the Italian center, which was turning left in column toward the second Austrian division of large wooden ships. The commander of the Austrian second division however avoided this attack by a turn to starboard, and after a brief skirmish with the Italian rear, which had turned to port to cut him off, he turned farther to starboard and formed a rough column to attack the Italian wooden ships. These in the meantime had been milling about aimlessly to the southward, despite orders from Persano to join battle.

From here on, the battle was a melee in which the movements of ships were mostly obscured by fog and smoke. Twice the *Affondatore* tried without success to ram the wooden *Kaiser*. With better luck the *Kaiser* struck the *Re di Portogallo* a glancing blow but was set ablaze by her gunfire. After a further attack by the *Affondatore,* the *Kaiser* was forced to withdraw toward Lissa with most of the other large wooden ships of the Austrian fleet following in her wake. In the meantime the Italian ironclad gunboat *Palestro* was set afire by shell and shortly after the battle blew up with the loss of almost all hands. The most spectacular action of all was the ramming of the *Re d'Italia* by Tegetthoff's flagship, the *Ferdinand Maximilian.* As the *Maximilian* groped about in the murk of battle, she came upon the *Re d'Italia* broadside to. The Italian ship had lost rudder control and was barred from going ahead by another Austrian ship. Backing down, she was dead in the water when the *Maximilian* at full speed plunged her ram into the side of the *Re d'Italia,* heeling her heavily to starboard. While the *Maximilian* backed slowly away, the *Re d'Italia* righted herself quickly and continued heeling to port as her own momentum and the weight of tons of water rushing into a great hole in her side capsized her and carried her to the bottom.

Shortly after noon Tegetthoff ordered his fleet to re-form in the vicinity of Lissa, and Persano, after several abortive efforts to renew the battle, retired to the west. Since the Austrian fleet had had several vessels damaged and was still inferior to the enemy, Tegetthoff did not pursue. Anyway, his mission was accomplished, for he had driven off the Italian fleet and prevented the seizure of Lissa. Despite their damages all his ships except the *Kaiser* were still fit for action, and even she was sufficiently refitted in 24 hours. His casualties amounted to only 38 killed and 138 wounded. On the Italian side, in addition to the losses in the amphibious operation, 667 men had been killed and 39 wounded, the new *Re d'Italia* and the *Palestro* had been sunk, and the *San Martino* had been badly damaged in the battle. Low on fuel, Persano withdrew to his base at Ancona, where the *Affondatore* later sank in a storm, probably as a result of battle damage.

The strategic lesson of the battle was perfectly apparent to naval critics of the age. By failing to seek out and destroy or neutralize the enemy battle force and thus gain command of the sea before involving himself in the amphibious operation, Persano had practically doomed himself to defeat from the start. Furthermore, he and his subordinates handled the amphibious operation with singular ineptitude, and in the course of it Persano made no preparation to cover himself against interference by the enemy fleet. Consequently he was forced to rush into battle pell-mell with no battle plan, and with his forces scattered and disorganized, and weakened by shore-based gunfire. On the Austrian side, Tegetthoff demonstrated how much can be done even with an inferior force by an aggressive leader who understands his objective and pursues it wholeheartedly with the means at his disposal.

The tactical lessons were not quite so clear and were hotly debated by contemporaries. On the one hand the failure of gunfire to sink any large armored ship seemed to demonstrate the effectiveness of armor against gunfire, while the sinking of the *Re d'Italia* by ramming seemed to establish the superiority of the ram over the gun. If so, the line-abreast formation would seem preferable to the line ahead for battle because it was better suited to ramming tactics. It even appeared that Tegetthoff had made a mistake in taking his first division through the gap in the Italian column instead of presenting a solid front to the enemy so that he could make best possible use of his ramming power. On the other hand it was noted that although repeated attempts at ramming were made by both sides, only the *Re d'Italia* had been sunk in that manner, and she had no way on at the time. So far as the effectiveness of armor was concerned, the ironclads had shown little more invulnerability than the wooden *Kaiser,* which survived a terrible shelling. Furthermore, the battle was no real test of the gun. Although Persano's apparent attempt to form column and cross ahead of the enemy formation to attack its left flank suggested that he understood how to take advantage of his vastly superior gunpower, the delay caused by his shifting his flag had spoiled his maneuver and brought on a melee in which accurate gunnery counted for very little. Anyway, the Italian gunnery throughout the action was wretched. So far as future developments in tactics and naval material were concerned, Lissa had actually changed nothing. As a British admiral put it: "In spite of the power of the ram, the gun is still the principal and dominating weapon of naval war."

THE CONTEST BETWEEN GUNS AND ARMOR

In 1865 the British navy had abandoned breech-loading guns for muzzle-loaders because of numerous accidents with breech mechanisms. But even muzzle-loading rifles like those of the ironclad *Bellerophon,* launched in that year, could penetrate 11.4 inches of wrought-iron armor. The largest muzzle-loader ever used in the Royal Navy, an 80-ton monster of 16-inch caliber installed aboard the *Inflexible* in 1881, could penetrate 24.3 inches of wrought iron. However, about this time the Royal Navy returned to breech-loading. Because the big muzzle-loaders had barrels which were too long to be withdrawn into their turrets, they had to be loaded outside, with consequent exposure of gun crew and ammunition to enemy fire. On the other hand the use of the interrupted screw principle for breech-closing mechanisms, discovered by an American naval officer and developed by the French navy, had largely overcome the dangers of breech-loading. A terrible gun explosion on the *Thunderer* in 1879 finally convinced the British Admiralty that muzzle-loaders were not inherently safer guns and led to the gradual adoption of breech-loading in the Royal Navy. The heaviest gun of the century, a breech-loading rifle of 16.25-inch caliber weighing 110 tons, first mounted in the *Victoria* of 1889, could penetrate 37.5 inches of wrought iron. But its power was exceeded by that of the 12-inch, 46-ton wire-wound guns of the *Majestic,* completed in 1896, which could penetrate 38.5 inches.

These great increases in gunpower were made possible by developments in metallurgy, chemistry, and mechanics. Wrought iron replaced cast iron in gun barrels, and steel replaced wrought iron for the strengthening sleeves that were shrunk on the liners of built-up guns. By 1881 naval rifles were being made entirely of steel. At the same time slow-burning "brown" powder, in which slightly charred straw was used as charcoal and the sulfur content was reduced, permitted the lengthening of gun barrels to secure higher muzzle velocity and greater range. In 1887 the French government adopted smokeless powder, or guncotton, made by nitrating cellulose—an improvement that was quickly copied by the rest of the world. The armor-piercing shell was improved to secure greater penetrating power by building a soft iron cap over the hard steel point of the main shell casing. When this soft cap smashed against an armor plate, it would stretch the metal around the point of impact to the limit of its elasticity, thereby greatly easing the passage of the hard shell casing through the plate. But the power of the great guns would only have brought destruction to their users had it not been for the concurrent development of hydraulic mechanisms that could absorb the force of their recoil—amounting to as much as 100,-000,000 foot-pounds—and return them to battery without a jar. As a result of all these technological improvements, toward the end of the century it became a rough rule of thumb that a naval gun could penetrate at battle ranges as many inches of the finest armor as its own caliber.

Even this degree of resistance in armor was achieved only by a long and complicated process of improvement in metallurgy. The very term "ironclad" indicates the nature of the material with which early models were protected. It first began to be a misnomer when compound armor, made up of iron plates covered with a steel face, was used on the turrets of the British *Inflexible,* designed in 1874. Her waterline belt of 24-inch wrought-iron armor could just be penetrated at close range by 16-inch muzzle-loading guns like her own. This was the ultimate in armor thickness. The complete use of compound armor in H.M.S. *Colossus,* designed in 1879, permitted the reduction of the waterline belt to 18 inches. Thereafter the introduction of nickel-steel armor made possible further gradual reductions in armor thickness, until the Harvey process for face-hardening steel by heat and water treatment, and the even better Krupp process of 1895, reduced capital-ship belt armor to its minimum thickness of six inches in the Royal Navy's *Canopus* class of 1897.

DEVELOPMENTS IN HULL DESIGN

Along with the improvement of armor ran a parallel evolution of the hulls built to carry it. In the early race with the French to build ironclads, the British had converted some wooden-hulled ships to carry armor, but their policy for new construction was to use iron for the hull, as they had in their first ironclad, the *Warrior.* The French, whose timber reserves were larger but whose iron industry was weaker than England's, continued to build wooden-hulled ironclads until 1872, when they took a long step ahead of the British by using steel combined with iron in the hull structure of the *Redoutable.* Having observed this partial use of steel in the French shipyards, the British Naval Constructor, Sir Nathaniel Barnaby, in 1875 challenged the steel makers of England to produce steel of sufficient quality for shipbuilding. The challenge was so well met by Sir William Siemen's open-hearth process, which permitted precise control of the alloy content of steel, that the British were able to design all-steel-hulled warships in 1879 and launch them in 1886—an example that the French were unable to follow until 1891.

Nevertheless, as gunpower outpaced armor resistance, no hull could carry sufficient armor to give a ship complete protection throughout its length. From the earliest days of the ironclad, designers had been obliged to compromise between inadequate protection everywhere and absolute protection in the most vital areas. The earliest ironclads, following the design of the sailing ship of the line, carried guns along nearly their entire broadsides. Since a primary function of the armor was to protect the guns and their crews, the armor had to extend along the entire broadside too. But as guns grew in size and power, and as steam propulsion and the ram seemed to increase the importance of bow fire, it was no longer deemed necessary to mount so many guns in broadside. Instead, designers began to concentrate the guns in a box-like structure about the central portion of the ship, around which the armor could then be concentrated also. Since there was less area to be armored, heavier armor could be used. Such ironclads were called "citadel" or central battery ships. A tendency in this direction was shown by the French *Magenta,* designed in 1859, but the

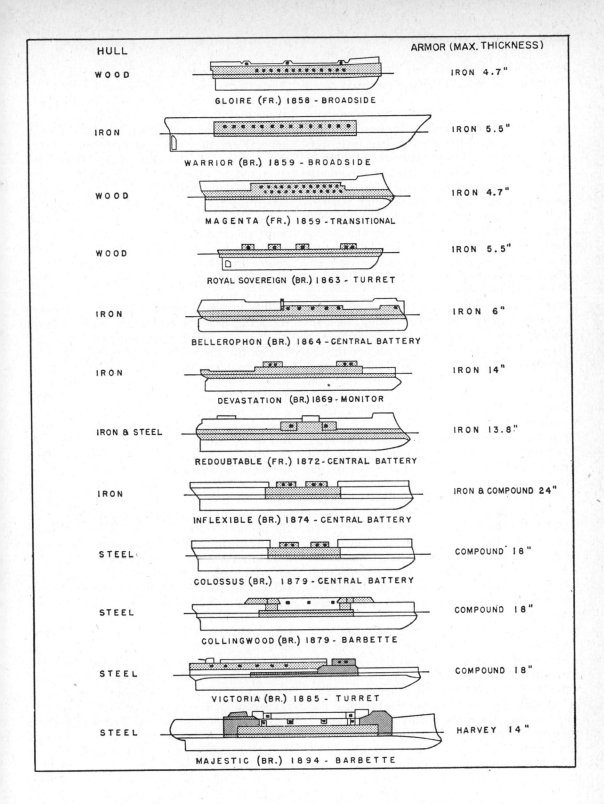

HULL		ARMOR (MAX. THICKNESS)
WOOD	GLOIRE (FR.) 1858 - BROADSIDE	IRON 4.7"
IRON	WARRIOR (BR.) 1859 - BROADSIDE	IRON 5.5"
WOOD	MAGENTA (FR.) 1859 - TRANSITIONAL	IRON 4.7"
WOOD	ROYAL SOVEREIGN (BR.) 1863 - TURRET	IRON 5.5"
IRON	BELLEROPHON (BR.) 1864 - CENTRAL BATTERY	IRON 6"
IRON	DEVASTATION (BR.) 1869 - MONITOR	IRON 14"
IRON & STEEL	REDOUBTABLE (FR.) 1872 - CENTRAL BATTERY	IRON 13.8"
IRON	INFLEXIBLE (BR.) 1874 - CENTRAL BATTERY	IRON & COMPOUND 24"
STEEL	COLOSSUS (BR.) 1879 - CENTRAL BATTERY	COMPOUND 18"
STEEL	COLLINGWOOD (BR.) 1879 - BARBETTE	COMPOUND 18"
STEEL	VICTORIA (BR.) 1885 - TURRET	COMPOUND 18"
STEEL	MAJESTIC (BR.) 1894 - BARBETTE	HARVEY 14"

19TH CENTURY DEVELOPMENTS IN BATTLESHIP DESIGN

earliest clear example was the British *Bellerophon,* of 1864. The type persisted down to the 1880's.

Another means of reducing the armor surface necessary to protect a ship was the monitor design. Since the monitor had little freeboard, it required heavy armor only along its waterline and on its turrets. But the greatly reduced freeboard made the ship less seaworthy, as the fate of the original *Monitor* had demonstrated. Nevertheless Captain Coles designed and built several large monitors for the Royal Navy. Unlike Ericsson however Coles refused to abandon sail entirely as motive power. Because of her low freeboard his *Captain,* completed in 1870, was not sufficiently stable to bear the weight of masts and sails in heavy weather. As a result she capsized at night in a squall on the Bay of Biscay, taking down with her the designer and most of her hand-picked crew, who had volunteered to serve in what was thought to be Britain's finest warship. Even after this disaster however the English did not entirely abandon the low-freeboard, turreted, monitor design. The mastless monitor *Devastation,* completed in 1873, was still considered a useful ship at the end of the century.

The advantages of the turret, which afforded all-around fire if properly mounted and full protection for gun and crew, were so manifest that it was early used in vessels other than the monitor type. The British *Royal Sovereign,* a wooden-hulled ship with full broadside armor designed by Coles, mounted four of his turrets on her main deck along the centerline. The *Huascar,* a single-turreted ship built in 1865 by an English shipyard for the Peruvian government, withstood 60 to 70 hits from the 38 guns of two British wooden frigates in an action off the Pacific coast of South America in 1877.

Despite the advantages of the turret, it did not at once become the universally accepted means of providing protection for main-battery guns. In fact many designers who liked the feature of all-around fire preferred the barbette, an open circular tower within which the gun revolved, because it was supposed to give better visibility for the gun

crew and thereby promote accuracy of fire. Barbettes were especially popular with the French, but many British ships mounted them too.

As barbettes and turrets came into more general use, they were mounted on the citadel portion of the ship. Often two were mounted at diagonally opposite corners of the citadel so that both could fire ahead or astern together. The citadel was now used to house the guns of intermediate caliber. Toward the end of the century the turrets or barbettes were usually spread out along the center-line of the ship, and the heavily armored citadel was eliminated.

After the increased power of the major caliber gun had forced designers to concentrate the heaviest armor in only the most vital areas of the ship, a greatly increased rate of fire in smaller caliber guns presented a new problem. By 1889 the Armstrong Company in England had produced quick-fire guns up to six inches in caliber, and their 4.72-inch could fire ten aimed shots in 48 seconds. It was useless to keep the big shells out of the vitals of a ship if the quick-firers could reduce her superstructure to scrap metal in a few minutes and make it impossible for her crew to operate her. To cope with this problem designers were forced to provide at least light armor protection throughout most of the ship. To save the weight of the additional armor surface, they had to reduce the thickness of belt and turret armor. Although this reduction was somewhat compensated by improvements in the quality of armor, toward the end of the century designers could no longer provide absolute protection for any part of the ship. The best that could be achieved was a reasonable degree of protection at battle ranges for guns, magazines, waterline, and machinery, and some protection for personnel elsewhere against quick-fire guns.

Besides armor and a well-directed fire from one's own guns, there was another means of protecting a ship against the enemy's fire—or at least of keeping it from sinking after it was hit. This was compartmentation. Even the *Warrior,* the first iron-hulled ironclad, was partially compartmented, and the system was early recognized as an important safety feature in merchant ships. In H.M.S. *Bellerophon* compartmentation was fully introduced in a naval vessel for the first time. Later ships were designed to carry coal in their outboard compartments in order to absorb the explosive force of shells that might penetrate them.

A feature closely related to compartmentation was the protective deck. Its main function was to guard the vitals of the ship against plunging fire. Located at the waterline, a full deck of armor sufficiently strong to stop plunging shells enclosed a space below of sufficient displacement to float the ship no matter how many holes were shot through the sides above. To deflect shells entering at or near the waterline the protective deck was given upward curvature from outboard to centerline. This feature was first introduced in the Italian *Duilio,* begun in 1872, and copied in the British *Inflexible,* designed in 1874. Such decks were the only protection of so-called "protected cruisers" in the last quarter of the century.

THE TORPEDO AND ITS CARRIERS

Although compartmentation was introduced into warship design as an adjunct to or substitute for armor, a strong impetus to its improvement was given by the development of automotive torpedoes, the first of which was designed in 1860 by the Englishman Robert Whitehead on the basis of research done by a Commander Lupis of the Austrian Navy. In 1867 the Austrian navy carried out official experiments with Whitehead's torpedo, to which its most important feature, a hydrostatic depth regulator, had meantime been added. Powered by compressed air, the early Whitehead was feeble and erratic in performance. In 1870 the speed of Whiteheads was only eight knots, and the total distance they could travel was only 400 yards. The effective range was only a fraction of that distance. But the power of the Whitehead increased steadily throughout the remainder of the century, and after gyroscopic

rudder control, an American invention, was introduced about 1885, its accuracy improved also. By 1898 its speed had increased to 30 knots and its effective range was about 500 yards. It was apparent too that it had by no means reached its technological limits.

The first use in action of a Whitehead torpedo had occurred much earlier. In the British attack on the mutinous Peruvian turret ship *Huascar* mentioned above, one of the British frigates had fired a torpedo, but the range was too great for the weapon to reach its target. Even earlier, special boats had been designed to carry torpedoes as their primary weapon. The earliest models carried spar torpedoes, which had to be brought by the boat into contact with the target, and Harvey towing torpedoes, which were so rigged that they could be swung out from the wake of the towing boat to strike the target ship. Experiments were made also with dirigible torpedoes which could be controlled by mechanical or electric cables, but these were mostly used on larger ships or for harbor defense and were generally unsuccessful. In the War of the Pacific, 1879-83, a dirigible Lay torpedo fired by the *Huascar* ran a circular course and was only prevented from striking its own ship by the timely action of an officer who jumped into the water and diverted it.

The torpedo saw extensive battle service in the Russo-Turkish War of 1877-78. The Russians used squadrons of torpedo launches, supported by fast steamers as tenders, against a Turkish fleet of ironclads based on the Black Sea and another Turkish force of monitors in the Danube River. The first certain success of the torpedo launches was achieved by spar torpedoes, which sank a small armor-clad in the Danube. Later a force of two tenders carrying six torpedo boats operated on the Black Sea with dubious results. In June 1877 the squadron made an attack with spar torpedoes upon four Turkish ironclads off the mouth of the Danube; it failed because the ships were protected by anti-torpedo nettings. Six months later the squadron attacked some Turkish ships near Batum and fired two Whiteheads, one of which probably dived and struck a rock, while the other failed to explode and was captured. The following month at the same place, according to Russian accounts, two Whiteheads fired at 80 yards scored hits and sank a 2,000-ton Turkish warship. All the torpedo actions of the war cost the Russians not a single man, but on the other hand the Turkish suffered no admitted loss to Whitehead torpedoes, despite their ships' lack of any quick-fire guns for close defense.

The Whitehead torpedo was not used again in warfare until the Chilean Civil War of 1891. The Chilean fleet of ironclads supported the Congress against the Presidential forces, which could muster only torpedo-gunboats. Thus the torpedo was already establishing itself as a weapon of dispute, employed by the weaker naval force in raiding tactics. On January 27 a steam launch from the Congressional ironclad *Blanco Encalada* fired a Whitehead torpedo at the Presidential armed steamer *Imperial,* missing its target. Three months later the *Blanco* herself was hit by one of two or three Whiteheads fired by a Presidential torpedo-gunboat squadron. In two minutes the *Blanco* became the first admitted loss of an ironclad to a torpedo. It should be noted however that the *Blanco* was at anchor and unprotected by nets, that although searchlights had been developed for use against torpedo boats the *Blanco* made no use of hers, and that she made only late and ineffective use of her quick-fire guns. Consequently the torpedo-boat was able to fire its torpedoes at a range of only 50 yards, and even so only one of two or three fired struck home. The action proved only that an unwary ship can often be sunk by surprise attack. In like manner the insurgent turret ship *Aquidaban* was sunk by one of several torpedoes fired from less than 400-foot range by a loyalist torpedo boat in a Brazilian revolution of 1893-94. Her sinking was the last torpedo action before the Sino-Japanese War.

Meanwhile the British navy had developed a series of craft called torpedo-gunboats or torpedo-catchers to combat the smaller torpedo boats. However, these turned out to be too large, unmaneuverable, and slow for their task. What was needed was a ship large enough to keep the sea in heavy weather and carry a substantial armament but at the same time small enough to have great speed and maneuverability. Such a vessel could be used for both torpedo and anti-torpedo work. The answer was the torpedo-boat destroyer. The first of these, the *Havoc,* launched in 1893, displaced 240 tons and had a speed of 26.7 knots. Before the turn of the century larger and faster destroyers were being built and their usefulness and versatility were becoming generally recognized.

IMPROVEMENTS IN PROPULSION

The surprisingly high speed of the first destroyer was made possible by developments in boiler and engine design that began after the American Civil War. As we have seen, early boilers were simply iron boxes reinforced internally by iron stay rods. As progress in metallurgy made it possible to build stronger box boilers, steam pressures rose from 20 to 40 pounds. At the same time the development of the fire tube boiler, in which numerous tubes carried the hot gases of combustion through the water in the boiler, increased efficiency by providing greater surface for heat absorption. However, there was a limit to the number of stay rods that could be built into a box boiler to strengthen it. The introduction of cylindrical boilers permitted the increase of steam pressures up to 60 pounds, and the locomotive type using forced draft achieved 155 pounds. The water-tube boiler, invented by Julien Belleville in 1855 and developed principally in France, further increased thermal efficiency. This type provided much greater heat absorption area than the fire-tube boiler by containing the water in steel tubes around which the gases of combustion passed. It was made practicable by the development of efficient salt-water evaporators. In the late 1880's the French installed water-tube boilers in battleships and armored cruisers. About the same time the British developed from American designs a water-tube boiler for use in destroyers. By the end of the century the newest ships of both the British and United States navies were using water-tube boilers capable of working pressures up to 250 pounds. To make full use of these higher steam pressures, compound or double-expansion engines, and later, triple-expansion engines had meantime been developed. In these the steam expanded in successively larger cylinders, instead of in only one cylinder, thus yielding more power to be applied through the piston-rods to the crankshaft.

As a result of all these improvements in engines and boilers, the horsepower of British battleships climbed from 5,200 in 1861 to 14,000 in 1892, with a resulting increase in speed from 14 to 18 knots, despite an increase in displacement from 9,000 to 14,000 tons. However, the type of ship that profited most from these mechanical developments was the cruiser. Often having nearly as great displacement as its battleship contemporaries but carrying smaller guns and lighter armor, the cruiser could accommodate sufficient machinery and fuel for both high speed and great range. The speed of British cruisers rose from 16.2 knots in 1868 to 24.0 knots in 1895, while at the same time their endurance increased from 2,800 miles to 25,000.

By the late 1890's the basic warship types of the 20th century had evolved, and their capabilities were nearly equal to those of similar types in World War I—in which, as a matter of fact, many 19th century ships fought. Battleships displaced up to 15,000 tons; they carried armor of face-hardened nickel-steel up to 14 inches in thickness, mounted breech-loading rifles up to 16.25 inches caliber in heavily armored turrets, and could make speeds up to 18.5 knots. Armored cruisers were often nearly as large as battleships; they carried armor up to six inches, mounted guns up to 9.2 inches, and could steam as fast as 24 knots. Protected cruisers displaced up to 5,600 tons, had armored decks up to 2.5 inches in thickness, mounted quick-firing guns as large as six inches, and could make as much as 20 knots. Destroyers were small—the largest not much over 400 tons—but they had made trial speeds up to 35.5 knots.

THE DECLINE OF THE UNITED STATES NAVY

During all but the last 15 years of this fertile period of technological advance in naval material the United States Navy was passing through a stage of decline and senescence. At the end of the Civil War the Federal Government had in service 700 ships displacing 500,000 tons and mounting 5,000 guns. By December 1870 this fleet had dwindled to 200 ships displacing 200,000 tons and mounting only 1,300 guns. Of these only 52 ships mounting 500 guns were in full commission. All of them were obsolete in comparison with the ships of European navies.

Perhaps the main reason for this deterioration was the concentration of American thought and energy on internal problems—reconstruction after the Civil War and the development of the West. Reinforcing this absorption in domestic affairs was a widespread feeling that American security was sufficiently guaranteed against European aggression by the 3,000-mile breadth of the Atlantic, which would greatly handicap the coal-burning ships of European navies operating in American waters without adequate supporting bases. With this safety factor in mind American politicians expected the Navy to use the traditional American naval strategy in the event of war: passive defense of seaports combined with offensive warfare against an enemy's commerce. They remembered the successes of American naval vessels and privateers against the merchant traffic of Great Britain in the Revolution and the War of 1812 and forgot that in both wars the Royal Navy had been able to operate at will along the American coast and blockade, sack, and occupy American cities.

To implement the strategy of harbor defense the Navy had left over from the war against the Confederacy a large number of small monitors and a few large seagoing ones. For warfare against an enemy's commerce a new class of fast steam-and-sail vessels, originally designed to cope with Confederate raiders like the *Alabama,* were completed. Their advanced engineering plants were the product of competition between the designs of private contractors and those of Chief Engineer Benjamin Franklin Isherwood of the Navy's Bureau of Steam Engineering. Regarding sail as only an auxiliary means of propulsion, Isherwood designed both ship and power plant to produce the maximum possible speed under steam. In 1868 the first of the class completed, the *Wampanoag*, achieved a maximum speed of 17.75 knots and a sustained speed of 16.6 knots on her trials.[1] Isherwood designed his ships in the best possible manner for their assigned task; like the American frigates of the War of 1812, they could outrun anything they could not outfight.

Yet the Navy Department rejected Isherwood's principles of design. In the year following the *Wampanoag* trials a board headed by Rear Admiral L. M. Goldsborough recommended that the ship be redesigned to carry more sail power at the expense of her steam power, and the Secretary of the Navy issued a general order requiring that all vessels of the Navy except tugs and dispatch vessels be fitted with full sail power. The *Wampanoag* and her sister-ship the *Ammonoosuc* were condemned as unfit for naval service and laid up. The Goldsborough board also recommended that four-bladed screws on naval vessels be replaced with less efficient two-bladed screws, which could be lined up vertically with the keel to increase speed when the ship was under sail. Many ships were so altered, and this policy was defended by Admiral of the Navy David D. Porter as late as 1871.

There were two related reasons for the Navy's emphasis upon sail power at the expense of steam. In the first place, the traditional American wartime strategy of commerce raiding would require ships to cruise individually at great distances from their home ports. Coal would be difficult to get and could therefore be used only sparingly.[2]

Furthermore, the Navy's peace-time mission was considered to be the showing of the flag in distant quarters of the world to protect American merchant ships and their crews against injury and interference by the uncivilized peoples of Asia and Africa. This mission, too, required ships that could operate independently over great distances for long periods without recoaling. However, the underlying reason for the sail-power preference was economy, which indeed was the basis for the general naval strategy. By denying the necessity of maintaining a strong navy of capital ships able to take offensive action against an enemy fleet, the defensive naval policy saved money. So strong was the economy motive in naval operations that commanding officers were ordered to enter in the log in red ink their reasons for getting up steam, and at one time the Secretary of the Navy even contemplated making them pay for the coal they burned if the reason seemed inadequate.

As the ships of the Navy aged, the expense of maintaining each became greater. Gradually a larger share of the annual naval appropriation found its way into the hands of contractors and suppliers for the repair of ships which should long ago have been surveyed. Navy yards flourished, while the forces afloat languished and their equipment became more obsolete.[3] The Navy rejected improvements like the interrupted screw breech block, Lieutenant Bradley Fiske's fire control devices, and the Howell depth-regulating torpedo, and permitted them to go by default to other nations. As late as 1884 the United States Navy was still using 9-inch Dahlgren smooth-bores and Parrott rifles—both muzzle-loading relics of the Civil War. In 1883 a French admiral who made a call on Captain Alfred Thayer Mahan aboard the screw sloop *Wachusett* on the Pacific station was struck by the outmoded armament of the ship. Noticing one of the ancient pivot guns, he murmured

[1] An English authority claims that her actual speed did not exceed 15 knots and that she was excelled by H.M.S. *Inconstant* before she was completed. See H. W. Wilson, *Ironclads in Action* (Boston, 1896), II, 254.

[2] The danger of a vessel that depended principally upon sail power and could make only moderate speed

under steam being run down and destroyed by a locally-based fast steam vessel does not seem to have entered into the calculations of the proponents of sail.

[3] See H. and M. Sprout, *The Rise of American Naval Power* (Princeton, 1942), 180, 181.

nostalgically, *"Ah! Capitaine, les vieux canons!"* [4] At a time when the British navy, though not at war, was active in every quarter of the globe, extending and protecting the Empire and supporting the rights and ambitions of its citizens, American naval officers were ashamed to meet even the officers of those small South American republics whose navies were more modern than their own.

NAVAL ACTIVITY IN THE YEARS OF DECLINE

Even with its obsolete ships and weapons the U. S. Navy performed its task of protecting American lives and property in distant parts of the world. At the very moment when the French admiral was reminiscing over Captain Mahan's old pivot gun, the mission of the *Wachusett* was to safeguard American lives and property in Chile during the long war between Chile and Peru. In 1881 a similar screw-sloop, the *Marion,* rescued the crew of the American whaler *Trinity* from Heard Island in the South Indian Ocean. That same year Commander R. W. Shufeldt usn negotiated a treaty with Korea that gave Americans trading privileges and provided for the protection of American seamen. Ten years before when the American trading bark *General Sherman* disappeared in the vicinity of Korea, Rear Admiral John Rodgers usn, commanding the Asiatic Squadron, investigated and took punitive action.

Throughout this period of material decay the Navy was active also in Arctic exploration, though with more loss than gain. U.S.S. *Polaris* was crushed in Arctic ice in 1871, happily without loss of life. The *Jeannette* Expedition eight years later was less fortunate. The steamer *Jeannette* had been purchased by the newspaper publisher James Gordon Bennett to explore the Arctic by a new route through Bering Strait, and Congress had authorized the United States Navy to refit and man the vessel. The expedition ended in disaster for ship and all but one

boat party under command of Passed Assistant Engineer Benjamin Melville. His long and arduous search of the Lena Delta in northern Siberia for his commander proved him a man of many parts besides engineering genius. Along with Commander Winfield Scott Schley, later commodore of the Flying Squadron in the Spanish-American War, Melville also participated in the Navy-commanded Greely Relief Expedition, which rescued Lieutenant A. W. Greely usa and the pitiful remnant of his exploring party from Ellesmere Island, where they had been marooned for nearly three years.

Much more important than Arctic exploration for the future of the United States Navy was the growing interest of naval officers in acquiring positions for advanced naval bases. Without coaling and repair bases, steam propelled warships simply could not operate in distant waters. In the Caribbean area a treaty to acquire the Virgin Islands was negotiated with Denmark as early as 1867, but was not ratified by the United States Senate. Later negotiations with the Dominican Republic were abandoned because of the political difficulties involved in the annexation of a territory inhabited by a large Negro population. In the Pacific Ocean area, efforts were more fruitful. Commander William Reynolds usn acquired Midway Island for the United States in 1867. A reciprocity treaty with Hawaii in 1875 which recognized the islands as "an American sphere of influence" was renewed in 1884 with the additional right to construct and maintain a naval base at Pearl Harbor. A treaty with Samoa for a naval station at Pago Pago, Tutuila, which Commander R. W. Meade usn made in 1872, was not ratified at that time, but a similar treaty was ratified six years later. Thus a start had been made in the direction of American naval control of the Pacific even before the Spanish-American War.

INTELLECTUAL PROGRESS

In the last 15 years of the 19th century the most important developments for the

[4] Captain A. T. Mahan usn Ret., *From Sail to Steam* (New York, 1907), 197.

future of the United States as a great naval power came in the realm of ideas. Rear Admiral Stephen Bleecker Luce USN, who had organized the Naval Apprentice Training System to train sailors for both the Navy and the merchant marine, had long felt that naval officers needed a school in which they could learn the art of naval warfare from the theoretical point of view by applying the techniques of analysis to the study of history. The report of a board which he headed recommended the establishment of a naval war college, which was to be more than a mere post-graduate school in the sense of continuing the practical professional training of the Naval Academy at a higher level. As a result of this recommendation the Naval War College was established in 1884 at Newport, Rhode Island in a building which had been the poor asylum. Besides the building, the most important acquisition of the new college was Captain Alfred Thayer Mahan, who at Luce's request was assigned as an instructor in October 1885.

Mahan had earlier published a book called *The Gulf and Inland Waters* about the operations of the Federal Navy in the Civil War, but nothing in it gave promise of the line of thought that he was to develop in the lectures he prepared for delivery at the War College. In fact, at the time Rear Admiral Luce asked him to come to the War College, Mahan believed the United States should avoid acquiring territorial possessions overseas, not only to save the expense of the large navy which would be necessary to protect them, but also to avoid the dominance of a powerful military caste over the democratic processes of the government. In line with these feelings he accepted the naval maxims of his time and country that commerce destruction and coast defense were the only tasks the United States Navy needed to perform in time of war.

However, as Mahan began to study history in preparation for his duties at the War College, he discovered that "control of the sea was an historic factor which had never been systematically appreciated and expounded." [5]

From this time on he had his vocation. Examining the situation and characteristics of nations that had been great sea powers, especially England, he perceived six factors he thought made the development of seapower possible: (1) geographic position, (2) physical conformation, (3) extent of territory, (4) number of population, (5) character of the people, and (6) character of the government.

The most important of these factors in the rise of English seapower had been the insular position of Britain off the coast of Western Europe. As an island nation England had enjoyed easy defense against rival land powers. Consequently she had been able to get along with only a small army and devote the bulk of her military expenditures to the maintenance of a large and powerful navy. Even more important, England's position flanking the North Atlantic sea lanes had enabled her to dominate the lines of sea communication between the countries of Western Europe and the resource areas of America, Africa, and Asia that were opened up by the explorers of the 15th and 16th centuries. In time of war England had therefore been able to interrupt her enemies' trade with these overseas regions and at the same time acquire colonies and trade for herself. The final result of this advantageous position, skillfully exploited, was the British Empire of the 19th century, and the complete dominion of the seas then enjoyed by the Royal Navy.

All the sea power factors that had made Great Britain mistress of the seas Mahan saw potentially present in the situation of the United States. The extent of the Atlantic and Pacific Oceans and the absence of strong rival powers to north and south made the country strategically an island from the point of view of defense. With an Isthmian canal constructed and the vast Pacific area developed, the United States would enjoy a dominant position on important trade routes. The country had sufficient good harbors, and the vast extent of its territory was no handicap to defense because it also had a large and rapidly growing population, a considerable part of which came from seafaring stock and followed the sea for a living. The

---

[5] *From Sail to Steam*, 276.

people of the country were inclined toward commercial pursuits and had a consequent tendency to trade upon the sea. Although the foreign commerce of the United States had diminished since the first half of the 19th century, when American clipper ships were supreme upon the trade routes of the world, the country could develop the steel shipbuilding capacity to win back from Great Britain the position it had lost to her in the second half of the century. All that was needed to bring these factors into harmonious coordination and develop a great American sea power to rival or surpass that of England was a government that understood the value of sea power and the importance of control of the sea to the security and prosperity of the nation. This last essential factor could be developed by persuasion.

But it would not suffice merely to convince the people and their government of the advantages of sea power and show them how it could be developed; it was equally important to show them how it should be exercised. According to Mahan the principal mission of a navy in warfare was to control the lines of sea communication in order to secure their use to one's own cargo vessels and transports while denying their use to an enemy's. In a conflict with another sea power that possessed a strong fleet of capital ships, such control could be achieved only by destroying or neutralizing the enemy's fleet with a more powerful fleet of one's own. Commerce warfare by fast cruisers might in part deny the use of the sea to the enemy's merchant marine, but it could not secure its use to one's own; it was merely an adjunct to the main objective of destroying the enemy's most powerful organized fighting force wherever it might be. But modern warships could not carry sufficient coal to cross an ocean and fight an enemy fleet on equal terms. Hence the need for overseas bases to extend the range of the fleet into any area where one's sea communications might be threatened. Since a base exists to support the fleet, and not the fleet to support the base, ideally a base should be self-sufficient. Hence bases are most favorably located in colonies, which can provide resources and are under

one's own control. Colonies in turn make trade more profitable, and thus nourish the merchant marine which is the *raison d'être* of sea power in the first place. Thus Mahan's line of reasoning led him from his original isolationist politics and defensive naval strategy to a position that was politically imperialistic and strategically offensive in concept.

The concrete result of Mahan's study and reflection was *The Influence of Sea Power upon History, 1660-1783,* a book published in 1890, in which he showed how the fortunes of the British Empire rose when her statesmen understood and used sea power correctly while those of France failed under misunderstanding and neglect. Two years later his *The Influence of Sea Power upon the French Revolution and Empire* continued the story to the end of the Napoleonic Wars. In 1905 he published a sea power analysis of the War of 1812. Meantime he had been writing numerous magazine articles, mostly for the *Atlantic Monthly,* in which he called to the attention of the American public the importance to their security of such measures as American ownership of an Isthmian canal and the acquisition of naval bases in Cuba and Hawaii.

Although Mahan's lectures at the War College had interested a number of naval officers in his ideas, his *Influence of Sea Power* did not immediately receive the acclaim in the United States that it was accorded in Europe, where his reasoned exposition of principles that many British statesmen had followed instinctively was flattering to the English. The German Kaiser also was so impressed that he ordered a copy placed in the wardroom of every ship of his new navy. Moreover, it was perhaps significant for the future course of history that more of Mahan's works were translated into Japanese than into any other language. In the United States however an adverse school of opinion was represented by the incumbent Chief of the Bureau of Navigation (who directed the assignment of officers) when he said: "It is not the business of a naval officer to write books." However, Mahan's ideas were already winning him influential friends;

on this occasion he was saved from sea duty to complete his second book on sea power by the intervention of Secretary of the Navy Benjamin F. Tracy. Even more important for the future influence of his ideas was the interest of Theodore Roosevelt, who became Assistant Secretary of the Navy in 1897, and Henry Cabot Lodge, the Chairman of the Senate Naval Affairs Committee. By the time Flag Captain Mahan returned from a European cruise with honorary degrees from Oxford and Cambridge, nearly everyone would admit that there was something to be said after all for naval officers writing books.

THE NEW NAVY OF THE UNITED STATES

Influential as Mahan's ideas became in the 1890's, it cannot be said that they brought about the rebirth of the United States Navy. That process had begun much earlier. Some tentative efforts at improvement were made 15 years before Mahan had even begun to think about sea power, when Secretary of the Navy George M. Robeson took it upon himself to use appropriations for maintenance and repairs to reconstruct old ships and build new ones. His bold misappropriations became the subject of a Congressional investigation which publicized the disgraceful condition of the Navy and spurred Congress in 1873 to authorize the construction of eight "steam vessels of war, with auxiliary sail power" totaling 8,000 tons. Under this authorization the Navy built three iron gunboats, four wooden corvettes, and the frigate *Trenton*.

Although these early beginnings were prompted more by a general awakening to the shameful decrepitude of the Navy than by any specific events, certain international incidents involving American merchant and naval vessels in the last three decades of the century helped the rebuilding program along by bringing home to the people of the United States how little naval power they had to defend the prestige of the nation when it was flouted by foreign powers. In 1873 a Spanish cruiser captured the American merchant ship *Virginius* in the act of running arms to Cuban insurgents and took her to Havana, where the Spanish authorities executed several dozen of the passengers, many of them Americans. An attempt to mobilize the fleet to support United States protests brought together only a few feeble relics. Continuing troubles with Spain over Cuba during the next decade helped to keep alive the country's concern about its naval weakness. In 1889 the rumor of a clash between American and German ships over Samoa prompted another stock-taking. Two years later a sailors' brawl which started in the True Blue Saloon at Valparaiso during a Chilean insurrection resulted in the killing of some American sailors on liberty from U.S.S. *Baltimore*. When hostilities with Chile threatened, the American public was surprised to find that it still had no armored cruiser or battleship in service.

Yet the reconstruction of the American navy had then been in progress since James A. Garfield became President in 1881. Conditions at that time had been peculiarly favorable to Congressional appropriations for a naval building program. The War of the Pacific, which was still going on, had shown that some small South American countries had navies stronger and more modern than that of the United States. Operations of the French de Lesseps Company in Panama threatened to put an Isthmian canal under European control. The United States had already acquired some territorial interests in the Pacific. Most important of all, the strong financial condition of the country made payment for a naval building program seem relatively painless. Determined to improve the condition of the Navy, William H. Hunt, Secretary under Garfield, appointed a board of officers to advise him what types and numbers of ships should be recommended to Congress.

The recommendations of the board were, to say the least, conservative. To use the large supply of ship timber on hand and provide employment in Eastern wooden shipbuilding yards, the board recommended construction principally of a large number of small wooden cruisers with steam engines and full sail power. A minority however, including Benjamin Isherwood, recommended construction of armored cruisers and seagoing armored warships. Next year the board went along in part with Isherwood's proposal by recommending the construction of several steel ships. As authorized by Congress in 1883 this program produced the steam-and-sail protected cruisers *Atlanta, Boston,* and *Chicago,* and the dispatch vessel *Dolphin*—popularly known as the "ABCD's." At the same time Congress encouraged the retirement of outmoded wooden ships by limiting the amount of money which could be spent on their repair to 30 per cent of the cost of a similar new vessel. A commission was also appointed to recommend elimination and consolidation of navy yards, which had mushroomed along the coasts with more regard for the constituencies of Congressmen than the requirements of the Navy. Some years later, to promote efficiency in procurement, all navy purchases were consolidated in the Bureau of Provisions and Clothing (afterwards renamed Supplies and Accounts), and the General Storekeeping system and property accounts for capital items were established.

As the shore establishment readied itself to support a new fleet, the forces afloat grew slowly in numbers and modernity, handicapped by American inexperience in warship design and lack of steel ship-building capacity. Plans for the cruiser *Charleston,* authorized in 1885, the Navy's first battleship, the *Texas,*[6] and the protected cruiser *Baltimore* of the following year had to be purchased in England. Although Congress desired to stimulate the growth of American warship building capacity by requiring domestic manufacture of these ships, their shafting had to be allowed as an exception. However, two years later an authorization for seven cruisers required that all parts without exception be manufactured in the United States.

Meantime a better understanding of the

strategic and tactical use of a modern navy had begun to develop slowly in the government. While the Congress was authorizing cruisers, the House Naval Affairs Committee was recommending seagoing battleships which could operate in defense of the entire coast. In 1886 Senator Matthew C. Butler of South Carolina derided commerce warfare and advocated a strong fleet of first-class battleships. Three years later the Navy Department established a "squadron of evolution" which organized all the new ships then in service into a single tactical unit. Next year Chairman Charles A. Boutelle of the House Naval Affairs Committee finally succeeded against strong opposition in getting authorization for three "seagoing, coast-line battleships," the *Indiana, Massachusetts,* and *Oregon.*

Although these ships and the later *Iowa* were designated "coast-line" by the Congress to indicate that they were intended for the defense of American waters and not for offensive action in an enemy's waters, some naval officers and politicians, following Mahan, had more aggressive ideas about the strategic function of a battle fleet. Secretary of the Navy Tracy in his Annual Report for 1889 wrote of the necessity to "beat off the enemy and threaten his coast," and in 1890 his Policy Board recommended in addition to a coast-defense fleet of battleships with limited coal capacity, a fleet of long-range battleships for offensive operations against an enemy. Finally in 1897 the organization of three first- and two second-class battleships and two armored cruisers into a powerful North Atlantic Squadron gave at least partial implementation to Mahan's concept of an offensive fleet.

Thus by the eve of the Spanish-American War the United States had acquired a navy which, though far from being the most powerful in the world, still had a respectable number of modern ships. The three battleships of the *Indiana* class each displaced more than 10,000 tons, carried armor up to 18 inches in thickness, mounted 13-inch guns in their main battery, and could make almost 17 knots. The larger *Iowa,* last bat-

---

[6] With the construction of the new fleet, the U. S. Navy began the practice of naming ships according to type—battleships taking the names of states, cruisers, the names of cities, and so forth.

tleship completed in time to fight, carried improved 15-inch armor and was somewhat faster. These ships compared favorably with the British *Majestic* class of 1896, which, though several thousand tons larger and therefore longer-range and slightly faster, carried lighter armor and smaller main and intermediate caliber guns. In all, the Navy had in service four first-class battleships, two second-class battleships, two armored cruisers, ten protected cruisers, and a considerable number of gunboats, monitors, and torpedo boats. Through the good fortune of not having been threatened with aggression by any naval power from 1865 to 1898 the United States had acquired this largely modern fleet without the tremendous expense of experimentation and obsolescence to which England and France had been put. In addition, through the teachings of Mahan, the American navy had at its disposal a body of strategic and tactical doctrine which showed how its new power could be effectively used.

23

The Spanish-American War

IF ANY SINGLE EVENT BE SE-lected to mark the emergence of the United States as a major power, perhaps no better choice could be made than the Spanish-American War of 1898. Lasting a little over a hundred days and costing some 3,000 American lives, this brief, one-sided conflict involved the United States in the complex problems of the Far East and served notice on the councils of Europe that henceforth in their deliberations American military power would have to be considered. For the Americans themselves it marked a turning point toward greater participation in world affairs and a more adventurous foreign policy.

Although the first major sea battle of the Spanish-American War was fought half a world away in the Philippines, the conflict arose from intolerable conditions in Cuba. Here a chronic state of revolution against Spanish misrule finally erupted into fiery rebellion in 1895. The *insurrectos,* vying in cruelty with their Spanish masters, set about a policy of deliberate devastation in which American property was not spared except for the payment of protection money, which in turn was expended to finance the revolt or to spread propaganda in the United States. Desperately determined to put an end to the havoc, the Spanish government early in 1896 sent to Cuba the ruthless General Valeriano Weyler, with orders to apply stern measures. Weyler's solution was to herd civilians into reconcentration areas, where they could not support the rebels. Here unhygienic conditions brought death to thousands, mainly women and children. The American public, already stirred by the skillful efforts of the Cuban junta in New York, reacted violently against the inhuman methods of "Butcher Weyler," and many urged that the rebel "government" be accorded recognition forthwith. Responding to the clamor, Congress passed a resolution demanding recognition of Cuban belligerency. Anti-imperialist President Cleveland ignored the resolution as an intrusion upon his executive powers, declaring that he would refuse to call out the army rather than go to war with Spain, but to the Spanish government he intimated that American respect for Spanish rule in Cuba might be "superseded by higher obligations, which we can hardly hesitate to recognize and discharge."

When a new, liberal Spanish ministry in 1897 recalled Weyler, modified the reconcentration system, and granted the Cubans a certain degree of autonomy, Americans began to lose interest in the Cuban cause.

Then, in February 1898, occurred two events which aroused public indignation in the United States as never before. One was the publication in the New York *Journal* of an indiscreet private letter written by Dupuy de Lôme, Spanish minister in Washington, and somehow obtained by the Cuban junta. In his letter the minister hinted at Spanish duplicity in discussions on pending trade agreements and referred to President Mc-Kinley as a "small-time politician." A week later, the battleship *Maine,* which had been ordered to Cuba to protect American lives and property, was torn apart by an explosion which killed 260 of her complement. The American public, later supported by the findings of a court of inquiry, believed that the explosion was external, caused by a mine planted and set off by the Spaniards. The New York *Journal* offered a $50,000 reward, never claimed, for the apprehension and conviction of the perpetrators. Though subsequent studies have shown that the explosion might well have been internal and accidental, the United States was brought to the brink of war.

Because in event of armed conflict with Spain, Cuba would be the primary military objective and Puerto Rico a secondary one, the bulk of the United States Fleet was concentrated in the Atlantic. To strengthen forces already there, the battleship *Oregon* made her history-making voyage from Puget Sound around South America to the Caribbean, a 15,000-mile passage completed in 66 days at an average speed at sea of nearly 12 knots. Her arrival raised the strength of the North Atlantic Squadron to five battleships and two armored cruisers, plus smaller types. Meanwhile, the Navy Department maintained only a small Asiatic Squadron in the Pacific, which was generally regarded as an area of lesser naval significance.

The effect of the *Maine* disaster was not lost upon the Spanish, who tried to appease American wrath and at the same time prepared for war. Upon learning of the explosion, the Spanish Minister of Marine alerted the fleet and advised Admiral Pasquale Cervera, commanding the main home force, to be ready to destroy the American base at Key West and then to blockade the American coast. To Cervera, constitutionally pessimistic, such an assignment appeared fantastic in the extreme, for his chief strength consisted only of five cruisers and a single battleship, all in poor shape. He pointed out his naval inferiority in comparison to the Americans, the absence of powerful Spanish bases beyond the Atlantic, and the probable lack of adequate logistic support for his fleet in Cuba and Puerto Rico. He expressed the opinion that the most practical naval strategy for his country in event of war would be to retain forces for defense of the homeland and asserted that his fleet could make the American coast a profitable military objective only if Spain could enlist a powerful naval ally capable of furnishing assistance. The Ministry thereupon modified its directive but insisted that the naval forces should at least defend Puerto Rico. On April 8, 1898 Cervera, still regarding his mission as hopeless, sortied from Cadiz and advanced to the Cape Verde Islands to await further political developments.

Word of the sortie of the Spanish home fleet caused a tremendous war scare along the American East Coast. Badly informed citizenry everywhere had visions of coastal bombardment and invasion by the enemy. Both Army and Navy received frantic calls for coast defense. Secretary of War Russell Alger afterwards remembered that "the calls made upon the department for immediate rescue from the advancing Spanish fleet were pathetic in their urgency. Telegrams, letters, and statesmen representing the imperiled localities poured into the War Department. They wanted guns everywhere; mines in all the rivers and harbors on the map." [1] Theodore Roosevelt later recalled that nervous Boston financiers, fearful for the safety of their investment securities, removed them 50 miles inland to Worcester for safer keeping.

No harm was done, and some nerves were calmed, by a general trundling out of obsolete Civil War guns to points along the coast, whence they were aimed futilely at the empty Atlantic. But demands for fleet pro-

[1] Russell A. Alger, *The Spanish-American War* (New York, Harper and Brothers, 1901), 38.

tection simultaneously of all parts of the East Coast were something else again, for a fleet is by reason of its mobility a weapon of attack. Even when its mission is defensive in purpose, its units should never degenerate into static platforms for guns. Undiscerning persons have misinterpreted the view of a navy as the first line of the nation's defense into the false concept of the "fortress fleet," by which warships sacrifice their mobility and capacity to concentrate, and become mere substitutes for coastal artillery. Such a concept was behind the clamor for the United States Fleet to be split up and its units distributed among the Atlantic ports as protection against the Spaniards. A fleet thus scattered and tied down is scarcely better than no fleet at all, for however weak the Spanish might prove, their state of concentration would give them an immense advantage over any individual American ships they might encounter. Assuming that Cervera could operate effectively so far from bases, he would be free to go where he pleased and destroy the split-up American fleet piecemeal.

The Navy Department was perfectly aware that the North Atlantic Squadron ought in the circumstances to operate as a unit. Even if Cervera should strike elsewhere than in the Caribbean, where he was expected, a fleet with its integrity preserved could still strike a retaliatory blow. Spreading the fleet thin along the coast, they knew, could prove military suicide; yet the clamor of the coastal cities for naval protection had to be satisfied. The solution was a compromise—the North Atlantic Squadron was divided into two main parts. One, under Acting Rear Admiral William T. Sampson, was based at Key West, poised and ready for offensive operations against Cuba and Puerto Rico. The other, the so-called Flying Squadron, was organized at Norfolk under the command of Commodore Winfield Scott Schley, as a mobile fortress fleet for the roving protection of the Atlantic seaboard. A smaller Northern Patrol Squadron of obsolete and generally useless vessels guarded the coast from the Delaware Capes northward.

Meanwhile, the Spanish Ministry was vacillating over American demands that Spain grant an armistice to the *insurrectos* and put an end to reconcentration—fearful of revolution at home if they capitulated and of war with the United States if they did not. By April 9, the Ministry had given in on both points. It was already too late however, for President McKinley had now come to realize that the Democrats with their cry of "Free Cuba!" would defeat him in the coming elections unless he put a definitive end to the unspeakable conditions in the Spanish colony. So he sent a war message to Congress on the 11th, requesting authority to use the Army and Navy. A week later Congress passed a joint resolution declaring Cuba free and independent, demanding the withdrawal of Spanish forces, and directing the President to use armed force to put the resolution into effect. A final clause, the so-called Teller Amendment, pledged that whatever the outcome the United States would not annex Cuba.

On April 22 the Navy Department directed Sampson to establish a blockade of Cuban waters from Havana around the western tip of the island to Cienfuegos on the south coast. On April 25 Congress declared a state of war to have existed since April 21. On the 29th Cervera's fleet left the Cape Verdes and steamed to the defense of Puerto Rico. Cervera was given "entire freedom of action as to route, port, and cases and circumstances in which battle should be sought or eluded." [2]

THE PHILIPPINE CAMPAIGN

No cries for coastal protection split the small American naval force in the Pacific. Indeed, few Americans were aware that Spain had possessions in that area. One man in Washington however knew very well that the Spanish owned the Philippines and had a fleet of sorts there. That was Theodore Roosevelt, Assistant Secretary of the Navy.

[2] Office of Naval Intelligence, *Notes on the Spanish-American War*, 10 vols. (Washington, 1899), VII, 65.

When trouble with Spain loomed, Roosevelt decided that the United States must be prepared to strike in the Pacific as well as in the Atlantic. Casting about for a man capable of striking a quick and effective blow against naval forces in the Philippines, he selected Commodore George Dewey and by neat wire pulling had him appointed Commander in Chief of the U. S. Asiatic Squadron.

Dewey at the time of his appointment was holding the routine and rather dull position of President of the Board of Inspection and Survey, but he had experienced extensive combat duty in the Civil War and had a reputation for aggressiveness—which perhaps is what mainly attracted Roosevelt. Dewey was much more than merely aggressive, however. Like his old commanding officer David Glasgow Farragut, he combined a keen eye for tactical situations with a capacity for meticulous care and attention to detail. Before leaving Washington he read everything he could find on the Philippines and studied all available charts of the surrounding waters. Urgently requesting the Navy Department to forward ammunition as soon as possible, he left for Japan in early December 1897. A month later he boarded the flagship *Olympia* at Nagasaki and assumed his new command.

Dewey soon moved his squadron to Hong Kong in order to be nearer Manila. Here he received a cablegram from Roosevelt, then Acting Secretary: "Keep full of coal. In the event . . . of war your duty will be to see that the Spanish squadron does not leave the Asiatic coast, and then offensive operations in Philippine Islands." Dewey needed no such prompting, for he was already furiously at work in preparation for his coming task. He purchased a collier and a supply steamer to serve as fleet train. He had his warships docked, the machinery overhauled, the underwater hulls scraped, and the white sides painted battle gray. The Commodore personally inspected all details, seeing to it that crews underwent daily drill and that all machinery was ready for sustained operation at a moment's notice. Lacking information on the Spanish fleet and fortifications in the

Philippines, he sent a spy to Manila and disguised his own aide as a tourist to pick up data from travelers arriving in Hong Kong. To by-pass British neutrality rules once war was declared, he arranged for a temporary anchorage at Mirs Bay in Chinese waters some distance up the coast.

On April 25, came a final cable from the Secretary of the Navy: "War has commenced between the United States and Spain. Proceed at once to Philippine Islands. Commence operations at once, particularly against the Spanish fleet. You must capture vessels or destroy. Use utmost endeavors." Dewey waited some 36 hours until the American consul arrived from Manila with the latest word on Spanish preparations. Then on the 27th Dewey sailed for the conquest of the Philippines.

In the American squadron were seven combat vessels: four cruisers, including the flagship *Olympia* (5,870 tons), the *Baltimore,* the *Raleigh,* and the *Boston;* two gunboats, the *Petrel* and the *Concord;* and the revenue cutter *McCulloch.* These vessels totaled about 20,000 tons [3] and carried some 100 guns, half of them larger than 4-inch. Six hundred miles away in the Philippines waited the fleet of Rear Admiral Don Patricio Montojo. Montojo's only modern vessel of any real consequence was the *Reina Christina* of about 3,500 tons and carrying six 6.2-inch guns. Another of his cruisers, the old wooden *Castilla,* was unable to move under her own power. In addition, he had five ships of 500 to 1,100 tons. Estimating that he would have no chance of defeating the American squadron in a battle of maneuver, Montojo planned to fight at anchor, using his ships as a fortress fleet to supplement shore batteries.

En route to the Philippines, the American squadron made final preparations for action, including battle drills in daylight and darkness, practice in fire fighting and damage control, and removal of practically all woodwork to lessen fire hazards. In the afternoon of April 30, after reconnoitering Subic Bay and finding the Spanish fleet not there,

---

[3] Compare with the 45,000-ton *Iowa*-class battleships in World War II.

Dewey remarked, "Now we have them," and headed for the passage south of Corregidor leading into land-locked Manila Bay.

Despite his outward assurance, the Commodore had inward qualms. He knew well enough that Manila was regarded throughout the Far East as impregnable and that all passages into the bay had been mined. Thirty years before, his old commander Farragut had damned the torpedoes and steamed into Mobile Bay. Since then of course mines had greatly improved, but Dewey, judging that there were no engineers in Manila skillful enough to place mines properly in the deep waters off Corregidor, determined to take his fleet in under cover of darkness. "Whenever I have been in a difficult situation, or in the midst of such a confusion of details that the simple and right thing to do seemed hazy," he wrote afterwards, "I have often asked myself, 'What would Farragut do?' In the course of preparations for Manila Bay I often asked myself this question, and I confess I was thinking of him that night when we entered the bay, and with the conviction that I was doing precisely what he would have done." [4]

A little after midnight when the American squadron had almost completed its passage into the bay without encountering any live mines, a few of the batteries on shore opened fire. "Well, well," said Dewey to Captain Charles Gridley, captain of the *Olympia*, "they wake up at last." Shells from the American ships quickly silenced the guns and the entire line passed through the strait unscathed. At dawn, May 1, Dewey's squadron was off Manila looking for the Spanish fleet and disdaining the city batteries, which opened fire but made no hits.

To spare the city bombardment by American guns, Montojo had placed his squadron off Cavite. Here Dewey found him and closed to 5,000 yards to conserve ammunition, since there was no nearby source of replenishment. Then at 5:40 AM the Commodore ordered, "You may fire when you are ready, Gridley." Firing steadily, the Americans passed and repassed the Spanish ships in a series of coun-

termarches reminiscent of Du Pont's tactics in Port Royal Sound. Several Spanish ships, including the *Reina Christina*, made futile attempts to advance but were sunk or driven

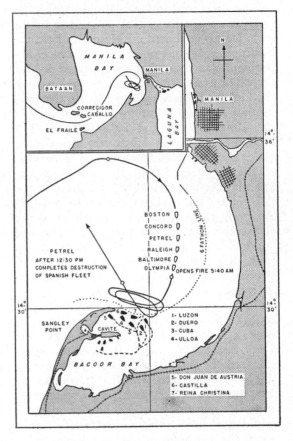

BATTLE OF MANILA BAY, MAY 1, 1898

back. When Dewey temporarily withdrew at 7:35 because of an erroneous report of ammunition shortage, the *Christina* and the *Castilla* had already been abandoned. At 11 o'clock Dewey resumed battle and in another hour of firing completed the annihilation of the Spanish squadron. When he lifted fire all of Montojo's warships were burned, sunk, or had been abandoned.

Spanish casualties, in the fleet and ashore on Cavite, were 381 killed or wounded. Dewey's squadron had suffered no fatalities and only seven wounded. The Americans, who had drilled regularly at gunnery, had

[4] *Autobiography* (New York, 1916), 50.

made at least 170 hits; the Spanish, who had had no practice at all, made only 15. The American victory was the result not only of superior power but even more of superior preparation. "The battle of Manila," said Dewey, "was won in Hong Kong harbor."

With no Spanish naval power left in the area, Dewey anchored off Manila to hold the Philippines against outside interference. His problem was somewhat complicated by the arrival of five German warships obviously on the lookout for a chance to pick up the Philippines for colony-hungry Germany should the United States not be interested. The United States however was very much interested. Some 11,000 Army troops were soon on the way from San Francisco to seize Manila and occupy the islands. En route to the Philippines the cruiser *Charleston,* escorting the troop convoy, made a bloodless capture of Spanish Guam, where the governor had not heard of the war. Less than a month later, the United States, with visions of growing empire, at long last annexed the independent Hawaiian Islands.

On August 13, 1898, under combined army and navy bombardment, Manila capitulated after a token resistance. Thereafter the Army, and the Navy as well, faced the three-year task of putting down an insurrection among the Filipinos, who had hoped for independence and not merely an exchange of imperial masters. Nearly half a century would pass before the United States would deem the Filipinos ready to govern themselves. Meanwhile, with the cession of the Philippines by the treaty of peace, the United States became permanently involved in the affairs of the Far East.

THE
CARIBBEAN CAMPAIGN

Admiral Sampson, intellectual, somewhat remote, but by no means lacking in aggressiveness, proposed opening hostilities against Spain with an amphibious assault upon Havana. By capturing the capital and military stronghold, he hoped to bring the conflict to an early end. Navy Secretary Long disap-

proved Sampson's proposal because the Army was far from ready and also because it was considered unwise to risk the American fleet against the guns of Havana while an enemy fleet was still at large. The accumulated experience of warfare suggested that before exposing one's ships to the perils of attack against a fortified coast one must either have gained command of the sea by destroying any enemy forces which might interfere, or else one must have the equivalent of two fleets, a Support Force to attack the coast and protect the invasion troops and a Covering Force to act as a shield to the beachhead and Support Force, fending off any approaching enemy fleet.

With the North Atlantic Squadron divided between Norfolk and the Caribbean, Long simply did not feel that Sampson had the strength for amphibious operations while Cervera's fleet remained intact. In this opinion he was seconded by the new Naval War Board. This board, composed in its final form of Admiral Sicard, retired commander of the North Atlantic Squadron, Admiral Crowninshield, Chief of the Bureau of Navigation, and Captain Mahan, the naval historian and philosopher, was intended originally as a mere intelligence agency but came in time to act as a central strategy board. As such, it served well to unify the efforts of the Navy, though it sometimes embarrassed local commands when it ventured into tactical directives. The Board was a great step forward from the somewhat hit-or-miss central directions in earlier wars, but no machinery had yet been developed which, like the Joint Chiefs of Staff in World War II, could coordinate Army and Naval operations.

When Cervera, on orders from Madrid, cleared the Cape Verde Islands on April 29, he was as gloomy as ever and with good reason. He knew that the combined North Atlantic Squadron included four battleships—the *Iowa, Indiana, Massachusetts,* and *Texas* —with a fifth, the *Oregon,* en route from the Pacific, plus the fast armored cruisers *Brooklyn* and *New York* and several smaller cruisers and some monitors. Against these he could oppose only four armored cruisers and two destroyers, all with boiler tubes in poor

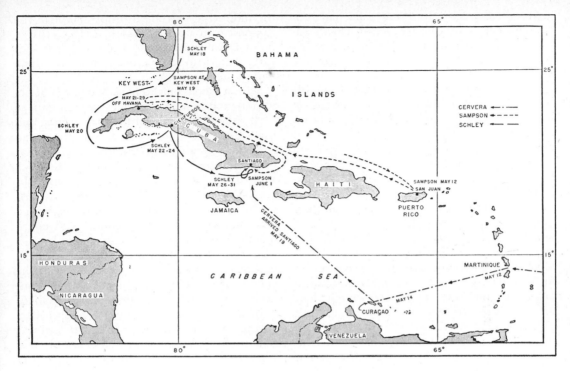

CARIBBEAN CAMPAIGN, MAY 3-JUNE 1, 1898

condition. Moreover, his best cruiser, the *Cristóbal Colón,* lacked her two 10-inch guns, and another, the *Vizcaya,* was slowed by a badly fouled underwater hull.

Sampson soon learned of Cervera's sortie and at once conceived the idea of going out to meet him at San Juan, Puerto Rico, where he believed the Spanish fleet would have to put in for coal. Mahan also had guessed that the Spanish would touch first at San Juan and had suggested placing scout cruisers in that area to detect Cervera and notify Sampson. The American fleet could then advance to San Juan and seek a decisive naval action. Sampson partially lifted his blockade of Cuba on May 3 and, on the basis of a mere guess regarding Cervera's destination, headed for Puerto Rico with the *Iowa,* the *Indiana,* the *New York,* two monitors, and a torpedo boat. Slowed down by the monitors, which had to be towed, Sampson did not reach San Juan until the 12th. Finding no signs of Cervera, he bombarded the port for an hour, taking eight casualties from

shore guns and doing only minor damage.

Mahan condemned Sampson's advance to Puerto Rico as an "eccentric movement." The main objective of American operations in the Caribbean was capture of Cuba by invasion, following defeat or blockade of the Spanish fleet. Until Cervera was located, therefore, Cuba was unquestionably the strategic center of the campaign. In the circumstances Sampson in abandoning Cuba was, using Mahan's terms, sacrificing his position at the strategic center for an eccentric operation of dubious advantage.

As a matter of fact, Cervera had outguessed Sampson by estimating that Sampson would do exactly what he did. While the North Atlantic Squadron was divided three ways—with Schley at Norfolk, Sampson at San Juan, and the *Oregon* circumnavigating South America, the Spanish made an end-run around Sampson's position and slipped into Cuba's back door. After crossing the Atlantic at less than seven knots, Cervera had applied for coal at Martinique. Refused assistance there by the French, he had proceeded on to Curaçao, where the Dutch authorities had proved more hospitable to his requests. Thence he proceeded straight for Cuba.

Sampson was already returning from his bootless advance to San Juan when he learned of Cervera's arrival in the Caribbean. He thereupon dropped his monitors behind and made full speed for Key West, arriving on May 18, a few hours after Schley's Flying Squadron had arrived from Norfolk. Believing that the Spanish fleet was bringing ammunition for defense of the capital, Sampson strengthened his blockade on Havana and sent the Flying Squadron, reinforced by the *Iowa,* around to the south coast of Cuba to blockade Cienfuegos, which was connected to Havana by rail. In the meantime, once more outguessing Sampson, Cervera had made directly for the isolated port of Santiago, far to the southeast. Here on the morning of the 19th he was received with congratulations when he steamed through the narrow channel into the harbor. He had achieved the incredible, but in reaching Santiago safely he had run through his bag of tricks. Though he found a certain amount of coal and other supplies there, he could think of nothing better to do than remain anchored in the harbor until the American blockade closed down on him nine days later.

Meanwhile Schley was taking his time getting to Cienfuegos. Once there he found he could not see inside the harbor, but he did see smoke and from that assumed that the Spaniards might be present. With evidence piling up that Cervera was elsewhere, Sampson sent Schley word by fast dispatch boat: "Spanish squadron probably at Santiago. . . . *If you are satisfied they are not at Cienfuegos,* proceed with all despatch, but cautiously, to Santiago de Cuba, and if enemy is there blockade him in port." [5] On the 24th Schley made contact with Cuban insurgents ashore and, determining at last that Cervera was not at Cienfuegos, headed for Santiago. Keeping down for a while to the 6-knot speed of one of his gunboats, which was having trouble in

the mounting seas, he did not complete the 315-mile run until the 26th. While still 20 miles from Santiago he made contact with three American scout cruisers, none of which had sighted Cervera.

Schley, who seems to have had a sort of obsession about fuel shortage, now began to worry about the state of his coal supply, and though he had a collier with him, the rough seas made coaling at sea impossible. So that night he ordered his squadron to head back toward Key West for recoaling. Delayed by engine trouble in his collier, he was overtaken by a scout cruiser next morning with a terse message from Washington: "All Department's information indicates Spanish division is still at Santiago. The Department looks to you to ascertain facts, and that the enemy, if therein, does not leave without decisive action." To which Schley replied: "Much to be regretted, cannot obey orders of the Department; forced to proceed for coal to Key West, by way of Yucatan passage; cannot ascertain anything respecting enemy." [6] Luckily, the seas soon calmed so that the Flying Squadron was able after all to take coal on board. Schley therefore returned to Santiago and took station off the harbor in the evening of May 28. The following morning the *Cristóbal Colón* was clearly visible anchored at the entrance, where she had been for the past four days. On June 1 Sampson arrived off Santiago, his squadron strengthened by the newly-arrived *Oregon,* and assumed over-all command. At last the parts of the North Atlantic Squadron had been brought together in one place.

The American vessels now took permanent blockading stations, with the battleships in a semicircle four to six miles off the entrance and smaller craft patrolling closer inshore. At night the ships closed in somewhat and a searchlight from one of the battleships played upon the harbor mouth. During the month-long blockade the fleet frequently bombarded the Morro and other shore batteries guarding Santiago harbor, and at night

---

[5] Winfield Scott Schley, *Forty-Five Years Under the Flag* (New York, 1904), 270.

[6] Schley communicated with the Department via dispatch cruiser to nearby Haiti, which had cable-telegraph connections with Washington. The dispatches are quoted from Schley, 278-9.

the experimental cruiser *Vesuvius* participated spectacularly but not very effectively by firing 1500-pound dynamite shells by compressed air from three fixed 15-inch tubes. In order to secure an advance base near Santiago for coaling, supply, and general maintenance of the blockading vessels, some 650 marines seized Guantanamo, Cuba on June 10 and in a week of fighting made good their position. These were the first Americans to fight on Spanish soil.

Cervera in the landlocked harbor of Santiago was harmless enough, yet his squadron still constituted a fleet-in-being whose mere existence exerted a restraining influence upon American operations elsewhere because there always existed the possibility that he might escape in a hurricane or at night. The United States could not exercise command of the seas around Cuba so long as there was any likelihood of Spanish warships suddenly appearing to interfere with landing or other operations. Sampson's fleet could not however penetrate the narrow, winding channel into the harbor because of mine fields planted there, and the mine fields could not be cleared because of the nearby shore batteries. Any attempt to run through the mines might result in a vessel in the middle of the attacking column being sunk and so splitting the fleet by blocking the ships already inside from those still outside. The alternative to going in and destroying Cervera's squadron was to plug the harbor entrance with a stopper which could not be by-passed at night or blown away by storms. For such a stopper Sampson chose a small collier and sent her in with a picked crew of seven under Naval Constructor Richmond P. Hobson to blow her up and sink her across the narrowest part of the channel. But the collier was detected by the Spanish, whereupon shore batteries opened fire and so smashed her steering gear that she drifted past the narrows and sank in a position where she would be only a minor obstacle.

With the failure of the harbor-blocking experiment it became clear that if the danger from the Spanish squadron was to be removed, it would have to be induced to come out and fight or Sampson's fleet would have to go into the harbor after it. Sampson therefore called on Washington for sufficient army troops to capture the shore batteries so that he could send in boats to clear the mines. The Army, eager to take part in the war which up till then had involved only the Navy and a few marines, quickly assembled 16,000 soldiers at Tampa, under command of Major General William R. Shafter. Shafter's orders from the War Department read in part:

> Proceed under convoy of the Navy to the vicinity of Santiago de Cuba, land your force at such place east or west of that point as your judgment may dictate, under the protection of the Navy, and move it onto the high ground and bluffs overlooking the harbor or into the interior, as shall best enable you to capture or destroy the garrison there, and cover the Navy as it sends its men in small boats to remove torpedoes [mines], or, with aid of the Navy, capture or destroy the Spanish fleet now reported to be in Santiago harbor.[7]

The fact that Shafter was given a choice of operations, when the Navy had asked for one specific task to be done, reveals serious lack of liaison between the War and Navy Departments. Moreover, Shafter and Sampson, who would have to work together closely in mutual support of each other, quite literally had no common superior below the level of the President of the United States.

Sailing from Tampa in mid-June in commercial transports escorted by naval vessels, the expeditionary force reached Santiago on the 20th. Included was the colorful Rough Riders cavalry with Theodore Roosevelt, who could not bear to remain behind his desk at the Navy Department when fighting was in prospect. Four days were consumed in leisurely, laborious landing operations at Daiquiri, 18 miles east of Santiago, with the Navy standing by to lend support and providing boats to ferry the troops to the beach.

Shafter in his one and only conference with Sampson had apparently accepted the batteries at the harbor entrance as his objective. Once ashore however he quite unaccountably plunged into the interior with his

---

[7] *Annual Report, Secretary of War*, 1898, I, 87.

troops and headed for the city of Santiago itself, some five miles from the sea. Hampered by rough bridle paths and barbed wire, the soldiers advanced slowly under the blazing tropical sun, many dropping out with heatstroke or typhoid fever. At San Juan Hill and El Caney the Spanish took a stand and inflicted on the invaders casualties amounting to nearly ten per cent. Alarmed, on the verge of retreating, Shafter, who was 63, weighed more than 300 pounds, and was confined to his tent with fever, sent Sampson an urgent message: "Terrible fight yesterday, but my line is strongly entrenched three-quarters of a mile from town. I urge that you make effort immediately to force the entrance to avoid future losses among my men." Thus the Army, which had been sent to enable the Navy to clear away mines to make an entrance, was asking the Navy to enter over live mine fields in order to assist the Army. Unable to reach an agreement with Shafter by messenger regarding the roles the Army and Navy should play, Sampson on Sunday July 3 steamed eastward along the coast for a personal interview with the General.

Before Sampson could put foot ashore however his differences with Shafter were resolved by Cervera himself. Though the situation looked grave enough to the Americans, it looked still more grave to the Spanish, who were convinced that Santiago was about to be captured and the fleet with it. Rather than see that happen, Governor General Blanco, at Havana, telegraphed Cervera to get out of port at any cost, and Cervera seized the opportunity of making his sortie while Sampson was off station in his flagship *New York,* and the *Massachusetts* was coaling at Guantanamo. The flagship *Maria Teresa* led the way at 9:35 AM, followed by the cruisers *Vizcaya, Cristóbal Colón,* and *Oquendo* and two destroyers. Sighting the smoke of the *Teresa* as she approached the entrance, the *New York* promptly came about, hoisted the signal for action, and sped westward trying to catch up with the running battle. We may imagine the consternation of Sampson as from a distance he watched his long-awaited battle being fought by Schley, whom he had left in tactical command during his absence.

Off Santiago harbor, the blockaders closed in, firing at the *Teresa* as she emerged. Then a curious thing happened. The *Brooklyn,* Schley's flagship, with the *Teresa* approaching as if to ram, swung to starboard across the bow of the nearby *Texas,* which had to back all engines to prevent a collision. Making almost a complete circle the *Brooklyn* finally headed west with the rest of the fleet, already pursuing the Spanish, who had broken through the blockade. Why the *Brooklyn* at first turned east instead of west, whether to avoid being rammed, to unmask the batteries of other American ships, or to open the range, was never satisfactorily explained, even by Schley, who stated merely that "it was the proper military maneuver under the circumstances" and that "it saved the day beyond any doubt." [8]

Soon the *Brooklyn* made good her loss in range and took the lead among the pursuers, with the *Oregon, Iowa, Texas,* and *Indiana* following. At the same time the little converted yacht *Gloucester* closed in on the two Spanish destroyers. Coming under concentrated fire from the American battle line, the *Teresa,* hit about 30 times, her steam lines severed, her wooden decks on fire, turned toward shore and beached herself six miles west of the harbor mouth.

The *Oquendo* and the *Vizcaya* next came under heavy fire, began to blaze, and likewise grounded. Only the *Colón,* last and swiftest of Cervera's cruisers, passed the range of American shells and made a genuine bid to escape. Her stokers spurred to unwonted activity by libations of cognac, she steamed away westward at 14 knots. After a 55-mile chase, when the alcoholic stimulation of her black gang had turned to drowsiness, the *Brooklyn* and the *Oregon* finally caught up with her and began making hits. At that, the *Colón,* only slightly damaged, struck her colors, steered for the beach, and surrendered. Meanwhile, the two Spanish destroyers, hotly engaged by the little *Gloucester,* had come under fire of the *Indiana* as she sped by. One destroyer was almost cut in

---

[8] Schley, 302.

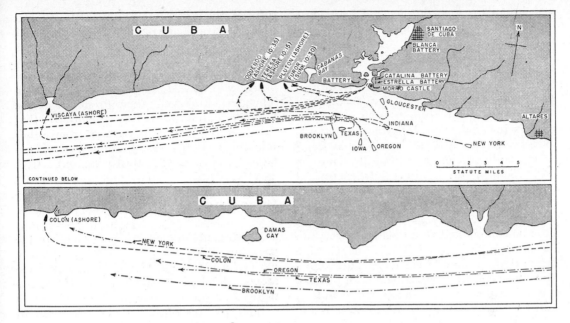

BATTLE OF SANTIAGO, JULY 3, 1898

two by a 13-inch shell; the other, heavily damaged by a smaller shell, sank after lowering her colors to the *Gloucester*.

As in the Battle of Manila Bay an inferior fleet had been annihilated by a superior, better-managed fleet. Spanish losses in the Battle of Santiago were 160 men killed and 1,800 captured, including Cervera himself. American losses were one man killed and one wounded.

The defeat of Cervera had far-reaching effects. Within a fortnight, Santiago, under naval bombardment and running short of food, became untenable, whereupon General Toral formally surrendered the city and his entire command of 22,000 troops to General Shafter. Spain's few remaining warships, en route to attack Dewey in Manila Bay, turned around in the Red Sea and headed back home to defend Spanish shores from a possible attack by the victorious North Atlantic Squadron. Now that the United States was in undisputed command of Caribbean waters, American expeditionary forces, with naval support, landed in Puerto Rico and headed for the capital. By the end of July, with United States forces victorious every-

where, the Navy laid plans for a cruise against the Spanish mainland, whereupon the Spaniards promptly sued for peace. In the final treaty, signed on December 10, 1898 in Paris, Spain relinquished all claim to Cuba and ceded Puerto Rico, Guam, and the Philippines to the United States.

THE SAMPSON-SCHLEY CONTROVERSY

For their services in the Spanish-American War, Dewey, Sampson, and Schley were all made permanent rear admirals. It would appear that there was glory enough for all, but bitter recriminations which eventually arose between the adherents of Sampson and Schley served in some measure to dim the renown of both.

In the first newspaper stories of the Battle of Santiago, genial, obliging Schley, a favorite of the press, received almost unanimous credit for the victory, though the preliminary planning had been done by Sampson, who had had the bad luck to be off station when the enemy fleet emerged. As newspapers began to reach the fleet off Santiago a week after the battle, Schley went to Sampson with a message which he asked him to transmit to the Secretary of the Navy: "Feel some mortification that the newspaper accounts of July 6th have attributed victory on July 3rd almost entirely to me. Victory was secured by the force under command Commander-in-Chief, North Atlantic Station [Sampson], and to him the honor is due." After reading the message carefully, Sampson said, "Schley, this is kind and generous; I will transmit it at once." He did, but that same day he wrote a secret message of his own to the Secretary in which for the first time he complained about Schley's procrastination in locating and blockading Cervera more than a month earlier. "This reprehensible conduct," wrote Sampson, "I cannot separate from his subsequent conduct, and for this reason I ask you to do him ample justice on this occasion."

Sampson's secret letter came out several months later when the promotions to rear admiral were being considered for confirmation by the Senate, and Secretary Long advocated that Sampson be advanced several numbers over Schley. Schley defended his conduct so well in a letter to the Senate Naval Affairs Committee that the inequity was canceled. Two years later however Schley's indignation was again aroused by the appearance of a third volume of Edgar Maclay's *History of the United States Navy,* the first two volumes of which were in use as textbooks at the United States Naval Academy. Maclay not only put the severest interpretation upon Schley's actions preceding the blockade but implied that Schley's turn-away to starboard in the *Brooklyn* was an act of cowardice. At this Schley requested a Court of Inquiry to determine what his war record had been.

For 40 days the Court held session under the chairmanship of Admiral Dewey. After 2,000 pages of testimony and findings had been assembled, the Court issued a majority and a minority report. The first found that Schley's conduct prior to June 1, 1898 "was characterized by vacillation, dilatoriness, and lack of enterprise" and concluded that "the turn of the *Brooklyn* to the eastward was made to avoid getting her into dangerous proximity to the Spanish vessels." The brief minority report just as vigorously praised and defended Schley's conduct.

Schley protested the majority findings to Theodore Roosevelt, then President of the United States. Roosevelt concluded that there was "no excuse whatever from either side for any further agitation on this unhappy controversy." So the matter rested.

LESSONS OF THE WAR

It was generally agreed that American naval gunnery, though superior to the Spanish, left much to be desired. Off Santiago, for example, the United States Fleet achieved a score of only a little over three per cent with major caliber shells, that is, 42 hits out of 1,300 rounds fired. Actually that was not especially bad in view of conditions of the battle and the primitive aiming methods then in use. American marksmanship, traditionally good, began to improve in postwar years with the development of scientific director fire and under the vigorous prodding of Rear Admiral William S. Sims.

The American Survey Board was incorrect in concluding that short range actions between major fleet types would continue and hence that rapid-fire secondary batteries would remain important in surface actions. Events were to prove that such batteries would find little use except in the yet-unforeseen function of antiaircraft defense.

The Survey Board, after careful examination of the Spanish wrecks at Santiago, recommended the reduction of wood aboard ship to an absolute minimum, a conclusion that Sampson regarded as the greatest single lesson of the war. The *Teresa, Vizcaya,* and *Oquendo* had experienced severe damage when their wood and pitch-seamed decks caught fire.

The difficulties and narrow escapes in pinning down Cervera underlined what such writers as Mahan had long emphasized, the importance of unified command, pursuit of a single objective, and maintaining a fighting force near the strategic center with its parts close enough together for mutual support.

Experiences in the Caribbean campaign revealed the need for a better amphibious doctrine. The landings at Daiquiri were carried out, as Theodore Roosevelt expressed it, "in a scramble." Against a well-defended coast they would almost certainly have been repulsed.

The Santiago operations also saw the introduction into the United States Navy of a new concept of the fleet train or service force. Three refrigerator ships furnished Sampson's fleet with fresh meats, fruits, and vegetables. The hospital ship *Solace* cared for the sick and wounded of Army and Navy alike. The first American hull repair ship, the *Vulcan,* handled 63 repair jobs while anchored off Guantanamo. These were the humble forerunners of the tenders and other auxiliary vessels which, operating as mobile service squadrons, freed the U. S. Pacific Fleet from fixed logistic bases in World War II.

The necessity for increased knowledge in naval engineering, for testing samples of material which might be useful both for naval and civilian purposes, and for a research and development center, led to the creation a few years after the war of the United States Naval Engineering Experiment Station at Annapolis. Rear Admiral George Melville, wartime Chief of the Bureau of Steam Engineering, was the chief promoter of this undertaking.

The Spanish-American War had provided a test under fire for the new "White Squadron" of the United States, and the accession of the Philippines, Guam, Hawaii, and Puerto Rico created a new need for, and interest in, a powerful navy to protect the expanded American empire. The fleets under Dewey and Sampson had won sweeping victories, but Mahan, pointing out errors and shortcomings, warned his countrymen that they could not "expect ever again to have an enemy so entirely inapt as Spain showed herself to be." [9]

---

[9] *Lessons of the War with Spain* (Boston, 1899), 157.

24

The Rise of Sea Power

in the Far East

WITH THE EMERGENCE OF Western European shipping upon the high seas at the end of the medieval period, East and West became linked together by sea power. The Portuguese, followed by the Dutch, the British, and the French, rounded Africa to found an immense trade empire in India and the Indies. Operating out of their bases in the New World the Spaniards, as we have seen, captured the Philippines, which remained in Spanish possession until 1898 when they came under the American flag.

The astonishing success of the Portuguese and their early successors can be ascribed in part to lack of effective and well-organized opposition. India was divided into a hundred separate principalities, frequently mutually hostile. Japan was suffering from centuries-long clan wars. China, in some respects highly civilized, could scarcely muster strength to police her own vast realms.

Yet navies and naval warfare were not unknown to the Far East when Europeans first arrived at the end of the 15th century. In 1273 and again in 1279 Kublai Khan had attempted to invade Japan from Korea and China. These were large-scale operations involving armies of 50,000 and 150,000 men respectively. The second expedition required the levy of virtually all the shipping in the Chinese Empire to lift the troops. Under the Mongol threat the Japanese temporarily abandoned their internecine strife and united to contain the enemy beachheads. Aided on both occasions by providential typhoons which scattered and sank much of the invasion fleet and thereby deranged the communications of the invaders, the Japanese were victorious. (Thus the "*kamikaze*," or "divine wind," became a part of the Japanese patriotic tradition.)

Not for over three hundred years was amphibious war to form an important part of Oriental history, except for the colonial exploits of Europeans. But in the late 16th century, the Japanese mounted large-scale invasions of the Asiatic mainland.

JAPANESE INVASIONS OF KOREA

The strong rule of the ex-stable boy Toyotomi Hideyoshi (1582-1598) [1] brought Japan a temporary respite from civil war. Eager to expand the Emperor's dominions, Hideyoshi made preparations to invade China via Korea. By new construction and a levy on the trading and fishing fleets, he created a naval and transport force adequate to carry more than 200,000 men across the Straits of Tsushima to Pusan (1592).[2]

In a five-week campaign the superior Japanese infantry defeated the Korean armies and occupied the country north of Pyongyang. But the Japanese naval dispositions were faulty, and Korea still had a formidable naval force at sea. Yi Sun Sin assumed command of the now united Korean fleet, and in a series of brilliant engagements defeated the three separate Japanese squadrons in succession.

The surprise—and the reversal of fortune —was complete. While the Japanese were prepared to receive a conventional attack from their despised foes and to destroy them with their samurai swords, they were unable to cope with a Korean onslaught spearheaded by a secret weapon designed and constructed by Yi Sun Sin himself. This was an iron-plated turtleback rowed galley fitted with artillery ports forward. The Korean commander's tactics were to use his invulnerable "dreadnought" to ram open a gap in the enemy line, while the rest of his force kept clear of the hazard of Japanese boarding parties and poured in a fire of small cannon, musketry, and flaming arrows.

By keeping his own fleet concentrated and taking advantage of Japanese dispersal, Yi Sun Sin was able to destroy the Japanese navy, and to cut off their armies on the beach from hope of reinforcement or supply from home bases. Hideyoshi made the

desperate gamble of attempting to reinforce his armies via the straits in the face of the Korean fleet, and lost. One hundred and twenty Japanese naval vessels and transports were destroyed by Korean naval forces, and most of the troops were drowned.

With the Japanese victorious on land and the Koreans unchallengeable at sea, a temporary stalemate ensued. But China, whose vassal Korea nominally was, finally bestirred herself to meet this threat on its Yalu frontier. Superior Chinese forces compelled a regrouping of the Japanese armies in the Pusan area, and the Japanese asked for a truce.

Without waiting for the promised Japanese evacuation, the Chinese armies withdrew, and the victorious Korean navy was partly disbanded. Hideyoshi profited by his enemy's injudicious haste to disarm himself. Protracting peace negotiations while he quietly prepared a fresh invasion force, after three years he was once more ready to strike.

In 1597 a new army under Kato Kiyomasa embarked in 200 ships and crossed the straits in a single day. A rejuvenated Japanese navy under Konishi was prepared to profit by past mistakes. It promptly secured the sea communications route from Kyushu to Pusan, and had little difficulty scattering such naval forces as the Koreans managed to dispatch to the area. But just as Hideyoshi had learned from the errors of the earlier campaign, so had the Chinese military command. The Chinese armies were promptly brought back into Korea and contained the Japanese advance south of Seoul. The front seesawed back and forth over a small area in southern Korea for over a year, with little important action undertaken by either adversary.

Then came the news of the death in Japan of Hideyoshi. The Japanese generals thereupon determined on immediate withdrawal from Korea. Yi Sun Sin, who had been called back from retirement to exercise naval command once more, profited by the Japanese fleet's encumbrance with transports, and furiously attacked the invaders. The ensuing battle has been called the Asiatic Trafalgar. The Japanese fleet, superior in numbers, barely avoided total disaster, and was de-

---

[1] As shogun, he was *de facto* dictator, though ruling "in the name of" the Emperor.

[2] The Japanese naval vessel of the day employed sail for cruising, but utilized sweeps for motive power in battle. Light cannon were carried, but boarding tactics were the Japanese specialty.

stroyed as an effective, organized force. For days after the engagement, badly battered naval vessels and transports staggered into the ports of Kyushu, but the losses were heavy and the check on Japanese seapower decisive. Three centuries were to elapse before the Japanese navy again ventured into Korean waters. Yi Sun Sin, like Nelson, fell in the battle which fittingly climaxed his career.

Like the relatively uncomplicated amphibious wars of antiquity, Hideyoshi's Korean campaigns illustrate certain strategic fundamentals in simplest terms. Foremost of these was the need of sea command as a prerequisite to troop transport. Significant also was the inability of sea power alone to defeat a self-sustaining opponent. Without the aid of Chinese armies, the Koreans though supreme on the sea would have faced long occupation of their country and probable ultimate defeat. There also appears to have been little effort made by either side to coordinate the operations of the land and sea forces.

By far the most notable aspect of the war was the leadership of Yi Sun Sin. Only a seaman who combined powers of command with professional skill of the highest order could twice have taken charge of forces depressed by defeat, weakened by inadequate logistics, and made them masters of the sea. This greatest of Koreans was never beaten in battle; his victories compelled the Japanese to shift to the defensive and reduced their capacity to resist the ultimate assault of the allies. His objective was always the enemy fleet and he seldom expended effort on diversionary operations. Few naval commanders have achieved surprise more consistently or more devastatingly, and few indeed have shown comparable ability to conserve effort to exploit every advantage to the utmost. He was a living embodiment of the offensive spirit in war.

After the death of Hideyoshi, the Tokugawa clan became supreme in Japan, but the intense nationalism of the unified archipelago was turned inward upon itself. Japan as a great trading nation might well have become a major sea power in the 17th cen-

tury, but instead the shogunate chose to discourage trade and exclude foreign influences of all sorts. A "bamboo curtain" would surround Japan for 250 years.

EUROPEAN POWERS IN THE FAR EAST

By the middle of the 17th century three European powers had established Far Eastern empires which were to nourish the economies of the mother countries for three centuries. The Portuguese had been virtually forced out of the East, but the English were well established in India, and the Dutch held unchallengeable sway in the East Indies. In 1605 the Dutch had dispatched a fleet from Java against the Philippines, but the Spaniards were more than capable of meeting this challenge, decisively defeating the invaders in a naval battle at Manila Bay.

Because of the nature of the universally-held mercantilist doctrines, which dictated exclusive trading privileges for the nationals of the colonizing country, the subsequent histories of India, the Indies, and the Philippines were almost completely separate. As detailed elsewhere, England was seriously but unsuccessfully challenged in India by France in the 18th century. Holland and Spain were both attacked in their Far Eastern holdings in the world wars of the 18th century, but for the most part enjoyed uninterrupted and exclusive commercial advantage from these colonies.

In the first half of the 19th century, the relative military advantage that the West enjoyed over the East was greatly increased by technological developments incidental to the Industrial Revolution, notably steam-powered ships and improved ordnance. Furthermore the new productivity of the West brought a new phase to the concept of imperialism. Whereas formerly control of the underdeveloped regions of the world had been sought mainly to insure sources of raw materials, now they were being eyed as great potential markets for cheap textiles and hardware. China, whose insulting treatment of foreigners and galling restrictions on trade

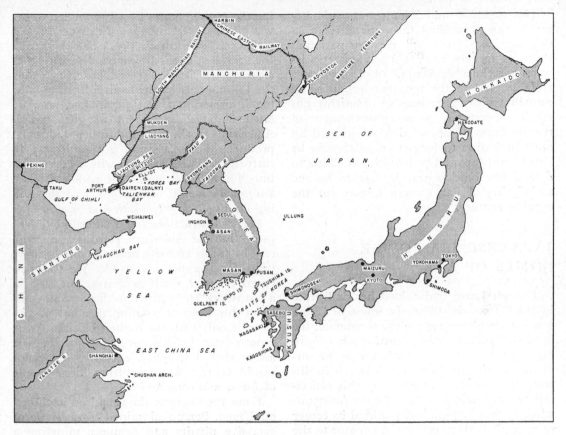

NORTHEAST ASIA, 1894-1905

had long been tolerated as the inevitable price of commerce with her, appeared to offer to the West the greatest unclaimed economic prize in the world.

In 1839 hostilities broke out between Britain and China (the "Opium War"). The technologically backward Chinese were repeatedly defeated, but the British, who made unsuccessful attempts at negotiation after nearly every battle, did not capture Chinkiang until 1842. The loss of this city, which because of its strategic location at the intersection of the Grand Canal and the Yangtze River controlled the communications of Peking with South China, frightened the Chinese into signing the Treaty of Nanking. The Nanking Treaty, and subsequent agreements with the Americans and the French, provided for the opening of five "treaty ports" to Western trade (Canton, Amoy,

Foochow, Ningpo, and Shanghai), and for a "fair and regular tariff." Hong Kong was ceded outright to Great Britain.

Fourteen years of troubled truce followed. Neither the Chinese nor the Western nations were satisfied. In 1856 Britain and France went to war jointly against the Chinese, and waged a campaign which culminated in the capture of the Taku forts defending the entrance to Tientsin. Thereby the road to Peking was opened. The Chinese once more sued for peace, and in the treaties of Tientsin (1858) made numerous further concessions, including opening further ports, permitting navigation of the Yangtze, allowing diplomatic missions in Peking, and admitting extraterritoriality. During a brief renewal of the war occasioned by Chinese reluctance to ratify the treaties, Peking itself was occupied.

The Nanking and Tientsin Treaties together largely defined the curious relationship between China and Western nationals that was to exist until 1945. These treaties were a serious weakening of Chinese sovereignty, and in the long run produced or contributed to a large number of mischievous results. Specifically, as an advertisement of the weakness of China, they constituted an open invitation to further encroachment by Russia and Japan. The inability of China to defend her borders was in fact to be the mainspring of Far Eastern history for the ensuing century.

JAPANESE SEA POWER COMES OF AGE

Though Japan maintained her deliberate isolation from the West, the lesson of China was not altogether lost on the shogunate; the harshest features of the exclusion edicts were modified in 1842 to permit succor to survivors of shipwreck and aid to vessels in distress. But for the United States this concession was not enough. After 1830 the American whaling fleet had gradually shifted its center of operations from below the equator to the North Pacific grounds off Hokkaido; hence the attitude of the Japanese became increasingly a matter of concern to the United States Department of State. The acquisition of California and the development of the Oregon territory made America a Pacific power. The prospect of a scheduled transpacific steamship service gave a special need for docking privileges in Japan, since the Island Kingdom lay directly athwart the great circle route to Shanghai.

Commodore Nicholas Biddle took the *Columbus* and the *Vincennes* to Tokyo in 1846 in an unsuccessful attempt to establish diplomatic relations. In 1849 Commander James Glynn in the *Preble* called at Nagasaki to repatriate 23 American seamen; Glynn's report after his return to the United States persuaded President Fillmore to make a determined effort to put an end to Japanese seclusion.

Commodore Matthew C. Perry, commanding the United States East Indian Squadron, was given special instructions to negotiate a treaty, and in addition a personal letter from the President to the Emperor of Japan. After a protracted fitting-out period during which the Commodore studied carefully all available information about Japan and accumulated a large assortment of gifts—typical American machinery and other industrial products—the expedition got underway in early 1853. The squadron which Perry took into Tokyo consisted of the paddle frigates *Susquehanna* and *Mississippi,* and the sailing sloops-of-war *Plymouth* and *Saratoga.*

Perry's instructions required him to obtain protection for American persons and property in Japan and free access to one or more ports for supplies and trade. He was prepared to use force if necessary, but only as a last resort. He planned to demand all courtesies due from one nation to another, and to treat only with the highest officials. As he reported to the Secretary of Navy, he was aware that a haughty, exclusive demeanor would secure most respect from "these people of forms and ceremonies."

From the moment the squadron anchored off Uraga, Perry maintained his attitude of excessive dignity and firmness, mingling a formally correct manner with an insistence on freedom of movement about the bay. He refused even to meet any dignitary below the rank of Prince of the realm. At the arrival of the Emperor's representative, the Prince of Idzu, Perry went ashore in a state procession and ceremoniously delivered the President's letter. He announced that he would return for the imperial reply the following spring. Returning to his flagship, he disregarded the protests of the authorities and steamed his squadron up Tokyo Bay to within six miles of the capital. After Tokyo's two million inhabitants had obtained a good view of the squadron the commodore took his leave for China. Perry's gifts as a negotiator nowhere showed to better advantage than in the timing of his departure. He wished to avoid pressing the Japanese for a decision when they had a valid reason to reject his demands for lack of discussion.

While the squadron wintered in China, its

strength now increased by the paddle frigate *Powhatan* and the sailing sloops *Vandalia* and *Macedonian,* the appearance of a Russian squadron at Shanghai caused Perry to expedite his second visit to Japan. He took his enlarged force back to Tokyo in midwinter. In negotiation Perry matched the Japanese representatives in obstinacy. The Council of State had hoped to put him off while preserving friendly relations. Perry finally convinced them that these were separate and irreconcilable policies: the Council must choose between a treaty and open war. Masahiro Abe, its senior daimyo and spokesman, reluctantly accepted the inevitable, for he well knew Japanese military weakness. But concessions were held to a minimum. The Treaty of Kanagawa, completed March 31, 1853 guaranteed protection to Americans and provided for the opening of Shimoda and Hakodate to American shipping. But there were no concessions on trade.

Perry's firm but judicious pressure had yielded the most that could have been obtained under the circumstances. That Townsend Harris two years later was capable of securing more generous terms stems from a fundamental change in attitude of the Shogun, who came to recognize that foreign trade offered the quickest means of promoting that technical and industrial revolution necessary if Japan was to insure its future security.

Neither treaty was popular with the nobles of Japan. The *tozama daimyo,* headed by the four great clans of Satsuma, Choshu, Hizen, and Tosa, chose to use foreign policy as a political weapon against their ancient enemy the Shogun. Their samurai committed a series of outrages climaxed in September 1862 by a murderous assault outside Tokyo on an English riding party. The Shogun was obliged to admit his inability to control his opponents or to secure reparation from the guilty Satsuma clansmen.

This crisis was immediately succeeded by a calculated gesture of defiance by Mori, lord of Choshu, the southern province of Honshu. Mori decided unilaterally to exclude all foreign vessels from his vicinity; he

emplaced 72 guns, including some 8-inch Dahlgrens, on his side of the four-mile narrows separating Honshu and Kyushu. Off the town of Shimonoseki he stationed three armed ships recently purchased from Americans. Mori's warlike intentions became apparent when, at dawn on June 26, 1863, his batteries opened fire on the American steamer *Pembroke* as she lay at anchor to the eastward, awaiting daylight to transit the uncharted strait. The merchantman hastily got under way and fled back to Yokohama, where it reported the incident to the American minister. In the next few weeks complaints multiplied.

In retaliation the 1000-ton *Wyoming*, sole United States naval vessel in the area, was sent to engage the batteries and the little fleet of the rebellious clansman. Early on July 16 the *Wyoming* entered the narrows and came under an accurate fire from Mori's guns. It was apparent that the batteries were ranged exactly on the channel. Observing that the Choshu steamer *Ko-shin* lay close inshore by the town of Shimonoseki and knowing that her draft was as great as the *Wyoming's,* Commander David S. McDougal shifted course out of the channel, and headed his ship to hug the northern bluffs under the batteries. The Japanese gunners tried in vain to depress their pieces sufficiently to hull their target as she steamed by close under them. Meanwhile the powerful 11-inch Dahlgren pivots and the broadside 32-pounders of the American vessel severely punished the shore batteries, dismounting several of the guns.

Once past the land batteries, the *Wyoming* with her superior armament destroyed the three-vessel navy of the daimyo in a matter of minutes. But in her maneuvering the American warship grounded at a spot where she was still under fire from the guns on shore. After some uneasy minutes during which the *Wyoming* took hits, McDougal succeeded in backing her off and in repassing the batteries without serious damage. The sloop reached the Bungo Channel with five killed and seven wounded.

Neither McDougal's punitive effort nor a bombardment of the Japanese batteries two weeks later by two French war vessels soft-ened Mori's determination to close the narrows. One month later a powerful British squadron under Rear Admiral Sir Augustus L. Kuper steamed to southern Kyushu to chasten the lord of Satsuma.

Six British war vessels, ranging in size from the 51-gun *Euryalus* to gunboats, appeared off Kagoshima to enable the British Chargé d'Affaires to deal directly with the daimyo. Negotiations came to nothing, and Kuper prepared to fight. In the teeth of an approaching typhoon he made a circuit of the harbor, sinking shipping and engaging the formidable Japanese batteries at ranges as short as 400 yards. The *Euryalus* carried 100-pounder Armstrong breech-loading rifles, and their shells, fired here for the first time in naval action, helped keep down the fire of the shore batteries. But the gunners ashore had the advantage of steady gun platforms. The *Euryalus* suffered heavy casualties—more than a quarter of her complement, including her captain and executive officer. As darkness fell the British squadron withdrew to the lee of Sakajima Island and rode out the typhoon at anchor. The violent winds of the storm meanwhile spread the fires which had been started in Kagoshima by the bombardment, and the whole city was gutted.

In spite of bitter political criticism in the House of Commons, the Admiralty supported Kuper. The validity of his judgment was confirmed by the fact that the daimyo presently paid the indemnity originally demanded. The Kagoshima bombardment engendered in the Satsuma samurai a great respect for naval power; they were to be foremost in building and commanding the navy of the new Japan.

The Daimyo of Choshu however still refused to accept the obvious fact that only by cooperation with the west could Japan hope to absorb the new technology requisite to maintain her independence. From behind his fortified headlands he continued to threaten bombardment of any vessel transiting the narrows between Kyushu and Honshu. In the summer of 1864 therefore, a joint international force of 17 ships under the command of Kuper assailed the fortified positions of the contumacious Japanese clansman. After laying down an overwhelming curtain of fire on the shore batteries, the fleet sent landing parties led by the British admiral. These forces spiked many of the guns, and dragged others down to their boats. Mori finally was obliged to bow to the inevitable; he signed an armistice requiring him to demilitarize the Shimonoseki waterway and to indemnify the powers for the cost of the punitive expedition just concluded.

The naval operations in Japan in 1863 and 1864 had a decisive influence on the course of the nation's history. The Choshu and Satsuma chieftains dropped their xenophobia and welcomed intercourse with the erstwhile foes, at least to the extent of acquiring western military techniques. They now turned their warlike energies against the Shogun; the coalition of *tozama* which they organized overthrew the house of Tokugawa and, during the course of a two-year civil war "restored" the Emperor. Under the "Meiji Restoration" the nation was westernized with a rapidity that amazed foreigners. The army and the navy were in the forefront of institutions that underwent reform.

The modernization of the navy was taken in hand even before the downfall of the shogunate, the first drydocks and slipways of the Yokosuka navy yard having been laid out in 1865. Officers were sent abroad to naval schools of all levels, principally in Great Britain and the United States.[3] From 1874 the Japanese commissioned foreign yards to construct warships of the latest types while not relaxing their efforts to construct improved imitations at home. While the protected cruisers *Naniwa* and *Takachiho* were building on the Tyne in 1885 the local dockyards could do no better than turn out the inferior clipper-bowed, bark-rigged composite corvettes *Yamato, Musashi,* and *Katsuragi*. By 1891 however they were able to launch the *Hashidate,* sister ship to crui-

---

[3] Beginning with two students admitted in 1870 the United States Naval Academy graduated Japanese in most of its classes for the next quarter century.

sers of the latest design delivered that year from the yards at La Seyne, France.

The strategic problem that confronted Japan after 1870 was in many respects analogous to that faced by Great Britain in the same period. Both nations occupied insular positions off continents which were liable to domination by one or a combination of dynamic land powers. Little strategic knowledge was required to recognize that Japan was in a dangerous position vis-à-vis Russia and China, and that what Japan had to fear most was the emergence of China as a naval power and the march of Russia toward ice-free ports. Strategically Japan was in a stronger position than either of her rivals; her strength was concentrated by the mere fact of her geographic situation. While she was weaker numerically than either of her antagonists, neither of them could deploy their full strength against her as long as she remained undefeated at sea. But the Japanese Pitts soon yearned for Napoleonic roles. They re-created the imperialistic ambitions of pre-Tokugawa days and steadily pursued a policy that aimed first to establish a defensive barrier off the east coast of Asia and then to exercise political control of the enclave formed by it. The new road to empire witnessed the annexation of the Bonins in 1876 and the Ryukyus three years later. Formosa and the Pescadores belonged to China and the central corridor, Korea, was nominally her vassal. Sakhalin, the northern flank, was Russian. The acquisition of all was necessary to complete the barrier.

China being the weaker was first to be attacked—in 1894. The conflict that followed is an instructive example of careful risk calculation in the use of war as a policy instrument. Operations against China were bound to succeed, but the intervention of foreign powers would be disastrous. At the time however Japanese statesmen correctly estimated that tensions and commitments elsewhere would make it impossible for any of the European powers to become involved. On the assumption that there would be no foreign intervention to complicate the strategic situation, the Japanese armed forces could move directly on the military objectives as determined by the national policy. Since the political objective was the elimination of foreign influence in Korea, the strategic plan was directed toward expelling Chinese military forces from the peninsula and preventing their return. The latter phase could best be achieved by military operations against Chinese concentrations in areas contiguous to Korea and by occupation of strategic positions commanding the land and sea approaches to the peninsula. The execution of the plan required a fleet strong enough to command the lines of communication with Korea, an overseas army strong enough to undertake offensive action, and a home army capable of providing for local defense and supplying reserves to the expeditionary force.

Having begun conscription in 1873, Japan had a well organized army. By 1894 she was able to put in the field seven first-line divisions, each numbering about 18,000 and complete with artillery. Behind each stood reserve cadres which when brought to strength in wartime would give the country a total force of 273,000 effectives. The Japanese were the first to use modern light artillery on a large scale, and this gave their divisions a high degree of mobility.

A well organized and well trained navy was available to cover the Japanese army's overseas line of communications. The fleet operated in two groups: the Main Squadron and the Flying Squadron. The former consisted of the three *Matsushima*-class protected cruisers, the largest in the navy, the armed cruiser *Chiyoda,* and the two old "armored vessels" *Fuso* and *Hiei.* The *Matsushimas* were relatively slow (15 knots sea speed) but heavily armed, carrying twelve 4.7-inch quick-firing guns in broadside in addition to their 12.6-inch guns. The *Chiyoda* was faster but was in the Main Squadron because she was armored with a 5-inch belt. Bringing up the rear were the obsolete *Fuso* and *Hiei,* "central battery" ships of an older generation mounting 6-inch to 9-inch guns. To make up a four-knot deficiency their captains were accustomed to "cut corners" during evolutions. The squadron's three heavy guns were powerfully reinforced with forty-four 4.7-inch quick-firers. Vice Admiral Sukenori Ito, the highly competent commander in chief of the fleet, also commanded the Main Squadron and flew his flag in the *Matsushima*.

The four faster protected cruisers operated together in the Flying Squadron, commanded by Rear Admiral Tsuboi in the 4,100-ton *Yoshino*. The flagship was the world's most modern light cruiser and could steam at 23 knots while the others could operate together at 17. Though the *Naniwa* and *Takachiho* each mounted two 10-inch guns, the bulk of Tsuboi's firepower depended on sixteen slow-firing 6-inch and twenty-two 6 and 4.7-inch quick-firers.

Fully equipped bases were located at Yokosuka, Kure, and Sasebo. The position of Sasebo near the Straits of Tsushima gave it exceptional strategic importance in a war with China. Until the capture of Port Arthur the Japanese were to be handicapped by the lack of advanced bases, having to send their ships to Japan for even minor repairs.

The defense establishments of China presented a quite different picture. Both the army and the navy were organized on a local rather than national basis. The army was huge on paper but was unable to campaign under modern conditions. The 356,000 troops stationed in north China were a heterogeneous crowd of "Green Standard Troops," "Braves" or volunteers, and "Bannermen," descendants of the Manchu conquerors, who received hereditary pensions but did little training. Despite their large numbers their unit of organization was the "camp" of 350 men. The army had some modern equipment, but the supply services were plagued with the traditional corruption. Shells were frequently filled with sand or cement, and lead rifle barrels were not unknown.

Four squadrons, named for the provinces they served, constituted the Chinese navy. Only the Peiyang or northern squadron participated in the war. It was formed about two German-built 7,400-ton battleships, the *Ting Yuen* and *Chen Yuen*. Completed in 1884, each was protected by a citadel of 14-inch iron-and-steel or "compound" armor

and carried four 12-inch guns in two open barbettes disposed on the beam in echelon. Theoretically these ships could fire all four guns directly ahead or abeam; in practice this was found impossible because of blast damage to the superstructure. In support of the battleships were three 2,900-ton armored cruisers protected with 9-inch side armor but each mounting the relatively weak armament of two 8-inch and two 6-inch guns. There were in addition ten light or protected cruisers carrying a greater number of 8-inch guns than Japanese ships of the type but fewer middle caliber guns. Their total number of quick-firers was limited to three 4.7-inchers. Nine gunboats and 14 small "second class" torpedo boats completed the squadron.

A few years before the war a group of foreign officers headed by Captain W. M. Lang RN had made the Peiyang force into a fairly efficient unit. But Lang's removal after his vain battle against graft was followed by the resignations of many foreigners; and though some remained, notably Commander Philo N. McGiffin, executive officer of the *Chen Yuen* and a graduate of the United States Naval Academy, it is the view of most historians that the squadron's operating standards declined. The commander in chief, Admiral Ting Ju Chang, early in his career had been a cavalry officer. He possessed personal courage in outstanding degree but his qualifications for naval command were slender, and he showed little grasp of strategic and tactical principles.

The Peiyang squadron had bases at Port Arthur on the Liaotung peninsula and at Weihaiwei on the extremity of Shantung. The former was greatly superior, being situated in a harbor well protected by sea and land and equipped with three drydocks and extensive repair shops. Weihaiwei had no docking facilities but its geography made it the squadron's home port. The anchorage behind Liu Kung Island, off the city, made attack by sea difficult, but essential repair facilities were lacking and the base was useful chiefly for its storehouses.

If Korea was a "dagger pointed at the heart" of Japan, it was also of great strategic importance to China. Its Yellow Sea coast flanked the sea approaches to Peking and the ports of north China. In spite of the weakness of her military organization, China was not without some strategic advantages. In a war of limited objectives she could if defeated at sea bring the weight of her armies to bear on Korea by land, though transport difficulties admittedly were greater. When war came however the Chinese went on the defensive from the outset, surrendering the strategic initiative to the Japanese.

OUTBREAK OF THE SINO-JAPANESE WAR

The pretext for war was furnished by a Japanese-fomented rebellion at Seoul in July 1894. When China moved in forces to restore order, Japan seized upon a treaty technicality to begin pouring troops ashore at Chemulpo (later renamed Inchon). Advancing to Seoul, the Japanese replaced the Korean king with a puppet "regent" and demanded that the Chinese withdraw from the peninsula. When China, instead of submitting to this demand, began rushing troops to Korea by sea, Admiral Tsuboi sortied from Sasebo with four cruisers and without formal declaration of war attacked the convoy, battering the cruiser *Tsi Yuen*, destroying one gunboat and capturing another, and sinking a troop-loaded transport. The Chinese force near Asan, thus deprived of reinforcements, was easily scattered by a Japanese detachment from Seoul. Japan had inaugurated the practice she was to employ in every subsequent war—strike first and declare war afterwards. Both sides issued declarations on August 1.

For the rest of the month while the Japanese army was being mobilized, Ito stayed at sea supporting the older ships that were guarding the terminus of the Seoul communication line at Chemulpo and the landing of the Fifth Division at Pusan. This was caution carried to excess since no enemy troops remained south of the Taidong River. The Chinese were if anything more cautious.

Following Ito's brief demonstration off Weihaiwei on August 10, during which the Japanese fired a hundred rounds at extreme range, the *Tsungli-yamen* (Foreign Office), which exercised control over Chinese military operations, sought to keep Ting's guns close to home territory. The squadron was forbidden to cruise south of a line from Shantung Point Light to the mouth of the Yalu. In apprehension the government also decreed that all troop movements to Korea should be made by land. The difficulties of transport thus imposed on the generals cost them the opportunity to occupy half of Korea. The Chinese navy also lost its chance to defeat the Japanese fleet, for Ting made little effort to cast off his leading strings and leisurely patrolled his confined area during the rest of the month. Ito meanwhile stayed close to his convoys and thus offered his opponent the advantage of initiative. He failed even to maintain a watching cruiser off Weihaiwei.

The rapid Japanese advance up the peninsula finally forced the Peking authorities to resort to the sea route to get timely reinforcements to Pyongyang, where 14,000 Chinese were digging in at the Taidong River crossings. Five chartered merchant ships were sent to Talienwan Bay to embark troops and artillery for transport to the Yalu River, and Ting was ordered to cover the movement. The squadron arrived at Talienwan on September 15. It comprised two battleships, two armored cruisers, two light cruisers, four gunboats, and an addition of two torpedo boats from the local units.

Before the transports put to sea Ting hoped to make a prior sweep in force as far as the Yalu to clear the area of enemies, but the news from Pyongyang was so threatening that he was dissuaded by the military commanders and the convoy steamed out of Talienwan Bay that night. The Yalu was reached next afternoon; the admiral detached a cruiser and large gunboat together with the two torpedo boats to accompany the transports up-river and cover the disembarkation. The rest of the force remained anchored off the mouth of the river.

THE BATTLE OF THE YALU RIVER

At ten o'clock the following morning, September 17, the crews were exercising at general quarters when heavy smoke banks were observed to the southwest. Ting ordered the squadron to get up steam. An hour later the squadron weighed anchor and headed for the still distant enemy at seven knots speed. The ships took stations abeam, the standard approach formation. Profiting from the experience of the *Tsi Yuen,* their crews had jettisoned unnecessary woodwork and rigging. Gun positions were sandbagged and ready ammunition was protected behind redoubts of sandbags and coalbags. But damage control was deficient in one important particular—excessive paintwork and burnish-

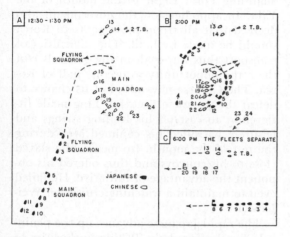

*BATTLE OF THE YALU RIVER
SEPTEMBER 17, 1894*

1. *Yoshino* (Tsuboi)	13. *Ping Yuen*
2. *Takachiho*	14. *Kwang Ping*
3. *Akitsushima*	15. *Yang Wei*
4. *Naniwa*	16. *Chao Yong*
5. *Matsushima* (Ito)	17. *Ching Yuen*
6. *Chiyoda*	18. *Lai Yuen*
7. *Itsukushima*	19. *Chen Yuen*
8. *Hashidate*	20. *Ting Yuen* (Ting)
9. *Fuso*	21. *King Yuen*
10. *Hiei*	22. *Chih Yuen*
11. *Saikio*	23. *Kwang Kai*
12. *Akagi*	24. *Tsi Yuen*

ing had made key connecting doors more decorative than watertight.

Ito arrived in the vicinity of the Yalu River in the course of a triangular search from the Taidong and Port Arthur. Since mid-August he had been engaged with troop convoy and only two days before had covered 30 transports which were landing General Nodzu's army at the mouth of the Taidong. On completing the task he had hurried northeastward, learning from spies that Ting and Chinese transports were at sea, but he had looked into Haiyun Island 90 miles east of Port Arthur on the day that the convoy had passed into the Yalu. Next morning when his squadrons were south of Talu Island off the Yalu, Ito and his staff sighted smoke to the northeast. It was then 11:30 and they soon afterward made out the Chinese squadron bearing down. The day was clear, the sea unruffled, and visibility excellent.

The Japanese fleet cruised in column of two divisions with Tsuboi leading in the *Yoshino.* Ito made few signals during the action and none which limited the independent action of his subordinate. The gunboat *Akagi* functioned as a dispatch boat and was stationed on the port quarter of the Main Squadron. It happened that the Chief of the Naval Staff, Vice Admiral Kabayama, was also present. He had come to inspect the fleet and now followed it into action, relying on the 14 knots speed of his ship, the converted merchantman *Saikio.*

The Chinese squadron was seen approaching in line abreast with the battleships *Ting Yuen* and *Chen Yuen* in the center. Ting's flag was flying in the former. The armored cruisers *King Yuen* and *Lai Yuen* flanked the battleships and the less powerful units were disposed equally on the wings. Ting's oldest and weakest cruisers, the *Yang Wei* and *Chao Yong,* he disposed on the right flank. Tsuboi led the Japanese column straight for the enemy's center, approaching from the Chinese left. At 12:50 when the range had closed to 6,000 yards, the Chinese battleships opened fire with their 12-inch guns without making hits. The Japanese Flying Squadron then changed course slightly to left, increased speed from ten to 14 knots, and bore down on Ting's exposed right wing, with Ito following in its wake.

At 3,000 yards the Japanese opened fire, and their van soon steamed across the bows of the *Yang Wei.* Tsuboi then changed course to the right and doubled the flank. The *Yang Wei* and *Chao Yong* were hit with a storm of 6-inch and 4.7-inch projectiles from the Japanese quick-firers and staggered out of the line in flames, one to go down shortly with nearly all hands, while the other was run onto Talu Island. It is likely that the rapid Japanese approach caught Ting unawares and that he found himself unable to form column before he was in difficulties.[4] With his left flank crumpling under Japanese fire he ordered a belated right turn, but the Chinese squadron soon lost all semblance of formation.

As Tsuboi rounded the end of the Chinese line he observed on his port bow four more enemy ships entering the area from the north. They were the cruiser *Ping Yuen,* the gunboat *Kwang Ping,* and two torpedo boats. To turn them aside Tsuboi reversed course 16 points to port. The maneuver was successful, and the Flying Squadron continued to circle and ran down the left side of Ting's squadron. Meanwhile Ito, who had continued around the Chinese flank, found himself on their right. Placed thus between two groups of the enemy, the Chinese rapidly disintegrated. The two rear ships left Ting's column and ran for Port Arthur heavily damaged. Reduced now to a strength of six against the Japanese ten, Ting proceeded to shoot out the battle with no attempt to ex-

ercise tactical direction. The protected cruiser *Chih Yuen,* holed with a 12.6-inch shell, steamed out to launch a torpedo attack on the *Yoshino* but was sunk with all hands under the concentrated fire of the squadron before she could get within the required 500 yards range.

A nucleus consisting of the Chinese battleships and two armored cruisers held together, and Ito made this his target. The Main Squadron circled round this group firing at a range of about 2,500 yards while Tsuboi steamed more widely through the area, confining his attention principally to stragglers and the disabled. At 3:26 one of the broadside 4.7-inch gun mounts on the *Matsushima* was struck by a 12-inch shell. Its explosion detonated ready ammunition and killed and wounded 100 officers and men. Fire swept through the battery deck and temporarily drove the crews away from the other broadside guns. As the big Canet gun (12.6-inch) had already been disabled by a hit under its platform from a ricochet, the flagship largely lost its fighting power. Ito transferred to the sister-ship *Hashidate.* About this time the armored cruiser *King Yuen* fell out from behind the battleships and became separated. Tsuboi's squadron took her under fire and in a few minutes sank her.

Throughout the afternoon the Japanese Main Squadron dueled the two battleships, which continued to fire slowly. Their superstructures were riddled, but the enemy's 12.6-inch shells do not appear to have hit the low-lying armor box which protected the vitals of each ship; though fires broke out frequently and the Japanese quick-firers caused many casualties among gun crews in exposed stations, offensive strength of the battleships was not greatly impaired. By 5 o'clock however their ammunition was running low; the *Chen Yuen,* for example, had by then shot away all her 6-inch and 12-inch shells, and no more than 25 steel solid shot remained to her main battery. Thirty minutes later when the opportunity for the annihilation of his antagonist lay within Ito's grasp he broke off the action, signaled Tsuboi to join up, and opened his distance from the Chinese to beyond gun range. When the

---

[4] Ting probably formed his fleet in line abreast for approach only, for with ten years experience of flag command he unquestionably realized the danger of fighting with his weakest units on the flank. Had he intended to fight an antagonist known to be faster in line formation, he doubtless would have stationed his heaviest units at the extremities of his line; for in addition to McGiffen he had with him as advisers several German officers. With his battleships in the center he needed only execute an eight-point turn to bring his ships into column with his heaviest units in the center, able to support either the van or rear with equal facility. Only from broadside could his ships deliver their maximum weight of fire.

firing ceased, the *Chen Yuen* had only three 12-inch shot left; these were loaded in the guns for a final salvo.

As the sun went down Ting formed his surviving ships into a column and limped off for Port Arthur. Four Chinese ships had been sunk, and of the two which had fled from the battle one failed to reach port. The retreating survivors consisted of the battleships, an armored and a protected cruiser, a gunboat and the two torpedo boats. Ito sent the *Matsushima* and two other cripples back to Japan. The squadrons kept each other in sight until dark, when contact was lost. Ito miscalculated Ting's destination and set course for Weihaiwei. Early next morning the much battered Peiyang Squadron reached Port Arthur.

Lack of aggressiveness in the final phases of the battle cost the Japanese a decisive victory. Ito broke off the action prematurely and he failed to intercept Ting at Port Arthur though he doubtless knew that only there could the Chinese repair battle damages short of going to Shanghai. Nor did the Japanese commander attempt to destroy the transports and gunboats still in the Yalu; at dawn on finding the sea empty he returned to his temporary base at the mouth of the Taidong River.

Like Jutland the battle of the Yalu River was at once decisive and indecisive. Though the Chinese lost five ships, their strongest units returned safely to base. But their morale was disastrously impaired, and they never again came out to dispute command of the strategic center or to threaten the communications of the Japanese expeditionary armies. Their fleet still existed however, and to eliminate the threat it became necessary for the Japanese later to undertake an amphibious campaign on a large scale. Of greater significance was the effect of the battle on foreign public opinion. The Japanese demonstrated a mastery of modern naval technology and for the first time established a standing among naval powers.

The battle was not without its lessons; some deficiencies in existing techniques were sharply evident. The quality of leadership shown by the Japanese was not above criticism. It will be recalled that Tsuboi as a division commander was granted greater independence of action than was usual at that time in western navies. His decision at the outset of the battle to lead diagonally across the Chinese front involved unnecessary risk, for this move would leave Japanese stragglers directly in the paths of their advancing opponents. This in fact did occur when the obsolete *Hiei* was left astern as Ito increased speed before beginning the turn around the Chinese right wing. To regain his station her captain "cut corners" right through the center of the Chinese fleet and passed at point blank distance between the *Ting Yuen* and *Chen Yuen*. He was lucky to escape with heavy damage. An attack on the Chinese left wing seemed logically to be indicated by the initial relative positions of the opponents. During the later phases Tsuboi's preoccupation with stragglers left Ito to fight the Chinese ironclads unassisted. In that respect the commander in chief failed to keep his striking power firmly in hand. While it is desirable to give the maximum opportunity to subordinates to exercise their initiative, it is no less incumbent on the fleet commander to keep the course of operations directed with maximum effect towards achieving the tactical objective. At the Yalu this should have been the destruction of the *Ting Yuen* and the *Chen Yuen*.

From the standpoint of naval technology the results of the battle were rather indecisive. In 1894 controversy over the rival claims of the big gun and armor filled a great deal of space in naval journals; the dispute was stimulated rather than settled by events off the Yalu. Armor appeared to have met a crucial test with complete success. Yet it was also true that the Japanese 12.6-inch guns did not actually hit Chinese armor and, conversely, that Ting's heavy guns were supplied with bad ammunition and therefore failed to destroy unarmored targets. Damage to several heavy guns in barbette mounts indicated a need for turrets despite the increased weights involved. Underwater attack was also seen to be in its infancy. The two Chinese torpedo boats early fired their six torpedoes without effect and remained out of the action thereafter.[5] Some Chinese ships were undoubtedly lost because their water-tight doors were ineffective. The deciding factor however was firepower. The Japanese had twice as many guns over 5-inch caliber (107 to 52) and 67 were quick-firing. The Chinese had only three of the latter. Being thus able to throw nearly triple the weight of metal in a ten-minute period, the Japanese could hardly have come away from the engagement without a large measure of victory.[6]

THE ADVANCE ON PORT ARTHUR

The troop movement from Talienwan Bay which cost the Chinese five warships gained them no compensating strategic advantage. On September 15 General Nodzu's division, which Ito the day before had landed at the Taidong, pushed inland to join Oshima's column below Pyongyang. Their combined force routed the Chinese army. The battle of

---

[5] The limited utility of the Whitehead torpedo at that date is shown by a report of the lieutenant commanding the torpedo boat *Foo Lung*. An attack was directed against the *Saikio* ". . . and at about 400 yards one torpedo was fired at her, but it deviated toward the right, the Japanese also steering to avoid the missile. . . . A second torpedo was fired and passed under her side about fifteen feet. . . . The Hotchkiss guns and Gatling guns were fired at her, she firing at us at the same time. . . . all the shots passing over our heads. . . . We ported the helm and passed her on our port side about thirty or fifty yards off, and fired the broadside torpedo at her, but it passed under her." Quoted in P. N. McGiffin, "The Battle of the Yalu," *Century Magazine* (August, 1895), 604.

[6] Admiral Sir Reginald Custance RN, pointing out that in the Battle of the Yalu as in the Battle of Lissa and later in the Battle of Tsushima "the winning fleet was worked in divisions," noted: "The conception grew out of a study of Nelson's Trafalgar memorandum. Its essence was to make the fleet flexible in the hands of the Admiral, and to enable any part to be moved by the shortest line to the position where it was most required." *The Ship of the Line in Battle* (Edinburgh and London, 1912), 103.

The success of the Japanese in using divided naval forces at the Yalu and subsequently at Tsushima unquestionably influenced their tactics in World War II, when Japanese naval forces almost invariably operated in divisions.

Pyongyang achieved the major political objective of the war: Korea came under Japanese control. Imperial Headquarters then proceeded to order further military measures which it considered necessary to preserve the gains and to secure a war indemnity. These were: to defeat the Chinese armies in Manchuria and North China, to destroy the Chinese fleet, and to insure continued Japanese control of Korean waters by acquiring a strategically located naval base.

Port Arthur was the obvious choice for the naval base. It lay at the head of the Yellow Sea on an extension of the 120-mile-long Liaotung Peninsula, and encircling hills concealed its harbor entrance. German engineers had constructed its forts and emplaced the 48 heavy Krupp cannon which commanded the approaches from all directions. Defensively however the fortress was weak in an important respect: it could be cut off by land, and if an enemy seized the base of the peninsula and also controlled the sea the defenders would be completely isolated.

A large scale siege operation having been decided on, General Oyama was placed in command and his Second Army was concentrated for embarkation at Sasebo. When the force sailed for the Liaotung on October 16, Nodzu's First Army attacked on the Yalu and penetrated 30 miles to Feng Huang on the baseline of the Liaotung Peninsula. The strategic effect of the advance was to contain Chinese military forces in south Manchuria. Ito's armada reached Pitzuo 90 miles east of Port Arthur on November 7. At the end of three days 26,000 troops of the fighting line and 13,000 auxiliaries stood on the beach. The fleet stayed by the transports until the landings were completed, an error of judgment on the part of Ito, for Ting's squadron might in the meantime have been bottled up at Port Arthur. The Chinese naval force left hurriedly for Weihaiwei two days after Oyama's arrival and kept well ahead of the belated pursuit.

The Japanese pushed rapidly down the south coast to Talienwan Bay, the only harbor at which a siege train and bulk stores could be put ashore. The last heavy guns were landed there on November 17 and the

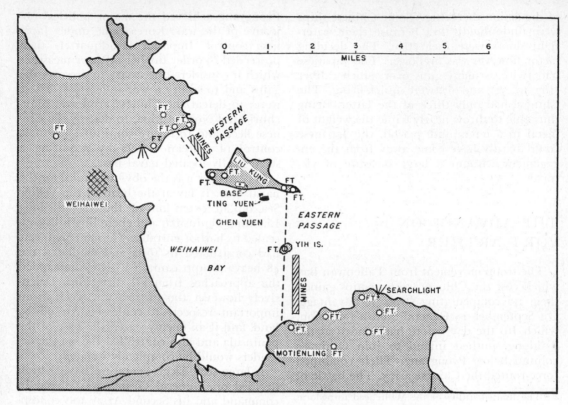

WEIHAIWEI, JANUARY 20 - FEBRUARY 12, 1895

assault on Port Arthur was made three days later. To the surprise of the world the forts were overrun in six hours. Ito was now provided with ample base facilities in the operations area. During December Nodzu moved across the base of the Liaotung Peninsula to the vicinity of Newchwang. Oyama's troops left Port Arthur shortly afterward and marched up the snow-covered coast to Kaiping, where they established contact with Nodzu. The First and Second Armies then went into winter quarters and prepared for a drive on Peking in the spring.

THE WEIHAIWEI CAMPAIGN: DESTRUCTION OF THE CHINESE SQUADRON

The Peiyang squadron at Weihaiwei threatened the flank of the projected attack. By the year's end reinforcements from the southern provinces had raised its strength to two battleships, four cruisers, six gunboats, and 15 torpedo boats. Since the Japanese navy could not eject Ting from a base so well fortified on its sea fronts, the army was ordered to cooperate. The attackers were confronted with the strategic problem of keeping the large Chinese army in Shantung away from Weihaiwei while they were capturing the mainland forts to force the Chinese squadron out or to open the channels to their own torpedo boats. Surprise, the greatest advantage inherent in an amphibious assault, was to be utilized to the full. The destination was kept secret, and to maintain intelligence security the Uji islands 140 miles south of Sasebo were selected for the staging point. An assault force of 32,500 men and 6,250 horses was assembled there under the command of Oyama, the victor of Port Arthur.

The physical features of Weihaiwei consisted of a bay lying between two capes five miles apart, with the island of Liu Kung dividing the entrance into a deep ship channel one mile wide on the west and a three-mile-wide inlet navigable by torpedo boats on the east. The Chinese warships lay behind Liu Kung, protected from sea attack but vulnerable from the land side of the bay. The channel entrances were guarded by modern forts on both sides and were closed by electric mines and a triple line of 3-inch steel hawsers buoyed on large timber crossties.

The 35 transports of Oyama's Third Army headed north from the Ujis and touched at Talienwan to pick up 15 additional ships carrying the artillery and engineers. While the last were embarking, Tsuboi on January 18, 1895 appeared off Tengchow, 70 miles to the westward of the true objective, bombarded the town, and landed a naval party of 2,000. Two days later Oyama's first wave was landed against some resistance at Yungcheng. The beachhead was 24 miles east of Weihaiwei and sheltered from northern gales by the projection of the Shantung promontory. By January 25 the whole army had been put ashore with six weeks' supplies, and it commenced the advance on Weihaiwei the next day. The fleet was at first divided between Yungcheng and Weihaiwei, but gales and extreme cold caused icing at gun muzzles and ports, and the blockading force was reduced in size. By day one cruiser watched the entrances; it was relieved after sunset by a patrol group consisting of the torpedo boats and one-third of the heavier ships.

The Japanese marched across the frozen rivers and reached Weihaiwei before the Shantung army could intervene. While the fleet on January 30 engaged the island and western batteries at extreme range, Oyama stormed the eastern forts and captured with them the firing station for the channel mines. When night came the eastern sections of the boom near the shore were removed; and although the channel at that point was made hazardous by rocks, a torpedo boat attack was planned for the following night. A gale sprang up on January 31 however, and all the Japanese ships were forced to run into Yungcheng for shelter. The bottled-up Chinese squadron could now have slipped out of port and run to the south with a good chance of clearing the Yellow Sea. It was an opportunity which a first class naval leader would not have neglected, but Ting failed to move.

Next day in a heavy snowstorm the Japanese captured the western forts, and Oyama secured the whole inner shore of the bay. The Chinese naval gunners now however did their best shooting of the war; aided by the island forts they kept down the fire of the Japanese land artillery. Ito's force then took up the weight of the offensive and launched a series of night torpedo boat attacks through the eastern inlet. Fifteen boats, ranging in size from 80 to 120 tons, were available. Beginning on February 2, the attacks were carried out under cold weather conditions of great severity. Some personnel at exposed stations on deck were frozen to death. The first attack was frustrated by the Chinese searchlights and heavy fire. Two nights later the second attack was made with two divisions, while the third created a diversion off the western channel. A boat was lost on the rocks and another by Chinese fire. Other boats reached positions for attack but frozen spray jammed many torpedoes in the tubes and no hits were made. The final attack was undertaken on February 5 with a single division, the others feinting in full force off the ship channel. Commander Machihara anticipated a suicide mission and told his men, "Our boats and our bodies are the enemy's." The division went close in to the Chinese anchorage and were able to launch seven torpedoes. They made four hits; the *Lai Yuen* capsized and sank, and the *Ting Yuen* had to be beached. Admiral Ting was left with but one major ship in serviceable condition.

The Chinese torpedo boat commanders showed themselves unable either to ward off the Japanese night attacks or to attack the blockading fleet. Ting ordered them to make a dash for freedom, and on February 7 they broke out of Weihaiwei. Only two managed to reach safety; the other 13 were captured or driven on the rocks.

With his base under fire from all sides and all his fleet except the *Chen Yuen* sunk, Ting on February 12 made arrangements for surrender and the personal safety of his crews and drank off a lethal dose of opium. The campaign had lasted 23 days. Ito sent the body of his late antagonist to Chefoo with full honors.

Two weeks after the fall of Weihaiwei the Chinese Manchurian army was decisively defeated at Liaoyang, and Viceroy Li Hung Chang opened negotiations for peace. The Treaty of Shimonoseki (April 17, 1895) was dictated by the victors. In addition to paying the full costs of the war, China ceded Formosa, the Pescadores, and Port Arthur.

The Sino-Japanese War was instructive to the victors and the foreign powers. It involved amphibious operations on a larger scale than had previously been undertaken in modern times. Japanese success was attained by skillful direction of naval and military forces to a common objective in accord with the principles of amphibious strategy, namely that the fleet support the army by preventing hostile troop movements while the army helped the fleet by hunting the enemy out of defended harbors.

25

The Russo-Japanese War

THE HOSTILITIES THAT BROKE out in 1904 between Russia and Japan first put steel navies to the test of extended operations under conditions of modern warfare. The mine, the torpedo, and the high explosive shell were used to such effect in this conflict as to mark a turning point in the technological revolution initiated by the shell-gun and iron armor in the Crimean War a half century before.

In the political sense too there was a historical connection. The Crimean War, by checking Russia's century-long quest for a warm water port in the Constantinople-Mediterranean area, brought about a new epoch in Russian policy. The Czar's government turned its attention to East Asia, and expansion there proceeded rapidly, if thinly. In 1858 the Treaty of Aigun with China enabled the Russians to consolidate all territory north of the Amur. Two years later, in requital for playing the role of "honest broker" at the negotiations ending the Anglo-French war with an exhausted China, General Ignatiev exacted the strategically important coastal region south of the Amur and east of the Ussuri. With the acquisition of this area, which she called the Maritime Province, Russia shifted her principal Pacific naval base from Petropavlovsk in Kamchatka to Vladi-vostok. But because the new port was closed by ice for three months each year, Manchuria and its warm water outlet, Port Arthur, on the Kwantung or southern promontory of the Liaotung Peninsula became the most attractive area for renewed Russian expansion.

These developments threatened to frustrate the national policy of Japan, which as already related aimed to dominate the mainland of Asia embraced within the arc of the Japanese island barrier extended to include Formosa and Sakhalin. In 1895 the Treaty of Shimonoseki following the victory over China brought the Mikado's government to within measurable distance of its goal, for it handed over Formosa and also Port Arthur to Japan. Russian reaction was immediate and effective: St. Petersburg secured the co-operation of the French and German governments in making a friendly *démarche* to Japan, warning that acquisition of the Chinese mainland would create a "permanent obstacle to peace in the Far East." The Japanese gracefully yielded to "the dictates of humanity" and forthwith proceeded to double their army and triple their navy.

Russian railroad policy was a source of further annoyance to Japan. Since the opening of the first Pacific railroad in the United States Russians had discussed prospects of a

431

trunk line to Vladivostok. The Czarevitch, later Nicholas II, turned the first shovelful on the Trans-Siberian Railway in 1891. Construction was pushed with unexpected rapidity: by 1895 less than a thousand miles remained uncompleted. This section, between Stretensk and Khabarovsk, would carry the line far to the northward along the bend of the Amur. Time, distance, and money would be saved by laying tracks through Manchuria, across the base of the Stretensk-Khabarovsk-Vladivostok triangle. Russia obtained the Chinese Eastern Railway concession in May 1896, permitting construction along that route in return for a treaty of alliance and for loans needed to pay China's war indemnity to Japan. Next year anti-foreign uprisings in Shantung, followed by the German acquisition of Kiauchau, offered the Russians an opportunity to demand the Liaotung Peninsula and the right to connect it with the Chinese Eastern Railway. They then secured a lease on Port Arthur and Talienwan, renamed Dalny, for 25 years, subject to renewal; and the historic question of a Russian warm-water port appeared to be settled definitively. It now remained only for Russian garrisons to establish control of the new South Manchurian Railway from Port Arthur to Harbin. The Boxer rebellion opportunely provided the occasion two years later and Russia extended her control over Manchuria.

The spread of Russian power in North Asia was regarded by the Japanese with resentment and apprehension. In 1875 under Russian pressure they had yielded their claim to southern Sakhalin; in 1895 on the pretext of safe-guarding Chinese territorial integrity they had been deprived of the best potential naval base on the Asiatic continent. Next they were compelled to stand by while Russia herself took Port Arthur and Manchuria and began intrigues to acquire a dominant position in the Korean court. To Japan a conflict appeared irrepressible. While six battleships and six heavy cruisers were building for her in Europe, her diplomats worked to insure that when war came the ring should be clear in the Far East. In 1902 they negotiated the Anglo-Japanese Alliance securing British aid

should an enemy be joined by another power. The Japanese government then demanded withdrawal of Russian troops from Manchuria under the terms of a Sino-Russian agreement of 1902. Evacuation was postponed and negotiations dragged on from August 1903 to February 1904. On February 6 Japan broke relations and began hostilities two days later without formal declaration of war.

The Japanese went to war in the face of some apparent disadvantages. They were compelled to undertake amphibious operations to capture territory that the enemy already possessed. Their first line and reserve troops totaled 435,000 against Russia's million, though most of the latter were at the other end of the Trans-Siberian Railway. In available naval strength Russia had a substantial preponderance: 15 modern battleships to six, and 38 destroyers to 21, though the Japanese had in addition 39 seagoing torpedo boats. In cruisers only did the Japanese have a margin of superiority: eight heavies (armored cruisers) to four, and 17 light (protected) cruisers to 15. Limited financial resources restricted Japan to a short war. Russia was economically more self-sufficient and had the further advantage of association in the Dual Alliance with France, the leading creditor nation of continental Europe. Such strategic handicaps however were to remain largely theoretical, for Japan possessed the incalculable advantage of having all her war material in close proximity to the strategic center. Besides the extensive base facilities at Yokosuka, Kure, Sasebo, and Maizuru the Japanese had 11 large commercial docking and repair establishments. Russia had virtually none in the Far East. Japanese morale too was an asset hard to overestimate. The patriotism of all classes was religious in fervor, and the ethical code of the ruling aristocracy derived from a military background beside which that of Prussia paled in comparison. The Russian people, on the other hand, knew little about the war and its causes and cared less.

In addition to her general lack of preparedness, Russia was handicapped by other strategic weaknesses. Her armies were split to hold sensitive frontiers in Europe and Asia, and their only line of communication was a single-tracked railroad interrupted at Lake Baykal by a train ferry in summer and sledge portage in winter. This division of force was paralleled in Russian naval dispositions. Three fleets of nearly equal strength were stationed in the Baltic, the Black Sea, and East Asia. The uncertain attitude of Japan's ally Great Britain contained the first of these in Europe until after the outbreak of war. As for the second, egress from the Black Sea was denied Russian warships by the London Treaty of 1870, closing the Dardanelles to foreign warships, and Britain's Mediterranean fleet stood ready to enforce the neutrality of the straits. Russia's Far Eastern squadron had no base that was both secure and convenient for operations. Since 1898 the Russians had heavily fortified Port Arthur, but they had not developed it as a naval base; the new docking and repair facilities were concentrated at the undefended commercial port of Dalny, 20 miles away. As in the Sino-Japanese War, Port Arthur was vulnerable to amphibious attacks on the peninsula in its rear. Vladivostok provided greater security. Its numerous channels and rocks made blockade difficult, and ice hampered naval operations from December through March. But both bases were contained within the arc of the Japanese archipelago.

Economic factors imposed an obvious line of strategy on the Japanese: hit first and hit hard. Their German-trained general staff hoped to achieve a quick victory of annihilation in Manchuria before the Russian army could be reinforced. Since troops had to be transported overseas and supplied from Japan, command of the Yellow Sea from the outset was essential.

Russia's strategy on the other hand was necessarily Fabian. Her military and naval staffs based their plans on delay—to avert a decision on land and sea and gain time to reinforce the armed forces in the Far East. The battleships based on the Port Arthur fortress would be a fleet-in-being threatening the sea lanes between Japan and Korea. It was widely believed in Europe, the experience of the Santiago campaign notwithstanding, that no government would commit trans-

ports to the open sea while an enemy fleet on its flanks threatened to dispute command. Four heavy cruisers would operate from Vladivostok to raid shipping on the Japanese coasts. In view of impending hostilities Admiral Alexiev, Viceroy of the Far East and commander in chief of all Russian forces there, ordered Admiral Stark, commanding the Port Arthur squadron, to send an observation group to Inchon, Korea. The cruiser *Variag* and a gunboat were dispatched accordingly. (See map, page 417.)

Japanese naval planning also followed obvious lines. The fleet would utilize its central position in the Korean Straits to keep the individual Russian squadrons divided and to defeat them in detail. When war came the high command decided that it was more essential to strike the Russian army quickly than to gain absolute command of the sea. A fleet-in-being, if contained, would not be permitted to hold up the immediate transport of troops. Again, as in the war with China, Japanese fleet operations were closely coordinated with those of the armies. Capture or neutralization of Port Arthur both to check a flanking threat and to secure the Yalu and Liao estuaries for transport became the immediate objective, closely related to the ultimate one of achieving the speedy and complete defeat of the main Russian field army in Manchuria.

THE OPENING OPERATIONS

From Sasebo on February 6, the day after the rupture of diplomatic relations, Vice Admiral Togo led the Japanese Combined Fleet to sea amid scenes of extraordinary enthusiasm. He determined to move with all force against the Port Arthur squadron, temporarily disregarding the heavy cruisers at Vladivostok. His main strength consisted of six homogeneous 12-inch gun battleships which he personally commanded, supported by four fast light cruisers under Vice Admiral Dewa. Also attached to his division were 19 destroyers and eight torpedo boats. The heavy cruiser force of six ships (armored cruisers), commanded by Vice Admiral Kamimura, was available for independent missions or for reinforcement of Togo's division in the battle line. Four older light cruisers under Vice Admiral Uriu[1] were assigned to Kamimura together with 18 torpedo craft—two divisions of destroyers and two of torpedo boats. The *Nisshin* and *Kasuga,* ex-Argentine heavy cruisers, were nearing Formosa en route to Japan from Genoa where they had been purchased while building.

Heihichiro Togo was 57 years old and had been commander in chief since the previous October. Diminutive in stature and taciturn to a degree unusual even in a class that cultivated stoicism as a virtue, he enjoyed a reputation for high professional skill and judgment. Reaching the Korean coast on February 8, Togo detached Uriu's squadron with the heavy cruiser *Asama* and eight torpedo boats to cover troop landings at Inchon and to deal with the Russian naval force there. The main body continued NW and at 10:30 PM sighted searchlight beams at Port Arthur. Ten Japanese destroyers stood in to attack while the other nine turned east toward Dalny where a portion of the Russian squadron was expected to be found.

Stark's force—seven battleships and six cruisers—lay at anchor however in the roadstead off Port Arthur. Alexiev had failed to inform its commander that Japan had broken relations, and no precautions against attack had been taken except to maintain a two-ship searchlight patrol and a picket of two destroyers, none of which had received orders to fire. The anchored ships were partially illuminated, their torpedo nets were stowed, the night was clear—for the attackers, conditions generally approximated those of target practice. The Japanese destroyers nevertheless lost touch with each other during the approach and, hampered by searchlight beams, delivered four uncoordinated attacks, most of the ten boats getting off their two torpedoes at ranges of about 800 yards. Two Russian battleships and a cruiser were hit and though flooding was controlled the larger ships grounded at the entrance to Port Arthur

as they were being taken in, completely blocking the channel to the rest of the squadron. As a result of confusion among the Russian crews and the fact that recoil cylinders in the best guns of the shore batteries had been drained for the winter, the attackers suffered no casualties or damage. Because destroyers were not then equipped with radio, Togo, keeping his battleships well out to sea for fear of attack by the 25 Russian destroyers known to be in the area, did not get word of the results obtained.

Dewa's cruisers closed Port Arthur at 8:00 the next morning and informed Togo by radio that Stark's ships lay outside the harbor unable to enter. The Japanese commander in chief himself arrived on the scene at noon but he had lost four valuable hours and the shore batteries had been restored to service. Had Togo arrived at dawn he might have closed decisively with 12 armored ships against 5. The subsequent long assault on Port Arthur would thereby have been rendered unnecessary and the concentrated Japanese armies might have achieved their decisive victory. For an hour Togo led his ships in a defilade and engaged in an artillery duel, but several 10-inch hits registered on his battleships by the cliff batteries helped dissuade him from closing. When the Japanese withdrew neither side had received serious damage.

While the destroyer attacks were in progress at Port Arthur Uriu carried out his assignment at Inchon and next morning dispatched an ultimatum to the two Russian warships, ordering them to come out or be destroyed. After a sharp 20-minute action with his superior opponent Captain Rudnev of the *Variag* had only two guns firing, and a third of his crew were casualties. He steered the burning cruiser back to harbor with engines only and, on rounding Wolmi-Do Island opened the Kingston valves. The Russian gunboat was not engaged but was likewise scuttled. The decision to station an unsupported force in a threatened area had cost the Russians a new cruiser and a serviceable gunboat.

When General Kuroki's Japanese First Army landed at Inchon in the middle of February Togo closed to provide battleship

---

[1] Sotokichi Uriu was graduated from the United States Naval Academy in 1881.

cover, leaving Kamimura to watch the Port Arthur force. The Russian armies held the line of the Yalu, their concentration point being at Liaoyang where the South Manchurian Railway crossed the south branch of the Liao River. Spring thaws bogged down Kuroki in a sea of mud and it was not until the end of April that he was able to storm the Yalu crossings, forcing his opponent, Kuropatkin, to retire toward Liaoyang. Togo, though he kept his main body close to Kuroki's depot at Inchon, made several attempts during these months to get at the Russian "fortress fleet." He sent in three groups of blockships, 27 in all, to close the entrance of Port Arthur, but all were sunk by Russian gunfire before they reached the channel or were run aground outside by crews blinded in the glare of searchlights. Destroyers made repeated unsuccessful night attacks, and in general support of these operations Togo on three occasions took his ships under the shelter of Liaotishan, the unfortified tip of the peninsula five miles south of Port Arthur, and bombarded the base with his 12-inch guns. Both sides introduced a modern aspect of war by laying mine fields in international waters, the Russians attempting to interdict approach to ports and beachheads on the peninsula, the Japanese aiming to seal Port Arthur. Within a week of the war's opening a Russian minelayer was sunk by one of her own mines off Dalny and the cruiser *Boyarin,* hastening to rescue survivors, ran on another and went down with heavy loss. For two months the Port Arthur squadron remained strictly on the defensive and had two cruisers, a minelayer, and a gunboat sunk, together with two battleships and another cruiser put out of action without doing damage or hampering enemy movements on the seas. But a change was at hand. On March 8, 1904 Vice Admiral Stephen Ossipovitch Makarov arrived at Port Arthur to take command of the Russian naval forces in Eastern Asia.

The new commander was the ablest officer of the Russian navy. He had written extensively on naval tactics and was a hydrographer of international reputation. He was also an accomplished seaman but it was in strong personal leadership that he brought to Port Arthur the quality most needed there. Announcing that "an ensign who knows what he is doing is of greater value to the country than a flag officer who carries out the letter of an order which he does not understand," Makarov set about with energy to restore morale, develop an aggressive spirit, and bring back the high standards of performance and material that had prevailed in the squadron when he had hauled down his flag there in 1897. On the day after his arrival his destroyers engaged the Japanese patrols and inflicted considerable damage. Togo quickly realized that his opponents had at last discarded their no-risks strategy.

Repairs to the Russian fleet were now pushed in earnest, a matter of some difficulty since the Port Arthur docks were too small to take the torpedoed battleships, and cofferdams had to be built around their ruptured plating. The rest of the squadron embarked on a rigorous schedule of training sorties and learned to work together, though on one occasion it meant the dismissal of an incompetent captain from his ship. On April 12 a Japanese mining force appeared in strength off Port Arthur and engaged the destroyer pickets. Makarov sent cruisers out in support and himself followed at top speed in the *Petropavlovsk* accompanied by the other four available battleships. He did not wait to bring out minesweepers. The 15-mile pursuit of Dewa's cruisers that followed was interrupted by Japanese battleships steaming over the horizon to cut off the retreat of the Russians. Makarov, outgunned, withdrew to the shelter of the coastal batteries and was passing the Lutin Rock, two miles from Port Arthur roads when his flagship struck a mine. Observers heard a muffled explosion followed by a roar. A burst of flame rent the superstructure and yellow smoke rose high in the air, shrouding the ship. The smoke rolled aside a minute later to reveal the quarter deck of the *Petropavlovsk* sliding into the sea. Thirty-two officers, including Makarov, and over 600 men went down in the ship. Prince Ukhtomsky, rear admiral second-in-command, led the squadron in a wide detour, but half an hour later as it again approached the channel another mine exploded against the *Pobieda*. This time magazines held and the battleship was brought into harbor. Makarov's death was an irreparable loss for Russia; very probably it was decisive on the outcome of the war. "With him" wrote a destroyer commander "all hope of rendering the squadron efficient was buried."

Rear Admiral Vitgeft, Makarov's successor, promptly resumed the defensive, but the Grand Duke Alexis, head of the navy, announced on April 30 that the Port Arthur force would henceforth be known as the "First Pacific Squadron" and that a "Second Pacific Squadron" would leave the Baltic at the end of July and arrive in the Yellow Sea four or five months later.

PORT ARTHUR BESIEGED

The Japanese now began to move with determination. By the beginning of May, Kuroki was across the Yalu and on his left the offensive against Port Arthur began. The Japanese Second Army landed at Pitzuo on Liaotung, Togo covering from his new base in the nearby Elliot Islands. The Japanese moved down the peninsula toward the fortress, and ten days later at the Battle of Nan Shan stormed the three-mile-wide neck connecting Kwantung and Port Arthur with the main body of the peninsula. During the battle Vitgeft lay at anchor in his base, failing to use his opportunity to make a surprise appearance and sweep the flanks of the assaulting columns with naval gunfire. Fate presented him with a still greater opportunity two days later. At 2:30 AM on May 14 Dewa's fast light cruiser *Yoshino* was rammed and sunk in the fog by her next astern. Later that morning the battleship *Hatsuse* on watch off Port Arthur struck a mine aft and filled her steering compartment. The *Yashima* nearby was shortly afterwards holed under the starboard coal bunkers by another mine. Both battleships were taken in tow but a third mine exploded against the *Hatsuse,* detonating a magazine and destroying the ship with heavy loss of life. In the afternoon the *Yashima* capsized and sank. With his battleship strength reduced by a third in a single

day Togo might effectively have been attacked by an enterprising opponent. But Vitgeft, though apprised of the situation, still swung at his anchors. With the promise of reinforcements he postponed all thought of action.

After the land battle at Nan Shan, the Japanese Third Army soon occupied Dalny and converted it into a military base for further operations. In June however, as the Japanese troops closed in on the main ring of forts about Port Arthur, Russian sea power intervened to stop their progress. The Vladivostok cruisers, under Rear Admiral Jessen, eluded Kamimura's patrol and reached the coast of Kyushu, where they captured and sank an unescorted merchantman carrying the Port Arthur siege train of eighteen 11-inch mortars. Nevertheless Alexiev ordered the naval forces to leave Port Arthur and concentrate at Vladivostok. With this decision Vitgeft was in strong disagreement. A preliminary sortie towards the Elliot Islands on June 23 had brought about a rapid concentration of Togo's forces, whereupon the Russians had withdrawn without firing a shot. Vitgeft believed that his naval brigade and the light ships' guns which he had landed were a significant element of the defense, and foremost in his mind was the prospect of reinforcement from the Baltic. His estimate was not wholly without validity. After the sortie of the 23rd the morale of the Russian squadron was low and its strength reduced by mine damage done to the battleship *Sevastopol*. A correct military decision would have kept Vitgeft at Port Arthur until its fall appeared certain and then launched his squadron at Togo to do as much damage as possible before the arrival of the Baltic fleet. Should the fortress hold out the Japanese would face a convergence of naval force that would out-number them by two to one, and they would in the meantime have been unable to leave the blockade in order to refit. The possibility of Russian reinforcement weighed heavily with Togo; his policy throughout the siege was to conserve his ships.

The pressure of world press comment unfortunately influenced the Czar to force Vitgeft's hand. Critical accounts of the squadron's apparent inactivity nettled the Imperial Court while news of Japanese gains by land alarmed it. Early in August, three months after the siege lines closed in, Japanese 4.7-inch shells began to fall in Port Arthur, accurately spotted by balloon observers. On receiving the news Nicholas II dispatched a personal order to Vitgeft: "Put out with full strength for Vladivostok." Seventy-two hours later, at dawn on August 10, 1904, the Port Arthur squadron, without attempting a feint toward Dalny to draw off Togo, made its dash for freedom. To get clear of the mine fields the column of six battleships, four light cruisers, and eight destroyers headed SW and lost four hours before it could set an easterly course for the Korean Straits. Dewa picked the refugees up at the turn and maintained contact until Togo's arrival. The Japanese commander in chief now had occasion to miss the four heavy cruisers which Kamimura had recently taken to the Tsushima Channel to search for Jessen's Vladivostok cruisers, but he summoned every combat ship in the Port Arthur area including the *Chen Yuen* and other relics of the China war and, coming himself with a column of four battleships and two heavy cruisers, sighted the Russians at noon.

THE BATTLE OF THE YELLOW SEA

Togo had a tactical plan, basically the simple concept of working up to full speed and then crossing and recrossing the enemy's "T" [2] until he should be annihilated or

---

[2] By crossing the "T," or capping the enemy, ships in column can achieve maximum concentration against opponents who are also in column. The maneuver is roughly equivalent to raking: the attacker, in crossing ahead nearly at right angles, is able to bring full broadsides to bear while the opponent finds his own after guns either "closed out" or able to fire only at the extremities of the attacker's column and at relatively long range. But even a considerably slower fleet can easily parry the threat by turning away during the attacker's approach or on contact, and this has made capping impracticable unless an opponent has fought in virtual blindness, as

driven back to port. The Japanese battle line steaming down from the NW crossed over ahead of the Russians nearly hull down and well beyond gun range. Reversing course Togo again crossed the Russians' "T" at an oblique angle and opened fire, but so anxious was he to conserve his ships that the range remained above 12,000 yards. Another course reversal to SE brought him back toward the oncoming enemy but Vitgeft turned to a parallel course. As the Japanese battle line pulled ahead, the Russian force made another course change and doubled back toward its wake. Togo promptly turned westward to keep his broadside bearing and thereby found himself completely outmaneuvered, for he was now on the wrong side of the Russians and steaming away from them. By the time the Japanese were back on an eastward course to continue pursuit, Vitgeft had gained a lead of some seven miles toward the Korean straits. Both sides maintained a steady fire at extreme range and damaging hits were scored in about equal numbers. The outcome now depended on the battle of the boilers. Towards sunset the Japanese pulled abeam of Vitgeft's fleeing column, but Togo could not yet overcome his reluctance to close. Five of the Japanese 12-inch guns were out of action and two Russian turrets were disabled.

The crisis came with unexpected quickness at 6:37. A 12-inch shell exploded against the foremast of the *Czarevitch* and its fragments swept the bridge. Every officer of the staff went down and among those blown overboard and never seen again was Admiral Vitgeft. Before the flagship's captain in the conning tower could inform the second-in-command, a second heavy projectile burst overhead, perforating the roof and killing or wounding everyone inside. The helmsman in falling grasped and spun the wheel,

---

for example in several night actions of World War II when the Japanese engaged radar-equipped American forces. Togo's official reports indicate that he attempted to cross the "T" rather with strategic objectives in mind, intending to turn the Russians away from their lines of advance or retreat. His basic battle tactic assumed an engagement in parallel columns and called for concentration on enemy division leaders.

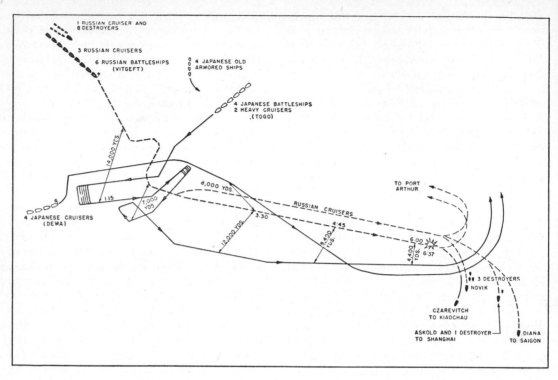

BATTLE OF THE YELLOW SEA, AUGUST 10, 1905

putting the ship into a wide left turn away from the enemy. The next two ships hung on but the *Peresviet,* fourth in line, turned left also to avoid collision with the flagship now coming round through 16 points. The last two battleships sheered off to follow the *Peresviet* and the Russian formation broke up in disorder. Rear Admiral Ukhtomsky in the *Peresviet* sensed the crisis and tried to transmit a follow-the-leader signal but found the halyards and radio antennae shot down. As the Russians turned NW in a confused group, Togo also grasped the situation and closed to 4,000 yards for the kill, his cruiser squadrons circling to close a ring around their opponents. But he shortly afterwards sighted Russian destroyers moving out menacingly from behind the engaged side of their battleships, and the fear of a torpedo attack in the gathering darkness overcame his resolution; he broke off pursuit and turned his battle line south to back up his cruisers. While the Russian battleships struggled NW, Reitzenstein, the cruiser admiral, also turned

south to break through the Japanese and signaled his division to follow. Three of them, accompanied by five of the eight Russian destroyers, fought their way through, two cruisers receiving enough damage to compel their seeking the nearest port.

During the night the Japanese torpedo flotillas made continuous but unsuccessful attacks on the Russian main body, and dawn found Ukhtomsky passing through his mine field and entering Port Arthur. He had only nine of the 18 ships that had sortied the day before. Of Reitzenstein's force, one cruiser reached Shanghai, where it was interned with a destroyer; another shared a similar fate at Saigon, Indo-China. The third Russian cruiser with three more destroyers reached Kiauchau to be joined shortly afterwards by the damaged *Czarevitch.* At the last port the German authorities disarmed all except the cruiser, which coaled and departed within 24 hours. This ship, the speedy *Novik,* ran up the east Japanese coast and into the Soya Straits between Hokkaido and Sakhalin. On leaving Korsakov in Sakhalin, where she had taken on more coal for the last lap to Vladivostok, she ran on the rocks and was sighted by Japanese cruisers; the crew opened her sea valves to avert her capture.

In the tactical sense, Togo's victory was something less than impressive. The excessive caution that had governed his movements in the early stages was equally manifest at the decisive moment of the action when he failed to follow up and destroy the confused mass of Russians. Togo also missed a great strategic opportunity. Because the siege of Port Arthur had been undertaken primarily to eliminate the threat to Japanese communications posed by the naval force sheltered there, annihilation of the Russian squadron on August 10 would have made capture of the fortress less urgent, if indeed necessary at all. And the troops thereby released might well have made good the lack of strength that cost the Japanese a decisive victory at Liaoyang a month later.

After its return to Port Arthur the reduced First Pacific Squadron ceased to be even a fleet-in-being. Its secondary batteries and a large proportion of its crews were incorporated in the land defenses. Meanwhile Alexiev, at Vladivostok, had sought to facilitate Vitgeft's escape by dispatching Jessen's three powerful cruisers to keep Kamimura occupied and, if possible, to join up with the Port Arthur battleships in the Korean Straits. Little effort was made to coordinate the timing however and Jessen failed to reach Tsushima until the 14th, four days after the Battle of the Yellow Sea. Moreover he ran into Kamimura, whose luck finally turned with this sighting of his elusive enemy. After the ensuing sea battle of Ulsan, Jessen escaped to the north but only after losing the *Rurik*, damaged and left behind to be sunk by the Japanese. A second heavy cruiser, the *Gromoboi*, grounded on rocks near Vladivostok shortly after. With but one cruiser and a few torpedo boats remaining, the Vladivostok squadron too was out of the war.

The satisfaction which the Japanese derived from the success thus far achieved on the sea was tempered next month by their failure to inflict a decisive defeat on the Russian army. In September their own field armies converged on Liaoyang for a final battle but General Kuropatkin, though defeated, skillfully extricated his forces and fell back on Mukden. Three weeks later the Japanese learned that the Second Pacific Squadron had departed from the Baltic for Port Arthur. The situation had become serious for them.

The war now took on a new aspect. General Nogi, commanding the Japanese Third Army facing Port Arthur, discontinued his orthodox tactics of siege approaches and ordered a general assault, introducing to the world the phenomena of the "banzai charge" and of human torpedoes blasting paths through barbed wire entanglements. But Russian resistance, if less spectacular, was equally desperate; and the besiegers, after the failure of the October attack and another in November, had lost 50,000 men. With the date of the arrival of the Russian fleet estimated at early January, the Japanese Third Army had now to make its supreme effort. The whole weight of the assault was shifted to one point, 203-Meter Hill, which provided an excellent view of the harbor. A ten-day attack at the cost of another 10,000 casualties —including Nogi's two sons—put the crest in Japanese possession on December 5. A forward observing post was set up and connected by telephone with the 11-inch mortar batteries. Within a week indirect fire had so heavily damaged the five Russian battleships and two cruisers in Port Arthur that their crews scuttled them at the buoys. Captain von Essen took the battleship *Sevastopol* and four destroyers to a boom-protected anchorage outside the harbor, but the reprieve was brief. In the fortress, Russian morale had been weakened by the death of General Kondratenko, second-in-command and the soul of the defense; Port Arthur surrendered on January 2, 1905 though not before von Essen had scuttled his ships to complete the death of the squadron.[3]

Russia now had to attempt with a remnant of her naval forces what she should have undertaken with her whole fleet earlier in

[3] The Japanese later raised four of the battleships and the two cruisers and incorporated them into their navy.

the war. From the first news of the Baltic fleet's sailing Togo was wholly occupied in preparing his squadrons for the coming battle. He sent ships to Japan for docking, he intensified target practice, and conducted fleet evolutions in the worst winter weather. He left but a skeleton force to guard Port Arthur, and the army took over virtually all offensive operations.

THE VOYAGE OF THE BALTIC FLEET

The defeat of Vitgeft in the Yellow Sea failed to shake the philosophic calm of the Russian navy department or to induce a sense of urgency in the fitting out of the naval reinforcements then being gathered in the Baltic. Vice Admiral Sinovie Petrovitch Rodjestvensky, Assistant Chief of the Naval Staff, had been appointed in May to command the Second Pacific Squadron and, having been given a free hand in the selection of his officers, he had obtained some of the best in the Russian navy. But his ships and crews were far from ready. The main strength of the squadron lay in the five 12-inch gun battleships completing at St. Petersburg, but it became necessary before the departure to detach the *Slava,* the least advanced in construction, and to use her fittings to get the other four ready. Additional battleships included the new but weaker *Osliabia* (10-inch guns) and two smaller ten-year-olds *(Sissoi Veliki* and *Navarin)* with old-type 12-inch guns. To the seven battleships were added three old heavy cruisers *(Dimitri Donskoi, Vladimir Monomakh,* and *Admiral Nakhimov)* built between 1882 and 1886 but recently re-engined and rearmed, four new light cruisers, and seven destroyers. Nine auxiliaries furnished the squadron with food, water, and repair facilities. The Russian government contracted with the German Hamburg-America shipping company to coal the fleet on its voyage to the Far East. Even had it possessed comparable efficiency, Rodjestvensky's force would still have been considerably inferior to the Japanese fleet. His battleships slightly outgunned Togo's but the three old

heavy cruisers were no match for the eight new Japanese, each of which was capable of standing in the line of battle.

The admiral selected to restore the naval situation for Russia was 57 years old, precisely the age of his opponent. He possessed both determination and intelligence, a combination unusual at that era in the Russian naval command, where chins were rather more prominent than foreheads, yet he lacked the gift of imagination. Rodjestvensky had never held a fleet command but he was an experienced staff officer. Curiously enough his own staff was both small and nominal; from its members he sought information but never advice. It came to be overburdened with the details of fleet housekeeping, and found neither time nor opportunity for analysis of the larger problems of war operations. His tactical ideas Rodjestvensky kept to himself, and even his flag officers were to enter battle with but an imperfect conception of what was in the mind of the fleet commander. It has been suggested that while Makarov surrounded himself with the best men of the squadron, Rodjestvensky deliberately dispersed his ablest officers through the fleet, so lacking in confidence was he in the capacity of the ships' complements.

Fitting out the squadron consumed four valuable months because of inefficiencies in the shore establishment; local problems were compounded by the more general ones of graft, news leaks, incipient political revolution, and court favorites in key positions. In the circumstances Rodjestvensky's attempt to administer the fleet single-handed imposed an impossible burden. He was in a sense driven in on himself, becoming ever more aloof and self-sufficient. Even his staff he held at arm's length. But the men behind the guns presented the gravest problem to the commander of the Baltic squadron. They were for the most part new conscripts and, though coming from the maritime Baltic provinces, had little knowledge of naval techniques. Time was lacking for systematic training before the squadron's departure; after that there was neither fuel nor ammunition to spare.

Additional problems crowded on Rodjestvensky's squadron from the hour of its departure from Libau on October 14, 1904. Engine room casualties plagued each division. Russia had no dockyards or coaling stations between the Baltic and Vladivostok, a distance of 18,000 miles, and the use of neutral ports depended on the interpretation of international law that each neutral was likely to make in the light of its own interests. It was hoped that the 70 German colliers sent from Europe would make the squadron independent of bases.

The voyage had barely begun when the squadron became involved in an international incident of the first importance that not only gave practical demonstration of the Russians' lack of training and confidence, but almost brought Great Britain into the war on the side of her ally Japan. On the night of October 21, the darkened squadron was steaming down the middle of the North Sea with gun stations manned when an auxiliary radioed that she was under attack by torpedo boats. Shadowy shapes visible from the warships seemed to corroborate the alarm. Without further investigation many of the ships opened fire on what proved to be a British trawler fleet properly lighted. In a brief but heavy fusillade, with some Russian ships firing on each other, a British fishing vessel was sunk, and the squadron continued on its way without attempting to rescue survivors. British cruiser divisions closed the Russians and kept them in sight all the way to Gibraltar, being called off only when the Czar's government agreed to submit the case to the Hague Tribunal.[4]

On arriving at Tangier on November 4, Rodjestvensky detached a force under Rear Admiral Folkersam—three light cruisers and nine destroyers, with the two smaller battleships for protection—to proceed through the Suez Canal to the squadron rendezvous at St. Marie, Madagascar. He was doubtful that his larger ships could enter the canal because of draft but wished to shorten the sea voyage for his lighter units. The other 16 ships pushed south around Africa and their progress, though hampered by frequent engine troubles, confuted the pessimistic predictions of foreign journalists and naval officers. The main Russian force met German colliers at Tangier, Dakar, Gaboon, and Luderitz Bay, the successive distances being somewhat less than 2,000 miles, and since each port was either French or German, the local officials made a liberal time allowance for coaling. Ever conscious of his need for haste, Rodjestvensky drove his subordinates hard and by instituting competition whenever possible he tried to speed fleet exercises and fueling.

Getting through a hurricane in good shape the Baltic squadron came to anchor at St. Marie on December 29, to learn that its government, fearful of pressing the French into a position of obvious unneutrality had agreed to a change of rendezvous to Hellville, a jungle shantytown on the isolated island of Nosy Bé off the northwest coast and 150 miles from the nearest telegraph-cable connection. Here Rodjestvensky arrived on January 9, to find Folkersam with the detached units already in the bay. The condition of the rejoined division did not encourage optimism. Admiral Folkersam lay ill of an advanced heart ailment. Revolutionary propaganda, fed on news of unrelieved Russian reverses picked up at coaling ports, had spread through the ships. The whole squadron was now made acquainted with what Rodjestvensky had learned at St. Marie: Port Arthur had just surrendered.

Rodjestvensky well understood that only by a rigorous routine of training and steaming at sea could the fighting spirit of his men be maintained against the corrosive combination of tropical heat, bad food, and bad news. He therefore planned to allow but 11 days for a final overhaul at Nosy Bé. The success of his mission depended on the speed with which he reached the Far East and hit the Japanese before they could dock or refit. Vladivostok was designated his new objective

---

[4] In its judgment on the "Dogger Bank Incident" the court found some extenuating circumstances to save Russia's face, but assessed damages of $330,000 to be paid to the families of the two killed and six wounded. The Russian government contended that the squadron's officers feared an attack by Japanese destroyers completing on the Tyne nearby. In reality the last foreign-built Japanese destroyer had left Europe more than a year before.

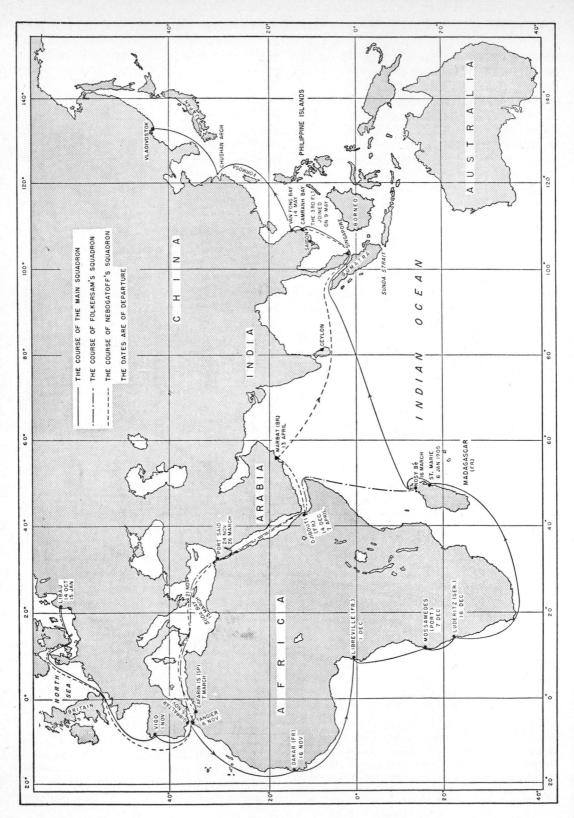

THE ROUTES OF THE BALTIC SQUADRON

and he was informed that a Third Pacific Squadron, coming from the Baltic under Rear Admiral Nebogatov, would join him off Madagascar. An additional reinforcement of two light cruisers, two destroyers, and three converted cruisers reached him while he lay at Nosy Bé.

The decision to send Rodjestvensky forward after the destruction of the Port Arthur squadron was inconsistent with the whole basis of Russian strategy. Both army and navy were agreed on the necessity of the defensive until it should be possible to move over to the offensive with overwhelming force. But the Baltic divisions had no edge whatever over their opponents, and it was hardly likely that the Japanese would permit them to slip safely into the Vladivostok haven. In guns of the heaviest caliber Togo's ships were nearly equal to those of Rodjestvensky and Nebogatov, and they enjoyed a three-to-two superiority in the fast-shooting middle calibers. The Russian naval ministry moreover was talking of organizing a Fourth Pacific Squadron to be sent out in April, and already, in December, it had approved a building program of 16 battleships, six heavy cruisers, 12 light cruisers, 150 torpedo craft, and a proportionate number of minelaying and service vessels. It was not too late to order Rodjestvensky to return to the Baltic; prudence indeed dictated such a course. But fear of ridicule abroad intervened. Of greater importance in deciding the issue, the Trans-Siberian Railway had been utterly unable to maintain an adequate flow of men and supplies to the Far East, and unless a similar constriction of Japanese communications could be achieved by spring, Kuropatkin's army would face disaster.

The breakdown of the Trans-Siberian Railway had a vital effect on the entire naval war. Rodjestvensky was warned of the resulting shortages at Vladivostok and was directed to retain his service force and detach only the empties. The squadron speed was thereby limited to 12 knots. As for Rodjestvensky's protest against reinforcement with any but large and powerful units, the Navy Ministry thought otherwise. Nebogatov had been sent out with what was available in the Baltic:

four reserve armored ships. Of these, the battleship *Nicholas I* was old and comparable in gun power to a heavy cruiser. Still weaker were the three 4,000-ton "coast defense battleships" armed principally with 9- and 10-inch guns. The small squadron steamed well however, and it had made a creditable passage to the Far East. Well handled, its armament would have added significantly to Rodjestvensky's strength, but it lacked trained seamen gunners.

Plans for an early start from Hellville were frustrated from an unexpected quarter, the Hamburg-America Line. The company abruptly terminated the coal contract, claiming danger to its ships should they go north of Madagascar.[5] Two months of negotiation in Europe were necessary to obtain the contract renewal and during this time the ships and men of the Baltic squadron deteriorated in the steaming heat of Madagascar. Spent in health and spirit, Rodjestvensky weighed for the China Sea on March 16, accompanied by four German colliers. The next stage of the voyage, extending over 5,300 miles, ranks as one of the great endurance feats achieved in the era of coal-burning warships. For three weeks the Indian Ocean swallowed up Rodjestvensky and he was neither observed nor heard from. Fuel was taken from the colliers at sea by means of specially constructed lighters. Entering the China Sea through the tortuous and less used Malacca Straits, the Baltic squadron eluded the Japanese scouts and anchored in Camranh Bay, Indo-China on April 14.

Protests from Tokyo impelled the French government to request the Russians to leave, but Rodjestvensky merely moved north 60 miles to Van Fong, where he stood in and out of the bay until May 9, when Nebogatov joined. The next four days were spent at anchor while inflammables were jettisoned and the fleet made ready for action. Rodjestvensky's tactical plan had already been issued and it reflected in its limitations the admi-

---

[5] The German state papers published after World War I furnish some evidence that the difficulty was initiated by the German government as a means of applying pressure on Russia to break the Dual Alliance.

ral's enforced preoccupation rather with the maintenance of his unreliable weapons of war than with their use in battle. It had a strong 18th century flavor. The approach would be made in column or line abreast. Battleships would fight in column; cruisers, also in column, would support the battle line or cover the convoy as directed. A purely defensive role was assigned the destroyers in daytime action and to the heavier ships at night. This tactical doctrine completely disregarded the concept of concentration.

The Second and Third Pacific Squadrons, 50 ships in all, steamed out of Van Fong Bay on May 14, 1905 for the final run to Vladivostok. Rodjestvensky had the choice of three routes from the China Sea: through the Korean, the Tsugaru, or the Soya Straits. The first was Togo's most likely point of concentration, and here too was Sasebo, the Japanese navy's principal operating base. The Tsugaru and the more remote Soya passages would afford more sea room for the approach, but would involve at least a thousand additional miles of steaming. The Japanese fleet meanwhile would enjoy the advantage of an interior position in the Sea of Japan. In addition to the known difficulties of fog and rocks the northern straits were suspected of having been mined, and so they were. Hampered by auxiliaries Rodjestvensky decided to take the shortest route—the Tsushima passage on the eastern side of the Korean Strait.

THE BATTLE OF TSUSHIMA

The Russian fleet rounded the eastern side of Formosa and, being out of the frequented routes, escaped detection. On May 23, near the Ryukyus, colliers came alongside for the last time and each ship was ordered to take only enough coal to insure good battle trim on the 26th, the day they expected to meet the Japanese fleet. As he approached the Chushan Archipelago near the mouth of the Yangtze River, Rodjestvensky detached five auxiliaries and sent them to Shanghai, hoping that their arrival would be interpreted by the Japanese as an attempt to mislead them into concluding that the Russian fleet was steering for the Korean Straits while in fact it went elsewhere. Soon afterwards Rodjestvensky turned northeastward and shaped a course for Tsushima, 400 miles distant. Speed was reduced to eight knots to enable the fleet to reach the island at noon on the 27th and cross the area of maximum Japanese concentration in daylight, thereby reducing the threat of destroyer torpedo attack. Fog and rain concealed the approach of the Russians on the 26th, and they maintained strict radio silence. Togo had estimated that his opponent would arrive that day in the southern approaches of the strait. As the afternoon gradually wore away and no contact reports came in, concern became manifest in the Japanese flag quarters in the *Mikasa*.

Since the fall of Port Arthur Togo had based his battleships and heavy cruisers at a secret anchorage near Masan, Korea. The light cruisers of Dewa and Uriu together with Kataoka's old veterans operated from Takeshiki on Tsushima and patrolled the straits northwest from the Goto Islands. Fifty miles beyond them a line of converted merchantmen covered the outer approaches. At 4:30 AM on the 27th one of these identified an illuminated hospital ship accompanying Rodjestvensky and a few minutes later made out his fleet. The warning radio call was taken in by all the Japanese patrols, and shortly after dawn the light cruiser divisions were shadowing the Russian fleet on the port side while one Japanese cruiser held on closely to starboard. By 6:30 the *Mikasa* with Togo aboard was steaming out of Masan anchorage followed by the Japanese battle line and the destroyer flotillas. The air was now filled with Japanese contact reports and Togo steered an easterly course to intercept the Baltic fleet abreast of Tsushima. A strong southwest wind drove spray over his fore turrets and piled green seas on his destroyers' turtleback forecastles. Observing the difficulties of the light craft Togo signaled them to take shelter at discretion in Takeshiki. This order would not interfere with the operation of the Japanese battle plan. The battleships and heavy cruisers in division columns would move like an articulated barrier across the Russian line of advance and turn back the oncoming enemy. Light cruiser divisions would engage the Russian cruisers and auxiliaries, and all gunnery ships would hand over the enemy to the destroyer flotillas at dark and withdraw to the north to give them a clear field. At dawn the next day the main units would sweep south to re-engage, and the pattern would be repeated until the Russian fleet should be annihilated.

Reaching the channel east of Tsushima an hour after noon without meeting any advanced Russian units, Togo turned and a few minutes later made out his own cruisers to the southwest. As he steamed toward them the Russian columns came into view eight miles away in the same direction. The day was gray but clearing and visibility was good. On sighting the enemy Togo, closely followed by Kamimura on his starboard quarter, changed to northwest to get across their van and attack their left flank. The Baltic fleet was observed to be steaming in four columns, the First Division of new battleships in the lead and to starboard, the smaller battleships of Folkersam's and Nebogatov's divisions in a single column to port.[6] The cruisers under Rear Admiral Enquist formed another column astern and covered the auxiliaries, which were also in column and to starboard.

At daylight Rodjestvensky had realized from the suddenly increased volume of Japanese radio traffic that his arrival had been made known to Togo. He then formed a column line of battle but at noon, desiring to change to an approach formation, ordered the van First Division to turn in succession to line abreast. The evolution was marred through misunderstood signals and at its conclusion the First Division found itself again in column but off to starboard of the others.

Togo crossed ahead of the Russian columns at 15,000 yards and at 2:02 turned his battle line left in succession. His ships, each of which was flying a huge battle ensign, now came down on the port bows of the Russians

___

[6] Folkersam had died two days before but the fact had not been disclosed to the fleet. His flag was kept flying in the *Osliabia* and her captain was directed to exercise command of the division.

and on opposite course. At this moment signal flags started up from *Mikasa's* bridge. They read: "The fate of the Empire depends on this day's battle. Let every man do his ut-

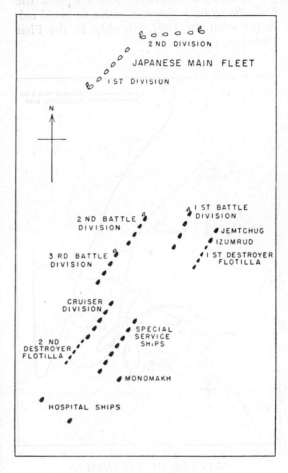

BATTLE OF TSUSHIMA:
THE MAIN FLEETS APPROACH, 2:05 PM

most." An exchange of broadsides in passing would have been indecisive. Within three minutes of his turn, therefore, finding himself only 10,000 yards from the *Suvorov*, Togo again led both divisions around to the left in succession nearly 16 points, steadying on a course slightly converging on that of the Russians. Neither side opened fire as yet. Rodjestvensky judged that the high trajectory coupled with rapid changes of range and deflection would prevent accurate fire and he therefore failed to order his squadron to shoot at the "knuckle" of the Japanese turn. Moreover he was absorbed during those minutes in getting his battleships back into single column, a maneuver which caused the *Osliabia* to back down in order to avoid colliding with the *Orel,* last ship in the First Division.

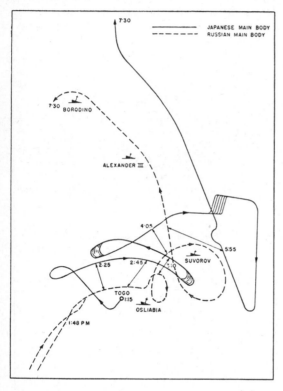

	JAPANESE MAIN BODY
	RUSSIAN MAIN BODY

BATTLE OF TSUSHIMA,
MAIN FLEET ACTION, MAY 27, 1905

At 2:08, as Togo's last ships completed the turn, the leading Russians opened fire at 7,000 yards. The Japanese replied two minutes later. Quickly selecting targets they concentrated on the division leaders *Suvorov* and *Osliabia.* In the meanwhile crowding and confusion in Rodjestvensky's Second and Third Divisions had prevented the rear ships from coming into action for ten minutes after firing began. Steaming at 14 knots to the Russians' ten, Togo drew ahead and came right gradually in an effort to cross the

"T" of his opponent. The Japanese fired high-explosive shells fused for instantaneous action, and their explosions quickly ignited paint fires. Soon after the action became general the crews in the leading Russian ships were driven from their guns by smoke. Even the Japanese occasionally lost their targets though the yellow Russian funnels stood out like beacons through the pall. The fires burned down to the basic red lead, and half an hour later when they had died down some Russian ships appeared to have been freshly coated. Togo's rear cruiser, the *Asama,* was hit above the steering compartment by a 12-inch shell at 2:30 and had to leave the line, well down by the stern. Twenty minutes later the *Suvorov* sheered to the right out of control, one funnel and a mast shot away and her upper works a shambles. She circled once and staggered off to the northeast, carrying Rodjestvensky out of the battle. As for the *Osliabia,* the other principal Japanese target, exploding shells had torn huge holes in her hull just above the waterline forward. Incoming seas then brought her down by the bow until the side gun ports were awash. Rapidly flooding through these she rolled over to port, hung on her beam ends for a few minutes and at 3:05 capsized and plunged with the loss of 600 of her 800 men. Thus ended the quarter hour which decided the issue of the battle; what followed was chiefly a mopping-up operation.

Togo's crowding tactics had now turned the Russian column to the right, past east, and he continued to pull ahead and toward southeast, both fleets turning in concentric circles with the Russians on the inner arc. But Togo overreached the Russian van and the *Alexander III,* now leading, turned left to break north across his wake. The Japanese 1st Division reversed course in two eight-point turns and again approached the Russian van to cross the "T," but the *Alexander III* came back to east and both columns passed on opposite courses exchanging broadsides. Kamimura however had remained some distance astern of Togo and on his original SE course. He now caught up with the Russians and thrust their van around to south before himself reversing to rejoin the battleships. Rodjestvensky's battle divisions, hardly more than fugitives now, continued their swing and lost both Togo and Kamimura in the smoke that hung heavily over the whole area. After they had again formed a ragged column the *Alexander III* at 3:40 set course for Ullung Island, a convenient rendezvous, and the Russian main body plunged blindly forward.

Some five miles to the northwest Togo and Kamimura were turning to sweep back eastward and in another ten minutes the column leaders of both fleets sighted each other and re-engaged. The second phase of the battle now began. Togo once more headed for a capping position and, as the Russians turned away eastward, the fighting squadrons converged on the *Suvorov*, still steaming slowly. During the next half hour she lay between the battle lines and was left a listing, blazing hulk—still shooting gamely with her last gun, a 12-pounder. The Russians were again turned south on their inner arc but Togo, having ordered his destroyers to make a torpedo attack, took his battleships north at 4:35 and after eight minutes lost all contact with the enemy.

The Japanese destroyers had already in this phase made an attack on the *Suvorov* but had been driven off by the secondary batteries of the nearby Russian battleships, though they claimed one hit. In the confusion they were unable to regroup for the fresh attack ordered by Togo. A lull therefore followed the separation of the fleets at 4:35, and some 90 minutes later the destroyer *Buiny* went alongside the *Suvorov* and removed Rodjestvensky, who was insensible from three head wounds. As she moved away, the *Suvorov's* men continued the battle with their single gun. Japanese destroyers launched renewed attacks soon after dark and made two more torpedo hits. At 7:20 the Russian flagship rolled over and sank without a survivor.

Twenty minutes after turning out of the battle Togo rejoined Kamimura and hurried south toward gunflashes on the horizon. The Japanese battle line missed the Russian main body in the smoke to westward but soon found itself heading into a battle of the light cruisers. All afternoon Enquist's division had closely covered the service force and, being comprised of new ships, used its speed advantage to head off Japanese cruiser attacks. The action had been continuous since noon but neither side had been able to inflict decisive damage. These craft held no attraction for Togo, who promptly turned north after bigger game. Kamimura meanwhile turned after Enquist's cruisers, which led him away from the convoy and later dropped him astern but so far to the west that he was unable to join up with Togo before dark, and so took no further part in the fighting.

The third phase of the action began at 5:55 as the north-steaming Japanese battleships again sighted the Russian main body bearing NW on their port bows. Togo turned in four points to close the range quickly before dark. But the Russians were still full of fight, and he now found himself running into heavy fire with all the advantages on the other side, since the sun was setting directly in the eyes of his pointers and his six ships were engaging ten. A quick turn to right opened the range another 2,000 yards and Togo came to a parallel course. The Russian column was steaming at full speed in spite of extensive damage to upper works. Togo's ships could barely keep pace; his stokehold force had been keeping steam for full speed since early morning and they were now obliged to clean fires.[7] But Togo could afford to wait, for the visibility was rapidly turning to his advantage. By 6:25 the Russians were silhouetted against the afterglow and now came under a very accurate fire. Again Japanese high explosive shells demolished superstructures and searched the interiors of their targets, starting new fires and driving crews away from the batteries. But the projectiles were not armor-piercing and they seldom penetrated main armor belts and turrets: their instantaneous fuses probably saved the Russians from complete annihilation. Had their turret gunners been able to shoot as well as the Japanese, the Russian battleships

---

[7] In coal-burning marine boilers of the period it was necessary to remove clinkers from each furnace at about eight-hour intervals. The operation unavoidably caused a drop in steam pressure.

might have made Tsushima something more of a fight.[8]

The crew of the *Alexander III,* leading the line, had been unable to check progressive

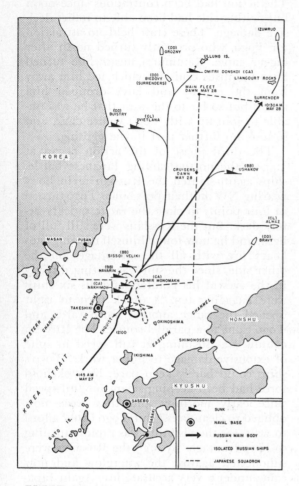

FLEET TRACKS, BATTLE OF TSUSHIMA

flooding, for her bows were nearly blown off and she was low in the water. At 6:40 with fierce fires revealing the loss of masts and smokestacks she turned left out of line and slowly capsized, carrying down all except four of her crew of 830. The Japanese battleships now concentrated on the new van ship *Borodino.* By 7:00 she was on fire in the

lowering night and presented an easy target to the Japanese range finders.[9] Twenty minutes later the *Fuji* landed a 12-inch shell which set off two magazine explosions. The *Borodino* suddenly capsized, floating bottom upwards for a few minutes. A single officer was picked up next morning by a Japanese fishing vessel. The loss of the *Borodino* broke up the Russian column. Signaling "Follow Me," Nebogatov led a disorganized mass of ships to the southwest. The Japanese battleships and cruisers now left the area according to plan, and steamed north at 14 knots toward the morning rendezvous near Ullung. With their departure the battle entered a fourth phase: a series of scattered and fiercely contested night torpedo actions.

The Russian fleet moved off to southward in three separated groups, Nebogatoff's squadron with the *Orel* leading, the cruisers and auxiliaries to port, and the battleships *Navarin* and *Sissoi Veliki* and the armored cruiser *Nakhimov* some distance astern. At dark the Japanese torpedo craft closed from all sides: 21 destroyers and 37 torpedo boats boring in continuously throughout the night to reduce the Russian crews to a state of exhaustion. The rear ships turned on searchlights and thus became targets for a concentrated attack. The *Navarin,* holed with four torpedoes, sank with all hands except three; a stern hit on the *Sissoi* caused her to settle slowly and sink next morning; the *Nakhimov* was torpedoed forward and, with speed reduced, was scuttled off Tsushima to prevent capture. Of the cruiser group, the *Monomakh* was hit and slowed with damaged engines; at daylight she too was scuttled as a Japanese cruiser came in sight.

One hundred and forty miles north of the previous day's battle area Togo's staff were sweeping their glasses over an empty horizon at dawn when a light cruiser division 60 miles to the south reported Russian ships. The Japanese battle divisions steered toward the contact and at 9:30 sighted the *Orel* and three of Nebogatov's battleships. The opening shots brought no response from the Russians save a hoist of international code flags

---

[8] The *Orel,* later captured, was heavily hit but her main armor was intact. Telescopic sights had been issued to the Russian squadron but many were unsuited to the gun mounts.

[9] Base line optical range finders were installed and used in the ships of both fleets.

on the *Nicholas I* announcing surrender. The cruiser *Izumrud* made off at high speed and escaped. As Admiral Nebogatov left the deck of his flagship to hand his sword to Togo he turned to the crew and said, "I am an old man over 60 and I do not care whether I live or die. I shall be shot for this, but that does not matter. You however are young, and you will be called upon some day to restore the glory and the lost honor of the Russian Navy. On these ships are 2,400 men whose lives are more important than mine." [10]

Of the separated Russian units, the crippled small battleship *Ushakov* steamed into the Japanese main body shortly after the surrender but refused to strike. She was then engaged by two of Kamimura's division, heavily hit, and scuttled. Two cruisers were driven ashore by gunfire later in the day; four destroyers were intercepted and sunk, two more were captured, including the *Buiny* with Rodjestvensky aboard, and another, out of fuel, was towed into Shanghai by a British merchantman. Four auxiliaries were sunk; three got away to neutral ports. Enquist's three cruisers broke out into the China Sea and were interned at Manila. Fifty-three Russian ships had left the Baltic; the converted cruiser *Almaz* and two destroyers reached Vladivostok; nine of the 12 armored vessels were sunk.

The battle of Tsushima was decisive in every sense of the word. It brought about the termination of hostilities. The grandiose Russian plans for reinforcing the Far Eastern armies had been made quite impracticable by the outbreak of internal revolution in January 1905. Both press and public as well as the high command had then put correspondingly high hopes in naval action, and they were ill prepared for the disaster at Tsushima. After that battle the Russian government recognized the paramount need for peace and retrenchment. It therefore welcomed the mediation of President Theodore Roosevelt, and its delegates at the Portsmouth peace conference obtained a treaty at the cost of Port Arthur and southern Sakhalin.[11] Had Togo lost the battle his nation would have experienced one of the greatest disasters in history; its army would have been isolated in Manchuria and its economic life lines severed. Russia would have imposed heavy terms and would have become master of the Far East and the world's greatest power.

From the naval point of view the battle was not without significance. The value of heavy armor was strikingly demonstrated and, conversely, the need of heavy guns. Togo's tactics appeared brilliant because the Russians fought without leadership and the Japanese retained the initiative throughout. Kamimura, like Collingwood at Trafalgar, was given a large measure of initiative and he used it effectively at critical moments. The Japanese commander in chief enjoyed a great advantage through having homogeneous ships with uniform tactical characteristics. The torpedo performed disappointingly. The Japanese fired over a hundred in the night action and secured seven hits. Its short range of a thousand yards still precluded its use as an effective daylight weapon.

As for strategy, the lessons of the war have never been more trenchantly summarized than in the words of President Roosevelt, addressed in a letter of March 3, 1909 to his successor, William Howard Taft:

Dear Will: One closing legacy. Under no circumstances divide the battleship fleet between the Atlantic and Pacific Oceans prior to the finishing of the Panama Canal. . . . It is nearly four years since the close of the Russian-Japanese War. There were various factors that brought about Russia's defeat; but most important by all odds was her having divided her fleet between the Baltic and the Pacific, and, furthermore, splitting up her Pacific fleet into three utterly unequal divisions. The entire Japanese force was always used to smash some fraction of the Russian force.[12]

---

[10] From *The Voyage of Forgotten Men,* by F. Thiess, copyright 1937, used by special permission of the publishers, The Bobbs-Merrill Company, Inc.

[11] A strong Japanese demand for a cash indemnity was rejected on the ground that Kuropatkin's army, though again defeated at Mukden in February 1905, was withdrawn intact and was still in the field.

[12] Quoted in William E. Livezey, *Mahan on Sea Power* (Norman, Oklahoma, 1947), 236-7. Roosevelt wrote the letter at Mahan's request.

26

The United States

Becomes a Naval Power

IN THE LIGHT OF THE WORLD political situation at present, the most significant naval development of the early 20th century was that the United States Navy came of age. The American people, acting through their elected representatives in Congress, finally determined to maintain a fleet consonant with America's wealth and commercial importance. Under the tutelage of Mahan and Roosevelt, the Navy finally achieved a long-term policy. The ambition and brilliance of officers like Fiske and Sims stimulated the service to become pre-eminent in tactical procedures and in material. It was in this period that the modern American navy was born—the navy that in World War II was to defeat Japan, and to render possible the invasions of Europe.

Yet in the perspective of 1900 or of 1914, the establishment of the United States as a naval power of the first rank did not appear to be a fact of great importance outside the Western Hemisphere. Though America's naval budget was generally somewhat larger than that of Germany, the fleet of the Kaiser was definitely the stronger in 1914.

The United States in that year, in fact, had the prospect of sinking to fourth rank as the French building program progressed. Throughout the pre-World War I period, Great Britain, mistress of the seas for centuries, successfully maintained her "two power policy." [1]

THE ANGLO-GERMAN NAVAL RACE

Yet Britain had much greater difficulty than hitherto in perpetuating her absolute naval superiority in European waters. In the rise of German sea power she correctly perceived the greatest threat to her security since the days of Napoleon. The signing of the Anglo-Japanese Alliance (1902), the creation of the Triple Entente with France and Russia (1907), and the gradual concentration of the British fleet in home waters all

---

[1] The British insisted that their fleet must have a statistical strength—in tonnage and in capital ships—equal to or greater than the combined totals of the second and third strongest powers.

stemmed from the presence of a formidable and growing naval rival across the narrow waters of the North Sea. The British naval estimates were composed with one eye on the German construction program. British diplomatic relations with France, Italy, Japan, and the United States were largely guided by the dictates of naval policy. From the British point of view, nothing was more important than maintaining her "margin of safety."[2]

Ostensibly, the German aim was not to grow stronger than Britain but rather to build a fleet able to "challenge" England, to induce that power to hesitate before involving herself in a continental war. For Germany suffered the fatal naval weakness of having strong potential enemies on her land frontiers. The German army was of necessity her "first line of defense," and consequently had first call on her defense budgets. Nevertheless, her building policy made the Anglo-German naval rivalry the commonly accepted prime fact of the period in contemporary eyes.

The guiding genius of German naval policy at this time was Alfred von Tirpitz, successively Chief of Staff of the Supreme Naval Command (1892), Secretary of State for Naval Affairs (1897), and Admiral of the Fleet (1911-1916). Politically astute, administratively able, he made sure that ship for ship the High Seas Fleet would match or outmatch any in the world. His long-range aim was to forge a fleet that could be a trump card in dealings with England. Ultimately he thought it would make Germany "worthy of a British alliance." He insisted on emphasizing the battleship line even at the expense of cruiser construction, and was an exponent of extensive compartmentation and extraheavy armor.

In the German naval estimates of 1900, which, by doubling the German capital ship line, is usually taken as initiating the Anglo-German Naval race, Tirpitz reluctantly accepted the "idea of risk." Well aware of how the news of the German plans would be received in England, he endeavored to promote a steady replacement and expansion program in the fleet. In fact, the 1904, 1906, and 1908 programs, which progressively reduced the retirement age of combatant vessels, considerably altered his plans for new construction, to which he succeeded in devoting a very large percentage of total naval expenditures.

In the British Navy the opposite number to Tirpitz was the brilliant, cantankerous First Sea Lord, Sir John Fisher, who fathered the *Dreadnought* design (see discussion below) and the battle cruiser type. Like Tirpitz a determined believer in material improvements, Fisher made his period of control one of those times during which the Royal Navy was pre-eminent in invention and innovation. Remarkable in his imaginative insights, Fisher could perceive the merits of radical untried designs and see better than most of his contemporaries the potentialities of weapons still in their pioneering stages. He encouraged and secured appropriations for seaplanes, airships, and a submarine fleet while most admiralties still regarded these weapons as scarcely more than toys. With the aid of naval budgets seldom less than equal to those of Germany and the United States together, Fisher was able to build incomparably the most powerful instrument of sea power the world had ever seen.

THE UNITED STATES ADOPTS A NEW NAVAL POLICY

Yet an ultimately greater sea power was already in an active stage of early growth. Up to 1898, the nations of Europe had regarded the United States as a distinctly minor naval power. American eyes had been focused on the western frontier. Politically nourished on the "minute man" and "gunboat" theories of military and naval policy for over a century, America had been simply unwilling to bear the burden of a substantial defense establishment. Professional experts

[2] Germany's naval expenditures between 1905 and 1914 increased steadily from £ 11,301,370 to £ 23,444,129 per year. In the same period, Britain's increased from £ 33,151,841 to £ 51,550,000.

in the European navies had freely predicted that the superior marksmanship of the Spaniards would make short work of the new and untried American ships, but the overwhelming and apparently easy victories of Dewey and Sampson made the world take the U. S. Navy seriously.

More important, they made the American people take it seriously. In developing the "new navy," the congressional partisans of sea power had felt it expedient in legislation and appropriations to designate the major fleet units as "seagoing *coast-line* battleships." This tacit concession to the antinavalist point of view was no longer necessary after 1898. The "monitor" type of vessel, favored by the "little navy" legislators from the Middle West and South as being both cheap and ill adapted to overseas meddling, had taken a large share of naval appropriations up to the turn of the century. But the last of the kind was commissioned in 1901.

From the time of the establishment of the Naval War College (1884), Admiral Alfred T. Mahan had been patiently documenting his major theses: it is sea power that has been responsible for the greatness of Britain, and a nation aspiring to world power must develop its merchant marine and its navy. With the publication of his first major work, *The Influence of Sea Power upon History*, in 1890, Mahan soon achieved a world-wide reputation. But this was largely the fame of a scholar among scholars, of a naval officer among naval officers. For several years after 1890 it would appear that few members of Congress, not to speak of the voting public at large, really read Mahan's books. His ideas, which were fundamental to United States naval policy in the 20th century, had to be relayed secondhand by the eloquence of such men as Theodore Roosevelt and Senator Henry C. Lodge to become politically effective. The Spanish-American War had the special importance of dramatizing the Navy and its role to the voting public.

Among all men, fundamental political attitudes are more apt to be determined by emotions than by reason. Changes in these emotional biases are more likely to be af-fected by concrete symbols than by ratiocinative argument. In a democracy, responsive to the deep currents of popular feeling, national policy can change almost overnight in response to new symbols. The victories at Manila Bay and Santiago, and the 15,000-mile epic voyage of the *Oregon* were such symbols. They furnished a popular emotional point of departure for an acceptance of the "big navy" policy that America was about to embark on.

Even before the war there had been something of a naval renaissance, dating from 1881. But in 1898 this was still in its early, experimental stages. The fleet, as a fleet, had not yet reached the standard of excellence of the best of the European navies. Naval policy was haphazard, short-term, and at the mercy of the accidents of political expediency.[3] Though the naval debates in Congress from 1898 to 1914 were often protracted and acrimonious, through this period there came to be a widely accepted goal of building policy—a Navy second only to that of Great Britain. Increasingly there was an awareness of the close relationship between naval policy and effective foreign policy. Congressmen as a group, though disagreeing often as to the implications of overseas political alignment, at least were generally in agreement on basic naval strategy—the Navy's proper role was to defeat the main force of any enemy rather than merely to raid commerce and aid in passive coast defense. United States building policy would be increasingly related to those of foreign navies—especially to those of Germany and Japan. After 1898, America had a genuine naval policy. America had become a naval power.

THE INFLUENCE OF THEODORE ROOSEVELT

The personal influence of Theodore Roosevelt, both as vigorous Assistant Secretary of the Navy (1897-1898) and as President (1901-1909) was enormously important in

---

[3] Note, for example, the needless and expensive maintenance of superfluous shore facilities.

giving definition and direction to America's naval policy. In an age when erudition was an uncommon attribute for a political figure, Roosevelt was a phenomenon. He was an omnivorous reader, with a keen appetite for history and monographs on international relations. He was at once a nationalist, an imperialist, and something of a militarist. For the Navy what was most important was that he had a good understanding of strategy and an abiding ambition to develop a fleet.[4]

In 1897 Roosevelt, as Assistant Secretary, burst into the placid bureaucratic routines of the Navy Department with all the enthusiastic vigor of a man with a mission. He scorned to dissemble his views, which were at this time at variance with the pacific attitudes of his superiors. He championed a big navy, to be maintained constantly on a near-war footing, and developed an uncompromising, expansionist foreign policy. He took pains to try to educate anyone who would listen—including Secretary Long and President McKinley. By his selection of George Dewey to command the Asiatic Station, and by his advice to and cooperation with that notable commander, Roosevelt forged the anchor link in the chain of events that was to lead to American possession of the Philippines, an event the full historical implications of which are not yet worked out.

Roosevelt's service in the field with the "Rough Riders," his subsequent governorship of New York, and his brief incumbency as Vice President turned out to be merely an extended recess from his concern with major national policy. In the fall of 1901 an assassin's bullet made Roosevelt the youngest President in American history. The brash young Assistant Secretary of the Navy of four years ago was Chief Executive of the United States. Whereas he had formerly been obliged to plead and cajole, he could now in a measure dictate. Through his own terms of office and that of his handpicked successor Taft, such was Roosevelt's prestige and personal force that his concept of correct foreign and naval policy was to a large degree the country's.

Even today something of a controversial figure, Roosevelt was unquestionably a very able and successful President. He had a clear understanding of how intimately diplomatic demands and the force-in-being to back them up are related—an understanding too few Chief Executives have possessed. He was generally successful in achieving the declared objectives of his administration in both domestic and foreign affairs. He had a strategic insight and technical knowledge of the Navy probably unmatched in United States history except by Franklin Roosevelt's in a later epoch. He left the sea service immeasurably stronger than he found it.

LESSONS OF THE SPANISH-AMERICAN WAR

The immediate lessons of professional interest gleaned from the Spanish-American War were carefully assessed by the Navy and its civilian chiefs. Mahan's first principles were vindicated. The ignorant outcries of the alarmed seaboard residents, which had compelled the diversion of first-rate fighting ships to the so-called "Flying Squadron" in Norfolk—away from the strategic center of operations in the Caribbean—suggested the imperative need for more widespread public understanding of naval strategy.

The war demonstrated the limitations as well as the strength of steam warships. Sailing vessels had been able to keep the seas for months at a time, but steam-driven warships with their insatiable furnaces could not outrun their bunker capacities. Schley's difficulties in coaling at sea in the relatively calm waters of the Caribbean demonstrated the importance of outlying coaling and repair bases to extend the radius of fleet action. The need of something more than an improvised fleet train was also indicated.

The gunnery of the American warships—particularly of the main batteries—was shown to be disappointing. The lack of success of United States ships in silencing Spanish forts at Santiago and San Juan confirmed

---

[4] In 1882, at the age of 24, Roosevelt had published his *The Naval War of 1812*, a precocious monument to its author's interests and to his firm grasp of naval first principles.

the long-standing opinion that guns afloat were no match for ordnance of comparable types ashore.

Finally, the difficulties of the Caribbean campaign suggested strongly the near impregnability of the continental United States to attack from overseas. An invading foreign fleet operating thousands of miles from its own bases would face in exaggerated form the difficulties and deficiencies the Americans experienced in the Caribbean.

From the point of view of Roosevelt and the "big navy" advocates, this security was a mixed blessing. On the one hand, it became possible to think of the fleet as potentially an instrument of tactical offense far from American shores. On the other hand, it gave cogency to the arguments of the anti-imperialist group in Congress who could not understand the need for a navy "second only to Britain's."

THE IMPERIAL LEGACY

Among the effects of the Spanish-American War was America's acquisition of a Caribbean and Pacific island empire. Cuba was temporarily under a protectorate, though the Platt Amendment had guaranteed it independence as soon as feasible. Puerto Rico became a permanent possession. The problem of what to do with the Philippines was finally resolved by occupying and taking possession of the whole archipelago. Guam in the Marianas was annexed. Indirectly the Spanish-American War was responsible for the annexation of Hawaii (1898) and American Samoa (1899). And it also doubtless promoted the prompt construction of the Panama Canal in the decade following.

America's new empire was the tangible reward for her possession of superior sea power. Strategically however it was a hostage to fortune. The Philippines particularly, 7,000 miles from continental United States, offered a defense problem which the American people were never to face squarely. Possession of the Philippines strengthened America's diplomatic position in the affairs of the Far East, but it increased the ultimate

likelihood of war with expansionist Japan.

The new American Empire enormously increased the Navy's responsibilities. Its potential area of operation was vastly expanded to include the entire Pacific Ocean. Overseas coaling stations and bases, and a canal across the Isthmus of Panama or Nicaragua became immediate necessities. The defense of the empire became a principal argument for the advocates of a big navy.

Directly following the war, there was no immediate restatement of naval policy in terms of these new problems. Occupation of Cuba and Puerto Rico, the Philippine Insurrection, and the Boxer Rebellion gave a coloring of "continuing emergency" to military and naval needs. But the improvised fleet of auxiliary cruisers recruited from the merchant marine were sold or returned to their owners. The peacetime "cruising stations" were instituted once more, and the wartime fleet organization was abandoned.[5] The General Board of the Navy was established in 1900 to provide a high level professional body to advise the Secretary. The impetus the war had given to shipbuilding had persisted until 1900,[6] but in 1901 Congress refused to authorize any ships at all. The reelection of McKinley and the continued secretaryship of Long gave every prospect of a continued policy of drift and compromise. The untimely death of McKinley in September 1901, because it elevated Theodore Roosevelt to the presidency, changed the character and direction of American naval development.

Roosevelt regarded foreign policy and naval policy as the warp and the woof of a seamless garment. It is evident from his writings and published speeches that from the first he had in mind clearcut diplomatic ends, and that he endeavored to fashion his weapons with these foreign policy objectives in mind. He believed in a continuum of pol-

[5] As the Sprouts point out, this was ". . . a surprising failure to profit from one of the most obvious lessons of the war." (H. and M. Sprout, *The Rise of American Sea Power*, 246.) The Bureau of Navigation apparently had no fleet policy, as such.

[6] 1898: three battleships, sixteen destroyers; 1899: three battleships, three armored cruisers; 1900: two battleships, three armored cruisers.

icy and did not hesitate to extrapolate existing relationships and trends into the future. He conceived of the President's role as that of dynamic leadership and policy-making, and that of Congress as a critic and ratifier of Presidential policy.

Roosevelt was typical of the American tradition up to that time in retaining the diplomatic ideal of "isolation from entangling alliances." But he had a better awareness than most that as a recognized first-class power, America could not ignore the affairs of other major powers.

ANGLO-AMERICAN RELATIONS

As an imperialist and an admirer of England, Roosevelt welcomed the developing confidence and mutual trust between Great Britain and the United States. Traditional "enemy" in ten thousand Fourth of July orations through the 19th century, England had evidenced a new friendliness in the last quarter of the century. After the strained relations prevailing before the settlement of the "*Alabama* claims" (1872), there had been no major quarrel. During the Spanish-American War, Britain alone of the major powers had shown positive sympathy. She had undertaken to guard American interests in Spain during hostilities. She had put no bar in the way of American acquisition of two warships building in English yards, originally on Brazilian order. She encouraged Canada to permit the transfer of revenue cutters from the Great Lakes to the Atlantic via the St. Lawrence River. The commander of the British squadron in Manila Bay, during the trying period between the naval battle and the occupation, gave moral support and tacit encouragement to Dewey.[7]

[7] The popular account current at the time had it that Captain Sir Edward Chichester RN placed his cruisers between Dewey's force and that of von Diederichs' German squadron. The Germans, who hoped to acquire part of the archipelago, had already aroused Dewey's wrath by failing to observe his blockade regulations. However, there is in fact no evidence that either Dewey or von Diederichs ever seriously considered starting a private war.

The Alaskan boundary dispute dragged on into Roosevelt's administration. A joint commission settled this problem in 1903 in an award wholly favorable to the United States. The Second Hay-Pauncefote Treaty (1901), which granted the United States unilateral control of the projected Isthmian Canal (and tacitly permitted fortification of it) was also an American diplomatic victory, widely and correctly judged to be evidence that Britain meant to meet the United States more than half-way in any clash of interest. The permanent withdrawal of the British West Indies squadron from Jamaica (1904-1905), though part of the long term policy of fleet concentration in home waters to overbalance the growing German strength in the North Sea, amounted also to an unspoken acknowledgment of American supremacy in the Caribbean. Responsible Britons and Americans were beginning to refer to the chance of any further war between the two countries as an "impossibility."

The implications for naval building policy of this relationship with Great Britain were important. Since England alone by virtue of her American bases (Halifax, Bermuda, Kingston) and the size of her fleet was in a physical sense able to wage a naval war in the Western Hemisphere, the certainty of her continued friendliness made America's continental security nearly absolute.

GERMAN-AMERICAN RELATIONS

It was Germany whose navy came to be the yardstick of American needs in congressional debate during the first decade of the 20th century. Germany, as last of the major nations of Europe to adopt an avowed imperialist policy, had aroused American suspicions and hostility on a number of specific occasions (Samoa, 1889; Manila Bay, 1898; Second Venezuela Crisis, 1902). The brutal efficiency of German development of their new colonies in Africa and at Tsingtao and the arrogant public utterances of the Kaiser made the American public distinctly unfriendly to the Hohenzollern Empire.

Furthermore, either Germany or the United States would be the possessor of the "navy second only to Britain's." In numbers of battleships and armored cruisers, the United States rose from fifth position in 1904 to second in 1907. But as a balanced fleet, Germany's seagoing navy was superior to that of the United States during most if not all of the pre-World War I period. In any event both the United States Congress and the American public regarded the relative rank of the United States Navy as a matter of great importance.

RELATIONS OF JAPAN AND AMERICA

Relations of the United States with Japan were generally good up to the 20th century. It was an American naval force that had "opened up" Japan in the mid-19th century. Many of the ranking officers of the Japanese navy who fought in the Sino-Japanese War (1894) and the Russo-Japanese War (1904-1905) had graduated from the U. S. Naval Academy. What Americans knew, or thought they knew, about the Japanese people came for the most part from Gilbert and Sullivan's *Mikado,* Puccini's *Madame Butterfly,* and the romantic writings of Lafcadio Hearn. The Japanese were judged to be a childlike, art-loving people, much given to artistic flower arrangement and water-color painting—deserving of American sympathy because they were in a measure protégés of America. Furthermore, as government officials and naval officers came to respect the professional efficiency of the Japanese services as shown in the Chinese War, Japan came to be regarded as a useful makeweight against Russian designs on North China and Korea. The Russo-Japanese War in Japanese history corresponds in a way to the Spanish-American War in United States history: it made the world realize that a new major power had emerged. At the beginning of this war, Japan was viewed as the underdog. The American administration and the American public wished Japan well, but with little confidence in her success. The

sweeping Japanese victories culminating in the fall of Port Arthur and the Battle of Tsushima compelled a new and soberer assessment of Japanese strength. For the first time in modern history an Oriental nation had decisively defeated a major western power in war. And this nation, highly disciplined, intensely nationalist, compulsively imperialistic, was very close to the new American possessions in the Philippines. The time might come when Japan would be an active threat to American interests in the Orient.

Furthermore, though Roosevelt's good offices had helped the Japanese to secure favorable peace terms in the Treaty of Portsmouth (1905), the Japanese demand for an indemnity was not met. The Japanese press and the Japanese public were inclined to feel that Roosevelt had helped to cheat them of the just deserts of their victory. In 1906 and the years following, the naval debates in the American Congress came to include frequent reference to Japanese as well as German naval building programs.

On the other hand, the Anglo-Japanese Alliance (1902) [8] was not viewed by the United States government as being in any way directed against the United States. Even in the light of the cordiality of American relations with England, this may seem strange. There is good evidence however that Roosevelt in 1905 entered into a secret agreement with the Japanese prime minister, by the terms of which the United States virtually became a secret third party to this treaty. This agreement involved a formal recognition by Japan of American sovereignty in the Philippines and an acknowledgment by America of Japan's sovereignty in Korea. It provided for "conjunct" action in the event of vaguely defined contingencies, presumably if British, Japanese, or American possessions were attacked by more than one power. [9] This agreement was never submitted to the Senate, where it would unquestionably have

[8] Which, *inter alia,* specified that either power, attacked in the Far East by *more than one* other power, could count on the naval assistance of the other.

[9] T. Dennett, "Roosevelt's Secret Pact With Japan," *Current History* (October 1924), 15.

received short shrift. On the other hand it was morally binding, at least so long as Roosevelt was President.

THE UNITED STATES NAVY EXPANDS

The century between 1815 and 1914 was the epoch of British ascendancy. Thanks to her fleet, England was able to maintain an effective and largely unchallenged police power over the entire world. Toward the end of the period however three new powers arose: Germany, the United States, and Japan. Each competed in its own sphere with Britain. It is not surprising that to some extent they should compete with each other as well. Certainly the growth of German and Japanese naval strength stimulated, indeed established, the vital pre-condition for American fleet expansion.

Various private industrial interests now had a stake in continued expansion. Shippers and exporters, and especially shipbuilders and steel companies not unnaturally favored a large navy. In 1903, these groups joined retired officers and disinterested citizens who were simply eager to increase the power of the United States in founding the Navy League of the United States.[10] As a prosperous organization with a limited and definite aim, it was immediately effective. It is impossible to say exactly how important it was in influencing legislation and in educating the public to accept the President's views on naval building policy, but there can be no doubt that its influence was a considerable one. As a lobbying organization, some of whose members had a pecuniary interest in achieving a bigger navy, the League was subject to attack by the Congressional minority of anti-naval partisans. But in its unwavering insistence on a consistent long-term policy, the League's influence was salutary. Beginning with 1903, the Navy Department began laying down two capital ships a year. Though there were exceptions in the ensuing decade, this came to be the norm of naval construction. Generally speaking, the building policy of the Taft Administration (1909-1913) continued the aims of Roosevelt's.

Some idea of the increased emphasis on the Navy can be gained from accompanying table.

FISCAL YEAR:	TOTAL FEDERAL EXPENDITURES:	NAVAL EXPENDITURES:	PER CENT OF TOTAL BUDGET *
1890	$318,040,711	$22,006,206	7.0
1900	520,860,847	55,953,078	10.8
1901	524,616,925	60,506,978	11.3
1905	567,278,914	117,550,308	20.7
1909	693,743,885	115,546,011	16.7
1914	735,081,431	139,682,186	19.0

* These budgetary percentages do not necessarily reflect the ratios of columns one and two.

Most of the increase in the costs of the naval establishment was due to the increase in the size and complexity of war vessels. In 1903, a first-line battleship cost $5,382,000. The *Delaware* and *North Dakota* of the 1907 program,[11] with standard displacement of 20,000 tons, cost $8,225,000 each. By the time of World War I, costs had soared (in the United States) to $15-20,000,000. But the typical first-line battleship at the turn of the century was less than 400 feet long, and displaced perhaps 10,000 or 11,000 tons. The *Pennsylvania,* building in 1914, was 600 feet long and displaced 31,400 tons.

In spite of the steady increase in its budget, the United States Navy never established supremacy over Germany before World War I. In the many published statements on the subject of the relative sizes of navies in the period, discrepancies stem from a lack of agreement as to the effective "life" of a war vessel. For example, it could be argued in 1914 that the United States had, built or building, 17 "first-line" battleships—vessels under ten years old. On the other hand, "big navy" men refused to count the older vessels in this total, and spoke of 11

---

[10] Similar organizations were already in existence abroad. The British Navy League was founded in 1894, and one in Germany in 1898.

[11] Commissioned in 1910. By some authorities these are regarded as the first American "dreadnoughts," though the earlier *Michigan* and *South Carolina* conform generally to the "all-big-gun ship" principle.

"dreadnoughts." In the Secretary's report for 1909, Britain's naval tonnage was listed as 1,758,350, the United States' as 682,785, and Germany's as 609,700. Yet Secretary Meyer was constantly warning that if the programs of his Department were not carried out, the United States would fall behind in the armaments race. In 1911 estimates, Germany was spending only $107,232,000 in comparison with the United States' figure of $129,248,000. France's estimates were $80,371,000 and Japan's $42,944,000.

On the other hand, *Brassey's Naval Annual* [12] for 1914 clearly viewed Germany's as the stronger fleet. In actual tonnage, Germany had forged ahead toward the end of this period. As of July 1, 1914 Germany had in commission 951,713 tons to America's 765,133 and France's 688,840 tons. Counting construction under way, Germany would be ranked relatively stronger, with 1,306,577 tons; France would have 899,915; the United States, in fourth place, would have 894,889 tons.[13] More suggestive of the real deficiencies of the U. S. fleet are the comparative figures for cruisers and destroyers. Britain had, built and building, ten battle cruisers; Germany, eight; Japan, four; the United States, none. Britain had 34 armored cruisers, the United States, 11. In other cruiser types, Britain had 91, Germany, 46; the United States 14. Britain had 188 destroyers; Germany, 154; the United States, 62. The obvious weakness of the United States building policy had been its dominant emphasis on capital ships.

The Roosevelt and Taft administrations and their professional advisers were of course well aware of this. Their reasoning was that battleships took up to four years to build,[14] and that smaller craft could be constructed in case of need in a much shorter time. Often Congressional opposition to increased expenditure could be mollified by canceling plans for smaller vessels as a compromise proposal. On the other hand, the resultant fleet was not immediately prepared to develop its maximum potential. And, in the sort of war it was called on to fight in 1917-18, this emphasis in building policy proved to have been especially unfortunate.

THE PANAMA CANAL

In the period 1898-1914, the Navy was called on from time to time to implement or to aid in promoting four major foreign policies of the United States. These were: (1) the acquisition of the Canal Zone, (2) maintaining the Monroe Doctrine and extending its scope, especially in the Caribbean area, (3) maintaining the "Open Door" in China, and promoting United States Far Eastern interests, and (4) helping to maintain the balance of power in Europe. On the whole, the Navy acquitted itself well in each of these missions.

The idea of an Isthmian Canal to connect the Caribbean and the Pacific is at least as old as Balboa, who first crossed the isthmus in the early 16th century. In the last quarter of the 19th century the de Lesseps company, which had already successfully completed the Suez Canal, undertook the mammoth engineering task of constructing a waterway across the narrow neck of the Isthmus of Panama. The tangled story of the French failure and the ensuing intrigues over the sovereignty of the canal right-of-way are too involved for retelling here. It is enough to observe that for a decade before the Spanish-American War expert opinion had come to support Mahan's view that such a canal was essential to enable the United States Navy to accomplish its mission. And obviously such a canal unequivocally under American sovereignty was preferable. There were two hurdles barring this: Colombian possession of the Isthmus of Panama and the Clayton-Bulwer Treaty (1850) with Great Britain, whereby England and the United

---

[12] *Brassey's Naval Annual* has a quasi-official authority, and may be taken as embodying British expert opinion.

[13] These figures are from the Office of Naval Intelligence, "Warship Tonnage of the Principal Naval Powers," *Navy Yearbook,* 1914 (Washington), 851.

[14] A conscious and rather successful effort to shorten the average building period was undertaken during this time. By 1914, capital ships took closer to two years than four to build.

States agreed to cooperate in building a canal and engaged not to fortify it.[15]

The *Oregon's* voyage through the Straits of Magellan during the Spanish-American War gave the American public an object lesson in the need for a canal. The acquisition of the Philippines and Hawaii, it was argued, meant that the United States must maintain a large Pacific fleet, or else have the canal to facilitate transit from one ocean to the other.

Secretary of State John Hay in 1900 concluded with the British ambassador the First Hay-Pauncefote Treaty, permitting American construction and ownership of the canal. Rejected by the Senate, this was followed by the Second Hay-Pauncefote Treaty of 1901, which also permitted fortification.

The remaining obstacle was the problem of securing treaty rights from Colombia. Hay signed a preliminary treaty with the Colombian chargé d'affaires in Washington (Hay-Herran Treaty, 1903), whereby the United States was to secure a six-mile wide transitway for $10,000,000 and a $250,000 annuity, but the Colombian senate refused to ratify the treaty.

Colombia's motivation was apparently a desire for more money. The French New Panama Canal Company was to receive $40,000,000 from the United States for its work and equipment. Its concession however ran out in October 1904, at which time all physical assets reverted to Colombia. From the Colombian point of view, the simple exercise of a year's patience appeared likely to be very profitable.

This was however a mistake, for it neglected the enormous conspiratorial talents of Philippe Bunau-Varilla, chief agent of the New Panama Company, who engineered a revolution in Panama from his headquarters in the old Waldorf-Astoria Hotel in New York. It also neglected the impatience of President Roosevelt, who was eager to "make the dirt fly."

Revolution in Panama was no novelty. According to Roosevelt's count, there had been 53 revolutions in 53 years. But this particular revolution had a synthetic look, for the patriot army of 500 men had cost $200 a head and was supplemented only by a reserve of 441 members of the Panama fire departments. Bunau-Varilla was however fairly confident that American support would sustain his patriotic efforts.

Under the terms of the Treaty of 1846 with New Granada (Colombia), the United States was pledged to maintain "perfect neutrality" and "free transit" in the Isthmus. On November 2, 1903 U.S.S. *Nashville* arrived at Colon. On November 3 the standard of revolution was raised ashore, and on November 4 the Republic of Panama was born officially. There was no overland route from Bogota. Colombian troops sent by water were politely told they could not land, since America had treaty obligations to uphold, and for them to proceed would obviously create an unneutral disturbance. The guns of the *Nashville* were an eloquent, unspoken argument. Presently the *Dixie* arrived with a force of marines for any necessary policing ashore. The United States recognized the fledgling member of the family of sovereign nations on November 6.

Bunau-Varilla, who never relinquished his French citizenship, now appeared in Washington as agent plenipotentiary for the Republic of Panama. On November 18, some 15 days after the revolution, the Hay-Bunau-Varilla Treaty conveyed to the United States a zone ten miles wide in perpetuity for $10,000,000 and a $250,000 annuity; the treaty was ratified by the Senate November 23. In 1921, $25,000,000 "conscience money" was paid to Colombia as a belated apology.

Whether this episode constituted "international piracy," as some liberal journals claimed, or simply an indirect exercise of a kind of "right of eminent domain," it was not calculated to increase the popularity of the United States in Latin America, particularly in Colombia. But in any event the organizing ability and technical skill of the U. S. Army Corps of Engineers and a decade of labor by a small army of workers produced the desired result. The canal was opened in August 1914 as the world was going to war.

---

[15] The discovery of gold in California had given topical interest to the subject at this time. An American company completed the railroad across the Isthmus in 1855.

The American navy had its priceless transit-way between the country's widely separated coasts.

THE NAVY IN THE CARIBBEAN

The prospect of the Canal's completion gave a new importance to the Caribbean. With the decay of the 18th century sugar trade, the area had become a cul-de-sac far removed from the important trade routes. Now it would become part of a vital sea artery in peace and war. In terms of strategic value, all Caribbean real estate went up. The Canal was a priceless asset, but only insofar as it was defensible—which entailed not only coast artillery but naval bases. Furthermore there must be bases far from the Canal itself to protect the entrance channels to the Caribbean. Equally important, no new footholds by foreign powers could be permitted, since these might become threats to the Canal. In a time when a naval war could be won or lost in an afternoon, the destruction of the locks of the canal could be the strategic equivalent of sinking half the United States Fleet.

Happily, intervention by foreign powers was contrary to the Monroe Doctrine, and any administration could count on over-whelming popular support in invoking it. But considering, as Roosevelt was inclined to do, that the western European powers and the United States had a mandate from "civilization" to impose moral rectitude on the "backward nations," he was unwilling that the Monroe Doctrine should become a shield behind which the less progressive Latin nations could allow anarchic disregard of the rights granted foreigners under international law. This dilemma Roosevelt resolved in 1904 by what has come to be called the "Roosevelt Corollary" to the Monroe Doctrine. The Roosevelt Corollary provided that the United States might feel obligated ". . . in flagrant cases of . . . wrong-doing or impotence [in Latin America] to the exercise of an international police power." In other words, if any situation appeared to demand intervention to protect lives or enforce treaty rights, the United States Navy and a force of marines would do the intervening. For the next 25 years and more, this policy was followed. European nations were glad enough to have their chestnuts pulled out of the fire on occasion, and the Caribbean countries, to which the Roosevelt Corollary in practice was held to apply, were too weak to make an effective protest. The Roosevelt Corollary was expressly repudiated by President Franklin D. Roosevelt's "Good Neighbor" policy in the early 1930's. United States relations with her Latin American neighbors have been notably friendlier since that time.

INTERVENTION IN LATIN AMERICA

In addition to the unilateral Roosevelt Corollary, treaty right permitted United States intervention in Cuba. Although the United States was morally and legally bound to speed Cuban independence, the geographic proximity of the island to continental America and to the Canal Zone gave the United States a legitimate and compelling interest in its political stability. Private American interests had a large stake in Cuba, particularly in the sugar industry. Furthermore the Cubans, though a gifted and vigorous people, had no experience with the institutions of democracy. Rather, they had a bitter tradition of revolution. It was reasonable to expect occasional violence and discord in the island.

This problem in prospect was provided for by the so-called Platt Amendment, which was at once an amendment to the Cuban constitution and the substance of a permanent treaty between Cuba and the United States. Among many other provisions, it provided for the right of intervention by the United States ". . . for the preservation of Cuban independence, the maintenance of a government adequate for the protection of life, property, and individual liberty . . ." It also provided that the United States should have the right to lease or buy naval reservations for coaling and repair.[16]

During a period of anarchy in 1906, Roosevelt intervened on the recommendation of the United States consul-general, and sent marines to Havana. This occupation lasted from 1906 to 1909, during which time an American civilian governor acted as chief executive. Again in 1912, President Taft sent in the marines. In 1917 Wilson refused to sanction revolution in Cuba, whereupon American marines formally occupied Santiago, and marine officers found themselves in the novel role of supervising a "free" Cuban election. Cuba's joint belligerency on the side of the Allies in World War I was a justification for maintaining a marine force on the island until 1922.

In the first quarter of the 20th century, small-scale intervention in various revolution-torn countries of the Caribbean area was common. Naval and marine forces were involved in both campaigning and governmental administration in Nicaragua, Haiti, and the Dominican Republic. Usually United States military occupation promptly brought law and order. Where the occupation was of long duration there were normally also spectacular improvements in public health measures and road building. Generally speaking, administration of civilian government functions by professional military men has tended to be fair but paternalistic—often resented more by neighboring countries than the ones occupied. To the stronger, stable countries of Latin America, this casual exercise of sea power by the United States was simply another evidence of "Yankee imperialism."

The most serious Latin-American imbroglio involving the United States during the 20th century occurred early in Wilson's administration. In Mexico, the idealist Madero had upset the Diaz dictatorship in 1911 but had been unable to establish a stable government. After two years of continued and confused revolution, Madero was murdered, apparently at the behest of Victoriano Huerta, who proclaimed himself provisional president. Wilson refused to recognize this government, discouraged recognition by other American nations, and lifted the embargo against shipments of munitions to private persons in Mexico. Considerable United States naval forces were stationed on both Mexican coasts.

On April 9, 1914 Mexican authorities arrested for no apparent reason a United States naval boat party loading gasoline at the pier in Tampico. The prisoners were promptly released, but Rear Admiral Mayo, commanding the U. S. squadron, demanded a formal apology and a 21-gun flag salute, which the Mexicans refused. President Wilson thereupon ordered a blockade of Mexican harbors and shortly afterwards directed the customs house at Vera Cruz to be seized. It looked as though the Second Mexican War was under way.

Supported by naval gunfire from the *Prairie, Chester,* and the *San Francisco,* a mixed force of marines and bluejackets fought their way into the city, occupying the customs house, cable office, and other waterfront buildings. Early on April 22, Rear Admiral Charles J. Badger, Commander in Chief of the United States Fleet, arrived with five battleships. The force ashore was powerfully reinforced, and the occupation of the entire city was accomplished by noon of the same day. Presently an army detachment came to take over the occupation.

Before hostilities could spread, a joint arbitration proposal by Argentina, Brazil, and Chile was accepted, and all-out war was averted. Huerta went into voluntary exile in July. American warships remained on station close off the Mexican coasts until November.

THE UNITED STATES NAVY IN THE FAR EAST

In the Philippines, a part of the native population under the leadership of Aguinaldo had risen in rebellion against the Spanish garrisons after the Battle of Manila

---

[16] The United States secured naval stations at Bahia Honda and Guantanamo for $2,000 per year. In 1913 the former was abandoned. The Guantanamo grant has since been extended and enlarged.

Bay but before the arrival of the American forces of occupation. Without treaty relations or indeed formal recognition by the United States, they regarded themselves as allies of the Americans. They were successful in gaining control of most of Luzon before General Merritt arrived to occupy the archipelago formally. Comparing their position to that of the Cubans, who had been promised independence, Aguinaldo and his lieutenants at first hailed the Americans as liberators. Their confidence was shaken when Merritt refused to permit the Filipino forces to share fully in the occupation of Manila. When the Filipinos realized that—at least for the time being—they had simply exchanged masters, they prepared for war anew. Hostilities broke out in February 1899, and for the next three years the United States Army (ultimately with a force of about 60,000 men) was obliged to fight a colonial jungle war. The Asiatic Squadron, considerably reinforced since Dewey's victory,[17] took an active part in the Philippine Insurrection, giving gunfire support to forces ashore, ferrying troops and supplies, furnishing landing parties, and establishing blockades.

The long-term prospects of the ill-equipped and badly supplied Filipino army were of course hopeless. But defeated in pitched battles, they broke into small units and conducted a guerilla campaign with the secret support of much of the population. Not until March 23, 1901 was Aguinaldo captured. Even then desultory bush fighting took place for over a year longer. In order to complete the pacification of the islands the exasperated army commanders were driven to a partial adoption of the "reconcentration" tactics of the despised Spanish General Weyler (in Cuba). The Philippine Insurrection cost the United States over $175,000,000 and the lives of 4,300 men. It

tied up a substantial part of the regular army and a fair portion of the fleet.

The United States Asiatic Squadron, preoccupied with its support mission in the Philippines, was abruptly called on in 1900 to participate in the defense of American lives and property in China. Chinese nationalism, deeply stirred by Russian, Japanese, and German aggression in North China, had given rise to a fanatical patriotic movement called the "Boxers"—pledged to the expulsion of all "foreign devils" from Chinese soil. The weak and corrupt government of the Dowager Empress gave tacit support to the Boxers. In late spring of 1900, the foreign legations in Peking began requesting military and naval support from their home governments. The United States sent the armored cruiser *Newark* to Tientsin and a 56-man reinforcement to the legation guard in the walled European compound of the city. Soon afterwards, the Boxers began attacks on the legation area. An improvised international relief column of 2,078 men under British naval command tried unsuccessfully in June to fight its way inland to Peking. About a hundred United States bluejackets under Captain McCalla of the *Newark* participated gallantly in this effort.

A second "international army" of 18,600 men, including 2,500 American soldiers and marines, succeeded after hard fighting in raising the siege of the legations on August 4, 1900. In September 1901 the Chinese government acceded to a joint allied protocol which engaged her to pay an indemnity of $333,000,000 in 39 annuities. The American share was later partly returned to the Chinese to provide for scholarships for study in the United States.

The Boxer Rebellion might well have been the excuse for a final partitioning of China into European dependencies and spheres of influence. American participation in the fighting however gave the United States a voice in the councils of the nations concerned. Secretary of State Hay made this the occasion of a new affirmation of his "Open Door" policy, calling on the powers to preserve China's territorial integrity, and to "safeguard for the world the principle of

[17] In February 1899, besides Dewey's old command, it consisted of the monitors *Monadnock* and *Monterey*, the cruiser *Charleston,* and the captured Spanish gunboats *Manila* and *Callao*. The *Oregon* and miscellaneous small craft joined shortly afterwards. Over the whole period there were numerous other reinforcements.

equal and impartial trade with all parts of the Chinese empire."

As noted above, the Japanese were at this time self-consciously emerging on the world stage. The Boxer Rebellion, in which Japanese troops had fought with bravery and skill beside the soldiers of western nations, probably helped to encourage Japan to make the challenge to expansionist Russia in 1904. The Japanese victory in the Russo-Japanese War gave further confidence to this proud people. Hence the action of the San Francisco School Board in 1906 in instituting segregation of Oriental school children was deeply resented by the Japanese people as an arrogant and undeserved imputation of inferiority. Magnified by yellow journalism both in Japan and in the United States, this became the occasion of a full-blown diplomatic crisis. Earlier in 1906, when there had been a near-crisis over the issue of Japanese seal-poaching in American territorial waters in the Aleutians, Roosevelt had ordered all capital ships of the Asiatic Squadron to stand by to leave for United States ports on order. He now ordered the armored cruiser squadron then on duty in the Far East to be replaced by lighter units, and to concentrate in home waters. These initial operational preparations for war happily proved needless. In the so-called "Gentlemen's Agreement" Japan engaged to restrict emigration to the United States, in return for which the city of San Francisco was persuaded to rescind its objectionable policy.

THE ROUND-THE-WORLD CRUISE OF THE U. S. FLEET

Roosevelt, equally enraged at Japanese truculence and at the state of California, wanted by a dramatic gesture to show Japan the power that lay behind the soft words of American diplomacy. This gesture he made with his order for a round-the-world cruise to be undertaken by the 16 first-line battleships. On invitation, Yokohama was included as a port of call. In the light of present-day technical knowledge and operating procedures, it is difficult to see this cruise in the perspective it offered to the world in 1910. To begin with, such a thing had never before been done. "Experts" freely predicted that breakdowns and fuel difficulties would make a fiasco of the attempt. Others suggested that for the battleship fleet to enter Far Eastern waters would be an unprovoked challenge to Japan. Congress at first demurred because of the extraordinary expense. Roosevelt's political instinct however was never more right. He brushed aside the difficulties and in December 1909 the battle line under "Fighting Bob" Evans steamed south from Hampton Roads on the first leg of its 46,000-mile, 14-month voyage.

In every way the cruise was an unqualified, spectacular success. The Japanese populace, as if to atone for their bitterness four years earlier, welcomed the American warships with what can only be described as delirious enthusiasm. In the Antipodes and in Middle Eastern and European ports of call, the fleet was hailed as exciting and tangible evidence not only of the might but of the good will of the United States. Material performed well; the predictions of the pessimists proved unfounded. The sustained steaming provided exceptional training and suggested improved operating procedures. And the performance of the fleet was a proud dramatization to the American people of their collective might.

From a technical and professional point of view, the cruise was an eloquent reminder of the need of an improved collier and supply service. For in war, the friendly offices of foreign powers would not be available. Further, the need of developed bases and coaling stations in the Pacific was made more apparent. The mere possession of islands was not enough. Expensive facilities were needed if any of these was to be regarded as a useful base in a strategic sense.

The problem of yards and bases, properly a purely strategic one, was during this period in fact still somewhat political. Tens of millions of dollars of appropriations were poured into needless and redundant shore facilities at home, and the really necessary installations overseas (where American "nationals" had no votes) were allowed to languish. In spite of vigorous efforts by Roosevelt and responsible naval officers, not until 1911 was an appropriation voted for Guantanamo; only the impending opening of the Panama Canal was a sufficiently eloquent argument. The problem of an offshore Pacific base was also postponed from year to year, and only in 1909 was work begun on Pearl Harbor. Minor installations at Olongapo and Cavite (on Luzon) were never developed into major facilities.

TECHNICAL DEVELOPMENTS IN THE NAVIES OF THE WORLD

Technical progress in guns, armor, engines, and hull design had been so rapid through the second half of the 19th century that it was not unusual for a ship to be obsolescent by the time she was commissioned. This breakneck rate of material improvement continued almost unabated through the first two decades of the 20th century.

The heavy gunnery vessel, the battleship, was the backbone of the fleet. A design revolution occurred in 1906 which relegated all previous battleships to a "second-class" or reserve status. The British Admiralty commissioned the secretly constructed *Dreadnought,* which proved to be the archetype of all subsequent battleships. Her predecessors had carried a main battery of four big guns in twin centerline turrets fore and aft, an intermediate battery of 6- to 8-inch rifles, and a secondary battery of smaller quickfiring, cartridge-loaded guns, which might include weapons of several different calibers. For example, the United States *Rhode Island*-class of battleships (1904) carried six different calibers. The *Dreadnought* was described as an "all-big-gun" ship. She carried ten 12-inch guns in five turrets (three centerline, one on each beam), and an anti-torpedo boat quick-firing battery of twenty-four 12-pounders. She thus had an effective main battery firepower 2½ times that of any other

existing battleship. This simplification of her ordnance also made for a less cluttered topside, and enormously simplified the problems of munitions stowage and fire control. The *Dreadnought* was somewhat larger than most earlier battleships, with a designed displacement of 17,900 tons.[18] She was 490 by 82 feet, with a loaded draft of 26½ feet. She carried eleven inches of armor on her belt and over the turrets and barbettes—more than any earlier British vessel. Her Parsons turbines had an indicated horsepower of 27,500; she clocked an impressive 21.5 knots in her speed trials. At £1,813,100 she cost more than any other war vessel constructed in Britain up to that time.

At once the admiralties of all the naval powers recognized the *Dreadnought's* superiority. All major navies scrapped or modified existing building plans, and turned to designing "dreadnoughts."[19] United States battleships increased in tonnage between 1898 and 1914 from 12,000 to 31,400 (e.g., the *Pennsylvania,* still an effective fighting ship in World War II). The cost of a firstline vessel nearly tripled.

In foreign navies, the battle cruiser type had by 1914 rendered the older "armored cruiser" obsolescent. This too was a British innovation, fostered by the energetic First Sea Lord, Lord John Fisher. The archetypes of the battle cruiser were the *Indomitable,* the *Inflexible,* and the *Invincible,* all launched in 1907, and commissioned in 1908 and 1909. These vessels were gunned like battleships, carrying eight 12-inch guns in double turrets on a 17,250 ton displacement; their hull dimensions were 530 by 78½ by 26; their test speed was 26 knots. They were designed as "cruiser-killers." They could outrun battleships and could outgun cruisers of the conventional type. Britain had built ten of them by the outbreak of World War I. Germany launched her first battle cruiser,

---

[18] The typical battleship built in 1900 was about 12,000 tons.

[19] United States naval experts still dispute whether the *South Carolina* (1908), mounting eight 12-inch guns, or the *North Dakota* (1908), mounting ten 12-inch guns, was the first American "dreadnought." The *South Carolina* was entirely designed before the British vessel was launched.

the *Von der Tann,* in 1909 (commissioned 1911), and had a total of eight built or building in 1914. Japan copied the type also. The United States and the other principal naval powers preferred to put their appropriations for major vessels into the slower but more heavily armored battleships.

The destroyer as a ship type may be said to have evolved rather than to have come into being as a sudden surprise unveiled by a single navy. Through the late 1880's and 1890's torpedo boats were simply built larger, faster, and more heavily armed so that they could outfight enemy torpedo boats as well as serve their primary function of torpedo attack. The Germans, who have a claim to pioneering the type, were building the first of their "D" boats as early as 1887—vessels just under 200 feet in length with designed speeds over 20 knots. These vessels were of course unarmored and lightly armed except for their torpedo tubes. Britain launched its first class of very fast (27-30 knot) vessels of this type in 1894-1895. In the United States Navy, the first destroyers were already highly evolved, displacing 420 tons and making over 28 knots.[20] In the first decade of the 20th century, the tactical use of destroyers as a "screen" for capital ships became doctrine in all navies. The destroyer flotilla also became a necessary adjunct to the scouting line. World War I was to demonstrate their value also in antisubmarine warfare.

Armor-making processes had improved enormously since the days when wrought iron plates backed with oak were the best protection available. The American "Harveyizing" process, involving heavily "carbonizing" the face of steel plates, had been refined and improved by Krupp (of Germany), whose secret processes included using a gaseous hydrocarbon as the carbonizing agent and introducing nickel or chromium in the alloy for the body of the plate. Germany, Britain, and the United States were in the van of progress in improving armor. In the United States, the Bethlehem Steel Company, the Midvale Steel Company, and the Carnegie, Phipps Company all produced naval armor of top quality.

Capped projectiles, increased gun calibers,[21] and improved propellants gave new advantages to the gun as opposed to armor. But the torpedo, as a means of "defeating" armor by striking below the armor belt, also received much technical improvement. Gyroscopic stabilization, introduction of alcohol heaters, and increased size made it a formidable and accurate weapon. Its range was also extended.

However, it remained manifestly impossible for any light surface vessel to survive in daylight the hail of shells a capital ship could bring to bear long before it closed to effective torpedo range. Hence all navies were interested in the American innovation, the true submersible or "submarine," which could launch its deadly underwater missiles at ranges of 2,000 yards or less. John P. Holland and Simon Lake independently devised workable submarines, the former as early as 1875. The French *Gymnote,* laid down in 1886 and launched in 1888, was the first commissioned submersible. The Italians and the Germans also built small experimental submarines in the 1890's. In 1888, the United States Navy solicited submarine designs; not until 1895 was the contract let for Holland's *Plunger.* So much was learned in the course of her construction that Holland proposed that the Navy take back the money so far advanced and not yet paid out and order an improved model instead. Hence the first commissioned American submarine was the *Holland* (1900), a tiny craft by modern standards, but even so a formidable weapon of war.

The *Holland* was only 54 feet long; submerged she displaced 74 tons. Her single screw was driven on the surface by a gasoline engine, and she had batteries and electric motor for underwater propulsion. She had a single, fixed torpedo tube and carried two "dynamite guns." [22] She incorporated most

---

[20] *Dale, Decatur, Lawrence, Paul Jones, Perry*—all launched in 1900.

[21] In 1900, the heaviest weapon installed in capital ships was the 12-inch gun. In 1914 the *Queen Elizabeth,* under construction in the British Navy, carried 15-inch guns.

[22] Similar to those on the *Vesuvius.*

of the hull design and stability features of modern submarines: a double hull, with ballast tanks exterior to the inner hull, hydroplanes, periscope, and conning tower.

Her test speed surfaced was seven knots. Her range was 1,500 miles. She could make nearly seven knots submerged for short distances at full power; at low speed she could cruise submerged about 50 miles. She could dive to 28 feet in eight seconds. Naval authorities were enough impressed at her trials to order five similar, slightly larger vessels from the builder. The English Vickers Company purchased rights to the Holland design; from Vickers in late 1900 the British Admiralty ordered five boats of the type.

In the ensuing decade all navies adopted the submarine as a fleet type. Bigger and bigger submarines were built, so that by 1914 the newer types were of 500 to 800 tons, capable of long voyages at sea. The problem of underwater navigation, nearly insoluble with magnetic compasses [23] became easy when the gyrocompass was perfected (1908). The German diesel engine (1909) was promptly and universally adopted for submarine surface propulsion, adding enormously to safety and cruising range.

The submarine had been conceived as a device primarily for attack on armored vessels. Ocean-going types were to be fleet vessels. Smaller submarines were for harbor and coast defense—inhibitors of close blockade. The potentiality of the submarine as a threat against merchant shipping was apparently entirely unrecognized. Certainly it was not appreciated by the Germans, who were slow to adopt the new weapon (1906), and who built relatively few of them before 1914. When World War I began, there was no weapon that could reach a submarine submerged below ramming depth: no admiralty had been much concerned to find one.

It is instructive to compare the submarine strength of the naval powers in 1914. Built and building, Britain had 97 boats with a total tonnage of nearly 50,000, Germany had

45 submarines with a total tonnage of 28,540, France had 86 submarines, and the United States, 49. Even Russia had more submarines than Germany.

Improvements in forging techniques and metallurgy had made possible the building of rifled naval ordnance of the largest size as early as the late 1880's. But fire control optical instruments, range clocks, and deflection calculators were not perfected until much later. Even in the World War I period only capital ships were equipped with adequate fire control. Furthermore as late as 1900 gunnery training and operating procedures were, at least in the United States Navy, inadequate to develop the potentiality of the weapons carried.

As in so many aspects of naval progress, the British were in the van of gunnery improvement. Admiral Sir Percy Scott RN, inventor of the "master sight" or director, devised an elaborate training routine based on a sort of "time and motion" study of a typical gun crew. He showed it was possible with the improved elevating gear then used to keep the gun "on target" throughout the roll of the firing ship. Earlier it had been the practice for the guns to be stationary, and hence on target at only one instant in the ship's motion. Scott devised a training aid called a "dotter" [24] which enabled gunners to practice continuous-aim fire under simulated sea conditions even when tied up to the dock. Rapidity of fire, as well as accuracy, was also stressed.

In the United States Navy, William S. Sims, who got to know Scott and his methods while on the China Station, became a single-minded zealot for improved gunnery. By the vigor and force of his personality, Sims, though still a junior officer, imposed his variant of Scott's system on the United States Navy. Roosevelt made him Inspector of Target Practice. The fact that his innovations worked converted even those officers who were personally resentful of Sims' methods. In 1898, optimum battle range for the big guns was thought to be about 6,000

---

[23] Changes in the magnetic field of the electric cables during submerged cruising caused unpredictable deviation.

[24] This device is described in some detail in Elting E. Morison, *Admiral Sims and the Modern American Navy* (Boston, 1942), 84-85.

yards. In World War I, effective director-controlled salvo fire at ranges over 20,000 yards was commonplace.

Of all weapons of war, none is so characteristically American as the airplane. The first successful heavier-than-air flight was made by Wilbur and Orville Wright at Kitty Hawk on Nag's Head in 1903. Military potentialities of aircraft were at once recognized by certain officials of the Army and the Navy. The destructive employment of planes was too remote to be anticipated at this time, but as a means of scouting and fire control at long ranges the invention was considered very promising. In 1910 and early 1911, Eugene Ely made successful takeoffs from a ship and landings on an improvised flight deck. The feasibility of the carrier was thus demonstrated. Glenn H. Curtiss developed and built the first seaplane in 1911. The same year the United States Navy purchased two planes from Curtiss, and one from the Wright Brothers. In 1912, Lieutenant T. G. Ellyson (Naval Aviator Number One) flew a plane from a compressed air catapult mounted on a barge in the Potomac. Rear Admiral Bradley Fiske, one of the most inventive and progressive officers in the service, proclaimed the practicability of the torpedo plane, and designed a workable torpedo release gear.

The first naval aviation unit was established at Annapolis. The Pensacola Naval Air Station was organized in 1913. Lieutenant John H. Towers made the first scouting flight in fleet exercises during that year. Scouting and spotting flights were made in combat during the Vera Cruz operation in 1914.

In invention and in trial-and-error pioneering, the United States Navy was well advanced. But for all that, neither Congress nor the Navy Department was prepared to take naval aviation seriously until World War I demonstrated dramatically the usefulness of aircraft in antisubmarine warfare. Up to 1917, appropriations for naval aircraft were inadequate even for a worthwhile research program.

In contrast, the British accepted the plane as an adjunct to operations as soon as flya-ble aircraft were available. Before World War I, Britain already had over 100 aircraft, mostly seaplanes, and had a fleet tactical doctrine for their employment in connection with patrol flotillas. She had six seaplane stations in commission. The Royal Flying Corps [25] stood prepared to test any aircraft brought to it, and stimulated manufacturing efforts in all possible ways. By January 1914, aircraft of the Naval Wing alone had logged 131,081 miles, with only two fatalities.

In 1914 Germany was most advanced in military aircraft of all types. She had four seaplane stations along her short coastline, and had over 500 airplanes. In 1913 a German pilot established an air endurance record of 16 hours, 20 minutes.

Other principal European powers had made some progress in military and naval aviation. The United States and Japan in 1914 were classified in *Brassey's Naval Annual* as "minor air powers" whose current development was not worth mention.

On the eve of World War I the attention of the experts was strongly drawn to airships—including the new "rigid" type perfected by Count von Zeppelin for Germany. The loss of the *L-1* and the *L-2* in successive disasters in 1913, far from discouraging the German admiralty, simply stimulated research into new protective devices. The Germans were apparently determined to hold their design lead in building "battle airships," as their big dirigibles were coming to be called.

Great Britain and the other European powers were fostering the development of local blimp and dirigible industries. In 1914, Winston Churchill, as First Lord of the Admiralty, announced in the House of Commons the order from the Vickers Company of Britain's first zeppelin-type rigid airship. The United States, in spite of her priceless monopoly of noninflammable helium gas, showed no official interest in this type of aircraft.

Space considerations preclude a detailed

---

[25] The British at this time allocated all aeronautical matters to the R.F.C., which had two branches, a Naval and a Military Wing.

description of all the technical improvements that enhanced the efficiency of navies between 1898 and 1914. It was a period of rapid development in the industrial arts; innovations and discoveries in chemistry, metallurgy, hydraulics, and electrical science helped to solve problems peculiar to the naval service. The obvious advantage of instantaneous communications made Marconi's "wireless" an object of early interest and experiment by most of the world's admiralties. By 1900, it was operational equipment in the British and the United States fleets. A host of developments in subsequent years enormously extended the range, selectivity, and dependability of this primitive radio apparatus. The first operational use of wireless appears to have occurred in the Boer War. The device proved itself in the Russo-Japanese War. Oil-burning capital ships were laid down.[26] Electrical and hydraulic gear on shipboard became more important as more and more heavy manual jobs were eased by the application of power. Improved ventilation of ships' spaces and increased utilization of refrigerated foods made shipboard life far more comfortable for the crews.

Many changes were to ensue after 1914: the development of the depth charge, underwater "listening" devices, the antenna mine. The carrier was to emerge as a type in the next decade. And of course the World War II period was to see a hothouse forcing of radical applications of science to new problems. But even so by 1914 the newest ships in the world's navies were beginning to acquire a "modern" look. And indeed some of them were to show real combat value 30 years later.

OTHER ASPECTS OF NAVAL GROWTH

In the early 20th century the shore establishment of all the world's navies grew in size, variety, and relative importance. Per-

manent ordnance proving grounds, air stations, off-shore bases, and vastly expanded "fleet schools" were added to the naval establishments of every country.

In the United States the lead offered by Stephen Luce a generation earlier was followed out. Whereas in the earlier 19th century it had been customary to recruit naval seamen from the merchant marine, it had increasingly become the practice to get landsmen, the younger the better, and to train them in the Navy's own schools. The increased complexity and variety of equipment on shipboard required more intelligent and better educated men. When Wilson's Secretary of Navy, Josephus Daniels, in 1913 held up the ideal of the Navy's being "a great university with college extensions ashore and afloat," he was giving recognition to what was already becoming an actuality. In the wooden ship days, illiterates could be taught to "hand, reef, and steer." But it takes a background of reading ability and mathematical skills to be capable of learning to man fire control apparatus, to run an engine room, to keep complicated electrical equipment in repair.

Simultaneously there was a gradual change in the basic problems of leadership by officers. The example of conspicuous personal gallantry has never lost its value, but superior intelligence and general administrative ability have become even more important than formerly.

In the United States Navy, administration was somewhat improved. After the Spanish-American War the General Board, set up as a professional advisory body to the Secretary, anticipated in part the office of the Chief of Naval Operations.

The growth of naval tonnage necessarily demanded increased personnel. However, the American navy was at this time notoriously undermanned, especially in the commissioned officer category. According to President Roosevelt, in 1902 the United States had fewer than half enough officers to fill the complements of ships in commission and building. Gradual increases in the numbers of Naval Academy graduates and of enlisted

---

[26] *Oklahoma* and *Nevada* (1914) in the United States Navy, and the *Queen Elizabeths* (1914-15) in the British service.

men were effected, but at the end of 1908, the United States not only had less than a third as many line officers as Great Britain; she had only about half as many as Germany, France, or Japan.[27] This was in spite of the fact that United States tonnage was only slightly less than Germany's and very much greater than Japan's.

TACTICAL AND STRATEGIC DOCTRINE

From the Spanish-American War to the outbreak of World War I, the only important fleet operations were in the Russo-Japanese War, considered in the previous chapter. However, both the Tripolitan War (Italy *vs.* Turkey, 1911-1912) and the First Balkan War (Turkey *vs.* Greece, Bulgaria, and Serbia, 1912-1913) were object lessons in the value of sea power. Italy and Greece, respectively, made effective use of their fleets in the Aegean area. Naval superiority conferred superior mobility to their forces and insured victory in both wars.

British naval doctrine through this period, as already sufficiently indicated, was one of increased concentration in home waters. New bases in Scotland, at Scapa Flow and Rosyth, were activated. As the military and naval planning of England and France tended to merge on the eve of world war, Britain even came to reckon on France's ability to keep naval dominance in the Mediterranean.

Roosevelt, as President, also took great pains to emphasize the sound doctrine of fleet concentration. The fleet as a unit might profitably be shifted from the East to the West Coast via the Panama Canal, but it must on no account be divided. The lesson of Tsushima would never be forgotten.

The growth of the world's navies in the years preceding the first World War was a costly tribute to the teaching of Admiral Mahan. He had shown how political potency and wealth had come to Great Britain

[27] Navy Department *Annual Report,* 1908, 12.

through her superior sea power. Britannia's secret weapon was the trident. And in 1914 Britain, by her tremendous expenditures, the technical excellence of her material, and her shrewd diplomacy, still appeared to grasp firmly her naval ascendancy.

However, Britain had rivals whose ultimate potential could predictably upset this superiority; Japan and the United States could be conciliated by diplomatic means and made into allies, tacit or actual. Germany, already the strongest military power in the world, was in a different category. Her mighty dreadnoughts were too close to home. Should Germany occupy Holland and Belgium, a strong German Navy operating from the mouths of the Rhine and the Scheldt would be a new pistol pointed at the heart of England. Then only the armored walls of two dozen battleships in the Grand Fleet could save England from invasion and defeat.

Because of this threat, England could no longer maintain her "splendid isolation." Perforce she had to bind herself into the complexities of continental power politics. Paradoxically, the new German fleet made England's safety depend in part on the French army.

THE END OF A WORLD APPROACHES

The outbreak of World War I has come to be the conventional historical division between one epoch and another. In the memories of the survivors of that war the very expression "pre-war" was to have an evocative, nostalgic quality. Partly this stemmed from the fact nearly every family in the combatant countries of Europe was touched by personal tragedy. Partly it derived from a growing recognition as the war dragged on that the whole pattern of civilization as formerly known was being smashed beyond repair. The unspoken assumptions of international law, the bases of peaceable intercourse among nations, were upset. Unrestricted submarine warfare, the use of poison gas, reprisals against civilian populations were—at first—outrages against the consciences of the liberals in all countries, including Germany. Yet these "crimes against humanity" engendered counters in kind, and in the end there were virtually no limits but military expediency to the devices or policies followed in prosecuting the war. All combatants poured out blood and treasure for more than four years, exhausting themselves, only to rebuild again less well. For when the guns were finally silent, few survivors could any longer believe in the inevitability of progress which had been the mainspring of so much 19th century thinking. The statesmen at Versailles were cynical and vindictive, for their experience left them no choice. That was the ultimate tragedy of the war, with all its ruinous consequences in subsequent years.

The student of military and naval history may fairly ask, Why was this war so infinitely more destructive, more cataclysmic, than any other since 1815? Part of the answer lies in the elaborate alliance system of Europe which could link an assassination in the Balkans to the mobilization of the British Fleet. Part lies in the nationalistic aims of Germany and of Russia. Part lies in the French desire to revenge the Franco-Prussian War.

But the enormous costs and casualty lists stemmed from a combination: a well-founded recognition that the combatants were fighting for their very existences, together with vastly improved weapons and vastly increased industrial capacity to create these weapons in enormous quantity. For more than a century Western man had been learning the discipline of the machine. Science, and the engineering techniques which batten on it, had greatly increased the productivity of every European economy. This could and did mean a gradual increase not only in total national wealth, but also in the standard of living of the European populations. But it also meant that gigantic war industries and huge armies could be and had to be developed, while a fraction of the work force was able to sustain basic civilian needs. It was, in fact, the economic richness of Germany and of England that made possible the full horrors of World War I. It was to be the economic richness of the United States that was to make possible the ultimate victory of the Allies, painful and partial as that turned out to be.

27

World War I:

Cruiser Actions

IN EARLY 1914 EUROPE COULD look back on 99 years of comparative peace. To be sure there had been wars, two or three of which—the Crimean War, the Austro-Prussian War, and the Franco-Prussian War, for example—had involved the great powers. But even these were comparatively brief in duration and localized in area of operations. In 1914 no man alive could remember what a true world war—involving whole populations in arms, hundreds of thousands of casualties, and the extirpation of empires—could mean in human terms. European wealth and culture flourished as never before in history. Scientific advance and progressive social legislation seemed to promise a new golden age in which men would live in peace and in comfort not even kings could command a few generations earlier. It was a time of optimism, of a belief in progress, of a confidence in the perfectibility of men.

THE CAUSES OF THE WAR

Yet later that year all Europe plunged into a bitter fratricidal war, a war which im-poverished England, bled France white, destroyed Imperial Germany, dismembered the Hapsburg Empire, and brought bloody revolution and civil war to Russia. World War I gutted the social, political, and moral order of most of continental Europe: it made possible Communism in Russia and Fascism in Italy and Germany. Out of World War I grew the inevitable World War II.

How could it be that responsible national leaders could have permitted this tragic violence? Who was responsible for the war?

In spite of the explicit "war guilt" clauses of the Versailles Treaty, it is obvious that no one person and no one nation was altogether responsible. Rather a multitude of little incidents, secret agreements born of fear, selfish prejudices dignified as "national patriotism" combined over many years to weave a web from which there could be no escape. Some of these underlying causes can be labeled and explained. Others embrace intangible mass psychological phenomena almost beyond the scope of the historian.

It is usual to emphasize nationalism and imperialism as important causes of the war. In the Balkans each of the ancient peoples

—Bulgars, Serbs, Romanians—aspired to greater nationhood and additional territory. Austria-Hungary was prepared to expand her empire at the expense of the disintegrating Turkish domain. Germany, late comer in the imperial race, sought territory and economic expansion anywhere and everywhere in the world.

Ancient animosities—the traditional hatred of Russian for Turk, of Italian for Austrian, of Frenchman for German—were always highly charged though latent. France particularly smarted over the humiliation of 1870. The provincial banners of Alsace and Lorraine, the "lost provinces," still hung decorated with black crepe in the Chamber of Deputies. The French army dreamed of vengeance over the barbaric Hun.

The implementation of nationalism and imperialist ambition had generated an unprecedented armaments race, on land and sea. The Germans, not content with the world's strongest army, elected to challenge the Mistress of the Seas as well, and forced on Britain colossal expenditures to maintain her two-power standard of naval strength. Only by budgeting almost twice as much as Germany each year after 1900 were the British able to maintain an over-all statistical naval superiority at an 8 to 5 ratio—a thin enough margin in the context of England's worldwide commitments.[1]

Of crucial importance among the causes of the war were the elaborate alliance systems which had grown up—each secured by a network of secret treaties, financial arrangements, and military "understandings." In 1914 the balance of power appeared to be approximately equal between the major power groupings—the Central Powers (Germany, Austria-Hungary, and Italy), and the Triple Entente (France, Russia, and Britain).[2] The origins of these alliance systems

go back to the German nation-builder Chancellor Otto von Bismarck, who engineered the secret Dual Alliance between Germany and her recent enemy Austria in 1879. Italy, which had been allied to Prussia in 1866, was in 1882 induced to join Germany and Austria in the Triple Alliance, by the terms of which each power engaged to fight if any other of the three were attacked by France.

Bismarck, who had no appetite for the prospect of war on two fronts, had taken good care to achieve a rapprochement with Russia. But in 1890 the young Kaiser, Wilhelm II, abruptly dismissed the aging "Iron Chancellor" from office. Almost at once, with less able hands at the helm, there arose threats to the German security system. France and Russia concluded the "Entente Cordiale" in 1891. Nurtured by French gold, this agreement gave way to a mutual defense pact in 1894, in which specific military pledges were given. Directed clearly against Germany, the Franco-Russian Alliance was, like the Triple Alliance, in theory defensive. But in practice it is often impossible to distinguish between aggressive and defensive war.

Britain from Napoleonic times to about 1900 had eschewed any but temporary wartime alliances. But as suggested earlier, this "splendid isolation" rested on two assumptions—that Britain's fleet be everywhere unchallenged, and that the European power balance be maintained. The containment of Germany—dynamic, militaristic, upsetting both these assumptions—became the focus of British diplomacy. The Boer War (1899-1902), besides pointing up the need for British military reforms, made clear to England that she had few friends in the chancelleries of Europe.

How Britain allied her Navy with the Japanese in the Far East, and tacitly abandoned the Caribbean to the growing United States Fleet has been told. In Europe her security now seemed increasingly to depend on a closer understanding with her ancient enemy France. In 1904 the thorny Moroccan

---

[1] The German challenge at sea was economic as well as naval. Though the Germans built excellent ships their merchant marine remained small compared to Britain's. According to *Lloyd's Register* in 1914, British flag operation accounted for 44 per cent of the world's shipping; the Germans had but 11 per cent.

[2] The term "entente" implies an agreement vaguer and less binding than an alliance. France was actually

allied to Russia. Britain's commitment to France was less absolute. Britain had no direct alliance with Russia.

question was the occasion of a new phase in Anglo-French relations. By the terms of the Anglo-French Entente in that year, France was to have a free hand in Morocco and Britain in Egypt—a bargain that aroused German wrath in later Moroccan crises. In 1907 Russia, under French diplomatic pressure, effected a definitive settlement with the British of three long-standing disputes relating to "spheres of influence" in Tibet, Afghanistan, and Persia. The way was cleared to an eventual wartime alliance. The entente between Britain and the Franco-Russian Alliance was not to produce a formally ratified military treaty prior to World War I, but through the decade 1904-1914 professional military and naval staff conferences—on a "when" and "if" basis—ironed out problems of joint wartime obligation. The French with good reason counted the British on their side in the assessment of the balance of power.

The proximate, immediate occasion of World War I was a double assassination in the Balkans. On June 28, 1914 at Sarajevo, capital of Bosnia, a Serbian "patriot" murdered Archduke Franz Ferdinand, Heir Apparent to the throne of the Austrian Empire, and his wife Sophia, while they were taking part in a parade. The Austrian Foreign Minister, emboldened by Germany's unqualified support,[3] fired off an ultimatum to Serbia demanding compensation and condign punishment to the guilty. These things Serbia could promise. But Austria also demanded Austrian policing of Serbian territory. This the Serbs refused. Russia, whose foreign office for a generation had been preaching "pan-Slavism" in the Balkans, had a mutual defense pact with Serbia. When Austria and Serbia mobilized, so did Russia. The Germans, whose strategy for a two-front war was to overwhelm the French first in a lightning thrust before Russia could fully mobilize,[4] felt compelled by circumstance to move at once. Austria declared war against Serbia on July 28. On August 1 Germany declared war

against Russia, against France on August 3, against Belgium on August 4. Kaiser Wilhelm II, bemused by his kinship with the English Royal Family and some idle talk by German professors about "Saxon solidarity," believed the English would maintain neutrality. The British government however felt bound by honor and interest to support France and defend Belgium. At midnight August 4 Great Britain declared war.

TECHNOLOGY, GEOGRAPHY, STRATEGY, AND TACTICS

To historians with a sense of drama the First World War may appear as a great human tragedy. To professional army and navy officers however the war, like all wars, had to be reduced to impersonal terms—to a matter of securing better machines and more of them, and to questions of morale, of strategy, of logistics.

The war was to reveal the difficulty of successful prewar prediction of weapons development and resultant changes in tactics. The Germans in 1914, for example, had not yet realized the immense potentiality of the submarine as a commerce-raider. The British, equally shortsighted, were woefully weak in the patrol craft—especially destroyers—which would be needed to defeat the submarine. No antisubmarine devices had been developed—neither listening gear nor depth charges.

Technological improvements in mines would enormously increase the scope and importance of this passive kind of warfare. Aircraft would come to fill a new and promising role, especially in the Allied war against the submarines. Serious weaknesses in the design of battle cruisers would be revealed. The heavily armored, heavily gunned dreadnought would remain the backbone of the fleet.

In the broadest sense, the grand strategy of World War I derives from the location of the opposed coalitions. Germany and Austria-

---

[3] The so-called "blank check." It has been suggested that if the Kaiser's government had counseled moderation, the war might have been prevented.

[4] The essence of the "Schlieffen Plan."

Hungary[5] occupied the "interior position" —a band of territory across Europe almost completely separating Russia from her western allies. The German command, utilizing the splendid system of railroads and highways that had been developed with military needs in mind, could quickly shift forces as needed from one front to the other. Utilizing the advantages inherent in the "exterior position," theoretically the Allies should have been able to apply simultaneous pressures on both fronts in a gigantic pincers operation. Practically, with no unified command and inadequate communications between the east and the west, the Allies were never to achieve this strategic ideal.

Naval grand strategy in the war was largely dictated by the geographic configuration of the British Isles and the north coast of Europe. Germany, which enjoyed the strategic advantage in the land struggle, was in a disadvantageous, off-center position in the sea war. The British Isles lay athwart Germany's natural seaways to the broad oceans. The superior British fleet was prepared to challenge any and every sortie. The North Sea itself was a watery no man's land, but even in it Britain with her margin of naval superiority was better able to afford bold scouting. Even German submarine operations were seriously hampered by geography. If they were to operate on England's western approaches, the U-boats would have had to run the gantlet of the Dover Patrol in the Channel or take the costly detour around the north of Scotland. Obtaining Belgian bases would shorten the period of maximum danger for submarine passage to and from the open sea. But the U-boats in World War I never enjoyed the advantage of bases in Norway and western France that they were to possess in World War II.

The short German North Sea coast was well protected by mines and submarines. The Kiel Canal opened in 1895 across the base of the Danish peninsula enabled the Germans to shift their fleet readily from the North Sea to the Baltic, and helped make any British venture into the Baltic a fool-

hardy enterprise. Throughout the war the Baltic was to remain a German lake, a valuable training area for the High Seas Fleet, and a priceless transitway for steel and timber from neutral Sweden.

The initial naval strategy of both sides was extremely wary. The German navy was subordinated to the German army. The Kaiser's hope was to win the war on land within a few weeks by defeating France while holding Russia in the east. German fleet policy therefore was to be one of a careful husbanding of her ships as a diplomatic force, valuable for bargaining at the expected peace table. The British Grand Fleet was also cautious, though for different reasons. It is true that Britain required sea control to keep open the ocean highways to her home islands, colonial areas, and the various fighting fronts, to eliminate enemy merchant shipping and keep the High Seas Fleet bottled up, and to maintain a rigorous long-range blockade against the Central Powers. On the other hand the Admiralty realized that the Allies had more to lose than to gain by risking a decisive naval engagement, and discounted the Allies' numerical superiority[6] in the face of suspected German technological advantages. Admiral Jellicoe, the gunnery expert who was appointed Commander in Chief of the Grand Fleet on August 4, 1914, went on record in a letter to the Admiralty that in fleet action he would decline to follow a deliberate tactical retirement of the enemy which might be purposed to lead him over mine fields and submarine ambush. He likewise would not seek a night encoun-

[6] At the outbreak of war the effective main fleet strengths of Britain and Germany, according to Admiral Jellicoe, were:

	DREAD- NOUGHTS:	BATTLE CRUIS- ERS:	CRUIS- ERS:	DESTROY- ERS:	SUB- MARINES:
Britain	20	4	21	42	9
Germany	13	3	17	88	24

These figures represent only the most modern vessels available in the strategic center of the maritime war. They do not take into account forces unassigned to fleet organizations, or obsolescent vessels. Britain had a relatively greater preponderance of naval strength in the outer seas than she possessed in the North Sea and adjacent waters.

[5] Presently joined by Turkey and Bulgaria.

ter; he considered that the factors of sheer chance and of German superiority in star shells and searchlights would make such a contest undesirably risky.

Thus at the outbreak of the war on opposite flanks of the 120,000 square miles of the North Sea—the prospective main naval area for surface action—the hostile fleets waited for opportunities to achieve limited victories against inferior forces. In the distant, secondary theaters of war the British had numerous organized squadrons—as in the Mediterranean and at Hong Kong. In contrast, the fewer German cruisers were scattered—several individual ships being in the Atlantic; one squadron, as well as individual vessels, under von Spee in the Pacific; and two cruisers in the Mediterranean.

In broadest terms, the titanic struggle to come, like the Napoleonic Wars a century earlier, was to be a war to the death between the world's greatest land power and the world's greatest sea power. According to the doctrines of Mahan, in any long drawn-out conflict the sea power was sure to win. But there were now men who predicted that the railroad, which had revolutionized land transportation, and the achievements of scientists in creating substitute materials—thereby defeating the blockade—had blunted the tines of the trident. Allied victory, as the account to follow will show, was in fact far from inevitable.

THE *GOEBEN* AND THE *BRESLAU*

The Mediterranean is one of the vital maritime arteries in the globe-encircling British transport system that ultimately pumps food, raw materials, and manufactured goods through the British Isles—the heart of the Empire. In 1914 British shipping in this area reached an annual value of $625,000,000. Red ensigns dotted the waters of the great inland sea as hundreds of merchantmen traversed the Suez Canal. As the summer of 1914 advanced, the Royal Navy was alerted to be prepared for trouble in the Mediterranean—trouble possibly involving

Germany, Austria, or Italy, or all three. Turkey might well have been added to the list of potential enemies.

To the north and east of the eastern basin of the Mediterranean the moribund Ottoman Empire, the "Sick Man of Europe," was slowly disintegrating. German influence in Turkey had been shrewdly and watchfully cultivated for some twelve years, and expanding Germany had high hopes of a successful economic thrust—a *"Drang nach Osten"*—into the undeveloped but potentially valuable Middle East. In 1902 Germany had secured a concession to construct a railroad from Constantinople to Bagdad. Shortly before the war a rising popular demand for modernization and reform in Turkey led to a very welcome invitation to Germany to furnish a military mission to train the Turkish Army. In December, German General Liman von Sanders arrived at Constantinople to assume the office of Inspector General of Turkey's land forces. German influence was very much on the ascendant.

Unknown to Britain was the secret alliance of August 2, 1914, which Germany had signed with Turkey on the very eve of war with the Allies. By the terms of this pact Turkey agreed to intervene at a propitious moment in any war in which Germany and Austria-Hungary might become involved. Meanwhile Turkish diplomats continued publicly to profess neutrality, and the British representatives in Turkey accepted these protestations in good faith. Consequently, the preoccupied British Admiralty had no particular fear or concern over the Eastern Mediterranean. The subsequent escape of the *Goeben* and the *Breslau* stemmed from British ignorance of this secret treaty and inaccurate British estimates of possible objectives of these warships.

Considerable naval forces were in the Mediterranean at the outbreak of war. In Pola on the Adriatic the Austrians had six battleships and two light cruisers. At the Austrian base also were the fast German battle cruiser *Goeben* and her consort, the light cruiser *Breslau*. Britain's force, under the command of Admiral A. Berkeley Milne, consisted of the Second Battle Cruiser Squadron (the *Inflexible, Indefatigable,* and *Indomitable*), four aging armored cruisers under Rear Admiral Troubridge, four light cruisers, and 14 destroyers. The French also had a large force in the western Mediterranean; these vessels however would play no part in the *Goeben-Breslau* incident.

When war began, the British Admiralty discounted Constantinople as a possible haven of the two German ships. The Admiralty dispatch of July 30 to Milne stressed the primary need of his assisting the French in the transportation of their Algerian army to Marseilles,[7] and only secondarily the importance of covering and bringing to action the German warships. Milne decided to keep one force close to the Adriatic to watch for enemy ships leaving Austrian ports, and to use another force to hunt down the cruisers at sea. Accordingly on August 2 he stationed Troubridge's four armored cruisers at the entrance to the Adriatic while he himself took two battle cruisers to search for and locate the Germans. Britain was not yet at war, hence Milne could do no more than merely keep track of his prey. He concentrated the remainder of his ships at Malta.

Early on August 4, just as Germany and France were going to war, German Admiral Souchon began coaling at Brindisi, then broke off to bombard the Algerian staging areas, sending the *Breslau* to fire on Philippeville and taking the *Goeben* against Bona, both with negligible results. Shortly afterwards Souchon received radio orders from the German High Command to proceed to Constantinople, thereby taking advantage of the secret alliance and the expected surprise of this move. The moment was especially propitious for the Germans, because the Turks were outraged at Britain's recent requisition of two battleships which had been building on Turkish order in British shipyards.

Late on August 4, just a few hours before Britain went to war against Germany, Souchon turned east after his African shore bombardment, and headed for Messina, Si-

cily to finish coaling. On the way he passed on opposite course the two British battle cruisers. During the night of August 5 and a part of the next day, he loaded his bunkers to the top. Meanwhile the light cruiser *Gloucester,* only British warship close to Messina, radioed to the fleet commander that the *Goeben* was there. But Milne was pursuing three separate and not altogether consistent objectives: interdiction of German interference with the French troop movement, prevention of the German cruisers' escape through the western Mediterranean, and preservation of Italian neutral rights by keeping his warships at least six miles from Italian territory. After weighing the Admiralty orders Milne decided to patrol between Sicily and Sardinia, and thereby occupy a central position with reference to Gibraltar, Marseilles, and Sicily.

At that time Souchon entertained no particular hope of escape. Believing interception by superior forces inevitable, he nevertheless cleared Messina in the late afternoon of August 6. Fortunately for him however Troubridge was well to the northeast, and Milne to the westward. Only the *Gloucester* was close enough to shadow the Germans that night; the next day she even exchanged long-range salvos with the *Breslau.* Conserving their coal, the *Goeben*'s engineers maintained speed of slightly less than 17 knots as the battle cruiser and her consort headed for the Aegean.

Meanwhile Troubridge's four armored cruisers, leaving their Adriatic station, had attempted to close the enemy, with hope of engaging at dawn, when their gunnery chances were believed best. Excessively cautious, Troubridge gave up the chase in the early hours of August 7 for he feared that he could not get within range until full daylight, when the bigger guns of the *Goeben* might well send his ships to the bottom, one after another.

Milne, wary of the prospect of a long fuel-consuming chase, on the night of August 6 steamed at half-speed to Malta to replenish his coal. On the next day he took his three battle cruisers in eastward pursuit at three-quarters speed—15 knots, over a knot slower

---

[7] A mission in which the French and British commanders signally failed to develop any coordinated plan.

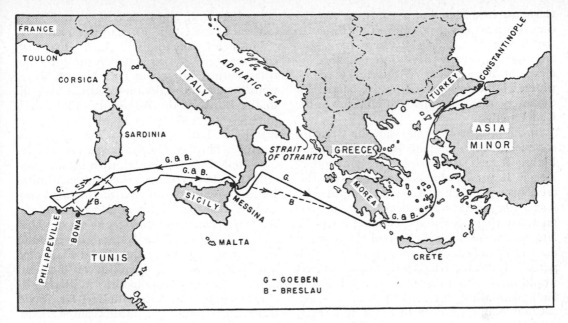

ESCAPE OF THE GOEBEN *AND THE* BRESLAU, *1914*

than the speed of the Germans he was pursuing. Souchon had an additional stroke of luck at this time when the Admiralty dispatch announcing war with Austria reached Milne. In the absence of orders from Whitehall to use his own discretion, Milne was obliged to implement previously issued orders on what he should do if conflict with Austria developed: he reversed course and headed back to support Troubridge in the Adriatic. A day later another message was received which corrected the previous oversight of the Admiralty, and Milne once more steamed east.

By now it was of course too late. Far ahead of pursuit, the Germans arrived at the Dardanelles on August 10, and then steamed slowly to Constantinople, to the delight of the German embassy and the chagrin of the British. In London there were outcries over "bungling in high places." The Admiralty convened courts-martial for the commanders. But Milne was supported by their Lordships in the measures he had taken. Troubridge also was exonerated for his failure to continue the pursuit on August 7. All the same, this abortive naval campaign illustrated the peril of inadequate diplomatic intelligence, and the penalty of divided objectives, inaccurate communications, and lack of command initiative.

The escape of the *Goeben* and the *Breslau,* seemingly an unimportant naval episode, was the first link in a chain of events that led to Turkey's entering the war soon afterwards, which in turn led to the Dardanelles failure of 1915. On August 13 the Turks announced the "purchase" of these two warships, although their original crews remained on board and Souchon remained their commander. Late in October the German admiral led a combined Turko-German squadron against the Russian Black Sea ports of Odessa and Novorossysk, laid mines off Sevastopol, and sank a Russian gunboat. This act of provocation, of course, resulted in war between Turkey and Russia.

HELIGOLAND BIGHT, AUGUST 28, 1914

Back in 1890 Great Britain had traded mile-long Heligoland in the North Sea to

Germany in exchange for Zanzibar. At that time German naval power was no threat to the British; Lord Salisbury and his associates could scarcely have foreseen the immense strategic value of this rocky island, which would provide a defensive barrier for the safety of the North Sea approaches to the Kiel Canal.

In the first weeks of the war, the Germans conducted regular patrols in Heligoland Bight. British submarines of Commodore Roger Keyes' command, cruising in this area, brought back to Harwich tempting information on the methodical nature of German scouting operations. Habitually in the late afternoon their light cruisers escorted destroyers to sea, where the smaller vessels patrolled until daylight; then the cruisers would meet them some 20 miles northwest of Heligoland, and shepherd them back home.

Commodore Keyes, a brilliant and enterprising officer, saw opportunity for the British fleet in this regularity and worked out a plan for taking the patrols by surprise. Using his submarines as bait, he would lure the Germans into the waters west of Heligoland, whereupon British surface vessels would sweep down from the north and then turn west like a giant sickle, cutting down any enemy units they encountered. Keyes believed that the British could thus smash the night patrol and with a little luck get their daytime reliefs as well. Such a timely victory would help make amends in home waters for the recent escape of the *Goeben* and the *Breslau* in the Mediterranean.

Submarine dispositions would be important. A few would be stationed off the Ems Estuary to watch for any German warships that might put to sea to provide reinforcement; three would be stationed a few miles west of Heligoland to attack targets of opportunity; three surfaced boats, breaking radio silence on all wavelengths, and acting as conspicuous as possible, would be positioned 40 miles farther west of Heligoland as decoys to draw German destroyers off in pursuit and into the trap. There would be strong British reinforcements on the periphery of the projected area of operations—cruisers and destroyers to the west, armored cruisers to the south, and light cruisers and battle cruisers of the Grand Fleet to the north.

Finding Commodore Reginald Tyrwhitt, commanding the two Harwich destroyer flotillas, enthusiastic about his proposal, Keyes went in person to London to submit his plan to the Lords of the Admiralty. The Admiralty accepted Keyes' general plan but at first limited his support to Tyrwhitt's two destroyer flotillas and the battle cruisers *Invincible* and *New Zealand,* with six armored cruisers held in reserve. Later, upon Admiral Jellicoe's pointing out that the planned concurrent landing of Royal Marines on the Belgian coast might bring out strong German surface forces, the Admiralty decided to send along ships from the Grand Fleet anyway. These were a squadron of six light cruisers under Commodore William R. Goodenough, and Vice Admiral Sir David Beatty's powerful First Battle Cruiser Squadron, comprising the *Lion,* the *Queen Mary,* and the *Princess Royal,* largest and newest of their type, displacing around 27,000 tons, carrying eight 13.5-inch guns, and making speeds up to 32 knots. To Beatty's squadron the *Invincible* and the *New Zealand* would be temporarily attached. Through an administrative mixup however neither Keyes nor Tyrwhitt got word of the Admiralty's change of heart. They put to sea prepared to make do with what they had, never suspecting that such formidable support was on the way.

Before daylight on August 28 the submarines, shepherded as far as Heligoland Bight by the destroyers *Firedrake* and *Lurcher*—the latter Keyes' flagship—took their dispositions, with the *E-6, E-7,* and *E-8* on the surface trying to attract attention. At the same time, to spring the trap, Tyrwhitt's 33 destroyers, together with the light cruisers *Arethusa* and *Fearless,* were coming down from the northwest. Behind Tyrwhitt at a distance came Goodenough's six light cruisers. Farther off and a little to the west were Beatty's five battle cruisers. At dawn Tyrwhitt's destroyers sighted Goodenough's cruisers and, taking them for an enemy force, prepared to attack. Luckily, Goodenough

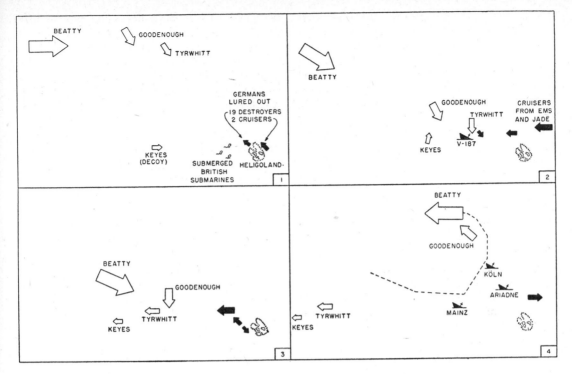

HELIGOLAND BIGHT ACTION, AUGUST 28, 1914

identified himself in time and a battle between friends was avoided.

The Germans, with some inkling of Keyes' plan but not suspecting the strength of his support, had 19 destroyers and the cruisers *Stettin* and *Frauenlob* at or near Heligoland. To the east and south they had five more cruisers: *Köln, Strassburg, Stralsund, Mainz,* and *Ariadne,* and inside Jade Roads some 60 miles away was the German Battle Cruiser Squadron. Each side was trying to trap the other, and if Tyrwhitt's flotillas had not had the backing whose presence he did not at first suspect, things might have turned out ill for him.

To all appearances Keyes' trap worked to perfection, for the German destroyers came out west of Heligoland as the British had hoped they would. It appears however that this was part of the German decoy plan, for when Tyrwhitt's flotillas swept down and gave chase, the enemy destroyers fled south at flank speed, and the cruisers *Stettin* and

Frauenlob darted out from behind Heligoland to engage the *Arethusa* and the *Fearless* and draw them within range of the guns on the island. The *Fearless* and her flotilla promptly took after the *Stettin,* which soon retreated under the Heligoland batteries, but the newly commissioned *Arethusa,* firing on the *Frauenlob,* found her guns jamming one at a time. At last, with one 6-inch gun operable, she got in a lucky shot which sent her opponent reeling back toward Wilhelmshaven with 50 casualties.

In disgust at his meager success, Tyrwhitt gave up the chase and signaled for the western sweep to begin, already a half hour behind schedule. On this westward course the *Fearless* flotilla encountered a lone German destroyer, the *V-187,* and quickly reduced her to flaming wreckage. The British destroyers stopped to pick up survivors, but the *Stettin,* misinterpreting what was going on, darted out from Heligoland and chased them away. One of Keyes' submarines, the *E-4,* thereupon fired at the *Stettin* and missed. At that the *Stettin* again retreated, and the *E-4* surfaced and took aboard two boatloads of Englishmen and their German prisoners which the British destroyers had left behind in their flight.

Goodenough's light cruisers meanwhile had arrived in the Bight west of Tyrwhitt's position without meeting any enemy. Observing the attack on the *V-187* in the distance, Goodenough detached two of his cruisers and sent them toward the scene of action to make sure the German destroyer would be sunk. Keyes, in the destroyer *Lurcher,* was also steering towards the action. Presently he saw the two light cruisers through the gathering mist and, taking them to be enemy, he reported that he was shadowing a pair of German cruisers. Goodenough, intercepting this message, headed with his four remaining ships to Keyes' assistance, but as he came into view Keyes thought four more enemy cruisers had arrived and called all the louder for help. In the confusion Goodenough tried to ram one of Keyes' submarines, and Tyrwhitt came dashing up to provide support against the non-existent enemy. An hour was lost before Keyes correctly identified the cruisers he was following and learned that not only Goodenough's light cruisers but Beatty's battle cruisers were in the area.

At last the British were ready to resume their westward run. The operation so far had been far from successful; the net had caught but one small vessel. Yet the delays were to be advantageous, for four fresh German cruisers were coursing toward the British concentration, little suspecting that British battle cruisers were just over the horizon. German Admiral von Ingenohl had ordered his battle cruisers to join in as soon as they could get over the Jade Bar, but high water was not until afternoon.

Beatty, who as Senior Officer Present had succeeded to over-all command of the British force, ordered the westerly retirement executed. British light units had already been milling around for a dangerously long time in a limited area near the enemy bases. Besides, Beatty was conscious of the real danger

of accidental action between Keyes' submarines and Goodenough's cruisers, as lack of adequate communications continued to plague the British. At this moment, the *Strassburg* and *Köln* burst out of the mists, as if to take advantage of the British dilatoriness. While they were engaged by the *Arethusa* and the *Fearless,* a third German cruiser, the *Mainz,* appeared on the scene, only to be driven off under a rain of shells from Goodenough's superior force. A few moments after Beatty had ordered Goodenough to send two cruisers to aid Tyrwhitt, Tyrwhitt sent a series of urgent signals for additional help. Beatty decided that a crisis had been reached. The time had come for him to strike.

Courageously disregarding the possibility of more substantial German strength than that reported, Beatty immediately took his five battle cruisers at full speed toward Tyrwhitt's hard-pressed force.

Beatty arrived within the hour, to sight the scattered German cruisers *Strassburg, Stettin, Köln,* and *Ariadne.* Leaving the already beaten *Mainz* to the British light cruisers, he chased the retiring *Stettin* and *Köln.* The *Lion* and *Princess Royal* poured salvos into the *Köln,* then continued east and brought the *Ariadne* under attack, driving her back into the mists, where she exploded and sank. Beatty, now feeling that he had approached as close to Heligoland as he dared, ordered a general retirement. As the battle cruiser line swung to port to reverse direction, they again located the injured *Köln* and quickly sank her, with only one man surviving of her crew. Meanwhile the *Mainz* had also gone down; Keyes' flagship rescued many of her survivors.

The action was over. The British steered for home, the *Arethusa* and one destroyer in tow. The *Stettin* and *Strassburg* fell back on the German battle cruisers, just now belatedly coming to the scene of the battle. The *Von der Tann* was able to pick up some survivors from the *Ariadne.* Time and tide had worked for the British, who had drawn first blood in North Sea surface action.

The British battle cruisers, as later at the Battle of the Falklands, had shown their usefulness in their designed function. Their speed and firepower had proved decisive against weaker vessels. The Germans had lost three light cruisers and a destroyer, suffering over 700 killed and almost 400 taken prisoner. The British experienced only slight material damage, and lost 35 men.

Strategically the action was not of crucial importance, but it prompted the Germans to mine the Heligoland area, and to supplement the two mine fields by increased numbers of patrol craft. For additional support they would in the future hold a battleship division in readiness and battle cruisers with steam up in Schilling Roads, unaffected by the tide—in case the British should make a second venture. The Kaiser, shocked at the defeat of his ships, determined to husband his surface forces and control their employment. He advised Ingenohl that loss of warships should be avoided, and that no sorties should be made without his personal approval.

The British Admiralty had been reminded of the danger of altering an operation order at the last moment, when the first phase of the original plan was already being executed and force commanders were unaware of important changes. They were fortunate in not having sunk or damaged some of their own vessels. They could hardly expect that their lack of coordination would ever again actually aid them in achieving success. Keyes' plan, first in the history of warfare to embrace combined operations of surface craft and submarines, had scarcely developed exactly as he had hoped. But he was proud of his force's scouting and rescue work.

Weather and tide each had played an important part in the battle. Sustained mists made identification of friend and foe difficult, and largely explained why contact between various vessels was frequently lost. Low tide over the bar at the entrance to the Jade River prevented the German battle cruisers from reaching Heligoland in time to make the contest one of more equal numbers and strength.

The Germans had failed to achieve concentration, feeding in their light cruisers piecemeal, three of them into the maw of superior forces. Furthermore, their scouting strength at sea had proved insufficient to determine the strength and location of their adversaries.

At a time when the German armies were rolling inexorably across northern France and Belgium, the news of the British victory at Heligoland Bight came like a tonic to the Allied peoples. At least it appeared that Britannia still ruled the waves.

CORONEL AND THE FALKLANDS

As in the Mediterranean, across the broader waters of the Pacific and South Atlantic lay important shipping lanes. Over these routes flowed Britain's trade with South America and much of the Orient, so it was an important British objective in the first few months of the war to clear these outer seas of German naval and merchant shipping and to suffer only nominal losses in the process.

Germany, which had acquired a naval base at Tsingtao, China during the 1890's, in 1913 had ordered Admiral Graf von Spee from Kiel to command her cruisers in the Pacific. Besides Tsingtao, certain of Germany's island colonies in the Carolines and Marshalls had been developed as coaling stations to supply its naval forces if war should come. Should need arise, German agents were also available in various neutral nations to make supply arrangements.

At the outbreak of the war, von Spee enjoyed a certain advantage of position. His fine cruisers, the *Scharnhorst* and the *Gneisenau*, happened to be at Ponape in the Caroline Islands on a training cruise—some 2,700 miles from both the British China Squadron at Hong Kong and the considerable Australian force at Sydney.

When the cruisers *Emden* and *Nürnberg* joined von Spee at Ponape in August 1914, the Admiral, after conferring with his captains, decided to make a war cruise to South America's west coast. He felt that if his squadron attempted to operate in the western or central Pacific it would be only a matter of time before superior British, Australian, or Japanese forces caught up with him. He also counted on the fact that in friendly Chile he could procure sufficient coal to continue operations. He dismissed commerce warfare as a suitable primary objective for the squadron as a whole, but two days after he put to sea from Ponape he detached the *Emden* and an attendant collier for raiding operations against British shipping in the Indian Ocean.

The German cruise to South America was relatively uneventful. Successive landfalls were made at Eniwetok, Majuro, and Christmas Island. In September, bombardments of Apia Harbor, German Samoa (which had been captured by New Zealanders), and Papeete in Tahiti produced negligible results. In mid-October he was at Easter Island, where he was joined by the cruisers *Dresden* and *Leipzig*. The former had already achieved some success in commerce destruction off the northeast coast of South America; the latter had just arrived from San Francisco. Receiving intelligence that the British cruisers *Good Hope, Monmouth,* and *Glasgow* were off the west coast of South America, von Spee proceeded thither at once.[8] By the end of October the augmented German squadron was cruising off Chile, with the *Leipzig* breaking radio silence in an effort to convince the British that only one German ship was in the area.

Meanwhile the British were more seriously alarmed at the danger of German surface raider incursions against their shipping in the South Atlantic. Steamers bound for Britain coursed through the Straits of Magellan with cargoes of wool, frozen meats, hides, wheat, and dairy products from Australia and New Zealand, and nitrates needed for explosives from Valparaiso. From the busy ports of Buenos Aires and Montevideo on the Plate Estuary came huge shipments of grain, meat, hides, and wool. Coffee from Santos, hides from Rio de Janeiro, cotton from Bahia, rubber and sugar from Pernambuco swelled the seaborne traffic to Liverpool and the Port of London.

On September 3 Rear Admiral Christopher Cradock had been appointed commander of the force of British cruisers operating off Pernambuco, near which the German cruisers *Dresden* and *Karlsruhe* had been raiding against shipping. The appearance of Cradock's cruisers patrolling the coast of South America buoyed the confidence of local shippers in the ability of the Royal Navy to maintain control of these sea lanes and to keep merchant ship losses at a minimum. By the middle of September however Cradock was advised by the Admiralty that when he had superior force he should search the Straits, being ready, as circumstances dictated, either to cruise to Valparaiso to destroy the German cruisers thought to be there or to return and cover the Plate.

A month later, in accordance with Cradock's own suggestion, the Admiralty ordered a division of forces. Rear Admiral A. P. Stoddart took charge of an east coast concentration off Montevideo—a battleship and five cruisers. Cradock to the south kept the slow 12-knot pre-dreadnought battleship *Canopus,* the cruisers *Good Hope, Monmouth,* and *Glasgow,* and the auxiliary cruiser *Otranto,* actually a mere armed merchantman. Winston Churchill, then First Lord of the Admiralty, assumed that no harm could come to Cradock, since "the old battleship . . . was . . . a citadel around which all our cruisers in those waters could find absolute security." [9] In effect, Churchill was imputing to the *Canopus* the role of mobile "fortress fleet" for the protection of Cradock's cruisers. Since Britain did not have sufficient naval numbers or strength to have powerful units of appropriate type in all seas, such makeshift arrangements were oc-

---

[8] In the light of what subsequently happened, it appears fortunate for the British that the Germans showed no inclination to use their naval forces against the Pacific shipping lanes, such as that from Sydney to Vancouver via Honolulu, or the route from Wellington via Cape Horn to the Plate Estuary. Through the newly opened Panama Canal during the last five months of 1914 passed 80 British merchant ships from the Pacific to the Atlantic.

[9] *World Crisis,* 4 vols. (New York, 1923), I, 449-450.

casionally unavoidable. Since Cradock did not, perhaps could not, employ the *Canopus* as Churchill anticipated, he found himself commanding a decidedly inferior force when he faced von Spee.

On October 21 Cradock left Port Stanley in the Falklands, passed into the Pacific via the Straits, and headed north, ordering the *Canopus* to join him at Juan Fernandez Island, west of Valparaiso. The fast *Glasgow*, which had gone on ahead, arrived off Coronel and heard German naval radio signals on October 29 and 30; the next day she identified messages as coming from the *Leipzig*. Von Spee's ruse was working.

Early on November 1 a German merchant steamer signaled von Spee that the *Glasgow* had anchored off Coronel, to the south. The German commander quickly headed for this area. Meanwhile Cradock's main body, hearing strong German radio signals, swept north seeking the *Leipzig*. So far, each commander expected to encounter only one opposing cruiser. Actually, the two squadrons approaching each other off the Coast of Chile included the vessels shown in the table.

advantages over their main antagonists, the *Good Hope* and the *Monmouth*. The German crews, who had served for three years, were famous for their excellent gunnery, the *Scharnhorst* having won the Battle Practice Cup in 1913 and placed second in 1914 to the victorious *Gneisenau*. Of great importance also was the German possession of a modified director system, not yet introduced by the British in their cruisers. This meant that the Germans could bring concentrated main battery fire on their target, whereas the independently directed British turrets could only by greatest chance achieve similar aim. British Admiral Sir Percy Scott's peacetime prediction had been that this advantage would give the Germans ". . . such a superiority in gunfire that if a British Fleet engaged a German Fleet of similar vessels, the British Fleet would be badly beaten in moderate weather, but annihilated if it was rough." [10]

By five o'clock von Spee, on opposite course and considerably inshore of the British, had closed up his line, slightly decreased his speed, and steered first southwest and then south. Cradock, with his force in

Name:	Type of Cruiser:	Displacement:	Belt Armor (inches):	Speed:	9.2:	8.2:	6:	5.9:	4.7:	4:	3:
Scharnhorst	armored	11,600	6	23.5		8	6				
Gneisenau	armored	11,600	6	23.5		8	6				
Leipzig	protected	3,250	—	23						10	
Nürnberg	light	3,450	—	24						10	
Dresden	light	3,600	—	24						10	
Good Hope	armored	14,000	6	24	2		16				14
Monmouth	armored	9,800	4	24			14				8
Glasgow	light	4,800	—	26.5			2			10	
Otranto	armed merchant cruiser		—	16					4		

Shortly after 4 PM the *Leipzig* sighted the British force, offshore and to the westward; not till 40 minutes later did the British identify the two van ships of the Germans, the *Scharnhorst* and the *Gneisenau*. These two cruisers cleared for action with significant

column, at about 6:04 vainly attempted to cross the German "T." Then, deciding to fight on a parallel course, he shifted to a southerly track, still to westward of the Ger-

[10] Percy Scott, *Fifty Years in the Royal Navy* (London, 1919), 255.

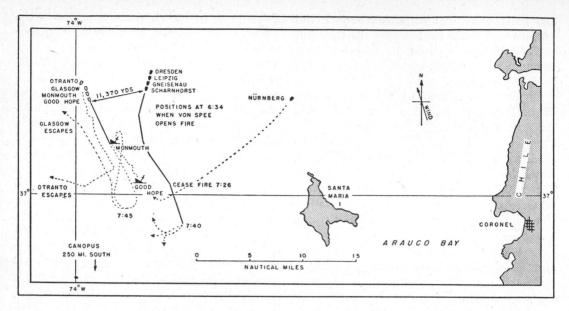

BATTLE OF CORONEL, NOVEMBER 1, 1914

mans. At 6:18 he sent what was to be his last message to the slow *Canopus,* then laboring some 250 miles to the south, "I am going to attack the enemy now." [11]

Carefully holding his fire until one minute after sunset, von Spee at 6:34 opened up at a range of 11,370 yards, benefiting from the silhouetting of the British cruisers by the sun's afterglow. Within five minutes superior German guns and instruments had obtained decisive hits, destroying the forward turret of the *Monmouth* and the forward turret and conning tower of the *Good Hope.* The heavy seas and strong southerly winds apparently interfered more with British than German gunnery. By 6:50 the *Monmouth* was limping south out of the battle line, fires raging within her hull; shortly afterwards her guns went silent. At 7:26 the two German van cruisers ceased their fire. A series of gusty rain squalls so limited their vision that they did not learn the fate of Cradock's flagship the *Good Hope,* which, after taking 30-odd hits from the *Scharnhorst,* was blown to pieces by an exploding magazine at about 8:00.

[11] Lloyd Hirst, *Coronel and After* (London, 1934), 105.

Von Spee, eager for the kill, directed his force to locate and finish off the enemy vessels. In the gathering gloom, the *Leipzig* actually charged at flank speed right through the *Good Hope* wreckage without realizing it. The *Nürnberg* chased and destroyed the crippled *Monmouth* at 8:58. Meanwhile the *Otranto* and the speedy *Glasgow* had escaped to westward.

Strategically, the Germans had gained but little. For a short time the nitrate, copper, and tin shipments from Peru and Chile were held up, but the Plate trade continued in undiminished volume. On the other hand the Germans had clearly won a tactical victory. Two second-rate British cruisers and all their crews had been wiped out, whereas von Spee's force had received only six inconsequential hits and had two men wounded. The German admiral had used shrewd tactics with superior force, and had taken skillful advantage of position, light, wind, and sea. Yet even in defeat, Cradock had lessened the chances of continued German success, for von Spee's squadron had expended 42 per cent of its 8.2-inch ammunition at Coronel. And there was no replenishment nearer than Germany. The battle gave tragic point to the strong recommendations of Scott and Jellicoe to hasten the extension of the director system of firing as quickly as possible in the British cruisers.

Kaiser Wilhelm, elated at the news of the German victory, awarded 300 Iron Crosses to his successful personnel, medals which they were not destined to receive. For von Spee's star had already passed its zenith. As soon as the British Admiralty heard the grim tidings, battle cruiser support suddenly was no longer reserved for waters considered more important to Britain than those touching South American shores. The peppery First Sea Lord, Admiral Sir John Fisher, acted promptly to restore British naval prestige and confidence. Admiral Sir Doveton Sturdee was ordered from the Admiralty to take the fast battle cruisers *Invincible* and *Inflexible* at their best possible speed to the Falkland Islands, where von Spee quite probably might next appear. Meanwhile to bolster defenses in the Falklands, the old *Canopus* was lightly grounded in Port Stanley harbor, for protection of the anchorage. Cruisers already there were joined on December 7 by Sturdee's force, which arrived 21 precious hours ahead of von Spee's dilatory approach.

Von Spee had been feted by pro-German residents at Valparaiso, where he received a dispatch from the Naval High Command recommending his return to Germany. The prospect of running out of ammunition made such a move inevitable sooner or later, but von Spee was resolved to do as much as possible for the German cause along the way. He slowly inched his way south around the tip of South America, spending three days coaling from a captured Canadian sailing ship. This was time he could never recover. On the morning of December 6 he held another conference with his captains, who by a vote of 3 to 2 recommended attacking Port Stanley in order to destroy the radio station, capture the British governor, and seize the coal stored there. The Admiral accepted the will of the majority.

Von Spee directed the *Gneisenau* and the *Nürnberg* to take station five miles off Pembroke Lighthouse at 8 AM on December 8. He thereby erred in separating his force,

hitherto concentrated, and also took a needless risk in scheduling this scouting mission so late in the morning that the Germans were sure to lose the advantage of surprise. By this time the British were carrying out

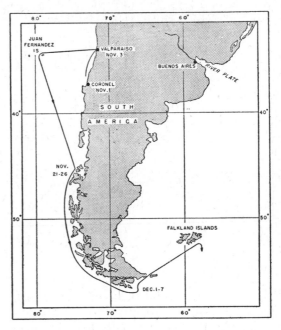

VON SPEE'S MOVEMENTS FOLLOWING THE BATTLE OF CORONEL

their plan of the day, which was "coaling ship." At 7:50 they first spotted the Germans from a high tower ashore. About 9:20 the *Canopus* opened indirect fire. Soon afterwards the two German cruisers, moving in toward the harbor entrance, recognized the tripod masts of British battle cruisers. As the British piped "action stations" and their engineers hastened to get up full steam, their opponents beat a hasty retreat and quickly gained a head start of some 15 miles. The sea was calm, the sky clear, and visibility good—all factors favorable to British engineering and gunnery. The *Glasgow* and *Kent* darted into the lead among the pursuers, but the British battle cruisers also soon increased their speed to 25 knots.

By 12:50 PM the British were within range of the rearmost German ship, the *Leipzig*. Von Spee, realizing that the battle cruisers

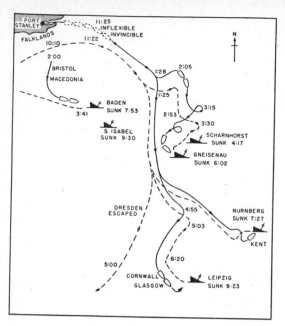

BATTLE OF THE FALKLAND ISLANDS
DECEMBER 8, 1914

The main action between the British battle cruisers and the *Scharnhorst* and *Gneisenau* began at 1:20 at 14,000 yards, some 1,000 yards outside the extreme range of the German ordnance. After various maneuvers at gradually decreasing ranges the British at about 3 PM obtained damaging hits on both German vessels. Von Spee made an unsuccessful effort to close the range, but the British sheered off. The issue was never in doubt. At 4:17 the *Scharnhorst* listed heavily to starboard, burning furiously forward and amidships, and then plunged to the bottom with her entire crew. The *Gneisenau* lasted longer, but by 5:30 her speed had been reduced to five knots. After receiving concentrated fire from both the battle cruisers and the *Carnarvon* her captain ordered her sea cocks opened, whereupon she quickly heeled over and sank. There were a few survivors, picked up by the British.

To the southwest the secondary action was scarcely less decisive. The *Kent* overhauled the *Nürnberg*, and, in mist and rain, at 3,500 yards range destroyed her. The *Glasgow* and the *Cornwall* sank the *Leipzig*, while the *Bristol* and the *Macedonia* were destroying two of the three German colliers.

The British squadron returned to Port Stanley triumphant, having sustained only slight battle damage and few casualties. Only two of the German ships had escaped, and they soon would be out of the war.

would quickly exploit their superior 12-inch guns, decided that his situation was hopeless if he kept his forces concentrated. He therefore elected to sacrifice his main units in order to render possible the escape of his three smaller cruisers. These deployed to the southwest, pursued by the *Glasgow, Cornwall,* and later the *Kent*.

Name:	Type:	Speed:	Guns by Size *(in inches):*					
			12:	8.2:	7.5:	6:	5.9:	4:
Invincible	battle cruiser	26.5	8					16
Inflexible	battle cruiser	26.5	8					16
Carnarvon	armored cruiser	23.0			4	6		
Cornwall	armored cruiser	23.5				14		
Kent	armored cruiser	23.0				14		
Bristol	scout cruiser	26.5				2		10
Glasgow	scout cruiser	26.5				2		10
Canopus	coast defense	16.5	4			12		
Macedonia	armed merchant cruiser	17.0				8		
Scharnhorst	armored cruiser	23.5		8			6	
Gneisenau	armored cruiser	23.5		8			6	
Leipzig	protected cruiser	23.0						10
Nürnberg	scout cruiser	24.0						10
Dresden	scout cruiser	24.0						10

The surviving collier was interned in Argentina the next month, and the *Dresden* was tracked down and blown up at Juan Fernandez Island in March 1915.

GERMAN SURFACE RAIDERS

Although the important instrumentality of commerce raiding in World War I was to be the German submarine, in the early part of the war only cruisers, and later specially-rigged auxiliary cruisers, carried out commercial raiding missions in accordance with the classical tradition. Individually some of these vessels were quite successful, but it is fair to say that their direct effect on the conduct of the war was not very great. The fact is that instantaneous world-wide communications by radio telegraphy made such cruises as that of the *Alabama* in the American Civil War no longer possible. It was always simply a question of time before a successful raider was run down or driven from the seas.

The effect of German surface raiders in 1914 was a mere pinprick to British maritime trade. By the end of January 1915, these vessels had sunk 217,590 tons of British merchant shipping; meanwhile Germany's own merchant marine had been reduced 246,358 tons either by sinking or capture. The British at this time were easily able to build new bottoms to replace those lost, an achievement which Germany was in no way able to duplicate.

The *Emden* and the *Karlsruhe* were the most successful of these early German commerce raiders, together sinking more than 145,000 tons of British shipping—approximately two-thirds of all that was accounted for by German cruisers through the first six months of war. (Of course when the later submarine campaigns began in earnest these surface ship records were eclipsed; several individual German U-boat commanders sank at least twice as much tonnage as had either of these cruisers.)

As related earlier, on August 14, 1914 von Spee had detached the *Emden* and a fast collier from his squadron, then in the Marianas. "Proceed to the Indian Ocean and wage cruiser warfare to the best of ability," he had ordered Captain Karl von Müller.[12] The *Emden* entered the Indian Ocean and on September 5 began raider operations against important Allied trade routes. Aided by a dummy stack to simulate the appearance of a four-stack British county-class cruiser, the *Emden* within a week had destroyed four British merchant ships and captured two others for use as a supply train. In alarm, the Australian government held up the sailing of the New Zealand and Australian army convoys.

Von Müller then shifted area, both to attack a fresh region of trade and to avoid being tracked down by superior enemy force. He turned to the west and struck against the Burma Oil Company at Madras, firing 130 shells and setting ablaze two quarter-million-gallon oil storage tanks. "I had the bombardment in mind purely as a demonstration to induce the Indians to demand their freedom, to ruin British trade, and to shatter British prestige...", von Müller later stated.[13] Although he scarcely succeeded in any of these objectives he may be said to be one of the naval pioneers in psychological warfare.

The *Emden* then cruised in the area south of Colombo, Ceylon, where she captured seven and sank six British merchantmen. After this von Müller coaled and cleaned ship's bottom at the lonely island of Diego Garcia. Here the seldom-visited inhabitants, who were British subjects, had received no news of the existence of war; this condition of ignorance the German visitors were most careful not to disturb. The makeshift overhaul of the *Emden* is a tribute to German ingenuity. But it also illustrates the difficulties of a raider whose country does not control numerous and accessible fixed bases.

On October 28 the *Emden* again made an attack on a land objective, this time against

[12] Erich Raeder, *The War at Sea*, 5 vols. (Washington, 1923), II, Part I, 12.

[13] *Ibid.*, 41.

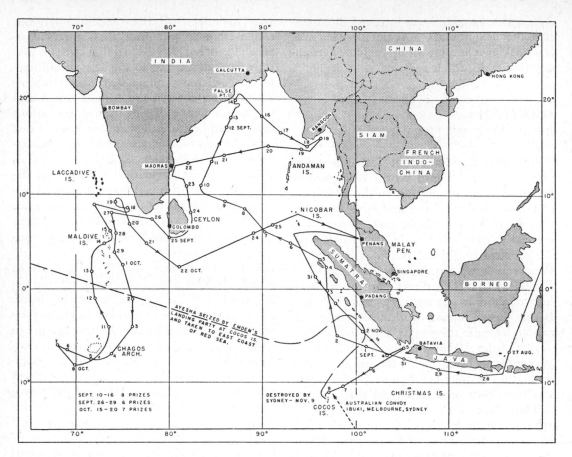

CRUISE OF THE EMDEN, *SEPTEMBER 1 - NOVEMBER 9, 1914*

Penang Harbor on the west coast of the Malay Peninsula. Here von Müller surprised and sank in the early morning hours the Russian light cruiser *Zhemchug* and the French destroyer *Mousquet.* This was the high tide of his success.

His next and final objective was to the southward, the British cable and radio station in the Cocos-Keeling island group. On November 9 a landing party from the *Emden* went over the side equipped to cut cable connections with Australia, South Africa, and the Dutch East Indies. However, the alert radio operator had ample time to send off a message that a strange ship was off the harbor entrance. Von Müller did not have the same luck as the *Goeben* and the

Breslau in having no powerful enemy within dangerous proximity when they were located. An Anzac troop convoy was only 50 miles away, en route to Colombo; an escorting cruiser, the *Sydney,* was detached to investigate the radio report. The Germans' first intimation of their danger was the sight of this superior enemy vessel charging over the horizon toward them at express speed. The *Sydney* made short work of the unfortunate *Emden.* She quickly established the advantage of her 6-inch guns over the 4.1-inch batteries of the German ship, and on the second salvo obtained two damaging hits. For an hour and a half the *Sydney* poured salvo after salvo into the *Emden,* which fought back bravely but futilely. At the end of this time the raider was a complete wreck, beached on a reef, her hull a sieve, her funnels demolished, foremast knocked over the side, and topsides a bloody shambles. "I held the greatest possible range in order to make use of the advantage of the greater range of my guns," victorious Captain Glossop of the *Sydney* later told interviewers.[14] As in the Falklands action the gunnery of the superior force had not been particularly good, but Glossop, like Sturdee, had adopted a no-risk policy, and did not need to care how much time or how many rounds it took to carry out his mission.

The *Emden* had performed creditable service for Germany in her three-month, 30,-000-mile cruise. She had sunk or captured 70,000 tons of Allied merchantmen. She had diverted scores of Allied warships from other important assignments to try to track her down, and she had delayed ship sailings in her known areas of operations.

The second outstandingly successful raider was the *Karlsruhe,* a new, fast cruiser of a transition type of engineering, with 12 coal-burning firerooms and four burning oil. At the start of the war she left the Bahamas to make an almost barren cruise in the Middle Atlantic. She then shifted to a more active and profitable area to the northeast of Cape San Roque, off Natal, Brazil on the main meat and grain trade route from South America to Europe. There between August 31 and October 24, 1914 she sank or captured 14 British ships.

Captain Kohler then decided to make a surprise attack against the Bahamas. As the *Karlsruhe's* bow was cutting its way through smooth water on the afternoon of November 4 she was suddenly torn in two by a terrific internal explosion of unknown origin, which killed the captain and 261 others. The Germans successfully concealed this loss from the British for many months, while Allied cruisers continued to search and sailings were arranged with due regard to her possible presence.

The *Karlsruhe* too had done well. The value of ships and cargoes which she had destroyed was estimated at about $1,500,-000. The Germans also derived two valuable war cruise lessons from her experiences. These were that a commerce-raider should limit the use of radio as much as possible to reception only, and that future surface cruisers should have seaplanes for scouting. As a result of the recommendation of Captain Kohler, the raider *Wolf,* which operated in 1916, was so equipped, and found this innovation very valuable.

Four other cruisers of commerce-destruction in 1914 merit mention, although their combined sinkings amounted to less than those of either the *Emden* or the *Karlsruhe.* The *Kronprinz Wilhelm* accounted for about 30,000 tons of British shipping before she sought internment in Norfolk in April 1915. It was simply the lack of German logistic and base support that caused this warship to seek neutral sanctuary rather than risk probable swift destruction. The *Dresden* sank 11,000 tons, and the *Leipzig* another 10,000 in operations before they joined von Spee's force. The *Kaiser Wilhelm der Grosse* was destroyed off Spanish Morocco in the first month of the war after having sunk 10,000 tons.

Taken as a whole, German surface cruiser warfare in 1914 was a failure—a gallant gesture perhaps, but not worth the cost in ships and men. After four months of combat, the British had pretty well tidied up the outer oceans. As the submarine menace was not yet serious, Winston Churchill was able to say that for the first time in the war the Royal Navy actually had a surplus of certain classes of vessels. Such adventures as the Dardanelles campaign became possible for the Allies. There was no serious threat to British sea lanes in the North Atlantic, the South Atlantic, the Pacific, or the Indian Ocean. Outside of the North Sea, only in the Mediterranean was there even the possibility of serious surface ship opposition. But the ominous shadow of the periscope was soon to darken and eclipse this temporarily serene naval outlook; it was in fact to threaten British survival.

---

[14] *Ibid.,* 99.

THE
DOGGER BANK ACTION,
JANUARY 24, 1915

Early in the winter of 1914-1915 there was some North Sea activity by both combatants but no significant encounter. In mid-December the German battle cruisers bombarded the Yorkshire coast, then returned safely to port. On January 19 Beatty's battle cruisers, supported by his own light cruisers and the Harwich destroyer and submarine force, made a fruitless sweep west of Heligoland Bight.

As a direct result of this British sortie and the continuation of their scouting operations in the Dogger Bank area, Admiral von Ingenohl ordered Vice Admiral Hipper to sea on January 23. Hipper's line was to consist of three battle cruisers and one armored cruiser; his support force would be a half dozen light cruisers and over a score of destroyers. Hipper's orders were to scout the Dogger Bank. The Germans hoped that in the early hours of January 24 this strong force might intercept and destroy any British scouts in the area.

Essentially, the German plan was a simplified version of the British operation plan in the Heligoland Bight action: to bring a superior concentration against enemy light units by securing surprise. However, unknown to the Germans, the British had by luck gained a secret advantage that almost precluded the possibility of their catching the British unawares. Early in the war, the Russians had captured the hulk of the German light cruiser *Magdeburg,* which had grounded in the Baltic. A Russian diver, recovering bodies in the shallow water around the vessel to give them suitable burial, brought up a dead German lieutenant still clutching the lead covers of a confidential publication. Further search on the bottom revealed a water-logged but still legible code book, including a grid of the North Sea similar to that used by German submarines in locating and transmitting chart positions. The Russian command wisely turned over this priceless find to the British Admiralty, then blessed with one of the finest intelligence services in the world. The result was that for most of the rest of the war, the British navy was well informed in advance whenever the High Seas Fleet planned an operation.

The Germans never radically changed their basic coding system. British radio direction finder stations, which dotted their east coast from Scotland to Kent, picked up a majority of German surface and submarine dispatches, pinpointed their origins, and quickly forwarded them to the Admiralty for decoding and possible action.

So it was that British radio intelligence intercepted and decoded the message to Hipper ordering a sortie. And so it was that 15 minutes after the Germans cleared the Jade in the late afternoon of January 23, Beatty was leaving the Firth of Forth with his five battle cruisers [15] and Commodore Goodenough's First Light Cruiser Squadron. Beatty's three newest battle cruisers had a few knots of speed advantage, and mounted 13.5-inch main batteries in contrast to Hipper's 11- and 12-inch guns. The Germans however had slightly heavier armor protection; and they possessed somewhat better shells, gun mounts permitting greater elevation, and superior fire control apparatus.

Beatty and Goodenough were directed to rendezvous with Commodore Tyrwhitt's Harwich force of three light cruisers and 30 destroyers early the next morning about 30 miles north of the Dogger Bank and some 180 miles west of Heligoland—the position where Hipper was expected to be at that time, calculated with remarkable accuracy. For protection of the British east coast, and for distant support to the intercepting force, seven obsolescent *King Edward*-class battleships put to sea from Rosyth. And Jellicoe brought the Grand Fleet out from its anchorage at Scapa Flow. As at Heligoland Bight the British were favored by the advantage of surprise and by a skillful plan which they took pains not to reveal, observing absolute radio silence until they should sight their adversaries. But in this second

---

[15] The *Lion* (flagship), *Tiger, Princess Royal, New Zealand,* and *Indomitable.*

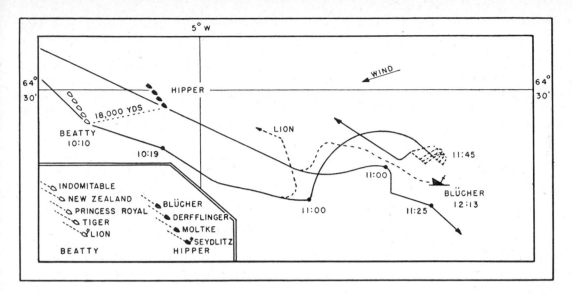

DOGGER BANK ACTION, JANUARY 24, 1915

North Sea encounter the British were once more to experience tactical confusion: failures in communications and a misinterpretation of Beatty's objective by his second-in-command were to snatch away the chance of a major victory.

Just before seven in the morning, on a calm sea with a light breeze from the northeast and good visibility, Beatty, Goodenough, and Tyrwhitt reached the intercepting position. A few minutes later, as if on order of the British Admiralty, Hipper's force came steaming northwest. Recognizing the telltale tripod masts of the British battle cruisers when about 25,000 yards distant, the Germans quickly reversed course and sped to the southeast, attempting to escape from Beatty and reach the haven of their base. Hipper's flagship, the *Seydlitz*, took the lead in the retreat, followed in order by the other battle cruisers, the *Moltke* and the *Derfflinger*, with the older and slower armored cruiser *Blücher*, whose side armor was from five to seven inches thinner than that of the battle cruisers, tagging along behind.

British engineering capabilities soon began to tell: the three new battle cruisers successfully met the challenge of Beatty's orders for more and more speed, increasing to 27, then 28, and finally 29 knots. As was to be expected, the slower *New Zealand* and *Indomitable* began to fall somewhat behind. A little before nine the *Lion* opened with slow and deliberate fire, following the post-Heligoland Bight fire doctrine. Ranging salvos splashed close to the unfortunate *Blücher,* as yet the only enemy within shot. As the British gained, the *Lion* obtained her first hit on the armored cruiser. Hipper's destroyers laid down a protective smoke screen, and the Germans shifted course to the east. For a time the smoke was to hamper the gunnery of both sides.

Presently the gap between the opposing forces was enough reduced that the *Lion* was able to shift target to the *Derfflinger,* number three in the German line, while the newly commissioned *Tiger* [16] took the *Blücher* under fire. As Beatty's force continued to gain on the enemy, the commander signaled by flag hoist, "Engage your opposite number." The *Tiger*'s captain, realizing there were five British vessels to four German, and erroneously assuming the rearmost, the *Indomitable,* was in range of her oppo-

---

[16] The *Tiger* in this action was the only British battle cruiser equipped with the director system of central fire control.

site, the *Blücher,* began counting from the rear forward. He concluded that the *New Zealand* was to fire on the *Derfflinger* and the *Princess Royal* on the *Moltke,* allowing the *Tiger* and the *Lion* to concentrate on the leading *Seydlitz.* He therefore laid his sights on the *Seydlitz.* Because of this faulty fire distribution the *Moltke* had no opponent for several minutes. Actually, the *New Zealand* took as target the *Blücher;* the *Princess Royal,* the *Derfflinger;* the *Tiger* and *Lion,* the *Seydlitz;* and nobody took the *Moltke.*

Meanwhile the retiring German battle cruisers all concentrated on the *Lion,* hoping thereby to knock her out. But before they succeeded, a 13.5-inch British shell struck the *Seydlitz* astern, penetrating an after turret and setting fire to charges in the reloading room below. Flames flashed through this turret, passing down into the ammunition chamber, into the adjacent ammunition space, and up into the other stern turret. In an instant 159 men died in these seared spaces. Smoke and flame rose 200 feet above the vessel. Explosion of her after magazines was only prevented by a petty officer's prompt action in flooding them.

Just after this the Germans obtained their first damaging hit on the *Lion,* ripping through the top of her "A" turret—the first indication that the horizontal armor protection of the British battle cruisers was inadequate. Within the next hour concentrated, accurate German fire put Beatty's flagship out of action and led to the series of events which were to permit Hipper to escape with the loss of only one vessel. The *Seydlitz* holed the *Lion's* port condenser feed-water tank with a hit. Later two *Derfflinger* shells struck her port side at the waterline, smashing in armor plate and causing extensive flooding. Shortly before eleven Beatty signaled the *Indomitable* to attack the *Blücher,* by this time a flaming hulk, listing and swinging out of line to the north, well behind Hipper's battle cruisers. Then the *Lion* was struck by several shells in quick succession, whereupon she was forced to secure her port engine, her speed dropped to 15 knots, and she took on a 10-degree list to port. At this moment her lookouts reported, "Submarines off the starboard

bow." This information, later proved false, caused Beatty to order his entire squadron to turn eight points to port.

The command crisis was now at hand. Beatty, as his flagship was obliged to fall out of the battle line, made three final flag signals: "Course northeast," "Attack the enemy rear," and "Keep closer to the enemy." With the line steaming almost directly into the wind, the flags were very hard to make out from positions astern of the flagship. Only the first two signals were seen and read by the other battle cruisers. Rear Admiral Archibald Moore, who assumed command, was well back in the line in the *New Zealand.* He completely misunderstood Beatty's intentions: to leave the already wrecked *Blücher* to the *Indomitable* and the light cruisers, and to press on with the *Tiger, Princess Royal,* and *New Zealand* after the three German battle cruisers, one of which was known to be severely damaged. Moore did not know that an imagined submarine contact had caused Beatty's port turn and supposed it was to make certain that the *Blücher* did not get away. Moreover he saw this cruiser bearing northeast, the course Beatty had last signaled. Obeying what he believed to be unequivocal commands, Moore led the entire line to join the light cruisers and overwhelm the *Blücher* in a tornado of shells. The chance of a major British victory was thereby lost.

Beatty was thunderstruck. As he later remarked to his Flag Captain, A. E. M. Chatfield, "Four we ought to have got . . . we had them beat, another half-hour would have done it, when the old *Lion* was done. My feelings when 'the merry hunt went heedless sweeping by,' and then swept in the wrong direction, was more than words can describe." [17] While Hipper was making good his escape the *Blücher* went down after a gallant, hopeless fight.[18] The British dragged

---

[17] *The Naval Memoirs of Admiral of the Fleet Sir Roger Keyes* (New York, 1934), I, 163.

[18] Before she plunged, an enterprising British photographer obtained one of the war's most vivid action shots, later widely publicized, showing her listing over on her port side, survivors clinging to her side, underwater hull exposed, and guns pointing crazily skyward.

260 shivering survivors from the icy water before a German plane appeared and began dropping bombs—the first air attack on naval craft of the war. A zeppelin also approached, and the rescue mission had to be abandoned.

Meanwhile Beatty transferred to the destroyer *Attack,* and began to close at flank speed on his retiring battle cruisers. Moore had broken off the action, and the line was on a northwesterly course. Beatty raised his flag in the *Princess Royal,* but concluded that now further pursuit would be fruitless as well as dangerous. The fleeing Germans had a long lead, and the High Seas Fleet might by now be well on the way. But the *Blücher* was gone, the *Seydlitz* badly damaged; almost a thousand German seamen had perished.

Technically victorious, as at Heligoland Bight, the British had lost a chance of a much greater victory because of faulty communications. The near-loss of the *Lion* should have taught a lesson, which in fact was not digested until after the experiences of Jutland: in long range action, high angle, plunging fire is most likely to produce hits on the horizontal surfaces of the target. Turret tops should carry at least as much protective armor as the vertical sides of the turrets and the barbettes, if not more. Also, flameproof scuttles between handling rooms and magazines are essential safety features. The Germans learned; the British did not. The British did however hasten to install directors and central fire control in all their battle cruisers. Engineering performance of the new British battle cruisers had proved superb.

On the other hand the Germans had good reason to be proud of the stoutness of construction of their battle cruisers. The *Seydlitz* in particular had taken the kind of punishment that might have been expected to sink a dreadnought. Yet she made it back to her anchorage under her own power at only slightly reduced speed. The *Seydlitz'* captain reported that his ammunition allowance had been insufficient, only 200 rounds remaining; he might even have run out if the action had not been broken off. His recommendation for more ammunition and more magazine space for the German battle cruisers was ap-

proved, and acted on. The German command strengthened their battle cruisers' side plating and turret tops, and improved their magazine systems and practices to reduce the chance of flashback.

Tactically, the Germans were obviously at fault in sending the obsolescent *Blücher* along with the faster battle cruisers. Hipper, in his action report, strongly recommended that in the future only fast, efficient vessels be included in the battle cruiser scouting force. In fact, of course, the sacrifice of the *Blücher* had contributed to Hipper's escape. The British had erred in placing their second in command in their next-to-slowest battle cruiser. There is considerable doubt that the *New Zealand* could have kept up in a prolonged chase.

The Dogger Bank action cost Admiral von Ingenohl his job. Incorrectly anticipating that the German battle cruisers would be engaging inferior British forces, he had not arranged to support Hipper. Earlier he had failed to have battle cruisers available for action at Heligoland Bight. Admiral von Pohl, who succeeded him in command of the German Fleet, was advised by the Emperor to be more cautious than his predecessor.

From the Heligoland Bight and the Dogger Bank actions the British had obtained substantial evidence of the pitfalls of deficient planning and faulty communications in battle. To be sure, in the earlier battle their failure to advise all commanders of their revised plan of operation had been less costly than might have been expected. In the latter, unintentional ambiguity in communications and the failure of signalmen to receive Beatty's all-important third message had limited the achievement. At Heligoland Bight, Beatty had made his bold decision to close, and it was simple to effect. But at Dogger Bank a more complex situation had been mishandled. As in many other naval engagements before and since, divided objectives and lack of clarity in communications trimmed the margin of victory. The need was apparent for more emphasis on operational training in command and communications. In wartime, of course, especially in new ships of new types, this is not easy to obtain.

Cruiser operations in distant and home waters in 1914 and 1915 had been unfavorable to Germany. Their single victory at Coronel had been more than canceled out by defeat at the Falklands. The British had inflicted humiliating ship losses in the North Sea, obtaining tactical victories and increasing the Germans' caution in employing surface units. The Kaiser's capital ships would now remain quietly in port until the spring of 1916. The Royal Navy, heir to the great traditions of Blake and Nelson, had met the new challenge of the Age of Steel, and driven the enemy from the seas.

28

The Dardanelles-

Gallipoli Campaign

WHEREVER ALLIED POLICY-makers turned at the end of 1914, some enemy power held the initiative. On the Eastern Front Germany and Austria had blunted Russia's initial offensive. German naval power centered on the Kiel Canal blocked trade between Russia and her western allies; and Turkey, by closing the Dardanelles, had completed Russia's isolation from the West. Turkey's decision to join Germany, moreover, influenced the Balkan States. Bulgaria, though still neutral, was leaning toward Germany, thereby threatening embattled Serbia and keeping Romania out of the Allied camp. Greece teetered on the fence, ready to be influenced either way. The Western Front had become an entrenched line meandering some 450 miles from Belgium's North Sea coast to the Franco-Swiss border. Defending this line had already absorbed French resources and demanded more men and munitions than Britain could afford. At sea the Allied picture was equally disturbing. The German High Seas Fleet was closer than the Grand Fleet to London and the Straits of Dover, and an advanced German naval base at Ostend threatened cross-Channel communications between England and France. The Allies clearly had to buttress the Western Front, shore up beleaguered Russia, and insure their vital sea lanes.

FLEET ASSAULT OF THE DARDANELLES— THE PROBLEM

Since Britain's navy remained the best Allied hope for regaining the lost initiative, the burden of devising an effective Allied strategy rested squarely upon the British Cabinet. However, neither the Cabinet nor any other agency was fully prepared for strategic planning. For some ten years both British military services had devoted maximum energy to producing weapons but had neglected the machinery for analyzing strategic problems or executing policy decisions in an effective manner. In short, Britain at the outbreak of war found herself with excellent military equipment but without techniques for making it produce satisfactory results. The Cabinet soon came to grips with this problem however and as a preliminary step delegated decision on all military policy to a streamlined sub-cabinet called the War Council. At Council meetings Prime Minister Herbert Asquith presided, and the armed forces were represented by Field Marshal Lord Horatio Kitchener, Minister for War, and by Winston Churchill, First Lord of the Admiralty. Since the Council, with no staff of its own, had to rely for staff work upon the War Office or the Admiralty, these two agencies tended to mold Council policy. Moreover, though not themselves members of the War Council, senior officers from both War Office and Admiralty attended meetings as professional advisers.

Lord Kitchener, refusing to delegate authority and acting as a sort of combined Secretary of War and Army Chief of Staff, was, in effect, the War Office. His monolithic control backed by his great prestige as England's foremost soldier gave his utterances weight before the War Council. Churchill's words carried no such weight, for the Admiralty had begun to shift to the decentralized organization soon to be adopted in the United States Navy Department. The position of the First Lord resembled that of the American Secretary of the Navy, while Admiral of the Fleet Lord John Fisher as First Sea Lord held a position similar to that later assigned to the U. S. Chief of Naval Operations. This evolution however had not progressed far enough to produce either clear lines of authority or smooth teamwork within the Admiralty. Here top officers still found themselves preoccupied with details of daily operations and thus too busy for orderly long-range planning. In consequence by the end of 1914 Admiralty policymaking became a contest of wills between 40-year-old Churchill and 73-year-old Fisher, and the War Council aggravated the conflict by frequently expecting Churchill to win Fisher's support. Lord Kitchener, on the contrary, so overshadowed his adviser from the War Office that he spoke alone for the Army. Thus in purely strategic decisions he held the balance of power, for he could support either Churchill, his Cabinet colleague, or Fisher, his opposite number in the armed services. It was these three men, all aggressive and determined, who conditioned the War Council's approach to a new Allied strategy for 1915.

Lord Kitchener focused his main attention on the static Western Front because he held that events there would decide the war. He favored any fleet operation that might distract German attention but insisted that no naval effort should divert either Allied troops or munitions from France. Lord Fisher also held that the decision must come in the west but instead of a massed assault on German trenches he favored expanding amphibious actions aimed first at Germany's sea flank in the North Sea, and later at her rear areas along the Baltic. Always aware of the danger from Germany's strong High Seas Fleet, Fisher strove to confine Britain's important naval effort to waters dominating German naval bases at both ends of the Kiel Canal. From the day he took office in November 1914 Fisher worked vigorously to promote a series of amphibious assaults along Germany's marginal seas which could lead eventually to a Russo-British landing on Baltic beaches behind Berlin. At first Churchill seemed to favor some of Fisher's sea-flank projects, but at the same time he wanted the fleet to neutralize a Turkish threat against the Suez Canal. However, by the end of 1914 it was clear that Kitchener would not approve Fisher's "Northern Project" because its amphibious assaults implied diverting Allied troops from France, and for different reasons Churchill too began to frown on the Fisher program. The Prime Minister shrank from the high initial losses inherent in all improvised amphibious assaults, and Churchill must have shared his view, for in December he wrote Fisher, "I am shy of landing under fire—unless there is no other way."

In Churchill's opinion the "other way" consisted in relying exclusively on the power of naval gunfire. He argued that conditions of war in 1914 invalidated lessons from the past and, like many other brilliant men, he placed absolute faith in a dramatic new weapon—in his case the heavy-caliber naval gun. Personal experience during the October Belgian campaign persuaded the First Lord that German siege artillery alone had eliminated strong forts, so he asserted that unsupported naval guns could destroy forts commanding Europe's marginal seas. Unfortunately Churchill's assumption rested on faulty evidence, for he had been too busy in Belgium to observe that German infantry supported the siege guns and occupied the forts immediately after the bombardment. Yet despite its faulty foundation, Churchill's radical gunfire doctrine enjoyed great surface appeal because it seemed to afford naval diversions that would neither cost many lives nor withdraw Allied troops from France.

And so the matter stood on New Year's Day 1915. The War Council refused to reject Army plans for a major 1915 effort on the Western Front, refused to approve any formal campaign against Germany's sea flank, and refused even to consider any project that diverted dreadnought strength from the Grand Fleet. In their collective effect these negative actions established a favorable climate for the Dardanelles decision.

THE DECISION

Positive decision of some sort became inevitable on January 2, 1915, when Russia asked for an immediate British diversion in the Aegean to weaken a Turkish advance through the Caucasus. The next day Kitchener induced Churchill to agree that the fleet could create a diversion at the Dardanelles without army support. Then Kitchener promised Russia that the Allies would make a show of force in the Aegean. Even though the War Council had not acted on the matter, Kitchener's action committed Britain to a purely naval operation against Turkey. Logic selected the Dardanelles as the Turks' most sensitive spot, and Kitchener had challenged Churchill to complete the job without army help. The Admiralty accepted Kitchener's challenge and began forthwith to grind out a tactical solution.

Lord Fisher moved immediately from his role as War Council adviser on strategic decision to the First Sea Lord's traditional job of submitting tactical plans. On January 4 he wrote "Dear Winston" an informal memorandum that recognized Constantinople as the campaign objective and outlined steps for securing it. The First Sea Lord assumed that Russia would cooperate in the assault on Constantinople. He proposed to supplement Russia's effort from the Black Sea with prompt Allied landings to secure both shores of the Dardanelles mouth, followed immediately by pre-dreadnoughts which would pass up the Straits and enter the Sea of Marmora below Constantinople. Fisher insisted that the pre-dreadnoughts could not fulfill their part of the mission unless at least 75,000 British troops supported them by dominating high land along the Straits. He asserted that weapons and supplies for the troops should be combat loaded in England, and that the troops should land immediately on reaching the assault area. (See map, p. 502.)

To emphasize the overriding need for mutual support between land and sea elements of an amphibious force, Fisher insisted that naval gunfire alone could not carry a fleet through the Straits. Success, he said, hinged on two conditions. The operation must begin promptly, and the combined force must have a single commander. "In the history of the world," Fisher concluded, "a Junta has never won. . . . You need *one* man." A few days after Fisher's analysis reached him, Churchill read a memorandum from Admiral Sir Henry Jackson, another of his Admiralty advisers. Jackson supplemented Fisher's analysis by focusing upon the objective. He said that even if ships should pass through the Dardanelles into the Sea of Marmora, they could win no substantial objective without support from ground forces protecting their supply line. In supporting this conviction Jackson said that unless ground forces controlled the high western shore of the Strait, mobile field artillery with plunging fire could shut out unarmed supply vessels and frustrate the effort to occupy Constantinople.

Despite this clear pattern of Admiralty staff advice for supporting ships with infantry, Churchill persisted in his assumption that naval guns alone would solve the Dardanelles problem. Without consulting his staff officers he telegraphed Vice Admiral S. H. Carden, British naval commander in the Aegean, for his opinion about forcing the Straits with naval firepower alone. Carden replied that he considered the prospects good, if he were allowed plenty of time and unlimited ammunition. This tentative answer prompted Churchill to ask Carden (in a wire that implied Fisher's approval) for a detailed plan. In reply Carden estimated that 18 heavy ships, 16 destroyers, and several minesweepers could begin to assault the Straits by mid-February of 1915. He set a month as the minimum time they might need to reach Constantinople, but offered no plan for taking or occupying the city. Indeed, he refused even to guess at the ammunition his limited objective would require. Carden summarized his plan by dividing the action it proposed into four separate steps:

(1) Destroy all forts at the Dardanelles entrance.

(2) Sweep mine fields as far as the Narrows, and reduce forts supporting them.

(3) Reduce forts and fixed torpedo tubes at the Narrows.

(4) Clear mine fields in the Narrows, eliminate mine fields and forts above the Narrows, enter the Sea of Marmora.

Carden's plan was far simpler than anything suggested by Admiralty staff officers but far less comprehensive. It assumed unlimited ammunition, ignored the danger from mobile artillery, merely sketched operations beyond the Narrows, and made no provision for taking or occupying Constantinople. Yet Carden's belief that unsupported naval gunfire could destroy the Dardanelles defenses coincided with Kitchener's wish and Churchill's assumption. So Churchill promptly set the Carden plan before the War Council—without any reference to the dissenting analyses by Fisher and others. The apparent simplicity of relying entirely upon naval gunfire appealed also to the War Council, for on January 13 it directed the Admiralty to ". . . prepare for a naval expedition in February to bombard and take the Gallipoli Peninsula with Constantinople as its objective." This directive did not set the Dardanelles campaign in motion, but was merely a War Council order that the Admiralty should prepare specific plans for a campaign aimed at Constantinople. A strict interpretation of the phrases "naval expedition" and "take the Gallipoli Peninsula" implied using infantry to support the fleet. Since Kitchener insisted that the army could spare no men, such support could come only from naval infantry. Thus in mid-January 1915 the War Council assigned to the Navy alone the job of clearing Turkish opposition from a sizable peninsula, merely as a preliminary step to the move against Constantinople.

Actually the Admiralty had some 12,000 naval infantrymen at its disposal. One-third of this force embraced four well-trained Royal Marine battalions, and an inexperienced Royal Naval Division provided eight additional battalions. For two weeks after the mid-January order, Fisher and many others pressed the view that fulfilling the War Council directive would require using this naval infantry to cooperate with the ships. Captain Herbert Richmond expressed their views in series of memoranda which stressed points raised in the following passage:

Until the batteries covering the approaches where you want transports to go are destroyed, you have not got command of the sea. . . . Also, until you have made navigation safe as regards to mines . . . , you cannot bring transports in. You cannot remove the mines except by sweeping, and you cannot sweep till the batteries are destroyed. . . . So long as there is an [enemy] army in the Gallipoli peninsula the Dardanelles Straits can never be a safe thoroughfare . . . , commanded as it would be by the field- and other guns entrenched on the heights. . . . The most recent experience . . . has shown that the capture of forts cannot be carried out by ships alone.

Yet in the face of such advice from his staff, Churchill refused to consider committing the Admiralty's naval infantry at the Dardanelles. He persisted in asserting that 20th century technology had invalidated all doctrine drawn from past experience. Finally the War Council resolved the issue at a meeting charged with suppressed drama.

On January 28, before the Council met, Prime Minister Asquith conferred with Churchill and Fisher about their differences over the Dardanelles plan. Asquith, apparently failing to perceive how important was the question of whether infantry should support ships, concluded that all of Fisher's objections flowed from the Admiral's obsession for a "Northern Project." So Asquith sided with Churchill at this conference and paved the way for the First Lord to say in full Council that the Admiralty approved Carden's plan. The War Council then directed the Admiralty to carry out Steps 1 and 2 of the Carden plan, and to pursue it further *only* if conditions inside the Straits should justify the cost. In reaching this decision the Council realized that it must supply enough troops to take and occupy Constantinople, if fleet units managed to reach the Sea of Marmora. During these deliberations Mr. Asquith did not call on Fisher for his opinion. Though the Admiral objected quietly to considering the Dardanelles project at that time, no councillor asked for his reasons. Once the Council reached its decision however, Fisher arose and moved toward the door, determined to resign as First Sea Lord. Before he reached the door, Kitchener overtook him, and after some earnest talk persuaded the Admiral to acquiesce. And thus was the decision reached for opening a route to Constantinople by using only the firepower of an Allied fleet.

This late January decision by the War Council closed two months' search for a 1915 strategy whereby the Allies might end a dangerous stalemate and seize the initiative. Through a series of negative decisions the Council had in mid-January made Constantinople a major 1915 objective. Yet two weeks later it converted the hope for quick and decisive action into a mere reconnaisance in force, to be broken off when it became too costly.

TURKEY'S SITUATION

Throughout its two months' deliberation the War Council had but a sketchy knowledge of events inside the Turkish Straits. The councillors knew that the Turkish government was disintegrating and that Germans had taken over many of its functions when Turkey joined the Central Powers. British intelligence reports suggested chaotic political conditions, exaggerated by friction between the German embassy staff and a German military mission sent to Turkey in 1913. Yet this very friction hampered the British, for some quirk of wartime intelligence furnished them messages between Berlin and its Turkish embassy, but denied them access to messages from the military mission to its superiors in Germany. So the War Council knew of the chaos in Constantinople, but not that General Otto Liman von Sanders, head of the German military mission, was emerging as the strong man who could keep Constantinople in Turkish hands.

Toward the end of 1914 General von Sanders foresaw an early collapse of the Turk campaign against Russia in the Caucasus, and expected its impending failure to inspire a Russo-Anglo-French attempt against Constantinople. Recognizing that city as the key to Turkish existence and a quiet Eastern Theater on Germany's flank, von Sanders bent all of his great energy to defending the capital. When 1915 dawned he was convinced that Constantinople could withstand either a Russian attack down the Bosporus or an Anglo-French attack up the Dardanelles. The three Allies could not win Constantinople, he reasoned, unless they coordinated simultaneous attacks from both directions—and even then only if Anglo-French ground forces should occupy Gallipoli. Thus von Sanders assigned a higher priority to defending the Bosporus and took command there in person. Immediately he withdrew troops from the coastal forts and trained them incessantly for a mobile campaign in which counterattacking infantry-artillery teams would disrupt any beachhead the Russians might establish.

Meanwhile Admiral Guido von Usedom

of the German embassy staff commanded the Dardanelles defenses. He did not anticipate an Allied landing on Gallipoli, so he invested his entire defensive strength in submarine mine fields and in the fortified positions that protected them. The forts, designed exclusively for fighting against ships, were not prepared to resist assault from the rear, nor did von Usedom hold out a mobile reserve to forestall enemy landing parties that might try to work behind his forts. Instead he complained bitterly to the German ambassador of severe shortages in mines, fortress ammunition, and experienced gunners, but help actually came from von Sanders. During an inspection trip through Asia Minor the General had army engineers repair bridges on roads leading to the Dardanelles so that field artillery might move there by land from the Bosporus. The work could not be completed till late February, but then field guns from von Sanders' army would reinforce the forts defending von Usedom's submarine mines, and offset his shortage of ammunition and fortress gunners. Yet so secretly did von Sanders act that no hint of his moves to bolster von Usedom reached the War Council. Thus, as Carden planned to destroy the Dardanelles forts by deliberate fire, von Usedom unexpectedly gained the means to make good his unbalanced defense.

So an odd twist of wartime intelligence, plus Churchill's refusal to support British ships with naval infantry, played right into von Usedom's hand. Defenses that intelligence reports called weak, grew strong as soon as von Sanders' Asiatic bridges came into use.

FLEET ASSAULT— PRELIMINARIES

After the War Council approved Carden's plan, it left all operational detail to Churchill and Kitchener. As before, the First Lord resisted staff pressure for sending Carden a large force of naval infantry, though he agreed that two battalions of Royal Marines should go out to the Aegean. Since the War Council had agreed that Army units ear-marked for taking Constantinople need not leave England till mid-March, Churchill's refusal to commit the naval infantry set March 20 as the earliest date for employing ground forces to cooperate with Carden's ships. Because he had so many details to handle, Churchill then put off preparing an advanced Aegean base to receive the troops, and Kitchener did not alert Army units for the Aegean till the Navy began activating a base to receive them. Nor did Kitchener require of his Quartermaster General the kind of combat-unit loading that was essential for any troops reaching the upper Aegean before an advanced base there could stage them. Considered collectively these negative decisions that deferred base development, troop movement, and combat-unit loading eliminated all possibility of modifying the Dardanelles plan before March 20. If unforeseen events forced Carden to use infantry in order to maintain schedule, he had to rely on his 2,000 marines supplemented by ships' landing parties.

Events leading directly to the Dardanelles assault began in mid-February when Commodore Roger Keyes joined Carden at Malta as his Chief of Staff. Keyes had only the four-day voyage from Malta to Tenedos for studying staff plans and renewing acquaintances with Carden's key officers. During the voyage Keyes had to refresh his knowledge of conditions inside the Straits and especially the area covered by Steps 1 and 2 of the plan, for conquest of the entire waterway depended upon the cost of completing those two phases of the operation.

As Keyes knew, the Dardanelles had all the characteristics of a river carrying water from the Marmora to the Aegean. Its streambed was 35 miles long and varied in width from 1,400 yards to four miles. At the mouth, Cape Helles on Gallipoli and Kum Kale on the Asiatic shore formed the entrance headlands. Two forts on each headland enjoyed interlocking fields of fire against approaching ships, both before and after they entered the Straits. Step 1 of the British plan called for destroying these forts by naval gunfire without infantry support. Once past the entrance headlands, the channel ran straight upstream for about 12 miles. Its steep western cliff offered many positions for small forts, broken ravines on the eastern bank provided ample cover for mobile field guns, and the channel itself could accommodate mines. Above this 12-mile stretch was the Narrows, a short dog-leg less than a mile wide and with a 5-knot current. High on the Gallipoli shore at the Narrows turn was Kilid Bahr plateau, mounting guns that dominated the approach. These guns, supplemented by others in Fortress Chanak directly across the channel, could fire some 12,000 yards downstream and protect the mine field. So to fulfill Step 2 of the plan, Carden's force had to neutralize fortress guns at Kilid Bahr and Chanak as well as smaller pieces on both sides of the channel, and then sweep the mines.

Keyes agreed with Carden's staff that conquest of the entire waterway hinged on controlling the Narrows, that sweepers must remove mines before heavy ships could reach the Narrows, and that Kilid Bahr was the key for unlocking the mine field. Only after solving this intricate problem could Carden decide whether Step 3 of the plan was feasible.

FLEET ASSAULT—STEP 1

When Admiral Carden reached Tenedos late on February 18 he wasted no time brooding over his awesome task. Early next morning he dispatched six old battleships to bombard the four entrance forts. After many hours of leisurely fire from comfortable ranges had provoked no effective reply, the *Vengeance* moved in. As she closed the headlands Turk gunners in the higher fort on each side quickly left their cover and opened a heavy fire. By the time supporting vessels drove those gunners back to cover, the sun was so low that Carden withdrew all ships to Tenedos. Undaunted by this setback, by a whole flight of telegrams from Churchill, or by five days of bad weather, Carden renewed the attack on February 25. This time he coordinated fire and movement. As support ships fired steadily from medium range,

other vessels moved in close and hammered the forts. By 4 PM all four entrance forts were deserted and Carden considered Step 1 complete. He returned the heavy ships to Tenedos, leaving Vice Admiral John de Robeck (his second in command) at the entrance to begin minesweeping early next morning.

Admiral de Robeck sent sweepers into the Strait at dawn on the 26th, but British battleships, working without shore observers to spot the fall of shot, failed to silence Turk field artillery, and the wooden sweepers fell back after a mere four-mile advance. As the sweepers withdrew in confusion de Robeck observed that the preceding day's bombardment had failed to destroy all guns in the entrance forts. Realizing that their crews could return and reopen fire, he organized a demolition party for each headland and radioed Carden for a marine battalion to support each party. Though the Admiral had two marine battalions available, he decided to withhold them till next day. But de Robeck refused to wait and in late afternoon sent away his parties without infantry support, only to have them repulsed by Turks already filtering back into the forts. Bad weather delayed the next try till March 4, when demolition parties supported by company-strength marine units failed again. As Keyes watched the hard fighting near Kum Kale on the 4th, he observed somberly that it was "an object lesson in the folly of procrastination in war."

Actually this procrastination had cost far more than even Keyes imagined. Late in February Admiral von Usedom had renewed his plaintive dispatches to Berlin, calling for more mines and fortress ammunition. When these requests fell into British hands they confirmed the Kitchener-Churchill assumption that naval gunfire alone could win the Dardanelles. Yet the British leaders did not know that on March 1 a field artillery regiment from the Bosporus moved over the bridges von Sanders' engineers had repaired, and began filtering into good positions on both sides of the Dardanelles. Their fire had played the major role in repulsing Carden's landing parties on the 4th.

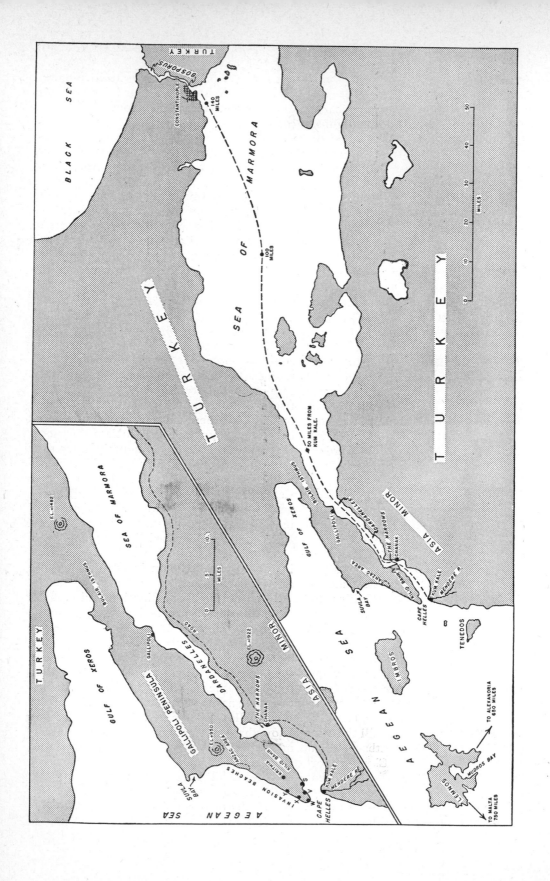

THEATER OF THE DARDANELLES-GALLIPOLI CAMPAIGN

Admiral Carden's fatal indecision about committing his marines grew in some degree from the fact that he too had begun to question the soundness of proceeding with naval gunfire alone. On February 19, after his initial bombardment failed, Carden began to look ahead toward Step 2 and the problem of destroying Turk guns on lofty Kilid Bahr. Several days later he telegraphed Churchill for an army unit from Egypt to land on Gallipoli and take the key plateau from its weak land side. The First Lord demurred and suggested that Carden land fleet infantry inside the Strait where it might scale Kilid Bahr's steep cliff. Unsatisfied with the Churchillian solution, the Admiral persuaded a visiting general from Egypt to offer 10,000 men for a landing on Gallipoli. At that point Kitchener refused, but authorized the general to lend Carden troops for a landing inside the Straits. By then Carden's experience on March 4 had convinced him that infantry could not land inside the Straits in the face of Turkish field artillery. Thus false optimism in London, engendered by incomplete information, frustrated Carden's belated effort to bring in the army ahead of schedule.

In that atmosphere Step 1 ended. Naval gunfire had shattered masonry and driven gunners to cover but had not dismounted all guns defending the entrance. Whenever Allied ships entered the Dardanelles after March 1, covering vessels stood by to neutralize the Turkish guns still emplaced.

FLEET ASSAULT—STEP 2

During the first week in March, while von Sanders' regiment of field artillery completed its movement into good firing positions on both sides of the waterway, Carden began the preliminaries to Step 2 of his plan. As in the initial bombardment on February 19, this effort comprised a series of uncoordinated attacks.

On the night of March 1-2, wooden sweepers covered by destroyers reached a point 9,000 yards below Chanak and Kilid Bahr, but increasing current and artillery fire stopped them there. During daylight hours battleships took up the fight. For two days the *Queen Elizabeth,* sent to the Straits for her shakedown, fired ineffectually across Gallipoli toward the Narrows forts. She had gotten off only 36 rounds when Turk field guns drove her out of range late in the second afternoon. Meanwhile other battleships entered the Straits. On March 7 two of these ships took station 12,000 yards below the Narrows, steaming back and forth across the channel till their fire completely dominated gun crews at the Narrows. Yet Carden failed to exploit this effective fire by using daylight sweeps to bring his battleships to short range. That night a single Turkish vessel, covered by darkness and the field guns, laid a string of 24 mines on the edge of the channel and directly athwart the course the bombarding battleships had used. Though ignorant of this achievement, Carden and his staff realized that they must devise more effective doctrine if they were to pass a 9,000-yard mine field against the 4-knot current.

With Churchill growling for results, Keyes finally induced his admiral to combine battleships, destroyers, and minesweepers in a series of night sorties, thereby applying inside the Straits the same kind of coordinated fire-and-movement he had used to weaken the entrance forts. Heroic effort on each night from March 10 through 16 produced meager results. Armored vessels suffered little from field artillery but could not neutralize it without shore spotters. The wooden sweepers were so battered, or their crews so demoralized, that 16 of the 24 mines laid on March 7 remained unswept and unsuspected. In the face of such difficulties the fleet effort approached its climax.

On March 16 Churchill wired Carden that the time had come for a determined and coordinated daylight assault, but he insisted that the Admiral should not risk a headlong rush through the Narrows. If this final fleet effort should fail to destroy both mine fields and batteries, Churchill's wire continued, Carden was to confer with General Sir Ian Hamilton about using troops to outflank Kilid Bahr. In spite of his strong professional opinion that Churchill's plan must fail, Carden replied immediately that the new assault would begin as soon as weather permitted. That decision marked Carden's final contribution to the campaign, for on the same day doctors insisted that he take an immediate and prolonged rest. The Admiral therefore resigned his command and the Admiralty put de Robeck in his place. The climactic operation both men had organized got under way on March 18.

At 11:30 AM on the 18th, as soon as light conditions permitted, six heavy British ships opened fire on the Turks from a support line 14,000 yards below the Narrows. Disposed across the Strait at regular intervals, these vessels kept their bows upstream and used power to offset the current, so that they kept fairly regular station without anchoring. Though de Robeck, Keyes, and the staff exuded confidence, many junior officers and seamen sensed impending disaster. Even without being told, they saw that this day's work differed from earlier sporadic dueling at long range. The Turks too must have sensed a crisis, for their field guns proved even more persistent and elusive than before. Midshipmen posted in the tops to spot the fall of shot found their own fire too slow to keep pace with the rapidly shifting enemy guns. Yet, despite irritating casualties from the field pieces or heavier damage from the forts, Britain's six mighty gun platforms kept position while their shells harassed gun crews at the Narrows.

Shortly after noon four obsolete French battleships moved through the British support line and closed gradually to within 9,000 yards of Chanak and Kilid Bahr. They fired for two full hours while heavy shells made a shambles of their superstructures. Finally the French began to withdraw on schedule so that the British might take up their work. During this maneuver the *Bouvet*, already low in the water, struck one of the mines laid on the 7th and sank abruptly. She had been so battered that British observers attributed her loss to a lucky Turkish shot. A second French ship took so much punishment that she nearly sank before beaching herself outside the Strait. Undaunted by these French losses, the British support ships continued their deliberate fire as four of their sisters moved forward and fired steadily for two more hours. By 4 PM the Narrows forts were so thoroughly cowed that de Robeck ordered his sweepers forward to clear the way for point-blank fire. But he had underestimated the mobile artillery still active on his flanks. Even before minesweeping kites began to trail, the field guns so battered the wooden sweepers that not even heroic volunteers could make headway against their fire.

Since Churchill's orders explicitly forbade any advance while mine fields remained unbreached, de Robeck had only one choice. He recalled the bombarding ships. Scarcely had they begun to withdraw when the *Irresistible* struck a second of the mines laid on the 7th. As tenders took off her crew under accurate fire from the shore batteries, the *Ocean* struck a third in the fatal string of mines. Recovering her crew, as well as survivors from the broken sweepers, provided a brilliant vignette of British seamanship, but both the *Irresistible* and the *Ocean* sank.

Undismayed by their losses Keyes and the staff considered the enemy beaten. Keyes attributed the entire failure to inadequate minesweepers and, belatedly, began to modify destroyers for sweeping mines. He estimated that his new force would be ready by April 4 and urged the Admiral to renew the attack then. De Robeck was less sanguine. He had lost three major bombardment vessels, while two French battleships, a British battle cruiser, and his entire force of minesweepers needed dockyard repairs. On March 19 he concluded that battleships could not pass the Narrows while mines remained unswept, that sweeping could not succeed as long as field artillery infested the shoreline, and that only a substantial ground force in possession of Kilid Bahr could suppress the field guns. De Robeck reasoned further that even if armored ships could pass into the Sea of Marmora without silencing the field guns, supply vessels essential for taking Constantinople would suffer the same fate as had his wooden minesweepers. No matter how de Robeck turned his problem, he came to the same conclusion that Churchill's Admiralty advisers had reached in January. He must have ground support on Kilid Bahr before passing the Narrows. And like von Sanders, de Robeck believed that his battle squadron could win no useful objective before Constantinople without a safe line of supply.

Even as de Robeck reached this bitter decision, Sir Ian Hamilton wired Kitchener that a fleet could not pass the Narrows till the Army held Kilid Bahr. After previously rejecting similar advice before the reinforcing field artillery had reached the Straits, Kitchener agreed on the 20th to let Hamilton land on Gallipoli if the Navy asked for army help. Then for a week Churchill simply could not bring himself to make the request. In a furious flight of telegrams he pressed his admiral for a final effort when improvised minesweepers were ready—though Churchill still insisted on breaching the mine field before any heavy ship passed the Narrows. But de Robeck held to his professional judgment that naval gunfire alone could not open the way to Constantinople. Finally, on March 28, the First Lord agreed to postpone fleet action inside the Straits until army units reached Kilid Bahr.

Though few recognized it at the time, these Kitchener-Churchill decisions marked the end of naval surface action inside the Dardanelles. Von Sanders' single regiment of field artillery had thwarted Britain's effort to master Constantinople by unsupported naval gunfire.

AMPHIBIOUS ASSAULT OF GALLIPOLI—STRATEGY AND LOGISTICS

When Kitchener and Churchill decided to send troops onto Gallipoli they effected a major change in British policy. Back in January the War Council had authorized a mere naval reconnaissance in force up the Dardanelles, with a clear proviso that British forces should withdraw if they met unexpected opposition. So the new decision converted a tentative approach into all-out action, and since the War Council did not even meet during March or April, Kitchener and Churchill took the drastic new departure on their own responsibility. In sum, this momentous March decision actually effected three separate changes. It modified Allied war policy significantly by requiring simultaneous ground action in both Eastern and Western Theaters. In the Eastern Theater the decision imposed a major change in strategy by shifting from a fleet drive up the Dardanelles to an amphibious campaign across the Gallipoli Peninsula. The Churchill-Kitchener decision also established an entirely new logistic situation in the Aegean Theater by requiring the ground commander to improvise an amphibious force, and the sea commander to support it from advanced bases created for a much simpler mission. Actually, the logistic implications of the decision proved most significant—though the entire calculated risk hinged upon Hamilton's amphibious assault, that assault could be no more effective than the logistic foundation that supported it.

Considering logistics in its narrow sense, the March decision posed problems of bases and effective lines for supply. These questions embraced requirements for docking facilities, transports, and the method of loading them, as well as necessary ammunition, food, water, and medical facilities. Yet in a broader sense logistics also included problems like finding the necessary military units and training each of them for a specific mission. Each aspect of logistics raised difficult questions for a theater command shared nebulously by a general and an admiral, but the troop problem was most critical. For in 1915 Britain had neither an amphibious force-in-being nor even a body of amphibious doctrine adapted to 20th century technology. So unless Hamilton could promptly improvise an effective amphibious force, Turkey would contribute substantially to the German cause merely by neutralizing ground strength diverted to Gallipoli from the Allied front in France.

Dilatory British action before mid-March on base development and troop movement had played right into Turkey's hand. When Hamilton left for the Aegean on March 13 he did not anticipate any ground action for at least a month. So he took out with him neither a staff nor plans for employing the force he would command. Nor did the army Quartermaster General receive orders to deliver Hamilton's troops in a state of combat readiness to the advanced base at Mudros harbor on the island of Lemnos. Yet one week after Sir Ian left England an entirely new situation required prompt landing on Gallipoli. When the troops began to arrive at Mudros they had no baggage because it had been stowed on slower transports. Guns were separated from ammunition, primers were separated from shells, and the advanced Aegean base had no dock or shore facilities for combat-unit loading. In such logistic circumstances Hamilton had no alternative. He withdrew the early arrivals from Mudros and re-routed his other transports to Alexandria, almost 700 miles away. In Egypt his battalions unloaded on open docks, sorted men and equipment into combat units, and reloaded. This difficult operation occupied all hands for a full month. It left no time for adequate staff organization, staff planning, or tactical rehearsal—a serious deficiency since the British committee system for amphibious command requires extensive pre-assault conference among transport, naval gunfire, assault, and command echelons. So the crying need for prompt action induced Hamilton to commit an unpracticed team upon the most difficult of all military operations, and then hope that intuitive common sense would solve any unexpected problems.

General Hamilton's orders from Kitchener forced him to take this desperate calculated risk in the full knowledge that its outcome must depend in a large degree on how skillfully the Turks used their month of grace. So Turkish logistics, in terms of both supply lines and training, also had a measurable influence upon Hamilton's success in amphibious assault. Thus, even during its logistical preliminaries, the campaign pitted Hamilton against von Sanders, whom the Turkish government sent to Gallipoli on the very day Hamilton began his fateful move from Mudros to Egypt.

When von Sanders reached his new command on March 26 he found the troops tied to forts or committed to a narrow belt along the Dardanelles, leaving Gallipoli open to assault from the Aegean. Immediately he began to apply the same tactical pattern he had worked out for defending the Bosporus. Field artillery that had preceded him remained along the Strait as the cornerstone of its defense, for as long as mobile guns dominated the waterway Allied craft could not sweep mines, and Allied ships could not reach the Marmora. Yet even if a few armored vessels should push through, von Sanders knew that no supply ships could follow while his guns covered the waterway. Then, to protect these guns against attack mounted from beaches on the Aegean, the General promptly divided his infantry among three key positions. Relying on small outposts to watch likely landing spots, he disposed the rest of his troops about the three central positions, ready for prompt action as soon as Hamilton showed his hand. Then while the British devoted a month to combat-unit loading, German engineers improved key roads, reinforcements marched down from the Bosporus, and von Sanders' infantry trained incessantly for night marches and hard fighting.

The defenders had barely completed this most essential preparation when Hamilton's transports began to filter back into Mudros harbor. In Asia von Sanders had two Turkish divisions near Kum Kale to fend off any move against that flank. At the Bulair Isthmus, where Gallipoli joins Europe, two divisions guarded his other flank and the two remaining divisions of Turkish infantry had to protect the whole of Gallipoli. One Gallipoli division established a reserve near Cape Helles at Krithia village and from that hub projected many small detachments to watch 45 miles of shoreline from the Cape to Suvla Bay. The second Gallipoli division continued its training near Kilid Bahr, ready to move promptly against any hostile force threatening that key terrain feature. These six Turkish divisions mustered a total of

45,000 effective riflemen. They lacked grenades or aircraft and were critically short of ammunition, entrenching tools, and artillery. Clothing was so scarce that company officers frequently commandeered sandbags to supplement the men's uniforms. Yet a month of hard training had instilled in them the conviction that all hands must stand firm and make do with what they had.

The waterway covered by this thin screen provided the interior line of communication such a defensive disposition required. It served both as a supply link to Constantinople and for converging reinforcements on any point Hamilton chose to assail. Yet, though the waterway remained von Sanders' main line of supply, the Asiatic road net his engineers had repaired provided a workable alternate route. If Hamilton tried to move up the Asiatic shore, Turks garrisoned in Asia Minor could use those roads to harass the British right flank. If British submarines cut the waterway north of Gallipoli or if Hamilton made Bulair a base for field guns to curtail Turk shipping, Kilid Bahr and her defenders could draw resources across the Strait from the Asiatic road net. Above Kilid Bahr the terrain was so rough that even should British troops seize Bulair they could not effect an overland raid against the anchor of von Sanders' defense, and broad shallows off the Aegean's shore eliminated Bulair itself as a potential advanced base for marching overland to Constantinople. So logistic factors made Kilid Bahr a fortress that the Allies had to crack before they could move effectively against Constantinople, and critical deficiencies in British logistic preparations worked powerfully in the defenders' favor.

AMPHIBIOUS ASSAULT OF GALLIPOLI— THE LANDINGS

The sense of tension that accompanied frantic preparation by both antagonists seemed to ease perceptibly as loaded British transports assembled in Mudros harbor. After their long bout with overwhelming logistic problems, both rank and file seemed almost relieved that combat would soon free them from the tedium of preparation. But as usually happens, the attacker experienced a fuller share of such relief than did the defender.

General von Sanders could not discover where Hamilton proposed to strike. So fervently did he want the Allies to walk into the traps prepared at Kum Kale or Bulair that the dispositions on both Turkish flanks left open the way for a determined British landing close to Kilid Bahr. As things turned out, von Sanders' dispositions fitted almost perfectly into the British tactical plan. Kitchener had ruled out an Asiatic landing and Hamilton was too sound a soldier to move into the dead-end at Bulair. So he turned both of the von Sanders traps to his own advantage. Sir Ian's tactical plan called for a realistic and prolonged feint against Bulair by his general reserve, 10,000 bluejackets comprising the Royal Naval Division. By this move Hamilton hoped to withhold from his main landing areas whatever Turkish force stood at Bulair. At the Asiatic extremity of von Sanders' line Hamilton alerted two French colonial divisions for a landing designed to occupy the Kum Kale batteries, and prevent them from firing across the Strait against the British landings on Cape Helles.

For his main effort Hamilton divided some 50,000 riflemen between two columns designed to converge on Kilid Bahr. To the north 30,000 men of the Australia and New Zealand Army Corps (Anzac) were to land below Suvla Bay and advance four miles (straight distance) due east to Kilid Bahr's upstream flank. There the Anzac could block any reinforcement from Bulair. Twelve miles south of the Anzac beaches 20,000 men of the 29th Division were to land on five narrow beaches surrounding Cape Helles and push across 12 miles of broken ridges toward Kilid Bahr. Unfortunately Hamilton failed to perceive the advantage of using a ten-mile corridor that ran from his northernmost Helles beach and offered the easiest land approach to Kilid Bahr, but in other respects his landing plan soundly exploited the Turk dispositions. It provided for a coordinated, concentric attack by 50,000 against a mere 15,000 Turks. Once British troops reached Kilid Bahr they could wipe out field artillery dominating the Straits. Then Allied ships could sweep mines, pass the Narrows, and outflank von Sanders' troops at Bulair. However, like all plans for coordinated, concentric action, Hamilton's project required both flexible and aggressive performance from everyone concerned.

As the last transports bearing the assault force completed their 50-hour voyage from Alexandria to Mudros, Sir Ian had to select a day for the great adventure. Unsettled weather and other factors combined to fix his lonely decision upon April 25. Throughout the 24th British soldiers and their equipment bounced across the choppy Mudros waters as they shifted from transports to the warships that would carry each unit to its assigned beach. All afternoon fighting ships filed out and set course for rendezvous points some seven steaming-hours away. Navy officers sharing in this final preliminary observed that the troops were cheerful to the point of lightheartedness.

Hamilton's landing plan required each ship to reach her rendezvous under cover of darkness and drop the troops into pulling boats before first light. The ten boats lifting each assault company were to form one tow behind a steam trawler. From a line of departure some three miles off shore each trawler would struggle toward the assigned beach till she grounded. Then the boats were to cast off and move under oars for about 50 yards to the shore. With the first wave ashore, trawlers were expected to recover their boats (the plan anticipated only slight boat damage), and return for the second wave. During both approach and landing two heavy ships standing off each beach were to stun defenders with naval gunfire. Indeed Hamilton's staff counted heavily upon this aggregation of more than 400 fleet guns to fulfill the mission that artillery normally performed in conventional ground action. On paper this landing plan looked sound, for it embodied the best practice similar British

forces had used successfully for more than 300 years. Yet the failure to rehearse left many critical problems for spot decision by officers who had never experienced amphibious assault on such a scale.

The climactic event so long anticipated finally got under way below Suvla Bay during the small hours of April 25. To exploit the surprise of a pre-dawn landing, the Anzac commander dispensed with preliminary naval bombardment. As the trawlers pushed slowly ashore through the blackness a pilot miscalculated the current, and led the entire first wave to shore some distance north of the beaches assigned. Despite the confusion it caused, this error was fortunate in one significant way. Turk guns bearing directly upon the beach Hamilton had selected proved so troublesome, even after gunnery ships took them under fire, that they might have disrupted the entire landing. Yet even this lucky accident created serious problems for the landed troops.

Hamilton had invoked such secrecy that a mere handful of the Anzac officers understood his plan and most of them remained afloat with the Corps commander. In consequence battalion commanders, sent into strange and mountainous terrain without adequate maps, could neither locate assigned objectives nor control their scattered units. By nightfall no battalion had reached the line assigned for its D-day advance, though a few smaller units managed to attain high ground from which they could move overland to Kilid Bahr. And they might well have succeeded had not Mustapha Kemal, then commanding a division of the general reserve, demonstrated the bold initiative that later enabled him to mold Turkey into an effective modern State.

At dawn on the 26th, while Kemal conducted a routine pre-breakfast inspection of one regiment in his command, a messenger reached him with a request for one company to reinforce an outpost opposite the most advanced British units. Perceiving instantly that the threatened position must hold at any cost, Kemal made sure that his troops had a full ammunition supply and then led the entire regiment toward the enemy without feeding his men or consulting any superior officer about committing the general reserve. Leading the forward element himself, Kemal reached the ridgeline just as the British attack began. After a day of seesaw combat for the ridge, he drove back the Anzac spearhead. Other reinforcements soon came to support Kemal's regiment and within three days the surprise Anzac assault became an entrenched beachhead with all rear areas under observation from Turkish lines on surrounding heights.

This unfortunate miscarriage did not, of itself, doom Hamilton's plan. His effective feint at Bulair held 15,000 Turks there for 48 hours, the French feint at Kum Kale delayed 15,000 more for three days, and the Anzacs themselves drew heavily upon von Sanders' general reserve. In fact fewer than 8,000 Turks remained free to confront the 20,000 Britons landing on Helles. Thus, even though Hamilton did not immediately grasp the fact, stalemate at the Anzac position simply converted the Helles Beaches into the only key for unlocking Kilid Bahr.

As Hamilton and his staff left Mudros aboard the *Queen Elizabeth* on April 24th, they reviewed mentally the five Helles Beaches that were to become so important on the morrow. The staff knew that Hamilton expected Major General Sir Aylmer Hunter-Weston, 29th Division commander, to exert tactical control from his own command ship. The plan focused the Division's main effort upon W and V Beaches, about a half-mile apart on the tip of Helles. Hunter-Weston expected four assault battalions to secure both W and V by 10 AM on the 25th, thus clearing an area to receive his five reserve battalions. As soon as they landed, this reserve was to provide the hard core of a general advance upon Krithia village, D-day objective in the Helles area. Because both W and V were narrow beaches, Hunter-Weston had assigned four additional battalions to three beaches that flanked W and V. East of the main landing area lay S Beach, just inside the Strait and somewhat more than a mile in the rear of Turk positions defending V Beach. Directly across the peninsula from S and to the west of W and V,

Beach X rose from the Aegean to high ground. This height then fell eastward for a very rugged half mile to the W Beach flank. A good two miles north of X, Beach Y sloped up from the Aegean to a low cliff. An easy mile due east of this cliff lay Krithia village, which sheltered all Turk reserves on Cape Helles. Y Beach also gave access to the ten-mile corridor leading directly to Kilid Bahr. Airline distance from Y to S, across the chord of Hunter-Weston's landing arc, was less than three miles. The four battalions earmarked for S, X, and Y expected to take high ground immediately above each beach and then wait for the reserve to land at W and V. When reserve battalions had deployed shortly after noon on D-day, battalions at S, X, and Y were to extend the line to its full three-mile length and join a general advance upon Hunter-Weston's D-day objective just beyond Krithia.

This Helles plan exploded into action as the sun rose on April 25. Ten heavy ships startled the sea gulls with a noisy bombardment, and steam trawlers began to shepherd their boats toward shore. For a full hour projectiles from two battleships and a cruiser, lying 2,000 yards offshore, bracketed Turk positions at W and V. Since the fleet enjoyed neither the fruits of detailed reconnaissance (precluded by Hamilton's secretiveness) nor forward spotting, they could not search out each strong point. So, with the target area masked by early-morning shadow, they damaged neither trenches on forward slopes nor barbed wire at the water's edge. When fire shifted inland ten minutes before the initial waves landed, the two companies of Turks defending each of the beaches had ample time to reoccupy their positions. Then all four companies of riflemen and a sprinkling of machine gunners lay quietly till the first assault boat at each beach touched bottom.

Three British assault companies rowed up to W Beach as helpless as an unsuspecting infantry column ambushed on the march. When the leading boat grounded, a hail of well-aimed fire all but wiped out men and boats. Fortunately, boats carrying the single company in close reserve eased to the west till a rocky outcropping masked Turkish fire. Then, imitating Wolfe's maneuver at Louisburg, the men clambered up to positions dominating enemy machine-gun and rifle pits. Though two small parties drove the Turks eastward, they could neither wipe out the defenders nor consolidate the beachhead. And the few remaining boats were too busy with wounded to bring in effective reserves. After a day of hard fighting, the weary men established a narrow perimeter at *W* strong enough to withstand counterattack during the night. But even that success came too late for the five reserve battalions to exploit *W* Beach on D-day.

Assault elements fared even worse at *V* Beach, where defenses echeloned up the sides of a natural amphitheater some hundred feet high. Because Hunter-Weston expected naval gunfire to stun the Turks defending at *V*, he had planned to supplement the conventional boat assault in battalion strength with two additional battalions in a landing ship improvised from an old collier. As she approached the beach this vessel towed three lighters which her commander hoped to rig as a floating gangway. Then, covered by deck-mounted machine guns, both battalions were to rush ashore and seize the high ground. But as at *W*, naval guns firing from 2,000 yards failed to disrupt the defenses at *V* Beach. The first blast of Turk fire wiped out the boated battalion. After bloody efforts to rig the gangway finally succeeded, one battalion from the collier suffered 70 per cent casualties trying to get ashore. The remaining battalion lay below decks all day while the collier's machine guns held the Turks at bay. After dark that battalion landed without casualty, and established a perimeter that withstood determined counterattack during the night. Needless to say, Hunter-Weston could not exploit *V* Beach on D-day.

While four companies of Turks, gradually reinforced from their reserve at Krithia, made a day-long shambles of *W* and *V* Beaches, landings on all three flank beaches went smoothly. At *S* Beach, inside the Strait, naval gunfire from 500 yards knocked out a battery on the Turk left flank and let British riflemen scramble up the cliff with very slight loss. But then Hamilton's obsessive secrecy betrayed his men. The successful battalion commander had no knowledge of the general plan. His orders were merely to join in the general advance, and he did not hear from Hunter-Weston all day. So at 8 AM he dug in and waited. Throughout the day, for lack of specific orders, 900 fresh British soldiers made no move to take in the rear a smaller Turk force that was stopping 3,000 of their comrades at *V* Beach only a mile away. Across Cape Helles at *X* Beach on the Aegean flank, naval gunfire from 500 yards stunned all 12 Turkish defenders. The assault battalion easily mounted a 40-foot cliff, and by 11 AM had disposed of a company from the local Turkish reserve. Elements of this battalion actually made contact with comrades on the left flank at *W*, but, like his colleague at *S*, the *X* Beach commander dug in his 900 fresh men and waited for a general advance. Meanwhile, two miles up the Aegean from *X*, two battalions landed at *Y* Beach without any opposition whatever. Since one of these units was a Royal Marine battalion and the other was from the 29th Division, there was some question as to which commander was senior officer present. The landing order had not settled this point and throughout the day neither lieutenant colonel assumed command of both units. Though the marine colonel strolled cross-country toward Krithia, by then denuded of reserves which had been rushed into the *W-V* pocket, neither commander took the initiative to capture the Division's D-day objective. Toward evening both battalions dug in just before Turk reserves drawn down from the north began a series of intermittent counterattacks that petered out at dawn.

While his D-day plans miscarried so painfully, Hunter-Weston remained afloat off *W* and *V*, holding with him the five battalions of his division reserve. Had things gone according to plan, the assistant division commander would have notified Hunter-Weston from *V* Beach as soon as it was ready to receive the reserve battalions. But the assistant commander died early in the firefight, and all day long the general had little more information about conditions ashore than could be collected visually from his ship. The collapse of his hope for winning *W* and *V* before 10 AM seemed to rivet Hunter-Weston's exclusive attention on those two unhappy beaches.

Actually the 29th Division had done far better than its commander realized. By 10 AM on D-day it had made good three out of five landing attempts, and its two unsuccessful assaults had drawn all local enemy forces into a deep pocket. With four fresh battalions ashore and five others ready to land over beaches he held, the general might well have taken firm hold of Krithia by nightfall. Indeed, during the morning Hamilton invited Hunter-Weston to make just such a move. When this polite message drew no reply, Hamilton's staff prodded him to repeat it in stronger language, only to have Hunter-Weston insist curtly upon following the original plan. At that point Hamilton refused to interfere any further with tactical decisions of the man who commanded the assault. During this exchange of messages about committing the division reserve, the *Queen Elizabeth* passed close enough to *Y* Beach for Hamilton's staff to observe the situation. Recognizing its unexpected opportunity, the Chief of Staff begged his general to bring down from Bulair the 10,000-man general reserve, land it at *Y* Beach early next morning, and exploit the easy corridor leading to Kilid Bahr. Hamilton rejected this move on the ground that it was far too early in the operation even to consider committing the general reserve. As a result of so many negative decisions, darkness on April 25 found the British hanging on grimly at *S, V, W, X,* and *Y.* The still sparse Turkish units on Helles fought hard throughout the night. When one hard-pressed company commander called plaintively for reinforcement, his senior curtly ordered him to keep fighting, and said that he wanted to find no Englishmen on Helles when April 26 dawned.

By daylight on the 26th, British troops at *Y* Beach had gotten out of hand. A clamorous stream of men wounded during the night

defense so frightened signalmen stationed at the beach that they called frantically for more boats than the situation required. Then as fast as the boats arrived wounded or stragglers filled them and pushed off. In a short time half of the force withdrew without orders. When the senior commander realized what had happened, he decided that too few men remained and abandoned the position. During the same day, forces that remained ashore managed to consolidate a line from *X* around the Cape to *S,* but Hamilton spent two more days getting ready to exploit his landing. By then von Sanders had gathered troops from Bulair and Kum Kale into an entrenched line at Krithia, and a stalemate set in.

STALEMATE

From May until the end of 1915 conditions on Helles recreated on a small scale the situation in France. Trench systems multiplied, rear echelons dug in, and both sides brought up guns. Each harassed the other continually with raids or gunfire. As this battle of fire continued, perhaps its most significant feature lay in von Sanders' skill at neutralizing the British naval guns. Almost invariably when a ship registered on one of his trenches, he used the cover of darkness to push that part of his line so close to British trenches that any fleet fire would endanger friendly forces. Such stubborn attrition depleted both armies, but Turk infantrymen expected fewer comforts than did the British and required smaller reinforcements.

The same kind of debilitating trench warfare obtained in the Anzac area until early August. On the 6th Hamilton, by then heavily reinforced, tried to shake loose his Anzacs for a drive straight through the mountains to Kilid Bahr. He set ashore two tired divisions on the Anzac left to support the breakout, but their assault spluttered out in a tragedy of errors. At its climax an Indian detachment topped a ridge overlooking the Strait, only recoil under an ill-timed salvo from their own supporting guns. Mustapha Kemal exploited this unhappy incident and forced the British back into an entrenched beachhead. Then the Anzac area relapsed again into the same kind of stalemate that shrouded the lines on Cape Helles.

This long period of costly vacillation ashore merely increased the gunfire and logistic missions required of the fleet. Until a single German submarine drove them to cover in late May, heavy ships stood close inshore each day to deliver call fire, and after the submarine scare confined battleships or cruisers to their bases, destroyers took up the daily fire missions. Fleet gunners worked hard at the job and improved measurably, but never managed to deliver an effective volume of fire beyond their own visual range. Weak facilities for communication, inadequately gridded maps, and a dearth of skilled fire observers all contributed to the unsatisfactory result, but experiments with aerial spotting produced the heaviest disappointment. Plane-to-ship radios functioned so rarely that, even when an airborne observer managed to spot the fall of shot, he usually had to land and send a message by destroyer in order to effect the necessary adjustment. Obviously, naval gunfire in such circumstances was neither sufficiently accurate nor rapid enough to inspire confidence. But the fleet offset its weak fire support by performing magnificently a myriad of logistical missions. Significant among them was the feat of constructing off Beaches *W* and *V* artificial harbors that anticipated the much larger structures at Normandy in 1944. Certainly the haggard British soldiers could not have held even their tenuous grip on Gallipoli without the ammunition, food, and water that the fleet pushed over the beaches regardless of weather. Indeed so busy was the fleet with gunfire and logistics that only its submarines made an independent contribution to the Gallipoli campaign.

From late April through December a handful of daring British submariners penetrated the Dardanelles for regular patrols in the Sea of Marmora. With barely enough speed to breast the surface current and too little endurance submerged to stay down for the whole passage, most of the tiny boats somehow managed to dodge both gunfire and mines. When the enemy laid a submarine net clear across the Narrows, the luckier boats broke through by sheer persistence and moved into the Marmora. There they sank supply ships, shot up trains, raided briefly ashore, and even sank vessels moored in Constantinople. Had von Sanders been forced to rely solely on waterborne supply, these submarines might well have proved the margin of British victory, but the Asiatic road net and a trickle of waterborne supply filled the defenders' minimum needs.

Proud as he was of the submarines, Commodore Keyes retained his conviction that armored surface ships too could pass the Narrows. As the army dug in deeper and the Turks withdrew most of their artillery from the Straits, he envisioned a truly coordinated ground-fleet action against Kilid Bahr. Throughout the dreary stalemate Keyes pressed steadily for sending destroyer-minesweepers and bombardment vessels through the Narrows to blast Kilid Bahr from upstream while the Army made one more determined drive across the peninsula. He insisted that no previous British effort had exploited the combined power of army and fleet, but he could not offset the handicap of a divided command, and his seniors in both services had lost faith in army-fleet assault. So the only Dardanelles-Gallipoli plan that envisaged a truly 20th century amphibious doctrine never materialized into action.

By December 1915 it was obvious that British arms would accomplish little at Gallipoli, so Kitchener ordered the peninsula abandoned. Fortunately staff officers in the Aegean had by then mastered the elements of modern amphibious cooperation, so their withdrawal was a masterpiece of sound planning and execution. Newly devised landing craft, forerunners of more efficient boats developed during World War II, contributed materially to their success. If Hamilton's April assault had enjoyed the same sound command, staff, and logistic support, it must certainly have succeeded.

THE AFTERMATH

The Dardanelles-Gallipoli Campaign was decisive in the Eastern Theater. In addition, its influence reached into the Western Theater, affected the structure of Britain's Government, and profoundly influenced postwar evolution of amphibious doctrine. Indeed the doctrinal evolution this year-long campaign foreshadowed is one of the most significant in modern times.

When 1916 dawned, Turks still controlled the waterway separating Russia from her western Allies, the last British troops were leaving Gallipoli, and Turkey no longer endured the isolation that threatened her existence as a modern state. Yet shrewd as he was in seizing every advantage the situation offered, von Sanders had been lucky. For lack of amphibious shipping Russia had refused flatly to cooperate with her western Allies in their drive up the Straits. Though a secret treaty promised Constantinople to Russia after the war, her Crimean armies watched idly while Britons entangled von Sanders' best units deep in Gallipoli, and other Czarist troops stood by as a Bulgarian alliance with the Central Powers touched off a campaign that doomed Romania and knocked Serbia out of contention. Forging this link connecting Turkey directly to Austria so strengthened the Central Powers that even after Britain transferred her Gallipoli force to Salonika the Allies could not mount a serious threat from the Aegean during the rest of the war. In addition to these military results many persons consider the Aegean fiasco as a contributing factor to the Russian revolution of 1917, for the heavy fighting Russia endured throughout 1916 without aid from the West certainly exaggerated conditions that doomed the Czarist regime.

Yet even beyond those significant by-products in the East, the 1915 Aegean campaign also exerted important influence upon developments in the Western Theater. On the land front Germany profited when action at Gallipoli drew Allied men and munitions from France but required no comparable German diversion from the Western Front, and the Aegean operation had an equally important impact on the western sea flank. While Britain sent her expendable ships to the Aegean, Germany's High Seas Fleet lay unharassed throughout 1915, husbanding strength for the climactic action finally to develop off Jutland. So when Britain lost expendable ships at Dardanelles-Gallipoli she drained the Grand Fleet of its vital reserves in trained manpower, thereby reducing materially its combat endurance.

Britain's Government also felt the impact of events at Dardanelles-Gallipoli. Lord Fisher's prevision of the gloomy outcome prompted his resignation as First Sea Lord in May. During the same month a wave of public dissatisfaction with progress in the war on all fronts produced a Cabinet shuffle that removed Churchill from the Admiralty. Despite the departure of two strong men however the net result here was sound, for problems raised by the Aegean campaign contributed materially to reorganizing Britain's top agencies for strategic and logistical planning—a development that fostered the eventual Allied victory.

Important as were its immediate effects, the Dardanelles-Gallipoli campaign had even greater impact on the evolution of amphibious doctrine and its eventual application in World War II. For instance, there is strong evidence that von Sanders' Gallipoli defense influenced German command decisions during the 1940's, and it is a strong presumption that many Japanese island commanders built their defenses on von Sanders' foundation. The Aegean experience certainly deterred British development of an amphibious force, while lessons drawn from that experience contributed measurably to amphibious progress within the United States Navy and Marine Corps.

Unfortunately a bitter controversy over responsibility for the Aegean fiasco still obscures these important amphibious lessons. For instance, most critics of the Royal Navy's failure to pass the Dardanelles assume that resolute acceptance of mine damage would have placed a substantial squadron in the Sea of Marmora, but they ignore the fact that in 1915 even the aggressive Churchill refused to let his admirals pass through un-breached mine fields. In effect Churchill con-curred belatedly in the conclusion reached by Fisher, Richmond, Carden, and de Robeck that mines commanded by mobile field bat-teries could not be swept until infantry si-lenced the guns. Yet one must observe that Carden's ships supported by the full com-plement of Britain's fleet infantry should have mastered the defenders before von Sanders had time to move in his regiment of field artillery. This premise leads to the con-clusion that the Royal Navy failed to im-provise the kind of amphibious force for which Jervis had spoken so eloquently a cen-tury earlier. Yet even this conclusion does not exhaust the amphibious lessons of the Dardanelles action, for though the all-big-gun ship did not emerge as the absolute amphibious instrument Churchill had en-visioned, the campaign revealed its potential for amphibious support. To give the modern floating gun platform full effect navies had to improve fire control techniques and de-velop a balanced magazine of projectiles, as well as a whole family of support craft. How-ever, as the brilliant Gallipoli evacuation suggested, 20th century seamen were learn-ing rapidly how to meet that challenge.

When the amphibious burden in the Aegean shifted to the army, Hamilton found himself forced to improvise assault units in a situation that required immediate action, and so had to afford von Sanders time to pre-pare skillful defenses. Yet in spite of the price this logistic lag exacted, the Gallipoli story leaves room for asserting that Hamil-ton's attack could have succeeded. Closer gunfire support, more initiative by battalion commanders, and prompt commitment of all reserves might well have given Hamilton a winning combination. Indeed, any one of those elements combined with the failure by von Sanders to post machine guns at W and V, or less initiative by Kemal, could have been decisive. Yet the very existence of so many simultaneous mischances is of itself significant. For each separate mischance con-tributes to the conclusion that in 1915 Brit-ish arms could not handle difficult amphibi-ous assignments because they lacked an amphibious force-in-being. However these same mischances provided evidence from which military innovators drew such 20th century amphibious concepts as integral command, thorough logistic and tactical planning, effective reconnaissance, realistic rehearsal, combat-unit loading, balanced fleet fire-support, armored assault craft, pow-erful ship-to-shore movement, early commit-ment of reserves, prompt and steady flow of supply across the beach, and aggressive ex-ploitation.

During a generation of trial-and-error ex-periment, the United States Navy and Ma-rine Corps refined these concepts against the background of lessons from Gallipoli. So even though it ended in failure, the Darda-nelles-Gallipoli campaign comprised the first large-scale effort to adapt time-tested am-phibious principles to the product of 20th century technology. And in that special sense it has become one of the two truly significant naval operations of World War I.

29

The Battle of Jutland

IN 1914 THE WAR'S CENTER OF gravity lay in the North Sea-Western Front area; it moved in 1915 to the Eastern Mediterranean and the Eastern Front. Early in 1916 both sides recognized that the decision must be obtained in the West. The Allies had achieved a considerable degree of unity and they planned to coordinate their military and, to a lesser extent, their naval operations. In Germany the strangle hold of Allied sea power had begun to produce shortages of strategic raw materials, and the High Command came to appreciate that time was fighting on the side of its enemies. General von Falkenhayn, Chief of the German General Staff, submitted an estimate of the situation to his government at Christmas 1915. In it he pointed out that the strategy of both the Pitts was being repeated; the island power, rendered secure by its naval strength, was able to draw on neutrals and colonies for the materials of war needed to keep its continental allies in the field. The defeat of this main enemy required an all-out offensive by land and sea and, since the German navy had been unable effectively to dispute command of the ocean lanes, the German army must achieve not merely a decision but a victory of annihilation over

Britain's allies. Of the latter, Russia appeared to Falkenhayn to be used up; Italy was immobilized behind the Alpine barrier; only France—"the sword of England"—remained. On February 21, 1916 at Verdun he launched the offensive that was aimed at breaking France by attrition.

German naval leaders were stung by the implications of Falkenhayn's appraisal. The surface fleet had been held at its bases by Imperial command since the Dogger Bank action, and submarines were severely restricted in response to pressure from President Wilson. For 12 months Tirpitz and Holtzendorff, Chief of the Naval Staff, with strong support from Falkenhayn, had pressed for removal of the unnatural leash. Their efforts were partially successful. The ailing von Pohl was removed on January 18 and Vice Admiral Reinhardt Scheer, an aggressive-minded nominee of Tirpitz, was appointed to command the High Seas Fleet. Three weeks later as the assault on Verdun gathered force, the Kaiser sanctioned offensive operations by his navy.

Scheer could afford to gamble for command of the North Sea. Defeat could not greatly worsen the strategic situation for the High Seas Fleet; with boldness he might gain much from his opponents' mistakes. His plans, like those of the army's General Staff, envisaged a strategy of attrition; they aimed to bring down the strength of the Grand Fleet to parity with his own. U-boats were to mine the vicinity of British bases and were to take up patrol areas off the entrance channels. With the aid of surface forces, skillfully baited traps would be set in hopes of enticing Admiral Sir John Jellicoe to divide his forces and so provide a chance for a portion to be cut off and destroyed. It was essential during surface operations that the commander of the High Seas Fleet have fullest possible information of the enemy; he therefore would rely heavily on airship and submarine reconnaissance.

Britain's naval strategy was determined by economic realities. The country was not only the chief entrepôt for Allied war supplies; it had also to import its own foodstuffs and basic raw materials. So while the principal active British naval effort was devoted to maintaining the blockade of Germany, the main fleet remained in its bases ready to intercept any threat to the nation's vital sea lanes. Periodically the Commander in Chief concentrated his forces and swept the North Sea. To dig the High Seas Fleet out of its fortified and mined base area was out of the question. Like Scheer, therefore, he also resorted to ambush, but with this difference: his objective was to bring on a decisive fleet engagement. The Grand Fleet he regarded as the instrument not merely of battle but of grand strategy—the very pivot of Allied action. His policy accordingly reflected an acute consciousness of responsibility; it was based on the rejection of avoidable risks, for he was, in Churchill's vivid phrase, "the only Allied commander who could have lost the war in an afternoon."

In 1916 there was a dearth of accumulated battle experience to serve as a tactical guide in the handling of dreadnought fleets. The one-sided action at Tsushima offered little of instructional value. But Jellicoe knew that he could annihilate the enemy in a day gunnery duel and, as long as the British fleet retained command of the strategic center, he was determined to fight under conditions

that would give him fullest use of this advantage. At whatever cost to his reputation the Grand Fleet must come out of an engagement preponderantly superior to the High Seas Fleet. In summarizing his tactical views for the Admiralty on October 19, 1914 Jellicoe had stated:

The Germans have shown that they rely to a very great extent on submarines, mines and torpedoes, and there can be no doubt whatever that they will endeavor to make the fullest possible use of these weapons in a fleet action, especially since they possess an actual superiority over us in these particular directions. It therefore becomes necessary to consider our own tactical methods in relation to these forms of attack. . . .

If, for instance, the enemy fleet were to turn away from an advancing fleet, I should assume that the intention was to lead us over mines and submarines, and should decline to be so drawn. I desire particularly to draw the attention of their Lordships to this point, since it may be deemed a refusal of battle, and, indeed, might possibly result in failure to bring the enemy to action as soon as is expected and hoped.

Such a result would be absolutely repugnant to the feelings of all British naval officers and men, but with new and untried methods of warfare new tactics must be devised to meet them.

I feel that such tactics, if not understood, may bring odium upon me, but so long as I have the confidence of their Lordships, I intend to pursue what is, in my considered opinion, the proper course to defeat and annihilate the enemy's fleet, without regard to uninstructed opinion or criticism.

The situation is a difficult one. It is quite within the bounds of possibility that half of our battle fleet might be disabled by underwater attack before the guns opened at all, if a false step is made, and I feel that I must constantly bear in mind the great probability of such attack and be prepared tactically to prevent its success.[1]

As in the days of sail, the over-all direction of British fleet movements originated at the Admiralty. Significantly however the old porticoed building, reminiscent of the era of Barham, was now joined in the rear to an annex larger than any other public building in Great Britain. The radio masts rising from its roof were more symbolic of the

---

[1] British Admiralty, *Battle of Jutland, Official Despatches* (London, 1920), 601-603.

problems at hand than the mantlepiece wind indicator which was still the most conspicuous feature of the historic Board Room, where decisions at the highest level continued to be made. The proximity of the Naval Intelligence Division was a principal reason for Admiralty control of operations. Here was the center of the radio direction finding network and the cryptanalysis section. In practice, the Admiralty ordered the disposition of fleets when German moves were impending. Otherwise, operations of the Grand Fleet were in the hands of its Commander in Chief, who remained at all times in full tactical control.

PRELIMINARY OPERATIONS

The new offensive strategy of the High Seas Fleet got under way with a bombardment of Lowestoft late in April 1916 by a German force of four battle cruisers and six light cruisers. An intended attack on Yarmouth to follow immediately afterwards was defeated by bad weather.

A month later Jellicoe attempted unsuccessfully to lure Scheer out to battle by sending the seaplane carriers *Engadine* and *Vindex*,[2] covered by Tyrwhitt's light cruisers, to attack the airship base on the Schleswig coast while battleships and cruisers of the Grand Fleet lurked beyond the horizon. The first attempt cost Jellicoe three of his five planes without achieving anything more than definitely locating the German hangars. Scheer left port with the main body of the High Seas Fleet, but the weather deteriorated with North Sea suddenness, whereupon his squadron guides turned back through mountainous seas without making contact. In a second similar raid a few days later, only two of the overloaded Baby Sopwiths managed to get off the water. One plunged through the antennae of a screening destroyer; the other dropped bombs but missed the hangars. Jellicoe waited about

during the day, but this time the German fleet failed to move from its anchorages.

In early May 1916 the German government agreed to the "Sussex Pledge" restricting its profitable submarine operations to the limitations prescribed by international law. Scheer protested by calling in the 30 boats under his command, for operations with the fleet. In his opinion the new curbs made the surface forces Germany's only practicable offensive weapon, and he accordingly decided to enlarge the scope of their hit-and-run strikes. He planned originally to bombard the important shipbuilding town of Sunderland at the mouth of the Tyne in an endeavor to draw out British naval detachments, which he would attack with submarines, airships, and surface forces.

Ship repairs delayed the fleet and bad weather grounded the airships until the end of May, when the German submarines were scheduled to leave their stations off the coast of England. So Scheer reluctantly abandoned the projected Sunderland raid and substituted a less hazardous strike at Allied patrols and shipping off south Norway, hoping to draw out scattered British fleet units. Here the Skagerrak provided a ready avenue of escape to Kiel should he be cut off from his North Sea bases. The German sortie was scheduled for May 31.

By a coincidence, Jellicoe was planning a sweep into the same waters in an effort to lure out the High Seas Fleet.

THE RIVAL FLEETS

The British Grand Fleet at this time enjoyed a comfortable superiority in tonnage, numbers, and weight of broadside.[3] The German High Seas Fleet, numerically strong enough to be a respectable foe, probably had a slight superiority in ship construction and in training. The line of battle of the two forces comprised the following:

---

[2] Converted Channel steamers, each with a hangar aft for four aircraft.

[3] The Battle Cruiser Force (scouting groups) was normally built around 10 battle cruisers. At this time Beatty had detached one for docking and his three oldest (under Hood) for target practice at Scapa Flow. Jellicoe had sent four fast battleships as replacements.

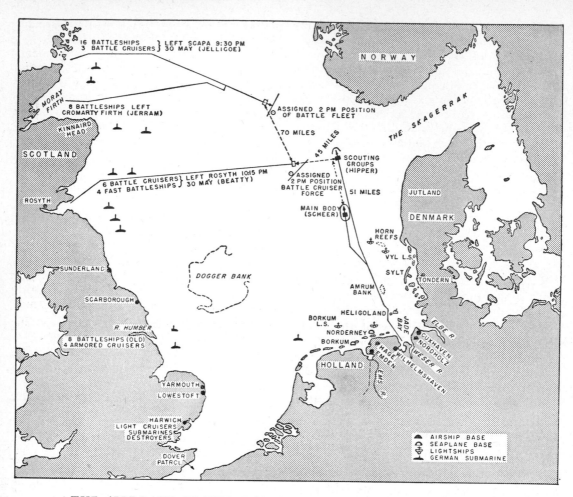

THE APPROACH OF THE FLEETS, MIDNIGHT-2:15 PM, MAY 31, 1916

	BRITISH:	GERMAN:
	Scouting Forces	
	(Beatty)	(Hipper)
Dreadnoughts	4	0
Battle cruisers	6	5
Light cruisers	14	5
Destroyers	27	30
	Battle Fleets	
	(Jellicoe)	(Scheer)
Dreadnoughts	24	16
Pre-dreadnoughts	0	6
Battle cruisers	3	0
Armored cruisers	8	0
Light cruisers	12	6
Destroyers	52	31

Discounting the German pre-dreadnoughts and the British armored cruisers as being of slight combat value, the comparison shows Jellicoe able to bring 37 capital ships (battleships and battle cruisers) against the German 21. In gunpower his margin was equally great: 344 of 12-inch to 15-inch could be brought against the 244 German 11- and 12-inch guns. The Grand Fleet also enjoyed a corresponding superiority in lighter units.

APPROACH AND FIRST CONTACTS

On May 30 the British Admiralty notified the British commanders of an impending

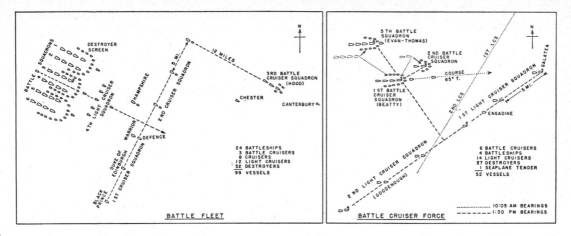

GRAND FLEET CRUISING FORMATIONS, MAY 31

movement by the High Seas Fleet. Jellicoe thereupon canceled his sweep and at 6 o'clock that evening received information that a German force intended the next day to enter the North Sea by the eastern swept channel off Horn Reefs. In a remarkable display of readiness and efficiency the Grand Fleet, pursuant to Admiralty orders, put to sea that very evening. The main body under Jellicoe proceeded on an easterly course from Scapa Flow. From Cromarty Firth came Rear Admiral Jerram with eight dreadnoughts, plus supporting units, to join Jellicoe's 16 dreadnoughts at sea the next day. From Rosyth came Vice Admiral Beatty with four dreadnoughts, six battle cruisers, and lighter units. Beatty was directed to sweep eastward, reaching position at lat. 56° 40' N, long. 5° E by 2 PM on May 31. If he made no contact with the enemy, he was to turn north and get in visual touch with Jellicoe, who at that time would be about 70 miles away. The combined force would then sweep toward Horn Reefs.

The various units of the Grand Fleet had cleared harbor toward midnight on May 30; Scheer with the German High Seas Fleet left Jade Bay some three hours later. On the morning of the 31st neither the British nor the German commander knew that the other was at sea. Jellicoe before leaving port had enjoined radio silence on the Grand Fleet. The German admiral had taken the precaution of having the guardship at Wilhelmshaven acknowledge all messages addressed to him, using the call sign of his flagship, *Friedrich der Grosse*. As a result Beatty and Jellicoe were incorrectly informed that the German fleet flagship was still at Wilhelmshaven. Scheer's airship patrol had been unable to get on station, and though Beatty had the *Engadine* in his light cruiser screen, the uncertain performance of the seaplanes made it necessary to save them for patrol when contacts were imminent. Two German submarines off Rosyth sighted Beatty but their reports were misleading, indicating that only small detachments were at sea.

The British Battle Fleet zigzagged at 14 knots speed of advance on a southeasterly course for the rendezvous with Beatty. The 24 battleships steamed in six parallel columns, or in "division line abreast," a cruising formation that would enable them to deploy into line of battle on either flank in minimum time. A destroyer flotilla screened each battle squadron, and eight armored cruisers steamed eight miles ahead of the main body, spread out on a 25-mile scouting line with the light cruisers between. Rear Admiral Hood's 3rd Battle Cruiser Squadron, in column and screened by destroyers, advanced 15 miles ahead of the cruiser line and was preceded by the light cruiser *Canterbury*.

To the southeast the High Seas Fleet

moved steadily at 16 knots up the Jutland coast. Vice Admiral Franz Hipper's Scouting Group I comprising five battle cruisers, screened by Scouting Group II of light cruisers and destroyers, led the way. Scheer's bat-

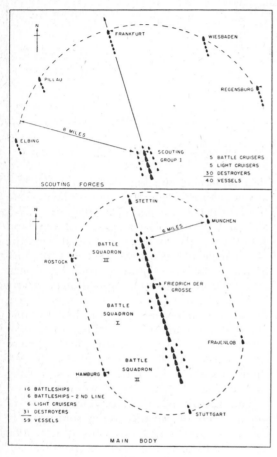

*HIGH SEAS FLEET
CRUISING FORMATIONS 2:15 PM, MAY 31*

tleships and light forces followed 50 miles behind with the powerful Squadron III of dreadnoughts in the van.

Beatty meanwhile had been zigzagging at some 19 knots on an easterly course with his three light cruiser squadrons disposed on a NE-SW scouting line 25 miles in length with the center eight miles in advance of his flagship *Lion*. At 1:30 PM on the 31st he changed formation preparatory to joining

Jellicoe, rotating the scouting line right to ENE-WSW and ordering Rear Admiral Evan-Thomas's 5th Battle Squadron of four dreadnoughts to take station five miles on his port beam. The scouting line would then be favorably located for maximum coverage on the sweep to Horn Reefs, and the 5th Battle Squadron would be in position to take its place in the van of Jellicoe's force as prescribed by the battle orders. (See diagram page 519.)

On reaching the designated position at 2:15 PM, most of Beatty's force in response to signal turned to a northerly course to join the main body according to plan. In the midst of these evolutions, while officers on the bridge of Evan-Thomas's flagship *Barham* were looking northward in anticipation of joining up, the light cruiser *Galatea,* at the northeastern end of the line, made out a column of smoke to eastward. Closing to investigate, the *Galatea* sighted a Danish merchant vessel, the *N. J. Fiord,* being stopped by two enemy vessels and flashed a warning by radio. This contact brought on the Battle of Jutland and probably cost the British a decisive victory, for had the *N. J. Fiord* not been stopped at that spot, it is likely the opposing forces would have met much farther north, with the Grand Fleet fully concentrated.

On receiving the *Galatea's* signal at 2:32, Beatty turned the battle cruisers to SSE to get between the enemy and his base. Heavy smoke pouring from the funnels of the battle cruisers as they prepared to increase speed obscured the turning signal from Evan-Thomas. When he got the *Galatea's* report at 2:38, however, he quickly grasped the situation and also turned to SSE. The distance between him and Beatty had meanwhile opened to nearly ten miles, but Beatty did not wait for the battleships to rejoin, for the High Seas Fleet battleships had been reported still in harbor, his six battle cruisers could stand up to the German five, and he yearned for another chance at Hipper, for he was convinced that ill luck had cheated him of an overwhelming victory in the Dogger Bank action.

While Beatty's 1st and 3rd Light Cruiser

Squadrons engaged Scouting Squadron II and drew it away to NW, Hipper, in the *Lützow,* turned his battle cruisers to SSW, and the British battle cruisers worked around to the NE, each commander moving to cut off the opposing light units and ignorant of the other's presence. Beatty at 2:47 ordered the *Engadine* to send up a seaplane reconnaissance. One aircraft was launched but the 1,000-foot ceiling prevented the observer from seeing British and German ships at the same time. After he had sent three reports of enemy light cruisers, the plane's fuel line broke, forcing the pilot to descend. He and his observer were the first fleet airmen to participate in a naval battle.

Beatty's easterly changes of course and his restriction of speed to 23 knots enabled Evan-Thomas to cut corners and reduce his distance. The German battle cruisers increased to 25 knots as Hipper turned W and then NW to support Scouting Group II.

THE BATTLE CRUISER ACTION

The dispersion of the scouting forces on both sides after 2:20 had resulted in an unexpected meeting of the battle cruisers. At 3:20 Hipper made out two columns of large ships—the two British battle cruiser divisions—forward of his port beam, and promptly steered to get across their line of advance. The *Princess Royal* sighted the Germans two minutes later, and at 3:28 Beatty changed course from NE to E to cut off the new enemy force. Hipper then countermarched to the right and recalled his light cruisers. At 3:45 the opposing battle cruiser squadrons were on parallel courses heading ESE, disposed on lines of bearing—Germans on the starboard quarter, British on the port—to keep each ship clear of its neighbors' smoke. Hipper now prepared to lead the British towards Scheer's guns. His destroyers were on his disengaged side, his light cruisers astern. The battle-wise Goodenough from his position at the southern end of the

scouting line closed to screen the battle cruisers when Beatty turned SSW. He refused to be drawn to the NW after the other light cruisers and maintained the 2nd Light Cruiser Squadron five miles ahead of Beatty, keeping his cruiser "eyes" on the southern horizon—in the direction of the German bases. Two flotillas of Beatty's destroyers

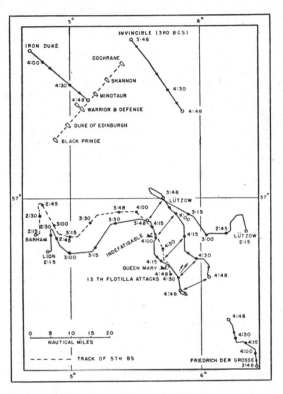

APPROACH OF THE FLEETS AND BATTLE CRUISER ACTION, 2:15-4:48 PM, MAY 31

pulled up on his battle cruisers to gain an attack position on their engaged bow.

When the battle cruiser forces closed to gun range, Scheer and Hipper were 47 miles apart, steaming toward each other. Jellicoe, 52 miles to the northwest, had been receiving information since the first contact. As early as 2:43 he had changed the line of bearing of his division guides to bring it to right angles with the enemy's bearing. He had gone up to 19 knots and now ordered steam for 20.

At 3:48 when the range between the battle cruiser forces was down to 16,500 yards, Hipper signaled to open fire, and salvos rippled down the German line. Atmospheric conditions at this time favored the Germans: the western horizon was clear, and the British vessels were silhouetted against a blue sky. Low-lying mists rendered visibility to the northeast extremely patchy, so that the British range finders were giving readings in excess of actual ranges. This caused Beatty to hold his fire so long that he lost the advantage of the greater range of his guns. Captain Chatfield of the *Lion* on his own responsibility ordered his gunnery officer to open fire. Both sides made slight changes of course to hamper the other's fire control, but in the first phase the Germans shot splendidly. They used their superior optical instruments to advantage and were early on their targets. Closely-grouped half-salvos fell at 20-second intervals.

Within four minutes the *Lion* was steaming through straddling water columns higher than the funnels and received her first two heavy hits. The range gradually decreased to 14,000 yards. About 4 PM the flagship barely escaped destruction from a penetrating 12-inch hit on the midships "Q" turret which blew off a roofplate. Ready charges ignited; fire flared down through the turret trunk into the handling room; the turret crew was wiped out. Only the sense of duty of the turret officer, a major of marines, who with his dying breath gave orders to close the magazine doors, prevented the flash from reaching the magazines. Presently a second powder fire roared through the open turret roof and rose higher than the mastheads. The prompt action taken by the doomed survivors of the initial blast saved the ship.

After 13 minutes of firing, the *Von der Tann* at 4:05 landed two salvos in quick succession on the *Indefatigable,* one on the quarter-deck abreast the after turret, the other under the fore turret. Two cordite fire balls leaped upward from the hull and the British battle cruiser rolled over and sank, leaving only three survivors.

Soon afterward things appeared to improve for Beatty, for at 4:05 the 5th Battle Squadron had closed to within firing range and her guns opened fire at 19,000 yards on the rear German ships. They soon reached the *Von der Tann,* knocking out her "A" turret and piercing her armor belt so that hundreds of tons of water poured into her hull. A 13.5-inch salvo from the *Queen Mary* then hit the *Seydlitz;* two shells struck her "C" turret and ignited powder charges, killing all hands in the turret and handling room. Four of the five German battle cruisers had been heavily hit. "Our fire began to tell," reported Beatty afterward, "the accuracy and rapidity of that of the enemy depreciating considerably." Hipper commented: "It was nothing but the poor quality of the British bursting charges that saved us from disaster." [4]

Beatty's optimism was premature. At 4:26 the *Derfflinger* dropped two salvos on the *Queen Mary* and exploded her magazines. Masts and stacks collapsed inboard, and the 29,000-ton battle cruiser broke in half and disappeared in a smoke pall that rose to a height of over a thousand feet. The *Lion*'s captain recalled that he and Beatty both looked around "in time to see the unpleasant spectacle. . . . Beatty turned to me and said, 'There seems to be something wrong with our bloody ships today,' a remark which needed neither comment nor answer. There *was* something wrong." [5]

The tactical reversal for the British was already being redressed however, for Evan-Thomas had come into full action and the salvos from his ships helped deter Hipper from closing to exploit his advantage after the destruction of the *Queen Mary*. At 4:23 the German battle cruisers were rapidly nearing their battle fleet and the decisive moment was at hand, when Hipper abruptly turned away 56 degrees to avoid torpedoes launched by British destroyers and passed out of effective range. Beatty had ordered the attack half an hour earlier, but the destroyers had difficulty gaining positions ahead

[4] Quoted in Rear Admiral W. S. Chalmers RN, *The Life and Letters of David, Earl Beatty* (London, 1951), 234.
[5] Admiral of the Fleet A. E. M. (Lord) Chatfield RN, *The Navy and Defence* (London, 1942), 143.

of the large ships, now steaming at 25 knots. Commander Barry Bingham in the *Nestor* led 12 destroyers across to attack the battle cruisers. The *Regensburg* and 15 destroyers came out to meet them and a series of "dog-fights" at ranges as short as a few hundred yards took place between the battle lines. After sinking two German destroyers Bingham pressed on toward the battle cruisers. Hipper continued turning away and at 4:30 was steering E, nearly at right angles to Beatty's line.

The action had been broken off at the decisive moment; three minutes previously Goodenough in the *Southampton* reported by searchlight: "Battleships to SE," and followed with a radio message which is quoted as a model contact report: "Course of enemy's battle fleet, N, single line ahead. Composition of van, *Kaiser* class. Bearing of center, E. Destroyers on both wings and ahead. Enemy's battle cruisers joining battle fleet from northward. My position lat. 56°29′ N, long. 6°14′ E." [6]

Hipper's turnaway gave Beatty a breathing spell and enabled him to get a better look at the developing situation. He held on his course and at 4:40 saw a long line of masts and funnels emerging from under smoke banks on the southern horizon and coming directly toward him. The whole situation had changed in an instant. Until the moment of receiving Goodenough's dispatch Beatty was unaware that the German battle fleet was at sea, though it was a possibility he always had in mind. [7] Now he was presented with an opportunity to turn the tables and lead the whole High Seas Fleet unsuspecting into Jellicoe's clutches. It was essential to prevent Scheer from receiving early warning of the Grand Fleet's approach; Hipper's scouting forces must be kept close to their battle fleet or headed away if they should approach Jellicoe too far in advance of their main body.

The *Lion* broke out a hoist for a 16-point turn in succession and the battle cruisers at 4:43 countermarched and headed at full speed to close Jellicoe by the most direct course. This well-timed maneuver kept the ships out of range of Scheer's guns. The 5th Battle Squadron now bore down on the opposite course, and as the *Barham* passed abeam, Beatty signaled the battleships to turn in succession. Because Evan-Thomas had not yet sighted the High Seas Fleet through the smoke, he delayed in executing the order. At 4:57 when he had steadied on the northerly course he was four miles behind Beatty and his ships were coming under fire from the Hipper's battle cruisers and Scheer's van battleships. The *Barham* and *Valiant* took the former under fire; the rear ships, *Warspite* and *Malaya,* engaged the latter. These fine new battleships gave out far more than they took, scoring five heavy hits to one during the first five minutes of firing.

Hipper in the meantime had counter-marched and come into position in the van of the battle fleet. Rather unaccountably he had recalled his destroyers, and they thereby missed a valuable opportunity to inflict torpedo damage on British capital ships and leave them crippled under the guns of the whole High Seas Fleet. Bingham now pressed in under heavy fire with the destroyers *Nestor, Nomad,* and *Nicator* to within 3,000 yards of the German battle cruisers and fired ten torpedoes. The *Seydlitz* was hit in the forward torpedo room, which quickly flooded, but she maintained her position in the line. So close was the action that the destroyers blazed away with their 4-inch guns, causing casualties among bridge personnel and damaging searchlights and radio antennae of the battle cruisers. They were followed by five more British destroyers, which made a second attack, getting off some shots at the van battleships also. The German vessels avoided the torpedoes by quick maneuvering, but the attacks helped ease the pressure on Beatty's withdrawing squadrons. The *Nestor* and the *Nomad* went dead in the water and were sunk under the concentrated fire of the German van battleships, but not before Bingham had fired his last torpedo.

---

[6] *Jutland Despatches,* 453.
[7] Chatfield, *The Navy and Defence,* 144.

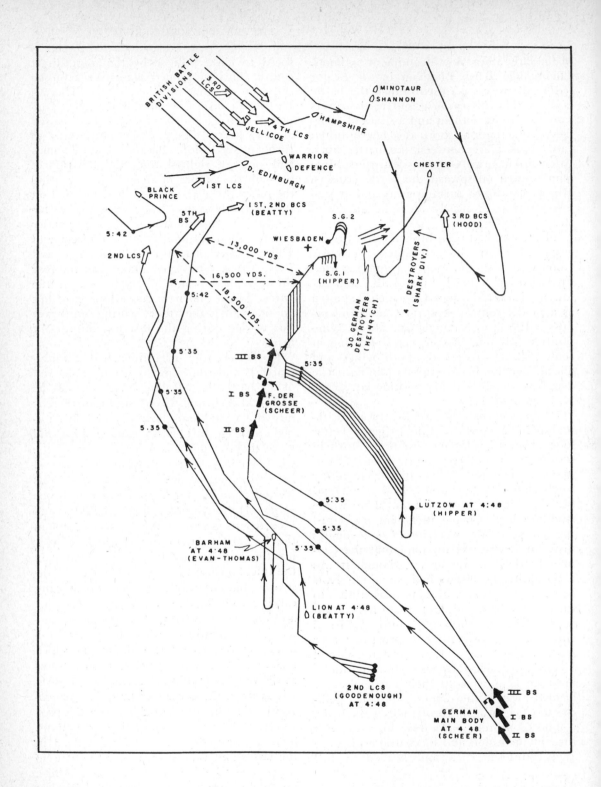

PURSUIT OF THE BRITISH BATTLE CRUISERS, 4:48-6:00 PM

THE PURSUIT OF THE BRITISH BATTLE CRUISER FORCE

From 4:50 to 6 PM the German fleet pursued the distant group of Evan-Thomas's battleships and the shadowy forms of Beatty's battle cruisers two miles farther ahead. Closer at hand and sharply visible at 16,000 yards, four smaller British ships moved on constantly changing courses, to the perplexity of Scheer, who reported that "their vague and purposeless hurrying to and fro led one to think that our fire had reached them and . . . had so surprised them that they did not know which way to turn next." [8] Had he grasped the significance of the erratic performance he would have shed some calm; they were Goodenough's scouts maintaining contact under fire of ten German battleships and reporting his position to Jellicoe. During the next hour the *Southampton* in the rear was missed within 100 yards by between 50 and 60 heavy shells, most of which burst on impact with the water and showered the decks with fragments. Her own guns, ranged for a maximum of 14,500 yards, were silent. Goodenough when later asked how he had escaped being sunk replied: "Simply by steering for the splashes of the last enemy salvo." [9]

The gun duel between the 5th Battle Squadron and the High Seas Fleet continued steadily. Evan-Thomas was steaming at 25 knots but Scheer's dreadnoughts at 22 knots converged on his course and kept within range. The Germans with many more ships made 17 hits; the British made 12, most of them on the battle cruisers. That the British battleships received no serious damage clearly demonstrated the value of their heavy armor. Toward the end of the hour the German fire became sporadic as the sun came out from clouds near the horizon and blinded the spotters.

When Jellicoe received Beatty's 3:45 dispatch informing him that the battle cruisers were about to engage Hipper, he changed to a SSE course to close and increased speed to 20 knots. At 4:05 he ordered Hood's 3rd Battle Cruiser Squadron, 27 miles ahead, to support Beatty. The three battle cruisers, with four destroyers, turned and headed on a southerly course at 25 knots.

The *Southampton's* 4:38 report gave Jellicoe his first intimation that the German battle fleet was at sea. He passed the information to his squadrons and at 4:51 sent the Admiralty the brief and stirring message: "Fleet action is imminent." His primary task now was to secure accurate information regarding the position, course, and speed of the enemy so that he could deploy his 24 battleships like a wall across Scheer's line of advance. The wall would then be advanced and rotated to fend the German fleet from its bases. With his battle cruisers and fastest battleships in the van Jellicoe believed that, like Togo at Tsushima, he could keep ahead of the enemy van and turn its direction of advance away from the path of escape. A stern chase, the contingency he so greatly feared, would in these circumstances be avoided. Should darkness fall he would maneuver to keep between the enemy and his base, eschewing the risks and uncertainties of night action, and be ready to use his gun superiority at dawn.

Such was Jellicoe's tactical doctrine, but many of his officers failed to be convinced of its soundness and advocated a more flexible system in the Nelsonian tradition.[10] Concentration could most easily be achieved, they argued, by independent squadron action, a method that possessed the additional virtues of requiring the exercise of initiative of subordinates and of bringing the Grand Fleet's numerical superiority to bear most fully. The principal difficulty confronting the "decentralizers" was communications. Operating procedures had not yet been devised to enable a commander in chief to re-

[8] Admiral R. Scheer, *Germany's High Seas Fleet in the World War* (London, 1920), 147.

[9] Quoted in Chalmers, *Earl Beatty*, 243. Actually his navigator carefully calculated the distance between the successive "walking salvos," steering from them when they moved away, and through them when they approached.

[10] See Vice Admiral K. G. B. Dewar RN, *The Navy from Within* (London, 1939), 265-281.

tain over-all tactical control when squadrons moved independently at high speeds in smoke-filled battle areas or beyond visual range. Under modern conditions it seemed that Nelsonian indoctrination of subordinates in the principle of the objective, no matter how thorough, was an inadequate substitute for firm central direction. There were also important subsidiary problems of target distribution and fire control which seemed to find their most satisfactory solution in terms of the fleet line of battle.

Jellicoe recognized that two fundamental conditions under which Nelson operated no longer prevailed: in the old French wars the admiral and all his captains could see all that happened all the time, and the enemy usually stayed to fight. The glorious tradition of Hawke was hardly more applicable: there had been no mine fields, smoke screens, or torpedo boats at Quiberon Bay. In working out tactics for the Grand Fleet, Jellicoe faced problems more akin to those of Monk and the Duke of York, 250 years before, when fleets put to sea in excess of a hundred sail. The historic arguments of the "melee" advocates and of the "formalists" once more appeared, clothed in modern garb. While it was generally agreed in 1916 that concentration by squadrons was desirable in theory, no one had produced a reliable scheme for giving it effect under conditions of war as they prevailed in the North Sea.

Beatty, on turning north to lure Scheer to the British battle fleet, dispatched a detailed report of his contact by radio. The message reached Jellicoe considerably garbled. This was the first of many misleading reports that were to go to the flagship *Iron Duke* while Jellicoe was steaming to intercept the High Seas Fleet. Beatty's given position varied as much as 20 miles from those reported by Goodenough, and none of these could be reconciled with radio fixes of the German fleet positions sent by the Admiralty. The British ships had been at sea for 17 hours, and separated components of the Grand Fleet had been subject to differences of tide and wind that magnified errors of dead reckoning. After they went into battle, frequent changes of course and hazards in-

cident to battle increased the difficulties of the navigators.[11]

Hood in steering for Beatty's force was considerably to the eastward and would have missed it altogether had not the light cruiser *Chester* stumbled on Hipper's light forces of Scouting Group II and lured them through the low-lying mist under the guns of Hood's battle cruisers. These opened a rapid and accurate fire with their 12-inch guns and quickly put the light cruiser *Wiesbaden* out of action in a position where she was to come under attack by practically every segment of the Grand Fleet. Scouting Group II quickly countermarched under a smoke screen, and Hipper switched his 30 destroyers to its support. British destroyers however absorbed the attack 7,500 yards from Hood's squadron, and at that range the nine torpedoes fired at the fast-moving battle cruisers were ineffective. The destroyer leader *Shark* was left sinking at 6:10 when the German destroyers withdrew, but the aggressive action of the British destroyers had caused the heavy German blow to fall in the air. Jellicoe's deploying battleships and Beatty's battle cruisers, then engaged in driving in Hipper's scouting forces, were both saved from torpedo fire.

At 5:30 Beatty, still leading the German scouting and battle forces northward, changed course some 45 degrees to starboard and opened fire on Hipper's ships at 15,000 yards in order to turn them away from the approaching British battle fleet. With visibility in his favor he inflicted heavy punishment, forcing Hipper to give way to the right, with Scheer's battleships following six miles astern. At 5:32 Beatty's van screening units sighted the *Black Prince*, Jelli-

---

[11] The officer working the *Lion's* flag plot recalled that a heavy shell hit just below the bridge: "At the same moment the chart table over which I was leaning, split in the center and the windows fell in, exposing the chart and myself to the full blast of a head wind. I placed both hands on the chart, but the wind was too quick for me, and before I realized what had happened, the chart was torn in two, and the business half of it flew through the window. I last saw it fluttering over the sea like a frightened seagull." From the personal narrative of Chalmers, quoted in his *Earl Beatty*, 241-242.

coe's southernmost cruiser, thereby establishing visual contact with the battle fleet. Judging that Jellicoe would deploy to the left, Beatty turned closer to Hipper, bending the enemy scouting forces still farther away from Jellicoe's advancing battle divisions and toward his port flank. Hipper thereupon temporarily reversed course and fell back on Scheer. As we have seen, Hipper was obliged to send to the aid of Scouting Group II the destroyers which he intended to use against Beatty. Exaggerated reports of the encounter between Scouting Group II and Hood's battle cruisers led Scheer to conclude that the British main body was much farther to the east than it actually was.

Hood, heading NW after engaging Scouting Group II, observed Beatty approaching directly ahead. Under cover of the destroyer battle, he countermarched into line at 6:17, three miles in advance of the *Lion*. Beatty had steamed across the heads of Jellicoe's deploying columns and had come around a full 90 degrees to course SE. He was now leading the 1st Division of British battleships and was working across the path of the German advance.

CONTACTS OF THE MAIN FLEETS

While Beatty was leading the High Seas Fleet to the north, the six British battleship columns steamed abreast to intercept. Jellicoe tried to resolve the discrepancies in his information, but these were so serious that any decision involved guesswork. He needed ten minutes to deploy the fleet from cruising formation into line of battle. Should he wait for actual contact before deploying in misty weather when gun range exceeded visual range, he risked coming under fire when his line was incompletely formed and the batteries of some of his ships were masked by their division mates. Successful deployment before contact required a preliminary flow of accurate information from his scouting forces, and this Jellicoe did not have. The armored cruisers of his own screen, furthermore, were unable to maintain the pace at

full speed, and the battleships by now were only six miles behind them. Jellicoe considered deploying on his right or western flank division, enabling Beatty's battle cruisers and fast battleships readily to take positions in the van. He estimated the time of contact with Scheer to be 6:20. After deploying into line the Grand Fleet would continue its easterly course to cross the enemy "T" or turn to the south and double the rear of the High Seas Fleet to prevent it from regaining its base.

It was a shock to the staff on the bridge of the *Iron Duke* when the *Black Prince* at the western end of the cruiser line at 5:42 reported enemy battle cruisers five miles ahead —only 11 miles from the Grand Fleet battleships. Jellicoe concluded correctly that the battle cruisers must be not enemy but his own, and received confirmation a minute later from the battleship *Marlborough* on the right flank. But the contact placed Beatty—and therefore the enemy—at least 11 miles farther west than had been anticipated. At 6:00 Beatty's ships were seen from Jellicoe's flagship five miles on the starboard bow heading east across the heads of the battleship divisions. Jellicoe signaled: "Where is the enemy's battle fleet?" Beatty, heavily engaged with Hipper and unable to see Scheer's column, replied, "Enemy battle cruisers bear to SE." To gain more ground to the westward, Jellicoe turned his divisions somewhat to starboard, putting them in line of bearing. But since he expected to sight the enemy momentarily, he quickly headed back to SE, directly for the expected point of contact and the course which kept his division guides directly abeam and in position for deploying most easily.

Jellicoe first intended to deploy to the right in the direction of the firing, but he realized that his oldest battleships were in the starboard battle squadron, and immediate contact would put him at a tactical disadvantage. He accordingly decided to deploy to port and work around between the German fleet and the coast. He hung on to his course until the last moment, waiting for a report from some ship which had both fleets in sight. The information came at 6:14

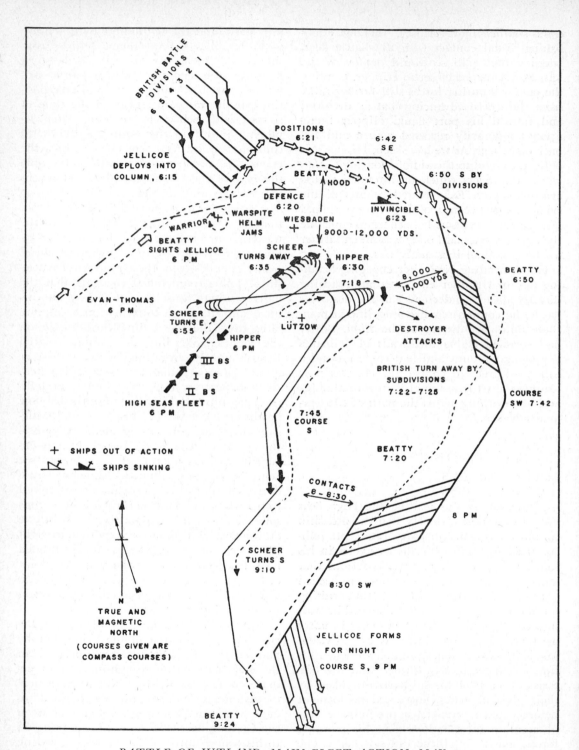

BATTLE OF JUTLAND, MAIN FLEET ACTION, MAY 31

when Beatty, having crowded Hipper's scouting forces back on Scheer's battle divisions, sighted the main body and signaled "Enemy battle fleet bearing SSW." Evan-Thomas confirmed the information at the same time. Jellicoe then ordered the British battleship divisions to deploy into single column with the port wing division leading on course SE by E.

At that moment Beatty's battle cruisers were steaming at high speed across the van of the British battleship division, making smoke which concealed the opposing battleship forces from each other. In advance of Jellicoe's dreadnoughts his armored cruiser screen was converging rapidly on Beatty and at the same time coming under enemy fire. Between the British and German forces lay the helpless *Wiesbaden* under attack by Beatty's destroyers. Here at "Windy Corner," as this general meeting point came to be called, "there was handling of ships . . . such as had never been dreamt of by seamen before." [12]

As the British battleships deployed, it became the duty of Jellicoe's armored cruisers to clear the range and pass over to the disengaged side of the battle line. The 2nd Cruiser Squadron on the left side of the scouting line promptly turned to port and crossed ahead of the deploying battleships. The *Duke of Edinburgh* and the *Black Prince* passed respectively ahead and astern of the six battle divisions; but the *Defence,* flagship of the 1st Cruiser Squadron, followed by the *Warrior,* made a wide turn to right, passing so close to Beatty's oncoming ships that the *Lion* swung sharply left to avoid collision. The squadron commander wanted to finish off the *Wiesbaden* and get in a final contact report on the German fleet. As the two armored cruisers passed down between the battle lines, they came under such concentrated fire from all guns of the *Lützow,* the *Derfflinger,* and four of Scheer's most powerful battleships that the *Warrior* staggered out of action and the *Defence* blew up with all hands.

Evan-Thomas, coming up four miles

[12] Quoted by Commander Holloway H. Frost USN, *The Battle of Jutland* (Annapolis, 1936), 305.

astern of Beatty and observing the deployment well advanced, turned his ships sharply left in succession at 6:18 to fall in behind the 6th Battleship Division in the rear. While executing this maneuver the *Warspite* jammed her helm and swung to starboard towards the German dreadnoughts. Quite by chance the *Warspite's* uncontrolled turn caused her to circle and draw enemy fire away from the shattered *Warrior*. But both the battleship and the cruiser were too badly crippled to continue in the line. The *Warspite,* saved by her thick armor decks, made it back to port under her own steam; the *Warrior* sank the next day while under tow. Meanwhile the luckless *Wiesbaden,* taken under fire by each British battleship and battle cruiser division, was reduced to a wrecked hulk without a gun in action. That night she rolled over and sank.

By deploying his 24 battleships from six columns of four each into a single column with the battle cruisers in the van and Evan-Thomas's three remaining battleships in the rear, Jellicoe brought the Grand Fleet into its long practiced battle formation. The evolution had put the British in the highly advantageous situation of steaming southward between the High Seas Fleet and the Danish coast, and across the only practicable line of German retreat. Both the poor visibility and the lateness of the hour made it imperative that Jellicoe lose neither time nor contact and turn decisively toward his enemy. Yet within a little more than an hour following his deployment order, he twice capped the "T" on the High Seas Fleet without quite realizing that he had done so and certainly without taking full advantage of his luck.

Hipper's Scouting Group I of battle cruisers, as we have seen, had been forced by Beatty's cruisers to fall back on Scheer's battle fleet, which they were now leading on course NE. By 6:21 Scouting Group I, converging through the haze on the head of Jellicoe's column, came within range of Hood's 3rd Battle Cruiser Squadron, then somewhat in advance of the main British line, and were taken under heavy fire. Hipper thereupon turned right to course SE to avoid being capped. In a brief, fierce engagement, Hipper's flagship *Lützow* was put out of action after receiving her 20th hit of the battle, and Hood's flagship *Invincible* was sunk. The *Invincible's* "Q" turret was pierced, and the flash from ignited powder charges passed down to the handling room and entered the magazine. Flames burst from her hull followed by two gigantic fireballs, her midship structure collapsed, and she broke in two and sank, taking down more than a thousand men including Admiral Hood. Hipper soon shifted from the disabled *Lützow* to a destroyer in order to transfer to another battle cruiser but became separated from his own force for three hours, during which time Captain Hartog of the *Derfflinger* assumed command of Scouting Group I.

When the van of Scheer's battleship column reached the waters where Hipper and Hood had engaged, Jellicoe's leading battleship divisions had already deployed on their easterly course. These now steamed across Scheer's bows delivering heavy fire all along the line. The leading German battleship *König*, hit twice, began to list. The battleship *Markgraf,* also hit twice, lost power in one of her engines. In reply the Germans could do very little, for all they could see to the north was a line of flashes from British gunfire. Conditions of visibility were not much better for the Grand Fleet. "Only three or four ships [were] in sight at a time from the van and center," wrote Jellicoe in his report. "Ships fired at what they could see when they could see it."

Here was a desperate situation from which Scheer had to extricate himself quickly or else take heavy losses without being able to retaliate. Luckily for the Germans they were well trained in just the maneuver needed to back out of such a spot. At 6:35 Scheer ordered a "battle turn"—a ripple movement beginning at the rear—180 degrees to the right. After completing this intricate reversal of direction without collision, he steadied on a southwesterly course.

Though several British battleships had observed Scheer's turnaway, they failed to report it to the Commander in Chief. Jellicoe

knew only that some German ships had appeared and then as suddenly disappeared into the mist and smoke. In any event, doctrine prescribed no countermeasure, for Scheer's fleet turn had not been considered practicable by British naval officers. Instead of turning to follow the Germans, Jellicoe maintained course for four minutes after his battleships had lost their targets and ceased fire. Then he changed the fleet course only one point to the right, to SE. Fortunately for the British the ever-vigilant Goodenough left the rear of the line and headed for the retreating German ships to keep them under observation, certainly a bold action since he would come under concentrated close-range fire should his ships break suddenly out of the mist and become clearly visible.

As the Grand Fleet continued to SE without finding targets, Jellicoe concluded that the range was opening. So at 6:50 he ordered the 24 battleships of his main body to turn south (to course 167°) by divisions. At that moment Scheer in the *Friedrich der Grosse,* after 15 minutes on the reverse course, was 12 miles SW of the British fleet. The German commander in chief now ordered his squadrons into another battle turn and headed east in single column for the enemy. The battered German battle cruisers resumed their places at the head of the line, less than 10,000 yards from the British battleships and closing them at right angles. It is not clear why Scheer put the battle cruisers in his van when undamaged battleships were available to lend power to his fighting front. He appears at this time to have been groping by instinct; and his reasons for turning again toward a concentrated enemy after he had barely completed disengagement he afterwards set forth in his memoirs in very general terms: "The maneuver would be bound to surprise the enemy, to upset his plans for the rest of the day, and if the blow fell heavily it would facilitate our breaking loose at night. The sight of the *Wiesbaden* helped also to strengthen my resolve to make an effort to render assistance to her and at least save the crew." [13]

---

[13] Scheer, *High Seas Fleet,* 155.

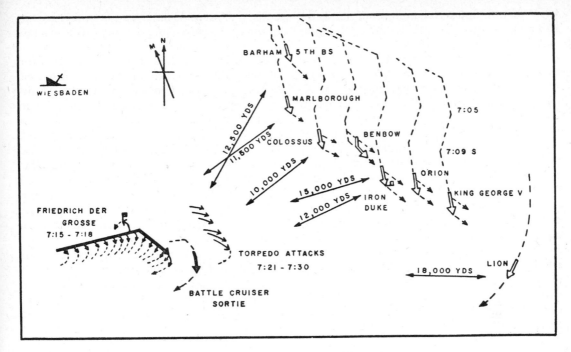

BATTLE OF JUTLAND: THE CRISIS, 7:15-7:25

At 6:55, when Scheer issued orders for the battle turn against Jellicoe, the German destroyer commodores ordered an attack; but the blow was deprived of full force by a further decision to detach eight destroyers—four to succor the *Wiesbaden* and the others to cover the *Lützow*. At 7:04 Goodenough sent the vital information that the German fleet was heading east. One minute later Jellicoe turned all his battleships 34 degrees toward the enemy, to course SSW.

The Battle of Jutland now moved to its crisis. The *Derfflinger* came into view of the British at 7:04 and was straddled by battleships capping the German line; the light cruiser *Regensburg* and the massed destroyers were also seen approaching from the west, nearly ahead. Jellicoe promptly at 7:09 pulled his battleships back to course S to put them in division columns; Scheer's battleships appeared out of the mist, and now the German van ships came under a deluge of British projectiles without being able to make more than a feeble response from their turrets. Forty-five minutes after his first es-

cape Scheer had cast aside all advantage and was marching his fleet into the maws of an unassailable antagonist. The German Official History admits that "this was against all the rules of the game"; total disaster was now within measurable distance.

Scheer from his position in the center of the line did not realize that the battle cruisers were already in the van and ordered them at 7:13 to turn and attack the enemy. One minute later he modified his order, directing the battle cruisers "to operate against the enemy van." Then at 7:15 he began to dispatch the order for a third 16-point battle turn by the fleet. Hartog before he received Scheer's orders realized that it was impossible to go on. His ships were under the most devastating fire yet experienced in the action and suffering heavy hits in rapid succession. He turned away to the southward and eventually steadied on course SE. During the ten minutes of his withdrawal, the *Derfflinger's* two after turrets were hit and burned out with few survivors; the *Von der Tann* was struck on the conning tower and all inside were killed. Some relief was afforded the stricken battle cruisers after 7:18 when the attacking destroyer flotillas advanced beyond them and covered them with smoke. In the meantime the German battle fleet was turning away, and Scheer kept on around to course W. The High Seas Fleet was now withdrawing at right angles to the course of the Grand Fleet.

When the British were firing most rapidly at the head of the German column, Jellicoe at 7:12 began maneuvers to rotate his fleet axis to the right to bring the powerful ships of his van battle squadron closer to the enemy. As the divisions turned intricately to form a single line ahead on the new bearing, the first group of German destroyers was discerned approaching in V-formation to attack. Four destroyers headed in to 7,500 yards at 7:21, fired 11 torpedoes and withdrew behind smoke. Nine more attacked three minutes later and got off 20 torpedoes. The British battleships opened with their secondary batteries, putting six destroyers out of action and sinking a seventh with a single heavy shell. A third wave was intercepted by the 4th Light Cruiser Squadron and broken up before it could get within effective torpedo range.

At the first torpedo splash, Jellicoe ordered the orthodox countermeasure, turning the battle fleet away 45 degrees, from S to SE, the ships of each sub-division twice turning two points in succession. Fourteen minutes later at 7:35 when the torpedoes were crossing the battle line, he swung back 56 degrees (five points) toward the German smoke screens and at 7:42 another 34 degrees (three points), coming eventually to course SW. His turnaway from the torpedoes cost Jellicoe 4,000 yards of range on the German fleet and a favorable opportunity to close decisively. But Scheer was also steering SW and Jellicoe believed himself again to be in position to fend his opponent from his base.

As Jellicoe steadied on course SW in single line ahead at 7:45 there remained a half hour till sunset and an additional hour of twilight. The battle cruisers were six miles on the starboard bow of the van battle division and on a parallel course, with the armored cruiser *Minotaur* midway between as communicating ship. The Grand Fleet was extended in a gradually curving formation 16 miles long. Beatty had not conformed to the battle fleet's turnaway and was keeping the German battle cruisers in sight. They however were still heading SW and he lost them behind the smoke of their van destroyers at 7:45. Five minutes earlier he had reported, "Enemy bearing NW" and now signaled Jellicoe: "Urgent. Submit van of battleships follow battle cruisers. We can then cut off whole of enemy's battle fleet," the last portion undoubtedly meaning "head off." A hitch in transmission held up delivery 20 minutes, but on receiving Beatty's first report at 7:59 Jellicoe immediately turned the battle fleet west by divisions to course 257°, and headed more directly toward the German fleet than the battle cruisers, a fact which deprived Beatty's second message of its significance. Meanwhile at 7:45 Scheer had brought the High Seas Fleet to course S. His battle cruisers now came abeam of the German pre-dreadnoughts, which had been in the van position since the 7:18 turnaway. Again Scheer's weakest units were leading his battle line, and the two fleets with their flagships 16 miles apart were converging at 45 degrees.

A little after 8 PM Beatty's light cruisers made contact with Hartog's and opened fire. Beatty, turning west to lend support, encountered Scouting Group I and with a series of salvos disabled the *Derfflinger's* last effective turret and wiped out the forebridge crew of the *Seydlitz*. As Hartog's battle cruisers disappeared to the west behind smoke, Beatty made out the German pre-dreadnoughts. After another rapid exchange of fire, the pre-dreadnoughts also swung away to the west.

Beatty's battle cruisers, which had fired the first British salvos five hours before, had fired the last of the day. Scheer had already turned the German battle fleet SW with the van and presently steadied on course S. Jellicoe had brought the British battle fleet to course SW and was preparing to take night dispositions. "Darkness was now rapidly setting in," said Jellicoe in his report; "the mist was increasing and it became necessary to decide on the future course of action. The British fleet was between the enemy and his base. . . . I rejected at once the idea of a night action between heavy ships, as leading to possible disaster, first, owing to the presence of torpedo craft in such large numbers, and secondly, to the impossibility of distinguishing between our own and enemy vessels. Further, the result of a night action under modern conditions must always be very largely a matter of pure chance. I was loath to forego the advantage of position which would have resulted from an easterly or westerly course, and I therefore decided to steer to the southward, where I should be in a position to renew the engagement at daylight." [14] Jellicoe changed course to S at 9 P.M. Twenty-four minutes later Beatty also headed south confident that the German fleet lay to the west cut off from its bases. The three groups were now steaming southward on nearly parallel courses: Beatty eight miles south of Scheer, Jellicoe nine miles abeam of the High Seas Fleet to the east.

THE NIGHT ACTION

Beginning at 9:17 the British battle fleet maneuvered into night cruising formation. The four battle squadrons took station one mile apart for visual identification. The 4th Light Cruiser Squadron preceded the battleship formation and Goodenough's 2nd Light Cruiser Squadron followed on the starboard quarter. Beatty's force, including besides the battle cruisers one armored cruiser squadron and two light cruiser squadrons, was distant 13 miles on the starboard bow of the battle fleet. Jellicoe stationed his seven destroyer flotillas five miles astern "in a position in which they would afford protection to the fleet from destroyer attack and at the same time be favorably situated for attacking the enemy's heavy ships." But the destroyers received little information on the battle cruiser and light cruiser dispositions and none at all on the enemy's estimated position and course. They had no attack or-

[14] *Jutland Despatches*, 20-21.

ders and no instructions other than the stationing dispatch.

Jellicoe's decision to decline night action was correct; his task was to bar the passage of the High Seas Fleet until dawn, which would come before 3 AM. He correctly estimated that of the three swept passages through the German mine fields, Scheer would attempt to reach the nearest, which passed close to Horn Reefs. So he maintained his southerly course at 17 knots and at 9:32 sent the fast fleet minelayer *Abdiel* to mine the Horn Reefs entrances.

Scheer at 9 o'clock had only five hours in which to break through the enemy interposed between him and his base. Determined at all costs to avoid another daylight battle, he characteristically chose the simple solution to his problem. Even though he was fairly sure that the Grand Fleet lay in his path, he took the risk of the shortest route home, concurring with his opponent that luck would prove friendly to the weaker side in a night encounter. At 9:30 he headed for the breakthrough. Shifting his crippled battle cruisers to the rear, he ordered the fleet to turn in succession to SSE 1/4 E and hold the course regardless of cost—"*durchhalten.*" His destroyers, dispatched radially from NW to S, missed the sector in which the British battle fleet was concentrated.

The general movement of the night action of May 31-June 1 may be visualized as a large "X" formed by the course tracks of the British and German fleets, with the latter moving down the NW-SE leg. A series of short and deadly encounters at point blank range flared up at intervals between 10:15 PM and 2 AM as the German battleships and cruisers passed a scant half dozen miles astern of the British battle fleet and forced their way through the screening light forces.

The confused night encounters began when the light cruiser *Castor* leading a flotilla of British destroyers sighted oncoming ships in the darkness. These were German light cruisers. They flashed part of the British recognition signal and then snapped on searchlights and opened fire, holing the *Castor* nine or ten times. The *Castor* replied

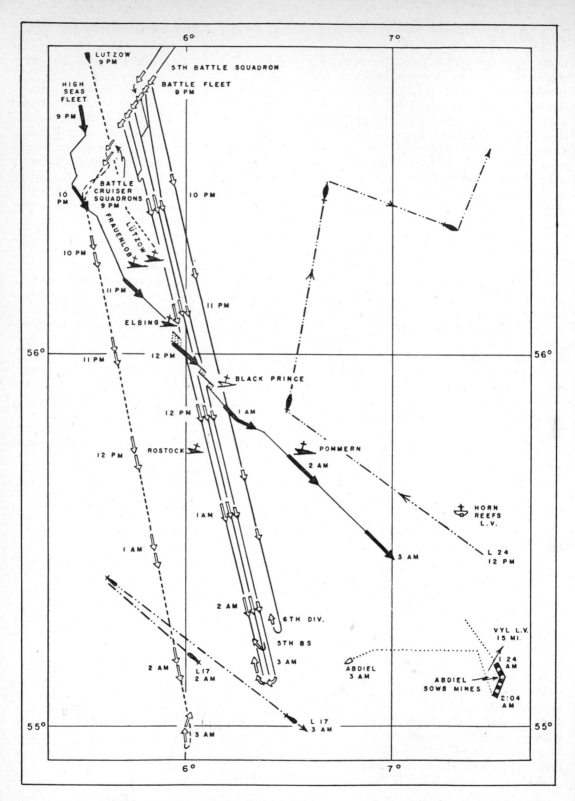

RETREAT OF THE HIGH SEAS FLEET, 9 PM - 3 AM, MAY 31 - JUNE 1

hotly, but the flotilla commander ordered the destroyers not to fire torpedoes, in conformity with fleet doctrine that in event of doubt big ships should fire and destroyers wait. Fifteen minutes later Goodenough's light cruisers were elbowed by Scouting Group IV. In the short, sharp engagement which followed, the *Southampton*, Goodenough's flagship, and the *Dublin* were heavily damaged by gunfire, and the German light cruiser *Frauenlob* was sunk by a torpedo. The torpedo officer of the *Southampton* recalled: "On the bridge the full glare of the searchlights of the leading enemy ship was on us, and we could see nothing, but I had already received enough impression of the general direction of advance of the enemy for the purpose of torpedo fire, so I passed down an order to the torpedo flat and waited impatiently for a reply. When it came through—the report 'ready'—I fired at a group of hostile searchlights, which were the only things visible." [15]

The German van reached the center of the British formation 11:45. The British 4th Flotilla was suddenly flooded by searchlight beams, accompanied by broadsides of 5.9-inch shells which left the flotilla leader *Tipperary* burning and helpless. A multiple high-speed collision involving the destroyers *Sparrowhawk, Broke,* and *Contest* followed, the first of these sinking some hours later. German losses were heavier: a torpedo hit the light cruiser *Rostock* and led to fatal flooding; the light cruiser *Elbing* in turning sharply away from the British destroyers ran into the bow of the battleship *Posen*. Once more in its history the ram proved more dangerous to friends than to enemies; the light cruiser continued on for a time but later went dead and was sunk by German destroyers.

This action was seen by Evan-Thomas's battleships *Malaya* and *Valiant* in the rear of the British battle fleet; but they sent no report to Jellicoe because, as a senior officer of the fleet later put it, "as it took place in full view of their own [squadron] flagship,

it would have been most improper of them to have done so." [16]

As the German battle line penetrated the British screen about midnight, heavy shells and secondary batteries quickly sank the destroyers *Ardent, Fortune,* and *Turbulent*. Searchlights suddenly illuminated the armored cruiser *Black Prince,* while four battleships concentrated fire upon her until she blew up with all hands. Despite what appear to have been numerous opportunities during the hours of darkness, the only effective counterattack by British destroyers was delivered by the 12th Flotilla beginning at 1:45 in the first light of dawn. Dashing down the German line on reverse course these destroyers fired 12 torpedoes. The battleships wheeled away to starboard, but two torpedoes found marks in the pre-dreadnought *Pommern;* her magazines were detonated and she blew up with the loss of her entire crew. The flotilla commander twice reported by radio, but jamming by the Germans prevented his vitally important dispatches from reaching the *Iron Duke*.

The last contact was made at 3:30 AM when the British light cruiser *Champion* and four destroyers sighted four enemy destroyers steaming south at full speed. The Germans fired torpedoes; the British replied with gunfire, hitting and disabling one destroyer, but neither side closed. The Germans had reason to avoid action; they were loaded with the survivors of the *Lützow,* which had been scuttled at 1:45.

The series of night actions at the Battle of Jutland resulted in large part from the fact that Jellicoe and Beatty had correctly estimated the German fleet's position but not its course. Many critics have expressed surprise that Jellicoe should have been so little suspicious of gunfire astern passing progressively from west to east. He decided that it was confined to scattered light units, and no information came from the light cruisers and destroyers concerned to alter his conclusion.

Incomplete intelligence from the Admi-

[15] H. W. Fawcett and G. W. W. Hooper, editors, *The Fighting at Jutland* (London, 1921), 303.

[16] *The Naval Memoirs of Admiral of the Fleet Sir Roger Keyes, Scapa Flow to the Dover Straits, 1916-1918* (New York, 1935), 62n.

ralty also confused the situation for the British commander in chief.[17] At 10:45 he received an obviously inaccurate report sent out at 9:58 putting the rear of the German fleet eight miles ahead of his own battleships. Had its source—the dead reckoning of a German destroyer—been mentioned, Jellicoe would have discounted the information. A second message, this time only too accurate, paraphrased three intercepts and stated that the German battle fleet was ordered home at 9:14, battle cruisers in the rear, and gave the course and speed. This was sent off at 10:44 and was handed to Jellicoe at 11:30. Shortly afterward two dispatches arrived from his light cruisers: one from the *Birmingham* announcing that the enemy's battle cruisers were steering south; the other—a jammed 10:45 dispatch from the *Southampton* via the *Nottingham* received at 11:38—putting Scouting Group IV to the west of the battle fleet's track.[18] In view of what appeared to him to be the Admiralty's poor record for reliability in the past 12 hours, Jellicoe disregarded the 10:44 message in favor of evidence submitted by his men on the spot. That he lacked adequate information from his subordinates was due to improper emphasis in training; that he failed to gage the probable route of the German fleet from other evidences is the measure of his responsibility as commander in chief for the outcome—it was the salvation of the High Seas Fleet.

Jellicoe turned the British fleet north at 2:30 AM. He had intended to close Horn Reefs at dawn, but the night action had so scattered his light forces that none were in sight. One Admiralty intercept now weighed heavily with him—a High Seas Fleet request for submarines. He concluded that it was "undesirable for the Battle Fleet to close the Horn Reef at daylight, as had been my intention when deciding to steer to the south-

ward during the night. It was obviously necessary to concentrate the Battle Fleet and the destroyers before renewing action." [19] Before this concentration had been effected, he received at 3:45 another Admiralty intelligence report announcing that the High Seas Fleet at 2:30 had been only 17 miles from Horn Reefs. Scheer had passed safely through the *Abdiel's* mine field, though his battleship *Ostfriesland* struck a mine farther south off the Vyl lightship and proceeded to port with difficulty. In failing to sweep to the entrance to the German mine fields at Horn Reefs Jellicoe missed bagging the *Seydlitz*. With 5,000 tons of water in her and her forecastle deck submerged, she lay grounded off Horn Reefs until 11:00 that night and was salvaged only by pumping vessels sent out from Wilhelmshaven.

The Grand Fleet looked on an empty sea on this "glorious first of June" and cruised over the battle area until noon, when it headed for its bases. At that time Scheer heard the cables of the *Friedrich der Grosse* rattling through the hawse in Jade Bay.

THE BATTLE OF THE BATTLE OF JUTLAND

From the moment that the fleets reached port a storm of controversy raged over the battle and its results. In its strategic sense Jutland was of minor importance. Scheer had successfully escaped annihilation by flight, and he was confirmed in his conviction that he could not hope to win a fleet action because of his opponent's superior strength. The British retained secure command of the North Sea, and the blockade of Germany and the reinforcement of the Allied armies continued unimpaired.

The ratio of fleet strength at the battle was 8 to 5 in favor of the British and the ratio of losses was approximately the same, but in favor of the Germans. Of the Grand Fleet, three battle cruisers, including two first line, three armored cruisers, and eight destroyers had been sunk, and magazine ex-

[17] For analysis see Admiral Sir R. Bacon RN, *The Life of John Rushworth, Earl Jellicoe* (London, 1936), 289.

[18] It was unfortunate for Jellicoe that the *Birmingham* saw the German cruisers heading south during a temporary turnaway from British destroyers, even more so that the Admiralty omitted the 9:54 intercept of Scheer's request for dawn airship reconnaissance at Horn Reefs.

[19] Admiral Sir J. R. Jellicoe RN, *The Grand Fleet, 1914-1916* (New York, 1919), 382-383.

plosions had raised British personnel losses to the inordinately high figure of 6,097. The Germans lost one old battleship, one battle cruiser, four light cruisers, and five destroyers. The blunt Admiralty communiqué released immediately after the battle made no attempt to conceal the losses; it was received by the British public and the Navy with bitter disappointment, the more so because both had been schooled in the Nelsonian tradition. For the moment the new German navy was left with a sense of achievement, but the moral effects of its excellent showing against the world's most powerful fleet were gradually dissipated by continued inactivity in port.

The material results of Jutland were more significant, if less publicized. German gunnery was seen to be of far higher quality than the British had previously been prepared to admit, though the vulnerability of the British battle cruisers compared with the German ships of the same class caused it to reflect less fairly on British gunnery proficiency than is warranted by statistics of the hits scored. The British learned at Jutland the lessons in damage control which the Germans had absorbed and utilized after the Dogger Bank action to increase the battleworthiness of their ships.

After his return to Scapa Flow, Jellicoe appointed committees from the fleet to analyze battle experience and make recommendations. The most significant achievement of the investigation was the redesign of the British armor-piercing shell and the adoption of a less sensitive bursting charge. It was shown that the destruction of the *Indefatigable* was probably due to insufficient armor protection of her magazines. Additional armor was worked on to turret tops and protective decks of all the capital ships of the Grand Fleet. The loss of the *Queen Mary* and *Invincible* was attributed to faulty fire precautions and the practice of passing ammunition through open magazine doors in action. Additional fire screens, baffles, and flameproof scuttles were installed, and other measures were taken to prevent the chance of downward flash from cordite in turrets. But some Grand Fleet officers believed that the development of the fast battleships of the *Barham* class made the British battle cruisers obsolete. They were quick to testify to the quality of German ships. Admiral Sir Roger Keyes stated it as his opinion that:

Our ill-fated battle cruisers were the offspring of Lord Fisher, who was obsessed by the belief that a combination of heavy long-range guns to annihilate, and high speed to keep out of the range of the enemy, were essential qualities for carrying out the functions of armoured cruisers, though he apparently did not foresee that in the normally low visibility of the North Sea his weakly protected ships might well receive vital injury before their speed would enable them to escape.

The Falkland Island action was fought in clear weather, and our battle cruisers, with their 12-inch guns, were able to keep outside the effective range of the slower German armoured cruisers, thus fully justifying Lord Fisher's contention. No doubt our battle cruisers could be relied upon to catch and destroy all existing armoured cruisers in good visibility; but in the meantime Admiral von Tirpitz, with a clearer vision than Lord Fisher, had been preparing the German answer to our battle cruisers, and after exhaustive and costly experiment he produced ships protected to withstand torpedoes and the heavy gunfire of our capital ships, and mounting guns of equally long range, though of lighter calibre than those of their British contemporaries. It is true that von Tirpitz also sacrificed a little speed to obtain protection, but Jutland most emphatically justified his wisdom.[20]

Jellicoe, as a former Director of Naval Ordnance, spared no pains to ferret out defects in material. The overhauling of tactical doctrine proceeded more slowly. By 1916 technological developments in land and sea warfare had made for maximum obscurity in the handling of armies and fleets and had undermined the basis of tactics—elasticity. The long range gun, high speeds of operation, the diversity of ship types, and above all the increase in the mass of material was unaccompanied by a corresponding extension of the fleet commander's "eyesight," which was later provided by the airplane. The fleets at Jutland have aptly been compared to bodies without arms. Concentra-

[20] *Keyes Memoirs*, 64.

tion, preferably in the single line of battle, was considered essential, and independent squadron action was accordingly held to a minimum. As Captain Liddell Hart has pointed out: "Thus however skilfully Jellicoe maneuvered his fleet he could not justly hope to paralyze his opponent's freedom of movement. And to pin an opponent is the vital prelude to a decisive maneuver; this dual act gives a double meaning to the old maxim—'divide to conquer.' The British fleet was all too truly 'one and indivisible.' " [21]

When Admiral Beatty assumed command of the Grand Fleet in November 1916, he directed attention to the importance of the offensive in destroyer tactics; he promulgated the doctrine of immediate attack and maximum torpedo fire. Direction of the light cruiser forces was unified under a single commander who was made responsible for the orderly development and reporting of contacts. Revision of the Battle Orders was taken in hand, and among other changes, divisions were directed to turn toward torpedoes. The name of the "Battle Orders" was itself changed as being too restrictive to initiative, and the Battle Instructions which followed merely defined the intentions and objectives of the commander in chief in battle.[22]

In retrospect it was recognized, within the British navy and without, that Jellicoe could have inflicted greater damage on the German fleet had he shown more aggressiveness and closed at every opportunity. It is certain that he would then have averted the renewal of the battle in books and pamphlets which has continued to the present. The effects of a decisive British victory at Jutland on the subsequent course of the war have been debated with equal vigor. That the British fleet could have opened the narrow Baltic entrances, close to German military concentrations in Schleswig and the naval base at Kiel, is doubtful. That the submarine offensives of 1917 and 1918 would have been crippled by lack of trained personnel recruited from the High Seas Fleet is controverted by the facts

of later history: after the outbreak of war in 1939, the U-boat force was rapidly expanded though the German surface fleet numbered but a fraction of Scheer's World War I command. But it cannot be gainsaid that the continued existence of the German fleet after Jutland required the continued concentration of the Grand Fleet and with it the immobilization of 100 destroyers that were urgently needed to fight U-boats in the Atlantic. It is true that the Grand Fleet destroyers were used extensively to convoy North Sea shipping but their radius of action necessarily was limited. In weighing Jellicoe's responsibility however, consideration must be given to the difficulty of destroying an enemy determined to employ every resource to escape. The four *Königs* had a two-knot advantage over the Grand Fleet battle line; the four *Kaisers* could hold their own. Had half of Scheer's battle fleet escaped, it would still have constituted, with new construction, a formidable fleet-in-being.

The Battle of Jutland did not greatly ease the problems of the Grand Fleet. On August 19, 1916 Scheer staged another Sunderland raid, using three fast battleships to fill up Hipper's still depleted squadron. The Grand Fleet put to sea but was detected by German scouting airships; Scheer retreated before reaching the English coast. In sweeping south to intercept the thrust the British lost the light cruisers *Falmouth* and *Nottingham* to submarines, a convincing proof of the increase in the power of the undersea boat since the beginning of the war. The depth charge had been put into production early in 1916 but a shortage of explosives in the British navy limited the number available for each destroyer. In October Jellicoe permitted Scheer to sweep to the center of the North Sea without taking the Grand Fleet out of port; it was the last offensive sortie aimed at reducing Britain's margin of naval superiority. A year later, in October 1917 German light cruisers twice raided convoys headed for Norway, sinking a large number of the ships and dispersing the escorting destroyers. The last cruise of the High Seas Fleet was undertaken in April 1918. Hipper's

[21] B. H. Liddell Hart, *A History of the World War, 1914-1918* (London, 1936), 380.

[22] *Earl Beatty*, 279-283.

battle cruisers advanced across the Skagerrak to attack the Norwegian convoy but missed contact. When the United States entered the war the morale of the German fleet received a heavy blow. Discontent among its crews in May 1918 erupted into the first of the mutinies which by October were to complete the destruction of its spirit and prepare it for submissive internment in December.

In retrospect Jutland stands out as the last great surface action fought mostly by daylight. It was as much a culmination of a certain type of naval warfare as Lepanto was the culminating engagement of galleys, and Trafalgar, the culminating engagement of sailing ships. When great fleets met again, as in the battles of the Philippine Sea and of Leyte Gulf in World War II, naval warfare had become enormously more complex—involving effective use of air, surface, sub-surface, and amphibious tactics all in a single vast operation.

30

The Struggle

for Command of the Seas

WHEN WORLD WAR I BEGAN, Britain could well believe that her Grand Fleet was ready for it. The battle concentrations effected during summer maneuvers had been quietly maintained by the Admiralty. Presently the transports of the British Expeditionary Force were being shepherded to France without incident. England enjoyed a better than eight-to-five statistical superiority in capital ships over Germany, and her diplomatic and strategic preparations had been such that the vast bulk of her battle line could be held in home waters ready for any ill-advised sortie by the German High Seas Fleet.

Yet the immediate missions of the British navy were not easy. Wars are not won by tables of comparative statistics. Whereas Germany could, and did, survive for years almost completely cut off from the world overseas, Britain was absolutely dependent on imported foodstuffs, merely to live.[1] Hence at all costs her navy must keep open the sea

lanes to Liverpool and the Thames Estuary. Britain, with almost half the world's merchant ship tonnage, could draw on the economic resources of most of the world—so long as she had uncontested control of the broad oceans. But for her to lose this control, even for a brief time, would spell defeat.

In the early months of the war, the British Admiralty was concerned to prevent the escape of heavy German units from the North Sea and to track down and destroy German cruisers and auxiliary cruisers that were overseas at the outbreak of the war. The Battles of Coronel and the Falklands were part of this phase of the British naval effort.

Offensively, the contribution of the Royal Navy was to be the unspectacular but inexorable blockade. The strategy that had defeated Napoleon a hundred years before was to be the strategy that ultimately defeated the Kaiser. Mines, aircraft, and submarines now made close blockade impossible, but geography conspired to render Germany easily blockaded from the North Atlantic. Because the British Isles lie athwart the German sea approaches, the Dover Patrol in the

[1] It is estimated that during the World War I period about 80 per cent of Britain's foodstuffs came from overseas.

Channel and the Grand Fleet in the Orkneys guaranteed the bottling up not only of Germany's combatant fleet but her merchant shipping as well.

If the role of the British navy was to *exercise* control of the seas, that of Germany was to *dispute* it. Initially, the German navy pinned high hopes on its far-ranging cruisers, and the *guerre de course* generally resorted to by the inferior naval power. The strategy of the High Seas Fleet was to attempt by hit-and-run raids, partial actions, and ambush to whittle down the British margin of superiority in the North Sea. Perhaps ultimately, on more nearly even terms, the High Seas Fleet could challenge the Grand Fleet in a fight to the finish.

The British fleet, imbued with the great tradition of Blake and Nelson, wished ardently for a showdown battle. Yet its commander had to be ever mindful that the Royal Navy was absolutely essential for the mere existence of the United Kingdom. The German fleet, which could better afford the risk of destruction, would nevertheless not be sacrificed in an utterly hopeless battle. Moreover, the Kaiser and his principal civilian advisers viewed the High Seas Fleet as a priceless bargaining card in the inevitable peace negotiations to come.

In the long run, the most serious operational naval effort the Germans were to make was their submarine offensive against the British and Allied merchant marine. This new and deadly version of commerce warfare, which gave a new dimension to the war at sea, was not anticipated by either belligerent before 1914. As noted earlier, submarines were originally designed either for coast defense or as fleet scouts. Generally accepted international law on the rules of search and seizure made their use against merchantmen and liners seem unlawful and inhumane in the eyes of the neutral world. Yet as the German Admiralty saw its cruisers swept from the seas and its battle line immobilized at Bremerhaven and Kiel, it turned inevitably to the one weapon and the one type of operation that appeared to permit the German navy a real chance of contributing importantly to a German victory—accepting the

risk, and then the certainty, that the United States would come into the war on the side of the Allies as a result of unrestricted German submarine warfare.

American participation proved to be a bigger factor than the German submarine campaign. But for all that, the German submarines brought the Fatherland to the very threshold of victory in 1917. During four years of war they sank more than 11,000,000 tons of Allied and neutral shipping, caused 85 per cent of British merchant losses, and sank five battleships, eight cruisers, and seven destroyers. From the point of view of strategic importance, the submarine campaign and the Allied countermeasures are the most fruitful study in the naval history of World War I.

1914

Initial German land strategy was to employ a modified Schlieffen Plan: to sweep through Belgium, capture Paris in one mighty surge, and thus put France out of the war. But in the Battle of the Marne, fought on Paris' doorstep, a hundred thousand British regulars, Kitchener's "Old Contemptibles," joined their ally and helped drive a wedge between two separated German armies.[2] The invaders were pressed back to the line of the Aisne River, and Paris was saved.

Allied sea power, which had made possible the presence of the British troops, provided the thin margin of Allied victory. By the end of September 1914 a quarter of a million troops, virtually all of Britain's professional army, had landed in France. Through the entire war, the "sea bridge" across the Channel was never to be successfully attacked by the German fleet. Even submarines were never a substantial threat against the troop-ferry. Germany was to learn all over again three decades later that Allied ability to transport millions of men and millions of

---

[2] General Alexander von Klück's First Army had earlier been weakened by withdrawal of certain divisions for a needless reinforcement of Field Marshal von Hindenburg on the Russian front.

tons of supplies to crucial war theaters is the single greatest contribution of sea power.

At the beginning of World War I, Germany had but 18 submarines on patrol in the North Sea. Each of these displaced slightly less than 900 tons submerged. It had a normal cruising speed of five knots and an emergency speed of ten, had four torpedo tubes and could carry six to ten mines. To expand this force as quickly as possible, the German admiralty placed orders for 49 new boats during the final months of 1914. Submarine operating bases were Heligoland, Emden, and the island of Borkum, off the mouth of the Ems River. The problem of additional bases closer to England was to be solved by the capture of Channel ports in Belgium and France.

German submarines initially struck only against British war vessels. The first victim was the cruiser *Pathfinder,* sunk by the *U-21* in the Firth of Forth on September 5, 1914. On September 22, the *U-9* in a matter of minutes sank the elderly British cruisers *Aboukir, Hogue,* and *Cressy.* These ships, patrolling together off the Dutch coast, were following a geometric patrol pattern at constant speed—an ideal set-up for the attacker. When the *Aboukir* was hit, the other cruisers slowed down to rescue survivors and in turn were picked off in quick succession. Their 1901 and 1902 hulls and compartmentation were defenseless against the improved and efficient German torpedo. They sank quickly, with great loss of life. This triple tragedy so dramatized the new threat to England that a vastly more extensive antisubmarine research and development program was put in hand by the British Admiralty. Later in the year, Britain lost four more war vessels to submarine torpedo attack.

The submarine threat forced a temporary withdrawal of the Grand Fleet, first to western Scotland, later to Lough Swilly in North Ireland, while the net and boom defenses at Scapa Flow were improved against underseas attack. The lowly submarine had diverted this powerful surface force away from its advanced base and from the maritime strategic center.

Since merchant shipping had not been subject to submarine attack, and because Britain's shipyards had been working around the clock, the year 1914 ended with England's over-all ship tonnage, merchant and naval, a half million tons greater than at the beginning.

1915

In 1915, the Western Front had settled down to a bloody stalemate; the fixed lines of trench warfare would not waver more than ten miles in either direction until 1917. The German naval authorities felt themselves driven to consider the wisdom of submarine warfare against British merchant shipping at the strategic center, England's home waters. On February 4, 1915, Admiral Hugo von Pohl, the new Chief of the Naval Staff, announced a "submarine blockade" of Great Britain and Ireland, to be effective two weeks later. Every British merchantman encountered within the barred zone would be liable to destruction. Neutrals were advised to avoid the blockaded area entirely.

There was a good deal of dissent within the German government over the wisdom of this policy. For example, Admiral von Tirpitz, who had not even been consulted in advance, denounced it as premature, impractical, and inviting American intervention. The "Grand Old Man" of the German Navy proposed instead a limited blockade of the Thames Estuary, for which Germany's 21 seagoing submarines were more nearly adequate. In any event, he counseled, a general blockade should at least be delayed until the Flanders bases were operational. His advice was disregarded.

The United States immediately made strong diplomatic objections to this violation of freedom of the seas and neutral rights. A submarine blockade, which clearly could not be conducted with proper regard to the accepted procedures of search and seizure, was unprecedented and illegal. Germany hinted in diplomatic exchanges that she might be persuaded to cancel this blockade if America could persuade England to agree to the limited contraband provisions of the Declaration of London of 1909. American Secretary of State Bryan knew too well however that there was literally no possibility whatever of Britain's blunting the edge of her best naval weapon, the blockade.

In the early hours of February 20, the U-boats took station in the North Sea and English Channel, and two days later off the Western Approaches to England. The results of their activity however soon proved this campaign premature, for submarine success against shipping was limited and Allied blockade measures became more stringent than ever. Rising American indignation reflected in notes of protest began to sound dangerously warlike.

The German armies meanwhile had provided the prospect of valuable submarine bases in Flanders. In October 1914 advancing German troops had pushed their right flank to the sea, deep in Belgian territory, and captured the important city of Bruges. There the German admiralty developed the main base for the Flanders Submarine Flotilla and prepared to use existing canals from this city to Zeebrugge and Ostend, both of which are Channel ports. By May 1915 five small minelaying UC boats of less than 200 tons submerged were ready for war cruises from the Bruges base. This force, excellently based for offensive operations, was eventually to account for almost one-fourth of all German submarine sinkings.

On May 7, 1915 the unarmed, unescorted Cunard liner *Lusitania*, steaming slowly off the coast of southern Ireland, was torpedoed and sunk by the *U-20*. Hundreds died, including 128 Americans—men, women, and children. At once the United States sent diplomatic dispatches to Germany protesting this murder of the innocent, asserting the right of her citizens to travel on the high seas, and demanding future safety from attack for liners. Germany did not yield. In the face of world-wide emotional revulsion, the German Foreign Office made a purely legal defense, claiming the presence of cartridges, shrapnel, and fuses in the vessel's cargo.[3]

In 1915 world public opinion was still strongly imbued with the gentlemanly ethics of "civilized warfare" as developed in the 18th and 19th centuries. Only uniformed soldiers and sailors were supposed to be killed. The lives and even the property of noncombatants were to be spared. Two "total wars" and the unscrupulous terrorism of the great dictatorships have coarsened the ethics of "civilized" men to accept almost any horror without revulsion. But in 1915 the German sinking of the *Lusitania* was a bad mistake. It was an important link in the chain of events leading to the American declaration of war two years later.

In mid-August the *U-77* sank the British White Star steamer *Arabic* some 60 miles off Kinsale. The loss of three American lives in this sinking further increased American wrath. In the face of what by now amounted to American threats of war, German opinion wavered. Tirpitz, who had come to change his mind on the question, von Pohl, and Bachman, Chief of Naval Staff, opposed any modification in submarine policy. Chancellor Theobald von Bethmann-Hollweg and Admiral Georg Müller of the Emperor's Naval Staff favored a conciliatory approach to the United States. All U-boats then in port were directed to remain at dockside until a definitive policy was agreed upon.

The decision was soon made. Ambassador Johann von Bernstorff notified Secretary Bryan that passenger liners would not in the future be sunk without warning, and that the commander of the *U-77* would be reprimanded. Germany thus ended her first submarine campaign on September 20, 1915. This respite for Allied and neutral shipping in the British coastal approaches lasted until March 1916. Meanwhile, on Tirpitz' recommendation, Allied shipping in the Mediterranean came under submarine attack.

The British blockade, instituted at the very beginning of the war, was made more effective during 1915. In the long run the abil-

---

[3] The German claim, for what it is worth, proved to have some merit, though it was vigorously denied by the British government at the time.

ity of the German Empire to carry on the war depended upon maritime import of a long list of vital raw materials. Britain had wisely refrained from ratifying the 1909 Declaration of London, which had proposed a very limited list of absolute and conditional contraband.[4] She therefore had no commitments to embarrass her aim of waging un-

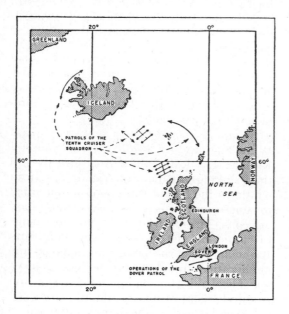

THE BLOCKADE OF GERMANY

trammeled economic warfare. Soon the Allied lists of contraband were enlarged, frequently by increasing the number of conditional commodities, then later by reclassifying many of these as absolute contraband. By October 1915, the Allies had declared 42 articles of trade to be absolute contraband, and 14 conditional.

Soon after hostilities began, the imports and exports of neutral Scandinavian countries increased sharply, indicating transshipment or release of equivalent commodities to Germany. For example, between 1913 and 1915 the value of Sweden's imports increased one-third, and her exports to Germany more than tripled. Denmark likewise profited by importing commodities for ultimate con-

sumption in Germany. This sort of thing Britain felt she could not permit, so she employed her sea power and her favorable geographic position to enforce her views on contraband. Sitting athwart the sea lanes of Europe, she used her Tenth Cruiser Squadron to intercept shipping in the waters north of Scotland and her Dover Patrol to plug the approaches through the Channel. In 1915 alone the Tenth Squadron stopped more than 3,000 vessels steaming to and from Scandinavia and sent 700 in to Scottish ports for further examination. The Germans themselves lent unwitting support to Britain's anti-contraband campaign, for after German mines had sunk 10,000 tons of British and neutral shipping in the North Sea in a single month, neutral vessels were willing enough to stop at British ports for sailing directions via swept channels—even though it meant a thorough check of their cargoes.

But by the fall of 1915, the blockade was beginning to show constrictive influence. The work of the Tenth Cruiser Squadron and the Dover Patrol was supplemented by other Allied measures. These included agreements with certain shipping companies whereby they promised to deny bunker coal to those who would not comply with Allied trade-control regulations and the establishment of British International Quota Commissions to limit the export of raw materials to Holland and Scandinavia. The Netherlands Oversea Trust was formed in 1914, a syndicate of importers who guaranteed not to re-export to Germany. Dutch trade quickly reflected this restriction, 1915 imports from overseas and exports to Germany both decreasing markedly. The United States likewise reduced her trade with neutral countries adjacent to Germany; prominent American exporters soon agreed to prevent shipment of copper—later of rubber and cotton—to any firm on the British "black list."[5] By late 1915 the flow to Germany of such strategic resources as copper, tin, rubber, cotton, wheat, wool, leather, and fats either had been stopped or substantially reduced. Blockade and the supporting techniques that to-

---

[4] Eleven articles in the first category; 14, in the second.

[5] A list of European firms suspected of German trade connections.

gether comprise "economic warfare" in the modern sense would not decide the conflict overnight, but they would slowly and inexorably reduce Germany's industrial power, her standard of living, and her civilian morale.

Meanwhile the British Admiralty was making limited progress in antisubmarine warfare. It had established 22 coast defense zones wherein auxiliary patrols, mostly former fishing boats, were responsible for combating torpedoes, mines, and torpedo boats. The most important defense zone was that guarded by the more heavily armed Dover Patrol, which had the dual function of visit and search of passing merchantmen and of defense of the Channel seaway, especially from Folkestone to Boulogne.

Operating from the North Foreland to Beachy Head, this patrol fulfilled its vital assignment of maintaining the safety of Britain's left sea flank. After the war the members of this force could point with satisfaction to the safe transportation to France of about 5,500,000 men and more than 100,000 safe crossings by merchant vessels. These operations were facilitated by effective trawler minesweeping. Fortunately, little surface opposition was encountered.

At the end of 1915 antisubmarine technology remained primitive. Captain Karl Bartenbach, Chief of the German Flanders Submarine Flotilla, later remarked, "Countermeasures were so insignificant in the year 1915 that a U-boat at sea could go to work exactly the way a pike goes to work in a carp pond." British scientists were conducting hydrophone experiments in the Firth of Forth and in Granton Harbor.[6] Depth charges armed with hydrostatic fuses had been perfected, but production of them was only beginning. Mine-bearing nets woven of steel wire were installed in the Dover area. These proved to be more of a psychological hazard than a genuinely effective device: submarines on occasion were "caught," but usually managed to work themselves clear.

U-boat losses were slight. Submarines out of Flanders bases almost nightly passed

through the Channel at low speed. Marker buoys showed the location of the nets, and at low tide the mines floated on the surface; however, in April the U-32 became entangled. Although it finally escaped, the German admiralty concluded this route was too dangerous for its larger submarine types, and ordered all of them thereafter to take the longer but safer passage north of Scotland. British and neutral merchantmen profited accordingly, for the big German submarines now consumed more time and fuel cruising on and off station and had less of both to devote to operations.

The Royal Navy tried various expedients in the antisubmarine war. Armed mystery ships or Q-ships, cleverly disguised as neutral merchantmen, would often endure shelling and simulate Abandon Ship while waiting for the most favorable moment to attack a surfaced submarine with point-blank fire. Fourteen Q-ships operated at sea in 1915 and sank three boats. Sometimes submarine hunted submarine. In June the British C-24 was submerged astern of a trawler used as a decoy. When the U-40 sighted the fishing boat and surfaced, the C-24 torpedoed her. Ramming tactics were employed whenever possible. One of the most famous of these attacks occurred on March 18, 1915, when the original Dreadnought by this means destroyed the U-29.

Italy's declaration of war against the Central Powers in the late spring of 1915 drew the attention of the German Admiralty to the Mediterranean. Both the fact that Germany's submarine campaign in the North Atlantic had been suspended and the belief that Allied antisubmarine measures in the Mediterranean were even less well advanced than elsewhere made an underseas campaign in those waters appear promising. Austria's little fleet of seven submarines, which began operations against Italy at once, sank two Italian cruisers and two submarines. Germany shipped nine of her coastal UB-boats and four UC minelayers by rail to Pola on the Adriatic and prepared for commerce warfare. In the fall of 1915 these German boats, concentrated south of Greece and of Crete, and southeast of Sicily, sank over a hundred

[6] The hydrophone was a mere underwater listening device, not an echo-ranging device like the later sonar and asdic.

unescorted and generally unarmed Allied merchantmen.

The year 1915 ended without either side gaining a decisive advantage in the submarine war—or elsewhere. British launchings made up all but a few thousand tons of merchant ship losses in all theaters. Germany on the other hand was not yet seriously pinched by the blockade, nor were her submarine losses severe. She finished the year with 68 seagoing boats in commission; her construction-to-loss ratio was almost five to one. German armies had pushed back the Russian hordes in the East but were still deadlocked on the Western Front.

1916

Early in 1916 various factors combined to make the Germans reconsider their earlier abandonment of unrestricted submarine warfare in the North Atlantic. General Ludendorff and Admiral Tirpitz had come to favor unrestricted warfare. Bulgaria's joining the Central Powers in 1915 encouraged some influential Germans to believe this would restrain remaining European neutrals from joining the Allies. They also believed that the most important neutral power, the United States, had become somewhat more sympathetic toward submarine warfare.[7]

Early in March 1916, the Kaiser showed a reluctant willingness to support the recommendation for unrestricted submarine warfare, but something changed his mind. Against the protests of General von Falkenhayn and without even consulting Tirpitz, he postponed the general campaign and ordered unrestricted underseas warfare only in certain limited areas. Deeply offended, Tirpitz promptly resigned.

---

[7] This curious belief may have been inferred, in part, from the January 18 note of the new American Secretary of State, Robert Lansing, to British Ambassador Spring Rice, which conveyed the opinion that Germany should not be deprived of a *proper* use of submarines in commerce warfare and that any armament of a belligerent merchant vessel must be considered offensive rather than defensive, and under international law, offensive armament compromised noncombatant rights.

Within two weeks a new German-American crisis arose. On March 24 the unarmed, unescorted French steamer *Sussex,* steaming slowly in the English Channel, was sunk by the *UB-29,* with injuries to three Americans. The United States immediately delivered a protest, advising that America would sever diplomatic relations with Germany unless submarine warfare were conducted in strict accordance with international law. The German Foreign Office quickly answered, promising no further destruction of passenger vessels without due warning and rescue of personnel unless resistance or escape were attempted.[8] Four days later Scheer in exasperation recalled his submarines from western waters, believing that these combat restrictions would make further cruises useless. For a second time the United States had induced Germany to alter her war plans. The German navy temporarily reverted to prewar submarine doctrine, using submarines with fleet units in joint operations against warships.

From May to September 1916 these occasional military thrusts were attempted, generally with meager results. Practically speaking, the German underseas force in this period existed simply as a part of a fleet-in-being. Scheer planned raids against such unfortified British east coast cities as Sunderland, in an attack pattern reminiscent of British planning before the Heligoland Bight Action. Surface units would be used as bait. Submarines would ambush any British forces lured out in chase. In late May a large number of U-boats were ordered to cover the English east coast ports. A dozen were so occupied when the Grand Fleet sortied for the sweep to the east which precipitated the Battle of Jutland. The German submarines scouted the British fleet and made reports to the German admiralty but were unable to make a single successful attack at this time. On August 19 two U-boats made a successful submerged attack on the cruisers *Nottingham* and *Falmouth.* During this period large minelaying submarines from the Elbe and smaller boats from Flan-

---

[8] The famous "*Sussex* Pledge."

ders were employed in British and French coastal waters. Such important French ports as Boulogne, Le Havre, and Cherbourg were made particular mining targets.

The tempo of Mediterranean submarine war continued to increase in 1916. In the middle of March Britain began to divert Australian and Far Eastern traffic from the shorter "middle sea" route via the Suez Canal to the longer but safer passage around the Cape of Good Hope. This meant that a steamer voyaging from Singapore to London via Capetown would navigate 3,500 miles farther and take perhaps two weeks longer en route than if it took the Mediterranean passage. This was however a wise anticipation of the German threat, for in the last half of 1916 German submarines increased in number at Cattaro from eight to 18, now including large U-boats and improved minelayers; these, concentrated on the western Mediterranean from Sicily to the French and North African coasts, sank 256 vessels amounting to 662,000 tons.

The situation of Allied merchant shipping and defensive measures at the end of the 1916 submarine campaigns was beginning to be alarming. British cumulative war launchings now were 700,000 tons behind losses. True, the Allied merchant fleet had been reduced only about five per cent, but the recent trend clearly was beginning to favor the submarine.

Definite progress had been made in research and production of detection gear and destructive devices. On July 7, 1916 an indication of forthcoming successes in 1917 and 1918 was the sinking of the *UC-7* while submerged, as a result of hydrophone detection and depth charge attack. Paravanes to ward off and cut loose moored mines now were available to many warships. Improved sloop minelayers had been added to the Grand Fleet. Merchantmen nearly all now carried guns manned by naval crews, for experience had shown that armed merchantmen had four times the chance for survival of unarmed vessels. But now that the submarine was being driven below the surface, it was more likely in the future to employ torpedoes rather than its previous tactics of sur-

face gunfire. A net barrier across the Strait of Otranto proved even less successful than the one at Dover. Q-ships had sunk only two submarines during the year.

Britain's economic warfare measures apart from blockade were improved and extended in 1916. Her greatly elaborated quota system brought an additional reduction of Sweden's and Holland's imports by one-third. The Tenth Cruiser Squadron and the Dover Patrol further increased their efficiency in visit and search of vessels. As German stockpiles of copper, tin, nickel, and cotton dwindled, Germany was forced to develop substitutes where possible. Her scientists in 1916 manufactured sufficient nitrocellulose from Baltic pine that their production of explosives did not lag. Certain other materials, such as iron, manganese, bauxite, lead, oils and lubricants, were at least sparsely available on the Continent, and no serious shortages of these developed. The German standard of living declined seriously however as a result of shrinking food imports and the poor harvests of 1916.[9]

As 1916 drew to a close, increasing pessimism in the German army allied itself to the German navy's faith in the submarines to bring a clear consensus in high service circles in favor of their unrestricted use. From the beginning of the war to February 1915, three British merchantmen were sunk for every German submarine destroyed. This ratio had increased to 15 to 1 by the end of 1916. Chancellor Bethmann-Hollweg, heretofore opposed, was also finally persuaded that unrestricted submarine warfare was necessary. American diplomatic action over the *Lusitania,* the *Arabic,* and the *Sussex* episodes had checked the submarine campaigns of 1915 and 1916, but now the High Command was ready to take the supreme gamble and disregard the danger of an American declaration of war. It was hoped in any event that the war would be won before the United States could make her weight felt in the balance.

This was a decision born of desperation. General Field Marshal Paul von Hinden-

---

[9] Germans still refer to the "turnip winter" of 1916-1917.

burg, now in supreme command of the German army, and his Chief of Staff Ludendorff both realized they were slowly losing the war simply because they were not winning. No longer could they afford a stalemate. By late summer they had given up hope of decisive results from the great Verdun offensive on the Western Front. Now the vigorous Allied counteroffensive on the Somme was draining their manpower, numerically inferior by a three-to-five ratio. In the long run the Allies were better able to sustain their 900,000 casualties from July to October than the Germans could their half million in the same period.

Restricted submarine operations had been resumed in the North Atlantic. In the Mediterranean the U-boats were more and more successful. Conditions appeared ripe for the *coup de grâce* to the staggering British merchant marine. On December 22, 1916 Admiral Henning von Holtzendorff of the Admiralty Staff wrote Hindenburg an important letter which was to become the basis of the final German decision. In this document, Holtzendorff categorically stated that the submarines if unleashed could force Britain to surrender within five months, from February through June, before the summer harvests could be reaped. He reviewed the situation of Britain's shipping and her food imports. His estimate was that 10,750,000 tons of cargo vessels, about two-thirds of this of British flag registry, were bringing food to Britain. Assuming that the U-boats could sink 600,000 tons monthly for five months, neutral shipping would be driven from the traffic by the frightful losses, and the surviving merchantmen and cargoes would be insufficient to prevent virtual famine in England. He also included a list of the specific strategic imports Britain must have which could be denied her: grains from the United States, Canada, Argentina, India, and Aus-

tralia; cotton from the United States and Egypt; wool and meats from Argentina and Australia; dairy products from Denmark and Holland; ores from Sweden and Spain; lumber products from Sweden. Previous German submarine results he regarded as encouraging. With never more than nine submarines on station at any one time, the U-boats had averaged monthly sinkings of 120,000 tons in the first campaign. In the second, they averaged 216,000 tons. In the Mediterranean, only six boats were sinking over 400,000 tons per month.

Holtzendorff dismissed possible counterarguments. American aid to the Allies, if given at all, would be too little and too late. Convoys as an Allied defensive measure were obviously not practicable or the British would already have employed them. Improved antisubmarine devices and tactics would be encountered, of course, but the large number and the improved efficiency of the underseas force Germany could throw into the campaign would outweigh enemy improvements.

These predictions were to prove entirely incorrect. At the time however the German High Command was persuaded. On January 9, 1917 the Kaiser ordered his 82 North Sea and Flanders boats to begin unrestricted submarine warfare on February 1. Cautious Bethmann-Hollweg commented ominously, "The U-boat war is the last card."

So German fortunes ashore and afloat were to sink or swim on the results of underseas warfare without restriction and with no regard for diplomatic repercussions. The submarine torpedo was to be pitted against the genius of the Allied scientists, against the convoy system, the hydrophone, the depth charge, the mine, and ultimately against the entire naval might of the United States added to that of Germany's current enemies.

31

American Participation

and Allied Victory

THE FAILURE OF THE GERman attack on Verdun and of the British Somme offensive in 1916 had again demonstrated the advantage of the defensive. Germany's strategy for 1917 was to exploit that advantage in the West by withdrawing to the shorter, well-prepared Hindenburg Line, while she gambled on the submarine to defeat England even at the risk of bringing the United States into the war. That gamble Germany was destined to lose. The irony of it is that she need not have gambled at all, for in March 1917, only a month after the declaration of unrestricted submarine warfare, a revolution broke out in Russia which took that country out of the war within a few months. With the troops thus freed from the Eastern Front Germany might have won the war without provoking the United States.

President Wilson, who had just won reelection in 1916 on the slogan "He Kept Us Out of War" had not yet received his second inauguration when on January 31, 1917, Germany proclaimed her blockade of Great Britain and Ireland by establishing a barred zone extending from Norway and the Faroes south to Cape Finisterre and westward about

400 miles beyond Ireland. Three days later Wilson severed diplomatic relations with Germany. After this, crisis quickly followed crisis in German-American relations. The Zimmerman note,[1] which the British had intercepted and turned over to the United States, caused grave concern. In March the President ordered armed guards placed aboard American steamers bound for the submarine zone. On April 2 Wilson grimly told Congress, "The right is more precious than peace, and we shall fight for the things we have always carried nearest our hearts." [2]

PLANS AND PREPARATIONS OF THE UNITED STATES

At the end of the war, charges by Rear Admiral William S. Sims and others regarding

[1] In mid-January Zimmerman, the German Foreign Secretary, had instructed the German minister in Mexico to attempt to form a German-Mexican alliance in event of war with the United States. He was to suggest to the Mexicans the possibility of their regaining Arizona, New Mexico, and Texas.

[2] Harold G. Black, *The True Woodrow Wilson* (New York, 1946), 169.

the unpreparedness of the United States Navy in 1917 led to a Congressional investigation. Evidence there adduced substantially supported the charges. At the beginning of 1917 only a third of the navy's vessels were materially fit and only ten per cent were adequately manned. Furthermore, the United States was seriously short of light vessels suitable for antisubmarine warfare. There was no plan which fitted the situation existing in 1917 and no arrangements had been made for cooperation with the British.

The explanation lies in part in America's interest during the prewar years in the Anglo-German naval building race, which emphasized capital ships, and in her determination to maintain a navy "second only to Britain's." In 1915 the General Board went beyond this concept to recommend a five-year program which would produce a navy second to none. Congress passed this bill in 1916, calling for its execution in three rather than five years. The 800,000 tons of new construction thus authorized was to comprise ten battleships, six battle cruisers, ten scout cruisers, 50 destroyers, and 67 submarines.

Admiral George Dewey, who was President of the General Board from its creation in 1900 till his death early in 1917, did not believe that the submarine would dominate naval warfare. The decision at sea, he believed, would be reached in an engagement of the main fleets of Britain and Germany. It was only after the indecisive Battle of Jutland that he tacitly acknowledged the growing importance of the German submarine by recommending that more cruisers, destroyers, submarines, and minesweepers be added to the United States Fleet.

Development of American naval war plans accompanied fleet expansion. American strategists were preoccupied with the Caribbean, scene of the United States' last naval war, subject of much of Mahan's writing, and now doubly important because of the recently completed Panama Canal. Because of the favorable climate, the Atlantic Fleet had from 1901 onward held its annual winter fleet exercises in these waters. In 1915 Bradley A. Fiske, then Aide for Operations, realizing that these exercises were little more

than drills in seamanship and navigation, persuaded the Department to develop the first American fleet war game, War Plan Black. For the purposes of this game it was supposed that the enemy had sent a fleet or squadron to the American coast, there to be engaged by the defenders. The fleet executed Strategic Problem No. 1 under this plan in October 1915, and a second one the following spring.

The hypothesis of the Black Plan, reasonable enough for a fleet exercise, bore no relation to the situation in 1917, for in order to threaten the American coast the blockaded German Navy would first have had to defeat the British fleet and then find bases from which to project its power into the western Atlantic. But during the 1916 hearings on appropriations before the House Committee on Naval Affairs, questions by Congressmen in regard to war plans were all based on the assumption that the United States would be fighting alone against a European nation which might create a Caribbean threat to the United States. Even after Jutland the General Board did nothing to alter strategic planning. If this seems startlingly shortsighted, it must be remembered that the nation in 1916 expressed its determination to keep out of the European war, and that there existed no experience such as was available in 1939 to suggest the probability of American involvement. As a consequence there were no arrangements for overseas bases, no plans for overseas transport and antisubmarine warfare, and there was a critical deficiency of vessels suitable for these functions.

In some respects however the United States Navy was better prepared than appeared on the surface, as was proved by its quick and efficient expansion to fulfill its wartime missions. In March 1915 Captain William S. Benson had become the first Chief of Naval Operations, with responsibility for fleet war plans and operations. Benson brought with him a broad experience in operations afloat, including duty as Flag Lieutenant of the Commander in Chief Atlantic Fleet, and Chief of Staff Pacific Fleet. He had also been a lecturer at the Naval War College. In his new office he made many important contributions to American preparedness—he required the Bureaus to report on their war readiness, he provided for naval inspection of merchant vessels to determine what alterations or repairs would be required to fit them for war service, he placed the Naval Reserve under the Bureau of Navigation, he gave full support to the Radio Communications Service and the development of codes, and he provided for the procurement of additional ordnance and ammunition when necessary. In 1915 the Navy established the Naval Consulting Board, which included such prominent scientists as Thomas Edison, Elmer Sperry, and Dr. William Coolidge, to study problems in technological research and development, particularly in antisubmarine warfare. The next year both the Naval Reserve Force and the Navy Flying Corps were authorized.

AMERICA'S EARLY EFFORTS: ADOPTION OF THE CONVOY

Just before America's break with Germany, Rear Admiral Sims had been detached as President of the Naval War College and ordered to England to study the shipping situation and recommend what services his navy best could perform in case of war. Arriving on April 9, 1917, after the United States had been at war three days, he promptly conferred with First Sea Lord Admiral Sir John Jellicoe and his associates. They advised him that the shipping situation was desperate. In February German submarines had sunk over half a million tons; they had increased this figure in March, and according to estimates they would exceed 900,000 tons in April. The Royal Navy frankly predicted British defeat by November unless the submarine could be conquered.

Sims at once informed his government of the gravity of the situation. It was clear that somehow the submarine would have to be dealt with and that American soldiers and supplies with safe naval escort must bring fresh strength to the stalemated Western Front. At the moment the United States possessed a regular army of only a quarter of a million men and only three naval transports. Obviously both services would require time. Soldiers and seamen had to be enlisted, trained, and equipped for overseas duty; an adequate transport and escort force had to be provided; ships and devices for antisubmarine warfare had to be developed and added to those of the Allies. With characteristic energy the United States threw itself into the task.

Warned by their experience with the submarine in 1915, British scientists had done much to meet the challenge of the U-boat. They had developed the depth charge, with a hydrostatic fuse to explode it at a predetermined depth, and the hydrophone, an underwater listening device which indicated the presence and direction (but not the range) of a submarine by the noise of its passage. This combination constituted a reasonably effective weapon against the U-boat in 1917.

But submarines could not be destroyed at sea rapidly enough to have a decisive effect on the war. Somehow shipping must be protected against the submarines which could not be sunk. Thus far the British had relied principally upon evasive routing and patrols. Evasive routing failed because, however successful it might be in the broad reaches of the Atlantic, the termini of the trade routes were fixed, so that submarines had only to lurk in the waters north or south of Ireland to find the ships coming to them. The British thereupon instituted patrols of these focal areas, but these were ineffective both because there were insufficient patrol vessels and because their usual effect was only to force a submarine to submerge until the patrol had passed.

The convoy was an ancient and well established method of protecting shipping, but the British had refrained from using it for several reasons: (1) they lacked sufficient escorts, (2) time would be lost in assembling the merchant vessels and in the longer turnaround, (3) the Admiralty disliked bunching targets for German surface raiders, and (4) it was supposed that merchant captains would have difficulty in keeping close station. But faced with the necessity of doing something, and under pressure from the civilian government, the Admiralty at last instituted the system. The first experimental

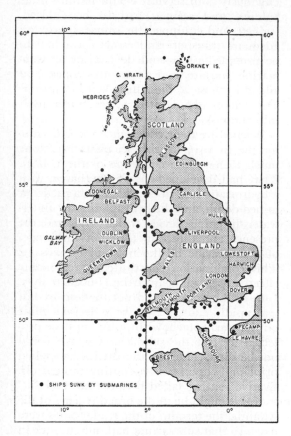

U-BOAT CAMPAIGN AGAINST THE
BRITISH ISLES, FEBRUARY 1918

convoy arrived safely in London from Gibraltar on May 20, 1917. By September the system was in general use.

One effect of the convoy system was to cause the U-boats to concentrate their operations in the waters around Britain. Previously they had ranged up to 300 miles to the westward to prey upon the virtually defenseless merchantmen, but now that ships were escorted, the submarines largely confined their activities to the waters within 50 miles of the European ports of debarkation. There was no serious attempt to disrupt the con-

voys, and while the U-boats occasionally hunted in pairs, there was no anticipation of the wolf-pack tactics of World War II. The nearest approach to a substantial campaign against the convoys was in May 1918, when several submarines operated within the Western Approaches, but they showed little coordination and sank only five out of 188 escorted vessels.

One of the most serious problems facing the Allies was the provision of escorts for the convoy system. Destroyers, the ideal escorts, were too much in demand for other purposes to be used extensively. About half of Britain's 200 destroyers operated with the Grand Fleet, and the remainder were stretched thin in critical operational areas, on patrol and other duties. About half of America's destroyers were likewise retained with the fleet in home waters. However, the United States made its first contribution to the naval war by dispatching Destroyer Division Eight under Commander Joseph Taussig USN from the Atlantic Fleet. Taussig reported to Vice Admiral Lewis Bayly RN in Queenstown, Ireland on May 4, 1917. The next three months brought the number of American four-stackers in Europe to nearly 40, and in addition numerous submarine chasers from the United States joined in the U-boat hunt. With their British counterparts, these destroyers and submarine chasers maintained the patrol areas and helped furnish escorts for the convoys, now growing rapidly in numbers. In mid-June 1917 the first all-American convoy sailed from New York and made a safe passage to St. Nazaire in France. By December the Cruiser and Transport Force of Rear Admiral Albert Gleaves USN was convoying about 50,000 American soldiers to France monthly.

The newly created United States Shipping Board quickly expanded the merchant marine, largely through rapid building of the famous Liberty Ships. Naval direction of these vessels was exercised by the Naval Overseas Transportation Service, which set up regular convoy schedules from ports on the east coast of the United States and Canada. Convoys for Great Britain cleared New York every 16 days; others bound for France sailed on different schedules. Ships received escort, or additional escort, as they approached known submarine zones. Vessels from South America and South Africa picked up an escort near Sierra Leone or Dakar, while ships from the Mediterranean received protection from Gibraltar on. A high degree of teamwork developed between escorting forces of the Allied nations. An American convoy, for example, had protection from Gleaves' cruisers until it reached the Western Approaches area, where a British, French, or American force would take over until the ships reached their destination. So successful was this service that not a single troopship or a single American soldier or marine out of more than two million men was lost on the eastward passage; only three vessels, under much lighter protection, went down on the westward voyage.

AMERICAN FORCES AND BASES IN EUROPE

In order to protect convoys as they approached Europe and to assist more effectively in fighting submarines in the waters around Britain, the United States developed and administered numerous bases in France, Great Britain, and Ireland. American naval aircraft operated from 27 of these European bases, for United States naval aviation had expanded rapidly after America's entry into the war. Starting with only 39 pilots in 1917, it grew by the end of the war to include almost 7,000 officers and more than 30,000 enlisted men, of whom approximately half were overseas. In the same interval its 54 planes were increased to more than 2,000. Of these about 500, mostly supplied by the British and French, were in Europe.

Their principal functions were antisubmarine patrols and the protection of convoys, but they incidentally discovered and destroyed numerous floating mines. In addition they operated directly against submarine bases. The Northern Bombing Group, comprising eight squadrons of land-type planes manned by naval and marine personnel, attacked the German submarine bases at Zeebrugge and Ostend and in 1918 were employed against other military objectives. From half a dozen bases in Britain and several in Ireland Americans flew patrols and covered convoys. Based in Italy other American aviators successfully attacked Austrian naval bases on the Adriatic.

Most important of the American overseas bases was that at Brest, established in the summer of 1917. On the best natural harbor on the west coast of France, it quickly replaced St. Nazaire as the funnel through which poured American troops and supplies. About 800,000 members of the American Expeditionary Forces made their first acquaintance with France at Brest. Other American sea and air bases dotted the Channel and Atlantic coasts of France from Dunkirk to Bordeaux. Destroyers operated from Brest, minesweepers from Lorient, and naval planes from Dunkirk and Calais. From these same bases the French operated their antisubmarine patrols, manning over ten per cent of all Allied patrol boats, including more than a hundred 110-foot, wooden-hulled submarine chasers turned over to them by the Americans. These vessels, built rapidly in the United States, were one of America's principal contributions to the war against the submarine. In addition, the French operated almost 20 per cent of the submarine force off Europe and about 400 naval planes.

Besides Sims' large staff in London, American enterprises in England included submarine chasers at Plymouth, naval aviators at Killingholme on the east coast, the Northern Bombing Group at Dover, and a base at Eastleigh for assembling personnel and repairing equipment. In 1918 minelayers were stationed at Scottish ports to lay the great North Sea Mine Barrage.

In Scotland, Rear Admiral Hugh Rodman's Battleship Division Nine, at one time or another comprising the *New York, Wyoming, Florida, Delaware, Arkansas,* and *Texas,* served from late 1917 with the British Grand Fleet as the Sixth Battle Squadron. These vessels were coal-burners and thus would make no demands on Britain's precious supply of imported oil.

In Ireland the Americans had destroyers

and submarine chasers at Queenstown. Later two new American oil-burning battleships, the *Nevada* and *Oklahoma,* and the older *Utah* were stationed at Bantry Bay as a precaution against heavy German surface raiders. Submarines at Bantry Bay and naval air stations at various strategic coastal points completed American installations in Ireland.

In the Atlantic, the United States operated a base at Ponta Delgada in the Azores for refueling submarine chasers and for air patrol. More important was the American force at Gibraltar, for about one-fourth of all Allied shipping passed through the Straits. This fleet of small craft, manned largely by United States Naval Reservists, assisted during the final 15 months of the war in escorting about 600 convoys without loss. These vessels performed more than two-thirds of the escort service from Gibraltar to Britain and one-quarter of that to French and Italian Mediterranean ports.

DEFEAT OF GERMANY'S 1917 SUBMARINE CAMPAIGN

Germany had started her 1917 submarine campaign with almost 150 boats, but the figure is deceptive. Through 1917 an average of only 23 boats operated from North Sea bases and ten from Flanders bases, and the number actually on station at any one time was even smaller. Losses of submarines, which had totaled only 25 in 1916, jumped to 66 in 1917. As a result German shipyards were able to achieve a net gain of only seven boats from February to July in 1917. At midyear German naval leaders desperately placed large orders for new construction, but it was too late to affect the course of the war. The net gain for the last six months of 1917 was only 14 boats.

Nonetheless these few boats during the first five months of the campaign sank more than the three million tons of shipping which German leaders had estimated would defeat England. Sinkings remained high throughout the year, but the total for the

last six months was somewhat less. In December the figure reached about 400,000 tons for the last time. In 1918 sinkings diminished steadily as the U-boat was brought decisively under control. Instrumental in achieving this result was the convoy system, but technological improvements in hydrophones and depth charges, a great increase in armed merchantmen, and extensive coverage by planes, airships, and balloons also played their part.

The single bright spot for Germany in the naval war of late 1917 was the Mediterranean. Operating from Austria's Adriatic bases, some 25 German U-boats destroyed a hundred thousand tons of shipping in February. They doubled this figure in April and did almost as well in the next two months. The Allies reinforced the Otranto patrol with additional destroyers, submarines, and aircraft, but succeeded in sinking only two submarines in the area in the entire year. Fortunately for the Allies, the Germans failed to concentrate in the Malta area, where the volume of shipping was heaviest and its vulnerability greatest; instead, they made most of their attacks at the extremities of the Mediterranean lifeline, and so missed many opportunities.

By late May the situation in the Mediterranean was as serious for the Allies as that in the Atlantic, but the institution of the convoy system improved matters immensely by early fall. In August 1917, months before the creation of a unified Allied command on the Western Front, Britain assumed the responsibility of administering a unified Mediterranean naval command. This ended the kaleidoscopic series of zones which had previously brought Suez-bound vessels successively into British, French, Italian, French, British, French, Italian, British, and French areas of responsibility. By October unbroken escort covered the whole route from Port Said to Britain. Now Indian and Far Eastern shipping could abandon the long, time-consuming voyage around the Cape of Good Hope for the more direct Suez-Mediterranean route to Britain and Western Europe.

By the end of 1917 Germany's challenge to Allied control of the seas had failed. On

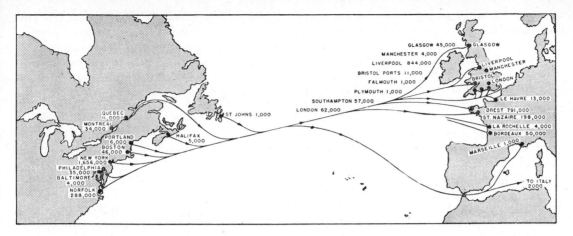

PORTS OF EMBARKATION AND DEBARKATION FOR UNITED STATES TROOPS

land however her prospects were distinctly encouraging. On the Western Front she had beaten off French and British attacks with heavy casualties. On the Italian Front the Austrians and Germans had broken through their opponents' line at Caporetto and had driven them back to the Piave, threatening Venice. The Eastern Front had almost ceased to exist. The revolution of March had marked the collapse of Russia's army, and the Communist revolution of November brought about her virtual surrender. With the German and Austrian divisions thus freed from the Eastern Front, Germany might yet win the war.

THE MILITARY CRISIS OF 1918 AND ALLIED VICTORY

The transfer of troops from the East gave Germany a numerical superiority of the Western Front for the first time since the Battle of the Marne in 1914. German strategy was to exploit this advantage to force a decision before the United States could make its weight felt. Ludendorff planned to attack along the Somme toward Amiens, drive a wedge between the British and the French, and roll the former back onto the Channel, the latter onto Paris. On March 21 he hurled a massive assault against the British and forced them back across the Somme, but failed to take Amiens. In this crisis the Allies finally agreed on a supreme commander in France and appointed the French General Ferdinand Foch to that post with the title of Marshal. Then, as their casualties mounted, they sent urgent appeals for aid from the United States.

There followed a race against time as the Americans attempted to transport enough troops to Europe to alter the balance before Germany could win the war. Increasing numbers of the A.E.F. arrived at Liverpool and Brest, beginning with a modest 50,000 in January, rising to 100,000 in April, a quarter of a million in May, and a record 300,000 in July. American transports, which included former German ships interned in American ports earlier in the war, were operated at full capacity, while the British assigned all available liners to the transportation of American divisions and actually carried a few thousand more troops than did United States vessels. Admiral Gleaves's force provided over four-fifths of the naval escort for the whole movement from the United States to Europe and all of that for the United States transports.

On the Western Front the crisis came on July 18, when Paris was threatened in the Second Battle of the Marne. American troops aided the weary French in checking the German drive and saving Paris. Then Foch struck decisively. The British and Belgians in the north, the French in the center, and the Americans to the south rolled back the enemy so swiftly that by November most of occupied Belgium and three-quarters of German-held France had been liberated.

While the fighting ashore was chiefly a matter for the army, American marines and seamen also played a part. Of the almost 25,000 marines who served in Europe, one out of every ten was killed in action. This casualty rate, much higher than that of the army, resulted from the bloody Château-Thierry, Aisne-Marne, St. Mihiel, and Meuse-Argonne campaigns. Most conspicuously gallant was the famous Fourth Marine Brigade, which in early June stopped the German advance at Belleau Wood in some of the fiercest fighting of the war. One-half of this Brigade fell in achieving victory, and the grateful French government perpetuated the memory of their valor by renaming this sector *Bois de la Brigade de Marine*. The French also cited the 5th and 6th Marine Regiments and the 6th Machine Gun Battalion for their performance in major campaigns of 1918. The use of the marines on the Western Front created a danger that they might be deprived of their unique function and assimilated into the army. The perception of this threat led to the subsequent creation of the Fleet Marine Force and its specialization in amphibious warfare which was to prove so important in World War II.

Part of the American navy went ashore during the Allied offensive of 1918 and struck at German logistics. Rear Admiral Ralph Earle, Chief of the Bureau of Ordnance, suggested sending to France large-caliber naval guns with a range of more than 22 miles—well beyond that of Allied army ordnance. Under command of Rear Admiral Charles P. Plunkett, five naval batteries of 14-inch guns on railway mounts, manned by American naval personnel, fought in the Meuse-Argonne campaign. Going into action in early September 1918, these naval batteries fired about 800 rounds at important railway yards, bridges, and ammunition dumps,

seriously disrupting the communications and supply of the retreating Germans.

VICTORY OVER THE SUBMARINE

The effectiveness of Allied antisubmarine measures increased steadily through the latter part of the war. Three-fourths of the 178 German U-boats destroyed were sunk in 1917 and 1918; about half of these were victims of depth charges and mines. As was to be expected, a majority of these submarines went down in the waters surrounding Great Britain, and most of them were bagged by the Royal Navy. Although United States warships definitely accounted for only four U-boats, their first kill, that of the *U-58*, was one of the most spectacular of the war. On November 27, 1917 the destroyers *Nicholson* and *Fanning* encountered this boat some miles off Ireland's southwest coast and closed in for the attack. A *Fanning* depth charge exploded near the stern of the submerged German and forced her to the surface. She sank seconds after the *Fanning* had rescued survivors, but not before an enterprising photographer had recorded the proceedings.

A prophetic trend in submarine warfare, of significance for World War II, was the success of the submarine as a killer of its own type. Twenty-eight undersea boats of the belligerents were victims, with the British achieving the remarkable record of 15 kills.

By late 1917 Britain, after more than three years of experiment, had produced the Mark H2 mine, while the Americans had developed a new antenna type. These improved mines made it possible to plan barrages to block the main routes used by the U-boats and to seal them in their bases. At the beginning of 1918 Rear Admiral Roger Keyes RN relieved Admiral Bacon in command of the Dover Patrol, and at once introduced such measures as maintaining continuous surface patrols and illuminating the area at night to discourage the German submarine practice of passing awash through the straits. By the end of January the second Dover

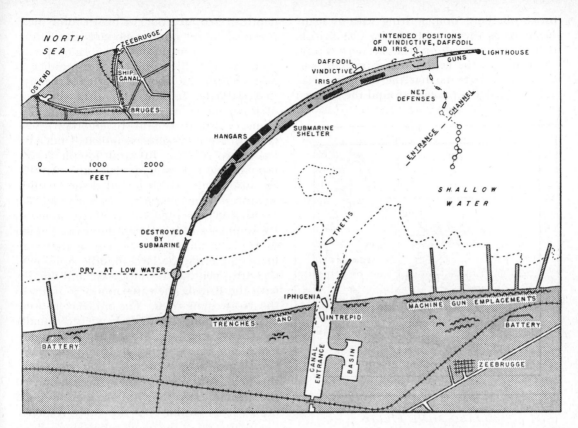

HARBOR OF ZEEBRUGGE, SHOWING GERMAN DEFENSES AND BRITISH BLOCKSHIPS

Mine Barrage, begun earlier by Bacon, was complete, extending from Folkestone to Cape Gris Nez. The effect was soon evident, for the Germans, after losing four boats, prohibited further use of this route.

Encouraged by this success, the Royal Navy and Marines determined to block the canals which reach the Channel at Zeebrugge and Ostend, thus sealing in the dangerous Flanders U-boat force, which had accounted for about one-quarter of British shipping losses and which was still operating some 18 boats. After R.A.F. raids had somewhat softened the two ports, two forces totaling 2,500 seamen and marines set out on April 22 for a simultaneous night descent on the two bases. The larger force, under Captain Alfred F. B. Carpenter RN, headed for Zeebrugge, whose harbor was formed by a long mole defended by artillery and connected to shore by a viaduct. The British planned to isolate the mole by blowing up a submarine under its viaduct, capture it by amphibious assault, and silence the guns, while they sank three blockships in the channel. Surprise and good timing would be essential for success.

Shortly before midnight the British, concealed by a smoke screen, crept in toward Zeebrugge. But a shift in the light northeast wind disclosed the force to an alert mole watch, and the defenders opened fire at short range. Just after midnight the landing party swarmed from the old cruiser *Vindictive* onto the mole and engaged the Germans in hand-to-hand combat, punctuated by a heavy explosion as the submarine *C-3* breached the viaduct. Shortly afterwards the three concrete-filled, obsolete cruisers entered the harbor. The *Thetis* failed to reach the channel, but the *Iphigenia* and *Intrepid* were sunk in approximate position. The attackers then broke off the action, retiring with as many survivors as they could rescue. The British, then hard pressed on the Western Front, claimed that the action was a brilliant success, but it appears that the Germans were able to dredge a passage around the scuttled

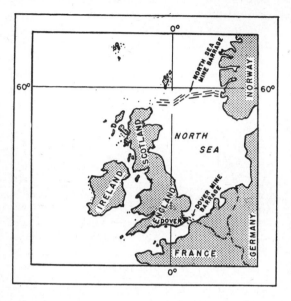

ALLIED MINE FIELDS

cruisers within a few hours, and that by mid-May no inconvenience to navigation remained.

At Ostend the Germans had moved the entrance buoy about a mile to the eastward, so that the British grounded their blockships harmlessly ashore. A second attempt to block Ostend on the night of May 9-10 also failed, but the failure was not really important. Other measures were bringing the submarines under increasingly effective control, and Allied successes ashore were soon to compel Germany to evacuate her Flanders bases.

The success of the Dover barrier encouraged the Americans and British to undertake to close the remaining U-boat route to the Atlantic by mining the North Sea from the Orkneys to Norway. The most extensive mining operation in history, this field would be 230 miles long and 15 to 25 miles wide, with mines spaced from the surface to a depth of 240 feet. Such a project was made practical by the development by the United States Navy's Bureau of Ordnance of the antenna mine, which reduced the number of mines required to about a quarter of the original estimate. In late May 1918 shipment of these mines began from Yorktown, Virginia to Inverness and Invergordon, Scotland, where they were assembled. Under the leadership of Rear Admiral Joseph Strauss USN, Captain Reginald Belknap's Mining Squadron One, which included the Spanish-American War veterans *Baltimore* and *San Francisco,* proceeded to lay these mines in the summer and fall. The Americans planted over 56,000 mines, 80 per cent of the total, first completing the large middle zone, next the area nearest the Orkneys, and finally, with the British, the easternmost 50 miles to the Norwegian coast. The minelayers were escorted mainly by destroyers, occasionally by cruisers and battleships, but the Germans made no serious attempt to interfere. By September U-boats were falling victims to this field. Although Germany later admitted the loss of only four submarines to these mines, it is possible that they were responsible for several of the many submarines which disappeared without trace. Checkmated in both the Straits of Dover and the North Sea, the Germans had little heart for continuing underseas operations in the waning days of a war already lost ashore. Soon naval mutiny would accompany military defeat.

In the Mediterranean, where submarines during the war sank over five million tons of shipping at the cost of only 17 boats, the British in 1918 took over from Italy the responsibility for the Otranto Patrol, but with little success. They increased the breadth of the surface patrol to 35 miles in order to force the U-boats to choose between a long submergence through the mine fields or the risk of surface and air attack, yet they sank only one submarine. In October, 1918, British and Italian cruisers and American submarine chasers with air support struck at the Austro-German base at Durazzo, Albania, some 50 miles northeast of the Straits of Otranto. They severely damaged the port and sank one U-boat. But at the end of the war Germany's 14 remaining boats were able to make their way safely out of the Mediterranean into the Atlantic.

In the summer of 1918 seven German cruiser-type submarines conducted an abortive campaign off the Canadian and United States east coasts, operating as far south as Cape Lookout, North Carolina. Logistically this area was extremely important, and had the Germans possessed the necessary strength and suitable bases they might have choked off American aid to the Allies at its source. As it was, the campaign was inconsequential, costing the Americans only a few steamers, tugs, and barges, without even menacing the convoys.

CONCLUSION

At the Armistice the United States could justifiably feel proud of the record of its naval forces. The United States had aided in the fight against the submarine by producing hydrophones, depth charges, and mines, by constructing submarine chasers and destroyers, and by far-flung operations, but its navy's principal contribution had been in escorting and supplying American ground forces in Europe. That these forces very probably had meant the difference between defeat and victory for the Allies offered little ground for self-congratulation, for they would have been meaningless had not the European Allies borne the brunt of four years of exhausting war. The United States Navy's creditable effort supplemented that of the Royal Navy, which had fought so long and so gallantly, and that of the other Allies.

The single greatest naval lesson of the war was the substantiation of Mahan's conviction that sea power perpetually influences history. Eventual control of the seas by the Allies, long disputed by Germany, enabled them to withstand and later to overcome the military might of the Central Powers. It appeared that sea power would be an essential adjunct to the defense or conquest of land masses in any world struggles in the foreseeable future.

32

Disarmament

and Rearmament

WORLD WAR I UTTERLY DE-stroyed the polity of Europe, so carefully nurtured through a hundred years of painstaking statesmanship. What survived was no brave new world but the wreckage of a social and economic order. Nor could anyone hope to restore that serenity and confidence in inevitable progress which had characterized the preceding century.

In the Allied states demobilization and rebuilding began at once. Munitions and shipbuilding programs were shelved. Obnoxious controls could be abolished. Dangerously inflated national budgets could be balanced. In the United States particularly, the tradition of isolationism made the people impatient to get back to what President Harding a little later was to call "normalcy."

POSTWAR OPERATIONS
OF THE
UNITED STATES NAVY

The immediate task of the Navy was to bring home from France the American Ex-peditionary Force—more than 2,000,000 men. All available ships—cruisers, battleships, cargo vessels, German steamers turned over to the Allies under the terms of the Armistice—were diverted to ferrying troops. Though as many as 340,000 men were transported in the single month of June 1919 at the peak of the program, it was nearly a year after the Armistice before all of America's citizen army was back on American soil. Another major chore was the lifting of the North Sea Mine Barrage, now simply a hazard to peaceful shipping. A fleet of 89 sweepers accomplished this difficult and dangerous task by September 1919.

In the Adriatic and in the Eastern Mediterranean the Allied navies had important quasi-diplomatic missions. The commander of the American Adriatic Squadron administered 300 miles of the Dalmatian coast until the Treaty of Versailles finally awarded the territory to the new state of Yugoslavia. Rear Admiral Mark Bristol, appointed American High Commissioner in Constantinople in 1919, for eight years skillfully mixed diplomacy and naval power. Bristol sent cruisers and destroyers to evacuate refugees in the Black Sea ports of Russia after the final Red victories, and cooperated in the evacuation of 262,000 Greeks from Asia Minor after the Turkish victory in the Greco-Turkish War.

Combined Allied expeditionary forces with strong naval support were sent to Archangel and Vladivostok to guard or destroy war materials that had been shipped there before the collapse of the Russian armies. In Siberia the well-founded fear that the large Japanese force intended to use the occupation as an excuse for permanent territorial aggrandizement kept the American army contingent and most of the United States Asiatic Fleet at Vladivostok until April 1920.

THE NEW ALIGNMENT OF POWERS

The prewar balance of power in Europe was destroyed. Germany was prostrate, presumptively disarmed for the indefinite future. The Hapsburg Empire and Turkey were dismembered. Russia was in the throes of a bloody civil war. Nor did the victors fare much better. France and Italy were on the verge of bankruptcy. Even mighty England, whose world-wide investments had earlier allowed her to levy tribute on the economic activities of the rest of the world, now found herself relatively poor. All the principal European combatants had suffered casualties so severe that they would experience a dearth of able leadership for a generation to come.

The effect of the war on Japan and the United States was quite otherwise. Japan, except for token forces, had limited her contributions to the Pacific area. The United States, which made a tremendous, all-out effort in the final months of the war, had nevertheless not experienced severe casualties. Even her colossal expenditures had been well within the capacities of the country. America, which in 1914 had been a "debtor nation," now found herself the world's foremost creditor. The industrialization of her economy had been accelerated and diversi-fied by the necessities of the war. Perhaps most important, the war had taught America and the world the miracles American industry could accomplish.

Great Britain had emerged from World War I still the world's strongest sea power. Her war losses in capital ships had been much more than made up by new construction. The United States Navy, which had shelved its ambitious 1916 building program in favor of the destroyers and patrol craft that the Allies needed to defeat the submarine threat, had increased in tonnage, but remained for the moment statistically inferior. And immediately after the Armistice there seemed to be a good expectation that the British would receive a powerful reinforcement in the form of ships from the defeated Germans.

THE END OF THE GERMAN FLEET

The Armistice had specified among other things that Germany must surrender immediately ten battleships, six battle cruisers, six light cruisers, 50 destroyers (of recent design), and all of her submarines. The larger units demanded were specified by name, and included the newest and finest vessels in the German navy. On November 21, 1918, with the Grand Fleet under Admiral Sir David Beatty lined up in parade ground regularity on either side of the huge anchorage, the German dreadnought line steamed slowly into Scapa Flow—a navy undefeated, but the navy of a defeated nation. These were the ships that had fought at Jutland—the *Friedrich der Grosse,* the *Koenig Albert,* the *Kaiser,* and the rest. There too were the battle cruisers—the *Seydlitz,* the *Moltke,* the *Derfflinger,* the *Von der Tann.* Tears streamed down the cheeks of the German officers and veteran ratings alike at this moment of humiliation. For them it not only signaled the end of a career; it seemed the end also of a tradition they had devoted their lives to building. The German submarines were ordered to Harwich. They came in one by one, and surrendered to Rear Admiral Sir Reginald Tyrwhitt's force. By January 1, 1919, 114 of the 158 submarines demanded had been delivered.

The Germans regarded their disarmed vessels at Scapa Flow as simply interned as hostages for their good behavior until the peace treaty could be arranged. Their officers and crews remained aboard without restriction. But the British and French, who disagreed about so much in writing the treaty, had no trouble in agreeing that Germany should never have the ships back. Indeed the question of division of naval spoils was informally canvassed.

The Versailles Treaty particularized the naval disarmament of Germany. In addition to the vessels already in British hands, the German Admiralty was to deliver its remaining eight dreadnoughts, eight more light cruisers, 42 more destroyers, and 50 torpedo boats. All these vessels would become the property of the Allies for such disposition as they might agree on. Furthermore, the future German navy was to possess no more than six pre-dreadnoughts, six light cruisers, twelve destroyers, and twelve torpedo boats. It was to have no submarines. All construction under way was to be broken up.

As soon as the news of the treaty provisions reached the interned German vessels at Scapa Flow, and their officers and crews came to realize that their compatriots were actually going to sign the treaty, they determined on the one course left open to them to strike back. At 11:15 AM, June 21, 1919, on signal from the *Emden,* every captain in the German fleet ordered the sea cocks opened. Almost before the British realized what was happening, the scuttled German vessels were sunk beyond salvage.[1] For all practical purposes, the German navy had ceased to exist.

This gesture, which in retrospect has a certain magnificence, had a peculiarly infuriating effect on British public opinion at the time. It was as though a hated criminal had forestalled the executioner by a secreted dose of cyanide. As condign punishment, Germany was compelled to deliver her remain-

[1] Only four vessels were salvaged—the cruisers *Emden, Frankfurt,* and *Nürnberg;* and the dreadnought *Baden.*

ing light cruisers, 300,000 tons of floating docks, and 42,000 tons of floating cranes, dredges, and tugs—in a word, practically everything still afloat in her silent harbors.

Professional opinion in the British navy, at least after the first reaction of anger, inclined somewhat to the view that the Germans by scuttling their ships disposed of a first class Allied headache. Quite apart from the probability of quarreling among the former allies over a proper division of the vessels, there were dozens of intractable technical problems that would have presented themselves had an effort been made to incorporate the German ships into other navies. There was the problem of guns and munitions, for example. Either the entire battery of each German ship would have had to be replaced, or else new manufacturing facilities would have to be created to suit the German calibers. Replacement parts for all the motive machinery would have to be specially cast or machined on order. On the whole, sinking the German fleet was certainly the easiest way to dispose of it. If the German crews chose to do it themselves, all the better.

POSTWAR BUILDING PROGRAMS

All through the war, the Japanese had pursued an active naval building program in their new yards, and immediately afterwards were pushing to completion several capital ships on the ways. On the other hand, French and Italian construction had been largely suspended during hostilities, and the empty national treasuries of those countries gave little prospect of a spirited renewal of large-scale building.

Of all the naval powers, only Britain's recent ally, the United States, seemed in any position to challenge Britain's naval ascendancy. Since the English at this time had been bred to regard mastery of the world's oceans as a natural prerogative, it did not immediately occur to them that their well-meaning American cousins would dream of a bigger fleet than theirs. Britain had had a long, tough war, and felt entitled to a period of relaxation. Certainly it would be less than friendly for the United States at such a time to bring on a naval armaments race.

This pardonable British prejudice however failed to take into account the stubborn, complex personality of the American President. A man of peace dedicated to the spirit of reform, he had nevertheless been the Commander in Chief of a great nation in time of war. To the common man the world over, Wilson emerged from the war period as the one compelling, truly great figure. What the cynical leadership in Europe's capitals could never quite realize about Wilson was the incredible fact that he always meant what he said. It might be naive to say, "The world must be made safe for democracy." But Wilson, saying it, dignified the phrase by his passionate sincerity. When at the peace conference he came to realize that Clemenceau and Lloyd George had always assumed he was merely spouting a good propaganda slogan, he withdrew his full confidence in them.

This aside on Wilson's character is germane to American naval policy in the immediate postwar period. For America had actually intervened in the war over maritime issues—to preserve neutral rights America had fought for a hundred years earlier. The second of Wilson's celebrated "Fourteen Points" had spelled it out:

Absolute freedom of navigation upon the seas, outside territorial waters, alike in peace and in war, except as the seas may be closed in whole or in part by international action for the enforcement of international covenants.

Literally interpreted, this seemed to deny the legality of blockade itself, to say nothing of the long-sanctioned belligerent right of search and seizure of contraband. The British, not unnaturally, had little enthusiasm for such a proposition. At their instance, the Allies did not even consider it at the peace conference. Wilson's reaction was analogous to Clemenceau's when he learned of the United States Senate's rejection of the French Treaty of Alliance—in effect, "If it can't be done by joint action then I'll go it

alone." In 1919, America's shelved 1916 building program was up for consideration by the General Board of the Navy. Wilson gave his personal blessing to a request to Congress for a new building program that would *double* the heavy 1916 schedule.

At the end of the war the United States had 16 post-dreadnought battleships, none more than eight years old. Though the British could count 42 capital ships in their navy, many of these were already obsolescent. Besides, after the experiences of Jutland, the nine battle cruisers in the total could be questioned as vessels worthy of a place in the line. For the United States merely to complete its original 1916 program, incorporating the lessons of the war in the new ships, would have provided 35 modern units, and a fleet qualitatively much superior to the battle-worn British Grand Fleet.[2] The entire proposed 1919 program would mean a fleet of over 50 first-line vessels, utterly eclipsing the British navy unless Parliament strained every resource of money and yard capacity to try to match the American schedule.

British popular and official reaction to the President's proposal was first one of incredulity, then of outrage. With the German fleet gone, it seemed to the English that such a naval building policy was pointed squarely at themselves. With much talk in government circles of their not having fought the war to relinquish their traditional sea supremacy to even the most trusted of allies, the British began to plan what would be needed to match or excel the American program.

President Wilson's exact motivation is not easy to fathom. It is unlikely however that he expected the entire 1919 program, even when authorized, ever to receive the necessary appropriations. Even for the rich United States, the cost would have been a serious burden, requiring a budget of wartime di-

---

[2] Besides the 16 vessels in commission, the *Idaho*, *Tennessee*, and *California* were nearing completion at the time of the Armistice. Of the 16 capital ships in the 1916 program, only the *Maryland*, *West Virginia*, *Colorado*, and *Washington* had been laid down.

mensions. And there was no compelling reason for such an increase.

Most probably, Wilson, irritated at the British attitude on the "freedom of the seas" issue and concerned over Japanese saber-rattling in the Far East, simply desired a much larger navy. He may well have assumed that Congress would automatically whittle down any administration request and hence asked for much more than he felt really essential. On the other hand, it has also been suggested that he intended to use the threat of completion of the 1919 program as a club over the head of the British, who did not then appear enthusiastic about Wilson's dream—the League of Nations. Since Wilson had made clear that he felt that any limitation of armament project should take place through the mechanisms of such a permanent organization, presumably an astronomical competitive building program would appear to England as an unattractive alternative to supporting the League of Nations.

THE BACKGROUND OF THE WASHINGTON CONFERENCE

Whatever Wilson intended, his vision of a new world order flickered out in the last year of his Presidency. Seriously ill, the League rejected by his own country, his party repudiated overwhelmingly in the 1920 election, he left the White House embittered at America's "sullen and selfish isolation."[3]

With popular support, Harding and the Republican Party had disowned the League, but the notion of disarmament appeared to have great public appeal. In early 1921 Senator Borah of Idaho introduced what was to become a joint congressional resolution favoring a tripartite disarmament conference; it passed the Senate unanimously, and the House by a vote of 332 to 4. Almost immediately the British Foreign Office intimated that it would be happy to follow America's lead in calling such a conference.

Accordingly Charles Evans Hughes, Harding's able Secretary of State, made informal overtures to the governments of Britain, Japan, France, and Italy.

All but Japan promptly replied with polite enthusiasm. The Japanese appeared reluctant. Diplomatic friction between Japan and the United States had been frequent and acute. During and immediately after the war Japanese territorial aims on continental Asia had become more blatant. With good reason the Japanese suspected that the conference was in part a device to abrogate the Anglo-Japanese Alliance, which for their part they wished to preserve. On the other hand, they were persuaded that the projected American naval building program was directed at them. And they, even less than the British, could scarcely afford an armaments race with the United States. Besides, it would be incompatible with the dignity of Imperial Japan to stay home from a major conference attended by all the other first-class powers. So, after a two-and-a-half-week delay, Tokyo announced it too would discuss naval disarmament and Far Eastern affairs in Washington.

THE WASHINGTON CONFERENCE

The conference met in Washington on November 12, 1921 with all the fanfare appropriate to the first international congress of this kind ever to be held in the Western Hemisphere. At the first plenary session, Secretary Hughes astonished his listeners and delighted the newspaper-reading public of the whole world by dismissing polite generalities, and laying the specific American proposals on the table at once.

Briefly summarized, these were: an agenda based on the existing strength of navies;[4] a ten-year "holiday" in capital ship construction; a scrapping program (with specific

---

[3] Speech of November 11, 1923.

[4] Defined to mean "ships built and ships building." To have admitted only ships built would have rendered permanent a British superiority that was no part of the American aim.

ships named) which would result in a 5:5:3 ratio as among the United States, Great Britain, and Japan. Moreover the scrapping schedule Hughes proposed went far beyond anything the foreign delegates had contemplated. Of America's postwar fleet, including vessels on the ways, the Secretary calmly proposed to scrap 30 ships, aggregating 845,750 tons.[5]

The British and the Japanese applauded Hughes with some sincerity at this point in his address. He had disposed of their countries' fears of a naval armaments race. But they were a bit premature. They listened in silence as the American Secretary went on to tell them what the United States would regard as a commensurate sacrifice. He enumerated 36 British and Japanese vessels with a total tonnage of 1,032,303 which must also be junked.

Hughes has been criticized for putting his cards face up on the table before the game began. But it was a calculated move, tremendously effective because totally unexpected. There is a real question whether the American aims in the conference were wise ones, but granting for the moment that they were, there is little doubt that this dramatic beginning to the conference vastly shortened the time of negotiation, and helped assure the acceptance of most of the American proposals. The reactions of the press and pulpit all over the world were tremendously enthusiastic. If Hughes' address was intended as an oblique bid for worldwide popular support, it was outstandingly successful.

The details of drafting the naval treaty of course fell to the technical committees, who by concession and compromise hammered out an acceptable text. France and Italy were included in the treaty. The aim was ultimate stabilization of the world's navies at 500,000 tons each for the United States and Britain; 300,000 for Japan; 175,000 each for Italy and France.

Other provisions of the treaty were: (1)

Japan might retain the new *Mutsu,* which Hughes had named for scrapping. In return for this concession, the United States and Britain each were privileged to finish two more ships of up to 35,000 tons. (2) The proposed 10-year capital ship building holiday would otherwise be respected. (3) Aircraft carrier allowances should be 135,000 tons for Britain and the United States, 81,000 for Japan, 60,000 each for France and Italy. (4) No capital ship would be completed with tonnage greater than 35,000,[6] no battleship gun exceed 16 inches in bore, no carrier exceed 27,000 tons,[7] no cruiser carry heavier ordnance than the 8-inch gun. In addition there were procedural rules for scrapping, replacement building, and subsidized construction of merchant marine auxiliaries. At Britain's behest, the treaty draft included a limitation on the use of submarines as commerce-raiders, as well as an agreement prohibiting the use of poison gas. These clauses were never binding however, for France refused to ratify them. An American effort to extend the ratios to cruisers and lesser naval types also came to nothing because of the reluctance of both Britain and Japan. The American delegation could not afford to be insistent because in existing strength of cruisers, America was not only far behind Great Britain, but also considerably weaker than Japan.

THE NON-FORTIFICATION CLAUSE

Also an integral part of the treaty was the controversial non-fortification clause, bitterly denounced by the professional representatives of the American navy. This provided that the Pacific powers were not to arm or

---

[5] This figure invites comparison with the 500,000 tons which became the legal limit to U. S. and British capital ship tonnage under terms of the Treaty.

[6] The British secured an exception for the battle cruiser *Hood,* which was nearing completion. With a designed tonnage of 41,000, she was for two decades the biggest warship afloat.

[7] An exception was allowed the United States, to permit completing the 33,000-ton *Lexington* and *Saratoga.* Providing they did not exceed their tonnage allowances, the other powers could exercise a similar privilege.

fortify bases in their island possessions, except that the Japanese might do as they chose in their home islands, and the Americans in the Hawaiian group. This provision did not apply to Australia or New Zealand. It did mean however that Britain was barred from fortifying Hong Kong, Borneo, the Solomons, and the Gilberts; Japan was barred from further fortifying Formosa or the former German possessions north of the equator which had been mandated to her—notably the Marianas (less Guam), and the Carolines; the United States was barred from fortifying Samoa, Wake, Guam, and, most important, the Philippines.

By agreeing to forego the development of adequately defended naval bases in Guam and the Philippines, it seemed to the American naval authorities that the United States was automatically forswearing the possibility of successful fleet operations in Asiatic waters and in effect underwriting Japanese naval supremacy in the Far East. Subsequent history has of course largely substantiated this view.

Yet in the context of the times, the willingness of the American delegation to surrender on this point is understandable. The Japanese were displeased at the imputation of inferiority implied in the 5:5:3 ratio. It is likely that the non-fortification clause was an essential part of their price of acceptance of the treaty. Secondly, there was a well-founded conviction on the part of the American delegation that it was bargaining away an empty right, one that Congress would probably either never exercise at all or else implement on too modest a scale to make any difference in event of war. After all, both Guam and the Philippines had already been American possessions for 23 years without anything much being done toward military and naval development. What real prospect was there of a change of American policy? On the other hand, there was good reason to think Japan would fortify her island possessions, in the absence of a treaty prohibition.[8]

---

[8] In fact, of course, the Japanese broke their word on this provision, but not until several years after the treaty.

THE NINE-POWER TREATY AND THE FOUR-POWER PACT

Finally, though the Disarmament Treaty was the most important product of the Washington Conference, it was of course related to the simultaneously negotiated Nine-Power Treaty and the Four-Power Pact.[9] The Nine-Power Treaty was essentially a multilateral endorsement of the "Open Door" policy: it reaffirmed the territorial integrity of China. The Four-Power Pact was designed to save face for Japan in the abrogation of the Anglo-Japanese Alliance. It provided that the signatory powers would "respect" each other's Far Eastern possessions.

Both of these treaties represented considerable triumphs for American diplomacy. In them Japan, the only nation at all likely to be harboring aggressive territorial designs in the Far East, agreed formally to policies inconsistent with aggression. Historic American aims were subserved by the joint action of many powers.

It is true that, under the pressure of Canada, Great Britain was more than willing to abandon the Japanese alliance. On the other hand the Japanese recognized that it was a cardinal American aim that they give up the specific guarantees of their alliance with England. The conference was a matter of compromise, and the Japanese in giving up a major security guarantee expected a security guarantee of another sort—the non-fortification clause in the disarmament treaty.

THE RESULTS OF THE WASHINGTON CONFERENCE

At the time, world opinion hailed the Washington treaties as a triumph of diplo-

---

[9] Nine-Power Treaty: United States, Great Britain, Japan, France, Italy, Netherlands, Belgium, Portugal, China.

Four-Power Pact: Great Britain, United States, Japan, France.

macy, a milestone in the world's progress to a millenium of peace. The treaties were ratified by the legislatures of the powers, and the world's navies settled down to a period of comparative stagnation in new construction.

The American State Department could count the conference a success in achieving its main goals:

(1) Great Britain gave official recognition to naval parity; (2) the Anglo-Japanese Alliance had ceased to exist; (3) Japan had accepted a statistical naval inferiority; (4) United States China policy was advanced; (5) a naval armaments race had been averted.

On the other hand, the disarmament treaty had, in failing to limit cruiser tonnage, to some extent simply diverted British and Japanese appropriations to lesser naval types, in which the United States was to become progressively more and more inferior. Furthermore, bemused by the prestige values involved, the American and the British delegations in seeking to weaken the comparative position of each other were being needlessly blind to the political realities of their time. Quite apart from considerations of blood, language, traditions, and recent wartime alliance, the two powers had a substantial identity of interest that made the possibility of war between them too remote to be worth serious consideration. Both had substantial hostages to fortune in the Far East. The possibility of Japanese aggression against British and American possessions was already real enough to have been the subject of a number of widely read books.[10] Even in the light of contemporary developments, it did not make sense for America and Britain to bargain themselves into a position that would allow Japan a free hand in the Far East even in the face of their joint power. Finally, and perhaps most damning, there is the criticism made particularly by the American naval service itself: the most obvious lesson of history is that treaties are more often honored in the breach than in the observance. The simple fact is that aggression has seldom been arrested by a "scrap of paper." The United States, dynamic and powerful, could easily have eclipsed Japan and even Britain in any armaments race. It may reasonably be argued that the naval limitations of the Washington Disarmament Conference were in fact a step along the path leading to the Pearl Harbor attack. Certain it is, in any event, that the naval treaty made no such contribution to world peace as its sponsors hoped.

LATER NAVAL DISARMAMENT CONFERENCES

After the Washington Conference, the heavy vessels of the American Navy were decimated in accordance with the provisions of the Washington treaty. Moreover, ten 7,500-ton, 6-inch gun, four-stack cruisers of the *Omaha* class were the only American vessels in the cruiser category fit to operate in a modern navy. Partly as a result of the currently strained relations with Japan,[11] President Coolidge countenanced the Naval Act of 1924, which provided for the eight 8-inch gun, 10,000-ton "treaty cruisers"—the *Northampton* class. This measure however was far from adequate to restore America's comparative strength in cruisers. At the time of the Geneva Naval Conference (1927), Japan had in commission or under construction 213,955 tons of modern cruisers, whereas the United States had but 155,000.[12]

The Geneva Conference, called by Coolidge specifically to impose the 5:5:3 ratio on cruiser tonnage, was a total failure. France and Italy refused to participate at all. The British delegation, agreeing in principle to the theory of parity with the United States,

---

[10] Of which Walter B. Pitkin's *Must We Fight Japan?* (1921) and Frederick McCormick's *The Menace of Japan* (1917) will serve as examples. See E. E. Tupper and G. E. McReynolds, *Japan in American Public Opinion* (New York, 1937), 156.

[11] The 1924 Immigration Act had revived the touchy racial issue so unsettling to the Japanese in 1906.

[12] The U. S. figure includes the unfinished *Northamptons,* of which only two had been laid down at the time of the Geneva Conference. Strictly speaking, the designation of all of these cruisers as being of one class is not quite accurate. There were a number of differences of design among the vessels.

insisted on a tonnage figure much higher than the American delegation deemed necessary. The British and American delegates also wrangled without reaching agreement over the size and gun calibers allowable to a cruiser, the British preferring more but smaller ships armed with 6-inch guns, and the Americans demanding the 10,000-ton allowance continued and the 8-inch caliber permitted.

Another fatal liability to the success of the conference has already been foreshadowed. In 1921-1922 at Washington, Hughes had based the capital ship ratio on "existing strength." For the American delegation at Geneva to have accepted a similar basis for a cruiser ratio would have meant acceptance of permanent inferiority not only to Britain, whose worldwide empire at least gave an excuse for a very large cruiser force, but also to Japan. The conference broke up without even a pretense at agreement.

The next attempt at naval disarmament came at the London Conference of 1930. Britain and the United States reached a compromise on the troublesome cruiser issue, each to be allowed 339,000 tons (more than the United States had afloat or authorized), and each to be allowed more of the cruiser type it preferred. Japan acceded to the London agreements conditional to an altered 10:10:7 ratio in cruisers, and parity in submarines. Submarine tonnage for all three powers was fixed at 52,700 each. The ban on capital ship construction was extended to the end of 1936. Since France and Italy had refused participation, it was felt necessary to include certain "escape clauses" permitting further construction in the event a nonsignatory power engaged in competitive building. Even in 1930 the auguries for navies regulated by the precise scales of diplomacy had ceased to be favorable.

Throughout the decade of the 1930's, the post-Versailles international political system was on greased skids sloping off to war. A General Disarmament Conference in 1932-33 at Geneva failed abjectly. The Second London Naval Disarmament Conference (1935-36) was a final effort at perpetuating the principle of treaty limitation of navies. The aggressions of Japan, Italy, and Germany, and their cynical contempt for existing treaties foredoomed the London Conference. Britain had already surrendered a principle to Germany in a bilateral naval treaty in 1935, by the terms of which Germany was "allowed" 35 per cent of Britain's naval tonnage, and parity in submarines.[13] Both France and Italy were engaged in substantial building programs. Italy refused participation at the start. The Japanese then demanded full parity in all categories. The American delegation demurring, the Japanese withdrew from the conference. The United States, Great Britain, and France finally signed a treaty so watered down with "escalator clauses" as to be virtually meaningless. For practical purposes, all treaty limitations of navies expired December 31, 1936.

AMERICAN BUILDING POLICY IN THE 1930's

American building policy entered a new phase beginning roughly with the inauguration of Franklin D. Roosevelt as President in 1933. Like Theodore Roosevelt earlier, Franklin Roosevelt showed a perception of the intimate relation between diplomatic and military strength. He recognized the true seriousness of the deteriorating world situation, and knew that navies cannot be improvised in the face of an emergency. Furthermore, again like the earlier Roosevelt, he had gained professional knowledge of the service as Assistant Secretary of the Navy and had a hobbyist's enthusiasm for the sea service.

The first substantial naval authorization of Roosevelt's first term came as a relief measure to assist the moribund steel and shipbuilding industries; section 202 of the National Industrial Recovery Act of June 16, 1933 authorized new construction in cruisers and lesser types to full treaty strength. On March 27, 1934, the Vinson-Trammel Bill

---

[13] This was of course a tacit admission by Britain that the Versailles Treaty was dead.

passed, providing for an eight-year replacement building program amounting to 102 ships. From 1934 to 1940, the American naval appropriations implementing the Vinson-Trammel program grew year by year, finally approaching a billion dollars annually. The Second Vinson Act of 1938 authorized an additional 20 per cent over-all tonnage increase. In addition to new construction, modernization of older vessels was undertaken; a new emphasis on naval aircraft and on carriers became apparent; new naval bases and air stations were established.

After the fall of France, in June 1940, the limiting factor in American defense expenditures ceased to be Congressional reluctance to underwrite the services' maximum programs: it was from then on simply the physical limitations of America's industrial capacity. By the time of the Pearl Harbor attack (December 7, 1941), the United States Navy had the following combat vessels in commission or on the ways:

	BATTLE-SHIPS:	CARRI-ERS:	CRUIS-ERS:	DESTROY-ERS:	SUB-MARINES:
In commission	17	7	37	171	111
Building	15	11	54	191	73

THE UNITED STATES MERCHANT MARINE

Virtually since the American Civil War, the American merchant marine has been at a competitive disadvantage in comparison with the shipping of other countries. In the 20th century, this has stemmed both from high construction costs and high costs of operation, which in turn have largely stemmed from high American labor costs. In those industries to which assembly-line techniques can be adapted, American capitalism can pay high wages and still undersell foreign competition in world markets. But neither the building nor the operation of ships lend themselves to the assembly line. In spite of high tariff protection, American ship building and operation could never compete effectively with that of other coun-

tries except with the additional crutch of federal subsidy. Up to 1936, this subsidy took the disguised form of a liberal government loan policy and of excessive payments for carrying the mails.[14]

In 1936, Congress passed an important Shipping Act, which established a five-man Maritime Commission under Rear Admiral Emory S. Land USN Ret., and initiated a new program of direct subsidy, both for construction and operation. The design of subsidized construction had to meet the approval of the commission, which examined it with the criterion of auxiliary use in wartime in mind. To qualify for subsidy, an operator had to carry crews two thirds of whom were United States citizens, and submit to certain investigatory and regulatory powers exercised by the commission.

Beginning in 1938, the Maritime Commission fostered a replacement program in the merchant marine which aimed to retire slow, obsolete craft at the rate of 50 ships per year. The following year this rate was stepped up. Under the forced draft of wartime, new construction was enormously increased. Yard capacity and the availability of shipyard workers were the only effective limiting factors after the Pearl Harbor attack. By September 1942, 300 tankers and 2000 standard-design Liberty and Victory ships had been contracted for. Even after allowing for large losses to submarines, the American merchant marine had a net growth by the time of the German surrender to over 30,-000,000 tons.

TECHNOLOGICAL PROGRESS

It is probable that the 15-year building holiday somewhat retarded advance in capital ship design. On the other hand, the *North Carolina* and the other battleships of the "new" battle line, launched shortly before and during World War II, represented an

---

[14] In addition, American shippers after World War I had been able to purchase surplus vessels from the government at bargain rates.

enormous advance over the *West Virginia* (1923), last of the treaty ships. The *North Carolina* was seven knots faster and possessed superior armor and much improved fire control. She also of course had a very much bigger and more effective antiaircraft battery. Other naval types made a more than commensurate advance.

In 1919-21 the collier *Jupiter* was converted into the *Langley* (19,360 tons), the first United States Navy aircraft carrier. Two battle cruiser hulls, which otherwise would have been scrapped under the Washington Treaty, were converted to the 33,000-ton *Lexington* and *Saratoga,* commissioned in 1928. It was on the flight decks of these three vessels that the operational techniques were worked out that were to make the United States Navy's air arm the world's finest. By December 7, 1941, as we have seen, America had seven carriers in commission, and eleven more on the ways.

The United States submarine service was expanded between the wars. The new and larger "fleet boats" were in the late 1930's already rendering obsolete the dependable old S-boats. Improved submarine rescue devices and methods were perfected.

Antisubmarine methods were the subject of a continuing research and development program. The Underwater Sound Laboratory developed "sonar," or underwater sound-ranging to replace hydrophone detection of submerged submarines.[15] Pioneer work in radar was also accomplished before the war. Both in underwater sound-ranging and in radar the British, working independently, duplicated American progress.

These and other scientific advances

changed standard tactics in important ways. Conversion of the fleet to oil fuel shortly after World War I led to the building of high speed naval tankers and an effective technique for fueling at sea. This in turn expanded the possible radius of action of the fleet, no longer dependent on closely spaced coal depots. Carrier aircraft and long-range naval reconnaissance planes effectively took over the traditional scouting role of cruisers. Much improved radio communication promised to increase effective operational control by the higher echelons of command.

As will appear in later chapters, there were deficiencies and failures in the United States Navy's technical development program, mistakes glaringly highlighted by the test of the war. But the miracle is that so much was done so well. It is probably fair to say that in 1941 a newly designed naval vessel represented man's supreme mechanical achievement up to that time.

THE BREAKDOWN OF COLLECTIVE SECURITY

Throughout the between-wars period, the diplomacy of the western democracies aimed at providing a collective security system. The original cornerstone of this system was conceived to be the enforcement of the Versailles Treaty, which undertook to insure the permanent disarmament of Germany, and the strengthening of the League of Nations. The Bolshevik threat was "solved" by the *"Cordon Sanitaire,"* a row of small buffer states along Soviet Russia's western border. France also by loans and diplomacy promoted a "Little Entente" (1924) of friendly states [16] in Middle Europe.

Joint international action was the order of the day. Besides the disarmament conferences described above, there were conferences on war debts and reparations, treaties of conciliation and of commerce.[17] Germany

---

[15] World War I hydrophones were not precisely directional and depended on the operator's picking up the sound of the submarine's motors or propellers. A skillful submariner could sometimes defy detection by shutting off all power and lying on the bottom. Sonar utilizes a self-initiated sound wave, which on striking a metal hull bounces back as a "return" or echo to the operator. Sonar is directional and it provides range data.

The British independently developed a similar device called asdic. Sonar and asdic may be bracketed with radar in wartime importance. Without them the British and American navies would have lost the Battle of the Atlantic.

[16] Yugoslavia, Czechoslovakia, and Romania, all of which had received territory from the dismembered Austrian Empire.

[17] Viz., Dawes and Young Plans, the Rapallo Treaty (Germany and Russia), and the Locarno Treaties.

entered the League of Nations after the Locarno Treaties (1925). Even Russia, outcast among nations, was at the behest of France admitted to the League in 1933. Through the decade of the 1920's, there seemed no good reason to think a new war inevitable. Probably most statesmen, and certainly most ordinary men, felt that diplomacy had displaced large-scale war for their lifetime at least.

But the apparent stability was extremely temporary. To Britain, France, and the United States, the *status quo* was satisfactory. For that very reason, their diplomacy was passive, and as the following decade was to show, comparatively impotent.[18] They failed to take effective joint action, and as war loomed nearer and nearer, their inadequate armaments and pacifistic populations emboldened the dictator-states to make more and more brazen demands. Russia too, which existed altogether outside the collective security system until about 1933 and was received grudgingly and suspiciously in the councils of the democracies afterwards, was preoccupied by a gigantic effort to build a modern state. Her influence in determining events was not important until after Munich (1938).

Japan, Germany, and Italy, the self-styled "have-not" nations, nationalistic, imperialistic, and opportunistic, came to assume the dynamic roles in the history of the 1930's. They were not satisfied with the *status quo,* and were prepared to risk war to remold their corners of the world.

The proximate causes of the aggressions of the Fascist countries in the 1930's may well be the alleged "injustices" of the Versailles Treaty (in the case of Germany), and the Great Depression that by destroying the means of livelihood of millions of men made them ready to follow any demagogue. But the deep-rooted underlying causes were the grandiose national objectives of Germany, Italy, and Japan—unchallengeable dominance in Middle Europe, in the Mediterranean, and in the Far East. For Hitler's Germany the immediate objective was the absorption of all German-speaking areas—Austria, Sudetenland, Polish Silesia, and Danzig; the ultimate objective was to subjugate the Balkans and the Ukraine. For Mussolini's Italy the short-term goal was an African empire comparable to France's—Ethiopia supplementing Libya, Eritrea, and Italian Somaliland—and a foothold on the east shore of the Adriatic—Albania, perhaps later a part of Greece. For Japan, the irreducible minimum was Manchuria; the more distant objective, hegemony over China, Malaya, and the East Indies.

In a sense World War II may be said to have begun on September 18, 1931, when a bomb explosion on the track of the South Manchurian Railway near Mukden signaled the beginning of the first "Chinese Incident," the invasion of Manchuria by the Japanese. The story of Japanese aggressions in the 1930's is summarized in a later chapter. At this point it is enough to say that the failure of the democracies to cope with this treaty-breaking threat to the general peace was a lesson not lost on Mussolini and Hitler.

Italy next broke the peace by the invasion and conquest of Ethiopia in 1935. It was not so much the intrinsic importance of Manchuria and Ethiopia to the democratic world that counted. Rather it was that these naked aggressions proved at once the impotence of the League of Nations at its designed function and the bankruptcy of the collective security system. With the advance connivance of the conservative governments of France and Britain, Mussolini manufactured a border incident at Walwal and made it an excuse for aggressive war. After a brave but futile fight the white-sheeted tribesmen of Haile Selassie were defeated. Meanwhile, popular support for the League proved surprisingly strong in Britain and France. The League did act to the extent of applying financial sanctions [19] and placing an embargo on munitions for the Italians. As could have been predicted, such measures were entirely ineffective in arresting a small-scale colonial war. Oil sanctions, which might have been effective, were not applied. Britain ostenta-

---

[18] This is perhaps unfair to France. However France was inherently much the weakest of the three great democracies.

[19] I.e., forbidding financial assistance or loans to Italy.

tiously moved a fleet into the Mediterranean, apparently for the purpose of allowing its personnel to watch Italian transports carry an army through the Suez Canal to Eritrea. About the only solace that friends of the League could distill from the sorry story was that the double-dealing foreign ministers of Britain and France—Hoare and Laval—were forced by popular indignation to resign.

The mere threat of oil sanctions, and the disturbing reports he received of public hostility to Italy in the democracies caused Mussolini to reassess his relations with Nazi Germany—with which Italy had recently been distinctly unfriendly. Up to 1935 Germany had been largely unarmed. But in that year, after some domestic massacres to consolidate his power at home, Hitler felt secure enough to denounce the Versailles Treaty and to announce to the world the rearmament of Germany. A rearmed Germany would be worth Italy's sympathetic attention, reasoned Mussolini. The Rome-Berlin "Axis" dates from 1936.[20]

Adolf Hitler, ignorant, fanatical, something of a paranoiac, yet unquestionably brilliant, came to power in Germany in 1933 pledged to cure unemployment and to destroy the Versailles settlement. By rearming Germany he did both. In 1936, in the face of French threats, he marched his new armies into the "permanently demilitarized" Rhineland—a necessary preliminary to defense of the industrial Ruhr should a major war develop later.

In the Spanish Civil War (1936-1939) both Hitler and Mussolini intervened on the side of the rebels with men and material—perhaps decisively. Though in the beginning popular sympathy in the democracies was 2 to 1 in favor of the Loyalist government, it was not the democracies but Russia that provided material assistance to the Loyalists, and that too little and too late.[21]

In early 1938 German rearmament had made Hitler bold enough to undertake his first really big gamble. With the cooperation of the Nazi party in Austria, he simply marched to Vienna and announced an *Anschluss*—a union of Austria with Germany. Not being challenged, later in the year he demanded of Czechoslovakia that she cede to Germany the German-speaking Sudetenland, a fringe of parishes along Czechoslovakia's borders.

Unlike the Austrians, the Czechs are primarily a Slavic, not a Germanic, people. They had military alliances with France and Russia. With mountainous frontiers, a good army, and a substantial armaments industry, they were prepared to fight. Nearly everyone in Europe expected war. Instead, the prime ministers of France and Britain flew to Munich for a personal conference with Hitler. The upshot was that France dishonored her commitment. In exchange for empty and false promises from Hitler, Daladier and Chamberlain bargained away the Czechs' freedom. Moreover Russia was able to claim later that because the western democracies had proved they could not be trusted, Russia herself had to look elsewhere for her security. But in the West such was the passionate hope for peace that cheering multitudes surrounded Chamberlain's homecoming plane at Croydon Airfield. The peace that he had so dearly bought was in fact to last a little less than a year.

AMERICAN PUBLIC OPINION IN THE 1930's

During the period 1930-1938, though the United States occasionally showed signs of a positive Asiatic policy, it shunned collective action in Europe. The American people unquestionably disapproved very strongly of Hitler, especially of his merciless persecution of the Jews, but they even more strongly rejected the idea of American commitments

[20] The German-Japanese "Anti-Comintern" Pact later in the year made Germany the kingpin in a Rome-Berlin-Tokyo axis. The term "Axis" was in common use from 1937 on.

[21] As the Spanish War dragged on to its miserable conclusion, the small Spanish Communist Party, by virtue of its determined and ruthless leadership, became the dominant group in the Loyalist government.

This of course made effective intervention by the democracies even less a political possibility.

that might lead to war. Indeed in the United States the self-evident failure of diplomacy to promote collective security in the 1930's stimulated a popular revulsion against the very practice of diplomacy. In 1934 headlines were made by the investigations of the Nye Committee in the Senate, which rehearsed in detail the well-known fact that American steel companies and munitions manufacturers had made handsome profits during World War I. World Peaceways and similar pacifist pressure groups promoted the erroneous conclusion that the war industries had been "responsible" for America's entrance into the war. The "merchants of death" propaganda thereby engendered helped make possible the neutrality legislation of the late '30's (1935-1941), which amounted to a deliberate surrender of the neutral rights the United States had twice gone to war to preserve.[22] As in Great Britain and France, in the United States there was a widespread feeling that no war was worth fighting. Contemporary literature reflected a profound cynicism about the motives and competence of World War I leadership.[23] A great many American students gave vociferous approval to the "Oxford Pledge," by which British undergraduates were swearing "under no circumstances" to serve King and country.

---

[22] The 1935 Neutrality Act forbade the sale or transport of munitions to a belligerent; the President might also prohibit Americans from travel on belligerents' ships.

The 1936 amendment prohibited loans to belligerents.

The 1937 Neutrality Act applied the earlier provisions to "civil strife" as well as war between nations. It permitted sales to belligerents of goods other than munitions on a "cash and carry" basis.

The 1939 Neutrality Act extended the "cash and carry" provision of the 1937 Act by lifting the embargo on munitions, and gave authority to the President to forbid American ships' entering designated "danger zones." The Neutrality Act of 1939 was repealed on November 13, 1941, a little over two weeks before Japan attacked the United States.

[23] Dozens of titles might be cited. Ernest Hemingway's A Farewell to Arms, C. S. Forester's The General, Erich Maria Remarque's All Quiet on the Western Front are examples from the novels. Plays and movies with a strong pacifist overtone reached nearly all of the population in the western democracies.

POPULAR THINKING ON GRAND STRATEGY

Along with a pacifistic and isolationist public opinion went a popular misconception of grand strategy that made many persons feel that in any event American participation was not necessary. Captain B. H. Liddell Hart and other military writers of reputation had severely criticized Allied generalship in World War I for useless sacrifice of men in trying to break the trench line. It was freely predicted that, if World War II came, the pattern of the Western Front would be the same except that this time the Allies, snug in the impregnable Maginot Line, would remain on the defensive. The Germans, finally driven to action by the relentless pressure of naval blockade, would break themselves on the Maginot barrier. The French and British land offensive, when it came, would be a matter of sweeping up the exhausted fragments of the *Wehrmacht*. In brief, the war would be won by a combination of the Maginot Line and superior British sea power. America could afford to keep hands off. In view of the fact that apparently the French general staff accepted this view, it is perhaps pardonable for a large part of the American public to have done so.

As everyone knows, the Maginot Line was to prove anything but impregnable. For that matter the role assigned to sea power in the prospective Allied strategy was not a realistic one. Sea power is a prerequisite to world power. It facilitates rapid shifting of forces among widely separated theaters of operations. Sea blockade can be decisive against an island nation dependent on imports for food and raw materials. But blockade cannot be decisive against a self-sufficient continental power with adequate internal communications. Hence naval supremacy alone was not enough to defeat Germany, even though German naval supremacy would have promptly defeated England. By the speedy development of synthetic oil and rubber industries, German scientists supplied at home the two bulky commodities their nation had previously lacked for waging war.

Hitler and his generals in planning for war were of course familiar with the theses of Mahan, but as the modest prewar German naval building program showed, the Nazis discounted the relevance of sea power to Germany's situation. The theoretical foundations of Nazi world strategy were in fact largely derived from Karl Haushofer's "geopolitical" writings,[24] which in turn were based on the ideas of the distinguished British geographer, Halford J. Mackinder.

"DEMOCRATIC IDEAS AND REALITY"

When in 1919 Mackinder published *Democratic Ideas and Reality,* he meant it as a warning to his countrymen. The book came nearer to being a blueprint for Nazi Germany. Briefly summarized, Mackinder's argument runs: (1) Contrary to the implications of Mahan's writings, sea power and land power have been alternately decisive in the long periods of history. (2) When land power has been ascendant, it has often been able to defeat sea power by taking its bases in land campaigns. (3) England's effective control of the seas gave her world hegemony until the 20th century, but now the steam and gasoline engines, and rail and highway networks are depriving the sea of its monopoly of bulk transportation; therefore England's inherent relative power has declined as compared to continental power. (4) Once it has achieved adequate communications and a high level of economic development, the center of the greatest land mass will be in a position to exert the greatest power. This "Heartland" comprises western Siberia and European Russia. (5) A vigorous people, armed with modern technology, may through control of the Heartland come to control the entire "World Island," i.e., Eurasia and Africa. (6) The superior resources and population of the World Island may well ultimately make possible domination of the fringe lands, i.e.,

Great Britain, Japan, Australia, and North and South America.

Writing shortly after the end of World War I, Mackinder expressed the view that the victorious powers had very narrowly escaped catastrophe. Had Germany confined her military effort to the Eastern Front, it is conceivable that, operating out of her strategic position in East Europe, she might have conquered the Heartland. Then after employing her advanced technical means to develop this area into a vast base for further military operations, she could have advanced in all directions to the oceans, taking the bases of sea power from the landward side. With the whole World Island as her base, she might have launched a new cycle of sea power to conquer the rest of the world. Mackinder warned that the defeat of Germany in 1918 did not permanently remove the danger. If Germany and Russia should combine by agreement, or by conquest of one by the other, they would be in a position to rule the world. He put his warning into a simple formula:

Who rules East Europe commands the Heartland:

Who rules the Heartland commands the World-Island:

Who rules the World-Island commands the World.[25]

Accepting the validity of Mackinder's views, Haushofer attempted to orient German territorial aspirations to the East. In the opinion of the Nazi geopoliticians, with a conquered Russia as a German base, Hitler could afford at last to defy the superior British fleet.

Herein lies the ultimate rationale of Germany's attack on Russia in 1941, perhaps also of the adventures of Rommel's *Afrika Korps* in Germany's North African campaign. Haushofer himself, through whom Mackinder's ideas reached Hitler, cannot be deemed responsible for the poor timing of the Russian campaign, since it was also part of his program that Germany should at all costs avoid another two-front war. But the

---

[24] Professor General Karl Haushofer was the founder and head of the *Institut für Geopolitik* in Munich. In addition to his writings, his personal influence with the Nazi hierarchy was important.

[25] *Democratic Ideals and Reality* (New York, 1919, 1942), 150.

idea of conquering Russia sooner or later, of making a large part of it a German colony, was at least thoroughly consistent with his program.

It is easy to criticize Mackinder.[26] The Heartland, the limits of which are vaguely defined, includes vast tracts of tundra and arid pasturage. Except insofar as its immensity furnishes space for defensive maneuvering, its size is more a liability than an asset. Control of such an area would not necessarily advance a program of world domination. Control of the centers of industry, wherever located, would still appear to be vastly more important. And over-all technological and industrial superiority seem more important still.

In any event, Mackinder never pretended to "prove Mahan wrong." He simply warned against a naive acceptance of an oversimplified version of Mahan's ideas. And as a mat-

[26] See, for example, *America's Strategy in World Politics* (New York, 1942) and other writings by Nicholas J. Spykman.

ter of interest, Mackinder himself was to acknowledge shortly before his death, in 1947, that a power combination centering in the North Atlantic and including Western Europe and North America might more than offset the rising power of the Eurasian Heartland.

At this writing, the struggle between the Communist-dominated "Heartland" and the "Fringe Lands" of the West is of course unresolved. Certainly improved internal communications and the increase of economic self-sufficiency through the development of synthetics have strengthened the Soviet Union in this long-term conflict. On the other hand, the extended radius of naval fire-power contributed by carrier aircraft, and the vastly increased raw material requirements of modern technology may more than counterbalance these new Soviet advantages. It is, in any event, probably safe to say that no oversimplified theory of the historical process can be a trustworthy basis for predicting the unpredictable.

33

Doctrinal Evolution
between World Wars

In the 19th century the United States Navy, as we have seen, made important contributions to the development of armor, armament, machinery, and similar materials of naval warfare. But in other respects it progressed more slowly because the American public lost interest in naval affairs and Congress curtailed naval funds. Consequently from 1886 until 1916 the Navy possessed a few modern vessels in each class, but never in sufficient number to conduct extensive maneuvers during peace. As a result it lagged during the years before World War I in developing either the tactical and logistic doctrines, or the techniques flowing from practiced teamwork, that are so essential in 20th century warfare.

Fortunately, experience during World War I convinced a number of key officers in the naval services of the need for developing doctrine and techniques, as well as material. Though scarcely noticed by the public, this new dynamism made of the years between world wars the most fruitful quarter-century in American naval history. This chapter focuses upon the doctrine and techniques that produced the two most significant instruments for naval combat to emerge from that period—the amphibious assault force and a balanced naval air force.

AMPHIBIOUS
FOUNDATIONS

The amphibious assault is a form of military combat which the attacker commences on water and carries ashore against a defender lodged close to the shoreline. It differs from conventional ground operations only in that the amphibious attacker advances in column (usually in transports), deploys into a line of boats, and comes under enemy fire while he is still water-borne; then he steps ashore almost at the moment when he comes to close quarters with the defender. Yet this difference is so significant that amphibious combat has always been the most difficult of military operations and has become increasingly difficult since technology began to complicate war.

In spite of these difficulties men have

576

fought amphibiously since the beginning of recorded history. We have seen already how extensively the British used amphibious techniques during their 18th century and early 19th century wars, as well as at Dardanelles-Gallipoli and at Zeebrugge in World War I. These British amphibious combats comprised what are now called "combined operations," for they required semi-autonomous army and navy units to form a temporary amphibious force with command responsibility divided equally between whatever senior army and navy officers happened to be present. Though this British arrangement worked acceptably in the era of ocean sailing vessels, it was not the only method, or even the first method, for organizing an amphibious force. During the centuries when major wars were confined to the Mediterranean there were army-centered amphibious forces whose ships were commanded by a general, and navy-centered amphibious forces whose infantrymen came under command of a navy flag officer. So when steam enforced marked changes in naval doctrines and techniques, there was ample precedent for three possible patterns of amphibious organization.

Distinguishing among these patterns is important because each separate form implies a different command doctrine. The army-centered amphibious force is unified, but its vessels are controlled by land officers rarely expert at handling ships in combat. The navy-centered force also is unified, but the participating elements are commanded by a sea officer whose experience rarely includes extensive combat command of infantry. And while the "combined" amphibious force enjoys the advantage of senior officers with experience in land as well as in sea combat, its command responsibility rests with a committee of at least two men. Selecting a form of amphibious organization therefore poses an option of difficulties. If one is to achieve the unified command essential for winning difficult objectives, he must devise some method for qualifying a general to command ships or for qualifying an admiral to command infantry.

As we have observed, the British steam navy retained the amphibious doctrine it had known under sail, and at Gallipoli British forces conducted a "combined" operation with command responsibility divided between General Hamilton and Admiral de Robeck. Possibly because they lacked any long tradition of "combined" operations under sail, United States forces experimented with all three forms of amphibious organization. During the Mexican War Commodore M. C. Perry conducted small navy-centered amphibious operations up several rivers, while Perry and Lieutenant General Winfield Scott mounted the "combined" operation against Vera Cruz as a preliminary to Scott's advance on Mexico City. During the Civil War Brigadier General A. E. Burnside led an army-centered amphibious attack on Roanoke Island in 1862. Three years later at Fort Fisher Admiral Porter and General Terry sent a "combined" attack against the land face of the fort while Porter mounted a navy-centered assault on its sea face. So in 1866, when the Navy took over from coast artillerists the role of front-line defender of the Western Hemisphere against any potential attack from Europe, officers then active had a body of amphibious experience on which to draw.

The steam vessels on which all navies had to rely for 40 years after 1866 enjoyed such limited operational range or combat endurance that they required a string of bases where warships might replenish coal supplies after three or four days of steaming. Since defense of the Western Hemisphere required the United States Navy to use advanced bases on Atlantic or Caribbean islands near the American coast, it had to develop some systematic method for making such bases available to its own ships while denying them to a potential European enemy. Because the cost of maintaining a permanent base on each outlying island was prohibitive, the Navy had to evolve the means for occupying on short notice an unfortified island, for improvising a base there, and for defending the position against attack from the sea. To occupy and defend even one outlying base required a larger force of trained infantry than the tiny regular army could muster on short notice during the late 19th century. So the steam navy's first amphibious problem—seizure and defense of an advanced island base—required it to develop naval infantry of a sort the United States had never possessed. This set of circumstances forced on the United States its first important amphibious decision: reliance upon a navy-centered amphibious force.

Shortly after 1880 alert navy officers began to give special attention to the problem of creating a force of naval infantry. For more than a decade many of them sought to expand the kind of bluejacket landing force Britons had evolved during the age of sail. But as the new ships devoted ever more space to machinery and placed increasing demands on their crews, it became clear that no major naval squadron could send away a bluejacket landing force without impairing its combat power. So in 1894, after a heated naval controversy, Congress stepped in and assigned to the Marine Corps the mission of providing units of fleet infantrymen that could establish and defend outlying bases.[1] And this Congressional decision provided a unique solution to the first amphibious problem confronting steam navies, for no other major naval power has developed such a specialized force of naval infantry.

The 1894 decision came none too soon; within four years the United States steam navy faced its first major test against a European force in American waters. Hard work between 1894 and 1898 produced the battalion of fleet marines which seized an advanced naval base at Guantanamo Bay, stood off a more numerous enemy, and made of Admiral Sampson's blockaders a "fleet that came to stay." Lessons from Guantanamo reinforced by unhappy experience with the Filipino Insurrection—which need not have occurred had Admiral Dewey's Asiatic Squadron possessed an adequate complement of fleet infantry—confirmed the wisdom of the 1894 Congressional decision. Since then the Commandant of the Marine Corps has been responsible for supplying trained units of naval infantry in the same way that Navy

type-force commanders became responsible, at a later date, for providing combat-ready submarines, destroyers, cruisers, and battleships. Thus in a sense the Marine Corps became the Navy's first type-force.

Establishing this type-force of fleet infantry created the need for amphibious doctrine and techniques. If exigencies of national security had enforced this need with sufficient urgency, the naval services might well have evolved an amphibious assault force long before they did. Even so, the succeeding 20 years witnessed real amphibious progress.

By 1900 conditions affecting world power had changed drastically. The United States emerged from the Spanish-American War as a world power whose industrial potential virtually insured America against invasion from Europe. Yet this very strength required her to join European powers in their competition for Asia's vast resources of raw materials, and Japanese aversion to the United States, position in the Philippine Islands called for a new military policy aimed at protecting the expanded national interest. Thus, though peace remained the chief objective of United States policy, extending her strategic boundary to the Philippines created a serious problem for the naval establishment. Almost before they had achieved a force capable of defending the Caribbean, the sea services had to evolve the means for sending a fleet to Philippine waters in the event Japan opened hostilities. So from as early as 1900 Japan became, in naval eyes at least, the nation's most threatening potential enemy, and after 1900 the naval services devoted a very large proportion of their energies to defending the United States position in East Asia.

Between 1900 and 1910 Marine Corps units constructed advanced-base defenses and other facilities at Guam and in the Philippines. Serving as fleet infantry under direct control of the Commander in Chief of the Asiatic Fleet, marines from those units fought near Manila, in the Leyte area, on Samoa, and in China. In the process Navy and Marine Corps officers hammered out fundamental doctrine essential for employing in-

[1] For detailed treatment of this problem, see W. H. Russell, "The Genesis of FMF Doctrine: 1879-1899," *Marine Corps Gazette,* April-July 1951.

fantry as an integral arm of the fleet. At the same time, regular tours of duty on combat vessels kept marine leaders in such close contact with navy officers that of necessity each group came to understand the other's problems. From such experience early in the century evolved the concept of complete tactical responsibility within a unified command. This set of "command relationships," as they came to be called, struck a nice balance between the loose "committee" system used by the British at Gallipoli and the rigidity of the over-centralized command system employed by the army-centered amphibious forces even then evolving in Germany and Japan.

While the Asiatic Fleet grappled with an immediate problem, other elements of the naval services strove to discover just what complement and equipment an effective Base Force should require. The General Board, the Office of Naval Intelligence, the Naval War College, Marine Corps Headquarters, and the North Atlantic Squadron all worked on the problem. As a result the Marine Corps in 1912 was able to establish a permanent Advanced Base Force at the Philadelphia Navy Yard. It comprised an infantry regiment reinforced by artillery and service units, all in a state of fire-department readiness for taking ship and moving to an area where an arm of the fleet should require a base. And in the years from 1912 through 1916 this fleet type-force of reinforced infantry gained valuable experience in a series of Caribbean police missions that required prompt naval action.

Despite the fundamental command relationships and the type-force of reinforced infantry American amphibians had evolved by 1916, there remained one more step before the United States could possess the foundation on which to build its amphibious power. In those prewar years, before aircraft began to threaten fleets or their bases, Pacific islands were so little developed that an armed force could establish an advanced fleet base merely by pre-empting an undefended island. In consequence early Marine Corps advanced-base units were not trained for assault against well defended beaches. Instead they

fulfilled missions very similar to those performed in World War II by naval Construction Battalions, and their few strictly tactical exercises trained the men to defend bases already won. As a result of this defensive posture, there was little urgency for developing special landing craft or for devising special logistic doctrine to meet amphibious requirements. Pleas by Marine Corps quartermasters for combat-unit loading fell on deaf ears. Moreover the Navy was not ready to experiment with special transports, the small craft required for ship-to-shore movement, or with doctrines for adapting naval gunfire to the role of supporting artillery. Colonel (later Major General) John A. Lejeune and a few other marines recognized the need for giving the fleet's new infantry type-force the capacity to attack as well as to defend. In 1916 they began to solve the problem by analyzing British experience at Gallipoli, but America's entry into World War I deflected their energies.

Curiously, it was the land war in Europe that supplied the naval services with the experience they needed to provide their amphibious force with the capacity for assault. In 1917 it seemed that the Navy could devote its main effort to moving convoys into Europe and that the Army Expeditionary Force would use overland transport already established by the Allies, but these two arms of the service required an advanced base capable of staging men and equipment from their ships into the army rear. When chaotic conditions at Brest threatened to offset America's contribution to the war, marines commanded by Brigadier General Smedley D. Butler (an Advanced Base veteran) quickly converted the port area into an efficient base. Experience there convinced a number of navy officers that their service should develop doctrines for streamlining cargo-handling at both ends of the sea lane, and the same experience confirmed conclusions reached earlier by individual Marine Corps quartermasters who had struggled with Advanced Base logistics. When contrasted with British experience three years earlier at Gallipoli, work at the "Brest beachhead" demonstrated that logistics dominate amphibious operations just as they do conventional combat on land or sea. Though the Brest experience did not translate immediately into improved amphibious doctrine, we shall see how the gradual emphasis on logistics which it sparked contributed mightily during succeeding decades. Many young marine officers who served at Brest made important contributions to logistic procedures the naval services were forced to improvise early in World War II.

Soon after Butler's men had organized Brest into an efficient base, other marines led by General Lejeune, and many less senior officers with Advanced Base experience, learned in combat to adapt the new 20th century weapons to age-old patterns for fire-and-movement. Their most significant experience flowed from using the Browning Automatic Rifle (BAR). This new weapon, issued to American ground troops in 1918, enabled the foot soldier to advance against defensive machine gun fire which had so long enforced a stalemate on the Western Front. Though all Allied armies contributed to driving the Germans out of France, such successful combat experience against first-class troops stimulated the aggressive spirit inherent in traditional Marine Corps doctrine. This aggressiveness coupled with the offensive power conferred on infantrymen by new automatic weapons like the BAR, taught a new generation of marines assault lessons that were to apply equally well in large-scale warfare, operations against guerillas, or the assault of defended beachheads.

When Japan's post-Armistice activity wrenched American military leaders away from their comfortable preoccupation with European affairs, Marine Corps combat experience in Europe completed the foundation for a new, Pacific-centered naval policy. Though it asserted itself slowly, the new capacity for infantry assault eventually became the keystone for amphibious operations during World War II. Combined with the "command relationships" and the type-force of reinforced infantry evolved during the Advanced Base period, as well as with logistic lessons learned at Brest, the new assault infantry techniques completed the foundation on which the naval services were to build

their amphibious doctrine for World War II.

In 1919 Japan again became America's most likely potential enemy. She had taken over the German-held islands of the Caroline, Mariana, and Marshall groups that flanked any line along which a United States fleet might advance to the Philippines, and was building a formidable navy capable of dominating Philippine waters. Unfortunately, very few American citizens recognized the impact of Japan's new position upon national policies, and a wave of anti-war feeling seriously hampered the naval effort to develop forces for protecting the nation's interests in East Asia. Yet public apathy did not deter thoughtful military leaders who recognized the danger, but rather added to their sense of urgency. It was this sense of urgency to provide a makeweight against the threat from Japan that stepped up the rate of amphibious development.

As we have seen, amphibious development in the United States sprang originally from the fact that 19th century steam warships could not operate very far from their supply of coal. Then this original impulse expanded in response to the problem of maintaining a fleet in Philippine waters. So it was natural that a renewed threat from Japan should revive interest in things amphibious, but this time there was a significant difference. During the Advanced Base period, officers dealing with an amphibious problem looked upon it as part of their routine professional work, and with only a vague sense that they were pioneering. After World War I, urgency supplied by the Japanese threat convinced many Advanced Base veterans that their earlier work, if adapted to the newer conditions, might contribute measurably to their country's security. In consequence American amphibians began to shift the direction of their efforts. For a few years after 1919 their efforts were ill organized, deriving more from individual initiative than from official policy, but almost imperceptibly the several threads drew together into a coherent policy deliberately fostered by the naval services.

Though this coherent policy was clear after 1933, few of the men responsible for it perceived clearly the goal of their own actions during the years immediately following World War I. Hindsight however reveals a pattern of action built around five separate steps that:

(1) Confirmed the United States concept for purely naval control of amphibious operations.

(2) Conferred a new offensive power upon amphibious infantrymen.

(3) Created a permanent type-force of reinforced naval infantry.

(4) Developed a body of amphibious doctrine adapted to 20th century requirements.

(5) Evolved techniques essential for implementing the new doctrine.

However dimly they saw their goal, military leaders of the United States did progress. When occupation forces returned from Germany in 1921 the first significant movement toward an effective amphibious force had already begun. In 1921 the Joint Board of the Army and Navy (early forerunner of the Joint Chiefs of Staff) issued a pamphlet outlining an amphibious doctrine based upon British experience with the "combined" army and navy force at Gallipoli. That same year the Navy organized a small fleet unit, called the Control Force, to revive the kind of small-scale exercises for testing amphibious techniques that had been conducted early in the century. Also in 1921 the Navy Department reactivated at Quantico, Virginia the old Advanced Base Force. Redesignated as the Marine Corps Expeditionary Force, it was considered an integral unit of the operating fleet and was expected to cooperate with the Control Force in amphibious exercises. There was also action at the planning level which stemmed from an extensive study, published by the Office of Naval Intelligence in 1920, of a projected transpacific campaign by United States forces. By the end of 1921 both Navy and Marine Corps planners developed a portfolio of war plans to implement the kind of operation suggested by the ONI booklet.

This promising start produced disappointing results. The Joint Board study did not mature, but served merely as a springboard for later work along quite different lines. Though the Control Force was well led,

budgetary limitations had restricted its immediate result to a series of amphibious problems studied at the Naval War College. A skimpy budget also hobbled the Marine Corps Expeditionary Force, but the Force did serve to focus attention upon a purely naval mission for the Marine Corps and provided tactical units for amphibious tests. Only the portfolio of war plans prepared in 1921 by Navy and Marine Corps officers was to exert direct influence upon the Pacific war a few long-sighted men foresaw even then.

These prophetic plans grew from the work of Lieutenant Colonel Earl H. Ellis USMC, a pioneer amphibian of the Advanced Base period. It provided for seizing fleet bases stretching westward from Pearl Harbor or Samoa, through which the United States might project her naval power as far as the Philippines. The Ellis war portfolio departed from earlier amphibious theory by recognizing that conquest of Pacific island bases from an aroused Japan would require offensive daylight action across well-defended beaches. Ellis insisted that no American force could operate in Asiatic waters without first wresting from Japanese control the bases it would need, and once such a fleet had fought its way to the threshold of Japan, Ellis foresaw two alternatives. Either purely naval forces might employ blockade to defeat Japan, or the navy could conduct an army expeditionary force to Japan and set troops ashore for a climactic campaign.[2]

Quite aside from its remarkably prophetic elements, Ellis' 1921 war portfolio had significant influence upon United States amphibious development between the World Wars. Once adopted by the naval services as their tentative plan for war the portfolio provided a blueprint for projected action across the Pacific, and so created the demand for an amphibious doctrine tailored to a real problem. In consequence each successful effort toward implementing this master plan became a link in the chain of development that gradually forged the United States amphibious force. Through its realistic insist-

---

[2] For a fuller account of Ellis and his work, see Lynn Montross, "The Mystery of Pete Ellis," *Marine Corps Gazette,* July 1954, 30-34.

ence on daylight infantry assault supported by naval gunfire, the Ellis war portfolio created the demand for an amphibious force as capable in its own field as balanced army units in conventional ground warfare. By creating this demand Ellis started a chain reaction that finally produced beach assault teams capable of exploiting the new offensive power conferred on amphibious infantry by the automatic rifle. Yet too few of Ellis' contemporaries grasped the implications of his hypotheses. Because thought-patterns based on conventional experience die hard, only slowly did a substantial group of marines perceive that the Corps' future rested on its continual development as a force of naval infantry. The few marines who grasped the Ellis concept worked skillfully, and there slowly developed in the Marine Corps Schools at Quantico a sense of the Corps' true mission.

One man who understood the implications of Ellis' work was Colonel Robert H. Dunlap usmc. Closely associated with Ellis during the Advanced Base period and a member of Admiral Sims' staff during World War I, Dunlap appreciated the amphibious problem and realized that the potential troop leaders of a future war should become proficient amphibians. As a step in that direction he published a clear analysis of the Dardanelles-Gallipoli campaign that laid down precise requirements for amphibious infantry. It should, he said, comprise a balanced force of all arms, carefully trained in advance for daylight assault of well defended positions and supported by painstaking staff planning. To drive his point home Dunlap insisted that United States naval forces might soon face conditions like those that had defeated the British at Dardanelles-Gallipoli. In effect he said that unless American naval men should learn by constant practice the techniques implicit in daylight landings under fire, many of them would experience a personal Gallipoli on some Pacific island.

The sense of urgency that produced the Ellis war portfolio and induced Colonel Dunlap to publish his analysis of Dardanelles-Gallipoli had a salutary effect. In 1922 and again in 1924 Navy and Marine Corps units tested the newest amphibious techniques in a series of exercises conducted at Culebra, a Caribbean island where Advanced Base amphibians had held similar maneuvers early in the century. The 1924 exercise at Culebra was the most ambitious effort since World War I. In addition to their usual ship-to-shore movement and tactical problems ashore, marines experimented with pontoon bridging equipment to improvise docks similar to those the British had used for supplying troops on Gallipoli. The entire force devoted more attention to logistics than in any earlier amphibious maneuver. Among the items of equipment tested was a single armored amphibious craft derived from the Beetle Boats the British had developed at Gallipoli in 1915. Some of the marines from Culebra joined fleet and army units in a similar exercise at the Canal Zone. Though the maneuver was crude, it provided the first intensive experiment toward efficient methods for transferring armed infantry from transports to boats, and it demonstrated that resourceful infantrymen could penetrate the conventional defense against amphibious assault. Brief as they had been, even these limited "laboratory" efforts toward improved techniques ended in 1924 because the Marine Corps Expeditionary Force shifted its entire strength to China as part of a marine division called there by threatening developments.

Amphibious experiment did not end completely however, for in 1925 army and navy units in the Hawaiian Islands conducted an exercise to test the British-type amphibious doctrine advocated by the Joint Board of the Army and Navy. Conducted near Pearl Harbor, this maneuver was a "combined operation" in which army and navy officers shared the top command as British officers had at Gallipoli. Though it presented a realistic problem and marked the first significant test of army and naval air units, the Hawaiian exercise proved disappointing. Yet if it did nothing else, the maneuver convinced key officers from all services that amphibious doctrine after the British pattern, as advocated by the Joint Board, would not produce an amphibious force capable of carrying out the

United States' basic Pacific war plan. This conclusion produced action. Though there is no clear record of any formal decision, all significant amphibious development in the United States after 1925 rejected the British doctrine of semi-autonomous "combined" forces commanded by what Lord Fisher had called a junta. Instead, the services implicitly accepted the command doctrine which gave full control to an admiral but assigned to the commander of reinforced infantry full responsibility for tactical employment of his troops. Thus, experience in the Hawaiian maneuver confirmed the purely American doctrine the naval services had been evolving for 30 years, and amphibious development in the United States became a purely naval mission after 1925.

During 1924 and 1925 a postwar trend at the Naval War College began to bear fruit. Several Navy and Marine Corps officers who had served in the "Brest beachhead," and others who worked at problems based on the Ellis war portfolio, came gradually to recognize that the basic plan for Pacific war could not succeed as long as United States military leaders expected combat commanders to improvise either tactical plans or their supply facilities. Studies looking toward a more effective Service Force and toward pre-planned organization for advanced bases, as well as for detailed staff planning of combat operations, slowly absorbed the Naval War College curriculum. This work coalesced about logistics and dominated work at the College for at least a decade after 1925. As a result officers trained at the Naval War College after 1925 were far better prepared to comprehend the problems inherent in an amphibious campaign than their predecessors had been.

Decisions flowing from the Hawaiian maneuver, and the emergence of logistics as the dominant study in the Naval War College, make 1925 the pivotal year in amphibious development between the world wars. By returning to lessons learned during the Advanced Base period and then supplementing those earlier developments by thorough logistic support, as well as with detailed staff planning, American amphibians carried the

evolution of modern amphibious doctrine into its final phase. Though many ideas from the earlier period persisted, they enjoyed official support after 1925 where before they had represented merely the thinking of individuals or of a few officers.

After 1925 the marine officers who understood how intimately their Corps' future was tied to the Navy began to exert measurable influence. Curricula at the Marine Corps Schools underwent steady revisions which saw problems devoted to amphibious assault gradually replace problems in ground warfare borrowed from the Army's school at Fort Leavenworth. As a result the Marine Corps Schools emerged slowly as the seedbed for maturing amphibious doctrine. At the same time officers rotating through the Corps Headquarters in Washington became increasingly aware that both naval services required a permanent type-force of reinforced infantry integral with the fleet. But just as the Marine Corps Schools and Headquarters began moving toward a solution, trouble broke out in Nicaragua during 1927 that absorbed virtually all of the Corps' energy for several years.

Even this interruption contributed to amphibious development, for the anti-guerilla operations in Nicaragua focused attention upon small-unit infantry tactics. Consequently it provided an opportunity for bringing up to date the fire-and-movement techniques evolved in 1918. Nicaraguan experience with small patrols, armed with rifle, BAR, and grenade, passed on to postwar marines a conviction that small efficient combat teams lay at the root of successful infantry assault. From just such teams as those nurtured in Nicaragua, the Corps built its amphibious assault forces in World War II.[3]

Nicaraguan experience also taught marines the value of close cooperation between air and ground elements of the same force. Since wiping out elusive guerillas required the ground force to operate in widely scattered units, small marine patrols faced severe hand-

[3] For detailed treatment of this development, see Lieutenant Lee M. Holmes, "Birth of the Fire Team," *Marine Corps Gazette,* November 1952, 16-24.

icaps. Repeatedly reconnaissance planes discovered guerillas lying in ambush and warned ground patrols. Frequently aerial bombing and strafing helped ground units to drive off numerically superior guerilla forces. Time and again aggressive pilots demonstrated the value of air supply and air evacuation of wounded. Though none of these incidents was part of a pre-planned cooperative effort, they demonstrated in dramatic fashion the kinds of assistance integrated air support could confer upon combat infantry. The growing conviction that close-support airmen were merely "infantrymen bearing other arms" opened a whole new field for aircraft in time of war. Specific Nicaraguan lessons in air-to-ground communication, close-support bombing or strafing, as well as in aerial supply or evacuation of wounded, all contributed measurably to the later elaboration of these techniques after World War II broke out.

By 1930, as relaxation of tension in China and Nicaragua gradually released marines in substantial numbers, the various threads of amphibious development began to assume a recognizable pattern. Interest at the Marine Corps Schools in evolving doctrine, Marine Headquarters' approach to a permanent type-force of fleet infantry, and Naval War College concern for a chain of island bases as well as a Service Force to support the combat fleet, all began to complement each other.

In the academic year 1930-31 the Marine Corps Schools completed its break with a ground warfare preoccupation dating back to 1917. Late in that year a naval gunfire problem based on British experience at Dardanelles-Gallipoli drew fresh attention to the example Colonel Dunlap had used to emphasize the need for an American amphibious doctrine. And at the same time informal cooperation with the Naval War College produced a well-rounded problem in amphibious assault. These steps induced the Commandant of the Marine Corps Schools to release four officers from teaching duties so that they might prepare a "Text for Landing Operations."[4] Relying heavily on tests at

Quantico with experimental landing craft, as well as experimental loading of a transport, this Barrett Committee prepared the working draft of an amphibious manual. Though never published, this work comprised the first formal effort to assimilate modern amphibious doctrine, and it provided a foundation for the fundamental amphibious manual published two years later.

While the Barrett Committee labored over its manual, the entire staff and student body at Marine Corps Schools devoted the academic year 1932-33 to amphibious studies. Divided into committees that functioned like the sections of an operational staff, they analyzed in detail the Dardanelles-Gallipoli campaign. Then the group devoted its full attention to the first formal Advanced Base Problem to be studied jointly by the Naval War College and Marine Corps Schools. This exercise followed closely the then-current plan for a possible Pacific war, a direct development from the 1921 Ellis war portfolio. And it aimed specifically at providing evidence from which naval planners could devise the structural details of an effective infantry type-force for the operating fleet.

Though work proceeded concurrently on the amphibious manual and on the force to implement it, the latter project matured first. Early in August 1933 Major General John H. Russell, Jr. (at the time Assistant Commandant of the Marine Corps and a pioneer amphibian of the Advanced Base period) began working with the Chief of Naval Operations upon procedures for creating the Fleet Marine Force, which was activated on orders from the Secretary of the Navy on December 8. Thus for the first time in its history the United States Navy acquired a permanent type-force of reinforced infantry dedicated to amphibious assault missions, and *assault* was the key concept that set this unit apart. For though the Marine Corps had always advocated aggressive performance of all missions, never before had it enjoyed for any protracted period specific designation as the fleet's front-line assault element. Yet important as was the mere existence of such a fleet marine

---

[4] Majors (USMC) Charles D. Barrett, chairman, L. H. Miller, and Pedro del Valle, and Lieutenant Walter C. Ansel USN comprised this committee.

force, it did not at once provide the fleet with the capability of establishing bases across the Pacific. The FMF needed a basic doctrine to guide its training as an arm of the fleet, and all other fleet elements to be involved in amphibious assault needed to perfect a myriad of techniques. So it was fortunate that doctrinal work at the Marine Corps Schools had paralleled efforts in Washington to create the new FMF.

General Russell knew of the Barrett Committee and its work toward an amphibious doctrine. In November 1933, shortly after he received an urgent request from the fleet for a manual to guide the planning and execution of amphibious exercises, Russell directed the Marine Corps Schools to work full time toward completing Major Barrett's project. Under Barrett's chairmanship the faculty and student officers at Quantico set up a quasi-staff organization and devoted almost a year to the problem. They made full use of published works and of the most recent amphibious directive issued by the Joint Board, but when it came to fitting all the material into a coherent system, the Quantico officers drew heavily upon 40 years of amphibious experiment by the naval services.

Late in 1934 the Marine Corps Schools produced the first United States manual to present a mature amphibious doctrine. Published as the *Tentative Manual for Landing Operations,* this work separated the doctrine into six elements which it described as: (1) command relationships, (2) naval gunfire support, (3) aerial support, (4) ship-to-shore movement, (5) securing the beachhead, and (6) logistics.

As used in the *Tentative Manual,* the term "command relationships" covered organization of the amphibious force as well as command doctrine. The manual provided that United States overseas expeditions should be conducted as part of a naval campaign, with the expeditionary force organized as a naval Attack Force commanded by a navy flag officer. This task force was to have two main components: the Landing Force comprising elements of the Fleet Marine Force, and the naval support groups (Fire Support Group, Air Group, Transport Group, and Screening Group). The Landing Force commander and the commander of each naval group was responsible directly to the Attack Force Commander, who had authority to make decisions affecting any of those subordinate units. Thus, instead of following the older "chain of command" concept the *Tentative Manual* adopted the "pyramid of command" doctrine. With very slight modification this doctrinal concept remained the fundamental basis for the organization and command of all American amphibious operations during World War II.

Though amphibious assault follows exactly the same pattern as offensive action in conventional ground warfare, the fact that so much of the troop movement takes place on water seriously complicates the problem of fire support for assault riflemen. Adapting naval guns to missions performed by ground artillery was a formidable task. Though naval fire control equipment was far more effective during the prewar years than that which forward artillery batteries could afford, the naval gun and its ammunition did not lend themselves readily to troop support. High muzzle velocity, flat trajectory, ammunition designed for sea battle, limited magazine capacity, and the problem of spotting targets invisible from the ship, all served to complicate the situation. The *Tentative Manual* analyzed these problems brilliantly and laid a solid foundation for effective naval gunfire support during World War II. But its specific doctrine required substantial development before naval guns were able to protect boated troops or infantry ashore against machine guns, mortars, or concealed guns.

The *Tentative Manual* also did pioneer work in spelling out for the first time the role of aircraft in support of assaulting infantry. It provided for preliminary visual or photographic reconnaissance, air cover over transports and boats from disembarkation through the ship-to-shore movement, and for airborne fire support of boat waves during the final 1,000 yards of their trip to the beach. The manual also provided for aerial fire support once the troops stepped ashore until artillery could be landed in sufficient strength to assume its conventional role. However, the whole problem of aerial fire support proved so complex that truly close air support of infantry did not materialize until 1944.

In the ship-to-shore movement the *Tentative Manual* provided for precise preliminary planning and rigid control of boat movement during the attack. Also it specified the organization of Boat Groups and Boat Waves, with special formations adapted to the various situations a landing force might encounter. Here the 1934 manual stimulated the successful prewar development of effective amphibious assault craft, and its basic pattern underwent little change throughout the war. For securing the beachhead the manual emphasized the techniques that permit infantry to survive in the twilight zone between full reliance on seaborne fire support and the landing of its own artillery. It gave special attention to establishing communication promptly between echelons ashore and those afloat, as well as to the complex problem of organizing supply and medical services in the shallow area immediately behind the front line. Here the 1934 doctrine suffered from a dearth of radio equipment that could withstand hard usage, as well as from the tendency of naval men in those years to assume that a single channel of communication would suffice. However, once communications technology caught up with amphibious requirements, the foundation laid in 1934 provided a sound basis for wartime solution of communications and supply problems.

In the field of logistics the manual laid heavy stress upon the overriding importance of tailoring all cargo loading to the requirements of the landed troops. Since assault forces usually comprised battalion units, the 1934 planners asserted that each assault battalion should occupy a single transport which would carry the battalion's assault equipment. This concept of "combat-unit loading" ran counter to the usual doctrine for loading cargo vessels because it implied stowing heavy equipment on deck with lighter material in the hold. Yet inconvenient as this practice was from the point of view of seamen, it was essential to the success of the entire operation. The manual's emphasis on this point gradually forced navy men to develop attack transports suited to amphibious needs. As transports improved, the original combat-unit loading doctrine underwent steady revision until it became by 1944 an important element in the successful drive across the Pacific to Luzon.

Supported by regular maneuvers which tested its theory, the *Tentative Manual for Landing Operations* underwent detailed modification until 1938, when the Navy adopted it as *Fleet Training Publication 167*. In 1941 the Army issued virtually the same text as a field manual. These two publications were refined steadily throughout the war, but remained the basic guides for both planning and training that produced all United States amphibious operations during World War II. The basic doctrine set down in 1934 withstood its prolonged trial by fire without fundamental change.

Revolutionary as it was, the 1934 doctrine owed much of its effect to searching and intelligent tests conducted both before and after war broke out. Beginning in 1935 the Naval War College, Marine Corps Schools, and units of the fleet took up the arduous task of refining the techniques that were to convert a doctrinal theory into the kind of practiced teamwork required for military success. Annual fleet training exercises from 1935 through 1941 provided continuing "laboratory" tests of the basic doctrine. Conducted at Culebra, the island of San Clemente near San Diego, and in 1941 at New River, North Carolina, these exercises refined amphibious staff work, stimulated the evolution of amphibious craft and radio equipment, underscored the need for improved gunfire and air support doctrine, and gave practical experience to thousands of marines, soldiers, and sailors. Though none of these exercises was sufficiently realistic to satisfy any interested participant, they improved in direct proportion to the quality of material available.

After 1934 Andrew Higgins took an active interest in developing small amphibious craft. The first Higgins assault boat appeared in the 1939 maneuver and in 1941 the first Higgins ramped boat performed well. Also in

1941 Higgins demonstrated an efficient tank lighter, forerunner of the LCM. A swamp vehicle built by Donald Roebling attracted Marine Corps attention in 1937. Roebling "Alligators" tested in 1939 developed into the tracked landing vehicle known as the LVT or amtrac, and in 1940 an armored amphibian designed by the Marine Corps went into production as the LVTA. Beginning in 1936 a trickle of old destroyers converted into transports afforded a stop-gap solution to an unsolved problem, yet not until 1941 did responsible navy officers perceive the need for the specialized attack transports developed during the war. The lack of an adequate naval gunfire range, and Navy reluctance to rotate its modern ships through amphibious exercises, hampered the development of naval gunfire techniques. But by 1941 the services began to train both navy and marine officers for duty with fire-control parties that would accompany the assault waves, and Marine Corps specialists began to supervise the gunfire training of several heavy ships. Creation of a naval gunfire range in Chesapeake Bay during 1942 and combat experience early in the war contributed heavily to the evolution of sound naval gunfire techniques early in 1944. In the same way limited material and unrealistic conditions delayed until after war began the achievement of sound techniques for close air support and the funneling of supplies over a beach.[5]

Yet despite their failure to implement the 1934 doctrine with adequate techniques before 1942, the amphibians worked a near-miracle. For the first time in United States history a military group proceeded logically from doctrinal theory through "laboratory" tests to the techniques which finally made possible what Major General J. F. C. Fuller has called "the most far-reaching tactical innovation of the war." By laying down first their sound doctrinal theory, the amphibians saved uncounted time and money that would have been required had they been willing to

wait for normal evolution to produce amphibious craft and related equipment in quantity, test the preliminary models in maneuvers, and then adapt their doctrine to whatever material the nation could afford them.

FOUNDATIONS OF NAVAL AVIATION

The development of a sound amphibious doctrine enabled the United States Navy in World War II to overcome and seize islands in the Pacific and beachheads for assaults on Africa and Europe. At the same time the development of naval aviation paved the way for control of the sea lanes in the face of land-based air, for destruction to be rained on ships and on land areas, and for preparation for and support of amphibious operations. It was the Navy which first developed the ability to carry air power over vast distances of the world and hurl it where needed in destructive raids or in support of land operations. It was aviation that finally conferred true balance upon the amphibious force, and both developments were products of the 20th century technological revolution. Because the special task of the naval aviator was adapting new mechanical equipment to his needs, his problems were largely financial and mechanical. He had to pry vast sums from Congress before he could begin to fly, and then he had to adapt each new engineering achievement to the needs of airmen operating far at sea.

This special set of circumstances imposed severe handicaps on naval aviation because the Navy had not by 1941 adjusted completely to the rapid changes inherent in technological revolution. Nor had many citizens accepted the startling fact that each new piece of naval equipment was obsolescent by the time it reached the operating fleet. In consequence, small groups of officers interested in the future of a special ship-type or weapon began to struggle vigorously for the funds their project required, and since there was frequently no top-level umpire within the Navy Department, each group had to

---

[5] For a more extensive account of amphibious maneuvers and the development of amphibious craft between the years 1935 and 1942, see Jeter A. Isely and Philip A. Crowl, *The U. S. Marines and Amphibious War* (Princeton, 1951), chapter 3.

press its claim before a Congressional committee. So the aviation pioneers found themselves from the beginning in conflict with big-ship proponents whose program soaked up about as much money as Congress was willing to appropriate for naval construction. Thus naval aviation was born and grew to maturity in an atmosphere of vigorous competition for funds. Gradually, as aviation took hold of the popular imagination, what began as an intra-service struggle before Congressional committees spilled over into the public press. Optimistic speculation about aircraft so stirred people that for the first time in the nation's history a pioneer naval minority won active support from a broad cross-section of public opinion. Though this swelling public debate provided naval airmen with an effective lever, it also seriously complicated the evolution of sound policies for sea-going aircraft. For the public acceptance of exaggerated claims, coupled with the high cost of producing improved planes and the very high rate of obsolescence, created a military dilemma wrapped in a cloud of public emotion.

This special circumstance that set aviation apart from other naval activities began to manifest itself even before World War I. Early in 1914 Congress recognized the Navy's need for an air arm, and naval aviation began to assume the shape we now recognize. During the next three years naval flyers pressed vigorously for more funds, as well as for recognition of the aerial bomb, torpedoplane, and aircraft carrier as adjuncts of a combat fleet. Unfortunately these efforts coincided with the need for keeping the surface fleet abreast of rapid developments in the European war, so claims for aviation funds fell on deaf ears and the United States entered World War I without planes or air weapons to compare with those current in Europe. Yet naval aviators had worked so well that when war came in 1917 the Navy had a rudimentary foundation for its aviation program. Hard work had produced effective training planes, a nucleus of competent aviators, and sound techniques for training citizens to fly. In addition, pioneer naval flyers had established good contact with the infant aircraft industry. As a result the Navy was able during World War I to expand its corps of pilots from 38 to nearly 7,000. And it induced industrialists to produce aircraft motors that satisfied essential needs. Thus by the end of 1918 naval aviation had passed its first harsh test, and in the process it had enrolled thousands of flight-conscious civilians in naval air reserve units, thereby winning friends among the population who fostered interest in naval aviation during the peacetime years.

In the theaters of war, air experience during 1917 and 1918 assured aviation a place in the postwar naval establishment. Well organized units had demonstrated the value of naval aircraft in antisubmarine work. Men from these units had tested the aerial bomb against enemy bases, and had briefly experienced logistic bombing close behind the front line of an enemy army. Individual flyers had begun to experiment with tactical techniques of air combat—including dive bombing and close support of infantry. In addition many American naval airmen had observed at first hand British experiments with the aircraft carrier, torpedo planes launched from towed lighters, and aircraft launched from battleship turrets; and they had noted various uses for captive balloons, free balloons, and dirigibles. Though none of this varied experience with new techniques was extensive enough to produce a clear-cut doctrine by the end of 1918, all of it contributed to the progress of naval aviation, and public interest which mushroomed during 1917-1918 served to make that progress far more rapid. Indeed it may well be that without such public interest generated by men returning from wartime aviation to all walks of life, the United States could not have developed a naval air arm capable of meeting the severe tests it faced from 1942 through 1945.

THE MORROW BOARD

Though one can scarcely overestimate the benefits that flowed from wartime enthusiasm for aviation, its after-effects created many new problems for the Navy. From 1880 through 1916 public interest in naval material had been limited to a very few persons outside the service, for only the occasional citizen had experienced duty with the fleet. But by 1920 this situation had changed radically. Aircraft appealed to American imagination far more than had the "all-big-gun ship," and millions of citizens held opinions about aviation matters confronting their navy. Consequently, instead of reaching postwar decisions in the objective atmosphere of a banker's inner office, naval policymakers found themselves subjected to constant pressures by articulate public groups. In such circumstances grappling with war's third dimension was far from easy. Yet the spotlight of publicity did produce one signal advantage. Each naval decision during 20 postwar years, and particularly decisions bearing on naval aviation, endured searching public scrutiny. So the policies that survived till 1942 had been tested far more exhaustively than had naval policy during any comparable period of the national history.

If not the first issue to attract popular attention after 1918, the problem of dividing funds between heavy ships and aircraft certainly generated the most heat. In the public mind this controversy soon came to transcend mere naval policy, and embraced the national policy toward all civil and military aviation. For it focused the first serious attention upon the question of a separate air force, a unit which could take over from the Navy its 50-year mission as the outlying bastion of American defense. With open or tacit support from some flyers in all branches of aviation, Brigadier General William D. Mitchell USA agitated the proposition that bombing aircraft had made steel battleships just as obsolete as wooden men-of-war. When newspaper controversy on this point reached white heat, the services attempted in 1921 a series of objective tests wherein planes bombed ships slated for the scrap heap.

As events were to prove, devising an objective mock combat between ship and plane was virtually impossible. In the interest of economy the services selected the captured German battleship *Ostfriesland* and several other vessels destined for scrapping. None of these ships afforded the kind of armored decks required to resist even the aerial bombs available in 1921, nor had they antiaircraft armament. And even if they had been designed and armed to resist aircraft, few Americans would have approved a genuine sham-battle in which combat crews manned the vessels under air attack. In consequence several flights of bombers attacked vessels lying at anchor in the Atlantic close to the exit from Chesapeake Bay. In order to assess accurately the results of the bombing, the Navy assigned officers to board each vessel immediately after each simulated attack. Thus they hoped to estimate accurately the effect of prompt damage-control. But this careful plan was not followed. Executing it required the land-based bombers to follow a rigid schedule arranged several days in advance, before weather conditions could be determined. When the test day came General Mitchell insisted that the weather required his squadron to take off ahead of schedule. Then, after the first bombing run, Mitchell radioed the observation parties to stand clear because, he said, the planes did not have sufficient gasoline to wait for evaluation of each strike. Instead, Mitchell insisted, the planes would complete all bombing runs as quickly as possible. So the *Ostfriesland* was sunk by aerial bombing as she lay at anchor, but without affording any objective evidence of the steps alert defenders might have taken to save her. And though General Mitchell insisted that his decisions were based on the safety of his airmen, most naval observers of the tests accepted his performance as a tacit admission that bombers could not sink a well-defended battleship.

However, despite its strident emotionalism, the Mitchell controversy did produce beneficial results. And the most significant benefit flowed from the creation in 1925 of a special Presidential board to recommend basic aviation policy for the United States. This Morrow Board held extensive hearings. Its findings established a pattern for United States aviation that produced effective working relationships among the armed services, civil aviation, and the aircraft industry.

With respect to naval aviation the Board

acted on advice from Rear Admiral William S. Sims USN Ret., who asserted that there could be no true progress until policymakers decided whether the Navy could dispense entirely with battleships or entirely with aircraft or whether it needed both. The Board held that a balanced 20th century navy had to rely on both ships and planes. The Morrow hearings also induced the Navy Department to reject several service suggestions for a separate naval air corps and to follow the pattern Congress had set in 1899 when seagoing engineers were integrated with the corps of navy line officers. In terms of national military policy, the Morrow Board advocated retention by the Navy of its traditional responsibility for defending America's marginal seas, even though that decision implied shore bases for naval patrol planes. And equally important was the Board's blueprint for orderly annual procurement of naval aircraft, a policy that induced industry to focus capital and energy upon creating planes adapted to specific military needs. Such decisions dispelled the most serious confusion engendered by the Mitchell controversy and established a firm foundation beneath the rapidly evolving naval air arm. But far-reaching as were the Morrow Board conclusions, they comprised merely an intermediate step. Much work remained to be done before naval aviators and their supporting elements could evolve the techniques, material, and doctrine required to convert broad policies into an effective instrument for two-ocean war.

TECHNIQUES, MATERIAL, DOCTRINE

After 1925, then, the fundamental problem facing policymakers for naval aviation lay in specifying the missions for naval aircraft, in bringing together the men and equipment for fulfilling such missions, and in welding those raw materials into a strong team.

From the earliest experiments with naval aircraft, most informed persons considered reconnaissance as the main mission for fleet planes, with spotting for big guns as an important secondary mission. Very early it became clear that sea-based fighter planes would have to defend aerial scouts or spotters against enemy aircraft. These related missions required so many planes that even before World War I navy men recognized the aircraft carrier as an essential prerequisite of an effective naval air arm. But the difficulties of operating planes from seaborne flight decks deferred extensive carrier experiment till wartime pressure induced Britons to convert an unfinished cruiser and a new liner into flight-deck cruisers, the *Furious* and the *Argus*. The Royal Navy thus produced the world's first aircraft carriers. Their existence forced the United States Navy to follow suit. In 1922 the *Langley* (converted from a collier) became the first American aircraft carrier. Because techniques for handling seaborne aircraft were so complex it was logical that fleet aviators and the *Langley*'s crew should spend six years mastering them. This program stressed landing, taking off, navigating, gunfire spotting, and aerial gunnery. Though individual pilots experimented with aerial bombs or torpedoes, carrier planes of that period were designed as fighters, scouts, or gunfire observers. And the six years of training produced a nucleus of aviators for the *Saratoga* and *Lexington*, built on battle cruiser hulls, when they joined the fleet in 1928.

Even while the *Langley* provided a floating laboratory for perfecting carrier techniques, thoughtful officers devoted increasing attention to the carrier's role in fleet combat. Among the most articulate of its proponents was Rear Admiral W. A. Moffett, Chief of the Bureau of Aeronautics. Early in 1922 Moffett's testimony before Congressional committees suggested very strongly that he looked toward aircraft carriers as capital ships of the future, for he advocated a gradual program whereby they would replace battleships. Though few other officers went quite so far at that time, the carrier question attracted serious attention at the Naval War College and before the General Board. Studies prepared in both agencies between 1922 and 1928 reflected genuine concern with the problem of defending the Philippines against any Japanese force strong in land-based aircraft. By 1927 the General Board had accepted the proposition that any United States fleet capable of operating successfully in Philippine waters must have an efficient carrier force whose planes could fulfill reconnaissance missions, spot for naval guns, and defend surface ships against hostile air attack. However, even by 1927 very few responsible officers had come to agree with Moffett that the carrier was emerging as a capital ship capable of offensive action against enemy ships or installations. Thus when the *Lexington* and the *Saratoga* were commissioned in 1928, service opinion had come to accept the carrier as an important fleet component but one still limited to reconnaissance or spotting missions.[6]

Scarcely had the Navy's first true fleet-type carriers shaken down when a few shrewd officers perceived that they opened a broader vista for seaborne aircraft. Soon after the fleet got under way for its regular maneuvers during the winter of 1928-29, Rear Admiral J. M. Reeves persuaded the commander in chief to approve a significant change in the plan for employing the *Saratoga*. Instead of advancing from San Diego toward the Gulf of Panama in a safe position behind the battle line, for which she was expected to scout, the big carrier made a wide sweep to seaward and approached Panama from the southwest. Barely outreaching the defending screen, the *Saratoga* launched a flight of planes while still nearly 200 miles at sea. Her aircraft pressed home an early morning raid that took the Canal defenders by surprise and then returned safely to their ship. Even though an umpire asserted that the *Saratoga* had been "sunk" by gunfire while her planes were airborne, the performance demonstrated forcefully that a properly defended carrier could assault targets far beyond the range of fleet guns.

As a result of such demonstrations, a growing number of aggressive officers gave serious thought to the carrier's offensive potential. In 1930 Lieutenant Commander Forrest P.

Sherman (who became Chief of Naval Operations 20 years later) advocated a fleet formation that anticipated the carrier-centered task force of World War II. And during the succeeding decade, as plane performance improved, squadrons of naval aviators bent more and more of their energies toward perfecting the techniques of carrier-borne assault. However, merely recognizing the carrier's offensive potential was not enough, for experienced officers knew that the Navy could not accept carriers as capital ships until the myriad techniques for projecting their offensive power were matured. And this maturing process embraced so many separate developments that World War II began before it was complete. Because the space limitations of a general history forbid presenting the story of each separate development, a summary of how dive bombing evolved must serve to illustrate the kind of problems overcome during this intricate process.

Fleet tests conducted as early as 1913 had demonstrated the feasibility of bombing naval objectives from the air, and heavy naval bombers served extensively during World War I. But the more missions they flew, the more pilots recognized their need for improved aiming techniques. Individual flyers from many of the warring nations observed the advantages of aiming the nose of a plane at the target, going into a shallow dive, and then releasing the bomb. After the war many pilots experimented extensively with this technique. In 1919 while serving with a Marine Corps squadron in Haiti, Lieutenant H. M. Sanderson USMC devised a crude bomb-release mechanism that permitted him to dive at a 45-degree angle down to about 250 feet before dropping his bomb. The squadron adopted Sanderson's glide bombing technique and refined it but did not as a regular practice achieve the sharper angle of descent required for true dive bombing. In 1923 Major Ross E. Rowell USMC trained with army pilots at Kelly Field and shared their experiments with true dive bombing. By 1927 when Rowell took command of marine aircraft squadrons in Nicaragua, he had gained enough confidence in dive bombing to establish it as a standard

---

[6] Gerald E. Wheeler, "Japan's Influence on American Naval Policy, 1922-1931," unpublished doctoral dissertation (Stanford University, 1954).

procedure in squadron operations. Rowell and his pilots used dive bombing against Nicaraguan guerillas with genuine effect. Toward the end of their mission they were able to dive steeply from 1,000 feet down to 300 feet, drop bombs as they pulled out, and then use tail guns for strafing the enemy as their planes withdrew. After returning from Nicaragua marine flyers did much to popularize dive bombing by conducting exhibitions at the large air shows. In fact they succeeded so well that many persons credit evolution of the German *Stuka* to ideas Ernest Udet developed after watching a marine exhibition at an air meet in Cleveland. Yet sound as was such experimenting by flyers in all of the armed services, effective wartime dive bombing had to wait on the evolution of a plane specially designed for the purpose. And the same kind of restriction hobbled the evolution of doctrines for using carrier-borne fighters and torpedo planes.

Six years of intensive development aboard the *Langley,* coupled with experience gained aboard the *Saratoga* and *Lexington,* produced by 1930 the dim perception of how carrier-borne torpedo planes, dive bombers, and fighters might conduct offensive operations. But to achieve what was then still an ideal required planes of far greater strength, range, and endurance, and there could be no real confidence until both the techniques and the doctrine had been tested thoroughly with aircraft that did not exist in 1930. Fortunately the United States possessed the capital, the engineering skills, and industrial capacity to foster development of such aircraft, but several practical factors impeded progress. First among these factors was the extremely high rate of obsolescence to which expensive aircraft were subject. Even a wealthy nation could not afford to mass-produce a particular model when designers promised far superior modifications within a short time. Yet there could be no sound evaluation of either flight technique or carrier doctrine until the fleet acquired enough planes to support full-scale maneuvers. So any decision about mass-producing a given model implied a seriously calculated risk. A second complicating factor flowed from vigorous public demand for

planes to match the performances an excited press attributed to foreign aircraft. In consequence, a decision to provide the fleet with enough planes to permit realistic maneuvers might well have alienated a large segment of public opinion if some single experimental plane produced abroad had surpassed aircraft operating with the United States Fleet.

Such factors combined to put naval policy-makers under great pressure, but they resisted the temptation to standardize too soon. For not until 1937 did Chance-Vought produce a single-wing scout bomber (SB2U) suitable for carrier operation, and only in 1941 did planes like the Grumman TBF and F4F or the Douglas SBD join the fleet in substantial numbers. So by waiting till industry produced true carrier aircraft susceptible of rapid refinement the policy-makers enabled American naval aviators to fight World War II from steadily improving planes that performed exacting assault missions. A more conservative decision would have held the Navy's pilots in the position of their German or Japanese contemporaries, who tried to adapt planes designed in the mid-1930's for missions conceived during the 1940's. Narrow as was this margin for American policy-makers, the decision to wait for aircraft that would support carrier assault proved correct.

Though they gained more publicity, problems inherent in producing assault aircraft were no more complex than those faced by men who designed carriers capable of serving as capital ships. When U.S.S. *Ranger,* the first American vessel conceived as an aircraft carrier, joined the fleet in 1934, carrier concepts had developed beyond her. Designed to support fleet reconnaissance aircraft, she was never modified for assault missions. Not until the *Yorktown* was commissioned in 1937 did the fleet acquire a third assault carrier. By then flight techniques and aircraft design had progressed far enough to justify steady building. The *Enterprise,* the *Wasp,* and the *Hornet* all were commissioned by the end of 1940. However, with the *Langley* long since converted to a seaplane tender, even such rapid construction gave the fleet only six assault carriers on Pearl Harbor Day. And the impact of the war in Europe deferred until after 1941 the development of mature teamwork among carriers, their aircraft squadrons, and surface ships of the fleet. At first glance this achievement seems small justification for so much effort expended between 1920 and 1942. Yet when one considers the bewildering welter of technological problems implicit in creating an entirely new naval instrument that could project its missiles more than 200 miles, the achievement assumes its true perspective. Wartime flyers justified the policy-makers' faith by learning rapidly in combat to exploit a unique contribution to naval armament.

Throughout the long controversial period that produced the carrier and her team of combat aircraft, long-range naval patrol planes kept pace with their shipborne sisters. The first transatlantic flight, by the United States naval patrol bomber NC-4 in 1919, stimulated navy and industrial engineers to convert bombing aircraft into large seaplanes with very long range and endurance. Originally conceived as a torpedo carrier, the naval patrol plane gradually became a scouting aircraft with exceptional range which could, in addition, bomb weakly defended targets. Preparing her for long water flight did much to call forth improved compasses, radios, navigating equipment, and flight instruments like the automatic pilot. Incidentally, many of these developments were soon adapted to smaller planes and so contributed to more efficient carrier operations. Hull structures developed for seaplanes before 1917 at the naval model basin in Washington proved so satisfactory that they required little significant change until after 1941, but as engines improved, patrol aircraft achieved constantly wider ranges throughout the 1930's. Even before the United States entered World War II, long-range naval flying boats like the Consolidated PBY proved invaluable to the Allies for submarine work or for shadowing German raiders. Throughout the Pacific war continually improved models fulfilled important reconnaissance, cargo-carrying, or air-sea rescue missions. Admittedly, these big flying boats failed to fulfill their proponents' dream of a sea- and air-worthy ship capable of performing difficult assault

missions, but had they done nothing else, reconnaissance missions the patrol planes completed during World War II more than justified all efforts devoted to their development.

Brief surveys like this must concentrate on trends that have produced successful combat instruments, and so they oversimplify a picture by slighting the less fruitful experiments. Those experiments are important too, because eventually they may justify their backers and because examining them helps one to understand how difficult were the decisions which produced combat-worthy equipment. Between the wars naval engineers conducted many promising experiments that failed to yield immediate results. For almost two decades the Navy worked to create efficient helium-lifted airships. Their advocates saw in such lighter-than-air craft the long range reconnaissance units that modern fleets require. In fact, engineers managed to build a rigid airship with long range and endurance which could launch and recover six light observation airplanes. But structural weaknesses and their vulnerability to enemy attack kept such dirigibles from replacing heavier-than-air patrol planes or seaborne aircraft carriers. And when three of the four experimental airships succumbed to squalls, the Navy transferred its funds to the more conventional planes and carriers. However, the costly experiments helped produce a whole family of small dirigibles and balloons that contributed measurably to anti-submarine work in World War II.

Another series of experiments during the 1920's and 1930's aimed at launching land-based patrol planes by catapult. As yet these efforts have not produced practical results, but one need only consider the logistic problems inherent in laying miles of concrete airstrips to perceive that the investment may yet pay off. Another series of important experiments that began immediately after World War I were directed towards the building of a practical helicopter. During the late 1920's however interest in this field shifted to the autogyro, which did not materialize as a usable wartime instrument. Yet closing out completely that line of endeavor would have deprived the naval services of one of their most promising postwar developments. In the same way there were hundreds of experiments in the field of radio and electronics. Though many of them fell short of providing usable gear in time for World War II, they contributed immeasurably to perfecting radar, or improving sonar and radio equipment, as well as to such postwar developments as television. And in large measure contacts between the Navy and scientists induced by the broad range of experimental work between the wars fostered the successful use of scientific methods for solving military problems implicit in defeating the submarine or evading antiaircraft fire.

Anyone who analyzes the two decades of aviation development between the world wars must conclude that change was the most predictable factor. Long-range seaplanes conceived as torpedo carriers finally emerged as efficient aerial scouts capable of piercing cloud or darkness. Carrier aircraft, originally considered for scouting or gunfire spotting, became the dive bombers, torpedo planes, and fighters that converted the carrier from a reconnaissance vessel into a capital ship. And the dive bombing technique originally perfected to assist marines on anti-guerilla patrols became the chief means for projecting the carrier's offensive power against an enemy nearly 300 miles away. Yet in the long view the greatest achievement of the United States Navy between 1920 and 1941 was the building of attitudes which encouraged continuing improvement after war broke out. One of the major bases of American success in World War II was the readiness of aircraft squadrons and carrier crews to perfect their teamwork even in the heat of combat.

34

World War II:

Atlantic Surface Actions

"It is peace in our time," said Britain's Prime Minister, Neville Chamberlain, as he returned from the Munich conference with Hitler. Less than a year later, at 0445 [1] on September 1, 1939, Nazi armies hurled themselves against Poland, and the holocaust of World War II began. The danger signs were unmistakable from the latter part of August when Hitler signed a non-aggression pact with Russia, a pact which freed him from the danger of Soviet intervention. To be sure, England and France had mutual aid treaties with Poland, but there was no reason to suspect that they would honor them any more than they had fulfilled their Munich-repudiated treaty obligations to Czechoslovakia. The German *Führer* planned a swift campaign which would smash Poland while England and France vacillated. He thus would present them with a *fait accompli*. But he reckoned without the change in temper of both leaders and people in the two Western countries.

This time he would be opposed, opposed with force to the utmost, force on land, on sea, and in the air. The British presented an ultimatum to Germany during the evening of September 1 and issued a final one at 0900 on the 3rd. At 1115 on September 3, 1939, in a broadcast to the nation, Prime Minister Chamberlain announced that His Majesty's Government was at war with Germany. France followed suit at once.

There was little that England or France could do to aid Poland. Germany unleashed a new kind of warfare on the Polish plains, a war of rapid movement, heavily mechanized, in which tanks were used to spearhead long lines of advance. Overhead, the *Luftwaffe* swept the ineffectual Polish Air Force from the skies and then roared in with their Stukas and Messerschmitts to wipe out Polish infantry strongpoints in the way of the onrushing German divisions. In a few weeks all was over. All was over on the Polish front, that is: the *Blitzkrieg*, or lightning war, tactics had done their work swiftly and well. All was not over in the west, however. The slow British and French mobilization

---

[1] This and the following chapters use 24-hour time, which came into universal use for military purposes in World War II.

was too late to aid Poland, but the governments of those countries could and did lay plans to meet any westward thrusts of the German *Wehrmacht,* the French primarily through the use of their armies sheltered behind the Maginot Line and the British through the use of their sea power.

Hitler had no wish to face a real war with Britain and France—at that time. He accepted the Russian occupation of half of Poland in an effort to keep the war localized; he hoped that he could persuade England and France to accept the situation and agree to peace, a peace that would give him time to build up his navy and undertake war in the west in 1944 or 1945. He had promised this much time to the head of the German navy, Grand-Admiral Erich Raeder. Thus after the Polish operation had been completed, Hitler refrained from any offensive action against the West. His abstention brought about what has been called the "Twilight War," the "Phoney War," and the "Great Bore War." German troops in the Siegfried Line faced French troops in the Maginot Line with only small skirmishes relieving the montony of the winter front.

THE WAR BEGINS AT SEA

At sea, the war began dramatically. On the very first day of English participation the passenger liner *Athenia,* loaded with American tourists returning from Europe, was torpedoed and sunk by the *U-30* with a loss of 112 lives, including 28 Americans. This sinking shocked America and Britain; it stunned Hitler and Raeder. Hitler had given instructions that the Hague Convention was to be strictly observed, hoping to lull the British into a false sense of security. To counter the adverse effect on world opinion, Hitler put out the story that the British First Lord of the Admiralty, Winston Churchill, had engineered the whole thing himself. Hitler caused the commanding officer of the U-boat to be severely reprimanded and for a considerable period of time greatly limited the operations of his undersea fleet.

German naval strategy was necessarily limited to commerce raiding, the traditional role of an inferior naval power, for Raeder had to undertake the naval aspect of the war before he was ready for it. By 1948, he had hoped to have a fleet which could challenge British supremacy at sea. But this was not to be. When the war opened, the German Fleet consisted of two battleships, the *Scharnhorst* and *Gneisenau* completed, two others, the *Bismarck* and *Tirpitz,* nearing completion; three pocket battleships,[2] the *Deutschland, Scheer,* and *Graf Spee;* three heavy cruisers, the *Hipper, Prinz Eugen,* and *Blücher,* and five light cruisers, the *Karlsruhe, Köln, Leipzig, Nürnberg, Emden,* and *Königsberg.* Twenty-six merchant ships were converted into armed merchant cruisers. A respectable number of destroyers, torpedo boats, mine sweepers, and auxiliaries completed the surface fleet. German submarine warfare, which was directed by Admiral Karl Doenitz, began operations with only 57 U-boats.

Raeder, making the best of the situation, planned to use his surface fleet to harry commerce—at first in accordance with the Hague Convention and with Prize Law. Twenty-one submarines were at sea even before the outbreak of war, and in a few weeks Raeder began to commit his surface vessels.

The British strategic plan was necessarily almost the converse of Germany's. The Royal Navy promptly blockaded the German North Sea coast and the exits from the Baltic, but in the main, England's vital task was to keep the sea lanes of communication open to all parts of the British Empire and across the North Atlantic to Canada and the United States. The Admiralty hurriedly established a convoy system, but as in World War I was considerably hampered by the lack of antisubmarine vessels to serve as escorts. The threat of German surface vessels breaking out of the Baltic Sea kept a goodly portion of the British Home Fleet on guard at Scapa Flow north of Scotland. Although the British surface fleet was far superior to that of Germany, England's world-wide com-

---

[2] The pocket battleship was a German experimental ship mounting 11-inch guns on a nominal 10,000-ton hull. It was supposed to be able to outrun a battleship and outgun everything else.

mitments and the absolute necessity of her importing not only munitions but also food-stuffs for daily living meant that the Royal Navy was spread thin. The concentration of strength at Scapa Flow caused by the German fleet-in-being further weakened the protection the British could give their lines of communication.

The German counterblockade of England was fought with all weapons which could be brought to bear—U-boats, surface raiders, and the *Luftwaffe*. Because these actions ran concurrently, to treat any part without reference to the others means an artificial separation of parts of the problem as it existed for the British Admiralty. However, for the purpose of analysis, it will be simpler if we break up our story and deal largely with the British and German surface actions in the Atlantic in this chapter and in another consider the U-boat campaign and Allied countermeasures.

THE *DEUTSCHLAND* AND THE *CITY OF FLINT*

Late in September 1939, the German pocket battleships *Deutschland* and *Graf Spee* slipped through the British blockade and set out to attack commerce in the Atlantic. The *Deutschland* took station between the Azores and the North American coast. By the middle of October she had sunk two merchant ships and committed a first class diplomatic blunder in seizing the American steamer *City of Flint*. This ship was put under a prize crew and sent to Murmansk and thence to Norway, where the Norwegian government interned the prize crew and restored the vessel to its master. In spite of the best efforts of the German Foreign Office, the incident caused a considerable strengthening of the anti-German sentiment in the United States. It also had the effect of turning Hitler's attention toward Norway, as he realized that Germany did not command Norway's territorial waters. Toward the end of November, the *Deutschland* returned to Germany, and her name was changed to *Lützow* to avoid repercussions on German morale in the event of her loss.

THE CRUISE OF THE *GRAF SPEE*

The three-month cruise of the *Graf Spee* was considerably more successful than that of her sister ship *Deutschland*. She sailed to carry out the instructions issued earlier by Raeder:

Task in the Event of War

Disruption and destruction of enemy merchant shipping by all possible means. . . . Enemy naval forces, even if inferior, are only to be engaged if it should further the principal task. . . .

Frequent changes of position in the operational areas will create uncertainty and will restrict enemy merchant shipping, even without tangible results. A temporary departure into distant areas will also add to the uncertainty of the enemy.

If the enemy should protect his shipping with superior forces so that direct successes cannot be obtained, then the mere fact that his shipping is so restricted means that we have greatly impaired his supply situation. Valuable results will also be obtained if the pocket battleships continue to remain in the convoy area.

The *Graf Spee* carried out these instructions punctiliously. She headed for the South Atlantic where she would claim a victim and then disappear. In general she operated in the area between Pernambuco and Cape Town, although in November she slipped over into the Indian Ocean south of Madagascar for a brief period. On the way back, she met the German supply ship *Altmark*, refueled, transferred prisoners, and then resumed her search for victims. The value of her voyage, completely apart from the 50,-000 tons she sank, is shown in the number of British ships which had to be assigned to chasing her. Out of Freetown, the British naval base on the western bulge of Africa, operated the carrier *Ark Royal* and the battle cruiser *Renown;* from Dakar two French heavy cruisers and the British carrier *Hermes* joined the search. The heavy cruisers *Sussex* and *Shropshire* were poised at the Cape of

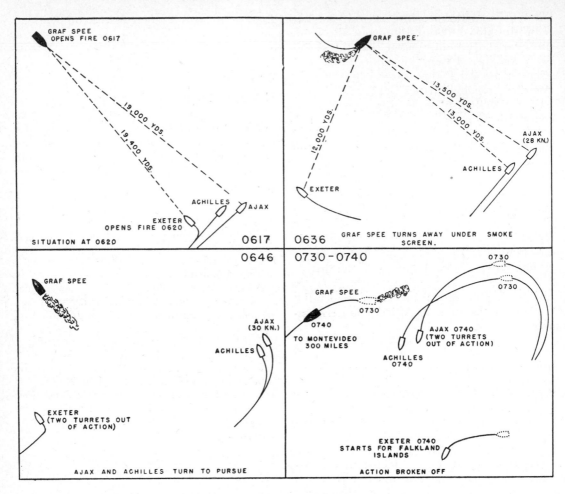

BATTLE OF THE RIVER PLATE, DECEMBER 13, 1939

Good Hope, and up and down the east coast of South America ranged Commodore Sir Henry Harwood's force consisting of the two heavy cruisers *Cumberland* and *Exeter* and the light cruisers *Ajax* and H.M.N.Z.S. *Achilles.*

Commodore Harwood's group, less the *Cumberland,* which was refitting in the Falklands, succeeded in intercepting the *Graf Spee* in the approaches to the River Plate on December 13. A very pretty tactical problem ensued. The *Graf Spee's* six 11-inch guns outranged the cruiser guns by nearly 10,000 yards. Not one of the cruisers could long withstand her fire. Their only opportunity would be to come in from widely diverging angles in order to force the *Graf Spee* to divide her fire. The cruisers would not be able to reply until they had passed through the danger zone from 30,000 yards, the range of the *Graf Spee's* guns, to about 22,000 yards, the extreme limit of the cruisers' main batteries. If the *Graf Spee* had been properly handled, she would have turned directly away from the cruisers, forcing them to a stern chase. Even with their speed advantage of about five knots, it would have taken the cruisers nearly half an hour to pass through the danger zone. Probably they would never have made it. As it happened however Captain Hans Langsdorff thought he had a cruiser and two destroyers to deal with and ran down to meet them. The three British cruisers were in column, the *Ajax* leading and the *Exeter* in the rear. At 0617, the *Graf Spee* opened fire, whereupon the *Exeter* turned to port to spread out the target so that the counterattack could be made from two directions at once. The two light cruisers continued toward the northeast. On the completion of her turn, at 0620, the *Exeter* opened fire at a range of 19,400 yards. The *Ajax* and the *Achilles* commenced fire a few minutes later, and the 6- and 8-inch shells from all three ships began to hit effectively. The *Graf Spee*'s shells also took their toll. Soon the *Exeter* received a hit which knocked out her "B" turret, destroyed bridge communications, and killed or wounded nearly everyone on the bridge. The German then shifted his fire to the two light cruisers and turned away under a smoke screen, apparently to make for the River Plate. As the *Ajax* turned in pursuit, the *Graf Spee* once more shifted fire to the *Exeter,* which was once again under control. By 0725, all her forward turrets were out of action, and at 0730 power was lost to the after turret. Meanwhile the *Ajax* had two turrets put out of action, and Commodore Harwood decided to break off the fight until night, when he would have a chance to make a torpedo attack. The *Exeter* started on the long voyage to the Falklands, while the wounded *Graf Spee* set her course for Montevideo, dogged by the *Ajax* and *Achilles*. Occasional exchanges of fire occurred all day, but there was never a chance to renew the action. A little after midnight, the *Graf Spee* entered Montevideo. There Langsdorff hoped to effect repairs and renew the fight at a later date.

Frenzied diplomatic activities on the part of the German consular representatives were unsuccessful in getting an extension in the 72-hour limit of stay in port for a belligerent ship. British propaganda was more successful in giving the impression of a large British fleet just offshore. Actually only the *Cumberland* had joined the battered *Ajax* and *Achilles*. Langsdorff requested instructions from Berlin and was given the option of fighting his way out or scuttling his ship. He decided on the latter course because of the shortage of ammunition aboard. Having landed his wounded and prisoners, he got under way on the afternoon of December 17 and headed out to sea. The British cruisers went to action stations, but before they could engage her, the *Graf Spee* was blown up and scuttled by her own crew. In spite of the permission given by Raeder to scuttle the ship, Langsdorff wrote a long letter justifying his actions and then shot himself. It was not until the spring of 1940 that the Germans again attempted to utilize surface raiders.

H.M.S. *ROYAL OAK* SUNK AT SCAPA FLOW

The anchorage of Scapa Flow had been the chief British base for the blockading fleet in World War I and was pressed into service for the same duty when hostilities opened in 1939. In October 1914 a false alarm that a U-boat was loose inside Scapa Flow had sent the Grand Fleet out to sea to escape torpedoing. As it turned out, that alarm was almost exactly 25 years premature. On October 14, 1939, the *U-47*, under the command of Lieutenant Gunther Prien penetrated the tortuous channel and sank the battleship *Royal Oak* at her anchorage. The operation had been planned by Admiral Doenitz himself, and Prien had been carefully selected as one of the most reliable Nazi U-boat commanders. Doenitz's confidence was well placed. Prien made his first approach on the morning of the 12th, lay on the bottom outside Scapa Flow all day, and came up in the evening to establish the position of the ship. He recorded in his log: "From 2200 to 2230 the English are kind enough to switch on all the coastal lights so that I can obtain the most exact fix." The next evening he started in, touching ground once in avoiding a blockship. At 0058 he fired a salvo of three torpedoes and turned to starboard toward the entrance. One torpedo was heard to hit. At about 0110 Prien again reversed course and came up to firing position once more. Another salvo started on its way at 0122, and in three minutes all torpedoes hit. The *Royal*

Oak sank almost at once, taking with her 786 officers and men. The *U-47* withdrew as she had entered and returned to Wilhelmshaven. Prien and his crew flew to Berlin for decoration at the hands of the *Führer*.

SINKING OF H.M.S. ROYAL OAK
OCTOBER 13-14, 1939

The flush of success of the operation against the *Royal Oak* caused Hitler to agree to Raeder's incessant proposals for a more vigorous prosecution of the naval war. He forthwith issued instructions to the fleet that all merchant ships that were clearly recognized as enemy could be torpedoed without warning, that passenger ships in convoy could be destroyed after warning, and that Italian, Spanish, Russian, and Japanese vessels were to be treated as other neutral vessels unless their governments would certify that they would not carry contraband goods.

THE CRUISE OF THE *SCHARNHORST* AND *GNEISENAU*

In late November 1939, the two battleships *Scharnhorst* and *Gneisenau* passed out into the Atlantic through the North Sea primarily to cover the return of the *Deutschland* from her mid-Atlantic raiding, and incidentally to see what they could pick up in the way of English commercial shipping. Instead they came upon H.M.S. *Rawalpindi*, a converted passenger liner armed with four old 6-inch guns and carried on the Admiralty List as an armed merchant cruiser. Her commander, thinking he had found the *Deutschland*, was under no illusions about the outcome of such a battle, but he accepted the odds against him. The *Scharnhorst* opened fire and the *Rawalpindi* replied as best she could, but in a few minutes the British ship was reduced to a helpless wreck. Before she sank, the two cruisers *Newcastle* and *Delhi* arrived on the scene but lost contact with the Germans in the dark and the heavy rain. The British Home Fleet sortied from Scapa Flow, but the two Germans, alarmed that their presence had been revealed and hence their usefulness lost, headed for home. Thus the hopeless fight of the *Rawalpindi* was not in vain, since these two powerful raiders were driven from the sea before they could get into the commerce lanes.

THE *ALTMARK* AFFAIR

The German supply ship *Altmark,* which had replenished the *Graf Spee* shortly before her final action off Montevideo, was serving as a floating prison for some 300 British seamen. The British were anxious to capture her, but she successfully hid in the South Atlantic for nearly two months. Gambling that the search had died down, the *Altmark* attempted to make her way back to Germany.

She was favored by the weather and was not sighted until February 14, 1940 in Norwegian territorial waters. A flotilla of destroyers under Captain Philip Vian in H.M.S. *Cossack* intercepted her at Jossing Fiord but did not take further action pending instructions from the Admiralty. When he received his orders, Vian sent two destroyers to board and examine the vessel, but two Norwegian gunboats met the small force and told Vian that the *Altmark* was unarmed, had been examined, and had received permission to proceed to Germany making use of Norwegian territorial waters. Accordingly, the destroyers withdrew for further instructions.

The First Lord of the Admiralty, Winston Churchill, sent orders for Vian to board the *Altmark,* using force if necessary in self defense. While the Norwegian authorities continued their protests, the *Altmark* made the first belligerent move by getting under way and attempting to ram the *Cossack,* which dodged and then ran alongside the German ship and sent over a boarding party. After a sharp hand-to-hand fight, the German crew surrendered. Examination revealed that the British prisoners were battened down in hatches and storerooms and that the ship had two pom-poms and four machine guns. Although the British had violated Norwegian neutrality in seizing the German ship, the Norwegian government had been equally guilty in its failure to make proper search before allowing a belligerent vessel to proceed under the protection of territorial waters. Hence, the British government was able to reject the Norwegian diplomatic protests.

Although Hitler had made the decision to invade Norway as early as December 14, 1939, the *Altmark* incident strengthened his determination. It also revealed to the British public a problem which had worried the Admiralty for some time, the fact that German ships were making free use of the three-mile zone off the Norwegian coast to enable their ships to break out far to the north under cover of fog or bad weather and thus escape the British blockade. Eventually the British decided on a desperate expedient, that of sowing mines in Norwegian waters. Lest the German reaction be to occupy Norway, the British prepared an expeditionary force to be used only in the event that the Germans did invade Norway; then it would land and assist the Norwegians in defense of that country. This force was embarked and ready when the mine laying force began operations.

THE INVASION OF NORWAY

By one of the major coincidences of the war, the British action in mining Norwegian waters took place at the very time that the invasion force from Germany was approaching Norway. On the morning of April 8, 1940, British destroyers mined the entrances to Narvik harbor in northern Norway; at the same time German forces were overrunning Denmark, and the next day descended on several parts of the Norwegian coast.

To support the invasion of Norway, the German High Seas Fleet had put to sea an advance force composed of the *Scharnhorst, Gneisenau,* and *Hipper,* leaving on April 7; the main body left the next day. The Polish submarine *Orzel* made contact with the invasion fleet and sank the transport *Rio de Janeiro.* About 300 German troops, rescued by fishermen, made their way from the sinking vessel to the Norwegian shore, but even this advance warning failed to save Norway. The German occupation was too well planned, and the fifth column work under the traitor Vidkun Quisling was too thorough. Only the British fleet could possibly break up the operation, and the warning was too late.

The Germans made simultaneous landings at several points along the coast. Where the fifth column work had been well planned, port and local defenses crumbled in the face of sabotage and subversion. At other points Quisling's men and Nazi "tourists" failed to overcome local resistance. At Oslo, the Norwegian defenders gave a good account of themselves. The minelayer *Olav Tryggvason* and two minesweepers faced an invasion force spearheaded by the cruisers *Emden* and *Blücher* and several destroyers. The *Olav*

Tryggvason accounted for a minesweeper and damaged two destroyers and the *Emden* before succumbing to the superior Nazi power. Shore gun and torpedo batteries sank the *Blücher,* and the other German ships retired. Capture of Oslo was achieved eventually by paratroopers and landings in the fiord, but not by direct assault at Oslo harbor.

In support of projected landing operations in Norway in the event of Nazi reaction to British minelaying activities in Norwegian territorial waters, the British had sent their fleet to sea a few days before the landing. By April 7, all the British Home Fleet was at sea. They were about 24 hours too late for effective opposition to the German landings.

At 0830 on April 8 the English destroyer *Glowworm,* one of the minelaying group, which had dropped back from its force to search for a man lost overboard, reported that it was engaging an enemy destroyer, then that it had sighted a second, and finally that it was engaging superior forces. After that there was silence. Not until after the war did the British learn her fate. After engaging the German destroyers for some time, the *Glowworm* found herself lured under the guns of the heavy cruiser *Hipper,* whereupon she retired behind a smokescreen. Suddenly emerging from the smoke, the *Glowworm* rammed the *Hipper,* tearing a hole 120 feet long in the side of the German cruiser. After she fell away from the *Hipper*'s side, the destroyer blew up. Forty survivors were rescued by the Germans. The captain of the *Glowworm* posthumously received the Victoria Cross for this action, which not only crippled the *Hipper* but enabled the Admiralty to make a shrewd deduction that a major German force was bound for Narvik. Accordingly, British forces were ordered to close on that area.

Near Narvik a running battle with the British battle cruiser *Renown* resulted in heavy damage to the *Gneisenau,* but she and her sister ship, the *Scharnhorst,* were able to pull out of range. Air and submarine attacks continued on the German forces, resulting in the sinking of the *Königsberg* by three bombs from aircraft of H.M.S. *Furious,* the first time a large naval vessel had been sunk in wartime by aerial bombs. The submarine *Truant* sank the cruiser *Karlsruhe* off Kristiansand; the following night the submarine *Spearfish* damaged the pocket battleship *Lützow* (ex-*Deutschland*), but she was able to make her way back to Germany for repairs and future operations.

At Narvik the British opened their counterattack to free Norway. Landing forces north and south of the city, they began a drive to take it from the rear. The Admiralty had received information that a German ship had already entered Narvik. Accordingly they sent an order to Captain B. A. W. Warburton-Lee, in command of the British destroyer force there, "Proceed to Narvik and sink or capture enemy ship. It is at your discretion to land forces, if you think you can recapture Narvik from the number of enemy present." Captain Warburton-Lee, in the *Hardy,* accompanied by the destroyers *Hunter, Havock, Hotspur,* and *Hostile* entered West Fiord. Here he was informed that six ships larger than his and a submarine had already entered the port. He decided nonetheless to press on, even though Rear Admiral Sir William J. Whitworth, commanding in the area, was unable to lend him any additional support. Warburton-Lee's force attacked at dawn on April 10, steaming up through snowstorms. In the approach phase, the *Hotspur* and *Hostile* were told off to engage the shore batteries while the other three ships pressed into the bay. There they found five German destroyers and 23 merchant ships. In the first attack, the *Hardy* torpedoed the German destroyer *Wilhelm Heldkamp,* killing the German commodore. Another Nazi destroyer was sunk and a third beached. Recovering from their surprise, the Germans straddled but failed to hit the *Havock.* The British ships retired under a smokescreen. Shortly they returned for a second attack, augmented by the *Hostile* and *Hotspur,* the latter sinking two merchant ships. A third attack was pressed home, but this time the fortunes changed. Warburton-Lee discovered three fresh German destroyers coming down on him from Herjangs Fiord. At a range of

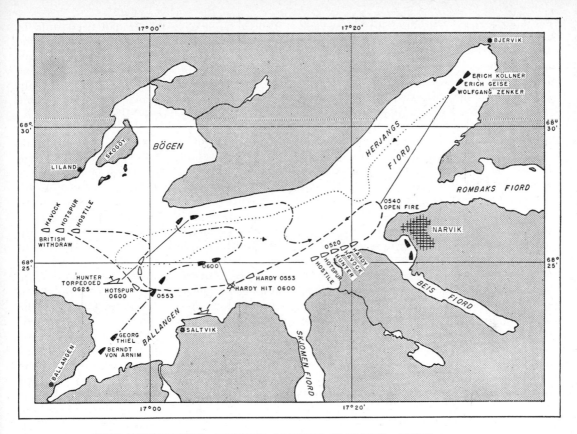

THE DESTROYER AMBUSH, NARVIK HARBOR, APRIL 10, 1940

10,000 yards he opened fire and turned away. The British ships commenced a retirement, keeping up a running fire, but ran into an ambush at Ballangen Fiord where two more Nazi destroyers were awaiting them. The *Georg Thiel* engaged the *Hardy,* and shortly afterward the English ship took a hit on the bridge which killed Warburton-Lee. The *Hardy* sank a few minutes later. Making a swing to the left, the *Georg Thiel* launched a spread of torpedoes at the *Hunter,* which also sank. The *Hotspur* and *Hostile* were both damaged, and, together with the *Havock,* made their way to the open sea. The damage the Germans had sustained made them helpless to follow. On the way out the three surviving British destroyers encountered the German ammunition ship *Rauenfels.* After a few salvos from their guns, the German blew up in a tremendous explosion.

A few days later, on April 13, a heavy British naval force including the *Warspite* and the carrier *Furious* finished off the work begun by Warburton-Lee, sinking eight destroyers which had survived his attack. The lesson of these two battles was plain. Warburton-Lee, much outnumbered, had accepted action in an area where the speed and maneuverability of his ships were restricted and in an area that afforded many chances for ambush. Effecting tactical surprise on his arrival, he did considerable damage, but was surprised himself by being caught between two forces, one of which blocked his way to the open sea.

The remainder of the story of the Norwegian expedition is easily told. The British landed a force near Narvik in an attempt to drive the Germans out of the area, but were unable to do so. Although British forces captured the city of Narvik on May 28, by that time the German drive through the Low

Countries and into France had so changed the strategic situation that the British had to evacuate Norway. All the forces that the Royal Navy could spare from other duties were sent to Narvik to cover the evacuation. Meanwhile the *Scharnhorst, Gneisenau,* and *Hipper* had left Kiel on June 4, accompanied by four destroyers to raid British installations on Narvik. Learning of the British evacuation plans on June 7, the German ships sought the transports. That afternoon the two battle cruisers *Scharnhorst* and *Gneisenau* came upon the carrier *Glorious* in the North Sea. She had been detached from her force and sent home to fuel, inadequately screened by two destroyers. The *Glorious* was completely surprised with no planes in the air. At 27,000 yards the Germans opened fire on the carrier, which struggled to get her torpedo bombers airborne, but before they could be launched, she was hit so severely that the planes could not get off. The two destroyers made a gallant effort to defend their helpless charge, launching torpedoes and making smoke to cover their own movements as well as those of the *Glorious.* In a few minutes, the *Ardent,* one of the British destroyers, was sunk, but before the other, the *Acasta,* suffered a similar fate, she managed to put a torpedo into the *Scharnhorst.* As a result of this hit, the two battle ships abandoned operations as the *Glorious* sank, and returned to Trondheim where the *Hipper* had already gone. The result was that the remainder of the British evacuation of Narvik was unopposed, and the British campaign in Norway came to an end.

THE FALL OF FRANCE

The disasters in Norway brought about the fall of the Chamberlain government in England. On May 10, the day that Hitler struck at the Low Countries, Neville Chamberlain offered his resignation as Prime Minister; he was succeeded by Winston Churchill, who had up to that time held office as First Lord of the Admiralty. Churchill set out to form a National Government with

ministers representing all parties, as contrasted to the Conservative Government of his predecessor. Under his direction the war was pursued with vigor and courage through the darkest hours when Britain stood alone.

Neither Holland nor Belgium was able to make a significant resistance to the *Blitzkrieg* of the Nazi forces pouring across the Rhine. Hitler, finally abandoning any thought of compromise peace with the west, had hurled his armies through the Low Countries as the Kaiser had done a quarter of a century before. Allied forces were forced back at point after point, overwhelmed as the Poles had been by the combination of air power and Panzer, or mechanized, divisions. Although the French and British air forces did their best, they were never able to stop the onrushing Germans, but on occasions they were able to achieve local air superiority. In spite of French objections, the British retained 25 air squadrons for home defense, refusing to commit everything to what was rapidly becoming a lost cause. As early as May 20, the Admiralty, recognizing that evacuation from the Continent would be necessary, began to organize shipping for an evacuation at Dunkirk near the Belgian border of France. Naval efforts were spontaneously aided by private boat owners who volunteered themselves and their craft for service. The Admiralty accepted these gladly, but there was hard naval planning as well. They hoped to rescue about 45,000 men in two days.

Hitler believed that his *Luftwaffe* would render escape impossible. He intended to paralyze the troops on the beach by repeated bombing and to sink the rescue ships as fast as they appeared. He reckoned however without three factors. Bombing of the troops was ineffective, the soft sand absorbing much of the force of the explosions. The R.A.F. was fully committed to protecting the Dunkirk beachhead; even the British Metropolitan Air Force, the last reserve that had been withheld from the defense of France, entered the battle. The third upset to Hitler's calculations was the presence in such large numbers of the evacuation ships and craft. There were simply too many targets. Pleasure boats, fishing craft, destroyers, mine-sweepers, trawlers—ships and boats of all types—shuttled from Dunkirk beach to English ports and then back to reload. When the operation was completed, 338,226 men had been safely delivered to England by 861 vessels, with a total loss of 243 sunk and many damaged.

THE PROBLEM OF THE FRENCH FLEET

Shortly after the Dunkirk evacuation, the French government sued for peace in spite of Churchill's efforts to keep France in the war, even if only to fight from the colonies. He went to the length of offering France union with England, the two peoples to share common citizenship. The French Assembly rejected this appeal and signed an armistice agreement with Hitler, who put the capstone on French humiliation by conducting the armistice proceedings in the same railway car that had been used for the German surrender in 1918. France was divided into two zones: occupied France, which included the Atlantic front and all of the northern part including Paris, and unoccupied France with a puppet government at Vichy under the aging Marshal Pétain, but dominated by the Nazi sympathizer Pierre Laval and his associates. Part of the reason behind Churchill's spectacular offer of union with France was his concern over the French fleet. The British simply could not afford to have the French navy surrendered to Germany to be used against them. With union, the fleet would have a legal pretext for carrying on the war against Germany. To be sure, some French ships were already in English ports—two battleships, four light cruisers, a few submarines, eight destroyers, and about 200 minesweepers and antisubmarine vessels. A battleship, four cruisers and some smaller ships were at Alexandria, where a strong British battle squadron guarded them. At Oran were the *Dunkerque* and *Strasbourg*, battle cruisers designed to be superior to the *Gneisenau* and *Scharnhorst*, and two battleships, several light cruisers, and a number of

destroyers, submarines, and smaller craft. At Algiers were four heavy and three light cruisers. The *Jean Bart* lay at Casablanca, but she was unfinished, lacking her guns. At Dakar was the *Richelieu*, nearer completion than the *Jean Bart*. At Toulon were many other French ships, but these the British could not hope to seize. Finally, in the West Indies at Martinique were the carrier *Béarn*, the cruiser *Émile Bertin*, the gunboat *Barfleur*, and six new tankers, and at Guadeloupe was the old training cruiser *Jeanne d'Arc*. The French navy was commanded by Admiral Jean François Darlan, a man of Nazi sympathies.

All of this amounted to a very nasty problem for the British. Hourly expecting invasion, hard put to fulfill existing naval commitments, the British were in no shape to cope with a fleet the size of that remaining to France. Accordingly, with many regrets at having to take arms against their former ally, the British government acted. On June 3, 1940, all French ships at Plymouth and Portsmouth were seized, peacefully except for a short scuffle aboard the submarine *Surcouf*. Most of the French sailors volunteered to man their former vessels and serve under the Free French flag, taking as their commander General Charles de Gaulle, who had established himself as head of the Free French Government in Exile in opposition to the German-dominated Vichy Government of Marshal Pétain.

With some of the French ships now in their hands, the British Admiralty turned their attention to securing or neutralizing the remainder of the French ships not actually in France. At Oran, prolonged negotiations between British Vice Admiral Sir James Somerville and French Admiral Marcel Gensoul came to naught, and the British attacked, sinking the battleship *Bretagne*, causing the *Dunkerque* and *Provence* to be beached, and damaging the *Strasbourg*, which escaped to Toulon. Admiral Sir Andrew Cunningham was more successful in his dealings with Admiral R. E. Godfroy at Alexandria, persuading him to avoid the tragedy of Oran and to incapacitate his ships for action by removing fuel, repatriating part of his crews, and removing the key parts of his gun mechanisms. At Dakar, the *Richelieu* was seriously damaged by air attacks from the *Hermes*.[3] The ships at Martinique were neutralized through the diplomatic efforts of President Roosevelt. Thus, although lacking complete success, the British were able to preserve their tenuous command of the sea, but at a cost of embittering their former French allies. This unfortunate by-product of their operations was to exact its toll at the time of Operation Torch, the invasion of North Africa in late 1942.

GERMAN PLANS FOR THE INVASION OF ENGLAND: OPERATION SEA LION

Jubilant over his swift conquest of France, Hitler paid scant attention to any idea of invading England, so confident was he that England would be forced to capitulate in a few weeks. In this belief he was encouraged by *Luftwaffe* commander Hermann Goering. Admiral Raeder however feared the situation was such that Hitler might suddenly order an invasion. Raeder regarded England as the chief foe, but had little confidence in the success of an invasion since he felt that he had inadequate resources and time to stage it. Although his exploratory soundings got no response, Raeder went ahead with preliminary planning in order not to be caught off guard when it became obvious even to Hitler and Goering that England had no intention of surrendering. Raeder was basically opposed to invasion; he thought it should be attempted only as a last resort, for he understood the difficulties far better than the army, which had commenced to show an interest in it. The army had millions of victorious troops on hand and no place to go with them. They eyed the English Channel and thought that crossing it would present no more problems than crossing a very wide river. Encouraged by the army, Hitler on July 16, 1940, issued a

directive for the invasion of England, Operation Sea Lion. This directive, drawn up by the army, showed little grasp of the naval problems involved. It ordered that the landing be made on a broad front extending from Ramsgate to a point near the Isle of Wight, a front of approximately 200 miles, and that it be ready to jump off by August 13. Patiently Raeder explained that landing on such a scale would require many harbors for preparation of the invasion fleet, that the French ones were too damaged for use, that the concentration of shipping in these harbors would infallibly reveal the plan to the British, and that in any event Germany did not have anything like the number of ships the operation would require. Raeder emphasized that the assault must be on a narrow front where there could be a reasonable hope of maintaining a supply line across the Channel. From his point of view the only possible landing sites lay between Dover and Beachy Head. To this proposal the Chief of the Army General Staff is reported to have stated, "I might just as well put the troops that have landed straight through a sausage machine." The navy replied that it wanted to put the troops ashore, on the beach, and not at the bottom of the sea. Hitler finally had to intervene personally to resolve the conflict. The plans, as finally worked out, were for landings in four main areas: Folkstone-Dungeness, Dungeness-Cliff's End, Bexhill-Beachy Head, and the Brighton-Selsey Bill. This compromise pleased no one, but both the army and the navy proceeded to draw up their plans in accordance with it.

In the meantime, everything depended on the *Luftwaffe*. All agreed that command of the air was an absolute prerequisite to an invasion attempt. The *Luftwaffe* unleashed heavy attacks against air installations in the south of England and other points to gain superiority over the R.A.F. The air effort was also intended to force England to sue for peace. The hope of sweeping its air force from the skies was vain. The British refusal to commit the 25 home defense squadrons to the Battle of France now paid off in the Air Battle of Britain. The British pilots shot down nearly two planes to each loss of their

[3] For further details on these operations see Chapter 35.

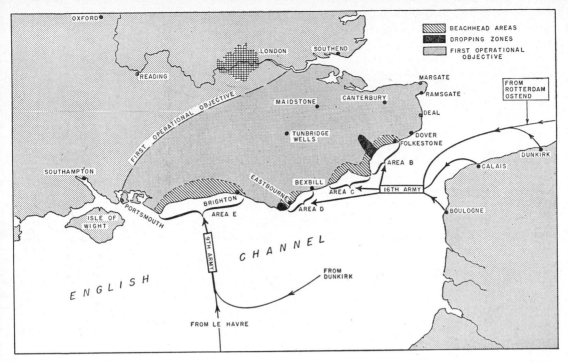

GERMAN PLANS FOR INVADING ENGLAND, SUMMER 1940

own. During the early critical period of the air war, the month of August 1940, the *Luftwaffe* was never able to whittle the R.A.F. strength down to an acceptable level for risking Operation Sea Lion. The day of decision for Sea Lion fell on September 14, 1940; on this day at a meeting of the Grand Council, after hearing reports from his commanders in chief, Hitler decided against giving the order to launch the invasion scheduled for September 28. This decision meant that there was little prospect that Sea Lion could be staged that year, since the next day when suitable tide and moon conditions could be expected was October 24, when bad weather could be expected to interfere. On October 12 Hitler decided to continue preparations for invasion in order to keep pressure on the British, but to postpone actual invasion indefinitely. This meant, of course, that Sea Lion was dead. Hitler was never wholeheartedly in favor of invading England, and there is good reason to believe he may have intended his preparations merely as a device to induce the British to surrender.

OPERATION MENACE: DAKAR

Situated far out on the western bulge of Africa, Dakar commands the narrows of the Atlantic; in Vichy hands, it posed a threat to commerce, so the British government planned an offensive operation to liberate it into the hands of the Free French. General de Gaulle was to command a landing force which would be supported by Free French warships as well as English ones. Through coincidence and a series of misfortunes, the Dakar operation came to naught. The coincidence was that just at this time three Vichy cruisers and three destroyers made the passage from Toulon to Dakar and strengthened its defenses so that the landing was hopeless in view of the limited amphibious doctrine of the time. The misfortunes were a series of mishandlings of the messages from the British destroyer *Hotspur*, which had sighted the Vichy force. Consequently, when the news reached the Admiralty, it was too late to intercept the French, who slipped into Dakar. Nevertheless, the investure was attempted. Several French ships were damaged, including the *Richelieu* and *Fort Manuel* on September 24, 1940. On the 25th, the British battleship *Resolution* was damaged by a torpedo fired from a Vichy submarine. On receiving this news, the Admiralty ordered the action broken off. The chief gain from the operation was that the *Richelieu* could not be repaired at Dakar and hence was powerless to operate against the British for some time to come. On the other hand, the operation seemed to the world to be a prime example of confusion, delay, and muddle.

SURFACE RAIDERS IN 1940

The pocket battleship *Scheer* made its debut into Atlantic waters in October 1940, followed a month later by the *Hipper*. Both stationed themselves in the North Atlantic in an attempt to break up the convoys from Halifax to the British Isles. The *Scheer* was looking for a convoy reported to have sailed from Halifax on October 27, and on November 5 her aircraft sighted eight ships on the horizon. The *Scheer* closed rapidly and first spotted the merchant ship *Mopan,* which she sank after taking off the crew. While the *Scheer* busied herself with this operation, the masts of Convoy HX 84, consisting of 37 ships, loomed up over the horizon. This was the very situation for which the *Scheer* had been sent to sea. With her superior speed and firepower, she might very probably have destroyed the entire convoy. Two things saved the day for the British: first, the lateness of the hour, for the sighting occurred at 1650, shortly before nightfall; second, the presence of the armed merchant cruiser *Jervis Bay*. Like her predecessor the *Rawalpindi,* the *Jervis Bay* was doomed to destruction under German guns, but she achieved her purpose. Pitting her 6-inch guns against those of the *Scheer* was suicidal, but it allowed the convoy to scatter. It took the *Scheer* nearly three hours to finish off the *Jervis Bay,* which had been able to broadcast

the alarm before turning to fight. Harried by the certainty that British forces would be converging on him, the German captain was able to overtake and sink only five ships of the convoy before he fled the area. The *Scheer* steamed rapidly south, refueled from a supply ship, made a brief appearance in the West Indies, and then disappeared into the South Atlantic and Indian Oceans, returning to Kiel in April 1941, having sunk 16 ships for a total of 99,000 tons.

The *Hipper's* cruise was not so fortunate. She attacked a convoy near the Azores, only to find it escorted by four British cruisers. After a brief action, the German cruiser managed to shake off pursuit and make her way home. In the spring of 1941, the *Hipper, Scharnhorst,* and *Gneisenau* again made brief sweeps into the Atlantic, sinking over 200,000 tons in two months of operation. By late March all three ships were in Brest.

THE *BISMARCK* BREAKS OUT

In mid-May 1941, British Intelligence and air reconnaissance provided information that led the Admiralty to suspect that the great German battleship *Bismarck* was ready for sea. The possible consequences were ominous. The U-boat campaign was at its height. A sortie of the *Bismarck,* possibly accompanied by the new heavy cruiser *Prinz Eugen,* combined with operations of the *Hipper, Scharnhorst,* and *Gneisenau* from Brest, would have the most serious consequences for the Atlantic lifeline. At this time 11 convoys, including one troop convoy, were at sea or about to sail. The concentration of German naval strength against them would have been calamitous. Although the three ships at Brest did not sail, and the *Prinz Eugen* accomplished nothing, it required all the available resources of the British navy to track down and sink the *Bismarck*.

This battleship, built in violation of treaty requirements, was regarded at the time as the most powerful battleship afloat. Mounting eight 15-inch guns in her main battery, she had a secondary battery of twelve 5.9's and an antiaircraft battery of sixteen 4.1's. She was reputed to displace nearly 45,000 tons. Her engines could drive her at 30 knots. Her armor was the most advanced on any capital ship, amounting in all to 16,000 tons dead weight. She had skillfully designed compartmentation to control flooding. The British were to discover how much punishment she could take.

News of the departure of the *Bismarck* and *Prinz Eugen* from Bergen was revealed by air reconnaissance. Admiral Sir John Tovey, Commander in Chief of the British Home Fleet, who had known of their passage through the Kattegat to Bergen and was anxiously awaiting news of their movements, immediately took steps to intercept the German ships. The Admiralty placed at his disposal all the warships that could be spared, stripping the convoys rather than let the Germans escape. Tovey had with him at Scapa Flow the battleships *King George V*, flagship, and *Prince of Wales* and the battle cruiser *Hood* in addition to destroyers and cruisers. In England were the carrier *Victorious*, which had not yet had her working-up cruise, and the battle cruiser *Repulse*. At Gibraltar, under the command of Admiral Sir James Somerville, the commander of the Oran operation, were the battle cruiser *Renown* and the carrier *Ark Royal*. The battleships *Rodney* and *Ramillies* were on duty escorting convoys in the Atlantic, and the battleship *Revenge* was at Halifax. All these ships played some part in tracking down and sinking the *Bismarck*.

In order to keep the various routes available to the *Bismarck* under observation and to have a force capable of striking at any of them, Tovey had to divide his force to cover all possible contingencies. Bad weather hampered his efforts. Because he had to keep the least likely passages under the lightest observation, he covered the passage between the Orkneys and the Faroes only by air search. He stationed a cruiser force in the passage between the Faroes and Iceland and headed thither himself in the *King George V* with the *Victorious* and *Repulse*. The heavy cruisers *Suffolk* and *Norfolk* patrolled the Greenland Strait, between Iceland and Greenland, supported by the *Prince of Wales* and *Hood*, en route at high speed from Scapa Flow, under the command of Vice Admiral L. E. Holland in the *Hood*.

The cruiser force of the *Suffolk* and *Norfolk*, flagship, Rear Admiral W. F. Wake-Walker commanding, first made contact with the *Bismarck* in the early evening of May 23 when a lookout on the *Suffolk* sighted her on an after bearing. The *Suffolk* immediately took refuge in a fog bank and began tracking the Germans by radar. The first report was amplified to two ships, and both the *Bismarck* and *Prinz Eugen* were accounted for. The *Suffolk* reported her find to the *Norfolk* and to Admiral Tovey, but because of radio interference, the latter did not receive the message and did not know that the Germans had been located until a later message from the *Norfolk* informed him of that fact. All during the night the two cruisers hung on to the German warships; it was not their business to fight but to keep track of them so that the big ships could bring them into action.

On board the *Hood*, Vice Admiral Holland calculated his intercept course and prepared for action at any time after 0140, May 24. Contact was not made until 0535, whereupon the *Hood* and the *Prince of Wales* advanced into action. Admiral Holland, maneuvering both his ships together, ordered a head-on approach which denied them the use of their after guns. The Admiral also ordered concentration of fire on the left-hand ship, believing, mistakenly, it to be the *Bismarck*. So convinced of the Admiral's error were the officers on the *Prince of Wales* that they decided to ignore the signal and fire on the right-hand ship. In three minutes, the Admiral apparently recognized his mistake, for he signaled for the two ships to shift targets to the *Bismarck*. It is doubtful if the *Hood* ever did so. Meanwhile the Germans had opened fire, concentrating on the *Hood*. To confuse the aim and to bring his after turrets to bear, Admiral Holland ordered a 20-degree turn to port, but scarcely had the ships begun to swing in response to the signal when the *Hood* disintegrated, hit in the magazine by a shell from the *Bismarck*. The

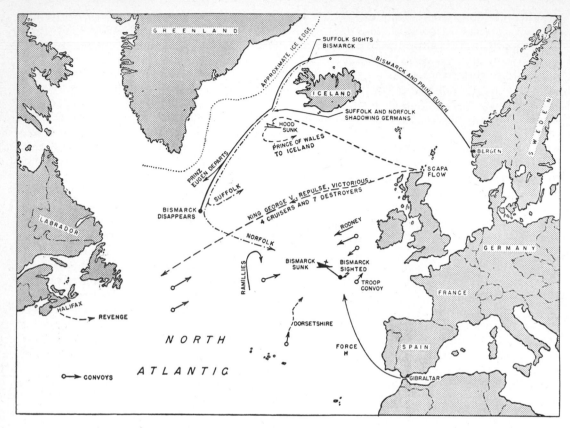

THE CHASE OF THE BISMARCK

Prince of Wales had to swing hard a-starboard to avoid the floating wreckage that was all that was left of the once-powerful *Hood*. The surviving British battleship now received the Germans' undivided attention. The situation had dramatically reversed. Tactical superiority had passed to the Germans. To make matters worse, the *Prince of Wales,* too new to have the mechanical difficulties worked out of her, was able to fire only about three guns a salvo. The *Bismarck* had just demonstrated what she could do. Rear Admiral Wake-Walker, who had been enjoying a ringside seat from the bridge of the *Norfolk,* suddenly found himself senior officer present with the full responsibility for the *Bismarck* on his shoulders. In view of the loss of the *Hood,* the inefficiency of and battle damage to the *Prince of Wales,* and the comparative weakness of his cruisers, he decided to resume the shadowing tactics in hopes of enabling Admiral Tovey's force to arrive on the scene.

The loss of the *Hood* can be blamed in large measure on British lack of readiness to spend money on conversion of older ships during the lean years of peacetime budgets. She was known to be weak to shell hits from a certain direction, but during the prewar years nothing had been done to strengthen her. When war came it was too late; as long as she could operate, she could not be spared. Also the tactics in the action showed a rigid formalism reminiscent of the *Fighting Instructions* of the 17th century. Such a code, after being discarded in the Napoleonic Wars, had been born again in World War I, as was most notably shown at Jutland. During the inter-bellum period the new fighting instructions had become more rigid, and Admiral Holland, by controlling the movements of the *Prince of Wales* and the *Hood* together, cut down their firepower. His bows-on approach was designed to close the range most rapidly, but he had all day before him and was already well within range when he signaled the turn for the approach. If he desired to close the range, he could have made a slower approach, which would have enabled him to bring all guns to bear, or he could have sent one ship at a time in rapidly while the other kept up its full broadside. Lastly, the close formation of the two British ships simplified the fire control problem of the Germans when the *Hood* was hit, for a change in deflection of only a degree or two brought their shells falling on the *Prince of Wales*.

THE *BISMARCK* DISAPPEARS

The Admiralty was watching the dispatch board with considerable interest as the news of the *Bismarck's* movements came in. Already they had ordered Admiral Somerville's Force H to sea from Gibraltar to participate in running the Germans down. They also summoned the *Rodney* and the *Ramillies* to break off from their convoys and join in the chase. When the news of the loss of the *Hood* reached the Admiralty, that office ordered all these vessels to search for the *Bismarck* and instructed the *Revenge* to proceed with all possible speed from Halifax.

After being dogged all day by the *Norfolk, Suffolk,* and *Prince of Wales,* the *Bismarck* suddenly turned on the *Suffolk,* which opened the range rapidly. This move was made to cover the departure of the *Prinz Eugen,* which escaped to the south and entered Brest ten days later. Once again the game of shadowing went on. Since the ships were by this time entering known U-boat waters, all British vessels were zigzagging. On the outward leg of one of these zigzags, the *Suffolk* lost radar contact and failed to regain it. Once more the *Bismarck* was loose —once again the chase boiled down to a following of the most likely probabilities. Three courses of action seemed to be open to the *Bismarck*. She was known to be trailing

oil from the encounter with the *Hood* and *Prince of Wales*. She might be in need of repairs. If so, she would head for Germany or for one of two French ports, Brest or St. Nazaire. Alternately, she might be heading for a rendezvous with a supply ship and then on to operations in whatever quarter of the globe she chose. The routes to Germany, to the Bay of Biscay, and to the mid or western Atlantic must be covered. Erroneously plotted radio direction finder signals led Admiral Tovey to believe that she was heading for the North Sea and Germany, so he steamed for several hours to attempt an interception in that area. Both he and the Admiralty had begun to have misgivings about this course of action, when a recomputation of the direction finder bearings aboard the *King George V* revealed a strong probability that the *Bismarck* was heading for a French port. A new dispatch from the Admiralty plotted the German battleship as being within a 50-mile radius of the position lat. 55° 15′ N, long. 32° 00′ W, about 600 miles southeast of Cape Farewell on the southern tip of Greenland. Admiral Tovey accordingly turned to attempt to intercept the *Bismarck's* probable course toward Brest, but his cruisers and the carrier *Victorious* held for home, being too short of fuel to continue. The damaged *Prince of Wales* was also ordered to proceed to England. Convoys were diverted to get them out of the probable danger area. The *Rodney's* course toward the North Sea was not immediately corrected, and she crossed ahead of the *Bismarck* on the afternoon of May 25. If she had been alerted, she could easily have intercepted. As it was, Admiral Somerville's Force H, consisting of the carrier *Ark Royal,* the battle cruiser *Renown,* and escorting ships, was now the only British force in position for an interception.

Realizing that the shortage of fuel for the smaller ships left the larger vessels exposed to submarine attack, the Admiralty decided that five destroyers could just be spared from Convoy WS 8B and one from the Irish Sea Patrol and sent them under Captain Vian of the *Altmark* affair to rendezvous with Admiral Tovey. During the night all forces raced toward the *Bismarck's* most probable position.

BISMARCKDÄMMERUNG

By the morning of May 26, the pursuers began to lose hope. The wind had increased during the night, forcing Somerville's ships to slow from 25 to 17 knots. The flight deck of the *Ark Royal* was pitching between 53 and 55 feet as measured by sextant observations, but in spite of the obvious difficulties and dangers of air operations, a search patrol set out from the carrier at 0835. Still no word of the *Bismarck*. Suddenly at 1030, a Catalina flying patrol from the Coastal Air Command broadcast a sighting of a battleship in position lat. 49° 33′ N, long. 21° 50′ W, approximately 750 miles west of Brest, steering course 150 at 20 knots. On all ships, plotting officers hurried with their work. It was no British battleship. The *Bismarck* was found.

On receipt of the news, Captain Vian in the destroyer *Cossack* decided to disregard his instructions to rendezvous with Sir John Tovey and turned with his five destroyers to intercept the *Bismarck*. Swordfish aircraft from the *Ark Royal* took over shadowing the German, but her position was too far ahead of any of the forces to make interception likely. Only an air strike from the *Ark Royal* could hope to slow her down until the heavy ships could come up. The strike preparations began immediately, while the cruiser *Sheffield* darted away at high speed to take up a station shadowing the Nazi battleship. Then came one of those near-tragedies of the war. The pilots, perhaps improperly briefed, and certainly impetuous, attacked the *Sheffield*, which had accompanied them from Gibraltar, under the impression that she was the *Bismarck*. Only highly skilled shiphandling averted a calamity. The next two strikes found the *Bismarck*, for the *Sheffield* had gone ahead and already located her. The pilots of these strikes had been briefed to fly to the *Sheffield* and take their departure from her. She would coach them on the target, which she did with alacrity. The results

of this strike were at first confused, and early reports led Sir John Tovey to believe that no significant damage had been done. However, it was eventually learned that she had been seriously hit and was heading in a northerly direction. Since this course was directly into the teeth of her enemies, the conclusion could only be that either the ship was having rudder difficulties or that damage was forcing her to take the heavy seas from that angle. In any event, the *Bismarck* was now running toward her pursuers. Darkness fell, and with it came Captain Vian and his destroyers to assist the *Sheffield* in shadowing. Vian saw no objection to attempting to put a few torpedoes into her as well. His first concerted attack the *Bismarck* drove off without damage either to herself or the destroyers by very accurate, radar-controlled fire. Captain Vian then stationed one destroyer on each bow and one on each quarter and took position astern himself. During the night each destroyer made several attacks on the *Bismarck* but obtained no torpedo hits because invariably the attacking destroyer had to break off the action before it could get to effective torpedo launching position.

Raeder had been making every effort to save the *Bismarck*. He summoned all available submarines to the area, but those closest had already expended all their torpedoes and could only watch impotently. By an odd chance, one U-boat passed within 400 yards of the *Ark Royal,* but, having fired her last torpedo the previous day, was powerless to harm the British carrier.

By morning the heavy British ships reached the scene of action. At 0847 the *Rodney* and *King George V* exchanged the first salvos with the *Bismarck* at a range of 25,000 yards. The *Norfolk,* which had sighted the German at 0815 and had coached the battleships on, was shadowing to the north. The *Bismarck,* although badly crippled, still had magnificent endurance and splendid fire control. Her third salvo straddled the *Rodney,* but soon the weight of British firepower began to tell, hitting the *Bismarck's* main battery director early in the action so that the accuracy of her fire diminished appreciably.

The British rapidly closed the range as one German gun after another fell silent. At no more than 4,000 yards, the *Rodney* pumped shell after shell into the battered German. The *King George V* did the same from slightly greater range. Still the *Bismarck* refused to sink. The *Rodney* fired two torpedoes and obtained one hit. From 4,000 yards the *Norfolk* launched four torpedoes with one probable hit. Still the *Bismarck* floated. At 1015, agonized that the German refused to sink, Sir John Tovey sadly directed the action broken off because of fuel shortage. Signaling the *Rodney* to fall in astern, he set his course for England.

The honor of actually sinking the *Bismarck* goes to the cruiser *Dorsetshire*. She had joined the action about half an hour before Admiral Tovey's departure and was at that time the only ship in the area with torpedoes remaining. On seeing the battleships discontinue the action, she began her run in. She fired two torpedoes at the starboard side of the *Bismarck,* one of which exploded directly under the bridge. Then she circled to the port side of the German and fired another torpedo. This one finally did the trick. Four minutes later, at 1040, the *Bismarck* capsized to port and quietly slipped under. The great chase was over. The *Dorsetshire* began to pick up survivors assisted by the destroyer *Maori,* but rescue operations had to be discontinued when a German U-boat appeared on the scene. The U-boat herself rescued five of the crew. All the rest, including Admiral Lutjens, were lost with the ship.

The story of the *Bismarck* reveals dramatically the effectiveness of the fleet-in-being. The bare chance that she might break out immobilized the services of at least two battleships, several battle cruisers, and their supporting vessels. All these ships had to be held ready should they be needed to track down the German battleship. Thus they had to be withheld from pressing duties elsewhere— North Atlantic convoy, the Mediterranean, the South Atlantic, and Indian Ocean trade routes. When she broke out she could disappear into the ocean wastes and strike at times and places of her own choosing. It required all the available resources of the British navy to run her down and sink her—five battleships, three battle cruisers, two aircraft carriers, as well as numerous cruisers and destroyers—in addition to extensive searches by the Coastal Air Command. Convoys lost parts of their escort, and no ships remained in Britain to oppose a sortie of the *Hipper, Scharnhorst,* and *Gneisenau* from Brest. The British had to ignore the escape of the *Prinz Eugen,* risking her getting in amongst their vital convoys. All this the *Bismarck* accomplished in her brief life. Her death meant that the British navy could resume its primary task of maintaining Britain's lifelines of communication.

THE MEDITERRANEAN THEATER

35

The Struggle

for the Mediterranean

DURING THE FIRST TWO YEARS of World War II the most important strategic factor affecting naval operations in the Mediterranean Sea was its geographic division into two basins by the Italian peninsula, the large island of Sicily, and the Tunisian peninsula in North Africa. The Strait of Messina between the toe of the Italian boot and Sicily is very narrow, and the Sicilian Channel between Sicily and Tunisia is only 80 miles wide and for the most part shallow enough to be mined. Therefore strong Italian sea and air forces based in southern Italy and Sicily should have been able to cut the British line of communications between Gibraltar at the western entrance to the Mediterranean and the British naval base at Alexandria in Egypt.

THE MEDITERRANEAN THEATER

The British realized the weakness of their supply line through the central Mediterranean and did not plan to rely upon it heav-

ily to maintain their position in North Africa and the Middle East if Italy entered the war. For the bulk of their supplies and reinforcements they would have to use the much longer route around the Cape of Good Hope and through the Red Sea and the Suez Canal. But the interior line of communications through the central Mediterranean would be available in emergencies when the gain in time might be worth the risk of losses.

The British might dispute Italian control of the central Mediterranean with forces operating out of their base on the small island of Malta only 55 miles south of Italian-held Sicily. Malta-based forces could give some protection to British shipping in the Sicilian Channel and, even more important, threaten Italian lines of communication to North Africa. From Naples, Italy's main port of embarkation, supply ships and transports would sail westward or eastward around Sicily to Tripoli and Benghazi in Libya, while shipping from Taranto and Brindisi would sail direct to the two main Libyan ports. All these routes were within easy reach of British surface ships, submarines, and aircraft based at Malta.

COLD WAR IN THE MEDITERRANEAN

Despite evidence of continuing Italian aggressiveness after Italy's seizure of Ethiopia in 1935, when Italy invaded Albania in April 1939 the British Admiralty had been taken completely by surprise. In fact, major units of the Mediterranean fleet were paying courtesy visits in Italian ports. The British immediately began to concentrate their fleet at Alexandria and within a week offered guarantees against aggression to Romania and Greece which only Greece accepted. In May the British and Turkish governments made a joint declaration of mutual aid against attack. In the same month Hitler and Mussolini proclaimed their Pact of Steel to aid each other in any military action. This strong public pronouncement was modified in secret however by the Cavallero Memorandum in which Mussolini told Hitler that Italy would not be ready for war for three years and asked him to postpone military action until 1942. Although Hitler agreed in principle, on August 11 the German foreign minister informed his Italian opposite number that Germany was about to attack Poland. When Mussolini asked Hitler for raw materials to help him fulfill his commitment under the Pact, Hitler declined and let him off by requesting only that Italy make threatening troop movements to pin down French forces. Consequently, when Germany invaded Poland in September, Mussolini proclaimed Italy's "nonbelligerence."

At the outbreak of war the British Mediterranean fleet consisted of one carrier, three battleships, three heavy cruisers, and some light cruisers and destroyers. Its first wartime tasks were the convoy of British merchant shipping and the establishment of shipping control over neutral vessels to prevent the movement of contraband to Germany. For such operations it was unnecessarily strong as long as Italy remained nonbelligerent. Gradually ships were de-tached for service on the vital Atlantic convoy routes, so that by the end of the year the Mediterranean fleet had been reduced to three small British cruisers and five old Australian destroyers.

But Mussolini was chafing under the restrictions of British shipping control, which he regarded as an intolerable affront, despite the conciliatory efforts of Britain to make it as painless as possible for Italy. Meeting Hitler at the Brenner Pass early in March 1940, he was evidently so impressed by German strength and plans that he promised to come in actively on Germany's side. At the end of the month he announced to the King and military leaders his concept of "parallel war," in which Italian operations would assist Germany indirectly but would be designed primarily to further Italian interests and would be carried out independently.

As the British began to see signs of coming Italian belligerency, they took measures to increase their security in the Mediterranean. In April they withdrew their merchant shipping from the area and agreed with the French to assume responsibility for control of the eastern Mediterranean with the assistance of a few French ships based at Alexandria, while the rest of the French fleet was to be responsible for the western Mediterranean. By early June the British naval force at Alexandria consisted of one carrier, four battleships, eight light cruisers, about 25 destroyers, and a dozen submarines. These were augmented by a French force of one battleship, three heavy cruisers, one light cruiser, and three destroyers.

However, Mussolini was not to be deterred. On June 5 he declared a 12-mile zone along the coasts of Italy, Albania, and his African colonies dangerous to neutral shipping, and within a week he announced that the Sicilian Channel had been mined and directed neutral shipping to use the Strait of Messina. Two days earlier the Italian admiralty had ordered all Italian merchant ships to Axis ports or neutral waters. The tardiness of this move cost Italy about one-third of her merchant marine, totaling 218 ships of 1,200,000 tons, when Mussolini finally declared war at midnight June 10.

THE OPPOSING FORCES

To combat the naval forces which the British Admiralty could spare for the Mediterranean Mussolini had a large and growing navy. Already on hand were four *Cavour*-class battleships built before World War I but recently modernized, seven heavy cruisers and 12 light cruisers, 60 destroyers, well over 100 submarines, and a large number of motor torpedo boats and antisubmarine craft. In addition the Italians planned to use various devices which they called *mezzi navali d'assalto*—"assault machines." These included pocket submarines, two-man piloted torpedoes, and explosive motor boats. Of the expected additions to the Italian fleet, the most important were the two new battleships *Littorio* and *Vittorio Veneto,* which were almost ready for service. Two more of these fast and powerful ships were in less advanced stages of construction.[1] Other combatant ships under construction included a dozen small cruisers, eight destroyers, and a dozen submarines.

The Italian navy not only was numerous but also enjoyed certain tactical advantages over the British Mediterranean forces. It far outnumbered the Mediterranean fleet in cruisers, especially of the 8-inch gun type. A large proportion of its ships were new, and most of them had greater speed than comparable British types. This speed advantage should have enabled the Italian fleet to make effective use of its central position between British forces based at Gibraltar and at Alexandria by falling upon one of them before the other could come to its support. In general the Italian fleet would be able to force action when it met inferior forces and avoid action in the face of a superior enemy. Finally and most important, in the central Mediterranean the Italian fleet would enjoy the support of strong air forces based in Italy and Sicily.

Nevertheless, the Italian navy had serious weaknesses. The fleet had no carriers or any air forces assigned directly to it for support, and the rigidity of organization among three

separate commands for land, sea, and air, all headed by a supreme command, made the coordination of the separate land-based air forces with the naval forces a cumbersome and time-consuming process. The ships of the fleet, though numerous and fast, were generally weaker in armor than comparable British ships, especially among the cruiser classes, and the older Italian battleships were outgunned by British battleships. The Italian ships were deficient in equipment too. They had poor sound gear, no radar at all, and no effective searchlight control for night action. Worst of all, the country itself lacked a sufficient industrial base to maintain a large navy in a long war. Much of the navy's new construction would never be finished, and the fleet would often lack fuel for combat operations.

On the other hand the British Mediterranean fleet had weaknesses too. In addition to its cruiser inferiority, it was so short of destroyers that at times the battle force could not go to sea because it could not be adequately screened. Although the battle force often had aircraft carriers in company, they carried few and obsolescent planes, and the fleet's land-based reconnaissance was weak. The British ships were inadequately armed with antiaircraft guns for operations in the central Mediterranean within striking range of the Italian air force, and the fleet supply of antiaircraft ammunition was short. The fleet's bases were also inadequately defended against air attacks and their harbors were insufficiently protected against Italian submarines and assault machines. Malta would obviously be unusable as a major fleet base, and berthing and repair facilities were inadequate at Alexandria.

Nevertheless, the Mediterranean fleet had one decisive strength. The much greater size of the Royal Navy as a whole in comparison with the Italian navy gave the British naval force at Alexandria what amounted to a strategic reserve. Though the Admiralty was often hard-pressed for surface forces in other theaters, more often than not it could make up losses suffered in the Mediterranean by sending reinforcements, if in the judgment of the War Cabinet the over-all strategic

[1] The *Roma* was completed early in 1943; the *Impero* was never finished.

situation justified such action. Therefore when the British Commander in Chief Mediterranean, Admiral Andrew B. Cunningham, found himself at war with a superior Italian fleet, he could afford to adopt a boldly aggressive policy. Even if he should lose his entire force and the Admiralty should be unable to replace it, the British would still have lost only a campaign. If the Italians should lose their fleet, they also would lose their war.

THE PROBLEM OF THE FRENCH FLEET

Admiral Cunningham was not slow to put his aggressive policy into action. On the day after Italy declared war he sailed from Alexandria with two battleships, five cruisers, one carrier, and nine destroyers to sweep the eastern Mediterranean as far westward as the south coast of Italy. He hoped to intercept Italian traffic to Libya or catch Italian fleet units at sea, but his force met no Italian surface ships. Outbound, one of his destroyers attacked an Italian submarine, and on the return voyage two of his cruisers stood in to the coast of Cyrenaica to shell Italian minesweeping and antisubmarine patrols off Benghazi and Tobruk. South of Crete an Italian submarine sank one of his cruisers. But except for one plane over Tobruk, neither the Italian air force nor the Italian fleet made an appearance.

Meanwhile French cruisers from Alexandria made a similar sweep of the Aegean Sea during which they met and chased off an Italian cruiser squadron. In the western Mediterranean a few days later French cruisers and destroyers from Toulon carried out a long-planned night bombardment of military objectives around the Italian port of Genoa. On June 20 the French battleship *Lorraine* at Alexandria joined forces with British cruisers and destroyers for a bombardment of the port of Bardia in Cyrenaica.

By this time French negotiations with Germany and Italy for an armistice were bringing relations between French and British naval forces to a crisis. The British government had consented to the negotiations provided the armistice involved no surrender of the French fleet. In the armistice as finally signed, Germany promised not to use the French ships, but all of them except a few designated for protection of colonial interests were to be recalled to France. Although Hitler had expressed himself in a conference with his naval high command as solicitous of French honor in the matter of the French fleet, the British War Cabinet was not aware of this, and in any event could not be sure that Hitler would not seize the French ships when he wanted them. Consequently they made plans and issued orders to their naval commanders in the Mediterranean to take action that would prevent French ships in North African ports from ever being used by the Axis. Though the story has been told in the preceding chapter in connection with Atlantic surface actions, it is repeated here in somewhat more detail, preliminary to considering the effect of these operations upon the Mediterranean theater.

At Oran Admiral Marcel Gensoul commanded a French squadron consisting principally of two battleships, two fast new battle cruisers, and six destroyers. At Gibraltar Vice Admiral Sir James Somerville, acting directly under the British Admiralty, commanded Force H: two battleships, one battle cruiser, an aircraft carrier, two cruisers, and a dozen destroyers. The Admiralty ordered Admiral Somerville to present Admiral Gensoul with an ultimatum. He could join forces with the British, sail to British ports or to a French port in the West Indies to have his ships disarmed, or sink his ships. When Force H arrived off Oran on July 3, Gensoul, incensed by the obvious threat of force, rejected the ultimatum and began to clear his ships for action. Somerville's force opened fire, capsizing one French battleship, setting fire to another which then ran aground, immobilizing the battle cruiser *Dunkerque* by a hit in the engine room, and damaging a destroyer. In this quick naval execution, 1,300 French sailors died. The battle cruiser *Strasbourg* and some destroyers managed to clear the harbor and escape to Toulon, despite a damaging attack by torpedo planes from the British carrier. Three days later at Oran the *Dunkerque* was further damaged by British torpedo planes.

At Alexandria the neutralization of French warships was handled more diplomatically. In the early days of the armistice negotiations Admiral Cunningham had informed the French Admiral René Godfroy that he could not permit him to obey an order to sail for France. On June 3 in accordance with his orders from the British Admiralty Cunningham asked Admiral Godfroy to join forces with him, disarm his ships where they lay, or scuttle them at sea. Godfroy accepted the second alternative and had begun to discharge the fuel from his ships when he heard of the ultimatum delivered to Admiral Gensoul at Oran. Having been ordered to sea by the French admiralty, he now felt obliged at least to stop discharging fuel. By ignoring a British Admiralty order for immediate action, Cunningham gained time to send his ships' captains in the morning to call on the captains of the French ships and win their support. On the afternoon of July 4 Godfroy finally consented to disarm his ships and reduce their crews.

A few other French fleet units remained to be accounted for. On July 8 at Dakar in French West Africa the battleship *Richelieu* was put out of action for a year by torpedo planes from a British carrier. In September a bombardment by Force H from Gibraltar in support of an unsuccessful Free-French landing at Dakar sank a destroyer and two submarines at a cost to the British of a battleship and two cruisers damaged. The battleship *Jean Bart* at Casablanca in Morocco was not molested because her main battery guns had not been mounted.

The action against the French fleet was as repugnant to the British as it was offensive to the French. No one can say whether it was necessary or not, but its effects were obvious. On the one hand it stiffened Vichy French resistance to the British and Free French in North Africa and Syria. On the other hand, for the time being at least the British did not have to worry that major units of the French fleet might join the Axis and tip the

scales of Mediterranean naval strength in favor of Italy.

WARFARE BETWEEN THE BRITISH AND THE ITALIANS

While the British were busy neutralizing the French fleet, Malta had become a serious problem. The air defenses of the island were very weak. In June 1940, of 112 heavy and 60 light antiaircraft guns authorized for Malta, only 34 heavy and eight light guns had been installed. The fighter defense, planned at four squadrons, consisted of four crated Gladiators intended as spares for the Fleet Air Arm at Alexandria. Although the Italian air force had not been active against the British Mediterranean fleet, it had early turned its attention to Malta. On June 11, the day after the Italian declaration of war, two waves of ten and 25 planes attacked Malta. During the rest of June Malta suffered 36 raids, the largest by 60 bombers escorted by fighters. On the 21st the floating drydock was sunk, and the submarines based at Malta had to leave temporarily. In early July the British decided to evacuate their women and children from the island and remove some supplies needed at Alexandria.

While covering the evacuation convoys, the Mediterranean fleet had its first action with the Italian fleet off Calabria, the toe of the Italian boot. The British force was disposed in three groups. A scouting group of five light cruisers was in the van, followed by the battleship *Warspite,* flagship, and destroyers, with the aircraft carrier *Eagle,* two slower battleships, and destroyers in the rear. The Italian force, heading northward toward Italy after escorting a convoy to Benghazi, consisted of two *Cavour*-class battleships, six heavy cruisers, 12 light cruisers, and destroyers under the command of Admiral Angelo Campioni, Commander in Chief of the Italian fleet.

Although the Italian force had been scouted by two flying boats from Malta on the morning of July 9, a strike launched by the *Eagle* was unable to find it.[2] In the afternoon the British light cruiser group found and was attacked by the Italian heavy cruisers, which were in turn driven off by the *Warspite*. The British cruisers then scored a hit on an Italian cruiser, and the *Warspite* engaged the battleships *Cavour* and *Cesare* in a long-range gunnery duel. When a hit at 26,000 yards slowed the *Cesare*, Admiral Campioni sent his destroyers in for a torpedo attack and retired behind a smoke screen. The *Warspite* and British cruisers drove off the Italian destroyers. A late afternoon air strike by the *Eagle* was unsuccessful, and the British forces beat off nine attacks by about 100 land-based planes of the Italian air force. At 1730 with his force within 25 miles of the Italian coast Admiral Cunningham abandoned the pursuit. Next day on the return trip to Alexandria the *Warspite* group endured 22 air attacks and the cruiser group 15 without suffering a hit.

The action off Calabria seemed to prove the soundness of Admiral Cunningham's aggressive policy. Although the Italian battleships mounted lighter main battery guns than the British battleships, they had more of them, and the two of them could have engaged the British flagship closely before the two slower British battleships could have got into action. The Italian force was greatly superior in cruisers. Although the British had a carrier within striking range, it had played an ineffective role up to the time of the surface action, and the Italians had at hand a vastly superior land-based air power. Yet the Italian admiral did not press the action.

Italian reluctance to engage approximately equal forces was displayed again on July 19 in the Battle of Cape Spada. When three British destroyers on an antisubmarine sweep northwest of Crete ran into two Italian light cruisers, they fell back upon the support of the British light cruiser *Sydney* and a destroyer, which were to the northward of them. When the Italians sighted the *Sydney* they retired to the southwest, although they had a 16-to-8 superiority in 6-inch guns and only a 16-to-20 inferiority in 5-inch guns.[3] In the pursuit the *Sydney* sank one Italian cruiser, but the other, although hit, escaped to Tobruk.

In the late summer and fall the supply and reinforcement of Malta and the British forces in Egypt continued without significant interference by the Italians. Convoys from Gibraltar via Malta to Alexandria brought troops and supplies to both bases. With one of these Admiral Cunningham got as reinforcements the battleship *Valiant* in response to his request to the Admiralty for another battleship to match his *Warspite* in speed and gun range, the armored-deck carrier *Illustrious,* and two antiaircraft cruisers. Meanwhile carriers of Force H from Gibraltar had been flying planes into Malta. By the end of the year there were 20 fighters, 12 torpedo planes, 20 bombers, and 11 reconnaissance planes at the base.

In early November the British Mediterranean fleet made a carrier-borne torpedo plane attack upon the Italian fleet at Taranto which foreshadowed in some respects though on a small scale the Japanese attack upon the United States Pacific fleet at Pearl

[3] Total relative gun power was theoretically about 4-to-3 in favor of the Italians.

---

[2] The characteristics of British carrier planes and the small number carried may explain the general ineffectiveness of carrier reconnaissance and strike operations in this and subsequent engagements:

Name:	Type:	Max. Speed: (m.p.h.)	Max. Height for Max. Speed: (feet)	Max. Range: (miles)	Number of Guns: (.303 cal.)	Bomb Load:
Gladiator	fighter	245	15,000	523	4	
Fulmar	fighter	253	10,000	820	8	
Swordfish	torpedo	139	5,000	528	2	1,500
Albacore	torpedo	163	4,800	521	2	1,500

In the Action off Calabria the *Eagle* carried only 17 Swordfish and two Gladiators. The *Illustrious* arrived in the Mediterranean with 22 Swordfish and 12 Fulmars. These numbers were often reduced by losses that could not be replaced immediately.

Harbor. In preparation for the raid Malta-based aircraft carried out a thorough reconnaissance of the harbor at Taranto, finally reporting on the evening of November 11 the presence of five battleships, including the two new ones, and three cruisers in the main harbor, and two cruisers and four destroyers in the inner harbor. A little after midnight 12 planes from the *Illustrious* dropped flares and attacked with bombs and torpedoes through intense antiaircraft fire. This and a similar strike about an hour later left the new *Littorio* listing with her forecastle awash and one *Cavour*-class battleship with her stern under water and another beached in the main harbor, and a cruiser and destroyer slightly damaged in the inner harbor, at a cost of two British planes and four airmen.

During the Taranto operation the balance of naval forces in favor of the British was further increased by a reinforcement of one battleship and two cruisers which joined the Mediterranean fleet from a Malta convoy. So great was the British preponderance now that Admiral Cunningham offered two of his older and slower battleships to the Admiralty for use on North Atlantic escort duty. The Italians, on the other hand, to escape further carrier attacks, moved their remaining battleships out of the eastern Mediterranean to Naples.

Under these circumstances it is not surprising that on November 27 an Italian force under Admiral Campioni consisting of the new battleship *Vittorio Veneto,* one *Cavour*-class battleship, six heavy cruisers, and 14 destroyers, though at sea in the western Mediterranean, missed an opportunity to fall upon either of two separated British forces from Alexandria and Gibraltar that were covering a Malta convoy. Unwilling to move too far from his land-based air support on the island of Sardinia, Campioni did not make contact with the British forces off Cape Spartivento until they had joined. The two battleships, one carrier, five cruisers, and ten destroyers of the combined British forces quickly drove off the Italian force in an action that damaged one British cruiser and one Italian cruiser and a destroyer.

During 1940 the war against supply lines in the Mediterranean by surface ships, submarines, and aircraft of both sides was more or less a draw. The Italians had been able to move more than 600,000 troops and 700,000 tons of supplies to Albania and support their attack upon Greece at the end of October with only negligible losses at sea. To North Africa they had sent 47,000 troops and 35,000 tons of material. In September Marshal Rudolfo Graziani's 215,000 troops in Libya attacked the 50,000 British troops of General Sir Archibald Wavell in Egypt, but the Italian offensive bogged down at Sidi Barrani only about 50 miles inside the Egyptian frontier. With the advantage of their safe exterior line of supply around Africa, the British, after their initial setback, had little difficulty building up their forces. During the last three months of the year they reinforced their army in Egypt with 76,000 troops from the home islands and 49,000 from India. In early December General Wavell launched an offensive from Sidi Barrani which rolled through Bardia and Tobruk in January and reached Benghazi on February 1. By February 9 the entire bulge of Cyrenaica was in British hands, and General Wavell's forces stood before El Agheila at the threshold of Tripolitania.

GERMANY TO THE RESCUE

The general situation in the Mediterranean area at the beginning of 1941 was very uncomfortable for Italy. In addition to the defeat suffered at the hands of the British in North Africa, the Italian army had been driven out of Greece and was being firmly held in Albania by the little Greek army. The Italian air force had been unable to neutralize Malta, and the Italian fleet had proved itself unwilling to stand up to British naval forces even in the central Mediterranean.

Concerned about the loss to Axis prestige resulting from Italian reverses, Hitler had decided at the end of 1940 upon three courses of action to relieve the pressure on his weak ally: (1) a German air fleet would reinforce the Italian air force in the central Mediterranean; (2) the German army would undertake an invasion of Greece through Bulgaria and capture the island of Crete; (3) German reinforcements would be sent to bolster the Italian front in North Africa.

During December and January the German Tenth Air Fleet of some 500 planes, specially trained in attack upon ships, moved from Norway to Italian airfields in Calabria and Sicily. Its tasks were to protect Axis communications with North Africa, prevent the passage of British convoys through the central Mediterranean, and neutralize Malta by air attack.

After a part of the German air reinforcements had already arrived, a British convoy of four cargo ships escorted by two battleships, one aircraft carrier, four cruisers, and destroyers of Force H passed Gibraltar January 6 en route to Malta and Greece. About the same time the battleships *Warspite* and *Valiant,* the carrier *Illustrious,* and seven destroyers of the Mediterranean fleet sailed from Alexandria to meet the convoy from Gibraltar and cover the movements of other convoys between Malta and Alexandria. In support of the operation Malta aircraft attacked the Italian fleet at Naples on the 8th, damaging a *Cavour*-class battleship and forcing the retirement of the other battleships there to Spezia in the Gulf of Genoa. On the evening of the 9th after daylight air attacks by Italian aircraft from Sardinia, the Gibraltar force turned back undamaged, leaving the convoy with three cruisers and destroyers to proceed to Malta. That night the cruisers drove off an attack by Italian destroyers, sinking one of them, but a British destroyer struck a mine and had to be towed to Malta. The next day Italian battleships from Spezia searched the western Mediterranean for Force H, which had long since passed out of their reach.

Around noon on January 10 the Alexandria force, which had joined the convoy from Gibraltar during the night, was attacked west of Malta by about 50 Stuka dive-bombers from Sicily. Unlike the Italian pilots, who attacked from high level, the Germans pressed home their attacks with great daring through very heavy antiaircraft fire. Concentrating on the *Illustrious,* they hit the carrier several times and knocked out her steering gear. Steering with her engines, the *Illustrious* headed for Malta, and despite an afternoon attack which started large fires, managed to make port that evening. Next day, en route to Alexandria, the cruisers *Gloucester* and *Southampton* were damaged by air attack, the latter so badly that she had to be sunk by her own force.

At Malta the *Illustrious* became the target of numerous air attacks. On January 16 she was hit again, and a cruiser and a merchant ship were also damaged, and again on the 18th and 19th the carrier was damaged. Nevertheless, the Naval Constructors at Malta succeeded in making temporary repairs to the *Illustrious,* and on the night of the 23rd she slipped out of the harbor and reached Alexandria without further damage. Since the *Illustrious* had to go to the United States for permanent repairs and the *Eagle* was unserviceable, the Mediterranean fleet would be without a carrier until the arrival of the *Formidable,* which the Admiralty had immediately decided to transfer from the South Atlantic.

While continuing air attacks on Malta at a rate of three or four a day with only brief periods of respite, the *Luftwaffe* did not neglect the eastern end of the Mediterranean front. At the end of January German aircraft from the Dodecanese Islands began dropping magnetic mines in the Suez Canal in such numbers that it had to be closed intermittently throughout the month of February. As a consequence the *Illustrious* and the *Eagle,* which was now to be transferred to the Indian Ocean, both had to be held at Alexandria where they were of no use, and the *Formidable,* which was to replace them, had to be held in the Red Sea. At the same time Force H at Gibraltar had to stop flying planes in to Malta for its defense because the presence of German heavy surface ships on the Atlantic sea lanes forced its employment there on escort duty.

Thus in the brief space of one month the intervention of the German air force in the

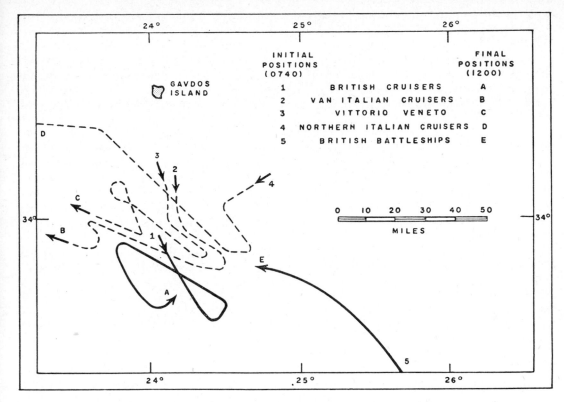

INITIAL
POSITIONS
(0740)

FINAL
POSITIONS
(1200)

1	BRITISH CRUISERS	A
2	VAN ITALIAN CRUISERS	B
3	VITTORIO VENETO	C
4	NORTHERN ITALIAN CRUISERS	D
5	BRITISH BATTLESHIPS	E

GAVDOS ISLAND

0   10   20   30   40   50

MILES

BATTLE OF CAPE MATAPAN, MARCH 28, 1941, MORNING ACTION

Mediterranean had completely changed the situation. The Mediterranean fleet had no carrier air support for operations in the central Mediterranean. The supply line from Gibraltar via Malta to Alexandria was now extremely hazardous. Even the exterior supply line around Africa was considerably hampered by the mining operations against the Suez Canal.

THE BATTLE OF CAPE MATAPAN

In spite of the favorable situation for Italy which the German air force had created, in March the Italian navy suffered another heavy blow from the Mediterranean fleet. Pressed by the German naval command, the Italians adopted a plan for a sweep by the new battleship *Vittorio Veneto*, three cruisers, and destroyers in the waters south of

Crete as far east as Gavdos Island off the south coast. At the same time five cruisers with destroyers were to make a sweep north of Crete. The whole force was to be commanded by Admiral Angelo Iachino, who had relieved Admiral Campioni as Commander in Chief in December.

During the morning of March 27 air search and cover which was to have been provided by the German and Italian land-based air forces proved ineffective, and about noon the Italian naval force was snooped by a Sunderland flying boat from Malta about 80 miles southwest of Sicily. Worried by these developments, the Italian naval command ordered the northern cruiser group to rejoin the main body before it could make its assigned sweep. Consequently on the morning of March 28 the *Vittorio Veneto*, screened by destroyers, was south of the west end of Crete steering southeast with a division of three cruisers and destroyers seven miles in the van and the northern group of five cruisers and destroyers 25 miles to eastward.

Warned by increased Italian radio traffic, the report of the Malta flying boat, and perhaps by the British intelligence service in Italy, Admiral Cunningham at Alexandria had taken measures to counter the Italian thrust. On March 27 he ordered a convoy en route to Greece to reverse course after dark and another due to leave Greece for Alexandria to remain in port. Vice Admiral H. D. Pridham-Wippel RN at Piraeus, the port for Athens, with four cruisers and destroyers was ordered to join Cunningham south of Crete on the morning of the 28th. Cunningham himself sortied from Alexandria with the flagship *Warspite* and two other battleships, the recently arrived carrier *Formidable,* and nine destroyers after dark on the 27th.

At dawn on March 28 a search plane from the Italian battleship *Vittorio Veneto* reported a force of British cruisers and destroyers 50 miles east of the Italian force. At 0740 the van Italian cruiser division sighted Pridham-Wippel's cruisers and gave chase, opening fire about a half hour later. Pridham-Wippel retired toward Admiral Cunningham's force, which was in the vicinity, until 0855, when the entire Italian force, having already gone somewhat beyond Gavdos, turned about and retired in their turn toward the northwest. Pridham-Wippel then came about to keep in touch. At 1000 the *Veneto,* which was now ahead and to starboard of the pursued Italian cruisers and steering the same course, came about to close the British cruisers from the north. Under fire from the Italian battleship, which slightly damaged one of his cruisers, Pridham-Wippel laid down a smoke screen and again retired.

Meanwhile Admiral Cunningham had sent a carrier air strike against the Italian cruisers at 0840 and another against the *Vittorio Veneto* at 1115. Although neither of these strikes scored any hits, after the second, Admiral Iachino retired to the northwest at 25 knots with the British battleships 55 miles astern in pursuit.

Shortly after noon Pridham-Wippel's cruisers joined the British main body, and for the next two hours the *Formidable* made repeated strikes against the Italian force in an effort to slow down some of the Italian ships so that the British battleships could overtake them. Finally at 1520 a torpedo hit in the port propeller stopped the *Vittorio Veneto* temporarily, but an hour and a half later she was making 19 knots. Late in the afternoon Admiral Iachino concentrated his force against further air attacks, stationing the original northern group of five cruisers 1,100 yards on the starboard beam of the *Veneto,* his other cruiser division on the port beam, and all his destroyers in an encircling ring as an antiaircraft screen. In this situation a final *Formidable* strike at sunset hit and stopped the cruiser *Pola* of the northern group. Unwilling to abandon a valuable ship, and believing the British force to be farther to the eastward than it actually was, Iachino detached the cruisers *Zara* and *Fiume* and four destroyers of the northern group to assist the *Pola.*

Earlier in the afternoon Admiral Cunningham had ordered Vice Admiral Pridham-Wippel to press on with his cruisers and attempt to make visual contact with the fleeing Italian force. At 2030 one of Pridham-Wippel's cruisers made radar contact with a large stopped ship, but Pridham-Wippel turned north to find the Italian main body. A little later Cunningham ordered eight destroyers to sortie in advance of his own battleship group. At about 2200 Cunningham's battleships sighted the stopped *Pola* close aboard on their port bow and two other cruisers to the westward crossing the bows of the British formation. Turning his battleships to starboard into line ahead, Cunningham opened fire at only 3,800 yards on the moving Italian cruisers, which burst into flames and stopped. Cunningham then made a further turn to the northward to avoid torpedo attack and left his remaining destroyers behind to deal with the Italian destroyers. At 2300 he ordered all forces not engaged to withdraw to the northeast. Fifteen minutes later the *Fiume* capsized and sank. After midnight the British destroyer

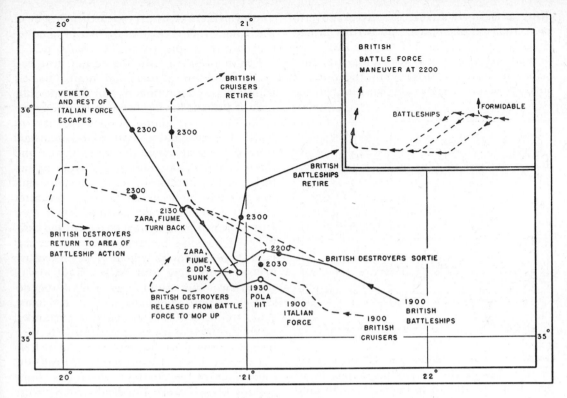

BATTLE OF CAPE MATAPAN, MARCH 28-29, 1941, NIGHT ACTION

Jervis sank the burning *Zara*, and the *Havock* found the *Pola* with all power, light, and gun control lost and her crew in a hysterical condition. The *Havock* and other destroyers of the group which had sortied earlier removed 236 prisoners from the *Pola* and sank her at 0320. During the whole rather confused melee of battleships, cruisers, and destroyers, two Italian destroyers had also been sunk.

The British had achieved a considerable tactical victory at almost no cost to themselves. Although the *Vittorio Veneto* escaped, three Italian cruisers and two destroyers were sunk. One British cruiser had been slightly damaged, and one plane and pilot had been lost. Belated air attacks by the *Luftwaffe* on the return trip to Alexandria failed to do any additional damage to the British force.

This disproportionate victory provided a much needed fillip to the morale of the Alex-andria fleet and the British public at a time when the Mediterranean situation seemed very dark. It had of course a converse effect upon Italian morale, with the important strategic consequence that the Italian fleet did not venture forth from the safety of its ports to interfere with the impending British naval operations in the waters around Greece and Crete.

THE GREEK ORDEAL

In the two months following its March victory off Cape Matapan the British Mediterranean fleet endured its most severe trial. When Italy invaded Greece in October 1940, the British had immediately established a fueling base for light forces at Suda Bay on the island of Crete. The Mediterranean fleet also took on the task of convoying supplies to Greece. However, in order to avoid inciting a German attack, the Greek government rejected the service of British armed forces on the mainland of Greece. After the German army moved by invitation into Bulgaria on March 1, 1941 with the obvious purpose of outflanking the position of the

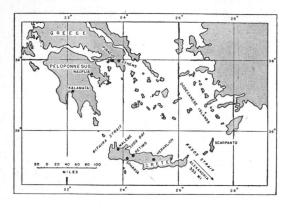

SOUTHERN GREECE AND CRETE

Greek army in Albania, the Greek government accepted the active participation of British troops and air forces in the mainland fighting. It then became the task of the Mediterranean fleet to transport three infantry divisions and an armored brigade from Egypt to Greece.

The first convoy sailed March 6, and others followed every three days. Italian explosive motor boats launched by two destroyers sank a British cruiser in Suda Bay on the night of March 26, and a few days later an Italian submarine sank another British cruiser which was escorting a convoy south of Crete. However, during a period of about six weeks 58,000 troops with their equipment and supplies were transported to Greece without loss.

They did not remain long. From Bulgaria the German army had invaded Yugoslavia and Greece on April 6. To the 800 supporting aircraft of the German Fourth Air Fleet, the Royal Air Force could oppose only 80 operational planes based in Greece, of which some were occupied on the Albanian front, and two long-range bomber squadrons flying night missions from Egypt. Outflanked and outnumbered, the Greek army retreated

southward. On April 21, with the consent of the King of Greece, the British decided to evacuate their forces from the mainland.

For this task the Mediterranean fleet had available seven cruisers, 20 destroyers, 21 transports, and a number of small craft. The port of Piraeus having been destroyed by the explosion of an ammunition ship early in April, the evacuation had to be managed from three beaches in the Athens area and three in the Peloponnesus. To avoid air attack the evacuating ships were ordered not to approach the beaches until one hour after dark and to leave by 0300. On April 27 a Dutch transport which delayed sailing from Nauplia was dive bombed and set afire, and later two destroyers which had picked up her survivors were sunk with a total loss of 500 troops and all but 42 men of the destroyer crews. The next day at Kalamata 7,500 troops out of 8,000 were left stranded when the temporary appearance of German troops in the town scared away the British evacuation force. Nevertheless, during the four days of evacuation operations some 50,000 British and Imperial troops were saved. In addition one cruiser, six destroyers, and four submarines of the Greek navy escaped to Alexandria.

Obviously the next German objective would be Crete. Lying only about 60 miles from the mainland of Greece, it was within easy range of German air forces based there, and an Italian airfield on the island of Scarpanto was only about 45 miles away to the eastward. The topography of the island as well as its proximity to Axis land-based air forces made naval support difficult. A central ridge of mountains traversed only by mule tracks ran its entire 160-mile length from east to west. On the south coast there was a small fishing village called Sphakia but no usable port. On the north coast British forces held Maleme airfield near the west end of the island, the fueling base at Suda Bay and Retimo airfield some 20 miles to the east, and Heraklion airfield about 50 miles farther eastward. To supply, defend, or evacuate these north coast positions, British ships would have to pass westward around Crete through Kithira Strait or eastward through Kasos Strait—both time-consuming passages in the face of nearby German air forces.

The defenses of the island were very weak, especially in planes and antiaircraft guns. The defending troops totaled more than 28,000, but the greater part of them had just been evacuated from Greece and were armed mainly with rifles and a low proportion of light machine guns. About 30 Royal Air Force and half a dozen Fleet Air Arm planes operated from the island until May 19, when heavy German air attacks forced their withdrawal to Egypt. Against these defending forces the Germans planned to use 16,000 airborne troops transported in 530 planes and 100 gliders, 7,000 seaborne troops, 430 bombers, and 180 fighters.

After four days of intensive bombing, the main assault began at 0700 on May 20 with heavy air attacks on the antiaircraft defenses of Maleme airfield. At 0800 gliders towed by transport planes landed troops west of the field, and 15 minutes later parachute troops jumping from airplanes began to land to the east. By the end of the day 5,000 airborne troops had landed, and Maleme field, though still under British artillery fire, was partly in German hands. Retimo and Heraklion fields had also been attacked, but less strongly, and the British forces there had held. Next day the Germans used Maleme airfield to build up their forces, even though many of their aircraft had to crash-land on the shell-pocked field.

For the sea defense of Crete Admiral Cunningham had divided his forces into three main groups. To the west of Crete two battleships with destroyers stood by to prevent interference by the Italian fleet. South of Crete two cruiser forces were stationed during daylight hours with orders to carry out sweeps north of Crete at night or when enemy forces were known to be at sea. On the night of May 20, while three destroyers bombarded Scarpanto airfield, the cruisers patrolled north of Crete without result. During the morning withdrawal heavy air attacks sank one destroyer and damaged a cruiser.

Next night the naval forces met with more success. A cruiser force which swept around the west end of the island met a German invasion force of small craft 20 miles to the northward and sank about 15 of them, drowning some 4,000 troops. Low on ammunition, the cruisers withdrew to the westward to join the battleship force. Meanwhile another cruiser force which had passed around the east end of Crete and swept to the northwestward sank several small vessels of another German convoy and drove it off. Since it was now daylight and the British ships were low on ammunition and already under heavy air attack, their commander did not pursue the convoy but instead retired to the southwest and asked for support from the battleship force. Before the forces could join, two cruisers were damaged, and at 1330 the battleship *Warspite* was hit and a destroyer was sunk by Axis planes. Of two cruisers sent to help the stricken destroyer, one was sunk by air attack in Kithira Strait at 1550. About an hour later another battleship was damaged, and in the next two and one half hours another cruiser was hit twice and finally sunk.

In a period of about 24 hours the naval forces defending Crete had lost two cruisers and two destroyers and had two battleships and three cruisers damaged by Axis aircraft. Although the Mediterranean fleet had prevented the seaborne invasion of the island,[4] on May 22 German airborne forces made Maleme airfield operational and began landing 20 troop-carrying planes and towed gliders per hour.

During the next few days the British forces continued to fare badly on sea and land. On May 23 two destroyers en route to Alexandria were sunk by air attack. On the 26th while making an air strike against Scarpanto airfield the carrier *Formidable* and a destroyer were badly damaged. Ashore German troops broke through to Suda Bay in the Maleme airfield area, and the British troops there began to retire across the mountains to Sphakia on the south coast. Late that night the British decided to evacuate their forces from Crete. Next morning another

[4] This accomplishment is disputed by a German claim that troops brought in by ship saved the airborne force from being defeated in the first few days.

battleship was damaged while covering the retirement of lighter forces that had landed troops and stores at Suda Bay. During the whole defense of Crete the Mediterranean fleet had lost two cruisers and four destroyers and had had two battleships, a carrier, three cruisers, and one destroyer put out of action.

Like the withdrawal from Greece, the evacuation of Crete had to be carried out during darkness. On May 28 three cruisers and six destroyers sailed from Alexandria for the Heraklion area, and although one cruiser was hit and forced to retire during the approach, the rest of the force embarked 4,000 troops that night. Homeward bound a destroyer lost steering control, probably as a result of a near miss the night before, and had to be abandoned, and air attacks sank a destroyer and damaged another and two cruisers. A bomb which exploded on the crowded mess deck of the cruiser *Orion* killed 260 troops and wounded 280. In the whole force a total of 800 troops were killed, wounded, or captured.

Evacuation from Sphakia on the south coast was naturally less costly. During the night of May 29 four cruisers, a fast transport, and three destroyers picked up 7,000 troops and got away with damage to only one cruiser. Meanwhile the British forces in the Retimo area had surrendered. The next night 4,000 more troops were evacuated from Sphakia with the loss of one cruiser.

In all about 17,000 troops were saved from Crete. Although the British had suffered about 13,000 casualties, their stubborn defense of the island had cost the Germans 400 planes and 15,000 to 20,000 troops, including 5,000 men of their only airborne division. After their Cretan experience the Germans were very reluctant to engage in any more airborne operations.

But the post-Crete situation of the Mediterranean fleet was not a happy one. Despite the arrival of reinforcements consisting of a battleship, two cruisers, and six new destroyers in early May, at the beginning of June only two battleships, three cruisers, and 17 destroyers were operational. The British supply line from Alexandria to Malta was now flanked to the northward by German air

forces based on Crete. As Malta grew weaker from lack of supplies, the Axis supply line to North Africa would become more secure. And in North Africa the German and Italian armies had already driven the British land forces back to Egypt.

BRITISH FLEET OPERATIONS IN SUPPORT OF THE IMPERIAL ARMIES

The British land offensive in North Africa which began at the end of 1940 had been helped materially by the support of the Mediterranean fleet. On January 3, 1941 the flagship *Warspite* and two other battleships, supported by cruisers and destroyers and covered by planes from the *Illustrious,* heavily bombarded the port of Bardia in Cyrenaica. The World War I monitor *Terror,* mounting twin 15-inch and eight 4-inch guns, and several 1915-vintage gunboats each with two 6-inch guns supplemented the fire of the battleships. In the middle of December the gunboat *Aphis,* supported by the *Terror,* had gone right into the harbor at Bardia and remained for half an hour. Two days after the battleship bombardment of Bardia, the monitor and gunboats, together with three minesweepers, four antisubmarine trawlers, and an assortment of small cargo vessels, were organized into an Inshore Squadron whose mission was to provide gunfire and logistic support on the sea flank of the Imperial Army. The Squadron was often assisted by five old Australian destroyers. In carrying on its work of clearing harbors and bringing up supplies for the army during the British advance, the Inshore Squadron suffered heavy losses from air attack and mines. By the end of February the *Terror,* two of the three gunboats, and four other small vessels had been sunk.

When Hitler decided at the end of 1940 to send reinforcements to North Africa, he did not consider it feasible to reopen the abortive Italian offensive against Egypt and the British fleet base at Alexandria. But Lieutenant General Erwin Rommel, whom he sent to command the *Afrika Korps,* was soon of a different mind. On March 30 he counterattacked General Wavell's forces in Cyrenaica, which had been greatly weakened by the transfer of reinforcements to Greece. Cutting across the bulge of Cyrenaica, Rommel's forces had surrounded Tobruk by April 11, and in May they took Sollum, just across the Egyptian border. There Rommel called a halt to consolidate his position.

Even before Tobruk had been surrounded, the British commanders in chief in Egypt had decided to hold the port as a threat to Rommel's line of communications. The supply of its garrison now became the task of the Inshore Squadron. Without air support to protect them from the 200 planes of the German Tenth Air Fleet now based in Libya, the little ships of the Inshore Squadron suffered continual losses. Nevertheless, they managed to move in 400 tons of supplies daily, sufficient to keep the garrison fighting, and Tobruk remained a thorn in the side of the Axis North African army.

To relieve the pressure on Tobruk as well as the main front at Halfaya pass, the British decided to strike a blow at Tripoli, the principal Axis port of supply for their North African forces. Admiral Cunningham resisted a War Cabinet proposal to sacrifice the battleship *Barham* and a large part of her crew in a combined bombardment and blocking operation, but he did arrange a surprise bombardment of Tripoli by the battle fleet on April 20 in conjunction with the escort of a convoy to Malta. The ships did heavy damage to the port and got away untouched.

It has been questioned whether maintaining Tobruk as a harassing position on Rommel's left flank was worth the cost. Far more important of course was the problem of supplying British forces on the Egyptian frontier. In early May as an emergency measure Force H from Gibraltar and the Mediterranean fleet escorted a convoy of four merchant ships carrying 200 tanks and other vehicles past Malta to Alexandria. One ship struck a mine and sank in the Sicilian Channel, but the rest, despite occasional light air attacks, reached Alexandria safely. For the bulk of their troops and supplies however the British forces in Egypt had to rely upon the long route around Africa. This was threatened by light Italian naval forces based in East Africa.

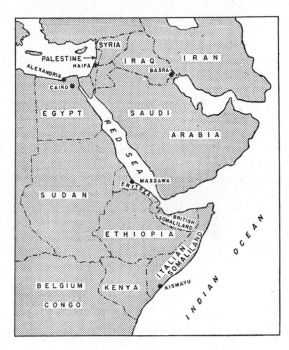

EAST AFRICA AND THE MIDDLE EAST

At the time of their entry into the war the Italians had had seven destroyers, two motor torpedo boats, five antisubmarine boats, and eight submarines based at Kismayu on the Indian Ocean and at Massawa in the Red Sea. In August 1940 an Italian army from Ethiopia seized British Somaliland. In January 1941 British forces from Kenya and the Sudan with fleet support began a campaign to drive the Italians out of East Africa. In February the Italians abandoned the port of Kismayu, and in early April British forces took Massawa while torpedo planes from the *Eagle* sank two Italian destroyers and drove one ashore. The remaining Italian naval forces in East Africa scuttled themselves or fled from the area. As a result the President of the United States was able under the Neutrality Act to proclaim the Red Sea open to American shipping.

Another threat to the eastern flank of the British army in Egypt and the fuel supply of the Royal Navy had developed meanwhile in the Middle East. In early April the pro-Axis Rashid Ali seized control of the government of Iraq. On the 18th, British naval forces under the Commander in Chief India supported a landing at Basra which quickly forced Rashid Ali to flee to Iran. By mutual agreement British and Russian forces moved into Iran in August to prevent its seizure by the Germans.

In Syria German agents, encouraged by the anti-British feelings of the Vichy-minded French colonial government, had been active too. Here the French had a small naval force of two destroyer leaders armed with five 5.5-inch guns and capable of 40 knots, three submarines, a sloop, and a patrol vessel. To oppose these the British Mediterranean fleet sent two cruisers and four destroyers to Haifa, Palestine. In early June a fast attack transport supported by another cruiser and two more destroyers landed British troops in Syria while other British and Free French forces advanced from Palestine. Three days later an armistice was signed. Before the fighting ended at sea however, one of the French destroyer leaders heavily damaged a British destroyer, and French aircraft severely damaged two others. Reinforced by two more cruisers, British ships and naval aircraft sank a destroyer leader en route to Syria with arms for the French and damaged the two that were already there. They also sank a submarine and two merchant ships.

In North Africa the Inshore Squadron kept up the supply of beleaguered Tobruk throughout the spring and summer. In August its overworked ships were further burdened by the task of removing 19,000 Australian troops from Tobruk and replacing them with a like number of other troops. By the end of October the Inshore Squadron had completed the exchange and at the same time had run in about 8,000 tons of stores for the garrison. Finally in November General Sir Claude Auchinleck, who had relieved General Wavell as Commander in Chief Middle East, launched an offensive which raised the siege of Tobruk on December 10

and reached Benghazi two weeks later. In the 242 days of the siege the Inshore Squadron had brought in some 33,000 troops, 92 guns, 72 tanks, and 34,000 tons of supplies. During the same period its ships had removed 34,000 troops, 7,500 wounded, and 7,000 prisoners. The entire support operation had cost two destroyers, one minelayer, 24 small naval vessels, and six merchant ships sunk, and seven destroyers, one attack transport, 19 smaller naval vessels, and seven merchant ships damaged.

THE MALTA STORY

Even before the British withdrawal from Greece, Admiral Cunningham, realizing the disruptive effect which surface forces operating from Malta could have upon the Axis supply line to North Africa, had based four destroyers there. On the night of April 16, 1941 this force destroyed an entire convoy of five supply ships and its escort of three destroyers with the loss of only one of its own destroyers. In May the remaining three destroyers were relieved by six new ones, but thereafter intensive aerial mining operations against the port greatly hampered operations. After a destroyer struck a mine and sank in the harbor, a cruiser and two other destroyers sent to Malta as reinforcements could not enter and were ordered on to Gibraltar. The rest of the Malta destroyers were soon called to the defense of Crete.

As a result of the losses incurred in the Greek debacle, no surface ships could be spared for Malta during the late spring and summer, but in other respects the Malta situation greatly improved, largely because of the transfer in June of the German Tenth Air Fleet from Sicily to Greece to replace half of the Fourth Air Fleet, which was being transferred to Russia. A July convoy of seven British supply ships was attacked by Italian aircraft, which sank a destroyer and damaged a cruiser and a supply ship, but all the supply ships reached Malta. An attack on the harbor by explosive motor boats and piloted torpedoes near the end of July was frustrated by the shore batteries, which destroyed all the Italian assault machines. In September another Gibraltar-Malta convoy of nine supply ships lost only one and suffered only minor damage to an escorting battleship. Meanwhile British submarines and aircraft kept up the work of interrupting Axis communications to North Africa. From July 1 through September 14 the Axis lost 53 supply ships totaling 202,300 tons as well as a cruiser, a destroyer, a submarine, and 19 small combatant ships. In October over 60 per cent of the supplies intended for the *Afrika Korps* were lost.

That same month two cruisers and two destroyers from England were sent to Malta and designated Force K. On the night of November 8 they intercepted a convoy of seven German supply ships escorted by two Italian cruisers and six destroyers bound from Messina to Tripoli and sank one destroyer and all seven supply ships. Another of the Italian destroyers was sunk by a British submarine the next day. About two weeks later a cruiser and a destroyer of Force K found two tankers escorted by two destroyers and sank both tankers while the escort ran away. At the end of November Force K was reinforced by two more cruisers and destroyers. In the middle of December four destroyers of Force K caught two Italian cruisers in the desperate expedient of rushing gasoline to Tripoli and turned them into blazing torches. By the combined action of British surface, submarine, and air forces, mostly based at Malta, 57,800 tons of Axis supplies for North Africa were sunk and 20,500 tons were damaged in the last three months of the year. Of 123,000 tons shipped, only 44,800 tons were delivered.

The German naval command had long been aware of the threat which British possession of Malta posed to Axis central Mediterranean communications and had repeatedly urged its capture. Unwilling to take the risk of airborne assault, especially after Crete, Hitler had never approved the project. But when the Italian navy and air force proved incapable of protecting the movement of supplies to North Africa from the attacks of Malta-based forces, Hitler decided to neutralize the island by air action alone.

In December he sent Field Marshal Albert Kesselring to Italy as Commander in Chief South with orders to gain control of the air and sea between southern Italy and North Africa. To accomplish this task the German Second Air Fleet of about 500 planes was ordered to Sicily.

Just as these measures were being taken, the British surface forces based at Malta suffered a serious reverse. On December 19 while trying to intercept an Axis convoy, three cruisers and four destroyers of Force K ran into a mine field off Tripoli which sank one destroyer and one cruiser and damaged two other cruisers. As a result of this disaster a big Axis convoy reached Tripoli safely.

Meanwhile the air assault on Malta was mounting in intensity. The Italians had been able to increase the number of air raids from 50 in October to 75 in November. Despite the arrival of additional fighters for the defense of the island on November 11, which cost the loss of the carrier *Ark Royal* to a submarine the next day, the scale of attack more than doubled to 175 raids in December. In the first four months of 1942 as German air reinforcements poured into Sicily, the monthly total of raids ranged between two and three hundred. At the end of March the British carrier *Eagle,* which had been flying in 12 Spitfires at a time for the air defense of Malta, was laid up for repairs. Early in April, at the personal request of Prime Minister Churchill, President Roosevelt made the United States carrier *Wasp* available to fly in its much larger capacity of about 60 Spitfires, but these were all destroyed within a few days. That month the tonnage of bombs dropped on Malta reached a high of 6,700, and the British were forced to withdraw the remnant of their surface ships that were still operational. Submarines continued to run in fuel and ammunition, but in early May the last Malta-based submarines retired to Alexandria. A second *Wasp* trip delivered 60 more Spitfires on May 9, just in time for a series of great air battles on that day and the next. But these afforded only temporary relief to the island. That same day Marshal Kesselring considered that his task of neutralizing Malta had been accomplished.

As Malta suffered from the air, its supply by sea became more difficult too. Back in early December 1941, the fuel situation had become so critical that the British decided to rush in a single supply ship escorted by three cruisers and seven destroyers. On a second trip the British convoy, reinforced by two cruisers and six destroyers from Malta, was intercepted north of Sirte by an Italian force of three battleships, two cruisers, and ten destroyers under the Commander in Chief, Admiral Iachino, which was covering a convoy to Libya. After about ten minutes of long-range fire by the new battleship *Littorio* and destroyer attacks and evasive maneuvers by the British force, Admiral Iachino broke off the action at sundown. Under cover of darkness the supply ship got through to Malta.

In March 1942 the supply situation at Malta became so desperate that all British North African forces concerted their efforts to get a convoy through. The Eighth Army made threatening attacks upon Axis airfields near Tobruk. The Royal Air Force attacked airfields in Cyrenaica and Crete, carried out air reconnaissance and strikes from Libya and Malta, and provided air cover for the convoy to the limit of its aircraft range. Royal Air Force planes and a naval air squadron bombed the Libyan port of Derna on the nights of March 20 and 21. The Mediterranean fleet could not provide battleship cover for the convoy because its last two battleships had been sunk in the harbor at Alexandria by Italian piloted torpedoes in December, but a covering group of three cruisers and destroyers was provided, and the four supply ships of the convoy were escorted by an antiaircraft cruiser and six destroyers. Six other destroyers made an antisubmarine sweep along the North African coast, in the course of which one destroyer was sunk; the remaining five reinforced the covering group. From Malta another cruiser and destroyer also joined the covering group.

During the morning of March 22 the convoy suffered intermittent air attacks without damage. In the afternoon an Italian force under Admiral Iachino consisting of the battleship *Littorio*, three cruisers, and four destroyers intercepted the British force north of Sirte. By adroit maneuvering, the use of smoke screens, and threatening destroyer attacks, the British admiral was able to keep his covering group between his convoy and the Italian force and hold off the superior enemy until sundown, when again Iachino retired to avoid a night action. All four supply ships arrived safely at Malta. Yet there was more honor than profit in the victory, for subsequent heavy air attacks upon the harbor so damaged the ships that only 5,000 of their 26,000 tons of cargo could be landed.

As the British supply difficulties increased and their Malta forces grew weaker, the Axis supply situation improved. Shipping losses dropped to ten per cent in January, and although they rose again to 25 per cent in March, this was still far below the 55-75 per cent range of losses during the last three months of 1941. In April 1942 Axis losses dropped again to 15 per cent and remained at that level in May, when 145,000 tons of supplies were safely delivered to the *Afrika Korps.*

From the latter part of January to the end of June General Rommel had need for all the supplies he could get. On January 21 he launched a counterattack against the Eighth Army at El Agheila that reached Benghazi before the end of the month. While Rommel paused to build up his forces, the German naval command continued to urge the capture of Malta, and Marshal Kesselring advised Rommel to wait until the island had been taken before renewing his offensive. But Rommel, like his *Führer,* was an opportunist. Before him stood the British fleet base at Alexandria and the Eighth Army's vast supply complex around Cairo. With these in his hands Malta would be useless to the British. Against the advice of Kesselring, a combined German and Italian airborne and amphibious attack force in Italy which had been preparing to capture Malta in June was dissolved and its troops were sent to North Africa to reinforce Rommel, and the greater part of the Second Air Fleet in Sicily was transferred to the Russian front. On May 26 Rommel resumed his offensive. His forces reached Tobruk on June 21, and this time there was to be no British stand. Axis forces broke through the Tobruk perimeter the next day, and by the end of June the *Afrika Korps* had crossed the Egyptian border and stood before El Alamein, only 60 miles from the Mediterranean fleet base at Alexandria.

THE TURNING OF THE TIDE

But Malta was not finished. In June the British Admiralty determined to push through simultaneous convoys from Gibraltar and Alexandria. Six supply ships escorted by cruisers and destroyers and covered by a battleship, two carriers, four cruisers, and 17 destroyers of Force H passed Gibraltar on the 12th. Air attacks next day scored no hits, but on the 14th a cruiser was damaged and forced to retire. At sundown Force H turned back, leaving the convoy to continue to Malta with one cruiser and nine destroyers. During the night an Italian naval force of two cruisers and five destroyers attacked the convoy and damaged two destroyers, one of which later sank. Daylight air attacks sank three supply ships, and upon arrival at Malta on the night of the 15th one destroyer was sunk and two destroyers, a minesweeper, and a supply ship were damaged by mines.

The Alexandria convoy of ten supply ships escorted by seven cruisers and 20 destroyers met even heavier opposition. Air attacks on June 14 sank one supply ship and damaged another. The next day one cruiser was damaged by a motor torpedo boat and another by air attack, and a destroyer was sunk by a submarine. Receiving reports that an Italian force of two battleships, four cruisers, and three destroyer squadrons was at sea to intercept him, the British admiral retired to the eastward. Further air attack damaged two more destroyers, one of which sank the next day. With its ammunition low and its destroyers short of fuel, the British force abandoned its mission and withdrew to Alexandria.

In spite of such heavy losses, the British continued their efforts to keep Malta in the fight. An August convoy of 11 supply ships escorted by two battleships, four carriers, seven cruisers, and 25 destroyers from Gibraltar fought its way through nearly every kind of opposition the Axis could muster except the Italian battle fleet. Two Italian cruiser divisions were sent out but later recalled before they had contacted the convoy; two of these ships were lost to a British submarine. However, Axis submarines, aircraft, and torpedo boats sank a carrier, a destroyer, and two cruisers, and damaged another carrier of the escort, and left only three sound and two damaged supply ships to struggle through to Malta.

Meanwhile the air reinforcement of Malta continued. Serviceable aircraft on hand rose from a low of 20 in May to a high of 165 in September. Even more important than the increase in numbers was the much greater range of the new torpedo planes being delivered. In 1939 the effective operating radius of Malta-based torpedo planes had been only 100 miles; in 1942 it had increased to 400 miles. Now torpedo aircraft could range as far west as Sardinia and as far east as Benghazi and Tobruk, making it impossible for Axis shipping to escape their attacks even by the most circuitous routing. As a result Axis shipping losses rose from a low of 15 per cent in July to a high of 40 per cent in October. Sinkings of tankers were especially damaging to the operations of the *Afrika Korps*. When Rommel launched a new offensive at Alam El Halfa on August 31, the loss of a tanker off Tobruk was so critical that Kesselring felt obliged to offer him some of his own air force reserves of aviation gasoline, which however were never delivered. Three more Axis tankers were sunk only a few days after the British started their final offensive in November. That month Axis shipping losses reached an all-time high of 77 per cent.

Rommel's offensive at Alam El Halfa failed. On August 13 General Sir Bernard L. Montgomery had taken command of the British Eighth Army with the determination that it must not suffer another reverse. Aware of the impending German attack, he made his dispositions to meet it, but when Rommel withdrew on September 3, Montgomery did not pursue him. With his own supply line to the eastward secure, Montgomery continued to build up his forces for a massive counterattack which began at El Alamein on October 23. After 11 days of furious fighting, the Eighth Army finally broke through the positions of the *Afrika Korps* and rolled on to the westward. Tobruk was in British hands again on November 13 and Benghazi on the 24th. On December 15 the Eighth Army reached El Agheila, and Rommel was in retreat toward Tunisia. Far to the westward British and American forces that had landed in Morocco and Algeria were advancing upon his rear. The tide of war in the Mediterranean had turned for the last time.

36

The Battle of the Atlantic:

U-boat Warfare

"THE ONLY THING THAT EVER really frightened me during the war was the U-boat peril." [1] So wrote Winston Churchill after the victory. From the Allied point of view, the Battle of the Atlantic was being won when nothing was happening. Every time a convoy arrived in port unscathed, the battle was that much nearer victory. When dramatic action took place at sea, the Allied cause came that much nearer defeat. This chapter tells of the men who kept the sea lanes open between the New World and Great Britain. Theirs was the dirty, dangerous, deadly dull job of keeping swift liners and plodding freighters moving across the sea lanes. If they succeeded in their task, no headlines proclaimed the victory; if they failed, they paid with their lives in the icy waters of the North Atlantic for their own deficiencies and for those of all who shared the blame for the lack of naval readiness for convoy duty. The victory was won by many people, by the merchant seamen who sailed in the freighters and tankers, by the stevedores who loaded and unloaded them, by the seamen, ratings, and officers who manned the escorting vessels, by the shipyards and shipyard workers who built both merchant ships and escorts, and by thousands of unheard of and unappreciated people on both sides of the Atlantic who plotted U-boat positions, routed convoys, organized sailing lists, experimented with new devices, and analyzed the results of previous actions. All of these properly have their part in the naval history of the Battle of the Atlantic, yet because their stories are too many and too complex to tell, only the broad principles can be presented here.

We have noted how Hitler at first observed the conventions of warfare in his submarine campaign. This was a stroke of luck for the British, for if the sinking of the *Athenia* had awakened them to the necessity for organizing convoys, the period of the Twilight War gave them time to get the convoys operating. Overseas trade is vital to England at all times; in wartime, the requirements of imports rise rather than decline because the additional requirements of armaments far

[1] Winston S. Churchill, *The Second World War* (Boston, 1949), II, 598.

outweigh the inevitable cutbacks of civilian goods. However, a convoy system has the effect of cutting the efficiency of the available shipping by about 25 to 40 per cent, first because all ships in a convoy are limited to the speed of the slowest member, and second because the task of loading and unloading is thrown out of gear. Either there are no ships in the harbor or there are more than can be afforded dockage, lighterage, and stevedoring. However, there was no help for it; the torpedoing of the *Athenia* caused the Admiralty to cancel previous plans for evasive routing, except for their fastest ships, and to set up their convoy routes as quickly as possible.

We have noted that at the outbreak of war, the German U-boat fleet numbered 57 boats. Of these, 30 were capable of sustained operations at sea. The others were coastal and might be expected to operate around the British Isles. That the German navy was so short of U-boats reflects Hitler's preoccupation with his *Luftwaffe* and army at the expense of the navy. During the period of Hitler's government, most of the naval funds were expended on surface ships under the grandiose plan for challenging Britain on the surface. But when war came this plan was so far short of fulfillment, that as we saw in a previous chapter the German navy was forced to employ its surface ships as raiders.

If Hitler had made inadequate preparations for an offensive submarine war in the Atlantic, the British Admiralty had been equally guilty of devoting insufficient thought and money to its antisubmarine fleet. A critical shortage of escorting vessels haunted convoy planners from the first. Only the most important shipping routes could be protected, some of them for but part of the way. However even the presence of a few escorts would force the U-boats to attack submerged and expend their precious torpedoes rather than have easy pickings from a leisurely surfaced attack. To keep the U-boats down and to afford antiaircraft protection as well, the British by the end of the first three months of the war had armed a thousand of their merchant ships. Ships sailing in convoy, even with a weak escort, had a mathematically

better chance of getting through than did the same number of ships sailing independently. By the end of September all ships outward bound from the Thames and from Liverpool were escorted for at least part of their journey; the same coverage was afforded all ships inward bound from Halifax, Gibraltar, and Freetown.

Thus began the Battle of the Atlantic, a battle for survival for England. Air power enthusiasts have stated that the air battle over Britain after the fall of France was the only battle in the entire war whose loss would have meant the loss of the war for England. That comment can better be applied to the Battle of the Atlantic. Without the food brought in by these unglamorous convoys, England would have been starved into capitulation, and without the fuel carried across the Atlantic at fearful cost in tankers, the Royal Air Force could not have left the ground to engage in the Battle of Britain.

Before proceeding further, it will be well to have a few terms before us, as these terms are necessary for the discussion of convoy operations. The word *convoy* has two meanings, first, it refers to all ships, whether merchant or warships, traveling together as a unit. Second, it refers in a more limited sense to the noncombatant ships for whose protection the convoy is organized. The *escort* refers to those warships whose duty is the protection of the convoy at sea. The *screen* refers to the antisubmarine vessels such as destroyers and corvettes. The *escort commander* is the senior officer of the escort and is in complete charge of the whole convoy, since he is responsible for its protection. In those convoys escorted by large surface ships, he would be the flag officer commanding the battleship or cruiser division present. If no large vessels are present, the escort commander is usually the commander of a destroyer squadron. The *convoy commodore,* who sails on a ship of the convoy itself, is responsible for internal discipline in the convoy. He was usually a retired flag officer of the Royal Navy or, in an American convoy, a reserve captain with experience in merchant shipping.

The Canadian navy cooperated with the

British navy from the beginning, and in mid-September 1939 the first of the transatlantic convoys sailed from Halifax bound for the United Kingdom.[2] Convoys in World War II were divided into two classes, "fast" convoys of $9\frac{1}{2}$ to 10 knots, and "slow" convoys of $6\frac{1}{2}$ to $7\frac{1}{2}$ knots average speed of advance. A typical transatlantic convoy of the period was made up of 45 to 60 merchant ships steaming in from nine to twelve columns, 600 yards between the ships in column and a thousand yards between the columns. The escort patrolled outside the formation. Early in the war it was customary to employ cruisers and battleships in the escort, but the practice was abandoned for two reasons. First, the Admiralty conceived it better to keep the surface fleet more concentrated to prevent a breakout of surface raiders rather than attempt to deal with them on the high seas; second, the heavy warships could provide no protection against the U-boat—the chief menace; instead they themselves required protection, adding to the burden of the already overtaxed antisubmarine ships.

The problems of the two groups of ships that make up the convoy are very different as is the seamanship training of the personnel. The merchant captain is unaccustomed to operating his ship in company with others. Years of training and experience have prepared him for a lone wolf role. Suddenly in wartime, he finds himself sailing with 40 to 60 other ships, forced to keep station, to zigzag or to change course when he is told to do so, all this at night without the benefit of lights or other aids to visibility. Outside the convoy he sees the snuffling little escort ships which seem to be running aimlessly over the ocean. Many merchant skippers found the discipline of sailing in convoy hard to bear. The escorts, on the other hand, were manned by people who were accustomed to operations in company with other ships and who were often unable to grasp the very real difficulties under which the merchantmen were operating. At first there was a serious degree of misunderstanding between merchant captains and their escorting commanders. Incidents of many kinds offended sensibilities on both sides. The passage of time however brought better understanding.

The customary box formation of the convoy was adopted for several reasons. First, it is the easiest one for station keeping; second, it minimizes the chances for collision during changes of course or zigzagging; and, third, it puts the greatest possible number of ships in easily maneuverable formation inside the area that a minimum escort can protect. The obvious disadvantage is that it bunches the targets. A torpedo shot almost at random at a convoy can scarcely avoid hitting a ship. In spite of this weakness, the box formation continued to be used throughout the war.

Escort doctrine changed many times during the war. Ideally the best protection against submarines is a circular screen completely enclosing the convoy. There were never enough escorts available to make this screen feasible, for the escorts must be close enough to each other so that their sound searches overlap, yet must be far enough to detect a submarine before it arrives at effective torpedo range. It required upwards of 30 destroyers to provide this kind of screen for a fast carrier task group in the closing months of the Pacific war; in the Atlantic, some convoys in the early months had to sail with only four or five escorts. At first, some effort was made to approximate a circle, stationing a ship off each corner of the box, with any additional ones in an arc ahead. To overcome the gaps in the sonar coverage, the escorts patrolled station, that is, steered sinuating courses around the general area of their stations in an attempt to cover all of the likely area some of the time rather than a very small area all of the time. In the event

[2] The designation of convoys during the war followed a kind of cryptic shorthand. A combination of letters and numbers was used which indicated the port of origin, the port of destination, and the particular number of the convoy. The principal convoy routes and their designations were: Halifax-United Kingdom, HX; United Kingdom-Halifax, ON; Sydney, Nova Scotia-United Kingdom, SC; United Kingdom-Sydney, ONS; Boston-Halifax, BX; Halifax-Boston, XB; Gibraltar-United Kingdom, GK; United Kingdom-Gibraltar, KG; United States-Gibraltar, USG; Gibraltar-United States, GUS; United Kingdom-North Russia, PQ; North Russia-United Kingdom, QP.

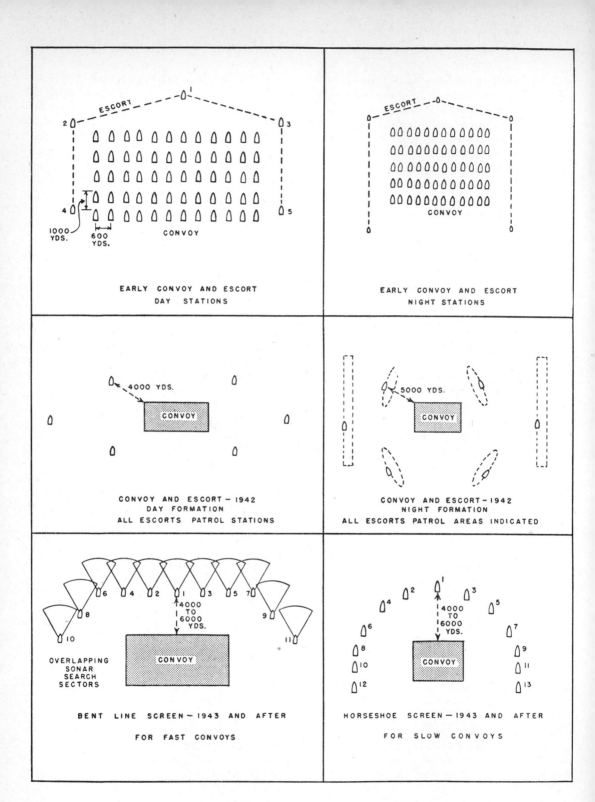

PRINCIPAL CONVOY FORMATIONS, WORLD WAR II

of an attack or sound contact, the standard doctrine was for one of the escort to attack the submarine to hold it down while the convoy escaped, but doctrine further stated that such an attack was not to be continued for more than one hour. This practice was ineffective, for it seldom resulted in a kill on a submarine, which was then left free to take action against the next convoy or even to catch up with the one it had been driven from. Later instructions directed a more persistent attack on a U-boat, even though it left the convoy temporarily more exposed.

From the point of view of a U-boat commander, the most favorable position for attack is within an arc of 45 degrees on either side of the bow of the convoy. This angle of attack means the shortest run for the torpedoes since the convoy is advancing toward them. The high relative speed gives the convoy little opportunity for evasive action, even if it sights the torpedo wakes or the submarine, and this angle of fire affords the greatest possibility of a torpedo hitting some ship. Other positions of attack in order of favorability to the attacker are from either quarter, either flank, dead ahead, and dead astern.

The screening dispositions adopted early in the war represented an attempt to protect the whole area. However, it rapidly became apparent that the position on the bow was the most dangerous, and screening doctrine changed to emphasize the degree of protection from that angle. As it eventually worked out, the bent-line screen provided the best answer that could be obtained. This formation protects both bows and provides additional ships ahead to pick up a submarine maneuvering into attack position on the bow or to give assistance on either bow if needed. At first the escorting ships were placed too close to the convoy so that it was possible for a submarine to fire torpedoes and dive before it was picked up on the asdic or sonar equipment of the escort. This problem was eased when the escorts moved out to a range of about five or six thousand yards. Occasionally with a very slow convoy it was still found necessary to protect the quarters with additional escorts. Under these conditions a horseshoe screen was used.

The principal weapons available at the time for combating the U-boat were the depth charge and asdic. Depth charges had been used in World War I and had changed little since then. Asdic is an underwater sound device which operates by training a supersonic sound beam in a given direction and listening for an echo which reveals the presence of an object in the water. Skilled operators learned to distinguish the sound returned by a submarine from that which bounced off a reef, a school of fish, or a thermal layer in the water. The device can be used for listening as well as for echo-ranging and is effective at a much greater range used in this manner, but its accuracy is greatly lessened. In the United States Navy the equivalent device is called *sonar*.

EARLY OPERATIONS

Ships escorted from Canadian ports were under the operational control of the Royal Canadian Navy until they reached an agreed Mid-Ocean Meeting Point (MOMP), usually about 20 degrees west longitude (south of Iceland) where they would meet a westbound convoy. The escorts would then exchange convoys, the Canadian vessels escorting their new convoy to Canada, while the HX convoy continued under the protection of the British navy to the British Isles. The Canadians had the longer route because usually lighter protection was required in the western Atlantic than from Iceland to England.

During the period of the Twilight War, Hitler's policy of attempting to avoid a showdown with England led him to restrict his U-boats; this led the British to a false complacency regarding the effectiveness of their antisubmarine methods. In September 1939 the British lost 26 merchant ships to U-boats, for a total of 135,522 tons; by January 1940, the sinkings by U-boats had dropped to two ships, although losses from other causes—such as air attack, collision in convoy, and fire at sea—amounted to about a hundred thousand tons. In the spring the curve of sinkings started up again, but after the fall of France in June 1940 the picture changed dramatically. The U-boat fleet moved its operating bases to Brest, St. Nazaire, Lorient and La Pallice on the western coast of France, adding several days to the time a U-boat could remain on patrol. Profiting from this gain and from the fruition of the U-boat building program in Germany, Admiral Karl Doenitz almost doubled the number of submarines continuously maintained in the North Atlantic.

With his additional facilities Doenitz instigated a vigorous program of anti-commerce warfare. Documents and sound gear from captured French ships enabled him to work out new methods of attack which paid off almost at once. The British were hard pressed to meet the new threat. Casualties among destroyers and other escort vessels during the Norwegian campaign and the Dunkirk evacuation had been heavy. No destroyers had been ordered in 1938; sixteen ordered in 1939 were in the building yards but could not be completed before the end of 1940. Since at that time there was an average of 2000 British merchant ships at sea, the need for escorts grew more pressing. Additional destroyers were ordered and two new types were authorized—corvettes and frigates. The former were vessels of less than a thousand tons, mounting one or two 4-inch guns, equipped with depth charges and asdic. The frigates were larger and improved versions, mounting more guns and having better seakeeping qualities than the corvettes, and also equipped with depth charges and asdic. Since these new ships would not be ready in any quantity until late 1940 or early 1941, and since significant numbers of destroyers could not be brought into service until middle or late 1941, the position of the British was desperate. Numerous trawlers and other kinds of small craft were equipped with asdic and with depth charges to engage in coastal patrol work. As early as May 1940, Churchill requested a loan of 40 or 50 American destroyers to tide them over the times ahead. Many difficulties intervened however and it was not until September that arrangements could be completed for the famous destroyers-for-bases deal.

THE UNITED STATES SHIFTS FROM NEUTRAL TO NONBELLIGERENT

When the European war broke out in 1939, a United States declaration of war—as remarked by a leading periodical—had as much chance of passing Congress as would a bill cutting Congressional salaries. In an attempt to avoid involvement President Roosevelt on September 5, 1939 established a Neutrality Patrol whose purpose was to keep belligerent activities from the Western Hemisphere. Early in October, the Pan-American Republics announced a neutrality zone running roughly 300 miles out into the Atlantic. All belligerents were warned against conducting military operations within that zone. The American Neutrality Act of 1937 had established the principle that belligerents could trade with the United States if they bought the goods with cash and carried them in their own bottoms. The thinking behind this was that the United States had been dragged into World War I by insisting on her neutral rights on the high seas, so the Act of 1937 abandoned many of those rights in the hopes that involvement would be avoided. At first the sale of munitions was prohibited, but in November 1939 the law was amended to allow the sale of munitions as well as other goods on a cash and carry basis. Although by language the cash and carry policy was strictly neutral, actually it favored the British, for their blockade allowed no German shipping on the North Atlantic.

The end of the period of Twilight War awakened the American Congress to the threat from abroad. Swiftly they passed legislation providing for a two-ocean navy and for the first peacetime draft bill in history. Events however were moving faster than legislation. Great Britain's desperate need for destroyers grew more evident every day. On the one hand Britain had to have the destroyers if she was to keep her sea lanes open. On the other, considerable doubt existed, in Washington as elsewhere, that Britain could survive the German onslaught. The prospect that the Royal Navy might be turned over to

Germany made it necessary for the United States to conserve every ship and to build new ones as rapidly as possible. Accordingly, President Roosevelt sought assurance from Churchill that the British fleet would never be surrendered to Germany. Churchill refused to make an unequivocal promise. The most he would say was that *he* would never do it; in the event of a British defeat, his government might be turned out of office and another group might use the fleet as bargaining chips at the surrender table.

Although this assurance was somewhat less than satisfactory to Roosevelt, he decided to take a calculated risk and attempt to transfer 50 American destroyers to the British flag. There was of course a risk that Germany would declare war on the United States, but Roosevelt thought otherwise, and as events turned out he was right. Hitler had no desire to make the mistake of the Kaiser and involve himself with the United States until he had cleaned things up in Europe to his satisfaction.

Lord Lothian, British Ambassador to the United States, concluded arrangements in late July 1940 for a deal whereby the United States would give 50 obsolete and obsolescent destroyers to Great Britain in return for 99-year leases on a series of bases running from Newfoundland to Trinidad. There was no thought that the trade was anything like a fair exchange. The value of the bases was enormous from both the monetary and strategic point of view. The value of the four-stack destroyers was more questionable. But they were the best that could be offered at the time, and with their aid, and with other American help, England was able to survive the period until her own escorts began to be less scarce. Final agreement was signed in September 1940, and delivery began shortly afterwards. By mid-April 1941 the 50 destroyers had been delivered, as well as ten *Lake*-class Coast Guard cutters well equipped for antisubmarine duty.

The American destroyers alone were not enough to solve Britain's problems of supply. In response to the destroyers-bases deal, Hitler on September 6, 1940 removed the last restrictions on U-boat warfare against British ships and accepted the possibility that some American ships might accidentally be sunk. He even toyed with the idea of seizing some of the Atlantic islands, but Raeder warned him that the German navy was in no position to mount such an operation.

In an effort to give further assistance to Great Britain in her struggle against Nazi Germany, President Roosevelt in December 1940 proposed the idea of Lend-Lease. The existing neutrality legislation banned American ships from carrying trade to belligerents and forbade private investors lending money or extending credit to warring governments. The idea of Lend-Lease was to give aid at a time when Great Britain had nearly exhausted her funds and at a time when her need for munitions was growing hourly. British ships would still have to pick up the goods; only the "cash" part of the "cash and carry" policy was to be changed. To avoid the embarrassment of the war debt problem which had poisoned Anglo-American relations after World War I, no formal accounting was to be kept, but Britain was to return all that was still usable after the cessation of hostilities. This proposal, unlike the destroyers-bases deal, required Congressional approval, which took place in March 1941 after extended hearings. Once again Hitler did not declare war.

The change from the Neutrality Act to Lend-Lease was another step in President Roosevelt's "all aid short of war" policy. In order to see how American efforts could best be directed to the common cause, and also to satisfy himself that Britain really could hold out, the President sent a party of Navy, Army, and Air Corps representatives to England in August 1940 for "exploratory talks" with their opposite numbers in that country. These discussions led to plans for cooperation in the Atlantic war in the event of American participation, and both sides generally agreed that Japan was to be held off as long as possible. This conference was followed by another in Washington in late January 1941 which resulted in the "ABC-1 Staff Agreement" which spelled out, first, America's "short of war" contribution, second, the action to be taken by the United States in the event she was forced into the war. Fundamental to this document was the basic concept that in the event of war with Japan, England and the United States would devote their primary effort to defeating Germany first. Germany, because of her proximity, the achievements of her scientists, who might produce a decisive weapon, and her military accomplishments thus far, was considered more dangerous to Anglo-American interests and survival. This basic strategic decision was never changed during the war, even though it later became possible to operate offensively in both oceans at the same time. Also included were such matters as command relationships in the various areas of the war and the allocation of areas of responsibility both on land and at sea. Also it was agreed that in the near future the United States would take over part of the responsibility for convoys in the North Atlantic.

To prepare for these new American responsibilities, the planning divisions of the United States Navy went to work extending earlier plans, and Rear Admiral Richmond Kelly Turner, director of the War Plans Division, informed the Chief of Naval Operations that the United States would be prepared to undertake convoy operations from North America to Scotland on April 1, 1941. The naval forces operating in the Atlantic were reorganized into the more appropriate title of Atlantic Fleet rather than Patrol Force on February 1, and Rear Admiral Ernest J. King was appointed its commander in chief and promoted to the grade of admiral. American naval bases were set up in England, one at Gare Loch in the Clyde River and one at Loch Ryan at the entrance to the Firth of Clyde; Londonderry and Lough Erne in Northern Ireland were also available in the event of war. By mid-June, the plans for American escort of convoys were changed. Instead of covering the whole route from North America to Scotland, the United States Navy was to concentrate on the segment from Argentia, Newfoundland, to Iceland. At Iceland, where the change of operational command (CHOP) would occur, British escorts would take over.

THE BATTLE OF THE ATLANTIC: JUNE 1940–JUNE 1941

Secure in his new U-boat bases in France, Admiral Doenitz intensified his attack on British shipping almost immediately after the fall of France. British ship losses mounted rapidly, with 638 ships sunk between June 1, 1940 and the end of the year. More than 700 British ships were sunk during the first six months of the following year. During these 13 months, when the average losses were 3.4 ships a day, the situation grew desperate from the British point of view. Over 5,700,000 tons of shipping were on the bottom. This was the most serious period of the entire war as far as British merchant shipping was concerned. The geographic situation favored the Germans. Not only did his French bases enable Admiral Doenitz to keep his U-boats on station longer than formerly, but Ireland's policy of neutrality denied to the British the air and naval bases in southern Ireland which were needed to keep adequate patrols over the entrance to the English Channel. All shipping to the British Isles had to be routed north of Ireland, enabling Doenitz to concentrate his U-boats in comparatively narrow passages. The Coastal Air Command, which operated under the tactical control of the Royal Air Force, made extensive patrols over these northern approach areas, attacking submarines from the air and flying air cover over entering and departing convoys, but still the losses mounted. Many expedients were adopted by the Admiralty. U-boat decoy ships ("Q-ships") were attempted with indifferent success. These ships, which had been used in World War I with some degree of effectiveness, looked like ordinary merchantmen, but when a submarine surfaced to attack, the crew would strip off gun covers and attack the U-boat. The use of these ships in World War II was rendered impracticable by the very tactics forced on the U-boats, that of attacking submerged, for these decoy ships could withstand a torpedo hit no better than the merchantmen they seemed to be, and they seldom had an opportunity to use their guns. A scheme which met with more success was to catapult expendable aircraft from merchant ships in outgoing convoys. These planes were intended primarily to counter attacks by Focke-Wulfe bombers operating from bases in Norway. This device proved fairly successful and was widely used in the early months of 1941.

By January of that year losses at sea, the crowding of docking facilities in the Clyde and the Mersey, and German air attacks on dockyard facilities in these and other areas had brought the arrival of laden cargo ships at British ports to less than half of what they had been in January 1940. Ships were being lost faster than new ones could be built to replace them. The British had acquired a large number of vessels from the Norwegian, Danish, and Dutch merchant marines, but were still falling far behind in the number of available bottoms. Even the fact that a ship got in with a cargo was not always an unmixed blessing, for the ship might not be available for another voyage without extensive repairs. By March 1941 nearly 1,700,000 tons of shipping were immobilized awaiting the attention of the repair facilities.

A considerable part of the success of the U-boat against shipping resulted from the Nazi wolf pack operations. Under this system U-boats, sometimes as many as 20 but more frequently from ten to 15, would be spread out across the likely shipping lanes. When a U-boat made contact on a convoy it would not attack at once but would report the contact, its size, composition, course and speed to Admiral Doenitz in his headquarters at Lorient. He would then direct the other members of the pack to a rendezvous with the convoy. In the meantime, the U-boat that had made the contact would shadow the convoy at extreme visual range. When night fell and the other U-boats had arrived on the scene, Doenitz would shift tactical command to the senior officer present. The wolf pack would then make a concerted attack, dive to escape detection, and attack again when things had quieted down. Unless the convoy managed to escape in darkness or bad weather, the wolf pack might shadow for several days on end, attacking each night under cover of darkness.

The U-boat wolf pack had several advantages from the German point of view. First, it helped to defeat the British efforts at evasive routing of convoys, for the spreading out of the U-boats meant that they covered a wide front and that they could quickly be massed where needed. The large size of the packs often rendered the escort helpless, for frequently there were more U-boats present than there were escorts, and the new U-boats then coming into service had a small enough turning circle to cut inside the larger escorts and enough speed on the surface to outrun the slower ones.

THE UNITED STATES WAGES UNDECLARED WAR IN THE ATLANTIC

Increasing effectiveness of air and sea attacks on U-boats in the Western Approaches area of Great Britain caused Admiral Doenitz to shift his U-boats out into the Atlantic. At the same time, in searching for ways of extending their radius of operation and for more reliable weather information, the Germans began landing weather observation parties on Greenland. The British earlier had found it necessary to assume the defense of Iceland in order to keep it from German hands. Now, with this newer threat, the United States moved to develop bases in Greenland and incidentally to drive the Germans out. In April 1941 President Roosevelt informed Churchill that the United States would extend its security patrol zone to the waters west of longitude 26 degrees west, which is bounded by a line extending from the east coast of Greenland, passing near the western tip of Iceland and south through the Azores. Since a week earlier a wolf pack had attacked a British convoy at 28 degrees west longitude, approximately a hundred miles within this zone, the new United States patrol area included waters the Nazis had set aside as hunting grounds. Thus incidents involving United States ships and German submarines became highly probable.

Three events of May 1941 brought about a further bold American step despite dangers of involvement in the war. First was the sinking of the neutral Egyptian ship *Zamzam* carrying about 150 American passengers. The second was the sinking in late May of the South Africa-bound American freighter *Robin Moor* by a U-boat which left without making any provisions for the safety of the crew. The third was the appearance of the *Bismarck,* which shocked American as well as British public opinion by her sinking of the *Hood.* On May 27, the very day the *Bismarck* was sunk, President Roosevelt declared an Unlimited National Emergency and announced to the country that more vigorous steps would be taken to keep the Germans from American waters.

The United States Navy found itself as ill prepared for antisubmarine war as the British had been in 1939. Admiral King has observed that the people in the Bureau of Ships had difficulty in interesting themselves in anything smaller than a destroyer of about 2,000 tons. The obvious need was for a smaller ship, especially designed for convoy work, which could be built more rapidly than destroyers at lower cost. While in many ways a destroyer is an ideal escort ship, it possesses many features not needed for that work but which are useful only when the destroyer is operating with the fleet. Speeds in excess of 25 knots are not required in escorting a 10-knot convoy. A destroyer is intended to be able to tackle anything afloat, under water, or in the air. Her high speed and offensive power are largely wasted in escort of convoy work. The answer was found in the destroyer escort, a smaller version of the destroyer, slower and especially designed for antisubmarine work. One of the great bottlenecks in building destroyers is the fitting of blades to the high speed turbines. This process has always resisted mass production, and although it was much speeded up during the war, it barely kept pace with the need for fleet ships. A serviceable substitute was found in the railroad diesel engine, and these were immediately put into mass pro-

duction for use in destroyer escorts. The British and Canadian navies began building these vessels at the rate of about eight a month, and in July 1941 the American shipyards started construction of them for the British at the rate of ten a month.

The German invasion of Russia in June 1941 added considerably to the problems of supply, for the Russians were also afforded Lend-Lease aid and had few bottoms in which to transport the goods. To discuss this problem and others, Prime Minister Winston Churchill met with President Roosevelt at Argentia, Newfoundland in August. The Prime Minister traveled to the meeting on the *Prince of Wales,* and the President, announcing that he was taking a fishing trip, voyaged on the Presidential Yacht *Potomac* to a rendezvous off Martha's Vineyard where he transferred to the *Augusta* for the remainder of the journey to Argentia, while the *Potomac* loafed along in the waters of New England to keep up the impression that the President was still aboard. This meeting enabled the Chiefs of Staff of the two countries to discuss plans for American escort of convoys and it produced the Atlantic Charter, a statement of the war aims of England and the United States.

For a considerable period of time American warships on Atlantic patrol had broadcast to the British the position of U-boats sighted although the Americans had refrained from attacking. After Admiral King's operation order describing such raiders as "potentially hostile," there was some doubt as to what course of action the Navy should take if it should sight a U-boat in the American zone of responsibility. That question was answered by the affair of the *Greer.* The United States destroyer *Greer,* proceeding on an independent mission to Iceland, was about 200 miles southwest of her destination when on September 4, 1941 she received a signal from a British plane that a U-boat was about ten miles ahead of her. The *Greer* went to general quarters and soon made sound contact with the submarine, keeping the contact for over three hours but not attacking. At length, harried by this and by depth charges dropped by the British patrol plane, the submarine turned and fired a torpedo at the *Greer,* which dodged and then counterattacked with depth charges. Thus the first shots were exchanged in the undeclared war between German and American naval forces. Although neither side was hurt, each burned with virtuous indignation. President Roosevelt issued a statement declaring, "From now on, if German or Italian vessels of war enter the waters the protection of which is necessary for American defense, they do so at their own risk."

The first convoy to sail under American protection was HX 150 bound from Halifax to the United Kingdom, consisting of 50 merchant ships. It was escorted from a point south of Argentia to a MOMP south of Iceland by the American destroyers *Ericsson, Eberle, Upshur, Ellis,* and *Dallas* with Captain Morton L. Deyo USN as escort commander. Although not attacked by U-boats, the convoy had an eventful voyage, suffering numerous breakdowns and losing one ship through fire.

In sharp contrast, convoy SC 48 fared badly from submarines on its voyage from Sydney, Nova Scotia, to the United Kingdom. About 400 miles south of Iceland, on October 16, this convoy ran into a wolf pack. Reinforcements to the escort in the form of five American destroyers, including the *Kearny,* a British destroyer, and a Free French corvette arrived. Because of close-in screening stations the U-boats were able to make six successful torpedo attacks from outside the screen the night the reinforcements joined. A brilliantly burning torpedoed ship silhouetted the *Kearny,* enabling a U-boat to put a torpedo into her. Excellent damage control kept her afloat, and she made Iceland under her own power. First blood in this undeclared war thus went to the Germans. Second blood occurred when the American four-stacker *Reuben James* was torpedoed about 600 miles west of Iceland on October 31. The ship sank in about five minutes, the first American naval vessel to be lost in the war.

The events just recounted led to two important changes in the American Neutrality Act. Passed in mid-November, these amendments allowed for the arming of merchant vessels and for their travel in the war zone. Now Lend-Lease goods could be carried to England in American ships. When we consider all these events, it is apparent that two months before the Japanese attack on Pearl Harbor, the United States was to all intents and purposes at war with Germany in the Atlantic, actually contributing more to the Allied cause at that time than she was able to do for some months after she officially entered the war.

THE UNITED STATES ENTERS THE WAR

The German government declared war on the United States on December 11, 1941, four days after the attack on Pearl Harbor. Italy followed suit the same day, and the Congress of the United States acknowledged the existence of a state of war with those two countries. This declaration, at least as far as the Atlantic was concerned, merely recognized the state of affairs as it then existed. The United States was already exerting herself to her full capacity in the Atlantic. It would take time before the American ships and planes then in production could have much impact on the Atlantic war. In fact, the United States had to reduce her aid materially in order to defend her own coasts and coastal shipping. To Admiral Doenitz, the situation changed drastically. Gone were the restrictions on attacking American ships. Hitler and Raeder decided the day after war was declared that they would attack American coastal shipping. This would have two important effects: first, it would cut down the flow of raw materials, especially oil, to the industrial eastern United States, and, second, it would spread the Allied escort ships even thinner by ultimately forcing a convoy system all the way from ports in the Gulf of Mexico, around the tip of Florida, up the east coast of the United States, and then across the North Atlantic to Britain. Doenitz was unable to institute this attack for a month however because of the losses he had been suffering in the Bay of Biscay in November and December at the hands of the Royal Navy. This delay gave the United States opportunity to mine or net principal harbor entrances, such as Chesapeake Bay, but it did not help the escort problem greatly. Sufficient escorts were simply not yet available.

On hearing the news of the raid on Pearl Harbor, Prime Minister Churchill visited Washington together with his Chiefs of Staff to work out with President Roosevelt and the American Chiefs of Staff the strategic direction of the war. Churchill recognized that American aid to Britain would necessarily be cut back for the time being as the United States began to grapple with her new responsibilities in the war. He recognized however the potential power of the New World and was confident of victory. This confidence is shown by the agenda of the Washington conference, which included preliminary plans for Operation Torch (the invasion of North Africa) and Operation Overlord (the invasion of Normandy).

Top military direction of the war was organized in the Washington meeting. The British representatives—the First Sea Lord, Admiral Sir Dudley Pound; the Chief of the Air Staff, Air Chief-Marshal Sir Charles Portal; and the former Chief of the Imperial General Staff, Field Marshal Sir John Dill— sat down with General George C. Marshall, U. S. Army Chief of Staff; General Henry H. Arnold, Chief of Staff of the Air Corps; and the newly appointed Chief of Naval Operations, Admiral Ernest J. King. These men, or their successors on the British side, and with the addition of Admiral William D. Leahy, Chief of Staff to the President, on the American side, constituted the Combined Chiefs of Staff. Although this first meeting was largely exploratory, and the first official meeting of the Combined Chiefs was not held until late January, this one laid the groundwork. On the shoulders of these men rested the burden of the military direction of global war.

Direction of the American effort in the war fell to the Joint Chiefs of Staff—the four top American military men, Leahy, Marshall, Arnold, and King. To King in particular the earliest burden fell, since it was at sea that

America could first challenge the Axis and first was challenged.

To meet these new threats, the United States Navy was extensively reorganized in the early months of 1942. King relieved Stark as Chief of Naval Operations in December 1941. Admiral Chester W. Nimitz relieved Admiral Husband E. Kimmel as Commander in Chief of the Pacific Fleet in the same month. King's old job as Commander in Chief of the Atlantic Fleet was taken over by Admiral Royal E. Ingersoll. In March 1942, because of confusion as to the division of function of the offices of the Chief of Naval Operations and that of the Commander in Chief, U. S. Fleet, the two offices were both vested in Admiral King, who became the first and only man ever to hold both titles. Also, because the Naval District organizations were primarily administrative commands, King found it desirable to set up operational commands known as Sea Frontiers which would conduct defensive operations in the waters they included. These commands were the Eastern Sea Frontier in the Atlantic, the Caribbean Sea Frontier, the Gulf Sea Frontier, the Panama Sea Frontier at the approaches to the canal, and the Western, Northwestern, and Hawaiian Sea Frontiers in the Pacific.

Since there were no escorts available for coastal convoys in the opening months of the war, such shipping during this time was run by leap-frogging along the coast during daylight hours and putting into harbor overnight. This system was workable off the northeastern part of the United States, where harbors are available about every 120 miles from Portland, Maine, down to Cape Hatteras; but farther south it was necessary to set up net-protected bases. No one pretended that this was a satisfactory solution. The U-boats, led by six of Doenitz's ace commanders and refueling from U-boat "milch cows," grew bold under this apparent immunity from attack and sank 82 merchant ships in the first four months of 1942 in the coastal area between the northern border of Florida and the northern tip of Maine. To assist in cutting down this slaughter, the British, reversing the deal by which they acquired 50 over-age destroyers, in February offered 24 of their best antisubmarine trawlers and ten corvettes with the latest asdic equipment aboard. The United States accepted this offer eagerly and gradually was able to institute a coastal convoy system. Until these convoys became effective, burning and sinking tankers and freighters were a common spectacle to resorters at the Florida beaches. Since the U-boats made a practice of silhouetting a passing ship against the glow of shore lights, local naval commanders sought to establish a "dim-out" of the bright lights of coastal cities; fearing loss of tourist trade, chambers of commerce resisted this idea until orders from the highest military authorities were stringently enforced.

As more escorting vessels were delivered to the American fleet, it became possible to plan an interlocking convoy system by which relays of escorts would cover merchant ships on their voyages. These escorts were at first concentrated in the dangerous waters between Cape Hatteras and Key West and later were extended northwards. By the end of May 1942 it was possible for a vessel to have some sort of coverage from Key West to Halifax and thence across the Atlantic. The escort doctrine as established by the United States at this time gives good indication of the actual practice:

While it is recognized that the strength of escorts may have to be meager, it should be borne in mind that effective convoying depends upon the escorts being in sufficient strength to permit their taking the offensive against attacking submarines, without their withdrawal for this purpose resulting in unduly exposing the convoy to other submarines while they are on this mission. Any protection less than this simply results in the convoy's becoming a convenient target for submarines. . . .

As a result of experience in the North Atlantic it now appears that the minimum strength which will afford reasonable protection is five escorts per convoy of 40 to 50 ships, of which all [the escorts] should make 18 knots (the maximum at which sound gear is usable), and be equipped with sound and depth charges, and two should be destroyers to permit ranging to the flanks and astern and rejoining without waste of time.[3]

Coastal convoy was not the whole answer to the U-boat threat off the eastern shore of the United States. Air and sea patrols played an important part. Operating out of east coast bases as well as the island bases acquired in the destroyer deal, patrol bombers spotted many submarines lying in wait for shipping. The direction of these air patrols brought to light a fundamental difference in command principles between Admiral King and General Marshall. The decision of this controversy was of considerable importance in the conduct of the war. General Marshall favored the point of view adopted by the British, whose Coastal Air Command operated under the tactical direction of the Royal Air Force but in close cooperation with the Royal Navy. Marshall wanted all land-based air, whether engaged in antisubmarine operations or not, to operate under army command. Admiral King believed that the Navy should have free use of any weapon it needed, and since antisubmarine work was a naval task, the planes should be under the operational control of the Navy. He argued, "that naval personnel are trained and skilled in things that have to do with the sea, and that consequently, 'economy of effort' will best be obtained by making full use of naval units and naval personnel in the activities in which they are perforce the most available and the most competent."[4] At length General Marshall, disturbed by the mounting shipping losses on the East Coast, acquiesced in the navy view and allocated a fair proportion of land-based planes to the Navy for antisubmarine work.

With the advent of the convoy system throughout the area of the Eastern Sea Frontier, from Jacksonville to Maine, Admiral Doenitz moved his U-boat operational area to the Caribbean and the Gulf of Mexico. Once again losses mounted, and once again the resources of the American navy were extended to the breaking point.

[3] As quoted in Samuel Eliot Morison, *History of*

United States Naval Operations in World War II (Boston, 1948), I, 256.

[4] Fleet Admiral Ernest J. King USN and Walter Muir Whitehill, *Fleet Admiral King, A Naval Record* (New York, 1952), 454.

The building of escorts was temporarily set back during this period by allocation of materials and building yard capacity to the construction of landing craft for Operation Sledgehammer, an amphibious assault on Brest or Cherbourg in late 1942 which both Prime Minister Churchill and President Roosevelt favored as a means of keeping a promise for a "second front" to relieve the pressure on Russia. These plans were eventually scrapped in favor of Operation Torch, the landing in North Africa. The escort program suffered severely in the meantime.

A partial answer to the shortage of escorts was tried from the earliest days of the war— the practice of arming merchant ships. Although the guns installed were of little use against submarines, they did often prove effective against aircraft attacks in European waters. To man these guns the navy assigned a group of men to sail in each merchant ship so armed. These naval gun crews were called the Armed Guard. Usually an ensign or lieutenant (junior grade) of the Naval Reserve was in command. Armed Guard was an unpopular duty both from the point of view of the danger involved and from the fact that friction often developed between the naval personnel and the merchant seamen. As time went on, each side grew to respect the other; with common danger grew common understanding.

No story of the Battle of the Atlantic can be called complete without at least a glimpse of a convoy in its hour of trial. Although the Halifax-United Kingdom route was most heavily traveled and suffered the most over-all losses, for sheer horror nothing can match the North Russian route, exposed as it was not only to U-boats but also to the *Luftwaffe* and the surviving ships of the German surface navy, including the mighty *Tirpitz*, a newer and better version of the *Bismarck*.

PQ 17

The Murmansk Run. These three words can still evoke a chill in the hearts of the men who successfully completed the passage.

It was opened from Scotland to Iceland to Murmansk and other North Russian ports to provide Lend-Lease assistance to Russia in sufficient quantity to aid her in the war. Russian rail facilities to the Persian Gulf were incapable of handling adequate amounts of supplies brought through that route. A trickle of supplies carried in Russian ships across the Pacific arrived at the front after the long trip on the Trans-Siberian Railway. But only Murmansk and Archangel offered the hope of significantly increasing the flow of munitions and supplies. To get to these ports, Allied ships had to pass through some of the most dangerous waters in the world, from Iceland to North Cape, not far from the German bases at Trondheim and Narvik, thence into the Barents Sea to their destinations. Submarines infested the route; German reconnaissance aircraft operating out of occupied Norway flew regular patrols that were backed up with fighters and bombers, and lurking in reserve for the final punch were the German surface units based in Norwegian ports and fiords.

Convoy PQ 17 sailed from Reykjavik, Iceland on June 27, 1942; destination, Archangel. The experiences of PQ 16 the previous month led everyone to believe that the going would be rough. It was. The convoy consisted of 33 merchantmen, three rescue vessels and a fleet oiler. The escort consisted of six destroyers, two antiaircraft ships, two submarines, and 11 trawlers, minesweepers, and corvettes. In addition there was a support force consisting of four cruisers, H.M.S. *London*, flagship, H.M.S. *Norfolk*, U.S.S. *Wichita*, and U.S.S. *Tuscaloosa*. Screening the support force were two American and one British destroyer and six corvettes. A covering force comprising H.M.S. *Duke of York*, U.S.S. *Washington*, H.M. Carrier *Victorious*, H.M. heavy cruiser *Cumberland*, H.M. light cruisers *Nigeria* and *Manchester*, two American destroyers, and six to nine British destroyers and corvettes, operated in the waters of the North Sea to deal with the German battleship *Tirpitz*, sister ship of the *Bismarck*, in the event she should enter the game.

Almost at once Convoy PQ 17 encountered

difficulties. One freighter ran aground in the Strait of Denmark and another was so damaged by ice that it had to turn back. On July 1, the convoy was spotted by German reconnaissance planes and the next day an attack by six U-boats was driven off by destroyers. The first ship loss to the Germans occurred on July 4, when the merchant ship *Christopher Newport* was hit by an aerial torpedo. A second ship was sunk the afternoon of the same day. Then came dreadful news. The battleship *Tirpitz,* the pocket battleship *Scheer,* the heavy cruiser *Hipper,* and several destroyers were at sea. The support force was withdrawn to confuse the enemy and the convoy was ordered to disperse. At this time they had passed North Cape; there was nothing to do but go on. Attacks from aircraft and U-boats intensified. At length, out of the 33 merchant ships that had left Iceland, 11 limped into Archangel and Molotovsk. Instead of being greeted with cheers, they were received with silence and resentment at the puny effort made by the Allies to aid Russia. It was only British and American propaganda that 33 ships had left Iceland.

At most perhaps 15 had sailed. Such were the relations between the Allies in 1942.

THE TIDE BEGINS TO TURN

The year 1942 was the height of the U-boat war in the Atlantic, and at its end the Allies were gradually winning. In April of that year, merchant ship construction at last passed the number of losses. Except for the month of November 1942, losses never again exceeded replacement. The Battle of the Atlantic continued; ships were still lost, but the means to win the war were assured of passage across the Atlantic. The downward curve in the effectiveness of the U-boat had begun, even though, as we shall see in a later chapter, some of the best means for its destruction had not yet been put into full or even partial operation. The year 1942 was, as Winston Churchill called it, "the end of the beginning." Henceforward the offensive strength of the United States could begin to make itself felt.

37

The Period

of Japanese Expansion

JAPAN STARTED DOWN THE road to World War II with the "Manchurian incident" of September 1931. Creating a pretext in an explosion on the Japanese-controlled railway, she launched a carefully prepared invasion that overran the country in three or four months. The seizure of Manchuria, bordering on Japanese-controlled Korea, was not merely a logical step in Japanese expansion. It was also a test of the world's reaction to aggression.

The American response was prompt. Henry Stimson, Secretary of State in the expiring Hoover administration, not only offered full American cooperation with the League of Nations in dealing with the affair but directly reminded Japan of her treaty obligations and declared that the United States would not recognize any situation in Manchuria brought about by force and in contravention of treaties. However, the League refused to support the firm stand of the United States, with the result that a year later Japan announced the creation of the puppet state of Manchukuo. There remained only the threat of interference by Russia,

which also had ambitions in Asia. This danger the Japanese met on November 25, 1936, when they signed the anti-Comintern pact with Germany, to which Italy adhered a year later.

By 1936 Japan was passing into the control of military extremists. They removed by assassination those moderate statesmen who objected to a policy of militarism and aggression. When the army was fully prepared, Japanese troops clashed with the Chinese at an outpost on Marco Polo Bridge near Peiping (Peking) and the invasion of China began.

The Japanese attempt to conquer China involved wholesale violations of the rights of Western powers. The United States was most directly affected by the sinking in late 1937 of the gunboat U.S.S. *Panay* in the Yangtze River by Japanese dive bombers. Although the Japanese government asserted (perhaps correctly) that the attack was a mistake made by over-enthusiastic pilots, circumstances seemed at the time to indicate that it was deliberate. But the United States was content to accept Japanese apologies and an offer of compensation, for war in 1937 was a considerably more sobering prospect than in 1898 when the *Maine* was sunk.

OIL AND APPEASEMENT

American public opinion condemned Japanese aggression, and the United States extended economic aid to China. Though Americans were little disposed to go to war in an area where the United States had slight direct interest, President Roosevelt refrained, in order not to deprive China of supplies, from invoking the 1937 Neutrality Act in the Sino-Japanese struggle. However this abstention worked both ways, for the Japanese too were receiving essential war materials from the United States. In July 1939 Secretary of State Cordell Hull gave the Japanese the necessary six months notice for the abrogation of the commercial treaty of 1911, thereby clearing the way for an embargo on munitions. This move and the announcement the next month of the Russo-German non-aggression pact had a temporarily sobering effect upon the Japanese. Moreover, Japan was rapidly "bogging down" in the Chinese hinterland, and her resources were being severely strained. Obviously the conquest of the continent was going to be difficult unless China could somehow be isolated from outside aid.

At this point the outbreak of the European war eased Japan's difficulties and presented new opportunities. The fall of France and of the Netherlands in the spring of 1940 left Indo-China and the Netherlands East Indies "orphaned" colonies and so weakened Britain's position that she consented in July to the closing of the Burma Road. The Imperial Japanese Navy, which had never been enthusiastic about the army's adventure on the mainland, now saw an opportunity for expansion into the East Indies area in order to obtain the oil, tin, rubber, and quinine which were obtainable nowhere else in the Far East. Japan had already worked her way south along the China coast and early in 1939 had occupied Hainan, an excellent base for a further move south. Shortly after the

fall of France, Japan made a series of demands upon the Vichy-controlled government of Indo-China, which yielded to Japanese occupation of the northern part of the country. In September 1940 Japan concluded with the Axis powers an alliance that was an obvious warning to the United States not to interfere in either Europe or Asia.

Since the termination in January 1940 of the old treaty of commerce, the United States had been free to embargo the shipment of strategic materials to Japan. American public opinion had long been overwhelmingly in favor of such a move, but the Roosevelt administration, warned by Ambassador Grew in Japan that abrupt termination of trade with the United States might cause the Japanese to invade the Netherlands East Indies, delayed action in the vain hope that supplying materials for aggression would somehow prevent aggression. In July 1940 Congress passed an act "for the strengthening of national defense" which provided for the licensing of exports. This stopped the sale of aircraft and aviation gasoline to Japan, but it was not till autumn that the export of iron and steel was cut off, and the State Department continued to license the export of oil until July 1941.

PLANNING FOR WAR

As it became apparent that Japan was preparing to move south, the United States attempted to concert plans with its potential allies. The first agreement of consequence was reached at the Washington Conference of January-March 1941, where it was agreed that if the United States and Britain should find themselves at war with Germany and Japan, the European Theater would be regarded as primary and that the Pacific Theater was to be the responsibility of the United States. At the Singapore Conference of April 1941, the divergence of American and British strategic thinking presented insuperable difficulties. British strategy centered on the defense of Singapore. The United States expected its small Asiatic Fleet to fall back southward to the Netherlands

Indies should it be forced to abandon the Philippines, but American strategists were unwilling to divert strength from the Pacific Fleet for defense of the Far East. To the Americans an offensive against the Marshall Islands seemed the best way to relieve pressure on Singapore. So the conference ended with only a recommendation for mutual support against aggression.

The Japanese advance in Indo-China was, in American eyes, the crucial issue. When on July 25, 1941, the Japanese announced that the Vichy government had admitted them to a joint protectorate of Indo-China—meaning that Vichy had surrendered the colony—the United States countered by freezing all Japanese assets in the United States, thus at long last shutting off the supply of oil. This move precipitated the final crisis. Japan had to have oil or see her military machine grind to a halt. In October the Konoye government fell, and a military government headed by General Tojo took over. The United States was already engaged in an undeclared war with Japan's ally Germany, and Roosevelt had already issued his "shoot on sight" order to the Atlantic Fleet. In November a special Japanese envoy, Saburo Kurusu, arrived in the United States to assist Ambassador Nomura in negotiations looking toward a resumption of the flow of oil. These negotiations led directly to Pearl Harbor.

UNITED STATES PREPARATIONS

The approach of war in the Pacific found the United States preparing but still unprepared. In 1938, in accordance with a directive of Congress, a board headed by Rear Admiral A. J. Hepburn had made a study of United States bases in the Pacific and had recommended an extensive program of development. Except for the fortification of Guam, most of the board's recommendations were adopted, and work was under way when war broke out.

It had long been the practice to keep the greater part of the United States Fleet in the Pacific, based on the West Coast. But after maneuvers in the spring of 1940 the fleet remained at Pearl Harbor with the hope of deterring Japan from further aggressive moves. After the outbreak of war in Europe there had been a constantly increasing need for naval forces in the Atlantic. In May 1941, because of the necessity for convoying Lend-Lease goods, Admiral Harold R. Stark, Chief of Naval Operations, transferred from the Pacific to the Atlantic three battleships, the carrier *Yorktown,* four light cruisers, and two squadrons of destroyers.

In recognition of the realities of the situation, at the beginning of February 1941 the Atlantic Squadron, as we have seen, was made the Atlantic Fleet, while the fleet at Pearl Harbor became the Pacific Fleet. The small American force in the Far East, commanded by Admiral Thomas C. Hart, was for purposes of international prestige designated the United States Asiatic Fleet. It was provided that one of these three fleet commanders should also act as Commander in Chief United States Fleet. At the time of the attack on Pearl Harbor Rear Admiral Husband E. Kimmel was Commander in Chief both of the Pacific Fleet and of the United States Fleet.

In the Atlantic the Axis powers had not a single operational carrier, and the greater part of the British fleet was concentrated against the comparatively small German navy. In the Pacific the United States faced the formidable Japanese navy practically alone. Yet at the time of the Pearl Harbor attack the United States Fleet was fairly evenly divided between the two oceans, with nine battleships in the Pacific and eight in the Atlantic, three carriers in the Pacific and four in the Atlantic. There were more cruisers in the Pacific but more destroyers in the Atlantic. True, the Atlantic Fleet lacked sufficient patrol craft and convoy escorts, but in the Pacific, even before the losses of Pearl Harbor, the fleet was inferior to the Japanese in every category, particularly in carriers, of which Japan had ten. The British had undertaken to reinforce Singapore, but the crisis in the Far East coincided with a desperate situation in the Mediterranean, where losses and damage had brought their forces to a low point. After considerable hesitation the Admiralty consented to send the new battleship *Prince of Wales* to join the battle cruiser *Repulse* at Singapore with the hope that the presence of two capital ships would have a deterrent effect upon the Japanese. The new aircraft carrier *Indomitable* was to have joined these two vessels, but during her shakedown cruise in the West Indies she was damaged by grounding in early November. The *Victorious* might have been sent, but the loss of the *Ark Royal* and the threat of the *Tirpitz* combined to convince the Admiralty that no carriers could be spared from the European theater. Thus left without carrier support, the only two Allied capital ships in the Far East were destined to be sunk within a few days of the outbreak of war. The Dutch had nothing heavier than light cruisers in the East. America's allies, it was clear, could do little to redress the unfavorable balance of power in the Pacific.[1]

The United States Pacific Fleet, besides being inferior in numbers, was unprepared for war. Antiaircraft armament was short in quantity and quality. The American 1.1-inch gun proved so unsatisfactory that the Navy had to turn to the foreign-designed Bofors and Oerlikon guns. Crews included many reservists with insufficient training. There was a serious lack of fleet auxiliaries. Planes were few and largely obsolete.

In the Far East the situation was even more grave. With Japanese on Formosa less than 300 miles to the north, in Hainan and Indo-China to the west, and in the Marianas and the Carolines to the east, the Philippines were almost surrounded. In July 1941 General MacArthur, then Field Marshal of the Philippine Army, was made Commanding General of United States Army Forces Far East. Thereafter there was a rapid build-up in the Philippines both of air and of ground forces, designed to enable the islands to defend themselves by the spring of 1942.

In event of war with Japan, it had long been planned for the tiny U. S. Asiatic Fleet to fall back to the Malay Barrier, for it could hardly expect to offer any significant opposition. But the increase of U. S. Army air strength gave hope that before long Luzon might be sufficiently secure to permit the fleet to continue operations from Manila. Admiral Hart suggested such a plan to the Navy Department, and on December 5 Admiral Tom Phillips RN arrived to discuss with the American commanders the possibility of basing British vessels there too. While the discussions were going on reports came of Japanese movements toward Malaya, whereupon Admiral Phillips left hurriedly for Singapore.

FINAL NEGOTIATIONS

There was never any real chance of success in the negotiations between the United States and Japan in the autumn of 1941. The United States was in no mood to recognize Japan's conquests in China or to condone further aggression. The militarists who

---

[1] As may be seen from the following table, total Allied forces in the Pacific were not greatly inferior to the Japanese in numbers except in the carrier category, which was the most important. Furthermore the Allies were divided, had serious logistic problems, and were inferior to the Japanese in training and readiness. The losses at Pearl Harbor and the sinking of the *Prince of Wales* and *Repulse* of course altered the balance completely.

ALLIED AND JAPANESE FORCES IN THE PACIFIC AND FAR EAST *

	Capital Ships:	Carriers:	Heavy Cruisers:	Light Cruisers:	Destroyers:	Submarines:
British Empire	2	—	1	7	13	—
United States	9	3	13	11	80	56
Dutch	—	—	—	3	7	13
Free French	—	—	—	1	—	—
Total Allied	11	3	14	22	100	69
Japanese	10	10	18	18	113	63

* From Capt. S. W. Roskill RN, *The War at Sea, 1939-1945*, I, (London, 1954), 560.

controlled Japan had no intention of abandoning their program of expansion and even less of surrendering any of their gains. However both sides wanted a little more time, and so the talks continued.

Throughout these negotiations the Americans enjoyed the remarkable advantage of being able to read the Japanese diplomatic correspondence, for the United States had succeeded in constructing machines for deciphering the Japanese "Purple Code" and had even given one to the British. As a result, Washington knew that the Japanese Foreign Office had set the latter part of November as a deadline for the conclusion of the talks, after which "things are automatically going to happen." Washington also knew that the Japanese were receiving information regarding the movements of the vessels of the Pacific Fleet and their berthing in Pearl Harbor, and that Japan was calling for more minute and more frequent reports in the late fall of 1941.

On November 26 the United States handed the Japanese a note that brought the negotiations to a crisis. Technically it was not an ultimatum, but rather a strong reiteration of American principles, including the demand that Japan evacuate China and support the regime of Chiang Kai-shek. While these demands were only just, it could scarcely have been expected that Japan would accept them. Deciphering of Japanese messages at once indicated that the Japanese regarded the American note as ending the conversations, though their ambassadors were to continue the pretense of negotiating "to prevent the United States from becoming unduly suspicious." On November 27 the Navy Department sent to Pearl Harbor a "war warning" indicating that the Department expected a Japanese move against the Philippines, Malaya, or Borneo. Apparently American officials were so hypnotized by Japan's obvious preparations to move southward that they overlooked her capability of striking in another direction as well.

By December 6 it was known in Washington that the Japanese were sending to their Washington embassy a message for the United States State Department breaking off diplomatic relations. Students of history were aware that in times past Japan had followed up such messages with a surprise attack on the opposing fleet, followed by a declaration of war. It was known too that Japanese diplomats in London, Hong Kong, Singapore, Batavia, Manila, and Washington were burning their secret documents and codes—usually done only when war is imminent. Thus by Saturday afternoon there was every reason to believe that war with Japan was only hours away. Then between 0400 and 0600 on Sunday, December 7, the Navy Department deciphered instructions to the Japanese ambassadors to deliver their message at 1 PM. One o'clock in the afternoon in Washington would be seven-thirty in the morning at Pearl Harbor.

THE ATTACK ON PEARL HARBOR

Admiral Yamamoto, Commander in Chief of the Japanese Combined Fleet, had as early as January 1941 proposed an attack on Pearl Harbor. Details had been worked out in the early fall, and the final decision to go to war was made at an Imperial Conference on December 1. Next day the date for the attack, already tentatively set for December 8 (east longitude date), was approved.

Essentially the decision was a gamble on an Axis victory in Europe, for few Japanese had any illusions about the outcome of the war should the United States be able to apply its entire strength to the Pacific. However, in the fall of 1941 Rommel was threatening Egypt and the German armies were near Moscow. It seemed likely that the United States would be forced to let the Pacific go more or less by default while it faced the greater danger of an Axis triumphant in Europe. In the meantime the Japanese would overrun Southeast Asia and would protect it and Japan by a defensive perimeter so strong that the United States would have to accept the *fait accompli*.

The attacking force, already at sea when the Imperial Council made its decision, consisted of six carriers—the *Akagi, Kaga, Soryu,*

Hiryu, Shokaku, and *Zuikaku*—escorted by two battleships, the *Hiei* and *Kirishima,* three cruisers, and nine destroyers. Its course lay well to the north, between Midway and the Aleutians, both to avoid American air patrols and to decrease the chance of meeting merchant shipping. Three submarines patrolled 200 miles in advance. Twenty-seven submarines, of which 11 carried planes and five carried midget submarines to penetrate Pearl Harbor, had gone ahead earlier.[2]

The day before the attack the Japanese carriers received last minute information about the ships in Pearl Harbor. The *Enterprise* and *Lexington* were at sea, much to the regret of the Japanese Air Operations Officer, who said he would rather sink the two carriers than all eight battleships,[3] but Vice Admiral Chuichi Nagumo, the task force commander, decided to launch the attack as planned. At 0530 on the 7th[4] two cruisers catapulted float planes for a preliminary reconnaissance. Forty-five minutes later from a position 230 miles north of Oahu, Nagumo began launching his first wave of 183 attack planes. From the Honolulu radio station, on which he was homing, the strike commander received a helpful report of the weather over Pearl Harbor.

At Pearl Harbor there was no suspicion of the death and destruction that were on the way. The warning of November 27 had indicated only that Washington expected Japan to make "an aggressive move" to the south. Accordingly Lieutenant General Walter C. Short, Commanding General Hawaiian Department, had taken precautions only against sabotage and had so reported to Washington. Admiral Kimmel had seen no reason to interrupt a very urgent training program.

The calm of what promised to be a fine Sunday morning was slightly disturbed at 0654 when the destroyer *Ward* after a two-hour search sank a midget submarine outside the harbor. This report started Admiral Kimmel on his way to headquarters but did

not lead to a general alert. Indeed, it was hardly a matter to concern the ships in the security of the harbor. Many officers were having breakfast, and preparations were being made to change the watch when the first Japanese planes appeared. Their hostile character was not appreciated until the first bombs fell at 0755.

The battleships moored east of Ford Island were the principal target. Despite the surprise, American sailors took station with an alacrity which impressed the Japanese pilots but did not seriously disrupt their plans. A torpedo attack on the battleships was followed closely by dive- and high-level bombing. The greater part of the damage resulted from this first attack, which was over by about 0830. Then after a brief lull came a second wave of 171 fighters and bombers, which concentrated on the ships that appeared to be the least damaged. By this time however the Americans were thoroughly alerted. The second wave suffered the greater part of the Japanese casualties, and a few pilots preferred to drop their bombs on Honolulu rather than face the antiaircraft fire above Pearl Harbor.

By the end of the attack the *Arizona* was a total loss. Moored inboard of the repair ship *Vestal,* which was too small to offer her any protection, she had taken several torpedo and several bomb hits early in the action. One bomb exploded in a forward magazine. Surrounded by burning oil, the battleship sank quickly, taking with her more than a thousand of her crew.

Of the ships moored in pairs, the outboard partners suffered severely from torpedoes. The *Oklahoma,* moored outboard of the *Maryland,* received three torpedo hits in the first moments of the attack and at once began to capsize. She too was a complete loss and was later raised only to clear the harbor. The *West Virginia,* outboard of the *Tennessee,* was also torpedoed early in the action, but prompt counterflooding prevented her capsizing, and her crew continued to fight as she settled to the bottom with only a moderate list. Their inboard partners fared much better. The *Tennessee* took two bomb hits and was threatened by burning

---

[2] These had no success whatsoever in the attack.

[3] The *Colorado,* ninth battleship of the Pacific Fleet, was on the West Coast for overhaul.

[4] Hawaii time (zone-plus-10½), west longitude date.

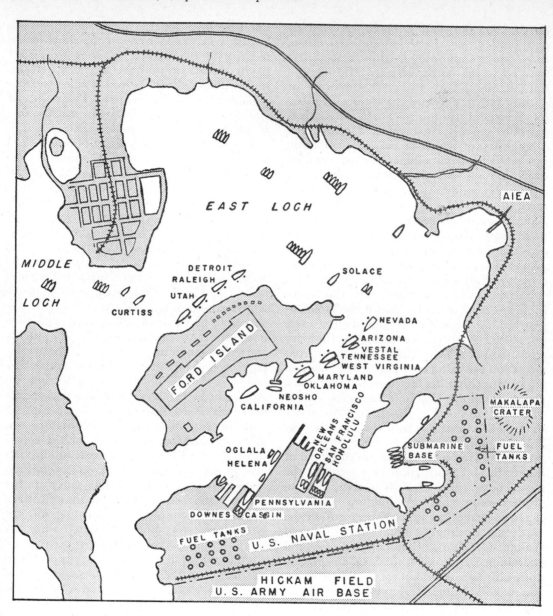

PEARL HARBOR, 0755, DECEMBER 7, 1941

oil from the *Arizona* but suffered only moderate damage. The *Maryland* escaped with only a couple of bomb hits.

The *California*, flagship of Vice Admiral William S. Pye, was moored singly. Hit by two torpedoes and a bomb, she later settled into the Pearl Harbor mud in an upright position. The *Nevada*, moored alone at the opposite end of "Battleship Row," was the only vessel to get under way. Although hit by a torpedo forward, she was able to sortie under a rain of bombs and finally beached herself to avoid the danger of being sunk in the channel.

The *Pennsylvania*, flagship of the Pacific Fleet, was in drydock. That saved her from torpedoes, and she put up such an effective fire that she suffered only a single bomb hit.

However, two destroyers, the *Cassin* and the *Downes,* in the dock forward of the *Pennsylvania,* were hit and were almost melted by burning oil, while the *Shaw,* in the nearby floating dry dock, had her bow blown off.

The lighter vessels moored north of Ford Island generally escaped damage. There only the old, defenseless target ship *Utah,* possibly mistaken by the Japanese for a carrier, was sunk. The light cruiser *Raleigh,* moored near her, received both a torpedo and a bomb hit but did not sink. The light cruiser *Helena,* at a pier in the Navy Yard, remained afloat after being hit by a torpedo, but the minelayer *Oglala,* moored beside her, was sunk by the explosion. The light cruiser *Honolulu,* in a dock also in the yard, was damaged by a near miss.

While the fleet had been the primary objective of the Japanese, they also simultaneously attacked the airfields in the area. There the Americans hastily improvised defenses, but they could not prevent the destruction of their planes, parked in compact rows as a precaution against sabotage. Altogether the Navy lost 80 planes; the Army counted only 64 of its 231 aircraft as "lost," but only 79 of the remaining planes were usable after the attack.

Most serious were the casualties, which totaled 4,575. The Navy and Marine Corps lost 3,077 killed and 876 wounded. The Army had 226 killed and 396 wounded.

The attack cost the Japanese fewer than 50 planes. Nine were shot down from the first attack wave and 20 from the second. On the return 50 crashed in landing, of which 20 were a total loss.

Although the American public could not at that time be told the full extent of its losses, the treacherous attack had the effect of uniting the people of the United States in a vigorous prosecution of the war which had been forced upon them. In many respects however the disaster was less than it first appeared, for the vessels sunk were of little immediate value. Line-of-battle tactics were outdated and the old battleships sunk at Pearl Harbor were too slow to accompany the fast carriers. Their chief use came in the last months of the war, after all but the *Arizona*

and the *Oklahoma* had been raised and refurbished, when they proved valuable for shore bombardment in the Fifth Fleet's advance across the Central Pacific. Moreover in concentrating on the battleships the Japanese had neglected the machine shops, so

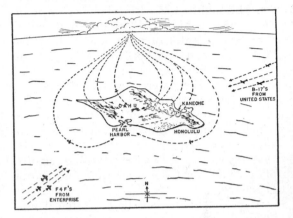

JAPANESE AIR RAID ON PEARL HARBOR
DECEMBER 7, 1941

that the repair facilities were substantially intact. But the greatest good fortune was that' the carriers had escaped. The *Saratoga* was on the West Coast, the *Lexington* was delivering planes to Midway, and the *Enterprise* was returning from having delivered planes to Wake. Besides the cruisers and destroyers accompanying these vessels, several others were at sea on various missions, and most of the lighter vessels in Pearl Harbor had escaped damage. The ships for fast carrier striking forces, the most effective naval weapon of World War II, were intact.

GUAM AND WAKE

Before the end of that tragic Sunday Admiral Kimmel received word that both Guam and Wake had been attacked by Japanese planes. Guam, in the southern Marianas, well over 3,000 miles from Hawaii and 1,500 from Manila, was practically defenseless. Since it was flanked by Japanese bases both to the north and to the south, nothing could be done to support it. The 365 marines and the few native troops had no weapons heavier than their side arms and a few .30 caliber machine guns. After planes from Saipan had bombed the island for two days the Japanese sent ashore some 5,000 men, who easily overwhelmed the defenders.

Wake however was quite a different matter. Although it was within bomber range of the Japanese Marshalls to the south, only about 2,000 miles of open sea lay between Wake and Pearl Harbor, with Midway halfway between. More than a thousand construction workers were engaged in building an air and submarine base on the little atoll. About 450 marines equipped with a dozen 3-inch antiaircraft guns and a half-dozen old 5-inch guns constituted the defense. On December 4, twelve F4F Wildcat fighter planes had been flown in from the *Enterprise*.

After the island had been "softened up" by bombers from Kwajalein in the Marshalls, a Japanese force of three light cruisers and six destroyers escorting several transports appeared at dawn on December 11. Major James P. S. Devereux, commanding the marines, held his fire until the bombarding destroyers were well within range. Then he opened up with his 5-inchers, and the Wildcat fighters took to the air. When the marines had succeeded in sinking two destroyers and in damaging two cruisers and two more destroyers, the Japanese limped away without having put a man ashore.

Meanwhile Admiral Kimmel had made plans and issued orders for the relief of Wake. The *Saratoga* force under Rear Admiral Frank Jack Fletcher was to cover the relief force directly while the other two carrier forces gave indirect support. But there were too many delays. The *Saratoga*, just arriving at Pearl Harbor from the West Coast, could not complete fueling and get under way till noon on the 16th. By the 21st she was only 600 miles from Wake, but she then paused for two days to refuel the destroyers of her group. There was hesitation at Pearl Harbor, where Admiral Kimmel had in the meantime been superseded, and the expedition was ordered to return.

The Japanese, quickly recovering from their initial repulse, sent against Wake on December 23 a new and stronger force covered by three heavy cruisers. At the same time Nagumo, returning from his attack on Pearl Harbor, had detached two of his carriers, the *Hiryu* and *Soryu,* to give air support to the landing. Planes from these carriers on the mornings of the 21st and 22nd destroyed the last planes on the island. Before light on the 23rd Japanese landing craft came ashore, chiefly at points where the marines' artillery could not be brought to bear, while the bombarding cruisers remained outside the range of the 5-inch guns. After a struggle against hopeless odds the marines were forced to surrender.

On Wake and at other American bases civilian construction workers had been exposed to enemy attack without having either the training or the legal right to defend themselves. To remedy this situation, the Navy early authorized the creation of "Construction Battalions"—the famous Seabees. Men of various construction trades were enlisted with appropriate ratings and were given military training. Often going ashore with the assault waves, these men performed vital functions in the Pacific war, from building bases and airfields to repairing equipment. In their hands the bulldozer became one of the instruments of victory.

COMMAND AND STRATEGY

The United States replied to the Japanese attack by declaring war on December 8. Thereupon Japan's allies, Germany and Italy, declared war upon the United States. The new situation led to several command and administrative changes in the Navy. In mid-December Admiral Kimmel was relieved of active duty, and in his place Admiral Chester W. Nimitz was appointed Commander in Chief Pacific Fleet.[5] The following April he was also made Commander in Chief Pacific Ocean Areas (CINCPOA),

[5] Admiral Nimitz could not arrive in Pearl Harbor until the end of the month. In the meantime Vice Admiral William S. Pye exercised command.

which gave him authority over the entire Pacific theater except for General MacArthur's Southwest Pacific Area. Nimitz was a tow-haired, blue-eyed Texan, of the Naval Academy class of 1905. Tactful and modest, sound in his judgment of men and events, he was to prove a thoroughly fortunate choice.

Admiral King's first instructions to Nimitz, on December 30, defined his tasks as:

1. Covering and holding the Hawaii-Midway line and maintaining communications with the west coast.
2. Maintaining communications between the west coast and Australia, chiefly by covering, securing, and holding the Hawaii-Samoa line, which should be extended to include Fiji at the earliest practicable date.[6]

In broader terms, American strategy was to hold against any further Japanese encroachment a line running from Dutch Harbor through Midway to Samoa; thence to New Caledonia to Port Moresby, New Guinea. To gain time for establishing this line Admiral Hart's Asiatic Fleet was to be sacrificed in a delaying action in the Netherlands East Indies.

BEGINNING THE ALLIED RETREAT

The U. S. Asiatic Fleet was in fact only a modest task force. Its flagship and most powerful vessel was the heavy cruiser *Houston*. She was seconded by the 17-year-old light cruiser *Marblehead*. When the light cruiser *Boise* arrived at Manila with a convoy on December 4 she was also "impressed" into the fleet. These vessels were supported by 13 flush-deck, four-stack destroyers of the 1917-18 class. Its 29 submarines were the strongest element of the fleet. Besides several auxiliaries there were a few river gunboats recently withdrawn from China. For reconnaissance the fleet had the 30 PBY's of Patrol Wing Ten, which operated from three tenders.

[6] Ernest J. King and Walter M. Whitehill, *Fleet Admiral King, a Naval Record* (New York, 1952), 353-4.

It had been fully expected that the Japanese would attack the Philippines, and Admiral Hart had dispersed his fleet accordingly. The *Marblehead* with eight destroyers and a tender had been sent south to Borneo in November. The *Houston* and the *Boise* were in the relatively safe waters of the central Philippines. Aside from submarines and auxiliaries, only five destroyers remained in the Manila area. (See map, page 662.)

Because of the difference in time, news of the attack on Pearl Harbor reached Manila at 0300 on December 8 (east longitude date). Admiral Hart hastily scribbled "Japan started hostilities—govern yourselves accordingly" for priority transmission to his fleet. Admiral Glassford, recently commander of the Yangtze Patrol and now Commander of the Asiatic Fleet Task Force, at once gathered several ships around the *Houston* and *Boise* and started south. For some reason never satisfactorily explained, the Army's 33 B-17's, of which only half had been transferred from Luzon to the comparative safety of Mindanao, were not sent to attack Formosa as the Japanese feared they might. The Army fully expected a dawn air raid, and American planes took to the air on an early alert. However bad weather over Formosa delayed the Japanese take-off, and when the pilots finally arrived over Luzon about noon they found the American planes again on their fields in neat rows. As in Hawaii, the aircraft were largely destroyed on the ground. With this initial Japanese success there vanished any real hope of repelling a Japanese invasion.

The attack on the Philippines was only one of several simultaneous Japanese moves in the Far East. Imperial Army troops which had been poised in Indo-China at once overran Thailand, where there was little resistance. At dawn on December 8 a force from Hainan landed at Singora on the Malay Peninsula; the next day more troops landed farther south at Kota Bharu and began a rapid advance toward Singapore. It was to meet this threat that Admiral Phillips took the battleship *Prince of Wales* and the battle cruiser *Repulse* north from Singapore, escorted by four destroyers. The carrier *In-*

domitable, which should have provided air cover, had been damaged by grounding, and the hard pressed Royal Air Force warned Phillips that it could provide no land-based cover. Nevertheless, feeling that the Royal Navy could not stand idly by in the hour of crisis, Phillips made the gallant decision to go ahead. He arrived too late to catch the Japanese transports at Kota Bharu; then acting upon a false report of a Japanese landing further south at Kuantan, he stayed too long within range of Japanese planes based in Indo-China. He had been shadowed for some time when the main attack came in a little before noon on December 10. Both the *Prince of Wales* and the *Repulse* took several hits, capsized, and sank. Admiral Phillips was among those lost.

The sinking of these two capital ships—the first ever sunk by aerial bombing while under way at sea—eliminated the possibility of serious naval opposition to the Japanese advancing on Singapore. By December 19 they had reached the Straits of Malacca.

On the same day that the Japanese sank the *Prince of Wales* they made a heavy air attack on the Cavite Naval Yard near Manila. They easily overcame American fighter opposition, after which they proceeded methodically to destroy the whole base with bombs. The merchant ships at Manila and most of the naval vessels fled to the south. Among those remaining were the tender *Canopus,* which remained to service the submarines as long as they could operate from Manila, and several small craft for local defense. The PBY's of Patrol Wing Ten were sent south, but not before a quarter of them had been lost.

This attack on Cavite on the 10th coincided with the first Japanese landings on Luzon, designed to secure airfields to support an advance on Manila. At Aparri on the north coast the Japanese, harassed by bad weather and by the remnants of the Army air forces, put their men ashore hastily and departed without unloading their heavy equipment. The same combination of bad weather, army planes, and local resistance delayed for a day an attempt to land on the northwest coast near Vigan. On the 12th the Japanese landed at Legaspi, on the southern "tail" of Luzon, in order to control San Bernardino Strait.

As General MacArthur expected, the main Japanese landing came at Lingayen Gulf, on the west side of Luzon above Manila. Japanese transports from Formosa entered the Gulf on December 21. American submarines, hampered by shoal water, had little success in intercepting. A few army planes and navy PBY's annoyed the convoy, but despite bad management the Japanese got their men ashore and overcame resistance with the help of the Vigan detachment, which had marched south to meet it. On Christmas Eve the Japanese put another force ashore on the east coast opposite Manila.

MacArthur, already withdrawing from Manila, declared it an open city and moved his forces in a wheeling movement toward Bataan, while the Navy hastily moved from the city such material as it could. Admiral Rockwell, Commandant of the 16th Naval District, moved into Corregidor, and on the 26th Admiral Hart left by submarine to join his fleet in the south. Five days later the last of the American submarines left Manila. On January 2 the Japanese entered the city unopposed. (See insert map, page 405.)

The stubborn defense of Bataan and Corregidor was important morally at a time when quick and easy enemy successes had become all too frequent, and it had the important practical effect of denying Manila Bay to the Japanese, but it did not delay their advance toward the Indies. As early as December 20 the Japanese had landed at Davao Gulf, on the southern side of Mindanao, which became an important base for further thrusts to the south. Within a few days the Japanese were on both Jolo and Borneo.

Thus in little more than two weeks from the outbreak of war the Japanese had moved past the Philippines, and the pattern of their multi-pronged southward advance was becoming clear. One line followed the Asiatic coast from Indo-China to Malaya and Singapore. A second thrust followed the west coast of Borneo south toward Sumatra. From Davao the Japanese advanced through both Makassar and Molucca Straits, taking important points along the way. Their ultimate objective was Java, richest and most highly developed of the Indies, with a population as great as that of England.

The Japanese advanced by a series of amphibious landings on islands that had almost no interior communications, so that control of the sea and air was decisive. Their method was to seize a key point where they could take over or develop an airfield which would provide air support for the next move. Allied defenses were spread so thin that the Japanese had little difficulty in building up a local superiority. For the most part they employed only modest forces and seldom required carrier support.

JAPANESE ADVANCE INTO THE INDIES

By early January 1942 the United States Asiatic Fleet had fallen back to the Netherlands East Indies. On the 10th British General Sir Archibald P. Wavell arrived in Java to take supreme command of the American, British, Dutch, and Australian (ABDA) forces in the area. Admiral Hart was given the naval command, while air and army commands went to the British and Dutch respectively.

The ABDA command never functioned smoothly, for besides the difficulty of two languages, it was complicated with four army, four navy, and six air organizations. Moreover, there was never any agreement on fundamental strategy: the British desired to use naval forces defensively to convoy reinforcements to Singapore, whereas the Americans wanted to create a striking force that might break up the Japanese advance. Eventually the Dutch insisted on a last-ditch stand, while the British preferred to save their forces for a more favorable moment.

As the Japanese advanced in a vast pincers movement on Java via the waters east and west of Borneo it appeared that the ABDA forces might be able to exploit their interior position by striking first at one and then at the other of the divided Japanese forces. But throughout January Allied naval vessels

were so much in demand for convoying that it was impossible to form a striking force. As a consequence, Admiral Hart had available only a few United States vessels when in late January Allied reconnaissance reported a Japanese convoy approaching the Borneo oil port of Balikpapan. On February 23 Admiral Glassford started up Makassar Strait with the *Marblehead,* the *Boise,* and the destroyers *John D. Ford, Pope, Parrott,* and *Paul Jones.* On the way the *Boise* tore a long gash in her bottom on a pinnacle rock and was out of the campaign for good, and the *Marblehead* was slowed by turbine trouble. So the four destroyers sped ahead without support for the first United States surface action of the war.

Approaching Balikpapan just after midnight through a haze of smoke from burning oil wells, the old four-stackers exploited their surprise by holding gunfire until their torpedoes had been expended. Steaming back and forth through the Japanese force for more than an hour, they sank a patrol craft and four of the dozen transports present, besides inflicting considerable damage on others. This raid, daringly conceived and skillfully executed, was the only successful naval action by Allied surface forces during the entire Netherlands Indies campaign.

The American vessels had been fortunate enough to escape detection by Japanese planes during the daylight portion of their run up Makassar Strait, but an attempt on February 1 to repeat their success showed what might be expected in the future. As they started north they found themselves shadowed by Japanese planes, and with surprise lost they had to abandon the project. Japanese control of the air prevented adequate Allied reconnaissance, while it enabled the Japanese to follow every move of Allied vessels. Air strength on Java was so meager that it was never possible to plan a naval operation with air support. More than once ABDA ships were turned back by Japanese planes before they could approach Japanese surface forces.

As a consequence, the ABDA naval forces were swung between the two arms of the Japanese advance without being able to

THE NETHERLANDS EAST INDIES AREA, 1942

1. Action off Balikpapan, January 24.
2. Madoera Strait, February 4.
3. Banka Island, February 13-14.
4. Badoeng Strait, February 19-20.
5. Java Sea, February 27-28.

strike effectively at either. While the British ships and the *Houston* were still engaged in convoying, the Dutch, acting upon a false report, sent their ships westward to Karimata Channel. In the meantime a strong Japanese force, supported by four carriers and two battleships, took Amboina, the chief Dutch stronghold on the east flank of the Indies. Soon afterwards the Japanese occupied Kendari, in southeastern Celebes.

By the first of February the British had thrown their last reinforcements into Singapore, after which several vessels were released from convoy duty. This made it possible at last to form an ABDA striking force, which was placed under the command of Dutch Rear Admiral Karel Doorman. In it initially were the two United States cruisers and four destroyers, the Dutch light cruisers *De Ruyter* and *Tromp,* and three Dutch destroyers.

On February 3 Japanese planes from Kendari made their first attack on Surabaya, the principal Allied naval base in Java, and destroyed most of the Dutch fighter aircraft in the vicinity. The vessels of the striking force fortunately escaped damage, and next morning Doorman led them forth with orders to make a night attack upon Japanese forces reported gathering at Balikpapan. As his ships sortied from the eastern end of Madoera Strait they were discovered by Japanese planes, which began a prolonged attack about 1000. The Dutch cruisers escaped with near misses, but the *Houston* received a hit which caused many casualties and put her after turret out of action for the rest of the campaign. The *Marblehead* took two hits and several near misses which jammed her rudder and left her barely afloat. Only the most strenuous exertions of her crew enabled her to make the port of Tjilatjap for temporary repairs before proceeding on a long voyage back to the United States.

In a few days Doorman had to turn his attention to the Japanese Western Force. With five cruisers and ten destroyers he rushed to the relief of the great oil port of Palembang in eastern Sumatra. The Japanese occupation force had already entered the river leading to Palembang when Doorman arrived off nearby Banka Island the night of February 13. Here the Allied force came under repeated air attacks. Although no Allied ship was hit, several were badly shaken by near misses, and Doorman was obliged to retire without accomplishing anything.

In mid-February Admiral Hart surrendered command of the ABDA naval forces to Dutch Vice Admiral Conrad Helfrich and returned to the United States, leaving Admiral Glassford senior United States naval officer in the area. Singapore surrendered on February 15. The Japanese were now ready to close the pincers on Java. Already they had started softening up the island by daily bombings which forced the practical abandonment of Surabaya as a naval base.

Doorman had just returned from Banka Island when word came that the Japanese were landing on the island of Bali at the opposite end of Java. Although this move had been expected, Doorman was not able to collect the vessels of his striking force in time to interfere. He determined however at least to hit the Japanese transports before they could withdraw. Because his ships were divided between Surabaya and Tjilatjap, he decided to attack in three successive waves.

When the two cruisers and three destroyers from Tjilatjap approached Badoeng Strait from the south on the night of February 19 there were only three Japanese vessels present, one transport and two destroyers. The two cruisers, both Dutch, sped through the Strait firing ineffectively. Advancing in their wake, the destroyers came under heavy fire. The Dutch destroyer *Piet Hein* was sunk by a torpedo, and the American destroyers *Ford* and *Pope* were obliged to turn back southward. The second wave, comprising the Dutch cruiser *Tromp* and four American destroyers, all from Surabaya, approached the Strait without any news of the first. The Americans attacked with both torpedoes and gunfire, but the dark shoreline and the smoke obscured their targets, and the *Stewart* was hit once. The *Tromp,* bringing up the rear, took several hits when she turned on her searchlight. By this time three more Japanese destroyers had come in from the northeast. In the heavy engagement which followed, the *Tromp* received several more hits but disabled one Japanese destroyer. When the third wave, of motor torpedo boats, arrived there were no Japanese to be found in the Strait. Because he failed to concentrate his greatly superior force Doorman accomplished little and incurred heavier losses than necessary.

By now Java was nearly isolated, and the Japanese set about cutting her last links with Australia. The Allies had been staging fighter planes from Australia to Java via Timor. On February 16 a convoy of reinforcements for Timor was turned back by Japanese planes. A few days later the Japanese occupied the island themselves. Then on February 19 Admiral Nagumo's carrier force raided Darwin, principal port of northern Australia. The city was completely surprised and there was little opposition when the Japanese planes arrived at 0930. In a prolonged attack they sank a dozen ships in the harbor, including the American destroyer *Peary* and two American transports, and virtually destroyed the docks and warehouses. The battered city was evacuated before nightfall, and the port of Darwin was abandoned as a naval base.

THE BATTLE OF THE JAVA SEA

By February 25 the Japanese were poised for the assault on Java. To the northwest Rear Admiral Jisaburo Ozawa was waiting at the Anambas Islands with 56 transports and cargo vessels and their escorts, which had come down from Camranh Bay, Indo-China. To the northeast Rear Admiral Shoji Nishimura was waiting in Makassar Strait with 41 transports and a cruiser-destroyer covering force. On February 25 a small Japanese force occupied Bawean Island, about 150 miles north of central Java, as an advanced observation base.

General Wavell, by this time convinced of the futility of attempting to defend Java, had departed on the 25th. With the ABDA command thus dissolved, Helfrich undertook to direct the naval defense. A vital need in this defense was air power. In a convoy which had departed Fremantle, Australia on February 27 bound for Ceylon were the United States aircraft tender *Langley* with 32 P-40's on deck and pilots aboard, and the freighter *Seawitch* with 27 crated P-40's in her hold. One of Helfrich's first acts upon assuming his new responsibilities was to order these two vessels diverted to Java.

A Japanese carrier force was operating south of Java to intercept such attempts at reinforcement, but it was land-based planes which discovered the *Langley* on the morning of February 27 when she was about 100 miles south of Java. The tender, which had been converted from a collier into the United States Navy's first aircraft carrier, now had only half a flight deck, so that she could not launch the planes she carried. In the ensuing attack she took repeated hits and had to be abandoned. The destroyers *Whipple* and *Edsall,* which had come out from Java to escort her, picked up survivors. These were transferred to the oiler *Pecos* and most of them perished when the *Pecos* was sunk a few days later by Japanese carrier planes. The *Seawitch* reached Tjilatjap on February 28. By that time the Battle of the Java Sea had been fought and lost, and it was too late to assemble her crated planes.

Allied submarines and the surviving planes of Patrol Wing Ten brought reports of the Japanese concentrations ready for a descent on Java. Admiral Helfrich thereupon stationed Allied submarines in positions for interception, and on the evening of the 25th Doorman led his striking force in a sweep along the north coast of Java to intercept any landing attempt. After two days of almost continuous patrol, punctuated by an air attack on the morning of the 27th, Doorman signaled, "Personnel have this forenoon reached the point of exhaustion," and started to put into Surabaya for rest and refueling. It was then that he received reports of Japanese transports west of Bawean Island. There was nothing to do but put about for the final battle.

As Doorman's force steamed from Sura-

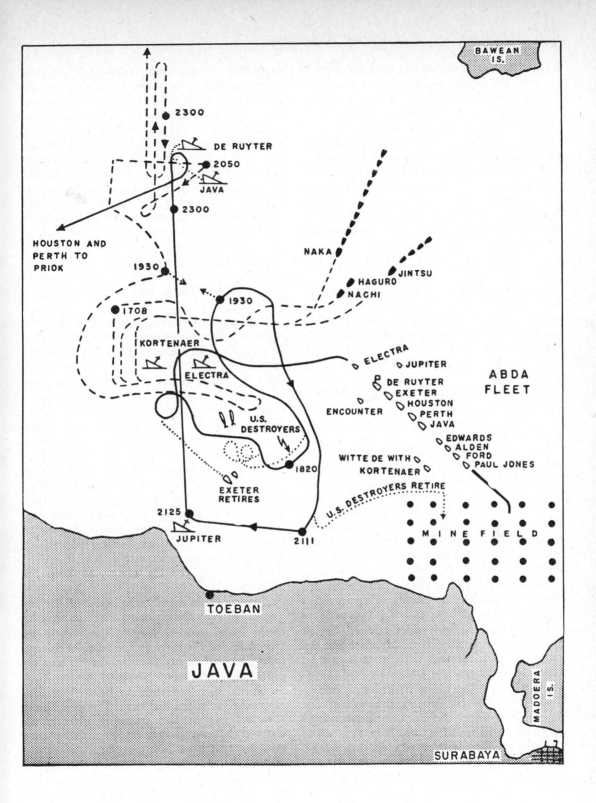

BATTLE OF THE JAVA SEA, FEBRUARY 27-28, 1942

baya into the Java Sea his cruisers were in column led by his flagship, the *De Ruyter*. Three British destroyers screened ahead, while two Dutch and four United States destroyers were astern and to port of the cruisers, endeavoring to work up to the port bow of the column (see diagram). These vessels were all that were available for the final defense of Java. A Western Striking Force of three British cruisers and two destroyers had been based at Tandjong Priok, the port of Batavia, in western Java. After an unsuccessful attempt to intercept the Japanese in Banka Strait on the 26th, these ships had withdrawn to Ceylon.

On paper Doorman's force was not greatly inferior to the Japanese forces which he actually encountered, though the Japanese could of course have brought up more had they been needed. But the Allied vessels were in poor repair from continuous operation—the *Houston's* after turret was still inoperative—and with no common doctrine and only the poorest of communications, they were condemned to primitive "follow the leader" tactics.

Nishimura, whose planes had kept him fully informed of Doorman's movements, had already ordered his transports to retire while he moved south with the light cruiser *Naka* and ten destroyers, accompanied by Rear Admiral Takeo Takagi's Covering Group, which consisted of the heavy cruisers *Nachi* and *Haguro* and a squadron of destroyers led by the light cruiser *Jintsu*.

About half an hour after leaving Surabaya Doorman sighted the enemy in two groups on his starboard bow, moving SW as if to cross his course. Both sides opened fire at about 28,000 yards. For about an hour the engagement continued with both forces on westerly courses, while Doorman made some effort to close the range in order to utilize his light cruisers. During this phase the Japanese enjoyed the important advantage of having air spotting for their fire, while Doorman had none. Nevertheless they scored only a single hit, a dud on the *De Ruyter*, though they straddled both that vessel and the *Exeter* repeatedly.

As the battle moved westward it approached the Japanese transports. To turn back the Allied force the *Jintsu* led her destroyer squadron down from the NW across the bows of Doorman's column for a torpedo attack. It was just at this moment that the *Haguro* scored an 8-inch hit on the *Exeter* which forced her to swing left out of column. The following vessels, assuming that Doorman had ordered a turn, swung to port also, thus throwing the Allied vessels into confusion and presenting their broadsides to the Japanese torpedoes. By good luck or good maneuvering all were able to escape except the Dutch *Kortenaer*. Caught by a torpedo on her starboard quarter, she immediately "turned turtle and folded up like a jackknife."

While Doorman circled to gather his cruisers into column once more, the *Perth* dashed in to lay smoke between the *Exeter* and the advancing Japanese destroyers, after which she fell in behind the *De Ruyter*. The British destroyers then covered the damaged cruiser by a counterattack in which the *Electra* was sunk by enemy gunfire. The Allied cruisers were meanwhile withdrawing on a southeasterly course, again engaging the Japanese heavy cruisers to the north. At about 1815, when the Japanese launched another torpedo attack, Doorman signaled the United States destroyers to "cover my retirement." Thereupon the *Edwards, Alden, Ford* and *Paul Jones* turned toward the Japanese for a long-range torpedo attack which scored no hits but forced the enemy to keep his distance.

Apparently in an effort to break off the engagement with the covering force so that he could make another stab at the transports, Doorman led his force to the east. In this attempt he had to act blindly, for he had no planes, and the reconnaissance reports from Surabaya were too stale to be of any use. Nevertheless when he turned north about 1830 he was in fact steaming directly toward the Japanese convoy. Japanese planes however had been following him constantly and marked his change of course with flares, so that the heavy cruisers of the covering force again had no difficulty in intercepting him. After a brief exchange in which the

Japanese enjoyed the advantage of aerial flares and superior starshells, the Allied cruisers at 1936 again broke off the action by turning away to the east and then withdrawing to the south. At about 2100, when the Allied force was some 50 miles from Surabaya, the four American destroyers, now without torpedoes and low on oil, returned to the port to refuel. There they found the *Exeter,* accompanied by the *Witte de With,* which had arrived a little before.

Doorman meantime had led the remainder of his force west along the north coast of Java, apparently hoping to outflank the Japanese Covering Group and intercept the transports if they came in for a landing. He had moved in this direction for about 15 minutes when there was an explosion beneath the British destroyer *Jupiter,* which began to sink slowly. The force had run into a Dutch mine field laid that afternoon without Doorman's knowledge. Turning north after this disaster, Doorman soon found himself again in the area where the *Kortenaer* had gone down, and he detached his last destroyer, the *Encounter,* to pick up survivors.

This left Doorman with only four cruisers for his final thrust toward the transports. It was not destined to succeed, for at about 2300 the two Japanese heavy cruisers appeared to port and began a duel on parallel courses at about 8,000 yards. After 20 minutes of firing the Japanese launched torpedoes which caught both the *De Ruyter* and the *Java.* The two Dutch cruisers burst into flames and soon had to be abandoned. As his flagship sank, Doorman signaled the *Houston* and *Perth,* all that remained of his Striking Force, to retire to Tandjong Priok, which they reached safely a little after noon next day.

THE RETREAT
FROM JAVA

The surviving Allied vessels were now divided with strong Japanese forces between. At Surabaya were the *Exeter, Encounter, Witte de With,* and five American destroyers —the four which had participated in the battle, plus the *Pope,* which had not been able to join in time. At Tandjong Priok were the *Houston,* the *Perth,* and the Dutch destroyer *Evertsen.* The problem now was how to withdraw from the Java Sea, for the Japanese controlled all the exits.

Of Doorman's Striking Force, the four American destroyers were the only ships to escape. Leaving Surabaya on the night of the 28th, they slipped through Bali Strait and after a brief skirmish with Japanese destroyers made their way safely to Australia. Because the *Exeter's* draft was too great to permit her to follow the same route, she was sent west to Sunda Strait. Accompanied by the *Encounter* and *Pope* [7] she set sail the evening of the 28th. To avoid the Japanese known to be near the Java coast, she swung wide toward Borneo, but next day the Japanese discovered the three Allied ships, and four heavy cruisers with destroyers converged on them. The two British vessels were overwhelmed. The *Pope* escaped for the moment, but was caught and sunk by planes from the light carrier *Ryujo* an hour later.

The *Houston, Perth,* and *Evertsen* left Priok on the evening of the 28th. They had almost reached Sunda Strait when an hour before midnight at Banten Bay they ran into the Japanese landing force which had previously been maneuvering off Banka Island. The Allied cruisers sank or forced the beaching of four loaded transports before they could be stopped by the covering forces. Then the two super-heavy cruisers *Mogami* and *Mikuma,* aided by the light cruiser *Natori* and ten destroyers, closed in. The *Perth,* hit by several torpedoes and many shells, went down first. The *Houston* fought on alone till, dead in the water and shot to pieces, she sank half an hour after midnight. The *Evertsen* escaped for a few hours, only to be sunk by Japanese destroyers in the strait.

A few Allied vessels were still based at Tjilatjap on the south coast of Java. On March 1, when it was apparent that nothing

---

[7] The Dutch *Witte de With* was unable to leave port because her propellers had been damaged by a depth charge which fell off her stern during the battle.

more could be done for the naval defense of Java, Admiral Helfrich authorized their withdrawal. A Japanese carrier-battleship force operating south of Java intercepted a few, including the United States destroyers *Edsall* and *Pillsbury* and the gunboat *Asheville,* but most reached Australia safely.

The Japanese had begun landing on Java on the night of February 28. Batavia and Surabaya fell quickly, and by March 9 the Japanese were in possession of the entire island. The ABDA forces had been expended to gain time, and they had bought little enough of that. But it is adversity which brings out the true quality of men and of navies. There is nothing finer in United States naval history than the performance of the United States Asiatic Fleet in the face of overwhelming odds.

HOLDING THE LINE
IN THE PACIFIC:
EARLY RAIDS

The defeat in the Java Sea marked the end of delaying actions, for the Japanese had now reached the line which the United States had determined to hold—if it could. As Admiral King put it in March 1942:

The plain facts of the matter are that we have not the "tools" wherewith to meet the enemy at all the points he is threatening;—Hawaii *must* be held—we must do what we can to maintain the line of communications with Australia.[8]

This meant first of all reinforcing the essential bases on the route to Australia and then a build-up of forces in Australia itself. Vice Admiral Herbert F. Leary had arrived in Australia in the first part of February to take command of an Anzac (Australia-New Zealand) Force, created on the recommendation of the Combined Chiefs of Staff after it became apparent that the ABDA forces were doomed. On March 17 MacArthur arrived at Darwin, designated at the request of the Australian government to take command of the Southwest Pacific Area, for which the

_____
[8] *Fleet Admiral King,* 373.

United States had recently assumed responsibility. Already he was dreaming of a return to the Philippines, but for the moment he was a general without an army.

Although the United States was on the defensive, its strategy was far from passive. As King put it, American policy was "hold what you've got and hit them when you can." For the present the hitting was to be done by the submarines and by the carriers. Immediately after the Pearl Harbor disaster the *Yorktown* had been ordered from the Atlantic to the Pacific. This would have brought the Pacific carrier strength up to four except that on January 11 the *Saratoga* was torpedoed by a Japanese submarine 500 miles southwest of Oahu. She was able to make port, but repairs kept her out of the war for five critical months.

The Japanese had covered the left flank of their advance into the Netherlands East Indies by occupying the British Gilbert Islands in December 1941 and by landing on January 23 at Rabaul, at the northern end of New Britain. If the United States was to protect its line of communications to Australia it must see to it that the Japanese did not use these bases to support further advances.

Early in January there was considerable apprehension at Pearl Harbor that the Japanese might move from the Marshalls and Gilberts against Samoa. Accordingly reinforcements were sent to the group escorted by the *Yorktown* under Vice Admiral Frank Jack Fletcher. There Fletcher was joined in the latter part of January by the *Enterprise* group, commanded by Vice Admiral William F. Halsey Jr., for a strike intended to neutralize Japanese bases in the Gilberts and Marshalls.

Six days after the combined force left Samoa, the *Yorktown* and her escorts were detached to hit Makin in the northern Gilberts and Jaluit and Mili in the southern Marshalls, while the *Enterprise* proceeded farther into the Marshalls. The attack, made on February 1, was only a modest success. The *Yorktown* found a paucity of military targets on her assigned islands, while bad weather hampered her operations and caused the loss of seven planes. The *Enterprise*

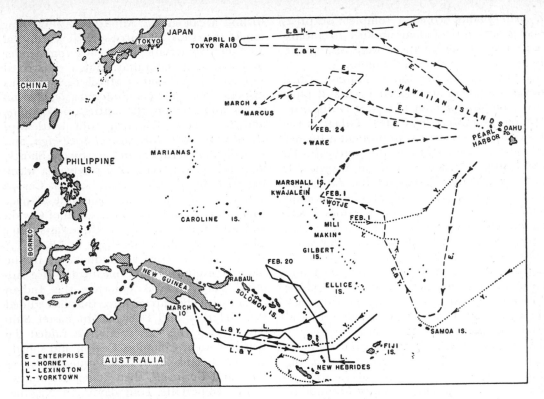

EARLY RAIDS BY UNITED STATES CARRIER FORCES

group fared a little better. At Taroa Island, Maloelap, two Japanese bombers got into the air and scored a hit on the heavy cruiser *Chester* of the bombardment group. At Wotje the bombardment group was unscathed and inflicted some damage on ships in the lagoon, while installations ashore were pounded both by its guns and by aerial bombs. Fog over Roi Island, Kwajalein Atoll, delayed the bombing attack until the Japanese were alerted, so that they were able to shoot down four of the attacking planes, but bombers and torpedo planes scored a few hits on warships in the Kwajalein lagoon.

At the time of the fall of Singapore in mid-February both the United States and the Australian governments were apprehensive that the Japanese might advance from Rabaul to attack New Caledonia and the New Hebrides. Consequently Vice Admiral Wilson Brown's *Lexington* group was temporarily assigned to Leary's Anzac force, and

Brown daringly offered to strike at Rabaul. On February 20, when his force was 350 miles east of the target it was attacked by Japanese bombers. American antiaircraft fire was ineffectual, but *Lexington* fighters successfully beat off the Japanese planes in the first action of its kind in the Pacific. With surprise lost, Brown had to abandon his strike.

The critical situation in the Southwest Pacific was responsible for an attempt to divert the Japanese by an attack on Wake. Departing from Pearl Harbor on February 14, Halsey's *Enterprise* group arrived off Wake on the 24th. Bad weather delayed the launching of planes until after the Japanese had discovered the surface bombardment group, but they had only three seaplanes on the island and were unable to counterattack effectively. After damaging the few installations on Wake, Halsey pressed on to attack Marcus Island, less than a thousand miles from Tokyo. In the attack of March 4, *En-*

terprise planes scored a complete surprise, losing only one of their number to antiaircraft fire, but again there were disappointingly few targets for their bombs.

By the time of the raid on Marcus, Allied naval forces had abandoned Java, and Japanese bombing of points in New Guinea, including Port Moresby, and of Tulagi in the lower Solomons seemed to portend a further advance to the south and the southeast. To check any such move, Admiral Brown was given a force built around the *Lexington* and *Yorktown* to make another attempt against Rabaul, which the Japanese were rapidly developing into a major base. Brown's force was already under way when word came that on March 8 the Japanese had landed at Lae and Salamaua, on Huon Gulf on the northern side of the New Guinea tail. Brown determined to attack these positions before the Japanese were well established. In order to achieve surprise he decided to launch his attack from south of Papua (southeast New Guinea), with the planes flying over the jungles of the interior and over the high Owen Stanley Mountains. The passage was difficult, especially for the torpedo planes, which had to nurse their heavy loads over a 7,500-foot pass, but these unusual tactics resulted in the greatest success yet scored by American carriers. The attacking planes sank a minesweeper, a freighter, and a converted cruiser and damaged several other vessels while losing only one of their number to antiaircraft fire.

While United States and Anzac forces were thus attempting to check Japanese expansion to the south and east, the British were facing a similar task in the west. In mid-January the Japanese had advanced from Thailand to begin their invasion of Burma. By early March Rangoon, the capital and key to lower Burma, had fallen, leaving the British the difficult task of withdrawing their army from upper Burma into India. In the latter part of March the Japanese protected the left flank of their advance by occupying the Andaman Islands, which put them in a position to threaten India. (See map, page 868.)

The Admiralty, which had been unable

to find a carrier for Admiral Phillips, now found three for his successor, Vice Admiral Sir James Somerville, the former commander of Force H at Gibraltar. When he arrived in Ceylon at the end of March he had at his disposal the carriers *Indomitable, Formidable,* and *Hermes,* the battleship *Warspite,* and the "Four R's," the old battleships *Resolution, Ramillies, Royal Sovereign,* and *Revenge,* plus cruisers and destroyers. Shortly after his arrival Somerville received a warning that the Japanese would attack Ceylon about the first of April. Somerville at once concentrated his force to the south of Ceylon and waited expectantly for three days, after which he withdrew his ships to "Port T," Britain's secret base at Addu Atoll in the Maldive Islands. In the meantime Vice Admiral Nagumo was entering the Indian Ocean with the carrier force that had raided Pearl Harbor and Darwin. On Easter Sunday, April 5, his carrier aircraft raided the British base at Colombo, Ceylon and shortly afterwards sank H.M. heavy cruisers *Dorsetshire* and *Cornwall,* then at sea attempting to join Somerville. Four days later Nagumo raided Trincomalee, Britain's other base in Ceylon, and that same afternoon sank H.M. carrier *Hermes* and an accompanying destroyer.

Meanwhile Vice Admiral Kurita had entered the Bay of Bengal with six heavy cruisers and a light carrier and pounced upon merchant shipping. In the first nine days of April 1942 Japanese air, surface, and submarine forces sank four British warships and 135,000 tons of merchant shipping.

After this disaster the "Four R's," which had proved only a handicap, were withdrawn to East Africa, while Somerville with the *Warspite* and two remaining carriers remained to cover sea communications between India and the Persian Gulf. But there was serious apprehension that his base at Bombay might not long remain secure, for it appeared that a Japanese invasion of Ceylon and India might be imminent. Churchill asked that the United States Navy undertake some action which might force the Japanese to draw their carriers back into the Pacific, and arrangements were made for

American vessels to join the British Home Fleet so that reinforcements might be sent to India.

British fears proved groundless however. The Japanese had no plans for the conquest of India. Moreover R.A.F. fighters based on Ceylon had taken a heavy toll of Nagumo's planes and pilots. His air groups were so badly cut up that in May Japan could send only two heavy carriers into the Battle of the Coral Sea, and in June many of the pilots who fought in the Battle of Midway were new to the fleet and inadequately trained.

It was only coincidence that the British plea for a diversion in the Pacific was followed by the most daring in the series of United States carrier raids, the Halsey-Doolittle raid on Tokyo on April 18. The plan was for the *Hornet,* accompanied by the *Enterprise* and a cruiser-destroyer screen, to carry 16 Army B-25's to within 500 miles of Japan. The planes, manned by volunteers, were to hit targets in Tokyo, Nagoya, Osaka, and Kobe, cross Japan and land on friendly airfields in China. However, while the carriers were still 650 miles from Japan they encountered Japanese picket boats that reported their presence. Rather than abandon the raid, Colonel James H. Doolittle USA decided to launch at that distance. Waves were breaking over the carrier's bows and the ships were pitching badly when Doolittle led his planes off. Not one of the pilots had even taken off from a carrier deck before; yet somehow every one succeeded in getting his big, heavily-loaded plane into the air.

By a remarkable coincidence the army pilots arrived over Tokyo about noon in the midst of an air raid drill with Japanese planes making mock attacks on the city, so that the Americans were scarcely noticed. There was only scattered opposition, and no plane was lost over Japan. But on arriving over China in the dark, 15 of the planes were lost in crash landings or when their crews abandoned them by parachute. The only plane to land safely was impounded by the Russians at Vladivostok. Of the 80 men who left the carrier, 71 survived the raid.

The physical effect of the raid on Tokyo was slight. Few of the Japanese public knew even that the city had been bombed, but Japan's rulers knew and were seriously disturbed. The raid was to have an important effect on strategic developments.

Indeed, none of the early raids inflicted significant damage, and there is no evidence that they diverted or delayed the Japanese in the slightest. However, their moral effect was important. These daring penetrations of enemy waters did much to dispel the gloom and defeatism engendered by Pearl Harbor and to create a feeling that the United States was fighting back.

DISPUTING JAPAN'S COMMAND OF THE PACIFIC

When the United States in 1922 agreed to a 5:5:3 ratio of capital ships with Great Britain and Japan, Japanese naval tonnage was only half that of the U. S. Navy. By construction in categories not limited by the disarmament treaties, Japan had built up to 73 per cent of American naval tonnage by 1936, when the treaties expired. By December 1941, Japanese naval tonnage was 81 per cent of American. But the U. S. Fleet then had to be divided between two oceans, and Japan's resulting naval superiority in the Pacific was greatly increased by the raid on Pearl Harbor and the torpedoing of the *Saratoga.* On top of this, the United States in compliance with the 1922 treaty had refrained from arming its islands in the Pacific while Japan had not. As a result, the Japanese early in World War II exercised command over vast reaches of the Pacific theater.

The United States and its allies, committed to employing their main effort against Germany, necessarily went on the defensive in the Pacific until America had generated sufficient power to shift to the offensive. In the meantime the Allied navies employed the means historically used by weaker powers to *dispute* the enemy's command of the sea: (1) suicide missions to delay the enemy's advance (by the ABDA forces off Java); (2) attacks on the enemy's communications and isolated fleet units (by submarines); and (3) raids on the enemy's bases (by carrier forces). It was clear however that such means were not enough, even for defense. Somewhere the Allied naval forces would have to take a stand, with all the power they could muster, against the Japanese expansion. In late spring of 1942 the United States Navy obtained definite information concerning enemy plans of advance and was thus enabled to take such a stand.

38

The Battle of the Coral Sea

THE CONQUEST OF THE Philippines, the Netherlands East Indies, Burma, and Malaya, completed by the spring of 1942, had required only about half the time the Japanese had anticipated and had cost them only a few thousand casualties. In the entire campaign they had lost no naval vessel larger than a destroyer. Seldom in history has so rich an empire been won at so small a cost.

The ease and rapidity of this conquest convinced many of the Japanese leaders that they had been too modest in their aspirations and too cautious in their planning. Chief among these was Admiral Isoroku Yamamoto, Commander in Chief Combined Fleet, who favored a more aggressive use of the Japanese fleet while Japan held the advantage. Yamamoto and his followers argued that instead of pausing to consolidate the new empire and to erect a defensive perimeter, as the strategic plan required, Japan should proceed at once to extend her control in the Pacific.

Specifically they urged three steps. First, Japan should take Port Moresby, in southeastern New Guinea, and Tulagi in the lower Solomons with the dual purpose of securing the Empire in the southeast and of preparing the way for a further advance in

that direction. Secondly, Midway and the Aleutians should be occupied in order to extend Japanese defenses in the central and northern Pacific and to force an engagement with the United States Fleet. Finally, the Japanese should seize New Caledonia, Fiji, and Samoa, which would cut the lines of communication between the United States and Australia. There was no immediate plan for the conquest of Australia, but with her communications cut and with many of her cities within range of Japanese bombers, her position would have been precarious.

Proponents of the accelerated program gained a strong argument in the Tokyo raid of April 18, 1942. The material results of this raid were negligible, but it made Japan's leaders acutely conscious of their lack of defensive positions to the east of Japan. The "Southern Resources Area" was protected by innumerable island barriers, but there simply were no island bases to the east of the homeland from which the Japanese could search for or intercept such raiders. The seizure of Midway and the western Aleutians was the best Japan could do toward filling this gap in her ring of defense.

So the new plan was adopted with all its fateful consequences. Its first step was to lead to the Battle of the Coral Sea, the second to

Midway. The threat of the third was to bring United States Marines to Guadalcanal. While the plan involved Japan in ultimate disaster, it must not be overlooked that the real cause of the failure was something the Japanese planners could hardly have anticipated— American knowledge of their plans. Without that knowledge it is difficult to see how the United States could have met the Japanese successfully at either Coral Sea or Midway.

PLANS AND PREPARATIONS

The first step in the new program, the occupation of Port Moresby, was necessary to the Japanese for the security of New Guinea and to provide a base for neutralizing Allied airfields in northern Australia. The simultaneous occupation of Tulagi, across the sound from Guadalcanal in the lower Solomons, would cover the flank of the operation by providing an advance seaplane base and would prepare the way for the subsequent advance toward the Fijis. Conversely, to the Allies the retention of Port Moresby was essential not only for the security of Australia but also as a springboard for future offensives.

New Guinea is shaped like a great bird, with the head to the west and the tail to the east. The Japanese, as we have seen, had occupied Lae and Salamaua, on the northern side of the tail, in March. But the rugged Owen Stanley Mountains, which form a sort of backbone for the bird, and the almost impenetrable jungle of the interior of the island made an overland attack on Port Moresby difficult. The obvious approach was by sea, around the tail of New Guinea through Jomard Passage.

According to the Japanese plan, the Port Moresby landing force was to sail from Rabaul, at the northeastern end of New Britain, in eleven transports with a destroyer screen. A smaller landing force was destined for Tulagi. A Support Force of two light cruisers with gunboats and other auxiliaries was designed to give direct support to both the Tulagi and the Port Moresby landings.

A Covering Force consisting of the 12,000-ton carrier *Shoho* with four heavy cruisers and a destroyer was first to support the landing on Tulagi, then turn back west in time to cover the passage of the Port Moresby force through the strait and to protect the landing. In addition, a Striking Force composed of two of the Pearl Harbor carriers, the sister ships *Shokaku* and *Zuikaku,* with a screen of four heavy cruisers and six destroyers, was to come down from Truk, the Japanese strong point in the Carolines, to deal with any United States forces that might attempt to interfere with the operation. A force of six submarines was to patrol the Coral Sea, and land-based aircraft were counted upon for scouting and support.

There were thus six separate naval forces engaged in this dual operation against Port Moresby and Tulagi. Such complex division of forces was typical of Japanese strategy throughout most of the war. So far, against a weak and disorganized enemy, it had worked well, and it was not inconsistent with concentration so long as the forces were properly coordinated and were sufficiently close together to render mutual support. But when the Japanese disregarded these two important conditions they met disaster.

At the Coral Sea some coordination was to be provided by a unified command. Vice Admiral Shigeyoshi Inouye, Commander Fourth Fleet, who at the beginning of the war had directed the capture of Guam and Wake, was to direct all forces, including land-based air, from Rabaul. Unfortunately for the Allies, their command was not integrated in the same manner. The battle was to be fought in General MacArthur's Southwest Pacific Theater, but it was understood that any fleet action would remain under Admiral Nimitz's strategic control. The result was that the land-based air and the naval forces were under separate commands without effective coordination.

Since the Pearl Harbor attack, the United States had broken the Japanese naval code and thus possessed the enormous advantage of accurate and rather detailed intelligence concerning the enemy's plans. Even so, it was

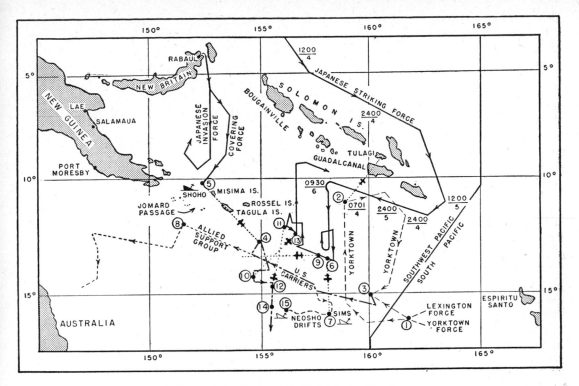

BATTLE OF THE CORAL SEA, MAY 4-8, 1942

1. May 1, 0623: *Yorktown* and *Lexington* meet.
2. May 4, 0701: *Yorktown* launches attack on Tulagi.
3. May 5, 0846: *Yorktown* rejoins *Lexington*.
4. May 7, 1000: Attack group launched.
5. May 7, 1150: *Shoho* sunk.
6. May 7, 0815: Japanese launch attack on *Neosho* and *Sims*.
7. May 7, 1230: *Sims* sunk.
8. May 7, 1425: Japanese planes attack Support Force.
9. May 7, 1615: Japanese launch night attack group.
10. May 8, 0900: U. S. carriers launch attack.
11. May 8, 0915: Japanese carriers launch attack.
12. May 8, 1118: U. S. carriers under attack.
13. May 8, 1058: Japanese carriers under attack.
14. May 8, 1956: *Lexington* sinks.
15. May 11, 1550: *Neosho* sunk by *Henley*.

not easy to gather sufficient forces to meet the Japanese threat to Port Moresby. The principal naval elements available were two carrier task forces: Rear Admiral Frank Jack Fletcher's *Yorktown* force, which had been operating in the South Pacific for some time, and Rear Admiral Aubrey W. Fitch's *Lexington* force, fresh from Pearl Harbor. From the Southwest Pacific Force came the *Chicago* out of Noumea, while Rear Admiral

J. C. Crace RN brought the cruisers H.M.A.S. *Australia* and *Hobart* from Australia.

These vessels were all that were available. The *Saratoga* was still in Puget Sound undergoing repairs for the torpedo damage she had suffered in January. The *Enterprise* and *Hornet* did not return to Pearl Harbor from the Tokyo raid till April 25. Although they were rushed on their way as soon as possible, there was little likelihood that they could reach the Coral Sea in time to play a part. Thus the Tokyo raid deprived the United States of half its Pacific carriers at a critical moment. Fortunately for the Allies; Japanese carrier strength had been similarly dissipated by the raid on Ceylon and the subsequent hunt for Halsey's Tokyo attack force, so that only two fleet carriers were available for Inouye's Striking Force. That seemed enough, for the Japanese had no way of knowing that the *Lexington* had been rushed south to join the *Yorktown* in the Coral Sea.

THE RAID ON TULAGI, MAY 4

The two American carrier forces, which had been ordered to join under Fletcher's command, made contact in the southeast Coral Sea on May 1. Instead of uniting his forces at once however Fletcher ordered them to fuel separately. Then on the evening of May 3 he received from MacArthur's headquarters news of the Japanese occupation of Tulagi, which had begun that morning. "This," said Fletcher in his action report, "was just the kind of report we had been waiting two months to receive." Being out of visual contact with the *Lexington* group, Admiral Fletcher did not know that it had completed fueling ahead of schedule, and he did not want to break radio silence. Consequently he made the daring decision to strike Tulagi with only the *Yorktown* group. This division of his forces at a time when attack might have been imminent could easily have proved disastrous. The Japanese Striking Force had not yet been reported, and the *Yorktown* might very well have run into the two enemy carriers during this move to the north.

But luck was with Fletcher. The Japanese apparently thought Tulagi too unimportant to attract an American attack. The Striking Force with its two big carriers was still north of the Solomons, while the little *Shoho* with the rest of the Covering Force, after seeing the troops safely ashore at Tulagi, had withdrawn to the northwest. Bad weather, extending almost to Tulagi, protected the

Yorktown from observation, while a southeast wind would permit the carrier to launch and recover planes while retiring.

Launching began soon after 0700 on May 4, and the attack continued throughout the day. Generally the strikes were badly coordinated, clearly reflecting American inexperience. By evening however the exuberant pilots felt they had dealt the Japanese a heavy blow. Actually, with an immense expenditure of ammunition (including 22 torpedoes, 76 half-ton bombs, some 12,500 rounds of .50 caliber and more than 70,000 rounds of .30 caliber) they had forced the Japanese to beach one destroyer, had slightly damaged another, and had sunk three minesweepers. It was, as Nimitz observed, a striking demonstration of the decline of efficiency under battle conditions and of the difficulty of accurately assessing results.

That evening the *Yorktown* began an uneventful withdrawal and on the morning of May 5 rejoined the *Lexington* group. The two forces steamed to the southeast during the day while the *Yorktown* group refueled from the oiler *Neosho,* then turned northwest during the night in order to close Port Moresby. Reports from MacArthur and from Nimitz of concentrations of Japanese ships in the Rabaul-New Guinea area indicated that the Japanese were ready to move. On May 6 Fletcher formally merged his two forces into one, with the two carriers operating within a single circular screen of cruisers and destroyers. Admiral Fitch, whom Morison called "the most experienced carrier flag officer in the Navy," was to be Commander Air, exercising tactical command during air operations. During the day the combined force steamed southwest to continue fueling.

Meanwhile the Japanese carriers had swung round the southern end of the Solomons on the evening of May 5 and on the 6th had penetrated into the Coral Sea. Their passage had been undetected because the Australians of MacArthur's Southwest Pacific Command had ceased to search the lower Solomons area after abandoning Tulagi, and the United States Navy's search from Noumea had not been extended to cover it.

Vice Admiral Takeo Takagi, commander of the cruiser division, was the senior officer and was technically in command of the Striking Force. However, Rear Admiral Tadaichi Hara, as commander of the carrier division, appears to have been responsible for some of the critical decisions of the battle.

Takagi's plan in coming around the Solomons was to catch the United States carriers in a sort of pincer movement. The whole Japanese advance into the Indies had been carried out by a series of such moves, and the double envelopment seems to have had a peculiar appeal to Japanese strategists. Had Japanese carrier search been better, Takagi might indeed have surprised the Americans and scored a decisive victory, for on the afternoon of May 6 he was rapidly overhauling Fletcher's force, which was proceeding slowly because of fueling. By 2000, just before the Japanese turned north, they had closed to 70 miles. Fletcher's morning search had been made before the Japanese came within range, and his afternoon search failed to discover them, apparently because of the bad weather. But the Japanese did no better. Relying on land-based search, Takagi apparently flew none from his carriers. A flying boat from Tulagi had in fact spotted the American force during the forenoon, but the report somehow never reached Tulagi. Thus the opportunity slipped away from the Japanese because of poor communications, and the Battle of the Coral Sea was postponed to another day.

ACTION OFF MISIMA, MAY 7

On the morning of May 7 the American task force was cruising on a northwesterly course south of the Louisiades, which form an extension of the New Guinea tail. Soon after launching the morning search, Fletcher detached the cruisers *Chicago, Australia,* and *Hobart,* and three destroyers under Admiral Crace to push on to the northwest to prevent the invasion force from passing through Jomard Passage. Fletcher fully expected his carriers to come under attack during the day and wanted to be sure that the Japanese invasion would be stopped even if his main force should be damaged or too heavily engaged to interfere. This did not seem unreasonable, but his action has been criticized on the ground that it weakened his screen at a time when attack was imminent, and it was after all the carriers that would decide the issue.

The *Yorktown's* search was incomplete because of bad weather to the northeast—which was just where the heavy Japanese carriers lay. To the northwest however the weather was clear, and reports soon began to come in from the scouts. At 0815 a pilot reported two carriers and four heavy cruisers in a position not far north of Misima Island. Fletcher at once ordered attack groups launched from both his carriers. The 93 planes were well on their way before the *Yorktown* scout returned and it was discovered that the report was an error due to improper coding—that the scout had meant to report two cruisers and two destroyers.

Fletcher was faced with a difficult problem. The Japanese were aware of his presence, perhaps of his precise position. He had good reason to believe that there were three enemy carriers in the vicinity—and he had just thrown the greater part of his offensive force at an insignificant target. He might very well find himself under attack without being able to strike back at the enemy carriers whenever they should actually be discovered. Should he recall his strike?

Fletcher made the courageous decision to let the attack proceed, probably thinking that with the Japanese invasion force in the area there must be some profitable targets. Then at 1022 came a report from Southwest Pacific headquarters of a carrier and many other vessels approximately 35 miles southeast of the point toward which the strike had been sent. The attack group had to alter course only slightly for the new target.

The first of the *Lexington* group sighted the *Shoho* just before 1100 and came in for the first attack ever made by American pilots on an enemy carrier. The Japanese screen was in extremely loose formation, and the antiaircraft fire was sporadic and ineffectual.

The *Shoho* had only three fighters in the air, but there were several on deck. A near miss blasted five of these overboard, but the *Shoho* succeeded in launching three of the remaining planes before the arrival of the rest of the *Lexington* group forced her to cease launching in order to take evasive action. At 1120 the *Lexington* bombing and torpedo squadrons made a particularly effective coordinated attack. When the *Yorktown* bombers arrived a moment later they found the carrier turning into the wind, "a perfect target." By the time they finished with her she was listing and burning so fiercely that the *Yorktown* torpedo planes were able to approach undetected under cover of the smoke. There were fewer hits than the attacking pilots claimed, but by Japanese count 13 bombs and seven torpedoes found their mark. That was more than the little *Shoho* could take. Three minutes after the last torpedo struck she went down.

The American carriers commenced landing their planes about 1240, and recovery was complete within an hour. Should a second strike be launched? Fletcher decided against it. He believed correctly that there remained two enemy heavy carriers in the area, and it seemed wise to hold his attack groups until they were located. Furthermore, there was reason to believe that the enemy knew his position, and it seemed likely that he would come under attack.

LOSS OF THE *NEOSHO* AND *SIMS*, MAY 7

Fletcher was quite correct in assuming that the Japanese knew his position. They failed to attack him on the 7th only because of a series of errors which by evening reached the fantastic.

Before 0900 on the 7th Inouye, directing the Japanese operation from Rabaul, had reports of two American carrier forces. One about 140 miles southeast of Deboyne Island was in fact Fletcher's force; the other, some 45 miles to the west of the first, was Crace's cruiser force, which of course contained no carrier. Then came a report from Takagi of a third United States carrier force in the eastern Coral Sea. This was a surprise. The two forces in the west were closer to the Invasion Force than Inouye had expected, and the third was totally unexpected. Actually this third force was the oiler *Neosho*, which had been detached from Fletcher's force the preceding evening and was proceeding in company with the destroyer *Sims* toward a rendezvous.

In the face of these developments Inouye ordered his Invasion Force to retire temporarily and directed the *Shoho* to launch an attack. For some reason never satisfactorily explained the *Shoho* failed to do so before 1100, when the American strike reached her and she had no further opportunity. At 0950 an attack group of navy planes took off from Rabaul to attack the westernmost of the United States forces. The Japanese pilots returned with reports that they had sunk a battleship and cruiser and seriously damaged a second battleship. Actually Crace's force of cruisers and destroyers survived without damage both this attack and another by B-26's from Australia, which mistook his vessels for Japanese.

The Japanese pilot's mistake in identifying the *Neosho* as a carrier had a serious effect on Japanese operations, for Hara at once launched a full attack on the hapless oiler and her escort. The *Sims* took three hits and went down with most of her crew. The *Neosho* absorbed seven hits, the crash of a suicide plane, and several damaging near misses. Several men who went overboard on the order to "stand by to abandon ship" were lost, but the fires were brought under control and the vessel remained afloat. An error in calculating her position unfortunately delayed rescue, so that it was not till May 11 that the destroyer *Henley* took off survivors and sank the hulk.

The discovery that he had revealed his presence by an attack on ships of only secondary importance caused Hara "much chagrin." In the meantime news of the sinking of the *Shoho* disclosed to him that the American carriers were to the west. He at once set course in that direction though the change necessitated breaking radio silence to inform his air attack group, which had not yet returned.

In Hara's estimation the situation was critical. The American carriers were in a position to threaten the Invasion Force, which it was his duty to protect. In mid-afternoon as he hurried westward he sent search planes out ahead but had to recall them before they reached the limits of their search in order to land them before dark. As night approached, the weather closed in, but Hara was determined to destroy the American carriers before they could damage the Invasion Force. Selecting 27 pilots best qualified in night operations, he sent them out at 1615 in the direction in which he estimated the American carriers lay. Sending an attack group close behind a search was a common Japanese practice, but this time there was no search.

It was not a bad gamble at that, for in the bad weather and poor visibility the Japanese planes actually passed near Fletcher's force without sighting it. The American combat air patrol, guided out by radar, intercepted the Japanese planes and shot down nine in a series of brief dogfights in the haze. An hour later, as the Japanese planes were attempting to return to their carriers, three flew alongside the *Yorktown* and crossed her bow, blinking in Morse code. Not long afterwards three actually attempted to join the landing circle. American gunners shot down one and drove the others off. The *Lexington*'s radar later showed planes circling as if for a landing about 30 miles to the east, which seemed to indicate that the Japanese carriers were very close indeed. Of the Japanese striking group ten had been shot down, and eleven others went into the water in attempting night landings on their carriers. Hara recovered safely only six of his 27.

The pilots of these planes reported the American carriers 50 or 60 miles away. Thus each of the opposing commanders was aware of the proximity of the other; both gave serious consideration to a night surface attack, and both abandoned the idea for similar reasons. Fletcher, having detached Crace's group that morning, did not feel that he could spare ships for a sufficiently strong raiding force, particularly in the absence of more precise information about the enemy. Hara, with only two heavy cruisers and six destroyers in his screen, was unwilling to send them against an enemy of unknown strength and thereby leave his carriers unprotected when an attack on them was possible. Thus the Battle of the Coral Sea was postponed still another day.

Actually the distance between the two forces was greater than either commander imagined, for postwar plots show that they were never closer than 95 miles.

THE BATTLE OF MAY 8

Thus far the two antagonists had been together in the Coral Sea for two days, and on both days they had come within a hundred miles of each other without exchanging blows. There was every likelihood that a decision would be reached on May 8, but on the evening of the 7th both commanders felt the enemy was uncomfortably close. During the night Fletcher withdrew to the south and west, while Takagi moved north.

For both commanders everything depended on locating the enemy as promptly as possible on the morning of the 8th. Three-quarters of an hour before dawn the Japanese launched a search to the southwest. It was almost half an hour later that the American search planes took off from the *Lexington*. Despite the difference in launching time however the two forces found each other almost simultaneously. At 0815 one of the *Lexington* scouts reported the Japanese carriers about 175 miles to the north of the American force. Minutes later Fletcher intercepted the report of a Japanese plane giving his position, course, and speed.

In other respects too the contest of May 8 started on curiously even terms. Each force contained two large carriers. The American screen, with five heavy cruisers and seven destroyers, was slightly stronger than the Japanese, and American antiaircraft was better. Fletcher had available 121 planes, Hara 122. The Americans were stronger in bombers, while the Japanese enjoyed a preponderance in fighter and torpedo planes. The Japanese pilots had had more combat experience, and their torpedoes were immensely better.

In another respect the Japanese enjoyed a significant advantage. By moving south through the night Fletcher had run out of the bad weather area in which he had been operating, and on the 8th his force lay exposed under clear skies. The Japanese remained within the frontal area, under the protection of clouds and rain squalls which were to prevent part of the American planes from finding their target and were to save the *Zuikaku* from attack altogether.

Essentially the battle consisted of a simultaneous exchange of strikes by the two carrier forces. Fletcher had notified Commander Southwest Pacific of the position of the Japanese, but no land-based planes appeared to take part in the engagement. Between 0900 and 0925 both American carriers launched their attack groups. That of the *Yorktown,* consisting of 24 bombers with two fighters and nine torpedo planes with four fighters, departed first. About 1030 the dive bombers found the Japanese carriers, about ten miles apart with their escorts in loose formation. While the pilots took cloud cover to await the arrival of the torpedo planes one of the Japanese carriers, apparently the *Zuikaku,* disappeared into a rain squall. Consequently the attack fell on the *Shokaku.*

When the torpedo planes approached from the southeast the SBD's began their dives. Although the attack was well coordinated it was only moderately successful. The torpedo planes failed to score. Their torpedoes were too slow and were dropped at too great a distance, so that the Japanese had little difficulty in avoiding them. The dive bombers succeeded in planting only two bombs on the *Shokaku,* one forward and one aft.

The *Lexington* group, which departed about ten minutes later than the *Yorktown's,* had difficulty in finding the target. The 22 planes of the bombing group after an unsuccessful search were forced by fuel shortage to turn back without sighting the enemy. Thus half Fletcher's bombers, his most effective type, failed to engage. Had these planes found the *Zuikaku* the Battle of the Coral

Sea might have ended differently. Of the *Lexington* group only the eleven torpedo planes, six fighters, and four scout bombers found the enemy. Again American torpedoes were utterly ineffective, but the bombers succeeded in adding another hit to the two already sustained by the *Shokaku.*

These three hits put the *Shokaku* out of action for the time being. Though her fires were soon brought under control and she was soon making 30 knots again, the damage to her flight deck prevented her recovering planes, so that Takagi shortly detached her for Truk.

The Japanese had sent off their group of 70 attack planes and 20 fighters at about the same time as the American launching. The American radar picked them up at a distance of about 70 miles. Thereupon Fitch, who had taken tactical command about 0900, launched additional fighters and, as a makeshift reinforcement for the antitorpedo patrol, eight SBD's. But fighter direction was badly handled; fighters were vectored out piecemeal, and despite the early warning only three of the 17 fighters in the air intercepted the enemy before the attack. At a distance of 20 miles, still having met no interference by American fighters, the Japanese planes divided into three groups, two of torpedo planes and one of bombers.

The two American carriers were together in the center of a circle of screening vessels. The *Yorktown* was a little north of the *Lexington* but changed her position slightly so that the *Lexington* would not be in her line of fire if the Japanese attacked from the sun. During the action the two carriers gradually drew apart.[1] Vessels of the screen followed the carrier that happened to be nearest. With the *Yorktown* went three cruisers and three destroyers, while two cruisers and four destroyers followed the *Lexington.* This was as evenly as the screen could have been divided, but the breaking of the circle left several vessels out of position and undoubtedly contributed to the Japanese success.

The *Yorktown* was the first to come under attack. Japanese torpedo planes approached

---

[1] In these days before the VT fuse, maneuver was more important in defense than antiaircraft fire.

on her port beam and quarter, but a full right rudder at flank speed put the carrier on a course parallel to their torpedoes. When more torpedoes were dropped on the starboard quarter a turn to port allowed them to pass harmlessly to starboard. Then came the bombers, diving out of the sun. The *Yorktown* took several near misses, one of which lifted her screws clear of the water, but there was only one direct hit. This penetrated her flight deck forward of No. 2 elevator and exploded between the third and fourth decks. There were several casualties, but the fires were quickly controlled and there was no reduction in the ship's fighting effectiveness.

The torpedo attack on the *Lexington* followed closely that on the *Yorktown* but was more skillfully executed, taking the form of an "anvil" attack on both bows simultaneously. Moreover, the *Lexington* had a considerably greater turning circle than the *Yorktown*. While turning to avoid torpedoes dropped on her starboard bow she received two hits on the port side which flooded three boiler rooms. The dive-bombing attack came almost simultaneously. Besides several near misses, the *Lexington* took two hits, one on the 5-inch ready-service locker on the port side, the other on her stack. Both bombs were small, so that the damage was not serious. The carrier had taken a 6-degree list as a result of the torpedo hits, but this was corrected by shifting oil. Her engines were unharmed, and her speed did not fall below 24 knots. To her pilots returning from their strike she appeared undamaged.

As the two American carriers began to recover their planes it appeared they had won the Battle of the Coral Sea. Both were operational with combat effectiveness essentially unimpaired except for a slight reduction in the *Lexington*'s speed. On the other hand, the *Shokaku* had been put out of action and was already withdrawing. Because the *Zuikaku* had been unable to take all the *Shokaku*'s planes, many had had to be jettisoned. Admiral Hara had only nine planes fit for further operations, while Fitch could still put into the air 37 attack planes and 12 fighters.

Even had Fletcher and Fitch been aware of this situation they would have had no opportunity to take advantage of it, for at 1247 there was an explosion deep inside the *Lexington,* caused apparently by the accumulation of vapor from ruptured gasoline lines touched off by a spark from a motor generator. At first the seriousness of the situation was not apparent, and the *Lexington* continued landing her planes. But at 1445 there was a second and more severe explosion. Fires passed rapidly out of control and the carrier was forced to call for assistance. The *Yorktown* took *Lexington* planes that were in the air, but there was no opportunity to transfer those already aboard the *Lexington.* With the ship burning furiously and shaken by frequent explosions there was no choice but to "get the men off." Abandonment was orderly, and after it was completed a destroyer was detached to sink the carrier. She fired five torpedoes to send the *Lexington* down at 1956.

In the meantime the remainder of the American task force, on orders from Nimitz, had commenced its withdrawal from the Coral Sea on a southerly course.

The Japanese pilots who returned from the attack reported sinking both United States carriers, and Hara was sufficiently sanguine to forward that estimate to his superiors. This comfortable belief undoubtedly influenced both Takagi's decision to detach the damaged *Shokaku* and Inouye's decision to withdraw the entire Striking Force. But even though he imagined both American carriers had been destroyed, Inouye still felt it necessary to postpone the Port Moresby invasion, apparently because he did not feel able to protect the landing force against Allied land-based planes.

However, Admiral Yamamoto, Commander in Chief Combined Fleet, did not acquiesce in this easy abandonment of the action. At 2400 he countermanded Inouye's order for the withdrawal of the Japanese Striking Force and directed it to annihilate the remaining American forces. Takagi thereupon put about and looked to the south and east for the retreating Americans. Fletcher was of course by this time safely out of reach, so that Takagi had to abandon his search about noon on the 10th.

RESULTS

Thus the first carrier battle of the war, the first battle in history in which the opposing ships never came within sight of each other, closed with the Japanese holding the field and the Americans in retreat. Tactically there is no doubt that Coral Sea was a Japanese victory, for the loss of the 30,000-ton *Lexington* far outweighed the sinking of the little 12,000-ton *Shoho,* and the Japanese destroyer and small craft sunk at Tulagi scarcely balanced the loss of the *Neosho* and *Sims.* Strategically however the United States had won. For the first time since the war began, Japanese expansion had been checked. The Port Moresby Invasion Force had been forced to withdraw without reaching its objective. Item one of the new, accelerated Japanese plan had been frustrated. Admiral Hara returned to port still believing that he had sunk two United States carriers, but with a consciousness that he had encountered a new kind of opposition and with a feeling that the war had somehow entered a new phase.

The battle had other important consequences. The strategic success helped the United States morally by taking some of the sting out of the surrender of Corregidor, which came on May 6, during the battle. More important, the damage to the *Shokaku* and the necessity for re-forming the battered air groups of the *Zuikaku* kept those two carriers out of the Battle of Midway, where their presence might well have been decisive.

The Japanese imagined that the conquest of Port Moresby was only postponed to a more favorable time, but the Battle of Midway was to make that postponement permanent.

39

Midway and the Aleutians

ON MAY 5, 1942, AFTER THE *Yorktown* had attacked Tulagi, but before the Battle of the Coral Sea was decided, Imperial Headquarters activated the second phase of Japanese basic strategy by ordering the Midway-Aleutian operation. The outcome of the carrier battle of May 8, far from causing any modification of these plans, seems actually to have encouraged the Japanese, for they believed that they had sunk both the *Yorktown* and the *Lexington*. A few days after the battle they sighted Halsey's *Enterprise* and *Hornet* in the South Pacific. Thus they felt certain that they would encounter no carriers in the Central Pacific.

JAPANESE PLANS

There was nothing petty in Japanese planning. The entire Combined Fleet, under the personal command of Admiral Yamamoto, was to be employed in a vast operation covering the Northern and Central Pacific. A carrier task force would strike in the Aleutians on June 3, after which occupation forces would land on Adak, Attu, and Kiska. This attack, to take place a day before that on Midway, was intended partially as a di-version. There would hardly be time for American forces actually to be pulled out of position, but the attack would at least confuse the American command.

At dawn on June 4 a second and larger carrier force, coming from the northwest, would bomb Midway Atoll, destroy the planes based there, and soften it up in preparation for the landing. Then on the night of June 5 the occupation forces, approaching from the southwest, would put some 5,000 troops ashore to take the island and convert it into a Japanese base.

The Americans, the Japanese believed, lacked the will to fight but would be forced either to defend Midway or to attempt to retake it. When the United States fleet sortied from Pearl Harbor it would cross one or the other of two lines of submarines that the Japanese had placed to the west and north of that base (see diagram, next page). These would inflict some losses on the American fleet and would give Yamamoto ample warning. The Japanese carrier force would then attack the Americans and might well maneuver to get between them and Pearl Harbor. Then Yamamoto's heavy surface ships of the Main Body, hitherto kept safely back to the northwest, would close in for the kill. The work of December 7 would be

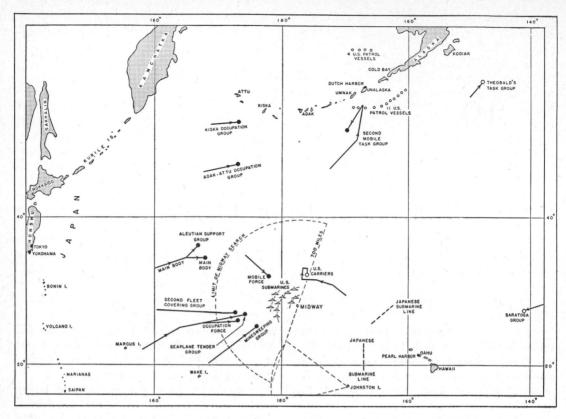

BATTLE OF MIDWAY, POSITION OF FORCES AT 2400 ON JUNE 3, 1942

completed and the United States fleet destroyed before it could be reinforced by new construction. The Japanese had no immediate plan for the occupation of Pearl Harbor. When the American fleet had been eliminated there would be ample time to think of that.

The fixed pattern of Japanese strategic thinking is evident when this plan is compared with that for the Coral Sea. Again there was a dual objective, again a multiplicity of forces, and again the Japanese were obsessed with the notion of pincer movements and envelopments.

The multiplicity of forces is even more striking when one examines the Japanese organization in detail. Vice Admiral Boshiro Hosogaya's Northern Area Force, destined for the Aleutians, contained three principal groups besides the command-supply group. Rear Admiral Kakuji Kakuta's Second Mo-

bile Group consisted of the two light carriers *Ryujo* and *Junyo,* two heavy cruisers, and three destroyers. The Adak-Attu Occupation Group was separate from that destined for Kiska and operated independently.

The Mobile Force for the central Pacific was commanded by Vice Admiral Chuichi Nagumo, who had conducted the Pearl Harbor and Ceylon raids. His carriers, the *Akagi, Kaga, Hiryu,* and *Soryu,* all veterans of Pearl Harbor, were screened by two fast battleships, two heavy cruisers, and twelve destroyers and were accompanied by their own oilers and supply ships. A little to the south and west of the Mobile Force was the Main Body. It was composed of seven battleships, including the *Yamato,*[1] flagship of Ad-

---

[1] The *Yamato* and her sister ship the *Musashi,* each 64,000 tons, were the largest battleships ever built. Their main batteries consisted of nine 18.1-inch guns, firing a 3,200-pound projectile, which was almost 50

miral Yamamoto, one light aircraft carrier, the *Hosho,* two seaplane carriers, two light cruisers and 13 destroyers. But even this force was divided. On June 3 the greater part, including four battleships and the two cruisers, turned north to become the "Aleutian Support Group." It was supposed to take a position about half way between the Aleutian and Midway forces, presumably to be able to give support in either area.

The Midway Occupation Force was commanded by Vice Admiral Nobutake Kondo, who as Commander in Chief of the Second Fleet had participated in the conquest of the Philippines and Indies. It consisted of five groups. Its twelve transports were screened by a cruiser, ten destroyers, and three patrol boats. The Close Support Group of four heavy cruisers and two destroyers was to cover the transports and support the landing. A powerful Second Fleet Covering Group, which Kondo retained under his direct command, was to assist in the same mission. It comprised two battleships, the light carrier *Zuiho,* four heavy cruisers, and eight destroyers. A Seaplane Tender Group was intended to set up a base on Kure, to the northwest of Midway. A Minesweeper Group would clear the way for the landings. These forces operated more or less independently. The Second Fleet Group was usually more than 50 miles to the north or northwest of the transports, while the Close Support Group was usually some 75 miles to the northeast.

The Japanese as usual sent an "Advance

Expeditionary Force" of submarines to scout ahead of the Combined Fleet. One boat went ahead to scout Midway, while four took positions off the Aleutians and two stationed themselves off Seattle. Most important of the submarine dispositions were two patrol lines designed to cover Pearl Harbor. One line of four submarines lay about 500 miles west of Oahu, while another of seven boats ran athwart the obvious route between Pearl and Midway, about half way between the two. These boats were to be on station by June 1.

Why did such a vast armada fail to accomplish its mission? There is no doubt that American intelligence of Japanese plans was a decisive factor. Even with ample warning Nimitz was barely able to get three carriers onto the scene in time. It is difficult to believe that without that warning he either could or would have done so. So one may say that the most obvious reason for the miscarriage of the plans of the Japanese was their failure to achieve the surprise on which they counted.

Now surprise is extremely important in naval and military operations and ought to be exploited whenever possible. Very often the weaker force has no alternative but to rely on surprise to achieve its ends. But the Japanese made the mistake of planning a major operation so that it depended on surprise when there was no necessity for their doing so. Even with the most complete warning, it is inconceivable that the three United States carriers could by any combination of luck and skill have defeated and turned back the seven carriers, eleven battleships, and the immense number of supporting vessels which the Japanese committed to this action *had the Japanese fleet been properly concentrated.* As it was, June 3, the day of the attack on Dutch Harbor and of the first contact in the Midway area, found the Japanese surface ships in no less than ten groups scattered all over the North and Central Pacific (see chart, opposite page).

Concentration of course does not require the massing of forces in a single group. In what, then, did the Japanese fail? First of all, they failed to pursue a single objective.

___

per cent heavier than a 16-inch projectile. One of the triple-mounted turrets weighed as much as a large destroyer, and the ships' side armor was more than 16 inches thick. Note that by comparison, the largest United States battleships, the 45,000-ton *Iowa* class, carry nine 16-inch guns.

Planning for these vessels began in 1934, even before Japan denounced the Washington Naval Treaty of 1922. After extensive experiments, final plans were drawn up early in 1937, and the two vessels were laid down that year, the *Yamato* at Kure, the *Musashi* at Nagasaki. A third vessel of the class was laid down at Yokosuka early in 1940, but after the Battle of Midway the hull was converted into the aircraft carrier *Shinano.* Construction was abandoned on a fourth unit of the class. The *Yamato* was completed in December 1941 and the *Musashi* eight months later.

The two carriers sent to the Aleutians might well have supplied the decisive margin in the Central Pacific. Had the Midway operation succeeded, the Japanese could have taken the Aleutians at their leisure. Without success at Midway the Aleutian operation lost its meaning.

In the Midway area itself the Japanese had some of the elements of concentration. Their forces were grouped concentrically about Midway, which they assumed was the strategic center. They had a unified command in Yamamoto, who could bring about coordinated action. But when the crisis developed Yamamoto found that his forces were too widely separated for mutual support. He found after a vain attempt that he simply could not bring the scattered groups together in time to retrieve the situation.

Fault may also be found with the more detailed arrangements of the Japanese. The carriers of the Mobile Force were inadequately screened. The vessels scattered elsewhere might profitably have been used to give them better protection. The Main Body after the departure of the Northern Support Group was for all its surface strength an ill-balanced, useless force. The Occupation Force, which approached Midway from the southwest under clear skies, was dangerously exposed. It did not have adequate air protection and might well have become a principal target for American forces. To have brought the Occupation Force forward before the United States fleet had been accounted for bespeaks utter callousness on the part of the Japanese command, which was more careful of its battleships than of its transports.

One of the most serious mistakes of the Japanese was in their handling of their submarines. On the assumption that the Americans were not likely to sortie from Pearl before the attack on Midway, Japanese submarines did not take station until June 1. The American carriers actually crossed their patrol line between Pearl and Midway, the *Hornet* and *Enterprise* on May 29, the *Yorktown* on the night of May 31. Had the Japanese submarines been on station in time there would have been no surprise at Midway and again the result might have been quite different.

UNITED STATES PREPARATIONS

Since the United States was intercepting and reading Japanese coded messages, American intelligence of the enemy's plans was remarkably complete. Nimitz's information indicated the Japanese objectives, the approximate composition of the enemy forces, the direction of approach, and the approximate date of attack. It was this knowledge that made the American victory possible, but in view of the meager forces available to meet the threat it must have seemed to the United States command very much like foreknowledge of an inevitable disaster.

The first decision confronting Nimitz was whether to let the Aleutians go by default or to reinforce them at the expense of the Central Pacific. He chose the latter course and sent to the area a force of five cruisers, 14 destroyers, and six submarines. These were under Rear Admiral Robert A. Theobald, who was also to command land-based air.

As for the Central Pacific, Midway itself was too small to support sufficient forces to repel an attack of the proportions of that impending. Lying at the northwest end of the Hawaiian chain about 1,100 miles from Pearl Harbor, the little atoll consists of two islands surrounded by a reef. Sand Island, the larger of the two, is only about two miles long, while Eastern Island, on which the runways were situated, is little more than half as large. However, everything possible was done to strengthen Midway's defenses. The beaches and surrounding waters were mined. The marine garrison was reinforced and given additional antiaircraft guns. Finally, air strength was increased to the limit of the island's facilities. For search there were approximately 30 PBY's. There was between Midway and Oahu a constant interchange of B-17's which left 17 on Midway on June 3. The marine squadrons were equipped with planes cast off by the carriers, which had more modern equipment. For defense they had 28 fighters, mostly old Brewster Buffaloes. For attack there were 34 scout bombers, divided between Douglas Dauntlesses and Vought-Sikorsky Vindicators. Most of the pilots for these planes had been rushed out from flight school and had not yet practiced dive bombing. There were four Army B-26's, jury-rigged for a torpedo attack for which they were utterly unsuited. The only really effective planes on the island were six TBF's, the first to reach the Pacific. It is a sad comment on America's unpreparedness that after six months of war this motley collection of planes was the best the country could provide for defense of a vital point.

The marines would undoubtedly have given the Japanese a warm reception had they come in for a landing, but it was clear that the fate of Midway depended in the final analysis on naval support. What could Nimitz assemble for the purpose? The *Lexington* had of course been sunk in the Coral Sea. The *Saratoga's* repairs had been completed and she was training on the West Coast, but there was delay in forming an escort for her, so that she left San Diego only on June 1 and did not reach Pearl till June 6, too late for the battle. The *Hornet-Enterprise* force had been hurriedly recalled from the South Pacific and arrived at Pearl Harbor on May 26. There illness compelled Halsey to relinquish command, and his place was taken by Rear Admiral Raymond A. Spruance, who had commanded the cruisers of the task force. Thoughtful, cautious, and modest, Spruance was in personality a striking contrast to the impetuous, colorful Halsey. But his unassuming manner concealed a brilliant mind and sound judgment, as the battle was to prove. The two carriers with a screen of five heavy cruisers, one light cruiser, and nine destroyers put to sea on May 28.

Fletcher's damaged *Yorktown* had also come back posthaste from the South Pacific. Repairs which would ordinarily have taken three months were compressed into three days, so that on the morning of May 30 she was able to put to sea with a screen of two heavy cruisers and five destroyers. The two carrier forces met northeast of Midway on June 2, and Fletcher, as senior, took command. However, after Fletcher's flagship, the *Yorktown,* was torpedoed on June 4, Spruance, who had retained Halsey's experienced staff, assumed local tactical command of both forces in the presence of the enemy.

These three carriers and their escorts were all that could be assembled. The United States had some old battleships on the West Coast, but they were too slow to accompany the carriers, there were no destroyers available to screen them, and they scarcely fitted the "attrition tactics" Nimitz had decided to employ. The British had three carriers in the Indian Ocean but could not be convinced of the need for them at Midway.

To backstop the carriers 19 submarines were assigned positions to cover the approaches to Midway. The *Cuttlefish* was stationed 700 miles west of Midway, where it was thought the Japanese might rendezvous. Three boats patrolled 200 miles to the west of the atoll. Six more 150 miles from the island patrolled an arc stretching from southwest to north, while two more were only 50 miles northwest of Midway. Others were stationed to support the carriers and to cover Oahu. Nimitz retained at Pearl Harbor the over-all command so that he could if necessary coordinate the movements of the submarines, the carriers, and the Midway planes.

The task that faced Fletcher and Spruance was appalling. Nimitz's instructions were: "You will be governed by the principle of calculated risk, which you shall interpret to mean the avoidance of exposure of your force to attack by superior enemy forces without the prospect of inflicting, as a result of such exposure, greater damage on the enemy." To fight cautiously, to meet a superior enemy force without unduly exposing one's own, is difficult in the highest degree. That Fletcher and Spruance were able to carry out these orders successfully was due primarily to their skillful exploitation of intelligence, which enabled them to turn the element of surprise against the Japanese. The American command perceived that air power was the key to the situation and correctly concentrated on the Japanese carriers. The position northeast of Midway was well chosen, since it placed the United States carriers on the flank of the Mobile Force, and the dispersion of the Japanese forces prevented any support from reaching that force in time.

THE ATTACK ON THE ALEUTIANS

Admiral Theobald, like a good many other officers, suspected that the information on which American intelligence estimates were based had been "planted" by the Japanese. He was particularly concerned that the threat of an attack on the western Aleutians might be designed to draw him away from the more important Dutch Harbor-Cold Bay area; so he decided to concentrate his forces for the defense of the latter. Inasmuch as his surface vessels were completely dependent for air cover on land or harbor-based planes, the most westerly base for which was the secret field at Otter Point on Umnak, he could scarcely have done otherwise, but this decision meant that his task force was destined never to make contact with the enemy.

Theobald directed his main force of five cruisers and four destroyers to rendezvous 400 miles south of Kodiak. The last ships did not arrive till the morning of June 3, a few hours after the Japanese had hit Dutch Harbor. At Makushin Bay, Unalaska, he stationed a striking force of nine destroyers to break up any landing the Japanese might attempt in the Dutch Harbor area.

Since the surface vessels could be used only if a favorable opportunity arose, the primary burden fell upon the planes, and they were all too few. The Navy had 20 PBY's for search. For defense the Army had about 65 pursuit planes, but little more than half these were at Cold Bay and Umnak, where they were needed. The principal striking power lay in the 20 Army bombers (chiefly B-26's) based at Kodiak, Cold Bay, and Umnak.

To provide early warning of the Japanese approach Theobald stationed his six submarines in likely positions for interception and placed 20 small vessels at a radius of 200 miles from Dutch Harbor, both to the south and in the Bering Sea. PBY's patrolled all the approaches, but their search was limited to 400 miles because of the scarcity of radar-equipped planes.

Somehow Kakuta's two carriers, approaching from the south-southwest, eluded submarines, picket boats, and planes. Although it was only an hour after midnight [2] of June 2-3, it was already a foggy half-light in Alaskan latitudes when the Japanese admiral launched 36 planes from a position about 165 miles south of Dutch Harbor. But the bad weather that had enabled him to escape detection now favored the Americans. The *Junyo's* planes wandered in the fog and returned to the carrier without finding the target. The *Ryujo's* group, emerging into locally clear weather over Dutch Harbor, scored almost complete surprise. Only the radar of the seaplane tender *Gillis,* lying at anchor in the harbor, gave the Americans a few minutes of warning. There was no fighter interception as the bombers "worked over" the buildings of Fort Mears, the radio station, and the oil storage tanks, while fighters strafed several PBY's on the water. Antiaircraft guns knocked down only two of the attacking planes.

On their return the Japanese sighted five destroyers of Theobald's force in Makushin Bay. Kakuta at once launched another strike at these targets, but worsening weather prevented the group from joining up. American P-40's from Otter Point shot down two, and none reached Makushin Bay.

After the attack on Dutch Harbor American patrol planes made strenuous efforts to discover the Japanese carrier force, but without success. Their failure was in part due to a belief that the attack had come from the Bering Sea, in part to the fact that Kakuta had retired to the southwest after his attempted strike on Makushin Bay. Then early on the 4th in accordance with his or-

---

[2] In this account both of the Aleutians and Midway, west longitude dates are used and zone-plus-12 time, which is local time for Midway and the central Aleutians.

ders he set course for Adak. However, unfavorable weather forced him to abandon this project, and he returned for a second strike on Dutch Harbor.

Kakuta had already started toward Dutch Harbor when at 0450 on the 4th an American PBY accurately reported his position. Thereafter American planes kept intermittent contact throughout the day. Kakuta had already launched his strike when the Americans began a series of sporadic attacks. However, none of the planes—PBY's rigged with torpedoes, B-26's, and B-17's—were really suited for operating against ships. Although the pilots attacked with great gallantry, they achieved nothing better than a few near misses at the cost of three planes, one of each type.

The Japanese striking group arrived over Dutch Harbor about 1600. During the next half hour it bombed and set fire to the new fuel oil tanks with some 22,000 barrels of fuel, the old station ship *Northwestern*, which had to be beached, a warehouse, and an empty aircraft hangar. Afterwards the *Junyo's* planes, making rendezvous over the western end of Unalaska, discovered the Army's secret airfield at Otter Point when American pursuit planes rose to shoot down four of them.

Meanwhile there were indications that the Japanese operations around Midway were going less well than in the Aleutians. Soon after launching his strike Kakuta had received from Yamamoto the order to join the Mobile Force immediately, and about the same time he was informed that the occupation of Midway and the Aleutians had been postponed. Kakuta waited till he recovered his planes more than two hours later before setting course to the south to join Nagumo. By that time Yamamoto, at the urging of his staff, had changed his mind about the Aleutian landings and authorized the occupation forces to proceed according to plan. However, Hosogaya, Commander of the Northern Force, made one modification. He canceled the landing on Adak. Apparently he considered it too risky to land only 350 miles from the newly discovered American airfield at Otter Point.

Soon after noon on June 6 about 1,250 men of a Special Naval Landing Force went ashore on Kiska, where they took prisoner the personnel of a small United States weather station. In the early hours of the following morning 1200 Japanese troops landed on Attu, "capturing" 39 Aleuts and an American missionary and his wife. It was not till June 10 that American patrol planes discovered the Japanese on the two islands.

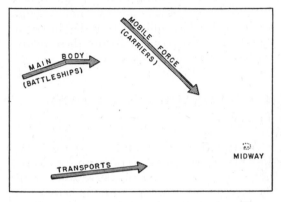

JAPANESE APPROACH TO MIDWAY,
JUNE 3

MIDWAY AREA—FIRST CONTACTS, JUNE 3

Midway's PBY's departed before dawn each morning to search the western sector to 700 miles. That distance was calculated to prevent any force which might be just out of range from reaching a launching position before the next day's search. During the last days of May and the first days of June coverage was excellent except in the critical area beyond 350 miles to the northwest, where weather was bad.

The first contact of the battle was made on the morning of June 3 when a patrol plane reported "two Japanese cargo vessels" almost 500 miles to the southwest. A little later another plane reported "six large ships in column" about 700 miles in the same direction. American commanders both on Midway and in the carriers surmised correctly that this was part of the Japanese Occupation Force. Since the main attack was expected from the northwest, the American carriers kept their position some 300 miles north-northeast of Midway, and the island forces for a while held their attack. Finally, a little after noon, when no new contacts had been made, nine B-17's with bomb-bay fuel tanks took off from Midway. Their attack, delivered about 1630, was ineffective. It was left for four radar-equipped PBY's which took off that night, each armed with a torpedo, to draw the first blood of the battle. Incredibly enough, one of these planes scored a hit that inflicted considerable damage on a Japanese oiler. Before these planes returned Midway was under attack.

THE ATTACK ON MIDWAY, JUNE 4

As American commanders expected, the Japanese carriers were approaching from the northwest under cover of the weather front. At 0430 on the 4th, half an hour before sunrise, at a distance of 240 miles from Midway, Nagumo sent off an attack group of 108 aircraft, made up of equal numbers of fighters, bombers, and torpedo planes. Weather was clear with scattered clouds and good visibility, and a southeast wind permitted him to hold his course while launching.

At Midway in the meantime patrol planes had as usual taken off at 0415, followed by the B-17's, which were put into the air to prevent their being surprised on the ground. At 0545 a PBY pilot reported in plain English, "Many planes heading Midway, bearing 320, distance 150." Five minutes later the Midway radar picked up the aproaching planes at a distance of 93 miles. But where were the Japanese carriers? The answer for which American commanders both on Midway and in the carriers were waiting came just two minutes later when a PBY pilot reported two carriers and their escorts, bearing 320° from Midway, distant 180 miles. This placed the Japanese about 40 miles southeast of their true position, an error which was to cause difficulty for the American carrier planes. The B-17's, then in the air, were at once directed to the enemy car-

riers, while the marine attack planes, the four B-26's, and the six TBF's, already warmed up and manned, took off to attack the same targets.

By this time the Japanese planes were approaching Midway. The marine fighters met them 30 miles out. "Each pilot made only one or two passes at the bombers and then spent the remainder of the time trying to shake from one to five Jap fighters off his tail," for the Zeke easily outperformed the American fighters.[3] Midway antiaircraft opened up as the Japanese formation came within range. The first bomb fell at 0630. Within the next half hour almost everything above ground was damaged; the power house was hit, the fuel tanks set afire, a hangar destroyed. Only the runways escaped injury. When it was all over the marine fighters were told to land. "Pitifully few" responded. Of the 27, fifteen were missing, and most of the dozen planes that returned were severely damaged. But they had helped see to it that a third of Nagumo's planes would never return to their carriers.

MIDWAY STRIKES BACK, JUNE 4

Midway's attack on the Japanese was carried out with high courage, but it was piecemeal, uncoordinated, and ineffective. It did however serve a useful purpose, for it distracted the Japanese at a critical time, prevented their launching, and thus helped make possible the success of the American carriers.

The B-26's and TBF's attacked at low altitude separately but simultaneously just after 0700. The Japanese ships made smoke, maneuvered radically, and threw up a heavy antiaircraft fire, while Zekes intercepted.

---

[3] Report of Major Verne McCaul USMC, Group Executive Officer, Aircraft Group 22, Second Marine Aircraft Wing, quoted in O.N.I. Combat Narrative, *Battle of Midway* (1943), 13.

The famous Japanese aircraft was called Zero until 1943. Thereafter Zeros with rounded wingtips were called Zekes and those with square wingtips were called Haps. Zeke however was the general term applied to all Zeros after 1943.

The American planes scored no hits. Five of the six TBF's and two of the four B-26's were shot down, while the three planes that returned were too badly damaged for further use.

It was almost an hour later that the marine scout bombing squadron, under Major Lofton R. Henderson, struck. Since the pilots were fresh from flight school, untrained in dive bombing, they were forced to make a more dangerous glide bombing attack. They scored no hits on their target, the carrier *Hiryu,* and only eight of the 16 planes returned to Midway. Six of these were badly shot up.

About 15 minutes later fifteen B-17's arrived. Bombing from 20,000 feet, the fortresses suffered no casualties and inflicted none. They were just departing when the second marine group arrived. Making a high speed approach at low level, they encountered such heavy antiaircraft and fighter opposition that they were unable to reach a carrier but dropped at a battleship instead. Again they scored no hits, and two planes made water landings before reaching Midway.

The first round of the Battle of Midway had clearly gone to the Japanese. They had pretty thoroughly smashed Midway. The island had sacrificed half its planes without damaging any enemy vessels in return. As Nimitz observed, "Most of Midway's fighters, torpedo planes, and dive bombers—the only types capable of making a high percentage of hits on ships—were gone." It was at this point that the United States carriers entered the battle.

THE UNITED STATES CARRIERS INTERVENE

When the Midway scout first reported the Japanese carriers at 0552 the American striking force was approximately 200 miles E by N of the Mobile Force. Fletcher immediately sent the *Hornet* and *Enterprise* toward the contact with orders to "attack enemy carriers when definitely located," while the *York-*

town continued on an easterly course in order to land the planes of her morning search.

Spruance in the *Enterprise* decided to close the range for an hour before launching in order to bring the enemy more safely within the 175-mile range of his torpedo planes. It was well he did so, for the distance was actually 25 miles greater than the report indicated. Finally, about 0700, when he estimated that he was 150 miles from the enemy and when there seemed a good chance of catching the Japanese refueling the planes which had struck Midway, he ordered launching.

In preparation for action the two carriers had separated, dividing the screening vessels between them. This was to avoid the error of the Coral Sea, where the *Lexington* and *Yorktown* had drawn apart under attack and had split the screening formation. The *Enterprise* put into the air 23 dive bombers, 14 torpedo planes, and ten fighters. The *Hornet* group consisted of 35 bombers, 15 torpedo planes, and ten fighters. To expedite the attack Spruance ordered the *Enterprise* bombers to proceed before the torpedo squadron was fully launched, and the *Hornet* bombers and torpedo planes, flying at different altitudes, became separated. Thus the attack force soon after its departure at approximately 0800 fell into four separate groups.

The *Yorktown* meanwhile had completed recovery of her search planes about 0630 and turned to follow the *Enterprise* and *Hornet.* Because Fletcher had expected four or five carriers in the enemy force and only two had thus far been reported he hesitated to commit the *Yorktown's* air group until the other enemy carriers had been accounted for. Finally, a little after 0830, in the absence of any further reports, he decided to launch half the *Yorktown's* planes. In the next half hour the carrier launched 17 dive bombers, twelve torpedo planes, and six fighters. Then, still concerned about the two or three enemy carriers that had not yet been sighted, Fletcher launched a search to the north and west a little after 1100.

Nagumo had up to this time been acting with admirable caution. Although his intelli-

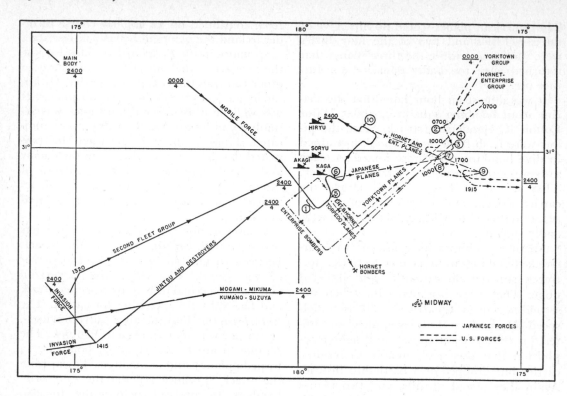

BATTLE OF MIDWAY, JUNE 4

1. 0705-0830: Midway planes and *Nautilus* attack Japanese carriers.
2. 0705: *Enterprise* and *Hornet* begin launching attack groups.
3. 0806: *Enterprise* and *Hornet* planes depart.
4. 0838: *Yorktown* begins launching.
5. 0920-1025: U. S. carrier planes attack Japanese carriers.
6. 1115: *Hiryu* attack group departs.
7. 1208: Japanese dive bombers attack *Yorktown*.
8. 1500: *Yorktown* abandoned.
9. 1530-1615: *Enterprise* and *Hornet* launch attack group.
10. 1701: *Hiryu* bombed.

gence led him to expect no naval opposition, he had sent only about half his available planes against Midway and had kept the rest on deck, armed with torpedoes, ready for action should any American vessels appear. Then, after his planes had departed for Midway, he had ordered his cruisers to catapult seven planes for a search to the east and south. These had departed at intervals through the next half hour, with the *Tone's* plane last to take to the air.

At 0700 Nagumo's strike commander, then returning from Midway, reported that an-

other strike at the island was necessary. Midway's torpedo attack, which came in almost immediately afterward, seemed to emphasize the point. By that time Nagumo's cruiser search planes had been gone for from two to two and a half hours and should have reached a radius of at least 200 miles. It seemed safe now to relax his precautions. At any rate, the planes from the Midway strike would soon be landing and would require servicing.

Therefore at 0715 Nagumo issued the fateful order, "Planes in second wave stand by to carry out attack today. Re-equip your-selves with bombs." It was just 13 minutes later that the *Tone's* scout reported ten American ships about 200 miles to the north-east. It is easy to imagine how different the Battle of Midway might have been had the *Tone's* plane been launched promptly so that this report might have come in half an hour earlier. Surface vessels 200 miles away did not constitute an urgent problem, but within a few minutes Nagumo changed course toward the contact, and at 0745 he sent his carriers the order, "Prepare to carry out attacks on enemy fleet units. Leave tor-pedoes on the attack planes which have not yet changed to bombs." It was not till 0820 that the *Tone* scout reported that one of the American ships appeared to be a carrier.

Nagumo was undoubtedly aware of the desirability of striking first, even though a single United States carrier against his four did not seem particularly dangerous. But he could not launch immediately because of the necessity of re-arming his planes. At the same time he was under attack by Midway planes from 0705 to 0830, taking evasive ac-tion which would have interfered with launching. Another distraction was provided by the submarine *Nautilus,* which had inter-cepted the Midway scout's first report of the Japanese carriers and had headed toward them. Between attacks by Midway planes she stuck up her periscope in the midst of the Mobile Force and fired two torpedoes to set off a grand confusion of circling destroyers and exploding depth charges. During all this turmoil Nagumo was attempting to recover the planes of his Midway strike, which began to arrive at 0738. The last of these was taken aboard at 0918, after which they had to be struck below and the fresh planes brought up. By that time it was too late, for the American carrier planes were upon him.

The *Enterprise-Hornet* planes had broken into four groups, while the *Yorktown's* made a fifth. Consequently whatever coordination was achieved in the ensuing attack was en-tirely accidental. The *Enterprise* fighters which were supposed to protect their car-rier's torpedo squadron had by mistake joined the *Hornet's* instead. Climbing to 20,000 feet en route, these fighters were above the Japanese force when both the *Hornet* and the *Enterprise* torpedo planes made their ill-starred attacks; but not receiving the pre-arranged signal for help, they circled un-til their fuel ran low, then returned to the carrier without having engaged in the battle.

Because of the scout's error in reporting the Japanese position, aggravated by Na-gumo's change of course to the northeast, the Mobile Force was not where the Ameri-can pilots expected to find it. The *Hornet's* dive bombers, flying at high altitude, failed to sight the Japanese and continued on to the southwest. However, "Torpedo 8," which was beneath the clouds, sighted the enemy carriers to the northwest at 0920 and imme-diately began its approach. Japanese fighters, which had been brought down to lower lev-els to counter the attacks by Midway planes, met them well out, and the veteran Japa-nese pilots easily overwhelmed the slow and clumsy torpedo planes. All 15 were shot down, probably before they were able to drop their torpedoes. Only one pilot sur-vived. He escaped strafing or capture by hid-ing under a floating seat cushion till dark. The *Hornet's* dive bombers continued to the southwest until their fuel ran low. Then 21 returned to the carrier, while the remaining 14 headed for Midway, where three crashed. All the accompanying fighters, which had shorter ranges, landed in the sea when their fuel was exhausted.

The *Enterprise* torpedo squadron arrived ten or 15 minutes after the *Hornet's.* Like Torpedo 8, it was without fighter protection, and it fared little better. The squadron split in an attempt to make an attack on both bows of the Japanese carriers, but the enemy turned to keep the planes on their quarter and prolong their approach. Zekes swarmed over them and shot down ten of the 14. Again there were no hits. But the sacrifice of the torpedo squadrons was not in vain, for their attacks drew the Zekes down to low al-titudes, and in their preoccupation with the torpedo planes the Japanese forgot to look up.

The *Enterprise* dive bombers, like the *Hornet's,* failed to find the enemy in the position expected, but Lieutenant Commander Clarence McClusky, Jr., the Air Group Commander, making "one of the most important decisions of the battle," turned north to fly the first leg of an expanding square. A little

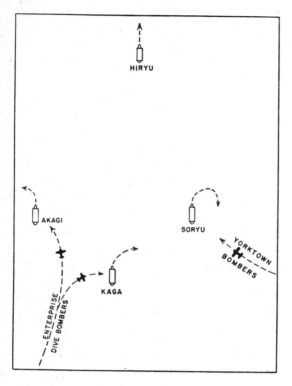

DISPOSITION OF JAPANESE CARRIERS AT TIME OF BOMBING ATTACK BY ENTERPRISE *AND* YORKTOWN *PLANES, 1020, JUNE 4*

after 1000, setting his course by a straggling destroyer, he was rewarded by a view of the Mobile Force. The four carriers were in a sort of diamond formation with the *Hiryu* somewhat off to the north (see diagram above). McClusky divided his attack between the two carriers in the southwest portion of the formation, which happened to be the *Akagi* and *Kaga.* Just as Spruance had hoped, their decks were covered with planes which they had been refueling and which they were now endeavoring to launch. Into the midst of these the American pilots dropped their bombs. There was no fighter

opposition until after they pulled out of their dives. By that time both carriers were burning. Off to the east the *Soryu* was also on fire, for the *Yorktown* planes had made a simultaneous attack.

The *Yorktown* air group had been launched more than an hour later than those of the *Enterprise* and *Hornet,* but rapidly clearing weather aided it both in joining up en route and in finding the enemy. Consequently its attack, without either group's being aware of it, coincided with that of the *Enterprise* dive bombers. Coming in from the east, the *Yorktown* planes concentrated on the nearest carrier, which was the *Soryu.* The torpedo squadron was slightly ahead. Despite the efforts of the six accompanying fighters, only five of the dozen planes survived to reach a dropping point, and only two returned to the carrier. They scored no hits. But the bombers, diving in from the sun, encountered no fighter and little anti-aircraft opposition. By the time the first 13 had completed their dives the *Soryu* was so completely aflame that the four remaining planes turned to other targets.

It was indeed fortunate for the Americans that they had caught the Japanese carriers refueling their planes, for they had no armor-piercing bombs, and the few hits they made would scarcely have been fatal had the Japanese been in a less vulnerable condition.

ATTACKS ON THE YORKTOWN, JUNE 4

Three of the four Japanese carriers had been put out of action, but the fourth, the *Hiryu,* standing off to the north, had escaped unscathed. A little after 1000 she started launching an attack group of 18 bombers and six fighters, followed an hour later by ten torpedo planes and six fighters. That seemed adequate to take care of the one American carrier which had thus far been reported to the Japanese command. In the meantime Nagumo had with difficulty been persuaded to transfer from the flaming *Akagi* to a cruiser, while Kondo was bringing his powerful Second Fleet Group from the transports, which did not seem to be threatened, to reinforce the screen of the Mobile Force.

The *Yorktown* had just completed launching her search planes and was refueling fighters of her combat air patrol and preparing to recover her striking group when about noon her radar picked up the *Hiryu's* planes at a distance of less than 50 miles. Refueling was hastily abandoned, planes on the flight deck were quickly launched with orders to clear the area, and returning bombers were waved away. The carrier's screen was in the standard circular disposition with a cruiser on either bow as the attack came in.

The combat air patrols of the *Enterprise* and *Hornet* had joined that of the *Yorktown* to make a total of 28 fighters. So effective was their interception that the Japanese attackers were split into small groups, and only about eight bombers succeeded in reaching the *Yorktown*. These scored three hits. One holed the flight deck, while another exploded on the fourth deck and forced flooding of the magazines in the vicinity. A third hit ruptured the uptakes, disabled two boilers, and extinguished the fires in all but one.

Repairs did not take long. Fires were quickly brought under control, the hole in the flight deck covered, and boilers relighted. The carrier was steaming at 20 knots and again refueling fighters when about 1430 her radar picked up the *Hiryu's* torpedo group only 40 miles away. Again refueling was suspended and the combat air patrol vectored out, but the *Yorktown* was still launching fighters when the attack developed.

The American fighters shot down a few of the Japanese before they came within range of the ships' guns. The *Yorktown's* screen, which after the first attack had been reinforced by two cruisers and two destroyers from Spruance's force, threw up a formidable barrage, but a few planes succeeded in penetrating it. The carrier avoided two torpedoes by maneuvering, but two more caught her amidships on the port side. Three fire rooms were flooded, and white smoke issued from her stacks as she slowed to a stop with a heavy list to port.

There was no power for shifting fuel or for counter-flooding, and as the list increased to 26 degrees there seemed to be imminent danger of the ship's capsizing. So at 1500 her captain ordered abandonment, and destroyers took off the crew. That evening the screening vessels departed, leaving only the destroyer *Hughes* standing by to sink the carrier if necessary to prevent her capture.

ELIMINATION OF THE *HIRYU*

Just as the attack on the *Yorktown* was drawing to a close, one of her scouts launched three hours earlier reported the *Hiryu* force approximately a hundred miles WNW. The *Enterprise* at once began launching an attack group of 24 bombers, of which ten were *Yorktown* refugees, while the *Hornet* launched 16. Both groups departed about 1600. There was no fighter escort, because it was felt that all fighters were needed for protection of the carriers.

The *Enterprise* group sighted the *Hiryu* at 1700. Off to the south three columns of smoke marked the other three Japanese carriers. There were a few Zekes in the air, and they shot down three of the bombers, but the others succeeded in planting four hits on the carrier. By the time the *Hornet* planes arrived half an hour later the *Hiryu* was burning so fiercely that it was no longer a profitable target; so they attacked the escorting vessels instead.

On the bridge of the flagship *Yamato* news of the disabling of the *Akagi, Kaga,* and *Soryu* had caused consternation, but Yamamoto saw no reason to abandon his plans, for he believed that the attack had been made at least in part by land-based planes. As yet he did not suspect that there was more than one American carrier present, and the *Hiryu* was dealing with that. Consequently he decided to proceed with the occupation of Midway with only a few changes in the disposition of his fleet. The Second Fleet, which was already on the way, would reinforce the Mobile Force. Midway transports were to retire to the northwest till the situation became clearer.

The Aleutian Support Group was to rejoin the Main Body.

It was not till 1300 that Yamamoto learned that the American force contained three carriers. He had just received a report that the *Hiryu's* planes had left one of these burning, but that still left two against the single *Hiryu*. It was on the receipt of this news that Yamamoto temporarily canceled both the Midway and Aleutian landings and recalled Kakuta's Second Mobile Force from Alaskan waters. With his forces united he would have three regular carriers to deal with the two remaining American carriers.

The *Hiryu* was meanwhile preparing to get off an evening strike with all her remaining planes—five bombers, five torpedo planes, and ten fighters. She had turned into the wind and was just commencing to launch when the *Enterprise* bombers attacked at 1701. Half an hour later Yamamoto learned that his fourth carrier was burning.

By this time there was little hope of saving any of the other three. The American submarine *Nautilus,* which had doggedly trailed the Mobile Force most of the day and had been in the midst of it twice, about 1030 sighted on the horizon three columns of smoke from the burning carriers. Closing, she came upon the *Soryu,* still burning but with her fires apparently under control and making two or three knots. The *Nautilus* slipped three torpedoes into her and left her completely aflame, to go down later in the evening. The *Kaga* blew up at 1925, when the flames reached her fuel tanks. The *Akagi* and *Hiryu* remained afloat till next morning, when Japanese destroyers took off survivors and sank the burning hulks with torpedoes.

MIDWAY, NIGHT OF JUNE 4

The United States had abandoned the *Yorktown,* and all the American air groups had suffered severely. The torpedo squadrons had been wiped out, and losses of both bombers and fighters had been heavy. Yet there were no enemy planes left to dispute the control of the air, and with it of the sea, exercised by the weary aviators of the *Enterprise* and *Hornet*. The action of June 4 had decided the Battle of Midway. But this was not immediately evident to most of the principals of the action, and indeed, had Spruance shown a little less judgment the battle might yet have moved on to a new climax and to another dramatic reversal of fortune.

On Midway itself the defenders awaited developments with considerable apprehension through the afternoon and evening of the 4th. They had received no clear reports of the success of the American carriers and knew only that the Midway planes had been so badly shot up that it was doubtful that they had inflicted any significant damage. Through the afternoon B-17's were dispatched in small groups as they became available to attack elements of the Mobile Force, but they scored no hits. On the report of a burning carrier 200 miles to the northwest, the eleven surviving marine dive bombers took off about 1900. They encountered rain squalls and failed to find the target. Eleven PT-boats which left about the same time on a similar mission had the same experience. Meanwhile refueling of planes by hand and preparations for repelling a landing continued through the night. When a Japanese submarine shelled Midway about 0130 it looked as if zero hour might be drawing close.

YAMAMOTO TRIES TO RETRIEVE THE BATTLE

Aboard the Japanese flagship Yamamoto clung doggedly to his plans of conquest. At 1915 he sent a message to his commanders: "1. The enemy fleet, which has practically been destroyed, is retiring to the east. 2. Combined Fleet units in the vicinity are preparing to pursue the remnants and at the same time occupy Midway. . . . The Mobile Force, Second Fleet and Submarine Force will immediately contact and attack the enemy." Yamamoto may have been confused as to the real situation, or he may have been whistling in the dark to sustain Japanese courage, but it was evident that he was determined to carry on the fight. An hour later he ordered the submarine *I-168* to shell Midway till 0200, when it would be relieved by a cruiser division from the Occupation Force.

Nagumo did not share his chief's offensive frame of mind. While things had been going well he had shown high competence, but since the bombing of his flagship he had revealed signs of shock and failing judgment. Now at 2130 he reported to Yamamoto: "The total strength of the enemy is five carriers, six cruisers, and fifteen destroyers. These are steaming westward. . . . We are offering protection to the *Hiryu* and are retiring to the northwest at 18 knots . . . ." Obviously Nagumo intended to continue his retreat. After a second communication in the same vein Yamamoto replied with the order: "Commander in Chief Second Fleet will take command of the Mobile Force excepting the *Hiryu, Akagi,* and the ships escorting them." Kondo, who had shown both good judgment and initiative in the crisis, was even then well on his way toward joining the remnant of the Mobile Force. He at once sent out orders for concentrating his force for a night surface action. For this he would have four battleships, nine cruisers, and 19 destroyers.

But this engagement, by which Yamamoto might yet have restored his situation, was not destined to take place. On the evening of the 4th Spruance, in reporting to Fletcher that his carriers were attacking the *Hiryu,* had asked, "Have you any instructions for further operations?" Fletcher, who had transferred to a cruiser after the abandonment of the *Yorktown,* responded, "Negative. Will conform to your movements." With the decision thus left to him, Spruance decided to set course to the east for the night. As he subsequently explained, "I did not feel justified in risking a night encounter with possibly superior enemy forces, but on the other hand, I did not want to be too far away from Midway in the morning. I wished to have a position from which either to follow up retreating enemy forces or to break up a landing attack on Midway. At this time the possibility of the enemy having a fifth CV somewhere in the area, possibly with his oc-

cupation force or else to the northwestward, still existed." [4]

By midnight Yamamoto had to face the facts. There were at least two American carriers still operational. They were retiring to the east, so that there was very little likelihood of their being forced into a surface action. Rather, his own vessels, if they persisted on their present courses, would almost certainly be caught by air strikes at dawn. Consequently at 0015 Yamamoto ordered Kondo's striking force, which had not yet united, to rendezvous with the Main Body. Two or three hours later he reluctantly issued an order canceling the Midway operation and ordering a general withdrawal to the west.

PURSUIT ON JUNE 5

So it was that the submarine's shelling of Midway was the Japanese swan song and not the prelude to invasion. But an incident of the early morning of June 5 delayed American recognition of the fact and contributed to making the 5th a day of fruitless pursuit, a blank day in the midst of the battle.

Spruance had not believed that the enemy would attempt a landing after losing his four carriers, but the possibility could not be disregarded. At 0215 the submarine *Tambor* reported "many unidentified ships" about 90 miles west of Midway. "This looked like a landing," as Spruance reported, "so we took a course somewhat to the north of Midway at 25 knots." Back at Pearl Harbor Rear Admiral Robert H. English, Commander Submarines Pacific Fleet, came to the same conclusion and pulled his boats in to a five-mile radius from Midway. So American forces were moving in the wrong direction for pursuit.

The *Tambor's* "unidentified ships" were four cruisers and two destroyers which had been ordered to relieve the *I-168* in shelling Midway. Shortly after the *Tambor's* report they received Yamamoto's retirement order and put about. It was after this turn that

---

[4] Admiral Spruance's report on the Battle of Midway, quoted in O.N.I., *Battle of Midway*, p. 36.

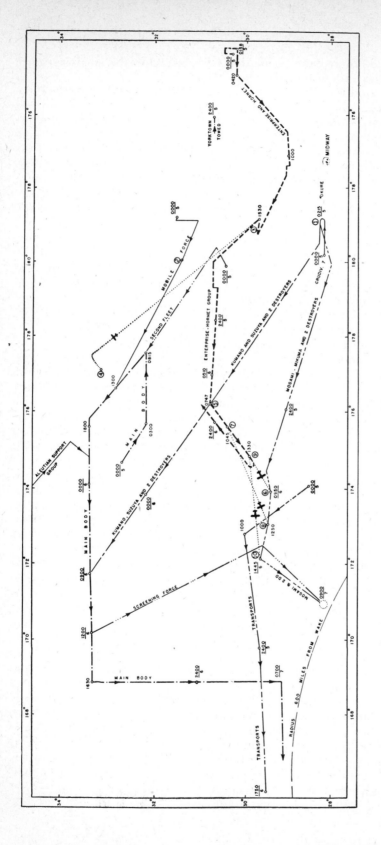

BATTLE OF MIDWAY, JUNE 5-6

JUNE 5

1. 0215: *Tambor* sights Crudiv. 7; *Mogami* and *Mikuma* collide.
2. 0719: Midway patrol planes report burning carrier (*Hiryu*), two battleships, cruisers and destroyers in this position.
3. 1500-1530: *Enterprise* and *Hornet* launch search-attack groups.
4. 1830: *Enterprise-Hornet* groups attack destroyer *Tanikaze*.

JUNE 6

5. 0757: *Hornet* launches attack group.
6. 0950: *Hornet* group attacks *Mogami*, *Mikuma*, and two destroyers.
7. 1045: *Enterprise* launches attack group.
8. 1250: *Enterprise* group attacks.
9. 1330: *Hornet* launches attack group.
10. 1445: *Hornet* group attacks.

a lookout sighted the *Tambor*. In maneuvering to avoid the submarine the heavy cruisers *Mogami* and *Mikuma* collided. The *Mogami*'s bow was damaged, and one of the *Mikuma*'s fuel tanks was ruptured so that she streamed oil. Before dawn the cruisers *Kumano* and *Suzuya* retired to the northwest, leaving the slower, damaged vessels escorted by two destroyers on a westerly course.

It was not till morning that the American commanders could be certain that the Japanese were in retreat. About 0600 the *Tambor* identified the vessels she was trailing as two *Mogami*-class cruisers and reported their westerly course. Between 0630 and 0800 Midway planes reported the few Japanese vessels within range, all on retirement courses. Besides the two damaged cruisers, mis-identified as "battleships" and now 125 miles to the west, they found the *Kumano* and *Suzuya* 175 miles to the northwest, and finally several ships to the northwest, including a burning carrier about 250 miles distant. This was the *Hiryu*, which sank shortly afterward, momentarily in the company of elements of Kondo's striking force, now hurrying to join Yamamoto to the west.

At the first report of the "battleships" to the west the twelve remaining marine dive bombers took off from Midway. Following the clearly visible oil slick, they found the two cruisers about 0800 and attacked at once. They made no hits, but Captain Richard E. Fleming USMC, commanding one of the two sections, dove his flaming plane into the after turret of the *Mikuma*, causing considerable damage. The Japanese were so engrossed in repelling this attack that they failed to notice a group of high-flying B-17's until their bombs began to burst around the vessels. Even so, the bombers scored no hits.

In the early afternoon two groups totaling twelve B-17's took off from Midway to attack the burning carrier to the northwest. It had of course gone down hours before. All they found was a "cruiser"—actually the destroyer *Tanikaze*, which had been sent to ascertain whether the *Hiryu* had sunk and was now scurrying back to Yamamoto. In the two attacks the Fortresses dropped eighty 500-pound bombs with nothing better than a few near misses.

Dawn of the 5th found the two American carriers about 130 miles northwest of Midway. As it became clear that the Japanese were in retreat, Spruance had to choose his targets from the ships reported by Midway patrol planes. He chose the group to the northwest, which although it was farther away, reportedly contained a carrier and two battleships. After steaming at 25 knots for several hours Spruance ordered a search-attack group sent out about 1500. All that the carrier planes found was the little *Tanikaze*, which they attacked with no more success than the army B-17's. Since these planes did not return till after dark Spruance had to take the risk of illuminating his force to recover them. For many pilots it was their first night landing on a carrier.

Spruance had ascertained that there were no Japanese forces for more than 250 miles ahead, and the carriers were approaching the bad weather area, into which it was futile to follow. Consequently he altered course to the west for the night and slowed to 15 knots to save fuel for his destroyers and to avoid overtaking any enemy battleships in the dark.

LAST CONTACTS, JUNE 6

June 6 dawned clear with a smooth sea and good visibility. *Enterprise* planes flying a dawn search to the west soon discovered the *Mogami* and *Mikuma* approximately 130 miles southwest of the American force. A southwest breeze facilitated launching and recovery as the carriers moved toward the contact.

In three successive attacks American planes made repeated hits on the two cruisers and put one bomb on the stern of each of the two accompanying destroyers. By the time of the third strike the carriers had closed to 90 miles, so that pilots could see both forces simultaneously. Despite a terrific battering the *Mogami* was able to stagger off to Truk, but she was out of the war for two years. The *Mikuma* went down a few hours after the last attack, taking a thousand men with her, but before she sank, two *Enterprise* planes took pictures of her which have been among the most widely published of World War II photographs.

On the evening of the 6th Spruance abandoned the pursuit. He had detached destroyers as their fuel ran low, so that he now had only four left. That was too few for safety in waters in which Japanese submarines had been reported. His aviators were exhausted from three days of continuous operations. Finally, it seemed unwise to come within air range of Wake, where he believed the Japanese had concentrated planes to be transferred to Midway. Consequently he turned back to the northeast toward a rendezvous for the first refueling of his force since May 31.

Again Spruance's caution was the highest wisdom, for Yamamoto, fleeing to the west with his scattered forces, had not yet given up hope of salvaging something from the operation. The attacks on the *Tanikaze* on the 5th and on the *Mogami* and *Mikuma* on the 6th told him he was being pursued and gave him some indication of the movements of the American force. At about noon on the 6th he dispatched a force of seven cruisers and eight destroyers to the south with the dual object of protecting the *Mogami* and *Mikuma* and of destroying the American carrier force. The commander of this "Screening Force" made preparations for an engagement during the night of the 6th, and the chart shows that he would probably have had it if Spruance had continued west. Meanwhile Yamamoto's Main Body was also moving south to join in the engagement, and planes were coming north from the Marshalls to reinforce Wake's striking power. Everyone was there except the victim.

END OF THE *YORKTOWN*, JUNE 7

The *Yorktown* had been abandoned on the afternoon of June 4. Her screening vessels withdrew in the evening, leaving only the *Hughes* to stand guard over the carrier, which was then stable with a list of about 24

degrees. On the morning of the 5th the firing of a machine gun from the port side of the *Yorktown* caught the attention of a lookout on the *Hughes*. An investigating party rescued two wounded men and discovered three secret coding devices that had been overlooked in the hasty abandonment of the vessel. But no one that morning noticed somewhere in the distance a Japanese cruiser-type plane, one of two that the fleeing Nagumo had that morning sent out for a search to the east. It reported the position of the abandoned carrier.

About noon the minesweeper *Vireo* arrived from Pearl and Hermes Reef, where she had been on patrol when Nimitz ordered her to go to the assistance of the *Yorktown*. She soon had the carrier under tow toward Pearl Harbor at about three knots, but that was more than the little vessel could maintain, and by morning of the 6th she was scarcely making steerageway. In the meantime five more destroyers had joined, and at daylight on the 6th the *Hammann* went alongside the carrier to put aboard a salvage party of *Yorktown* officers and men.

During the day the party made considerable progress. They reduced the list by two degrees and were lowering the water level in some of the flooded compartments. The *Hammann* was secured forward along the *Yorktown's* starboard side to supply foamite for fighting fires and power for the pumps. The other destroyers were circling the carrier as a precaution against submarines.

At 1335 the wakes of four torpedoes were sighted to starboard. These had been fired by the *I-168*, which after shelling Midway on the early morning of the 5th had received orders to go after the carrier reported by Nagumo's plane. After searching for a day and a half she had just found the *Yorktown*. There was no time for the *Hammann* to pull clear. One torpedo broke her back, while the other two passed under her to explode against the carrier. The *Hammann* went down at once, and underwater explosions killed many of her crew in the water. Some of the destroyers picked up survivors while others went after the submarine. They succeeded only in damaging the boat, which later limped back to Kure for repairs.

The *Yorktown* remained afloat for some time, riding low in the water but with her list partially corrected. In the early morning of June 7 she turned over to port and sank.

AFTERMATH

Spruance had refused to pursue the Japanese further on the night of June 6, but Yamamoto did not give up. After refueling on the 7th he formed a "Diversion Force" of two cruisers and a destroyer to attempt by radio deception to lure the Americans within range of Wake planes and into a submarine trap. At the same time he hoped that Nimitz might send a force to the Aleutians. So he created an "Aleutian Late Support Group" of the small carrier *Zuiho,* two battleships, two heavy cruisers, and eight destroyers to reinforce the Northern Force.

The latter scheme almost worked. The *Enterprise* and *Hornet* refueled on the 8th and 9th. Several vessels in the screen were replaced, and on June 11 the *Saratoga* delivered plane replacements to the two carriers. They then proceeded north under orders to join Admiral Theobald on the afternoon of the 12th. But on the morning of that day Nimitz, remembering Yamamoto's penchant for setting traps, recalled his carriers to Pearl Harbor. So there was no Aleutian finale to the Battle of Midway.

RESULTS

Midway was essentially a victory of intelligence. In attempting surprise, the Japanese were themselves surprised. But beyond this, the Japanese made serious errors which the American command skillfully exploited while making few indeed of its own. Like Coral Sea, the battle was entirely a contest of air power. The Japanese were never given an opportunity to employ their immense superiority in surface ships.

The American performance, while not without faults, showed a more professional touch than at the Coral Sea. Better tracking by scouts and more rapid communications would have paid handsome dividends. The pursuit phase of the battle could have been immensely more profitable had there been an earlier realization that the Japanese were in retreat. Prompter and more determined damage control might well have saved the *Yorktown.* The poor performance of American torpedoes and the inferiority of American planes were again demonstrated, but these defects of material more than compensated by the courage of American pilots.

For the Japanese it was the first major defeat since the 16th century. Against the *Yorktown* and *Hammann* they had to list four carriers and a heavy cruiser sunk. The United States lost 150 planes, but the Japanese carriers took down with them their entire complement of 253 aircraft. While 307 Americans died in the battle, 3,500 of the Emperor's subjects, including a hundred first-line pilots, lost their lives. This loss of experienced pilots was not the least important consequence of the battle, for it began a process of attrition that was eventually to prove fatal to Japan.

The battle marks a turning point in the war. It removed the margin of superiority that had enabled the Japanese to take the offensive at will. For the United States it ended the purely defensive phase of the war and introduced a period in which American arms could take some initiative.

The Japanese concealed their defeat not only from their public but even from officials in responsible positions. They deleted mention of it from war diaries and reports, but they could not undo its effects.

40

The Allied Offensive

against North Africa and Italy

By EARLY SUMMER 1942 AXIS forces appeared well-nigh invincible in the European war. The Germans had reopened their offensive on the Russian front, reconquered the territory lost during the winter, and thrust toward Stalingrad on the Volga. There they could disrupt the flow of oil from the Caucasus and the Persian route for American supplies to Russia. In North Africa, forging ahead toward Egyptian territory, Rommel's tanks appeared to have the momentum that would carry them through to Cairo and the Suez Canal. Malta persisted indeed as an outpost of what was once Britain's Mediterranean lifeline of Empire, but supplies for the British Eighth Army were to reach the Nile Delta only by the circuitous route through the South Atlantic, around the Cape of Good Hope, and up the Indian Ocean to the Red Sea and Suez. Under these conditions, a cross-Channel invasion by the Allies, which the Combined Chiefs of Staff were then planning, might never be possible if something was not done soon to halt the Axis. President Roosevelt and Prime Minister Churchill were agreed that plans for a major European offensive would have to be pigeonholed, at least temporarily, in favor of more immediate counteraction.

CONCEPTION OF THE NORTH AFRICAN INVASION

French territory in North Africa offered an unusual opportunity to the Allied cause. Morocco, Algeria, and Tunisia were unoccupied by the Germans and loyal to the Vichy government, with which the United States had maintained relations in one of the most difficult and successful diplomatic ventures of the entire war. While the British had supported the Free French under de Gaulle and aroused the enmity of many French patriots by their attacks on the French fleet at Oran and Dakar, the United States had appointed Admiral William D. Leahy ambassador to Vichy and through him exerted influence to stiffen French resistance to any German effort at domination of French Africa. Cultivating good-will through the Murphy-Weygand agreement for American economic aid

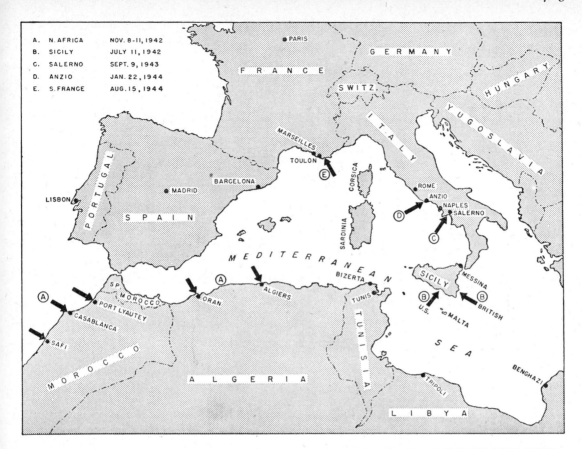

A.	N. AFRICA	NOV. 8-11, 1942
B.	SICILY	JULY 11, 1942
C.	SALERNO	SEPT. 9, 1943
D.	ANZIO	JAN. 22, 1944
E.	S. FRANCE	AUG. 15, 1944

AMPHIBIOUS OPERATIONS IN THE NORTH AFRICA-MEDITERRANEAN THEATER

to the peoples of North Africa and using its representatives and control officers to locate the French leaders who could be counted on to cooperate in a major effort to defeat the Axis powers, the United States had been fighting a delaying action by means of diplomacy.

At last, on July 25, 1942, after every alternative was rejected as either ineffective or at that time beyond the capabilities of the United States and Great Britain, the Combined Chiefs of Staff decided to gamble on an amphibious invasion of French North Africa. Unquestionably the ghost of Gallipoli discouraged rashness among the planners. Failure would inevitably lead to German occupation of the Atlantic ports of Casablanca and Dakar, eminently suitable for U-boat bases. The vast raw material resources of French Africa would then go to the Nazi war machine; possibly all France would be occupied, and Gibraltar as well. But these dire possibilities were overweighed by the need for positive action, for a token "second front," and the likelihood of slight French opposition to the landings, of trapping Rommel between the Eighth Army and invading forces, and of splicing the Mediterranean lifeline.

The immediate objectives would be the three major North African ports that were west of the effective range of the *Luftwaffe*—Casablanca on the Atlantic and Oran and Algiers on the Mediterranean. Once those cities were secured, the invasion forces would have to race the Germans for occupation of the strategic centers of Tunisia—the port cities, Bizerta and Tunis. Best utilization of available ships and manpower determined the various assignments. American Task Force 34, which would transport about 35,-

ooo troops directly from the United States to the target area, was to capture Casablanca. The Central Task Force of about 39,000 American troops with British naval support, all staging from the United Kingdom, would

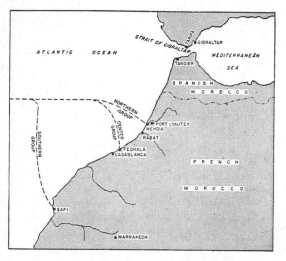

AMERICAN LANDINGS IN FRENCH MOROCCO, NOVEMBER 8, 1942

invade Oran. The Eastern Task Force of about 49,000 American and 23,000 British troops with British naval support, also staging from the United Kingdom, would take Algiers.

All preparations had to be telescoped into a few months. Lieutenant General Dwight D. Eisenhower USA was appointed Commander in Chief Allied Expeditionary Force; Admiral of the Fleet Sir Andrew B. Cunningham RN, Commander in Chief Mediterranean, was in over-all naval command. D-day, postponed once, was set for November 8, 1942, the latest date on which landings across beaches open to the ground swell of North Atlantic storms were deemed feasible. With the utmost secrecy the expeditionary armies were trained, assembled, and embarked. While en route they received the cheering news of the Eighth Army's great victory over Rommel at El Alamein on November 5.[1]

[1] That battle, in Winston Churchill's opinion, "marked the turning of 'the Hinge of Fate.' It may almost be said, 'Before Alamein we never had a victory. After Alamein we never had a defeat.'" Win-

Even at the last moment no one could be certain of the kind of reception the French would give the expeditionary forces. Through the efforts of Robert D. Murphy, the American Consul-General in Algiers, a secret meeting was held in late October between Major General Mark W. Clark USA and the French military commanders in Algeria. It seemed likely that the French army officers in Africa would offer only token resistance, especially after Murphy persuaded General Henri Giraud that he should permit himself to be spirited away from the Riviera by submarine and join the Allied leaders in the invasion, for Giraud was considered a man of sufficient authority and popularity to rally the French to the United Nations' cause. There was no success in winning over the French navy however, and that was especially serious because coastal defense batteries were commanded by naval personnel. The French navy proved tenaciously loyal to Admiral Jean Darlan, Pétain's Anglophobic heir-apparent. Darlan, the father of his country's modern navy, could not forget that his great-grandfather had been killed at Trafalgar or forgive the British attacks on his fleet at Oran and Dakar. The Toulon fleet was at his disposal as well as a number of warships scattered along the African coast. This uncertain situation took a strange turn on November 5 however when Darlan flew to Algiers to be at the sickbed of his son and thus placed himself, by design or by accident, in a position to exert an immediate influence on the course of events. Darlan's exact motives may never be known. The fact is that when Giraud failed it was Darlan, under Allied pressure, who issued the cease-fire order that terminated French resistance in Algeria and Morocco.

PREPARATIONS FOR THE INVASION OF FRENCH MOROCCO

Even before the North African campaign received official approval Rear Admiral H.

ston Churchill, *The Second World War*, 6 vols. (Boston, 1950), IV, 603.

Kent Hewitt USN, in command of the Amphibious Force Atlantic Fleet, assembled his staff and initiated planning for a major assault across 4,000 miles of ocean. When the Western Naval Task Force (Task Force 34) was created, he was placed in command. Troops had to be landed on the Atlantic coast of French Morocco—in the north at Mehdia to capture Port Lyautey and its airport, in the center at Fedhala en route to Casablanca, the Moroccan metropolis of about a half million population, and in the south at Safi to provide facilities for bringing tanks ashore and to control communications with Marrakech, a native city of over 200,000 population. These attacks, if successful, would win control of the coastal plain between the Atlas Mountains and the sea with a major port for handling logistic support (via the railroad to Oran) of subsequent operations in Tunisia or in Algeria itself, should the Germans close the Mediterranean by forcing Spain into the war or by seizing Gibraltar.

Because the United States Marines had been assigned to the Pacific theater, it was necessary to train Army troops for assault landings, and because of U-boats operating off the Atlantic coast and the detailing of all available Allied escort vessels to convoy duty, the amphibious training exercises had to be conducted in the sheltered waters of Chesapeake Bay, while the gunfire support vessels practiced nearby. Not until August 1942 was Major General George S. Patton, Jr. USA appointed to command the land forces. Though by then there was neither time nor experience essential for working out a true joint plan, somehow Task Force 34 met its schedule and on October 28 made rendezvous in mid-Atlantic. This armada of 102 warships, transports, and train, covering over 500 square miles of ocean, would exploit control of the sea to gain a toehold beneath *Festung Europa*. To mislead the enemy, part of the attack group sortied from Hampton Roads and turned south; the next day the remainder proceeded as if from the Chesapeake to England. These forces later joined with the covering groups out of Casco Bay, Maine and the air group, consisting of the carrier *Ranger* and four escort carriers with screen,

out of Bermuda. Their transatlantic track, curving well south of the usual sea routes, followed an irregular course that could be altered to avoid known U-boat positions and short-cut if the invasion timetable was threatened by delays from weather or breakdowns.

After an uneventful passage during which final briefing kept all hands furiously occupied, adverse weather reports from London and Washington forced Admiral Hewitt to consider delaying the entire Atlantic coast invasion or undertaking a poor substitute—an alternative plan for landings on the Mediterranean coast of French Morocco as prelude to an overland campaign against the original objectives. A decision had to be made before TF 34 reached the point where it would divide into three separate forces, each bound for its own target. The task force aerologist, Lieutenant Commander R. C. Steere USN, who had made Moroccan coastal weather and sea conditions his special study for the preceding six months, advised that the heavy seas would subside by November 8, leaving surf conditions poor, though not impossible, with the weather probably getting worse after that date. Admiral Hewitt decided to proceed on schedule.

THE CASABLANCA ATTACK

The entire French Moroccan campaign resembles a dress rehearsal where mistakes tend to overshadow solid accomplishments. At Casablanca the plan called for the midnight arrival of the transports in the disembarkation area off beaches north of Fedhala. That area was beyond range of Casablanca's major coastal battery on Point El Hank and of the 15-inch guns of the new but inoperative battleship *Jean Bart,* which had been moored in the harbor at Casablanca since the fall of France.

Silencing these heavy guns and protecting the landing operations from sorties by French warships known to be in Casablanca was the responsibility of the *Massachusetts* covering force. The Army's preference for a dawn attack—0400 H-hour—imposed on inexperienced sailors and infantrymen the task of accomplishing a ship-to-shore movement in total darkness. Once landed, the troops were expected to overrun Fedhala and quickly drive south to capture Casablanca so that the city's port facilities would be available for a fast support convoy scheduled to arrive on D-plus-5 day. Tactical surprise would probably be lost as soon as the French received President Roosevelt's radio announcement of the arrival of the Allies, to be repeatedly broadcast beginning at 0100, the H-hour of the Mediterranean assaults. It was hoped however that the French might then welcome, rather than oppose, the invaders.

All available landing craft concentrated on loading the first assault wave from the lead transports. H-hour had to be postponed an hour, and succeeding delays turned the later landings into daytime assaults covered by naval gunfire. Boats overturned in the rising surf, drowning soldiers who were borne down by their 60-pound packs. Troops were landed on the wrong beaches, and 46 per cent of the landing craft were lost through poor handling and because salvage facilities were inadequate. The only serious resistance came from shore batteries, located on either flank, and from a few French aircraft. The former were soon silenced by the support ships, and the latter were driven off or destroyed by American carrier planes covering the landings. By noon of D-day Fedhala's small harbor was in American hands and landing craft were re-routed to its quieter waters, thus averting complete chaos on the beaches. By 1700 the exhausted boat crews had ferried 40 per cent of the troops ashore.

Three major problems confronted Admiral Hewitt during the operation. The first was the unsatisfactory landing of both troops and supplies. Experienced boat handlers, adequate craft (such as the LST's, LCM's, and LCI's, still abuilding) and proper beach discipline were sorely lacking. The transports and cargo ships simply had to wait off the beaches until they could be laboriously unloaded. The second problem, protection of the landing area from U-boats, was thus aggravated. Neither a quickly-laid mine field nor the destroyer screen could prevent two

U-boat attacks and the loss of four transports on November 12 after their troops and most of their cargo had been landed. The third problem centered on French naval resistance. When the invasion began, the pro-Allied French general in command of the Casablanca area, who had been told of the invasion only the evening preceding D-day, was at Rabat, the capital of French Morocco, trying to win over the Resident General. In the meantime, Vice Admiral F. C. Michelier in Casablanca had been alerted by his superiors and was prepared to resist, believing at first that the attack might be another British raid rather than an American invasion.

Thus it was that the El Hank batteries and the *Jean Bart* were ready to open fire when the American covering force approached Casablanca in battle formation shortly after dawn on D-day. The first action was a brush between American spotting planes and French aircraft. Then at 0700 the French opened fire at 20,000 yards and were immediately answered by the *Massachusetts* and a cruiser. After 20 minutes of firing, during which the United States ships were not damaged, the *Jean Bart's* turret was jammed by a hit on the barbette and three French submarines in the harbor were probably sunk. Eight other French submarines sortied from Casablanca at about this time, while the American covering force broke off action and withdrew to the west, ceasing fire when erroneously told that some naval shells were dropping among American troops. The French admiral immediately availed himself of this opportunity to send seven destroyers on a sortie toward the landing area. These 36-knot craft were coming into range and had actually sunk one American landing craft before they were driven back by the flagship *Augusta*, the *Brooklyn,* and destroyers of the screen. Making excellent use of smoke, the French ships escaped, only to attempt another attack about 1000 when joined by the light cruiser *Primauguet.* All eight ships, with one exception, were sunk or severely damaged, and an afternoon raid by three small French ships was quickly driven back. But the El Hank battery was still active and two days later the *Jean Bart* suddenly came to life again with a burst of fire from her repaired turret which almost caught the *Augusta.* Shortly afterwards dive bombers from the *Ranger* scored direct hits with three 1000-pound bombs that caused the French battleship to settle into the mud of the shallow harbor with her decks awash.

On land, General Patton's troops, holding a 180-degree arc around Casablanca, planned their final assault for the morning of November 11. Fortunately for both sides, the French admiral in command received orders to cease resistance just before the attack and arrange for a conference later that day. Then it was learned that French North Africa had joined the fight against the common enemy. French honor had been saved and within a few hours the French and Americans were working together to restore Casablanca's port facilities so that the city might become a major rear base for the campaign opening in Tunisia.

MOROCCO SECURED

Of the three landings in Morocco, that at Safi in the south had the most spectacular success. In the blackness before H-hour, despite debarking troubles caused by a heavy ground swell and the inevitable errors of inexperienced personnel, the crucial phase of the assault was conducted according to plan. Two old razeed fourpipers, the *Bernadou* and the *Cole,* each carrying about 200 assault troops, led the landing craft directly into the breakwater-protected harbor. The French had been alerted and there was a lively exchange of fire through which the *Bernadou* slowly steamed without taking a serious hit and drove the French gunners to take cover so that the *Cole,* bringing in the first assault wave, was able to come directly into the quay without a single casualty. While French batteries that might have shelled the ships were silenced in the early morning hours by the *New York* and *Philadelphia,* the American troops ashore took over key positions in the town. That afternoon, after the seatrain had brought in a load of tanks, all objectives of the amphibious operation were attained. Subsequently most French planes in the area

were destroyed on the ground by carrier aircraft, and a half-hearted French effort at counterattack was stopped en route from Marrakech. By the time resistance officially ceased the Army's tank forces were on their way by road toward Casablanca while a string of gasoline-carrying landing craft accompanied them along the coast shepherded by the *Cole.* The entire operation had been carried out with dispatch. All ships were completely unloaded in three days and only one landing craft was lost.

By contrast the northern landings were the least satisfactory. There the objective was Port Lyautey and its all-weather airstrip, the only one in northwest Africa. Plans called for landings on both sides of the Wadi Sebou, a navigable river that connected Port Lyautey with the sea. The initial assault was intended to overwhelm the village of Mehdia and its ancient fortress, the Kasba, that guarded the mouth of the river. The troops would then penetrate inland to Port Lyautey, a mere three miles away, while forces landed north of the river outflanked the city from that side. The *Dallas,* another razeed fourpiper, was to proceed with raiders up-river to the airfield and support the army operations.

On D-day everything went wrong. Darkness, delays, and inexperience "turned the debarkation into a hit-or-miss affair that would have spelled disaster against a well-armed enemy intent upon resistance," as Brigadier General L. K. Truscott, Jr., the army commander, later reported.[2] Attempting to penetrate the boom across the river, the *Dallas* was driven off by shore batteries, while troops already landed were stopped by the defenders of the Kasba. Delays in boating troops, confusion, and error in landing on designated beaches, and poor beach discipline grew worse as the weather deteriorated and resistance from French troops, shore batteries, and aircraft stiffened. By the end of the second day less than 50 per cent of the troops had landed. To these failures was added General Truscott's refusal to use the

<hr>

[2] Samuel Eliot Morison, *History of United States Naval Operations in World War II,* 14 vols. (Boston, 1947), II, 123.

warships for any appreciable amount of heavy gunfire support.

On November 10 the situation suddenly changed. By that time a net-cutting party had severed the river boom so that the *Dallas* was able to break through in the pre-dawn darkness and then proceed upstream by daylight under the guidance of an expert French pilot to land her troops on the airfield without a single casualty. At about the same time the Kasba surrendered to a landing team that had been supplied with howitzers, and long range shelling from the old battleship *Texas* turned back French reinforcements advancing toward the Port Lyautey area. After resistance officially ended on the morning of the 11th, eight of the unloaded transports were sent south to Casablanca, where port facilities were then available.

Thus the Moroccan "dress rehearsal" was completed and the gamble won. Critics who believe that greater Allied confidence in the French and a daylight approach in force would have resulted in no opposition forget the risks involved—not so much in Morocco, to be sure, as in the simultaneous Algerian phase of the operation.

THE ANGLO-AMERICAN INVASION OF ALGERIA

When the Allied forces staged from England steamed past Gibraltar into the Mediterranean, the fact that some major move was under way could no longer be concealed from the Axis powers. At that moment the Germans appear to have been so concerned with the Russian front and with Rommel's campaign that they had no plans for countering a sea-borne invasion that might strike at any one, or several, possible objectives. By forcing the Germans to wait and see what would happen, Allied sea power had wrested the initiative from the Axis.

The Royal Navy's Force H, consisting of three battleships, a battle cruiser, two large carriers, four light cruisers, and 17 destroyers under Vice Admiral Somerville, guarded the amphibious forces from any action the Italian navy, the French fleet at Toulon, or

the Nazis might take. One transport was torpedoed off the African coast by a U-boat, but most of its personnel arrived safely, if tardily, at their objectives after a long open-sea voyage in landing craft and an escort vessel. Otherwise the Eastern Naval Force arrived off Algiers without incident. This force, directed from a British "headquarters ship," prototype of the later American command ship (AGC),[3] consisted of three light cruisers, two carriers, three auxiliary antiaircraft cruisers, a monitor, 13 destroyers, and 17 smaller warships screening and supporting the transports carrying 23,000 British and 10,000 American troops so organized because of French bias as superficially to resemble an all-American force.

The plan for the capture of the city of Algiers called for simultaneous landings on three flanking beach areas, two to the west of the city and one to the east, and, as at Safi, a raid by two destroyers to seize port facilities and shipping in the harbor. In the relatively quiet waters of the Mediterranean the debarking of troops began auspiciously enough with the first wave making its landings practically on schedule against little or no opposition. As the day progressed however the weather worsened and at 1800 all further landings were canceled. By that time poor boat handling reached such prodigious heights that the Eastern Task Force lost 90 per cent of its landing craft and was roundly taken to task by army commanders for gross inefficiency.

Even so, British and American troops ashore captured airfields on both sides of Algiers and with support planes flown in from Gibraltar were preparing to advance against Algiers, had not all resistance ended by noon the next day on orders from Admiral Darlan. This victory was largely the work of Robert Murphy, who had convinced Darlan that he should act on his own responsi-

---

[3] Admiral Hewitt had found the *Augusta* unsatisfactory as a command ship at Casablanca, feeling that cruisers should be free to perform their proper functions as gunfire support or screening ships and that the commander needed a ship of his own with adequate communication facilities and accommodations for the amphibious staff.

bility. The diplomatic triumph ashore allowed unloading of troops and supplies to be completed in Algiers itself and paved the way for launching the Allied drive on Tunisia.

In the meantime the two destroyers had failed completely in their efforts to take over the port. Confused by darkness and strange waters, the *Broke* and *Malcolm* had missed the entrance on their first try. On her second the *Malcolm* was severely damaged by shore batteries and forced to retire. The *Broke* did get into the harbor and landed her raiders, but they were pinned down by small arms fire and captured while the *Broke* herself escaped from her untenable position so damaged that she sank the next day while under tow.

The most severely opposed of any of the Allied landings was that made at Oran by the Center Task Force. Because of ill-will engendered by the British attack on French naval forces at Oran in 1940, American troops, some 39,000 strong, had been selected for this operation, with a Royal Navy escort and screen of a battleship, a large carrier, two escort carriers, an antiaircraft cruiser, 13 destroyers, and more than a score of smaller warships. The plan was almost identical to that for Algiers. Simultaneous landings were to be made on two beach areas west of the city and, the major effort, on beaches east of the city at the town of Arzeu. Two converted U. S. Coast Guard cutters, which had been given to Great Britain earlier in the war, would carry raiders into the harbor to seize port facilities. After the troops ashore had captured outlying airfields, American planes would fly in and an enveloping attack would climax the operation.

The action at Arzeu opened favorably when Rangers got ashore undetected and captured the shore battery installation at Fort de la Pointe. Only sporadic and ineffective resistance followed once tanks were debarked from two prototype LST's. Those vessels, converted shallow draft tankers with bow ramps, illustrated clearly the advantages to be gained in amphibious operations through the use of ships capable of bringing heavy equipment directly to the beach.

French resistance ceased in the Arzeu area by late afternoon. On the beaches west of Oran where landings were largely unopposed, the Army—aided by a third LST—got tanks ashore, making it possible to achieve inland objectives after considerable hard fighting.

Satisfaction over the success of the landings was somewhat tempered by the disaster that overtook the cutters filled with raiders attempting to enter Oran harbor. There had been a serious dispute at high command levels concerning the timing of this strike for H-hour-plus-2. Pointing out that by that time French destroyers in the harbor would certainly be alerted and could make the attack suicidal, American naval officers had suggested in vain that it was better to wait until the Army had entered the city and could support the operation. The *Walney,* the first cutter to enter, bulled her way in under heavy fire; coming into point-blank range of a French destroyer, she blew up and sank with 75 per cent casualties among her sailors and troops. The *Hartland* followed with even worse luck. Half of her people were killed when, forced topside by fires and explosions, they were mowed down by machine-gun fire. The ship was abandoned and all survivors were captured. When the French forces belatedly obeyed Darlan's cease-fire order on November 10 and Americans took over the city, the inner harbor was clogged with sunken shipping. Again the French navy had resisted with all its power, upholding its honor with a regrettable loss of lives and ships.

THE TUNISIAN CAMPAIGN

With Morocco and Algeria on their side, the Allies had valuable rear base areas, but it was Tunisia, separated from Europe by only the 100-mile wide Sicilian Channel, that was the true strategic goal. The Germans worked swiftly to keep it out of Allied hands. By 11:30 AM on the invasion D-day, November 8, the Nazis forced the Vichy Cabinet to accept their offer of air support from Sicily and Sardinia. "This caitiff decision," as

Churchill branded it, "enabled the Germans to take the quick decisive action of occupying airfields in Tunisia, with all its costly consequences upon our campaign." [4] Then the Germans took over unoccupied France and attempted to gain possession of the Toulon fleet. Meanwhile, on the Allied side, Admiral Darlan was doing all he could to bring French forces and territory over to the Allied cause. He ordered the Toulon fleet to sortie to North Africa with the aid of British warships that stood by to render aid, but the French admiral at Toulon delayed until threatened by the approaching Germans. Then he finally settled the issue by scuttling his ships in the harbor. Darlan also sent orders to Admiral Esteva, the senior French officer in Tunisia, but unhappily for the Allies German planes landing on Tunisian fields carried a more convincing argument. Although British forces did reach the Algeria-Tunisia border on the 12th, the next day when several thousand German troops landed in Tunisia from transport planes it was apparent that the Allies could look forward to no easy victory. There was however some consolation in the information that Dakar had joined the Allies on November 23 without a shot being fired and Rommel was fleeing westward with the British Eighth Army in close pursuit.

Hitler's decision to hold what he could of North Africa may have been foolish in the long run, for the six-month campaign that followed was more expensive to the Germans than to the Allies. At the end of the year heavy rains in Tunisia had mired the Allies so badly that they pulled their forces back to better defense positions, while out in the desert Montgomery's advance was delayed until supplies could catch up with him. Despite temporary setbacks caused largely by inexperienced personnel—the Army's counterpart of the Navy's landing craft troubles —General Eisenhower was able to get the offensive rolling again in the spring even though, by air alone, the Germans had brought in 40,000 troops and 14,000 tons of supplies. While the American forces drove east—it was then that General Patton's armored divisions first distinguished themselves—the British Eighth Army fought its way north through the fortified Mareth Line. Rommel, broken in health and spirit, was ordered home by Hitler. By April 7 British Eighth Army and American patrols met, having crossed 2,000 miles of Africa between them, and by May 13 the Tunisian campaign was over. Almost 250,000 prisoners were taken; Allied air, surface, and submarine forces had sunk 433,000 tons of Axis shipping; few, if any, Axis troops escaped across the straits to Sicily. The first British trans-Mediterranean convoy since 1941 left Gibraltar on May 17 and reached Alexandria on May 26 without a loss. Reeling back from the Russian offensive at Stalingrad and driven out of Africa, the Nazis were clearly on the road to defeat.

THE STRATEGIC DECISION TO INVADE SICILY

Meeting with their staffs at Casablanca in January 1943, President Roosevelt and Prime Minister Churchill reaffirmed the general goals of Allied policy and conferred on means for attaining their announced objective, the "unconditional surrender" of the Axis. American military opinion was averse to any diversion of strength that would cause postponement of a major cross-Channel attack, whereas the British, advocating the invasion of Sardinia, insisted that the Axis must not be allowed six to eight months' freedom from attack in the west, the minimum time considered necessary for building of even a limited assault on the French Channel coast. These discussions were greatly influenced by assurances made to Stalin that the Allies would open a second front and also by the known fact that the Nazis had 44 divisions in France. The final decision reached at Casablanca was a compromise in which the American leaders agreed to action in the Mediterranean, if a worthwhile target were chosen, but with the understanding that no operation to be scheduled for 1943 would be

---

[4] Churchill, IV, 623.

allowed to interfere with adequate preparations for the liberation of France in 1944.

The "main lines of offensive action" thus
determined at Casablanca for the European
theater of operations have been succinctly
stated by Churchill as follows: [5]

In the Mediterranean
(a) The occupation of Sicily with the
object of:
(i) Making the Mediterranean line of
communications more secure.
(ii) Diverting German pressure from
the Russian front.
(iii) Intensifying the pressure on Italy.
(b) Creating a situation in which Turkey could be enlisted as an active ally.

In the United Kingdom
(c) The heaviest possible air offensive
against the German war effort.
(d) Such limited offensive operations as
might be practicable with the amphibious forces available.
(e) The assembly of the strongest possible force in constant readiness to reenter the continent as soon as German
resistance had been weakened to the required extent.

To command the Sicilian campaign General Eisenhower was raised to four-star rank
with General Sir Harold R. Alexander his
deputy. Naval forces would again be under
Admiral Cunningham and air under Air
Chief Marshal Arthur W. Tedder. Basing
estimates on assumed completion of the Tunisian campaign by the end of April, staff
officers were ready by mid-March with a general preliminary estimate, but decisions concerning the time and place of the landings,
the coordination of British and American
air, sea, and land forces, and the strategy for
the land fighting on Sicily were delayed or
repeatedly revised. D-day was set for July 10,
when there would be a moon for paratroopers which would set in time for pre-dawn
landings covered by darkness. The assault
would be made simultaneously by eight reinforced divisions. The Western Naval
Task Force (Vice Admiral Hewitt) would

land the 228,000-man Seventh Army (Lt. General Patton) on the south central coast, and
the British Eastern Naval Task Force (Vice
Admiral Sir Bertram Ramsay) would land
the 250,000-man Anglo-Canadian Eighth
Army (Lt. General Bernard L. Montgomery)
on beaches extending from the southeast corner of the island north almost to Syracuse.

The American forces, staged through almost every available French African port in
the Mediterranean from Bizerta westward,
were embarked in and supported by a total
of 580 ships of all types and carried with
them 1,124 landing craft. The British, staged
from the eastern Mediterranean and Tunisia, required 818 ships, including the tactical force of combat ships, and 715 landing
craft. Each force was supplied with LST's,
LCT's, LSI's, and LCI's and improved landing boats and vehicles that could take men
and heavy equipment ashore so rapidly that
the invasion in its initial stages need not be
dependent upon the immediate capture of
harbors.

The most serious problem that army and
navy planners faced, because of an irreconcilable difference of opinion on tactical doctrine, was obtaining the cooperation of the
land-based air forces. The air forces considered their job was to destroy enemy communications and knock out the enemy's air
power, including airfields, so that there
would be no need for local air support; the
army and navy, on the other hand, wanted
the kind of tactical air support that the
Ranger had supplied off Casablanca and that
was to become routine in Pacific amphibious
operations. Although a tactical air force of
400 planes was assigned to support the Sicilian landings, it was to be controlled from
the rear area with no assurance that priority would be given to army and navy requests for aid.[6] In other words, half a mil-

---

[5] From Churchill, IV, 692.

[6] Samuel Eliot Morison makes the bitter comment: ". . . the real reason that the Allied Air
Forces refused to coöperate was the current doctrine
of their leaders that they should not coöperate; they
did not wish to support ground or naval forces at
a beachhead. The top air commanders of both countries were trying to prove that air power, alone and
uncoordinated, could win the war. They almost
managed to prove the opposite." Morison, IX, 17.

lion troops and over 3,000 ships and landing craft would have the part-time support of 400 planes along a hundred miles of coast as compared with as many as 700 naval planes supporting the assault on a single unreinforceable atoll in the Pacific. Although General Patton wanted aircraft carriers assigned to the operation, Admiral Hewitt felt that such a request could not really be justified in view of the great demand for carriers elsewhere and the presence of abundant land-based air power on Malta and recently captured Pantellaria, both within easy range of the target beaches.

Of the efforts made to conceal Allied plans from the enemy, the most dramatic by far was the British ruse that convinced Hitler the attack would come in Greece with a secondary assault on Sardinia. British intelligence dropped a carefully prepared corpse into the sea off the Spanish coast to wash ashore near Cadiz. Major William Martin, as the corpse was called, had his pockets filled with choice misinformation that quickly fell into the hands of German agents. The result was the movement of German troops and mine craft to the Peloponnesus, despite the unshaken conviction of the Axis military leaders that the real Allied objective was Sicily.

The Italians and Germans did however make extensive preparations to meet an invasion across the narrows of the Mediterranean. Two German divisions were sent to Sicily shortly before the attack (Mussolini rejected Hitler's offer of three more). With coastal defenses of the major cities strengthened, anti-invasion exercises were held at Gela, where an Allied landing was correctly expected, mobile forces were billeted in strategic positions, and a total of about 350,000 troops, of whom 60,000 were Germans, awaited the D-day attacks.

THE AMPHIBIOUS ASSAULT ON SICILY

As D-day approached, the Allied Air Forces made raid after raid on Axis airfields in Sicily, forcing both the Germans and the Italians to abandon their Sicilian fields and base their remaining aircraft on Sardinia or in the Naples area. The beach areas were intentionally neglected by the Allied bombers —a practice that actually tipped off the Germans to the likely invasion beaches, rather than deceiving them—and neither troop concentrations nor shore installations received much attention. The net result of the air raids however was beneficial. The Allies almost achieved control of the air over the target area, badly disrupted the Sicilian transportation system, and reduced the already low morale of the Italian forces.

The American task force concentrated its attacks on three groups of beaches in the Gulf of Gela. The western flank at Licata was assigned to the *Joss* force, the center at Gela to the *Dime* force, and the eastern flank at Scoglitti to the *Cent* force. Auguring well for the success of the undertaking was the skill with which the ships maintained their routes from the African ports to the departure points off Malta. Even when heavy weather made up on the night of July 9 and the landing ships plunged slowly through the seas, the general pattern of the attack force was maintained. In fact, the degree of professional improvisation which characterized Operation Husky leaves the impression that in this vast amphibious operation there was such remarkable confidence, self-reliance, and cooperation among army and navy personnel that success looked easier than it really was. The Axis troops realized that attack was imminent but the foul weather convinced them that they had at least another 24 hours to wait. So it happened that the initial landings received less immediate opposition than the enemy would otherwise have been capable of offering.

At Licata the night landings were pushed forward so vigorously that the troops attained their first-day objectives ahead of schedule. LST's, LCI's, and DUKW's proved their worth in getting men and heavy equipment (especially divisional artillery and tanks) ashore in the face of severe enemy fire. At Gela the worst bottleneck was the beach itself, where supplies piled up in mountains of confusion, with both space and beach personnel in such short supply that loaded landing craft frequently had to return to their ships. Worst of all were the Scoglitti landings, which were open to heavy seas. Landing craft casualties there approached the most costly of the Moroccan landings and the restricted beaches became so clogged that it was necessary to seek better beaches in more protected waters.

The American landings in Sicily illustrated fully the modern conception of amphibious operations, i.e., exploitation of control of the sea by transporting, landing, and fully supporting an army of such size that it can acquire a beachhead from which a major land campaign can be staged. All these elements were present in the Moroccan invasion but only after Gela did the army rely on gunfire support from ships as an integral part of the attack plan. Details for gunfire support had been worked out in training sessions in Africa, so that gunfire support teams going ashore with the troops soon had an opportunity to prove that the navy's ships were just as accurate, just as dependable, and much more mobile than the army's heavy artillery. At Gela, after having stopped a counterattacking tank column with salvos fired at a 5-mile range as directed from a naval spotting plane, the *Boise* had the rare opportunity of giving a front row repeat performance for General Patton's benefit. On D-day morning Patton went ashore and, learning that the German counterattack was being spearheaded by a rapidly approaching tank column, climbed into an observation post from which he could get a clear view of the Gela plain. There were the Germans, just a few miles off and no artillery between them and the beaches. A naval liaison officer at Patton's side got word through to the *Boise,* which promptly dropped 38 rounds of 6-inch shell on the road. Captured Germans later inquired about the secret American anti-tank gun, unequaled by anything in their armies. Turning back the attack with almost 4,000 rounds on D-day alone at Gela was only the high point of many gunfire support missions.

Naval gunfire might have been even more effective had it been possible to have better spotting from the air. As the fighting progressed, the ground observers were sometimes blinded by the smoke of burning wheatfields and houses, and were always limited in their field of observation; the float

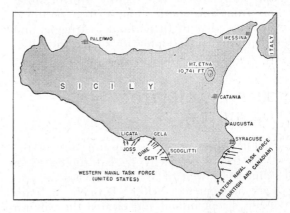

INVASION OF SICILY, JULY 11, 1942

planes from cruisers and battleships—"sitting ducks" for the Messerschmitt fighters that the Nazis sent over—were soon shot down. Absence of air cover likewise resulted in the sinking of a destroyer, a particularly valuable LST, and an ammunition ship.

Poor liaison with the air force resulted in the most publicized disaster of the campaign. With moderate success paratroopers had been dropped behind the Gela front before the landings were made and another drop from 144 transport aircraft was scheduled for evening. No one in the assault force heard of this until late afternoon or in time to get the flight routed away from the ships. When the transports did come over, their arrival coincided almost exactly with a major enemy raid and 23 Allied planes were shot down by antiaircraft guns on shore and afloat.

The British landing in four different beach areas extending from the American right flank to the vicinity of Syracuse met with very light opposition. Since most of the Italians they encountered were eager to surrender, the worst troubles for the British came in the form of heavy seas, rough beaches, and stevedoring problems. The great success of their attack was the speedy capture of Syracuse. British paratroopers seized a key bridge by which the city is approached from the south and held it against everything the Italians could throw at them during D-day. That evening 19 survivors of the 160 who made the drop were relieved by the vanguard of the Eighth Army coming up from the south. The British occupied Syracuse that night without a struggle, and when Augusta fell a few days later, the Allies possessed two of Sicily's best ports.

THE EVACUATION OF SICILY

The Allies hoped to capture most of the Axis troops on Sicily by entrapping them somewhere west of Mt. Etna in a great pincers movement. While Patton's Seventh Army swept inland and cleared the western end of the island, Montgomery's Eighth Army would drive north across the Catania plain and capture Messina to cut the Axis escape route across the narrow straits to Italy. The Germans, deciding immediately that the invaders could not be thrown back into the sea, determined on "tactics of attrition and delay" to make the Allied victory as expensive as possible. While two Panzer divisions poured into Sicily as reinforcements, the Axis stopped the British in their tracks before Catania and began pulling the German forces to the eastern half of the island. At the same time the Americans pursuing disintegrating Italian units across the island, took 20,000 prisoners, and on July 22 entered Palermo, Sicily's principal north-coast port, practically unopposed.

The depressing news from Sicily, climaxed by a 560 plane raid on Rome itself, finally caused the King of Italy on July 25 to make the popular move of deposing Mussolini and taking him into "protective custody." Marshal Badoglio, the new head of government, announced that he would continue the war. No one took this announcement seriously, the Nazis even considering seizing Italy by a *coup d'état* but settling on a continuation of the delaying action in Sicily with the important modification that the three German

divisions there were to be evacuated. Thus the objective of the campaign shifted, and though the Allies were successful in occupying the entire island by August 17, the Nazis were not prevented from evacuating their three divisions—about 45,000 German soldiers with their equipment as well as over 60,000 Italians made good their escape to Italy.[7]

General Montgomery believed a frontal attack on Catania would be so expensive in casualties that he requested and received approval for a new plan of attack, a left-flank wheeling movement hinged on Catania. Unfortunately this move took time and removed his army from the flat coastal plain—where tanks were most effective and troops could be supported by naval gunfire—to the easily defended mountainous terrain. By contrast, Patton's drive from Palermo along the rugged coast to Messina progressed rapidly because of a series of amphibious end runs which took the American troops around the Nazi strong points set up to delay them. Most disappointing was the Allied failure to break the escape route across the straits. Credit must be given the Germans for their skill in withdrawal and in their maintenance of the pretense of greater military strength in the straits than actually existed. On the other hand, both the Royal Navy and the Allied Air Force were deterred from bolder action by the fact that the straits were beyond the range of land-based fighters and that the air and sea commanders were looking ahead to the build-up of forces for the invasion of Italy.

The Sicilian campaign had, in fact, been a major triumph for the United Nations. With less than five per cent casualties, Operation Husky had achieved all objectives in just over a month's time. Most, if not all, aims of this action as set forth at the Casablanca Conference were achieved. Turkish neutrality, if not active participation, was as-

---

[7] Morison is outspoken in his criticism of this Allied failure to trap the enemy. While admitting that the terrain around Mt. Etna favored the Germans, he emphasizes the fact that "the Allies had two superior elements, sea and air power, which might and should have more than compensated for the terrain. These they failed to use intelligently." IX, 202.

sured, convoys could now steam through the Sicilian Channel with little to fear from Nazi air attack, air bases on Sicily would extend the effective range of Allied aircraft well up the boot of Italy, and most important, the Axis was cracking. Soon Germany would be fighting alone against overwhelming odds.

SALERNO

At the Conference held by President Roosevelt and Prime Minister Churchill in Washington just as the Tunisian campaign was concluded, American and British differences of opinion on proper objectives in Europe again came to the fore. The invasion of Italy appeared to be the inevitable next step after Sicily; if Italy were knocked out of the war, the British argued, the Nazis would be forced to send their own troops to replace the Italian divisions in the Balkans, and an Allied cross-Channel invasion would then be feasible. So it was agreed that Italy would be next, but with the important proviso that only forces already available in the Mediterranean should be used. Later when beaches south of Naples in the vicinity of Salerno were selected as being within extreme range of Allied air support flown from Sicily and adjacent to a great port, plans were drawn up for a new kind of operation, a "limited" attack, not the heaviest blow the Allies could strike but the heaviest they cared to strike in that area at that time.

Meanwhile the fall of Mussolini and the victory in Sicily had been followed by peace feelers from the Italians. Remembering the disapproving public reaction to the "Darlan deal," Allied leaders were not exactly welcoming the Italians to their bosom. After lengthy negotiations, it was decided that announcement of the surrender of Italy would be timed to coincide with the Salerno landings on September 9. Unfortunately for the Allies, the brief time spent in re-grouping forces for the invasion had given the Nazis an opportunity to make adequate preparations to take over in Italy.

The team of Eisenhower, Alexander, Cunningham, and Tedder was carried over from the Sicilian operation, while Admiral Hewitt commanded all amphibious forces and Lieutenant General Mark Clark, the newly formed Fifth Army. The Allied forces would be divided for the landings into a primarily British Northern Attack Force of two divisions and an American Southern Attack Force of like strength. Greatly improved arrangements were made for air cover to be supplied by land-based craft in a constant daylight patrol subject to the direction of an air officer aboard the task force flagship and by naval planes flying from five escort carriers. Great difficulty was experienced however in obtaining firm commitments of men and equipment, so that changes were being made in the operation plan even after departure for the beachhead. One objectionable feature was that the transports would have to debark troops ten miles off the beaches to allow time for minesweepers to go in and clear mines with which the Nazis had sown the Gulf of Salerno. Another complication arose from the Army's provision that there should be no pre-landing naval bombardment, on the grounds that it would make tactical surprise impossible.

There were other troubles, not at all connected with the invasion plan as such. Priority for certain equipment had to be given to General Montgomery who, after crossing the straits at Messina on September 3, was working his way up the toe of the Italian boot. While the Salerno task force was en route, one of the gunfire support cruisers was detached to join Admiral Cunningham's force, which would occupy the great naval base at Taranto when the Italian fleet steamed out to surrender at Malta under the terms of the armistice. And, finally, General Eisenhower's radio announcement of the armistice on the eve of the landings made it next to impossible for officers to convince their Salerno-bound troops that, though Italy might be out of the war, the Germans would offer plenty of resistance.

The Germans had, indeed, estimated that the Salerno beaches were among the most likely for an Allied landing. Three days before D-day they moved in the 16th Panzer Division and an Italian coastal division, prepared machine-gun positions and beach obstacles, and planted artillery on the mountain rim overlooking the plain. By D-day all the beaches were mined, another Panzer division had been ordered to break off contact with Montgomery's forces and hurry north, and tanks were gathered at strategic points to hurl the invaders back into the sea.

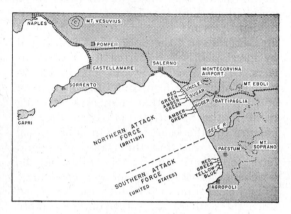

INVASION OF ITALY (SALERNO)
SEPTEMBER 9, 1943

For once the approaching task force was enjoying perfect weather. While the pickets took their assigned positions guided by bearings on extinct volcanos rising behind the beaches, the troops were boated with a minimum of confusion. Led by the overworked minesweepers, they found their destinations in most instances with fair accuracy. With that misleading prelude, what followed for the next full week was one of the most vigorously opposed amphibious assaults of World War II. Ready and waiting, the Germans contested the landings from the water's edge. Troops were pinned down, landing craft were damaged, and the gunfire support ships were assailed as never before in the Mediterranean. At the end of D-day with all the designated beaches occupied, the Fifth Army had successfully landed, but the situation was far from satisfactory, for the Germans were throwing in reinforcements faster than the Allied troops could be put ashore. By D-plus-3 day the Germans had 600 tanks assembled for a final thrust and threatened to cut the Allied forces in two. On D-plus-4

day the situation looked so bad that General Clark requested Admiral Hewitt to prepare plans for evacuating either the northern force and relanding it with the southern, or vice versa. No major Allied landing had ever been so close to defeat. Fortunately for the Allies the crisis passed and success followed because of their own hard fighting and Rommel's holding back of Nazi divisions available in northern Italy. Marshal Kesselring's counterattack did not have the weight to carry through to the beaches. "On 16 September, in order to evade the effective shelling from warships," Kesselring later recorded, "I authorized a disengagement on the coast front . . ." [8]

During that critical week at Salerno, working effectively with control parties ashore and with pairs of Mustang (P-51) fighters supplied by the air forces, gunfire support ships had pounded the Nazis with 11,000 tons of shells. Time and again tank attacks were broken up, troops scattered, and artillery silenced by the ships' guns. At the height of the fighting the Royal Navy, called upon for additional ships, augmented the fleet with the battleships *Valiant* and *Warspite* and six destroyers. By this time the Germans, realizing the need of destroying the ships as well as the troops ashore, introduced a new weapon, the radio directed glide bomb. A fighter raid would be sent over at low altitude to decoy the Allied air cover and then a bomber would come in at high altitude, drop its bomb, and direct it against the target. One heavy bomb ripped through the light cruiser *Savannah,* blowing out a section of her bottom and forcing her withdrawal for major repairs. The *Warspite* was also severely damaged. Some transports and landing ships were sunk by glide bombs and three destroyers by U-boats which had joined the attack on the beachhead.

Although the beaches were saved, the goal of the campaign could not be achieved until strength was built up for a break-out and the capture of Naples. The Germans meanwhile, deciding to withdraw to a prepared defense line along the Volturno River, de-

_____
[8] Morison, IX, 296.

molished the harbor of Naples with what appeared to be vengeful wrath and slowly retreated, permitting American forces to enter Naples on October 1 and push forward to the Volturno by the 6th. There the new battle line formed while the Navy's experts, who had cleared the wreckage from the harbors of Algeria and Tunisia, went to work to restore Naples as a major port and Allied base.

STALEMATE AT ANZIO

The surrender of Italy had proved disappointingly small help to the Allies, who now found themselves engaged in a major land campaign of slight strategic importance and conducted through terrain and weather that heavily favored the defenders. By early October, with all northern Italy securely under Nazi domination, Marshal Kesselring could count on 19 divisions to hold the 11 that the Allies had been able to land. All that month and November too, the Allies devoted themselves to reinforcing the Eighth and Fifth Armies for a heavy attack which, when it came, promptly bogged down in the mud and cold winter rain.

United Nations leaders meeting for the Cairo Conference at this very time reached agreement for some kind of "end-run" to outflank the German defense and lead to the capture of Rome, but the Americans absolutely refused to make any Mediterranean commitments that would interfere with the cross-Channel invasion. Only Churchill's persistent optimism regarding over-all gains that could be effected through victory in Italy buoyed up the project. The goal was Anzio, 37 miles south of Rome and separated from it by the Alban hills. Here a British and an American division would land on January 22 in coordination with a major attack by the Fifth and Eighth Armies on the Gustav Line. From its very conception, the operation was plagued by ambiguity, largely because the military leaders could not reconcile Churchill's hopes with the fact that two Allied divisions were to land where they were more likely to be met by superior German force than by Allied troops driving through from the south.

Rear Admiral Frank J. Lowry USN and Major General John P. Lucas USA had plans prepared by January 12 and ten days later conducted an almost perfect series of landings that achieved virtually complete tactical surprise. By the evening of D-day 36,000 men were ashore; casualties, including missing, were fewer than 150. Part of the credit for the ease of the landing was due to the launching of a costly but unsuccessful major attack on the Gustav Line that pulled German reinforcements south. General Lucas has since been criticized for failing to send an armored force barreling straight through to Rome. No Allied commander knew that the way was momentarily wide open; nor, on the other hand, was anyone quite prepared for the power of the German reaction. Heavy bombing of communications by the Allied Air Force did not prevent Kesselring from moving up troops that effectively sealed off the beachhead. Even though many ships were damaged and some lost to mines or heavy air attacks,[9] and the debarkation schedule was delayed by a severe storm on D-plus-4 day, almost 70,000 men, over 25,000 tons of supplies, 500 guns, and 237 tanks had been landed in the first week of the operation. But that was not enough: four months of fighting were to follow. With their heavy guns in the hills just beyond range of the gunfire support ships, the Germans devoted six divisions to sealing off the beachhead, so that the Allies had to expend additional men and ships in maintaining an LST ferry service for supplies between Naples and Anzio.

Finally, on May 25, when an attack by 20 Allied divisions had finally broken the Gustav Line, contact was made between advance patrols from the seven-division force at Anzio and the vanguard of the southern Allied forces. Kesselring skillfully withdrew his army to prepared positions north of Rome and on June 4 the Allies made their triumphant entry into the Eternal City. Properly taken as a symbol of heroic tenacity, the

---

[9] British: 2 cruisers, 3 DD's, 3 LST's, 1 LVI, and a hospital ship; United States: 1 minesweeper, 1 minecraft, 1 LST, 2 LCI's, 3 LCT's and 2 Liberty ships.

Anzio operation, costing over 25,000 casualties, was nevertheless a strategic mistake. Instead of breaking the military stalemate at the Gustav Line, it became a military liability, rescued by, not the rescuer of, the Fifth and Eighth Armies. Two days after Rome fell, the landings at Normandy made the Italian front a mere backwash of the war.

THE SIGNIFICANCE OF THE MEDITERRANEAN CAMPAIGNS

Anglo-American utilization of sea power and Italo-German lack of appreciation of sea power are both clearly illustrated in the Mediterranean campaigns. With the entrance of Italy into the war and the fall of France, the Axis had it within its power to seal off the Mediterranean by utilizing the time and forces that Hitler tied up while contemplating Operation Sea Lion. This strategic blunder apparently rests upon German contempt for the Italians and the German attitude that in Greece and North Africa they were simply pulling Mussolini's chestnuts out of the fire. The tenacity of British resistance in that theater revealed however that England saw more clearly the worldwide implications of the Mediterranean struggle than did the continental-minded Nazis. Hence the specific reasons for victory are found in Axis errors as well as in United Nations' strength. The Germans themselves later came to believe that lack of aircraft carriers cost them their defeat. Possibly so, but to that must be added poor Italian morale and an overextension of available forces. The importance of the war with Russia made it difficult for many Germans to feel that fighting in the Mediterranean could be more than a sideshow.

From the Allied point of view the Mediterranean offered opportunities for limited offensive action, a taking of the initiative with its choice of objectives and of utilizing available power most effectively until strength had been built up for a vital blow. As part of this process the technique of amphibious operations was perfected and equipment developed, both of which were essential to the subsequent success at Normandy.

41

The Campaign against Rabaul,

Phase I: Guadalcanal and Papua

THE BATTLE OF MIDWAY jarred the Japanese into realizing they were not prepared after all to assault points within attack range of Allied naval bases. Their relatively easy conquests of Wake, the Philippines, and the East Indies had led them to believe that their expeditionary forces were invincible. But their setback in the Coral Sea and the disastrous outcome of their attempt to occupy Midway made them pause and re-estimate their strategic planning. In the face of respectable opposition Japan was evidently not prepared to isolate major targets by seizing command of the sea and air. So Tokyo went on the defensive, temporarily canceling the order for invasion of New Caledonia, Fiji, and Samoa. The immediate and imperative task was strengthening the defense perimeter.

To the Bismarcks came Vice Admiral Gunichi Mikawa with a force of cruisers and destroyers. More planes and equipment arrived to buttress airdromes in New Guinea, the Bismarcks, and the Upper Solomons. Yet there still remained the Allied base at Port Moresby. The Imperial Navy had signally

failed to eliminate that threat. Now the army would have a try, striking from the north coast of Papua across the Owen Stanley Mountains. To cover the flank of this operation and to provide air support for a later renewal of Japan's march to the southeast, a landing field would be constructed on Guadalcanal, 20 miles south of the Japanese seaplane base at Tulagi.

To the Allies the results of Midway spelled opportunity. Now that the enemy was off balance and his preponderance of strength cut down, the time had come to block his advance by an offensive-defensive move. Where to strike depended upon probable future enemy thrusts. In estimating Japan's next line of advance, the Allies now had to work in the dark, for their most important source of information regarding Japanese plans had suddenly been cut off. An American newspaper correspondent with the fleet at Midway had learned about the United States Navy's intelligence based on code breaking. Afterwards he published a story showing such detailed knowledge of the Combined Fleet's dispositions and objectives

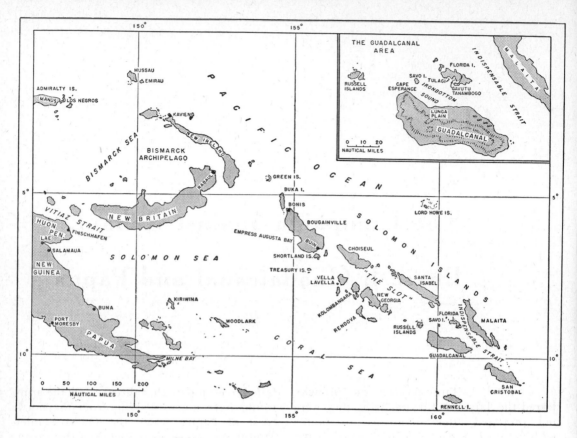

THE APPROACHES TO RABAUL

that the Japanese guessed what had happened and promptly changed their code. The Allies thus lost a priceless advantage, which American cryptanalysts finally restored several months later by breaking the new code.

However as early as February Admiral King, without benefit of inside information, had pointed out the growing Japanese base at Rabaul as the probable springboard for the next enemy advance. To counter any move from this quarter against the American communication line to Australia and also to provide a jumping-off place for an Allied drive through the Solomons and the Bismarcks, he started work on a base on Efate in the New Hebrides. He then set up a separate command in the South Pacific, subsidiary to Nimitz' Pacific Ocean Areas, and appointed Vice Admiral Robert L. Ghormley Commander South Pacific Force and Area.

Leaving Washington with a specific understanding from King that he was to prepare for offensive operations, Ghormley established headquarters at Auckland, New Zealand and promptly began work on another New Hebrides base on Espiritu Santo.

Meanwhile General MacArthur, under direct cognizance of the Joint Chiefs of Staff, had assumed command of the adjacent Southwest Pacific Area with headquarters at Brisbane, Australia. After Midway, MacArthur not only eagerly accepted King's proposal for an advance on the Bismarcks but startled the Joint Chiefs by offering to go in and recapture Rabaul in a single stroke. For this assault he would require big bombers and a naval force including at least two carriers to provide fighter support. Moreover, since his three army divisions were neither trained nor equipped for amphibious warfare, he asked for the 1st Marine Division to spearhead the attack.

King protested sending scarce carriers and amphibious troops across the reef-strewn Solomon Sea against a large land mass guarded by airfields. He favored a step-by-step approach and argued that since the initial invasion would have to be carried out by marines transported and supported by the Pacific Fleet it ought to be under naval command. After debating the matter for several days, the Joint Chiefs of Staff on July 2, 1942 issued a directive which substantially followed King's proposals. The opening operations, seizure and occupation of the Santa Cruz Islands, Tulagi, and adjacent positions, would be under the general strategic command of Admiral Nimitz. As soon as a base had been secured in the Tulagi area, the strategic command would pass to General MacArthur, who would coordinate a naval move up the Solomons with an army thrust up the Papuan Peninsula to Salamaua and Lae. The two Allied advances would then converge on Rabaul. Target data for the initial invasions, called Operation Watchtower, was set for August 1.

PLANNING "OPERATION SHOESTRING"

Admiral Nimitz, anticipating the Joint Chiefs' directive, had almost completed basic planning for Operation Watchtower by the first week in July. Admiral Ghormley would exercise strategic control, with Vice Admiral Frank Jack Fletcher, of Coral Sea and Midway fame, in tactical command of the Expeditionary Force. From King's staff, where he had headed the War Plans Division, came Rear Admiral Richmond Kelly Turner to command the Amphibious Force. The 1st Marine Division, which would make the assault, was to be commanded by Major General Alexander A. Vandegrift, who had learned the business of fighting in the jungles of Nicaragua and the theory of amphibious assault on the staff of the Fleet Marine Force in its germinal first years.

A month was of course an uncomfortably brief period in which to assemble forces, work out details, and complete training and rehearsals for so complex an operation as an amphibious assault. Moreover, adequate reinforcements and proper air and surface support were hard to come by. The invasion of North Africa, planned for November, had top priority for everything. MacArthur could spare no men. South Pacific bases would have to be stripped of part of their defense forces to provide garrison troops to follow up the marines. Little wonder that the somewhat baffled participants in Operation Watchtower soon began to call it "Operation Shoestring."

While Fletcher and Turner were conferring with Nimitz at Pearl Harbor there came the startling news that an American patrol plane had sighted an airstrip under construction on Guadalcanal. This information put a more urgent complexion on the Watchtower project. Nimitz, Turner, and Fletcher agreed that Guadalcanal would have to be included in the Tulagi-Santa Cruz invasion plan. Ghormley and MacArthur, in conference at Melbourne, argued for postponement until enough force could be built up to carry out the march on Rabaul in one continuous movement. But King and Nimitz would defer the invasion no more than a week and set D-day definitely for August 7. They saw a quick move into the southeastern Solomons as now doubly imperative. The airfield must be captured from the Japanese before it could be completed; otherwise planes from the new enemy base could not only endanger and perhaps turn back an approaching Allied fleet but imperil the Allied base at Espiritu Santo as well. King saw clearly that the Guadalcanal airstrip had become the strategic center of the invasion. Whoever first put it into operation might well be the victor.

In the latter part of July the strategic situation took another turn when a Japanese convoy landed troops near Buna mission on the Papuan Peninsula directly opposite Port Moresby. Whatever concern this invasion caused MacArthur's staff, it could only have been taken as a happy sign in the South Pacific command. Japanese attention was focused on the old target of Port Moresby, not upon the end of the Solomons chain. Rabaul was looking southwest instead of southeast. Surprise was possible.

THE ALLIED INVASION

Steaming from points as widely separated as Wellington, Sydney, Noumea, San Diego, and Pearl Harbor, the various components of the Watchtower Expeditionary Force on July 26 assembled at sea some 400 miles south of the Fijis. Admiral Ghormley, then shifting his headquarters to Noumea, could not be present. He at no time saw the fleet over which he exercised an ambiguous control or met all his top commanders to discuss operation plans. Admiral Fletcher however held council aboard the *Saratoga,* where he created some consternation by stating that under no circumstances would he permit the carriers to support operations beyond the fourth day.

After a chaotic rehearsal of landing operations in the Fijis, the expeditionary fleet steamed westward into the Coral Sea—Turner's Amphibious Force of transports carrying the 1st Marine Division, escorted by cruisers and destroyers; and a Support Force including the carriers *Saratoga, Enterprise,* and *Wasp* and their screening vessels. In the Coral Sea the fleet shaped course due north and headed for Guadalcanal through rain squalls that grounded all planes, including Japanese search patrols.

Guadalcanal, part of the drowned volcanic mountain range forming the Solomons, rises steeply in the south from a narrow coastal flat. Only on the north coast are there plains broad enough to provide level ground for airfields, and here only is there an extensive break in the surrounding coral reef. Here on Lunga Plain, mostly rain forest traversed by numerous creeks and small rivers, and broken here and there by coconut plantations and grassy fields, the Japanese had landed and begun their airdrome. Onto Lunga Plain the marines would necessarily follow. Under a clearing sky in the early hours of August 7, the Carrier Force moved into position south of Guadalcanal while the Amphibious Force slipped up the west coast, split into two groups around little Savo Island, and entered Ironbottom Sound.[1]

In darkness shortly after 0600 fire support vessels of the south group began the bombardment of Guadalcanal, guns seeking out enemy shore batteries and supply dumps. Then came planes from the carriers to add to the destruction. With dawn just breaking over the scarcely ruffled Sound, the convoy commander signaled, "Land the landing force," and Higgins boats, ramp boats, and tank lighters began to hit the water. Loading completed, the boats advanced to the line of departure, marked by two destroyers 5,000 yards from the beach. On signal for the run-in, the destroyers gave the Guadalcanal coast a final bombardment with their 5-inch guns and then lifted fire just before the first landing craft grounded in the dark volcanic sand.

By nightfall August 7 the landing boats had put 11,000 marines ashore on Guadalcanal, and the beach was cluttered with great piles of supplies. One combat team had advanced west along the shoreline, while a second was penetrating the jungle in a southwesterly direction. Most of the 2,000 or so Japanese on the island, chiefly laborers, had fled westward during the bombardment, but a few determined warriors had remained behind to snipe and to man machine guns. These the marines encountered and destroyed on the second day of their advance. In mid-afternoon of the 8th, one marine team had entered the main Japanese base, taking possession of machine shops, electric power plants, and considerable stores of provisions, firearms, and ammunition. A little later the other team occupied the airstrip, the future Henderson Field.[2]

On the north side of Ironbottom Sound operations did not proceed so smoothly. Here the objectives were three small islands

---

[1] This body of water, between Guadalcanal and Florida Islands, was originally named Savo Sound but was renamed in memory of the many vessels sunk there in 1942 and 1943.

[2] Named in honor of Major Loften Henderson, commander of the marine bombing squadron in the Battle of Midway.

lying inside a bight of the larger Florida Island: Tulagi, a two-mile-long ridge rising abruptly from the Sound, and Tanambogo-Gavutu, a pair of islets joined by a narrow causeway. In this area, despite naval bombardment and bombing and strafing by carrier aircraft, which quickly knocked out all the enemy seaplanes, the marines ran into trouble.

On Tulagi, by picking an unlikely beachhead, the invaders got ashore easily enough. It was only when they reached high ground that they found an enemy so well dug in that they had to dislodge him the hard way with machine guns, mortars, and grenades. Gavutu had to be taken by amphibious assault in the face of heavy small-arms fire, for this island, rising sheer out of a broad coral shelf, could be invaded only by way of the seaplane ramp. An attempt to take Tanambogo on August 7 was thrown back. Before these three little islands could be secured on the 8th, Vandegrift had to double the 1,500 marines he had originally sent against the 750 defenders.[3] This used up all his reserves and meant that the Santa Cruz phase of Operation Watchtower would be postponed and eventually abandoned.

The Watchtower amphibious operations, despite hasty planning, had proceeded with surprising smoothness, proof that Fleet Marine Force doctrine and training had been sound. But the Tulagi-side invasions had brought out grave deficiencies in American air and naval gunnery support. Part of the trouble resulted from poor communications with ground forces, but naval gunfire also suffered from faulty doctrine based on the expectation that the defending troops would be exposed or only lightly protected. Against such defenders an area fire, using thin-skinned, high-capacity ammunition can be deadly, but it accomplished little against the Japanese on the northern islets, for they were well protected in caves and sunken pillboxes. They merely took cover until the burst of fire was over. What

was needed against such defenses was deliberate, carefully-aimed, long-sustained, high-trajectory fire using armor-piercing as well as high-capacity shells—destructive fire, in short, instead of mere neutralizing fire. This fact was only slowly recognized, and the lesson had to be re-learned at Tarawa.

TURNER DECIDES TO PULL OUT

Admiral Turner's chief worry as he planned the amphibious phase of Operation Watchtower was what enemy aircraft might do to his vessels off the beachheads. He began to find out a few hours after the first landing when bombers and fighters from Rabaul appeared over Ironbottom Sound. Alerted by a coastwatcher,[4] the American carriers sent in a strong combat patrol which soon decimated and routed the intruders. Warned the following morning of approaching torpedo planes, Turner had his transports and screening vessels in cruising formation and maneuvering at top speed when they arrived. He could thus baffle the attackers by keeping the keels of his ships in line with the approaching aircraft, obliging them to swing away at low altitude for a better angle and thereby become easy targets for antiaircraft gunners. Caught between the devastating fire of more than 50 vessels and the air patrol swooping down from above, the torpedo planes were almost wiped out.

The Expeditionary Force came through the air attacks rather better than many would have ventured to predict—21 American fighter planes lost, two destroyers dam-

[3] Japanese figures approximate, from J. A. Isely and P. A. Crowl, *The U. S. Marines and Amphibious War* (Princeton, 1951), 124-5, and John Miller, Jr., *Guadalcanal: The First Offensive* (Washington, 1949), 65-67.

[4] The Australian coastwatchers manned a network of small radio stations along the coasts of the Bismarcks and the Solomons. Established before the war and incorporated into the Australian navy in 1939, some remained after the Japanese invasion; others returned later. Operating in concealment usually with portable radio equipment and assisted by loyal natives, they were of inestimable value in warning Allied commands of enemy ship, troop, and plane movements. A similar New Zealand network operated in the Gilberts, the Ellices, the Fijis, and the more easterly islands. Many coast watchers were captured or killed by the advancing Japanese.

aged, a transport set fatally ablaze. But the long absence of the cargo vessels from their anchorages had utterly confused an already critical logistics problem. By the evening of August 8 some of the vessels were no more than 25 per cent unloaded, so Turner accepted the necessity of remaining in Ironbottom Sound at least two more days. Then came two bits of information that abruptly changed his mind. The first was news that Fletcher, citing heavy loss of fighter planes and a need for refueling, had sought and obtained permission from Ghormley to withdraw the carrier force from the Guadalcanal area.[5] The second piece of news came from MacArthur's headquarters. That morning an Australian pilot on air patrol had sighted Japanese vessels heading to enter the passage—later known as the Slot— through the major Solomons. Instead of immediately sounding a radio alert, as he had been instructed to do, he spent several hours finishing his patrol, returned to base, and had his afternoon tea before making a contact report. Not sure what he had seen, he identified two of the vessels as probably "seaplane tenders." Turner, accepting this identification, concluded that the enemy force was en route to set up a seaplane base in the Central Solomons. With his Amphibious Force stripped of carrier support and at the same time menaced by probable new dangers from the air, he decided that he had no choice but to withdraw the following day. He therefore sent for General Vandegrift and British Rear Admiral V. A. C. Crutchley, the screen commander, to come to his flagship to hear his decision and help him make plans.

Crutchley, speeding to the rendezvous in

the cruiser *Australia,* had drawn up no battle plan for countering a surface attack and had designated no one to the over-all command of the cruisers and destroyers in his absence. These vessels, in second condition of readiness, were divided several ways. Light screens of destroyers and minesweepers covered the Guadalcanal and Tulagi beachheads, where the transports were anchored. One cruiser-destroyer group patrolled the passage between Savo and Florida Islands, another patrolled the passage between Savo and Guadalcanal, a third patrolled the east channels—a satisfactory arrangement for protection against submarines but not for much else. Just northwest of Savo was a radar patrol of two destroyers. (See diagram.) There were no picket vessels patrolling the outer approaches to Ironbottom Sound.[6]

THE BATTLE OF SAVO ISLAND

The Japanese force sighted by the Australian plane in the morning of August 8 was composed of five heavy and two light cruisers and a destroyer, under command of Admiral Mikawa. Mikawa's objective was Ironbottom Sound; his mission, to smash the Allied transports and break up the invasion by a night attack.

For years the Japanese navy had been training to offset superior opposition by making use of foul weather and darkness. Many of their major training operations had been carried out in the stormy North Pacific, where day and night they trained under conditions of such extreme severity that, it is said, between 50 and 100 men were killed in each exercise. For night work they developed superior binoculars, highly dependable star-

---

[5] Fletcher, having already lost two carriers since the outbreak of war, was understandably loath to risk further losses, but opinion is divided as to whether his situation off Guadalcanal was as critical as he implied. He still had 78 fighter planes and all his ships—except destroyers, which could be fueled by the carriers —had at least 50 per cent fuel on board. Vessels of the *Saratoga* group were filled to 75 per cent or more of capacity. Nimitz, calling Fletcher's withdrawal "most unfortunate," suggested that he might have solved his fuel problem by sending the carrier groups southward one at a time for refueling.

[6] The Naval War College analysts criticize the disposition thus: (1) The North and South Patrol Forces were not close enough together for quick mutual support; they could have maneuvered more effectively in a single column. (2) The picket screen was inadequate in that the two destroyers were too close to the cruiser forces for timely warning, and at the extreme ends of their sectors they would be 20 miles apart. *The Battle of Savo Island, August 9, 1942, Strategical and Tactical Analysis* (U.S. Naval War College, 1950), 58-60.

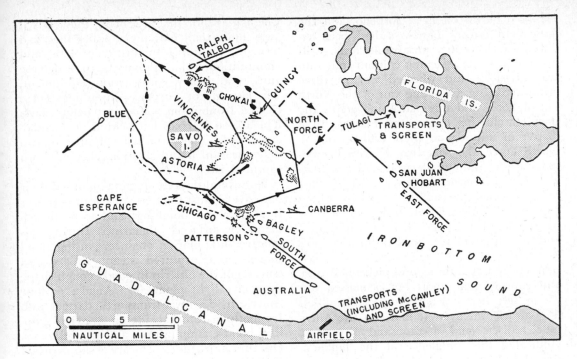

BATTLE OF SAVO ISLAND, AUGUST 9, 1942

shells and parachute flares, and the most lethal torpedo in the world—the 24-inch Long Lance, which could carry a thousand pounds of explosive 11 miles at 49 knots, or 20 miles at 36 knots.[7] Because limited resources made Japan a weak base for naval operations, they counted on surprise coupled with adverse forces of nature to give them the advantage over better-based adversaries.

After he had been sighted from the air, Mikawa entered the Slot with foul weather closing in and headed directly for Guadalcanal. Late in the evening two of his cruisers launched float planes which proceeded ahead to report the location of ships in Ironbottom Sound. Some Allied vessels which saw the planes tried to warn the flagship but were defeated by static; others assumed, since no general alarm had been sounded, that the aircraft must be friendly. A few minutes be-

fore 0100, when Mikawa's force was heading for the passage between Savo and Cape Esperance, Japanese lookouts dimly made out the hull of picket destroyer *Blue*. Promptly the entire force prepared for action, training all guns. But there was no reaction from the picket, which steamed tranquilly away. Mikawa, puzzled, suspecting trickery, detached his destroyer to watch the *Blue* and engage her if she should attempt to follow him. Then he entered the Sound.

Not since the Pearl Harbor attack had American or allied forces been taken so unaware. As the Japanese planes overhead eerily illuminated the area with parachute flares, Mikawa's cruisers dashed past the South Patrol Force firing shells and torpedoes. The destroyer *Patterson* sounded the alarm by voice radio: "Warning! Warning! Strange ships entering harbor!" but it was too late. Before the Allied vessels could bring their guns to bear or the surprised torpedomen could insert firing primers, the American cruiser *Chicago* had had part of

---

[7] The contemporary American torpedo was 21 inches in diameter and carried a 780-pound charge three miles at 45 knots, 7.5 miles at 26.5 knots. Through the first two years of the war the exploder mechanism remained notoriously undependable.

her bow blown off by a torpedo, and the Australian cruiser *Canberra* had been reduced to a blazing, unsalvable hulk. Still unscratched, the attacking column split into two divisions and wheeled north,[8] three cruisers passing across the van of the North Patrol Force and three steaming across the rear, searchlights open, guns blazing. In a matter of minutes all three cruisers of the North Force, the American heavies *Vincennes, Astoria,* and *Quincy,* were afire and sinking. The *Vincennes* however with her last salvo smashed the staff chart room of the Japanese flagship *Chokai,* killing 30 men. At 0220 Mikawa ordered "All ships withdraw," and his attack force headed up the Slot. North of Savo Island one of his cruiser divisions encountered the second picket destroyer and concentrated upon her a massed fire which left her superstructure a shambles. The attack was over. It had cost the Allies four cruisers and a thousand lives and vindicated the confidence of the Japanese that the night was their friend.

Mikawa, mindful that he had not carried out his mission, considered returning to Ironbottom Bay to blast the transports. But he decided against it lest the American carrier planes catch him within easy range after dawn. He need not have worried, for Fletcher had already retreated far to the southeast. The Japanese attack force retired up the slot unmolested.

HENDERSON FIELD PUT INTO OPERATION

The roar of battle had scarcely died away before the American sailors and marines returned to their backbreaking task of unloading cargo. After dawn, alarms of air raids that never materialized twice sent all ships into the open Sound for evasive maneuvers. So when the transports and cargo vessels

weighed anchor that afternoon, they carried away more than half the supplies they had brought, including quantities of food and ammunition and all radar sets, coast defense guns, and heavy construction equipment. The last ship of Turner's Amphibious Force cleared Ironbottom Sound just before dark. The 16,000 marines left behind on Guadalcanal and Tulagi would be limited to two daily meals of B and C rations eked out with captured rice.

For several days the Japanese limited their offensive against the new American positions to light aerial bombings and to bombardments by surfaced submarines. During this relative lull, marine engineers, using hand shovels and captured steam rollers and trucks, got the airstrip in good enough shape to receive light planes. On August 15 four American destroyer-transports darted into Ironbottom Sound bringing aviation gasoline, bombs, ammunition, and ground crews. On the 20th an escort carrier approached Guadalcanal from the southeast and flew in marine corps planes—19 F4F's and 12 SBD's. From that moment the tide began to turn in favor of the Allies.

PREVIEW OF A FAILURE

The Japanese, with nearly everything in their favor, lost Guadalcanal through bad strategy, bad tactics, and faulty intelligence. Their determined but fruitless drive to recapture their lost position, which precipitated no fewer than six sea battles and three important land battles, forms one of the most complex campaigns of the war. Yet when one considers just what the Japanese were trying to do and why they failed, the whole struggle falls into an easily comprehended pattern. So it is well to preview the campaign as a whole before considering the individual operations.

In the period between the departure of Allied naval forces from Guadalcanal and the completion of Henderson Field, the Japanese possessed the strategic advantage but lacked sufficient troops in the South Pacific for an immediate counter-invasion.

[8] "Wheel: To alter course in such a manner that upon completion all ships will be in their former relative positions." John V. Noel, Jr., *Naval Terms Dictionary* (New York, 1952), 240. In a wheeling column, the vessels change course one at a time in the same water.

Their fleet however was still superior. Their base at Rabaul, backed by the still more powerful base at Truk, lay 560 miles northwest of Guadalcanal, with an intervening aircraft staging base on Buka Island and excellent positions for other bases in the Upper and Central Solomons. The nearest Allied airfield and anchorage was the still-primitive base at Espiritu Santo, 560 miles southeast of Guadalcanal across open water. The retirement of Fletcher and Turner left the Japanese in command of the sea around and the air over the island, but they were not prepared to make their control permanent by seeking out and engaging the Allied fleet in the Coral Sea. Their experience at Midway made them wary of this classic means of isolating the target. They would disregard the teachings of Mahan and begin by putting men ashore to destroy the American occupation force and recapture the airfield. Then carriers would approach to send in planes in order to seize control of the air over the island. Under cover of this land-based air, fleet units would move in to take command of the waters around Guadalcanal.

Four times the Japanese tried to capture the island by means of this topsy-turvy strategy; each time the attempt led to a land battle, a sea battle, or both. The first Japanese counterattack, in August, produced the Battle of the Tenaru River on land and the Battle of the Eastern Solomons at sea. The second, in September, brought about the Battle of Bloody Ridge but no sea battle. The third, in October, precipitated the Battle for Henderson Field and the Battle of the Santa Cruz Islands. The fourth and last, in November, resulted in the Naval Battle of Guadalcanal but no land battle. American operations to halt enemy surface forces en route to Ironbottom Sound brought about two additional naval conflicts, the Battle of Cape Esperance in October and the Battle of Tassafaronga in November, actions less notable for strategic results than for the tactical lessons they provide.

Of the numerous explanations for Japan's four failures to recapture Guadalcanal the following are the most important: (1) The Japanese, grossly underestimating the number of American troops on Guadalcanal, for two months directed their major strength against Papua. When they learned the truth and switched emphasis it was too late. In the reinforcement race they could never get sufficient preponderance of manpower on the island to wrest the airfield from the entrenched Americans. (2) Japanese tactics, especially on land, were too complex. Hoping to divide and surprise the Americans they so divided their own strength that the elements more often than not failed to coordinate and were themselves surprised. (3) Japanese strategy was too inflexible. By repeating the same attack plan four times with little variation, they rendered their moves predictable and failed to achieve the surprise on which they placed so much value.

THE BATTLE OF THE TENARU RIVER AND THE BATTLE OF THE EASTERN SOLOMONS

On August 7, 1942, the day of the Allied invasion of Guadalcanal, B-17's from Port Moresby raided Rabaul, thereby sharply reminding Tokyo that Papua must not be neglected just because of the new threat developing in the Solomons. Urgent requests for help brought convoys of Japanese infantry speeding towards Rabaul from all over the Western Pacific. By mid-August 16,000 troops had arrived or were on the way. Of these, 10,000 were promptly dispatched to reinforce the lodgement at Buna for the march across the mountains to Port Moresby. The rest were earmarked for Guadalcanal, where the Japanese believed that no more than one or two thousand Americans had landed.

The Japanese reinforcements, besides being too few and too late, were rendered ineffective by being committed in driblets. On succeeding nights in mid-August destroyers landed 500 troops on Guadalcanal west of American positions and 900 east. A day later 1,500 more sailed from Rabaul in an Occupation Force commanded by Rear

Admiral Raizo Tanaka, of whom we shall hear more. To protect the Occupation Force, the entire Combined Fleet proceeded from Truk as a Supporting Force under Vice Admiral Nobutake Kondo. The remaining 3,000 or so troops would be sent down from Rabaul after Tanaka's force had landed.

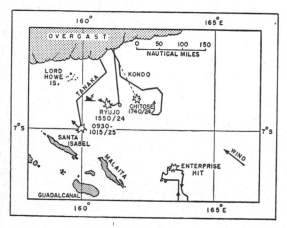

BATTLE OF THE EASTERN SOLOMONS
AUGUST 22-25, 1942

Informed by coastwatchers and by Mac-Arthur's air patrol of stepped-up Japanese activity, Ghormley sent Fletcher with the carrier forces to guard the American positions in the Solomons. On August 23, as Tanaka and Kondo reached the edge of an overcast that had concealed their advance, Fletcher sent the *Wasp* force south to refuel. With the *Enterprise* and *Saratoga* forces he then took station 150 miles east of Guadalcanal. By that time, unknown to the Japenese commanders, the chief segment of their advance force had been eliminated. The 900 troops east of the American perimeter on Guadalcanal had attacked prematurely and been wiped out almost to a man in the 16-hour Battle of the Tenaru River, which cost the marines 35 killed and 75 wounded.

August 24 found the Japanese sea forces out from beneath the overcast on a southerly course—Tanaka 250 miles due north of Guadalcanal, with Kondo, his main strength concentrated in the sister-carriers *Shokaku* and *Zuikaku,* 40 miles to the east covering his flank. Far in advance was a Diversionary

Force with the light carrier *Ryujo,* whose unhappy mission was to strip herself of planes to neutralize Henderson Field and then remain as a decoy to attract American attention while the larger Japanese carriers sent their squadrons against Fletcher's forces. Fletcher took the bait, sending 30 bombers and eight torpedo planes, which sank the *Ryujo* in a well-coordinated attack. Absence of these aircraft temporarily weakened his striking power but left his defenses unimpaired, for his outsize combat air patrol of 53 F4F Wildcat fighters remained with the fleet.

When American patrol planes located the big Japanese carriers to the north, Fletcher promptly made preparations for an attack from that quarter. He turned fighter-plane direction over to Rear Admiral Thomas Kinkaid's *Enterprise* force and, hoping to divide the enemy, withdrew with the *Saratoga* force ten miles to the southeast. As radar detected the approaching Japanese attack groups, the remaining bombers and torpedo planes of both American carriers were ordered to take to the air and seek out the hostile fleet, while the fighters stacked themselves over the American forces and on the line of approach of the enemy planes. Kinkaid's Wildcats quickly broke the enemy formations and shot down half a dozen bombers before they could begin their dives. The rest, ignoring the distant *Saratoga,* swooped down upon the *Enterprise* force, where they ran into a blistering antiaircraft fire which no torpedo planes and few bombers penetrated.

Three determined bomber pilots however bored through the fire to make direct hits in quick succession on the flight deck of the *Enterprise,* killing 74 men, knocking out two elevators, wrecking compartments, and blasting holes in her side. Six minutes after the first attack on the carrier the battle was over, and a small remnant of the attacking squadrons was fleeing northward with the Wildcats in hot pursuit. The Americans had lost only 15 planes. Within an hour damage control parties aboard the *Enterprise* had corrected her slight list and she was steaming south at 24 knots landing aircraft. The American air attack squadrons meanwhile had missed the main enemy carrier force and instead struck a detached group, sending the seaplane carrier *Chitose* flaming out of action.

At midnight Kondo, having lost a carrier and 90 planes, withdrew towards Truk. But Tanaka's Occupation Force steamed doggedly southward through the night to become the morning target of Henderson Field bombers, which severely damaged the light cruiser *Jintsu* and so crippled a transport that it had to be scuttled. Not long afterwards B-17's from Espiritu Santo struck the Occupation Force and sank a destroyer. Rabaul thereupon acknowledged the failure of this first attempt to recapture Guadalcanal by recalling Tanaka and canceling the operation.

THE BATTLE OF BLOODY RIDGE

The defeat of August 24-25 caused scarcely a pause in Japanese activities. On the 28th four destroyers approached Guadalcanal with additional reinforcements, but Henderson Field bombers dived on them at sunset, sinking one and damaging two others. Thereafter the Japanese timed their approaches more cautiously. Hovering up the Slot until dark, destroyers and small transports darted into Ironbottom Sound each night so regularly that marines nicknamed them the Tokyo Express. After putting men and supplies ashore they would lob a few rounds of shells at the airstrip and be back up the Slot out of reach of marine bombers before light. Allied vessels, after night sinkings of two destroyer-transports by Japanese destroyers, shunned the Sound after nightfall as conscientiously as the enemy shunned it after dawn. Thus the Allies, under protection of Henderson Field, commanded the waters around Guadalcanal by day, and the Japanese commanded these waters by night. Every surface action in Ironbottom Sound thereafter resulted from contacts made when Allied warships out-stayed the sun.

Even by day Allied vessels were not immune from enemy air attacks staging out of Rabaul, one of which sank a destroyer-transport in late August. But marine corps aviators soon made the air above Guadalcanal unhealthful for the enemy—especially after Grumman (Wildcat) pilots solved the problem of the darting Zekes by operating in mutually protecting pairs.[9]

By September 10 the Japanese had 6,000 troops on Guadalcanal, divided characteristically between positions east and west of the American perimeter. The time had come for the second drive to recapture the island. The Imperial Army commander ashore, accepting the official underestimate of American forces, reported that he had sufficient strength for an attack. Thereupon Kondo's carrier-battleship-cruiser fleet again departed Truk, and a new D-day was set for September 12. The Japanese troops, after chopping a trail through the jungle, at nightfall on the 12th struck with their main force along the high ground, subsequently known as Bloody Ridge, which led from the south directly to Henderson Field. But their move had been anticipated and marines were waiting for them with mortars and machine guns backed by 105 mm. howitzers. The American lines held through the night and the next day. When darkness came on the 13th, the marines opened and maintained a continuous barrage of shells which the Japanese for lack of artillery could not counter. Just before midnight Imperial Army troops launched a final banzai attack which carried them perilously close to the airfield before it collapsed under withering massed fire. By first light the Japanese were in disorderly retreat. Planes taking off from Henderson Field at dawn peppered the jungle with strafing fire, helping to bring enemy losses to

---

[9] Said one pilot: "The Zero could outmaneuver, outclimb, outspeed us. One Grumman against one Zero was not an even fight, but with mutual support two Grummans were worth four or five Zeros." Quoted in Robert Sherrod, *History of Marine Corps Aviation in World War II* (New York, 1952), 83. Apparently the tactical innovation of operating fighter aircraft in pairs was first employed by Major General Claire Chennault's "Flying Tigers" in the China-Burma-India theater. Another advantage enjoyed by the flyers on Guadalcanal was of course early warning from the coastwatchers, which enabled them to get altitude.

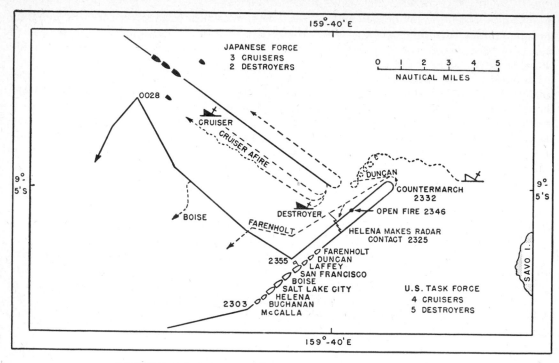

159°-40' E

JAPANESE FORCE
3 CRUISERS
2 DESTROYERS

0   1   2   3   4   5
NAUTICAL MILES

0028

CRUISER

CRUISER AFIRE

9°
5'S

DUNCAN

COUNTERMARCH
2332

OPEN FIRE 2346

BOISE

DESTROYER

HELENA MAKES RADAR
CONTACT 2325

FARENHOLT

9°
5'S

FARENHOLT
DUNCAN
2355   LAFFEY
SAN FRANCISCO
BOISE
SALT LAKE CITY
HELENA
2303   BUCHANAN
McCALLA

U.S. TASK FORCE
4 CRUISERS
5 DESTROYERS

SAVO I.

159°-40' E

BATTLE OF CAPE ESPERANCE, OCTOBER 11-12, 1942

1,500. American casualties were 40 dead and 103 wounded.

Once more Kondo's fleet retired on Truk. The second attempt had failed.

ATTRITION IN THE CORAL SEA

During the race to supply Guadalcanal following the Battle of the Eastern Solomons, the American carrier forces patrolled the Coral Sea, protecting the communication line from Espiritu Santo. In these dangerous waters a Japanese submarine fired a torpedo into the *Saratoga,* putting her out of action for the three crucial months to follow. Two weeks later, in mid-September, two submarines torpedoed the *Wasp,* the fast battleship *North Carolina,* and the destroyer *O'Brien* all within a quarter of an hour. The two torpedoes which struck the *Wasp* ignited open fuel lines and at the same time broke her water mains so that effective fire fighting was impossible. Captain Forrest P. Sherman,

her commanding officer, after vainly attempting to confine the fires by turning her undamaged stern into the wind, at length ordered Abandon Ship, and a destroyer sank the flaming derelict with torpedoes. The *North Carolina,* with a 32-foot underwater rip in her hull, made Pearl Harbor for repairs, but the *O'Brien* broke up and sank before she could reach drydock. That day's series of calamities left the Allies only one operational fleet carrier, the *Hornet,* and one undamaged new battleship, the *Washington,* in the whole Pacific. Luckily the convoy which the *Wasp* and the *Hornet* had been supporting reached Guadalcanal safely. Aboard were 4,200 troops, Turner's last marine reserves, which he had withdrawn from the defense of Samoa.

TOKYO SHIFTS EMPHASIS

The Japanese were making no better progress on Papua than they were making on Guadalcanal. Their troops based on Buna had penetrated a 6,500-foot-high pass of the Owen Stanley Mountains, descended the southern slope, and come within sight of Port Moresby, only to be stopped short by MacArthur's Australians. An attempted lodgement in Milne Bay at the eastern tip of New Guinea had been hurled into the sea by Americans and Australians who got there first. Frustrated on both fronts, the Japanese concluded that they had to make a choice of objectives. Guadalcanal, they decided at last, was the greater threat. So they went on the defensive in Papua and began rushing all available reinforcements down the Slot by Tokyo Express, sometimes as many as 900 troops a night. Admiral Yamamoto, with advance headquarters at Truk, had decreed that the carrier fleet would not again be committed in close supporting operations until Henderson Field had been captured. The Imperial Army was determined that if manpower could prevent it, there would be no repetition of the August and September fiascos.

Additional manpower became also the pressing requirement of the Allied South Pacific command because the Americans were losing their initial numerical advantage as increasing numbers of Japanese reached Guadalcanal. It is a measure of Ghormley's desperation that he stripped his New Caledonia garrison of 3,000 United States Army troops and embarked them to reinforce Vandegrift's marines. Task forces built around the *Hornet* and the *Washington* cleared the way for the convoy, and a cruiser-destroyer force under Rear Admiral Norman Scott advanced to derail the Tokyo Express.

THE BATTLE OF
CAPE ESPERANCE

Warned that an enemy group of three cruisers and two destroyers was coming down the Slot, Admiral Scott towards midnight on October 11 placed his force of four cruisers and five destroyers in an intercepting position outside the strait south of Savo. One of his cruisers, equipped with the new SG surface-search radar, detected the oncoming enemy group, but before her commanding officer could warn the admiral, Scott ordered a reversal of course by column movement and led with his flagship, the *San Francisco*. This threw out of line his three leading destroyers, which raced up the flank of the column to regain the van (see diagram).

As Scott's cruisers completed their countermarch, the Japanese, who had no radar, blundered head-on at right angles into range of every gun of the American force, which promptly opened fire, sinking a cruiser and a destroyer and setting another cruiser ablaze. Scott, without realizing it, had neatly capped the Japanese "T," but his tactical advantage was somewhat offset by the unhappy position of his van destroyers, which were caught between the opposing forces. The *Laffey* managed to get out of this predicament without a scratch, but the *Farenholt* was holed by two American shells, and the *Duncan,* furiously battered by friend and foe, caught fire and sank.

The surviving Japanese vessels fled up the Slot with the Americans in pursuit. The *Boise,* upon snapping on her searchlight to find a target, took six hits which opened her hull and sent her blazing out of line. An exploding magazine then reduced her topside to a shambles and at the same time silhouetted the *Salt Lake City,* which received two hits. Scott's force thereupon concentrated on the undamaged enemy cruiser and battered her with shellfire as she retreated to the northwest.

It was an American victory at an hour when, to paraphrase Jervis, a victory was very essential. In the general jubilation few ventured to point out that it was to some extent an accidental victory, won despite dubious tactics. Had the Japanese been a little earlier they might have capped the American "T," or caught Scott's column bent double with half its guns masked. Scott blinded himself by choosing a flagship equipped with obsolescent short-range radar. He neither used his destroyers for scouting ahead nor released them to attack with torpedoes, their primary night weapon. Instead of turning together or by divisions he countermarched in disputed waters, thereby masking his fire for 15 perilous minutes. He led the countermarch with his cruisers, thus interposing his van destroyers between his own force and the enemy. His battle plan called for searchlight illumination, which provided enemy guns with a point for aim. Yet because he won a victory his tactics were not only widely condoned but even imitated.

GETTING READY FOR THE OCTOBER SHOWDOWN

The American convoy with the reinforcements from New Caledonia reached Ironbottom Sound in the morning of October 13, discharged soldiers and cargo, and got safely away. But these reinforcements were soon to be offset by an enemy convoy bringing 4,500 troops down from the Upper Solomons. To pave the way and knock out American air power on Guadalcanal, battleships *Kongo* and *Haruna* on the night of October 13-14 systematically pounded the Henderson Field area for an hour and a half with hundreds of high-capacity shells, churning up the landing strip and destroying half the aircraft on the island. Two air raids the next day and a bombardment by heavy cruisers the following night added to the destruction. Only a few planes were left to oppose the Japanese convoy, which reached Guadalcanal in the early hours of the 15th. The new arrivals brought the enemy garrison up to 22,000, the majority fresh troops, to oppose 23,000 Americans, mostly battle-worn, malaria-ridden marines. As the Imperial Army forces confidently prepared for what they regarded as the inevitable recapture of the airdrome, Admiral Kondo brought down from Truk the most powerful battleship-carrier concentration since the Battle of Midway.

In the face of these vast enemy preparations morale in the South Pacific reached a new low. Part of the general lack of confidence grew out of command problems that had haunted the Guadalcanal operation from the beginning. Now Turner was finding fault with Vandegrift's perimeter defense, insisting that American troops should go on the offen-

sive from a number of points along the coast of Guadalcanal. Vandegrift for his part felt that he was getting inadequate support from the fleet. Ghormley, who from the beginning had had his doubts about the invasion, seemed able neither to resolve these differences nor to instill confidence in his subordinates. Nimitz therefore relieved Ghormley of the South Pacific command, replacing him with the confident and aggressive William F. Halsey.

Halsey promptly called a conference at Noumea and settled the disagreement on strategy in favor of Vandegrift, to whom he said, "Are we going to evacuate or hold?" "I can hold," said Vandegrift, "but I've got to have more active support than I've been getting." "All right," replied Halsey. "Go on back. I'll promise you everything I've got." [10] Halsey next directed the *Washington* force to put a halt to the enemy reinforcement and bombardment of Guadalcanal. Then he daringly ordered Kinkaid, who had recently relieved Fletcher, to take the two carrier forces, one centered around the *Hornet* and the other around the hastily-repaired *Enterprise*, to the waters northeast of Guadalcanal.

THE BATTLE FOR HENDERSON FIELD AND THE BATTLE OF THE SANTA CRUZ ISLANDS

The Japanese launched their drive on October 20. It quickly became apparent however that this was to be no easy march to Henderson Field. The well-entrenched Americans refused to give ground. The three lines of the Japanese advance got out of phase. After the army command had thrice notified Kondo's carriers that they might approach and send in planes, and each time postponed the hour, Yamamoto at Truk lost patience. He warned the army that the fleet was running

[10] From *Admiral Halsey's Story*, by William F. Halsey and J. Bryan III (New York: McGraw-Hill Book Company, Inc., 1947), 117. Copyright, 1947, by William F. Halsey. Copyright, 1947, by The Curtis Publishing Company.

out of fuel and would have to retire unless Henderson Field were soon captured.

In the early hours of the 26th, PBY's from Espiritu Santo reported that Kondo was heading northward, away from the Guadalcanal area. Kinkaid's two carrier forces had by this time reached the vicinity of the Santa Cruz Islands, within striking range of the Japanese fleet. Admiral Halsey noted all this on his operations chart at Noumea and just before dawn flashed the electrifying order: "Attack—Repeat—Attack." Search planes promptly left the deck of the *Enterprise* and began the day auspiciously by locating the major enemy carrier group and with a pair of 500-pound bombs blasting a hole in the flight deck of the light carrier *Zuiho*.

Thereafter events worked increasingly to American tactical disadvantage. Kinkaid, whose experience prior to Operation Watchtower had been with battleships and cruisers, adopted Fletcher's plan of controlling all fighter-direction from the *Enterprise*, but with less precision and certainly with less luck. Because the Japanese got the jump on him by putting a strike in the air 20 minutes before the Americans launched, Kinkaid had to accept battle over his own decks before his fighters attained altitude; and as ill fortune would have it, the enemy concentrated on the *Hornet* force while the *Enterprise* was ten miles away. Five bombs struck the *Hornet*'s flight deck, some penetrating deep into the hull before detonating. Two torpedoes exploded in her engine spaces, severing electric cables and water mains and flooding fire rooms. Listing, ablaze, without power or communications, the carrier went dead in the water. Meanwhile, far to the northwest, the *Hornet*'s bombers were exacting vengeance by fighting their way through strong Japanese air patrols to cripple the heavy cruiser *Chikuma* and put the carrier *Shokaku* out of the war for several months.

An hour later a second Japanese air strike found the *Enterprise* force unready and in a state of some confusion because a submarine had just torpedoed the destroyer *Porter*. Accuracy and volume of antiaircraft fire, especially from the new battleship *South Dakota*, limited damage this time to three bomb hits on the flight deck of the *Enterprise*. After a

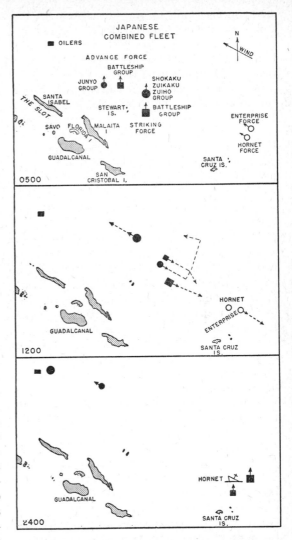

BATTLE OF THE SANTA CRUZ ISLANDS
OCTOBER 26, 1942

third morning attack had damaged two more of his ships, Kinkaid ordered the *Porter* scuttled, and the *Enterprise* force retreated to the southeast.

Left thus without fighter cover, the *Hornet* became the target of repeated afternoon air attacks. When another torpedo and two more bomb hits made her blaze afresh and heel over dangerously, the force commander ordered the carrier abandoned. He then withdrew, leaving two destroyers behind to sink her. These expended all their torpedoes and more than 400 shells without producing any effect except to start new fires. After dark, when the American destroyers had departed, ships of Kondo's fleet approached the burning derelict. Unable to take her in tow, they sent her down with four Long Lances.

Though tactically the Americans had got the worst of this battle, in the long run it worked to their strategic advantage. Kondo had lost 100 planes; Kinkaid, 74. This disparity was more one-sided than the bare numbers indicate, for the Japanese were to be quickly outmatched by the upsurging American pilot training and aircraft construction programs. Not again would the Combined Fleet risk its carriers in close support of the Solomons campaign. The Japanese carrier forces were to retreat ever westward until forced into battle many months later to protect their Marianas defense line. By that time the advantage would be all with the Americans, who following the Santa Cruz Islands battle re-studied carrier tactics and sacrificed the flexibility of individual carrier groups in favor of putting several carriers in a single group to take better advantage of the superior American antiaircraft fire.

Though the fleet at a heavy price had won important long-term gains, it was the American soldiers and marines on Guadalcanal who saved the immediate situation. They held firm while the enemy attack rose to a crescendo and finally died out on the 26th. Henderson Field remained in American hands, and Japanese casualties were perhaps ten times the American losses. Enemy ground force would no longer pose a serious threat.

GETTING READY FOR THE NOVEMBER SHOWDOWN

Convinced that they had barely missed recapturing Guadalcanal, the Japanese in early November duplicated their October preparations, but at a swifter pace. The night-running Tokyo Express sped up operations until Imperial Army forces on Guadalcanal outnumbered the Americans by several thousands. These piecemeal reinforcements however

were merely a preliminary to the 13,500 troops which the persistent Admiral Tanaka was about to bring down from the Shortland Islands in a Reinforcement Group of 11 transports escorted by 11 destroyers. Exactly as in October, a battleship group and a cruiser group would bombard Henderson Field on successive nights and bombers would raid by day. To provide some air cover for Tanaka's transports, Kondo's carriers would maneuver north of the Solomons, but they were under orders to avoid a naval engagement.

Halsey, informed of Japanese activities by air reconnaissance and other intelligence sources, did his best to make good his promise to Vandegrift. He would somehow find more troops for the defense of Guadalcanal, he would do everything possible to prevent the further bombardment of Henderson Field, and he would exert every effort to intercept Japanese reinforcements. Arrival of fresh troops from New Zealand and the United States enabled him to strip the remainder of his island garrisons and rush 6,000 soldiers and marines to Guadalcanal escorted by Turner's surface forces. By direct intervention of President Roosevelt, additional cruisers, destroyers, and submarines were ordered to the South Pacific; bombers and fighter planes were flown in from Hawaii and Australia. Finally, as the November showdown became imminent, Admiral Kinkaid set out from Noumea with the *Enterprise* force, now including the *Washington* as well as the *South Dakota,* taking along a tender so that repair to the damaged carrier could continue at sea. The Battle of the Santa Cruz Islands had taught Halsey caution also, for he directed Kinkaid under no circumstances to take the *Enterprise* into the waters north of the Solomons.

Though Turner beat Tanaka to Guadalcanal, he did not arrive undetected by the enemy. Bombers struck repeatedly at the American troop convoy in Ironbottom Sound. On November 12, a pilot crashed his burning plane into the *San Francisco,* knocking out a gun director and killing or injuring 50 men. Some of the bombers were from the carriers, for Kondo had already brought his fleet down from Truk to a position north of Santa Isabel Island. Thence he had dispatched Vice Admiral Hiroaki Abe southward with the first Bombardment Group, including battleships *Hiei* and *Kirishima*. Tanaka's Reinforcement Group was on the point of departing the Shortlands for its dash down the Slot.

Notified by scout planes of the approaching battleship force, Turner at sunset withdrew the convoy to the east. Since the *Enterprise* force, coming up from the south, was still nearly two days' steaming away, he ordered five cruisers and eight destroyers of the escort to separate from the convoy and return to Ironbottom Sound under command of Rear Admiral Daniel J. Callaghan to break up the impending bombardment of the airfield. Here surely was a David sent against a Goliath, for Admiral Abe besides his two battleships had a cruiser and 14 destroyers. Happily for the Americans, Abe's vessels were armed chiefly with bombardment rather than armor-piercing shells. Otherwise the United States force could hardly have avoided annihilation.

Callaghan, who had served as Ghormley's chief of staff until Halsey's arrival, was a courageous and devoted officer but was little prepared for the sort of action he was about to encounter. He neither issued a battle plan nor provided for means of scouting ahead; and, in imitation of Scott in the Battle of Cape Esperance, he retained his destroyers at the ends of his cruiser column instead of using them for a high-speed torpedo attack against the enemy. Also like Scott he chose for his flagship the *San Francisco* with her inferior radar. Scott, now second in command, led the column of cruisers in the *Atlanta,* which also lacked SG radar.[11]

THE NAVAL BATTLE OF GUADALCANAL

Under a moonless but starry sky, Callaghan's force passed back through the eastern channel and re-entered Ironbottom Sound. His vessels had almost reached the waters north of Lunga Point, when Abe's Bombardment Group, without radar, entered the sound through the passage south of Savo with a pair of detached destroyers scouting out ahead. The two forces were thus heading toward each other at high speed when the *Helena* detected the enemy 14 miles away and warned the flagship by voice radio. Callaghan thereupon ordered two successive column movements to the right which put him on course due north. He apparently hoped by this maneuver to reproduce Scott's capping position of the month before. But the leading destroyer *Cushing,* suddenly espying enemy scout destroyers dead ahead, swung out of line and threw the van into disorder. Callaghan's cruisers then wheeled left to avoid their own destroyers, and Japanese and American ships intermingled.

There followed a half-hour melee which for confusion and fury is scarcely paralleled in naval history. All formations broke and the engagement became a series of individual ship duels with each side at one time or another firing on its own vessels. From this midnight brawl the contending forces at length managed to extricate themselves, but both had been desperately hurt. Dawn revealed the extent of their injuries. The Japanese had lost two destroyers; and Abe's flagship *Hiei,* riddled by more than 50 shells, was helpless north of Savo, where aircraft from Henderson Field struck her again and again until she sank. Admirals Callaghan and Scott and most of the members of their staffs had been killed. Four American destroyers had been lost. The cruiser *Portland* and a destroyer were unnavigable. The cruiser *Atlanta,* flame-gutted, and shelled by friend and foe, had to be sunk. All but one of the other American vessels were damaged. The cruiser *Juneau,* while retiring from battle with a weakened keel, was torpedoed by a submarine and went down, carrying nearly 700 of her crew. Yet the Americans, despite overwhelming odds and faulty tactics, had by sheer valor carried out their mission. Abe's battleships had been turned back; Tanaka's transports returned to base.

[11] Cruisers *Portland*, *Helena*, and *Juneau* and destroyers *O'Bannon* and *Fletcher* carried long-range SG radar.

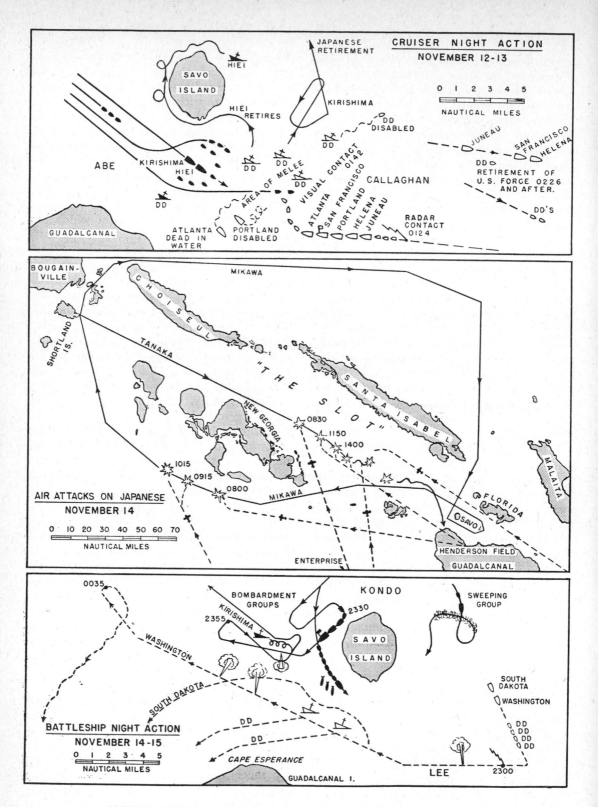

NAVAL BATTLE OF GUADALCANAL, NOVEMBER 12-15, 1942

The frustration of their intended battleship bombardment interrupted the Japanese schedule scarcely at all. Down came Mikawa from the Shortlands with his Cruiser Bombardment Group and in the early hours of the 14th carried out his bombardment of Henderson Field, achieving considerably less damage than Abe might have done with his 14-inch guns. The fortunes of war were turning against the Japanese however, for Kinkaid's force had at last arrived within flight range of the Solomons.

Daybreak on November 14 disclosed two Japanese forces to American search planes— Mikawa's Cruiser Bombardment Group south of New Georgia Island on a westerly retirement course and Tanaka's Reinforcement Group once more in the Slot approaching Guadalcanal. Bombers from Henderson Field and from the *Enterprise* first struck Mikawa, sinking one cruiser and damaging three others. Then, joined by B-17's from Espiritu Santo, they struck repeatedly at Tanaka's lightly-protected transports. By evening seven of them, carrying about 1,000 troops each, were sunk or sinking.

The complicated Japanese scheme was now becoming absurd as well as tragic. The transports were the heart of their whole November offensive, yet they had come down the Slot shielded by a mere handful of destroyers and a meager cover of fighter planes operating at near extreme range out of the Upper Solomons and from the decks of Kondo's carriers maneuvering far to the north. In his extremity Tanaka now rose to a sort of magnificence. With remarkable if perhaps foolhardy tenacity he pushed on towards Guadalcanal with four severely damaged transports, all he had left of his convoy. Meanwhile, Kondo himself with the *Kirishima,* four cruisers, and nine destroyers was heading down from the north to redeem Abe's failure of two nights before by blasting Henderson Field with a really effective bombardment.

At the same time up from the south came the *Washington,* the *South Dakota,* and four destroyers, detached from the *Enterprise* group with orders from Halsey to protect the field. The American force, under command of Rear Admiral Willis A. Lee in the *Wash-*

ington, reached Guadalcanal first, and late in the evening under a setting moon passed into Ironbottom Sound through the passage north of Savo. Though Lee had detected nothing, Kondo had seen Lee and characteristically divided his force into three groups, two to attack and the third to keep the Americans under observation (see diagram).

As Lee's force, in column with the destroyers leading, turned west towards Cape Esperance, the battleships made radar contact with the shadowing group and chased it away with a series of salvos. But one of the bombardment groups had passed west of Savo where it could not be detected by American radar. It now attacked Lee's van with shells and torpedoes, sinking two of his destroyers and putting the other two out of action. To avoid hitting the disabled vessels the *Washington* shifted to port and the *South Dakota* swung to starboard towards the enemy. This accidental separation of the American battleships occurred at a critical moment, for Kondo was about to strike again. His main Bombardment Group, the *Kirishima,* two heavy cruisers, and two destroyers, which had been maneuvering northwest of Savo, emerged and took the nearby *South Dakota* under fire, so wrecking her superstructure that she was obliged to retire.

The *Washington* was thus left to face the entire Japanese force. Lee, with the advantage of radar fire control, at which he was expert, accepted the challenge and quickly evened the score. With his 5-inchers and long guns, he concentrated on the *Kirishima.* Seven minutes and 50 shell hits later the Japanese battleship was helpless and turning in circles. Lee continued for a while to the northwest to attract the enemy away from his cripples and then withdrew to the south pursued by destroyers fruitlessly expending torpedoes.

Kondo now gave up, ordered the *Kirishima* and a disabled destroyer scuttled, and left the area. But tenacious Tanaka, who had steamed unflinchingly through the embattled waters, continued on to Guadalcanal, where he beached his four bomb-riddled transports. After dawn American planes and ship and shore artillery quickly smashed them to pieces

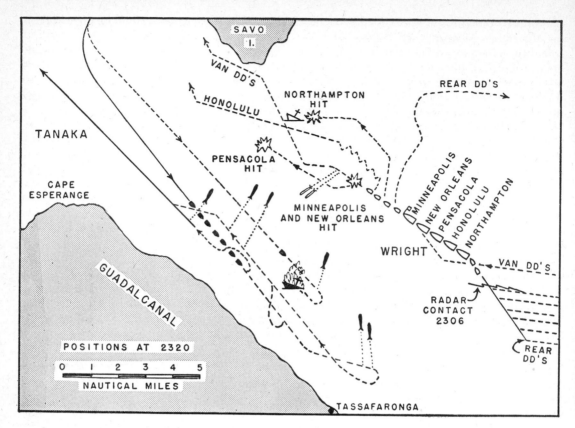

BATTLE OF TASSAFARONGA, NOVEMBER 30, 1942

—but not before the surviving troops had landed.

Japan's final attempt to recapture Guadalcanal had ended in fiasco like all the rest. Thereafter Yamamoto risked no more capital ships in the Solomons defense.

THE BATTLE OF TASSAFARONGA

Following the collapse of their November attack the Japanese went entirely on the defensive, maintaining their garrison on Guadalcanal merely as a holding force to keep the Americans occupied while they prepared a new defense line by constructing a pair of airfields in the Central Solomons. In the meantime Admiral Tanaka contrived a streamlined Tokyo Express of fast destroyers which kept the garrison supplied by dropping floating drums of material offshore and then darting back up the Slot before daylight. To derail this new express Halsey assigned to Admiral Kinkaid a force of cruisers and destroyers.

Kinkaid, an able tactician with surface forces, prepared a detailed battle plan designed to secure him from the errors his predecessors had made. Not for him was the blind approach or the single unbroken column. In night engagements he would use float planes for early warning and for parachute flare illumination when needed. His destroyers were to speed ahead to make a surprise torpedo attack and then turn away. His cruisers, holding off at 12,000 yards from the enemy, were to open with their guns the moment the torpedoes hit. But Kinkaid was detached for duty elsewhere and it fell to his successor, newly arrived Rear Admiral Carleton Wright, to execute this admirable plan.

Warned that Tanaka was about to begin

operations, Wright approached Guadalcanal on November 30 and that evening took his force through the east channel—four destroyers in the van, followed by five cruisers. Two additional destroyers, which joined too late for briefing, were tacked uselessly to the rear of the column. Forming line of bearing inside Ironbottom Sound, the cruisers swept westward with the destroyers on their flanks. Meanwhile Tanaka with eight destroyers had entered the Sound from the opposite direction; but of this Wright was unaware, for the seaplanes which were to give him warning had been unable to rise from the water because of the dead calm.

At 2306 Wright's flagship made radar contact with the Japanese, whereupon the cruisers promptly resumed column formation and wheeled to parallel the enemy. Now was the moment to release the van destroyers, but Wright hesitated because he could get no clear radar data. Tanaka's force, speeding past on an opposite course, merged with the nearby shoreline. When at last Wright ordered his van destroyers to fire torpedoes, the moment of opportunity had passed. The range was opening rapidly and none of the torpedoes found a target. The cruisers however opened fire on a picket destroyer somewhat nearer than the others and sent her down in flames.

The other Japanese destroyers had now reversed course by divisions. Since the Americans had no flashless powder, their gun flashes provided Japanese torpedo directors with a point of reference. Tanaka's well-drilled team released a score of deadly Long Lances at the extended American track. Because they were well aimed and ran hot, straight, and normal, and Wright's cruisers maintained course and speed, the torpedoes inevitably found their targets. Every one of the cruisers except the *Honolulu* took one or more hits. The *Minneapolis* and the *New Orleans* had their bows ripped away. The *Pensacola,* her after engine room flooded, three of her turrets knocked out, was quickly wreathed in oil fires. Worst hit of all was the *Northampton*; as water poured into her gashed-in side and blazing oil drenched her decks, the crew abandoned ship and she heeled over and sank. By that time Tanaka's

seven surviving destroyers, virtually undamaged, were far up the Slot.

This brief battle, which besides vitally needed cruisers cost the Americans 400 lives, provided a sort of textbook on how not to combat the powerful and accurate Japanese torpedo. In the hard school of the Solomons American commanders studied the lesson well, re-discovering flexibility and concentration tactics much as Rodney, Howe, Jervis, and Nelson restored concentration tactics to the Royal Navy in the Golden Age of sailing ship warfare.

GUADALCANAL SECURED

In December the malaria-ridden veterans of the 1st Marine Division together with their commander, General Vandegrift, were evacuated to Australia, and Major General Alexander M. Patch USA took command of the Guadalcanal garrison, which was soon raised to corps strength by the arrival of an additional army division directly from the United States. In January 1943 Patch had 50,000 soldiers and marines [12] under his command. The Japanese had assembled an equal number of reinforcements at Rabaul, but when the success of PT boats and aircraft against Tanaka's streamlined Express made it clear that these could not be committed, Tokyo at long last concluded that Guadalcanal would have to be abandoned.

In mid-January Patch, unaware that the enemy had already conceded defeat, began an all-out drive westward from the American defense perimeter. The Japanese, using cleverly sited artillery, gave ground stubbornly, fighting for time to carry out their evacuation plan. This they achieved by means of a grandiose and neatly-timed stratagem. While transports and destroyers assembled at Rabaul and in the Upper Solomons, Admiral Kondo brought the Truk battleship-carrier fleet once more to the waters north of Guadalcanal. As the Japanese had expected, all this activity caught Halsey's attention. What did it portend? Was the enemy, after failing four times, about to make a fifth attempt to recapture the island? If so, the South Pacific at

---

[12] Of the 2nd Marine Division.

long last had power aplenty to turn him back. Halsey promptly dispatched to Guadalcanal an additional troop convoy supported by five task forces, including two large and two escort carriers and three fast battleships. But no fleet action ensued, for Kondo had brought his fleet down not to do battle but merely to create a diversion. Instead, the Japanese struck from the air. At night, using parachute flares and floating lights, torpedo planes from the recently-constructed airfield on New Georgia succeeded in sinking the cruiser *Chicago*. Evidently the enemy had developed yet another technique for turning the night to his advantage.

As the main body of Patch's troops advanced westward along the north coast of Guadalcanal, a battalion was ferried around to a new beachhead west of Cape Esperance. The newly-landed troops then advanced eastward to meet the approaching main body in order by a double envelopment to nip off the enemy's communication line with the coast and seal him up in the jungle for annihilation. But when the American forces made contact on February 9, they found that the quarry had slipped through their fingers. While American attention had been diverted elsewhere, a score of destroyers in three high-speed night runs down the Slot had carried away the 12,000 half-starved survivors of the Imperial Army garrison. Thus on a note of mingled frustration and triumph for both sides the Guadalcanal campaign came to an end.

PAPUA SECURED

While the Americans were tightening their grip on Guadalcanal, Allied forces a thousand miles to the west were with equal difficulty and equal success wresting from the enemy the peninsula of Papua. Here too the Japanese were defeated by insuperable problems of communication. Those troops who had labored through pestilent jungle and over the rugged Owen Stanley range in a futile attempt to capture Port Moresby had paid for their advance by ever lengthening their supply line, a rough mountain trail over which food and ammunition had to be carried by manpower. By bombing and strafing this trail, Allied planes reduced the attackers to starvation.

Thus when MacArthur launched his counterattack it was against an enemy already demoralized by fatigue, disease, and hunger. While the Australians turned the enemy transmontane advance into a retreat and then into a rout, American soldiers flew over the mountains to an airstrip on the north coast of Papua and thence proceeded by motor launch to a lodgement southeast of the Japanese position centered on Buna. In November 1942 the Americans made contact with the Australians, who by this time had pursued the decimated enemy back over the mountains and into their Buna defense area. Thenceforth the Allied situation in Papua was the reverse of that on Guadalcanal, for in Papua it was the Allies who were assaulting a perimeter—fighting along matted jungle trails, across fields of man-high kunai grass, and through dense mangrove swamps. But the Papuan campaign was little affected by sea power. A strong naval force might quickly have turned the tide either way by supporting rapid waterborne reinforcement and by repeated bombardment. Neither side however ever ventured ships into this area of uncharted waters and hostile airfields.

The Japanese tried first to reinforce and then to evacuate Buna by means of night-running barges, but American PT boats made such attempts too costly. MacArthur's troops, supplied initially by airdrop, soon hacked out landing fields in the grassy plains so that a regular airlift could be set up. From then on Allied strength in the Buna area steadily increased while the enemy's waned. Yet despite everything MacArthur could send against them, the Japanese held their bit of coastline until late January 1943. Then at length their defenses collapsed, less from outside pressure than from starvation and disease within.

The long and critical preliminaries were over. South Pacific and Southwest Pacific forces had each captured a base that the Japanese had intended to use as a springboard for further aggression. For the Allies two roads to Rabaul were now open.

42

The Campaign against Rabaul, Phase II: the Central Solomons and Huon Peninsula

WITH THE CAPTURE OF GUA-
dalcanal in the Solomons and Buna on the
north coast of Papua early in 1943 the Allies
had completed Phase I of their campaign
against Rabaul. The shift to Phase II—the
coordinated dual advance via the Solomons
and via New Guinea—could not be rushed.
It would require strengthening bases, training new forces, and, not least important, developing an offensive psychology. Since General MacArthur proposed to advance along
the northern New Guinea coast by a series
of waterborne leaps, the Southwest Pacific
command would have to acquire a respectable force of naval and amphibious craft. The
South Pacific meanwhile had to train the
43rd Army Division to operate as an amphibious corps while the 1st and 2nd Marine
Divisions were undergoing rest and rehabili-
tation from the rigors of the Guadalcanal
campaign.

DEVISING A
PACIFIC-WIDE STRATEGY

In March 1943 Admiral King clarified
naval organization by inaugurating a numbered fleet system whereby United States
fleets operating in the Atlantic and the Mediterranean would bear even numbers, and
those in the Pacific would bear odd numbers. Under this plan Halsey's South Pacific
Force became the U.S. Third Fleet, with Halsey in direct command; and Turner's amphibious team became the Third Amphibious
Force. MacArthur's miniature Naval Forces
Southwest Pacific became U.S. Seventh Fleet,
under Vice Admiral Arthur S. Carpender
(later succeeded by Vice Admiral Kinkaid),
with amphibious craft and support designated as Seventh Amphibious Force, under
Rear Admiral Daniel E. Barbey. The Central
Pacific Force, based on Pearl Harbor, would

become the U.S. Fifth Fleet, commanded by Vice Admiral Raymond A. Spruance. In July 1943 Turner was to be transferred from the South to the Central Pacific to organize a new Fifth Amphibious Force.[1]

Two weeks after King's fleet reorganization the Joint Chiefs of Staff issued a directive specifying the tasks of Phase II. MacArthur's task was to control Huon Gulf and Peninsula and to invade New Britain. Halsey's was to invade Bougainville Island and there establish airfields whence bombers accompanied by fighters could strike regularly at Rabaul. Before either commander could move upon his assigned objective, he would have to advance his land-based bomber range by establishing new forward airfields. To this end, MacArthur would occupy Kiriwina and Woodlark Islands, and Halsey would invade the Central Solomons. Since the dividing line between Halsey's and MacArthur's areas of command lay just west of Guadalcanal, Phase II would see South Pacific forces penetrating the Southwest Pacific Area. This led to a curious command set-up, with Halsey in effect wearing three hats. He would look to MacArthur for general strategic direction, but as Commander Third Fleet and Commander South Pacific Area he would plan the details of his own operations and be responsible to Nimitz, who was Commander in Chief Pacific Fleet and Commander in Chief Pacific Ocean Areas.[2]

There was thus no supreme commander of the campaign against Rabaul. This odd command relationship was only the first that had to be devised whenever forces of the Southwest Pacific Area operated with any part of Nimitz' broad command. Certain naval officers early proposed a permanent solution. Pointing to the successful joint operations against North Africa under the supreme command of General Eisenhower, they suggested that the entire Pacific theater be placed under Admiral Nimitz. The idea had merit but it could never be put into effect for a variety of reasons, not the least of which was the military reputation and towering stature of MacArthur himself, for MacArthur had captured the imagination of the world by his defense of the Philippines and by his promise to return. On the other hand, the Joint Chiefs would not give the sole command to MacArthur because, as we shall see, they did not agree with his strategy.[3]

Looking forward to Phase III of the Rabaul campaign, Admiral King questioned whether it would be necessary after all to expend time and lives in the capture of fortress Rabaul. At far less cost, once Phase II had been completed, Rabaul could be bombed into impotence while advancing

---

[1] The fleets would be divided into task forces, task groups, and task units as operations required. Thus TU 31.2.3 would be a component of TG 31.2, which would be a component of TF 31, which would be a component of the Third Fleet. For command and administrative purposes ships of the same type continued to be organized into squadrons and divisions. The Central Pacific Force did not officially assume the title Fifth Fleet until 1944, but for the sake of simplicity this narrative follows the informal practice of calling it Fifth Fleet from the beginning of operations in 1943.

[2] One purpose of this arrangement was to preserve the flexibility of the Pacific Fleet. As Commander in Chief Pacific Fleet Nimitz could freely shift naval forces between the Third and Fifth Fleets and elsewhere in the Pacific Ocean Areas as operations required. Over the Seventh Fleet, which was not part of the Pacific Fleet, he had no such control. Had the Third Fleet been placed in the Southwest Pacific

chain of command it also would have been outside Nimitz' control.

[3] Not all military analysts believe that the whole Pacific theater should have been placed under a single officer. The proponents of separate area commands argue that the strategic problems of the various areas of the Pacific were on too vast a scale for one person to grasp. They decry uncritical adherence to "unified command," regarding it as desirable only within a geographic entity that gives coherence to operations. General Marshall, a believer in almost unlimited unity of command, proposed at the time of the Normandy invasion that all forces operating against Germany—land, sea, and air, whether approaching from the Atlantic or the Mediterranean—be placed under one officer. The British Chiefs of Staff objected, stating: "There must be some limit to the responsibilities which Allied Governments can delegate to a single soldier." Prime Minister Churchill, agreeing with his Chiefs, questioned ". . . whether any single officer exists who would be capable of giving decisions over the vast range of problems now being dealt with by the British and American governments assisted by the Combined Chiefs of Staff." (Quotations from Winston S. Churchill, *The Second World War,* V, 301.)

RABAUL NEUTRALIZED AND BY-PASSED

Allied forces broke through the barrier of the Bismarcks and captured the Admiralty Islands on the far side. Occupation of these islands would obviate the need to capture Rabaul for Allied use because in the Admiralties there was ample level ground for airfields and base installations, and here also was Seeadler Harbor, one of the finest anchorages in the Pacific. In the end the common sense of King's proposal was to win general consent. Rabaul would be neutralized, not captured.

What then? The Joint Chiefs were agreed that Japan must be cut off from her source of oil and other materials in the East Indies area, that she must be brought under sustained air attack, and that an invasion of her home islands might be necessary. The surest way of accomplishing these ends and also cutting off Japan from the Asiatic continent was, they believed in 1943, by occupying the coast of China. It remained to choose the best route, and MacArthur was ready with an answer. After the reduction of Rabaul, he argued, South Pacific and Southwest Pacific forces should combine under his command, thrust the enemy back the whole length of New Guinea, and, first seizing the Palau Islands to clear the Allied flank, leap to Mindanao in the Philippines and proceed through the Philippines to China.

To the Joint Chiefs' planners MacArthur's New Guinea-Philippines approach looked like a roundabout road to the objective, with the added disadvantages that it would be by way of readily defended land masses and that the Allied right flank and line of communication would be threatened by enemy bases in the Central Pacific. Why not a drive directly across the Central Pacific? This would remove the threat to MacArthur's flank, likely provoke the Japanese into a decisive fleet action, more quickly sever the enemy's communications with the Southern Resources Area, and place American forces in position for an earlier attack on Japan. The means would soon be at hand, for American shipbuilding, aircraft, and training programs were getting into high gear.

MacArthur protested that the proposal for a Central Pacific drive ignored the advantages conferred by using Australian bases. British officers expressed concern lest any stepped-up drive in the Pacific draw forces from the attack on Europe, which was and remained the primary Allied objective. In May however the Combined Chiefs approved both MacArthur's plan for an advance in New Guinea and the concept of a drive across the center. They also authorized operations against the Japanese-held islands in the Aleutians and tentatively planned to have a British fleet cooperate by breaking through the Straits of Malacca to join the Americans in the final drive on China.[4] This was to be the program for 1943-1944, but the Joint Chiefs wisely kept the plan flexible by not settling details far in advance. Opportunities as they arose would determine how the program would be executed. For the time being, enemy-occupied Attu and Kiska would be attacked and isolated in the North, MacArthur and Halsey would continue their drive on Rabaul in the South, and Nimitz would prepare to invade the Gilberts and Marshalls at the Center.[5]

Advancing simultaneously along more than one line towards the objective is a wartime strategy usually reserved for the stronger antagonist, for it undeniably risks defeat in detail. But a dual or multiple drive also confers great advantages: it can keep the enemy off balance and under continuous pressure, it obliges him to divide his forces and leaves him in doubt where the next attack will come, and it is a means of achieving strategic concentration by bringing one's main strength against part of the enemy forces while the enemy is held at other points.[6]

[4] Strategic planning for the Pacific theater was delegated by the Combined Chiefs to the American Joint Chiefs, but all major decisions requiring reallocation of men and material between theaters were subject to review by the Combined Chiefs.

[5] The Aleutians, Gilberts, and Marshalls campaigns are narrated in Chapter 44.

[6] Mahan's definition of strategic concentration: "The specific method of so distributing your own force as to be superior to the enemy in one quarter, while in the other you hold him long enough to permit your main attack to reach its full result." *Naval Strategy* (Boston, 1918), 49.

BEGINNING THE
TACTICAL REVOLUTION

The year 1943 was to see the transition of Allied night surface fighting away from the inept tactics that had produced the midnight brawl in the cruiser action of the Naval Battle of Guadalcanal and had turned American cruisers into a shooting gallery in the Battle of Tassafaronga. In Vella Gulf and off Bougainville American commanders would fight three of the most skillfully conducted battles of any war. Part of the reason was the arrival in the South Pacific of some of the smartest tacticians in the United States Navy—notably Commanders Frederick Moosbrugger and Arleigh Burke and Rear Admiral Stanton Merrill, all of whom were to make their names in the Solomons. Another reason was that dependable radar became generally available to the fleet, and fleet personnel learned to use it effectively. In 1943 most American warships carried SG radar as standard equipment. The scopes were housed in a special compartment known as radar plot, where contacts were plotted and analyzed. Gradually other information, from radio and lookouts, began to be correlated here, and radar plot became the Combat Information Center (CIC). Possession of the CIC gave the Allies an enormous advantage over the Japanese, whose radar, still primitive by American and British standards, had at this time been installed in only their largest vessels.

American destroyer commanders had long been agitating to be released from the cruiser line so that they might use their torpedoes at close range. There was nothing new about the idea; it was standard doctrine. Beatty, Hipper, and Scheer had released their destroyers at Jutland; Doorman had done it in the Java Sea battle; and Kondo had brilliantly demonstrated what could be done with detached destroyers in the night battleship action of November 14-15, 1942. Still, American force commanders remained reluctant to divide their forces in darkness. They could not forget that the Allied forces had been divided in the Battle of Savo Island and that

subsequently Americans had twice fired on their own vessels at night.

In some respects the tactical discussions of 1943 were a continuation of the formalist-melee debate that began in 17th century England. The Formal School preferred the unbroken line in order to insure tight and continuous control by the commander; it stressed the defensive and sought to minimize risk. The Melee School, stressing the offensive, accepted risks and some loss of central control in order to attain tactical concentration. Though the experience of the centuries had revealed the shortcomings of a rigid line rigidly controlled, American commanders were loath to take chances when confronted with an enemy obviously trained and armed for night fighting.

Development of the CIC and radar recognition devices however gradually gave Allied officers confidence in their ability to split their forces after dark without losing control. Commander Burke, most vocal of the destroyer men, insisted that it must be done and called for "an act of faith" on the part of task force commanders. Then he demonstrated his worthiness of such faith with some of the smoothest ship handling thus far seen in the Solomons. As his destroyer division swept past, officers used to tune in on his voice circuit for the pleasure and instruction of listening to his precise commands.

Rear Admiral Merrill was one task force commander who not only favored splitting up his divisions to attain optimum use of all his weapons but went on to devise maneuvers and drill his team to produce the perfect night attack. By use of radar he intended if possible to lead his cruiser-destroyer column undetected across the head of the approaching enemy. He would then release his van and rear destroyer divisions for flank torpedo attacks on opposite bows of a single enemy column, or on different columns if the enemy were divided. The destroyer divisions would then turn away together to avoid enemy torpedoes and their own cruiser fire. On a retirement course, again paralleling the enemy, the destroyers would be in position to use their guns when the cruisers opened up. The cruisers meanwhile would have turned together and be poised to open fire at optimum range just as the American torpedoes struck. The maneuvers could be repeated if necessary until the enemy had been put to flight.

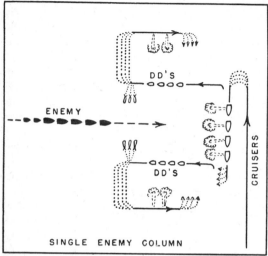

SINGLE ENEMY COLUMN

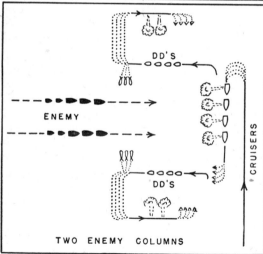

TWO ENEMY COLUMNS

*MERRILL'S BATTLE PLAN
FOR NIGHT ATTACK*

Again and again Merrill's force practiced these intricate tactics against the old battleships backing up the line at Efate. Night conditions were at first simulated; then as the force gained in skill and confidence, the exercises were conducted in darkness at speeds up to 35 knots. This was the sort of drill that could at long last wrest the advantage of night operations from the enemy.

GETTING READY FOR PHASE II

A continuing threat to Guadalcanal and its overseas communications was the pair of Japanese airfields in the Central Solomons, one at Munda Point on New Georgia Island, the other at the mouth of the Vila River on nearby Kolombangara Island. As a step preliminary to seizing or neutralizing these fields, Turner's Amphibious Force occupied the Russell Islands, 65 miles northwest of Henderson Field. Here small craft bases were established, and an airstrip was constructed to extend the reach of Allied bombers farther up the Slot.

Before and after the Russell Islands occupation, the Munda and Vila fields were regularly bombed from the air by day and by night. At the same time a pair of cruiser-destroyer task forces under Rear Admirals Stanton Merrill and Walden L. Ainsworth took turns making night runs to subject the airstrips to prolonged bombardment. During one such run in early March, Merrill's well-drilled team made naval history by sinking two Japanese destroyers by radar-controlled gunfire. Japanese supply problems were greatly complicated by air attacks on shipping, by mining of the waters about New Georgia and Bougainville, and by submarines operating in the vicinity of the Bismarcks. Such Allied activities in the first half of 1943 cost the enemy six submarines, eight destroyers, and a dozen transports.

Not least among the conditions which sped the advance and cut down the losses of South Pacific forces was the buildup and reorganization of Allied air forces in the Solomons. Henderson Field was expanded into a complete bomber base surrounded by three fighter strips. Five miles to the east Carney Field, a bomber base bigger than Henderson, went into operation on April 1. By this time there were on Guadalcanal more than 300 planes of every variety, under the operational command of Rear Admiral Marc A. Mitscher.[7] Operating together were bombers and fighters of the Royal New Zealand Air Force and of the United States Army, Navy, and Marine Corps.[8] To this heterogeneous but closely-integrated force, known as Air Command Solomons—Airsols for short—was to fall the major burden of neutralizing Rabaul. Airsols and its New Guinea counterpart, Lieutenant General George C. Kenney's Fifth Army Air Force, were destined within a few months to win command of the air over the whole Eastern New Guinea-Solomons-Bismarcks area.

JAPANESE REACTION

Tokyo's immediate reaction to the expulsion of Japanese troops from Guadalcanal and Papua was to draw in Rabaul's defenses to a line running from Salamaua in New Guinea to Munda airfield. Imperial Army forces under General Hotishi Imamura would defend New Guinea, while infantry, naval air, and surface forces commanded by Vice Admiral Jinichi Kusaka assumed the major responsibility of guarding the Central and Upper Solomons. Admiral Yamamoto, with an eye on the growing Fifth Fleet at Pearl Harbor, planned to retain his Combined Fleet at Truk, counting on the Americans to over-extend themselves eventually and so give him an opportunity to strike a decisive blow at sea.

The night-running Tokyo Express again went into high gear, pouring troops and supplies into the Central Solomons. Reinforcing the Lae-Salamaua area in New Guinea was more risky, involving passage over open seas partly by daylight. Nevertheless on the last day of February 1943 Kusaka dispatched on the Rabaul-to-Lae run some 7,000 troops in eight transports escorted by eight destroyers. This convoy, resembling in make-up Tanaka's ill-fated Reinforcement Group of the

preceding November, came out from under a weather front in the Bismarck Sea north of New Britain on March 2 and there was quickly pounced on by Kenney's American and Australian aircraft. A small Japanese combat air patrol operating at long range out of Lae, Gasmata, and Rabaul was utterly unprepared to deal with the newly-devised Fifth Air Force low-level attack technique, in which slow-fused bombs were dropped alongside enemy vessels to crush in their sides by mining effect after the attacking plane had pulled out of range of the explosion. For three days the Battle of the Bismarck Sea continued, until all of the transports and four of the destroyers had been sunk and about 25 Japanese planes had been shot down. Some of the surviving troops made their way to New Guinea in boats and on rafts but at least 3,000 lost their lives. After more sinkings of Japanese vessels in the next few days, the Japanese High Command decided to send no more convoys to New Guinea. Any further reinforcements or supplies would have to go by submarine or by barge from Cape Gloucester.

Alarmed by the deteriorating situation, Yamamoto himself came to Rabaul to direct an all-out air offensive on which he reckoned to snarl up Allied plans. By stripping some 200 planes from the Imperial Third Fleet—Vice Admiral Jisaburo Ozawa's carrier force—and adding them to his land-based planes he built up the most powerful Japanese air armada of the war and sent it first against shipping in Ironbottom Sound and then against targets in Papua. Its achievements were by no means negligible: a destroyer, a corvette, and two cargo vessels sunk, 12 Allied planes destroyed. But these results had been attained at the cost of 40 Japanese aircraft and a heavy loss of first-line carrier aviators which rendered the Imperial Fleet considerably less battleworthy than before.

Nevertheless Yamamoto was pleased. Exaggerated reports from his flyers convinced him that he had dealt the Allies a severe blow. So he set out with his staff on a triumphal air tour of Upper Solomons bases to inspect defenses and raise the morale of the defenders. Unfortunately for the Japanese, the Ameri-

[7] Relieved in July by Major General Nathan F. Twining USA.

[8] Newly arrived was the F4U Corsair fighter, with which the marines could at last outmaneuver the wily Zeke.

cans were again reading their coded radio messages and thus had the naval Commander in Chief's complete itinerary. Counting on Yamamoto's known passion for punctuality, Admiral Mitscher dispatched from Henderson Field a squadron of long-range army P-38's to shoot him down. Yamamoto was precisely on schedule over southern Bougainville and so were the P-38's. Just as two Japanese bombers filled with high-ranking dignitaries were coming in for a landing, the American fighters dived and sent them down in flames. Admiral Yamamoto died in his seat, his samurai sword between his knees. To the Japanese navy the loss of its most able and colorful commander was the equivalent of a major defeat.

Yamamoto's successor, Admiral Mineichi Koga, directed frequent air raids against Guadalcanal but with steadily diminishing success, for the Imperial Navy had expended its best flyers. The ineptitude of the new, hastily-trained aviators was spectacularly demonstrated in mid-June, when nearly two dozen attacking bombers and 70 Zekes were shot down over Guadalcanal at a cost of six American fighters.

INVADING THE CENTRAL SOLOMONS

The first objective of South Pacific forces in Phase II of the campaign against Rabaul was the airfield at Munda, a snout of land projecting out of the south coast of New Georgia Island. Possession of Munda would not only remove a major threat to Guadalcanal and a barrier to further Allied advance but it would also enable the Allies to neutralize Vila airstrip on Kolombangara, just across funnel-shaped Kula Gulf, and it would advance Airsols' bomber line 125 miles closer to Rabaul.

Munda was tricky to get at, for the only possible beaches in the vicinity were within easy artillery range of Rendova Island five miles to the south. But the Japanese failed to see their advantage: they had no artillery and only some 300 soldiers on Rendova. So on June 30, timed to coincide with a triple in-

vasion by MacArthur in the New Guinea area, Kelly Turner's Third Amphibious Force put ashore on Rendova several thousand soldiers and marines who wiped out the enemy garrison and turned American guns on Munda.[9] Then, under cover of their own artillery, they began ferrying troops over to New Georgia for the march on the Japanese airfield. So far all had gone smoothly, for Airsols planes had chased enemy aircraft away whenever they had appeared. Only one Allied vessel, Turner's flagship *McCawley*, had been seriously damaged. But once the troops entered the New Georgia jungle the picture changed abruptly. Confined to narrow trails by swamps and flooded rivers, they were brought almost to a standstill by concealed snipers. When they succeeded in moving again they came up against a ring of strong points, camouflaged dugouts capped by tough-fibered coconut logs and coral and covered with dirt—almost impervious to anything but point-blank artillery fire. Evidently this was to be no repetition of the American invasion of Guadalcanal and the easy march to Henderson Field, for inside the Japanese perimeter were 4,500 veteran jungle fighters, and though the U.S. Third Fleet prevented them from being reinforced from the Upper Solomons, additional Japanese troops did slip over from Kolombangara.

What was expected to be a four-day battle turned into a six-week campaign with a great pouring in of American reinforcements until 32,000 soldiers and 1,700 marines had been committed. Coordinated use of air and naval bombardment with artillery, tanks, and flame-throwing infantry were required to reduce the Japanese fortifications and capture the airfield. Then the invaders spent six more weeks pursuing the surviving defenders, who generally succeeded in working their vanishing act, slipping away by water to Kolombangara as the pincers closed. The campaign against Munda cannot be classed as one of the more successful Allied operations. The Americans, in view of their relatively safe

---

[9] Several smaller landings were also made on and about New Georgia to provide a small craft staging base and an airstrip for close fighter support and to cut off Japanese waterborne reinforcements.

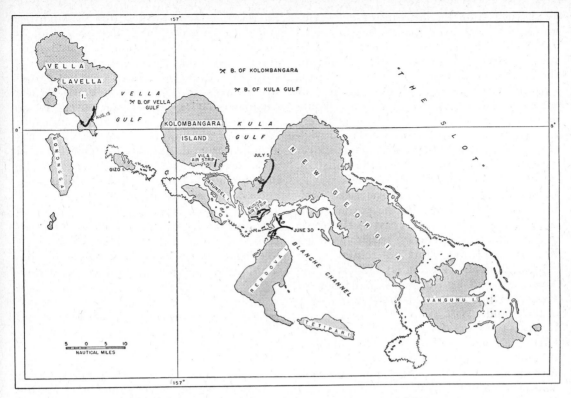

OPERATIONS IN THE CENTRAL SOLOMONS, 1943

overwater supply line, their command of the air, and their immense superiority in numbers, might have been expected to achieve their objective more swiftly.

Long before the end of the New Georgia Campaign, Halsey's staff had begun planning the next move up the ladder of the Solomons. Original plans had called for a continuation of the "island hopping" campaign, which would bring Allied forces next against Kolombangara and the Vila airfield. Admiral Kusaka, who suspected and indeed hoped that this would be the next Allied target, had been reinforcing Kolombangara for weeks, making an assault on that island an increasingly unattractive prospect. But Halsey, noting the build-up of enemy strength, decided not to play Kusaka's game. He would by-pass Kolombangara and invade lightly-held Vella Lavella beyond. Such a move would be distasteful to an army commander, who dreads leaving a strong enemy force in his rear, but the naval commander can sometimes out-

flank the enemy with impunity provided that in so doing he can isolate him, cut his communications, and leave him to "wither on the vine." Farragut demonstrated this fact when he by-passed the Mississippi forts to take New Orleans. Kinkaid had recently proved it in the Aleutians by going past Kiska to take Attu.

The landings on Vella Lavella, begun on August 15, were carried out by forces under Rear Admiral Theodore S. Wilkinson, who had succeeded to the command of the Third Amphibious Force upon Admiral Turner's departure for the Central Pacific. Transports, LCI's, and LST's landed 4,600 soldiers and marines the first day and 1,700 more during the following week.[10] The enemy attacked

[10] The **LST** (landing ship, tank), the **LCT** (landing craft, tank), and the **LCI** (landing craft, infantry) were large *beaching craft,* permitting a shore-to-shore expedition by transporting men, vehicles, and supplies from one beach to another. The smaller *landing craft* were generally carried aboard transports to make ship-to-shore landings.

persistently from the air, causing a few casualties and blowing up one LST, but antiaircraft fire and Airsols fighters operating from Munda repulsed or destroyed most of the attacking planes.

Wilkinson avoided the heavy casualties of the Munda drive by invading at Barakoma on the southeast coast of Vella Lavella, where there were no enemy forces. Here the invaders established a defense perimeter within which Seabees began constructing an airstrip. When it became apparent that there was to be no counterattack on the American position, troops moved out of the perimeter in both directions along the coast to entrap or destroy the small enemy garrison which Rabaul made no effort to reinforce. In September New Zealanders relieved the Americans and by October 1 had pocketed about 600 Japanese in the northwest corner of the island.

With the American landings on Vella Lavella Kusaka's defense in depth collapsed. When the Japanese had foreseen the necessity of evacuating Guadalcanal, they had held on there until they could complete and fortify Munda airfield. The campaign against Munda gave them time to build up forces on Kolombangara, and these were counted on to delay the Allied advance while Bougainville was strengthened. Now by his end-run Wilkinson had rendered Kolombangara impotent and was directly threatening Bougainville. A last-ditch fight for Vella Lavella was out of the question, for Imperial Headquarters refused to commit any more troops to the Solomons. To reinforce Bougainville Kusaka would have to evacuate both Kolombangara and Vella Lavella.

Daylight evacuation of the Japanese garrisons was of course impossible, for between dawn and dusk Third Fleet units, supported by Airsols, controlled the waters about the Central Solomons. Command of the waters did not automatically pass to the Japanese at dusk as it had in the early days of the Guadalcanal campaign, for American night fighting techniques had greatly improved—though not to the point that the Americans were ever quite sure of control by night. The Japanese waited until late September and the dark of the moon. Then by destroyer, submarine, and swift armored barge they undertook to carry away the Kolombangara garrison of about 10,000 in five nights. American destroyers sent out to intercept were not particularly successful. There was no battle, for the Japanese, having lost 40 destroyers in 14 months, now generally turned tail and ran. Americans did however succeed in damaging a destroyer and sinking a submarine and about a third of the barges. The rest of the barges eluded 5-inch shellfire by fishtailing and scattering. Despite their losses the wily Japanese escape artists succeeded in evacuating nine-tenths of the Kolombangara garrison. With scarcely a pause they then set out to evacuate their 600 troops on Vella Lavella. This, as we shall see, led to a surface action.

FLEET SUPPORT OF THE CENTRAL SOLOMONS CAMPAIGN

Besides bringing invasion forces to the beachheads, transporting supplies and reinforcements, and bombarding enemy positions, the Third Fleet had the responsibility along with Airsols of cutting enemy communications with rearward bases. Interception of the resurrected Tokyo Express was assigned to Merrill's and Ainsworth's cruiser-destroyer forces. Merrill made no contact with Japanese surface units during the Central Solomons Campaign, but in July Ainsworth twice met the enemy in the same waters a little after midnight and fought the battles of Kula Gulf and Kolombangara with similar tactics and similar results.

Ainsworth entered both battles in the usual nighttime formation with cruisers in the center and destroyers in the van and rear. In both, his cruisers closed to within 10,000 yards of the enemy, fired at almost machine-gun rapidity for five minutes and then turned away together to avoid enemy torpedoes. In each, the Allied force, though much the stronger, sank only one vessel—a destroyer in the first, a light cruiser in the second. In each, an American cruiser was tor-

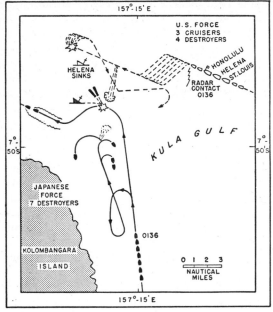

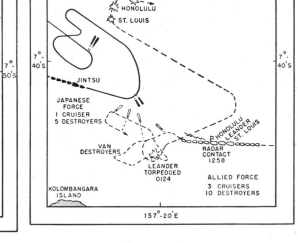

BATTLE OF KULA GULF
JULY 5-6, 1943

BATTLE OF KOLOMBANGARA
JULY 12-13, 1943

pedoed on the turnaway—in the Battle of Kula Gulf the *Helena*'s bow was blown off by three torpedoes, and the remainder of the cruiser jackknifed and sank; in the Battle of Kolombangara the New Zealand cruiser *Leander* was put out of action. In both battles, Japanese destroyers withdrew to reload their torpedo tubes and came back to fight again—in the first battle, the rearmed destroyers fired salvos of torpedoes at American vessels engaged in picking up survivors of the *Helena* but missed; in the second, the returning destroyers torpedoed the cruisers *Honolulu* and *St. Louis* and so battered the destroyer *Gwin* that she had to be sunk.

It is important to understand why Ainsworth failed to achieve a victory in either of these two similar actions. Despite his advantages of long-range radar and 6-inch guns, he came in close, making himself an easy visual target. He then waited too long to open fire and so permitted the enemy to take careful aim and release torpedoes that reached his position just as he was reversing course. His radar operators, as was usual in this period, selected only the largest or nearest target in-

stead of providing for effective distribution of fire. The more than 2,000 rounds of 6-inch shell which his gunners pumped out in five minutes were, like area fire against shore targets, more spectacular than accurate. And because Ainsworth was unaware that the Japanese had a torpedo reloading device aboard, he was not alert against counterattack. Still, his turnaway after firing, though belated, was sound tactical doctrine, and in the Battle of Kolombangara he held his cruiser fire until after his van destroyers had advanced and launched torpedoes. By these techniques, at least, he improved upon the American night surface tactics of 1942.

Convinced that Ainsworth's force was smashed, Rear Admiral Shoji Nishimura, whom we last met in Makassar Strait and whom we shall meet again, came steaming down the Slot a few nights after the Battle of Kolombangara with a strong cruiser-destroyer force looking for Merrill. Merrill's ships were not out that night, but a PBY "Black Cat" picked up Nishimura by radar and flashed the word to Guadalcanal, whence came night-flying bombers to sink two of his destroyers and damage a cruiser and send him reeling back to the Shortlands. After that the Japanese steered clear of the Kula Gulf route to their base at Vila, choosing rather to thread the ticklish passage south of Kolombangara. Here American PT boats

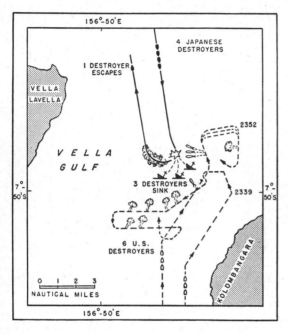

BATTLE OF VELLA GULF
AUGUST 6-7, 1943

sank one enemy barge and battered several others but proved no barrier to the Tokyo Express of heavier types.

Admiral Wilkinson decided in early August to put larger craft on the new enemy reinforcement route. Because Merrill's force was too far away and Ainsworth's was depleted by the July battles, he ordered to the area what he had available, Commander Burke's division of six destroyers. Burke had worked out an ingenious plan for just such a mission, but like Kinkaid the preceding November he was detached on the eve of battle to assume a higher command. Luckily his successor was Commander Moosbrugger, who adopted the essential features of Burke's plan and carried them out with such skill and sense of timing that in the Battle of

Vella Gulf he achieved a little classic of naval warfare.

Warned by a search plane that the Express was en route, Moosbrugger's destroyers entered Vella Gulf from the south at 2200, August 6, two columns in line of bearing, and advanced northward hugging the coast of Kolombangara to avoid visual or radar detection. A little before midnight four enemy destroyers crowded with troops for Vila entered the Gulf from the north and soon registered themselves on American radar scopes. Moosbrugger's first division thereupon raced past the enemy column on a parallel and opposite course, launched torpedoes, and then promptly turned away together. The other division meanwhile came about on a "T"-capping course across the van of the enemy column. Just as the torpedoes struck their targets, both American divisions opened up with gunfire. Under this neatly-timed triple blow three of the Japanese destroyers exploded, hurling 1,800 soldiers and sailors into the water and creating such a pyrotechnical display that PT boatmen 30 miles away in Kula Gulf thought a volcano had erupted on Kolombangara. The one enemy destroyer to escape was able to do so only because the torpedoes that slid under her hull failed to detonate. None of the American vessels was damaged. The Battle of Vella Gulf provides a perfect example of tactical concentration achieved by divided but mutually supporting forces. Americans at last had outperformed the Japanese at their own specialty.

The Battle of Vella Lavella, two months later, was a by-product of the Japanese evacuation of Vella Lavella Island. Tactics on both sides were poor, and so far as the Americans were concerned it was a repetition of the Battle of Tassafaronga in miniature. In the late evening of October 6, Captain Frank R. Walker, commanding destroyers *Selfridge*, *Chevalier*, and *O'Bannon*, made contact with six Japanese destroyers in two divisions escorting small craft. As Walker advanced to attack, the nearer enemy division missed a chance to cross his "T" and then masked its own fire by approaching in line of bearing. The Americans fired 14 torpedoes and a hail of shells at the nearest enemy vessel, which burst into flames and presently blew up. By this time the Japanese had turned away under a smoke screen. Walker might properly have turned away also but he chose to maintain course—with predictable results. The *Chevalier* and the *Selfridge* both had their bows blown off by torpedoes and in the confusion the *O'Bannon* rammed the *Chevalier*. The timely arrival of Third Fleet reinforcements obliged the enemy destroyers to retreat, but while the Americans were looking after their crippled vessels and sinking the helpless *Chevalier,* the Japanese small craft proceeded to Vella Lavella and succeeded in carrying out another evacuation.

The Japanese had completed their mission and won the battle, but this was the last battle they were to win in World War II. And their victory did not alter the fact that the Allies now held the Central Solomons, with airfields close enough to support a jump to Bougainville.

CAPTURING HUON PENINSULA

During the spring of 1943 Kenney's Fifth Air Force hammered away at Salamaua, Lae, and Finschhafen, Japanese strong points guarding Huon Peninsula, while Australian troops marched overland by jungle trail towards Salamaua. Then, on July 30, timed to coincide with United States Third Fleet landings on Rendova and New Georgia, the Seventh Fleet placed troops ashore without opposition on Kiriwina and Woodlark Islands flanking the Papuan Peninsula and at Nassau Bay 17 miles south of Salamaua.[11]

Admiral Barbey's heterogeneous Seventh Amphibious Force staged the island invasions in style, proceeding from Milne Bay with destroyers, transports, and beaching craft. But because no one was yet ready to risk valuable Allied ships in the inner reaches of the Solomon Sea, the Nassau Bay operation was a mere 40-mile night run up the coast with troops of Lieutenant General

[11] The war moved so swiftly westward that airfields constructed on Kiriwina and Woodlark proved of little value.

Walter Krueger's Sixth U. S. Army carried in PT's and landing boats. Four such night runs established a beachhead from which the Americans proceeded up the coast to make contact six miles from Salamaua with the Australians moving from the interior.

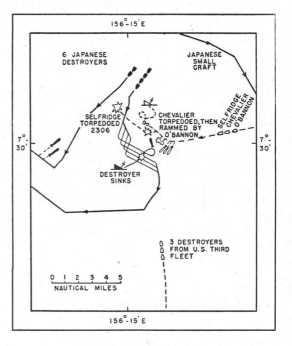

BATTLE OF VELLA LAVELLA
OCTOBER 6-7, 1943

With communications from Rabaul practically interdicted by the Fifth Air Force and by barge-hunting American PT boats, the Japanese had no recourse but to reinforce threatened Salamaua with troops drawn from Lae. This precisely suited MacArthur's plans, for he was about to take a leaf from Halsey's book and by-pass the more southerly base. In preparation for this offensive move, survey of the dangerous reefs went on apace and Kenney's planes ranged as far west as Madang and Wewak destroying enemy planes.

In the night of September 3-4, Barbey's Amphibious Force at last penetrated the Solomon Sea, moved across Huon Gulf past Salamaua, and after dawn put nearly 8,000 Australians ashore east of Lae in the face of an enemy air attack. The next day army transport planes from Papuan bases flew over the jungle to drop 1,700 American paratroops, who quickly seized a Japanese airstrip west of Lae. Thousands of Australian soldiers were then flown in to the captured field and began advancing on Lae from one side to meet their seaborne compatriots moving in from the other. The Japanese thereupon abandoned Salamaua and attempted to take a stand at Lae, which however soon became untenable under the pounding of American destroyer guns. So, as the pincers closed, the Imperial Army evacuated Lae also, took to the jungle, and began a disastrous month-long march northward across Huon Peninsula. (See map, page 743.)

From captured Lae, Barbey in late September carried a brigade of Australians 65 miles around the tip of the peninsula for pre-dawn landings north of Finschhafen. This invasion took the enemy completely by surprise. Expecting the Allied forces to march overland, they had deployed most of their troops south of the town. Only a handful of Japanese marines guarded the northern approaches. These the Australians quickly pushed aside and took possession, whereupon the rest of the Japanese pulled inland to a nearby mountain range and girded themselves for a counterattack at a favorable moment.

In a series of quick strokes MacArthur had captured Huon Peninsula, thereby completing his conquest of the northeast coast of New Guinea from Milne Bay to Vitiaz Strait. The quick acceleration of the Southwest Pacific advance, in such striking contrast to the painful march on Buna, resulted in part from the addition of a touch of sea power in the form of Barbey's makeshift amphibious force. It was also made possible by the diversion of Japanese strength in the vain attempt to stop Halsey's march through the Central Solomons. But Barbey's leapfrog advance along the coast, unlike Wilkinson's end-run around Kolombangara, did not render the by-passed enemy impotent, for he could, albeit with difficulty, be reinforced over land.

After the reduction of Finschhafen came a period of consolidating gains in the New Guinea area. Japanese airfields and strong points along the river valleys had to be cleaned up, and the enemy forces in the mountains behind Finschhafen in due course would have to be attended to. Meanwhile, Barbey's destroyers hunted submarines in and about Huon Gulf, a dangerous business which resulted in the sinking of the destroyer *Henley* in early October; and Kenney's planes continued weakening Japanese air power based on enemy fields newly brought within their reach. MacArthur's command would have its hands full for a while making good its summer conquests.

43

The Campaign against Rabaul, Phase III: Rabaul Neutralized and By-passed

THE STRATEGIC PICTURE IN the South Pacific was abruptly changed in August 1943 when the Combined Chiefs concurred with Admiral King in deciding that Rabaul was to be neutralized and by-passed rather than captured. On the basis of this decision the second phase of the campaign may be considered ended with Halsey's conquest of the Central Solomons and MacArthur's occupation of Huon Peninsula. Phase III would see Southwest Pacific forces breaking through the barrier of the Bismarcks, while from an encircling ring of captured bases Allied planes battered the Japanese stronghold into impotence.

MacArthur's advance to Finschafen in September had brought him nearly abreast of Vitiaz Strait. Evidently if he intended to push farther west along the New Guinea coast he would have to secure a base on the far side of the strait in order to prevent air or surface attack on his sea communications. This was to be achieved in three steps. First, MacArthur's Fifth Air Force planned to carry out a series of heavy attacks on Rabaul. This was intended to lessen the very genuine risks of the second step, which was Halsey's invasion of Bougainville to establish airfields closer to the Japanese stronghold. A sustained aerial campaign from the new fields against air power and shipping in the Bismarcks would facilitate step three, capture of Cape Gloucester on the eastern side of Vitiaz Strait.

General Kenney launched the three-step plan in mid-October by hurling 349 planes against Rabaul in the most massive air attack thus far seen in the Pacific. In the following weeks he struck again and again. The blasting of the Bismarcks barrier was under way. The next move was up to Halsey.

ON TO BOUGAINVILLE

On and near fiddle-shaped Bougainville, northernmost and largest of the major Solomons, were 60,000 Japanese. Most of them were on the southern plain at the Buin anchorage and the Kahili airfield, in the nearby Shortland Islands, and in the far north at Buka and Bonis. The Munda campaign had shown how desperately the Japanese would defend their airdromes, which when captured were rarely adequate. As a consequence the Allies had invaded Vella Lavella at an undefended point and built their own airfield while troops set out along the coasts to encircle the enemy garrison. On Bougainville the South Pacific Command introduced a new refinement. Between Buin and Bonis stretched a high mountain range flanked by marshy coastlands, all weakly defended and connected with the north and south by only the most primitive of jungle trails. Admiral Wilkinson's Amphibious Force planned to by-pass the nest of bases around southern Bougainville and land the assault troops half way up the west coast at Cape Torokina in Empress Augusta Bay. Here the invaders would lay out airstrips, establish a powerful perimeter, and wait for the Japanese to come to them.

For the Bougainville operation Halsey had sufficient troops—General Vandegrift's I Marine Amphibious Corps, comprising the 3rd Marine Division, the 37th Army Infantry Division, and a brigade group of New Zealanders. Shipping however was in short supply because of the concurrent Mediterranean campaign and because Nimitz was about to unleash the United States Fifth Fleet in the Central Pacific. Wilkinson would have to cram his first echelon landing force into a dozen transports, escorted by 11 destroyers. Merrill's Task Force 39, cruisers and destroyers, was available to pave the way and cover the beachhead; and a single carrier group, including the *Saratoga* and the light carrier *Princeton,* under Rear Admiral Frederick C. Sherman, was on loan from the Fifth Fleet to supplement Airsols. Some gloomy observers, comparing the new venture to the Guadalcanal invasion, dubbed it "Operation Shoestring No. 2." Though the means were indeed in some respects scanty, adequate air support and improved defense techniques made a world of difference.

In mid-October Airsols began an accelerating series of bombing attacks which soon made enemy airfields on Bougainville unusable. At dawn on the 27th, destroyer-transports and beaching craft began putting 6,000 New Zealanders ashore on the Treasury Islands south of Bougainville. These quickly overran the small Japanese garrison and began setting up long-range radar and preparing a staging base for small craft en route to Empress Augusta Bay. That night some of the same destroyer-escorts landed 700 marines on Choiseul Island to attract Japanese attention away from the invasion area. Merrill's TF 39 provided further diversion by bombarding the Buka and Bonis airfields. Then while Merrill raced back south to bombard the Shortlands, Sherman's carriers sent in planes to continue the pounding of the Buka and Bonis fields.

While Japanese attention was thus diverted in several directions, Wilkinson's amphibians entered Empress Augusta Bay at daybreak on November 1. Here was another beach where the invaders might have gone ashore standing up had the surf conditions been less difficult and the naval gunfire support been more effective. Airsols controlled the air, and on shore there were fewer than 300 defenders, armed only with rifles, machine guns, and one 75 mm. artillery piece. But although four destroyers worked over the landing areas, the enemy's fire appeared undiminished when the invaders headed for the beach. Nevertheless by holding down the defenders with machine guns mounted on the landing craft, more than 7,000 marines got ashore in the first wave. Then followed the difficult and dangerous task of taking enemy pillboxes one by one. The troublesome 75 mm. gun was at length captured by a lone marine who charged into the emplacement through the gunport and killed or dispersed the gunners at the cost of his own life. The much feared air attack from nearby Rabaul came promptly, but the enemy planes achieved only minor damage before Airsols fighters chased them away. American losses during the day were limited to 70 men killed. By nightfall the Amphibious Force had marked up a new record by putting ashore 14,000 troops and 6,000 tons of supplies. In the early evening the transports pulled out of Empress Augusta Bay, and four minelayers began laying a protective mine field north of Cape Torokina.

THE BATTLE OF
EMPRESS AUGUSTA BAY

The Imperial Eighth Fleet reacted to the landings in Empress Augusta Bay much as it had 15 months before when the marines had landed in Ironbottom Sound. Down from Rabaul to smash the American transports came a hastily-assembled force of two heavy and two light cruisers and six destroyers under Rear Admiral Sentaro Omori. This attack force was early spotted by Airsols patrol planes, which promptly and accurately reported their find to South Pacific headquarters and continued tracking.

The only force available to stop Omori was TF 39. Though the crews were exhausted after having carried out two bombardments in the past 16 hours, Admiral Halsey had no choice but to order them to Empress Augusta Bay. Merrill was at last to have an opportunity to put his battle plan to the test, though not under optimum conditions. He was fortunate in having Arleigh Burke, now Captain Burke, as commander of his Destroyer Division 45, for the two had operated together and saw eye to eye in tactical matters. But Desdiv 46, his other four-destroyer division, would be at a disadvantage, for it was so new as a unit that Commander Bernard Austin had not yet had an opportunity to exercise his ships in formation.

On receiving Halsey's order, Merrill's four light cruisers left the vicinity of Vella Lavella with Desdiv 46 and headed northwest. Desdiv 45, which had gone to Kula Gulf for refueling, finished topping off at record speed and set out in pursuit. Burke caught up with the task force before midnight and took the van while Austin's division dropped back to the rear. At 0227 November 2, as the force was approaching the Torokina beachhead on course 345° with the three divisions in line of bearing north to south, the flagship *Montpelier* detected the enemy

18 miles away coming down from the northwest. Merrill thereupon shifted to course due north, which brought his ships into a stretched-out version of the usual column formation for American cruisers and destroyers going into night action.

In accordance with his oft-rehearsed plan, Merrill intended to release his destroyer divisions for torpedo attacks on the flanks of the enemy. With his four cruisers he would block the entrance to Empress Augusta Bay and by continuous fire from his 6-inch guns and a series of simultaneous reversals of course gradually force the enemy westward in order to gain sea room for maneuver and to permit any damaged American vessels to retire on the disengaged side. He would match radar against Japanese eyes, fighting his cruisers at long range, out of easy reach of the Long Lances. Caution was imposed upon him by the fact that TF 39 was now the principal surface force in the whole South Pacific. Cruisers had to be hoarded. He dared not risk them in an attempt to annihilate the enemy in an all-out battle. He would have to limit himself merely to repulsing the attackers from the beachhead.

Omori was advancing in intense darkness under a rain squall in three columns, the two heavy cruisers *Myoko* and *Haguro* in the center, flanked by the light cruisers *Sendai* and *Agano,* each leading three destroyers. His immediate objective was the American minelaying group off Cape Torokina, which Japanese planes had identified as a cruiser and three destroyers.

As soon as the enemy appeared in his radar scopes Burke swung left according to plan and led Desdiv 45 on an attack course toward the flank of the northern enemy group. The American cruisers then reversed course together, and Merrill detached Desdiv 46 to strike the southern enemy group.

At 5,600 yards on the *Sendai's* port bow, Desdiv 45 fired half salvos of torpedoes and turned away together. None of the torpedoes found targets, for the Japanese had changed course. The *Sendai* had seen the TF 39 cruisers, had launched torpedoes, and had warned Omori, who ordered his divisions to wheel south to form a line of battle.

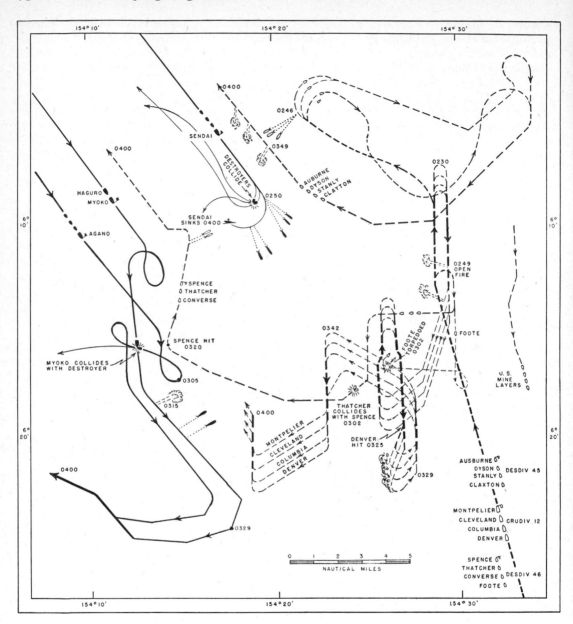

BATTLE OF EMPRESS AUGUSTA BAY, NOVEMBER 2, 1943

"My guppies are swimming!" Burke had reported at the moment he launched. Merrill then began to count off the six minutes it would take the torpedoes to complete their run, but when CIC reported the enemy change of course, he at once ordered his cruisers to open fire. Forty-eight guns promptly began to roar, taking as their tar-get the nearby northern group, which replied with shells that fell forward and short. Maneuvering to avoid the concentrated 6-inch fire, two of the Japanese destroyers collided, and the *Sendai* began to blaze and fell out of line with a jammed rudder. The Americans had handily won the first round, but Desdiv 45 had become separated on the turnaway. It would take Burke an hour to locate and reassemble his vessels and bring them back into the battle.

Because of Omori's change of course the TF 39 cruisers at 0251 turned together to course 200° in order to close the range. It now appeared that Austin's destroyers had been released prematurely, for Merrill's advance to the southwest brought them within the cruisers' line of fire. Moreover, the destroyer *Foote* had become separated.[1] In racing west to rejoin Desdiv 46, she cut across the path of the oncoming cruisers so that the *Denver* had to sheer left to avoid a collision.

To clear Desdiv 46 and close on the *Sendai* group, the cruisers at 0302 turned north. Almost at once they had to swing right to avoid hitting a vessel dead in the water. It was the *Foote* again. Still heading west she had been struck by one of the *Sendai*'s torpedoes, which had demolished her stern.

At 0310 Merrill turned south once more, thus completing the first loop of a huge figure eight. The waters of the South Pacific were now witnessing a new high in ship handling. Barking his orders by TBS through the roar of gunfire, Merrill kept his cruisers in perfect order—zigzagging and swinging back and forth across the enemy's line of fire to present him constantly changing problems in range and deflection. Through 30 minutes of rapid maneuver Merrill managed always to be somewhere else when the enemy's shells or torpedoes arrived.

To take advantage of his 8-inch guns, Omori, like Merrill, wanted to fight at long range, but he was having difficulty locating the Americans. So he began a complete loop, thereby sadly confusing the *Agano* group, which vaguely tried to conform. Then as he steadied again on a southerly course, American 6-inch shells began to fall all around him. One of the *Agano* destroyers, while dodging, collided with the *Myoko* and had a piece of her bow sheared off. Then six shells, four of them duds, hit the *Haguro*. By this time Japanese planes arriving over the American cruisers were dropping red and white parachute flares. These, reflecting off the low cloud ceiling, combined with star shells to turn the night into an eerie twilight and thereby rob Merrill of some of his radar advantage.

Now at last Omori saw Merrill and advanced southeast to close the range. The *Myoko* and the *Haguro* launched ten torpedoes and fired salvos of shells, three of which hit the *Denver* but failed to detonate. Merrill thereupon turned away, making smoke. At this point Omori ceased fire and withdrew. His explanation was that he thought he had sunk all the American cruisers, but this is manifestly absurd. If that had been true, then the way was wide open for him to carry out his mission of sinking the transports, which he supposed were still in Empress Augusta Bay. Instead, at 0337 he ordered a general retirement in order, he afterwards explained, to be out of easy range of Airsols planes by dawn. Perhaps the real reason for his withdrawal lies in another of his later statements: "The analysis of reports indicated that there were at least seven heavy cruisers and 12 destroyers opposing us." [2]

While Merrill and Omori were dueling it out, Austin's division was suffering one unlucky break after another. The *Foote,* as we have seen, was early put out of action. Then, while the other three destroyers were maneuvering frantically to avoid being silhouetted by starshell and to clear the line of fire of their own cruisers, the *Spence* sideswiped the *Thatcher*. Though both vessels suffered heavy topside damage, Desdiv 46 proceeded westward at high speed until it was 6,000 yards on the port bow of the enemy center group, in perfect position to carry out a torpedo attack against the Japanese heavy cruisers. At that moment the *Spence* was temporarily slowed down by a shell hit at the water line. Immediately afterwards, the CIC evaluator became disoriented and reported to the division commander that the *Myoko* and *Haguro* were "friendly."

With no time to check, Austin turned north to go after the *Sendai,* which was turning in circles but still firing. A couple of his

---

[1] When Desdiv 46 had countermarched to conform to the cruisers, the *Foote* had turned at once instead of following in column.

[2] *Interrogations of Japanese Officials,* II, 340.

destroyers launched torpedoes and apparently made hits, but the cruiser was still afloat as he headed northwest in pursuit of her two collision-damaged destroyers, which had been standing by. The *Sendai* was evidently reserved for Burke. After having cruised far and wide to reassemble his scattered division, Burke sped in from the east at 32 knots and sent the *Sendai* down at last in a hail of shells. Then because radar recognition was working badly that night he set out in hot pursuit of Austin.[3] Presently Austin's division opened fire on the Japanese destroyers, one of which caught Burke's attention. "We have a target smoking badly at 7,000 yards, and we are going to open up," Burke warned by TBS. "Oh-oh, don't do it," replied Austin, "that's us." And so the two Japanese destroyers got away, and Burke turned his fire on the *Spence*. "Hope you are not shooting at us," said Austin. "Sorry," Burke responded, "but you'll have to excuse the next four salvos as they are already on the way." [4] After such loss of opportunity and near disaster the two division commanders at length located each other and with special satisfaction joined forces in sending down the last of the Japanese cripples in the area, the destroyer whose bow had been ripped off by the *Myoko*. Except for the lost *Sendai* the remainder of Omori's force was making best speed for Rabaul.

Because dawn was breaking, Merrill ordered his divisions to leave off the chase and to rendezvous for better defense against the inevitable air attack. Leaving three destroyers behind to salvage the torpedoed *Foote*, he headed south with the rest of TF 39. At 0800 the Japanese struck—a hundred carrier bombers and fighters from Rabaul. By a combination of accurate antiaircraft fire and deft ship handling, the Americans shot down 17 attacking planes and avoided all but two rather inconsequential bomb hits. Before the enemy planes could come in for a second

strike, Airsols fighters arrived and chased them away, shooting down eight more.

The American performance in the Battle of Empress Augusta Bay was not without flaws, particularly in the accuracy and distribution of radar-controlled gunfire, but Merrill had brilliantly carried out his mission of repulsing the enemy from the beachhead. His night victory demonstrated the soundness of the tactical doctrine and practice that his predecessors had been groping for. On a smaller scale Merrill's battle plan was as much a culmination and landmark as Nelson's Memorandum. To paraphrase Sir Julian Corbett's comment on the Battle of Trafalgar, the Battle of Empress Augusta Bay seems to gather up and coordinate every tactical principle that had ever proved effective in the night actions of the Solomons.

CARRIERS AGAINST RABAUL

Incensed at Omori's poor showing in the Battle of Empress Augusta Bay, Admiral Koga promptly relieved him of his command. Then, wasting no time, he sent Vice Admiral Takeo Kurita south from Truk with a stronger, better integrated cruiser-destroyer force from the Imperial Second Fleet to redeem Omori's failure. Had Kurita proceeded directly to Bougainville he might have smashed the beachhead. Certainly he could have sunk any shipping he found in the Torokina area. But he chose to stop by Rabaul for refueling and that proved his undoing, for Airsols B-24's sighted him approaching the New Britain base on November 4 and flashed a timely warning. "This," stated Halsey, "was the most desperate emergency that confronted me in my entire term as Comsopac." [5] The oncoming fleet was too strong for Merrill, even if he had been within reach and his crews fresh. The only force available to stop Kurita was Sherman's *Saratoga-Princeton* group, then fueling south of Guadalcanal. With grave misgivings at the

---

[3] Morison thinks Burke was tracking the *Sendai* destroyers, but these were almost certainly slowed down by collision damage whereas, as Merrill pointed out in his action report, Burke's targets were traveling at 34 knots, Austin's speed.

[4] Morison, VI, 315, 318.

[5] *Halsey's Story* (New York, 1947), 181.

prospect of sending carriers against a powerful base, Halsey ordered Sherman to proceed northwest at high speed. At the same time he directed Airsols to lend Sherman every bit of support it could.

Halsey's perilous resort succeeded beyond the most sanguine hopes of anybody in the South Pacific command. On the morning of the 5th, as Sherman maneuvered under a concealing cloud cover off Empress Augusta Bay, Airsols fighters from Vella Lavella arrived and took over the job of combat air patrol. The carriers were thus able to strip their decks, putting nearly a hundred planes into the air. Striking from clear skies over Rabaul, Sherman's bombers bored in through a steel curtain of antiaircraft fire. Their target was Kurita's Second Fleet force, which had anchored in Rabaul's Simpson Harbor only two hours before. At a cost of only ten aircraft, the American dive bombers and torpedo planes put Kurita out of business, damaging six cruisers and two destroyers.[6] There would be no surface attack against the amphibious shipping in Empress Augusta Bay.

Elated at the success of his experiment, Halsey prepared to try it again on a larger scale. From the U.S. Fifth Fleet, then poised to invade the Gilberts, he borrowed another carrier group, including the *Essex,* the *Bunker Hill,* and the *Independence,* under Rear Admiral Alfred E. Montgomery. On November 11 he sent both Sherman and Montgomery against Rabaul. The *Saratoga* and *Princeton* attacked first from the waters north of Bougainville but were foiled by nasty weather. Montgomery's carriers had better luck. Striking from south of Bougainville under Airsols fighter cover, they launched 185 planes, which thrust aside defending Zekes to hit shipping once more in Simpson Harbor. Kurita had prudently departed but there were other targets. The Americans sank a destroyer, torpedoed another, sheered off the stern of a light cruiser, and played havoc among transports and cargo vessels.

This time Admiral Kusaka located the source of his attackers and struck back. In the afternoon 120 Japanese planes swooped down from the north and headed for Montgomery's carriers. Their raid cost them heavily and achieved next to nothing. The opposition of carrier fighters plus land-based combat patrol plus intense antiaircraft fire was simply too formidable for them. The new American formations, with several carriers grouped together within a ring of escorts, here proved its superiority in achieving concentrated firepower. The Japanese lost a third of their aircraft without damaging a single ship. American losses in both attack and defense were limited to 11 planes.

Having made a potent contribution in the campaign against Rabaul, Sherman's and Montgomery's carrier groups sailed away to participate with the Fifth Fleet in opening the drive across the Central Pacific.

BURKE MAKES USE OF HIS BATTLE PLAN

In the afternoon of November 24 Captain Burke, then heading for Bougainville with a squadron of five destroyers, received a message from Admiral Halsey: "Thirty-One-Knot Burke, get this. Put your squadron athwart the Buka-Rabaul evacuation line. . . . If enemy contacted, you know what to do."[7]

The Japanese Army command at Rabaul believed that the American landing in Empress Augusta Bay was a temporary expedient and that the real objective was Buka. So the Imperial Navy was ordered to rush more soldiers to the area and bring away the airmen. A Tokyo Express of two destroyers and three destroyer-transports was told off to do

---

[6] Included was the heavy cruiser *Mogami.* Newly repaired from her battering at Midway, she had to return to Japan for another major repair job.

[7] As paraphrased (for cryptographic security) by Morison. By this message Halsey's operations officer, Captain Harry R. Thurber, conferred upon "31-knot Burke" the nickname that soon became known around the world. The prefix was a gentle jibe at Burke's repeated reports that he was "making 31 knots" with a force thought capable of no more than 30 knots sustained speed.

the job. This was the movement that Halsey wanted stopped, and Burke knew very well what to do. Here at last was an opportunity to make personal use of his destroyer battle plan.

The Battle of Cape St. George which occurred that night was a sort of duplication of the Battle of Vella Gulf followed by a

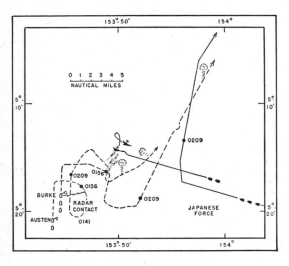

*BATTLE OF CAPE ST. GEORGE
NOVEMBER 25, 1943*

chase. Reaching the interception point a little before 0100, Burke made radar contact with the two vessels of the enemy screen. Then while Commander Austin with two destroyers covered, Burke led his other three towards the enemy's flank, fired 15 torpedoes at his extended track, and turned away. The Japanese destroyers, having seen nothing, plowed unsuspectingly ahead. Both blew up as Burke's torpedoes reached them at the calculated point. Austin thereupon opened fire and swung in to finish them off. By that time Burke was away after the loaded transports. He sank one with shell-fire and chased the other two to within 60 miles of Rabaul before turning away to clear the area while it was still dark.

Americans had won another night classic, proving that the victories of Vella Gulf and Empress Augusta Bay were the result of sound doctrine and not mere luck.

ESTABLISHING THE TOROKINA PERIMETER

Though the Japanese committed all available troops in the Empress Augusta Bay area to throw back the American invasion, Vandegrift's soldiers and marines moved steadily forward. The tank-artillery-troop combination which had finally cracked the Munda defenses proved equally effective on Bougainville. To these was added the first really successful close air support of the war as marine pilots, directed by radio from ground liaison parties, bombed and strafed just ahead of the American line.

Airsols and the Third Fleet saw to it that the Tokyo Express did not resume operations, while the Third Amphibious Force, despite vicious and damaging air attacks out of Rabaul, in two weeks brought 34,000 men and more than 23,000 tons of supplies to the expanding perimeter. The I Marine Amphibious Corps in another month of hard fighting pushed the defense line inland and laterally along the coast until it enclosed some 36 square miles. Within this area Seabees worked rapidly to complete a fighter strip near the beach and two bomber strips farther inland.

In December, the 3rd Marine Division, having completed its assignment, began pulling out and the XIV U.S. Army Corps took over the perimeter defense. Not until March 1944 did the Japanese army, after dragging their artillery over mountains and along jungle trails, come up against the American position. Stripped of air and naval support by that time, they attacked in vain, taking heavy losses. The Allies were on Bougainville to stay.

MACARTHUR'S BREAKTHROUGH TO THE WEST

By Christmas 1943 two steps in support of MacArthur's projected breakthrough had been completed. The Fifth Air Force had thrown its full weight against Rabaul. Airsols bombers, supported by fighters from the new Bougainville perimeter, had then tremendously stepped up the offensive. Now that the enemy had his hands full defending himself, the time evidently had come to secure Vitiaz Strait. But the fact, unknown to the Allies, was that the strait had already been rendered reasonably secure. The first two steps in the campaign had so far exceeded expectations as to make the third superfluous, for the whole Bismarcks defense system had been brought to the point of collapse. Not realizing that the door to the west stood open before him, MacArthur in late December ordered the 1st Marine Division into western New Britain.

Supported by guns of the Seventh Fleet and planes of the Fifth Air Force, the Guadalcanal veterans stormed ashore near Cape Gloucester. Fighting through swamps in the monsoon rain they captured the enemy airfield in less than a week. Then they shattered the defending 65th Imperial Army Brigade and chased the survivors back to the Rabaul area, where they bottled them up. By that time MacArthur's forces had long since crashed through the Bismarcks barrier by land and by sea.

Australian troops had dislodged the Japanese holed up in the mountains back of Finschhafen and were pushing them westward along the coastal trail towards Sio, where there were 12,000 more Japanese. Beyond Sio was the Imperial Army air base at Madang, and 170 miles beyond Madang was the Japanese Eighteenth Army headquarters at Wewak. The Australians were thus rolling the enemy back on his sources of supply and reinforcement, a situation not at all to MacArthur's liking.

But there was a sea power solution to this strategic dead end. Between Sio and Madang was the village of Saidor, where there were no Japanese at all. So MacArthur ordered Barbey to complete his amphibious support of Cape Gloucester as quickly as possible and rush American troops by sea to Saidor to plug the enemy coastal communication line. Using his Cape Gloucester task force, Barbey early on the second day of January 1944 landed 2,400 American soldiers at Saidor,

with more to follow. The sorely reduced Japanese Army Air Force did not react until mid-afternoon, after all the American vessels had got clean away.

Cut off from supplies and reinforcements the Japanese abandoned Sio to the Australians. When they assembled on the coast 37 miles to the west to be evacuated by sea, they got such a murderous pounding from Seventh Fleet destroyers that they turned inland and set out on foot for Madang by way of the jungle. Two thousand of them, starved and diseased, died on the way. No campaign in the Pacific theater more clearly demonstrates the advantages of sea control to troops operating near a coast.

KNOCKING OUT RABAUL

Though Rabaul was stunned by the Allied air offensive in the fall of 1943, it remained far too powerful to be entirely by-passed. The 90,000 Japanese there began to go underground, scooping out subterranean barracks, shops, and hangars. Though the fleet had left, Kusaka retained some small craft and more than a thousand seagoing barges. All carrier planes had been withdrawn, but at the five airfields in the Rabaul area and at the other Bismarck bases at Gasmata and Kavieng there still remained nearly 300 serviceable aircraft. This was more striking power than MacArthur or Nimitz cared to have athwart their communication lines as they advanced westward.

So with the completion of the Torokina fighter strip in mid-December Halsey launched an all-out air offensive to pound the Bismarcks into final impotence. Escorted by fighter planes from Bougainville, Airsols bombers based on Munda and Vella Lavella struck regularly at Rabaul. In January, as the bigger fields became operational at Torokina, the bombers were able to strike from there and so step up the raids to one or more a day. By February they were averaging a thousand sorties a week. For a while Admiral Koga continued to rush planes to Rabaul at the expense of Truk. But after the U.S. Fifth Fleet raided Truk on February 17-18, he gave up the air defense of the Bismarcks as too costly. He not only cut off aircraft reinforcements but even withdrew fighter planes and ground forces for use where there was a better prospect for air defense. U. S. Third Fleet destroyer squadrons now moved freely along the Bismarck coasts, demonstrating Allied control of the sea and air by bombarding Japanese shore installations. Fortress Rabaul had been knocked out.

But to assure that the enemy should not again make use of his extensive facilities in the Bismarck Archipelago, Halsey and MacArthur completed their ring of steel. In February Wilkinson's Third Amphibious Force, in the neatest of a series of neat landings, placed New Zealand assault troops ashore on the Green Islands northwest of Bougainville. After the New Zealanders had killed off the small Japanese garrison, Seabees built on the major island of the atoll a fighter strip only 115 miles from Rabaul and within range of Kavieng and Truk. A month later the Third Fleet put the 4th Marine Regiment ashore on Emirau Island 70 miles northwest of Kavieng. By this time MacArthur's forces had captured the Admiralty Islands almost due west of Kavieng. The boxing in of Rabaul was complete.

THE ADMIRALTIES—AN END AND A BEGINNING

MacArthur continued to oppose the concept of a dual drive across the Pacific, his own and Nimitz', though the Combined Chiefs of Staff had accepted the plan at the Washington conference in May 1943, confirmed it at the Quebec conference in August, and confirmed it again at the Cairo conference in December. As late as February 1944 he was arguing that such a plan made for two weak thrusts by divided forces under divided command. Even if, as he urged, all South Pacific forces should be added to his own, the requirements of the Central Pacific drive might delay his return to the Philippines until March 1945.

While these discussions were still under

way, the U. S. Fifth Fleet demonstrated its speed and reach by raiding Truk and the Marianas and seizing Eniwetok, all within a week. Clearly the Southwest Pacific Command would have to show more speed, or MacArthur would find his resources draining away to the swift-moving Central Pacific drive. So MacArthur, after conferring with Halsey, advanced D-day for the Admiralties from April 20 to April 1. Then came General Kenney with another suggestion. The Fifth Air Force had severely hurt the already weakened enemy air power on New Guinea with a stunning raid on Wewak. A few days later a B-25 had spent an hour and a half over the Admiralties without noting any signs of occupation. Evidently the Japanese had already evacuated the islands. Why not send in a reconnaissance in force? If it met little or no opposition, that would be the invasion. Otherwise they could pull out. MacArthur jumped at the suggestion and in the afternoon of February 25 issued orders for a thousand soldiers to be landed on Los Negros, easternmost of the Admiralties, on the 29th.

There was great stirring about in the Seventh Fleet to assemble the necessary vessels for the accelerated operation, but on the afternoon of the 27th two cruisers, 12 destroyers, and three loaded destroyer-transports set out from a point near Buna. At that moment came a startling bit of information. A small reconnaissance party which had slipped ashore on Los Negros for a closer look reported by radio that the place was "lousy with Japs." There were in fact nearly 5,000 Japanese on the islands. Here was a grave situation, for it is an axiom of amphibious war that assaulting troops should outnumber the defenders by at least three to one. But MacArthur, counting on his control of the sea and the air, decided to go ahead and make the gamble.

It paid off. Under the eyes of MacArthur and Seventh Fleet Commander Vice Admiral Kinkaid, watching from the bridge of a cruiser, the troops landed without opposition on the east coast of Los Negros, and there they stayed. At first bad weather kept Kenney's planes from doing much, but Seventh Fleet guns took over and put on a demonstration of close support unlike anything hitherto seen in the whole Rabaul campaign. "The Navy didn't support us," said a brigade commander ashore; "they saved our necks!" [8]

In little more than an hour the invaders had overrun an airstrip, about which they drew a tight defense perimeter. While the fleet, and later Fifth Air Force B-25's and P-40's, were holding the enemy at bay, navy task groups in succeeding days poured fresh echelons of troops with artillery and Seabees with bulldozers into the perimeter. On March 15, after Seeadler Harbor had been swept for mines, troops were carried across the harbor in landing craft and put ashore on Manus Island westward of the main Japanese strong point. By the end of the month 4,000 Japanese had been killed or captured as against about 300 Americans killed, and work on the naval and air base was under way. Such was the advantage conferred by command of the sea and air.

Development of the base facilities in the Admiralty Islands (or simply Manus, as they came collectively to be called) was the responsibility of the South Pacific Command, its last cooperative effort with MacArthur's Southwest Pacific forces. The South Pacific Area, left far behind by the war, was being gradually reduced to garrison status. Its army forces, plus a few warships, were allotted to MacArthur; its marine and naval forces went to Nimitz. MacArthur had hoped to enlist Halsey to command his fleet. "If you come with me," he had said, "I'll make you a greater man than Nelson ever dreamed of being." [9] But Admiral King had other plans: Halsey was ordered to Pearl Harbor for a seagoing command under Nimitz.[10]

For MacArthur the capture of Manus marked the end of one campaign and the beginning of another. Even before the islands were secured he was planning a tremendous 400-mile leap westward to Hollandia, a movement not inappropriately named Operation Reckless. Beyond Hollandia he would leap forward again and again until at length he reached the Philippines in fulfillment of his promise: "I will return."

THE NEW STRATEGIC PICTURE

Among the numerous advantages accruing to the Allies from the 20-month campaign against Rabaul, two stand out: it reduced Japanese air power to the point where it was no longer a serious threat; it gained for the United States time to build up weapons and trained manpower for a swift advance across the Central Pacific in 1944.

While the Japanese naval air arm was being cut to pieces in defense of Rabaul and the Solomons, MacArthur's Southwest Pacific air forces, in supporting actions and in strikes on Lae, Madang, Wewak, and beyond, were whittling down Imperial Army air power in New Guinea. Japan lost nearly 1,000 naval planes trying to recapture Guadalcanal and nearly 2,000 more defending the Upper Solomons and Rabaul. Figures for Imperial Army losses are uncertain but they must have been nearly as great. Japan's aircraft industry made up the losses in planes by pushing production up to 1,700 a month, but replacing competent air crews could not be rushed. As training was curtailed, losses mounted.

When Airsols, the Fifth Air Force, and U. S. Pacific Fleet carriers combined efforts in support of the Bougainville invasion they very nearly wiped out the Japanese carrier planes temporarily committed to the defense of Rabaul. In less than two weeks the Imperial Third (Carrier) Fleet was stripped of half its fighters, 85 per cent of its dive bombers, and 90 per cent of its torpedo planes. After that Admiral Koga had no choice but to withdraw his Third Fleet from the Pacific. Like Yamamoto before him, Koga dreamed of catching Nimitz overex-

[8] Morison, VI, 447.

[9] *Halsey's Story*, 186.

[10] The plan which had brought Halsey and MacArthur into close cooperation during the advance on Rabaul was given the code name Elkton, after the small Maryland town of quick marriages. At the same time the tentative plan for operations westward after the reduction of Rabaul was prophetically named Reno.

tended and winning the war in a single great naval battle as Togo had done in 1905. But there was to be no repetition of the Battle of Tsushima. Nimitz' drive across the center would allow the Japanese at most six months to train new carrier pilots before they were forced into battle against American pilots with a minimum of two years' training and 300 hours' flying time.

The Americans owe their Pacific victories of 1944 in large part to the wearing away of Japan's air power in 1942 and 1943. The fruitless draining away of her planes and crews to the South Pacific left her defenses everywhere vulnerable. Not until the innovation of the kamikaze suicide corps would the Japanese again find any effective means of aerial counterattack, and then it would be too late.

The dual advance across the Pacific inevitably became a race for the China coast. In accordance with estimates submitted by MacArthur and Nimitz, the Joint Chiefs set up a schedule of advance: Southwest Pacific forces would invade Hollandia in April, Mindanao in November, and Luzon in February 1945; Central Pacific forces would invade the Marianas in June, the Palaus in September, and Formosa in February.

MacArthur knew the penalty for falling behind, and it was unthinkable—he might miss his heart's desire of liberating the Philippines; the Philippines might very well be by-passed. Nothing of the sort must be allowed to happen. He would invade Mindanao on schedule, he grimly told General Kenney, even if he were "down to one canoe paddled by Douglas MacArthur and supported by one Taylor cub." [11]

---

[11] *The Army Air Forces in World War II*, IV (Chicago, 1950), 615.

44

The Aleutians,
Gilberts, and Marshalls

WE NOW HAVE TO TURN OUR attention briefly away from the principal maritime theaters of World War II and consider the campaign in the Aleutians. In this arena of fog, foul weather, and perpetual frustration, nothing that was done had any influence upon the outcome of the war except insofar as it drew men and material away from the areas of decision.

When Admiral Yamamoto set out in mid-1943 to push Japan's defense perimeter eastward and so signally failed at Midway, he set up bases on Attu and Kiska at the western extremity of the Aleutian chain as roadblocks to Allied advance. But the Combined Chiefs of Staff, mindful of logistic complications, early rejected plans for an advance on Japan via the icy Aleutians; and even the Army Air Forces lost their enthusiasm for the northern route once they had got a taste of arctic weather. Besides, such an approach was strategically unsound because it would leave intact Japan's principal external source of strength, the oil-rubber-rice shipping line from the East Indies, which she had gone

to war with the United States to establish.

As matters turned out, the best Allied strategy in the north would have limited operations to pounding down the enemy-held islands from the air until the victory had been won elsewhere. But the Combined Chiefs, anticipating the timely entrance of the Soviet Union into the Pacific war, wanted the Aleutians cleared as a route for staging aircraft into Siberia.[1] So the Joint Chiefs planned in due course, when enough ships and men should become available, to recapture Attu and Kiska.

EARLY OPERATIONS IN THE ALEUTIANS

In the meantime the North Pacific Force under Rear Admiral Robert A. Theobald

---

[1] Soviet vessels carried lend-lease goods from the West Coast of the United States to Vladivostok throughout the war in the Pacific. The Japanese, anxious to avoid trouble with the Soviet Union, were careful not to interfere.

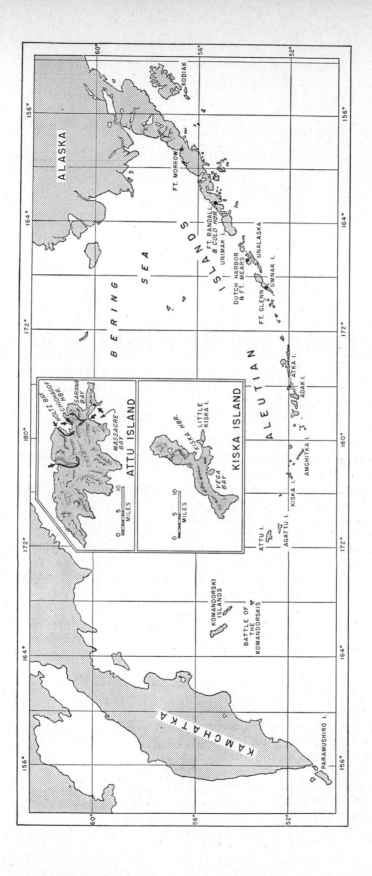

THE ALEUTIAN THEATER

did what it could to add to the discomfort of the Japanese. Until the exigencies of the Guadalcanal campaign called them southward, fleet submarines in the Aleutians staged a fruitful campaign against shipping to and from the enemy bases. In August 1942 an American cruiser-destroyer force finally penetrated the fog to give Kiska its first pounding from the sea. For several months thereafter the job of harassing the Japanese-held islands was left in the hands of Canadian and U. S. Army air forces, which raided them whenever weather permitted.

During the winter, the Americans moved westward along the Aleutian chain and occupied Adak and Amchitka, the latter only 65 miles east of Kiska. On each of these islands they constructed airfields in record time so that fighter planes could escort bombers in stepped-up attacks which soon cut off Kiska from all surface contact with Japan. In order to isolate the more westerly Attu, Rear Admiral Charles H. McMorris in mid-February 1943 led a cruiser-destroyer group in a bombardment of the island and then, proceeding southwest to patrol the enemy supply line, had the satisfaction that night of sinking an ammunition ship en route to Attu. Two other enemy vessels fled back to the Japanese base at Paramushiro in the northern Kuriles.

Realizing that the last Japanese surface supply line to the Aleutians could not much longer be maintained, Vice Admiral Boshiro Hosogaya early in March rushed to Attu a convoy escorted by his entire North Area Force, unloaded, and got safely back to Paramushiro. Later the same month he tried it again, but his luck had run out, for this time McMorris's task group, the light cruiser *Richmond,* flagship, the heavy cruiser *Salt Lake City,* and four destroyers, was patrolling in an intercepting position south of the Russian Komandorski Islands. Contact between the two forces resulted in the Battle of the Komandorskis, last of the classic daytime surface actions—the sort of battle which most navies were particularly prepared to fight and which would not be fought again, at least in this war.

THE BATTLE OF THE KOMANDORSKIS

An hour before sunrise on March 27,[2] the American task group made radar contact with the Japanese convoy to the north, and McMorris promptly gave chase, little guessing that he was in pursuit of a force considerably stronger than his own. As Hosogaya made out the approaching American vessels in the first light of dawn, he ordered his two transports to retire to the northwest and hastened to put his four cruisers and four destroyers between the Americans and their Aleutian bases.

When McMorris had closed the Japanese enough to see how greatly he was outnumbered, he still had the option of retiring southeast towards friendly airfields or engaging the enemy. Disregarding the odds, he chose the latter, radioed for help from the Eleventh Air Force, and set out in pursuit of the transports, knowing full well that he would have to run a gantlet of shells and torpedoes. Just as the sun was beginning to rise, the Japanese, ten miles away, launched a spotting plane and shattered the morning calm with a series of salvos. In reply, 8-inch shells of the *Salt Lake City* shook up Hosogaya and his staff with a pair of damaging hits in the superstructure of the flagship *Nachi.* The other Japanese heavy cruiser *Maya* however returned the *Salt Lake's* fire with such vigor that McMorris temporarily abandoned his attempt at overtaking the transports and turned away to the southwest with the enemy in hot pursuit.

There followed a three-hour chase that is chiefly remarkable for how little the Japanese accomplished. They lost their speed advantage by zigzagging in order to use their after turrets, which would be masked in a bows-on approach; and the Americans avoided hits by expert salvo chasing—steering toward the enemy's shell splashes so that in correcting his aim he would miss again. The Japanese destroyers in this action showed none of the aggressive daring that had shattered the Allied formation in the

----
[2] East longitude date.

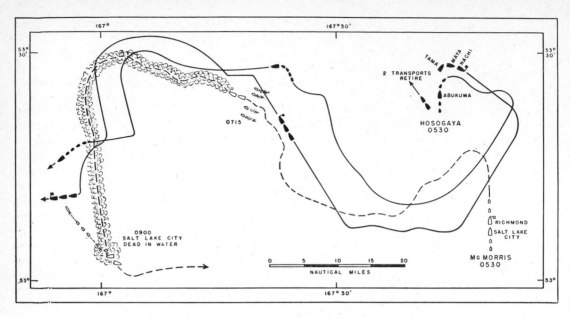

BATTLE OF THE KOMANDORSKIS, MARCH 27, 1943

Battle of the Java Sea. For the most part they merely trailed behind uselessly out of action in company with the light cruiser *Abukuma.*

A little after 0600 the *Salt Lake City,* chief target for the Japanese shells, had taken two superficial hits which did not prevent McMorris from gaining somewhat on his pursuers. He presently swung to the right and again went after the transports. But the Japanese took an intercepting course and closed the range, forcing the Americans to turn off to the west. There followed some of the hottest fighting of the battle, at such close range that the American destroyers could make good use of their guns. Their 5-inch shells, said Hosogaya's air officer afterwards, "landed aboard like rain." [3]

The *Salt Lake City* was soon in trouble, taking water from a new shell hit and having trouble with her steering gear. So McMorris ordered his destroyers to fall behind and make smoke. Thus concealed, he presently headed south with the sole aim of saving his outnumbered vessels.

Another hit flooded the *Salt Lake's* after

---

[3] *Interrogations of Japanese Officials,* I, 99.

engine room and sea water in the fuel oil extinguished her burners so that just before 0900 she went dead in the water. In this desperate situation, McMorris retained one destroyer to make smoke around the wounded cruiser and ordered the other three to delay the pursuing enemy with a suicide torpedo attack. The three expendables, headed by the *Bailey,* reversed course at once and steamed boldly into the blazing guns of the Japanese cruisers. Severely damaged by two 8-inch shells, the *Bailey* launched five torpedoes—at extreme range lest she be sunk before she could complete her mission. She then turned back, followed by her consorts.

From what looked like a hopeless predicament, the Americans suddenly found themselves extricated. Hosogaya had already broken off action and was heading for the Kuriles. He could not see the *Salt Lake City* through the smoke, and his spotting plane, which might have informed him of his opportunity, had fled the area at the first taste of American antiaircraft fire. He was disgusted with the performance of his destroyers and fearful of Allied bombers, which were already overdue. Besides, he was low in fuel and ammunition and two of his cruisers were severely damaged. So he took his entire convoy back to Paramushiro, where his displeased seniors relieved him of his command. Thereafter only submarines attempted to get supplies through to Attu and Kiska.

The *Salt Lake City* soon had her fires relighted, and McMorris's victorious task group headed for Dutch Harbor. Seven Americans had been killed and seven were seriously wounded, but Japanese casualties were more than twice as great. En route the American task group met the Eleventh Air Force bombers, which as a result of foul weather and a series of mishaps, had taken off too late to do any good.

RECONQUEST OF ATTU

Rear Admiral Thomas C. Kinkaid, who in January 1943 had relieved Admiral Theobald, had for some time been pressing for the early recapture of Kiska. But the Joint Chiefs of Staff, concerned with building up strength in the Solomons-New Guinea area for the push on Rabaul, could not for several months let him have the ships and men he needed. So Kinkaid took another look at the reconnaissance reports and decided that he could temporarily by-pass Kiska and with a much smaller force seize the more distant Attu. His estimate was correct, for the 2,600 defenders of Attu were fewer than half the number on Kiska, their airstrip was unfinished, and they had no coast defense and few antiaircraft guns. When the Joint Chiefs accepted the substitution, Admiral Nimitz ordered north the old battleships *Idaho, Pennsylvania,* and *Nevada* for extra gunfire support and set May 7 as target date.

Designated to carry out the assault, the 7th Infantry Division, United States Army, which had been training in the Nevada desert, moved to the California coast for amphibious exercises. In late April the division sailed away to the Aleutians and a kind of warfare for which it had had little realistic preparation. At dawn on May 4 the Attu Assault Force, comprising three battleships, six cruisers, 19 destroyers, five transports,

and the escort carrier *Nassau,* under the command of Rear Admiral Francis W. Rockwell, sortied from Cold Harbor into rising seas.

After two postponements because of heavy surf, Rockwell's force in the afternoon of May 11, 1943 landed 1,000 troops without opposition near Holz Bay on the north coast of Attu and 2,000 more at Massacre Bay on the south coast. The northern and southern invasion forces were to advance and meet in the mountainous interior and then force the Japanese into the eastern tip of the island, where fleet guns and planes from the *Nassau* could pound and strafe them into submission. But the Japanese, instead of retreating eastward, holed up in the mountain passes and by use of concealed artillery prevented the juncture of the American forces until 11,000 soldiers, including the entire reserve, had been put ashore.

As days passed with the stalemate on Attu unbroken, Admiral Kinkaid at Adak became uneasy. He had never intended that the Assault Force should remain so long in the invasion area. Two cruiser-destroyer groups guarding the approaches were more than enough to take care of Japanese forces based on Paramushiro, but what if the Combined Fleet should come to the relief of beleaguered Attu?

As a matter of fact, Admiral Mineichi Koga, the new commander in chief, was already steaming north with a formidable force including three battleships and two cruisers. In Tokyo Bay he picked up three carriers and five more cruisers. Then, instead of heading at once for Paramushiro and collecting the not inconsiderable naval force there, he paused at Tokyo "to await developments."

On May 16 Kinkaid, his patience exhausted, replaced the army general in command of ground forces on Attu, and thereafter the invasion picked up momentum. In justice it must be said however that the fault was not entirely with the troops or their commander, for fleet support was not all it might have been. The battleships stood off six to eight miles from shore delivering a neutralizing fire that would drive the enemy temporarily to cover but leave him and his positions largely intact. This was, after all, only the third Allied invasion of World War II. The lessons of Sicily, the Upper Solomons, and of Tarawa were yet to be learned.

By the end of May the remnant of Japanese defenders on Attu had been forced into the highlands near the north shore, where fleet guns proved more effective against them. When they had used up their store of shells and most of their bullets, they threw away their lives in a massive banzai charge, so typical of Japanese desperation tactics and so incomprehensible to the Western mind. Before dawn on May 29, a thousand Imperial Army troops, many armed only with knives or bayonets, came silently down from the hills. At first light they threw themselves howling through a gap in the American lines, overran two command posts, and broke into a medical station, where they butchered the sick and wounded. At last brought to bay, some 500 of the attackers committed suicide by holding hand grenades against their heads or chests. Surviving Japanese made further attacks that day and the next morning until all the defending garrison except 28 captives had killed themselves or been killed. American losses in the Attu campaign were about 600 killed and 1,200 wounded. Nearly 1,500 more had been put out of action because their shoes and clothing, not to speak of their training, had been ill-suited to the cold, damp climate of the Aleutians.

The only attempt of the Japanese to support their troops on Attu was by submarines, which made no hits, and by aircraft from Paramushiro, which were generally defeated by fog but which did succeed in shooting down two army fighters at the cost of five Japanese torpedo bombers. Admiral Koga and the Combined Fleet contributed nothing at all. Had Koga proceeded at once to Attu, he might have inflicted on the Americans an Aleutian Battle of Savo Island. But at Tokyo he paused so long that he not only did not hurt the Americans in the north, but he did not get back south in time to oppose Admiral Turner's easy invasion of Rendova Island at the end of June.

SURPRISE AT KISKA

In preparing for the assault on Kiska, set for mid-August 1943, the North Pacific command put to good use the hard lessons learned at Adak. In six weeks Eleventh Air Force planes dropped 1,200 tons of bombs on the island. Battleships, cruisers, and destroyers bombarded the Japanese main camp and harbor. At Adak 29,000 United States and 5,300 Canadian troops under Major General Charles H. Corbett USA, equipped to a man with tested Arctic gear, practiced landings and maneuvered across the muskeg. This huge force, carried in numerous transports and supported by nearly a hundred men-of-war, left Adak August 13 under the command of Admiral Rockwell. With the expeditionary force went several high-ranking observers, including an Assistant Secretary of War. Before dawn on the 15th, gunnery support vessels were off Kiska thundering away at enemy positions. At first light, LST's, LCI's, and LCT's moved to the beach and disgorged their troops. There followed the greatest anticlimax of the war. The Japanese escape artists had carried out another evacuation. Three weeks before, while fog covered the area, cruisers and destroyers had slipped in and carried away the entire Kiska garrison.

How, despite elaborate measures to keep Kiska blockaded, had the Japanese escape been possible? The American blockading force shortly after midnight on July 26 had got into a hot half-hour battle with an "enemy" that showed up on radar screens. After the battleships and cruisers had expended some 500 rounds of 14-inch and an equal quantity of 8-inch shell, the commanders began to suspect that the pips were radar phantoms. And so they were—return echoes from mountains in the Aleutians more than 100 miles away. As a result of high-speed maneuvering in "The Battle of the Pips," the entire force had been obliged to move east to refuel. This had given the Japanese their opportunity to slip in and evacuate.

Aviators had noted the sudden absence of antiaircraft fire but it was supposed that the Japanese had merely withdrawn into the hills to hole up for the expected invasion. Though the press mockingly played up "the great assault" and faces were red in the services, all were relieved at the saving of lives. Two bits of American soil had been redeemed from the enemy, and the United States had acquired bases from which bombers could strike the northern Kuriles.

His mission completed, Kinkaid, promoted to vice admiral, was relieved by Vice Admiral Frank Jack Fletcher, whom he had relieved a year before as Commander Carrier Forces in the South Pacific. Kinkaid now went to assume command of the U. S. Seventh Fleet under MacArthur.

STRATEGY OF THE CENTRAL PACIFIC DRIVE

The decision of the Combined Chiefs of Staff to open a new line of advance across the Central Pacific marked the victory of one strategy over another. General MacArthur's plan for a single line of advance would have made carrier air power auxiliary to land-based aircraft. MacArthur, it will be recalled, favored driving toward Japan entirely by way of the large land masses bordering the southwestern and western Pacific. In these areas troops could be transported by sea to a succession of relatively unopposed beachheads and landed under cover of army planes from airstrips at the take-off points. The Navy would have the secondary roles of transport and convoy, of guarding communication lines, and of securing the flank of the Army's advance by neutralizing enemy bases in the Central Pacific.

Naval leaders, while recognizing these as traditional fleet missions, regarded the MacArthur plan as wasteful of carrier air power. Carriers, they believed, had made possible a new kind of warfare. Freed from a mere auxiliary role, the aircraft carriers might be used continuously to gain command of the sea over ever-increasing areas. This sort of advance would require capture in the Central Pacific of islands so small that assault of strongly-defended beachheads would be inevitable, but it would open up less round-

about lines of communication and more speedily bring the war into Japanese waters. While forces moving along the New Guinea-Mindanao Axis were limited in their successive advances to the range of fighter-escorted bombers, forces on the Central Pacific Axis, by taking their mobile airfields with them, could make tremendous leaps, invading any point to which reasonably secure communication lines could be established.

To comply with the Combined Chiefs' decision in favor of opening a Central Pacific drive, the Joint Chiefs in June 1943 directed Nimitz to draw up a plan for invasion of the Marshall Islands the coming November. Nimitz however pointed out that there were sound and urgent reasons for taking the Gilbert Islands first. The Guadalcanal and North African operations had demonstrated the need for thorough photographic air reconnaissance preceding each invasion, and it was then thought that only large land-based planes were suitable for such work. Unless American airfields were established in the nearby Gilberts, he believed, the Marshalls could not be properly photographed. Moreover, capture of the Gilberts would permit land-based air support of the Marshalls operation and also eliminate a potential threat to American communications with the Marshalls and with the South and Southwest Pacific. Convinced by these arguments, the Joint Chiefs directed Nimitz to invade the Gilberts in November 1943 and the Marshalls in early 1944.

POWER FOR THE NEW DRIVE

The arrival at Pearl Harbor of the first of the new 32-knot *Essex* class of heavy carriers in the spring of 1943 was a token that American industry was catching up with the problem of arming a two-hemisphere conflict. Despite the requirements of the war against the European Axis, it would evidently be possible before long to mount an all-out offensive in the Pacific. By autumn there were in the Fifth Fleet and available for the Gilberts operation six heavy and five

ACROSS THE PACIFIC

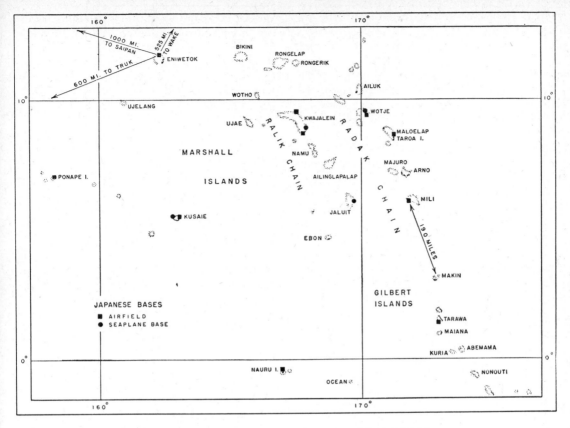

THE MARSHALLS AND THE GILBERTS

light carriers, eight escort carriers, five new battleships and seven old ones, nine heavy and five light cruisers, 56 destroyers, and 29 transports and cargo vessels, together with ample landing and beaching craft. Commanding this considerable fleet was austere, exacting Vice Admiral Raymond A. Spruance, who had demonstrated his brilliance as a tactician at Midway and, since then, his high competence as a strategist as Deputy Commander in Chief of the Pacific Fleet and Pacific Ocean Areas.

The main striking arm of the new Fifth Fleet was the Fast Carrier Task Force, the greatest concentration of power in naval history. The specific task of the carrier force was preparing the way for and supporting amphibious operations—the first, by pre-invasion raids on the target area and by distant strikes to isolate the beachhead; the second, by providing tactical support for the assault troops and by intercepting enemy air and surface threats to the amphibious forces. The Fast Carrier Task Force operated normally in four task groups, each of which at full strength typically contained four heavy or light carriers surrounded by a ring of support vessels—one or two fast battleships, three or four cruisers, and 12 to 15 destroyers. Always flexible, the carrier groups could operate together or independently, and they could detach surface vessels to form battle line or to carry out special missions. Such was the great floating air base that was to lead the way across the Pacific to the shores of Japan. The Fast Carrier Task Force commanded by Rear Admiral Charles A. Pownall in the Gilberts operation however was only a miniature version of the armada which later wiped out resurgent Japanese naval air power and helped shatter the Imperial Combined Fleet.

The amphibious arm of the Fifth Fleet was the Fifth Amphibious Force, organized and commanded by Rear Admiral Richmond Kelly Turner. In an invasion this force controlled transports, cargo vessels, landing and beaching craft, and LSD's (landing ships, dock) and also the destroyers, escort carriers, cruisers, and old battleships assigned for close support. The Amphibious Force could be split into two or more Attack Forces, and in the event of an impending major fleet action it could transfer cruisers and destroyers as needed to the fast carrier groups. As the war progressed escort carriers and gunnery vessels of the Amphibious Force tended to take over tactical support of the troops, leaving the fast carriers and their escorts as a Covering Force for interceptions.

Troops assigned to the Fifth Amphibious Force were designated V Amphibious Corps. Commanding the Corps was Major General Holland M. Smith USMC, whose typical reaction to an inept or slovenly performance had won him the nickname "Howling Mad." Though he was as stubborn and outspoken as Kelly Turner, the two made a durable team, for both were amphibious experts and each recognized and appreciated the special qualifications of the other.

Finally, the Fifth Fleet had its own Land-Based Air Force, composed of army, navy, and marine corps planes under the operational control of Rear Admiral John H. Hoover. From bases on Canton and in the Ellice Islands B-24's carried out photographic reconnaissance and raided the Gilberts and neighboring islands. After the reconquest of the Gilberts, these aircraft were to move into the newly-captured bases in order to bomb and photograph the Marshalls.

Such was the United States Fifth Fleet of World War II—less a fleet in the traditional sense than a complex system for projecting power across great distances. But striking power was not enough. To thrust across the reaches of the Central Pacific, seizing command of the sea as it went, the Fifth Fleet had to have mobility and strategic momentum to an unprecedented degree. It could not, like fleets of the preceding hundred years, be closely tied to rearward bases for supply, refueling, and upkeep. The Fast Carrier Force, at least, would have to go to sea and remain at sea—as fleets had done before the transition from sail to steam. All this had been foreseen, and the means were at hand.

The principal instrument that restored to fighting ships their old sea-keeping capacity was Vice Admiral William L. Calhoun's Service Force Pacific Fleet and its mobile service squadrons. These squadrons were seagoing logistic bases, comprising oilers, tenders, ammunition barges, repair ships, floating drydocks, provision ships, hospital ships, and half a dozen other auxiliary types, requiring nothing more elaborate than the relatively quiet waters of a lagoon to open shop and set about servicing the fleet. In addition, fleet oilers accompanied the amphibious forces, and roving groups of oilers maneuvered in designated areas to which combat vessels could repair for topping off. These were the means by which the Fifth Fleet was freed from fixed bases and was enabled to maintain command of the seas it conquered. The mobile supply and maintenance base, in the phrase of Samuel Eliot Morison, was the "logistic counterpart to the airplane carrier." [4] After the Fast Carrier Task Force left Pearl Harbor for the conquest of the Marshalls in early 1944, it did not return as a whole until after the end of the war. The restoration to the Fleet of the endurance and reach of sailing ship days was one of the great logistic achievements of World War II.

RECONQUEST OF THE GILBERT ISLANDS

As the new carriers—*Essex, Yorktown, Lexington, Princeton, Belleau Wood,* and *Independence*—reached the Pacific, together with new support vessels of all types, they were formed into task groups and sent

---

[4] VII, 107.

against live targets for warm-up and training. In the late summer and fall of 1943, they struck Marcus, the Gilberts, and Wake.

Alerted by all this activity, Admiral Koga hastened from Truk to the Marshalls with his entire Combined Fleet. But when nothing further happened, he decided it was a false alarm and returned to Truk, whence he dispatched most of his carrier aircraft to the defense of Rabaul. Then in early November, as we have seen, Halsey's South Pacific forces invaded Bougainville, and Rabaul was heavily attacked by Airsols and by Montgomery's and Sherman's task groups on loan from the Fast Carrier Task Force. Virtually stripped of its carrier planes and crews, the Combined Fleet no longer had the power to attack.

The Americans, unaware of Japanese weakness at sea, took elaborate care to achieve surprise, in order to gain a foothold in the Gilberts before the enemy fleet could strike. So as not to disclose the target, Hoover's B-24's delayed regular raids on the invasion area until mid-November, when the Fifth Fleet was already at sea en route to the assault.

Like most island groups in the Central Pacific, the Gilberts are an archipelago of atolls, each a perimeter of coral islets surrounded by a fringing reef and enclosing a lagoon. The objectives of the Fifth Fleet, from north to south, were the atolls of Makin, Tarawa, and Abemama.[5] To assault Makin Atoll came a Northern Attack Force from Pearl Harbor, with troops of the 27th Army Infantry Division. The rest of Admiral Turner's Fifth Amphibious Force, designated the Southern Attack Force, picked up the 2nd Marine Division at Wellington, New Zealand, rehearsed landing operations in the New Hebrides, and then headed for Tarawa Atoll. The submarine *Nautilus,* carrying a single company of marines, set out to scout lightly-held Abemama, which was to be invaded after Makin and Tarawa had fallen.

At the appropriate moment in the intricate pattern of approach, the four task groups of the Fast Carrier Task Force set out for their assigned supporting and covering positions—two from Pearl Harbor and the two from the South Pacific that had just completed their raid on Rabaul. While the carrier groups were pounding away at the Gilberts and nearby enemy strong points, the Northern and Southern Attack Forces made contact at sea and moved on parallel courses toward Makin and Tarawa, prepared to land troops simultaneously on the morning of November 21, 1943.[6]

Though Tarawa was known to be the strong point of the Gilberts, Makin received the bulk of the American air and surface support and the personal attention of Turner and Holland Smith. Because of its exposed position near the Japanese-held Marshalls, a one-day victory was deemed essential here so that the fleet could be quickly withdrawn from dangerous waters. Fleet guns and carrier aircraft so pounded little Butaritari, main island of the atoll, that the 6,500 assault troops were able to walk ashore without opposition from the 800 defenders. In the interior however the invaders aroused the wrath of Holland Smith by losing momentum and bogging down.

Responsibility for the slowdown has been attributed to poor leadership and faulty indoctrination of the 27th Division, which after long garrison duty in Hawaii was seeing combat for the first time. Over-age officers had unrealistically trained the division in continental-style warfare, in which troops, advancing under a barrage, do not proceed until the enemy is wiped out by artillery. Such tactics, of course, are out of place in island warfare, where speed keeps the enemy off balance and permits him little opportunity to dig in, and where isolated pockets of resistance are by-passed and left to the rear echelons to clean up.

Under the circumstances it is not surprising that whole companies of the 27th Division were held up for hours by a few snipers or a machine gun or two. By November 24 however sheer numbers had conquered the island at the cost of 64 Americans killed and 150 wounded. All the defenders were wiped

---

[5] Often, but incorrectly, spelled Apamama.

[6] East longitude date.

out except three Japanese soldiers and about a hundred Korean laborers.

The capture of Abemama was not expected to present much of a problem, but nobody foresaw that the tiny atoll would fall

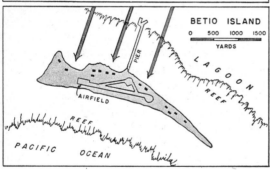

THE ASSAULT ON TARAWA,
NOVEMBER 21, 1943

into American hands without preparatory bombardment and even without a regular assault. When the marine scouts put ashore from the *Nautilus* found only 25 defenders, they called on the submarine for gunfire support and went ahead and captured Abemama themselves.

Interest in the Gilberts operation centers chiefly on Tarawa, where at the cost of heavy casualties the Americans learned the techniques that were to carry them across the

powerfully defended beaches of the Central Pacific. The storming of Tarawa proved a bitter school for amphibious assault, completing the lessons of the Solomons and New Guinea operations, and the prewar exercises of the Navy and the Fleet Marine Force.

The main target for Rear Admiral Harry Hill's Southern Attack Force was narrow, two-mile-long Betio, only fortified island in the Tarawa Atoll and strong point and administrative center of the Japanese-held Gilberts. Major General Julian C. Smith commanded the amphibious corps, and Colonel David M. Shoup led the assault. Only about 6,500 troops were assigned to capture a beachhead from the 4,800 defenders of Betio, but these troops were 2nd Division marines, seasoned veterans of Guadalcanal. Some 11,-000 additional marines—artillerymen, tank troops, engineers, and division and corps reserve—were available, and all would be committed before the tough little island was captured.

The special strength of Betio lay in the difficulty of its approaches and the nature of its defenses. The island was surrounded by a wide shelf of coral barely submerged at low tide. On this shelf the Japanese had laced concrete, coral, and metal obstacles together with barbed wire to force approaching craft into lanes covered by shore-based artillery. Along the beach ran a four-foot-high barricade of coconut logs enclosing an airfield and an intricate system of pillboxes and shelters which only heavy caliber armor-piercing shells could penetrate. About the perimeter of the island, coast defense guns and machine gun emplacements were sited to cover all approaches with blistering crossfire.

Against a small island so strongly manned, the possibility of an unopposed landing was out of the question. Lack of sufficient troops, and the requirement of speed to release the fleet quickly, ruled out invading adjacent islets to set up supporting artillery as had been done in the New Georgia invasion. The marines would have to go in against some of the most formidable defenses in the Pacific and take their beachhead by sheer assault. Thanks to extensive photographic reconnaissance, the American commanders knew very well what they were up against, and the more experienced officers did not count heavily on the effectiveness of a week of bombing by Hoover's land-based planes or of raids by the Fast Carrier Task Force immediately preceding D-day. They placed their hopes mainly on close-range pre-invasion gunfire from Hill's three old battleships, four cruisers, and nine destroyers. It was doubtless an instance of whistling in the dark when a naval officer announced to the press regarding Betio: "We do not intend to neutralize it. We do not intend to destroy it. Gentlemen, we will obliterate it." [7]

Preparations for the assault began badly at sunrise on November 21; because of a misunderstanding and faulty communications, carrier planes were nearly half an hour late over the target. After a few minutes of scattered bombing, the aircraft departed so that the delayed naval bombardment could begin. Then Hill's fire support vessels opened up and in two and a half hours poured into Betio nearly 3,000 tons of projectiles which gunnery officers fondly believed constituted destruction fire. The results were spectacular —the whole island appeared to be aflame and an enormous pall of dust and smoke billowed into the air. Betio was hurt, no question about that; but, as events were to prove, it was not hurt badly enough.

Despite the steady pumping in of shells, there had not been sufficient gunfire, and what there was had generally been the wrong sort. Because of the close range, the trajectory was too flat for projectiles to hit low-lying defenses on a flat island; plunging fire with armor-piercing shells was needed to penetrate the six-foot-thick overheads. As at Tulagi and Gavutu the gunners were delivering area fire rather than point fire; they were thus achieving mere neutralization rather than the destruction which the situation required. The aerial bombing had been too brief and too random, and bullets from strafing planes which passed over the beach fortifications just ahead of the first assault wave had no more effect than a shower of

pebbles. In short, the preparation was unrealistic for fortress Betio. It was the sort that achieves optimum results only against an exposed or lightly-protected enemy who can be hurt by bullets and by shell and bomb fragments. Lastly, the landing force, concealed from the fleet by smoke, was off schedule and still 15 minutes from the beach when the distant gunnery ships ceased fire. This respite permitted the Japanese to mass on the lagoon side of the island, toward which the marines were advancing.[8]

The first three assault waves reached the beach without prohibitive losses because they were carried across the coral reef in versatile amtracs,[9] which operate as easily ashore as afloat. Later waves, in more conventional landing craft, were grounded at the edge of the reef by a sustained low neap tide that no one had foreseen. From that point they had to wade in to the beaches under murderous fire. A few Sherman tanks, discharged by LCM's at the outer edge of the reef, made the shore; but LCVP's bringing artillery had no choice but to retract and wait for the tide to rise. Nearly a third of the 5,000 Americans who reached Betio or the reef on D-day were casualties. By nightfall some troops had penetrated the interior but many got no farther than the log barricade, and here they spent the hours of darkness with their dead. But the situation was not so desperate for the Americans as it seemed, for half the Japanese defenders had been killed by the naval bombardment and the survivors could not coordinate because their telephone communications had been cut.

During the night, artillery and more tanks were brought ashore, and after daylight call strikes from carrier aircraft and call fire from the gunnery vessels developed remarkable accuracy. Towards noon on November 22, General Julian Smith committed the corps reserve,

---

[7] J. A. Isely and P. A. Crowl, *The U. S. Marines and Amphibious War* (Princeton, 1951), 220.

[8] Radio aboard Hill's flagship, the *Maryland,* was knocked out every time the old battleship fired a salvo. This sort of breakdown in communications was avoided in subsequent operations by the introduction of the special Amphibious Force Flagship (AGC), usually a converted cargo vessel fitted with Flag quarters and elaborate communications apparatus.

[9] Short for amphibious tractor, officially LVT (landing vehicle, tracked).

and these rushed ashore over Betio's broad western beach, which had just fallen to the marines of the right flank. There then followed two days of mopping up—clearing out pillboxes, shelters, and gun emplacements with flamethrowers and charges of TNT. When victory was at length attained on the 24th, the defenders had been practically wiped out. More than a hundred Korean laborers survived, but all the Japanese except 17 captives had been killed. Of the 18,000 American invaders, marine and naval, a thousand had been killed and twice as many wounded.

The demands of the defense of Rabaul had so drained Japanese planes from the Central Pacific that the American carriers were able to shield the Gilberts invasion forces from all air attacks during the battle for Butaritari and Betio. The only important raid during the first six days was directed against one of the fast carrier groups, and succeeded in putting the light carrier *Independence* out of action with a single torpedo. Japanese submarines however penetrated to the amphibious forces. One was rammed off Tarawa by the destroyer *Frazier*. Off Makin two days later another fired a torpedo into the escort carrier *Liscome Bay*. The blast set off her stored aircraft bombs, which simply blew the little carrier apart. Of her crew of about 900, nearly 650 were killed in the explosion or in the flaming oil that spread out from her shattered hull. The loss of so many men must be counted as part of the price of taking Makin. Had the conquest of that lightly-defended atoll been the one-day affair Turner and Holland Smith intended it to be, the *Liscome Bay* and other support vessels could have been withdrawn from dangerous waters before the enemy submarines arrived. Nowhere has the Navy's insistence upon speed in amphibious assault been more sharply vindicated. Two days after the islands had been secured, Japanese planes at last began reaching the Marshalls from Truk and Rabaul. These aircraft staged a series of night raids on the Northern Attack Force, but they were completely foiled by Admiral Turner's skillful maneuvering and by interceptor planes from the American carriers.

A nation shocked by the cost in lives of the brief Gilberts campaign could not be expected to understand at once that here was a new kind of warfare in which lasting control over a large area was purchased at the price of many losses over the first few days. The hard rind of the Japanese defense perimeter had been penetrated. Bases were secured for photographing and neutralizing the Marshalls. The recovery of the Gilberts opened the way for an all-out offensive in the Central Pacific, as great a turning point in the Pacific war as the victory at Midway, which had permitted the Allies to shift from the simple defensive.

Perhaps the greatest benefit derived by the United States from the assault on Betio was that it shocked the Navy into inaugurating a revolution in support tactics and material. Though the mistakes at Tarawa were generally unforeseeable, officers of all ranks criticized their part in the invasion with ruthless honesty. The whole system of surface and air support was overhauled. The techniques of naval bombardment and aerial bombing were re-studied with the object of attaining greater precision. Underwater demolition teams of expert swimmers were trained to reconnoiter and destroy submerged obstacles. Not again in the Pacific would invading American or allied troops have to fight their way onto beaches against anything like the odds they met at Tarawa.

INVASION OF THE MARSHALL ISLANDS

In the next American invasion, the air of uncertainty and trepidation that had marked the planning for the Gilberts assault was replaced by well-founded assurance. The enemy's weakness on the sea and in the air had been revealed, and the Navy had worked out new techniques for overcoming his beach defenses. The measure of the new confidence was Admiral Nimitz' bold decision to by-pass the Japanese bases on Wotje, Maloelap, Mili, and Jaluit and send the Fifth Fleet directly against the great Kwajalein Atoll, center of the Marshall Islands defense system.

The attack on the Marshalls was begun by

land-based planes operating from the new American airfields in the Gilberts. Towards the end of January 1944, an expanded Fast Carrier Task Force, now designated Task Force 58, arrived in the invasion area under command of Rear Admiral Marc A. Mitscher with 750 planes to step up the destruction. While one carrier group set about neutralizing the by-passed eastern Marshalls and another raided Eniwetok to the west, the remaining two groups won local command of the air at a stroke by destroying every plane on Kwajalein in a single massive raid. That night battleships of TF 58 moved in to bombard the shores, and the following day planes and ships began working over island defense installations.

The attack forces of the Fifth Amphibious Force were on the way: nearly 300 vessels bringing 53,000 assault troops—half soldiers and half marines—and 31,000 garrison troops. As this armada approached the Marshalls, a Special Attack Group under Rear Admiral Hill peeled off and proceeded to occupy undefended Majuro Atoll in the Eastern Marshalls. Into Majuro's lagoon followed a mobile service squadron prepared to look after the needs of the naval forces. Thus was set up the first of a series of temporary forward bases which freed the fleet from immediate dependence upon Pearl Harbor and extended its reach step by step across the Pacific.

On January 31 the Northern Attack Force, under Rear Admiral Richard L. Conolly, and the Southern Attack Force, under Admiral Turner's direct command, reached Kwajalein Atoll and added their guns and escort carrier planes to those of the fast carrier groups to step up the three-day intensive preparation. The Navy's meticulous study of the Tarawa assault now paid off. The primary invasion targets, Roi and Namur, a pair of islands connected by a causeway at the north end of Kwajalein lagoon, and Kwajalein Island, 40 miles to the south, were pounded with four times the weight of bombs and shells that had been hurled against Betio. Aircraft picked their targets and bombed precisely. Gunnery ships varied range and trajectory and shifted from high-capacity to armor-piercing shells as the situation re-

quired. There was no notable confusion between point and area fire. An officer who went ashore after the assault reported that the island he visited looked as if it had been raised to 20,000 feet and then dropped.

On February 1, troops seized islets near Roi-Namur and near Kwajalein Island to permit entry of amphibious vessels into the relatively calm lagoon and to site artillery to cover landing beaches. The main assaults followed the next day. There were now tracked vehicles aplenty to carry the troops over the reef, amtracs supplemented by the Army's equally versatile DUKW's.[10] These were carried to the line of departure by LST's, out of which they crawled fully loaded under their own power. The first wave of landing craft was led by armed, flame-throwing amphibious tanks and was accompanied to the beach by shallow-draft LCI's converted into gunboats by the addition of rocket racks and 20 mm. and 40 mm. guns. Preceding the first wave, underwater demolition teams searched ahead for mines and submerged obstacles. Fire from offshore gunnery vessels continued to pound the beaches until parachute flares dropped by air observers signaled that the initial wave was within 500 yards of the shore. Such were the new amphibious techniques born out of the agony of Tarawa. It is scarcely surprising that there was no opposition at the Marshalls beachheads.

Major General Harry Schmidt's new 4th Marine Division, lifted directly from San Diego to the Marshalls by the Northern Attack Force, had had little opportunity to practice landings. Their assault on Roi-Namur from the choppy waters of the lagoon was marred by confusion and poor timing. Once ashore however these inexperienced marines showed the effect of sound basic training by forging ahead rapidly. On Roi they advanced to their D-day objective line in 20 minutes, there consolidated, and completed the conquest before nightfall. Namur presented a greater problem, for this island was more built up than Roi and had been less thoroughly flattened. Here tank-infantry teams kept pushing the enemy, allowing him

---

[10] Known also as amphibious trucks or amtrucks.

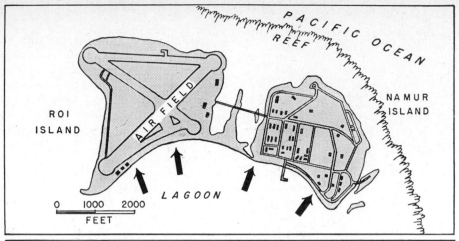

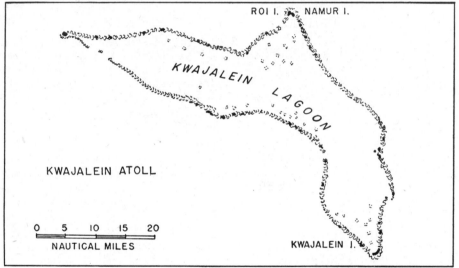

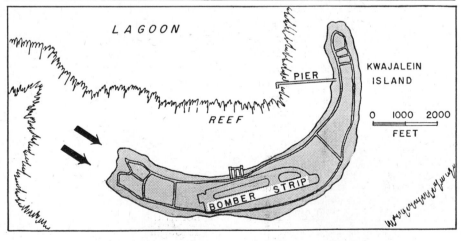

THE ASSAULT ON KWAJALEIN

no time to dig in. Strong points were by-passed, to be cleaned out by support troops using demolition charges and flamethrowers. Namur was secured by noon of the second day.

On Kwajalein Island, at the southern end of the lagoon, Major General Charles H. Corlett's 7th Infantry Division made an almost flawless landing. Mild seas in this area helped, but the efficient assault was mainly the product of rigorous rehearsals Corlett had put his division through since it fumbled on Attu. Once ashore however the soldiers advanced slowly in comparison with the marines on the northern islets. This was partly a matter of army tactics, but mainly it was because the 7th Division was unable to invade its island on a broad front, as the marines had done. Rough surf and heavy defenses had ruled out a landing on the ocean side of the southern island, and an assault on the concave lagoon beach would have exposed the invaders to flank fire from the shore. So the soldiers were obliged to land at the western end. This meant that they had to advance the whole length of the island while presenting a narrow front that could be resisted by a relatively small force. After three days of deliberate advance under a barrage of shells and aerial bombs, the invasion forces squeezed a few hundred surviving defenders into the northern tip and began the final mopping up. By the afternoon of the following day, February 5, all organized resistance had ended on Kwajalein Island.

Of the 8,700 defenders on Roi-Namur and Kwajalein, fewer than 300 captives survived. Some 42,000 American invaders had gone ashore in about equal numbers in the two areas, where they suffered losses of 372 killed and about 1,600 wounded.[11] The casualty rate for the Marshalls was thus below five per cent, reflecting the increased power and improved techniques of the Fifth Fleet since

Tarawa, where the rate was 17 per cent. Except for a few hits from coast defense guns, the fleet was unscratched. Evidently the bitter lessons of Betio had been well learned.

Because he had not had to commit the 8,000 troops of the corps reserve, Admiral Spruance could push on without delay to seize Eniwetok Atoll. Here he planned to set up another logistic base to support his next westward jump. But Eniwetok, largest of the western Marshalls, was in an exposed position, only a thousand miles from Saipan, less than 700 from Truk, less than 600 from Ponape. To prevent interference with the new operation, these Japanese bases had to be neutralized. That was quite an order and might have been considered too risky before American carrier and land-based air power had so brilliantly demonstrated its capabilities by isolating Kwajalein.

When the Americans had penetrated the Japanese defense perimeter with their capture of the Gilberts, Tokyo had set up a new, more restricted perimeter stretching south through the Marianas and the Palaus to western New Guinea. Garrison troops on the islands east of the new defense line were given the suicide mission of delaying and weakening American forces so as to allow Japan time to build up its depleted air power. With the fall of Kwajalein, Admiral Koga felt so exposed at Truk that he withdrew Admiral Kurita's surface fleet to the Palaus and ordered Admiral Ozawa's virtually planeless carrier fleet to Singapore.

Meanwhile pilot training went on apace in Japan. As soon as crews for land-based aircraft had attained enough skill to fly so far, the planes were fed south along the new inner defense chain and to outposts in the Carolines. In this manner the Japanese began building up power along the restricted perimeter to destroy any invading force which might approach. By mid-February 1944, 365 planes were at Truk, and 200 more were ready to take off from Japan for the Marianas.

That was the situation when TF 58 sortied from Majuro and Harry Hill's Eniwetok Expeditionary Group left Kwajalein. While one group of the Carrier Force remained near

---

[11] By far the greater percentage of American casualties was suffered on Kwajalein Island. The rushing tactics of the marines had apparently proved more economical of men than the methodical advance of the soldiers. Most army commanders in the Pacific recognized that by-passing isolated pockets of resistance is sound doctrine in island warfare and acted accordingly.

Eniwetok to support the assault, the other three headed southwest for Truk. Bombers of the Seventh Army Air Force were already reaching out 900 miles from Tarawa to take the fight out of Ponape with a series of sharp blows.

Truk, an archipelago of islands surrounded by a coral reef, provides one of the world's finest anchorages. Its reputation for impregnability under Japanese mandate had won it such names as "the Japanese Pearl Harbor" and "Gibraltar of the Pacific." Task Force 58 exploded that reputation and at the same time proved the ability of the fast carriers to beat down major enemy positions at vast distances from any friendly base. While Mitscher's planes hit Truk repeatedly on February 17, Spruance led the 45,000-ton *Iowa* and *New Jersey,* with two heavy cruisers and four destroyers, in a sweep around the archipelago to sink enemy ships escaping through passages in the perimeter reef. To catch any vessels that might elude Mitscher's planes and Spruance's guns, Nimitz had sent ten submarines to patrol the area. During the night of February 17-18, carrier aircraft, exploiting a newly-developed technique, bombed vessels in Truk lagoon by radar. At dawn the carriers, already beginning to withdraw, launched a final all-out attack. At the cost of severe torpedo damage to the carrier *Intrepid* and 25 planes shot down, the Americans during this raid destroyed about 200 enemy aircraft, damaged 70 more, sank 15 naval vessels including two light cruisers and four destroyers, and sent down 24 merchant vessels and five tankers.

"Impregnable Truk" had been proved a myth. Japan's maritime investment during the 20 years of her mandate had gone into her fleet and not, as many had supposed, to building up an oceanic Maginot Line. By smashing the air power of Truk, TF 58 had both isolated Eniwetok and completed the neutralization of Rabaul. Airsols planes on February 18 encountered not a single enemy aircraft over the Bismarcks.

Following the successful raid on Truk, Admiral Mitscher with two groups of TF 58 set out for the Mariana Islands. Detected by a Japanese patrol plane in the afternoon of February 22, Mitscher's force was attacked by aircraft through the night. Rather than lose time by turning into the wind to launch fighters, the Americans defended themselves with gunfire alone. So effective were their radar-aimed, VT-fused antiaircraft shells that not a ship was hit. The speedy approach paid off handsomely, catching the enemy air defenses awkwardly off balance. Vice Admiral Kakuji Kakuta, commanding the Marianas Air Base Force, had just moved about 150 torpedo bombers in from Japan in advance of the fighter squadrons. After sunrise on the 23rd, TF 58 planes struck at Guam, Tinian, and Saipan and wiped out the bombers before the fighters could arrive to protect them. As important to the Americans as this destruction of Marianas air power were aerial photographs taken of airfields and of beaches suitable for assault.

While Mitscher and Spruance were pounding down enemy bases, Hill's force captured Eniwetok, using methods similar to those employed at Kwajalein. But whereas the assault troops at Kwajalein had outnumbered the defenders 5 to 1, the ratio at Eniwetok was only a little over 2 to 1. So the three occupied islands of the atoll had to be taken one at a time. Three battalions of marines overran Engebi and Parry each in a single day. The two battalions of the 27th Infantry Division put ashore on Eniwetok Island however got off to such a slow start that one of the marine battalions had to be rushed in to take over the brunt of the fighting. Three days were required to secure Eniwetok Island, partly because the invasion force, discovering belatedly that it was defended, had given it inadequate preparatory bombardment, and partly because of the diverse tactics of the soldiers and the marines. Evidently the officers of the 27th Division had learned little from the criticisms of their slowdown on Makin.

Back at Kwajalein Atoll, the Americans had begun moving out from their lodgements on Roi-Namur and Kwajalein Island to clear the enemy from all his positions in the chain of islets surrounding the lagoon. The by-passed bases in the eastern Marshalls—Wotje,

Maloelap, Mili, and Jaluit—were kept neutralized by occasional air raids. Cut off from all supply and reinforcement except by submarine, they could create no serious problem in the rear of the American advance.

The almost perfect invasion of the Marshalls had extended the reach of the Fifth Fleet far across the Pacific, demonstrated the power of carrier-based air, and forced the enemy into retirement behind a restricted perimeter. For their achievement, and in recognition of their increased responsibilities in an expanding fleet, Spruance, Turner, Holland Smith, and Mitscher were each awarded an additional star.

In Admiral Mitscher, Nimitz had found a carrier force commander worthy to complete the Spruance-Turner-Smith team. With little of the colorful command personality of a Halsey or the icy intellect of a Spruance, soft-spoken, gnomelike little Marc Mitscher proved to be one of the most effective commanders of the war. His success derived in part from professional competence, for he had been a pioneer in naval aviation and had grown up, as it were, with the carriers. But added to this were utter integrity, an intuitive sense for calculated risk, and warm consideration which inspired intense loyalty from his associates. From the time he took over the carriers in early 1944, Admiral Mitscher stayed with them through every important action till the end of the war. He became, as much as any, an indispensable man.

45

The Dual Advance

to the Philippines

AFTER THE SWIFT CONQUEST of the Gilberts and Marshalls by the United States Fifth Fleet, there was never again any serious objection raised to the concept of a separate Central Pacific drive. The Joint Chiefs of Staff now assigned to Admiral Nimitz his next objective: occupation of Saipan, Tinian, and Guam in the Marianas. From bases in these islands submarines could step up attrition of tankers and freighters plying the Japanese lifeline from the Southern Resources Area, and the Army Air Forces could employ their new long-range B-29 bombers in strikes directly against Japan. D-day for Saipan was June 15, 1944, little enough advance notice for General Holland Smith to prepare assault forces and for Admiral Turner to plan amphibious operations against so formidable a target.

Meanwhile General MacArthur's Southwest Pacific forces were completing their conquest of the Admiralties and preparing to leap 400 miles westward to Hollandia, on the northeast coast of New Guinea. They would thus by-pass the Japanese Eighteenth Army, about 20,000 survivors of the march from Huon Peninsula, then moving into Wewak. But the leap to Hollandia would carry the Seventh Amphibious Force beyond the range of Fifth Air Force fighter planes and at the same time expose it to flank attack from the western Carolines. So the floating airfields of the Fifth Fleet, then temporarily unemployed, were called upon to neutralize the Carolines, to lend direct support to the new invasion, and to protect the amphibious shipping of the Seventh Fleet.

TASK FORCE 58
SUPPORTS MACARTHUR

Toward the end of March 1944 three carrier groups of TF 58 departed Majuro and headed for the Palau Islands in the western Carolines. Detection of this westbound force by a search plane from Truk stimulated the Japanese into extraordinary activity. When Admiral Koga had pulled back to the Mariana-Palau-Western New Guinea line, he had declared that this was to be his last retreat—he would hold the new line at all costs. Esti-

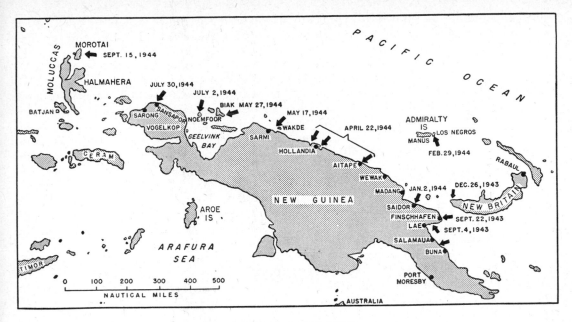

THE NEW GUINEA CAMPAIGN, 1943-1944

mating that the Allies were now about to attack his new defense perimeter, Koga summoned planes from the Marianas and carrier forces from Singapore and ordered his surface fleet to sortie from the shelter of the Palaus and stand by for trouble.[1] Then he set out with his staff in two planes for new headquarters at Davao in Mindanao. En route the planes ran into bad weather and crashed. The Combined Fleet was once more without a commander in chief.

All Koga's hustle and bustle was to no avail. As March was turning into April, TF 58 struck the Palaus, destroying most of the defending aircraft and sinking practically all the shipping that had not departed. Before the Combined Fleet could assemble for counterattack, TF 58 had also raided nearby Yap and Woleai and was well on its way back to the Marshalls. The western Carolines were at least temporarily neutralized; MacArthur's right flank was safe.

In mid-April the fast carriers were again at sea, this time in direct support of the Hollandia landing. On the return passage, the

carrier aircraft gave Truk another pounding which left it so helpless that bombers from Eniwetok and the Admiralties had no further trouble keeping it neutralized. Before returning to base, TF 58 detached cruisers to bombard the central Caroline island of Satawan, and Lee's battleships, formed into battle line, shelled Ponape in the eastern Carolines.

HOLLANDIA AND WESTWARD

For the Hollandia operation Admiral Barbey's Seventh Amphibious Force, divided into three attack groups, sortied from Manus supported by light escort carriers on loan from the Fifth Fleet. After setting a course toward the Palaus to mislead the enemy, the groups split in the evening of April 21 and headed toward their separate objectives. The Eastern Group, with the escort carriers, proceeded to Aitape, 125 miles southeast of Hollandia, and there put American soldiers ashore against almost no resistance from a surprised enemy. The landing force quickly began construction of an aircraft staging base and, in

---

[1] As the fleet sortied, the American submarine *Tunny* blew the bow off Koga's flagship, the super-battleship *Musashi*.

order to contain the Japanese Eighteenth Army, set about plugging the coastal road between Wewak and Hollandia. For the latter task the invaders were quickly reinforced to corps strength—and none too soon, for the enemy soon advanced from Wewak and attacked. While warfare raged in the jungle, Allied PT boats and planes kept the Japanese from using the coastal road or sending supplies by barge; and with the aid of Australian spotting planes, Seventh Fleet cruisers and destroyers bombarded the enemy's inshore supply line. Thus deprived of food and ammunition, the initial Japanese counteroffensive at length collapsed with heavy losses, but the American garrison at Aitape nevertheless had its hands full until the end of the war.

Barbey's Central and Western groups went ashore some 20 miles apart in the Hollandia area. Thanks to a series of massive bomber raids by General Kenney's Fifth Air Force, which had destroyed nearly 500 enemy planes in the area, and to vigorous support by TF 58 and Seventh Fleet gunnery vessels, these landings also were made virtually without opposition. The objective here was three Japanese airfields behind the coastal Cyclops Mountains. The invaders from the beachheads penetrated southward around the ends of the range and, advancing from east and west, took the fields by double envelopment.

General MacArthur was now launched upon his drive to capture Japanese airstrips and convert them to his own use, ever advancing his bomber line until it could cover his invasion of Mindanao. Determined to maintain momentum, he issued his next invasion order only five days after the Hollandia landings. The new targets were two airfields 120 miles northwest of Hollandia, one on the New Guinea coast near Sarmi, the other on nearby Wakde Island. This double operation, successfully carried out by MacArthur's well-balanced infantry-navy-air force team, demonstrated the typical features both of coastal invasion and of small island assault —the soldiers met little resistance on the mainland beach but ran into heavy resistance in the interior; on Wakde on the contrary they found the beachhead strongly defended, yet

cleared the island of enemy in a little over two days. A week later army engineers had lengthened the Wakde airstrip for use by heavy bombers, just in time to support MacArthur's next westward leap.

MacArthur was not so naive as to suppose that the Japanese would let him continue his swift westward advance without at some point making an all-out effort to block his progress. The anticipated reaction came at the end of May 1944, when the Americans invaded Biak—a large island in New Guinea's Geelvink Bay. Though Biak was east of Japan's inner defense perimeter, it was so uncomfortably close to the Philippines that the Japanese felt compelled to take drastic action. They therefore put into effect a plan designated the *Kon* Operation.

As a first step the Japanese drained their Central Pacific bases of much of their airpower, rushing planes to New Guinea from Japan, from the Marianas, and from the Carolines. Seventh Fleet antiaircraft fire kept the new arrivals from achieving much on and around Biak, but the hostile planes greatly weakened Biak's air defense by damaging or destroying upwards of 60 Allied aircraft parked on Wakde. They might have done more had not the Japanese aviators from healthier climes to the north almost at once and without exception succumbed to New Guinea malaria and jungle fever. Even those who survived were out of action through the crucial month of June.

But the Japanese had another string to their bow. From the First Mobile Fleet, then massed at Tawitawi, south of the Philippines, Admiral Ozawa released surface units to reinforce Biak. The Tokyo Express was running again. The first reinforcement group prudently turned back after being sighted by a submarine and by a plane from Wakde. A second was chased away from the Biak area by a cruiser-destroyer force under Rear Admiral V. A. C. Crutchley RN. To support the third attempt, Ozawa sent his superbattleships *Yamato* and *Musashi* and several cruisers and destroyers under Vice Admiral Matome Ugaki. This formidable force on June 11 assembled at Batjan in the Moluccas, just west of New Guinea, for a quick run to Biak, where Ugaki intended to land his troops, smash Allied positions, and if possible hunt down and destroy the United States Seventh Fleet.

Apparently MacArthur had overreached himself. A new and more terrible Battle of Savo Island seemed inevitable. But the very day Ugaki reached Batjan, the whole strategic picture changed abruptly for the Japanese. A thousand miles to the northeast, the U. S. Fifth Fleet attacked the Marianas preparatory to invading Saipan, which was within bomber range of Japan itself. The Japanese at once abandoned Biak to its fate, dropping the *Kon* Operation in favor of the *A* Operation, the long-awaited counterattack against the Fifth Fleet. Ozawa sortied from Tawitawi to do battle; and Ugaki, leaving his transport units at Batjan, headed northeast to join the main body of the First Mobile Fleet in the Philippine Sea.

Here was a situation dramatically illustrating the relative advantages of interior and exterior position in warfare. Had Ozawa defeated Spruance at the Marianas, he might have taken advantage of his interior position by turning south, advancing on a straight line through the Japanese-held Carolines to smash MacArthur's forces at Biak before a weakened Fifth Fleet could come the long way around east of the Carolines to lend assistance. But the Marianas-based planes on which Ozawa had counted to offset Spruance's carrier-based air superiority had largely been drawn south within range of the deadly New Guinea mosquito by MacArthur's advance to Biak. It was Ozawa who was defeated in the great sea-air Battle of the Philippine Sea off the Marianas on June 19-21, 1944, and the dual thrust by the Allies, which gave them the exterior position, ended with both Saipan and Biak in Allied hands. Allied forces had attained strategic concentration by holding part of the enemy force in one quarter while bringing their main attack against the enemy in another quarter. Such concentration may be achieved by either interior or exterior position; but the exterior position, being fraught with the greater peril, is generally reserved to the stronger power.

Ozawa's defeat took the pressure off MacArthur. In early July his forces invaded Noemfoor Island without outside interference. Naval gunfire supporting this landing was so thorough that the surviving Japanese defenders were too stunned to offer organized resistance. At the end of July, Southwest Pacific forces went ashore at Cape Sansapor near the western end of New Guinea. There was no opposition at the beachhead and no reaction from the enemy for several weeks.

In a little more than three months General MacArthur's forces had advanced 550 miles from Hollandia to Cape Sansapor, seizing five enemy air bases en route. No campaign of the war had been carried out with more expert planning, better teamwork, or more competent execution. Only the Moluccas and the Talaud Islands now stood between MacArthur and Mindanao, 500 miles to the northwest.

We must now backtrack a little in time in order to follow the Central Pacific Axis of the dual Allied advance.

ACROSS THE CENTER

June 1944 saw unleashed the most titanic military effort in history. Almost simultaneously, American forces in the Pacific and predominantly American forces in Europe cracked the inner defense lines of Japan and of Germany. For sheer magnitude the cross-Channel invasion of France is without rival, but the assault on Saipan nine days later was scarcely less complex, for the Saipan operation required projecting overwhelming power more than three thousand miles westward from Pearl Harbor and a thousand miles from Eniwetok, the most westerly American anchorage in the Central Pacific. Yet whereas planning for the Normandy invasion had been under way for more than two years, Spruance, Turner, and Holland Smith and their staffs had had only three months to plan and organize the expedition against the Marianas.

On June 6, Task Force 58, with Admiral Spruance in the *Indianapolis* and Admiral Mitscher in the *Lexington,* left Majuro and headed for the Marianas, followed at a considerable distance by the amphibious forces, which included 535 ships, carrying more than 127,000 assault troops, two-thirds of them marines. As this armada departed the Marshalls, other American forces were al-

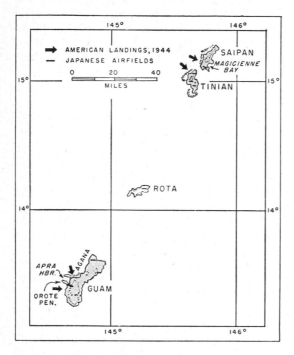

THE SOUTHERN MARIANAS

ready en route from the United States with nearly 40,000 garrison troops to take over when the invaders had completed their conquest.

During the advance of the Fifth Fleet, U. S. Army Air Force planes created a diversion and cut down Japanese air power by striking repeatedly at enemy bases in the Carolines, as far west as the Palaus. On June 11, when TF 58 had reached a point 200 miles east of Guam, Mitscher hurled his carrier air groups against the southern Marianas. Enemy plane losses were heavy and retaliation was light, partly because, as we have seen, most of the Japanese air power in the Central Pacific had been drained away southward in defense of Biak. (See map, page 794.)

On June 13 Mitscher detached his seven

battleships under Vice Admiral Willis A. Lee to begin the naval bombardment of Saipan and Tinian. On the 14th he detached two carrier task groups northward under Rear Admiral Joseph J. Clark to raid Iwo Jima and Chichi Jima in order to cut air communications from Japan and thereby complete the isolation of the Marianas. The other two carrier groups steamed around to west of the island chain to lend direct support to the invasion of Saipan.

THE ASSAULT ON SAIPAN

Mountainous, 12-mile-long Saipan could not be bombarded into impotence as the flat islets of Kwajalein Atoll had been. Yet because the Japanese were certain to react violently to an invasion of the Marianas, the island had to be seized quickly from its 32,000 defenders. The proposed solution was to strike for a broad, deep beachhead from which the marine invaders could seize the main airfield and drive straight across the island.

On June 14 the old battleships and other gunnery vessels of the amphibious force relieved Lee's battleships off Saipan and began a methodical bombardment, while demolition teams blasted passages through the coral reef. On the morning of the 15th, transports and tractor groups bringing 43,000 marines of the 2nd and 4th Divisions moved into position off the beachhead on the relatively flat southwest coast.

After a final two-hour naval bombardment, interrupted by a half hour of air strikes, eight battalions of marines in amtracs advanced towards the beach on a four-mile front. LCI gunboats gave close support and the fleet plowed up the beachhead area with a tremendous barrage. Despite its intensity however, the preparatory bombardment had not been thorough enough, for still intact behind the beach and on the flanks were numerous mortar and machine gun nests backed by well-sited artillery in the hills. In the face of heavy enemy fire, casualties among the landing forces mounted. By nightfall the marines had penetrated inland only about half the distance the planners had counted on for the first day.

The next morning, informed by a submarine report that a Japanese fleet was approaching, Admiral Spruance postponed the intended early invasion of Guam. Admiral Turner thereupon ordered ashore the 27th Infantry Division and directed the Guam Attack Force to stand by in the event even more troops should be needed on Saipan.

By June 17, the American offensive, now amply supported by tanks and artillery, had overcome fierce Japanese resistance and begun to roll. The next day the 4th Marine Division reached the east coast, and the 27th Division captured the main airfield. On the 19th, as the fleets joined battle in the Philippine Sea to westward, the two marine divisions began to pivot for a drive to the north.

THE IMPERIAL NAVY PREPARES TO COUNTERATTACK

In 1944, with the tide of war turning ever more against them, Japanese naval leaders, becoming obsessed with a false parallel between the Russo-Japanese War and World War II, looked to a new Battle of Tsushima to extricate them from their difficulties. On assuming command of the Combined Fleet in May, Admiral Soemu Toyoda announced his determination to seek the decisive naval battle that had been the last great hope of his deceased predecessors, Yamamoto and Koga. He then organized his swiftest combat ships into a carrier-centered First Mobile Fleet, evidently in imitation of the American Fast Carrier Task Force, and stationed it at Tawitawi between the Philippines and Borneo, under the command of Vice Admiral Jisaburo Ozawa, Japan's top naval air officer.

Toyoda had selected Tawitawi for two reasons. From the remarkable wells of nearby Tarakan, pure but highly volatile oil could be pumped directly into the bunkers of his fuel-hungry vessels. And from this position he could quickly dispatch the Mobile Fleet to defend the inner defense perimeter, for he assumed that the Allies were committed to a

single line of advance, via the New Guinea-Mindanao Axis. But Tawitawi proved an unfortunate choice. When captured documents on New Guinea revealed to the Allies the existence and location of the new carrier fleet, American submarines converged upon the Celebes Sea and the Philippine Islands in such numbers that Ozawa dared not leave port for maneuvers. And since there was no airdrome on or near Tawitawi suitable for them to use, his aviators, who had been sent to the carriers with a minimum of basic training, ceased training altogether and merely loafed, losing their fighting edge.

In June, as we have seen, surface units under Vice Admiral Ugaki detached themselves from the Mobile Fleet and hastened to the relief of Biak. Then came Mitscher's air attack on the Marianas. Evidently the great naval battle, so long anticipated, was at hand —though not in the Southwest Pacific, where the Japanese had expected it to take place. Toyoda at once suspended the Biak operation and ordered Ozawa and Ugaki to rendezvous in the Philippine Sea to "attack the enemy in the Marianas area and annihilate the invasion force."

Ozawa, estimating correctly that TF 58 was nearly twice as strong as the Mobile Fleet on the surface and more than twice as strong in the air, was acutely conscious of the inadequate training of his flyers.[2] But he was aware also of his advantages. Because of the easterly tradewind, he was almost sure to have the lee gage, which would permit him to launch and recover planes while advancing on the enemy; he counted on the assistance of land-based aircraft from Rota, Guam, and Yap; and his carrier planes, unhampered by armor and self-sealing fuel tanks, gave him a profitable attack range of more than 300 miles, while optimum range for the Americans was only a little over 200 miles. Moreover he had appraised Spruance as a

[2] Mobile Fleet: 9 carriers, 5 battleships, 13 cruisers, 28 destroyers, 473 planes. Task Force 58: 15 carriers, 7 battleships, 21 cruisers, 69 destroyers, 956 planes. The Japanese had gathered extensive intelligence about the United States Fifth Fleet from captured documents, from daring air reconnaissance over the Marshalls, and from interrogation of downed American aviators.

cautious man who would not be lured from a covering position off the Saipan beachhead. That was exactly the way he wanted it, for TF 58 would thus remain tethered within range of air attack from the Marianas. At the same time Ozawa could hold off out of reach of Mitscher's planes while sending his own carrier aircraft to attack TF 58. The Mobile Fleet air groups could then proceed to nearby Guam, there refuel and rearm, hit TF 58 again, and return to their carriers with fuel to spare. It was on this finesse that Ozawa counted to achieve victory.

In the afternoon of June 18, planes from the Japanese carriers located TF 58 some 200 miles west of Saipan. Ozawa thereupon began to take disposition for an attack the next morning. Under Vice Admiral Takeo Kurita, a Van Force consisting of three circular groups, each centered on a single light carrier, advanced to a position 300 miles west of TF 58, just outside the extreme attack range of the American planes. A hundred miles to the rear of the Van Force, that is to say a hundred miles farther from the Americans, was the Main Body under the direct command of Admiral Ozawa. This consisted of two circular groups each centered on three carriers—six carriers in all, five heavy and one light. Most of the heavy surface ships were in Kurita's Van, for this force with its con-

centration of antiaircraft fire was expected to absorb the first shock should the aircraft of TF 58 manage to attack. Ozawa's disposition had a certain logic, but as in the Battle of Midway the Japanese divisions were too widely separated for mutual support, and the heavy carriers were poorly protected against possible submarine attack.

"The fate of the Empire rests on this day's battle. Let every man do his utmost," Admiral Togo had announced to his fleet just before the Battle of Tsushima. And from Japan Admiral Toyoda had repeated Togo's exhortation to the Mobile Fleet, now going into action. As dawn grayed the skies over the Philippine Sea on the morning of June 19, 1944, more than 300 Japanese carrier planes prepared to take off against TF 58, in order to duplicate by other means Togo's exploit of 39 years before.

SPRUANCE COVERS THE BEACHHEAD

On June 14 the situation of the U. S. Fifth Fleet superficially but rather startlingly resembled that of the Japanese Combined Fleet two years earlier, when it had advanced on Midway with results so disastrous to itself. The Saipan Attack Force was heading in for the assault. The Floating Reserve and the Guam Attack Force were maneuvering east of the Marianas awaiting the outcome of the Saipan invasion. Half of TF 58, including Mitscher's and Spruance's flagships, was steaming to a covering position west of Saipan; the other half, under Clark, was moving northwest for a strike at Iwo Jima and Chichi Jima, 500 miles away. The parallel would have been exact had the Japanese, with advance intelligence of American intentions, brought their full carrier fleet strength undetected to the Marianas before the Americans arrived. Then while the Fifth Fleet was divided several ways, the enemy carriers might conceivably have struck at the two task groups west of Saipan before the rest of the Fifth Fleet could come to their support. The Japanese might thus have defeated the two American groups as decisively as the Ameri-

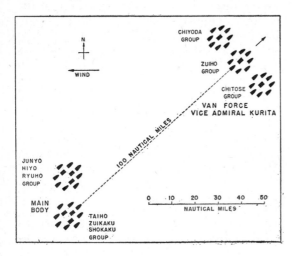

DISPOSITION OF MOBILE FLEET, JUNE 19

cans defeated Nagumo's Mobile Force on June 4, 1942.

But the relative state of military intelligence in 1944 was such that nothing of the sort occurred. The American attack on the Marianas took the enemy completely by surprise, and Spruance knew very well where the Japanese fleet was. United States submarines were on station off Tawitawi and in the Philippine Sea keeping close watch on the Mobile Fleet and on all approaches to Saipan. When the submarine *Redfin* reported Ozawa's sortie on the 13th, Spruance guessed that a battle was imminent, but he was not alarmed. Coolly calculating the enemy's rate of advance, he in due course postponed the invasion of Guam, transferred eight cruisers and 21 destroyers from the Saipan Attack Force to TF 58, deployed Turner's old battleships and escort carriers so as to delay any enemy units that might slip past the fast carrier force, and ordered Clark's two raiding groups to complete their strikes on the 16th and rendezvous with the rest of TF 58 on the 18th.

Coastwatchers kept Spruance informed by radio of the progress of Ozawa's Main Body as it threaded its way through the Philippines. On June 15 a submarine reported Ozawa debouching from San Bernardino Strait, and an hour later another submarine sighted Ugaki's battleship force on a northeasterly course in the Philippine Sea. These reports established that the Japanese fleet was in at least two widely separated divisions; and since the rendezvous of Ozawa and Ugaki on the 17th went unobserved, Spruance remained uncertain whether the enemy had massed his forces or was employing the tricky strategy of divided force which had characterized most of his operations up till that time. Two contacts by the submarine *Cavalla* on the 17th indicated that the Japanese were still advancing on the Marianas; but because the *Cavalla* had sighted only part of the Mobile Fleet, Spruance continued to suspect that not all Japanese forces had been accounted for.

In the morning of June 18, Clark's two raider groups rejoined TF 58, whereupon Spruance ordered his seven fast battleships,

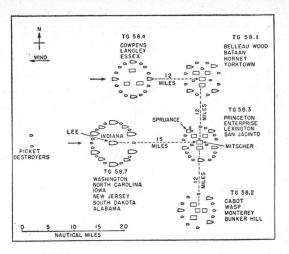

DISPOSITION OF TF 58, JUNE 19

plus four heavy cruisers and 14 destroyers, detached from the carrier task groups to form a circular Battle Line under Vice Admiral Lee, to be ready for a surface engagement should opportunity offer. The five task groups thus formed, all in circular formation, then deployed for safe maneuver with 12- to 15-mile intervals between groups. Lee's Battle Line took the position nearest the enemy's expected line of advance. Like Kurita's Van Force in the Mobile Fleet, it was to employ its concentration of antiaircraft fire to shield the more distant carrier groups.

During the period of expectant waiting, Spruance maintained a covering position near the Marianas and the Saipan beachhead, advancing westward by day and retiring eastward by night so as to prevent any enemy diversionary force from passing him in darkness. Through the daylight hours of the 18th, TF 58 shaped the usual westerly course towards the last enemy contact, feeling out ahead with search planes. The carrier aircraft found nothing; equally fruitless was aerial reconnaissance by PBY's out of the Admiralties and PBM's from a tender off Saipan. At nightfall, having developed no further intelligence regarding the enemy, Spruance ordered TF 58 to reverse course and head back east. Two hours later he received from Pearl Harbor radio direction-

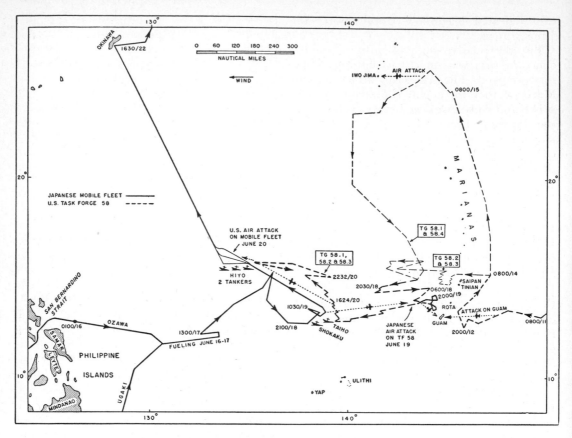

BATTLE OF THE PHILIPPINE SEA, JUNE 19-21, 1944

finder bearings that placed the Mobile Fleet 355 miles WSW of his own position. Admiral Mitscher then proposed by TBS that TF 58 again reverse course in order to be within attack range of the Japanese by dawn, for he guessed Ozawa's intention of using airfields on Guam to extend his reach.[3]

After an hour-long discussion with his staff, Spruance a little after midnight rejected Mitscher's proposal. His orders were to cover the invasion of Saipan. In the light of these orders and of good strategy TF 58 had to be considered primarily a Covering Force. As such, with battle imminent, it should be close enough to Saipan to shield the beachhead from the enemy but far enough out to avoid embroiling the amphibious forces in the action. Recalling that the Japanese had used flanking forces in the battles of the Coral Sea and of Midway and in actions off Guadalcanal, Spruance sought a position where no enemy units could get behind his back to strike at the invasion forces off Saipan. Through the night therefore he continued to close the Marianas, accepting the risk of placing himself between enemy carriers and enemy airfields—and within range of both.

Dawn on June 19 found TF 58 ninety miles SW of Saipan, 80 miles NW of Guam. Ozawa, with his forces deployed three to four hundred miles WSW of TF 58, could have wished for no better set-up to execute the

---

[3] Mitscher's flagship was at the center of TG 58.3; Spruance's, in the circumference of the same group. Though Mitscher was tactical commander of TF 58, Spruance, as Commander Fifth Fleet, had to concur in all decisions that might affect the entire fleet. In view of his broader responsibilities, it is understandable that Spruance would view the military picture more broadly than Mitscher did.

grand finesse on which he counted to reverse the course of the war and rescue the Empire from defeat.

THE BATTLE OF THE PHILIPPINE SEA: ACTION OF JUNE 19— "THE MARIANAS TURKEY SHOOT"

Had Ozawa realized that TF 58 had already reduced Japanese air power in the Marianas to no more than 30 operational planes, that Clark had destroyed aircraft reinforcements coming down from Japan, and that the aviators sent to the relief of Biak were in no condition to return, he might have been less sanguine about the approaching battle. For he had counted on the island-based planes to strike first and achieve at least 33 per cent attrition of the American fleet before his carrier-squadrons went into action. Aircraft based on Guam did attempt an attack early on June 19, but TF 58 planes pounced on them as they were taking off, shot down a few, and then turned their attention to 19 reinforcements arriving from Truk. In this early morning skirmish, 33 Hellcats destroyed 30 Japanese fighters and bombers. That ended the participation of land-based air in the Battle of the Philippine Sea.

For several hours Mitscher, lacking reliable information of the enemy's whereabouts, simply awaited attack while his aggressive-minded task group commanders fretted. Finally at 1000 radars in Lee's Battle Line detected aircraft at 150 miles, approaching from the west. This, the first of four raids launched by the Mobile Fleet, consisted of 69 planes, including only 16 fighters. Even allowing for his unrealistic expectation of help from the Marianas, it is curious that Ozawa should have sent so few planes. He had 430 carrier aircraft, 222 of which were Zeke fighters. He was not ignorant of American strength, and from air reconnaissance made that morning he knew that his fleet was safely beyond attack range of TF 58.

Mitscher at once ordered all his dive bombers and torpedo bombers into the air. Throughout the day whenever Japanese planes appeared from the west, the American bombers orbited to the east, attacking airstrips on Guam and keeping them virtually unusable. While the enemy planes were regrouping 70 miles away, American fighter directors operating with superb efficiency vectored out more than 450 Hellcats and stacked them at high altitude, whence they swooped down on their neophyte opponents, shooting down more than half and scattering the rest. A few Japanese aircraft penetrated as far as the American Battle Line, where they were blasted with deadly VT-fused ammunition. One bomber made a near miss on the *Minneapolis;* another hit the *South Dakota,* causing 50 casualties but not impairing her fighting efficiency. Only 27 Japanese planes returned to their carriers; all but one of the American planes returned.

Ozawa continued to expend his strength piecemeal. His second raid, 128 planes, was met by Hellcats 60 miles out and cut down to half size. Survivors took further heavy losses over the Battle Line. A few reached the carrier groups and with two near misses damaged an elevator and started small fires in the carrier *Bunker Hill.* Only 31 planes of this raid returned to the Mobile Fleet. Of the 47 planes of the third raid, most failed to find TF 58. They caused no damage and took only seven losses. The 82 planes of Ozawa's final raid became scattered. One group was intercepted far out and cut in half; another reached the American carriers and did minor damage with near misses but was very nearly wiped out. The third group headed for Guam, jettisoning bombs. Here Hellcats intercepted them and shot down 30. Nineteen survivors were wrecked in attempting to land on the cratered runways. Only 11 planes of this final raid returned to their carriers.

During this eight-hour decimation of Japanese air power, which American flyers called the "Marianas Turkey Shoot," other disasters were overtaking the hapless Mobile Fleet. Two American submarines had slipped through the weak screen of the Japanese rear echelon and attacked the heavy carriers. The

Albacore put a single torpedo into Ozawa's flagship, the new *Taiho*. Three hours later the *Cavalla* fired three torpedoes into the veteran *Shokaku*. From ruptured tanks and bunkers, gasoline fumes and explosive vapors from the crude petroleum of Tarakan seeped through the vessels. Damage control parties worked valiantly, but they had developed no techniques adequate to deal with such a situation. In mid-afternoon both carriers blew up with tremendous loss of life. Among the survivors were Ozawa and his staff, who transferred from the sinking *Taiho* to a cruiser and thence to the carrier *Zuikaku*.

Ozawa ordered a general retirement to the northwest for refueling, grimly intending to resume battle the next day, for he believed reports from his flyers that TF 58 was badly crippled. When the tally was in and he learned that his carrier planes had been reduced to an even hundred, the tough little admiral's only reaction was to postpone the proposed attack till the 21st.

THE BATTLE OF THE PHILIPPINE SEA: PURSUIT PHASE, JUNE 19–20

Night had descended before TF 58, then 35 miles west of Rota, had recovered the last of the planes from the Turkey Shoot. Now that the enemy's wings were clipped, Spruance was ready to advance on the Mobile Fleet. Leaving one carrier group behind to cover the Saipan beachhead and to keep Guam and Rota neutralized, Mitscher moved S by W through the night. The choice of course, based on a misestimate of the enemy's position, was unfortunate, for though the Americans were making five knots better speed than the Japanese, they closed the range only slightly. After a fruitless search to westward after daylight on the 20th, Mitscher changed course to NW, but because he was obliged to turn into the easterly wind several times to launch search planes, he ceased to gain on the enemy.

As the day wore on it appeared that the

hoped-for counterstroke would not be delivered after all. Not a single American carrier plane had yet seen the Mobile Fleet, and Mitscher had received no information on Ozawa's position since the *Cavalla* had reported her attack on the *Shokaku* at noon the preceding day. At last toward 1600 the long-awaited word came through. A pilot 280 miles away, at the extreme edge of his search sector, had finally sighted the enemy.

"Well," said Mitscher, "can we make it?" [4]

"We can make it," replied his air operations officer after a pause, "but it's going to be tight."

Admiral Mitscher was grimly aware that the Mobile Fleet was far beyond the acceptable attack range of American carrier planes, that a strike at this distance would have to be made at twilight, and that the flyers would have to head back into darkness against a head wind and make night landings, for which few were trained. With feelings of almost paternal affection for his aviators, he had always sought to minimize the risks of their necessarily risky calling. Yet now, with the enemy at last within his reach, he had no alternative but to attack. "Launch 'em," said he firmly.

THE BATTLE OF THE PHILIPPINE SEA: TWILIGHT AIR BATTLE AND NIGHT RECOVERY, JUNE 20

The flyers were quickly briefed, with orders to concentrate on the Japanese carriers. Then they raced for their planes. A full deck-load strike was in the air by 1630. Thereupon TF 58, having turned into the wind for launching, resumed course toward the enemy in order to close the range for recovery of its returning aircraft. A little over two hours after take-off the American aviators sighted an oilslick, where enemy fueling operations

---

[4] All direct quotations for June 20 are from J. Bryan and Philip Reed, *Mission Beyond Darkness* (New York, 1945), written in part aboard the *Lexington* directly following the battle.

had been hastily broken off. Next they saw an oiler group and, 40 miles beyond this, the three divisions of the Mobile Fleet scattering fanwise to the northwest. While a few planes attacked the oilers, sinking two, the rest split and went after the enemy carrier groups. Speeding past their targets, they circled back in order to put the setting sun behind them.

The northern Japanese group, which had lost the *Shokaku* and the *Taiho,* now included only one carrier, the *Zuikaku,* serving as flagship. Dive bombers set the carrier afire with several bomb hits and strafed the deck and island, killing an officer standing beside Admiral Ozawa on the bridge. Flames roared up so fiercely that Abandon Ship was ordered —and then rescinded as the fires were brought under control. The southern group, Kurita's Van Force, put up an intense anti-aircraft fire, but 16 American bombers accompanied by eight fighters bored in, damaged a battleship and a cruiser and with one bomb ripped up the flight deck of the carrier *Chiyoda* and set her afire. The only Japanese carrier actually sunk in this action was the *Hiyo,* of the center group. This kill of the day was achieved by Avengers which dropped out of a cloud and succeeded in releasing torpedoes at a low altitude, one, possibly two, of which found their mark. Ablaze and racked by internal explosions, the *Hiyo* gradually settled at the bow and went down.[5]

Ozawa had managed to get 75 planes airborne, and these survivors of the Turkey Shoot had given a good account of themselves. Antiaircraft guns and swift-darting Zekes had shot down 20 American aircraft, but Japanese casualties had been much heavier. When the sun set on June 20, losses aboard the battered carriers and in the air left the Mobile Fleet only 35 planes. Japanese naval air power had been struck a blow from which it could not recover.

Their mission completed, the American air groups headed back toward TF 58. Fuel gages in a few of the bombers and torpedo planes were far below the half-full mark; some showed perilously close to empty. Pilots with badly damaged craft were among the first to go down. Those who in the excitement of battle had neglected fuel-conserving measures soon followed. Others wasted fuel in a fruitless attempt to outspeed nightfall. One group took a formal vote by radio to ditch together instead of each continuing until his fuel was exhausted. "O.K.," said the chairman, "here we go."

Mitscher had spread out his three carrier groups to allow more maneuvering room for recovery operations. As the minutes ticked past he prowled restlessly between Flag Plot and Flag Bridge. It was up to him to make another hard decision. If he lighted up the task force he would unquestionably save many a desperate pilot who otherwise must make a water landing, but he would also risk exposing 100,000 men and billions of dollars worth of ships to attack by prowling enemy aircraft and submarines. A little after 2000 Air Plot announced the approach of the first of the returning planes, whereupon the task force turned into the east wind to take them aboard. Mitscher went back into Flag Plot, took a seat, and puffed thoughtfully on a cigarette. At length he said to Captain Burke, his chief of staff, "Turn on the lights." [6] Then he went back to the bridge. On went running lights, truck lights, and glow lights to outline the flight decks, while 5-inch guns of the screen fired star shell, and searchlights pointed straight upward as homing beacons.

Landing signal officers, gesturing with fluorescent batons, waved in the first few planes smoothly enough, but as newly-arrived aircraft swarmed into the landing circles, the officers were obliged to wave off far more than they landed. When planes exhausted their last drops of fuel and went down, destroyers moved busily through the fleet seeking survivors. Ordered to land wherever they could find a flight deck, some pilots shopped through the fleet for an uncrowded landing circle. One desperate pilot disregarded a wave-off from the *Lexington* and

---

[5] Thereby restoring confidence in the American aerial torpedo, which had performed poorly at Midway.

[6] Arleigh ("31-Knot") Burke, who had made his reputation with the destroyers in the Solomons Campaign, had joined TF 58 at Mitscher's request just before the raid on the Palaus.

crashed into six newly-landed planes, killing two men and injuring half a dozen others. Two planes in quick succession disregarded signals and crash landed on the *Bunker Hill,* killing two men and injuring four. Aboard the *Enterprise* a fighter and a bomber landed together and incredibly did not crash, the fighter's tail hook catching the second cable and the bomber's, the fifth.

Since the battle over the Mobile Fleet, 80 American aircraft had ditched or crashed on landing. After completing recovery of planes at 2232, TF 58 resumed course NW and through the night proceeded at 16 knots along the path of the returning flyers. By this means destroyers and float planes rescued more than three quarters of the 209 aviators who had made water landings.

Spruance estimated that the two hours the American force had spent on an easterly course plus the subsequent slow speed to facilitate rescues had permitted the fleeing enemy to get beyond reach of a second air strike. This opinion was confirmed after dawn when long-range Avengers found the Mobile Fleet making 20 knots on a north-westerly course 360 miles away. Task Force 58 continued northwest through the day on the 21st in a fruitless search for cripples, but at sunset Spruance ordered the pursuit abandoned, and the task force turned back east.[7]

THE BATTLE OF THE PHILIPPINE SEA: SPRUANCE'S DECISION

Though Admiral King emphatically concurred with Admiral Spruance's decision to remain close to Saipan until the enemy's wings had been clipped, Spruance himself regretted that his responsibilities had kept him tethered to the beachhead. "It would have been much more satisfactory," he afterwards

said, "if, instead of waiting in a covering position, I could have steamed to the westward in search of the Japanese fleet." [8]

With this point of view Samuel Eliot Morison has since ventured to disagree.[9] He points out that if Mitscher had moved into attack range of the Mobile Fleet on June 19, his planes would have encountered the heavy antiaircraft fire of Kurita's Van Force while the Japanese heavy carriers were still a hundred miles away. By remaining on the defensive near the Marianas, TF 58 had all its fighter planes available for interception. These aircraft, with able assistance from Lee's Battle Line and the carrier groups, shot down most of the Japanese planes at near the limit of their attack range and destroyed the planes on Guam as well. Thus, says Morison, TF 58 on the 19th was at the optimum position to hurt the enemy. True, most of the Japanese carriers got away, but without trained aviators their only function thereafter was to decoy Admiral Halsey the following October into doing what Admiral Spruance refused to do in June. In the light of subsequent events it is clear that the Marianas Turkey Shoot made the defeat of Japan inevitable.

CONQUEST OF THE SOUTHERN MARIANAS

As the two marine divisions on Saipan pivoted for their drive to the northwest, Holland Smith ordered the 27th Infantry Division to the center of the new front. But the hesitant leadership and deliberate tactics which had slowed down this division on Makin and again on Eniwetok now brought it so nearly to a standstill that the inner flanks of both marine divisions became more and more exposed as they pressed forward. His patience exhausted, General Smith summarily replaced the 27th Division's commanding general.

Thereafter, well supported by naval guns and carrier aircraft, the Americans advanced

---

[7] Since submarines *Albacore* and *Cavalla* had not stayed to observe the results of their marksmanship on June 19, and reports from the flyers were often conflicting, American evaluators could assume with confidence that only one Japanese heavy carrier had been sunk and two or three light carriers damaged.

[8] "The Victory in the Pacific," *Journal of the Royal United Service Institution* (November 1946), 549.

[9] VIII, 315-316.

together up the narrowing north peninsula, where the enemy was deeply entrenched in a network of fortified caves and underground defenses. At the end of the first week in July, some 3,000 Japanese, finding themselves being forced into an ever-diminishing perimeter, struck out in a desperate early morning banzai charge, broke through a gap in the 27th Division front, and surged forward nearly two miles before the Americans halted them with fearful slaughter. Holland Smith thereupon withdrew the army troops into reserve. Three more days of fighting carried the marines to the northeast tip of the island. That ended organized Japanese resistance on Saipan, but several thousand enemy soldiers still had to be routed from by-passed caves and ravines before Admiral Spruance could declare the island secure.

All through the Saipan campaign, bombers and navy guns had been intermittently softening up nearby Tinian. As the campaign came to an end, most of the artillery on Saipan, nearly 200 field pieces, was placed hub to hub on the southwest shore to take over bombardment of the northern half of Tinian while the ships and planes continued working over the rest. By western standards the defending garrison of the smaller island in this hopeless situation might properly and laudably have surrendered to avoid fruitless sacrifice of life, but here, as elsewhere, stern Japanese military tradition required that the defenders fight to the last man.

Because Tinian's two best landing beaches, one in the southwest and one in the east, were heavily mined and fortified, Admiral Turner chose to invade over two very narrow beaches on the northwest coast. Achieving a secure landing through these restricted corridors required surprise, speed, and new logistic techniques. On July 24, while the 2nd Marine Division staged a mock assault on the southern beach to bemuse the defenders, the 4th Marine Division was transported to the area off the northwest beaches. From LST's amtracs carried the invaders ashore in 15 closely spaced waves. This assault was, as it were, the Saipan invasion turned sidewise, making up in momentum what it lacked in breadth. Once ashore, the marines fanned

out quickly, while amtracs and DUKW's carried supplies directly to dumps. The surprised Japanese offered some resistance with rifle fire and a few shells, but by nightfall the 4th Division and part of the 2nd, amply supplied with tanks and artillery, had established a perimeter a mile wide and more than a half mile deep. The complete success of this risky assault attests to the flexibility which American amphibious techniques had attained by mid-1944.

Because the canefields of generally flat Tinian offered little opportunity for the Japanese to take protective cover, the marines abandoned their usual rushing tactics for a methodical advance behind artillery barrages. Now for the first time planes used the deadly napalm fire bomb to destroy pockets of enemy resistance. At the end of a week the two divisions had reached the southern end of the island. Here among caves and rough terrain the Japanese made a final stand, and though Tinian was declared secure on August 1, three more months were required to clear out the last of the concealed enemy.

Twenty-five-mile-long Guam was the largest and best fortified of the Marianas. Here, the Japanese garrison of 19,000 had set up defenses, from obstacles offshore to gun emplacements in the terraced hills, more complex and complete than anything the Americans had encountered thus far in the campaign. Yet the conquest of Guam proved relatively easy because Rear Admiral Conolly, Commander Guam Attack Force, and Major General Roy S. Geiger USMC, commanding the new III Amphibious Corps, studied and expertly applied the lessons of Saipan. American carrier planes and underwater demolition teams did their work well, but the gunnery vessels were downright superb. Thirteen days of sustained, methodical naval bombardment demoralized the garrison and rendered the island relatively defenseless.

In the morning of July 21, 1944, the III Corps arrived off the west coast of Guam and headed for shore in amtracs under a rolling naval barrage. The 3rd Marine Division landed north of Orote Peninsula, and the 1st

Provisional Marine Brigade,[10] followed by the 77th Infantry Division, landed to the south. From the two beachheads the invaders advanced into the hills. Despite enemy artillery and desperate banzai charges, more senseless and fruitless than usual, the 3rd and the 77th Divisions forced their way to a meeting in the hilly interior, sealing off Orote Peninsula, which the 1st Marine Brigade captured, thereby enabling the Americans to use the Orote airfield and nearby Apra Harbor.

The surviving Japanese now abandoned their positions and hastily retreated to the northeast. Thither they were pursued by the invaders, the marines on the left and the army on the right, with the fleet providing call fire by day and harassing fire and star shell illumination by night. Throughout the advance, Army, Navy, and Marine Corps teamed together in complete harmony and with mutual respect. On August 10 Guam was declared secure, though as on Saipan there were still at large detached bands of Japanese, some of whom did not surrender until long after the end of the war.

The conquest of the southern Marianas had cost the lives of 5,200 American soldiers and marines, but for each American killed, ten Japanese had lost their lives. A score of Pacific Fleet amphibious and support craft had been struck off Saipan and Tinian by enemy planes and shore batteries. In general the damage had been light, but a torpedoed LCI had to be scuttled, and several larger vessels including the *Maryland* were obliged to withdraw for repairs.

Such losses cannot be considered severe in view of the enormous advantages to the Americans in gaining positions athwart the enemy's inner defense perimeter: jumping-off points and logistic bases for further conquests westward; a break in Japan's direct air staging line to New Guinea and the Carolines; a base for stepped-up submarine attack on Japanese communications with the Southern Resources Area; and, above all, airfields from which the new B-29's could blast the industrial concentration in the Tokyo area.

---

[10] Nucleus of the future 6th Marine Division.

In late November 1944 a hundred of the big bombers winged north from Saipan to bring the war home to the enemy.

No such demonstration was needed to convince the Emperor and high Japanese and military officials that the loss of the Marianas marked the beginning of the end for them. The Tojo government fell and was succeeded by a cabinet to whom the Emperor made known his desire for early peace negotiations. Yet so binding was the Japanese military code, so rigid the demands of Oriental "face," that for a whole year no official could bring himself to initiate steps for ending hostilities. On the Allied side, the goal of "unconditional surrender" set by Roosevelt and Churchill forbade the proffering of terms which might have served as bases for negotiations.

NEW STRATEGIC DECISIONS

Between the two Allied lines of transpacific advance—via New Guinea and via the islands of the Central Pacific—the Japanese-held Carolines now formed a deep salient, 1,600 miles from Ponape in the east to the Palaus in the west, with Truk about half way between. To seal off this salient from reinforcement and thereby protect the Allied inner flanks, Admiral Nimitz proposed capturing bases in the western Carolines—Yap, Ulithi, and the Palaus. While the Spruance-Turner-Smith team was busy conquering the Marianas, he ordered Admiral Halsey up from the South Pacific to take over planning and execution of this new operation.

When Halsey arrived at Pearl Harbor he soon found himself involved in another decision: Where next? MacArthur, as always, favored an invasion of the Philippine Islands; some naval officers preferred invading Formosa or the China coast. Late in July, President Roosevelt, at a conference in Hawaii, weighed General MacArthur's argument that there were moral and political as well as strategic reasons for not by-passing the Philippines. Concurring with the General, the President directed the Central Pacific and the Southwest Pacific commands to combine forces in a single gigantic operation directed against Mindanao.

Halsey objected to the western Carolines operation as both too costly and unnecessary, but Nimitz overruled his dissent, for now that an early return to the Philippines had definitely been decided upon, he regarded capture of the nearby Palau Islands as doubly imperative. He did however agree to by-pass the main island, Babelthuap, and confine operations to the smaller Peleliu and Angaur in the south, where from captured airfields American planes could neutralize the rest of the island group and cover the right flank of the Philippines invasion force. The landing on Peleliu was set for September 15, 1944. On the same date MacArthur's Southwest Pacific forces were to invade Morotai, half way between New Guinea and Mindanao. A month later MacArthur planned to seize the Talaud Islands, half way between Morotai and Mindanao. The invasion of Mindanao was to be in November. (See map, page 774.)

With the securing of the southern Marianas, Admirals Spruance and Turner and General Holland Smith returned to Pearl Harbor to rest from their labors and to plan future operations. In late August, while Halsey was en route in his flagship *New Jersey* for a rendezvous with the Fast Carrier Task Force, he officially relieved Spruance. The Central Pacific Force thereupon became the United States Third Fleet, and TF 58 became TF 38, with Admiral Mitscher remaining in command. Under Halsey the amphibious craft were assigned to Vice Admiral Theodore Wilkinson, Commander Third Amphibious Force, and the Central Pacific invasion troops were assigned to General Geiger's III Amphibious Corps.

MOROTAI AND THE WESTERN CAROLINES

The concurrent mid-September invasions by the Southwest Pacific and by the Central Pacific forces provide a study in contrasts. Except for the hazard and inconvenience of natural beach obstacles, the capture of Morotai proved to be one of the easiest of the war; while the intricate defenses of Peleliu made the invasion of the Palaus one of the most difficult and costly assaults up to that time.

Admiral Barbey's Seventh Amphibious Force, carrying 28,000 army troops, by-passed heavily garrisoned Halmahera, largest of the Moluccas, and took lightly held Morotai by surprise. While Third and Seventh Fleet carrier planes and Allied land-based aircraft isolated the target, a two-hour naval bombardment sent the few hundred defenders scuttling to the hills. A rough, almost impassable coral reef and mud flats into which troops sank to their hips, obliged the invaders to abandon their original beachhead and seek out a somewhat better landing site. But, despite further delays caused by torrential rains and lack of coral suitable for surfacing, engineers had two bomber fields and a fighter strip ready on Morotai in time to cover the left flank of the Philippines invasion.

Simultaneously, nearly 500 miles to the northeast, the 1st Marine Division was finding rough going on Peleliu. The operation here was a small scale duplicate of the Saipan operation, with inadequate naval bombardment and a bitterly contested beachhead. As on Saipan the marines, after capturing the airfield on the southern plain, pivoted to the left and advanced up a hilly northeast peninsula. Here the Japanese had withdrawn into an elaborate system of more than 500 natural and artificial caves, mostly interconnected, some fitted with steel doors and all skillfully camouflaged or concealed by vegetation.

As the marines penetrated this maze of caverns, their losses rose. Clearly the Japanese had studied and were applying the lessons of the Marianas. They made no banzai charges but, employing a carefully calculated defense in depth, sold their lives dearly. To counter such opposition more American troops were needed. The 81st Infantry Division had stood by as a floating reserve through the first phase of the Peleliu assault, but since Major General William H.

Rupertus, commanding the 1st Marine Division, asked for no help, the infantrymen had proceeded to invade nearby Angaur Island and distant Ulithi Atoll. Fortunately, Angaur proved to be lightly defended and Ulithi not defended at all. General Geiger was able to detach one regiment from the Angaur operation and rush it across to Peleliu—over the protests of General Rupertus, who disliked mixing soldiers and marines. Bazookas, demolition charges, and long-range flamethrowers provided an eventual answer to the new Japanese resourcefulness found on Peleliu, but clearing out the enemy was a slow process, costly in American lives.

The bloodless seizure of Ulithi gave the Pacific Fleet another broad, island-ringed lagoon to serve as an important anchorage and logistic base, supplementing Majuro, Kwajalein, and Eniwetok. It must be acknowledged however that Halsey had been right about the Palaus. They were probably not worth the 10,000 casualties they cost. The airfields on Peleliu and Angaur were not operational in time to support the initial assault on the Philippines, and the Japanese simply did not possess sufficient air power to make use of the Palaus even had they retained possession of them.

A SHIFT IN STRATEGY

On September 11, Admiral Halsey joined TF 38 and observed air strikes against the central Philippines in strategic support of the impending invasions of Morotai and Peleliu. The results were startling. At the cost of eight planes and ten men, TF 38 destroyed at least 200 enemy aircraft and sank a dozen freighters and a tanker.

Convinced by these results that the central Philippines were "a hollow shell with weak defenses and skimpy facilities" [11] Halsey sent to Nimitz an urgent message recommending that the planned seizure of Yap and the Palaus be abandoned forthwith and that the ground troops for those operations be turned over to MacArthur for an invasion of the

central Philippine island of Leyte at the earliest possible date. Nimitz, willing to bypass Yap but insisting upon the capture of the Palaus, forwarded Halsey's recommendation to the Joint Chiefs of Staff, then meeting with Roosevelt, Churchill, and the British chiefs of staff at the second Quebec conference. The Joint Chiefs thereupon radioed for MacArthur's opinion. When MacArthur concurred in the speed-up plan,[12] they ordered the proposed landings on Yap, the Talaud Islands, and Mindanao abandoned and set October 20, 1944 as target date for the invasion of Leyte.

While these messages concerning high strategic policy were flashing around the world, TF 38 deployed to support both the Morotai and the Palau landings. Nimitz turned the Third Amphibious Force over to MacArthur's Southwest Pacific command and ordered the Eastern Attack Force, then en route to Yap with the XXIV Army Corps, to shape course instead for Manus. As supporting naval forces were released from the Palau-Ulithi operation, these too headed for Manus and Hollandia. The U. S. Third Fleet was thus stripped down virtually to TF 38. Practically everything else was added to the Southwest Pacific Forces in preparation for the assault on Leyte.

THE THIRD FLEET PAVES THE WAY

While the enormously augmented Southwest Pacific Forces were assembling for the coming invasion, Halsey set out with the Third Fleet to soften up the enemy. After destroying more hundreds of aircraft and sinking numerous vessels in carrier air strikes against the central and northern Philippines, TF 38 headed north and churned up the airstrips on Okinawa. Halsey next swung back south, feinted at Luzon with a fighter sweep, and then moved in for an attack on Formosa.

---

[11] W. F. Halsey and J. Bryan, *Admiral Halsey's Story* (New York, 1947), 199.

[12] Actually the MacArthur reply was sent by his staff in his name and without his knowledge, for the General was then at sea en route to Morotai observing strict radio silence.

Anticipating this move, Vice Admiral Shigeru Fukudome, commanding Japanese air forces in the area, had already begun assembling additional aircraft. Avoiding Admiral Kakuta's mistake in bringing unescorted bombers to the Marianas the preceding February, Fukudome brought to Formosa only fighter planes. His night-operating torpedo bombers, designated the Typhoon Attack Force,[13] he left in southern Japan ready when called upon to attack the Third Fleet via the Ryukyus. Fukudome thought that by this disposition of force he was setting a trap for Halsey similar to the one Spruance had set for Ozawa in the Battle of the Philippine Sea. He would meet the full force of the American air attack with a concentration of fighter planes operating over their own antiaircraft batteries on Formosa. Then when he had stripped the Third Fleet of planes, as Ozawa had been stripped in the Marianas Turkey Shoot, the Typhoon Force would counterattack and destroy the defenseless American fleet.

Fukudome was caught in his own trap, for the Japanese aviators were not sufficiently trained to deal with experienced, well-drilled American flyers. Attacking first on the morning of October 12, TF 38 aircraft in two days destroyed nearly every plane on Formosa, knocked down hangars, blew up supply dumps, and sank nine freighters and six tankers at a cost of 43 American aircraft. When hurried repairs to Okinawa airfields permitted the Typhoon Force late on the 13th to begin staging through, the Japanese torpedo bombers likewise took heavy losses. They succeeded however in torpedoing cruisers Canberra and Houston,[14] which had to be taken in tow. Elated by this moderate success and in the darkness mistaking their own flaming aircraft for burning American vessels, the Japanese aviators flashed the

word back home that they had sunk 11 carriers, two battleships, and three cruisers. They thereby set off victory celebrations in Japan, and Radio Tokyo broadcast the fictitious Japanese triumph to the world. Taking advantage of the enemy's fond delusion, Halsey set a trap of his own. He temporarily withdrew the bulk of the Third Fleet from Formosan waters, leaving behind the damaged cruisers and a single carrier group as bait to lure out the Mobile Fleet and thus precipitate a sea battle.

Admiral Toyoda took Halsey's bait. He sent all his better-trained carrier air squadrons to help Fukudome's Typhoon Force complete its supposed victory and ordered out Vice Admiral Kiyohide Shima's Second Striking Force of cruisers and destroyers "to mop up remaining enemy elements." But long-range Japanese search planes, quartering the seas for a final check, at length found all the groups of the U. S. Third Fleet and reported none noticeably impaired. So Admiral Halsey's trap was exposed, and Admiral Shima prudently retired to the Ryukyus. Fukudome's planes got in one last lick however, firing another torpedo into the battered Houston. That ended the "Battle off Formosa." Both damaged American cruisers, saved by efficient damage control, at length reached Ulithi under tow.

The rest of the Third Fleet, having wiped out the greater portion of Japanese land-based air power and the only effective part of Japanese carrier air power, proceeded to station off Leyte to support the invasion of the Philippines. Neutralization of Formosa as a staging base had by this time been taken over by the B-29's of Major General Claire L. Chennault's Fourteenth Air Force operating out of airfields in western China.

At last the two lines of advance, via the Southwest Pacific and via the Central Pacific, were merging in a single operation. A number of military commentators and analysts have suggested that to achieve coordination in the common effort, all forces should have come under a single local commander. Instead, the nearest commander of all forces present was the President of the

---

[13] So called because they were "to be used in total darkness or in very bad weather," another example of Japanese reliance on night and foul weather to offset numerical inferiority. Shigeru Fukudome, "Strategic Aspects of the Battle off Formosa," U. S. Naval Institute Proceedings (December 1952), 1285-1295.

[14] The second cruisers in World War II of the same name. The U.S.S. Canberra was the first American warship to be named for a foreign city.

United States, half a world away in Washington.

THE INVASION OF LEYTE

General MacArthur and his staff had less than a month in which to assemble forces from all over the Pacific and to plan for the invasion of Leyte. Vice Admiral Kinkaid's Seventh Fleet, expanded to more than 700 ships, Australian and American, would transport and provide close support for Lieutenant General Walter Krueger's Sixth Army, an invasion and occupation force of close to 200,000 American troops. Admiral Halsey's Third Fleet was to furnish strategic support and launch strikes as the situation required. Lieutenant General Kenney's Fifth Air Force would operate from airfields on Leyte as soon as these were ready. In late September, while the Third Fleet anchored briefly at Ulithi preceding the raid on Okinawa, Halsey and members of his staff flew to Hollandia and spent three days with MacArthur and Kinkaid working out details for close coordination between the Third and Seventh Fleets.

On October 11 and 12, 1944, the first elements of the Leyte assault forces sortied from Hollandia and from Seeadler Harbor in the Admiralties. On the 17th, advance units of the fleet, in order to secure the flanks of the oncoming invasion forces, put United States Rangers ashore on the islands guarding the entrance to Leyte Gulf. At the same time minesweepers and underwater demolition teams began their important preparatory work off the Leyte beachheads, while destroyers, cruisers, and old battleships under Rear Admiral Jesse B. Oldendorf and escort carrier groups under Rear Admiral Thomas L. Sprague came in for a three-day pounding of Japanese coastal defenses.

In the early hours of October 20, the amphibious attack forces entered the Gulf and steamed to positions for the assault—Admiral Barbey's Seventh Amphibious Force off Tacloban, capital of Leyte, and Admiral Wilkinson's Third Amphibious Force 11 miles farther south. At the same time one regimental combat team was lifted down to Panaon Island to seize a base whence PT boats could command the southern entrance to Surigao Strait. After a final bombardment of the shoreline and interior, troops headed for the marshy beaches in a variety of craft —LCPR's, LCT's, LST's, and even amtracs, which had been loaded aboard Third Amphibious Force vessels for the canceled invasion of reef-surrounded Yap. The only opposition to the assault came from mortars in the hills to which the Japanese had retreated. These the cruisers soon silenced with fragmentation projectiles. Before the day ended, both gulf beachheads had expanded well inland, and the northern beachhead enclosed the Tacloban airstrip.

Early on the 20th the Japanese had begun a series of minor air attacks which, while never seriously threatening the invasion, somewhat delayed unloading. One enemy plane, coming undetected through a rain squall, dropped a torpedo which tore a hole 25 feet across in the hull of the light cruiser *Honolulu*. More ominous, though less damaging, was the attack on H.M.A.S. *Australia*, for the pilot of an armed bomber deliberately crashed into her superstructure.

A few hours after the first landings on Leyte, General MacArthur, accompanied by Philippine President Sergio Osmeña and members of his cabinet, came ashore. Stepping up to a Signal Corps radio microphone the General broadcast his speech of liberation for all Filipinos to hear: "This is the Voice of Freedom, General MacArthur speaking. People of the Philippines! I have returned. By the grace of Almighty God our force stands again on Philippine soil, consecrated in the blood of two peoples. As the line of battle rolls forward to bring you within the zone of operations, rise and strike. . . . Rally to me. Let the indomitable spirit of Bataan and Corregidor lead on!"

46

The Battle for Leyte Gulf

THE BATTLE FOR LEYTE Gulf, touched off by the American invasion of the Philippines in October 1944, is for complexity and magnitude without parallel in naval history. Lasting four days, covering an area of nearly 30,000 square miles, it was really a whole series of battles and subsidiary actions. Among these the most important were the Battle of the Sibuyan Sea of October 24, and the Battle of Surigao Strait, the Battle off Cape Engaño, and the Battle off Samar on October 25. When the long-drawn-out conflict at length subsided, the Imperial Japanese Navy no longer existed as an effective fighting force, and the Americans commanded the Pacific.

ACTIVATING THE
SHO OPERATION

When the Americans broke Japan's inner defense perimeter by seizing the southern Marianas, the Imperial High Command readjusted its strategy in preparation for last-ditch defense. The home islands had of course to be defended, but almost equally vital to Japanese security were the Philippines, Formosa, and the Ryukyus. Behind the screen of these offshore islands the tanker fleet, though heavily depleted by American submarines and carrier aircraft, could still transport from the East Indies to Japan a trickle of the oil without which conduct of modern war is impossible.

All the efforts of the surviving tankers however were not enough to provide fuel for the Mobile Fleet in home waters, where Admiral Toyoda wanted to keep it united while he set about offsetting the fearful losses of the Marianas Turkey Shoot. So Toyoda perforce split up the fleet. Retaining the so-called Main Force of carriers in Japan for repairs and pilot training, he sent Vice Admiral Takeo Kurita with the First Striking Force of surface vessels to operate in the Singapore area, where oil was plentiful. At the same time he ordered Vice Admiral Kiyohide Shima's small Second Striking Force down from defense duty in the Kuriles to supplement the inadequate carrier screen.

Toyoda hoped to reunite the Mobile Fleet before the Americans struck again, but for lack of fuel and lack of trained carrier pilots, he made no more plans to send the fleet out to meet the enemy. Instead, he would let the Americans come to him, whereupon he would strike first with massed land-based air power and then seek a decision with his concentrated fleet. This new plan, called the *Sho* (Victory) Operation, was worked out in four variations, one for each area where the

Americans might be expected to strike next: *Sho* 1, for defense of the Philippine Islands; *Sho* 2, for defense of Formosa, the Ryukyus and Southern Japan; *Sho* 3, for defense of the main Japanese home islands, Kyushu, Shikoku, and Honshu; *Sho* 4, for defense of the northernmost home island, Hokkaido. If at the time of the next American assault all of Japan's sea power could be massed at the point of impact under cover of all of Japan's land-based air power, which would strike a first, devastating blow, then Japan might yet hope for a new Battle of Tsushima to turn the tide of war—provided of course that enough Japanese carrier pilots could be trained in time to complete the destruction begun by the land-based air force and further provided that the Americans made many mistakes and the Japanese few or none. Chances were slight that the Imperial Forces would be favored by such optimum conditions, but on this desperate improbability the Japanese based their last hopes.

The *Sho* Operation began to come apart at the seams in mid-October, when Halsey's sweep over the Philippines and to the north still further cut down Japan's thin margin of tankers and transports and destroyed 800 planes, including carrier aircraft that Toyoda had ill-advisedly committed to the defense of Formosa. Shima, as we have seen, sortied from the Inland Sea to mop up the "remnants" of the U. S. Third Fleet and then hastily retired to the Ryukyus when he learned that the Formosa-based aircraft had by no means shattered the Americans as Japanese pilots had reported.

On October 17, when United States Rangers landed in Leyte Gulf, the Mobile Fleet was dispersed as follows:

(1) The Main Force of the Mobile Fleet, commanded by Vice Admiral Jisaburo Ozawa, in the Inland Sea between Honshu and Shikoku. The Main Force included the heavy carrier *Zuikaku*, Ozawa's flagship, the light carriers *Zuiho, Chitose,* and *Chiyoda,* with 116 planes in all; the *Hyuga* and the *Ise,* converted battleships with flight decks aft but never actually used as aircraft carriers; and a light screen of cruisers and destroyers.

(2) The First Striking Force of battleships, cruisers, and destroyers, commanded by Vice Admiral Kurita, at Lingga Roads near Singapore. This force was organized in three sections, each centered on a battleship division. The First Section contained the battleship *Nagato* and the mighty 64,000-ton, 18-inch superbattleships *Yamato* and *Musashi;* the Second Section contained the older battleships *Kongo* and *Haruna;* and the Third Section contained the older battleships *Yamashiro* and *Fuso.*

(3) The Second Striking Force, consisting of three cruisers and seven destroyers, commanded by Vice Admiral Shima, at Amami in the Ryukyus.[1]

Though the Mobile Fleet, as a whole, was under the nominal command of Vice Admiral Ozawa, Admiral Toyoda, as Commander in Chief Combined Fleet, retained in his own hands the strategic command of all naval forces in the *Sho* Operation.

With the landing of the Rangers, the Japanese High Command immediately activated *Sho* 1. Though they knew that the Imperial Fleet was vastly outnumbered and that their land-based air was now entirely inadequate for the grandiose concentration they had planned, they had no thought of not putting up a fight. For if they lost the Philippines they must lose everything. The Mobile Fleet would be permanently divided, and they would have no means of supplying Kurita's force with ammunition or Ozawa's and Shima's forces with fuel. The fleet could be defeated in detail and Japan blockaded.

So Toyoda took advanced headquarters in southern Formosa, in order to maintain close radio contact with his forces in the Philippines area. Kurita's First Striking Force began moving northeastward with orders to head for Leyte Gulf, eluding the United States Third Fleet if possible, engaging and defeating the Seventh Fleet if necessary, in order to sink the Allied transports in the Gulf and destroy the troops on the beach. Shima's Second Striking Force headed for the Pescadores, west of Formosa,

---

[1] Administratively the Main Force was designated Third Fleet; the First Striking Force, Second Fleet; and the Second Striking Force, Fifth Fleet.

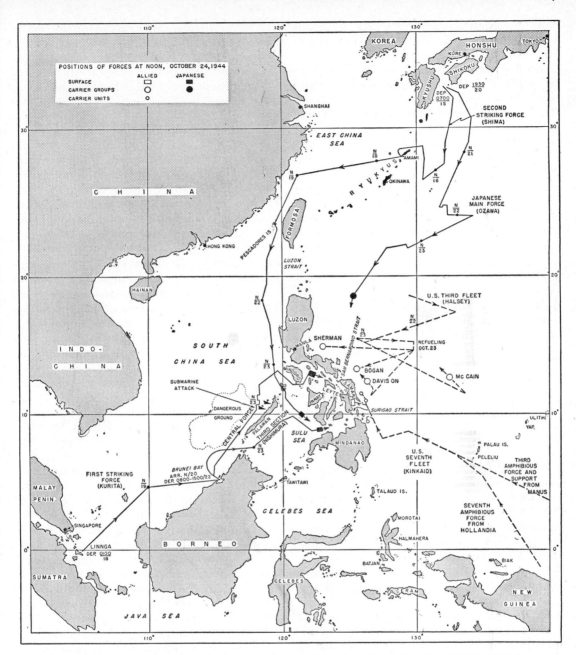

APPROACH OF ALLIED AND JAPANESE NAVAL FORCES TO LEYTE GULF,
OCTOBER, 1944
Unless otherwise indicated, the daily positions are as of 1200 hours

and thence shaped course southward to as-
sist Kurita. At the same time Ozawa's Main
Force prepared to sortie from the Inland
Sea. The Main Force could offer little direct

assistance in the impending battle, for the
training of new carrier pilots was so far from
complete and losses of aviators over Formosa
had been so severe that there remained few

flyers sufficiently skilled to land on flight decks. In this extremity the Japanese carriers were ordered to commit suicide by decoying the Third Fleet away from the vicinity of Leyte Gulf, leaving the transports and beachhead open to attack by Kurita's surface force. Toyoda, who had correctly guessed that Spruance would not let himself be drawn away from Saipan, now estimated that the bellicose Halsey, captivated by the possibility of a carrier battle, might well be lured away from Leyte. It was assumed that in serving as bait the Main Force would be destroyed. Such was the humiliating final mission of the once-formidable carrier force which had opened the war in the Pacific by attacking Pearl Harbor.

The First Striking Force entered Brunei Bay, North Borneo, at noon on October 20, just as MacArthur was gaining a foothold on Leyte. At Brunei Kurita's ships refueled and then, in line with the usual Japanese strategy of operating in divisions, split up. The First and Second Sections (five battleships, twelve cruisers, and 15 destroyers), under Kurita's direct command, left Brunei early on the 22nd and shaped course west of Palawan Island with orders to cross the Sibuyan Sea, penetrate San Bernardino Strait, and attack Leyte Gulf from the north at dawn on the 25th. The Third Section (two old battleships, the heavy cruiser *Mogami,* and four destroyers) under Vice Admiral Shoji Nishimura sortied that afternoon and headed via the Sulu and Mindanao Seas for Surigao Strait in order to strike at Leyte Gulf from the south in coordination with Kurita's attack from the north. Shima's Second Striking Force, coming down from the Pescadores, was ordered to assist in the attack via Surigao Strait but with no clear directive how or to what extent it was to cooperate with Nishimura's Third Section. By this time Ozawa's Main Force had sortied from the Inland Sea and was en route for the Philippines. Thus at one time four separate Japanese forces were converging on Leyte. The success of so complex an operation depended upon teamwork and perfect timing. These in turn depended to a large extent upon good radio communication; but

the transmitter in Ozawa's flagship, *Zuikaku,* cranky from the beginning, at length fell silent without Ozawa ever realizing that he was not making himself heard by the widely-scattered segments of the Mobile Fleet.

FIRST BLOOD

Kurita's First and Second Sections, which together we shall call the Central Force, soon ran into trouble. An hour after dawn on October 23, the Central Force was attacked off Palawan by the *Darter* and the *Dace,* two of the American submarines assigned to patrol the approaches to the Philippines. Kurita's flagship, the heavy cruiser *Atago,* was hit by four torpedoes from the *Darter* and sank in 20 minutes. Two more torpedoes, passing under the *Atago*'s stern, so severely crippled the heavy cruiser *Takao* that she was obliged to return to Brunei escorted by a pair of destroyers. Just as the *Atago* was going down, the *Dace* put a spread of torpedoes into a third heavy cruiser, the *Maya,* whose magazines ignited and blew her apart in a series of searing blasts.

From the sinking *Atago* Kurita and his staff managed to escape to a destroyer and transferred thence to the *Yamato,* which became the new flagship. Early on the 24th the surviving vessels of the Central Force passed south of Mindoro Island into the Sibuyan Sea. Kurita, shaken by his experience of the day before, realized that the presence of his force was now known to the Americans and that he was coming within easy attack range of Halsey's carriers eastward of Luzon.

Nearly 200 miles to the south, in the Sulu Sea, Nishimura's Third Section, with Shima's Striking Force trailing some 60 miles behind, was also coming within range of Halsey's carrier planes. The main phase of the battle was about to begin.

DISPOSITION OF THE ALLIED FORCES

During the first stages of the Leyte invasion, Allied naval forces, almost entirely

American, were disposed in three layers off the beachhead.

Inside Leyte Gulf was the greater part of the enlarged Seventh Fleet, including the two amphibious forces of transports, cargo vessels, and amphibious craft, and also a fire support group of six old battleships and cruisers and destroyers, commanded by Rear Admiral Jesse B. Oldendorf. Here also were Commander Seventh Fleet Vice Admiral Kinkaid in the communication ship *Wasatch,* and General MacArthur in the cruiser *Nashville.*

Far down in Surigao Strait were 39 PT boats guarding the approaches to Leyte Gulf from the south. To the east just outside the Gulf were three Seventh Fleet carrier task units commanded by Rear Admiral Thomas L. Sprague. These units, which included 18 escort carriers screened by destroyers and destroyer escorts, were on antisubmarine, antiaircraft, and ground support patrol. East of Luzon were the combat vessels of Admiral Halsey's Third Fleet, now stripped down to TF 38, commanded by Admiral Mitscher.[2] The four task groups making up TF 38 were at this time commanded by Vice Admiral John S. McCain and Rear Admirals Gerald F. Bogan, Frederick C. Sherman, and Ralph E. Davison. These groups, though not uniform, averaged 23 ships each—two heavy carriers, two light carriers, two new battleships, three cruisers, and 14 destroyers. Halsey, in the *New Jersey,* was with Bogan's group; Mitscher, in the *Lexington,* was with Sherman's.

Because the landings on Leyte had been successfully carried out without hindrance from the Japanese fleet, Halsey seized the opportunity to refuel and rearm his ships and to relieve his exhausted crews. Intending to replenish one task group at a time, he had already dispatched McCain's group towards Ulithi when he received the *Darter's* report of Kurita's approach from the west. Evidently the Japanese fleet was about to strike after all. Halsey let McCain's group

---

[2] Because the Third Fleet had thus been temporarily stripped down to build up the Seventh Fleet, the titles Third Fleet and TF 38 are sometimes used interchangeably in this chapter.

continue southeastward, but at once ordered his other three groups to rendezvous with oilers for refueling and then to head in closer to the Philippines. Fanning out during the night, the groups by first light on October 24 had reached their assigned positions 125 miles apart—Sherman's off Luzon, Bogan's off San Bernardino Strait, Davison's off Leyte Gulf. Before 0630 planes were away from all three groups, searching north, west, and south.

THE BATTLE OF THE SIBUYAN SEA

Towards 0900 on the 24th, aircraft from Davison's group discovered Nishimura's Third Section in the Sulu Sea and attacked at once, slightly damaging the old battleship *Fuso* and a destroyer without however cutting down the speed of either. A little later a single plane sighted Shima's Second Striking Force also in the Sulu Sea, but this was assumed to be merely a detached portion of Nishimura's command. Halsey's interest in these small southern forces was overshadowed by news of much bigger game farther north, for Bogan's flyers had sighted Kurita's Central Force south of Mindoro, about to enter the Sibuyan Sea. Leaving the southern groups to Kinkaid and the Seventh Fleet, Halsey ordered Davison and Sherman to close at best speed on Bogan, at the center, and to concentrate their full air power upon stopping Kurita. "Strike—Repeat—Strike" he signaled. At the same time he directed McCain to reverse course and refuel at sea in order to be available for whatever might develop.

From the carrier decks of the Third Fleet task groups, five air strikes attacked Kurita's Central Force on the 24th as, without air cover, it doggedly plowed across the Sibuyan Sea toward San Bernardino Strait. By midafternoon all five of Kurita's battleships had been hit; and the heavy cruiser *Myoko* and the superbattleship *Musashi* had been put out of action and were retiring westward, the latter escorted by two destroyers. The final attack of the day concentrated on the

Musashi, which at length capsized, carrying down 1,100 men, half her complement.[3]

Complaining bitterly by radio about the lack of air support which had left him open to crippling attack, Kurita at length ordered his Central Force to reverse course and head back west.

ATTACKS ON SHERMAN'S TASK GROUP

Kurita lacked air support because Japanese flyers had been ordered not to cover his or any other sea forces. The Imperial High Command now based its dwindling hope of success on Ozawa's decoy tactics, which were counted on to clear the way to Leyte Gulf for Kurita, and on aircraft attacks directly against the American carriers. The hastily-trained Japanese pilots, it was believed, had a better prospect of hitting the enemy's ships than of hitting the enemy's planes over their own ships. To carry out this phase of the *Sho* Operation, Vice Admiral Fukudome had come south, adding the remnants of his Formosa air force to the hundred or so operational planes already on Luzon. Early in the morning of October 24, a Japanese search plane sighted Sherman's task group through scattered squalls and reported its find. Supposing that this group was the entire United States Third Fleet, Fukudome launched against it every plane he could muster.

Sherman's group detected the oncoming Japanese planes just as his carriers were about to launch a strike of their own against Kurita's Central Force. So Sherman postponed his strike, returned his bombers and torpedo planes to the hangar decks, and scrambled every available fighter, while his

task group retired under a rain squall. As in the Marianas Turkey Shoot, the highly trained, experienced American pilots decimated their neophyte opponents. During the air battle not a single Japanese aircraft got close enough to Sherman's carriers to attack. A little before 1000 however, when the air had apparently been cleared of hostile planes and the task group was emerging from the overcast to take the fighters aboard, a lone bomber dived out of a cloud and bombed the light carrier *Princeton.* Planes igniting on the hangar deck spread fires and set off ammunition that ripped up the flight deck in a series of rending explosions. In the circumstances Sherman did not close on Bogan as Halsey had directed. Instead he left several cruisers and destroyers standing by the burning carrier and maneuvered the rest of his group within support range. Late in the morning his remaining carriers at last got off their postponed strike against Kurita, achieving one of the most successful attacks of the day.

Search planes from Ozawa's Main Force, now operating off Cape Engaño to the north, had by this time also located Sherman. At 1145 Ozawa launched a strike of 76 planes, which included most of the operational aircraft he had left. An hour later American radar detected their approach, just as Sherman was about to launch a second attack against the Central Force. This time he launched the strike at once and then scrambled his fighters to ward off the new attack. In this raid one American vessel was slightly damaged from a near miss. Of Ozawa's attacking aircraft, some 30 fled to Luzon, three got back to their carriers, and the rest were lost.

The fires in the *Princeton* meanwhile were getting more and more out of hand. In mid-afternoon her bomb magazine blew up, blasting off most of her stern and after flight deck. The *Birmingham,* then close alongside, was swept by debris and chunks of plating which killed more than 200 of her crew and injured nearly twice as many others. It began to appear that the crippled carrier could not be saved.

---

[3] The *Yamato* and the *Musashi* had been built with a fatal flaw. To offset the weight of the heavily-armored main hull, the bulkheads in the forward and after parts of the ship and in the lower decks were left weak. The *Musashi* was dragged down by her flooded bow compartments. Capt. K. Matsumoto and Comdr. M. Chihaya, "Design and Construction of the Yamato and Musashi," *U. S. Naval Proceedings* (Oct. 1953), 1113.

HALSEY LEAVES
THE BEACHHEAD

It must be emphasized again at this point that under the command set-up and the operation orders in force at the time of the Leyte invasion, Admiral Halsey, Commander Third Fleet, and Admiral Kinkaid, Commander Seventh Fleet, operated almost independently of each other. Such cooperation as was achieved between these local commands resulted from the spirit of teamwork and not from any effective coordinating agency. Halsey was responsible to Nimitz at Pearl Harbor, and Nimitz was responsible to the Joint Chiefs of Staff in Washington. Kinkaid was responsible to MacArthur in Leyte Gulf, and MacArthur was responsible to the Joint Chiefs. There was no over-all commander at the scene of action.

The decision for divided command, made in Washington, was out of Nimitz' hands, but at least in his Operation Plan he specifically directed Halsey to cooperate with his opposite number. "Necessary measures for detailed coordination of operations between the Western Pacific Task Forces [Third Fleet] and forces of the Southwest Pacific [Seventh Fleet]," he directed, "will be arranged by their respective commanders." Halsey, as we have seen, made an effort to carry out this directive by flying to Hollandia in September for a three-day conference with MacArthur and Kinkaid. It would appear that the plans for cooperation were far from complete however, for throughout the Battle for Leyte Gulf Halsey and Kinkaid remained uncertain of the exact degree or area of responsibility the other was assuming.

It was clear that the Seventh Fleet, which had escorted the invasion forces to Leyte, was to furnish close support for the assault, but which fleet was to provide cover, that is, fend off hostile naval forces from the beachhead? Kinkaid had designated a segment of his fleet as a "Close Covering Group," but that appears to have been merely a loose use of the term *cover*. On the other hand, Nimitz' Operation Plan directed Halsey to "cover and support forces of the Southwest Pacific in order to assist in the seizure and occupation of objectives in the central Philippines." On the basis of a similar directive, Spruance the preceding June had felt it his responsibility to remain near Saipan, "close enough to the transports and beachhead to intercept any enemy force which tries to interfere and far enough away to avoid embroiling the escort and close-in support in the ensuing battle."

Kinkaid thought Nimitz' directive required the Third Fleet to protect the transports and supply ships. The job of the Seventh Fleet, said he, ". . . was to land troops and keep them ashore. The ships were armed accordingly with a very low percentage of armor-piercing projectiles. The CVE's carried anti-personnel bombs instead of torpedoes and heavy bombs. We were not prepared to fight a naval action." [4] But Nimitz' Plan also directed: "In case opportunity for destruction of [a] major portion of the enemy fleet offer or can be created, such destruction becomes the primary task [of the Third Fleet]." From this, Halsey concluded that the mission of the Third Fleet was offensive, not defensive. "It was not my job to protect the Seventh Fleet," he later wrote. "My job was offensive, to strike with the Third Fleet." [5]

On October 24, as we have seen, Halsey massed all his available air strength against Kurita's formidable Central Force "on the assumption that the Seventh Fleet forces could take care of the smaller southern force." [6] Kinkaid, apparently without protest, took over the task of blocking Surigao Strait, on the assumption that Halsey would continue blocking Kurita's passage through San Bernardino Strait.

By afternoon on the 24th, despite terrific punishment from the air, Kurita was still boring eastward, evidently intent upon breaking through San Bernardino under cover of darkness. So at 1512 Halsey sent

---

[4] Quoted in Walter Karig *et al.*, *Battle Report*, IV (New York, 1948), 422.
[5] *Admiral Halsey's Story*, 219.
[6] Halsey's action report in Cominch *Confidential Information Bulletin No. 22*, 12.

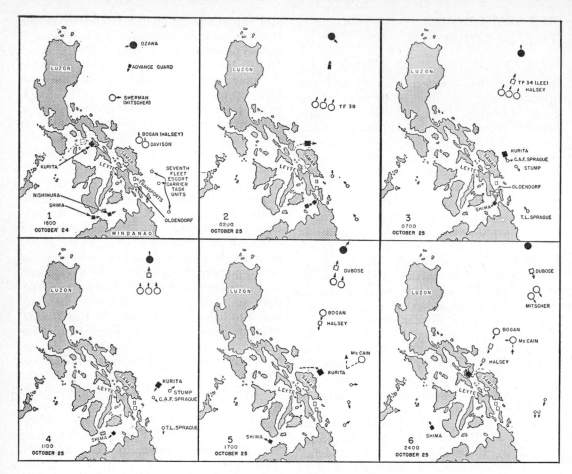

FLEET MOVEMENTS, BATTLE FOR LEYTE GULF

to his subordinate commanders a radio message stating that battleships *New Jersey* (fleet flag), *Iowa, Washington,* and *Alabama,* plus two heavy cruisers, three light cruisers, and 14 destroyers "will be formed as TF 34 under Vice Admiral Lee, Commander Battle Line. Task Force will engage decisively at long ranges." "This dispatch," said Halsey, was "intended merely as a warning to the ships concerned that *if a surface engagement offered,* I would detach them from TF 38, form them into TF 34, and send them ahead as a battle line." [7] But though the

order was marked as a battle plan and not as an executive message, Halsey must have realized that it was ambiguous, for two hours later he got on TBS and told his commanders, "If the enemy sorties [through San Bernardino], TF 34 will be formed when directed by me."

One curious feature of the situation during the Leyte invasion was that Halsey was not directed by his orders to obtain the concurrence of either Kinkaid or MacArthur in carrying out any of his operations, nor was he required to advise them of any changes in his plans. He had not included Kinkaid among the addressees of his 1512 message,

[7] *Admiral Halsey's Story,* 214. The above and other encoded messages in this chapter follow Halsey's security paraphrase.

After the war it was suggested in several quarters that in military orders *shall* should invariably be used

for an order; *will,* to denote mere futurity. The ambiguous *will* in Halsey's 1512 message was cited to bolster the suggestion.

but it was intercepted and decoded by communicators aboard the *Wasatch* and shown to him.[8] Kinkaid assumed that it was an order requiring immediate execution. He did not of course hear the short-range TBS clarification. Neither did Mitscher, with Sherman's carrier task group, which was still far to the northwest trying to save the *Princeton*. Mitscher, like Kinkaid, assumed from the 1512 message that TF 34 had been formed.

Since early morning Halsey had been haunted by the thought that not all the pieces in the Japanese jigsaw puzzle had been accounted for. Discovery of Kurita's force in the Sibuyan Sea and Nishimura's force in the Sulu Sea suggested a pincer movement on Leyte Gulf—but what about the carriers? Surely in a naval attack of such magnitude the enemy would use what Halsey still assumed to be his strongest weapon, the carrier force. Since it was almost certain that the carriers had been in Japanese waters at the time of the Leyte invasion, it could almost be taken for granted that they were now at sea, coming down from the north to coordinate with the Japanese Southern and Central forces in their grand convergence on Leyte Gulf.

Ozawa's Main Force was indeed to northward, as we have seen. Bent on suicide, it was doing its utmost to attract American attention—making smoke, breaking radio silence on various frequencies, and even sending forward an advance guard of surface vessels in a fruitless attempt to contact and engage the Third Fleet. Through the morning and early afternoon Sherman, whose responsibility it had been to search to the north, had sent out no scout planes because he was preoccupied with warding off air attacks and with fighting fires in the *Princeton*. At last, late in the day, his scout bombers found the Japanese Main Force only 190 miles away to the NNE and flashed back the word. As soon as his staff had evaluated the reports, Mitscher passed the information to

Halsey. Mitscher then ordered the *Princeton* to be abandoned, and Sherman sent in a cruiser to sink her with torpedoes.

Now that Halsey at last had all the pieces of the Japanese puzzle in his hands, the picture seemed to confirm his first impression, that the Southern Forces heading for Surigao, the Central Force heading for San Bernardino, and the Main Force coming down from the north were all moving toward a rendezvous in the vicinity of Leyte Gulf for an attack on the transports. He had no intention, he said, of standing by for a test of his theory but determined if possible to thwart the massing of hostile forces. To achieve this he had a choice of three battles. The Southern Forces he felt he could ignore, for Kinkaid had much more than enough strength to take care of them. The far more formidable Central Force was a real threat, but a day of air strikes had left it battered and mauled, and latest reports indicated that it had reversed course and was retreating to the west. Accepting his pilots' overoptimistic estimate that it was now too damaged to win a decision, Halsey concluded that the Central Force also could be left to the reinforced Seventh Fleet. That left the Northern Force, fresh and undamaged, with carriers which presumably gave it a combat range hundreds of miles wider than the others. Halsey had no way of knowing that the carriers were virtually without planes or that Ozawa had come south as a mere decoy with the specific aim of drawing him away from Leyte Gulf. Hostile carriers were in his opinion, and in the opinion of practically all Allied commanders at that time, the principal threat in any naval operation. By destroying them he believed he could remove any serious threat from the sea.

So Halsey selected destruction of the Northern, or Main, Force as his principal objective. How best to meet this antagonist again offered him a choice of three alternatives:

1) He could guard San Bernardino Strait with his whole fleet and wait for the Main Force to strike. This he rejected because it would permit the carriers to extend their range by using their Philippines airfields

---

[8] Halsey could have anticipated that Kinkaid would intercept and read his 1512 dispatch, for "eavesdropping" (decoding radio messages not addressed to oneself) was a common practice.

much as the Mobile Fleet had attempted to use the airfields of Guam in the Battle of the Philippine Sea.

2) He could guard San Bernardino with TF 34 while striking the Main Force to the north with his carrier groups. This he rejected because, over-estimating the enemy's surface strength and his shore-based and carrier air power, he believed that together they might inflict far more damage on a divided fleet than on the Third Fleet intact.

3) He could leave San Bernardino unguarded and strike the Main Force with his whole fleet. This alternative he accepted, for, as he said, "It preserved my fleet's integrity, it left the initiative with me, and it promised the greatest possibility of surprise. Even if the Central Force penetrated San Bernardino and headed for Leyte Gulf, it could only hope to harry the landing operations. It could not consolidate any advantage because no transports accompanied it and no supply ships. It could merely hit and run." [9]

Thus, in a situation not unlike that faced by Spruance on June 19, Halsey on October 24 decided to abandon his covering position off the American beachhead and go out to meet the enemy carrier force. His decision made, he went into Flag Plot just before 2000, put his finger on the charted position of the Japanese Main Force 300 miles away, and said to Rear Admiral Robert B. Carney, his chief of staff, "Here's where we're going. Mick, start them north."

Carney promptly sent off a series of radio messages: to McCain, ordering him to close at best speed; to Davison and Bogan, ordering them to shape course due north; to Sherman, ordering him to join the Davison and Bogan groups at midnight as they dashed past. To Kinkaid he radioed in Halsey's name: "Central Force heavily damaged according to strike reports. Am proceeding north with three groups to attack carrier force at dawn."

Kinkaid, supposing that TF 34 had been formed and was guarding San Bernardino Strait, interpreted this latest dispatch to mean that Halsey was sending three *carrier*

groups north. Kinkaid had already sent most of the gunnery vessels of the Seventh Fleet south to close Surigao Strait and destroy the approaching Japanese Southern Forces. So secure was he in his assumption that San Bernardino was blocked by TF 34 that he did not even bother to send adequate air searches to check on the movements of the Japanese Central Force.

Meanwhile Kurita had turned back east and was once more heading for San Bernardino. From his advance base on Formosa, Admiral Toyoda had radioed to the entire Mobile Fleet: "Trusting in Divine Assistance, all forces will attack," by which he meant that the raid on Leyte Gulf was to be carried out despite any obstacles whatever, even if it meant the sacrifice of the Imperial Navy.

While the surface combat strength of the United States Seventh Fleet was moving south to block Surigao Strait and the bulk of the Third Fleet was advancing on the Japanese Main Force to the north, Kinkaid, Mitscher, and even Nimitz at Pearl Harbor remained under the erroneous impression that San Bernardino was safely blocked by TF 34. In fact, on receipt of Halsey's 1512 message, Mitscher's staff had worked out a battle plan whereby one carrier group of TF 38 would be left behind to provide air cover for the four Third Fleet battleships off the Strait, while two battleships proceeded northward for a night gunnery attack on the Main Force, to be followed up by an air attack by two TF 38 carrier groups at dawn. Thus both Kurita's and Ozawa's forces would be met by superior American forces. But Mitscher, possibly calling to mind the rejection of his advice by Spruance four months earlier, refused to allow his staff to transmit this gratuitous suggestion to Halsey.

When Sherman's task group joined Bogan's and Davison's at midnight, October 24-25, Mitscher's chief of staff, Commodore Arleigh Burke, inquired over TBS: "Is Admiral Halsey there?" and was startled to receive an affirmative answer. Until that moment he was fairly certain that TF 34 had been formed and left behind to block Kurita.

---

[9] *Ibid.,* 217.

Thirty-seven minutes later the Japanese Central Force emerged from San Bernardino Strait into the Pacific behind Halsey's back. Kurita fully expected to run into an ambush, but the only vessels standing between him and the thin-skinned American transports were in the three small Seventh Fleet escort carrier units operating eastward of Leyte Gulf. Though Toyoda's decoy plan had succeeded, Kurita did not know it then or later, for the radio transmitter aboard the Main Force flagship had now broken down altogether. Ozawa's dawn announcement that Halsey was on his tail would not be heard by other commanders of the Mobile Fleet.

THE BATTLE OF SURIGAO STRAIT

Though the Seventh Fleet gunnery vessels carried few armor-piercing shells and were low in fuel and ammunition after supporting the Leyte invasion, Admiral Kinkaid, as we have seen, accepted the task of intercepting the Japanese forces coming up from the south. Because he had undertaken the unusual burden of commanding both the fleet and the amphibious forces, he did not assume tactical command in person. In the afternoon of October 24 he alerted the PT boats guarding the southern end of Surigao Strait and assigned the Seventh Fleet combat forces to Rear Admiral Oldendorf with orders to prepare for a night engagement.

Oldendorf, like Togo at Tsushima, decided to exploit the geographical advantages of his position by letting the enemy come to him. And in view of his immense superiority of force, he determined not merely to repulse but to destroy his antagonist. To that end, and to conserve fuel and ammunition, he planned for a short and decisive action at close ranges. His six old battleships, mostly veterans of the Pearl Harbor attack, he placed cruising back and forth at a stately five knots, across the northern end of the Strait where it opened into Leyte Gulf. Then he extended the flanks of his battle line with cruisers, on east-west courses somewhat

farther south. One destroyer squadron he sent down the Strait as pickets across the enemy's line of advance. His remaining three destroyer squadrons he retained for torpedo attacks on the enemy's flanks as he ap-

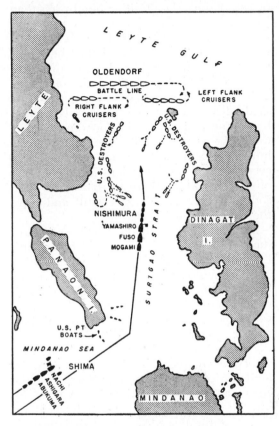

OLDENDORF'S TRAP, BATTLE OF SURIGAO STRAIT, POSITIONS AT 0330, OCTOBER 25, 1944

proached. Any hostile force entering Surigao Strait from the south would thus have to run a gantlet of torpedo fire, first from PT boats and then from destroyers, and at last come under "T"-capping shellfire from battleships and diagonal fire from cruisers. In all naval warfare no more deadly trap had ever been set.[10]

[10] It should be noted that Oldendorf's disposition of his forces was a sort of static version of the "perfect battle plan" used by Merrill in the Battle of Empress Augusta Bay, November 2, 1943.

Across the Mindanao Sea toward this perfect ambush sped Nishimura, unwarily and ahead of schedule as if seeking his own destruction. By racing to enter Surigao Strait hours before the time assigned, he sacrificed all possibility of joint action with Kurita—or with Shima, then trailing him by less than 30 miles, trying vainly to catch up. Since Nishimura, taciturn by nature, kept his counsel and was killed in action that night, it may never be known why he chose to disregard orders and logic in order to go it alone. One of his surviving officers has suggested that he sped ahead because he preferred a night battle and because he did not want to come under the command of his rival, the younger but senior Shima. It is more probable however that he was overoptimistically counting on Ozawa's Main Force to draw the Allied combat forces out of Leyte Gulf and leave the transports at his mercy.

An hour after midnight Nishimura's force successfully fought its way past the Seventh Fleet PT boats, hitting three with gunfire and so smashing another that it had to be beached. Not long afterwards the *Louisville's* radar detected the advancing Japanese, whereupon Oldendorf unleashed his destroyer squadrons, which silently sped down the sides of the Strait. Concealed from radar detection by the shoreline, the destroyers fired torpedoes as they came abreast of the enemy and then reversed course. A few minutes later the Strait was lit up by brilliant flashes as the torpedoes found their targets. Nishimura's flagship, the battleship *Yamashiro,* simply blew apart as her magazines exploded. One Japanese destroyer went down at once; the rest were put out of action. The battleship *Fuso* and the cruiser *Mogami* continued doggedly northward, firing wildly right and left. Just before 0400 these two survivors came within 15,000 yards of the American Battle Line. It was for this Oldendorf had been waiting. He gave the signal, whereupon the guns of his six battleships and eight cruisers opened fire almost simultaneously. Under a hail of shells the *Fuso* began to sink, and the *Mogami,* attempting to reverse course, caught fire and went out of control.

During this brief but deadly bombardment a division of American destroyers, maneuvering to avoid Japanese torpedoes, swung out into the middle of the Strait between the opposing forces and came under fire from both sides. One destroyer, the *Albert W. Grant,* hit by 27 shells from friend and foe, was put out of action with a loss of nearly two score of her crew. This was the sole damage inflicted on Oldendorf's force during the battle.

Shima's Second Striking Force had by this time fought its way into the Strait past the PT boats, which put the light cruiser *Abukuma* out of action. Shima could see tracers and the flash of gunfire, but in the thickening smoke of the upper Strait he could make out no vessels at all. At 0420 his radar detected targets to the north, whereupon Shima turned to fire torpedoes. On the turn his flagship, the *Nachi,* rammed into the *Mogami* as she loomed out of the smoke. At this, he sent his destroyers north for a fruitless torpedo attack and then withdrew southward, with the crippled *Mogami* limping along in his wake.

Of Nishimura's and Shima's forces, four cruisers and five destroyers, some badly crippled, fought their way back past the American PT boats and regained the Mindanao Sea. At Oldendorf's request, planes from the Seventh Fleet escort carriers struck these fugitives after daybreak, sinking the *Mogami* and scattering the rest. Army bombers later discovered and sank the damaged *Abukuma.*

Oldendorf had virtually destroyed Nishimura's Third Section, as he planned, but his ships had failed to make contact with Shima's Striking Force, which slipped into and out of Surigao Strait without being detected except by the PT boats. Nevertheless the threat to Leyte Gulf from the south had been removed by dawn of October 25. While the Seventh Fleet cruisers and destroyers were far down in the Strait finishing off three of Nishimura's battered destroyers however there came an electrifying report: Kurita's Central Force had penetrated San Bernardino and was attacking one of the escort carrier units off Samar. The transports in Leyte Gulf were now in deadly peril from the north.

THE BATTLE OFF CAPE ENGAÑO

In the dark early hours of October 25, while Kurita was cruising eastward along the north coast of Samar, and Nishimura and Shima were advancing into Surigao Strait, Halsey and Mitscher, with the task groups of Bogan, Davison, and Sherman, were speeding north in pursuit of Ozawa. A little after 0200 American search planes scouting ahead of TF 38 made brief contact with two separate enemy surface groups. These were the advance guard and the main body of Ozawa's Main Force, which the day before had split apart in the frustratingly difficult task of attracting American attention, and were now heading on converging courses for a 0600 rendezvous. On receiving word of this contact, Halsey at last formed TF 34, including all six of the battleships then attached to the Third Fleet. With this force he set out in advance of his carrier groups, intending to complete the work of Mitscher's planes by sinking cripples and stragglers and any other Japanese vessels he could overtake.

As dawn was breaking, search planes followed by a deck-load strike of 180 aircraft took off from the American carriers. Not until an hour and a half later did the TF 38 scouts regain contact with the Japanese Main Force—one heavy carrier, three light carriers, two carrier-battleships, three light cruisers, and eight destroyers. The American attack groups, quickly vectored in, arrived in sight of the enemy ships a little after 0800. What followed was too one-sided to be of much tactical interest. Hellcats shot down most of the dozen or so fighter aircraft that came out to meet them, while the American bombers and torpedo planes bored in through intense antiaircraft fire to drive home their strike. The attacking air groups promptly sank a destroyer, made bomb hits on all three carriers, and torpedoed the cruiser *Tama* and the heavy carrier *Zuikaku*. The light carrier *Chitose,* burning and exploding, soon went down. The damaged *Tama,* unable to keep up with the formation, was ordered to proceed alone to Okinawa. As the *Zuikaku,*

steering erratically, also began to fall behind, Admiral Ozawa shifted his flag to a cruiser in order to continue the battle. A second American air strike at 1000 found the Main Force widely scattered. The torpedo planes and bombers concentrated on the damaged light carrier *Chiyoda* and left her dead in the water, afire and listing.

By this time Admiral Halsey, forging ahead with TF 34, scanning the horizon for masts of Japanese stragglers, was having his attention diverted more and more from the impending surface action. At 0410 that morning Admiral Kinkaid had radioed Halsey: "Am now engaging enemy surface forces in Surigao Strait." Then, to reassure himself, he added a question: "Is TF 34 guarding San Bernardino Strait?" It is part of the bad radio communications bedeviling this whole battle that Halsey did not receive Kinkaid's message until 0648. He then promptly replied: "Negative. TF 34 is with our carriers now engaging enemy carriers." This reply dumbfounded Kinkaid; and his amazement quickly turned into alarm, for immediately after receiving Halsey's message he was handed a radio call for help from Rear Admiral Clifton A. F. Sprague, commanding one of the three small escort carrier task units off Leyte Gulf. Kurita had suddenly appeared and was attacking Sprague's little carriers, then cruising near Samar Island.

Kinkaid thereupon began sending Halsey that series of messages which at first puzzled and then exasperated him, intent as he was upon destroying the Japanese Main Force. Adding to Halsey's growing irritation was the fact that Kinkaid's messages were usually belated in reaching his hands and were not received by the Third Fleet in the order in which they were originated.

At 0800 Halsey received the reassuring but much delayed news from Seventh Fleet: "Enemy vessels retiring Surigao Strait. Our light forces in pursuit." Good! Then the Seventh Fleet, having removed the menace from the south, was able to give Leyte Gulf whatever cover it needed—so Halsey supposed. Twenty minutes later came startling information: "Enemy battleships and cruisers reported firing on TU 77.4.3 [Clifton

Sprague's task unit] from 15 miles astern." So the Japanese Central Force had penetrated San Bernardino Strait after all! Halsey wondered how the Seventh Fleet had let itself be surprised, why the escort carrier planes had not detected the approaching Japanese. But he was not alarmed. "I figured," he said, "that the eighteen little carriers had enough planes to protect themselves until Oldendorf could bring up his heavy ships." [11]

Eight minutes later came an appeal from Kinkaid: "Urgently need fast battleships Leyte Gulf at once." At that time flash reports of the first attack on the Main Force were coming in, telling of several crippled Japanese vessels for the big guns of the battleships to finish off. Halsey quickly weighed these conflicting calls to action and made his decision. By TBS he directed Vice Admiral Willis A. Lee, commanding TF 34: "Close enemy at 25 knots," whereupon the big ships, including Halsey's *New Jersey,* picked up speed to the north, away from Leyte Gulf. Halsey then radioed McCain's task group to go to the aid of Sprague and notified Kinkaid that he had done so. A few minutes later came Kinkaid's fifth message: "Our escort carriers being attacked by four battleships, eight cruisers, plus others. Request Lee cover Leyte at top speed. Request fast carriers make immediate strike." Halsey now began to fume. "I had already sent McCain," said he. "There was nothing else I could do except become angrier." [12]

Then came a sixth message, which was in fact Kinkaid's third message much delayed: "CTU 77.4.3 under attack by cruisers and battleships 0700 11-40 N 126-25 E. Request immediate air strike. Also request support by heavy ships. My old battleships low in ammunition." Low in ammunition! Now for the first time Halsey realized that the gunnery ships of the Seventh Fleet were in no condition to defend the Gulf. But what could he do, from a distance of 350 miles? To Kinkaid he reported his position, showing that it was impossible for him to lend assistance, and repeated that he had ordered McCain

to come to the aid of the Seventh Fleet at best possible speed. The fast battleships of TF 34, followed by three carrier groups, continued to the north, intent upon overtaking and sinking the damaged Japanese vessels just over the horizon.

Kinkaid, increasingly alarmed at the situation off Samar, now decided to send a shocker. At 1000 Halsey received from him an unencoded message: "Where is Lee? Send Lee." Kinkaid had sent the message in plain English both to startle Halsey out of his complacency and to scare Kurita. He succeeded in both objectives.

If Halsey had been shocked by Kinkaid's plain-language dispatch, it was nothing compared to the sensation he felt when he received a message immediately afterwards from Nimitz at Pearl Harbor. Nimitz had sent: "Where is Task Force 34?" But the Pearl Harbor communicator had put in as padding (to increase difficulty of enemy cryptanalysis) the words: "The whole world to know." Such plausible padding is of course strictly contrary to regulations. The very plausibility of the padding led Halsey's communicator to make the second blunder. He typed up the padding as part of the message. The dispatch placed in Halsey's hands read: "The whole world wants to know where is Task Force 34."

"I was as stunned as if I had been struck in the face," says Halsey. "The paper rattled in my hands. I snatched off my cap, threw it on the deck, and shouted something I am ashamed to remember." In a rage he ordered TF 34 to change from course 000 to course 180—from due north to due south. "At that moment the Northern Force, with its two remaining carriers crippled and dead in the water, was exactly 42 miles from the muzzles of my 16-inch guns. . . . I turned my back on the opportunity I had dreamed of since my days as a cadet. For me, one of the biggest battles of the war was off, and what has been called 'the Battle of Bull's Run' was on. I notified Kinkaid. . . ." [13] At 1115 Task Force 34 came about and headed south. Halsey de-

[11] *Admiral Halsey's Story,* 219.
[12] *Ibid.,* 220.

[13] *Ibid.,* 220-1. Halsey was often referred to in the press (but not by his intimates) as "Bull" Halsey.

tached four cruisers and ten destroyers, sending them back to their original groups in TF 38. Then, as he passed TF 38 he picked up Bogan's carrier task group to provide air cover.

Mitscher, with Sherman's and Davison's groups, continued to the north to launch the final air strikes against the Japanese Main Force. The third strike of the day, 160 planes, took off a little after noon. With orders to "sink the carriers," the bombers concentrated on the light carrier *Zuiho* and the heavy *Zuikaku*. Battered and set afire by many hits, the *Zuikaku*—last survivor of the carriers which raided Pearl Harbor and veteran of the battles of the Coral Sea, the Eastern Solomons, the Santa Cruz Islands, and the Philippine Sea—rolled over to starboard in mid-afternoon and sank. A final air strike finished off the *Zuiho* an hour later.

Now that three of the enemy carriers had been sunk; and the fourth, according to aircraft reports, was apparently helpless, Mitscher decided to send a surface force ahead to finish off cripples. This was to be no casual mission, for the enemy still had two converted battleships—and Halsey had taken all the American battleships south with him. On receiving word from an aircraft pilot that the hermaphrodites *Ise* and *Hyuga* had retired towards Japan, Mitscher detached four cruisers and 12 destroyers northward under Rear Admiral Laurence T. Dubose. These ships, pausing to sink the lone and helpless *Chiyoda*, last of Ozawa's carriers, were outsped by most of the retreating Main Force. After dark however Dubose's force overtook a group of three enemy destroyers and sent one down in flames with a gunfire-torpedo attack. Farther to the north the cruiser *Tama* and a destroyer, limping home separately alone, were sunk by submarine wolfpacks which Admiral Lockwood had ordered to cover all likely escape routes.

Ozawa, minus his carriers, but with ten of his 17 vessels, returned to Japan. His decoy mission had succeeded beyond his most hopeful expectations. Yet luring the U. S. Third Fleet north did the Japanese little good, for Ozawa could never get the word through to Kurita.

THE BATTLE OFF SAMAR

Amazed at his luck at finding no ambush awaiting him on his entry into the Pacific, Kurita, his force reduced to four battleships, eight cruisers, and eleven destroyers, moved eastward in a night search disposition until 0300, October 25. Then he wheeled southeast and proceeded down the coast of Samar. As dawn approached, he signaled his vessels to form in a circular antiaircraft disposition about the flagship. At this time Kurita began to receive disturbing radio reports that the attack via Surigao Strait was ahead of schedule and that Nishimura's force had been shattered. That was the last word he had from the Southern Forces, and of course he heard nothing at all from Ozawa, to the north.

With the coming of sunrise the Central Force began to detect aircraft by radar, and a little later the lookouts began to report masts looming up over the horizon. At this, Kurita increased speed and presently identified his opponent as "a gigantic enemy task force including six or seven carriers accompanied by many cruisers and destroyers." This was not an unwelcome surprise to Kurita and his officers, who had from the beginning opposed expending the surface fleet on mere empty transports. "A severe blow at the enemy carriers would cut off their advance towards Tokyo and might be a turning point in the war," wrote Kurita's chief of staff. "If the Kurita Force was to be expended, it should be for enemy carriers. At least that would be an adornment for the record of our surface fleet, and a source of pride to every man." [14] Now by an incredible piece of good fortune, so the Japanese thought, they had brought their heavy surface vessels undetected within gun range of part of Halsey's Third Fleet. At 0700 Kurita opened fire.

As a matter of fact, Halsey was by then 300 miles to the north engaging Ozawa's Main Force. What Kurita had seen in the morning haze was a task unit of six little 18-knot escort carriers, three destroyers, and four destroyer escorts commanded by Rear

---

[14] Rear Admiral Tomiji Koyanagi, "With Kurita in the Battle for Leyte Gulf," *United States Naval Institute Proceedings* (February, 1953), 121.

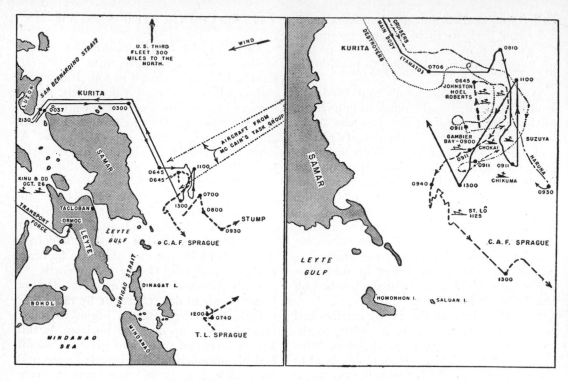

BATTLE OFF SAMAR, OCTOBER 25, 1944

Admiral Clifton A. F. Sprague. This was one of the three Seventh Fleet task units patrolling off the mouth of Leyte Gulf. A second, of similar composition, under Rear Admiral Felix B. Stump, was just over the horizon to the southeast. The third, under the group commander, Rear Admiral Thomas L. Sprague, was 120 miles to the south, off Mindanao. These vessels alone barred Kurita's entrance into the Gulf.

On receiving an aircraft contact report and immediately afterwards sighting Japanese pagoda masts to the northwest, Admiral Clifton Sprague changed course to due east in order to launch aircraft into the northeasterly wind and yet close the enemy as little as possible. He next ordered all his planes launched, armed with whatever they had aboard. Then, as enemy 14-, 16-, and 18-inch shells began to straddle his carriers, he directed his screening ships to make smoke and headed for the cover of a nearby rain squall. In plain language Sprague radioed for help, knowing very well that his baby flattops and

his thin-hulled escort vessels were by no stretch of the imagination a match for the swift Japanese surface fleet. "It did not appear," said he, "that any of our ships could survive another five minutes of the heavy-caliber fire being received." [15]

There followed one of the most remarkable chases of naval history, climaxed by a surprise ending. Concealed by rain, Sprague's unit, having launched all planes, turned right and headed south. Kurita's heavy cruisers, which had been pursuing on an easterly course, now likewise turned south and began coming up on the left flank of the American formation. At the same time, Japanese destroyers began advancing on the American right flank. Thus boxed in, the carriers could no longer turn into the wind to launch or receive planes, and it was evident that the enemy vessels with their superior speed would soon be in position to force the Ameri-

[15] C. Vann Woodward, *The Battle for Leyte Gulf* (New York, 1947), 168.

cans into the Japanese Battle Line, which was pursuing dead astern.

In this desperate situation Sprague ordered his three destroyers and four destroyer escorts to reverse course and attack the entire Japanese Central Force. This was to be, as one destroyer commander announced to his crew, "a fight against overwhelming odds from which survival could not be expected." [16] Plowing northward under a hail of heavy-caliber shells, the little ships resolutely pressed home their attack, dodging into smoke screens and rain squalls for such protection as these could afford. Destroyers *Johnston* and *Hoel* and destroyer escort *Samuel B. Roberts* were sunk, and two of the remaining escort vessels were heavily damaged.

The desperate foray was worth the cost. American torpedoes put the heavy cruiser *Kumano* out of action. More important, they broke up the Battle Line, causing the flagship *Yamato* to lose seven miles in evasive maneuvers so that Kurita was not again to get a clear picture of the tactical situation. The confusion in the Central Force was compounded at this point by its own destroyers, which circled away under attack from Sprague's carrier planes, and by the battleship *Haruna,* which sighted Stump's task unit on the horizon to the southeast and sped away towards this new objective intent on a private battle of her own.

The Japanese now enjoyed a brief respite from attack. During the lull, the heavy cruisers, followed by the battleship *Kongo,* pressed ever closer on the American left flank, forcing Sprague's unit to shift to course SW, towards Leyte Gulf. The little carriers during this phase began to take numerous 8-inch hits. That they were not all sunk can be attributed only to the enemy's failure to press on aggressively, taking advantage of his superior speed, and to his use of armor-piercing shells, which for the most part passed through the unarmored carriers without exploding. Carrier *Gambier Bay* however took two hits below the waterline, apparently from the *Kongo*. She lost power, began to list, and at 0900 rolled over and sank.

---

[16] *Ibid.,* 175.

At this point, when Sprague's unit again appeared on the verge of extinction, the situation was saved by the only really coordinated air attack of the battle. Most of the aircraft came from Stump's task unit, which not only launched 31 Avengers and 28 Hellcats of its own but also serviced and launched refugee planes from the other two units. Under this concerted attack, Kurita's heavy cruisers *Chokai* and *Chikuma* were crippled and put out of action. The Japanese destroyers at length fired torpedoes but at so great a range that none reached the American vessels. The Japanese battleships scattered to evade torpedoes dropped by the American planes, and the whole Central Force, already widely dispersed, fell into increasing confusion.

Admiral Kurita, who had lost touch both with the American task unit and with most of his own force, concluded that his prey had escaped and decided that the time had come to bring order out of chaos. So at 0911 he headed north, signaling his ships once more to converge on the *Yamato*. Thereupon the two remaining Japanese heavy cruisers, then almost within point-blank range of Sprague's carriers, reversed course; the *Haruna* broke off her private pursuit of Stump; and the *Kongo* and the destroyers abandoned their attack and swung left toward the distant flagship.

Sprague's task unit, bewildered by the sudden retreat of the enemy vessels, which a few minutes before seemed to have every advantage on their side, steamed on towards Leyte Gulf, just 25 miles away.

THE KAMIKAZES STRIKE

With Kurita's turnaway, the Seventh Fleet escort carriers had escaped annihilation by what at the time seemed a miracle, and remained until after the war a profound mystery to the American forces. The hazards of the day were however by no means ended, for on October 25, the Japanese carried out the first successful operations of the newly-organized Kamikaze ("Divine Wind") Special Attack Corps, composed of suicide-minded aircraft pilots and taking its name from the typhoons that in 1273 and 1279 saved Japan by scattering Kublai Khan's invasion fleets.

When word of Kurita's apparently suicidal advance towards Leyte Gulf reached the Japanese air forces in the Philippines, Vice Admiral Takajiro Onishi, commanding the 2nd Air Fleet, decided that the time had come for his aviators to take similarly desperate measures. Evidently ill-trained flyers piloting bombers were not elusive enough to penetrate American air defenses and turn back the Allied attack, but the inexperienced Japanese aviators might yet succeed if they flew highly-maneuverable Zeke fighters armed with light bombs directly into their targets. Onishi personally put the proposition before his aviators at Mabalacat Airfield on Luzon and received immediate and wholehearted response. Admiral Fukudome followed Onishi's example, organizing Special Attack Corps within the 1st Air Fleet. Soon units of volunteer human missiles were set up throughout the Philippines. At last, when it was too late, the Japanese had improvised a new and terrifying means of disputing America's growing command of the sea.

Following the American invasion of Leyte, the Special Attack Corps sortied four successive days but because of bad weather, or out of sheer ineptitude, failed to find a target. On the 24th, the limited success of the conventional attack against Sherman's carrier task group off Luzon underlined the growing necessity for better methods and more certain results. Clearly if the kamikazes had a better method, the time to demonstrate it had arrived. The next morning they staged their first successful unit attack.

At dawn on October 25, six Special Attack planes took off from Davao, Mindanao and, winging almost due north, discovered T. L. Sprague's carrier task unit off Leyte Gulf. Out of an overcast at about 10,000 feet the Zekes dived directly, some almost vertically, at the escort carriers just as they were launching planes for a strike against Kurita's Central Force, then engaging C. A. F. Sprague's task unit to the north. The planes heading for the carriers *Petrof Bay* and the *Sangamon* were deflected by antiaircraft fire, but the

Sangamon was slightly damaged by an exploding bomb when one of the kamikazes hit the water. Carriers *Suwannee* and *Santee* were both struck by planes whose exploding bombs tore gaping holes in their flight decks. In the midst of the ensuing confusion, the *Santee* was also torpedoed by an undetected Japanese submarine. The torpedo blasted in the *Santee's* hull, flooding several compartments and causing her to list. Despite these attacks, the damaged carriers kept station in the formation and by means of quick emergency repairs resumed flight operations within a couple of hours.

A half hour or so after Kurita's Central Force had broken off action, the escort carriers of C. A. F. Sprague's battered northern task unit were attacked by five kamikazes out of Mabalacat Field. One of the Zekes narrowly missed the *White Plains*, which eluded the diving plane with a hard left rudder. Another struck the *Kitkun Bay* a glancing blow that did minor damage. Two more crashed into the *Kitkun Bay*, already scarred by 15 shell hits, and started fires. The fifth, armed with a bomb under each wing, struck the *St. Lô* amidships. The plane skidded overboard, but at least one of the bombs penetrated to the hangar deck, where it exploded among the parked planes, setting them afire and touching off further explosions which ripped up the flight deck and apparently blew out a section of the bottom. Less than half an hour after being hit, the *St. Lô* rolled over and sank almost vertically by the stern. Leaving his remaining escort vessels to pick up survivors, Sprague withdrew towards Manus with his carriers. "We had been through so much by then," he said afterwards, "that it didn't seem to matter whether we had escorts with us or not."

KURITA'S RETIREMENT

What meanwhile was Kurita doing? Shortly after 0900, it will be recalled, he broke off action with C. A. F. Sprague's task unit and headed north, ordering all his vessels to converge on the flagship. Up until that time his radio and other communications had been so congested that he had little real knowledge of the tactical situation. He had not realized how near his advance units had been to overtaking the Americans. Now, beginning to get the picture a little more clearly, he was less immediately concerned with his lost opportunity than with the extent of his injuries, and ordered his more heavily damaged vessels to retire. This the *Kumano* and a destroyer did, but the *Chokai* and the *Chikuma,* hopelessly crippled, had to be sunk.

Presently came a final attack from the American escort carrier planes, some of which had made use of an unfinished airstrip on Leyte for servicing. Worst hit in this raid was the heavy cruiser *Suzuya,* which caught fire and began to blow apart as the flames reached her torpedo mounts. When it became clear that she could not be saved, one of Kurita's destroyers removed her crew and sent her down. Of the ten heavy cruisers which had steamed out of Brunei Bay with the Central Force, only two were still afloat and battleworthy.

Despite his losses and the escape of the American task unit, Kurita believed he had done a good morning's work and had fulfilled a substantial part of his mission. Relying on his captain's reports, he radioed Toyoda that of the "gigantic task force" he had encountered, his vessels had "definitely sunk" three or four carriers—one of the *Enterprise* class, two heavy cruisers, and a number of destroyers.

By 1100 the Central Force was back in formation under clear skies and had almost reached the point where the battle had begun four hours before. No enemy ships or planes were to be seen. Still full of fight, Admiral Kurita signaled another reversal of course, whereupon his ships wheeled again and once more headed for Leyte Gulf. During the next hour the Central Force, on a southwesterly course, was not attacked, but Kurita gradually began to lose enthusiasm for entering the Gulf. After five days, he reasoned, the Allied transports surely would have been unloaded, and with plenty of warning they must by now have withdrawn under escort of the United States Seventh Fleet. From Nishimura and Shima he could

expect no help, for the Southern Forces apparently had met with disaster. He thought he had met part of the U. S. Third Fleet, but where was the rest of it? There was no word at all from Ozawa to enlighten him on that score. On the other hand, intercepts of plain language radio dispatches gave a startling picture of what the Americans were up to. Kurita received the impression that powerful air forces were assembling on Leyte and that Third Fleet carrier groups were converging on him from all directions. Though the horizon was empty, he felt surrounded. In the circumstances Leyte Gulf might easily prove a trap instead of an opportunity. At any rate, he definitely preferred fighting the next battle in the open Pacific.

Kurita's orders, like Halsey's, gave him the option of engaging enemy carrier forces if opportunity offered. From Manila that morning had come a false radio report of American carriers to the northeast of Samar. After due consideration Kurita and his staff concluded that these non-existent carriers were their most profitable objective. With the aid of Japanese planes based on Luzon, they might yet win a decision—or at least die gloriously fighting capital ships instead of sinking empty transports. At 1300 therefore the Central Force again reversed course. Like Halsey the day before, Kurita headed north in search of carriers.

Not long afterwards came the first of several attacks by carrier planes from the east. These were from McCain's group, which on orders from Halsey had headed for Samar. Striking from extreme range, McCain's aircraft did no crippling damage to the Central Force, but they secured many near misses which perforated the bulges of all the major Japanese vessels, causing them to trail oil.

At Kurita's request, nearly every available plane on Luzon made rendezvous with the Central Force in the late afternoon for a coordinated attack on the supposed American carrier group. No trace of any such force however was to be found by ships or aircraft. By this time Kurita's destroyers were low in fuel, and he and his staff were utterly exhausted after three days under attack from surface, subsurface, and air. Toward sunset the Central Force shaped course for San Bernardino, and at 2130, October 25, it passed back through the strait. One vessel, the destroyer *Nowake,* having stopped to remove the crew from the *Chikuma,* trailed far behind the others.

THE END OF
JAPANESE SEA POWER

The massed power which Halsey had assembled off Luzon at the end of October 24 was split four ways in the evening of October 25. Mitscher's forces in the north were divided, with Dubose's cruiser-destroyer group advancing ahead of the carrier groups to pick off cripples and stragglers from Ozawa's Main Force. In an attempt to beat Kurita to San Bernardino Strait Halsey further divided the Third Fleet by detaching from his southbound vessels his two fastest battleships, the *Iowa* and the *New Jersey,* together with three light cruisers and eight destroyers. With this detachment he raced ahead, but the race was futile for when Halsey arrived off San Bernardino Strait a little after midnight the Central Force had already passed through. The fast battleships of the Third Fleet had steamed 300 miles north and then 300 miles back south between the two major enemy forces without quite making contact with either. Still outside the Strait however was the destroyer *Nowake.* Not worth battleship fire, this lone vessel became the target of Halsey's cruisers and destroyers, which converged upon her and sent her down with shells and torpedoes.

At dawn on the 26th, Bogan's carrier group coming down from the north and McCain's group coming in from the east made rendezvous off Luzon. From here they launched a series of air strikes against the Central Force as it retreated westward across the Sibuyan Sea. Kurita, with four battleships, two heavy and two light cruisers, and seven destroyers, had made best possible speed through the night and was off Panay before coming under attack. Here a little before 0900 seventy-three Third Fleet planes struck the Central Force, further damaging

the *Yamato* with two bomb hits and stopping the light cruiser *Noshiro* with a torpedo. A second strike an hour and a half later sent the *Noshiro* down. Other aircraft sought out Kurita's stragglers, sinking a destroyer and putting more holes in the crippled *Kumano*.

Meanwhile the battle-weary escort carriers of the Seventh Fleet were having their hands full in the Leyte area. At about noon on the 26th, kamikazes struck once more at Admiral T. L. Sprague's task unit. Two Zekes hit the damaged *Suwannee,* starting fires and bringing the two-day total of casualties aboard this carrier to 143 killed and 92 wounded. The nearby *Petrof Bay* again avoided damage by putting up a heavy screen of antiaircraft fire which tore an attacking Zeke "almost completely to pieces" and diverted its dive from her flight deck harmlessly into the sea. Planes from Admiral Stump's task unit, in the meantime, were striking again and again at a Japanese transport force which had landed troops on the west coast of Leyte during the heat of battle the day before. Though Stump's aircraft had expended all their torpedoes and heavy bombs on the 25th, they attacked persistently with contact bombs, rockets, and guns until they sank the light cruiser *Kinu* and a destroyer, the entire escort of the convoy.

This attack ended the Battle for Leyte Gulf.

SUCCESS AND FAILURE
AT LEYTE GULF

The Battle for Leyte Gulf was unquestionably an overwhelming victory for the United States Navy.[17] Between October 23 and 26, the U. S. Third and Seventh Fleets, with some assistance from submarines and army bombers, sank 26 Japanese combat vessels: three battleships, four carriers, ten cruisers, and nine destroyers. American losses in the same period were six combat vessels: one light and two escort carriers, two destroyers, and a destroyer escort. In other terms, the

---

[17] Assisted by four Australian cruisers in the Battle of Surigao Strait.

Japanese lost 305,710 tons of combat shipping; the Americans, 36,600 tons. Of tonnage committed, the Combined Fleet lost nearly half; the U. S. Navy, less than three per cent. At the end of the battle the Imperial Navy had ceased to exist as a fighting team, whereas the Americans had clearly secured command of the sea over the entire Pacific basin. Though the Allied fleets would still have their hands full conducting amphibious assaults and supporting forces ashore, they would not in this war again partake in a true fleet engagement.

That the abortive *Sho* Operation cost the Imperial Navy half its dwindling strength was no surprise to Admiral Toyoda, for it had been activated as a suicide mission. Yet despite these losses, the transports in Leyte Gulf, which were the main target of the entire operation, had not been touched. The principal cause for Japanese failure was lack of air power. Chiefly this was a question of shortage of trained pilots—and that shortage goes back to the heavy Japanese air losses in the Battle of Midway, the grinding attrition in the Rabaul campaign, the devastating blows of the Battle of the Philippine Sea, and Toyoda's decision to commit what air power he had to the defense of Formosa. Yet the Japanese might have achieved something had their forces been better coordinated. As it was, their land-based air and their four naval forces operated almost independently in a complex operation in which coordination was imperative. Nishimura failed to cooperate with Shima or with Kurita, and Ozawa failed to get the word to Kurita that he had lured Halsey away from Leyte Gulf. Thus Kurita, left alone, unsupported and uninformed, wavered and stumbled when victory of a sort was within his grasp.

The United States Navy also achieved less than a full measure of victory when, despite overwhelming power, it let six enemy battleships and numerous supporting vessels elude destruction. The fleets cannot be said to have been handled with utmost efficiency when the main American surface strength cruised fruitlessly north and then south through the most critical hours of the battle, leaving inferior forces in contact with the enemy's two main forces. Here also the failure was lack of coordination, an essential feature of military concentration. American naval forces did not fully coordinate, did not achieve a clear understanding of their respective areas of responsibility. Who or what was to blame? It is a little too simple to write the whole matter off as a classic example of divided command. After all, the Japanese naval forces also failed to achieve coordination, though they had a single, over-all commander in Admiral Toyoda, who did his best to unravel the complexities of the vast operation from his advance headquarters on Formosa.

Had the Americans had an effective coordinating agency, probably a certain amount of confusion might have been avoided, but it is questionable whether any agency could have maintained control over so complicated and far-flung a battle. Part of the trouble arose of course from unrecognized ambiguities in orders issued before and during the battle, part resulted from failures of radio communication, part can be attributed to errors in judgment. But even had these faults been avoided, no adequate machinery existed for preventing operations at cross purposes in a battle so huge and complex. No previous experience had prepared the commanders to foresee events or evaluate data in so involved and gargantuan a series of actions as the Battle for Leyte Gulf.

47

Submarines in the Pacific

WHILE THE CLASH OF FLEETS and assaults on defended beachheads inevitably hold the center of attention in any study of naval operations in the Pacific theater of World War II, the unremitting pressure applied by American submarines was no less effective in bringing about the collapse of the Japanese Empire. Their success shines all the more brightly in contrast to the Japanese failure and does not suffer in comparison with the achievements of the U-boat in the Atlantic. The sinking by American submarines of Japanese tonnage, both merchant and naval, had much to do with the reduction of the Empire to the hollow shell that, in a military sense, it proved to be in 1945. The figures tell the story: taking Japanese merchant tonnage as their principal target, submarines sank 1,113 vessels in this category displacing about 4,800,000 tons, out of a total of 2,346 vessels displacing about 8,600,000 tons sunk by all agents, American and allied. In addition, American submarines sank a sizable portion of the Japanese navy: 201 vessels displacing about 540,000 tons out of 686 vessels displacing about 1,960,000 tons sunk by all agents. In other terms, American submarines destroyed roughly 56 per cent of all Japanese merchant tonnage and 28 per cent of all Japanese naval tonnage sunk in World War II.[1]

This record becomes all the more astonishing when one considers that the submarines of the United States Navy began operations in World War II hampered by an over-conservative doctrine and a defective torpedo. Before the raid on Pearl Harbor, the Navy had not expected to war on merchantmen, for the United States had entered World War I in protest against unrestricted submarine warfare. That self-imposed limitation, promptly scrapped once war was declared in 1941, and an exaggerated estimate of what aircraft could do against submarines, had limited the scope of peacetime planning and practice. However, the early decision to attack any and all enemy vessels and the trial and error of wartime patrols soon produced a realistic doctrine. Thereafter the American submarine was hampered only by the deficiencies of the torpedo with which it was obliged to work for two years.

---

[1] Joint Army-Navy Assessment Committee, *Japanese Naval and Merchant Shipping Losses during World War II by All Causes* (Washington, 1947), vi, vii.

826

TORPEDO TROUBLE

For American submariners these were two years of frustration and disappointment. Time and time again they cruised thousands of miles into the teeth of enemy defenses and returned with torpedoes expended and little or nothing to show for their labors. In a sense these years were spent in finding where the trouble lay. Three incidents will serve to illustrate.

In November 1942 the *Seawolf* found an 8,000-ton transport at anchor in Davao Gulf in the Philippines and got off four torpedoes. Of the three that missed, one was set to run at 18 feet depth and the other two at four feet. A fourth, set at eight feet, exploded prematurely but close enough to heel the transport far over. In disgust Lieutenant Commander Frederick P. Warder withdrew and reloaded his bow tubes with officially obsolete torpedoes. When he got one off it exploded on contact and sank the transport.

In December 1942 the *Sargo,* under Lieutenant Commander Tyrell D. Jacobs, found plenty of targets on her first patrol. She made eight day-submerged attacks and fired 13 torpedoes. All 13 missed.

In July 1943 Lieutenant Commander L. R. Daspit, commanding the *Tinosa,* stopped a 19,000-ton tanker with two torpedoes fired at an oblique angle. To be sure of finishing her off he shifted to a position 875 yards on her beam. From this supposedly ideal position he fired nine more torpedoes; all hit, and all failed to explode. Daspit then wrathfully took his last torpedo back to Pearl Harbor to be examined.

During the early part of World War II, S-class submarines normally carried the officially obsolete Mark 10 torpedo; fleet-type submarines carried the heavier, faster, and more intricate Mark 14. Both were weapons of fantastic complexity, 21 inches in diameter and weighing more than a ton. Steam, generated by spraying water through an alcohol torch, passed into turbines to supply propulsion. Gyroscopic controls determined the course of the torpedo, and a hydrostatic valve reacting to water pressure determined the depth of the run. Ejected from the torpedo

tube by air pressure, the torpedo in response to settings made before firing was designed to curve to the desired course and level off at the desired depth. The forward part of the torpedo, or warhead, contained the charge and the exploder. To avoid premature explosion from the shocks of firing and the turns and twists of course and depth seeking, the exploder remained inoperative until the torpedo had run 450 yards. The Mark 14 could transport its ship-destroying charge 9,000 yards at 31.5 knots, or 4,500 yards at 46 knots, and explode by magnetic induction without ever touching the target. There is little wonder that so complicated a weapon, inadequately tested, often operated less than perfectly.

The causes for faulty performances by American torpedoes were finally discovered, but fixing the blame was not simple. Specifically, the Bureau of Ordnance is responsible for designing torpedoes, and its station at Newport, Rhode Island was its only torpedo testing agency in the years before World War II.[2] Yet it would be less than fair to saddle either the Bureau or its testing agency with the whole blame. Certainly a partial cause was the traditional reluctance of the American people to spend an adequate sum for war material during peacetime. When each torpedo cost around $10,000, the Newport Naval Torpedo Station was operating on an annual budget of $70,000. While poverty-haunted Japan was freely expending live torpedoes to attain its lethal and dependable Long Lance, the United States was firing unarmed underwater missiles and then retrieving them for further tests. The practice at Newport was to replace the warhead and exploder with a water-filled exercise head. At the end of a practice run, the water was expelled by compressed air, whereupon the lightened torpedo rose to the surface for easy recovery. To avoid damage to torpedo or target, the torpedo was set, not to hit, but to pass under the target.

Beyond the blunt fact that the torpedoes

[2] The extensive facilities at Alexandria, Virginia remained closed from 1923 until the outbreak of World War II. This partially explains the torpedo scarcity in the early days of the war.

often did not work, the first trouble to be recognized was inaccurate depth running. The Mark 10 was found to run consistently four feet deeper than its setting and hence presented no real problem, but the standard Mark 14 deviated unpredictably. When reports of the Mark 14's erratic performance reached Rear Admiral Charles A. Lockwood USN, then commander of submarines in the Southwest Pacific, he began to send inquiries to the Bureau of Ordnance. The Bureau at first stood firm on the basic design and attributed the failures to improper handling. So Lockwood ran a test of his own to find out where the fault lay. He had a submarine fire three Mark 14's at a fishnet from 850 yards. The first two, set for ten feet, cut the net at 25 to 18 feet. The third, set at zero, cut at 11. Informed of these results, the Bureau replied that they proved nothing since the test had been conducted with improper conditions of trim. Lockwood thereupon repeated the test with trim conditions improved. This time three torpedoes set to run at ten feet pierced the net at 25. Again Lockwood reported his findings. This report, together with letters on the same subject from Admiral King and from Rear Admiral Robert H. English, Commander Submarines Central Pacific, finally induced the Bureau to recheck its technical data. Not long afterwards it officially confirmed that the Mark 14 tended to run some ten feet deeper than its setting.

This announcement explained the torpedoes' baffling habit of passing far under the target vessel, revealed by bubbles rising in and beyond the ship's wake, but correction of depth settings still did not produce a dependable weapon. It merely revealed, or underscored, other deficiencies. Torpedoes with corrected settings tended to go off too soon or not at all. The duds were heartbreaking enough for submarine skippers who had cruised for weeks and at last had a fat target in their sights only to register a zero. But the prematures led to erroneous and misleading reports, for an explosion between the submarine periscope and the target looked like a kill and was often reported as such. Moreover the skipper, supposing he had made a kill, often failed to take measures against

depth charge counterattack. The cause of the prematures and duds was ultimately traced to the Mark 6 exploder used in the Mark 14 torpedo.

The killing charge in a torpedo warhead (early in World War II it was TNT, later replaced by the more powerful torpex) is not easily set off; a primer and a booster charge are necessary. To trigger this series, an exploder mechanism such as the Mark 6 drives a firing pin into the primer cap. Since the chain of explosions, once started, was relied on to finish the job, the logical place to look for firing trouble, it would seem, was in the exploder, which determines when to fire and must start the chain effectively.

The Mark 6 exploder had been developed in 1925, when nobody believed that the United States would ever engage in unrestricted submarine warfare. It was designed therefore to operate against warships only—preferably very large warships. For such targets with side armor extending below the waterline the most lethal point of detonation was supposed to be under the hull. Here the explosion would have to be triggered by the ship's magnetic field. Once the magnetic exploder had been built, its developers thought they had found the perfect weapon against all types of steel ships, for the target was thereby in effect expanded to the limits of its magnetic field; a near miss would be as good as a hit. Submariners were directed to fire their Mark 14's not *at* but *under* enemy vessels—ten feet under the keel of a battleship, five feet under the hull of lighter types. Until depth settings had been corrected in line with the Bureau's announcement, the torpedoes had been passing too far under the hulls for the exploder to be activated.

There were several fallacies in the theory of magnetic firing. For one thing, experiences in World War II revealed that ships sank less often from loss of buoyancy than from loss of stability; a torpedo hit in the side which caused them to roll over led to quicker flooding than a blast against the bottom of the hull. For another, the magnetic field of a ship varies according to all sorts of factors including variations in the earth's magnetic field. Lastly, the magnetic exploder, involving induction coils for generating electromagnetic force and vacuum tubes for amplification, was highly sensitive to shock. The developers of the Mark 6 must have realized that magnetic triggering was not altogether dependable, for they took the precaution of retaining the contact firing device also. By the time the Mark 6 was issued in 1941, both Britain and Germany had developed a similar magnetic device, tried it in combat, and withdrawn it because of erratic performance.

Aside from the inherent undependability of the Mark 6, the extreme secrecy with which it was surrounded led to mishandling by well-intentioned but uninformed submarine crews. Many a skipper called for a shallow setting in order to fire directly at the hull of his target rather than under it, on the theory that if the magnetic exploder failed to work, the contact exploder would do the trick. But the horizontal component of a ship's magnetic field is often so much wider than the vertical that a shallow-running torpedo might blow up as much as 50 feet away from the hull. The *Seawolf's* torpedo that rolled its target without inflicting damage was doubtless such a premature.

Deeply concerned over increasing reports of prematures, Admiral Lockwood, who had succeeded Admiral English as Commander Submarines Central Pacific, in April 1943 descended upon Washington. After speaking his piece to Admiral King he addressed a meeting of submarine officers from all Bureaus. "If the Bureau of Ordnance can't provide us with torpedoes that will hit and explode . . .," said he, "get Bureau of Ships to design a boat hook with which we can rip the plates off the target's sides!" [3] This comment, widely repeated, brought protests from the Chief of Ordnance but it also led to constructive action.

Meanwhile, in July 1943 Admiral Nimitz ordered destroyers and submarines in his command to inactivate the magnetic portion of the Mark 6 exploder. As a result prematures were practically eliminated in Nimitz'

theater. They continued to plague submariners in the Southwest Pacific until Admiral Ralph Christie, commander of submarines in that area, followed Nimitz' example in March 1944.

There still remained the problem of duds. For example, July 1943 was the month of the *Tinosa's* frustrating experience with the big tanker. When she returned to Pearl Harbor the experts examined Daspit's last torpedo and found nothing wrong. Thereupon Admiral Lockwood went into action again, and sent a submarine out to fire two torpedoes against underwater cliffs in the Hawaiian Islands. One exploded; the other was duly recovered and examined. It was found that the firing pin, which moved perpendicularly to the long axis of the torpedo, had not hit the primer cap hard enough.

With this clue, Lockwood ordered ten dummy warheads with exploders to be dropped from 90 feet onto a steel plate. Seven of these failed to fire, and examination showed clearly why. When direct impact crushed in the warhead, the guide studs were bent, squeezing the firing pin and preventing it from sliding athwartships at full force against the primer cap. Improvements in studs and pin overcame this, and as Lockwood put it, "At last—almost two years after the beginning of the war—U. S. submarines went to sea with a reliable torpedo."

This solution adds an ironic postscript to the story of the *Tinosa* attack. The submarine had fired too well for a kill. The first hits, the ones that crippled the tanker, had been delivered at an oblique angle that crumpled the warhead only slightly and did not bend the guide studs. It was only when the *Tinosa* took up an "ideal" firing position abeam that the firing pin jammed on impact and the target became to all intents invulnerable.

THE ELECTRIC TORPEDO

Just as the United States Navy was solving the problems connected with the steam-turbine torpedo, the electric torpedo appeared and threw a new set of problems into the

[3] Vice Admiral Charles A. Lockwood USN, *Sink 'Em All: Submarine Warfare in the Pacific* (New York, 1951), 85.

laps of the experts. Early in 1942 the Navy had turned over to the Westinghouse Electric and Manufacturing Corporation a captured German electric torpedo with the request that the company copy it for eventual mass production. But making an exact copy proved impractical—for one thing, the dimensions of the German torpedo were such that it could not be adapted for firing from American torpedo tubes. The project lagged until Admiral King ordered the Naval Inspector General to investigate. The Inspector General in his report found the Bureau of Ordnance competing rather than cooperating with commercial firms, but he also noted that the Bureau had not been provided with capable and experienced submarine officers to push the project and provide guidance. Partly as a result of this report procedures were corrected and electric torpedoes soon began to come off the production line.

Submariners did not take instantly to the new torpedo. Now that the various shortcomings of the Mark 14 had at last been eliminated, it seemed like asking for more trouble to introduce a new model. Besides, electric torpedoes were slower than the steam-turbine types (28 or 30 knots to 46). But their obvious advantages soon overcame the skepticism with which they had been received: their engines left no tell-tale wake of exhaust bubbles, their initial dive was shallower and their over-all depth control was better, and they had an impact exploder that worked. Moreover they cost far less and could be produced much faster.

Inevitably the new weapon showed up deficiencies which had to be corrected. The storage batteries generated explosive hydrogen with no means for venting. The steel rudder posts rusted and produced erratic or circular runs. The weak tail vanes were sometimes knocked off in firing. Cold sea water lowered the battery temperature, causing the torpedo to run slow. As quickly as such weaknesses were recognized steps were taken to eliminate them, sometimes by ingenious devices—the hydrogen menace for example was removed by means of a red-hot chrome wire which burned off the gas as fast as it formed.

As the electric torpedo came into wide use in 1944 and 1945 the American submariner had at last a weapon to match his mettle. In the last six months of the war 65 per cent of torpedoes expended were electric.

SPECIAL MISSIONS— U.S.S. *NAUTILUS*

World War I demonstrated the capabilities of the submarine for raiding communications, and that was the submarine's principal task in World War II. The nature of the war in the Pacific however made new and unexpected demands upon underwater craft. The success with which they carried out numerous special missions proved them more versatile than anyone had suspected. Some idea of the variety of these missions can be gained from the wartime history of U.S.S. *Nautilus*.

The *Nautilus*, the *Argonaut*, and the *Narwhal*, all built during the 1920's, were the three largest submarines ever to serve in the United States Navy. Their surface displacement of better than 2,700 tons exceeded that of a 74-gun ship of the line at Trafalgar, and their length, over 370 feet, was greater than that of any ship Lord Nelson ever saw. In general, the Navy preferred smaller submarines for their agility and their efficiency as commerce-destroyers; the 1,525-ton *Flasher*, for example, sank 100,000 tons of shipping in little over a year, nearly five times the record of the *Nautilus* for the entire war. Yet the size of the *Nautilus*, a drawback in some respects, made her one of the most versatile of all submarines. The outbreak of war in the Pacific found her undergoing a thorough modernization at Mare Island. When the work was completed she moved out to Pearl Harbor and operated from there through most of the war.

At the time of the Battle of Midway in mid-1942 the available submarines of the Pacific Command were deployed in three groups, two covering Pearl Harbor and the third patrolling along lines of bearing radiating fanwise west from Midway. The *Nautilus* was in this Midway group, operating along the 310-degree line. At 0710 on the morning of "the Glorious 4th of June" her commander, Lieutenant Commander William H. Brockman, through his periscope saw planes bombing something in the distance and changed course toward the scene of action. Three-quarters of an hour later he began to make out masts on the horizon, but a plane suddenly swooped down out of nowhere and began dropping bombs, whereupon Brockman submerged without further ado. Presently he brought the *Nautilus* up again to periscope depth. A look around revealed four Japanese warships at close range. Before he could take action the *Nautilus* was subjected to renewed air attack, and a nearby destroyer came charging in for a kill. Brockman lost no time in diving to 90 feet. Then he and his crew sat out the inevitable depth bomb barrage. The attack failed to rupture the submarine's hull but released a hot torpedo from one of her deck tubes—these were a peculiarity of the *Nautilus*—by knocking out the retaining pin.

Nothing daunted, Brockman bobbed up again as soon as the coast seemed reasonably clear. This time he found himself in the midst of an enemy fleet and quickly fired two torpedoes at a battleship. One stuck in the tube and the other missed the target; a battleship returned the compliment by firing a salvo at the inquiring periscope. The battleship's screening vessels were closing in by this time, so down went Brockman to weather another depth charge attack. At his next rise to periscope depth he sighted a carrier under air attack but was soon driven under by a persistent destroyer. The *Nautilus* had been bobbing up and down in the middle of the Japanese Mobile Force during the hottest minutes of the Battle of Midway, when carriers *Kaga, Akagi,* and *Soryu* were under attack by American carrier bombers.

It was nearly 1000 when the *Nautilus* ventured up to periscope depth again. By then the Mobile Force had passed on, but from beyond the horizon three pillars of smoke were towering into the sky. Brockman made for the nearest. Gradually he made out the source, a Japanese carrier, burning but on an even keel, making two or three knots, and about to pass a towline to a nearby cruiser. Though his batteries were dangerously low from all the diving, Brockman decided to attack and slowly closed the interval. Just before 1400 from a range of 2,700 yards on the carrier's island side he fired three torpedoes. All three struck, and flames blossomed the whole length of the ship. Then the carrier's escorts converged on the *Nautilus,* which submerged to 300 feet and remained down until her crew counted the last of 42 depth charges dropped on them that day.

At 1800 the *Nautilus* was once more up to periscope depth. The stricken carrier was now alone, glowing and wreathed in smoke. Presently a series of terrific blasts shook the submarine as the carrier settled exploding beneath the surface. At last, with the sea to herself, the *Nautilus* surfaced to recharge her exhausted batteries. A few days later Brockman was told that his submarine had finished off the 17,500-ton *Soryu,* damaged earlier that day by carrier-based dive bombers.

After refueling at Midway, the *Nautilus* resumed her interrupted patrol. On June 25 she found and sank a destroyer in Japanese home waters. Sinking two warships before finding her first merchantman was hardly a typical beginning.

Early in August the *Nautilus* was again at Pearl Harbor, where she joined the *Argonaut* in taking aboard Colonel Evans F. Carlson and two companies of marines for a commando raid on Makin in the Gilbert Islands. This was at the time of the Guadalcanal invasion, and the Makin operation was intended as a diversion—to attract Japanese forces away from the Solomons. The marines got ashore without opposition at dawn on August 16. Soon however they began to encounter Japanese arriving by foot, on bicycles, and by truck—all in a very inhospitable mood. On request, the *Nautilus* opened fire in the general direction of the fighting, but lacking spotters to pin-point targets in this area she shifted fire to the lagoon and sank a small transport and a patrol boat. Japanese aircraft forced both submarines to submerge several times during daylight hours, but on two successive nights they took aboard what were presumed to be all the surviving marines.[4] Tactically the landing party had done a brilliant job, wiping out the small garrison on Butaritari Island, destroying installations, and picking up useful intelligence material. From the strategic point of view however the operation was a failure. Not only were the Japanese not diverted from Guadalcanal; they began to build up formidable defenses in the Gilberts, especially on Tarawa, which were to cost the lives of many Americans in the full-dress invasion a little more than a year later.

For these two patrols and a third during which she sank three merchantmen in Japanese waters, the *Nautilus* and her crew received a Presidential Unit Citation.

In the last days of December 1942 they went to Bougainville to evacuate a party of Allied refugees—14 nuns, three married women, three children, and nine men—who came aboard New Year's Eve to as festive a welcome as the circumstances permitted. In May of the next year the *Nautilus* became a troop carrier again as she and the *Narwhal* reconnoitered in the Aleutians in preparation for the American recapture of Attu. The two big submarines disembarked 214 Army Scouts into rubber boats off Attu at 0300 on the 11th, and the *Nautilus* stood by until dawn, showing an infrared light to guide the reconnaissance party to the beach of the Japanese-infested island.

Officers in Naval Intelligence had for some time been considering the use of submarines for photographic reconnaissance, and at least one submarine (the *Pompano*) had photographed shorelines through her periscope while reconnoitering. To the *Nautilus* however went the distinction of carrying out the first mission with photography as the primary task. Her new skipper, Commander W. D. Irwin, was given orders to survey the shores of Makin, Tarawa, and Abemama preliminary to the Gilberts invasion. With an

enlisted photographer and several cameras aboard and her lower sound room equipped as a laboratory-darkroom, the *Nautilus* left Pearl Harbor in mid-September 1943 to secure data on beach conditions and Japanese defenses at the target islands. The navy cameras proved inadequate to the task. Luckily the executive officer, Lieutenant Commander R. B. Lynch, a photography enthusiast, had his German Primarflex along, and it did the job. His photographs proved the most useful advance intelligence on Tarawa obtained from any source. The success of the mission convinced the Navy of the feasibility and usefulness of submarine photoreconnaissance, and the special techniques worked out aboard the *Nautilus* set the pattern for future operations.

The actual invasion of the Gilberts found the big boat in the area with the threefold job of lifesaving, weather reporting, and more transport work. Lifeguard patrol for downed aviators was a new task, pioneered by the *Skate* when she picked up six men from the *Lexington* after a raid on Wake Island. The *Nautilus* patrolled off Tarawa as ordered on D-minus-two and D-minus-one days, finding no airmen in distress. Switching to her second job, she sent off a report on local surf conditions in the evening of the second day and then began to withdraw along a preassigned track. But the invasion fleet by now was closing the island, and the destroyer *Ringgold* came booming down on the *Nautilus* at 25 knots. A 5-inch shell ripped into the submarine's superstructure but luckily failed to explode. Irwin ducked under, nervously because he was in shallow water, and when the tracking stopped went on to his third job, landing 78 marines of an amphibious reconnaissance company on Abemama. As will be recalled, the marines, finding the Japanese garrison not too big and certainly not too tough for them to handle, proceeded to capture the atoll without reinforcements. The *Nautilus* had a major part in this unpremeditated operation, bombarding enemy shore positions and taking off casualties.

The *Nautilus* sank a transport in March 1944 and then was transferred to the South-

[4] Actually nine marines were left behind. They were later captured by the Japanese and taken to Kwajalein, where they were beheaded. After the war Vice Admiral Koso Abe, who ordered the execution, stood trial for committing atrocity and was hanged on Guam. Witness for the prosecution was a Marshallese native who had watched the beheadings from nearby bushes.

west Pacific Area, where Lieutenant Commander G. A. Sharp took over as skipper. Here she began to carry out guerilla supply missions to the Philippines. In September 1944, as she pulled away from Cebu after unloading, she went hard aground on Luisan Shoal. After fruitlessly blowing all his main and variable ballast, Sharp sent the crew topside to sally ship,[5] also to no avail. He then sent ashore about 40 tons of cargo, blew 5,900 gallons of reserve fuel overboard, jettisoned 190 rounds of 6-inch ammunition, and blew the gasoline tanks dry of ballast. Five and a half hours after grounding the submarine pulled free with all engines backing at emergency speed.

The *Nautilus'* last important duty was like her first: operating with the fleet as a scout and advance patrol, this time in connection with the impending Battle for Leyte Gulf. But no more *Soryus* came her way; this time the chief blows were struck by other submarines, notably the *Darter* and the *Dace.* When the *Darter* grounded immovably the *Nautilus* was assigned the melancholy job of destroying her with 55 six-inch shells fired at point-blank range.

Versatile as the *Nautilus* was, no one ship could perform all the special missions which fell to the lot of American submarines. Some of them acted as minelayers, especially in the early part of the war when torpedoes were in short supply. Early in 1942 submarines removed key personnel and even the national gold reserve from the Philippines. And later that year when the marines were hardpressed on Guadalcanal the submarine *Amberjack* turned tanker and brought in a load of aviation gasoline.

SUBMARINES VERSUS THE JAPANESE NAVY

Enemy warships of course were fair game for submariners throughout the war. In January 1942 the *Gudgeon* achieved the first

officially confirmed sinking of an enemy warship by a United States submarine; her victim was another submarine, the 1,700-ton Japanese *I-173*.[6] In the course of the Pacific War American submarines sank 25 enemy submarines, including two U-boats that ventured into the Java Sea from their regular hunting grounds in the Indian Ocean. Dutch boats sank at least two more. American submarines sank 39 Japanese destroyers, though these were low-priority targets until late in the war. Among larger types they sank nine light and four heavy cruisers, a battleship, and nine carriers, and put two additional heavy cruisers permanently out of action.

The first major victim was the carrier *Soryu,* already heavily damaged by American carrier planes before the *Nautilus* sank her during the Battle of Midway. Except for this feat, the work of the dozen American submarines operating off Midway was something of a disappointment. The only other one to affect the battle at all was the *Tambor,* the sight of whose periscope caused the cruisers *Mogami* and *Mikuma* to collide.

During the first phases of the Guadalcanal campaign close liaison was lacking between surface and sub-surface forces because the submarines came from General MacArthur's Southwest Pacific command and the surface ships from Admiral Nimitz' Pacific Fleet. Among the many flaws in disposition of forces that led to tragic Allied losses in the Battle of Savo Island was the absence of submarines on the route between Rabaul and Guadalcanal. No American submarines were in position to intercept Mikawa's cruisers as they came down for their attack, but the leaky old *S-44,* patrolling off New Ireland under the command of Lieutenant Commander J. R. Moore, caught them as they returned from their victory. Moore fired four torpedoes at the heavy cruiser *Kako;* all four hit, and—because they were obsolete Mark 10's—they exploded. The 8,000-ton victim of the 850-ton submarine went down quickly, the only large warship sunk by an S-boat during the war. The achievement of Moore and

---

[5] "Evolution aboard ship in which crew runs from side to side together, causing ship to roll slowly. Used to extricate ship in ice or aground." John V. Noel, Jr., *Naval Terms Dictionary* (New York, 1952).

[6] This was not the first submarine sunk, however; a Dutch submarine had got one earlier.

his crew may have helped to gain the victory on Guadalcanal. By alarming the Japanese over the possibility of submarine attack, the *S-44* may well have slowed down the speed of reinforcement, and it was this Japanese tardiness that permitted the United States Marines to get firmly established on the island.

For the invasion of the Gilbert Islands, Admirals Nimitz, Spruance, and Lockwood worked together as a team. They decided that enemy surface opposition to the landings must emanate from Truk, that it would probably swing north to avoid land-based air searches from Guadalcanal, and that it would have to refuel in the Marshalls. So five of the ten submarines available took station in the Carolines—three near Truk, the others farther east. Three more were in the Marshalls covering the likely Japanese bases for refueling—Kwajalein, Eniwetok, and Wotje. The ninth submarine lay 300 miles west of Tarawa and sent daily weather reports from D-minus-five until D-plus-four day. The tenth submarine was the *Nautilus* on her threefold mission.

Since no Japanese surface forces went to the Gilberts, the submarines had little to do except attack whatever merchantmen and convoys came their way. Nevertheless two of the boats were lost. The *Corvina,* off Truk, was sunk by a Japanese submarine—the only American submarine so destroyed during the whole war. The *Sculpin,* in the eastern Carolines, was detected while closing in on a convoy. She underwent a depth charge attack from the convoy escorts that brought her to the surface, where her crew fought her deck-guns as long as they could and then scuttled her.

Aboard the *Sculpin* was Captain John P. Cromwell USN. Considering that a wolf pack might be needed in those waters, Admiral Lockwood had sent Captain Cromwell to take command. Because he possessed important information about the Gilberts landings and other war plans and feared that the Japanese might extract that information through torture, he elected to go down with the submarine. For his decision he was post-

humously awarded the Congressional Medal of Honor.

The deployment of submarines for this operation seems to have impressed Admiral Spruance favorably, for he adhered to the same pattern thereafter. Instead of having a scouting line at sea, he placed submarines in the narrow waters through which the enemy had to sortie in order to approach the place of battle. Unlike the Japanese at Midway, he got his submarines to their stations early enough for them to be of value. Moreover a doctrine of submarine employment in connection with fleet operations began to take shape:

1. Submarine concentration to cut the enemy's supply lines to the target areas.

2. Submarine photographic reconnaissance of beachheads marked for amphibious landings and enemy military or naval installations marked for future reference.

3. Submarine lifeguarding during air strikes.

4. Submarine scouting duty in the target area and off enemy bases to report enemy movements and intercept and attack enemy forces which sortied to oppose the attacking United States forces.

5. Submarines stationed to intercept and attack fugitive shipping attempting to flee the target area.[7]

For the Marshalls landings of January 1944 not one but four submarines performed photoreconnaissance. Again three submarines took stations off the approaches to Truk, and this time two of the three sank destroyers. The deployment of the other available submarines for this operation was patterned on that of the Gilberts operation.

For the three big carrier strikes at Truk, Saipan, and Palau in early 1944, the pattern was varied somewhat, since Spruance believed that his opposition would come not from surface units but from the enemy's land-based air, while the surface units and the merchant shipping present would flee the areas. Consequently he stationed his submarines on the escape routes, where they did some damage. Off Truk the *Skate* sank the light cruiser *Agano,* and the *Tang* got a

[7] Theodore Roscoe, *United States Submarine Operations in World War II* (Annapolis, 1949), 361.

cargo ship. At Saipan the *Sunfish* got two merchantmen and the *Tang* got four. Off Palau the *Tullibee* was sunk by her own circling torpedo,[8] and apparently most of the Japanese shipping escaped through the area assigned to her. It was on this occasion however that the *Tunny* put her two torpedoes into the superbattleship *Musashi*.

Before the American invasion of the Marianas in June 1944 Admiral Lockwood, of the Pacific Fleet, and Admiral Ralph Christie, of the Seventh Fleet, positioned their submarines at the request of Admiral Spruance. Their deployment was nothing less than brilliant. Three boats were watching the Japanese fleet assembled at Tawitawi; others were off the principal straits through which it would have to pass to reach Saipan; four more were patrolling the Philippine Sea in 90-degree arcs inside and centered on the corners of a great square. Still others were in motion, relieving patrollers or returning to base after relief; two of these transients played major roles in the development of the battle. There was also a wolf pack on routine patrol—the *Shark II,* the *Pilotfish,* and the *Pintado*—called Blair's Blasters after group commander Captain L. N. Blair usn.

On May 31, 1944 the submarine *Silversides,* patrolling an adjacent area, informed the Blasters that a convoy was coming their way, apparently heading from Honshu to Saipan. By the time the *Silversides* had joined forces with the wolf pack, two more convoys had appeared in the area. Early on June 1 the *Pintado* picked off a freighter from the first of the three convoys. All that day and for several days thereafter the wolf pack chased the third convoy, but the *Silversides,* her torpedoes expended, had to withdraw. Late on June 2 and again on the morning of June 4 the *Shark* sank a cargo ship. On the evening of June 5 she got two more, one a passenger-cargo vessel of 7,000 tons. That same night the *Pintado* sank two ships. As a result of these sinkings half a division of Japanese reinforcement troops was drowned, and many other soldiers reached the Marianas without guns or battle gear.

The Japanese commander on Saipan had to ration munitions. Blair's Blasters had enormously lessened the opposition American assault troops would have to overcome.

From June 6 through June 9 the submarine *Harder,* under Commander Samuel D. Dealey, set a remarkable record in the vicinity of Sibutu Strait, which lies between the southern islands of the Sulu Archipelago and the northern coast of Borneo. According to the official postwar assessment the *Harder* sank three destroyers and damaged at least two more. On the morning of June 10 the *Harder* was patrolling one of the three stations off Tawitawi in the Sulu Sea when she witnessed the sortie of Admiral Ugaki's battleship force for the relief of Biak and radioed a timely warning to Allied commands.

As a result of the *Harder*'s destroyer-shoot, Admiral Toyoda in Tokyo believed that the Tawitawi anchorage was surrounded by a great force of submarines. Nervous as to the safety of the Mobile Fleet, he initiated the *A* Operation as soon as he heard of the preliminary moves toward Saipan. Thus it is probable that the *Harder*'s operations got Admiral Ozawa to sea too soon and simplified the job of American reconnaissance. The Japanese carrier force moved northward on June 13; the *Redfin* saw it go and flashed the contact report that caused Admiral Spruance to postpone the invasion of Guam and prepare for the impending Battle of the Philippine Sea.

On the evening of June 15, 1944 two more American submarines made contacts. The *Flying Fish,* patrolling off San Bernardino Strait, sighted Ozawa's Mobile Fleet; the *Seahorse,* on her way to a patrol station, encountered Ugaki heading northeast. When the *Seahorse* developed engine trouble, Admiral Lockwood ordered his nearest available submarine to take over. This was the *Cavalla,* under Commander H. J. Kossler—another transient proceeding to relieve the watch on San Bernardino Strait. Early on June 17 the diverted *Cavalla* made a contact of her own, this time on a tanker convoy heading for Ozawa's rendezvous point. Kossler failed to realize that these

---

[8] Reported by a survivor picked up by the Japanese and released from prison camp at the end of the war.

tankers could lead him to the Japanese fleet for he could hardly guess that Ozawa was still in the vicinity. Having arrived in the Philippine Sea 24 hours ahead of schedule, the Mobile Fleet had spent a day in aimless, fuel-consuming maneuvers. So the *Cavalla* made her contact report and headed for the Philippines again, only to be turned back by a peremptory order from Admiral Lockwood. Although unable to pick up the tankers again, the *Cavalla* found Ugaki and reported him as he steamed northward to the rendezvous. The report stated that she had seen "15 or more large combatant ships." It was the discrepancy between this report and the 40 large Japanese ships already known to be in the Philippine Sea that kept Admiral Spruance close to the Saipan beachhead on the supposition that there was more than one Japanese fleet in the area.

As a result of the *Cavalla*'s second report, Lockwood made some changes in the disposition of his submarines, the chief one being that the four boats patrolling from the corners of a square shifted southward by about a hundred miles. Now that the approximate location of the Japanese forces was known, the admiral gave his submarines permission to shoot first and transmit contact reports afterwards. Thus the *Albacore*, assigned to the southwest corner of the new square, found herself in the right place and with the right orders on the morning of June 19, when, it will be recalled, she sank the carrier *Taiho*. Sixty miles farther along, the Japanese were spotted by the ubiquitous *Cavalla*. Freed at last from the necessity of sending contact reports, she promptly put three torpedoes into the *Shokaku* and sent her down.

Before the next big fleet operation, the Palau campaign, the submarine *Burrfish* made a combined photographic and landing-party reconnaissance of Yap Island. Because three of the five men put ashore on Yap were lost, the landing-party reconnaissance mission, rarely employed by the United States Navy, was abolished for good.

Admiral Halsey's ideas of submarine deployment differed from Admiral Spruance's. Although Halsey agreed that the narrow seas should be patrolled, he placed considerable

reliance on a scouting line in the open ocean. So while four boats guarded important straits, nine formed a scouting line between the Philippines and Palau. It was really a double line; two of the submarines from each of three wolf packs formed the first line of six, and the third submarines formed the second line, each boat in "safety" position behind its own packmates. These two lines—"Halsey's Zoo"—made no important contacts during the operation. Preferring the Spruance system, Admiral Nimitz never again granted permission to form such a line.

The story of submarine operations at the time of the Battle for Leyte Gulf has already been told in considerable detail. There were some of Lockwood's submarines north of the Philippines, where they harassed the Japanese fleet and scored some hits. But the big responsibility was that of the Southwest Pacific submarines: in addition to the achievements of the *Dace* and *Darter*, which sank two of Admiral Kurita's heavy cruisers and put a third out of action, the *Bream* did severe damage to a fourth heavy cruiser, the *Aoba*, which had been detached by Kurita for special duties and was not intended to take part in the battle. As Admiral Ozawa's surviving cripples limped homeward after the battle, the Central Pacific's *Jallao* sank the light cruiser *Tama*, already damaged by the air strikes.

In operations less closely associated with the surface fleet American submarines achieved several more successes against large warships; the three most noteworthy were the sinkings of the carriers *Chuyo* and *Shinano* and the battleship *Kongo*.

The *Chuyo* was relatively small and old, but her sinking came late in 1943 when the frustrations resulting from defective torpedoes were still fresh in the submariners' minds and when no large Japanese man-of-war had been sunk by a submarine for 16 months. The *Sailfish*, which broke this run of bad luck, had previously had her own share of trouble; she was the *Squalus*, victim of the memorable disaster in 1939, now raised and rechristened. On her tenth war patrol (but her first with Lieutenant Commander R. E. M. Ward as skipper) she ran into a typhoon off Japan. At 1745 on December 3, 1943 Ward had recorded, "Tremendous seas, 40-50 knot wind, driving rain, and visibility, after twilight, varying from zero to 500 yards." Just before midnight he made radar contact with a large target. At 0012 he was in position to fire four tubes, with which he scored one hit on the 20,000-ton *Chuyo* then returning from Truk to Japan in company with a cruiser and a destroyer or two. The carrier was hurt, but she limped through the gale at from two to five knots. At 0552, in morning twilight with the weather improving slightly, the *Sailfish* fired another spread of three; again one of them hit, this time stopping the *Chuyo* dead in the water. At 0748 Ward saw and identified his victim for the first time; at 0940 he fired a spread from his stern tubes. At least one more torpedo hit the target, and the *Chuyo* sank at 0948, unobserved by the *Sailfish,* which had been driven deep by the carrier's escorts.

The 31,000-ton *Kongo,* which went down about a year later, was the only battleship sunk by an American submarine, although by that time Japanese warships of other categories were becoming fairly usual targets. The *Sealion II* (Commander Eli T. Reich) encountered her victim 40 miles north of Formosa. The first radar contact showed the target so far distant that the officer of the deck mistook it for land, but he called the skipper when a further contact showed the target moving nearer. It was just past a November midnight, the sky overcast but visibility fair. Identifying the contact as comprising at least two battleships, two cruisers, and several destroyers heading for Japan, Reich elected to make a surface approach using radar. By the time he had gained the desired attack position and made his first visual contact with the enemy force at about 0245, the sea was rising, whipped by a night wind. At 0256 Reich fired six bow torpedoes at the leading battleship, at a range of 3,000 yards. Throwing the rudder hard right, he brought his stern tubes to bear on the second battleship and got away three torpedoes at 0259. Then he took the *Sealion* away from there at flank speed. To his great disappointment

the task force continued on its course at 18 knots. Taking water over the bridge and a good deal down the conning tower hatch, the *Sealion* chased. At 0450 the battleship at which the bow tubes had been fired slowed to 12 knots and dropped astern of the task force with two destroyers standing by. Shortly afterwards this ship, the *Kongo,* went dead in the water. As the *Sealion* maneuvered into attack position, a flash of light, presumably from the explosion of the battleship's magazines, illuminated the entire sea, and the *Kongo* sank. The *Sealion* immediately began to pursue the other battleship but was unable to overtake her in the now heavy seas. Only after the war did the *Sealion's* crew learn that one of the stern-tube torpedoes fired at 0259, missing its intended battleship target, had sunk a destroyer. All the torpedoes used in this attack were Mark 18 electrics.

Even this achievement was overshadowed about a week later when the *Archerfish* sank the *Shinano.* There is a story to the effect that once, as the Japanese were launching a big carrier before cheering crowds, a submarine fired a torpedo into her so that she kept going right on down to the bottom. The story is not literally true, but the *Archerfish* (Commander J. E. Enright) did almost as well. The *Shinano* was of 68,000 tons displacement, one of the largest warships in the world. Begun as a sister ship to the superbattleships *Yamato* and *Musashi,* she had been converted into a supercarrier instead. She was commissioned on November 18, 1944 and sunk ten days later. When the *Archerfish* found her 150 miles south of Tokyo, she was on her way to the Inland Sea for fitting out in comparative safety from air attack. The American submarine made radar contact with the carrier and her four escorts at 2048. A stern chase ensued, which the *Archerfish* must inevitably have lost had the target not zigzagged. At 0300 a radical change in the Japanese base course put the submarine ahead of the carrier, and a zig at 0316 made the position perfect except for a rather large gyro angle. At 0317, with range 1,400 yards and a 70-degree starboard angle, Enright fired a spread of six Mark 14 torpedoes, at least four of which took effect.

The *Shinano* should not have sunk, but she did. The crew was inexperienced and the ship unready for sea. Doors that should have been watertight had no gaskets; water poured through them and through unsealed conduits. Steam pumps had not yet been installed and piping was incomplete. There were too few hand pumps. When the morale of the crew failed also and discipline broke down, the loss of the ship was inevitable. It is fitting that an American submarine should climax the undersea campaign against Japanese warships by sending down the new queen of the Imperial Navy before she had an opportunity to come into action. It is also ironic because Japan no longer had any use for such a vessel. She had freely expended the bulk of her remaining fast carriers as mere decoys in the Battle for Leyte Gulf because she lacked trained pilots for carrier aircraft.

COMMERCE DESTROYING: THE BIG ACHIEVEMENT

"Execute unrestricted air and submarine warfare against Japan." So read the directive issued to American submarine forces on December 7, 1941. This directive reversed the long-standing opposition of the United States Navy to attacks on non-combatant vessels without prior warning and removal of crews. But for the United States to have adhered to such a point of international law when pitted against an enemy who obviously had no intention of so restricting himself would have put the Navy at a fatal disadvantage. In the eyes of American naval leaders Japan, by her attack on Pearl Harbor without previous declaration of war, had placed herself outside the formal limitations of warfare.

Besides, the old distinction between combatant and non-combatant vessels had become blurred by the nature of 20th century warfare. The rule against unrestricted sea warfare had been intended to apply to merchantmen, but during World War II Japanese merchantmen ceased to exist as such.

All vessels were impressed into the national service. Every tanker bringing oil, every freighter bringing rice or tin to Japan or carrying provisions and munitions to her island bases was as vital to her conduct of warfare as an armed warship. Overcrowded Japan cannot survive without imports even in peacetime, and in 1942 she had to meet the enormously stepped-up requirements of warfare, including the maintenance of her far-flung garrisons. In December 1941 Japan possessed barely the 6,000,000 tons of merchant shipping required to supply her home islands and her bases. In August 1945, despite a frantic shipbuilding program, she had left only 1,800,000 tons. As we have seen, American submarines accounted for 4,800,000 tons, or more than half of all merchant tonnage sunk; British and Netherlands submarines contributed another 100,000 tons. This was the great contribution of submarines to victory in the Pacific—a strangling blockade, isolating the bases from the home islands and the home islands from their sources of supply, gradually but surely starving the Empire into impotence.

During the first two years of the war all the vast area of the Pacific inside Japan's defense perimeter was closed to Allied surface ships and aircraft. Within this area were the oceanic communication lines on which the Japanese depended to carry on the war: the lifelines between the Southern Resources Area and Japan and between Japan and her forward bases—Rabaul, Truk, Tarawa, Kwajalein, and the rest. But the submarine could and did go virtually anywhere; by the end of 1942 patrols near the home islands were becoming routine.

The submarine war against Japanese communications got under way slowly, for in the early months even the large American fleet boats (named for fish) lacked reliable equipment. Their torpedoes were faulty; their radar, if they had any, was the rudimentary SD type, good for little more than helping a lookout spot aircraft; the PPI (position plan indicator) had yet to be invented. To be sure, the TDC (torpedo data computer) had become available, but it was new and unfamiliar. Moreover early American tactical doctrine was based on an overestimate of what planes could do against submarines. Submerged sound attacks were stressed, and attacks at periscope depth were discouraged where there was any probability of detection by aircraft. As a result of these shortcomings, all American submarines together during the first four months of the war sank only about as much tonnage as the single boat *Flasher* was to get in 1944. However, this slow start had the advantage of lulling the enemy into a false sense of security. The Japanese at first set up no effective convoy system and for months did not trouble to arm their cargo vessels.

As better equipment such as the SJ radar came into use, and submarine commanders gradually freed themselves from overcautious doctrine, the rate of kills rose sharply. The Japanese, shocked by their losses, hastily improvised convoys and countermeasures, bringing the effectiveness of their antisubmarine warfare to a peak in 1943. This was the year however in which Admiral Lockwood struck at the heart of the Japanese war effort by assigning high priority to tankers, thereby bringing the Japanese oil supply under heavy attack.

To deal with the convoys, American submarines adopted the German style of operating in wolf packs. Because Japanese convoys were small in comparison to Allied convoys in the Atlantic, American wolf packs rarely comprised more than three submarines. Each pack had a commander—usually of the rank of commander or captain—and the pack generally took its designation from the commander's name, e.g., "Blair's Blasters," "Ed's Eradicators," "Roach's Raiders," and the like. Initial wolf pack tactics called for a boat on each flank of the convoy and a third to trail behind to get stragglers. Such station-keeping on a sharply maneuvering convoy proved so difficult however that doctrine gave way to improvisation on the spot. As the ST radar came into use, coupled with a really dependable torpedo, submariners tended to jettison attack doctrine altogether and make themselves virtuosos of undersea warfare. They made kills at all hours, from all depths and angles, including "down the throat" and "up the kilt"—difficult shots from dead ahead and dead astern.

Despite Japanese use of escort vessels and mine fields and their much-touted magnetic airborne detector, American submarines continued to range and kill everywhere. Not all came home; 52 were lost, mostly without a trace. But the vast majority of the patrols were successful, mainly through skill and daring but partly because the Japanese failed to equip their planes and escort ships with radar until it was too late.

With the increasing destruction of Japanese shipping, especially of vital tankers, the efficiency of Japan's war machine declined ever more sharply. On the eve of the Philippine Sea battle, it will be recalled, scarcity of oil in the home islands forced the Mobile Fleet to base at Tawitawi. After the battle Admiral Ozawa took his fleet to Japan for repairs and ammunition, but here he found an acute shortage of fuel. So the fleet had to be divided, and Admiral Kurita took most of the surface vessels back south where there was oil aplenty but few repair facilities and no stores of ammunition. The Imperial Fleet was thus caught in two widely separated parts when the Americans invaded the Philippines, precipitating the last great clash of fleets in the Battle for Leyte Gulf. Even then the Japanese might have achieved something had they been able to use their carriers as combat ships rather than as mere decoys. But the carriers were powerless to strike because Japan, largely for lack of aviation fuel, could never train enough replacement pilots to offset the heavy losses which began with the Battle of Midway. Thus American submarines, patiently tracking and destroying oil-bearing ships from the East Indies, divided the enemy's sea power and rendered him incapable of maintaining his air power.

THE FAILURE OF JAPANESE SUBMARINES

Before the Japanese submarines were diverted in significant numbers to non-combat duties, they scored some important kills in the United States Fleet. At Midway the *I-168* sank the crippled *Yorktown* and the destroyer alongside her. Late in 1942, in the space of three months, submarines operating on the Allied supply line to Guadalcanal sank the carrier *Wasp,* finished off the damaged cruiser *Juneau,* mortally wounded the destroyers *O'Brien* and *Porter,* and crippled the battleship *North Carolina.* Through the rest of the war however only two more large warships were sunk by Japanese submarines—the escort carrier *Liscome Bay* in 1943 and the heavy cruiser *Indianapolis* in the last month of hostilities.

Like the Americans, the Japanese often sent their submarines on special missions, some of them peculiar to the Imperial Navy. Such was the practice of "piggy-backing" small attack devices into effective range—midget submarines, aircraft, and *Kaitens,* i.e., torpedoes steered by suicide crews. Midget attacks were carried out early in the war on Pearl Harbor, Madagascar, and Sydney. Though at Madagascar they sank a tanker and damaged H.M. battleship *Ramillies,* their general performance was so poor that they were not used after the middle of 1942. Submarine-launched aircraft carried out some successful photoreconnaissance missions, and one of them dropped several incendiary bombs in the forests of Oregon, but difficulties of launching and recovery precluded widespread use of aircraft-carrying types. The war was ending before Japan began to commission its *I-400* class of monster 3,500-ton submarines, intended to bring three planes apiece to within range of the Panama Canal. The *Kaitens* also came too late, for by the time they went into operation highly-developed Allied antisubmarine devices were able to keep them from doing major damage.

The Japanese often used their submarines on nuisance raids of little strategic value. Once or twice they refueled flying boats for raids outside their normal cruising radius. In 1942 they caused some excitement along the Pacific Coast of North America by sinking a few ships and shelling Vancouver Island, Astoria and the shore north of Los Angeles. Several submarines tried to establish liaison with Germany but only the *I-8* made the round-trip to Europe successfully.

The poor showing of the Japanese submarines in contrast to the magnificent achievement of American boats deserves analysis. The two opposing underwater forces were about equal in numbers at the outbreak of war: the Japanese had a few more submarines than the Americans, but this advantage was offset by boats from the Netherlands fleet. The small, obsolete Japanese RO-class was greatly inferior to the corresponding American S-boat, but their modern I-class was certainly no mean antagonist in comparison with the American fleet types. Technical deficiencies of the Japanese boats of course account to some extent for their comparative ineffectiveness: until late in the war they had no radar and their sound gear was extremely inefficient, leaving them far more vulnerable to countermeasures than German U-boats. The main trouble however was simply strategic blindness on the part of the Japanese High Command. They never used their submarines in a regular campaign against merchant shipping, apparently failing to understand the central place of logistics in modern war.

When the Germans pointed out the extraordinary effectiveness of the submarine as a commerce-raider and urged that Japan use her underwater fleet against Allied communications, the Japanese invariably replied that they would risk their submarines only against warships. So while American submarines were wearing down Japanese fighting potential by unremitting attacks on their lines of supply, Japan sent her boats after well-protected fleet units but disregarded the far more vulnerable tankers and cargo vessels on which the Allied fleet depended.

With the inauguration of the Allied flanking strategy, the desperate Japanese sidetracked even this objective. To supply their by-passed and isolated garrisons, they began using submarines as cargo carriers. Gradually, to the disgust of their submariners, their best boats were pressed into such routine service. Thus while the United States and its allies were lengthening their overwater communication lines more and more by seizing and operating bases ever nearer Japan, the effectiveness of Japanese submarines steadily declined. Never in the long history of warfare has a primary weapon been used with less grasp of its true potential.

"THERE'LL ALWAYS BE AN *ENGLAND*"

The ineffectiveness and vulnerability of the Japanese submarines in the latter half of the war is well illustrated by their operations in connection with the Marianas invasion. The Japanese knew very well that the Americans were about to strike again, and they correctly guessed that the next blow would be along the line of Japan's inner defense perimeter. Aside from these conclusions their estimates were all wrong. They set up an apparently formidable submarine defense screen, but the screen proved not to be formidable at all—worse, it was in the wrong place. MacArthur's landing on Biak Island led them to expect that the next Fifth Fleet operations would be against the Palaus instead of the Marianas, for it was the Palaus that Nimitz had hit in support of MacArthur's invasion of Hollandia. Confident that the Americans would come that way again, the Japanese sent submarines to operate north of the Admiralties. In setting up their screen they not only selected the wrong area; they also failed to allow for improvements in American countermeasures. By mid-1944 the war against the U-boat was drawing to a close, and destroyer-escorts capable of throwing weapons forward—by means of such devices as the "hedgehog" and the "mousetrap"—were beginning to move to the Pacific. Of no fewer than 25 I-boats and RO-boats operating in connection with the Marianas campaign, 17 were sent to the bottom by American destroyers, destroyer escorts, and aircraft.

The exploits of the destroyer escort U.S.S. *England* (Lieutenant Commander W. B. Pendleton) in May 1944 demonstrate the impotence of Japanese submarines against the new type of attack. Alerted by the news that an American destroyer division had sunk a submarine near Green Island, Admiral Halsey ordered the destroyer-escorts *England*, *Raby*, and *George* from Ironbottom Sound to the Bismarcks-Admiralties area. The next day the group made contact north of the Solomons with the 2,600-ton *I-16* on a cargo-carrying mission out ahead of the main line of Japanese submarines. The *England* made five hedgehog attacks and obtained five hits, whereupon she was rocked by a terrific explosion as the I-boat blew apart. Proceeding NW the group ran into the main defense line of seven RO-boats. Here in three successive days, May 22, 23, and 24, the *England* sank *RO*'s *106, 104* and *116*. Ordered to proceed to Seeadler Harbor to take on more hedgehog ammunition, the group towards midnight of the 26th made radar contact with *RO-108*. The group commander gave the *Raby* first chance at this submarine, but she lost contact and the *England* made another kill. Joined by a fourth destroyer escort bringing the needed ammunition, the *England's* group returned to the hunting grounds, where they were integrated into a hunter-killer group of destroyers and an escort carrier. When this combined group made contact with the *RO-105* in the early hours of May 31, the officer in tactical command deliberately ordered the *England* to stand aside in order to give the other ships an opportunity to score. When these missed, in came the *England* once more and blew up the RO-boat with another hedgehog salvo. In ten days she had sunk six submarines. This unparalleled achievement received no special attention in the Pacific theater, but when the report reached Washington, Admiral King made sure that the name of the champion would not be forgotten. "There'll always be an *England* in the United States Navy," he signaled.

"TAKE HER DOWN!"

One more story must be told, for without it no account of submarines in the Pacific can be complete. In February 1943 the American submarine *Growler* was patrolling near the Bismarcks. At 0110 she sighted an enemy ship and began a surface run. As the range closed, the target—a 2,500-ton Japanese gunboat—sighted the submarine, reversed course, and rushed at her. The *Growler*'s radar operator below decks noted the enemy's change of course immediately, but her skipper, Commander Howard W. Gilmore, and the other six men on the bridge did not see the maneuver in the darkness. The command, "Left full rudder!" came too late to avoid collision; the *Growler* plowed into the Japanese gunboat at 17 knots. All hands were knocked down by the impact. As the submarine, which had heeled far over, righted herself, the gunboat sprayed the bridge with machine gun bullets. The junior officer of the deck and one of the lookouts were instantly killed; Commander Gilmore was severely wounded. Clinging to the bridge frame, he made his voice heard: "Clear the bridge!" The four other living men scrambled as best they could through the hatch. Then came Commander Gilmore's last command, "Take her down!"

For this "distinguished gallantry and valor," Commander Gilmore was posthumously awarded the Congressional Medal of Honor. His last words have taken their place in naval tradition beside those of Captain James Lawrence of the frigate *Chesapeake*.

There is much more for Americans to recall with pride about the Pacific submarines of 1941-1945. The *Flasher,* as we have noted, sank over 100,000 tons of enemy shipping, all but 850 of it in a single year. The *Tautog* sank the most ships, 26. Only three ships in the entire United States Navy won two Presidential Unit Citations apiece; two of these were submarines: the *Guardfish* and the *Tang.* Once the problem of the defective torpedoes was solved, American submarines did an amazingly efficient job. Such incidental services to the war effort as the special missions were of great value. The submarine sank more warship tonnage than any other agent except carrier-based air. And in the destruction of merchant shipping the submarine was supreme. Until American aircraft obtained bases relatively near the Japanese home islands and the life line to the East Indies, the submarine alone could strike at shipping in those waters. Thus it played the major role in disrupting Japanese logistics, and for a great part of the war it played this role virtually alone.

48

The Defeat of Germany

WHILE AMERICAN SUBMA-rines were throttling Japan in the Western Pacific, the Nazis were growing desperate over their failure to starve Great Britain into submission. Geography imposed a far more difficult problem on the Germans than it did on the United States in cutting supply routes, for Japan's main lines of communication were restricted to a comparatively narrow channel between the east coast of Asia and the island chain including the Philippines, Formosa, the Ryukyus, and Japan itself. In the Atlantic, the communication lines crossed the open ocean, and Allied defense measures were strong enough to keep the majority of U-boats at a distance from the focal areas around the British Isles.

Nonetheless, after a midwinter lull, the early months of 1943 brought a sharp upturn in the rate of Allied cargo ships sunk in the North Atlantic. In March, 95 ships displacing 567,401 tons were sent to the bottom, a figure comparing to the darkest hours of 1942. Although the peak of the submarine menace had passed, few of the men who had to go to sea derived comfort from that fact. On North Atlantic convoy runs, the hunter and hunted continued their grim game of hide and seek, with death the penalty for carelessness or lack of vigilance. Echelons of

German wolf packs lurked along the supply routes in such numbers that evasive routing was useless. For the first five months of 1943, an average of 110 submarines operated in the convoy lanes on any given day in the Atlantic. They could not be eluded; a convoy had to fight its way through

ALLIED VICTORY IN THE BATTLE OF THE ATLANTIC

The Casablanca Conference in January 1943 took up the question of the supply routes across the Atlantic and agreed unanimously that the defeat of the U-boat was the chief problem confronting the Allies in their war against the Axis. The Combined Chiefs of Staff considered five methods for combating the menace: (1) bombing of European factories that produced parts for U-boats, (2) bombing of U-boat assembly plants, (3) bombing of U-boat bases and refitting yards at Lorient, Brest, and other places on the French coast, (4) tracking down and sinking U-boats at sea, and (5) defeating the purpose of the U-boat by convoying all ships in an endeavor to hold losses down to an accepta-

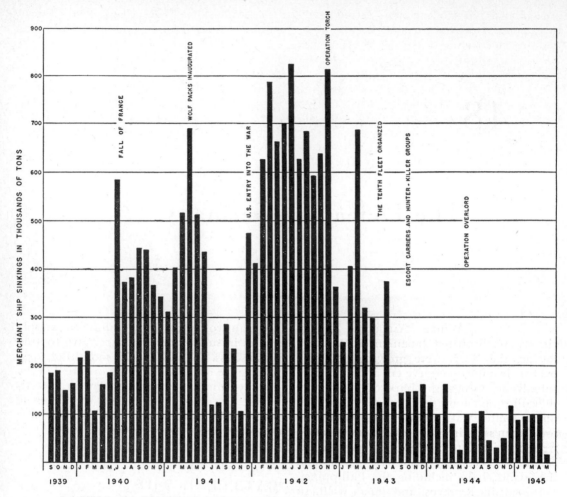

BATTLE OF THE ATLANTIC: MERCHANT VESSEL LOSSES TO U-BOATS

ble figure. Some of these methods had been in effect since the beginning of the war, but they could be improved upon and new ones adopted. The British were inclined to stress destroying the U-boats at sea, while the American navy put more faith in destruction of German capacity for building U-boats and in improved convoy systems. Actually, improved convoy defense resulted in the accomplishment of the British aim as well, for escorts began to strive harder for kills whenever contact was made on a submarine.

Early in 1943, it became apparent that the American phase of the antisubmarine war needed more centralized direction. The sea frontier commands, often working effectively

within their prescribed geographical limits, were not well coordinated. Conflicting doctrine was being promulgated by some of the subordinate commands, so that personnel going from one geographical area to another were often confused to the point of losing effectiveness. As a result, in May 1943 Admiral King established the Tenth Fleet, actually a paper organization, which was given operational control over all existing antisubmarine activities in the Atlantic. This in effect reduced the sea frontier commands to the level of task forces, but the additional flexibility of the new organization outweighed all objections. Under unified command, forces could be rapidly shifted from an area of inactivity to one more immediately threatened. Doctrine became standardized, and the effectiveness of the new organization became apparent almost at once with the increased number of U-boats destroyed.

An earlier chapter noted the British expedient of flying expendable aircraft from tankers fitted with catapults. This device, which had had some measure of success, was only a temporary expedient until the escort carrier could be developed and put into production. With these small, easily-built carriers, the Allies were able to afford air cover to convoys in areas outside the range of land-based planes. No longer was there a gap in the mid-Atlantic area where U-boats could hunt with comparative impunity. The escort carriers offered two new methods for protection of shipping. Some of them sailed with the convoys to provide a combat air patrol, to search for and attack submarines on the surface, and to coach the surface antisubmarine vessels onto a submerged U-boat. Escort carriers also operated in hunter-killer groups to make the hunter become the hunted. Such a group typically consisted of an escort carrier and a half-dozen destroyers and destroyer escorts which had no escort responsibilities but were used rather to move into the scene of U-boat operations and hunt them down and destroy them before they could attack. The aircraft, armed with the new rockets and equipped with airborne radar, succeeded outstandingly in locating U-boats and either sinking them or driving them down, whereupon the surface units would take over. Increasing numbers of antisubmarine vessels meant that coordinated search and attack techniques could be developed and refined. Sinkings of U-boats mounted sharply as these hunter-killer groups took to sea.

Radar proved to be one of the most important inventions in defeating the U-boat campaign. Early in the war radar sets had been in too short supply for use on more than a handful of escorting ships, but by the spring of 1943, enough progress had been made so that aircraft could be supplied with special light-weight search equipment. This almost at once defeated the U-boat practice of running surfaced across the Bay of Biscay at night en route to and from their hunting grounds, and traversing these waters submerged meant loss of operating time on the Atlantic stations.

The new radar puzzled the Germans. Earlier models had operated on comparatively low frequencies and could be detected and jammed, but a shift to microwave frequencies defeated both the detection and jamming equipment on which the Nazis were relying. As a result Doenitz, who had replaced Raeder in January 1943 as Commander in Chief of the German Navy, was forced to call his U-boats in from the North Atlantic area, where Allied air cover was the rule, to the area west of the Azores, where it was the exception, to try to pick off shipping bound for Gibraltar. He also attempted the expedient of putting increased antiaircraft armament on the U-boats and instructing them to fight it out on the surface, but this merely resulted in increased U-boat sinkings.

The predictable result of the withdrawal of the U-boats from the North Atlantic area was an increased flow of shipping to Great Britain. After late June 1943, the British Admiralty allowed merchant ships which could make 15 knots or better to cross the Atlantic independent of convoy protection, thereby speeding up the flow of goods and releasing escorts for better protection of slower convoys and for independent hunter-killer work.

Admiral Doenitz however did not consider that he had lost the Battle of the Atlantic. He pinned his hopes on five developments: (1) an increase in the antiaircraft armament on his U-boats, (2) an increase in the use of mine warfare, (3) the use of the acoustic torpedo, which would "home" on a ship's screws, (4) the expected introduction of the Walther-type U-boat propelled by hydrogen peroxide and capable of high underwater speed for a short period of time, and (5) the addition of the snorkel underwater breather device. We have already noted the failure of the first of these. The thin hulls of the U-boats proved no match for aircraft rockets. Mine warfare proved no more successful since the mines had to be laid in focal areas, and these the allies routinely swept. The acoustic torpedo promised greater success, for the screws of a ship cannot be silenced, but Allied scientists came up quickly with the answer in the form of a device called the "foxer," a noise-maker towed behind a ship. This device made so much noise that it drowned out the screws and diverted the acoustic torpedo into exploding uselessly against the foxer.

The Walther-type U-boat was a rather long range solution; it was not expected for use before 1944, and production difficulties so held it up that none was actually used in the war. This boat had great promise and conceivably could have put an entirely different complexion on the Atlantic war if the Germans had managed to develop it in time. A few were captured at the time of the German surrender, some going to the Western Allies and some to the Soviet Union.

The most immediately successful of these devices was the snorkel, an exhaust tube to the surface with an automatic closure valve to prevent flooding. When running on snorkel, a submarine can operate its diesel engines and yet be submerged except for the tip of the snorkel, which is very difficult to detect from a surface ship, either visually or by radar. This meant that a submarine could operate indefinitely at snorkel depth with a very slight chance of detection and could even recharge batteries for complete submergence without ever exposing more than the tip of the snorkel tube. A second advantage to the snorkel boats was that detection by asdic or sonar became increasingly difficult because the propagation characteristics of a sound wave in water result in the wave being bent gradually downward. It was easy for a snorkeling boat to lie in wait above the sound beam, whereas before the advent of this device, the U-boats customarily operated on the surface or submerged to a greater depth for optimum listening characteristics.

The change to snorkel tactics might have been serious to the Allies if they had not already found the answer to it in carrier aircraft, which could not only detect the faint wake of the snorkel but could often see the whole silhouette of the submarine at snorkel depth. The effectiveness of hunter-killer groups increased as ahead-thrown weapons were perfected, and from 1944 on, the U-boat campaign went from bad to worse from the German point of view. The loss of French bases after the Normandy invasion added greatly to German difficulties, and although the Germans abandoned the deep Atlantic to concentrate around the approaches to the British Isles, attempting to hide from sonar detection by lying on the bottom behind the shelter of reefs or wrecks, sonar proved flexible enough to deny the Nazis this last resort. Sinkings of Allied shipping diminished steadily until May 8, 1945, when Admiral Doenitz sadly called upon his beaten U-boat fleet to proceed to port or to surrender to Allied surface ships.

Thus ended the fierce, dirty, ruthless Battle of the Atlantic. Although it cost more in Allied effort and resources to destroy the U-boats than it did in German effort and resources to employ them, the relative economic strength of the two sides makes the comparison almost meaningless. The German U-boat campaign very nearly succeeded. As it was, the U-boats destroyed about 3,000 ships, amounting in all to more than 14,000,000 tons of shipping, against a loss of 994 German U-boats and 116 Italian submarines, but the Allied effort was able to surmount these losses. The U-boat campaign had to win swiftly or not at all. Once Allied production and ship-building programs matched the rate of sinkings, the U-boats were beaten. By the end of 1942, this had been achieved. Thereafter the U-boats fought merely to delay the build-up of men and materials in Africa and Europe. They could not halt the process.

Near the end of the war, U-boats changed their tactics and began to go after the escorts. By this time escort vessels were plentiful and no serious consequences resulted, but if the submarines had tried the scheme back in 1940-1942, when escorts were pitifully short, they might well have crippled Allied shipping in the North Atlantic. Unprotected or too lightly protected convoys merely offer conveniently bunched targets. Rather than thus offer themselves for destruction in wholesale lots, transports and freighters would have had

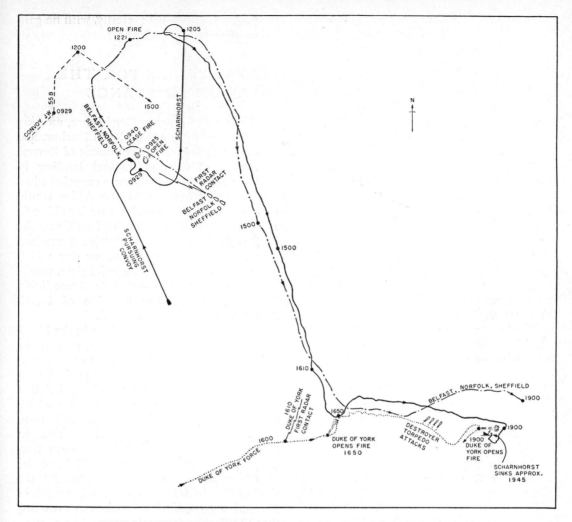

THE SINKING OF THE SCHARNHORST, *DECEMBER 24, 1943*

to proceed independently, employing evasive routing—certainly a poor alternative to well-guarded convoys. Britain's heavy losses early in the war, with weakly escorted convoys and with some ships forced to sail alone, illustrate what the U-boats might possibly have achieved had they earlier selected escorts as their main targets.

THE *SCHARNHORST'S* LAST CRUISE

With the declining effectiveness of the U-boat campaign, Hitler and Admiral Doenitz

decided to reverse the policy which had kept the surface ships of the German navy idle since 1942. On Christmas Eve of 1943, the battleship *Scharnhorst* set out from Norway to intercept a convoy bound for north Russia. But the convoy had been diverted to the northward, and the battleship met instead a cruiser scouting force of the British Home Fleet. In the morning of December 26, H.M.S. *Belfast* made radar contact with the German and opened fire, joined by the *Sheffield* and the *Norfolk;* but foul weather so reduced the speed of the British cruisers that they soon lost contact. Vice Admiral Robert Burnett, judging that the *Scharnhorst* would make for the convoy, headed to intercept and again made radar contact a little after noon. Destroyers which Burnett now sent in to attack with torpedoes were defeated by high seas, but the threat was enough to make the battleship head for Norway. This suited Burnett exactly, for the German line of retirement provided a perfect intercept course for the battleship *Duke of York* and the cruiser *Jamaica*, under command of Admiral Sir Bruce Fraser, Commander in Chief of the British Home Fleet. The *Belfast, Sheffield,* and *Norfolk* made no further attempt to engage, contenting themselves with shadowing the German. By late afternoon the two British forces were both in the area of expected contact. Because in those latitudes it was already pitch dark, Burnett illuminated with starshell, whereupon the *Duke of York* and the *Jamaica* sighted the *Scharnhorst* and immediately engaged at 12,000 yards. A high-speed eastward chase developed until the 14-inch shells of the British battleship began to take effect and the *Scharnhorst* lost speed. British destroyers then further slowed her with torpedo attacks. Ordered to sink her with torpedoes, the *Belfast* and the *Jamaica* attacked in concert with destroyers and sent the *Scharnhorst* down off North Cape a little before 2000.

That the *Scharnhorst* was mishandled is evident. She was superior to the three British cruisers which first engaged her and stood a good chance of fighting it out with them to a successful conclusion. If she had done so and then continued toward the convoy, interception by the *Duke of York* would have been impossible, at least until after the *Scharnhorst* had wreaked havoc among the freighters. Her running to the eastward to regain the Norwegian ports meant that she was running toward the most likely route for the approach of British reinforcements. In running for safety, the *Scharnhorst* adopted the course that offered the least probability of inflicting damage to the British and offered the greatest risk to herself. She had been sent out with a specific task, that of inflicting the maximum damage to the convoy. Her abandonment of her task meant that she was expended uselessly, with no gain to compensate for her loss.

PREPARATIONS FOR THE INVASION OF FRANCE

The first Washington Conference, meeting shortly after the attack on Pearl Harbor, had planned a return to the continent of Europe by means of a cross-Channel landing in France. However, the plan was canceled when it became apparent that the Allies would lack the strength for such an undertaking in 1942. The Combined Chiefs of Staff and the Prime Minister and the President realized that an unsuccessful assault, or one which had to be evacuated after a brief time, would be destructive to Allied morale. Accordingly Operation Torch, the invasion of North Africa, was substituted instead.

Once committed to operations in the Mediterranean, there was temptation, among the British especially, to continue to make that theater the major Allied effort against Germany. But the Russians, mindful of Allied promises, pressed for some operation which would draw more divisions from the Eastern front. The British and Americans thought also in terms of exerting pressure on Germany where that pressure would have the greatest chance of decisive results. By the time of the Cairo Conference the last week in November 1943, final agreement was reached that the decisive operation would be a cross-Channel invasion of France as originally planned, and at the Teheran Conference a few days later, where President Roosevelt and Prime Minister Churchill met with Marshal Stalin, the date was fixed for as soon after May 1, 1944 as possible. During both conferences perplexity arose over who would command Operation Overlord, as the cross-Channel undertaking was henceforth known. When it was being tentatively planned for 1942 or 1943, the Combined Chiefs had reached an understanding that the supreme commander of any large operation would be of the same nationality as the majority of the troops. Since at the earlier date British forces would necessarily predominate, Churchill had promised the command to Field Marshal Sir Alan Brooke; but as it became obvious that by May 1944 American troops would outnumber the British, Roosevelt and Churchill agreed that the supreme commander should be an American. At first the President planned to give the command to General George C. Marshall, Chief of Staff of the United States Army. Admiral King and others protested this selection, stating that Marshall could not be spared from the Joint and Combined Chiefs of Staff. On the second anniversary of Pearl Harbor Roosevelt made his decision and appointed General Eisenhower to command Operation Overlord. For his task Eisenhower was issued the broadest of directives:

You will enter the continent of Europe and, in conjunction with the other United Nations, undertake operations aimed at the heart of Germany and the destruction of her armed forces. The date for entering the Continent is the month of May, 1944. After adequate channel ports have been secured, exploitation will be directed towards securing an area that will facilitate both ground and air operations against the enemy.

The significant part about this directive is that it provided for nothing less than ending the war. All previous operations in Europe had had more limited objectives, for Allied commanders realized that decisive results could be obtained only by a drive on Germany from the West. Operation Overlord however was conceived on a scale that would permit carrying out the ultimate objective. Although the initial landings were to be made with only a few divisions, plans called for the establishment on the continent of Europe of a force of well over a hundred Allied divisions before the coming of winter.

When Eisenhower arrived in London, he found that a vast amount of spadework had already been done. For nearly two years Lieutenant General Sir Frederick Morgan of the British Army had toiled at planning the invasion. General Morgan had at that time been named as Chief of Staff to the Supreme Allied Commander (Designate), and his organization, COSSAC, had done all that could be done pending the appointment of the actual commander. They had surveyed possible landing beaches from Norway to the Spanish border, with special attention to those on the English Channel. These beaches offered the shortest routes across water and hence the quickest turn-around of Allied shipping in the assault. COSSAC had considered and dealt with problems as diverse as the tactical control of the Strategic Air Command in England and the availability of landing craft. On the solid foundation of General Morgan's work rested a great deal of the success of Operation Overlord.

It will be well to look briefly at the large plan so that Overlord can be seen in its proper perspective. Even though it was the largest amphibious assault ever mounted, it was but a part of the over-all strategy against Germany. In the spring of 1944 Germany was fighting on the defensive on two fronts. The Allied landings in North Africa, with the subsequent invasion of Sicily and Italy, had pushed the German forces north of Rome, where the front stabilized. A significant portion of the German forces were thus tied down in northern Italy and were unavailable for use elsewhere. In Russia, where the beaten German armies were being driven back to the Fatherland, 151 divisions faced the Soviets. Although the diverse Allied forces far outnumbered anything that would be used in the invasion of France, they had the strategic effect of a holding force as far as Overlord was concerned. Germany could not spare troops from the Russian front to bolster her defenses of France. Indeed, Germany's Western Army Command in France was raided to provide replacements in the East.

Allied leaders agreed that the invasion of western Europe would catch the German *Wehrmacht* between two great forces that would be able to crush it, but disagreement arose between the British and American Chiefs of Staff over the best way to exploit German weaknesses. The British, as we have noted, favored building on the base of conquests already accomplished in the Mediterranean while the Americans continued to favor a cross-Channel operation aimed at the heart of Germany. The British objected in part to the loss of strategic initiative to forces in Italy—a loss necessitated by the over-all priority that would have to be given to the cross-Channel buildup. As a kind of compromise with this view and also because it would cover the flank of Normandy and would cut off the southwestern part of France, Operation Anvil, an assault on the Marseille-Toulon area simultaneous with the assault on Normandy, received the go-ahead. Early planning conceived of Anvil as being a three-division assault, the same initial strength as that planned for Normandy, but there were not enough landing craft available for so vast a double operation. When Eisenhower demanded a five-division assault for Overlord, Anvil had to be reduced to a one-division attack and postponed to the middle of August so that landing craft assigned to it could first be used in Overlord. This expedient together with the reallocation of one month's production designed for the Pacific brought the number of landing craft for Overlord to the just acceptable minimum. So short was the supply that the loss of three LST's to German motor torpedo boats during an invasion rehearsal brought the reserve force of landing craft down to zero.

Planning for Operation Overlord was perhaps the most complex problem in the history of warfare. The problem had to be attacked from both ends at once, from the point of view of strategic desirability and from the point of view of logistic feasibility. Under the first consideration, SHAEF (Supreme Headquarters, Allied Expeditionary Force) planners had to consider where and when to invade; under the latter, whether the supplies, equipment, and personnel could be provided and transported to carry out the strategic aims. The choice of the landing area was the basic problem on which all else depended. General Morgan had considered various sites and had finally recommended an area in Normandy between the mouth of the Orne River and the Cotentin Peninsula. He had further recommended that if feasible a simultaneous assault on the east shore of Cotentin would be desirable inasmuch as it would provide for the early isolation of the great port of Cherbourg at the tip of the peninsula. General Eisenhower accepted his

choice of landing area including that on Cotentin after having enlarged Morgan's plan to a five-division assault. As SHAEF planners recognized from the beginning, the selected landing area was not ideal. The Germans expected that the assault would take place in the Pas de Calais area, which offered the shortest sea route and hence the quickest turn-around of landing vessels. This area also offered the best natural beach conditions and was geographically closest to the Dutch and Belgian ports and to the Ruhr, the industrial center of Germany. It suffered from the drawbacks that the Germans expected the landing in that region and hence had made elaborate preparations to throw an assault force back into the sea, and that the beach area which could be exploited in a reasonably short period of time was too narrow to support operations on the scale planned after the landing phase was complete.

The Normandy area had good beach conditions for part of its length, was somewhat sheltered by the natural breakwater of the Cotentin Peninsula, and was in range of fighter planes based on England. It offered good possibilities for a breakout on both flanks. A thrust to the sea in the west would neutralize German forces in the Brest Peninsula, while a wheeling movement on the left flank would provide opportunity for capture of important French channel ports, notably Le Havre. Recognizing that the capture of French ports could not be immediately accomplished, and that the Germans realized the supreme importance of ports to the Allies and hence would destroy their facilities before evacuating them, the Allies decided to construct artificial harbors in the beachhead area to expedite unloading of the deluge of supplies required.

As plans for Operation Overlord finally crystallized, they called for three paratroop divisions to be dropped the night before D-day to cut German communication lines and disrupt beach defenses. Then on D-day itself, five divisions would make nearly simultaneous landings from the sea. Five beach areas were set up, Utah and Omaha, under American responsibility, and Gold, Juno, and Sword, under the British. Preceding the actual landing the beaches and their defenses would be subjected to heavy aerial and naval bombardment.

GERMAN DEFENSE PLANS

Despite German knowledge that invasion of France was likely, the Western Front remained very much the stepchild of the German *Wehrmacht*. Hitler's attention was concentrated on Russia, and despite two orders that bade his western armies defeat the enemy, he paid little attention to the changing situation in the west. Marshal Gerd von Runstedt, charged with the responsibility for the defense of the western coast of Europe, began the construction of a series of "impregnable" concrete casements with which he eventually hoped to sweep every possible landing beach. His aim was to defeat the Allies at the water's edge, or if they did gain a foothold to have such strong defenses in depth that no beachhead could be exploited. Because of shortages of labor, materials, and trained construction workers, the work on the casements and on the beach obstacles was not pursued with vigor. In early 1944 Marshal Ernst Rommel of North African fame was assigned responsibility for the defense of the supposed invasion area. Under his energetic direction, fortifications were greatly strengthened. In addition to the emplacement of many concrete casements, Rommel also devised two other kinds of obstacles that might have been disastrous to the Allies had he had time and materials to complete his plans. First, he planned four rows of beach obstacles on which landing craft would impale themselves. Fortunately for the Allies, the two rows that would have been effective at low tide were not installed. All the obstacles were intended to be mined, but the mining was not completed by D-day.

Rommel's second scheme was directed against possible paratroop landings. He planned to set captured artillery shells on top of stakes set into the ground so close together that no glider could land without setting off at least two of these improvised

mines. As a further precaution, the shells were to be wired together so that men on the ground would stumble into them and be unable to operate effectively. Again however only a part of this scheme was carried out. In addition of course Rommel placed great emphasis on more conventional methods of defense—the usual beach obstacles, land mines, sea mines, and gun emplacements. He recognized that the topography of certain parts of northern France, with their numerous, almost impenetrable hedgerows, would make almost impossible the kind of war of movement for which he was famous, so he concentrated on strengthening the beach lines as much as he could and bent his attention toward building up a strategic reserve with which to oppose the landings. In this however he ran into great difficulties. First, the pressure for troops on the Russian front left him with few available reserves, and the effort to be as strong as possible on the beach lines ate into what reserve strength he was able to assemble. Also his mobility suffered for lack of motorized vehicles. Nor were things improved from his point of view by the combined bombing and sabotage of railroads that left them all but useless for troop movements at the time of the landings. It is somewhat ironic to see pictures of the inventors of the Blitzkrieg proceeding to the battle area on bicycles.

PREPARATIONS FOR D-DAY

The target date for the invasion of France had been set for May 1, 1944, with the understanding that the actual date would be determined by the physical conditions of tide, weather, and availability of equipment. In order to get an additional month's production of landing craft, General Eisenhower, with the concurrence of the Combined Chiefs of Staff, postponed the target date to June 1. This was about as late as the invasion could well take place, for the Allies needed all the summer campaigning weather they could get in order to consolidate the conquest of

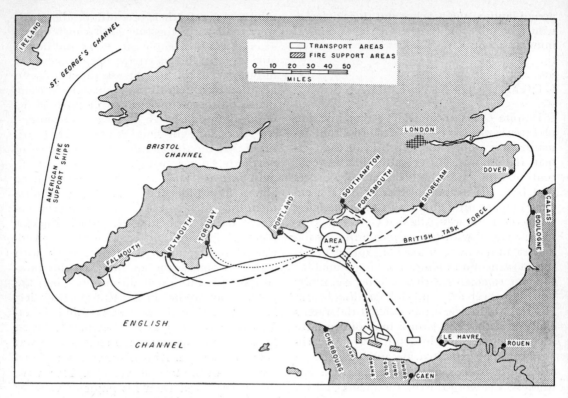

SEA ROUTES FOR OPERATION OVERLORD, JUNE 6, 1944

France. With the June 1 target date in mind, members of the SHAEF staff began to look for the combination of natural conditions most favorable for the landing. They desired to cross the English Channel during the hours of darkness, to land near low tide so that underwater obstacles would be exposed, to have a minimum of 30 minutes or a maximum of 60 minutes of daylight before their chosen tide conditions so that pre-landing bombing and naval gunfire would be effective. In addition they desired a moonlit night preceding D-day so that the airborne divisions would be able to organize and reach their assigned positions before sunrise. For a three-day period once a month these conditions would be met. A fortnight after this three-day period they would all be met again except for the moon which would then be in its new phase. The earliest date after June 1 that fulfilled the conditions was June 5, with June 6 and June 7 also suitable. D-day was

thus set for June 5, 1944, with H-hour at approximately 0630.[1]

THE NAVAL PLAN

The naval forces bore large responsibilities for Operation Overlord. They had to transport the assault troops to the beaches and land them with their equipment. They had to provide shipping to handle the enormous flow of supplies across the Channel—600 to 700 tons a day per division in addition to the mechanized equipment. They had to act as floating artillery until the guns could be established ashore. They had to provide for the orderly and timely arrival of reinforcement troops and their supplies and equipment, and they had to make provision for the evacuation of casualties. They had to

---

[1] Because of differences in the times of the tide, H-hour varied slightly from beach to beach.

keep German naval forces out of the Channel. They had to sweep lanes through the mine fields and clear the beaches of obstacles that would impede the landing and deployment of troops ashore.

Over-all naval command was assigned to British Admiral Sir Bertram Ramsey, since the British had far the greater naval force committed to the operation. Five task forces were organized to shepherd the troops to the five assault beaches. Two of these, Task Forces U and O, consisted of American ships under the command of Rear Admiral Alan G. Kirk usn; these forces would provide for Utah and Omaha Beaches respectively. Three British task forces, G, J, and S, under Rear Admiral Sir Philip Vian, held the naval responsibility for Gold, Juno, and Sword Beaches respectively. Provision of transport, wharfage, and the requirements for reasonable security added greatly to the naval problem. When Operation Neptune, as the naval phase of Overlord was called, got under way, vessels came from points as widely separated as the Thames Estuary and Northern Ireland. The timing of these forces to arrive on schedule was most intricate; any disruption could prove disastrous.

SOFTENING UP
"FESTUNG EUROPA"

SHAEF planners believed that they could attain nearly complete command of the sea and of the air on D-day. Only on the ground were the Germans expected to have strength commensurate with what the Allies would thrust against them. Hence, for several months before invasion, the Allies did all in their power to soften up the defenses in Europe to pave the way for the troops. General Eisenhower early demanded and obtained control of all strategic bombing, both the British Strategic Air Command and the American Eighth Air Force, based in England. These forces were directed to attack as first priority oil stores and oil refineries, then to bomb beach and harbor defenses, and, just before D-day, to cut rail lines and roads leading from inland to the coast. To avoid tipping the Germans off on the landing site, heavier raids were made in the Pas de Calais area than in the actual invasion region. Strong efforts were made to organize the French Underground for sabotage and for actual fighting against the Germans once the landings had taken place.

ON THE BRINK

Weeks before D-day the entire southern part of England became an armed camp, sealed off from the rest of the country. No one was allowed to cross the line in either direction without a special pass. Stores of all kinds crowded the depots, offering tempting targets to German bombers that never came. As early as May 31, troops began to embark in the boats and ships that would carry them across the Channel. By June 4 everything was in readiness; nothing more could be done. It was now a matter of weather. Because some of the ships had to be at sea by the 3rd to make the landing on schedule on the 5th, any decision on cancelation had to be taken no later than the early morning of the 4th.

Allied Commanders met with General Eisenhower at 0400 on the morning of June 4 to hear the weather reports. They were discouraging. High winds, low clouds, and high waves were combining in the target area. Air support would be impossible, landing of troops most hazardous, and gunfire undependable as a result of the storm conditions. When he had considered all factors, Eisenhower made the decision to postpone the invasion for 24 hours.

A mighty coiled spring already unwinding had to be stopped, wound up again, and readied for release the next day. That this was done without loss or serious consequence is a tribute to the skill and adaptability of everyone who played a part in the event. The next morning, the commanders met again as hurricane winds whipped the command tent. Faces were gloomy. It was inconceivable that the day could prove favorable for Overlord. Only one more day's postponement would be possible; after that, everything would have to be stopped for at least two weeks, more

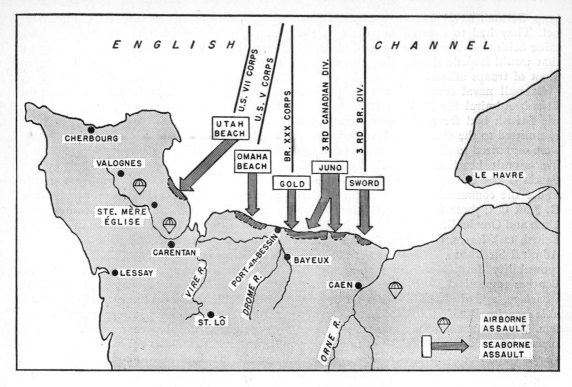

THE NORMANDY BEACHHEAD, JUNE 6, 1944

probably a month. Security would be lost; the whole world would know that something had gone wrong, and morale would suffer severely.

To the commanders' amazement, the weather experts brought in word that a period of good weather of at least 36 hours duration would prevail over the landing beaches on the morning of June 6. This unexpected break in the storm had the added advantage, as it turned out, of catching the Germans completely unprepared, for they considered a landing impossible under the conditions prevailing.

Once the decision was made, Operation Neptune gathered momentum. From all ports all along the south coast of England, from the east and the west, and from Ireland the invasion armada put to sea. Five swept channels were provided from Point Zebra south of the Isle of Wight to the Transport Area about ten miles off the beachhead. These channels were further divided into fast

and slow routes, one for the invasion forces— the slow, lumbering LCM's, LCI's, LCT's, LSM's, LCA's, LST's, and the like; the other, for the faster combat vessels. Along each channel were provided guide ships to assist the small craft with navigation. All ships from whatever staging area proceeded to Point Zebra before crossing the Channel. Here final adjustments were made in assignments and departure was taken for the great enterprise.

THE NORMANDY LANDINGS

The first troops to land were three airborne divisions dropped on the night of June 5-6. The British 6th Airborne Division dropped in the area between Caen and Coburg, east of the Orne River, with the task of preventing German reinforcements from moving in on the scene of the landing. The

American 82nd and 101st Airborne Divisions landed behind Utah Beach. Their assignment was to seize control of the causeways crossing the swamp that separated Utah Beach from the inland. By dawn, all three divisions were approaching their assigned objectives.

Shortly after midnight on June 6 more than a thousand British and Canadian bombers raided coastal batteries between Le Havre and Cherbourg. Just at dawn about as many American heavy bombers followed up this attack, concentrating on the beach areas. As soon as they had passed, medium and light bombers attacked gun positions and machine gun nests. When these retired, the naval bombardment forces opened up. In the American sector, the U.S.S. *Texas, Nevada,* and *Arkansas* engaged the heavy defenses with their 14-inch guns, while the cruisers U.S.S. *Tuscaloosa, Quincy, Augusta,* and H.M.S. *Bellona, Glasgow, Hawkins, Enterprise,* and *Black Prince,* assisted by the French cruisers *Montcalm* and *Georges Leygues,* the Dutch gunboat *Soemba,* 34 American destroyers, and five destroyer escorts, took on the lighter beach targets. In the British sector H.M. battleships *Warspite, Nelson,* and *Ramillies* provided the big guns, assisted by the cruisers H.M.S. *Belfast, Arethusa, Danae, Scylla,* and *Dragon,* and numerous destroyers, to shatter smaller targets. In the transport area, boats entered the water and the assault waves formed up.

At Utah Beach the American 4th Infantry Division went ashore against light opposition. Here, loss of control vessels marking the line of departure, combined with lack of clear reference points and a southerly tidal set, caused the landing to be made three-quarters of a mile south of the intended beach. As it turned out, this accident proved fortunate for the Allies, for the beach obstacles were lighter in the actual landing area than in that designated in the Neptune plan. By the end of the day, the 4th Division had established a beachhead six miles deep, had made contact with the 101st Airborne Division, and was ready to press across the base of the peninsula to link up with the V Corps in the vicinity of the Vire Estuary. Afloat

however things did not go quite so well. An undiscovered enemy mine field sank several small ships before safe waters could be found.

Omaha Beach, about ten miles in length, was the scene of the hardest fighting of the day. Because of rough water some amphibious tanks, intended to clean up beach obstacles, landed in far less strength than was expected, and others foundered as they tried to make shore. The first wave of troops hit the beach at 0635, five minutes late, and were immediately pinned down by heavy fire in the front and threatened by the rapidly rising tide from the rear. These troops, the American 1st and 29th Divisions, elements of the V Corps, piled up on the shore line, unable to move, as other waves pushed in behind them, competing for the already crowded beach space.

By mere chance, the German 352nd Division, perhaps the best trained and most experienced combat division in France, was in position to oppose the landing in the area of Omaha Beach. For five desperate hours, American troops were pinned down on a few yards of beach while fleet and aircraft combined efforts to open a path inshore for them. Consideration was given to landing later waves planned for Omaha on the adjacent Gold Beach, where the opposition was lighter, but gradually the situation eased at Omaha. Small groups of men began to rush across the sands to the beach exits to knock out pillboxes and machine gun nests. Destroyers ran as close to the beach as they could, blasting paths for the infantry still huddled on the shore. By 1300 general advance was possible, and by nightfall the V Corps occupied a line approximately a mile inshore.

Gold Beach, where the British 50th Division landed, presented few problems in comparison to Omaha. By the end of the day the 50th had captured Port-en-Bessin and had cut the road between Bayeux and Caen. At Juno Beach the 3rd Canadian Division stormed ashore under stiff resistance which they were able to overcome on schedule. At Sword Beach sea conditions interfered with the landings, but casualties were fewer than expected, and the British 3rd Division began

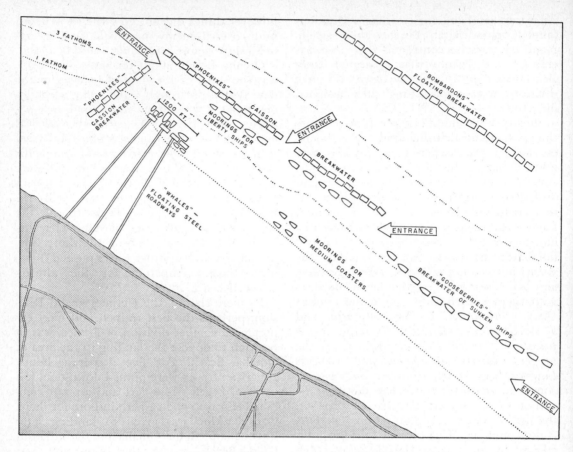

"MULBERRY A," OMAHA BEACH

to advance toward Caen, the first major objective of the campaign, and toward the Orne River to establish contact with the 6th Airborne Division, which had been dropped in that area the previous night.

The evening of June 6 saw another great project started, as perhaps the strangest fleet ever to sail from any harbor anywhere got under way from British ports. Included were tired old merchant ships (code name: Gooseberries) on their last voyage, huge concrete caissons (Phoenixes), enormous cruciform steel floats (Bombardons) with only their heads visible above the surface, and quantities of tugs and other auxiliaries. This was Operation Mulberry, which was to provide harbors where none existed—one in the British area and one in the American.

Mulberry A, commanded by Captain A. D.

Clark USN in a submarine chaser, arrived off Omaha Beach at dawn on the 7th after a 5-knot crossing. Construction began that afternoon with the sinking of a line of Gooseberries in an arc out from shore. To extend the line of Gooseberries beyond the shallows, lines of Phoenixes next were sunk with their flat upper surfaces left protruding above the surface. Outside the artificial harbor, or Mulberry, thus formed was moored a row of Bombardons to act as a floating breakwater. Inside, extending from the beach, were metal piers (code name: Whales) constructed to rise and fall with the tide.

By June 17, D-plus-11, Mulberry A was ready to receive ships. Here and at Mulberry B in the British zone, which was ready about the same time, unloading proceeded very rapidly. This happy state of affairs did not last long however, for two days later the worst storm in the English Channel for half a century roared in from the west. In spite of frantic struggles on the part of Clark's men, Mulberry A was so badly battered that it had to be abandoned. Mulberry B, better sheltered under the lee of Cap de la Hève, survived the storm with comparatively minor damage, and all shipping had to be routed through there. It proved of incalculable value in supplying the troops ashore.

It had never been contemplated that the Mulberries, even both of them, could supply the demands of the Allied Armies in France. The early seizure of a major port was essential. Hence the right flank of the Overlord forces, after driving across the Cotentin Peninsula, executed a wheeling movement and began an all-out drive on Cherbourg. By June 22 the United States VII Corps was outside the city, which was attacked on three sides by land, on the fourth from the sea, as well as from the air by heavy bombing raids. Gunfire from the U.S.S. *Nevada* and from British and American cruisers provided artillery support to the troops. On June 26 the city fell, although one pocket holding out in an arsenal in the outer harbor did not capitulate until three days later. Though limited use of the port was made early in July, so thorough had been the German demolition of the port facilities that it was August before the Allies could effect enough repairs for traffic to be handled through it in volume.

About five miles south of Sword Beach lies the small city of Caen. Pre-invasion planning had visualized the capture of this city on D-day. However, into this area Rommel poured all available reserve strength and made it the focal point for his defense of the continent. Rommel feared that a breakthrough at Caen and a crossing of the Orne on a wide front would permit Allied troops to execute a massive wheeling movement to their left and advance to the capture of Le Havre, after which they would continue to drive on to the Pas de Calais region where, he thought, they would be joined by the main Allied assault across the narrowest point of the English Channel. Hence to the German strategy Caen was all-important.

Because of the stiff resistance at Caen, Allied forces to westward drove to the south and captured Caumont, about 20 miles inland, and then were able to flank Caen from the west. On July 8 the city fell, but a week-long battle ensued for the high ground to the south. Then only were the Allies able to begin their swing toward Falaise as the first step in their plan to wheel to the left for a drive on the channel ports, Paris, the Low Countries, and the Ruhr.

BREAKOUT

The first breakout of the beachhead resistance line was a giant thrust aimed at St. Lô, preluded by heavy artillery bombardment spearheaded by the United States VII Corps, and supported on the west by the VIII Corps. Capitalizing on the breakthrough the American XIX Corps and the V Corps moved down in the direction of the city of Avranches. Once there the attacks fanned out to the south, west, and east. The effect of this was to seal off the Brittany Peninsula and to establish a broad front for advance toward the east. By August 14 all of France northwest of the landing area was in Allied hands except for a pocket south of Caen, including the cities of Falaise and Argentan. A pincers movement involving the British Second Army, and the American First and Third Armies converged on this pocket, which was soon cut off and seized. Thus by August 15 the Normandy landing had broken out and was moving in a concerted, well-planned operation through Northern France in the direction of Paris and Germany.

OPERATION DRAGOON—LANDINGS IN SOUTHERN FRANCE

As we have seen, the original plan for attacking France called for a landing in the Marseilles area to coincide with the landings

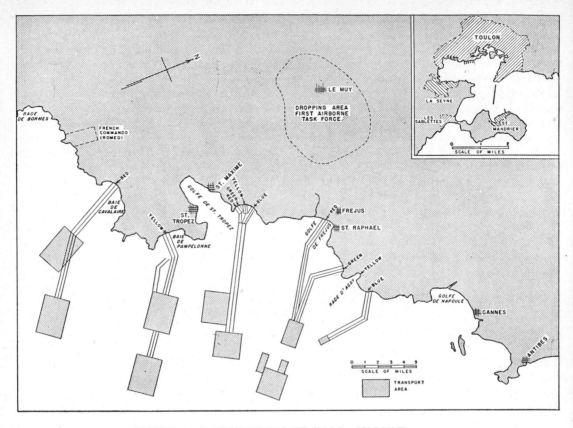

INVASION OF SOUTHERN FRANCE, AUGUST 15, 1944

in Normandy. We have noted how those plans had to be abandoned because of the shortage of assault shipping. Now, with Overlord successfully launched, the necessary shipping could be spared to the Mediterranean, and the invasion of Southern France could take place. The original code name Anvil was changed to Dragoon, and the landings were set for August 15. Vice Admiral H. Kent Hewitt usn, in command of the naval invasion forces, worked closely with the army and air commanders, Major General Alexander M. Patch and Brigadier General Gordon P. Saville, to coordinate the operation plan. Three landings were planned, at St. Raphael, St. Maxime, and St. Tropez, and a fourth was to be carried out by parachute drops behind the lines. The plan called for this force, elements of three infantry and one airborne division, to be reinforced to ten-division strength and then to drive up the

Rhone Valley to make contact with the United States Third Army in the vicinity of Dijon.

The beach situation here was far easier than it had been in Normandy. A comparatively steep gradient and small tidal range made placement of underwater obstacles difficult, the beach areas were more sheltered from the action of the sea than those in the north, and the time of year augured well for good weather in this region.

The naval forces were organized into groups corresponding to their landing areas of responsibility. As usual, fire support was furnished by large ships—American, British, and French battleships and cruisers. Heavy bombing raids from Italian bases cooperated with the landing, but because of the shortage of fighter bases within reach of the target areas, tactical air support was flown from escort carriers as at Casablanca and in the Pacific. Seven British and two American escort carriers participated in clearing obstacles in the path of the advancing troops.

At St. Tropez and St. Maxime the landings proceeded without difficulty against such light opposition that at the end of D-day, the invaders had secured objectives scheduled for D-plus-2. Similarly, at Green Beach near St. Raphael the opposition was negligible. But at Red Beach, five miles west of Green Beach and separated from it by a small cape, defending fire reached such proportions that the first wave was turned back. Rear Admiral Spencer S. Lewis USN, naval assault commander in that area, ordered the fire support ships to give the beach another going over with their guns. Then the assault waves tried again, and again they were turned back. On his own initiative, since Major General J. E. Dahlquist, commanding general of the St. Raphael assault troops could not be reached, Admiral Lewis ordered the troops assigned to Red Beach to be landed on Green Beach and then work back to Red Beach along the shore, attacking the German defenses from the rear. General Dahlquist heartily approved the plan when he learned of it, and he was able to capture Red Beach that night.

Toulon, once France's chief Mediterranean naval base, fell to combined land and air assault supported by naval guns ten days after the landings. The chief naval interest here was the systematic reduction of a fort at the harbor entrance, which was armed with 340-mm (roughly 13-inch) guns taken from the French battleship *Provence*. Curiously enough, the first ship to engage this battery was the *Provence*'s sister ship *Lorraine*. After nearly two weeks of bombardments—three days after Toulon fell—the garrison capitulated. The harbor of Toulon was quickly repaired and was in use three weeks after it had been seized. Marseilles, France's second largest city and greatest seaport, capitulated the same day as Toulon, after stubborn resistance.

Lieutenant General Jacob L. Devers' Sixth Army Group had already begun the drive up the Rhone. This Group, consisting of Lieutenant General Patch's U. S. Seventh Army and General de Lattre de Tassigny's French First Army, captured Sisteron on August 20; Avignon, five days later; Lyon, September 3; and on September 11 made contact with elements of General Patton's Third Army from Normandy. Thus the two great thrusts combined, sealing off from Germany all of southwestern France, including Vichy. The Sixth Army Group next wheeled to the east and drew up in a line along the German frontier from the Swiss border for a distance of about 80 miles where their left flank was in contact with the right flank of the U. S. Third Army.

THE NEW BLITZ

German and Allied scientists had for many months been engaged in a battle of invention seeking to arrive at a decisive weapon. Basic strategic decisions resulted in these two groups diverging in the direction of their efforts. In the United States the early promise of the Manhattan Project caused the Allied scientists to concentrate on the development of the atomic bomb; in Germany major efforts were directed toward the production of the airborne missile. Fortunately for the Allies, neither of the two weapons the Germans put into production was ready before D-day in Normandy. But soon after the landings the German V-1 began falling on London. This was a pilotless, jet-propelled, winged projectile. When at last the British began to learn how to cope with the V-1, mainly by the use of VT-fused shells, the Germans shifted to the first long-range rocket ever to be used in wartime, the V-2, swifter and deadlier than its predecessor. These rockets sped faster than sound; usually the explosion was the first evidence that the V-2 had been on the way. There was next to no defense against the V-2's. They were capable of destroying a large part of London, particularly if, as the Allies feared, the Germans produced an atomic warhead for them. Hence one of the prime objectives of the British forces in Europe was the early capture of the rocket launching platforms in northern France and the Lowlands.

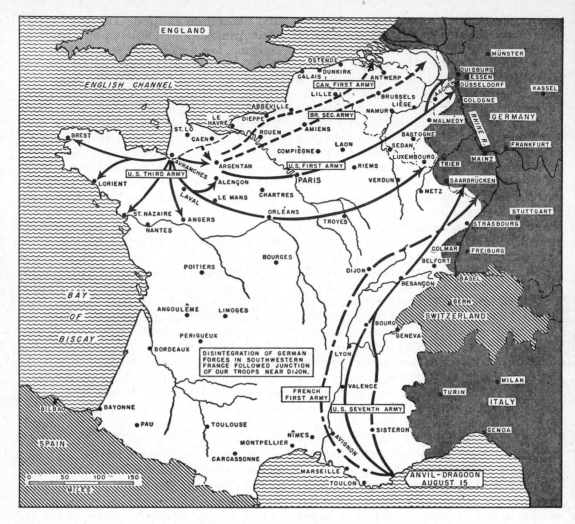

THE DRIVE INTO GERMANY, 1944

THE GERMAN COLLAPSE IN FRANCE

Faced with the success of the Allied landings in Normandy and in southern France, the German situation in France became desperate. Having committed the bulk of their defenses to the beach areas, Germany had no strategic reserves to hold back Allied thrusts once a breakout had been effected. Paris fell on August 25, and the Germans continued their retreat toward the east, pursued by a three-pronged Allied thrust. General Bernard Montgomery's British and Canadian armies

drove to the Dutch border. General Omar Bradley's First Army smashed through to the German border near Aachen and was the first Allied force to set foot in the Fatherland. General George Patton's Third Army raced on to Metz and thence into Luxembourg. Since this advance meant ever-lengthening supply lines for the Allies, the time was bound to come when the advancing divisions would outrun their logistic support. It came shortly after the fall of Paris; at that time military operations were several weeks ahead of the schedule laid out in the Overlord plan while the supply phase was behind schedule.

In an effort to shorten supply lines and to open up additional ports for Allied use, General Eisenhower ordered a drive up the Channel coast aimed at Antwerp and Amsterdam. With Antwerp in Allied hands, it would be possible to make a bridgehead over the Rhine in the Arnhem region. This plan was pushed with vigor, but stiff fighting developed around Arnhem. On September 17 one British and two American airborne divisions attacked the Arnhem area, and although they did not establish the bridgehead over the Rhine, they did succeed in capturing territory to protect Antwerp.

Serious German resistance to the loss of France was not encountered until December of 1944, when the Germans counterattacked in force in the region of Ardennes in what has been popularly called the "Battle of the Bulge." This was a vast gamble to which Hitler committed the troops hitherto reserved for the defense of the Fatherland. At one point, the German forces pushed the Allies back for nearly 50 miles, but with overpowering strength on both sides of the penetration, Eisenhower was able to crush the German counteroffensive. Once the Battle of the Bulge was over, the next problem to face the Allies was that of crossing the Rhine.

CROSSING THE RHINE

SHAEF planners expected that the retreating Germans would destroy every bridge across the Rhine River. To surmount the difficulties of this crossing, they called once again on the Allied navies to support one more amphibious landing, the last of the European war. As luck would have it, Allied troops found the Ludendorff Bridge across the Rhine at Remagen intact. General Bradley immediately rushed five divisions across the bridge, establishing a narrow beachhead on the east bank. This bridge, supplemented by floating "Treadway" bridges, was the target of German guns and aircraft, but the combination was able to sustain traffic for a considerable period of time. In addition, the United States Navy during March 1945 provided assault boats—brought overland—and trained assault crews to carry troops across the Rhine at several points. Despite the swift current and heavy fire from the Germans in the Third Army area alone, a U. S. Naval Unit ferried approximately two complete divisions and their supporting equipment in a period of less than two weeks.

GERMANY SURRENDERS

The first Allied objective in Germany was the capture of the industrial Ruhr, which was reduced by mid-April 1945. Spearheads driving eastward swiftly approached Russian forces pressing westward. Although Winston Churchill desired that the Western Allies should capture Berlin because of political considerations, General Eisenhower considered that Berlin had lost its strategic value and aimed two thrusts, one to the northeast by the British armies to seize German ports, and the other eastward toward Leipzig in order to cut the German homeland in two. He feared that remnants of the German forces would barricade themselves in the mountainous regions of southern Germany and would drag out a futile resistance which would blur the effect of Allied victory. Eisenhower's plan was carried out, and the Russians had the honor of seizing Berlin. Just before the end, Hitler, after hearing of Mussolini's death at the hands of a mob, shut himself up in his Chancellery and committed suicide. On May 7, 1945 Marshal Alfred Gustav Jodl placed his signature on a document stating, "We, the undersigned, acting on behalf of the German Supreme Command, agree to unconditional surrender of all our armed forces on land, on sea, and in the air, as well as all forces which at present are under German command . . ."

So ended World War II in Europe. Once again Germany's bid for world power had been turned back. As in 1914-1918, Germany had sought to draw her military power from the resources of Europe and had pitted her predominately land forces against the combined sea and land forces of the Western Allies. As in 1914, Germany realized that her only chance of neutralizing the land power which sea power could transport to the battle scene was to disrupt sea lines of communication. In both wars, Germany turned to the U-boat fleet; in both wars, the U-boat campaign was first resisted, then neutralized, and finally crushed. In World War II more than 30,000 seamen lost their lives in keeping the sea lanes open under U-boat attack, and 14 million tons of shipping went to the bottom. Yet those sea lanes had to be kept open, for Germany could not be defeated at sea; it required massive land armies converging from the east, south, and west to drive Hitler to death at his own hands amid the ruins of his *Wehrmacht* and his country. The land armies could not have been brought to bear against the Germans without the means of transporting them, and of supplying them once they were on the scene of battle. Even the air assault that paved the way for the foot soldiers was dependent on the sea. Every drop of gasoline which powered bombers of the Strategic Air Command and the Eighth Air Force, and the fighters that escorted them, had to be brought in by plodding tankers. Foodstuffs, war material of all kinds—most of the planes themselves—arrived in Europe by sea. Sea power permitted England to become a vast base for further operations. Sea power lifted men and supplies from this base and hurled them against the Germans and Italians wherever they were needed. Sea power did not win the war, but without sea power the Allies could not have won.

49

The Dissolution

of the Japanese Empire

DEPENDING UPON ONE'S POINT of view, operations in the Pacific theater during 1944 can be described in several ways. General MacArthur for example never ceased to think of his own series of landings along the coast of New Guinea as the principal line of advance toward the Philippines and Japan. He regarded the conquests of Nimitz' Central Pacific forces as useful chiefly for clearing the right flank of the Southwest Pacific drive; hence he was critical of the leap from the Marshalls to the Marianas while the Carolines were left in Japanese hands. Many naval officers regarded the drive across the Central Pacific as the main line of advance and considered MacArthur's operations as useful principally for clearing the left flank of the Central Pacific forces and for protecting Australia. Almost certainly the truth lies between these extremes: the Allied advance to the Philippines was along two distinct but mutually supporting lines, enjoying the advantages and running the risks of the exterior position.

The campaign against Rabaul, by destroying Japan's carrier air power, enabled the Fifth Fleet to seize the Gilberts without having to fight off any significant counterattack. The Fifth Fleet raid on the Palaus removed the Japanese fleet from MacArthur's path. MacArthur's invasion of Biak pulled out of the Central Pacific land-based aircraft that otherwise would have resisted the Fifth Fleet assault on Saipan. The Fifth Fleet, by invading the Marianas, drew Ugaki's battleships away from their intended attack on MacArthur's forces on Biak and attracted the Mobile Fleet into the Philippine Sea, where the "Marianas Turkey Shoot" stripped it of planes. The Third Fleet raids on Formosa and Luzon so weakened Japan's air power that it could make no immediate resistance of any consequence to MacArthur's invasion of Leyte. The two Allied advances across the Pacific had operated as a team—partly by chance, it must be admitted—each relieving the other of a portion of its burden.

HOW TO DEFEAT JAPAN

As the war in the Pacific moved towards its inevitable conclusion, Allied leaders propounded various theories as to how Japan could most quickly and economically be made to surrender. Many submariners held the view that submarines could do the job alone, as U-boats had twice nearly defeated England. The scientists and military men involved in the Manhattan Project were convinced that once they produced the atomic bomb Japan could not long hold out—especially after the development of the B-29, capable of carrying the bomb, and the American conquest of the Marianas, which provided airfields within range of the target. Others pointed to the coming defeat of Germany or the promised invasion of Manchuria by the Russians as the final blow that would convince Japan that further resistance was futile. There was undoubted merit in all these views, yet the majority of Allied military leaders and statesmen adhered to one or a combination of three other theories. For convenience we may call these the Army theory, the Navy theory, and the Air Forces theory, provided we understand that none of the three was advocated exclusively by any one service or branch.

The Army theory regarded the invasion of Japan as a necessary step in breaking the Japanese will to resist. Military history supported this point of view, for in the past nations generally had capitulated only after invaders had occupied a substantial portion of their territory, including the capital. In World War II the Italians had sought terms after the invasion of Italy and before the occupation of Rome, but Germany was to hold out until after the fall of Berlin. The Army theory gained wider acceptance after the American conquest of Saipan, for here even Japanese civilians had committed suicide in wholesale numbers rather than surrender. This sort of fanaticism convinced many officers that nothing short of physical seizure of the home islands could make the Japanese stop fighting.

The Navy theory was as old as naval history; the means proposed for defeating Japan was blockade. True, no major nation had ever been defeated by blockade alone, but Japan, like England, was peculiarly vulnerable. An island nation, overpopulated and lacking internal resources for carrying on modern warfare, she was absolutely dependent upon imports. She had gambled all she had won by warring on the United States in order to obtain unimpeded access to the essential oil, rubber, and other products of the East Indies. With the recapture of the Philippines and the virtual destruction of Japanese sea and air power, Allied air, surface, and subsurface forces operating from Luzon would be able to interdict the flow of materials from the Southern Resources Area and gradually render Japan incapable of fighting.

The Air Forces theory was that Japan could be defeated by continuous bombing of her cities and industries until she lacked the will and the means to make war. The Marianas were within bomber range of Tokyo, but airfields still nearer Japan would have to be captured for such strategic bombing to achieve maximum effect.

In line with the Allied policy of "unremitting pressure" on Japanese military and naval power, the Joint Chiefs of Staff directed operations to put into effect all means of defeating the enemy—and all except actual invasion of the home islands were carried out.

THE NAVY FINDS NEW OBJECTIVES

The Battle for Leyte Gulf was the Trafalgar of World War II. Halsey and Kinkaid in 1944, like Nelson in 1805, had finally obliterated the enemy fleet as an effective fighting force. There would be no more stand-up battles at sea in this war. Moreover the United States Navy in bringing the Army to the Philippines had apparently assured the success of the Navy's primary objective of cutting Japan's communications with the Southern Resources Area.

After Trafalgar the Royal Navy had been at loose ends, not quite knowing what to do with its fighting fleets. In consequence it had spent several years engaging in all sorts of eccentric operations before it found its true function—putting the Army on the Continent and keeping it supplied and reinforced where it could come actively to grips with Napoleon.

After Leyte Gulf the United States Navy had no doubts about its further function. Before World War II the Navy had fought only a few actions which even by liberal interpretation could be called fleet engagements. In the American Revolution Benedict Arnold with a makeshift little squadron had challenged the British on Lake Champlain; there were several lake actions in the War of 1812 but two only were of consequence; in the Spanish-American War American squadrons had destroyed Spanish squadrons at Manila and at Santiago. None of these were typical naval battles. For the most part, aside from blockade duty and attacks on enemy communications, bases, and isolated fleet units, the Navy throughout its history had operated in support of the Army. In the Mississippi campaign of the Civil War the two services had worked together "like the blades of a pair of shears." In World War I the Navy had devoted itself almost exclusively to assuring that the Army should be transported safely to France and adequately supplied there. Consequently the United States Navy entered World War II with a well-established tradition of cooperating closely with the sister service. After the Navy had attained its own major objective in late 1944 it continued to assist the Army and the Army Air Forces to attain theirs. The Twentieth Air Force was hampered because fighter planes lacked sufficient range to support the big bombers in the long flight from the Marianas to Japan. So following the Battle for Leyte Gulf Admiral Halsey prepared to take the Third Fleet north for a joint raid on Tokyo. He did not make the move however for it soon appeared that the Sixth Army still required the assistance of the Third Fleet in the Philippines campaign.

THE LEYTE CAMPAIGN

Tipped off by the Allied invasions of the Palaus and of Morotai that the Allies would next invade the Philippines, the Japanese High Command sent thither their smartest army commander, General Tomoyuki Yamashita, conqueror of Manila and Singapore. After surveying the situation Yamashita concluded that the coming assault would be against the southern or central Philippines. He planned therefore to fight a delaying action in the invasion area while building up forces on Luzon for a final showdown. But when the Americans landed on Leyte in October 1944, the High Command decreed that the decisive battle for the Philippines must be fought there. So Yamashita began rushing in reinforcements to the 16,000 Japanese troops already on the island, and the Mobile Fleet began converging on Leyte Gulf. The crushing defeat of the Imperial Navy on October 23-26 did not change the basic Japanese plan.

The decision to take a stand on Leyte is merely another example of the Japanese policy of making allies of darkness and foul weather. The northeast monsoons of November and December lose most of their moisture in the eastern Philippines. Consequently fair weather prevailed over the airfields of Luzon while torrential rains turned Leyte into a quagmire that minimized the American advantage of superior land-based air power and mechanical equipment. On Leyte the Americans found only one usable airstrip and could not construct others because engineers and machines had to be diverted to keeping open the rough roads which were fast becoming mere trails of knee-deep mud. The Seventh Fleet escort carriers could not alleviate the awkward situation because the Battle for Leyte Gulf had left them battered and short of planes and personnel. So Admiral Kinkaid asked Admiral Halsey to hold his Third Fleet in Philippines waters a month longer, and Halsey reluctantly agreed. During the ensuing operations Admiral McCain assumed temporary command of TF 38 in order to give Admiral Mitscher a much-needed rest.

In late October and in November 1944, Third Fleet aviators, striking mainly at Luzon and other areas on the fair weather side of the Philippines, destroyed about 700 Japanese planes and sank three cruisers, ten destroyers, and numerous auxiliaries and smaller types. At the same time General MacArthur ordered marine air groups up from Bougainville to lend close support to his troops and borrowed others from Peleliu to cope with wily Japanese night bombers.

Despite all efforts the Americans could not gain command of the air in the Leyte area. Kamikazes struck repeatedly at the Third and Seventh Fleets, damaging six of Halsey's carriers and hitting two battleships, two cruisers, two attack transports, and a score of cargo vessels in Kinkaid's command. During the same period Yamashita was able to pour at least 35,000 reinforcements into Leyte. The American counter was to rush in three more divisions and a regimental combat team under escort by the Seventh Fleet. The struggle for Leyte became, like the earlier struggle for Guadalcanal, a reinforcement race, with troops on the island fighting under almost primitive conditions in mud and jungle with the air advantage generally favoring the Japanese.

Seventh Fleet PT boats occasionally slipped around west of Leyte, where they succeeded in sinking a few troop-bearing barges, but they accomplished little against larger types. After the Third Fleet carriers had withdrawn from the Leyte area, Kinkaid sent three of the new *Sumner*-class 2,200-ton destroyers around for a night attack on shipping in Ormoc Bay. They achieved at least a footnote to tactical history by operating in line abreast in order to present minimum gun targets while using their two forward twin 5-inch mounts. In 14 action-packed minutes they sank a destroyer, damaged another, set fire to a troop-loaded transport, and smashed shore installations. Without air cover however the American destroyers fell easy victims to Japanese planes—the *Cooper* was sunk and another was damaged.

The land campaign for Leyte was in a sense won by American submarines and car-

rier aircraft, for they had not left the Japanese enough transports to keep ahead in the reinforcement race. By December seven United States army divisions, numbering 240,000 troops, were on Leyte, and the Japanese had been pushed into the northwest peninsula. To seal them off Seventh Fleet units on December 6 ferried the 77th Infantry Division around to the western side of the island. The landing, made at night four miles south of Ormoc, was unopposed, but after dawn kamikazes began attacking the convoy. Despite cover by army fighters, crashing suicide planes so damaged the destroyer *Mahan* and the destroyer-transport *Ward* that both had to be scuttled. A few days later, kamikazes hit the first resupply convoy, sinking the *Reid* and heavily damaging another destroyer.

Meanwhile the 77th Division moved northward up Ormoc Valley and on December 21 met the 1st Cavalry Division pushing south. Though destroying the sealed-off Japanese troops would require several more months, General MacArthur declared that all organized resistance had ended. By this time about 50,000 Japanese had been killed and 400 captured; the United States Sixth Army had lost about 3,000 men.

THE MINDORO OPERATION

Long before Leyte was secured MacArthur's staff had begun planning for the recapture of Manila. First however airfields would have to be obtained on one of the western Philippine islands, nearer Luzon and outside the rainy area. So in mid-December the Third Fleet, after two weeks' rest at Ulithi, again stood to eastward of the Philippines and struck repeatedly at Luzon airfields in preparation for an American landing on Mindoro Island, 300 miles northwest of Leyte. Meanwhile a Seventh Fleet invasion convoy carrying 12,000 combat and 6,000 service troops set out on a roundabout voyage via Surigao Strait and the Mindanao and Sulu Seas. The amphibious force was accompanied by its own close air support, escort carriers screened by old battleships and cruisers, which someone dubbed the Slow Carrier Task Force.

The enemy reacted vigorously to the advance of the Mindoro Attack Force, sending out the remnants of their Second Striking Force from Indo-China ports and attacking with more than 150 kamikazes. One suicide plane hit the convoy flagship *Nashville,* killing or injuring a third of her crew and forcing her to return to Leyte; another seriously damaged a destroyer, which also had to turn back. However with tactical cover by the escort carrier planes and strategic support from Halsey's fast carriers, the invaders went ashore on Mindoro without opposition. Later, suicide planes succeeded in sinking two LST's at the beachhead, but by this time the army engineers, including many Australians, had two airstrips under construction.

Discovery of the presence of the escort carriers sent the Second Striking Force scuttling back to port, but after the American convoy had departed the Japanese ships came out again for a night bombardment of the new airfields. They were detected on their approach, and planes and PT boats from Mindoro counterattacked, sinking one destroyer and damaging several other ships. Though the Japanese got in their bombardment, it was brief and did little damage. By midnight the Striking Force was heading west and did not again approach the Philippines.

Third Fleet support of the Mindoro operation was cut short by a typhoon which battered Halsey's carrier groups for nearly 48 hours, doing as much damage as a major battle. Three destroyers were sunk and 146 airplanes were lost. Damaged more or less seriously were seven carriers, a cruiser, six destroyers, two destroyer escorts, and a fleet oiler.

LINGAYEN GULF

General MacArthur, ever determined to advance at maximum speed in order to keep the enemy off balance, had already directed Admiral Kinkaid and General Krueger to proceed with the invasion of Luzon. The main assault was to be in Lingayen Gulf north of Manila, where the Japanese had landed three years before. MacArthur first ordered the new invasion to be carried out on December 20, 1944, just five days after the landing on Mindoro, but when his army, navy, and air commanders all protested that this gave them too little time for preparation, he reluctantly postponed the operation to January 9. Except for a few additional ships newly arrived from the United States, the Lingayen invasion force was about the same as for the assault on Leyte—i.e., the Sixth Army and the Seventh Fleet supplemented by the Third Amphibious Force from the Pacific Fleet. This time however the responsibilities of the supporting forces were more precisely defined. Submarines scouted everywhere except in the actual path of the invasion force. Bombers from the Fourteenth Air Force, operating from airfields in western China, were to strike at Formosa and search the China Sea. B-29's of the Twentieth Air Force, operating out of the Marianas, would raid Japan and search to the north of Luzon. The Far East Air Force (an amalgamation of the Fifth and Thirteenth Army Air Forces), operating from Morotai, Leyte, and Mindoro, would cover the convoys and bomb southern Luzon. Halsey's Third Fleet, still stripped down to TF 38, would bomb airfields on Formosa and northern Luzon and patrol the seas north, east, and west of the Philippines.

By New Year's Day 1945 the various forces assigned to conduct and support the Lingayen landing were converging on the Luzon area. The Third Fleet was on course NW out of Ulithi to strike Formosa. The Seventh Fleet, comprising nearly 700 ships, was approaching from a variety of places—Admiral Oldendorf's heavy bombardment vessels from Kossol Passage in the Palaus; Admiral Wilkinson's Third Amphibious Force, carrying the XIV Corps, from Bougainville and Cape Gloucester, New Britain; and Admiral Barbey's Seventh Amphibious Force, bringing the I Corps, from Hollandia and other ports of New Guinea. The Seventh

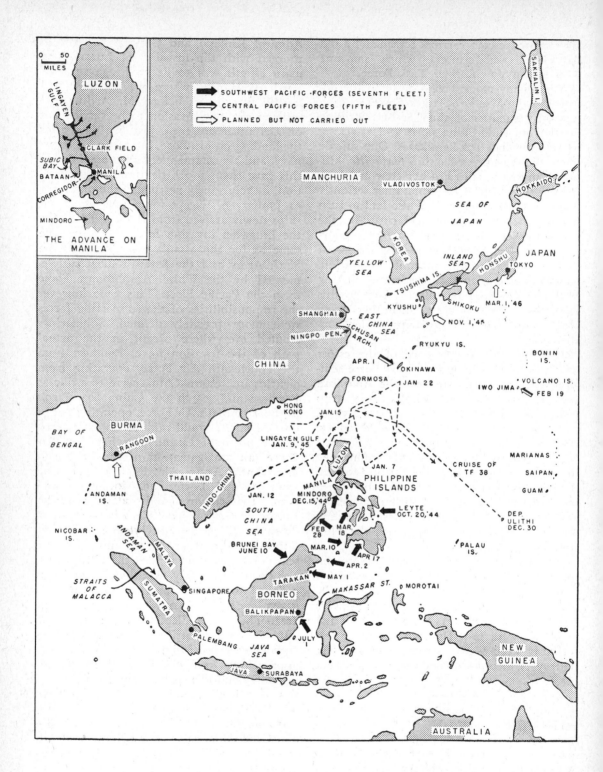

FINAL OPERATIONS OF THE WAR AGAINST JAPAN

Fleet picked up additional ships in Leyte Gulf and swept down through Surigao Strait and across the Mindanao Sea. Then with Oldendorf's supporting forces far out ahead it shaped course northward for Luzon.

Japanese aircraft sighted the oncoming Seventh Fleet in the Sulu Sea, and soon afterward the kamikazes began to strike. The first victim was the escort carrier *Ommaney Bay*, hit west of Panay on January 4. Aflame and torn by internal explosions, she had to be abandoned and scuttled. The next day as Oldendorf's force stood off Manila, kamikazes attacked in wholesale lots, damaging escort carriers *Savo Island* and *Manila Bay*, H.M.A. cruiser *Australia*, two destroyers, and an LCI gunboat. On the 6th heavy ships and minesweepers entering Lingayen Gulf underwent an even more sustained attack. After suicide planes had crashed into the *New Mexico*, the *California*, the *Columbia*, the *Louisville*, the already-damaged *Australia*, and several smaller types, Oldendorf ordered his ships out of the Gulf. "Consider use of additional air power urgent and vital," he signaled Kinkaid.

So Halsey was asked to leave off his attack on Formosa and bring TF 38 south at once. Moreover he was asked to extend his reach beyond his assigned sector of northern Luzon and hit the Clark Field complex of air bases, which the Far East Air Force obviously had not succeeded in knocking out. Halsey complied and at a cost of 28 planes put nearly all the airfields on Luzon at least temporarily out of action. When Oldendorf's heavies re-entered the Gulf on the morning of January 7, no kamikazes were to be seen. Luckily the gunnery vessels did not have to wait for minesweeping operations but could proceed at once to bombard the shore. Filipino guerillas, using rowboats, had already cleared nearly 400 mines from the Gulf.

Although there were no more kamikaze attacks on a scale sufficient to interrupt operations, sporadic raids were made by two or three planes at a time. As the amphibious forces neared Luzon they too came under attack; the escort carrier *Kadashan Bay* and a transport were damaged on the 7th. The next day, just off Lingayen Gulf, the escort carrier *Kitkun Bay* was put out of action by a lone kamikaze, and inside the Gulf the *Australia* was hit twice more. On the morning of the landing the *Columbia* was hit again and a destroyer was crashed. That afternoon a kamikaze dived into the *Mississippi*, and the unhappy *Australia* took her fifth hit.

Despite the rough reception they had received, Oldendorf's bombardment ships had done their work well, forcing the Japanese to flee the area. The assault troops landed without opposition and quickly established a beachhead four miles deep. Only then did enemy mortars and artillery open up from nearby hills. Battleship guns and carrier aircraft however kept this counterattack down to a minimum.

That night, while the American ships in Lingayen Gulf lay under a protective blanket of smoke, the enemy went into action with a new set of terrifying tricks. Six 20-foot powerboats carrying depth charges and mines sped through the fleet releasing their explosives against the sides of ships and then speeding away. In this manner two LCI's were sunk and three LST's and a destroyer were damaged. During the same night naked Japanese swam out to the fleet with demolition charges strapped to their backs. But their approach was detected by the Americans, who went after them in whaleboats, using machine guns, rifles, and knives. None of the human torpedoes found a target and none survived.

THE LONG CRUISE OF TF 38

Meanwhile TF 38 had hit Formosa again, sinking nine ships and destroying 47 planes. Then Halsey daringly took his force through the strait between Luzon and Formosa into the South China Sea—forbidden waters for three years to all Allied naval units except submarines. In 11 days TF 38 cruised 3,800 miles in this inner sea, unmolested by enemy forces on, above, or below the surface. On January 12, Halsey's planes hit the coast of Indo-China, wrecking nearly a hundred planes, sinking 40 ships, including the light cruiser *Kashii,* and smashing warehouses, docks, locomotives, and oil storage tanks. On the 15th the carrier squadrons hit Takao on the inner side of Formosa, destroying 34 enemy planes and disabling eight ships. The next day they struck in the Hong Kong area but took heavy losses from intense antiaircraft fire. Then while the Japanese radio was jubilantly announcing that the United States Third Fleet was bottled up in the South China Sea, Halsey slipped back through Luzon Strait at night under an overcast and re-entered the Pacific.

Before returning to Ulithi to turn his fleet over to Spruance in accordance with the plan for alternating commands, Halsey struck again at Formosa. This time the Japanese located their attackers and struck back. The light carrier *Langley* was hit by two 100-pound bombs which did moderate damage, and suicide planes crashed into the heavy carrier *Ticonderoga* and the destroyer *Maddox.* The *Langley* continued operations, but the kamikaze victims had to retire to Ulithi. Task Force 38 now moved northwest for a vital part of its mission—photo-reconnaissance of Okinawa in preparation for an impending American assault. On January 25 the task force steamed back into Ulithi Lagoon, having achieved a fantastic score of destruction and dispelled all lingering illusions among Allied leaders that the Imperial Japanese Navy still had the wherewithal to put up a fight.

THE ADVANCE TO MANILA

On Luzon, in the meantime, the I Corps was pressing upon Japanese positions in the hills north of Lingayen, where Yamashita had elected to take a stand with the bulk of his forces, while the XIV Corps was deploying on the Central Plain preparatory to seizing Clark Field. On January 28 the Americans began the actual assault on the air base. The next day a Seventh Fleet attack group put 35,000 soldiers ashore northwest of Subic Bay to prevent the Japanese

from withdrawing into Bataan Peninsula. These troops met no opposition, for native guerillas had already cleared the area of enemy. Two days later two regimental combat teams landed south of Manila Bay and advanced on the city through cheering crowds of Filipinos.

On the Central Plain seven squadrons of newly-arrived marine dive bombers dispelled the skepticism of army commanders by successfully providing close air support for the advancing XIV Corps and covering its otherwise unprotected left flank. On February 1 the final drive for Manila got under way. Two days later Americans reached the city, which was defended by 16,000 naval troops and 5,000 soldiers. There followed a solid month of fighting, street by street and house by house, until the last of the Japanese garrison had been killed or captured.

Before Manila fell operations were initiated to secure the harbor. Sweepers braved the fire from Japanese fortifications in order to clean up the hundreds of mines planted by the enemy. In mid-February 2,000 paratroops and as many amphibious assault troops landed on the island fortress of Corregidor. Conquest of Corregidor proved an unexpectedly costly and time-consuming operation, partly because army intelligence had estimated the enemy garrison at 850, whereas there were actually seven times as many Japanese on the island. The Rock was declared secure in early March. Conquest of the other harbor islands extended into April.

THE LIBERATION OF THE PHILIPPINES

While General Krueger's Sixth Army was pursuing General Yamashita's 100,000 surviving troops into the mountains of northern Luzon, Admiral Kinkaid's Seventh Fleet, now stripped of the Third Amphibious Force, cooperated with General Robert L. Eichelberger's Eighth Army in clearing the enemy out of the rest of the Philippines. The first step was to capture and convert to Allied use all air bases and ports from which the Japanese might conceivably dominate lines of sea communication.

The long island of Palawan was the first objective. Late in February 1945, while the last Japanese were manning their defenses in Manila, 80 ships carrying 8,000 men of the 41st Division steamed from Mindoro to Puerto Princesa on Palawan's east coast. The preliminary bombing and bombardment sent the 2,000 or so Japanese defenders scurrying to the hills so that the landing was unopposed. Possession of the harbor and the nearby airfield gave the Americans increased control over three important sea lanes: the two straits connecting the South China Sea and the Sulu Sea, and Palawan Passage, the channel between Palawan and a vast area of uncharted shoals to the west known as Dangerous Ground.

The next American move, two weeks later, was against positions dominating the passage between the Sulu and the Celebes Seas. The first landings were in the vicinity of Zamboanga at the tip of the western tail of Mindanao. When the Japanese attempted to contest this beachhead with machine guns, mortars, and artillery, the *Boise* moved in and routed them with her fifteen 6-inch guns. Subsequently troops were put ashore without opposition on the islands of Basilan, Tawitawi, and Jolo in the adjacent Sulu Archipelago, thereby completing the isolation of the Japanese in the central Philippines and providing airfields for close support of a projected assault on Borneo.

In March the Seventh Fleet conducted amphibious operations against the islands of Panay, Negros, Cebu, and Bohol. The landings, preceded by bombardment, were unopposed, but the beaches on Cebu were thickly sown with land mines, and the 7,000 Imperial Army troops on Negros held out for three months in the hills. By the end of May additional landings had been made around the coasts of northern Luzon to squeeze Yamashita into an ever-more-restricted area. Other amphibious operations had been carried out on the north and south coasts of Mindanao. From these beachheads troops advanced and joined, splitting the Japanese forces and preventing them from

achieving a united front. On Mindanao, as in many other parts of the Philippines, the destruction of the enemy was enthusiastically completed by guerilla forces. Here Colonel Wendell W. Fertig USA, evacuated from Bataan early in the war to build airfields in the southern islands, had raised a guerilla army of 25,000 men. Supplied by American submarines, his forces had already conquered 95 per cent of Mindanao before the Eighth Army arrived. Nevertheless the slow, tedious, costly task of cleaning out pockets of Japanese resistance continued until, and in some places long past, the official termination of the war.

THE ROYAL NAVY

It will be recalled that following heavy losses resulting from Vice Admiral Nagumo's raid in the Indian Ocean, Admiral Sir James Somerville had withdrawn the British Eastern Fleet to Kilindini, East Africa. Early in 1943 the Joint Chiefs of Staff considered how this reduced force might be built up again and put to work. At the Washington conference in May they presented to the Combined Chiefs a strategic plan which in essence received the approval of Churchill and Roosevelt. American sea, land, and air forces under MacArthur would advance via New Guinea to the Celebes Sea. Here they would meet the Royal Navy, which was to have advanced through the Straits of Malacca and recaptured Singapore. The combined fleets would then proceed via the South China Sea to Hong Kong, which they would occupy with Chinese help and use as a sea and air base for operations directly against Japan. This ambitious project fell through because of new Japanese successes in China and Britain's inability to disengage naval forces from the Mediterranean. In its place was substituted the plan for a second line of advance across the Central Pacific. Nevertheless the Joint Chiefs continued urging the British to undertake offensive operations against the East Indies if only to divert a certain amount of enemy pressure away from Allied forces in the Pacific.

After the surrender of Italy, the Royal Navy at last felt able to release some units from the Mediterranean to the Eastern Fleet, and Nimitz in early 1944 further strengthened Somerville by lending him the carrier *Saratoga.* As a result the Eastern Fleet was able to shift back from Africa to Ceylon and go on a limited offensive. In April and May the *Saratoga* and H.M. carrier *Illustrious,* escorted by Australian, Dutch, and French surface vessels, raided Japanese bases on and around Sumatra and then proceeded to Java for a blow at Surabaya. In the succeeding months Somerville's revitalized fleet staged several further raids on Sumatra and on the Nicobar Islands. By the fall of 1944, with the invasion of western Europe completed and the U-boat virtually defeated, ships of the Royal Navy had nowhere to seek employment except in the Eastern Fleet.

The Combined Chiefs of Staff considered three possibilities: the Royal Navy should (1) limit operations to the Bay of Bengal and launch amphibious operations in support of the Burma campaign and for the recovery of Singapore, (2) i.itiate operations to recapture the Netherlands Indies and cover MacArthur's left flank, or (3) join the United States Pacific Fleet in the campaign against Japan. At first Prime Minister Churchill seemed to favor completion of tasks (1) and (2) before considering (3). In this point of view Admiral King heartily concurred for he saw endless difficulties in meeting the logistic requirements of the Royal Navy along with those of the rapidly expanding United States Pacific Fleet. At the London conference of the Combined Chiefs in June 1944 he agreed that the British fleet should not operate north or east of the Philippines. In his opinion the Royal Navy could most profitably be used to recover the oil fields and refineries of Borneo and Sumatra. This would provide the British and American fleets in the Far East with a handy source of fuel at an enormous saving in tankers.

At the second Quebec conference in the fall of 1944, when the wars in Europe and in the Orient appeared to be rushing toward a conclusion, Churchill apparently changed his mind. He now offered the British fleet for operations in the Pacific under American command.

"I should like," replied President Roosevelt, "to see the British fleet wherever and whenever possible."

Admiral King interposed to say that a paper had been prepared for the Combined Chiefs, who had the matter under active study.

"The offer of the British fleet has been made," repeated Churchill. "Is it accepted?"

"Yes," said Roosevelt.[1]

As a result of this decision, the fastest and best ships of the Royal Navy proceeded to the Pacific to join the main attack on Japan, while the older and slower vessels went on the offensive in the Bay of Bengal. The conquest of Borneo was assigned to the Australian army and elements of the Seventh Fleet, including Australian cruisers, under the over-all command of General MacArthur.

En route to join Nimitz' forces, carriers of the newly-designated British Pacific Fleet on January 24 and 25, 1945 launched strikes against oil refineries in the Palembang area of southern Sumatra in order to cut down the supply of gasoline reaching Japanese air forces in Burma. Left behind in the Bay of Bengal were H.M. battleships *Nelson* and *Queen Elizabeth* and the French *Richelieu* and cruisers, escort carriers, destroyers, and submarines, which together were now called the East Indies Fleet, commanded by Admiral Sir Arthur Power.

The first task of the East Indies Fleet was to support the Burma campaign by covering the sea approaches and by an amphibious assault on Rangoon. So rapidly was the situation ashore turning in favor of the British however that the Japanese evacuated the city before the assault could be launched. Nevertheless the stepped-up Allied operations in the Bay of Bengal so impressed the enemy that they ordered to Singapore the lim-

---

[1] Ernest J. King and Walter M. Whitehill, *Fleet Admiral King* (New York, 1952), 569. Winston S. Churchill, *The Second World War* (Boston, 1953), VI, 154.

ited naval forces they had left in the Java Sea-South China Sea area and began to evacuate the rest of the East Indies to strengthen Sumatra and Malaya, leaving behind in most places only a small police force.

From Singapore in May the heavy cruiser *Haguro* and a destroyer slipped into the Andaman Sea to run in supplies to the Japanese army in south Burma. On the return passage the cruiser was attacked and damaged by a bomber from an escort carrier, and five British destroyers sped to the Straits of Malacca to intercept her. In a well fought night action the destroyers, eluding the *Haguro's* superior fire, surrounded the cruiser and sent her down with torpedoes. Three weeks later a British submarine sank the heavy cruiser *Ashigara* southeast of Singapore. These sinkings left only two major Japanese warships in the East Indies, the heavy cruisers *Myoko* and *Takao*, both seriously damaged in the Battle for Leyte Gulf. The *Myoko* had received from an American submarine further damage that put her out of action, and the *Takao* was rendered useless for combat by a midget British submarine that penetrated Singapore's harbor defenses.

THE BORNEO CAMPAIGN

The activation of the East Indies Fleet and the resultant movement of Japanese forces to the west immensely lightened MacArthur's problems in invading Borneo. On May 1, 1945 Admiral Barbey's Seventh Amphibious Force, including American and Australian cruisers, put Australian troops ashore without opposition on Tarakan Island off Borneo's east coast. Six weeks later Barbey's force took more Australians around to Brunei Bay and put them ashore in another unopposed landing.

These invasions were preliminary to the July 1 assault on oil-rich Balikpapan on the Makassar Strait. At this important port the Japanese had left behind a sizable garrison, and the harbor area was protected by a thickly sown mine field and by guns emplaced in caverns along the shore. To sup-

port the operation against this formidably defended point, the Seventh Fleet assembled in Makassar Strait three escort carriers and seven cruisers, including H.M.A.S. *Shropshire* and *Hobart*, and the *Tromp*, only cruiser left in the Netherlands Navy after the Battle of the Java Sea. Because shoals along the coast prevented the gunnery vessels from working in close, the minesweepers came under heavy fire from the shore. The fire support ships, doing their utmost to keep down casualties, hurled some 32,000 rounds of shells at the coastal defenses—more than had been fired at Leyte or at the Lingayen Gulf beachhead before the landings. Land-based bombers joined the carrier planes in blasting the gun emplacements, yet so well protected were they that together with mines they succeeded in sinking five minesweepers and damaging 12 more. Despite all opposition however, underwater demolition teams swam in to remove beach obstacles as planned, and the invasion proceeded on schedule.

Though the Australians got ashore without losing a single man, they met considerable resistance in the interior. For a week the cruisers remained offshore to provide fire support. There followed two more weeks of attack and counterattack before the last of the Japanese had been killed or had fled the area. Then the invasion forces began moving up the coast to seize oil wells and refineries to the north. By this time the forces landed at Brunei had secured all northwest Borneo, and oil for the Seventh Fleet was flowing from the wells of Tarakan.

"UNREMITTING PRESSURE"

The Allied policy of "unremitting pressure" on Japan produced an exceedingly close schedule of operations in late 1944 and early 1945. The Spruance-Turner-Smith team was to take over the Central Pacific Force from Halsey at the completion of the assault on Luzon and proceed to capture Iwo Jima in the Volcano Islands and Okinawa in the

Ryukyus. The original plan, worked out by the Fifth Fleet staff while the Central Pacific Force was operating against the Philippines under the title of Third Fleet, called for the invasion of Iwo Jima on January 20, followed by the invasion of Okinawa on March 1.

The unforeseen difficulties and delays of the Leyte campaign spoiled the Fifth Fleet's tight schedule. Part of the plan was for Halsey to disengage from the Philippines operation as soon as the Leyte beachhead was secure, join the Twentieth Air Force in a raid on Tokyo, and then turn over the fleet to Spruance. As we have seen, Halsey was obliged to forego the Tokyo raid and operate in support of the Philippines campaign three additional months, and MacArthur had to postpone the invasion of Luzon from December 20 to January 9. Moreover the Fifth Fleet, when Spruance assumed command at Ulithi on January 26, 1945, was somewhat under anticipated strength as a result of the Battle for Leyte Gulf, the kamikaze attacks, and the December typhoon. Obviously the new operations would have to be postponed, but long delay was out of the question because machinery was already in motion for staging a massive invasion of the Japanese home islands in the fall, and the success of this invasion was in a large measure dependent upon long-sustained air operations involving both Iwo Jima and Okinawa.

In late November 1944, B-29's of the Twentieth Air Force, operating out of Saipan, had begun attacking the Tokyo area. The results had proved less than satisfactory because the 3,000-mile round trip required cutting bomb loads from a possible ten to three tons, and lack of fighter plane support obliged the bombers to make fuel-consuming climbs to around 28,000 feet, an altitude from which precision bombing was impossible. Enemy bases in the Volcano and Bonin Islands, lying between the Marianas and Japan, further impeded the bomber operations by warning Tokyo of the approaching B-29's and sending fighter planes up to attack them en route. Capture of Iwo Jima, almost exactly half way between Saipan and Tokyo, would not only enable American aircraft to put an end to this nuisance but also provide a base for fighter planes and medium bombers within range of Japan, a way station for B-29's in need of refueling, a refuge for damaged bombers, and a base for air-sea rescue.

Iwo Jima was too small to serve as a major airdrome. Okinawa, on the contrary, would provide ample space for numerous airstrips and supporting installations within 400 miles of Japan. But the assault on Iwo would have to come first so that the Marianas-based bombers could reduce the hazards of the Okinawa operation by a series of massive raids on aircraft and aircraft factories in Japan. The assault on Iwo Jima therefore was scheduled for mid-February, with the invasion of Okinawa to follow six weeks later.

To direct this tightly-scheduled double operation Fleet Admiral Nimitz shifted from Pearl Harbor to advance headquarters on Guam. Because the Fifth Fleet now contained two amphibious forces and two amphibious corps, Vice Admiral Kelly Turner and Lieutenant General Holland Smith had been raised an echelon in command. Turner was now Commander Amphibious Forces Pacific Fleet; Smith, Commanding General Fleet Marine Force Pacific. Vice Admiral Marc Mitscher resumed his command of the Fast Carrier Task Force, back to its old title of Task Force 58.

THE CAPTURE OF IWO JIMA

The Japanese took for granted that the Americans would eventually assault the Volcanos or the Bonins and had selected Iwo Jima as the probable target because it provided the best terrain for airfields and was the most readily assailable of the numerous islets in the area. So on this tiny volcanic ash heap they established a garrison of 23,000 troops under the command of able Lieutenant General Tadamichi Kuribayashi, who set out to make Iwo the most formidably defended eight square miles in the Pacific. In achieving this goal he was abetted by the terrain. The broad northeast end of the island was a plateau of lava for the most part tortured into fantastic hills and ravines and fall-

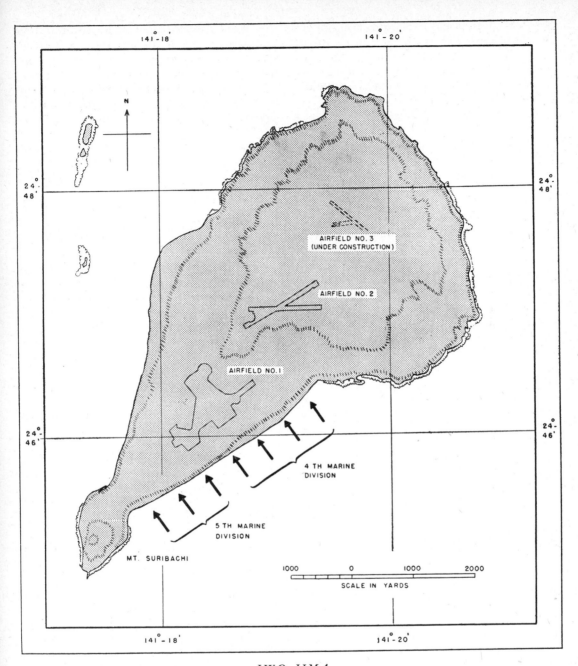

IWO JIMA

ing off into steep escarpments at the shoreline. At the opposite end stood a dormant
volcano, 550-foot Mt. Suribachi. These two
heights flanked the only possible landing
beaches, on the sides of the tapering southwest peninsula; on them Kuribayashi con-

centrated his artillery where it could enfilade
the beaches and the ridge between. On the
high ground he set up more than 400 pillboxes and blockhouses interconnected by
passages tunneled through the lava.

To prepare the way for the coming assault

B-24's of the Seventh Air Force, also operating out of the Marianas, hit Iwo Jima almost daily without achieving any important effect except to stimulate the defenders to greater exertions in their underground burrowing. Pinpoint precision was required to hurt Kuribayashi's type of defenses, and high-level bombing was not noted for precision, particularly where, as in the Bonin-Volcano area, haze or cloud cover is almost continuous. During the air campaign the Japanese brought in supplies as before, maintained two airfields on the island, and began construction on a third airfield.

Even hard-bitten marine commanders were startled by what air photoreconnaissance revealed about Kuribayashi's preparations on Iwo Jima. Assigned to make the assault, they asked for no less than ten days of preparatory naval bombardment. They, like the Navy, had learned in the school of experience that rapid pouring in of shells, with resultant clouds of obscuring smoke and dust, could not knock out well-built defenses. The fleet had to take its time, locate actual targets, and using a variety of shells and trajectories, endeavor to pinpoint fire from different angles. Unfortunately the speeded-up timetable of the war could allow only a three-day bombardment and, as events were to prove, that was not enough.

The delay in opening fire on Iwo Jima stemmed partly from the necessity of isolating the island by a carrier strike in the Tokyo area. Because of Halsey's late return to Ulithi, TF 58 could not rest its crews, rearm and replenish its ships, and reach Japanese waters before mid-February. On the 16th, the Fast Carrier Task Force, with Spruance and Mitscher aboard, arrived off Tokyo and sent in planes in the first fleet attack on Japan since the Halsey-Doolittle raid of early 1942. In the strikes of February 16 and 17 bad weather limited destruction to 40 or 50 enemy planes and minor damage to airfields. The raids did however distract Japanese attention briefly away from Iwo, on which Rear Admiral W. H. P. Blandy's Amphibious Support Force of gunnery and escort carriers opened fire on the 16th.

Despite rain and mist over the island and the necessity of lifting fire to avoid hitting minesweepers and underwater demolition teams, the Support Force performed extraordinarily well in the limited time allowed. The known targets had been mapped in advance, and with the help of aerial photoreconnaissance each was checked off as it was destroyed; others were added to the control map as they were discovered. Kuribayashi had wisely ordered his men to hold their fire until the actual invasion. As a result the American minesweepers had not been molested, but when the underwater demolition teams moved towards the beach accompanied by a formidable array of LCI gunboats, certain trigger-happy Japanese must have assumed that the assault had begun. At any rate, they opened fire, damaging 11 of the gunboats and sinking one. They thereby revealed the location of many previously unsuspected shore-defense guns, and these were duly marked down for destruction. The old battleship *Nevada* began counterbattery against the new targets at once, and other gunnery vessels followed suit. During the preparation the carrier aircraft did valuable service in spotting gunfire and burning off camouflage and concealing vegetation with napalm drops. Though their bombs were generally too light to be effective, their 5-inch rockets proved capable of penetrating the enemy installations with deadly effect.

Following the raid on Tokyo TF 58 turned back to join the bombardment of Iwo. At the same time Rear Admiral Harry Hill's Iwo Jima Attack Force approached, bringing in nearly 70,000 marines under Major General Harry Schmidt USMC, the new commanding general of the V Amphibious Corps. Also with the Attack Force were Secretary of the Navy James Forrestal, who came as an observer, and General Holland Smith, to provide a corps rank equal to that of Admiral Turner, who took over Blandy's Support Force during the actual invasion.

On D-day, February 19, the supporting ships shifted from destructive fire to massed neutralizing fire in order to drive the defenders underground. After 175 planes had roared over and dropped their bombs the fleet resumed the bombardment, throwing up clouds of dust that obscured the sun. Already about 500 landing craft, carrying marines of the 4th and 5th divisions, were moving to the line of departure. At 0830 the first wave, 68 armored amtracs carrying machine guns and 75 mm howitzers, headed for the beach. The naval guns thereupon shifted fire to provide a rolling or box barrage, while more than 50 combination gunboats and rocket ships advanced to furnish close support.

The momentum attained by this powerful assault was expected to carry the first waves well beyond the beach, but at the shoreline they were brought to a virtual halt by an unforeseen obstacle. The shore, rising steeply from the water, was of volcanic ash so soft that the treads of many of the amtracs sank in without taking hold. Succeeding waves of landing craft could not be beached at all. Many were thrown broadside to the shore and swamped. Wreckage piled up along the beaches. Newly arriving craft had their propellers damaged or their bottoms smashed in. LST's and LSM's in the follow-up waves, unable to beach themselves or find purchase with their anchors, collided and added to the confusion.

Fortunately the continuous neutralizing fire from the fleet kept the enemy on the flanks of the beach quiet for an hour while the marines scrambled ashore as best they could. Deprived of most of their armed amtracs, the troops crawled up a series of terraces towards the island's spiny ridge in the face of machine gun fire and grenades from isolated pillboxes. During the hour of relative enemy inactivity armored bulldozers got ashore, flattened out the steepest parts of the beach, and cut sloping roads in the terraces for tanks, which soon moved in to support the troops.

By the time the enemy guns on the flanks opened fire, the invaders had climbed the second terrace and were putting pillboxes out of action with flame throwers and 75mm tank guns. The marine right wing, nearest the northeast plateau, remained pinned down through the 19th by heavy and sustained artillery fire, but the center got as far as Airfield No. 1, and the left surged across the narrows, isolating Mt. Suribachi. This the marines had achieved with no other cover than sparse vegetation and depressions in the churned-up ash. The cost was high: of the 30,000 troops put ashore the first day, more than 2,300 were casualties by nightfall.

On the 20th, marines of the center captured Airfield No. 1, those on the right penetrated the high ground to the northeast, and the regiment on the extreme left began the assault on the mountain. The capture of Suribachi required nearly three days of blasting or burning out pillboxes and sealing up interconnected caves with grenades, flamethrowers, rockets, and demolition charges. On the morning of the 23rd the volcano was surrounded, and a patrol had reached the summit and raised the American flag.[2] Meanwhile the 4th Division and two regiments of the 5th Division had pivoted to the right and begun the assault on the plateau. As the battalions that had suffered the most casualties were relieved, the 3rd Marine Division, in reserve, began to be committed, moving in between the other two divisions. On the right and left flanks of the line now stretching across the island northwest to southeast, troops did well to advance a hundred yards a day. Those at the center spent three days under intense crossfire attaining the center of Airfield No. 2.

Throughout this advance into the plateau area and the subsequent fighting among the crevices, gullies, ledges, and caverns of the high ground, the fleet added call fire to the barrage from artillery ashore, and at night cut down the effectiveness of Japanese infiltration by starshell and searchlight illumination. Carrier air support was unusually effective, particularly during the first four days, while TF 58 stood off Iwo Jima. Coordination of these various supporting arms reached a new high, reflecting improved communication procedures and sound training based on experience. Nevertheless most of Kuribaya-

[2] Towards noon the marines raised a second and larger flag, visible to the entire island and to the fleet and a source of inspiration to all the Americans. Secretary Forrestal and General Smith witnessed this flag raising from the foot of the mountain. The newspaper photographer Joe Rosenthal took a picture of the second raising, producing the most frequently copied and reproduced of all war photographs.

shi's well-concealed strong points had to be taken by infantry supported by tanks at close range.

There was no immediate counterattack from Japan because the Imperial High Command was hoarding its few remaining warships and 10,000 planes to defend the home islands and adjacent areas. In the late afternoon of the 21st however kamikazes swept down from the north and crashed into five ships of the Fifth Fleet. The *Saratoga,* hit by three suicide planes and as many bombs, burst into flame. Though her casualties amounted to nearly 300, she was at length saved by expert fire fighting and damage control, but she had to retire to the United States for extensive repairs. Aboard the escort carrier *Bismarck Sea,* fires started by two crashing suicide planes ignited ammunition, which blew off her stern with a tremendous explosion. She rolled over and sank with the loss of 350 of her crew and all her aircraft.

Instead of the estimated five days, the capture of Iwo Jima required nearly a month of vicious fighting and mutual slaughter. Even after the island had been declared secure, hidden Japanese came forth and made a final attack. At length however all the enemy garrison except 200 prisoners were killed. For once, casualties among the assault troops approximated losses among the defenders: more than 5,500 marine, navy, and army personnel killed and three times as many wounded. Except for a too-brief naval bombardment and unforeseen difficulties at the beach, no assault in the Pacific had been devised more thoroughly or carried out with more precision. Yet nowhere had the invaders suffered anything like so high a casualty rate. Clearly Japanese advances in the science of defense were not far behind American progress in the techniques of assault.

Before the battle was over, Iwo was proving worth the high cost of its capture. After fighters began operating from Airfields No. 1 and 2 in mid-March, B-29's could proceed from the Marianas with full bomb loads, pick up an escort of P-51's from Iwo, and attack Japanese industrial centers with improved precision from low altitude. En route to and from Japan they were virtually immune from attack. If the big bombers were damaged or out of fuel they now had a haven for emergency landings, and if they were forced down at sea they could expect rescue by Iwo-based seaplanes.

The stepped-up air campaign against Japan got under way even before the captured airfields on Iwo were usable, for on February 25 Task Force 58 cooperated with 200 B-29's in a massive raid on Tokyo. The result was two square miles of the enemy capital burned out, about 150 Japanese planes destroyed, two aircraft plants gutted, and two railroad trains demolished. From the Tokyo area TF 58 shaped course southwest to raid and photograph Okinawa on March 1 and then proceeded to Ulithi to get ready for the next invasion.

THE OKINAWA CAMPAIGN

In mid-March TF 58 again departed Ulithi and returned to Japanese waters to pave the way for the coming assault on Okinawa. On the 18th and 19th the carriers launched a series of strikes at planes and airfields on Kyushu and at the remnants of the Japanese fleet in the Inland Sea. At a cost of 116 American aircraft, these raids damaged several enemy warships and destroyed so many planes that the Japanese were helpless to counterattack for several days after the Okinawa invasion began.

Aircraft from Japan struck back repeatedly. Part of a suicide plane, already hit by antiaircraft fire, slightly damaged the carrier *Intrepid.* The carriers *Enterprise, Yorktown, Franklin,* and *Wasp* were struck by bombs, but only the *Franklin* was seriously damaged. A bomb, penetrating to her hangar deck while she was launching aircraft, set off fires and explosions that took the lives of 800 of her crew. While the *Franklin,* saved by an extraordinary feat of damage control, headed for the United States and a major repair job, the rest of TF 58 prepared to lend direct support to the impending assault.

On March 23, TF 58 planes struck at Okinawa. On the 24th Vice Admiral Lee's Battle Line from TF 58 joined Rear Admiral Blandy's Amphibious Support Force in opening the naval bombardment. On the 26th a special amphibious attack force seized the tiny Kerama Islands 15 miles west of southern Okinawa in order to obtain a handy seaplane base and anchorage. The Kerama attack force also unexpectedly removed a serious threat to the American transports by capturing some 350 explosives-bearing plywood powerboats similar to those the Japanese had used earlier in Lingayen Gulf. Also on the 26th a marine reconnaissance battalion went ashore in the Keise Islands still nearer southern Okinawa to find sites for setting up 155 mm guns on the Japanese flank.

For the main invasion, assembled from such distant points as Leyte, Saipan, Guadalcanal, and Espiritu Santo, came Vice Admiral Turner's Joint Expeditionary Force: 318 combatant and 1,139 non-combatant ships bringing 182,000 assault troops. Included were the III Amphibious Corps, comprising the 1st and 6th Marine Divisions; the XXIV Army Corps, composed of the 7th, 77th, and 96th Infantry Divisions; the 2nd Marine Division, as a demonstration force; and the 27th Infantry Division, as a floating reserve. These seven divisions made up the Tenth Army, commanded by Lieutenant General Simon Bolivar Buckner, Jr. USA.

Final American estimates had placed 65,000 Japanese troops on Okinawa. Actually the defenders under Lieutenant General Mitsuru Ushijima numbered more than 100,000, of whom 77,000 were regular Imperial Army troops and the rest were naval personnel and Okinawan laborers and draftees. In an attempt to draw the enemy away from the scheduled invasion beaches, Lee bombarded the southeast coast, and on D-day the 2nd Marine Division made a realistic feint at the same coastal area.

It is unlikely that these diversions deceived Ushijima, and if they did it made little difference, for the power of the assault demonstrated at Iwo Jima had decided him not to contest the landing. Here was the ultimate tribute to the amphibious doctrine developed during World War II and in the ten years preceding. Whereas students of warfare had concluded following the Gallipoli fiasco of World War I that an amphibious assault in the face of modern coastal defenses was next to impossible, the hard-fighting Japanese had now come to the conclusion that no sort of coastal defenses could stop a properly launched amphibious assault—and that trying to stop one could only be a costly and losing venture. Ushijima had deployed the bulk of his forces on a line running east-west across the narrows of southern Okinawa. He planned to meet the enemy here and to protract the campaign as much as possible so as to expose the supporting Allied naval forces to prolonged attack from airfields in Japan. By such attrition optimistic Japanese officers hoped to cut deep into the strength of the Pacific Fleet and thereby improve Japan's chances for survival.

Involved in the final preparations were Lee's new battleships, Blandy's old battleships, and bombers from the Marianas, the Philippines, and China, and from the Fifth Fleet. Task Force 58 covered the approaches from Japan, and at the other end of the line Task Force 57 covered the approaches from Formosa and kept the intervening islands neutralized.

Task Force 57 was the British Pacific Fleet, commanded by Admiral Sir Bruce Fraser.[3] Newly arrived via Sydney and Manus, the British task force included four carriers, two battleships, five cruisers, and ten destroyers —about the strength of one task group of TF 58. Though the British carriers had nearly the same displacement as American *Essex*-class carriers, they could accommodate only about half as many planes, their logistic force was not designed to service them in long-range operations, and their closed-in hangars slowed operations and proved uncomfortable in tropical waters. In the Okinawa campaign however their armored flight decks gave them a special advantage, rendering them less vulnerable to kamikaze attack than the contemporary American carriers with wooden flight decks and armored hangar decks.

When the Tenth Army went ashore in a high-powered assault on the west coast of

---

[3] Admiral Fraser joined Admiral Nimitz on Guam, leaving operational control of TF 57 to Vice Admiral Sir Bernard Rawlings.

southern Okinawa on the morning of April 1 the troops met little resistance. In the course of the day 50,000 soldiers and marines landed, and advance elements, pushing ahead against only light opposition, seized two airfields. By the morning of April 3 they had

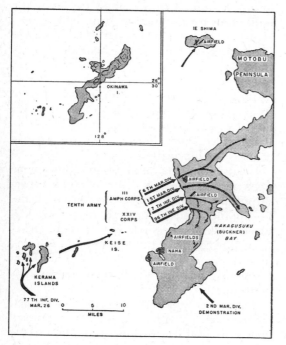

OKINAWA

thrust across to the east coast. Turner and Buckner attributed absence of resistance at the beachhead to the strength of the naval support, but when days passed revealing little evidence of organized enemy defense some officers began to suspect a trap.

While most of the XXIV Corps wheeled to the south and the 1st Marine Division secured the area opposite the beachhead, the 6th Marine Division advanced up the long northeast axis of the island. Here also they met only scattered resistance until they entered the rugged hills of the Motobu Peninsula, where the enemy fought back for several days. Capture of the peninsula provided high positions for artillery bombardment in support of the invasion of nearby Ie Shima by American forces seeking another airfield. By the end of

the third week, the marines had secured all of north Okinawa.

The XXIV Corps meanwhile had come up against the main Japanese force north of Naha. In this area Ushijima, taking advantage of terrain, had fortified three parallel east-west lines to provide defense in depth. In place of the old system of individual pillboxes and blockhouses, he had organized each hill and ridge into a fortress by siting artillery for massed fire and linking all defenses together with trenches and tunnels. Along the first enemy defense line the battle remained relatively stalemated for several days while fleet and shore artillery blasted away in vain against the Japanese positions. After north Okinawa had been captured, the 27th Division reserves relieved the marines in that area, and the III Amphibious Corps took over the left (west) flank of the American line. By this time the Japanese, under steady pressure, had begun to give ground. Ushijima's forces in 11 weeks of intensive warfare were gradually compressed into the southern tip of the island, but they skillfully maintained their line to the end, permitting no flanking.

On April 6 the Japanese of the home islands, recovered somewhat from the shock of the carrier attacks on Kyushu and the Inland Sea, began their counterattack. The Imperial Second Fleet, comprising the mighty *Yamato,* the cruiser *Yahagi,* and eight destroyers, took aboard the last 2,500 tons of fuel that Admiral Toyoda could find in Japan and sortied from the Inland Sea under the command of Vice Admiral Seiichi Ito. Obviously this was to be a suicide mission, but as Toyoda afterwards explained, ". . . nothing was to be gained by letting those ships lie idle in home waters, and besides it would have been contrary to the tradition of the Japanese navy not to have sent them. . . ." [4] At the same time 355 kamikazes in old planes rigged for suicide attacks prepared to take off from Kyushu. The common target of both was the 1,200 ships of Turner's amphibious force supplying and supporting the troops on Okinawa.

[4] *Interrogations of Japanese Officials,* II, 316.

Half the suicide planes were intercepted and shot down by air groups from TF 58 before they reached Okinawa, but many came over the amphibious force, where perhaps a hundred more were destroyed by antiaircraft fire and by fighter aircraft from the escort carriers. Many crashed into the ships however and damage was widespread. The chief victims of the attack were the Fifth Fleet radar pickets, rings of destroyers and smaller craft encircling Okinawa at a distance to give early warning of approaching aircraft. Because a large proportion of the kamikazes had been assigned the task of hitting this warning screen, the picket ships came under especially heavy attack and three of them were sunk.

Warned by submarines in the late afternoon that the Imperial Second Fleet had sortied, Admiral Spruance kept TF 58 cruising through the night in an area a hundred miles east of Okinawa. Before dawn on April 7 he began moving north for the kill. Shortly after first light American planes relocated the Japanese ships on a westerly course, and PBM's from the Kerama Islands kept them under surveillance. At 1000, when the Second Fleet was directly north of Okinawa, Mitscher launched his air groups. Two hours later the carrier planes struck in overwhelming force, sending down the *Yamato,* the *Yahagi,* and a destroyer, and so damaging the rest of the destroyers that two more had to be scuttled. This attack ended the last sortie of surface warships from Japanese home ports.

After the opening attack, suicide planes continued to strike regularly and viciously at the fleet and shipping off Okinawa.[5] During the two months in which the Fifth Fleet operated in close support of land operations, four American and three British fleet carriers were damaged. Mitscher's flagship, the *Bunker Hill,* lost nearly 400 of her crew in one attack and had to retire to the United States for repairs. Altogether 36 American ships were sunk, none larger than a destroyer.

[5] A new weapon introduced by the Japanese during this period was the *Baka,* an explosive-loaded, jet-propelled miniature plane. Released from the undercarriage of a bomber, it could be guided into the target by a suicide pilot.

Of the 368 damaged, many were beyond salvage. Requiring more or less extensive repairs were ten battleships, 13 fleet and escort carriers, five cruisers, and 67 destroyers. About 5,000 naval personnel were killed and almost as many more were wounded.

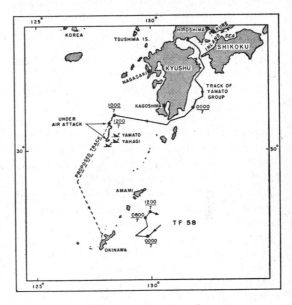

LAST SORTIE OF THE IMPERIAL JAPANESE FLEET, APRIL 6-7, 1945

To a large extent TF 58, by remaining on the defensive off Okinawa, served as bait to attract the kamikazes away from the transports and the land forces. Some officers protested that this was a misuse of carriers, that carrier forces should exploit their mobility in offensive action, diverting enemy strength by surprise attacks in unexpected quarters. As a matter of fact, TF 58 three times approached Kyushu to raid airfields in attempts to cut down the kamikaze menace; but for the most part it remained off Okinawa, and TF 57 remained off north Formosa except when refueling and replenishing.

Spruance's use of the fleet for static defense resembled his strategy off Saipan the preceding June, and his reasons were the same: he regarded protection of the beachhead as his principal duty. He would not leave the area until enough airfields out of range of enemy fire had been obtained on Okinawa for land-based planes to take over the protection of the troops. Moreover he would not relieve his picket vessels until the army had established an effective radar screen ashore. Gradually these conditions were fulfilled. As soon as the two airfields in the beachhead area became operational, marine fighters were based there to provide close air support for the troops. The arrival of 32 army fighters at the Ie Shima airfield in mid-May was taken as a sign that the Navy's "fortress fleet" operations could soon be suspended.

On May 27 Halsey relieved Spruance, McCain relieved Mitscher, and Hill relieved Turner. As the Fifth Fleet resumed its old title of Third Fleet, Halsey ordered his new flagship, the *Missouri,* to drop a few 16-inch shells on the enemy positions on Okinawa. "I just wanted to leave my calling card," he said. He at once got in touch with the army about pushing the radar network program, and on his recommendation a marine air group was ordered up from the Philippines to operate from Okinawa's airfields. Nimitz then took Hill's amphibious force and Buckner's Tenth Army under his direct command, thereby freeing TF 38 as a striking force. Halsey promptly advanced on Japan and sent air strikes against Kyushu on June 3 and 4. But bad weather and improved Japanese antiaircraft fire cut down the effectiveness of the raids; only 77 enemy aircraft were destroyed at a cost of 18 American planes. Then a typhoon struck Halsey's force, wrenching off the bow of the cruiser *Pittsburgh,* damaging 32 other ships, and destroying 142 planes. Three days later TF 38 again struck at Kyushu. It then retired to Leyte Gulf to prepare for a series of July attacks against the Japanese home islands.

After TF 38 left Okinawa, the land campaign dragged on for three more weeks before the island was declared secure. Some 7,400 prisoners were all that remained alive of the Japanese garrison. About 7,600 American troops were dead or missing, and more than 31,000 were wounded. Including losses in the fleet, the total number of Americans killed in the Okinawa campaign ran well over 12,000. In exchange for such heavy casualties, the Allies had won a position from which to bring air power to bear heavily against the industrial centers of southern Japan and a base for completing the blockade and for staging at least part of the invasion of the home islands.

PRE-INVASION OPERATIONS AGAINST JAPAN

In early 1945 two methods for ending the war in the Pacific were under consideration by Allied leaders: (1) intensified aerial bombardment and absolute blockade, the latter to be achieved by "encirclement," i.e., by capture of the Chushan Archipelago and the nearby Ningpo Peninsula south of Shanghai and of the southern tip of Korea and the nearby Tsushima Islands, or (2) direct assault on the home islands. On May 25 the Joint Chiefs of Staff after long deliberation decided upon direct assault. Kyushu was to be invaded on or about November 1 ("Operation Olympic"), with an assault on Honshu ("Operation Coronet") and an advance into the Tokyo plain to follow on or about March 1, 1946.

General of the Army MacArthur, newly designated Commander in Chief United States Army Forces Pacific, was to command the invasion. His orders specified however that if it became necessary for him to control the amphibious assault he should do so through the appropriate naval commanders. At last the Central Pacific Force was to be separated into two fleets in fact as well as in name: the amphibious and close support forces were designated Fifth Fleet and assigned to Admiral Spruance; the Fast Carrier Task Force together with the British carrier force was designated Third Fleet, under Admiral Halsey, with the mission of staging pre-assault strikes and providing strategic cover.

Troops for Operation Olympic were assigned to the Sixth Army, to be composed of four corps of three divisions each. The objective was to capture and hold southern Kyushu for development into a naval and air base for the subsequent invasion of Honshu. While one army corps feinted at Shikoku and then stood by as a floating reserve, two army corps would invade the east coast of Kyushu, and the V Amphibious Corps (comprising the 2nd, 3rd, and 5th Marine Divisions) would go ashore on the west coast to seize Kagashima and Kagashima Bay in order to secure a harbor.[5]

The Japanese, correctly estimating the American plan, expected to rely heavily on suicide tactics to repel the invasion. Half of the 10,000 aircraft in Japan were to be set aside for kamikaze use. When these had been expended, whatever orthodox planes and pilots were left would become kamikazes. For launching the suicide aircraft little airfields were constructed all over Japan. These fields were simple affairs—hard to find, hard to hit, easily mended, for the most part capable only of launching aircraft but not of receiving them back. As always the Japanese intended to make maximum use of foul weather and darkness.

In preparation for Operation Olympic American and allied forces set about tightening the blockade and stepping up the bombardment of Japan. Submarines slipped through the mine fields to operate in the shallow Sea of Japan. Fleet air wings based on Okinawa and the Kerama Islands scoured the East China Sea for enemy shipping. In this they were soon joined by army bombers which not only attacked ships and convoys operating between Japan and the continent but also mined the Korea Straits. The Twentieth Air Force from the Marianas and the Eighth Air Force newly established on Okinawa went on an ever-mounting campaign to smash Japanese industry. This meant burning out great areas of the major cities, sometimes by means of night saturation attacks using napalm drops, for under

Japan's decentralized manufacturing system much of the detailed work was done in small workshops and even in private homes. By June the B-29's were appearing over Japan in waves of 500 or more, and in Tokyo and other large cities there were huge burned-out areas.

To extend the destruction beyond the reach of land-based bombers, Halsey's Third Fleet, after raiding Tokyo on July 10, began striking targets in and around northern Honshu and Hokkaido. While the carrier planes were smashing coastal shipping, inter-island railroad ferries, and other targets of opportunity, the Battle Line detached itself to bombard manufacturing towns along the coast. On July 17 Halsey's 105 men-of-war were joined by 28 British warships, designated TF 37. This combined fleet, the most powerful striking force in history, then raided the naval bases at Yokosuka in Tokyo Bay and at Kure on the Inland Sea, heavily damaging or sinking the remnants of the once-mighty Imperial Japanese Fleet.

After another blow at Tokyo on July 30, the Third Fleet withdrew briefly to ride out another typhoon. On August 9 it was on the prowl once more in Japanese waters, hitting airfields in northern Honshu, where most of Japan's remaining aircraft were being hoarded. After further battleship bombardment of shore targets, the fleet turned back south on the 13th for another strike against Tokyo. On August 15, when one carrier strike was already over Honshu and another had just been launched, the Third Fleet received the order to "cease fire"—Japan had surrendered. Admiral Halsey thereupon recalled the newly-launched attack wave but added that if the planes encountered Japanese aircraft on the return they were to take no chances. They were to shoot them down "not vindictively but in a friendly sort of way."

THE JAPANESE SURRENDER

On June 22, 1945 Emperor Hirohito of Japan at a meeting of his Supreme War

---

[5] Estimates made by Army Air Forces intelligence at the time of the decision to invade Japan placed six Japanese divisions comprising 115,000 troops on Kyushu, with 2,500 aircraft available for support. Final joint estimates just before the Japanese surrender upped these figures to 14 divisions, 590,000 troops, and 7,000 aircraft. Actual figures in August 1945 were 14 divisions, 710,000 troops, and 10,000 aircraft.

Council gave utterance to what others in authority had been unwilling or afraid to state officially: Japan must work out a plan to end the war. It was high time. Because of the strangling blockade the nation's production of war materials was coming to a standstill, and hunger was beginning to stalk the land. Clouds of American bombers were turning Japan's cities to ashes. In April the Soviet Union had made the ominous announcement that it would not renew its Neutrality Pact with Japan. In May the surrender of Germany had dispelled the vain hope that some "decisive weapon" might yet be obtained from that quarter and at the same time released the combined forces of the Allied world for use in the Pacific War. On the very day the Supreme Council met, Okinawa, the last outpost, had fallen to the Americans.

Ending the war was not simple because powerful factions in Japan and in the armed forces abroad favored a war to the bitter end, and neither the rulers nor the people would accept a peace that did not preserve the imperial system. Negotiations therefore had to be carried out in secret, and terms short of "unconditional surrender" had to be obtained. Since of the major powers only Russia was even ostensibly neutral with respect to the Pacific War, it was appropriate that peace feelers should be extended through Moscow. The Supreme Council hoped also by bringing the Soviet government into the negotiations to obtain a new neutrality commitment from Russia in exchange for concessions in Manchuria. But when the Japanese ambassador at Moscow approached the Russian foreign office on the subject of peace terms he was informed that no official action could be taken at that time because Premier Stalin and Foreign Minister Molotov were about to depart for Potsdam to confer with the other victors over Germany.[6]

On July 26 however the governments of the United States, Britain, and China made it clear in the Potsdam Proclamation that for Japan "unconditional surrender" was to apply only to the armed forces. The Proclamation further stated that Japan was to be stripped of all her territorial gains and possessions except the four home islands and that points in Japan would be occupied until a "peacefully inclined and responsible government" had been established in line with the people's desires expressed in a free election. Nothing was said about the fate of the Emperor or the imperial system because the Allied governments had not yet made up their minds on that point.

The Potsdam Proclamation came a little too suddenly for the Supreme War Council, for they had not yet received the hoped-for commitment from the Soviet Union, they had not settled disagreements among themselves, and they had not taken steps to prepare the people for surrender. But because some inkling of the situation had already reached the newspapers, the Premier decided that it was advisable to release the Potsdam terms to the Japanese press and radio, with the added statement that the Imperial Government was withholding comment. By a quirk of the Japanese language however, foreign governments and press understood by the Premier's statement that his government had contemptuously rejected the terms.[7]

While the Council was still awaiting word from the Soviet Union, the United States reacted militarily to the supposed rejection. On August 6 a B-29 from the Marianas dropped an atomic bomb which seared and flattened a major part of the city of Hiroshima. On the 8th the city of Nagasaki was similarly devastated. That same day the Soviet Union declared war on Japan, and the Red Army marched into Manchuria.

These startling events both ended the procrastination of the Supreme Council and solved one of its most difficult problems. Until then the members had been at a loss how to present the facts to a nation long deluded

---

[6] Though Stalin did not inform his colleagues at Potsdam of the Japanese request for terms until July 28, President Truman and Secretary of State Byrnes already knew about it, for American intelligence had broken the coded exchange of radio messages between the Japanese Foreign Minister and the Japanese Ambassador at Moscow.

---

[7] The ambiguous word that led to the misunderstanding was *mokusatsu* (*moku:* to be silent; *satsu:* to kill), meaning literally "to kill with silence" but subject to several interpretations.

with propaganda tales of fictitious triumphs. There was a strong chance under the circumstances that any attempt to surrender would precipitate mutiny in the armed services and civil war among the people. But the power and mystery of the new bomb and the advance of the Red Army persuaded all but the most hot-headed that further resistance was useless. "I do not think it would be accurate to look upon use of the atomic bomb and the entry and participation of Soviet Russia into the war as direct causes of termination of the war," said a member of the Supreme Council afterwards, "but I think that those two factors did enable us to bring the war to a termination without creating too great chaos in Japan."[8]

By mid-August the Japanese and the Allied governments had reached agreement. The Allies somewhat reluctantly accepted the condition that the imperial system should remain unimpaired, but made two stipulations of their own: that during the occupation the Emperor must submit to the authority of the Supreme Allied Commander in Japan, and that the Japanese people should decide his ultimate status through free election. A general cease-fire was issued by both sides on August 15.

On September 2 aboard the *Missouri* in Tokyo Bay, with ships of the United States Third Fleet standing by, the Japanese Foreign Minister, acting for the Emperor and the Imperial General Headquarters, signed the instrument of surrender. General of the Army MacArthur then signed the acceptance as Supreme Commander for the Allied Powers. Fleet Admiral Nimitz next affixed his signature as Representative for the United States, followed by Representatives of the United Kingdom, China, the Soviet Union, Australia, Canada, France, the Netherlands, and New Zealand.

Soon afterwards General MacArthur moved into headquarters in Tokyo to direct the occupation.

---

[8] *Interrogations of Japanese Officials*, II, 320.

50

The Uneasy Peace

EVEN BEFORE THE SURRENDER of the Imperial Japanese forces the War and Navy Departments of the United States began to feel terrific pressure "to bring the boys home." Negligent of requirements for occupation forces, and unaware of other vast commitments inevitable in a postwar world, the American public forced upon the Congress a swift demobilization which in a few months reduced the vast fighting forces of the United States to near impotence. The Navy hastily arranged "Operation Magic Carpet," employing all types of ships in transport service. Cots and hammocks were rigged on the hangar decks of carriers, which ran shuttle services across both the Atlantic and the Pacific. In one such crossing, the *Lake Champlain,* crowded with troops, set a speed record for the Gibraltar-New York crossing, but even that seemed too slow to the troops aboard and to the American public.

SOVIET EXPANSION

Even in a world in which friendly relations among victorious allies were certain, such swift disarmament would have been unwise. In 1945-1946 however such a happy state was far from reality. Before the defeat of the common enemies, the leaders of the Soviet Union had given unmistakable evidence that the war and its end had made no difference in their long-range plans for a world Communist empire. They were ready to resume their permanent war against capitalism.

The result of the swift American demobilization was a power vacuum. The Soviet Union, making only a token demobilization, now had power to move into areas which could not be contested by the United States other than by diplomatic protest or by the use of the atomic bomb. Short of these extremes there was no practicable way to oppose Soviet expansion or to hold the U.S.S.R. accountable for violations of agreements reached in conferences at Yalta and Potsdam. Already a limitation in American strategy was becoming apparent, a limitation which for several years was to hamper the United States in its international relations. To be effective, particularly against an expansionist state, diplomacy must be backed up with power in order to enforce the will of the protester, or at least to bring about a reasonable compromise, which is, of course, a partial defeat for the expanding nation. By the spring of 1946, the United States had too few men under arms to supply its garrison forces and have any force left as a support for diplomacy. American public opinion was solidly against more war, even in the face of outrageously bold Soviet violations of war-time agreements. A good many people in the United States were suffering pangs of con-science over the use of the atomic bomb against Hiroshima and Nagasaki. Hence, the Soviet's calculated risk that the United States would not employ this terrible weapon against its former ally was shrewdly judged, and the United States was nearly impotent to take any effective steps to hold Russia to the terms of the wartime agreements or to keep her from territorial expansion.

RUSSIA'S STRATEGIC PICTURE

A study of the globe will reveal that in the over-all strategic picture, Russia enjoys the advantage of interior position with respect to the areas that were to come into dispute. On both littorals of the Eurasian land mass exist countries over which Russia sought control. These countries were, generally speaking, weakened from the efforts of World War II, and occupation or partial occupation had disrupted the governments and the econo-mies of these countries. Germany, France, Finland, Belgium, Norway, the Netherlands, and Italy on the Atlantic side had all under-gone defeat and occupation, and the conse-quent instability of these countries seemed a natural opportunity or series of opportuni-ties for Russia. On the Pacific side, the Kremlin saw its opportunity in China and Korea. Korea had been under Japanese rule for years; China had not been beaten by Japan, but large areas had been occupied; a Communist movement was already making headway in China, and the Nationalist Gov-ernment of Chiang Kai-shek was weakened by corruption and venality. Into both these coastal areas the Soviet Union planned to move, but was prepared apparently to draw back when opposed by significant force or when there seemed to be the risk of global war.

Immediately off both the Atlantic and the Pacific shores of this vast continent are situ-ated island powers which in hands unfriendly to Soviet expansion could serve as great dangers to any Russian military operation against the littoral areas. The British Isles in the Atlantic had already proved their useful-ness as air and naval bases in the war against Germany and Italy. Japan, in a similar posi-tion off the Pacific coast of Eurasia, controls the sea entrances to Russia's only Pacific ports, and bombers based on Japan would offer a serious threat to the Soviet lines of communications between European Russia and the coastal cities of Siberia. Both of these island groups off the continental mass were under the control of powers which the Soviet Union deemed unfriendly to her national aims. However, lacking a navy which could compete with that of either the United States or Great Britain, the Soviet could not readily threaten these island groups as it could the continental nations of Western Europe and Southeast Asia.

Another dangerous opportunity for Russia existed in the Middle East. The large de-posits of oil in Iran and Iraq offered tempt-ing bait to any nation whose civilian or mil-itary components were large oil consumers. Again however these areas are coastal in a large sense. They lie within the reach of the Mediterranean Sea, the Red Sea, and the Persian Gulf, and at a somewhat greater dis-tance from the Indian Ocean.

THE WEAKNESS OF THE WESTERN WORLD

In this strategic situation, with the Soviet Union in firm and expanding control over the center of the largest land area in the world, with the littoral countries weakened in military power and torn by internal dissension, and with island groups off the shore in both oceans affording necessary bases for air and naval operations and for staging areas for ground troops, the Western Powers, especially the United States and Great Britain, sought a means of living with this new threat. It was not immediately recognized as a threat. Large numbers of peo-

EUROPE AS SEEN FROM THE KREMLIN

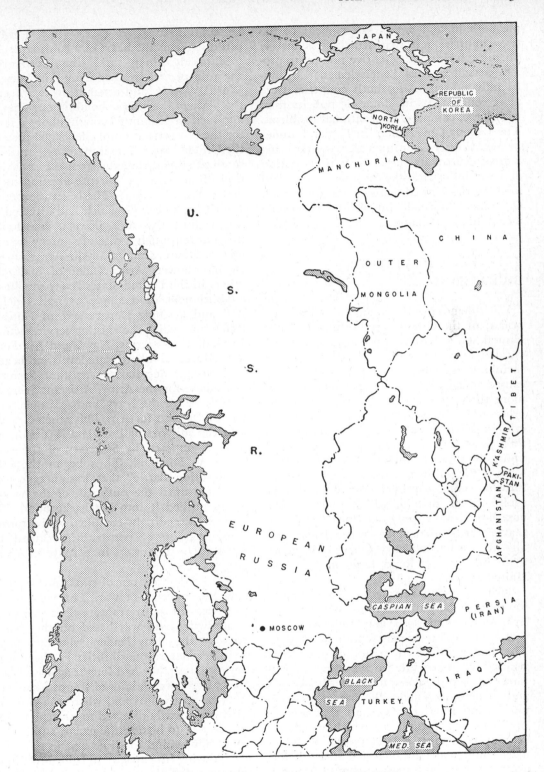

ASIA AS SEEN FROM THE KREMLIN

ple both in and out of government in the two countries felt that Russia was merely pursuing legitimate defensive policies to protect herself against "encirclement" by unfriendly powers. Also, both countries were more concerned with domestic policies than with large, complex, international problems. The Labour Government in England, under Prime Minister Clement Attlee, was devoting a great deal of its energy to nationalization of basic industries—the railroads, coal, and steel. In the United States, there was a rush to resume "normal" life, by which people meant life as it had existed before the war.

THE UNIFICATION BATTLE

With demobilization, came about a reappraisal of the defense establishment of the United States. Unification had long been advocated by many military leaders, and the shrinking of budgets to peace-time levels caused a mad scramble for each service to get more than its share at the expense of the others. The Navy in particular came in for criticism. The maintenance of ships, or even their preservation in "mothballs" was looked upon by some members of Congress and some of the public as needlessly extravagant, for what would ever be the use of naval ships again? Great Britain, which possessed the next largest navy—only one-third the size of that of the United States—was a friend and ally. Russia had no navy to speak of; hence there was no use for a large navy in the United States.

Such arguments revealed a lack of understanding of the purposes of a navy; they suffer from the common layman's misconception that a navy exists primarily to fight another. The better informed critics of the Navy pointed out that while we would need naval forces to keep the communication lines open and to deny an enemy the use of its communication lines, this was all that a navy could do in a future war which would inevitably be against a land power. Unless a navy could make its offensive strength felt against a large land mass, it should properly

be subordinated to those services which could strike at the heart of a continent.

Thinking along these lines, recognizing the role played by the Army Air Corps in World War II, and attempting to integrate the place of the atomic bomb in our strategic and tactical planning brought about a desire for the reorganization of the armed forces of the United States. The idea of reorganization received special impetus from the consideration of the strategic picture existing at the end of World War II. The institution of the Joint Chiefs of Staff, which had directed the war against the Axis powers, was looked upon as too much a case of strategy by committee. Hence, General of the Army Dwight D. Eisenhower, Army Chief of Staff, and others in the United States Army sought the establishment of a single over-all chief of staff and a single Department of National Defense in which the existing services should be made three, Army, Navy, and Air Force, but reduced to subordinate levels and headed by Assistant Secretaries—Assistant Secretary of Defense for the Army, Assistant Secretary of Defense for the Navy, and Assistant Secretary of Defense for Air. This scheme, which won the support of President Truman, was strongly opposed by Secretary of the Navy James V. Forrestal. Thus began the great "Unification Battle" that was to rage from this time until the outbreak of the war in Korea pushed it into the background. The story is exceedingly complex, and unfortunate intrusion of personalities caused the issues to be forgotten in a spate of name-calling.

The battle grew out of two fundamentally different concepts of war. The view of the Army was in many respects close to that of its air wing, and was based on the experiences of the army leaders who had borne their heaviest responsibilities in the war in Europe. Here they had fought against a land mass where large bodies of troops faced each other on vast fronts and where the effort by air was primarily directed to strategic bombing, that is, to hitting the enemy's industrial targets far behind the lines and in this manner reducing his capacity to fight. Most high-ranking naval officers had had their most important experience in the Pacific, in a war of movement over vast distances against an island empire and against objectives whose area and whose garrisons were tiny in comparison to those encountered in Europe, and where tactical air support played an enormous part.

This is not to say that either group was too narrow to be able to appreciate and understand the war as it had been fought on the other side of the globe, but intellectual understanding is one thing and wholehearted acceptance is another. All were convinced that the most likely—indeed, the only possible—enemy was Soviet Russia, or a Russian inspired satellite, but methods proposed for countering the threat differed. The Army and its air component, the Army Air Corps, felt that the only realistic possibility was to plan on the basis of an all-out war with Russia. The United States obviously could not hope to match the number of soldiers that Russia could place in the field, but the advantage in troops could be neutralized by strategic bombing, for if the factories behind the lines could be knocked out, the huge armies of the Soviet (200 divisions or more) could not long be supported in the field. This strategic bombing concept was based largely on the fact of American possession of the atomic bomb, which it was believed would prove a powerful deterrent to war.

The Navy's point of view, shared by Secretary Forrestal and the Chief of Naval Operations, Fleet Admiral Chester Nimitz, was that strategic bombing, even with the atomic bomb, could not alone win a major war. Sooner or later, ground forces would have to move in, and they would require support of two kinds: direct air support in battle, usually called tactical support, and logistic support, which would require shipping and protection of shipping. The navy men also felt that the danger was not so much that a big war would break out in the immediately foreseeable future, but that the United States would be unable to oppose the piecemeal taking over of countries on the littorals of Eurasia, having nothing between protest and the atomic bomb as a counter to this kind of move. Mr. Forrestal opposed the idea of the single Chief of Staff on the grounds that the officer who filled this post would be in the position of being oversold on the potentialities of one service only, and that the consequent loss of flexibility would embarrass or even cripple the war potential of the United States.

Out of these different concepts came differing methods of planning for another war.

The airmen were convinced of the deterrent effect of the atomic bomb and of the effectiveness of strategic bombing. They prepared to assume the Navy's traditional role of the First Line of Defense, even though almost all of their planning was offensive or at least retaliatory in nature. They pinned their faith in the B-36 bomber which was capable, they said, of delivering an atomic bomb anywhere in the world and of bombing from 40,000 feet. In their opinion the major portion of the defense funds of the United States should be devoted to the air arm with the other services substantially reduced.

The view of Secretary Forrestal was that there should be "balanced forces." This phrase, unfortunately, was subjected to almost immediate misunderstanding. His critics leaped to the conclusion that he meant each service should get an equal part of the defense budget. This was far from Forrestal's thinking. By "balanced forces" he meant balanced in capability, so that each would be able to function capably and to coordinate with the others. In this manner, he hoped to achieve flexibility and the capability of responding to threats in ways of the nation's own choosing, without having to depend on the all-out destructiveness of atomic warfare.

Inter-service rivalry aggravated, and in some ways obscured, the points at issue between the armed forces. Budding Air Force enthusiasts sought control over all aviation, no matter how used. Whether their view was the simple one that each service should have control of all weapons in its particular field —the Air Force, all air; the Army, all ground troops; and the Navy, all ships—or whether their fears that air expenditures by the Navy and the Army would offer budgetary competition or needless duplication and expense, their view found widespread support both in Congress and among the public.

The idea of letting the Air Force win the next war by strategic bombing was as appealing to the public as it was appalling to the navy leaders. The Navy felt that such a rigid strategic plan would invite disaster and that it would also make it impossible for the naval establishment to carry out its mission. The Navy needed to duplicate or at least adapt two types of military force which would come under the control of other services if the air force view prevailed. It needed a highly mobile body of troops, trained in sea-to-land operations, which could be used to seize, protect, and garrison bases needed for naval operations, and to protect American lives and interests in troubled areas in the world. To this end, the Marine Corps had been formed and its achievements had become a part of the national heritage of the United States. The other requirement of the Navy was for an air arm which would be under naval control and which could be used to support the naval mission.[1]

At least in the mind of the general public, there was never any idea of entirely doing away with the Marine Corps. But it was felt that there should not be two land armies in the United States with identical missions. This criticism resulted from the widespread employment of marines on the division scale in the Pacific and on the multidivision scale on Iwo Jima and Okinawa. Army leaders tended to feel that such employment of marines was a usurpation of the Army's proper function. In the same way, Air Force enthusiasts felt that the air arm properly belonged to them and that the Navy was stepping out of line in its employment of air. Although the Navy perhaps had the need of carrier-based air for its antisubmarine operations in mid-ocean, the Air Force argued that it should not have control of land-based air, whatever its mission, or of combatant air, even carrier-based, that was not directed against strictly naval targets.

At first glance, the idea of complete functionalism as the criterion for division seems attractive. In this way the Navy would handle all ships, the Army all troops, and the Air Force all aircraft. However, such a division would result in a lack of flexibility, a rigidity in military operations which could be overcome only by the closest on-the-scene cooperation of the respective commanders in a given operation.

To illustrate, we can examine the role of the Navy under these conditions. A navy has three main functions—to defend its own territory against sea-borne attack, to control the strategic sea lanes of communication, and to carry the attack with its logistic requirements across the seas to an enemy. Each of these missions requires a degree of command of the sea; at times this command may be tenuous and strictly limited in area, as in the case of a convoy whose escort commands only the water through which the convoy is passing; at other times it is much broader. However if significant strategic use is to be made of the sea routes of the world, and if the oceans are to be used as highways of attack, it follows that the nation desiring to employ these weapons must exercise a substantial degree of command of the sea.

To a very real degree since World War I, and to some extent even earlier, command of the sea has become three-dimensional. When Farragut damned the torpedoes in Mobile Bay, he was at least recognizing an effort to dispute command of the sea by means of underwater attack from moored mines. Blake, St. Vincent, Decatur, Nelson, and the rest had to contend only with the surface. But mines, torpedoes, and especially submarines have greatly complicated the problem of the navy that seeks command of the sea in wartime, for command must also extend to the sub-surface. In the same way, the airplane has extended the problem to the air, and the air and sub-surface may be exploited on a hit-and-run basis by a force that does not command the surface, as sailors on the Murmansk run found to their cost in World War II. There, under attack by both the U-boats and the *Luftwaffe*, there was comparatively little safety for a convention-

---

[1] The Navy had fought this battle during World War II when the Army sought to control antisubmarine patrols flown from the east coast of the United States (see Chapter 36).

ally escorted surface convoy.[2] But a nation wishing to use the sea lanes for large-scale transport of strategic materials *must* command the surface, the sub-surface, and the air above the surface to such a degree that the losses the enemy can inflict are kept to an acceptable minimum. This command not only requires a high degree of flexibility in the employment of naval weapons, but also requires that it adopt weapons of other services, notably troops and aircraft, if it is to accomplish its role. It needs troops to seize and hold bases required for operations, and it needs aircraft to be able to dispute the enemy's command of the air. In addition, the airplane is one of the best instruments for detecting submarines. To this end, not only carrier-based air is needed, but also land-based air for detection of submarines and for searching for other naval targets. To hold a carrier near a coast to do a task that might be accomplished by shore-based planes is to negate the chief advantage of the carrier, its mobility.

For these reasons the Navy opposed the unification bill being pushed by the Army and its air component. Yet there were many things to be said for unification. In World War II there had been difficulties arising from lack of unified command; the Battle for Leyte Gulf is the best-known example—presumably the new bill would preclude such experiences. It was possible through unification moreover to eliminate waste and duplication among the services.

THE NATIONAL DEFENSE ACT

After a long and sometimes bitter fight the Unification Bill was passed by the Congress and was signed by President Truman in the spring of 1946. Secretary of the Navy Forrestal became the first Secretary of Defense and set about administering the law that he had managed to keep within reasonable limits

despite the efforts of extremists. Under its terms the armed forces of the United States were reorganized into the Department of Defense, headed by the Secretary of Defense, who would sit in the President's Cabinet. Three sub-departments were created, the Department of the Army, the Department of the Navy, and the Department of the Air Force. Each service was to be headed by its own secretary, who would not be of cabinet rank. The Air Force was given responsibility for strategic bombing and for combatant operations in support of land armies. The Navy retained not only its carrier aviation but also its land-based reconnaissance wing and a Marine Corps of limited size. The Army was left its traditional tasks pretty much unchanged.

"THE GREAT DEBATE"

Matters rested in fairly peaceable fashion until bitter acrimony again broke out among the services in 1948. The quarrel seems to have originated in the projected budget, which was set at $16 billion for defense. Air Force spokesmen charged that the Navy was attempting to edge its way into the field of strategic bombing by requesting new, larger carriers and carrier planes capable of transporting the atomic bomb. Naval supporters responded with an attack on the B-36, on which the Air Force was basing its strategy. A series of articles in the popular magazines succeeded in selling the public the idea of an easy victory through strategic atom bombing. In the naval view, this projected plan was not only inflexible but was nearly suicidal. Tempers flared. The B-36 was attacked as a vulnerable crate lacking the capability to press home an attack. Air Force supporters retorted that the aircraft carrier was obsolete, that it was too vulnerable to land-based air, to submarines, and to weather conditions. So the argument raged. Secretary of Defense Louis Johnson, who had succeeded Forrestal, accepted the Air Force view in the main and added fuel to the flames by his decision to cancel the 60,000-ton carrier *United States,* then under con-

---

[2] The German surface forces did dispute these runs, but inflicted minor losses in comparison to those inflicted by the submarines and the dive bombers.

struction at Newport News. Tempers grew so hot in this so-called "Great Debate" that it seemed to many that the whole affair was out of hand. The debate ended, as far as the public was concerned, in a victory for the Air Force in the dismissal of the Chief of Naval Operations, Admiral Louis Denfeld, and his replacement by Admiral Forrest P. Sherman, but the dispute was effectively ended only by the outbreak of war in Korea, with its immediate problems and more liberal budgets.

THE TRUMAN DOCTRINE AND THE MARSHALL PLAN

It is now time to back-track in order to examine in detail the strategic picture of the world. Even before the end of World War II it was apparent that there would be every prospect of trouble with Russia, conceivably leading to war between the United States and the Soviet Union. The United States had stood by somewhat helplessly as the Soviets expanded to the Baltic and into the Balkans and threatened the Middle East. The first major trouble came over Iran, but serious consequences were averted through the action of the United Nations. In the spring of 1947 President Truman proclaimed a new policy in regard to United States relations with Russia, a policy of helping free peoples everywhere "against aggressive movements that seek to impose upon them totalitarian regimes" and "of supporting peoples who are resisting attempted subjugation by armed minorities or by outside pressures."

Although the Soviet Union was not mentioned by name, there was no doubt that this policy was directed against her. At this time, Greece and Turkey were both threatened by Soviet aspirations. In Greece civil war was in progress, the rebels receiving substantial aid from Yugoslav sympathizers across the border and even aid from the Yugoslav government itself. At that time Yugoslavia was considered to be a Russian puppet government acting with the approval of and in support of the Russian Politburo. Russia also demanded of Turkey the rights to—indeed complete control of—the Dardanelles. The Truman Doctrine effectively served notice on the Soviet Union that the United States would clearly support Greece and Turkey against any expansion by Communist forces into their territory. American supplies and munitions and American military advisers were sent to aid the Greek government. Visits of American naval forces to the Mediterranean, begun in 1946, were stepped up to serve as a diplomatic show of force. Again serious trouble was avoided.

In early June 1947 Secretary of State George C. Marshall, speaking at Harvard University, proposed a scheme for reconstruction of European countries through their own efforts, supported by American economic aid. This program came to be called the Marshall Plan, and was translated into the European Recovery Program. This plan, which at first met with enthusiastic response, was later viewed with a certain degree of hostility in Congress. The Soviet Union denounced the plan as American economic aggression and not only refused to participate but also kept any of its satellites from accepting American assistance.

COUP IN CZECHOSLOVAKIA

Ever since the end of World War II Czechoslovakia had been governed by coalition governments, which despite Soviet influence had maintained respect for civil liberties. Then in a sudden *coup d'état* in 1948, the Communist party under Prime Minister Klement Gottwald seized complete control of the Czech government. This coup, the first seizure by force of a peaceful government by Communists, served to awaken many people to the ferocity and determination of Communist aggression.

Because of this action and because of deteriorating relationships with Russia, American defense officials began to press for a revival of Selective Service and also for universal military training. These two proposals touched off bitter congressional debate. At length, in June 1948, the Selective Service Act was passed, but Congress balked at universal military training. The Selective Service Act was later rewritten to act as a substitute for universal military training by providing obligated service in the reserve components in addition to prescribed tours of active duty.

THE BERLIN BLOCKADE

The most dangerous situation to confront the United States since the end of World War II occurred in June 1948, when to all intents and purposes, the Soviet Union clamped down a blockade on Berlin, preventing all material from entering or leaving by road, rail, or canal. This blockade resulted partly from the division of Germany into four zones of occupation after World War II. The Russian Zone contained all of Berlin, but the capital itself was also under quadripartite rule in a manner similar to that of occupied Germany itself. Hence, the three western powers, France, Great Britain, and the United States, held their Berlin garrisons as on an island surrounded by Soviet-held territory and by Soviet troops. The Soviet Union obviously had as its aim the complete ousting of the Western Powers from Berlin. The ostensible reason given for the blockade was the imminence of a western currency reform in the western zones, which the Russians said was sure to disorganize the East Zone currency. The blockade became so tight that no land or canal traffic was allowed to flow between the western zones and Berlin.

This situation presented United States leaders with a grave problem. Russia, obviously making a major bid for supremacy in Germany, was forcing a show of strength. On the reaction of the Western Powers depended not only the fate of Germany but also that of the free world. It was clear that if the free nations backed down now, Russia would assume they were acting from fear and would proceed to further and even more serious aggression. The challenge was clear. How could the West respond? In his diary, Secretary Forrestal outlined the alternatives:

1. Decide now to withdraw from our position in Berlin, in concert with the other Western powers, at an appropriate time in the future, presumably when a constituent assembly for a Western German government is called on September 1, and plan accordingly.

2. Decide at this time to retain our position in Berlin by all possible means, including supplying Berlin by convoy or using force in some other manner, such action to be only as a last resort after utilizing all diplomatic and other means without force to avoid war, but accepting the possibility of war as a consequence if necessary.

3. To maintain our unprovocative but firm stand in Berlin, utilizing first every local means, and subsequently every diplomatic means, to obtain recognition and assertion of our rights while postponing ultimate decision to stay in Berlin or withdraw.[3]

The second of these alternatives was adopted, but rather than resort to force by sending an armed train or truck convoy overland, an airlift was attempted. This proved successful, and by the end of the year, about 7,000,000 tons of supplies were delivered to the former German capital, seven-tenths of it in American planes and three-tenths in British. The Russians did not oppose the airlift in any serious way although Russian fighters occasionally made dry runs on airlift planes. The American and British pilots were careful to stick to the routes prescribed in the original agreement on Berlin in 1945. The Soviets clearly did not wish to resort to force unless the Western Powers used it first, as would be inevitable if an armed convoy were sent through. United States navy as well as air force planes were used in the airlift to supply foodstuffs, medical supplies, and coal. The blockade came to an end early in May 1949, when the Western Powers and Russia agreed to hold a conference on Austria. In the 11 months of the blockade the Anglo-American airlift transported over a million and a half tons of supplies.

[3] Walter Millis, editor, *The Forrestal Diaries* (New York, 1951), 453.

THE NORTH ATLANTIC TREATY ORGANIZATION

As the cold war progressed from insult and vilification to such dangerous phases as the Berlin Blockade, the United States and several of the western European nations began to realize that their national security was at stake and that military cooperation between free countries was essential to combat the Soviet threat. Hence in 1949 the United States and 11 other nations agreed upon a treaty, the North Atlantic Pact, by which it was provided that the member nations would consider an attack on any one of them as an attack against them all. The signatory nations were Belgium, Canada, Denmark, France, Iceland, Italy, Luxembourg, the Netherlands, Norway, Portugal, the United Kingdom, and the United States. The year after its inception NATO invited Greece and Turkey to become members.

The language of the treaty had to be very carefully chosen in order to keep within the limitations of the United Nations Charter, especially Article 53, which provides for United Nations action in times of aggression and excepts regional action under such circumstances. When Russia later charged that the North Atlantic Pact violated Article 53, Secretary of State Dean Acheson pointed out the provisions of Article 51 and 52 which allow each member state to take whatever action it deems necessary in self-defense. Another hurdle that the pact had to face was ratification in the United States Congress, which jealously guarded its constitutional power to declare war. Some members charged that the decision would no longer be up to Congress but would rest with any of the signatories who fancied themselves attacked. In spite of this opposition, the Senate ratified the treaty in July 1949, by a vote of 82-13.

The teeth of the pact are in Article 5, which states:

The parties agree that an armed attack against one or more of them in Europe or North America shall be considered an attack against them all:

And consequently they agree that, if such an armed attack occurs, each of them, in exercise of the right of individual or collective self-defense recognized by Article 51 of the Charter of the United Nations, will assist the party so attacked by taking forthwith, individually and in concert with the other parties, such action as it deems necessary, including the use of armed force, to restore and maintain the security of the North Atlantic area.

Provisions of the treaty also called for a command organization of military forces to be made available for military operations as necessary. The employment of this force was to be directed by a council known as the North Atlantic Council, which was to sit in continual session in London. This council represented the political planning level and was to be responsible for grand strategic direction. Below the council came the military level, divided into three basic commands with provision for others as might be necessary. Those commands were to be Supreme Allied Commander Europe (SACEUR), Supreme Allied Commander Atlantic (SACLANT), and the Canada-United States Regional Planning Group. To implement the program, the United States passed a billion dollar grant-in-aid for military equipment needed under the proposed arrangement. At a meeting in London in May 1950, it was agreed that in order to avoid duplication of effort, each nation should concentrate on a part of the defense machine. For example, Great Britain was to concentrate on jet tactical aircraft and naval vessels; France, on light artillery and infantry weapons; and the United States, on strategic bombers and naval forces. In December 1950, General of the Army Dwight D. Eisenhower was appointed SACEUR, and in January 1952, Admiral Lynde D. McCormick USN was named to command the naval forces and to become SACLANT. The actual operation of setting up a military force met with considerable difficulty because of national pride and national rivalries and because of the economic impact of armament budgets on countries still trying to recover from the economic disruptions of World War II.

THE FAR EAST

At the end of World War II, the victorious allies seemed to have nothing to fear. Japan was badly beaten; the other eastern powers were allied to the common effort. Yet within five years, all of China was shut off from the Free World behind a "Bamboo Curtain" like the Iron Curtain in Europe, and outright war was in progress in the Far East. China was gradually lost through civil war. Step by step the Communists won territory until at length the Nationalists fled to Formosa and established a temporary government seat there. Similar civil war broke out in Indo-China in 1946. In Korea, the artificial division of the country at the 38th parallel led to open warfare in June of 1950.

CHINA

The government of Chiang Kai-shek, which had fought the war against Japan, came under severe criticism both inside and outside China. Charges of corruption and mismanagement were loud and severe. Local unrest bred by uneven distribution of food and other consumer goods was seized upon by Chinese Communists who concealed themselves under the disguise of "simple agrarian reformers." As time went on, the Communists under Mao Tze-Tung became well organized and were armed with surrendered Japanese weapons, with captured Chinese Nationalist weapons, and with American weapons originally supplied to Chiang but sold by unscrupulous persons, some of them inside the Nationalist government itself. In the course of events, sporadic guerilla fighting spread into organized civil war between the Nationalists and the Communists.

Attempting to halt the deterioration of the situation in China, the United States supplied more money and arms to the Nationalists and sent a special representative to strive to resolve the conflict. General of the Army George C. Marshall was chosen for this mission; his instructions were to attempt to bring about a coalition government of the Nationalists and the People's Party—as the Communists called themselves. The efforts of Marshall met with very little success. American marines, which had been in China since the end of the war, were withdrawn, and the Communists gained strength as time went on. By October 1948, they had occupied all of Manchuria, and during 1949 and 1950 took over the rest of the country. The Nationalist Government moved to Taipeh, Formosa in December of 1949.

Mao immediately established a *rapprochement* with Soviet Russia, and a 30-year pact of "friendship, alliance, and mutual assistance" was signed by the two Communist powers on February 15, 1950. Thus, within five years, nearly 500 million persons came under the domination of the Communist world. An American "White Paper" issued late in 1949 pointed out American efforts to stem the tide, noting that equipment for 39 divisions and over two billion dollars in aid had been given to the Chinese Nationalists and that most of the arms and money had gone ultimately into the hands of Mao and his followers. The loss of arms and money was serious enough, but loss of China behind the "Bamboo Curtain" was to have consequences of the utmost gravity.

KOREA

At the Potsdam Conference it had been decided that Russia would occupy North Korea and the United States South Korea. The actual line of demarcation, the 38th parallel, was decided on the spot as a convenient division line, no one on the non-Communist side expecting that it was more than a temporary expedient. In the last four days of World War II, Russian forces moved into North Korea and seized Japanese forces there. Immediately the Soviets began organizing Socialists and Communists in their zone and set up the Korean People's Interim Committee as the basis of a government in opposition to the Democratic Party of Kim Koo and Syngman Rhee. Much political maneuvering ensued, with the Russians refusing to recognize Rhee and his party or even to allow the United States and, later, United Nations officials to visit north of the 38th parallel. In September 1947, the Soviet Union, having organized the North Korean government and army to its liking, proposed that all occupation forces be withdrawn by January 1948. This proposal was rejected. The United Nations named a commission to hold free elections in all of Korea in 1948, but the members of that commission were summarily refused permission to enter North Korea. Making the best of a bad situation, South Koreans established in South Korea the Republic of Korea with Syngman Rhee as president and the capital at Seoul. This government was elected in July 1948, and on August 15, the United States turned the government over to the Republic. American troops were withdrawn by the end of June 1949.

In May 1948, the Communists of North Korea proclaimed the People's Democratic Republic of Korea with its capital at Pyongyang. Shortly after this the Russians withdrew, leaving behind them a well organized and trained North Korean army. The United States had left South Korea with nothing more than a police or constabulary force to keep order but lacking the organization, equipment, and training for fighting against an army. Thus, the situation was ripe for the North Korean attack on South Korea in June of 1950.

INDO-CHINA

As early as 1941, a nationalist movement began to gather strength in French Indo-China, but Japan's occupation of that territory during World War II prevented any fulfillment of the Indo-Chinese desire for independence. When Japan's forces were withdrawn in 1945, the Nationalist drive was renewed, and met with some degree of sympathy in Paris. The French government recognized the Vietnam Republic of Annamese Nationalists in 1946, but following a series of Communist-inspired guerilla raids, withdrew its recognition. The Viet Minh Communist forces under General Ho Chi Minh had early sought to exploit the power va-

cuum caused by the withdrawal of Japanese troops, and these activities caused the French to station an expeditionary force there, including elements of the famed French Foreign Legion, almost as soon as the Japanese moved out. When France recognized the new anticommunist Provisional Government of Vietnam in June 1948, civil war broke out. The French diverted a large proportion of their national income to maintaining forces in Indo-China and were thereby weakened in fulfilling their commitments to the European Army. The United States extended economic aid to the French in Indo-China without producing decisive results. The issue was further clouded by the fact that many anticommunists are also anti-French. Further, because there was no distinct territorial division as in Korea, no well-defined battle lines could be drawn.

JAPAN

Unlike Germany and Korea, Japan was not divided between occupying powers at the end of the war. The Allied Command named the United States as the occupying power and General of the Army Douglas MacArthur as Supreme Commander. By the terms of the surrender, Japan agreed to a democratic government and to free elections. Under the direction of General MacArthur, a cabinet headed by Baron Kijuro Shidehara granted the franchise to women, lowered the voting age from 25 to 20, and dissolved the vast family and corporate trusts that had constituted much of Japan's economic and military strength. A new constitution was ratified and became effective May 3, 1947. Under it Japan renounced her right to wage war and the idea of the divinity of the emperor, and also abolished the House of Peers. A new Diet became the "highest organ of state power and sole law-making authority."

In American strategic planning for the Far East, Japan was established as one of a series of key positions running from Japan through Okinawa and Formosa to the Philippines. Areas of friction with the Russians developed over the Kurile Islands and fishing rights in the waters between Japan and Siberia. Further friction developed from Russia's efforts to organize a Communist party in Japan. Although small, the party was well organized and so active that on June 6, 1950, General MacArthur ordered the government to ban Communist members of the Council from public activities "for perversion of truth and incitation to mass violence."

NAVAL DEVELOPMENTS

With the deterioration of relations between the Western Powers and Russia following World War II, it became necessary for military planners in the West to consider Russia as the most likely future enemy and to base plans and policies on that assumption. Accordingly, heads of naval forces set in motion plans and programs to counter Russia's known or suspected capabilities. It was perfectly obvious that no nation could challenge the sea power of the United States, for her navy in terms of tonnage was larger than that of the rest of the world combined. However, Russia could choose the traditional role of an inferior naval power, that of commerce raiding, depending largely on submarines. At the end of the war, Russia secured not only several of the latest German Type XXVI U-boats, but also the persons and services of several top designers responsible for the type. The Type XXVI had been developed too late to be of war service to Germany, but its menace was real. Powered by hydrogen peroxide, it was a limited submersible, not requiring surface air for its propulsion unit and capable of high speed submerged, if only for a short period.

War planners among the non-Communist powers had to assume that in a future war, Russia would embark on wide scale submarine operations, not only against commerce but against naval forces as well. In 1950 Russia was known to have approximately 350 operational submarines in contrast to the 57 with which Germany started World War II. Armed with new acoustic torpedoes and equipped with the snorkel, even the conventional boat was a threat, while the probability of encountering Type XXVI boats or improvements on them presented western naval planners with very grave problems.

To meet these problems required much imagination and boldness in a time when national feeling was concentrated on peace. Officers and men of the United States Navy were being released from active duty so fast that it was sometimes difficult to get ships to ports where they could be decommissioned. The first step taken in the United States to prepare for possible future trouble was to organize a strong reserve of both ships and trained personnel. Some ships that had outlived their usefulness or whose cost of maintenance would exceed their replacement value were disposed of to navies of allied nations. Others were sold outright to private citizens. Some were scrapped. A few were used as target ships in atomic tests at Bikini Atoll in the Marshall Islands. Most ships which were worth retaining in the fleet but which had to be decommissioned for want of funds and personnel were put in "mothballs." [4]

The establishment of an adequate, well-trained Naval Reserve was of utmost importance. Drilling units were set up in the various naval districts, some with drill pay for 48 drills a year. The Organized Reserve consisted of units with authorized complements of 200 enlisted men and 15 officers. In addition there were many volunteer specialized units in electronics, intelligence, base construction (seabees), aviation, and many others. Fourteen days' paid training duty afloat or ashore annually was authorized for reservists in these programs. Some of these cruises were on fleet ships, others on district ships, usually destroyer escorts assigned to the various naval districts and kept in par-

---

[4] "Mothballing" was intended to preserve ships from the deterioration usually considered inevitable in long periods of idleness. Gun mounts were covered in a moisture-proof "cocoon" of vinylite plastic. Machinery spaces were sealed and electrically dehumidified. Ships' records were transferred intact to storage, and propulsion machinery was greased and otherwise protected from moisture. The success of the program became apparent with the outbreak of war in Korea when the mothballed ships were returned to full service in a matter of a few weeks.

tial commission with a skeleton crew aboard. The reservists would fill out the crew and help take the ship to sea.

The active fleet operations were extended to include the navy's traditional role of implementing diplomacy as in the case of the Sixth Fleet's operations in the Mediterranean. Beginning in 1947 the Sixth Fleet remained on continuous duty in that area, showing the flag and helping to support western interests. One large carrier—the *Midway,* the *Franklin D. Roosevelt,* or the *Coral Sea*—was always on duty there; a second carrier, several cruisers and destroyers completed the carrier task force. In addition there was maintained an amphibious force of transports carrying the Fleet Marine Force. Logistic supply was handled primarily from the United States on a simulated wartime basis. This force existed not only as an arm of diplomacy but as a force to strike offensively in time of war, to protect American lives and interests, to act as goodwill ambassadors, and to keep control of all that vital waterway, essential for western communication lines. With the establishment of NATO and EDC, joint naval operations came into increasing prominence. Combined signals and tactics were developed for joint operations of ships of NATO navies and joint maneuvers were successfully held on several occasions.

The American navy spent much time and effort in combating the submarine menace for future operations. Hunter-killer groups, sonobuoys, high frequency radio direction finders, sonar, and other devices were refined and improved.

Developments were also extensive in naval aircraft design and operation. The jet fighter completely replaced the old propeller-driven types. Jet bombers became common, and the speed of aircraft, both fighter and bomber, far outstripped anything available in the war years. *Essex*-type carriers gradually received strengthened flight decks to accommodate jet planes and heavier bombers. One of the most radical changes in design was the so-called "canted" carrier deck, which was developed by the British and was installed in U.S.S. *Antietam* and other United States car-

riers. The landing section of the deck was angled about eight degrees to port so that a plane coming in for a landing would not crash through the barriers into planes parked on the forward part of the flight deck. This kind of angling also permitted simultaneous landing and launching operations from one carrier, planes being sent off forward at the same time others are landing aft.

Construction after the war reflected the increased emphasis on destroyer and carrier types. New carriers were authorized, such as the *Forrestal* and the *Saratoga* of 59,900 tons. Destroyer leaders such as the *Mitscher,* 3,500 tons, and the *Norfolk,* 4,500 tons, represented new trends in escort thinking. Great Britain built a new carrier *Ark Royal,* while Russia was reported to have two battleships and eight heavy cruisers of the *Sverdlov* type under construction. A milestone in naval construction was passed with the launching of U.S.S. *Nautilus,* the world's first atomic-powered submarine, whose construction was directed by Rear Admiral H. V. Rickover. This vessel was designed to have high underwater speed and her endurance submerged was to be limited only by that of her crew. She represented the first true submersible—capable of sustained operations at complete submergence.

Changes in munitions were also of prime importance. Depth charges and ahead-thrown antisubmarine weapons were redesigned to speed sinking time so that a submarine would not be able to twist away while these projectiles were dropping through the water. Automatic 6- and 8-inch guns were developed and installed on cruisers. Automatic 3-inch guns began to replace 40 mm mounts as antiaircraft weapons. In the field of rocket weapons both the Army and the Navy conducted extensive developmental programs. For ground-to-air weapons the Army developed *Nike,* a slim, pencil-shaped missile about 15 feet long, which would automatically seek out and destroy an enemy bomber. The Navy's equivalent weapon, the *Terrier,* was designed to be launched from shipboard. In the realm of air-to-air guided missiles, the Air Force's *Falcon* and the

Navy's *Sparrow* were like the old aircraft rockets except that they could be guided to the target.

The helicopter was another important development in the Navy's aircraft program. Its flexibility of operation and the small space needed for landing and take-off meant that it could operate successfully from cruisers and battleships as well as carriers. It made a good scout and was able to relieve destroyers of some of the more onerous mail-delivering duties as well as the duty of plane guard in carrier operations. In Korea these craft played many other important roles from air strike control planes to rescue missions. Supply or evacuation of isolated positions was but one of the vital services they performed. The lives of many wounded were saved by these "whirly-birds" operating from hospital LST's and hospital ships, for they were able to pick a wounded man up from an advance dressing station and fly him directly to the hospital ship.

THE ATOMIC BOMB

After the dropping of the atomic bombs on Hiroshima and Nagasaki in the closing days of the war, it became imperative for military leaders to have more exact knowledge of this weapon. They needed to know how to use it effectively in offense and they needed to know its capabilities and limitations so that some countermeasures might be taken to minimize its effects in the event that an enemy used it. For this purpose "Operation Crossroads" was scheduled as a test of the atomic bomb against naval ships. The venture became a joint experiment of the War and Navy Departments. Under the command of Vice Admiral William H. P. Blandy USN, tests were conducted at Bikini Atoll in the Marshall Islands, about 190 miles east of Eniwetok and 250 miles northwest of Kwajalein. Over 200 ships, 150 airplanes, and 42,000 men were involved in the test. Seventy-five ships were placed in the target area to provide data for study of blast damage and radiation contamination. The target

ship, the *Nevada*, was in the center with four other battleships, the *Pennsylvania*, the *Arkansas*, the *New York*, and the Japanese *Nagato*, ranged around. Two carriers, the *Saratoga* and the *Independence*, were included as well as the cruisers *Pensacola*, *Salt Lake City*, the German *Prinz Eugen*, and the Japanese *Sakawa*. In addition there were other cruisers, destroyers, attack transports, submarines, and various smaller vessels. Each of the ships contained scientific instruments, an assortment of equipment, and live animals to measure or reflect the effects of the blast and subsequent radiation. Drone airplanes were prepared to fly through the cloud and send back scientific data. Drone boats were to take samples of the water after the explosions.

Test Able, a drop from *Dave's Dream*, a B-29 piloted by Major Woodrow P. Swancutt, took place on July 1, 1946 at 0900 Bikini time. The damage was summarized by an evaluation board set up by the Joint Chiefs of Staff. A destroyer and two APA's sank at once, and another destroyer capsized and sank later. The Japanese cruiser *Sakawa* sank the next day. The *Independence* was wrecked and gutted by fire. The submarine *Skate*'s superstructure received extensive damage. The superstructures of the *Nevada*, *Arkansas*, and *Pensacola* were badly wrecked. Casualties would have been very high among exposed personnel, but the animal survivors indicated some measure of protection from radiation would be afforded crew members below decks.

Test Baker, held at 0825 on July 25, 1946, was an underwater explosion. The bomb was suspended below *LSM 60*, which disintegrated from the blast. Also sunk were the *Arkansas*, the *Saratoga*, an LST, an LSM, and an oiler, while the destroyer *Hughes* and the APA *Falcon* were beached to prevent them from sinking. One submerged and three surfaced submarines went permanently to the bottom. The Japanese battleship *Nagato* sank five days later. The water of the lagoon was so dangerous from radioactivity that four days after test Baker it was unsafe for personnel to spend any "useful length of time" on the target vessels. Subsequent tests were held at a new test area in Eniwetok Atoll.

The United States did not long enjoy the monopoly on the atomic bomb. Partly as a result of the work of traitors and partly as a result of Soviet scientific knowledge, the Russians developed an atomic bomb of their own several years ahead of the time western scientists thought possible. They successfully exploded the prototype somewhere in the Caucasus area in September 1949. Detection of radioactive particles in the stratosphere led to American knowledge of this explosion, an event confirmed by the Russians a short time later. The fact of Soviet possession of atomic weapons caused military and political leaders to take another look at the world strategic picture. They had scarcely begun this process when a new development brought war from a hypothetical to an actual condition. The militarized North Koreans recklessly flung down the gauntlet; the response was up to the free world.

51

The Korean War

THE UNEASY PEACE ENDED abruptly on the morning of June 25, 1950 when North Korean troops crossed the 38th parallel in an invasion of the Republic of Korea. Unlike previous border skirmishes, this was invasion—full scale and without warning. Nothing, it seemed, could save free Korea.

The Communist leaders had, they thought, chosen shrewdly in their efforts to fill the gap in their holdings in Asia, to point a dagger at the heart of Japan, where General Douglas MacArthur prevented their customary subversion, and incidentally to test the determination of the Western world to resist their aggression. Spokesmen for the State Department of the United States had publicly intimated that Korea was not important to American strategic defense. The implication seemed clear: the United States would not seriously oppose the invasion of South Korea.

North Korean troops, well trained in conventional infantry tactics, excelled in camouflage, infiltration, and night operations. Even if the forces of the United Nations should intervene, the physical aspects of Korea and the primitive but effective North Korean logistic organization were of a kind greatly to hinder a force that put great emphasis on the use of machines, both for supply and for attack, and whose striking power could most quickly be brought to bear through sea and air power. The mountainous terrain and the extremes of heat and cold, mud and dust, typhoon and rainy season would limit the effectiveness of mechanized warfare. In logistics North Korea had an organization almost invulnerable to United Nations forces; it later proved nearly impossible to interdict the flow of supplies without physical possession of the supply routes or the supply bases. The North Korean soldier could live off the land. Conscripted peasants could carry supplies, ammunition, and other requisites over back roads while giving the appearance of harmless refugees. The 1,500-mile-long Korean coastline offers many places for concealment, but few opportunities for amphibious landings where combined sea, air, and land power can best be brought to bear. The east coast of Korea has few adequate harbors, while the west is protected in many areas by vast mud banks and tide ranges. The mountainous terrain would assist a foot-borne and foot-supplied army by offering easy cover, opportunities for ambush, and protection from air attack. The

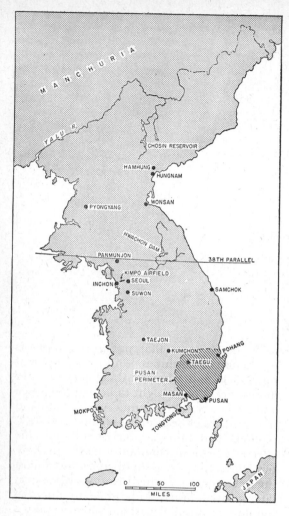

KOREA

conclusions. They miscalculated however in several important respects. On June 25 (New York time), the day after the Reds crossed the border, an emergency meeting of the United Nations Security Council convened in New York. Without a veto, by grace of a Russian boycott, the Security Council condemned the North Korean act as a breach of world peace and forthwith ordered military sanctions. To the United States fell the direction of military operation. President Truman delegated responsibility for the "police action," as he later called it, to the American Joint Chiefs of Staff, who, in turn, named General of the Army Douglas MacArthur to have operational control in the Far East in addition to his responsibility as Supreme Commander, Occupied Japan. On June 27, President Truman ordered the United States Seventh Fleet, based on Japan, to neutralize Formosa—to prevent the Chinese Communists from attacking that island and to prevent the forces of Generalissimo Chiang Kai-shek from attacking the mainland. In addition the Seventh Fleet was to operate under the orders of General MacArthur in attacks on military targets, at first in South Korea, later at targets located in North Korea as well.

NAVAL OPERATIONS

Early naval operations in Korean waters included evacuation of civilians and Americans at Inchon and Pusan. Merchant freighters, protected by American and South Korean naval forces, picked up thousands of refugees at both ports. The U. S. destroyers *Mansfield* and *De Haven* stood by off Inchon, and Korean patrol craft looked after Pusan. The *De Haven* saw further action in a bombardment of Samchok on the east coast shortly afterwards. With the cruiser *Juneau,* she broke up a troop landing which the Reds had made from motor barges.

The first ship-to-ship action of the war took place off Pusan. Three South Korean ships, two YMS's and one PC, discovered what turned out to be a North Korean troop transport attempting to seize the port of

same mountainous terrain would greatly handicap a mechanized army, adding immeasurably to its vastly greater logistic problem.

THE UNITED NATIONS INTERVENES

Some such reasoning process as this may well have formed the basis for the North Korean—or Communist Chinese or Russian —"Enemy Capabilities" section of their Estimate of the Situation. If this is true, events soon proved the soundness of many of their

Pusan. The strange vessel flew no colors and refused to answer repeated challenges. Searchlight illumination revealed her identity, and she was sunk after a short gun battle.

As the days passed, it became evident that South Korean ground forces and Allied naval and air forces alone could not stop the advance of the North Korean armies. Allied ground forces would also be needed, so General MacArthur was authorized to strip Japan of occupation forces to furnish troops for the action in Korea. Transportation of these men from Japan to Korea was handled by air and by LST's for the most part. During this operation two aircraft carriers in the area, U.S.S. *Valley Forge* and H.M.S. *Triumph,* sent interdiction and close air support strikes over Korean territory. This was to be the pattern of operations for some time to come—shore bombardment by cruisers and destroyers and air strikes by the carrier groups. Escort of supply ships to Pusan became advisable in face of reported submarine sightings in Korean waters. Speculation over Russian intentions with their Vladivostok-based submarines caused deep concern in the early days of the war. Commitment of submarines would very certainly mean great difficulty in support and reinforcement of ground forces already in Korea, and it might well mean that World War III was at hand. Fortunately this menace never materialized, for submarines, although occasionally spotted in the area, never engaged in any offensive actions.

THE REDS DRIVE SOUTH

South Koreans, lacking tanks and combat aircraft, fell back before the invaders in a hopeless rout. Smashing past Suwon, the Reds sent flanking drives to the east just as the first American troops, two battalions of the 24th Infantry Division, arrived from Japan. Digging in, falling back from one road block to another, the American troops managed to slow the Red drive and caused the Communists to overestimate American strength. As a result the invaders deployed across the country instead of smashing through to Pusan as they well might have done.

As the Americans retreated from Taejon to Kumchon, an important rail and road junction, they received strong support on their right flank from the Republic of Korea army which had somewhat recovered from its panic and was fighting effectively in the east. In the west however defenses were non-existent, and in a few days the Red invaders had reached the southwestern corner of Korea, where they wheeled and began a drive east to Pusan. In sight of Masan, only 30 miles from the vital port of Pusan, they were stopped by a small, determined force of the 24th Infantry. Instead of reinforcing this drive, the Communists chose to maintain pressure on the center, where they met strong Allied resistance. Hence their drive slowed down and the Americans were able to dig in and hold the Pusan Perimeter.

REINFORCEMENTS ASSEMBLE

It quickly became apparent that the forces then in the Far East were insufficient for the task at hand. Unless speedy reinforcements arrived, the United Nations troops might well be pushed out of Korea entirely. To this end, General MacArthur requested the "immediate dispatch of one Marine Regimental Combat Team with comparable Marine Air Unit for tactical support" from the United States. Other nations of the 53 that condemned North Korean aggression began to send either military forces or supplies or both. By the end of the year, 19 nations had offered military help and 21 were giving supplies and medical aid. Chiang Kai-shek repeatedly demanded that he be allowed to use his forces currently on Formosa, but Allied leaders considered that this would result in spreading the war. By far the heaviest burden for both military forces and logistic support fell on the United States. A new carrier task group under the command of Rear Admiral Walter F. Boone USN was hastily assembled in Hawaiian waters. This group included, besides the heavy carrier *Philippine Sea,* the cruisers *Toledo* and *Helena,* ten destroyers, five submarines, and four oilers.

Manpower became an increasing problem; many ships were short not only of wartime complements but were not even up to authorized peacetime strength. General MacArthur's request for a Marine Regimental Combat Team was followed by requests for a full Marine Division. He received assurance from Washington toward the end of July that one would be forthcoming. On its timely arrival depended whether the United Nations could hold in Korea. To fill manpower shortages personnel of the Army, Navy, Air Force, and Marine Corps were pulled out of duty stations in the United States and rushed to Korea. Their places were taken by reservists who either volunteered or were recalled to active duty. Many reservists too found themselves Korea-bound.

Already boxed in within a small perimeter around the port of Pusan, the United Nations forces could no longer trade space for time. Taejon had fallen; Taegu was threatened. Driving to Mokpu, the North Koreans, as we have noted, had reached the southwest tip of Korea. They then began to close to the eastward and the southward, compressing still further the narrow field of operations around Pusan. In an attempt to reinforce the armies in the field, on July 18 the United States 1st Cavalry Division made an unopposed amphibious landing at Pohang, 70 miles north of Pusan. Approximately 10,000 men, 2,000 vehicles, and 2,800 tons of bulk cargo were put ashore. The newly landed troops got into action two days later, assisting the badly battered 24th Infantry Division.

The Pusan Perimeter as finally established was enclosed by a line beginning on the south coast of Korea at Tongyong, about 25 miles west of Pusan, proceeding northerly for approximately 80 miles, around Taegu, and thence easterly to a point south of Pohang, which had to be given up after the 1st Cavalry Division's landing there. The situation grew so desperate that General MacArthur ordered the 1st Provisional Marine Brigade directly to Pusan, canceling its plans for landing first at Japan for reorganization. The marines reached Pusan on August 2, followed a day later by the Army's 2nd Infantry Division and the 5th Regimental Combat Team. Since the United Nations did not have sufficient force to hold the perimeter at all points, the marines were employed as a mobile reserve to be rushed to the scene of any attack before a breakthrough could be exploited.

PLANNING OPERATION CHROMITE

By the end of the third week in August, the North Korean drive seemed to have lost its push; hence on the 23rd General MacArthur called a conference of naval leaders in the Far East—Admiral Forrest C. Sherman, Vice Admiral C. Turner Joy, and Vice Admiral Arthur D. Struble—to discuss the possibilities of an amphibious assault on Inchon. MacArthur had first directed planning for a landing in the Inchon area in the early days of the war, but the deteriorating situation on the Korean mainland had forced cancelation of these plans. Now, in August, they were revived. Determined to take advantage of the mobility afforded him by his sea power, MacArthur pointed out how a landing well up the peninsula would cut off supplies for the bulk of the North Korean army, 90 per cent of which was engaged in South Korea. Inchon, the port of Seoul, very nearly the only possible port for a large-scale amphibious landing, presented almost insurmountable difficulties. In the first place, the only approach to the area is through Flying Fish Channel, a long, narrow, tortuous channel with irregular three-to-five knot currents. The approaches to the harbor itself are commanded by the island fortresses of Wolmi-do and Sowolmi-do. The difficulties of the harbor meant that the reserve ships would have to stand off 30 miles from the assault vessels, approximately three times the distance customarily considered the maximum. Greater than all these difficulties loomed the matter of the tide. The tidal range at Inchon—one of the greatest in the world, 29 feet on the average and on occasion rising to 36 feet above low water—nearly precluded the proposed landing, yet paradoxically made it possible because it afforded deep water over the mud flats that make up a large part of Inchon's waterfront. LST's need 29 feet of water for proper maneuvering, and this depth of water could be assured only for a period of about three days once a lunar month. Thus, the moon set the date for the Inchon landing. The proper tide conditions would obtain on the three days beginning September 15; such conditions would not again be encountered until the middle of October—too close to the Korean winter. Accordingly September 15 was set, leaving just over three weeks for planning an operation more difficult than most of those encountered in World War II, when preparation for amphibious operations had customarily taken months. In view of the short period of time remaining, planning for Operation Chromite was begun without delay.

At once, Lieutenant General Walton H. Walker [1] was warned that the Marine Brigade would be withdrawn from the Pusan area in the immediate future for an amphibious landing. General Walker was understandably reluctant to let it go since it was in combat and he had no replacement. The brigade was released however at the personal order of General MacArthur and became the nucleus for the 1st Marine Division which was to spearhead the Inchon landing. No replacements were offered General Walker because none were available. The risk of weakening the Pusan Perimeter was foreseen, but nothing could be done about it; the risk had to be taken if the Inchon landing was to succeed. Only the command of the sea exercised by the United Nations naval forces made such a speedy redeployment possible and the risks acceptable.

The marines from Pusan were to be reinforced by others coming from the United States, and from these two sources the 1st Marine Division was organized. This division, with the 7th Infantry Division, the 187th Airborne Regimental Combat Team and a Korean Marine Corps regiment, comprised the X Corps, which was to make the assault. The operation was placed under the tactical direction of Vice Admiral Struble, Commander Joint Task Force Seven. The Attack Force, TF 90, was under the command of Rear Admiral James H. Doyle. Escort carriers were to fly close support missions, while the cruisers and destroyers of the Covering Force supplied artillery assistance. Deep support air strikes were to be flown from the carriers *Philippine Sea, Valley Forge,* and *Boxer,* under the command of Rear Admiral Edward C. Ewen in the *Philippine Sea.* Logistics were the responsibility of Captain Bernard L. Austin, Commander Task Force 79.

One of the pressing needs was for intelligence information on the landing area. Air Force, Marine, and Navy planes flew photo-reconnaissance missions, but on-the-spot information was vital. Accordingly an intelligence team led by Lieutenant Eugene F. Clark USN landed near Inchon. His reports, especially on the feasibility of the landing beaches and on the strength of the defenses on Wolmi-do played an important part in the planning.

It seemed that all the work of preparation was to be lost when a typhoon boiled up through Japan, hitting Kobe especially hard, where the First Marine Division had debarked three days earlier. The typhoon, with winds up to 110 knots, not only imperiled ships but, worse, cost 24 hours of the precious time needed for the arduous tasks of unloading mixed cargoes and combat-loading assault vessels. Another delay like this would postpone the landing until the middle of October, the next period of flood tide. Anxious weather observers carefully checked for disturbances. A very few days later, they spotted a depression about 200 miles west of Saipan. By September 8, this depression had blown up into another typhoon whose predicted track crossed that of Joint Task Force Seven. As if this were not bad enough, a new

---

[1] General Walker had replaced Lieutenant General William F. Dean in command of the Eighth Army in Korea after Dean had been captured in the defense of Taejon.

danger loomed: a South Korean patrol vessel on station near Inchon sank a North Korean minelayer. Had it already laid its mines? No one knew. Mines in Flying Fish Channel would make Operation Chromite nearly impossible. Not only would detection be difficult in the muddy water, but even a small ship sunk in the channel would effectively block it.

On September 11, the second typhoon began a slow turn to the north. Taking a chance that the northerly curve would continue, Admiral Doyle ordered the Transport and Advance Attack Groups to get underway from Kobe, one day ahead of schedule. Because rough weather impeded the passage, the extra time was all to the good.

CAPTURING THE HARBOR ISLANDS

The first job to be done at Inchon was to neutralize the islands of Wolmi-do and Sowolmi-do. The plan as finally carried out was to send a cruiser-destroyer force to draw fire from Wolmi-do in order to reveal batteries and to knock them out. This effort was to be made on D-minus-2 and D-minus-1 days. Then on the morning of D-day, marines would occupy Wolmi-do. The main landing on the city itself would take place that evening at the peak of the tide.

The destroyer-cruiser force, under Admiral John H. Higgins, started up Flying Fish Channel at 0730 on D-minus-2 day. The cruisers *Toledo, Rochester,* H.M.S. *Kenya* and H.M.S. *Jamaica* peeled off at stations ranging from 20,000 to 14,000 yards out. Destroyer Squadron 9, *Mansfield, De Haven, Lyman K. Swenson, Collett, Gurke,* and *Henderson,* continued up the channel and anchored in a line to the west of Wolmi-do, with the nearest ship approximately 800 yards from the island. On the way in, the *Mansfield* spotted a mine field, whereupon the *Henderson* was detached to investigate and destroy the mines. As the destroyers were standing in, carrier planes from TF 77 attacked Wolmi-do. Their strikes lifted at 1300, at which time the destroyers opened

fire, the cruisers joining in as gun emplacements were revealed. The *Collet* was hit five times during the hour-long bombardment, the *Gurke* three times, and the *Lyman K. Swenson* once. At 1400 the destroyers withdrew, the tide having swung them around to head for the open sea. The next day saw the bombardment repeated, this time for an hour and a quarter. At the end of two days' cruiser and destroyer bombardments, and heavy strikes from carrier aircraft, Wolmi-do was considered softened up enough for the landing the next morning.

H-hour for Wolmi-do was 0630 on the morning of September 15. The time was chosen to give the 3rd Battalion of the 5th Marine Regiment the maximum daylight time for the capture of Wolmi-do before the main landing at Inchon scheduled for 1730. To arrive on schedule at Wolmi-do the transports and their supporting ships had to navigate Inchon channel at night—the moonless night of the spring tide. Unaccountably, the Reds had not extinguished the light on Palmi-do, about half way down the channel, and this provided a useful check for the 19 ships making the assault. The troops were embarked in LSD *Fort Marion* and in destroyer transports *Diachenko, Horace A. Bass,* and *Wantuck.* The supporting ships, the six destroyers which had bombarded Wolmi-do, were making their third trip up the channel. In addition there were three rocket landing vessels and four cruisers. The *Mansfield* led the column in, navigating without difficulty by radar. The ships were all in position by 0500 and the landing force was ordered into the boats at 0540. At 0545 bombardment commenced and proceeded without incident except for the difficulty of the rocket vessels in maintaining station in the $3\frac{1}{2}$-knot current. The first wave left the line of departure at $0627\frac{1}{2}$ and landed on Green Beach on the west side of the northerly projection of the island at 0631, one minute late. The second wave landed five minutes later, followed in ten minutes by landing craft from the *Fort Marion*. By 0701, the flag was hoisted from the highest point of the island and at 0807, Wolmi-do was pronounced secure. Sowolmi-do, next on the

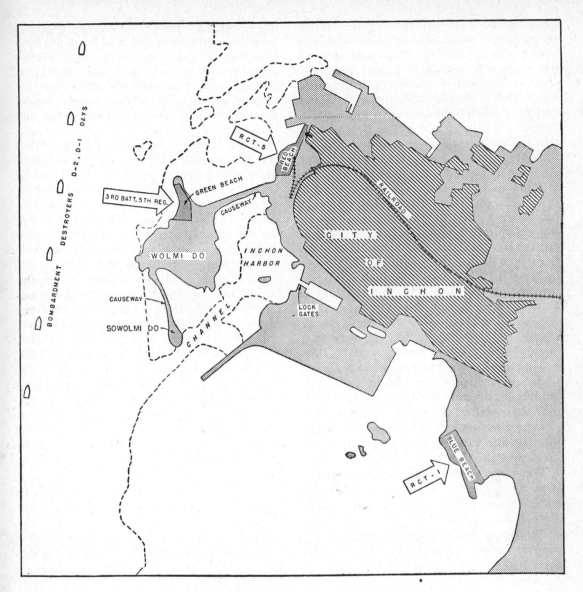

THE ASSAULT ON INCHON

schedule, was difficult to approach because the long causeway connecting it to Wolmi-do could be swept by a single enemy machine gun, Horatio-at-the-bridge style. However, at the request of the marines, one of the support ships sprayed Sowolmi-do with 40 mm fire, and the marines were able to cross while the Reds were seeking cover from this fire. Thus, Wolmi-do and Sowolmi-do were captured with comparative ease at small cost,

and the biggest man-made obstacle to the landing was removed.

THE INCHON LANDING

The main landing was next to get underway. It was something unique in marine history. Never before had the marines made an amphibious landing into the heart of a large city.[2] Nowhere except in downtown Inchon could heavy equipment—tanks, bulldozers, and trucks—be landed. Two landing areas had been selected: Red Beach, 1,000 feet wide, immediately to the north of the causeway connecting Wolmi-do to the mainland, and Blue Beach, in the outskirts to the south. No one knew much about Blue Beach except that it was narrow and too muddy to support heavy equipment. Everything known about Red Beach was bad, for here the potential difficulties of the invaders were increased by two special conditions. In the first place, tidal conditions at Red Beach made it as easy for the defenders as for the invaders to figure out the time of landing. It had to be no later than 1730 so that the area might be secured before the LST's came in at high water, approximately an hour later. It could not be earlier, for then the tide would not be high enough to allow the landing craft to get ashore. In the second place, the very word "beach" was a misnomer, for at Red there was no beach whatever, only sea walls designed to keep out the highest tides. The landing craft would not be able to discharge over these walls. All carried scaling ladders, but there was no way of knowing in advance whether the ladders and grappling equipment were the right sort for the task.

The preliminary bombardment began at 1645, a combination of cruiser and destroyer guns, rockets, and carrier aircraft strikes. Task Force 77, the fast carrier force, flew deep support and interdiction strikes. Close support for the landings came from marine flyers based on the escort carriers *Sicily* and *Badoeng Strait*. The bombardment was successful only in part. Large gaps were blown in the sea wall at Red Beach, but the wall was not entirely demolished. The large hill in back of Red Beach, appropriately called Cemetery Hill for the simple reason that it was Inchon's principal cemetery, came in for a special pounding, since it was here that the Communist troops had dug in and prepared their gun emplacements. The first wave hit the beach on schedule at 1730, with the land-

ing unopposed except for natural obstacles over the rubble of the sea wall. Not until the fourth wave was landing did the defenders open up with any serious opposition, but by that time, the troops already ashore were becoming effective in seizing enemy strong points. There was some confusion as the marines tried to make their objective line, about 1,000 yards inland, including Cemetery Hill and Observatory Hill next to it. Although the officers had been briefed on the layout of Inchon's streets, some men got lost and all were in danger from snipers and falling rubble. However by 2000, when darkness fell, the marines had attained their objective line and had sent probes 500 yards beyond it without meeting resistance.

At 1830, eight LST's started in for the beach; the 1,000-foot area could accommodate no more. The situation was far from ideal, for the landing area was under fire, and the LST's carried oil, gasoline, napalm, and ammunition. The thin sides of an LST offer little protection for such a cargo, but it had to be landed to keep the marines supplied through the night. Remarkably enough, all eight ships got safely in and began unloading. If the sea wall had hampered the small landing craft, it nearly blocked the LST's. Only the two ships on the flanks could lower their ramps sufficiently to discharge cargoes through the bows. The ramps of the others slammed down on the wall with their outboard ends six feet above the ground on the far side. The situation improved as the bulldozers from the LST's at each end of the line knocked down parts of the sea wall to enable the other ships to unload. The bulldozers also took care of pillboxes and other defensive emplacements, so that with the marine advances the beach rapidly became a safer place for unloading.

At Blue Beach the 1st Marines went ashore against light resistance and seized control of the rail line to Seoul. Because of the mud flats, LST's in this area had to wait for the morning tide. By that time the logistic problem was becoming simplified, first, by the arrival of more LST's at Red Beach, and then by the discovery that the conventional port

---

[2] In 1946 Inchon had a population of 216,000.

facilities of Inchon could be used with a minimum of repair. At 1730 on September 16, just 24 hours after the landing, Major General Oliver P. Smith USMC set up his command post ashore near the force beachhead line. The landing phase of the operation was concluded, with total marine casualties of 21 killed and 186 wounded.

The invasion was a superb example of teamwork and adaptability under adverse circumstances. American forces had complete control of the sea and air and by exploiting these media were able to land a major assault against a major city offering excellent opportunities for concealment. In spite of the ample warnings that the Communist forces had received of the imminence of a landing in Inchon, they had not given sufficient thought or care to the disposition of troops in the city. The few mines encountered in Inchon harbor had been outside the channel routes, although natural conditions determined that United Nations ships must use the channels. The sporadic mining merely indicated that the North Koreans had not been effectively prepared for the possibility of an amphibious assault.

On D-plus-2 day, the two assault regiments began the advance on Seoul. They met with only scattered resistance, so effective had been the carrier interdiction strikes. Although the Reds made a suicide stand near the Kimpo Airfield, this did not seriously delay the marines. On September 21 the amphibious phase ended, and over-all command passed from Admiral Doyle, commanding TF 90, to the Commanding General X Corps, Major General Edward M. Almond USA.

PUSAN BREAKOUT

On D-plus-1 day, the Eighth Army under General Walker began a major offensive in the area of the Pusan Perimeter. This offensive, together with the landings at Inchon, placed the North Korean forces in an impossible military situation. The mountainous terrain, on which they had counted, now worked to their disadvantage, for the mountain ranges determined that adequate supplies could be brought to the Perimeter area only via the Seoul-Taejon road or via the east coast road. The Inchon landing brought the former under fire, while Allied naval forces interdicted use of the latter.

Cut off from their sources of supply, attacked both in front and behind, the North Koreans literally had no way to turn. The situation was true military surprise. Even though the Inchon landing could have been and probably was foreseen by the Reds, there was nothing they could do. Their forces were in a position from which they could not extricate themselves. When the advance forces of the Eighth Army coming up from Pusan made contact with elements of the X Corps 25 miles south of Seoul on September 26, the war between the United Nations and North Korea was over. Not that the fighting had ceased, but the North Korean troops were finished; they had no hope of victory. Those below the line of junction of the two United Nations forces were cut off; those above were disorganized and were only a small proportion of the total number of North Korean soldiers. The landing had "pulled the drawstring" on Korea, cutting off the last hope of a North Korean victory; short of Chinese intervention, all that remained was mopping up.

Nowhere is there a better illustration of General MacArthur's dictum that four times out of five a force is defeated when its main supply line is cut, or, as Alfred Thayer Mahan put it 60 years earlier, that "communications dominate war."

Even before the success of military operations in South Korea became apparent, political questions began to loom very large. The question of the intent of the United Nations directive in regard to the Korean War came to be paramount. Were the United Nations forces simply to liberate South Korea? Were they to proceed into North Korea to punish the aggressor? Were they to occupy all of North Korea? If they did the last, would the Red Chinese intervene? These questions caused concern not only at Lake Success, New York—at that time the United Nations Headquarters—but also in the American State Department, the British Foreign Office, and in ministries of the 53 nations that had condemned Communist aggression in Korea.

The 38th parallel had long ceased to be a dividing line as far as naval and air operations were concerned, but the decision to cross it with ground troops was not made lightly. Most of the non-Communist nations in the United Nations believed that sanction had been given to drive North Korean troops as far as necessary to insure that South Korea would be safe from future attack. For this purpose, it was necessary to move into North Korea to prevent North Korean forces from regrouping and rearming and launching an attack at some later date.

The Russian group, of course, opposing any operations at all in Korea, attempted to deny United Nations forces permission to cross the 38th parallel. In this attempt, Andrei Vishinsky received support from Prime Minister Pandit Nehru of India, who argued against crossing the parallel, but for different reasons. First, he thought that by this action, United Nations troops might become aggressors themselves and that crossing the line might bring Communist China and even Russia into the war. He further showed in the course of debate that he had no great love or admiration for Syngman Rhee, the President of South Korea. At length the United Nations authorized the crossing of the 38th parallel in order to attempt to end the capability of North Korea to remount an aggressive drive to the south.

While the Eighth Army, breaking out of the old perimeter in all directions, mopped up the liberated countryside, ROK (Republic of Korea) troops advanced into North Korea via the east coast road.

DRIVING NORTH

The Eighth Army, advancing north from Seoul towards Pyongyang, capital of North Korea, met strong resistance and was temporarily brought to a standstill. On the United Nations right flank however, the ROK's met little more than token resistance. Racing up the east coast, they advanced a hundred miles beyond the 38th parallel in ten days. In order to exploit the enemy's weakness in the east, MacArthur prepared to shift General Almond's X Corps from the Seoul area around to the opposite coast of Korea to begin a second line of advance on Pyongyang. To spearhead this move the 1st Marine Division moved by sea from Inchon on the west coast for an amphibious assault on Wonsan on the east coast.

The situation was so fluid however that plans were not able to keep up with events, for the Eighth Army captured Pyongyang on October 19, while the marines were not able to land at Wonsan until the 26th, after it had been taken from the rear by the ROK's. Mines had caused the delay. The North Koreans had mined Wonsan harbor as they should have mined Inchon. Instead of the five days of minesweeping operations allowed in the operation plan, the job had taken 15 days. During the extra time, the transports had steamed up and down off Wonsan in what the marines called "Operation Yo-yo." It was somewhat anticlimactic for them to land quietly, especially when they found that the First Marine Air Wing was already there and had been entertained the previous night by a USO show featuring Bob Hope.

The rest of the X Corps soon arrived at Wonsan and proceeded to clear the area of enemy and to push on to Hamhung.

THE NEW WAR

With the advance of United Nations forces into North Korea, there came increasing hints that the Red Chinese might intervene. General MacArthur's intelligence chief, Major General Charles A. Willoughby, had estimated that the Chinese would not enter the war in significant numbers, even though they might send "volunteers." He argued that if they had intended to intervene in force, they would have done so while the Allies had their backs to the sea. On the strength of this estimate, MacArthur sent General Walker's Eighth Army northward from Pyongyang and General Almond's X Corps north from Hamhung. As these two forces drove toward the Yalu, they were separated from each other by 80 miles of mountainous terrain, so that liaison between them had to be handled through Tokyo.

Into this breach the Chinese hurled their armies, though their own territory was not threatened. The bitter cold of late November found both American drives in full retreat after efforts at mutual support had failed. The Eighth Army fell back, trading space for time, past Pyongyang, past the 38th parallel, and past Seoul, until it managed to stabilize a new line across Korea. In the meantime, Almond's X Corps retired in the direction of Hungnam.

During the drive toward the Yalu, elements of the 1st Marine Division had reached the Chosin Reservoir. There the Chinese surrounded them, threatening them with total extinction. The marines, as at Guadalcanal and Bougainville, depended on their perimeter defense and held their position until they could organize for retirement southwards. This retreat, through difficult terrain, through snow and cold, under constant attack and harassment, has come to be known as one of the great retreats of history. The marines, skillfully supported by carrier aircraft from the U. S. Seventh Fleet, fought their way through eight Chinese divisions, brought out most of their equipment and the survivors of three army battalions which had also been cut off in the Reservoir area. On December 11, sixteen days after the Chinese had first attacked the Eighth Army in force and 13 days after they had swept down upon X Corps positions, Almond's forces had reached Hamhung and Hungnam, where they were safe under the protection of Seventh Fleet guns and planes. In the long march the marines had suffered more than 7,000 casualties, nearly half of which were the result of frostbite and exposure. Enemy losses probably amounted to 25,000 killed and half as many wounded.

HUNGNAM—AN AMPHIBIOUS OPERATION IN REVERSE

The Hungnam evacuation or embarkation—it was called both, depending on the optimism of the speaker at the moment—had as its aim the saving of life and the orderly retirement from an impossible military situation. Unlike Dunkirk, Hungnam represented no military rout, for the retirement was carried out with a minimum of confusion and loss. Task Force 90, reconstituted for the operation under the command of Rear Admiral James J. Doyle, included 76 transport vessels—navy transports and cargo ships, USMT's and chartered merchant vessels. The Gunfire Support Group consisted of two heavy cruisers, the *Saint Paul* and the *Rochester,* eight destroyers and three LSMR's. Close support strikes were again flown from the escort carriers *Sicily* and *Badoeng Strait,* joined by the light carrier *Bataan.* The *Missouri* employed her big guns to support the Gunfire Group and she also operated with TF 77, the fast carrier task force, now increased to include four attack carriers, the *Leyte, Philippine Sea, Valley Forge,* and *Princeton.*

The first phase of the Hungnam operation was the limited evacuation of Wonsan where the 3rd Infantry Division was waiting. In addition, it seemed to observers on the spot that the entire population of Wonsan—about 75,000 and another 20,000 from the outlying districts—was attempting to get aboard the merchant transports in Wonsan harbor. Of course only a few could be accommodated, and when the ships left, approximately 20,000 were still seen milling around the waterfront area.

The "amphibious operation in reverse" at Hungnam lasted two full weeks, from December 10 to 24. Gunfire and carrier strikes kept the Reds back, actually creating a "no man's land" troops could not penetrate. Transports were loaded not only with men but also with heavy equipment of all sorts—trucks, tanks, bulldozers, ammunition, artillery, stores, and great numbers of civilian refugees. Altogether in that two-week period, Task Force 90 evacuated approximately 100,-000 troops, 90,000 Korean refugees, 17,500 vehicles, and 350,000 tons of bulk cargo. During this time the Fast Carrier Task Force flew strikes at the Red supply lines, operating in conditions of great difficulty because of icy decks, molasses-thick lubricating oil, and freezing winds that made carrier operations all but impossible. In spite of such difficulties, the Hungnam operation was brought to a successful close on Christmas Eve as the Underwater Demolition Teams blew up port facilities and waited for stragglers before embarking in the *Catamount*, the last ship out of Hungnam.

OTHER NAVAL OPERATIONS

We have outlined the land operations from the time of the Chinese intervention through the Hungnam evacuation; at sea nothing very dramatic was going on, yet the operations of the United Nations naval forces during this time were of great significance. Repeated bombardment of coastal roads forced the Reds to rely on inland roads and trails. Carrier strikes successfully interdicted use of the inland trails, roads, and railroads by day, so that the Red advance was considerably held up as they were forced back on night operations and infiltration tactics.

Perhaps the most significant naval air operations came about as a result of the complex political situation. In spite of the open intervention of Communist China in the Korean war, General MacArthur received orders that Manchurian territory was to be immune from attack or even territorial violation. Shortly after the Chinese intervention, the Reds had begun to use aircraft in a militarily significant way, employing Russian-built MIG-15 jets, which flew from bases in Manchuria. The denial of permission for United Nations planes to fly over Manchuria, even for a moment, meant that the MIG's had a sanctuary; if they were attacked by Allied jets, they broke contact and streaked across the Manchurian border while Allied

planes had to break contact about ten miles from the border to have room to turn so that they could avoid inadvertent crossing. Repeated requests for permission to cross the Yalu in "hot pursuit" were refused. The question of "hot pursuit" came to play an important part in later political discussions and activities.

As soon as the Red Chinese intervened, an important question arose concerning the bridges across the Yalu. General MacArthur had previously regarded the southern bank of the river as the limiting line for his operations. Yet to leave the Yalu bridges intact was to invite disaster by affording unimpeded passage of Chinese troops across the river. He made the decision to destroy the bridges, but his political directives were unchanged. He now assumed however that the mid-point of the river was the dividing line and set out to destroy only the Korean half of the bridges, thereby preserving Manchurian territorial integrity and also achieving his objective of denying the bridges to the Reds. How to destroy the bridges presented a problem. It had to be done by air, for there were no demolition teams in the area. Yet the Fifth Air Force pilots were not trained in the type of precision bombing required for this kind of operation. The task was given to the navy carrier pilots; it was no easy one. A bridge is a difficult target to hit and a more difficult one to destroy. A hole in the bridge roadway can be patched easily. It is necessary to hit one of the main supporting members. When there is only half a bridge to aim at, the task is even more difficult. Moreover, only two routes of approach to the bridges could be used, from either side, exactly parallel to the river bank. Any other route of approach would result in crossing the border either on the run-in or the pull-out. This limitation of mobility imposed on the planes meant that the Red defenders could concentrate their antiaircraft weapons along the north bank of the Yalu, and put up extremely heavy fire that the Allied planes would have to penetrate.

Seven bridges spanned the Yalu, all of them ruggedly built. Against the odds mentioned above, against fire from the Manchurian side of the river, and against MIG attacks, dive bombers from the *Philippine Sea,* the *Leyte,* and the *Valley Forge* in ten days of strikes knocked down three of the Yalu bridges, including the main railroad bridge at Manpojin.

Another operation of carrier planes in the Korean War is of interest. In mid-spring 1951, the decision was made to destroy Hwachon Dam on the Yalu in order to flood the valley below it and also to knock out Manchurian hydroelectric plants. Several unsuccessful strikes were flown by conventional bombers, but even their largest bombs could not successfully penetrate the concrete of the dam. When the problem was put up to the Navy, it was solved very quickly and simply—torpedoes. Using a weapon new to the Korean War, navy attack bombers dropped torpedoes into the lake above the dam, aiming them at the flood gates. A single strike succeeded in penetrating the dam and releasing the pent-up waters.

THE DISMISSAL OF GENERAL MACARTHUR

When the Red Chinese intervened, the Korean War became, as General MacArthur later called it, a new war. Once the position of the Eighth Army had become fairly stabilized south of Seoul, the X Corps was integrated into the new line. The United Nations land forces were at last placed under a unified command in the person of Lieutenant General Matthew B. Ridgway, who had succeeded General Walker, killed in a jeep accident.

MacArthur pressed for new instructions, new directives to enable him to cope with the changed situation. But pressure from European allies, especially France and Britain, who were fearful of expanding the war, was received with sympathy in the United States State Department, and their view prevailed with the President. No new directives were forthcoming except to reinforce the old ones regarding the sanctity of the Manchurian border.

So General Ridgway began Operation Killer, whose announced aim was not to capture, or re-capture territory, but to inflict maximum casualties on the Reds. Operating along the new line the United Nations army, better supplied with weapons, with superior air power, and using superior tactics, began methodically chewing up the Communist army. In the process Ridgway pushed his line again towards the 38th parallel, at length attaining a new stabilized line above Seoul on the west and thence northeasterly to a point well above the parallel on the east.

General MacArthur, chafing at the limitations imposed upon his freedom of action, had made his views on these matters known as early as August 1950, in a speech prepared for delivery at the annual meeting of the Veterans of Foreign Wars. Specifically he sought the right to cross the Manchurian border in "hot pursuit," to bomb Red supply bases and airfields in Manchuria, to institute blockade of the China coast, and to use the troops of the Chinese Nationalists on Formosa, either in Korea or against China itself in order to take the pressure off Korea.

At the order of the President, this speech had been withdrawn, but not in time to prevent publication of copies released to the press. The fact that General MacArthur was out of sympathy with national policy of the United States in regard to the Korean war was well known, and he was particularly reminded of a presidential order that all statements by him must be cleared with the Joint Chiefs of Staff. This reminder was dated March 24, 1951. However on the 20th General MacArthur had written in answer to a letter from Joseph W. Martin, Jr., Minority Leader in the House of Representatives, a statement of his own views, which Martin read in the House. This letter reveals his views so well that excerpts from it are worth quoting.

My views and recommendations with respect to the situation created by Red China's entry into war against us in Korea . . . are well known and clearly understood, as they follow the conventional pattern of meeting force with maximum counter-force as we have never failed to do in the past. . . .

It seems strangely difficult for some to realize

that here in Asia is where the Communist conspirators have elected to make their play for global conquest, and that we have joined the issue thus raised on the battlefield; that here we fight Europe's war with arms while the diplomats there still fight it with words; that if we lose the war to communism in Asia the fall of Europe is inevitable, win it and Europe most probably would avoid war and yet preserve freedom. As you pointed out, we must win. There is no substitute for victory.

Nothing MacArthur said later was more than an amplification of the ideas contained in this letter. Its release appeared to the President to be a violation of orders on the part of the General. Summarily, Mr. Truman ordered MacArthur's immediate relief from all his duties in the Far East, replacing him with General Ridgway. The President's dispatch was released to the press in advance of delivery to General MacArthur, so that the General first heard of it on a news broadcast.

On his return to the United States MacArthur received a tremendous ovation from the public everywhere he went. Public opinion, not fully aware of the dangers of Russian involvement under the Sino-Russian mutual defense pact of 1950, was strongly sympathetic with the General's point of view. He was invited to address a Joint Session of Congress, at which time he elaborated the views already presented in his letter. A committee to investigate the relief of General MacArthur held lengthy hearings. The inquiry broadened its scope into an investigation of the conduct of the Korean War and agreed that the President had a right to remove the General, but that the method of removal was unwise, that the General had never violated directives, that there was no serious disagreement between him and the Joint Chiefs of Staff, that the Secretary of State had assumed military functions, his advice overruling that of the Joint Chiefs

of Staff, and that there had been a lack of adequate support from the other nations involved in the United Nations effort. The conclusion reached was that cessation of hostilities based on a restoration of the *status quo* at the 38th parallel would be a victory for aggression.

PEACE TALKS

In spite of this conclusion, when Russia's Jacob Malik proposed in June 1951 that armistice talks might profitably be held, United Nations leaders agreed. Vice Admiral C. Turner Joy was named as chief delegate for the United Nations forces, while North Korean General Nam-Il led the Communist truce party. Early the Communists tried to twist the situation to their advantage, making it appear as though the United Nations forces had been beaten. But skilled diplomacy and a rigid insistence on United Nations rights brought about an end to such attempts. For more than two years the peace talks dragged on, involving discussion and haggling over the line of demarcation between the two forces. Was it to be the 38th parallel? So the Communists said. The Allies insisted on a militarily defensible line based roughly on the then existing battle zone. The issue of the return of prisoners of war held the discussion up for many months. Eventually however agreement was reached, and the armistice was signed at Panmunjon on July 27, 1953.

Hostilities ceased 12 hours later, troops withdrawing from the agreed buffer zone. Thus ended the third largest war in American history, with no clear-cut victory on either side and with neither side completely satisfied with the situation, but willing to accept it as the end of a conflict unprofitable to the policies of both the Communist and non-Communist worlds.

52

Cold War and Hot Peace

THE END OF THE WAR IN Korea brought no real peace to an apprehensive world. Shooting stopped in that hapless land, but not all over the earth. In Indo-China the French grimly resisted the advance of the Red forces of Ho Chi Minh. Mao Tse-tung, with hordes of Chinese troops blooded and trained in Korea, cast avid eyes on the island of Formosa. Russia, blowing hot and cold in the war of nerves with the West, alternated protestations of peaceful intentions with attacks on American aircraft in various parts of the earth. While the people of the world waited there came local war and the constant threat of global war.

With the election of President Eisenhower, new direction came to the United States Department of State and Department of Defense. The members of the Joint Chiefs of Staff who had directed the war in Korea gradually fulfilled their terms and were replaced by others who proceeded to take what came to be called a "New Look" at the strategic situation all over the world.

The first consideration was that Russia had apparently decided to shift the emphasis from Europe to Asia. The period before the Korean War had, as we have noted, been disturbed by threats to the peace in Iran, Greece, Turkey, and Germany itself. The outbreak of war in Korea marked the beginning of the new Soviet emphasis on the Far East. There Russia saw her opportunity for extensive territorial gains to world Communism through the use of the armed forces of other nations. Stirring up discontent through well indoctrinated native agents in key places, training military forces in troubled countries, and equipping them with arms and munitions marked the new Soviet tactics in the hot peace both before and after Korea. The Korean Truce left the Communists in a position of strength vis-à-vis the West. The United Nations had shown that they feared beyond all things any extension of the Korean War. They had not used atomic weapons. Any effort that they might make against further aggression would be at worst on a pattern with Korea, which had left the Reds no worse off than before and which they extolled as a victory for Communism. Taking up the cry, Communist propaganda agents, specifically directing their attack on the United States as the only Western nation that had considered bolder steps in Korea, proclaimed that the glorious Chinese armies had defeated the once mighty power of America. Seizing on the hated word "colonialism," Red spokesmen identified the United States with the worst colonial practices of the 19th century. Allying themselves with and engulfing the nationalist causes, the Reds were soon ready to undertake further expansion.

The strategic picture was further complicated by the development of the hydrogen bomb. In 1950 President Truman ordered the Atomic Energy Commission to proceed to develop a thermonuclear weapon. Extensive experimentation had indicated that such a weapon was feasible, provided a hot enough "match" could be applied to start the fusion process in heavy hydrogen. Calculations indicated that such a temperature could be provided by an atomic bomb to light off the explosion.

On November 1, 1952 United States Joint Task Force 132 detonated a hydrogen nuclear explosion which observers reported as the most violent blast ever made by man. The target island in Eniwetok Atoll completely disappeared, and the explosion was visible from 50 miles away. The bomb was estimated to have an explosive force equivalent to five million tons of TNT, or, to put it another way, to be 25 times as powerful as the original atomic bomb dropped on Hiroshima. In March 1954, two other hydrogen bombs were set off at Eniwetok. A Japanese fishing boat approximately 75 miles from the blast was so contaminated that the boat's crew was in a critical condition for a considerable period of time, and one man died as a result of the radioactivity. A B-29 flying about 20 miles from ground zero was flipped over on its back by the force of the blast. On the basis of figures released concerning this blast, which had an explosive force of 40 megatons (equivalent to 40 million tons of TNT), we can deduce that the area of total destruction from such a blast would be bounded by a circle with a radius of 12 miles, that serious blast damage would extend up to 40 miles and dangerous radiation over 100 miles from the explosion, while wind-borne radioactive fall-out would extend even farther.

The United States did not long enjoy a monopoly of this fearsome weapon. The Russians had sources of information within the atomic energy program itself—notably the British physicist Klaus Fuchs, who supplied Soviet scientists with vital information. At the end of August 1953, the Atomic Energy Commission announced that Russia had exploded a hydrogen bomb a few days before.

The new defense establishment of the United States also had to take into consideration other developments in political as well as military fields. A NATO conference which convened in Lisbon in February 1952 considered means of realizing plans for developing Western strength, and adopted a "firm and vigilant" policy to discourage Russia from aggressive war. The Council set as its goal the organization and equipping of 4,000 tactical aircraft and 50 divisions for use by the end of 1952 and laid plans for further expansion in later years. Specific quotas were allocated to each country in the number and kind of troops and equipment. The Council also approved the use of West German troops in the projected European army, and on this issue came many of the subsequent difficulties, particularly with France, which feared any move to rearm the Germans.

In May of 1952, the foreign ministers of France, West Germany, Italy, Belgium, Luxembourg, and the Netherlands signed a treaty establishing the European Defense Community, which soon came to be known by its initials, EDC. This organization was intended to supplement NATO and was to be bound to it by treaties which to all intents and purposes made it a subsidiary of that organization. The EDC actually provided for the establishment of armed forces as a European army. Enthusiasts planned to have 43 divisions available for use by the end of 1954. This schedule ran into immediate difficulties when the treaty came up for confirmation in the various parliaments. In France especially the National Chamber of Deputies held back from ratification and eventually in the summer of 1954 by a procedural vote effectively killed any chance of French ratification of the treaty. As a result EDC was dead, for it was predicated on the assumption of France and Germany together furnishing the bulk of the ground forces. So discussions began almost at once among the leaders of England, France, Germany, and the United States on proposals for the rearmament of Western Germany.

On the other side of the world, the non-Communist powers sought to construct mutual defense agreements in Asia similar to those in Europe. The first step in this program occurred in September 1951 when the United States, New Zealand, and Australia signed a treaty to create a military and psychological bulwark against Communist aggression in the Pacific. This treaty, known as the ANZUS (Australia, New Zealand, United States) Pact, differed little from the NATO one in that it pledged that an armed attack on the territory or against the armed forces of any one of them would be considered as an attack on them all, and each would "act to meet the common danger in accordance with its constitutional processes." Many proposals were subsequently forthcoming to create a Southeast Asia Treaty Organization (SEATO) on the model of NATO, with other countries joining the basic ANZUS organization.

All of these considerations profoundly affected the thinking of the men charged with responsibility for the defense of the United States. As many countries vacillated, as even Great Britain, America's stanchest ally in World War II, showed increasing signs of hesitation, American leaders came to lean more and more on the concept of "massive retaliation." The United States Strategic Air Command was strengthened, and additional aircraft carriers of the *Forrestal* class were authorized so that the United States would have the power to deliver atomic and hydrogen bombs anywhere in the world if the Communists stepped over the lines set by the containment policy that had directed American planning for some years. This dependence on the "massive retaliation" policy probably kept all-out war from materializing, but it suffered from the very lack of flexibility which Secretary of Defense James Forrestal had foreseen as early as 1946. Determined not to get in more peripheral wars on the type of Korea, and fearing the consequence of global nuclear war, the United States was unable to oppose the new thrusts the Communist forces soon launched in the Far East.

The first real test came in the spring of 1954 when the civil war in Indo-China stepped up in intensity. The siege of Diênbiênphu, in which the beleaguered French forces of General de Castries held out against hordes of Red attackers, won the sympathy of the Western world, but sympathy was not enough. Diênbiênphu fell at length, and with it went all hope of the Western world saving much from the ruins of their influence in that country. In a truce that represented a clear victory for the Communists, Indo-China, already divided into three territories—Vietnam, Laos and Cambodia—was further divided into North (Communist) Vietnam and South (Free) Vietnam, with the Communists in a favorable position because of pockets of Communist sympathizers to penetrate and eventually take over South Vietnam.

The truce in Indo-China was agreed to by the French and Vietnamese partly because of the American decision not to intervene in the struggle. During the siege of Diênbiênphu, intervention was seriously considered only to be rejected by the United States National Security Council, as a part of the basic decision to avoid any more "little wars."

Apparently emboldened by the Red success in Indo-China, the Chinese began to show further signs of belligerence. Chinese leaders made open threats to invade the island of Formosa, which was under protection of the guns of the United States Seventh Fleet. Actual bombardment of Nationalist-held islands near the coast of China stirred up a near-crisis in American military policy over the issue of whether the United States was also committed to fight for the preservation of such places as Quemoy. Again the decision was for inaction, although the commitment to guard Formosa and the Pescadores Islands was confirmed by a pact signed in November 1954 with Chiang Kai-shek. Chinese reaction to the announcement of the pact was a further statement that Formosa was a part of China and a warning to the United States of the gravest consequences if she opposed "legitimate" efforts of the Reds to seize that island.

With America seemingly firmly committed to a policy of war of words and diplomatic notes in the Pacific, the Reds began to stir up further trouble in Indonesia, Thailand, Malaya, and elsewhere. External pressure and internal sedition were the methods used with

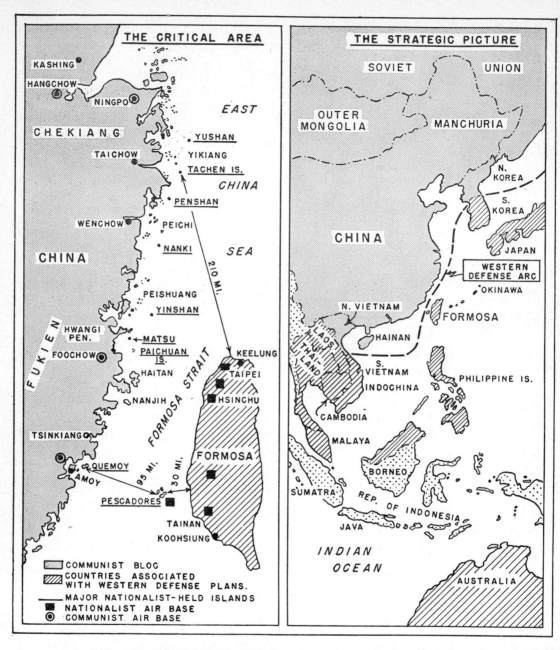

THE STRATEGIC PICTURE IN THE FAR EAST, EARLY 1955

the aim of bringing these territories into the Communist orbit. In Korea itself the Communists openly defied the West, violating the Korean Peace Treaty by bringing additional combat aircraft and airmen into North Korea, by blocking the work of United Nations Inspection Teams and by holding Allied prisoners of war in spite of agreements for their return. The Reds apparently felt that the United Nations, particularly the United States, would not again open the war over such peace treaty violations.

When Red China announced that she was holding as spies 13 American airmen, some captured during the Korean War and some shot down by her planes during routine patrol missions over the ocean, a new challenge was presented to the United States. One vocal party in Congress, led by the Republican Majority Leader, Senator William F. Knowland, proposed that the United States institute a blockade of Communist China. A majority of the members of the Joint Chiefs of Staff also favored blockade, but the proposal was rejected by President Eisenhower, who pointed out that a blockade was an act of war. Instead, negotiations for the release of the Americans were put up to the General Assembly of the United Nations.

About this time, Russia entered an apparently new phase in her international diplomacy. Less belligerent ever since the death of Stalin, Russia espoused the policy of "peaceful coexistence" and began to talk more pleasantly to foreign diplomats. Many observers interpreted this as Russia's two backward steps in her strategic manner of advancing three steps and then backing up two. The peaceful face was particularly apparent in Europe; tension remained in Asia.

FORMOSA AGAIN

In mid-January 1955 the Red Chinese launched a successful amphibious assault on the tiny island of Yikiangshen, about 215 miles north-northwest of Formosa and about 20 miles off the coast of China. This seizure was accompanied by threatening overtures directed toward the nearby Tachen Islands and by renewed promises on the part of the Reds that they would capture Formosa in spite of the protective cover of the United States Seventh Fleet. President Eisenhower, taking cognizance of the threat to the peace, sent a message to Congress asking for authority to use American military forces as he saw fit in the defense of Formosa and the Pescadores Islands and such other areas as were considered necessary for the defense of Formosa. After a brief debate Congress granted this power, and the Senate also ratified a treaty with Chiang Kai-shek providing for the defense of Formosa.

The immediate concern became the evacuation of the Tachen Islands, and the larger question was whether such islands as Matsu and Quemoy would be defended by the armed forces of the United States. During the operations around the Tachen group several skirmishes took place between ships and aircraft of the Chinese Nationalists and Communists. In an attempt to stop these clashes, several nations proposed a cease-fire agreement, but Chou En-lai, Premier of Red China, flatly rejected the idea of a cease fire and reiterated his challenge to the United States, promising to "liberate" Formosa. Under such ominous conditions, the United States Seventh Fleet successfully carried out the evacuation of the Tachens.

NAVAL DEVELOPMENTS

Two great problems faced the naval leaders of the United States in the mid-1950's. As emphasis shifted from the surface ship to aircraft, from piloted to guided missiles, and from conventional explosives to atomic and thermonuclear weapons, there came increasing information about the naval plans of Russia. Since the end of World War II, as we have noted, Russia had concentrated on building up her submarine forces. Then in the early 1950's the emphasis shifted as Russia began to build surface ships, especially fast cruisers with a wide operational range and battleships of an advanced design. The problem of how Russia intended these kinds of forces to fit into her strategic plans for war in the future remained a puzzle to American planners. If Russia seriously intended to dispute command of the sea with these conventional type ships, the resources of the United States Navy would be more than adequate to meet the threat, especially when the Americans could also bring carrier-based air to attack such vessels. Yet Russia's building program so far as revealed indicated no plans for aircraft carriers of her own.

The second great problem was of more immediate concern to the United States—the almost simultaneous obsolescence of its ships. By far the greatest part of the American Navy, both the active and reserve fleets, was built during World War II or in the years immediately preceding. Over 90 per cent of the ships were ten years old in 1955, if not older. Many of them had been driven hard in World War II and again in the Korean War, some ships having steamed nearly half a million miles since they were built. Machinery was wearing out and some hulls were showing evidences of metal fatigue. Turbine blades had become pitted. In addition the ships, originally designed for World War II operations, had been modified and re-modified, but were still not well suited for post-Korean War conditions. The proliferation of electronic gear had consumed space to such an extent that living spaces became more crowded. The necessary wiring had penetrated decks and water-tight bulkheads in makeshift ways so that water-tight integrity became threatened in many places. Even the modification to such ships as the *Essex*-class carriers which provided them with stronger flight decks did not answer the basic problems of the aging hulls of the ships themselves. What were needed were new ships, designed with new tasks and new equipment in mind, designed from the keel up as modern ships.

Many alterations were performed on existing hulls. The angled carrier deck became standard for large carriers, then designated attack carriers. Some destroyers, designated DDE's, were modified to serve as special anti-submarine ships; others had extensive radar installations and were intended for use as radar picket and fighter direction ships. Many large vessels were equipped with an extensive shower spray system that could wash down all topside spaces in the matter of a few minutes. This invention was not intended to ease the traditional burden of sailors of washing down the decks but to provide a means for rapid decontamination of ships caught in radioactive spray from an atomic explosion.

A few new ships were authorized, including all-rocket and guided missile ships built on battleship hulls. The amphibious command ship of World War II and the Korean War was redesigned onto a cruiser hull, the *Northampton* being the first of this class. Four *Forrestal*-class carriers had been authorized by the end of 1954, and the prototype was launched in December of that year. All of these had the capability of handling 90 A4D long range, atomic bomb-carrying jet bombers.

CONCLUSION

To the vocal minority who insist that sea power has come to the end of its usefulness as a military weapon, there are clear and unequivocal answers. If by sea power, we mean the ability to keep the lines of communication open between distant areas of the world, there is no doubt that sea power can and must continue to fulfill this vital mission. If by sea power we mean the ability to carry attack to the enemy shore, to land armed forces in the face of atomic and thermonuclear weapons and to deliver those weapons against a large land mass, there may be a different answer. So long as sea power has the capacity to control all three dimensions in tridimensional war at sea, then it can make its force felt at long distances from its point of origin, over water or over land, and its point of origin can move rapidly from one point to another to concentrate force. With thermonuclear weapons however war has become so absolute that perhaps no weapon can be decisive. Sea power offers flexibility in projection of force and for swift retaliation in attack. Where land bases may well be neutralized by enemy bombs or by political decisions, the carrier force at sea at the beginning of hostilities can hope to evade detection and be in position to launch a devastating counterattack. Fleets of submarines carrying guided missiles with atomic warheads may cripple a nation whose defenses are concentrated merely against attack from the air. Until tested in the crucible of combat no weapon can be written off. The navies of the world may yet prove to be decisive.

Bibliography

THE ORIGINS OF WESTERN SEA POWER (Chapter 1)

GENERAL

The Cambridge Ancient History, 12 v.; New York: The Macmillan Company, 1928-1939 (the most authoritative and useful modern treatment). Grundy, George B., *A History of the Greek and Roman World;* London: Methuen & Co., 1926. The writings of *Plutarch;* The Loeb Classical Library, formerly published in the United States by The Macmillan Company and more recently by the Harvard University Press. Rodgers, Vice Admiral William L. USN (Ret.), *Greek and Roman Naval Warfare;* Annapolis: U. S. Naval Institute, 1937. Rose, J. Holland, *The Mediterranean in the Ancient World;* Cambridge: Cambridge University Press, 1933. Shepard, Arthur M., *Sea Power in Ancient History;* Boston: Little, Brown, & Co., 1924. Torr, Cecil, *Ancient Ships;* Cambridge: Cambridge University Press, 1894.

GREECE

Arrian, Diodorus Siculus, Herodotus, Polybius, Quintus Curtius, Thucydides, and *Xenophon;* The Loeb Classical Library editions (see *supra*). Bury, John B., *A History of Greece to the Death of Alexander the Great;* London: Macmillan & Company, Ltd., 1931. Godolphin, F.B.R., ed., *The Greek Historians,* 2 v.; New York: Random House, 1942 (contains Herodotus, Thucydides, Xenophon, and Arrian unabridged). Grote, George, *History of Greece,* 12 v.; New York: Harper and Brothers, 1854-1856. Grundy, George B., *The Great Persian War;* New York: Charles Scribner's Sons, 1901. Grundy, George B., *Thucydides and the History of His Age,* London: Murray, 1911. Hutchins, Robert M., ed., *Great Books of the Western World,* 54 v.; Chicago: W. Benton, 1952 (Herodotus and Thucydides are given in volume VI and Plutarch in volume XIV). Polybius, *The Histories* (W. R. Paton, trans.), 6 v.; New York: G. P. Putnam's Sons, 1922-1927. Tarn, William W., *Hellenistic Military and Naval Developments;* Cambridge: Cambridge University Press, 1930.

ROME (INCLUDING THE EASTERN EMPIRE)

Appian, Dio Cassius, Julius Caesar, Livy, Polybius, Suetonius, and *Tacitus;* The Loeb Classical Library (see *supra*). Bury, John B., *A History of the Eastern Roman Empire;* London: Macmillan & Company, Ltd., 1912. Dodge, Theodore S., *Hannibal;* Boston: Houghton, Mifflin Co., 1891. Ferrero, Guglielmo, *The Greatness and Decline of Rome* (A. E. Zimmerman, trans.), 5 v.; New York: G. P. Putnam's Sons, 1909. Foord, Edward A., *The Byzantine Empire;* London: Adam and Charles Black, 1911. Gibbon, Edward, *Decline and Fall of the Roman Empire* (available in Hutchins, ed., *Great Books,* v. XL-XLI; also condensed as *The Portable Gibbon,* New York: Viking Press, Inc., 1952). Gibbon, Edward, and Ockley, Simon, *The Saracens;* London: Frederick Warne & Co., Ltd., n.d. Lewis, Archibald R., *Naval Power and Trade in the Mediterranean, A.D. 500-1100;* Princeton: Princeton University Press, 1951. Mommsen, Theodor, *History of Rome* (W. P. Deiberon, trans.), 4 v.;

London: Richard Bentley, 1867. Starr, Chester G., *The Roman Imperial Navy, 31 B.C.-A.D. 324;* Ithaca: Cornell University Press, 1941. Thiel, J.H., *Studies of the History of Roman Sea Power in Republican Times;* Amsterdam: North-Holland Publishing Co., 1946 (contains a thorough discussion of the history of the *corvus*).

THE RISE OF ENGLISH SEA POWER (Chapters 2-13)

GENERAL

Navy Records Society, London (the nearly 100 volumes published by this society, some of which will appear below, are invaluable collections of source and authoritative materials on the British navy). Abbott, Wilbur C., *The Expansion of Europe;* New York: Henry Holt & Company, Inc., 1924. Albion, Robert G., *Forests and Sea Power: The Timber Problem of the Royal Navy, 1652-1862;* Cambridge: Harvard University Press, 1926. Baker, J. N. L., *History of Geographical Discovery and Exploration;* London: George G. Harrap & Co., Ltd., 1931. Beazley, C. Raymond, *The Dawn of Modern Geography*, 3 v.; London: John Murray, 1897-1906 (covers the period to 1420 only). Branch, W. J. V., and Brook-Williams, E., *A Short History of Navigation;* Annapolis: Weems School of Navigation, 1942. Brendon, J. A., *Great Navigators and Discoverers;* London: George G. Harrap & Co., Ltd., 1929. *Bulletins of the Campaigns, 1793-1832*, 25 v.; London: *The London Gazette*, 1794-1833. Callender, Sir Geoffrey A., *The Naval Side of British History;* London: Christophers, 1924. Callender, Sir Geoffrey A., *Sea Kings of Britain*, 3 v.; London: Longmans, Green, & Company, 1911-1915 (a history of British naval operations from the Armada to Trafalgar, built around the careers of outstanding naval leaders). *The Cambridge Medieval History*, 8 v.; New York: The Macmillan Company, 1911-1936 (many students of naval history may prefer *The Shorter Cambridge Medieval History*, 2 v.; Cambridge: Cambridge University Press, 1952). *The Cambridge Modern History*, 13 v.; New York: The Macmillan Company, 1903-1911. Clowes, Sir W. L., *et al.*, *The Royal Navy: A History from the Earliest Times to the Present*, 7 v.; London: Sampson Low, Marston & Co., Ltd., 1897-1903. Corbett, Sir Julian S., *England in the Mediterranean: A Study of the Rise and Influence of British Sea Power within the Straits, 1603-1713*, 2 v.; London: Longmans, Green, & Company, Ltd., 1904. Corbett, Sir Julian S., ed., *Fighting Instructions, 1530-1816;* London: Navy Records Society, 1905 (this and the following book together contain most of the Fighting Instructions which established British tactics in the age of sail, as well as elucidations from contemporary authorities and Sir Julian's analyses). Corbett, Sir Julian S., *Signals and Instructions, 1776-1794;* London: Navy Records Society, 1908. Duro, C. F., *La Armada Española*, 9 v.; Madrid, Sucesores de Rivadeneyra, 1895-1903. Fortescue, Sir John, *A History of the British Army*, 13 v.; London: Macmillan & Co., Ltd., 1899-1920. Gravière, Edmund Jurien de la, *Guerres Maritimes sous la République et l'Empire*, 2 v.; Paris: Plon, 1853. Hakluyt, Richard, *The Principal Voyages, Traffiques, & Discoveries of the English Nation*, 12 v.; New York: The Macmillan Company, 1903. Hewson, J. B., *A History of the Practice of Navigation;* Glasgow: Brown, Son, & Ferguson, 1951. Jouan, René, *Histoire de la Marine Française;* Paris: Payot, 1950. Lewis, Michael, *The Navy of Britain: A Historical Portrait;* London: George Allen & Unwin, Ltd., 1948 (highly readable; made up of histories of various aspects of the British navy—ship construction, officers and rank, armament, tactics, and so forth). Mahan, Alfred T., *The Influence of Sea Power upon History, 1660-1783;* Boston: Little, Brown, & Company, 1890, 1918, 1935 (still the most complete and thought-provoking analysis of the influence of sea power in the age of sail). Mahan, Alfred T., *The Influence of Sea Power on the Wars of the French Revolution and Empire*, 2 v.; Boston: Little, Brown, & Company, 1901. Marshall, John, *Royal Naval Biography*, 12 v.; London: Longman, Rees, Orme, Brown, & Green, 1823-1825. Montross, Lynn, *War Through the Ages;* New York: Harper and Brothers, 1946. Oman, Sir Charles W. C., *The Art of War in the Middle Ages;* Ithaca: Cornell University Press, 1953. Penrose, Boies, *Travel and Discovery in the Renaissance, 1420-1620;* Cambridge: Harvard University Press, 1952. Richmond, Sir Herbert W., *The Navy as an Instrument of Policy, 1558-1727;* Cambridge: Cambridge University

Press, 1953. Richmond, Sir Herbert W., *Statesmen and Sea Power;* Oxford: The Clarendon Press, 1946. (These two works by Sir Herbert, the first of which is a continuation and refinement of the second, provide a thought-provoking analysis of the interrelationships between naval operations and politics.) Rivera y Casares, P. D. de, *Historia de la Organizaciones Navales de España y Francia;* Madrid: Editorial Alhambra, 1932(?). Rodgers, Vice Admiral William L. USN (Ret.), *Naval Warfare under Oars;* Annapolis: U. S. Naval Institute, 1939. Rose, J. Holland, *Pitt and the Great War;* London: George Bell & Sons, Ltd., 1911. Thomazi, A., *Napoleon et ses Marins;* Paris: Editions Berger-Levrault, 1950. Tramond, J., *Manuel d'Histoire Maritime de la France;* Paris: Challamel, 1916. Yonge, C. D., *The History of the British Navy,* 3 v.; London: Richard Bentley, 1866.

THE REVIVAL OF SEA POWER THROUGH THE ARMADA CAMPAIGN (CHAPTER 2)

Beazley, C. Raymond, *Prince Henry the Navigator;* New York: G. P. Putnam's Sons, 1895. Du Chaillu, Paul B., *The Viking Age,* 2 v.; New York: Charles Scribner's Sons, 1889. Corbett, Sir Julian S., *Drake and the Tudor Navy, with a History of the Rise of England as a Maritime Power,* 2 v.; New York; Longmans, Green, & Company, Ltd., 1898. Corbett, Sir Julian S., *The Navy during the Spanish War, 1585-1587;* London: Navy Records Society, 1894. Diedo, Girolano, *La Battaglia di Lepanto.* Duro, Cesario Fernandez, *La Armada Invencible,* 2 v.; Madrid: Rivadeneyra, 1884-1885. Gravière, Edmond Jurien de la, *La Guerre de Chypre et la Bataille de Lépante,* 2 v.; Paris: E. Plon, Nourrit, et Cie., 1888. Kendrick, T. D., *A History of the Vikings;* New York: Charles Scribner's Sons, 1930. Laughton, Sir John Knox, ed., *State Papers Relating to the Defeat of the Spanish Armada,* 2 v.; London: Navy Records Society, 1894. Morison, Samuel Eliot, *Admiral of the Ocean Sea: A Life of Christopher Columbus;* Boston: Little, Brown, & Company, 1942. Motley, John L., *The Rise of the Dutch Republic,* 3 v.; New York: Harper and Brothers, 1856. Williamson, James A., *The Age of Drake;* London: A. & C. Black, Ltd., 1938. Williamson, James A., *Maritime Enterprise, 1485-1558;* Oxford: Oxford University Press, 1913. Williamson, James A., *Sir John Hawkins: The Time and the Man;* Oxford: Clarendon Press, 1927.

THROUGH THE ANGLO-DUTCH WARS (CHAPTER 3)

Beadon, Roger, *Robert Blake;* London: Edward Arnold & Co., 1935. Penn, C. D., *The Navy under the Early Stuarts, and Its Influence on English History,* London: J. Hogg, 1920. Tedder, Arthur W., *The Navy of the Restoration;* Cambridge: Cambridge University Press, 1916.

THE ANGLO-FRENCH WARS THROUGH 1748 (CHAPTER 3)

Clark, G. N., *The Dutch Alliance and the War against French Trade, 1688-1697;* Oxford: Oxford University Press, 1934. Graham, Gerald S., *Empire of the North Atlantic: The Maritime Struggle for North America;* Toronto: University of Toronto Press, 1950. Owen, John H., *War at Sea under Queen Anne, 1702-1708,* Cambridge: Cambridge University Press, 1938. Richmond, Sir Herbert W., *The Navy in the War of 1739-1748,* 3 v.; Cambridge: Cambridge University Press, 1920.

THE SEVEN YEARS' WAR (CHAPTER 4)

Corbett, Sir Julian S., *England in the Seven Years' War: A Study in Combined Strategy,* 2 v.; London: Longmans, Green, & Company, Ltd., 1918. Molyneux, Thomas More, *Conjunct Expeditions;* London: R. and J. Dodsley, 1759. Richmond, Sir Herbert W., *The Navy in India, 1763-1783;* London: Ernest Benn, Ltd., 1931. Tunstall, Brian, *Admiral Byng and the Loss of Minorca;* London: Philip Allan & Co., Ltd., 1928. Willson, Beckles, *Life and Letters of James Wolfe;* London: Heineman, 1909.

THE AMERICAN REVOLUTION—INCLUDING THE ACTIVITIES OF THE FRENCH NAVY (CHAPTERS 5-6)

Clark, W. B., *John Young;* Baton Rouge: Louisiana State University Press, 1953. Clark, W. B., *Lambert Wickes;* New Haven: Yale University Press, 1932. Clark, W. B., *Nicholas Biddle;* Baton Rouge: Louisiana State University Press, 1949. James, W. M., *The British Navy in Adversity;* London: Longmans, Green, & Company, Ltd., 1926. Knox, D. W., *A History of the United States Navy;* New York: G. P. Putnam's Sons, 1936. Lewis, Charles Lee, *Admiral de Grasse and American Independence;* Annapolis: U. S. Naval Institute, 1945. Lorenz, Lincoln, *John Paul Jones;* Annapolis: U. S. Naval Institute, 1943. Middlebrook, L. F., *History of Maritime Connecticut during the American Revolution,* 2 v.; Salem: The Essex Institute, 1925 (for a picture of a state navy). Neeser, R. W., *A Statistical and Chronological History of the United States Navy;* New York: G. P. Putnam's Sons, 1936. Paullin, C. O., ed., *The Out-letters of the Continental Marine Committee and the Board of Admiralty, 1776-1780,* 2 v.; New York: Naval History Society, 1913-1914. Stevens, B. F., ed., *Facsimiles of Manuscripts in European Archives Relating to America, 1773-1783,* 24 v.; London: Malloy & Sons, 1889-1898 (the basic source for documents). Trevelyan, Sir George O., *The American Revolution,* 4 v.; London: Longmans, Green, & Company, Ltd., 1899 (the classical history of the Revolution). Ward, Christopher, *The War of the Revolution,* 2 v.; New York: The Macmillan Company, 1952 (a recent authoritative study).

THE WARS OF THE FRENCH REVOLUTION: OPENING EVENTS (CHAPTER 7)

Burne, Alfred H., *The Noble Duke of York;* London: Staples Press, 1949 (early operations in Holland). Rose, J. Holland, *Lord Hood and the Defence of Toulon;* Cambridge: Cambridge University Press, 1922. Tonnele, Jean, *L'Angleterre en Méditérranée;* Paris: Charles-Lavauzelle, 1952.

ENGLAND AT BAY, 1797 (CHAPTER 8)

Closmadeuc, G. Thomas de, *Quiberon, 1795;* Paris: Plon, 1899. Debrière, Edouard, *1793-1805 Projets et Tentatives de Débarquement aux Îles Britanniques,* 4 v.; Paris: Chapelot, 1900-1902. Jackson, T. S., *Logs of the Great Sea Fights,* 2 v.; London: Navy Records Society, 1899-1900. James, Sir William, *Old Oak: The Life of John Jervis;* London: Longmans, Green, & Company, Ltd., 1950. Mahan, A. T., *Types of Naval Officers,* Boston: Little, Brown & Company, 1901. Pellew, George, ed., *Life and Correspondence of Henry Addington, Viscount Sidmouth,* 3 v.; London: John Murray, 1847. Smith, D. B., *The St. Vincent Papers,* 2 v.; London: Navy Records Society, 1921 and 1926.

ENGLAND RE-ENTERS THE MEDITERRANEAN (CHAPTER 9)

Anderson, R. C., *Naval Wars in the Levant, 1559-1853;* Princeton: Princton University Press, 1952. Barrow, John, *Life and Correspondence of Admiral Sir William Sydney Smith,* 2 v.; London: Richard Bentley, 1848. Bunbury, Sir Henry (Sir John Fortescue, ed.), *Narratives of Some Passages in the Great War with France;* London: Peter Davies, Ltd., 1927. Carlan, J. M., *Navios en Secuestro: La Escuadra Española del Oceano en Brest (1799-1802);* Madrid: Instituto Historico de Marina, 1951 (for the details of Spanish assistance to France). Corbett, J. S., and H. W. Richmond, eds., *The Spencer Papers,* 4 v.; London: Navy Records Society, 1913-1914 and 1923-1924. Garcot, Maurice, *Kléber;* Paris: Berger-Levrault, 1936. *Histoire de l'Expédition Française en Egypte,* 10 v.; Paris: Denain, 1830-1836. Hoskins, H. L., *British Routes to India;* New York: Longmans, Green, & Company, 1928. Knox, D. W., ed., *Naval Documents Related to the Quasi-War with France,* 7 v.; Washington: Government Printing Office, 1935-1938. Maurice, Sir J. F., ed., *The Diary of Sir John Moore,* 2 v.; London: Longmans, Green, & Company, Ltd., 1904 (shows the development of British amphibious practice). Nicolas, Sir Harris, ed., *Dispatches and Letters of Lord Viscount Nelson,* 7 v.; London: Henry Colburn, 1846 (essential for any study of the naval history of the period). Puryear, V. J., *Napoleon and the Dardanelles;* Berkeley: University of California Press, 1951.

ATLANTIC FRONT, 1798-1802 (CHAPTER 10)

Anderson, R. C., *Naval Wars in the Baltic during the Sailing Ship Epoch;* London: Gilbert Wood, 1910 (best work in English on the Russian navy). Bruun, Geoffrey, *Europe and the French Imperium, 1799-1814;* New York: Harper and Brothers, 1938. *The Cambridge Modern History,* cited *supra,* Chapters 2-13, "General," has an entire volume on Napoleon and his era. Napoleon I, *Correspondence,* 28 v.; Paris: Plon avec Dumain, 1857-1859.

THE TRAFALGAR CAMPAIGN (CHAPTER 11)

British Admiralty Bluebook, *The Tactics of Trafalgar;* London: H. M. Stationer's Office, 1913. Corbett, J. S., *The Campaign of Trafalgar;* London: Longmans, Green, & Company, Ltd., 1910. Désbrière, Edouard, *Trafalgar;* Paris: Chapelot, 1907. Knox, D. W., ed., *Naval Documents Related to the United States Wars with the Barbary Powers,* 7 v.; Washington: Government Printing Office, 1939-1945. Leyland, John, ed., *The Blockade of Brest, 1803-1805,* 2 v.; London: Navy Records Society, 1898 and 1901. Máhan, A. T., *The Life of Nelson,* 2 v.; Boston: Little, Brown, & Company, 1907. Marliani, M. de, *Combate de Trafalgar;* Madrid: Impreso de Orden Superior, 1850. Thomazi, A., *Trafalgar,* Paris: Payot, 1932.

POST-TRAFALGAR: THE BRITISH COME TO GRIPS WITH NAPOLEON (CHAPTER 12)

Creswell, John, *Generals and Admirals;* London: Longmans, Green, & Company, Ltd., 1952 (able treatment of the Walcheren fiasco). Hamilton, Sir R. V., ed., *The Byam Martin Papers,* 3 v.; London: Navy Records Society, 1898, 1900, and 1902 (Baltic and Spanish theaters). Napier, W. F. P., *History of the War in the Peninsula, 1807-1814;* Philadelphia: Carey & Hart, 1842 (the classic work on the Spanish War). Parkinson, C. N., *War in the Eastern Seas, 1793-1815;* London: George Allen & Unwin, Ltd., 1954. Ross, John, *Admiral Lord de Saumarez,* 2 v.; London: Richard Bentley, 1838 (Baltic operations, 1807-1814). Waite, Richard A., *Sir Home Riggs Popham,* microfilmed typescript of Harvard University Ph.D. dissertation, 1942 (coastal operations off Flanders, and so forth; Waite is an apologist for Popham, especially in the Argentine adventure).

WAR OF 1812 (CHAPTER 13)

Adams, Henry, *The War of 1812;* Washington: *The Infantry Journal,* 1944. Davies, Godfrey, *Wellington and His Army;* London: Basil Blackwell, 1954. James, William, *Naval Occurrences of the Late War between Great Britain and the United States of America;* London: Thomas Egerton, 1817. Smith, W. H., *Life and Services of Captain Philip Beaver,* London: John Murray, 1829.

THE NINETEENTH CENTURY (Chapters 14 and 15)

NEW NAVAL WEAPONS (CHAPTER 14)

Bathe, Greville, *Ship of Destiny;* St. Augustine, Fla.: n.p., 1951. Baxter, James Phinney, *Introduction of the Ironclad Warship;* Cambridge: Harvard University Press, 1933. Bennett, Frank M., *The Steam Navy of the United States;* Pittsburgh: Warren and Co., 1896. Lady Bourchier, *Memoir of the Life of Admiral Codrington;* London: Longmans, Green, & Company, Ltd., 1873 (Battle of Navarino). Brodie, Bernard, *Sea Power in the Machine*

Age; Princeton: Princeton University Press, 1941 (the fullest general treatment).   Bushnell, David, letter to Thomas Jefferson, *Transactions of the American Philosophical Society,* IV (old series), 303-312.   Chapelle, Howard I., *History of American Sailing Ships,* and *The History of the American Sailing Navy;* New York: W. W. Norton & Company, Inc., 1935, 1949.   Cowie, J. S., *Mines, Minelayers and Minelaying;* London: Oxford University Press, 1949.   Dahlgren, J. A., *Shells and Shell Guns;* Philadelphia: King and Baird, 1856.   Dickinson, H. W., *Robert Fulton, Engineer and Artist: His Life and Works;* London: John Lane, The Bodley Head, Ltd., 1913.   Parkinson, C. Northcote, *Edward Pellew, Baron Exmouth, Vice Admiral of the Red;* London: Methuen & Co., Ltd., 1934 (action at Algiers, 1816).   Preble, George Henry, and Hammersley, L. R., *A Chronological History of the Origin and Development of Steam Navigation;* Philadelphia: L. R. Hammersley, 1883.   Robertson, Frederick Leslie, *The Evolution of Naval Armament;* London: Constable & Company, Ltd., 1921.   Tennent, Sir J. Emerson, *The Story of The Guns;* London: Longmans, Green, & Company, Ltd., 1864.

THE MEXICAN WAR (Chapter 15)

Bancroft, Hubert Howe, *History of the Pacific States,* XXII; San Francisco: The History Company, 1886 (background information for the conquest of California).   Bayard, S. J., *A Sketch of the Life of Commodore Robert F. Stockton;* New York: Derby and Jackson, 1856 (partisan, but contains interesting primary source material on the conquest of California, in appendices).   Conner, P. S. P., *The Home Squadron under Commodore Conner in the War with Mexico;* Philadelphia: n.p., 1896 (reprints memoir of Vera Cruz landing by W. G. Temple).   DeVoto, Bernard, *The Year of Decision, 1846;* Boston: Little, Brown, & Company, 1943 (Kearny's side of the Frémont-Kearny controversy).   Henry, Robert Selph, *The Story of the Mexican War;* Indianapolis: The Bobbs-Merrill Company, 1950.   Nevins, Allan, *Frémont: Pathmarker of the West;* New York: D. Appleton-Century Company, Inc., 1939 (Frémont's side of the Frémont-Kearny controversy).   *Report of the Secretary of the Navy, 1846;* Washington: Government Printing Office, 1847 (Vera Cruz Landing).   *Senate Executive Document 33, 30th Congress, 1st Session;* Washington: Government Printing Office (record of Frémont's court-martial).   Smith, Justin A., *The War with Mexico,* 2 v.; New York: The Macmillan Company, 1919.

THE CRIMEAN WAR (Chapter 15)

Bazancourt, Baron C. de, *The Crimean Expedition to the Capture of Sebastopol,* 2 v.; London: Sampson Low, Son, and Co., 1856 (French side).   Daly, Robert W., "Nakhimov: Black Sea Admiral," *Marine Corps Gazette,* April 1953, 54-61 (Battle of Sinope).   Furse, Col. George Armand, *Military Expeditions beyond the Seas,* 2 v.; London: William Clowes & Sons, Ltd., 1897.   Heath, Sir Leopold George, *Letters from the Black Sea during the Crimean War, 1854-1855;* London: Richard Bentley and Son, 1897 (British view).   King-lake, William, *The Invasion of the Crimea,* 8 v.; Edinburgh: William Blackwood & Sons, Ltd., 1863-1887.   Russell, William Howard, *General Todleben's History of the Defence of Sebastopol: a Review;* New York: D. Van Nostrand Company, Inc., 1865 (Russian side).   Russell, William Howard, *The War,* 2 v.; London: George Routledge & Sons, Ltd., 1856.

THE CIVIL WAR (Chapters 16-21)

GENERAL

Battles and Leaders of the Civil War, Johnson, R. U., and C. C. Buel, eds., 4 v.; New York: The Century Co., 1887-1889.   *Official Records of the Union and Confederate Armies in the War of the Rebellion,* 128 v.; Washington: Government Printing Office, 1880-1902.   *Official Records of the Union and Confederate Navies in the War of the Rebellion,* 128 v.; Washington: Government Printing Office, 1894-1922.   Porter, D. D., *Naval History of the Civil*

War; New York: Sherman Publishing Co., 1886. *The Rebellion Record,* Moore, F., ed., 11 v.; New York: George Putnam's Sons, 1861-1864, and Van Nostrand, 1864-1868. *Report of Joint Committee on the Conduct of the War,* 9 v.; Washington: Government Printing Office, 1863-1866. Scharf, J. T., *History of the Confederate States Navy;* New York: Rogers and Sherwood, 1887. Thompson, R. M. and Wainwright, R., *Confidential Correspondence of G. V. Fox,* 3 v.; New York: Naval History Society, 1918-1919. Welles, G., *The Diary of Gideon Welles,* 3 v.; Boston: Houghton Mifflin Company, 1911. West, R. S., Jr., *Gideon Welles: Lincoln's Navy Department;* Indianapolis: The Bobbs-Merrill Company, 1943.

THE BLOCKADE AND THE CRUISERS (CHAPTERS 17 AND 21)

Bradlee, F., *Blockade Running during the Civil War and the Effect of Land and Water Transportation on the Confederacy;* Salem: Essex Institute, 1925. Bulloch, J. D., *The Secret Service of the Confederate States in Europe,* 2 v.; New York: George Putnam's Sons, 1883. Ellicott, J. M., *The Life of John Ancrum Winslow;* New York: George Putnam's Sons, 1902. Owsley, F. L., *King Cotton Diplomacy;* Chicago: University of Chicago Press, 1931. Robinson, W. M., *The Confederate Privateers;* New Haven: Yale University Press, 1928. Semmes, R., *Memoirs of Service Afloat;* New York: P. J. Kenedy & Sons, 1869. Soley, J. R., *The Blockade and the Cruisers;* New York: Charles Scribner's Sons, 1883. Schwab, J. D., *The Confederate States of America, 1861-1865: A Financial and Industrial History;* New York: Charles Scribner's Sons, 1901. Watson, William, *The Adventures of a Blockade Runner;* London: T. Fisher Unwin, 1892.

THE BATTLE OF THE IRONCLADS (CHAPTER 18)

Bennett, F. M., *The Monitor and the Navy under Steam;* Boston: Houghton Mifflin Company, 1900. Church, W. C., *The Life of John Ericsson,* 2 v.; New York: Charles Scribner's Sons, 1891. Lewis, C. L., *Admiral Franklin Buchanan;* Baltimore: The Norman, Remington Company, 1929. (See also Baxter, *Introduction of the Ironclad Warship, supra,* Chapter 14, "New Naval Weapons.")

THE MISSISSIPPI CAMPAIGN (CHAPTERS 19-20)

Butler, B. F., *Autobiography and Personal Reminiscences;* Boston: A. M. Thayer, 1892. Farragut, L., *The Life of David Glasgow Farragut;* New York: D. Appleton Co., 1879. Fiske, John, *The Mississippi Valley in the Civil War,* Boston: Houghton Mifflin Company, 1900. Mahan, A. T., *Admiral Farragut;* New York: D. Appleton Co., 1892. Mahan, A. T., *The Gulf and Inland Waters;* New York: Charles Scribner's Sons, 1883. Walke, H., *Naval Scenes and Reminiscences of the Civil War;* New York: F. R. Reed & Co., 1887. West, R. S., Jr., *The Second Admiral: A Life of David Dixon Porter;* New York: Coward-McCann, 1937. (See also Lewis, *Admiral Franklin Buchanan, supra,* Chapter 18, "The Battle of the Ironclads.")

LATER NAVAL DEVELOPMENTS (Chapter 22)

FOREIGN

Barnaby, Sir Nathaniel, *Naval Development in the Century;* Toronto: Linscott Publishing Co., 1904. *Brassey's Naval Annual;* Portsmouth: William Clowes & Sons, Ltd., 1886-present. Clowes, Sir William Laird, *Four Modern Naval Campaigns;* London: Unit Library Ltd., 1902. Colomb, Cdr. P. H. RN, "Lessons from Lissa," *Journal of the Royal United Service Institution;* XI (1867), 104-126. Wilson, H. W., *Ironclads in Action,* 2 v.; Boston: Little, Brown & Co., 1896. (See also Brodie, *Sea Power in the Machine Age, supra,* Chapter 14, "New Naval Weapons.")

UNITED STATES

Long, John D., *The New American Navy*, 2 v.; New York: The Outlook Co., 1903 (useful for administrative changes).   Mahan, A. T., *From Sail to Steam;* New York: Harper and Brothers, 1907 (autobiography).   *Mahan on Naval Warfare*, Westcott, Allan, ed.; Boston: Little, Brown & Company, 1948 (a valuable compendium of Mahan's principal writings on strategy and tactics).   Puleston, Capt. W. D. USN, *The Life and Work of Captain Alfred Thayer Mahan;* New Haven: Yale University Press, 1939.   Sprout, Harold and Margaret, *The Rise of American Naval Power;* Princeton: Princeton University Press, 1944 (the most useful general work on political, strategic, and tactical developments).   (See also Bennett, *The Steam Navy of the United States, supra,* Chapter 14, "New Naval Weapons.")

THE SPANISH-AMERICAN WAR (Chapter 23)

GENERAL

Annual Report of the Secretary of the Navy, 1898; Washington: Government Printing Office, 1898.   *Annual Report of the Secretary of War, 1898;* Washington: Government Printing Office, 1898.   *Appendix to the Report of the Chief of the Bureau of Navigation, 1898;* Washington: Government Printing Office, 1898.   U. S. Naval Intelligence Office, *Information from Abroad: Notes on the Spanish-American War;* Washington: Government Printing Office, 1898-1900.   Chadwick, French E., *The Relations of the United States and Spain: The Spanish-American War;* New York: Charles Scribner's Sons, 1911.   Mahan, A. T., *Lessons of the War with Spain and Other Articles;* Boston: Little, Brown & Company, 1899.   Mayo, Lawrence S., ed., *America of Yesterday, As Reflected in the Journal of John Davis Long;* Boston: Little, Brown & Company, 1923.   West, Richard S., Jr., *Admirals of American Empire;* Indianapolis: The Bobbs-Merrill Company, 1948.   Wilson, Herbert W., *The Downfall of Spain;* London: Sampson Low, Marston & Co., Ltd., 1900.   (See also Long, *The New American Navy, supra,* Chapter 22, "United States.")

PHILIPPINES CAMPAIGN

Dewey, George, *Autobiography of George Dewey;* New York: Charles Scribner's Sons, 1913.   Fiske, Bradley A., *From Midshipman to Rear-Admiral;* New York: The Century Company, 1919.   Sargent, Nathan, *Admiral Dewey and the Manila Campaign;* Washington: Naval Historical Foundation, 1947.

CARIBBEAN CAMPAIGN

Record of Proceedings of a Court of Inquiry in the Case of Rear-Admiral Winfield S. Schley, U. S. Navy; Washington: Government Printing Office, 1902.   Alger, Russell A., *The Spanish-American War;* New York: Harper and Brothers, 1901.   Clark, Charles E., *My Fifty Years in the Navy,* Boston: Little, Brown & Company, 1917.   Evans, Robley D., *A Sailor's Log, Recollections of Forty Years of Naval Life;* New York: D. Appleton-Century Company, 1901.   Goode, William A. M., *With Sampson through the War;* New York: Doubleday and McClure Company, 1899.   Schley, Winfield S., *Forty-Five Years under the Flag;* New York: D. Appleton & Co., 1904.   Sigsbee, Charles, *The "Maine," An Account of Her Destruction in Havana Harbor;* New York: D. Appleton-Century Company, 1899.

SEA POWER IN THE FAR EAST (Chapters 24 and 25)

GENERAL

Ballard, R. N., *The Influence of the Sea on the Political History of Japan;* New York: E. P. Dutton & Co., Inc., 1921.   Falk, E. A., *Togo and the Rise of Japanese Sea Power;* New

York: Longmans, Green, & Company, 1936.   Hudson, G. F., *Europe and China,* London: Arnold, 1931.   Morse, H. B., *The International Relations of the Chinese Empire,* 3 v.; London: Longmans, Green, & Company, Ltd., 1910-1918.   Morse, H. B., and H. F. Macnair, *Far Eastern International Relations,* Houghton Mifflin Company, 1931.

RISE OF, TO 1870 (CHAPTER 24)

Alden, C. S., *Lawrence Kearny, Sailor Diplomat;* Princeton: Princeton University Press, 1936.   Brown, D., "The Impact of Firearms on Japanese Warfare, 1543-1598," *Far Eastern Quarterly* (May, 1948).   Clowes, W. L., *The Royal Navy, A History,* VI-VII; London: Sampson Low, Marston & Co., Ltd., 1901 (only available source for some naval operations of the Opium War and the China Wars of 1857-1860).   Cole, A. B., ed., *With Perry in Japan;* Princeton: Princeton University Press, 1942.   Dennett, T., *Americans in Eastern Asia;* New York: Barnes & Noble, Inc., 1941.   Dulles, F. R., *China and America;* Princeton: Princeton University Press, 1946.   Eldridge, F. B., *The Background of Eastern Sea Power;* Melbourne: Georgian House, 1945.   Fairbank, J. K., *Trade and Diplomacy on the China Coast 1882-1854,* 2 v.; Cambridge: Harvard University Press, 1953.   Hansard, A. C., "Early Days in Japan," *U. S. Naval Institute Proceedings,* XXXVII (March, 1911); 141.   Marder, A. J., "From Jimmu Tenno to Perry: Sea Power in Early Japanese History," *American Historical Review,* LI (October, 1945); 1.   Murdock, J., *A History of Japan,* 3 v.; London: Kegan Paul, Trench, Trubner & Co., 1925.   *Narrative of the Expedition of an American Squadron to the China Seas and Japan;* Washington: Government Printing Office, 1856.   Okuda, T., "The Bombardment of Kagoshima by the British Fleet, August, 1863," *Journal of the Royal United Service Institution,* LVII (November, 1913); 1485.   Ouchterlony, J., *The Chinese War (1839-1841);* London: Saunders and Otley, 1844.   Paullin, C. O., "Early Naval Voyages to the Orient," *U. S. Naval Institute Proceedings,* XXXVII (March, 1911: 239, 255; June, 1911: 387).   Prestage, Edgar, *The Portuguese Pioneers;* London: A. & C. Black, Ltd., 1933.   Sadler, A., "The Naval Campaign in the Korean War of Hideyoshi, 1592-1598," *Asiatic Society of Japan Transactions* (June, 1937).   Satow, E., *A Diplomat in Japan;* Philadelphia: J. B. Lippincott Company, 1921.   Takekoshi, Y., *Economic Aspects of the History of Civilization of Japan,* 3 v.; New York: The Macmillan Company, 1930.   Treat, P. J., *Early Diplomatic Relations between the United States and Japan;* Boston: Houghton Mifflin Company, 1921.   Underwood, H. H., *Korean Boats and Ships;* Seoul: Chosen Christian College, 1934.   Walworth, A., *Black Ships Off Japan: The Story of Commodore Perry's Expedition;* New York: Alfred A. Knopf, Inc., 1946.

SINO-JAPANESE WAR (CHAPTER 24)

Marble, F., "The Battle of the Yalu," *U. S. Naval Institute Proceedings,* XXI (1895), No. 3; 479.   McGiffin, P. N., "The Battle of the Yalu," *Century Magazine,* L (August, 1895); 585.   Porter, R. P., *Japan, The Rise of a Modern Power;* London: Oxford University Press, 1914.   Wallach, R., "The War in the East," *U. S. Naval Institute Proceedings,* XXI (1895), No. 21; 691.   Wilson, H. W., *Battleships in Action,* 2 v.; New York: Little, Brown, & Co., 1928.   "Vladimir" (pseud. Volpicelli, C.), *The China-Japan War;* London: Sampson Low, Marston & Co., Ltd., 1896.   (See also Wilson, *Ironclads in Action,* II, *supra,* Chapter 22, "Foreign.")

RUSSO-JAPANESE WAR (CHAPTER 25)

"Battle of the Sea of Japan," *Journal of the U. S. Artillery,* XXIV (July-August, 1905); 72.   Cotten, L. A., "The Naval Strategy of the Russo-Japanese War," *U. S. Naval Institute Proceedings,* XXXVI (March, 1910); 41.   Fuller, J. F. C., *Decisive Battles: Their Influence on Civilization and History,* chap. 24; New York: Charles Scribner's Sons, 1940.   Great Britain, Committee of Imperial Defence, Historical Section, *Official History of the Russo-Japanese War,* 3 v.; appendix, 3 map cases; London: H. M. Stationery Office, 1910-1920.   Hoadley, W. T., "The Battle of the Sea of Japan." *U. S. Naval Institute Proceedings,* XL (July-August, 1914); 152.   Hoadley, W. T. (trans.), "The Battle of the Yellow Sea: Official Version of the Japanese General Staff," *U. S. Naval Institute Proceedings,* XL (September-October, 1914); 153. Jane, F. T., *Heresies of Sea Power;* London: Longmans, Green, & Company, Ltd., 1906. Jane, F. T., *The Imperial Russian Navy;* London: Thacker, 1899. Jane, F. T., *The Imperial Japanese Navy;* London: Thacker, 1899. Klado, N., *The Battle of the Sea of Japan;* London: Hodder & Stoughton Ltd., 1906. Kladre, N., *The Russian Navy in the Russo-Japanese War;* London: Hurst and Blackett, 1905. Lloyd, A., *Admiral Togo;* Tokyo: Kinkodo, 1905. Mahan, A. T., "Retrospect upon the War between Japan and Russia," *Naval Administration and Warfare;* Boston: Little, Brown, & Company, 1918. Maltzahn, K. von, *Der Seekrieg zwischen Russland und Japan;* Berlin, 1912-1914. Mizuno, H., *This One Battle;* Tokyo: Daitoa Shuppan Kabushiki Kaisha, 1944 (reflects the Japanese illusion then current that a new Battle of Tsushima might extricate them from their desperate situation, as narrated in chapter 45 of this history). "Naval Attacks upon Port Arthur," *Journal of the U. S. Artillery,* XXVII (January-February, 1907); 54. Nebogatoff, "Battle of Tsushima," *Journal of the Royal United Service Institution,* L (October, 1906); 1262. Nojine, E. K., *The Truth about Port Arthur;* London: John Murray, 1908. Novikov-Priboy, *Tsushima;* London: George Allen and Unwin, Ltd., 1936. Ogasawara, N., *Life of Admiral Togo;* Tokyo: Saito Shoin, 1934. Semenoff, V., *Rasplata;* London: John Murray, 1909 (Cruise of Rodjestvensky); *The Battle of Tsushima;* London: John Murray, 1906. Theiss, F., *The Voyage of Forgotten Men (Tsushima);* Indianapolis: The Bobbs-Merrill Company, 1937. White, R. D., "With the Baltic Fleet at Tsushima," *U. S. Naval Institute Proceedings,* XXXII (June, 1906); 597. Whitton, F. E., *The Decisive Battles of Modern Times;* London: Constable & Company, Ltd., 1923.

THE UNITED STATES BECOMES A NAVAL POWER (Chapter 26)

Bailey, T. A., *Theodore Roosevelt and the Japanese-American Crises;* Stanford University: Stanford University Press, 1934. Bywater, H. C., *Navies and Nations;* Boston: Houghton Mifflin Company, 1927. Callcott, W. H., *The Caribbean Policy of the United States, 1890-1920;* Baltimore: Johns Hopkins Press, 1942. Davis, G. T., *A Navy Second to None;* New York: Harcourt, Brace & Company, Inc., 1940. Evans, R. D., *An Admiral's Log;* New York: D. Appleton & Co., 1910. Fiske, B. A., *The Navy as a Fighting Machine;* New York: Charles Scribner's Sons, 1916. Miller, R. J., *Around the World with the Battleships;* Chicago: A. C. McClurg & Company, 1909. Montague, L. L., *Haiti and the United States, 1714-1938;* Durham: Duke University Press, 1940. Morison, E. E., *Admiral Sims and the Modern American Navy;* Boston: Houghton Mifflin Company, 1942. O'Gara, G. C., *Theodore Roosevelt and the Rise of the Modern Navy;* Princeton: Princeton University Press, 1943. Perkins, D., *Hands Off: A History of the Monroe Doctrine;* Boston: Little, Brown & Company, 1941. Roosevelt, T., *Autobiography;* New York: Charles Scribner's Sons, 1929. (See also Brodie, *Sea Power in the Machine Age, supra,* Chapter 14; Evans, *A Sailor's Log, supra,* Chapter 23; Fiske, *From Midshipman to Rear Admiral, supra,* Chapter 23; Puleston, Mahan, *supra,* Chapter 22; Sprout, *Rise of American Naval Power, supra,* Chapter 22.)

WORLD WAR I (Chapters 27-31)

GENERAL

History of the Great War, Based on Official Documents: Corbett, Julian S., and Henry Newbolt, *Naval Operations,* 5 v. (London: Longmans, Green, & Company, Ltd., 1920-1931); Fayle, C. Ernest, *Seaborne Trade,* 3 v. (New York: Longmans, Green, & Company, 1920 and 1923); Hurd, Archibald, *The Merchant Navy,* 3 v. (New York: John Murray, 1921-1929). Bingham, Barry, *Falklands, Jutland, and the Bight;* London: John Murray, 1919. Churchill, W. S., *The World Crisis,* 4 v.; New York: Charles Scribner's Sons, 1923-1927 (available also in condensed one-volume edition). Keyes, Roger, *The Naval Memoirs of Admiral of the Fleet Sir Roger Keyes;* New York: E. P. Dutton & Co., Inc., 1934. Scheer,

Reinhard, *Germany's High Sea Fleet in the World War;* London: Cassell & Co., Ltd., 1920.
Wilson, H. W., *Battleships in Action, II;* Boston: Little, Brown & Company, 1926.

CRUISER ACTIONS (Chapter 27)

Fisher, John A., *Memories and Records,* 2 v.; New York: George H. Doran Company, 1920.
Hirst, Lloyd, *Coronel and After;* London: Peter Davies, Ltd., 1934. Milne, A. Berkeley,
The Flight of the 'Goeben' and the 'Breslau,' London: E. Nash, 1921. Pocchammer, Hans,
Before Jutland; London: Jarrolds, Publishers, Ltd., 1931. Raeder, Erich, *Cruiser Warfare
in Foreign Waters,* 2 v.; Newport: U. S. Naval War College, 1923-1935. Scott, Percy, *Fifty
Years in the Royal Navy;* London: George H. Doran Company, 1919. Tirpitz, Alfred, *My
Memoirs,* 2 v.; New York: Dodd, Mead and Company, Inc., 1919. Verner, Rudolf, *The
Battle Cruisers at the Action of the Falkland Islands;* London: J. Bale, Sons & Danielsson,
1920. Young, Filson, *With the Battle Cruisers;* London: Cassell & Co., Ltd., 1921.

THE DARDANELLES-GALLIPOLI CAMPAIGN (Chapter 28)

Ansel, Walter C., "Naval Gun Fire in Support of a Landing," *Marine Corps Gazette,* XVII
(May, 1932); 23. Ansel, Walter C., "Naval Gunfire in Support of Landings," *Naval In-
stitute Proceedings,* LVIII (July, 1932); 1001. Aspinall-Oglander, Cecil, *Roger Keyes;*
London: Hogarth Press, 1951. Aspinall-Oglander, Cecil, and Becke, A. F., *Official History,
Military Operations, Gallipoli,* 4 v.; London: William Heinemann, Ltd., 1929. Bacon,
R. H., *The Life of Lord Fisher of Kilverstone,* 2 v.; New York: Doubleday & Company,
Inc., 1929. Callwell, C. E., *The Dardanelles;* Boston: Houghton Mifflin Company, 1924.
Dardanelles Commission, *First Report;* London: H. M. Stationery Office, 1917. Hamilton,
Ian, *Gallipoli Diary,* 2 v.; New York: Doran, 1920. Keyes, Roger, *The Fight for Gallipoli;*
London: Eyre and Spottiswoode, Ltd., 1941. Marder, Arthur J., *Fear God and Dread
Nought, The Correspondence of Admiral of the Fleet Lord Fisher of Kilverstone;* Cam-
bridge: Harvard University Press, 1952. Marder, Arthur J., *Portrait of an Admiral: The
Life and Papers of Sir Herbert Richmond;* London: Jonathan Cape, Ltd., 1950. Mason,
A. T., "An Introduction to the Gallipoli Campaign," *Marine Corps Gazette,* XX, (February,
1936). Oxford and Asquith, Herbert Henry Asquith, Earl of, *Memories and Reflections,*
2 v.; Boston: Little, Brown & Company, 1928. Liman von Sanders, Otto, *Five Years in Turkey;* Annapolis: U. S. Naval Institute, 1927. Wester-Wemyss, Rosslyn, *The Navy in the
Dardanelles;* London: Hodder & Son, 1924.

THE BATTLE OF JUTLAND (Chapter 29)

Bacon, R. H., *The Life of John Rushworth, Earl Jellicoe;* London: Cassell & Co., Ltd.,
1936. Bellairs, C. W., *The Battle of Jutland,* London: Hodder & Stoughton, Ltd., 1920.
Bywater, H. C., "Gunnery at Jutland," *U. S. Naval Institute Proceedings,* LI (September,
1925); 1780. Chalmers, W. S., *The Life and Letters of David, Earl Beatty;* London: Hodder & Stoughton, 1951. Chatfield, A. E. M., *The Navy and Defence;* London: William
Heinemann, Ltd., 1942. Cruttwell, C. R. M. F., *A History of the Great War, 1914-1918;*
London: Oxford University Press, 1936. Fawcett, H. W., and Hooper, G. W. W., eds.,
The Fighting at Jutland; London: Hutchinson & Co., Ltd., 1920. Frost, H. H., *The Battle
of Jutland;* Annapolis: U. S. Naval Institute, 1936. Frothingham, T. G., *The Naval His-
tory of the World War,* II; Cambridge: Harvard University Press, 1924. Gibson, L., and
Harper, J. E. T., *The Riddle of Jutland;* New York: Coward-McCann, Inc., 1943. Gill,
C. C., *What Happened at Jutland: the Tactics of the Battle;* New York: George H. Doran
Company, 1921. Groos, O., *Der Krieg in der Nordsee,* V; Berlin: E. S. Mittler & Sohn, 1925.
Liddell Hart, B., *A History of the World War, 1914-1918;* New York: Little, Brown & Co.,
1935. Von Hase, G. O. I., *Kiel and Jutland;* London: Skeffington & Son, Ltd., 1921.
Jellicoe, J. R., *The Grand Fleet, 1914-1916;* New York: George H. Doran Company, 1919.
Pastfield, J. L. R., *New Light on Jutland;* London: William Heinemann, Ltd., 1933. Raw-
son, G., *Earl Beatty, Admiral of the Fleet;* London: Jarrolds, Publishers, Ltd., 1930. Von

Schoultz, G.   *With the British Battle Fleet: War Recollections of a Russian Naval Officer;* London: Hutchinson & Co., Ltd., 1925.   Waldeyer-Hartz, H., *Admiral von Hipper;* London: Rich and Cowan, Ltd., 1933.

THE STRUGGLE FOR COMMAND OF THE SEAS; AMERICAN PARTICIPATION AND ALLIED VICTORY (CHAPTERS 30 AND 31)

SUBMARINE AND ANTISUBMARINE WARFARE

Carnegie Endowment for International Peace, *Official German Documents Relating to the World War,* 2 v.; New York: Oxford University Press, 1923.   Gayer, A., "Summary of German Submarine Operations in the Various Theaters of War from 1914 to 1918," W. P. Beehler, trans., *U. S. Naval Institute Proceedings,* LII (April, 1926); 621.   Gibson, R. H., and Maurice Prendergast, *The German Submarine War, 1914-1918;* New York: Richard R. Smith, Inc., 1931.   Jellicoe, John R., *The Crisis of the Naval War;* London: Cassell & Co., Ltd., 1920.   Jellicoe, John R., *The Submarine Peril;* London: Cassell & Co., Ltd., 1934. Michelsen, Andreas, *Der U-Bootskrieg, 1914-1918;* Leipzig: K. F. Koehler, 1925.   Spindler, Freiherr, "The Value of the Submarine in Naval Warfare," *U. S. Naval Institute Proceedings,* LII (May, 1926); 835.

BLOCKADE

Bacon, Reginald, *The Dover Patrol 1915-1917,* 2 v.; New York: George H. Doran Company, 1919.   Guichard, Louis, *The Naval Blockade, 1914-1918;* New York: D. Appleton Co., 1930. Tupper, Reginald G. O., "The Blockade of Germany by the Tenth Cruiser Squadron," *Journal of the Royal United Service Institution,* LXVII (February, 1923); 1.

MINELAYING

Belknap, Reginald R., *The Yankee Mining Squadron;* Annapolis: U. S. Naval Institute, 1920.   Cowie, J. S., *Mines, Minelayers, and Minelaying;* London: Oxford University Press, 1949.

U. S. NAVY IN THE WAR

Annual Report of the Secretary of the Navy, 1914-1919; Washington: Government Printing Office, 1914-1919.   Gleaves, Albert, *A History of the Transport Service;* New York: George H. Doran Company, 1921.   Kittredge, Tracy B., *Naval Lessons of the Great War;* New York: Doubleday, Page & Company, 1921.   Sims, William S., and Hendrick, Burton J., *The Victory at Sea;* New York: Doubleday, Page & Company, 1920.

OSTEND AND ZEEBRUGGE

Carpenter, Alfred F. B., *The Blockade of Zeebrugge;* Boston: Houghton Mifflin Company, 1922.   Frost, Holloway H., "The Attack on Zeebrugge," *U. S. Naval Institute Proceedings,* LV (March, 1929); 177.   Schultz, Karl, "The British Assault on the German Bases Ostend and Zeebrugge," *U. S. Naval Institute Proceedings,* LV (July, 1929); 573.

DISARMAMENT AND REARMAMENT (Chapter 32)

Atwater, E., *American Regulation of Arms Exports;* New York: Columbia University Press, 1941.   Buell, R. L., *The Washington Conference;* New York: D. Appleton Co., 1922. Bywater, H. C., *Navies and Nations;* Boston: Houghton Mifflin Company, 1927.   Davis,

F., *The Atlantic System: the Story of Anglo-American Control of the Seas;* New York: Reynal & Hitchcock, 1941. Davis, H. I., ed., *Pioneers in World Order: An American Appraisal of the League of Nations;* New York: Columbia University Press, 1944. Engely, G., *The Politics of Naval Disarmament;* London: Williams and Norgate, Ltd., 1932. Grew, J. C., *Report from Tokyo: a Message to the American People;* New York: Simon and Schuster, Inc., 1944. Johnstone, W. C., *The United States and Japan's New Order;* London: Oxford University Press, 1941. Levine, I. D., *Mitchell, Pioneer of Air Power;* New York: Duell, Sloane & Pearce, Inc., 1943. Miller, H. B., *Navy Wings;* New York: Dodd, Mead & Company, Inc., 1937. Perkins, D., *America and Two Wars;* Boston: Little, Brown & Company, 1944. Rippy, J. F., *The Caribbean Danger Zone;* New York: G. P. Putnam's Sons, 1940. Sprout, H. and M., *Toward a New Order of Sea Power;* Princeton: Princeton University Press, 1940. Strakhovsky, L. I., *Intervention at Archangel;* Princeton: Princeton University Press, 1944.

DEVELOPMENT OF AMPHIBIOUS AND NAVAL DOCTRINE (Chapter 33)

MARINE CORPS

Holmes, Lee M., "Birth of the Fire Team," *Marine Corps Gazette,* November, 1952. Isely, Jeter A., and Crowl, Philip A., *The U. S. Marines and Amphibious War;* Princeton: Princeton University Press, 1951. Russell, W. H., "The Genesis of FMF Doctrine: 1879-1899," *Marine Corps Gazette,* March-July, 1951. Smith, Holland M., "Amphibious Tactics," *Marine Corps Gazette,* June, 1946 through March, 1947. Smith, Holland M., and Finch, Percy, *Coral and Brass;* New York: Charles Scribner's Sons, 1949.

NAVAL AND MARINE AVIATION

Morrow Aircraft Board, *Hearings before the President's Aircraft Board,* 4 v.; Washington: Government Printing Office, 1925. Paine, Ralph D., *The First Yale Unit,* 2 v.; Cambridge: The Riverside Press, 1925. Sherrod, Robert, *History of Marine Corps Aviation in World War II;* Washington: Combat Forces Press, 1952. Turnbull, Archibald D., and Lord, Clifford L., *History of United States Naval Aviation;* New Haven: Yale University Press, 1949. Wilson, Eugene E., *Air Power for Peace;* New York: McGraw-Hill Book Company, Inc., 1945. (See also Fiske, *Midshipman to Rear Admiral, supra,* Chapter 23, "Philippines.")

WORLD WAR II AND AFTER (Chapters 34-50)

HISTORIES

BRITISH

United Kingdom Military Series, *History of the Second World War,* J. R. M. Butler, ed.; London: H. M. Stationery Office (the official British history; included in the series are: Captain S. W. Roskill, *The War at Sea,* 3 v. projected, 1954- ; and Major General I. S. O. Playfair, *et al., The Mediterranean and Middle East,* 6 v. projected, 1954-). Churchill, Winston S., *The Second World War,* 6 v.; Boston: Houghton Mifflin Company, 1948-1953 (all the strengths and weaknesses of a history written by a major participant who is also a gifted writer and observer). Cresswell, Captain John RN, *Sea Warfare, 1939-1945;* New York: Longmans, Green & Company, 1950. James, Admiral Sir William R. RN, *The British Navies in the Second World War;* New York: Longmans, Green & Company, 1947. Richards, Dennis, and Saunders, Hilary St. George, *Royal Air Force 1939-1945,* 3 v.; London: H. M. Stationery Office, 1953-1954.

FRENCH

De Belot, Rear Admiral Raymond, French Navy (Ret.), *The Struggle for the Mediterranean, 1939-1945;* Princeton: Princeton University Press, 1951.

UNITED STATES ARMY

U. S. Department of the Army, Office of the Chief of Military History, *The United States Army in World War II,* 96 v. projected; Washington: Government Printing Office, 1947- (the official Army history, which also contains a good deal of Marine Corps history in the volumes concerning operations in the Pacific theater). Eisenhower, Dwight D., *Crusade in Europe,* Garden City: Doubleday and Company, Inc., 1948.

UNITED STATES ARMY AIR FORCES

U. S. Office of Air Force History, *The Army Air Forces in World War II,* Craven, W. F., and J. L. Cate, 7 v. projected; Chicago: University of Chicago Press, 1948- (the official Air Forces history). *U. S. Strategic Bombing Survey;* Washington: Government Printing Office, 1945-1947. (This series goes far beyond the limits suggested by the title, especially in the volumes published by the Naval Analysis Division. Students of naval history will be particularly interested in *Interrogations of Japanese Officials,* 2 v., *Campaigns of the Pacific War,* and *The Allied Campaign against Rabaul.*)

UNITED STATES NAVY

Karig, Walter, and others, *Battle Report,* 5 v.; New York: Rinehart and Co., 1944-1949 (a "non-technical narrative of the Navy's war, as much as possible in the words of the men who participated in the actions described"; stresses the human-interest side). Connery, Robert H., *The Navy and the Industrial Mobilization in World War II;* Princeton: Princeton University Press, 1951. Morison, Samuel Eliot, *History of United States Naval Operations in World War II,* 14 v. projected; Boston: Atlantic, Little, Brown & Company, 1947- (an unofficial history, written by a major historian with the active cooperation of the U. S. Navy; accurate and readable). Office of Naval Intelligence, U. S. Navy, *Combat Narratives* (Confidential); Washington: Government Printing Office, 1942-1945. Roscoe, Theodore, *United States Destroyer Operations in World War II;* Annapolis: U. S. Naval Institute, 1953. U. S. Naval War College, *Strategical and Tactical Analyses* (Confidential); Washington: Bureau of Naval Personnel, 1947. (See also *U. S. Strategic Bombing Survey, infra,* "Air Forces.")

UNITED STATES MARINE CORPS

U. S. Marine Corps, Historical Section, *Operational Narratives of the Marine Corps in World War II;* Washington: Government Printing Office, 1947- (this Marine Corps monograph series when completed will cover all operations in which United States marines participated, from Guadalcanal to Okinawa). (See also Isely and Crowl, *The U. S. Marines and Amphibious War, supra,* Chapter 33, "Marine Corps"; Sherrod, *History of Marine Corps Aviation in World War II, supra,* Chapter 33, "Naval and Marine Aviation"; *supra,* Chapter 33, "Aviation"; and Merillat, *The Island,* and Sherrod, *Tarawa, infra,* "The War in the Pacific.")

BIOGRAPHIES, MEMOIRS

Cunningham, Admiral of the Fleet Viscount Andrew B. RN, *A Sailor's Odyssey;* New York: E. P. Dutton & Co., Inc., 1951. *The Forrestal Diaries,* Walter Millis, ed.; New York: Viking Press, Inc., 1951 (James Forrestal's notes covering his terms of office as Secretary of the Navy and Secretary of Defense, mid-1944 to early 1949). King, Fleet Admiral Ernest

J. usn, and Whitehill, Walter M., *Fleet Admiral King: A Naval Record;* New York: W. W. Norton & Company, Inc., 1952 (particularly useful for insight into the workings of the Joint and Combined Chiefs of Staff). Leahy, Fleet Admiral William D. usn, *I Was There;* New York: McGraw-Hill Book Company, Inc., 1950 (valuable for inside story of high-level conferences). Sherwood, Robert E., *Roosevelt and Hopkins;* New York: Harper and Brothers, 1948. (See also *General Kenney Reports, Admiral Halsey's Story,* and *The Magnificent Mitscher, infra,* "The War in the Pacific.")

SUBMARINE OPERATIONS

BRITISH

Chalmers, Rear Admiral William S. rn, *Max Horton and the Western Approaches;* London: Hodder and Stoughton, Ltd., 1954. Lipscomb, Commander F. W. rn, *The British Submarine;* London: A. and C. Black, Ltd., 1954 (second half of book deals with British submarine operations in World War II).

JAPANESE

Hashimoto, Mochitsura, *Sunk: The Story of the Japanese Submarine Fleet, 1942-1945;* London: Cassell and Co., Ltd., 1954.

UNITED STATES

Beach, Edward L., *Submarine;* New York: Henry Holt and Company, Inc., 1952. Lockwood, Vice Admiral Charles A. usn (Ret.), *Sink 'Em All;* New York: E. P. Dutton and Co., Inc., 1951. Pratt, Fletcher, "The Torpedoes that Failed," *Atlantic Monthly,* June, 1950 (see also Admiral R. W. Christie's rejoinder in a letter to the editor, December, 1950). Roscoe, Theodore, *United States Submarine Operations in World War II;* Annapolis: U. S. Naval Institute, 1949.

HITLER AND THE GERMAN NAVY

U. S. Office of Naval Intelligence, *Fuehrer Conferences on Matters Dealing with the German Navy,* 3 v.; Washington: Government Printing Office, 1946. Martienssen, Anthony T., *Hitler and His Admirals;* New York: E. P. Dutton and Co., Inc., 1949.

BRITISH NAVAL ENGAGEMENTS

Campbell, Commander A. B. rn, *The Battle of the Plate;* London: Herbert Jenkins, Ltd., 1940. Grenfell, Captain Russell rn, *The Bismarck Episode;* New York: The Macmillan Company, 1949. Grenfell, Captain Russell rn, *Main Fleet to Singapore;* New York: The Macmillan Company, 1952. Strabolgi, Lord rn, *The Battle of the River Plate;* London: Hutchinson and Co., Ltd., 1940. Woodward, David, *The Tirpitz;* London: William Kimder, 1953.

PEARL HARBOR ATTACK

Pearl Harbor Attack, Hearings before the Joint Committee, Seventy-Ninth Congress, 40 v.; Washington: Government Printing Office, 1946. *Narrative Statement of Evidence at Navy Pearl Harbor Investigation,* 3 v.; Washington: Navy Department, 1945. Kimmel, Rear Admiral Husband E. usn (Ret.), *Admiral Kimmel's Story;* Chicago: Henry Regnery Co., 1955 (the commander in chief of the U. S. Pacific Fleet at the time of the Pearl Harbor attack defends his record). Kittredge, Captain Tracy B. usnr (Ret.), "The Muddle before Pearl Harbor," *U. S. News and World Report* (December 3, 1954) (contains text of orders and letters between Washington and Pearl Harbor before the 1941 attack).

THE WAR IN THE PACIFIC

Bryan, Joseph, and Reid, Philip, *Mission Beyond Darkness;* New York: Duell, Sloan and Pearce, 1945 (the story of the long flight of aircraft from the *Lexington II* on the second day of the Battle of the Philippine Sea; written in part aboard the *Lexington II* directly following the battle).   Butow, Robert J. C., *Japan's Decision to Surrender;* Stanford University: Stanford University Press, 1954.   Field, James A. Jr., *The Japanese at Leyte Gulf;* Princeton: Princeton University Press, 1947.   Halsey, Fleet Admiral William F. usn, and Bryan, J., III, *Admiral Halsey's Story;* New York: McGraw-Hill Book Co., Inc., 1947.   Johnston, Stanley, *Queen of the Flat-tops;* New York: E. P. Dutton & Co., 1942 (carrier *Lexington I* in the Battle of the Coral Sea).   Kenney, George C., *General Kenney Reports,* New York: Duell, Sloan and Pearce, 1949.   Merillat, Herbert L., *The Island, a History of the First Marine Division on Guadalcanal;* Boston: Houghton Mifflin Company, 1944.   Sherman, Frederick C., *Combat Command: the American Aircraft Carriers in the Pacific War;* New York: E. P. Dutton and Co., 1950.   Sherrod, Robert, *Tarawa: The Story of a Battle;* New York: Duell, Sloan and Pearce, 1944.   Taylor, Theodore, *The Magnificent Mitscher;* New York: W. W. Norton & Company, Inc., 1954.   Willoughby, Charles A., and Chamberlain, John, *MacArthur, 1941-1951;* New York: The McGraw-Hill Book Company, Inc., 1954.   Woodward, C. Vann, *The Battle for Leyte Gulf;* New York: The Macmillan Company, 1947.   (See also *U. S. Strategic Bombing Survey, supra,* "Air Forces," and numerous articles in the *Naval Institute Proceedings* and the *Marine Corps Gazette*.)

ALLIED AMPHIBIOUS OPERATIONS, AFRICA AND EUROPE

Edwards, Commander Kenneth rn, *Operation Neptune;* London: Collins, 1946 (a British account of the naval phase of the Normandy Invasion).   Mordal, Jacques, *La Bataille de Casablanca;* Paris: Librairie Plon, 1952 (a French account of the American invasion of Morocco).   Morgan, Lieutenant General Sir Frederick, *Overture to Overlord;* Garden City: Doubleday and Company, Inc., 1950 (planning for the Normandy Invasion).   Stanford, Alfred, *Force Mulberry;* New York: William Morrow and Company, 1951 (installing the artificial harbors off the Normandy beaches).

THE KOREAN WAR (Chapter 51)

Geer, Andrew Clare, *The New Breed: the Story of the U. S. Marines in Korea;* New York: Harper and Brothers, 1952.   Karig, Walter, *et al., Battle Report,* VI; New York: Rinehart and Co., 1952 (a continuation of the World War II series).   Marshall, S. L. A., *The River and the Gauntlet;* New York: William Morrow and Company, 1953 (the story of the defeat of the Eighth Army in November 1950, based on Marshall's new technique of group interrogations; vivid and revealing).   Thomas, R. C. W., *The War in Korea, 1950-1953;* Aldershot: Gale and Polden, 1954.   U. S. Army Department, Historical Division, *Korea—1950;* Washington: Government Printing Office, 1952.

Index

Index

A

A4D jet bomber, 922
Aaron Manby (mer)(U.S.), 261
"ABC-1 Staff Agreement," 641-42
ABDA forces, 661-64, 668, 672
Abdiel (AM)(Ger), 533, 536
Abe, Hiroaki (Japanese adm), 735
Abe, Koso (Japanese adm), 832n
Abe, Masahiro, 419
Abemama, 777, 778, 832
Abercromby, James (Br gen), 80
Abercromby, Sir Ralph (Br gen): at
   Aboukir, 173-7; death of, 175;
   Helder Expedition, 180-81; West
   Indies, 135
Aboukir, Bay and Point:
   amphibious assault on (1801), 172-
   77, 232; *diagram*, 174
   naval battle (Nile), 163-168
Aboukir (Cr)(Br), 542
Abukuma (CL)(Jap), 770, 816
Acasta (DD)(Br), 604
Acheson, Dean, 896
Achille (74)(Fr), 213
Achilles (CL)(NZ), 598-99
Acre (see St. Jean D'Acre)
Across the Pacific, *map*, 774
Actium, 17
   Battle of, 18, 31; *diagram*, 18
Adak, 683, 684, 689, 769, 771, 772
Adamant (50)(Br razee), 155
Adams, Charles Francis, 312
Adams, John, 160, 162
Addington, Henry, 187, 191-93, 199,
   201, 203-5
Addu Atoll, 670
Admiral Nakhimov (CA)(Ru), 440,
   448
Admiralty Islands, 744, 764-65, 786,
   787, 794, 804, 841
Aegatian Islands, Battle of, 15
Affondatore (turret ram)(It), 383,
   386
Africa, circumnavigation of:
   by Phoenicians, 24; by Portuguese,
   25-27; *map*, 26
Afrika Korps, 628, 631, 632, 633, 634
Agamemnon (64)(Br), 144
Agano (CL)(Jap), 757, 759, 834
AGC, 708; *defined*, 779n
Agrippa, 17, 18
Agrippina (collier)(Conf), 313
Aigun, Treaty of, 431
Ainsworth, Walden L. (U.S. adm),
   746, 750-51, 752
Air Command Solomons (Airsols),
   747, 748, 750, 756, 757, 760, 761,
   762, 763, 765, 777, 784
Aircraft carrier development, 570,
   590-93, 900, 922
Aisne-Marne Campaign, 556
Aix, Island of, capture, 74
Aix-la-Chappelle, Treaty of, 65, 67
Aix Roads, 81; Battle of, 229-31,
   232; *map*, 231
Ajax (CL)(Br), 598-99
Akagi (gunboat)(Jap), 424

Akagi (CV)(Jap), 654, 684, 694, 695,
   696, 697, 831
Akitsushima (Pr Cr)(Jap), 424
Alabama (raider)(Conf), 311, 312-15,
   393, 487; Battle with *Kearsarge*,
   314-15
Alabama (BB)(U.S.), 812
"*Alabama* Claims," 310, 455
Albacore (SS)(U.S.), 796, 798n, 836
Albatross (gunboat)(U.S.), 360, 361
Albemarle, Duke of (see Monk,
   George)
Albemarle, Earl of (Br gen), 88
Albemarle (ironclad)(Conf), 329
Albert, Prince Consort of England,
   308
Albert W. Grant (DD)(U.S.), 816
Alden (DD)(U.S.), 666
Alecto (paddle-wheeler)(Br), 263
Alert (16)(Br), 242
Aleutian Islands, 673, 683, 684, 686,
   688-9, 701, 767-73, 832
   operations in, 767-73
      and Battle of Midway, 688-89
   Theater, *map*, 768
Alexander, Czar of Russia, 190-91,
   210, 223, 225, 237, 251, 252
Alexander, Sir Harold R. (Br gen),
   711, 715
Alexander of Macedon (The Great),
   2, 9-11, 16, 28
Alexander III (BB)(Ru), 446, 447,
   448
Alexandria, Egypt, 11, 17, 165, 221,
   617, 628, 632, 633; founding of,
   11; British capture of, 221
Alexandria, La., 363-4
Alexiev, Yevgeny Ivanovich (Ru
   naval off), 433-36, 439
Alfred (24)(U.S.), 102
Alfred, King of England, 22
Algeciras, Battle of, 176-77, 235n;
   diagram, 177
Alger, Russell, U.S. Secretary of
   War, 402
Algeria, Decatur's treaty with, 271-
   72; French attempt at conquest,
   272-73; invasion of, 708-709; U.S.
   war with, 271
Algiers, 29, 51, 161, 199, 272-73, 703,
   704
   Exmouth's attack, 272-73
      map, 272
   invasion of, 708
   peace with, 199
   tribute system, 161
Alhandra Flotilla, 236
Ali, Mehemet, Viceroy of Egypt, 274,
   277
Ali Pasha, 30, 31-32
Ali, Rashid, 630
All-big-gun ship, 457n, 464, 589
Allemand, Zacharie Jacques (Fr
   adm), 221; promoted to command
   Toulon fleet, 231; at Aix Roads at-
   tack, 230-31
Allen, Joseph, quoted, 104
Alliance (32)(French), 105, 160
Alma, Battle of the, 292
Almaz, (Cr)(Ru), 449

Almond, Edward M. (U.S. gen), 911,
   912, 913
Alphea (10)(Br), 243
Altmark (AKA)(Ger), 597, 600-601,
   611
Alvarado, capture of, 284
Amberjack (SS)(U.S.), 833
Amboina, 45, 663; massacre at, 45
American Revolution, 90-125
   British campaigns; *map*, 94; of
      1777, 95
   British strategy, 91-92
   colonists' strategy and resources,
      92
   French entry into, 96
   Spanish entry into, 96
   and the West Indies, 100, 102
American Turtle (SS)(U.S.), 257, 262
Amherst, Lord Jeffrey (Br gen), 80,
   81-2; in Quebec campaign, 81-2
Amiens, Peace of, 192-3; broken, 199-
   201
Ammonoosuc (gunboat)(U.S.), 394
Amphibious assault, defined, 576
Amphibious command ship (see AGC)
Amphibious doctrine, 576-87
Amphibious operations:
   Abemama, 778, 832
   Aboukir, 172-77
   Admiralty Is., 764-65
   Algeria, 708-09
   Anzio, 717
   Attu, 771
   Betio, 778-80
   Bougainville, 755-57
   Buenos Aires, 89
   Cape Gloucester, 763
   Central Solomons, 748-50
   Cherbourg, 75-76
   Dardanelles-Gallipoli, 505-12
   Eniwetok, 784
   Ferrol, 183
   Fort Fisher, 377-81
   France (World War II), 848-59
   French Morocco, 704-08
   Gilbert Is., 776-80
   Guadalcanal, 722-23
   Guam, 799-800
   Havana, 88
   Helder, 180-81
   Hollandia, 787-88
   Inchon, 909-11
   Iwo Jima, 874-78
   Kiska, 772-73
   Kwajalein, 781-83
   Leyte, 804, 865-66
   Lissa, 384-85
   Louisburg, 80-81
   Makin, 777, 831-32
   Manila, 88
   Manus, 764-65
   Marianas, 789-800
   New Georgia, 748
   New Guinea, 740, 753-54, 762-63,
      787-89
   New Orleans, 88
   Normandy, 854-57
   Okinawa, 878-82
   Papua, 740, 753-54
   Peleliu, 801-02

941

C

K

N

T

V

W

Due